P9-DXG-203

Prentice Hall

LITERATURE
Timeless Voices, Timeless Themes

Copper

Bronze

Silver

Gold

Platinum

The American Experience

The British Tradition

PROGRAM ADVISORS

The program advisors provided ongoing input through-out the development of Prentice Hall Literature: Time-less Voices, Timeless Themes. Their valuable insights ensure that the perspectives of the teachers throughout the country are represented within this literature series.

Diane Cappillo
Language Arts Department Chair
Barbara Goleman Senior High School
Miami, Florida
Facilitator at the University of Miami/Dade County Public Schools Summer Writing Institute. Past president of the Dade County Council of Teachers of English.

Anita Clay
English Instructor
Gateway Institute of Technology
St. Louis, Missouri
*Former supervisory positions:
Middle School Team Leader Chairman, High School English Department; Coordinator Effective and Effi-cient School; Coordinator, Writing Across the Curricu-lum Project.*

Nancy M. Fahner
Language Arts Instructor
Charlotte High School
Charlotte, Michigan
Recipient of Charlotte Teacher of the Year Award 1992. Currently working on School-to-Work Curriculum Development.

Terri Fields
Language Arts and Communication Arts Teacher, Author
Sunnyslope High School
Phoenix, Arizona
Recipient of both Arizona Teacher of the Year and U. S. WEST Outstanding Arizona Teacher awards. Member of the Northern Arizona University Center for Excellence in Education Advisory Council. First place award for educational writing from National Federation of PressWomen.

Argelia Arizpe Guadarrama
Secondary Curriculum Coordinator
Phar-San Juan-Alamo Independent School District
San Juan, Texas
Recognized by Texas Education Agency for work on Texas Assessment of Academic Skills. Recipient of National Recognition of Positive Avenues for Student Success Program.

V. Pauline Hodges, Ph.D.
Teacher and Educational Consultant
Forgan High School
Forgan, Oklahoma
Formerly Language Arts Coordinator
Jefferson County, Colorado
Denver Professor in English Education/Reading, Colorado State University. President-elect of the National Rural Education Association. Recipient of Oklahoma Foundation for Excellence Award for Secondary Teaching 1993 and Outstanding Educator Award from the Colorado Language Arts Society.

Jennifer Huntress
Secondary Language Arts Coordinator
Putnam City Schools
Oklahoma City, Oklahoma
National trainer for writing evaluation, curriculum integration, and alternative assessment strategies. Instructor of language arts methods classes at Oklahoma City University.

Angelique McMath Jordan
English Teacher
Dunwoody High School
Dunwoody, Georgia
Teacher of the Year at Dunwoody
High School, 1991.

Nancy L. Monroe
English and Speed Reading Teacher
Bolton High School
Alexandria, Louisiana
Past president of the Rapides Council of
Teachers of English and the Louisiana Council
of Teachers. National Advanced Placement
Consultant.

Rosemary A. Naab
English Chairperson
Ryan High School
Archdiocese of Philadelphia
Philadephia, Pennsylvania
English Curriculum Committee.
Awarded Curriculum Quill Award by the
Archdiocese of Philadelphia for the
development of effective strategies
for the teaching of writing and the
integration of technology and writing.

Ann Okamura
English Teacher
Laguna Creek High School
Elk Grove, California
Participant of the College Board
Pacesetters Program. Formerly K–12
District Resource Specialist in Writing,
Foreign Languages, Lay Readers,
District Writing, Competency Assessment,

and the Elk Grove Writing Project. A
fellow in the San Joaquin Valley Writing
Project and California Literature Project.

Jonathan L. Schatz
English Teacher/Team Leader
Tappan Zee High School
Orangeburg, New York
Creator of a literacy program to assist students
with reading in all content areas.

John Scott
English Teacher
Hampton High School
Hampton, Virginia
Recipient of the Folger Shakespeare Library
Renaissance Forum Award. Master Teacher
in Shakespeare who produces workshops for
professional development at the local, state,
and national level. Selected to participate in four
National Endowment for the Humanities teacher
programs.

Ken Spurlock
Assistant Principal
Boone County High School
Florence, Kentucky
Former English Teacher at Holmes High School
and district writing supervisor. Past president of
Kentucky Council of Teachers of English.

LITERATURE
Prentice Hall
Timeless Voices, Timeless Themes

GOLD

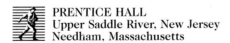

PRENTICE HALL
Upper Saddle River, New Jersey
Needham, Massachusetts

ISBN 0-13-434056-6

3 4 5 6 7 8 9 10 02 01 00 99 98

PRENTICE HALL
Simon & Schuster Education Group

STAFF CREDITS FOR PRENTICE HALL LITERATURE
(in alphabetical order)

Advertising and Promotion: Judy Goldstein, Carol Leslie, Rip Odell, Rob Richman, Ann Shea

Business Office: Emily Heins

Design: Laura Jane Bird, Sarah Carroll, Annemarie Franklin, Monduane Harris, Jim O'Shea, AnnMarie Roselli, Gerry Schrenk

Director of Language Arts: Douglas McCollum

Editorial: Ellen Bowler, Pam Cardiff, Megan Chill, Barbara W. Coe, Donna C. DiCuffa, Elisa Mui Eiger, Amy E. Fleming, Philip Fried, Rebecca Z. Graziano, James S. Jeglikowski, Jacqueline M. Regan

Electronic Publishing: Gregory Myers, Cleasta Wilburn

Manufacturing: Katherine Clarke, Rhett Conklin

Market Research: Eileen Friend, Joan McCulley

Marketing: Glenn E. Bell, Jean Faillace, Belinda Loh

Media Resources: Martha Conway, Libby Forsyth, Melanie Jones, Vickie Menanteaux, Maureen Raymond, Melissa Shustyk, Keirsten Wallace

National Language Arts Consultants: Linda Alexander, Kelly Ford, Karen Massey, Gail Witt

Permissions: Doris Robinson

PrePress Production: Kathryn Dix, William J. Hanna

Production: Christina Burghard, Holly Gordon, Elizabeth Torjussen

Technology: Rick Hickox

Art/Photograph Credits begin on p. 995.

ACKNOWLEDGMENTS

Grateful acknowledgment is made to the following for permission to reprint copyrighted material:

Margaret Walker Alexander
"Memory" from *For My People* by Margaret Walker, copyright 1942 Yale University Press. Reprinted by permission of Margaret Walker Alexander.

Rudolfo A. Anaya
"A Celebration of Grandfathers," copyright by Rudolfo Anaya, from *New Mexico Magazine,* March 1983. Reprinted by permission of the author.

(Acknowledgments continue on p. 991.)

Looking at Universal Themes

Spine Tinglers

Unit

2

Looking at Universal Themes

Challenges and Choices

Looking at Universal Themes

Unit 3

Moments of Discovery

Unit 4

Looking at Universal Themes

The Lighter Side

Looking at Universal Themes

Visions of the Future

Unit

6

Short Stories

Nonfiction

Unit 8

Drama

Unit 10

The Epic

Complete Contents by Genre

SHORT STORY

DRAMA

FOLK TALES AND MYTHOLOGY

Complete Contents by Genre (continued)

Complete Contents by Genre (continued)

POETRY (CONTINUED)

Complete Contents by Theme

Complete Contents by Theme (continued)

MOMENTS OF DISCOVERY

PERSPECTIVES

Complete Contents by Theme (continued)

VISIONS OF THE FUTURE

THE WORLD AROUND US

WORKING IT OUT

Prentice Hall

LITERATURE

Timeless Voices, Timeless Themes

The Storm, 1893, Edvard Munch, ©1997 The Museum of Modern Art, New York

Spine Tinglers

Turn the page to enter a world of suspense and mystery. Here, extra-ordinary events are commonplace, and desperate acts or unexplained phenomena can change the course of a life forever. Experience these stories, poems, and essays—if you dare! Your heart will race, your fists will clench, and your spine will tingle.

Guide for Reading

Edgar Allan Poe *(1809–1849)*

One of the first great American storytellers, Edgar Allan Poe blazed the trail for writers like Stephen King.

To this day, writers of spine tinglers point to Poe as the master of horror.

Poe's dark imagination may have its roots in his troubled childhood. Both of his parents died before he was three, and he was raised by John Allan, a wealthy Virginia merchant.

A Bitter Break While attending the University of Virginia, Poe amassed gambling debts, which his stepfather refused to pay. Forced to leave school, Poe later attended the United States Military Academy at West Point. Within a year, however, he was expelled for academic violations, causing an irreparable break with his stepfather.

The Downward Spiral Poe found brief happiness when he married Virginia Clemm. Tragically, however, Clemm succumbed to tuberculosis in 1847. Poe, heartbroken over the death of his wife, became increasingly antisocial. In 1849, he was discovered in a delirious condition on a Baltimore street. Three days later he was dead at the age of forty.

The Story Behind the Story

This story has its roots in Poe's experiences in the First Artillery at Fort Independence. Soldiers told a story about a bullying officer who killed a younger officer named Robert Massie in 1817. Massie's friends avenged his death by leading the killer into the dungeons. There, they chained him to the floor and sealed him inside to die a horrible death. The story was confirmed in 1905 during renovations to the fort. Behind a wall, workmen found a skeleton, chained to the floor, with tatters of a military uniform hanging from the bones.

◆ Build Vocabulary

PREFIXES: *pre-*

The word *precluded* in this story begins with the prefix *pre-*, which means "before." The prefix *pre-* can help you unlock the meanings of words in which it appears. You can determine, for example, that *precluded* refers to something happening before something else. It actually means "made something impossible in advance."

WORD BANK

As you read this story, you will encounter the words on this list. Each word is defined on the page where it first appears. Preview the list before you read.

precluded
retribution
accosted
afflicted
explicit
recoiling
termination
subsided

◆ Build Grammar Skills

PRONOUN CASE

Pronouns help writers avoid repeating names. The use of pronouns is especially important in this story because there are only two characters.

Pronoun case refers to the different forms a pronoun takes to indicate its function in a sentence.

Subjective case pronouns—*I, we, you, he, she, it, they*—are used when the pronoun performs the action or renames the subject. In this example, *I* renames *it*.

It is I.

The objective case—*me, us, you, him, her, it, them*—is used when the pronoun receives the action of the verb or is the object of a preposition.

       subject   obj. of prep.

In this respect *I* did not differ from *him* materially.

The Cask of Amontillado

◆ *Literature and Your Life*

CONNECT YOUR EXPERIENCE

Often, it doesn't take much to spark a desire for revenge. It can start with a simple insult, an unresolved dispute, even an unhappy loser in a hard-fought game. You encounter these situations in books, movies, television programs, and in real life. Sometimes, as in this story, a quest for revenge can get out of hand.

Journal Writing Think about why some people become obsessed with revenge and jot down all the reasons that come to mind. Then note some of the negative consequences of such an obsession. If possible, cite examples.

THEMATIC FOCUS: SPINE TINGLERS

In this spine-tingling tale, suspense builds about how far one character will go in his quest for revenge against another character. As you read, you may find yourself wondering: How far will a character go to satisfy such a desire?

◆ Background for Understanding

CULTURE

The mask you see on this page might remind you of Halloween, but it's related to a different cultural custom. Masks and costumes are an important part of Carnival—a mad, wild celebration that precedes Lent, a period of fasting and penance before Easter. Because the masks and costumes of Carnival hide a person's real identity, many people feel free to enter into the Carnival spirit and loosen their usual rules of behavior. This week-long celebration of costumes, food, and dancing serves as the setting for "The Cask of Amontillado," providing cover for a gruesome act of revenge.

HISTORY

Much of the action in this story takes place in underground burial chambers known as catacombs. These long passages and side tunnels with hollowed-out cavities along the walls stretch out like hidden cities of the dead. Until recent centuries, many wealthy European families had their own catacombs beneath the family manor. In these stone vaults beneath their homes, families held funerals for their dead, surrounded by the bones of ancient ancestors. The most extensive known catacombs are the early Christian catacombs outside Rome.

◆ Literary Focus

MOOD

As the two characters in this tale descend into the depths of the catacombs, you can't help feeling that something sinister is about to happen. Poe creates this eerie, suspenseful **mood**, or feeling that the reader experiences, with carefully chosen words and details, such as *drops of moisture trickle among the bones* and *torches glow dimly in the foulness of the air*. Notice the many other descriptive details that contribute to the mood in Poe's classic tale of horror.

Jot down the details and the effect that they create in a graphic organizer like this one.

Detail		Effect
_____	→	_____
_____	→	_____
_____	→	_____

Reading for Success

Literal Comprehension Strategies

Your first goal in reading is to understand what the writer is saying. Reaching this goal is easy when the writer writes clearly, simply, and directly. Sometimes, however, the writer may use words you don't understand or may construct sentences that don't seem to make sense right away. Don't worry. There are strategies you can use to understand what a writer is saying.

Reread or read ahead.
▶ Reread a sentence or a paragraph to find the connections among the words or to connect the ideas in several sentences to make sense.
▶ Read ahead. A difficult word or idea may become clearer as you go on.

Use context clues.
Context refers to the words, phrases, and sentences that surround a word. You can often use clues in the context to figure out the meaning of a word. Look, for example, at this sentence from "The Cask of Amontillado":

> I continued, as was my wont, to smile in his face ...

The word *wont* may be unfamiliar to you, but the words "I continued" provide a clue that *wont* is something the narrator does regularly, a habit or custom.

Break down confusing sentences.
▶ Read sentences in meaningful sections, not word by word.
▶ Figure out the subject (what the sentence is about). Then determine what the sentence is saying about the subject. Sometimes you may need to rearrange the parts of a sentence or to take other groups of words out of the way to do this.

Look at the first sentence in "The Cask of Amontillado." You will find it easier to understand if you break it down and rearrange it like this:

> I had borne the thousand injuries of Fortunato as best I could, but I vowed revenge when he ventured upon insult.

Paraphrase.
Restate a sentence or a paragraph in your own words.

Summarize.
As you read, review and state the main points of what has happened. Notice important story details and fit them into your picture of what is happening.

Look for signal words.
Signal words show relationships among ideas, such as time or importance.

As you read the following story, look at the notes along the sides. The notes demonstrate how to apply these strategies to a work of literature.

The Cask of Amontillado[1]

Edgar Allan Poe

The thousand injuries of Fortunato I had borne as I best could, but when he ventured upon insult I vowed revenge. You, who so well know the nature of my soul, will not suppose, however, that I gave utterance to a threat. At *length* I would be avenged; this was a point definitely settled—but the very definitiveness with which it was resolved precluded the idea of risk. I must not only punish but punish with impunity.[2] A wrong is unredressed when retribution overtakes its redresser. It is equally unredressed when the avenger fails to make himself felt as such to him who has done the wrong.

It must be understood that neither by word nor deed had I given Fortunato cause to doubt my good will. I continued, as was my wont, to smile in his face, and he did not perceive that my smile *now* was at the thought of his immolation.[3]

He had a weak point—this Fortunato—although in other regards he was a man to be respected and even

> **Break down** this difficult sentence by changing the word order, putting the subject first: I had borne the thousand injuries of Fortunato as best I could . . .

> Use **context clues** to discover that *unredressed* means "not made right" or "not made even." One clue is the narrator's stated intent, to punish; another clue is his statement that retribution (punishment) shouldn't catch up with the punisher.

1. **Amontillado** (ə män′ tə ya′ dō) *n.*: A pale, dry sherry.
2. **impunity** (im pyoo′ nə tē′) *n.*: Freedom from consequences.
3. **immolation** (im′ ə lā′ shən) *n.*: Destruction.

◆ **Build Vocabulary**

precluded (prē klood′ id) *v.*: Prevented; made impossible in advance

retribution (re trə byoo′ shən) *n.*: Payback; punishment for a misdeed or reward for a good deed

Critical Viewing Explain how the context of a story might make a festive mask such as this one appear sinister. **[Explain]**

feared. He prided himself on his connoisseur-ship[4] in wine. Few Italians have the true virtu-oso[5] spirit. For the most part their enthusiasm is adopted to suit the time and opportunity, to practice imposture upon the British and Austrian millionaires. In painting and gemmary, Fortunato like his countrymen, was a quack, but in the matter of old wines he was sincere. In this respect I did not differ from him materially; I was skillful in the Italian vintages myself, and bought largely whenever I could.

It was about dusk, one evening during the supreme madness of the carnival season, that I encountered my friend. He accosted me with excessive warmth, for he had been drinking much.

The **signal words** "It was about dusk" indicate that he's finished with background and is starting to tell the story.

The man wore motley.[6] He had on a tight-fitting parti-striped dress, and his head was surmounted by the conical cap and bells. I was so pleased to see him that I thought I should never have done wringing his hand.

I said to him, "My dear Fortunato, you are luckily met. How remarkably well you are looking today. But I have received a pipe[7] of what passes for Amontillado, and I have my doubts."

Summarize these sentences to note that the narrator is glad to meet Fortunato. He can now put his plan for revenge into effect.

"How?" said he. "Amontillado? A pipe? Impossible! And in the middle of the carnival!"

"I have my doubts," I replied: "and I was silly enough to pay the full Amontillado price without consulting you in the matter. You were not to be found, and I was fearful of losing a bargain."

"Amontillado!"

"I have my doubts."

"Amontillado!"

"And I must satisfy them."

"Amontillado!"

"As you are engaged, I am on my way to Luchesi. If any one has a critical turn it is he. He will tell me—"

---

4. **connoisseurship** (kän´ ə sʉr´ ship) *n.*: Expert judgment.
5. **virtuoso** (vʉr´ chōō ō´ sō) *adj.*: Masterly skill in a particular field.
6. **motley** (mät´ lē) *n.*: A clown's multicolored costume.
7. **pipe** (pīp) *n.*: Large barrel, holding approximately 126 gallons.

"Luchesi cannot tell Amontillado from sherry."

"And yet some fools will have it that his taste is a match for your own."

"Come, let us go."

"Whither?"

"To your vaults."

"My friend, no; I will not impose upon your good nature. I perceive you have an engagement. Luchesi—"

"I have no engagement—come."

"My friend, no. It is not the engagement, but the severe cold with which I perceive you are afflicted. The vaults are insufferably damp. They are encrusted with niter."

"Let us go, nevertheless. The cold is merely nothing. Amontillado! You have been imposed upon. And as for Luchesi, he cannot distinguish sherry from Amontillado."

Thus speaking, Fortunato possessed himself of my arm; and putting on a mask of black silk and drawing a roquelaure[8] closely about my person, I suffered him to hurry me to my palazzo.

There were no attendants at home; they had absconded to make merry in honor of the time. I had told them that I should not return until the morning, and had given them explicit orders not to stir from the house. These orders were sufficient, I well knew, to insure their immediate disappearance, one and all, as soon as my back was turned.

Read ahead to find out that *absconded* means "sneaked away." The paragraph says that all the attendants have gone.

I took from their sconces two flambeaux, and giving one to Fortunato, bowed him through several suites of rooms to the archway that led into the vaults. I passed down a long and

---

8. **roquelaure** (räk´ ə lôr) *n.*: Knee-length cloak.

◆ Build Vocabulary

accosted (ə kôst´ id) *v.*: Greeted, especially in a forward or aggressive way

afflicted (ə flikt´ id) *v.*: Suffering or sickened

explicit (eks plis´ it) *adj.*: Clearly stated

winding staircase, requesting him to be cautious as he followed. We came at length to the foot of the descent, and stood together upon the damp ground of the catacombs of the Montresors.

The gait of my friend was unsteady, and the bells upon his cap jingled as he strode.

"The pipe," he said.

"It is farther on," said I; "but observe the white webwork which gleams from these cavern walls."

> **Paraphrase** this paragraph this way: Fortunato looked at me with watery and unfocused eyes, which showed that he had been drinking.

He turned towards me, and looked into my eyes with two filmy orbs that distilled the rheum of intoxication.

"Niter?" he asked, at length.

"Niter," I replied. "How long have you had that cough?"

"Ugh! ugh! ugh!—ugh! ugh! ugh!—ugh! ugh! ugh!—ugh! ugh! ugh!—ugh! ugh! ugh!"

My poor friend found it impossible to reply for many minutes.

"It is nothing," he said, at last.

"Come," I said, with decision, "we will go back; your health is precious. You are rich, respected, admired, beloved; you are happy, as once I was. You are a man to be missed. For me it is no matter. We will go back; you will be ill, and I cannot be responsible. Besides, there is Luchesi—"

"Enough," he said; "the cough is a mere nothing; it will not kill me. I shall not die of a cough."

"True—true," I replied; "and, indeed, I had no intention of alarming you unnecessarily— but you should use all proper caution. A draft of this Medoc will defend us from the damps."

Here I knocked off the neck of a bottle which I drew from a long row of its fellows that lay upon the mold.

"Drink," I said, presenting him the wine.

He raised it to his lips with a leer. He paused and nodded to me familiarly, while his bells jingled.

"I drink," he said "to the buried that repose around us."

"And I to your long life."

▲ **Critical Viewing** Analyze how the contrast of light and dark contributes to the mood of this photo. **[Analyze]**

He again took my arm, and we proceeded.

"These vaults," he said, "are extensive."

"The Montresors," I replied, "were a great and numerous family."

"I forget your arms."

"A huge human foot d'or, in a field azure; the foot crushes a serpent rampant whose fangs are imbedded in the heel."

"And the motto?"

"Nemo me impune lacessit."[9]

"Good!" he said.

The wine sparkled in his eyes and the bells jingled. My own fancy grew warm with the Medoc. We had passed through long walls of piled skeletons, with casks and puncheons[10] intermingling, into the inmost recesses of the catacombs. I paused again, and this time I made bold to seize Fortunato by an arm above the elbow.

"The niter!" I said; "see, it increases. It hangs like moss upon the vaults. We are below the river's bed. The drops of moisture trickle among the bones. Come, we will go back ere it is too late. Your cough—"

"It is nothing," he said; "let us go on. But first, another draft of the Medoc."

I broke and reached him a flagon of De Grâve. He emptied it at a breath. His eyes flashed with a fierce light. He laughed and threw the bottle upwards with a gesticulation I did not understand.

I looked at him in surprise. He repeated the movement—a grotesque one.

"You do not comprehend?" he said.

"Not I," I replied.

"Then you are not of the brotherhood."

"How?"

"You are not of the masons."[11]

"Yes, yes," I said; "yes, yes."

"You? Impossible! A mason?"

"A mason," I replied.

"A sign," he said, "a sign."

"It is this," I answered, producing from beneath the folds of my *roquelaure* a trowel.

"You jest," he exclaimed, recoiling a few paces. "But let us proceed to the Amontillado."

"Be it so," I said, replacing the tool beneath the cloak and again offering him my arm. He leaned upon it heavily. We continued our route in search of the Amontillado. We passed through a range of low arches, descended, passed on, and descending again, arrived at a deep crypt, in which the foulness of the air caused our flambeaux rather to glow than flame.

At the most remote end of the crypt there appeared another less spacious. Its walls had been lined with human remains, piled to the vault overhead, in the fashion of the great catacombs of Paris. Three sides of this interior crypt were still ornamented in this manner. From the fourth side the bones had been thrown down, and lay promiscuously upon the earth, forming at one point a mound of some size. Within the wall thus exposed by the displacing of the bones, we perceived a still interior crypt or recess, in depth about four feet, in width three, in height six or seven. It seemed to have been constructed for no especial use within itself, but formed merely the interval between two of the colossal supports of the roof of the catacombs, and was backed by one of their circumscribing walls of solid granite.

It was in vain that Fortunato, uplifting his dull torch, endeavored to pry into the depth of the recess. Its termination the feeble light did not enable us to see.

"Proceed," I said: "herein is the Amontillado. As for Luchesi—"

"He is an ignoramus," interrupted my friend, as he stepped unsteadily forward, while I followed immediately at his heels. In an instant he had reached the extremity of the niche, and finding his progress arrested by the rock, stood stupidly bewildered. A moment more and I had fettered him to the granite. In its surface were two iron staples, distant from each other about two feet, horizontally. From one of these depended a short chain, from the other a padlock. Throwing the links about his waist, it was but the work of a few seconds to secure it. He was too much astounded to resist. Withdrawing the key I stepped back from the recess.

"Pass your hand," I said, "over the wall; you cannot help feeling the niter. Indeed, it is *very* damp. Once more let me *implore* you to return. No? Then I must positively leave you. But I must first render you all the little

---

Summarize: They are going deeper into these burial vaults, where there are hollowed-out sections in the walls.

Break down these sentences and **paraphrase** them: Fortunato tried unsuccessfully to feel the depth of the recess, but the light was too feeble to enable us to see the end.

Read ahead to clarify what *fettered* means and what has happened here: Fortunato is chained to the wall.

---

9. *Nemo me impune lacessit:* Latin for "No one attacks me with impunity."

10. **puncheons** (pun´ chənz) *n.*: Large barrels.

11. **masons:** The Freemasons, an international secret society.

▲ **Critical Viewing** How does this costume compare with your image of the costume worn by Fortunato? **[Compare and Contrast]**

the pile of bones of which I have before spoken. Throwing them aside, I soon uncovered a quantity of building stone and mortar. With these materials and with the aid of my trowel, I began vigorously to wall up the entrance of the niche.

I had scarcely laid the first tier of the masonry when I discovered that the intoxication of Fortunato had in a great measure worn off. The earliest indication I had of this was a low moaning cry from the depth of the recess. It was *not* the cry of a drunken man. There was then a long and obstinate silence. I laid the second tier, and the third, and the fourth; and then I heard the furious vibrations of the chain. The noise lasted for several minutes, during which, that I might hearken to it with the more satisfaction, I ceased my labors and sat down upon the bones. When at last the clanking <u>subsided</u>, I resumed the trowel, and finished without interruption the fifth, the sixth, and the seventh tier. The wall was now nearly upon a level with my breast. I again paused, and holding the flambeaux over the masonwork, threw a few feeble rays upon the figure within.

A succession of loud and shrill screams, bursting suddenly from the throat of the chained form, seemed to thrust me violently back. For a brief moment I hesitated, I trembled. Unsheathing my rapier, I began to grope with it about the recess; but the thought of an instant reassured me. I placed my hand upon the solid fabric of the catacombs, and felt satisfied. I reapproached the wall; I replied to the yells of him who clamored. I reechoed, I aided, I surpassed them in volume and in strength. I did this, and the clamorer grew still.

attentions in my power."

"The Amontillado!" ejaculated my friend, not yet recovered from his astonishment.

"True," I replied; "the Amontillado."

As I said these words I busied myself among

◆ Build Vocabulary

recoiling (ri koil´ iŋ) *v.:* Staggering back

termination (tʉr mə nā´ shən) *n.:* End

subsided (səb sīd´ id) *v.:* Settled down; became less active or intense

It was now midnight, and my task was drawing to a close. I had completed the eighth, the ninth, and the tenth tier. I had finished a portion of the last and the eleventh; there remained but a single stone to be fitted and plastered in. I struggled with its weight; I placed it partially in its destined position. But now there came

from out the niche a low laugh that erected the hairs upon my head. It was succeeded by a sad voice, which I had difficulty in recognizing as that of the noble Fortunato. The voice said—

"Ha! ha! ha!—he! he! he!—a very good joke, indeed—an excellent jest. We will have many a rich laugh about it at the palazzo—he! he! he!—over our wine—he! he! he!"

"The Amontillado!" I said.

"He! he! he!—he! he! he!—yes, the Amontillado. But is it not getting late? Will not they be awaiting us at the palazzo, the Lady Fortunato and the rest? Let us be gone."

"Yes," I said, "let us be gone."

"For the love of God, Montresor!"

"Yes," I said, "for the love of God!"

But to these words I hearkened in vain for a reply. I grew impatient. I called aloud—

"Fortunato!"

No answer. I called again—

"Fortunato!"

No answer still. I thrust a torch through the remaining aperture and let it fall within. There came forth in return only a jingling of the bells. My heart grew sick; it was the dampness of the catacombs that made it so. I hastened to make an end of my labor. I forced the last stone into its position; I plastered it up. Against the new masonry I reerected the old rampart of bones. For the half of a century no mortal has disturbed them. *In pace requiescat!*[12]

---

12. *In pace requiescat:* Latin for "May he rest in peace!"

Guide for Responding

◆ Literature and Your Life

Reader's Response At what point in the story did you find Montresor most disturbing? Explain.

Thematic Focus Poe's tale is a spine-tingling exploration of one man's obsession with revenge. Why do you think revenge is a popular subject for suspenseful movies, novels, and stories?

Journal Writing Explore how this story influenced your answer to the question: What happens when a desire for revenge gets out of hand?

☑ Check Your Comprehension

1. Why does Montresor hate Fortunato?
2. How does Montresor persuade Fortunato to follow him to the catacombs?
3. What specific steps does Montresor take to ensure that his plan works?
4. What happens to Fortunato at the end of the story?

Guide for Responding (continued)

◆ Critical Thinking

INTERPRET

1. In what ways are Montresor and Fortunato alike? How are they different? **[Compare and Contrast]**
2. What character traits make Fortunato such an easy prey for Montresor? **[Analyze]**
3. Which of Montresor's words and actions could have revealed his plan to Fortunato? **[Infer]**
4. Why does Montresor feel justified in carrying out his plan against Fortunato? **[Infer]**
5. Why does Montresor keep urging Fortunato to turn back? **[Infer]**

EVALUATE

6. Montresor acts as judge and executioner in this story. Explain whether you think individuals are ever justified in taking justice into their own hands. **[Evaluate]**

APPLY

7. If you were on the jury of Montresor's murder trial, would you agree to a plea of innocent by reason of insanity? Explain. **[Make a Decision]**

◆ Reading for Success

LITERAL COMPREHENSION STRATEGIES

Review the reading strategies and the notes showing how to comprehend a writer's words and meanings. Then apply them to answer the following:

1. Using context clues, identify the meaning of *gesticulation* on p. 8.
2. Summarize what has happened in the paragraph beginning, "Pass your hand . . ." on p. 8.
3. Paraphrase the paragraph on p. 9 that begins, "A succession of loud and shrill screams . . ."

◆ Literary Focus

MOOD

The eerie, sinister **mood,** or atmosphere, adds to the suspense of Poe's story. Poe creates this mood with descriptive details the way movie makers use visual effects.

1. Find three or four specific images that contribute to the story's eerie mood.
2. Using a scene from the story, explain how you would create a movie scene with an eerie mood.

◆ Build Vocabulary

USING THE PREFIX *pre-*

The prefix *pre-* means "before" or "in advance." Define each of these words. Incorporate the definition of *pre-* into each answer.

1. preview   2. precondition   3. precaution

USING THE WORD BANK

In your notebook, write the letter of the word that is the best antonym, or opposite, of the first word.

1. precluded: (a) prevented, (b) aided, (c) started
2. retribution: (a) reward, (b) disaster, (c) assignment
3. accosted: (a) sought, (b) retreated, (c) discovered
4. subsided: (a) increased, (b) created, (c) challenged
5. afflicted: (a) weary, (b) skeptical, (c) blessed
6. explicit: (a) unnecessary, (b) vague, (c) impatient
7. recoiling: (a) unfastening, (b) releasing, (c) advancing
8. termination: (a) height, (b) beginning, (c) extension

◆ Build Grammar Skills

PRONOUN CASE

When you use pronouns, be careful to choose the correct form, especially when using pairs of pronouns or when pairing a pronoun with a proper noun.

The **subjective case** is used when a pronoun is the subject or renames the subject. The **objective case** is used when the pronoun receives the action of the verb or when it is the object of a preposition.

Practice In your notebook, write each of these sentences. Choose *I, he, we, me, him,* or *us* to complete each one.

1. Fortunato and _____?_____ ran into each other at Carnival.
2. No one followed_____?_____to my home.
3. It was time to settle the score between _____?_____and_____?_____.
4. _____?_____and_____?_____reached the end of the catacombs.
5. _____?_____two entered the catacombs together, but only one would return.

Build Your Portfolio

 ## Idea Bank

Writing

1. **Monologue** Write a brief monologue—a speech delivered by a single character—in which Montresor explains the "injury" he has suffered at Fortunato's hands. **[Performing Arts Link]**

2. **Opening Argument** Create the prosecution's opening argument for the murder trial of Montresor. **[Social Studies Link]**

3. **Letter to Edgar Allan Poe** Respond to the story by writing a letter to Poe. Explain whether you found the characters believable and the ending satisfying.

Speaking and Listening

4. **Casting Discussion** With a small group, discuss actors who would be good choices to play each of the characters in "The Cask of Amontillado." Through discussion, agree on one actor that the group would recommend for each role. Present your recommendation and reasons to the class. **[Performing Arts Link]**

5. **Resolving Interpersonal Conflicts** Montresor's evil plot of revenge arises from a conflict between him and Fortunato. With a small group, brainstorm for situations that could cause conflicts among you and your friends. Then take turns role-playing constructive resolutions.

Projects

6. **Pantomime** With a partner, convey the plot of the story through facial expressions and broad gestures, but not words. **[Performing Arts Link]**

7. **Storyboard** Create a storyboard that outlines the main events in the plot for a movie version of "The Cask of Amontillado." **[Art Link]**

 ## Writing Mini-Lesson

Description of a Set

Imagine that "The Cask of Amontillado" is being made into a movie. Choose one of the settings in the story and write a description of a set design that incorporates Poe's descriptive details and your imagination.

Writing Skills Focus: Precise Details

Use **precise details** to create a vivid picture of your set. For example, if a tree is tall, tell *how tall.* If the setting is damp, use words like *clammy* or *humid* to indicate whether the dampness is cool or warm.

Poe uses precise details to create an image of a specific crypt of a certain size. With these precise details, you can imagine how Fortunato looks standing in the crypt because you know how big it is compared with a person.

Model from the Story

Within the wall thus exposed . . . we perceived a still interior crypt or recess, in depth about four feet, in width three, in height six or seven.

Prewriting Set designers usually make a sketch of the set. Drawing to scale—using one size to represent another (1/4 inch to represent a foot)—helps keep the dimensions of the set in proportion. Make a sketch or model to work out details of sizes, colors, and placement.

Drafting Begin your description with a few striking images that will capture the mood you want the set to convey. Refer to your sketch as you draft.

Revising Try making a second sketch of your set based on the details provided in your draft. This will help you discover places where you may need to add precise details to complete the picture.

PART 1 *In Suspense*

New Moon, New York, 1945, George Ault
Museum of Modern Art, New York

Guide for Reading

Richard Connell *(1893–1949)*

Some authors have a wide variety of jobs before they settle on being a writer. Others seem destined from the start to be writers. Richard Connell belongs to the second category.

Connell began his writing career as a sports reporter —at the age of ten!

Wartime Experiences By the time he was sixteen, Connell had graduated from reporting on sports to editing his father's newspaper in Poughkeepsie, New York. He continued his involvement in journalism at Harvard University, where he was an editor for the *Daily Crimson*. After enlisting in the army during World War I, Connell served as editor for his division's newspaper. The wartime events that Connell reported are echoed in the experiences of Rainsford in "The Most Dangerous Game," who fought in the trenches of France during World War I.

Hollywood Hotshot After the war, Connell changed his focus from journalism to fiction and movie screenplays. In 1924, he published his unforgettable short story "The Most Dangerous Game."

A year later, he settled in Beverly Hills, California. Many of his popular stories were soon made into movies. The film version of "The Most Dangerous Game" was released in 1932 and has been the inspiration for a number of other adventure movies. Connell's success as a screenwriter continued throughout the remainder of his life, and he received two Academy Award nominations for his work.

◆ Build Vocabulary

RELATED WORDS: FORMS OF *SCRUPLES*

You can increase your word power by learning other forms of a word. For example, in this story you learn the noun *scruples*, referring to the uncomfortable feelings one has about something one thinks is wrong. By adding the suffix *-ous*, meaning "having" or "full of," you form the adjective *scrupulous*, which means "having scruples."

palpable
indolently
bizarre
naive
scruples
blandly
grotesque
futile

WORD BANK

As you read "The Most Dangerous Game," you will encounter the words in this list. Each word is defined on the page where it first appears. Preview the list before you read the story. What other words can you form from the words in the list?

◆ Build Grammar Skills

PAST AND PAST PERFECT TENSES

The **tense** of a verb indicates the time of the action. "The Most Dangerous Game" is told in the past tense. Sometimes it's important to indicate when two events in the past occurred in relation to each other. The **past perfect tense** shows that an action took place before another action in the past.

In this passage from the story, Richard Connell uses the past perfect tense.

> past   past perfect
> ...he *stopped* before he *had swum* fifty feet.

To form the past perfect tense, use *had* with the past participle of the verb.

The Most Dangerous Game

◆ *Literature and Your Life*

CONNECT YOUR EXPERIENCE

Some competitions, like a one-on-one basketball game, can be relaxed and friendly. Others can be fierce. If one side takes the competition more seriously than the other, the situation can become unpleasant—or even dangerous. Sometimes, as in this story, a competition gets so intense, it becomes a life-or-death situation.

Journal Writing Describe the most memorable competitive situation you have ever experienced or seen. How did it make you feel?

THEMATIC FOCUS: IN SUSPENSE

Competition can sometimes be so intense that it frightens you. This suspenseful adventure story is sure to send shivers down your spine as you wonder whether the hero has what it takes to win a life-threating competition.

◆ Background for Understanding

CULTURE

Both of the main characters in this story are big-game hunters, people who enjoy hunting large wild animals, such as bears, for sport. For hunting enthusiasts, big-game hunting is the ultimate test of their skill, pitting them against large, often dangerous, animals in unfamiliar, exotic surroundings. In recent times, this sport has become the subject of controversy as populations of big-game animals have dwindled.

◆ Literary Focus

SUSPENSE

When you read a spine-tingling story, you just *have* to find out what happens next. This feeling of curiosity, uncertainty, even anxiety about the outcome of events is called **suspense**. Writers can create suspense by placing characters in tense, risky, or unpredictable situations. Often, writers provide hints about events to come while withholding enough information to keep readers guessing. As you read "The Most Dangerous Game," pay attention to the unsettling events and details that create suspense and look for clues to the story's outcome.

◆ Reading Strategy

CONTEXT CLUES

An author's choice of words can increase your enjoyment of a story by making people, places, and situations more vivid and lifelike. Occasionally, however, an author might select a word that is unfamiliar. Don't reach for the dictionary the minute you see an unfamiliar word. Often, you can determine its meaning from its **context**; that is, the words, phrases, and sentences that surround it. Try to use context clues to determine the meaning of the word *appraising* in this passage from "The Most Dangerous Game."

> . . . he found the general studying him, *appraising* him narrowly.

The key clue to the meaning of *appraising* is the word *studying*. From this context clue, you can guess that the word *appraising* is close in meaning to the word *studying*. You might then ask yourself why the general is studying the other man closely, and you could conclude that the general is trying to figure the man out, or is evaluating him. Thus the word *appraising* means "evaluating."

The Most Dangerous Game

Richard Connell

"Off there to the right—somewhere—is a large island," said Whitney. "It's rather a mystery—"

"What island is it?" Rainsford asked.

"The old charts call it 'Ship-Trap Island,'" Whitney replied. "A suggestive name, isn't it? Sailors have a curious dread of the place. I don't know why. Some superstition—"

"Can't see it," remarked Rainsford, trying to peer through the dank tropical night that was palpable as it pressed its thick warm blackness in upon the yacht.

"You've good eyes," said Whitney, with a laugh, "and I've seen you pick off a moose moving in the brown fall bush at four hundred yards, but even you can't see four miles or so through a moonless Caribbean[1] night."

"Not four yards," admitted Rainsford. "Ugh! It's like moist black velvet."

"It will be light in Rio," promised Whitney. "We should make it in a few days. I hope the jaguar guns have come from Purdey's. We should have some good hunting up the Amazon.[2] Great sport, hunting."

"The best sport in the world," agreed Rainsford.

"For the hunter," amended Whitney. "Not for the jaguar."

"Don't talk rot, Whitney," said Rainsford. "You're a big-game hunter, not a philosopher. Who cares how a jaguar feels?"

"Perhaps the jaguar does," observed Whitney.

---

1. **Caribbean** (kar´ ə bē´ ən): The Caribbean Sea, a part of the Atlantic Ocean, bounded by South America, Central America, and the West Indies.
2. **Amazon** (am´ ə zän´): Large river in South America.

◀ Critical Viewing How does this painting create a feeling of suspense? [Analyze]

◆ Build Vocabulary

palpable (pal´ pə bəl) *adj*.: Able to be touched or felt

Peering Through the Jungle, Larry Noble, Sal Barracca & Associates

"Bah! They've no understanding."

"Even so, I rather think they understand one thing—fear. The fear of pain and the fear of death."

"Nonsense," laughed Rainsford. "This hot weather is making you soft, Whitney. Be a realist. The world is made up of two classes—the hunters and the huntees. Luckily, you and I are the hunters. Do you think we've passed that island yet?"

"I can't tell in the dark. I hope so."

"Why?" asked Rainsford.

"The place has a reputation—a bad one."

"Cannibals?" suggested Rainsford.

"Hardly. Even cannibals wouldn't live in such a God-forsaken place. But it's gotten into sailor lore, somehow. Didn't you notice that the crew's nerves seemed a bit jumpy today?"

"They were a bit strange, now you mention it. Even Captain Nielsen—"

"Yes, even that tough-minded old Swede, who'd go up to the devil himself and ask him for a light. Those fishy blue eyes held a look I never saw there before. All I could get out of him was: 'This place has an evil name among sea-faring men, sir.' Then he said to me, very gravely: 'Don't you feel anything?'—as if the air about us was actually poisonous. Now, you mustn't laugh when I tell you this —I did feel something like a sudden chill.

"There was no breeze. The sea was as flat as a plate-glass window. We were drawing near the island then. What I felt was a—a mental chill; a sort of sudden dread."

"Pure imagination," said Rainsford. "One superstitious sailor can taint the whole ship's company with his fear."

"Maybe. But sometimes I think sailors have an extra sense that tells them when they are in danger. Sometimes I think evil is a tangible thing—with wave lengths, just as sound and light have. An evil place can, so to speak, broadcast vibrations of evil. Anyhow, I'm glad we're getting out of this zone. Well, I think I'll turn in now, Rainsford."

"I'm not sleepy," said Rainsford. "I'm going to smoke another pipe on the after deck."

"Good night, then, Rainsford. See you at breakfast."

"Right. Good night, Whitney."

There was no sound in the night as Rainsford sat there, but the muffled throb of the engine that drove the yacht swiftly through the darkness, and the swish and ripple of the wash of the propeller.

Rainsford, reclining in a steamer chair, indolently puffed on his favorite brier. The sensuous drowsiness of the night was on him. "It's so dark," he thought, "that I could sleep without closing my eyes; the night would be my eyelids—"

An abrupt sound startled him. Off to the right he heard it, and his ears, expert in such matters, could not be mistaken. Again he heard the sound, and again. Somewhere, off in the blackness, someone had fired a gun three times.

Rainsford sprang up and moved quickly to the rail, mystified. He strained his eyes in the direction from which the reports had come, but it was like trying to see through a blanket. He leaped upon the rail and balanced himself there, to get greater elevation; his pipe, striking a rope, was knocked from his mouth. He lunged for it; a short, hoarse cry came from his lips as he realized he had reached too far and had lost his balance. The cry was pinched off short as the blood-warm waters of the Caribbean Sea closed over his head.

He struggled up to the surface and tried to cry out, but the wash from the speeding yacht slapped him in the face and the salt water in his open mouth made him gag and strangle. Desperately he struck out with strong strokes after the receding lights of the yacht, but he stopped before he had swum fifty feet. A certain cool-headedness had come to him; it was not the first time he had been in a tight place. There was a chance that his cries could be heard by someone aboard the yacht, but that chance was

◆ **Build Vocabulary**

indolently (in´ də lənt lē) *adv.*: Lazily; idly

slender, and grew more slender as the yacht raced on. He wrestled himself out of his clothes, and shouted with all his power. The lights of the yacht became faint and ever-vanishing fireflies; then they were blotted out entirely by the night.

Rainsford remembered the shots. They had come from the right, and doggedly he swam in that direction, swimming with slow, deliberate strokes, conserving his strength. For a seemingly endless time he fought the sea. He began to count his strokes; he could do possibly a hundred more and then—

Rainsford heard a sound. It came out of the darkness, a high screaming sound, the sound of an animal in an extremity of anguish and terror.

He did not recognize the animal that made the sound; he did not try to; with fresh vitality he swam toward the sound. He heard it again; then it was cut short by another noise, crisp, staccato.

"Pistol shot," muttered Rainsford, swimming on.

Ten minutes of determined effort brought another sound to his ears—the most welcome he had ever heard—the muttering and growling of the sea breaking on a rocky shore. He was almost on the rocks before he saw them; on a night less calm he would have been shattered against them. With his remaining strength he dragged himself from the swirling waters. Jagged crags appeared to jut into the opaqueness, he forced himself upward, hand over hand. Gasping, his hands raw, he reached a flat place at the top. Dense jungle came down to the very edge of the cliffs. What perils that tangle of trees and underbrush might hold for him did not concern Rainsford just then. All he knew was that he was safe from his enemy, the sea, and that utter weariness was on him. He flung himself down at the jungle edge

Hat, Knife, and Gun in Woods, David Mann, Sal Barracca & Associates

▲ **Critical Viewing** Based on this painting, predict what is going to happen in the story. **[Predict]**

and tumbled headlong into the deepest sleep of his life.

When he opened his eyes he knew from the position of the sun that it was late in the afternoon. Sleep had given him new vigor; a sharp hunger was picking at him. He looked about him, almost cheerfully.

"Where there are pistol shots, there are men. Where there are men, there is food," he thought. But what kind of men, he wondered, in so forbidding a place? An unbroken front of snarled and ragged jungle fringed the shore.

He saw no sign of a trail through the closely knit web of weeds and trees; it was easier to go along the shore, and Rainsford floundered along by the water. Not far from where he had landed, he stopped.

Some wounded thing, by the evidence a large animal, had thrashed about in the underbrush; the jungle weeds were crushed down and the moss was lacerated; one patch of weeds was stained crimson. A small, glittering object not far away caught Rainsford's eye and he picked it up. It was an empty cartridge.

◆ **Reading Strategy**
What context clues would you use to determine the meaning of the word *lacerated*?

"A twenty-two," he remarked. "That's odd. It must have been a fairly large animal too. The hunter had his nerve with him to tackle it with a light gun. It's clear that the brute put up a fight. I suppose the first three shots I heard was

The menacing look in the eyes did not change. The revolver pointed as rigidly as if the giant were a statue.

when the hunter flushed his quarry[3] and wounded it. The last shot was when he trailed it here and finished it."

He examined the ground closely and found what he had hoped to find—the print of hunting boots. They pointed along the cliff in the direction he had been going. Eagerly he hurried along, now slipping on a rotten log or a loose stone, but making headway; night was beginning to settle down on the island.

Bleak darkness was blacking out the sea and jungle when Rainsford sighted the lights. He came upon them as he turned a crook in the coast line, and his first thought was that he had come upon a village, for there were many lights. But as he forged along he saw to his great astonishment that all the lights were in one enor-

mous building—a lofty structure with pointed towers plunging upward into the gloom. His eyes made out the shadowy outlines of a palatial château;[4] it was set on a high bluff, and on three sides of it cliffs dived down to where the sea licked greedy lips in the shadows.

"Mirage," thought Rainsford. But it was no mirage, he found, when he opened the tall spiked iron gate. The stone steps were real enough; the massive door with a leering gargoyle[5] for a knocker was real enough; yet about it all hung an air of unreality.

He lifted the knocker, and it creaked up stiffly, as if it had never before been used. He let it fall, and it startled him with its booming loudness. He thought he heard steps within; the door remained closed. Again Rainsford lifted the heavy knocker, and let it fall. The door opened then, opened as suddenly as if it were on a spring, and Rainsford stood blinking in the river of glaring gold light that poured out. The first thing Rainsford's eyes discerned was the largest man Rainsford had ever seen—a gigantic creature, solidly made and black-bearded to the waist. In his hand the man held a long-barreled revolver, and he was pointing it straight at Rainsford's heart.

Out of the snarl of beard two small eyes regarded Rainsford.

"Don't be alarmed," said Rainsford, with a smile which he hoped was disarming. "I'm no robber. I fell off a yacht. My name is Sanger Rainsford of New York City."

The menacing look in the eyes did not change. The revolver pointed as rigidly as if the giant were a statue. He gave no sign that he understood Rainsford's words, or that he had even heard them. He was dressed in uniform, a black uniform trimmed with gray astrakhan.[6]

"I'm Sanger Rainsford of New York," Rainsford began again. "I fell off a yacht. I am hungry."

---

3. **flushed his quarry** (kwôr´ ē): Drove his prey into the open.

4. **palatial château** (pə lā´ shəl sha tō´): A mansion as luxurious as a palace.

5. **gargoyle** (gär´ goil) *n*.: Strange and distorted animal form projecting from a building.

6. **astrakhan** (as´ trə kan´) *n*.: Fur made from young lambs.

The man's only answer was to raise with his thumb the hammer of his revolver. Then Rainsford saw the man's free hand go to his forehead in a military salute, and he saw him click his heels together and stand at attention. Another man was coming down the broad marble steps, an erect, slender man in evening clothes. He advanced to Rainsford and held out his hand.

In a cultivated voice marked by a slight accent that gave it added precision and deliberateness, he said: "It is a very great pleasure and honor to welcome Mr. Sanger Rainsford, the celebrated hunter, to my home."

Automatically Rainsford shook the man's hand.

"I've read your book about hunting snow leopards in Tibet, you see," explained the man. "I am General Zaroff."

Rainsford's first impression was that the man was singularly handsome; his second was that there was an original, almost bizarre quality about the general's face. He was a tall man past middle age, for his hair was a vivid white; but his thick eyebrows and pointed military mustache were as black as the night from which Rainsford had come. His eyes, too, were black and very bright. He had high cheek bones, a sharp-cut nose, a spare, dark face, the face of a man used to giving orders, the face of an aristocrat. Turning to the giant in uniform, the general made a sign. The giant put away his pistol, saluted, withdrew.

"Ivan is an incredibly strong fellow," remarked the general, "but he has the misfortune to be deaf and dumb. A simple fellow, but, I'm afraid, like all his race, a bit of a savage."

"Is he Russian?"

"He is a Cossack,"[7] said the general, and his smile showed red lips and pointed teeth. "So am I."

"Come," he said, "we shouldn't be chatting here. We can talk later. Now you want clothes, food, rest. You shall have them. This is a most restful spot."

Ivan had reappeared, and the general spoke to him with lips that moved but gave forth no sound.

"Follow Ivan, if you please, Mr. Rainsford," said the general. "I was about to have my dinner when you came. I'll wait for you. You'll find that my clothes will fit you, I think."

It was to a huge, beam-ceilinged bedroom with a canopied bed big enough for six men that Rainsford followed the silent giant. Ivan laid out an evening suit, and Rainsford, as he put it on, noticed that it came from a London tailor who ordinarily cut and sewed for none below the rank of duke.

The dining room to which Ivan conducted him was in many ways remarkable. There was a medieval magnificence about it; it suggested a baronial hall of feudal times with its oaken panels, its high ceiling, its vast refectory table where twoscore men could sit down to eat. About the hall were the mounted heads of many animals—lions, tigers, elephants, moose, bears; larger or more perfect specimens Rainsford had never seen. At the great table the general was sitting, alone.

"You'll have a cocktail, Mr. Rainsford," he suggested. The cocktail was surpassingly good; and, Rainsford noted, the table appointments were of the finest—the linen, the crystal, the silver, the china.

They were eating *borsch*, the rich, red soup with whipped cream so dear to Russian palates. Half apologetically General Zaroff said: "We do our best to preserve the amenities of civilization here. Please forgive any lapses. We are well off the beaten track, you know. Do you think the champagne has suffered from its long ocean trip?"

"Not in the least," declared Rainsford. He was

◆ Literary Focus
What is your impression of the general? Can he be trusted?

◆ Reading Strategy
How can you use context clues to determine the meaning of *amenities*?

---

7. **Cossack** (käs´ ak): Member of a people from southern Russia, famous for their fierceness.

◆ **Build Vocabulary**

bizarre (bi zär´) *adj.*: Odd in appearance

finding the general a most thoughtful and affable host, a true cosmopolite.[8] But there was one small trait of the general's that made Rainsford uncomfortable. Whenever he looked up from his plate he found the general studying him, appraising him narrowly.

"Perhaps," said General Zaroff, "you were surprised that I recognized your name. You see, I read all books on hunting published in English, French, and Russian. I have but one passion in my life, Mr. Rainsford, and it is the hunt."

"You have some wonderful heads here," said Rainsford as he ate a particularly well cooked filet mignon. "That Cape buffalo is the largest I ever saw."

"Oh, that fellow. Yes, he was a monster."

"Did he charge you?"

"Hurled me against a tree," said the general. "Fractured my skull. But I got the brute."

"I've always thought," said Rainsford, "that the Cape buffalo is the most dangerous of all big game."

For a moment the general did not reply; he was smiling his curious red-lipped smile. Then he said slowly: "No. You are wrong, sir. The Cape buffalo is not the most dangerous big game." He sipped his wine. "Here in my preserve on this island," he said in the same slow tone, "I hunt more dangerous game."

Rainsford expressed his surprise. "Is there big game on this island?"

The general nodded. "The biggest."

"Really?"

"Oh, it isn't here naturally, of course. I have to stock the island."

"What have you imported, general?" Rainsford asked. "Tigers?"

The general smiled. "No," he said. "Hunting tigers ceased to interest me some years ago. I exhausted their possibilities, you see. No thrill left in tigers, no real danger. I live for danger, Mr. Rainsford."

The general took from his pocket a gold cigarette case and offered his guest a long black cigarette with a silver tip; it was perfumed and gave off a smell like incense.

"We will have some capital hunting, you and I," said the general. "I shall be most glad to have your society."

"I have hunted every kind of game in every land. It would be impossible for me to tell you how many animals I have killed."

"But what game—" began Rainsford.

"I'll tell you," said the general. "You will be amused, I know. I think I may say, in all modesty, that I have done a rare thing. I have invented a new sensation. May I pour you another glass of port, Mr. Rainsford?"

"Thank you, general."

The general filled both glasses, and said: "God makes some men poets. Some He makes kings, some beggars. Me He made a hunter. My hand was made for the trigger, my father said. He was a very rich man with a quarter of a million acres in the Crimea,[9] and he was an ardent sportsman. When I was only five years old he gave me a little gun, specially made in Moscow for me, to shoot sparrows with. When I shot some of his prize turkeys with it, he did not punish me; he complimented me on my marksmanship. I killed my first bear in the Caucasus[10] when I was ten. My whole life has been one prolonged hunt. I went into the army—it was expected of noblemen's sons—and for a time commanded a division of Cossack cavalry, but my real interest was always the hunt. I have hunted every kind of game in every land. It would be impossible for me to tell you how many animals I have killed."

---

8. **cosmopolite** (käz mäp´ ə līt´) n.: Person at home in all parts of the world.

9. **Crimea** (krī mē´ ə): Region in southwestern Russia on the Black Sea.

10. **Caucasus** (kô´ kə səs): Mountain range in southern Russia.

The general puffed at his cigarette.

"After the debacle[11] in Russia I left the country, for it was imprudent for an officer of the Czar to stay there. Many noble Russians lost everything. I, luckily, had invested heavily in American securities, so I shall never have to open a tea room in Monte Carlo or drive a taxi in Paris. Naturally, I continued to hunt—grizzlies in your Rockies, crocodiles in the Ganges, rhinoceroses in East Africa. It was in Africa that the Cape buffalo hit me and laid me up for six months. As soon as I recovered I started for the Amazon to hunt jaguars, for I had heard they were unusually cunning. They weren't." The Cossack sighed. "They were no match at all for a hunter with his wits about him, and a high-powered rifle. I was bitterly disappointed. I was lying in my tent with a splitting headache one night when a terrible thought pushed its way into my mind. Hunting was beginning to bore me! And hunting, remember, had been my life. I have heard that in America business men often go to pieces when they give up the business that has been their life."

"Yes, that's so," said Rainsford.

The general smiled. "I had no wish to go to pieces," he said. "I must do something. Now, mine is an analytical mind, Mr. Rainsford. Doubtless that is why I enjoy the problems of the chase."

"No doubt, General Zaroff."

"So," continued the general, "I asked myself why the hunt no longer fascinated me. You are much younger than I am, Mr. Rainsford, and have not hunted as much, but you perhaps can guess the answer."

"What was it?"

"Simply this: hunting had ceased to be what you call 'a sporting proposition.' It had become too easy. I always got my quarry. Always. There is no greater bore than perfection."

The general lit a fresh cigarette.

"No animal had a chance with me any more. That is no boast; it is a mathematical certainty. The animal had nothing but his legs and his

---

11. **debacle** (di bäk´ əl) n.: Bad defeat—Zaroff is referring to the Russian Revolution of 1917, a defeat for upper-class Russians like himself.

instinct. Instinct is no match for reason. When I thought of this it was a tragic moment for me, I can tell you."

Rainsford leaned across the table, absorbed in what his host was saying.

"It came to me as an inspiration what I must do," the general went on.

"And that was?"

The general smiled the quiet smile of one who has faced an obstacle and surmounted it with success. "I had to invent a new animal to hunt," he said.

"A new animal? You're joking."

"Not at all," said the general. "I never joke about hunting. I needed a new animal. I found one. So I bought this island, built this house, and here I do my hunting. The island is perfect for my purpose—there are jungles with a maze of trails in them, hills, swamps—"

"But the animal, General Zaroff?"

"Oh," said the general, "it supplies me with the most exciting hunting in the world. No other hunting compares with it for an instant. Every day I hunt, and I never grow bored now, for I have a quarry with which I can match my wits."

◆ Literary Focus
Predict what Zaroff is going to identify as the "most dangerous game."

Rainsford's bewilderment showed in his face.

"I wanted the ideal animal to hunt," explained the general. "So I said: 'What are the attributes of an ideal quarry?' And the answer was, of course: 'It must have courage, cunning, and, above all, it must be able to reason.' "

"But no animal can reason," objected Rainsford.

"My dear fellow," said the general, "there is one that can."

"But you can't mean—" gasped Rainsford.

"And why not?"

"I can't believe you are serious, General Zaroff. This is a grisly joke."

"Why should I not be serious? I am speaking of hunting."

"Hunting? General Zaroff, what you speak of is murder."

The general laughed with entire good nature. He regarded Rainsford quizzically. "I refuse to believe that so modern and civilized a young man as you seem to be harbors romantic ideas about the value of human life. Surely your experiences in the war—"

"Did not make me condone cold-blooded murder," finished Rainsford stiffly.

Laughter shook the general. "How extraordinarily droll you are!" he said. "One does not expect nowadays to find a young man of the educated class, even in America, with such a naive, and, if I may say so, mid-Victorian point of view.[12] It's like finding a snuff-box in a limousine. Ah, well, doubtless you had Puritan ancestors. So many Americans appear to have had. I'll wager you'll forget your notions when you go hunting with me. You've a genuine new thrill in store for you, Mr. Rainsford."

"Thank you, I'm a hunter, not a murderer."

"Dear me," said the general, quite unruffled, "again that unpleasant word. But I think I can show you that your scruples are quite ill founded."

"Yes?"

"Life is for the strong, to be lived by the strong, and, if need be, taken by the strong. The weak of the world were put here to give the strong pleasure. I am strong. Why should I not use my gift? If I wish to hunt, why should I not? I hunt the scum of the earth—sailors from tramp ships—lascars,[13] blacks, Chinese, whites, mongrels—a thoroughbred horse or hound is worth more than a score of them."

"But they are men," said Rainsford hotly.

"Precisely," said the general. "That is why I use them. It gives me pleasure. They can reason, after a fashion. So they are dangerous."

"But where do you get them?"

The general's left eyelid fluttered down in a wink. "This island is called Ship-Trap," he

▲ **Critical Viewing** What might it be like to hunt in an environment such as the one pictured here? **[Speculate]**

answered. "Sometimes an angry god of the high seas sends them to me. Sometimes, when Providence is not so kind, I help Providence a bit. Come to the window with me."

Rainsford went to the window and looked out toward the sea.

"Watch! Out there!" exclaimed the general, pointing into the night. Rainsford's eyes saw only blackness, and then, as the general pressed a button, far out to sea Rainsford saw the flash of lights.

The general chuckled. "They indicate a channel," he said, "where there's none: giant rocks with razor edges crouch like a sea monster with wide-open jaws. They can crush a ship as easily as I crush this nut." He dropped a walnut on the hardwood floor and brought his heel grinding down on it. "Oh, yes," he said, casually, as if in answer to a question, "I have electricity. We try to be civilized here."

"Civilized? And you shoot down men?"

A trace of anger was in the general's black

---

12. mid-Victorian point of view: A point of view emphasizing proper behavior and associated with the time of Queen Victoria of England (1819–1901).
13. lascars (las´ kərz) *n.*: Oriental sailors, especially natives of India.

◆ **Build Vocabulary**

naive (nä ēv´) *adj.*: Unsophisticated

scruples (scroo´ pəlz) *n.*: Misgivings about something one feels is wrong

♦ Literary Focus

How are Rainsford's remarks affecting the general? How might this affect future events?

eyes, but it was there for but a second, and he said, in his most pleasant manner: "Dear me, what a righteous young man you are! I assure you I do not do the thing you suggest. That would be barbarous. I treat these visitors with every consideration. They get plenty of good food and exercise. They get into splendid physical condition. You shall see for yourself tomorrow."

"What do you mean?"

"We'll visit my training school," smiled the general. "It's in the cellar. I have about a dozen pupils down there now. They're from the Spanish bark San Lucar that had the bad luck to go on the rocks out there. A very inferior lot, I regret to say. Poor specimens and more accustomed to the deck than to the jungle."

He raised his hand, and Ivan, who served as waiter, brought thick Turkish coffee. Rainsford, with an effort, held his tongue in check.

"It's a game, you see," pursued the general blandly. "I suggest to one of them that we go hunting. I give him a supply of food and an excellent hunting knife. I give him three hours'

He need not play the game if he doesn't wish to. If he does not wish to hunt, I turn him over to Ivan.

start. I am to follow, armed only with a pistol of the smallest caliber and range. If my quarry eludes me for three whole days, he wins the game. If I find him"—the general smiled—"he loses."

"Suppose he refuses to be hunted?"

"Oh," said the general, "I give him his option, of course. He need not play the game if he doesn't wish to. If he does not wish to hunt, I turn him over to Ivan. Ivan once had the honor of serving as official knouter[14] to the Great

White Czar, and he has his own ideas of sport. Invariably, Mr. Rainsford, invariably they choose the hunt."

"And if they win?"

The smile on the general's face widened. "To date I have not lost," he said.

Then he added, hastily: "I don't wish you to think me a braggart, Mr. Rainsford. Many of them afford only the most elementary sort of problem. Occasionally I strike a tartar.[15] One almost did win. I eventually had to use the dogs."

"The dogs?"

"This way, please. I'll show you."

The general steered Rainsford to a window. The lights from the windows sent a flickering illumination that made grotesque patterns on the courtyard below, and Rainsford could see moving about there a dozen or so huge black shapes; as they turned toward him, their eyes glittered greenly.

"A rather good lot, I think," observed the general. "They are let out at seven every night. If anyone should try to get into my house—or out of it—something extremely regrettable would occur to him." He hummed a snatch of song from the Folies Bergère.[16]

"And now," said the general, "I want to show you my new collection of heads. Will you come with me to the library?"

"I hope," said Rainsford, "that you will excuse me tonight, General Zaroff. I'm really not feeling at all well."

"Ah, indeed?" the general inquired solicitously. "Well, I suppose that's only natural, after your long swim. You need a good, restful night's sleep. Tomorrow you'll feel like a new man, I'll wager. Then we'll hunt, eh? I've one rather promising prospect—"

---

14. **knouter** (nout′ ər) n.: Someone who beats criminals with a leather whip, or knout.
15. **tartar** (tär′ tər) n.: Stubborn, violent person.
16. **Folies Bergère** (fô lē ber zhär′): Musical theater in Paris.

♦ **Build Vocabulary**

blandly (bland′ lē) adv.: In a mild and soothing manner

grotesque (grō tesk′) adj.: Having a strange, bizarre design

Rainsford was hurrying from the room.

"Sorry you can't go with me tonight," called the general. "I expect rather fair sport—a big, strong black. He looks resourceful—Well good night, Mr. Rainsford; I hope you have a good night's rest."

The bed was good, and the pajamas of the softest silk, and he was tired in every fiber of his being, but nevertheless Rainsford could not quiet his brain with the opiate of sleep. He lay, eyes wide open. Once he thought he heard stealthy steps in the corridor outside his room. He sought to throw open the door; it would not open. He went to the window and looked out. His room was high up in one of the towers. The lights of the château were out now, and it was dark and silent, but there was a fragment of sallow moon, and by its wan light he could see, dimly, the courtyard; there, weaving in and out in the pattern of shadow, were black, noiseless forms; the hounds heard him at the window and looked up, expectantly, with their green eyes. Rainsford went back to the bed and lay down. By many methods he tried to put himself to sleep. He had achieved a doze when, just as morning began to come, he heard, far off in the jungle, the faint report of a pistol.

General Zaroff did not appear until luncheon. He was dressed faultlessly in the tweeds of a country squire. He was solicitous about the state of Rainsford's health.

"As for me," sighed the general, "I do not feel so well. I am worried, Mr. Rainsford. Last night I detected traces of my old complaint."

To Rainsford's questioning glance the general said: "Ennui. Boredom."

Then, taking a second helping of crêpes suzette, the general explained: "The hunting was not good last night. The fellow lost his head. He made a straight trail that offered no problems at all. That's the trouble with these sailors; they have dull brains to begin with, and they do not know how to get about in the woods. They do excessively stupid and obvious things. It's most annoying. Will you have another glass of Chablis, Mr. Rainsford?"

"General," said Rainsford firmly, "I wish to leave this island at once."

He nodded toward the corner to where the giant stood, scowling, his thick arms crossed on his hogshead of chest.

The general raised his thickets of eyebrows; he seemed hurt. "But, my dear fellow," the general protested, "you've only just come. You've had no hunting—"

"I wish to go today," said Rainsford. He saw the dead black eyes of the general on him, studying him. General Zaroff's face suddenly brightened.

He filled Rainsford's glass with venerable Chablis from a dusty bottle.

◆ Literary Focus
What idea has just come to Zaroff's mind?

"Tonight," said the general, "we will hunt—you and I."

Rainsford shook his head. "No, general," he said. "I will not hunt."

The general shrugged his shoulders and delicately ate a hothouse grape. "As you wish, my friend," he said. "The choice rests entirely with you. But may I not venture to suggest that you will find my idea of sport more diverting than Ivan's?"

He nodded toward the corner to where the giant stood, scowling, his thick arms crossed on his hogshead of chest.

"You don't mean—" cried Rainsford.

"My dear fellow," said the general, "have I not told you I always mean what I say about hunting? This is really an inspiration. I drink to a foeman worthy of my steel—at last."

The general raised his glass, but Rainsford sat staring at him.

"You'll find this game worth playing," the general said enthusiastically. "Your brain against mine. Your woodcraft against mine. Your strength and stamina against mine. Outdoor chess! And the stake is not without value, eh?"

"And if I win—" began Rainsford huskily.

"I'll cheerfully acknowledge myself defeated if I do not find you by midnight of the third day," said General Zaroff. "My sloop will place you on the mainland near a town."

The general read what Rainsford was thinking.

"Oh, you can trust me," said the Cossack. "I will give you my word as a gentleman and a sportsman. Of course you, in turn, must agree to say nothing of your visit here."

"I'll agree to nothing of the kind," said Rainsford.

"Oh," said the general, "in that case— But why discuss that now? Three days hence we can discuss it over a bottle of Veuve Cliquot, unless—"

The general sipped his wine.

Then a businesslike air animated him. "Ivan," he said to Rainsford, "will supply you with hunting clothes, food, a knife. I suggest you wear moccasins; they leave a poorer trail. I suggest too that you avoid the big swamp in the southeast corner of the island. We call it Death Swamp. There's quicksand there. One foolish fellow tried it. The deplorable part of it was that Lazarus followed him. You can imagine my feelings, Mr. Rainsford. I loved Lazarus; he was the finest hound in my pack. Well, I must beg you to excuse me now. I always take a siesta after lunch. You'll hardly have time for a nap, I fear. You'll want to start, no doubt. I shall not follow till dusk. Hunting at night is so much more exciting than by day, don't you think? Au revoir,[17] Mr. Rainsford, au revoir."

General Zaroff, with a deep, courtly bow, strolled from the room.

From another door came Ivan. Under one arm he carried khaki hunting clothes, a haversack of food, a leather sheath containing a long-bladed hunting knife; his right hand rested on a cocked revolver thrust in the crimson sash about his waist. . . .

Rainsford had fought his way through the bush for two hours. "I must keep my nerve. I must keep my nerve," he said through tight teeth.

He had not been entirely clear-headed when the château gates snapped shut behind him. His whole idea at first was to put distance between himself and General Zaroff, and, to this end, he had plunged along, spurred on by the sharp rowels of something very like panic. Now he had got a grip on himself, had stopped, and was taking stock of himself and the situation.

He saw that straight flight was futile; inevitably it would bring him face to face with the sea. He was in a picture with a frame of water, and his operations, clearly, must take place within that frame.

"I'll give him a trail to follow," muttered Rainsford, and he struck off from the rude paths he had been following into the trackless wilderness. He executed a series of intricate loops; he doubled on his trail again and again, recalling all the lore of the fox hunt, and all the dodges of the fox. Night found him leg-weary, with his hands and face lashed by the branches, on a thickly wooded ridge. He knew it would be insane to blunder on through the dark, even if he had the strength. His need for rest was imperative and he thought: "I have played the fox, now I must play the cat of the fable." A big tree with a thick trunk and outspread branches was nearby, and, taking care to leave not the slightest mark, he climbed up into the crotch, and stretching out on one of the broad limbs, after a fashion, rested. Rest brought him new confidence and almost a feeling of security. Even so zealous a hunter as General Zaroff could not trace him there, he told himself; only the devil himself could follow that complicated trail through the jungle after dark. But, perhaps, the general was a devil—

An apprehensive night crawled slowly by like a wounded snake, and sleep did not visit Rainsford, although the silence of a dead world was on the jungle. Toward morning when a dingy gray was varnishing the sky, the cry of some startled bird focused Rainsford's attention in

---

17. **au revoir** (ō´ rə vwär´): French for "until we meet again."

◆ **Build Vocabulary**

futile (fyōōt´ əl) adj.: Useless; hopeless

that direction. Something was coming through the bush, coming slowly, carefully, coming by the same winding way Rainsford had come. He flattened himself down on the limb, and through a screen of leaves almost as thick as tapestry, he watched. The thing that was approaching was a man.

It was General Zaroff. He made his way along with his eyes fixed in utmost concentration on the ground before him. He paused, almost beneath the tree, dropped to his knees and studied the ground. Rainsford's impulse was to hurl himself down like a panther, but he saw the general's right hand held something metallic—a small automatic pistol.

The hunter shook his head several times, as if he were puzzled. Then he straightened up and took from his case one of his black cigarettes; its pungent incense-like smoke floated up to Rainsford's nostrils.

> # Something was coming through the bush, coming slowly, carefully, coming by the same winding way Rainsford had come.

Rainsford held his breath. The general's eyes had left the ground and were traveling inch by inch up the tree. Rainsford froze there, every muscle tensed for a spring. But the sharp eyes of the hunter stopped before they reached the limb where Rainsford lay; a smile spread over his brown face. Very deliberately he blew a smoke ring into the air; then he turned his back on the tree and walked carelessly away, back along the trail he had come. The swish of the underbrush against his hunting boots grew fainter and fainter.

The pent-up air burst hotly from Rainsford's lungs. His first thought made him feel sick and numb. The general could follow a trail through the woods at night; he could follow an extremely difficult trail; he must have uncanny powers;

only by the merest chance had the Cossack failed to see his quarry.

Rainsford's second thought was even more terrible. It sent a shudder of cold horror through his whole being. Why had the general smiled? Why had he turned back?

Rainsford did not want to believe what his reason told him was true, but the truth was as evident as the sun that had by now pushed through the morning mists. The general was playing with him! The general was saving him for another day's sport! The Cossack was the cat; he was the mouse. Then it was that Rainsford knew the full meaning of terror.

"I will not lose my nerve. I will not."

He slid down from the tree, and struck off again into the woods. His face was set and he forced the machinery of his mind to function. Three hundred yards from his hiding place he stopped where a huge dead tree leaned precariously on a smaller, living one. Throwing off his sack of food, Rainsford took his knife from its sheath and began to work with all his energy.

The job was finished at last, and he threw himself down behind a fallen log a hundred feet away. He did not have to wait long. The cat was coming again to play with the mouse.

Following the trail with the sureness of a bloodhound, came General Zaroff. Nothing escaped those searching black eyes, no crushed blade of grass, no bent twig, no mark, no matter how faint, in the moss. So intent was the Cossack on his stalking that he was upon the thing Rainsford had made before he saw it. His foot touched the protruding bough that was the trigger. Even as he touched it, the general sensed his danger and leaped back with the agility of an ape. But he was not quite quick enough; the dead tree, delicately adjusted to rest on the cut living one, crashed down and struck the general a glancing blow on the shoulder as it fell; but for his alertness, he must have been smashed beneath it. He staggered, but he did not fall; nor

> ◆ *Literature and Your Life*
> Relate Rainsford's feelings to your own experiences of playing a game with someone who is much better at it than you are.

did he drop his revolver. He stood there, rubbing his injured shoulder, and Rainsford, with fear again gripping his heart, heard the general's mocking laugh ring through the jungle.

"Rainsford," called the general, "if you are within the sound of my voice, as I suppose you are, let me congratulate you. Not many men know how to make a Malay mancatcher. Luckily, for me, I too have hunted in Malacca. You are proving interesting, Mr. Rainsford. I am going now to have my wound dressed; it's only a slight one. But I shall be back. I shall be back."

When the general, nursing his bruised shoulder, had gone, Rainsford took up his flight again. It was flight now, a desperate, hopeless flight, that carried him on for some hours. Dusk came, then darkness, and still he pressed on. The ground grew softer under his moccasins; the vegetation grew ranker, denser; insects bit him savagely. Then, as he stepped forward, his foot sank into the ooze. He tried to wrench it back, but the muck sucked viciously at his foot as if it were a giant leech. With a violent effort, he tore his foot loose. He knew where he was now. Death Swamp and its quicksand.

His hands were tight closed as if his nerve were something tangible that some one in the darkness was trying to tear from his grip. The softness of the earth had given him an idea. He stepped back from the quicksand a dozen feet or so, and, like some huge prehistoric beaver, he began to dig.

Rainsford had dug himself in in France[18] when a second's delay meant death. That had been a placid pastime compared to his digging now. The pit grew deeper; when it was above his shoulders, he climbed out and from some hard saplings cut stakes and sharpened them to a fine point. These stakes he planted in the bottom of the pit with the points sticking up. With flying fingers he wove a rough carpet of weeds and branches and with it he covered the mouth of the pit. Then, wet with sweat and aching with tiredness, he crouched behind the stump of a lightning-charred tree.

He knew his pursuer was coming; he heard the padding sound of feet on the soft earth, and the night breeze brought him the perfume of the general's cigarette. It seemed to Rainsford that the general was coming with unusual swiftness; he was not feeling his way along, foot by foot. Rainsford, crouching there, could not see the general, nor could he see the pit. He lived a year in a minute. Then he felt an impulse to cry aloud with joy, for he heard the sharp crackle of the breaking branches as the cover of the pit gave way; he heard the sharp scream of pain as the pointed stakes found their mark. He leaped up from his place of concealment. Then he cowered back. Three feet from the pit a man was standing, with an electric torch in his hand.

◆ Literary Focus
How does Rainsford feel after his efforts? How does this passage make you, the reader, feel?

His hands were tight closed as if his nerve were something tangible that some one in the darkness was trying to tear from his grip.

"You've done well, Rainsford," the voice of the general called. "Your Burmese tiger pit has claimed one of my best dogs. Again you score. I think, Mr. Rainsford, I'll see what you can do against my whole pack. I'm going home for a rest now. Thank you for a most amusing evening."

At daybreak Rainsford, lying near the swamp, was awakened by a sound that made him know that he had new things to learn about fear. It was a distant sound, faint and wavering, but he knew it. It was the baying of a pack of hounds.

Rainsford knew he could do one of two things. He could stay where he was and wait. That was suicide. He could flee. That was postponing the inevitable. For a moment he stood

---

18. **dug himself in in France:** Had dug a foxhole to protect himself during World War I.

there, thinking. An idea that held a wild chance came to him, and, tightening his belt, he headed away from the swamp.

The baying of the hounds drew nearer, then still nearer, nearer, ever nearer. On a ridge Rainsford climbed a tree. Down a watercourse, not a quarter of a mile away, he could see the bush moving. Straining his eyes, he saw the lean figure of General Zaroff; just ahead of him Rainsford made out another figure whose wide shoulders surged through the tall jungle weeds; it was the giant Ivan, and he seemed pulled forward by some unseen force; Rainsford knew that Ivan must be holding the pack in leash.

They would be on him any minute now. His mind worked frantically. He thought of a native trick he had learned in Uganda. He slid down the tree. He caught hold of a springy young sapling and to it he fastened his hunting knife, with the blade pointing down the trail; with a bit of wild grapevine he tied back the sapling. Then he ran for his life. The hounds raised their voices as they hit the fresh scent. Rainsford knew now how an animal at bay feels.

▲ **Critical Viewing** Imagine Rainsford at the edge of the cliff. What will result from his leaping into the crashing waves? **[Speculate]**

He had to stop to get his breath. The baying of the hounds stopped abruptly, and Rainsford's heart stopped too. They must have reached the knife.

He shinnied excitedly up a tree and looked back. His pursuers had stopped. But the hope that was in Rainsford's brain when he climbed died, for he saw in the shallow valley that General Zaroff was still on his feet. But Ivan was not. The knife, driven by the recoil of the springing tree, had not wholly failed.

"Nerve, nerve, nerve!" he panted, as he dashed along. A blue gap showed between the trees dead ahead. Ever nearer drew the hounds. Rainsford forced himself on toward that gap. He reached it. It was the shore of the sea. Across a cove he could see the gloomy gray stone of the château. Twenty feet below him the sea rumbled and hissed. Rainsford hesitated. He heard the hounds. Then he leaped far out into the sea. . . .

When the general and his pack reached the place by the sea, the Cossack stopped. For some minutes he stood regarding the blue-green expanse of water. He shrugged his shoulders. Then he sat down, took a drink of brandy from a silver flask, lit a perfumed cigarette, and hummed a bit from *Madame Butterfly*.[19]

General Zaroff had an exceedingly good dinner in his great paneled dining hall that evening. With it he had a bottle of Pol Roger and half a bottle of Chambertin. Two slight annoyances kept him from perfect enjoyment. One was the thought that it would be difficult to replace Ivan; the other was that his quarry had escaped him; of course the American hadn't played the game—so thought the general as he tasted his after-dinner liqueur. In his library he read, to soothe himself, from the works of Marcus Aurelius.[20] At ten he went up to his bedroom. He was deliciously tired, he said to himself,

as he locked himself in. There was a little moonlight, so, before turning on his light, he went to the window and looked down at the courtyard. He could see the great hounds, and he called: "Better luck another time," to them. Then he switched on the light.

A man, who had been hiding in the curtain of the bed, was standing there.

"Rainsford!" screamed the general. "How in God's name did you get here?"

"Swam," said Rainsford. "I found it quicker than walking through the jungle."

The general sucked in his breath and smiled. "I congratulate you," he said. "You have won the game."

Rainsford did not smile. "I am still a beast at bay," he said, in a low, hoarse voice. "Get ready, General Zaroff."

The general made one of his deepest bows. "I see," he said. "Splendid! One of us is to furnish a repast for the hounds. The other will sleep in this very excellent bed. On guard, Rainsford. . . ."

He had never slept in a better bed, Rainsford decided.

---

19. ***Madame Butterfly:*** An opera by Giacomo Puccini.
20. **Marcus Aurelius** (ô rē´ lē əs): Roman emperor and philosopher (A.D. 121–180).

Guide for Responding

◆ *Literature and Your Life*

Reader's Response What do you admire about Rainsford? What don't you admire? Why?

Thematic Focus Sometimes, as in this story, competition is too intense. What are some of the potential consequences (aside from the ones in this story) of a competition that gets too fierce?

Group Discussion Discuss with a group what you can learn from this story about competition.

☑ Check Your Comprehension

1. How does Rainsford come to Ship-Trap Island?
2. What, according to Zaroff, is the most dangerous game? Why?
3. Explain how Zaroff's treatment of Rainsford changes during the course of the story.
4. Describe three of the tricks Rainsford uses to elude Zaroff. What is the outcome of each trick?
5. Why does Zaroff think that Rainsford "hasn't played the game"?

Guide for Responding *(continued)*

◆ Critical Thinking

INTERPRET

1. Is Zaroff "civilized"? Why or why not? **[Analyze]**
2. Why does Rainsford call himself "a beast at bay"? **[Infer]**
3. How does Rainsford's attitude toward hunting compare with Zaroff's? **[Compare and Contrast]**
4. How does this experience change Rainsford? Explain. **[Analyze]**

APPLY

5. Do you think that Rainsford will continue to hunt? Why or why not? **[Hypothesize]**

EXTEND

6. What kind of careers, other than hunter, would be good for someone with Rainsford's skills and attitudes? **[Career Link]**

◆ Reading Strategy

CONTEXT CLUES

For each passage from the story, give the meaning of the italicized word and explain what **context clues** helped you determine its meaning.

1. He heard [the sound] again; then it was cut short by another noise, crisp, *staccato*.
   "Pistol shot," muttered Rainsford, swimming on.
2. To Rainsford's questioning glance the general said: "*Ennui*. Boredom."

◆ Literary Focus

SUSPENSE

Richard Connell builds **suspense**—uncertainty and excitement about the outcome of events—by placing Rainsford in a dangerous, unpredictable situation and by hinting at events to come.

1. Find three details from the beginning of the story that provide clues about Zaroff's hobby. Explain how these clues help create suspense.
2. How does the description of Rainsford's first night in the château create a sense of dread?
3. What are the three most suspenseful events that occur? Explain how these incidents build on one another to create mounting tension.

◆ Build Vocabulary

RELATED WORDS: FORMS OF *SCRUPLES*

Considering forms of the word *scruples*, answer these questions.

1. What word would describe a person who does *not* feel misgivings about doing things others consider wrong?
2. Which character in this story would you describe with this word?

USING THE WORD BANK

In your notebook, complete each sentence with a word from the Word Bank.

1. The farmer was ___?___ about big-city ways.
2. "Surrender now," commanded the conquering general. "Resistance is ___?___."
3. The silence was so ___?___ she thought she could cut it with a knife.
4. He sprawled on the couch ___?___, munching popcorn and watching television.
5. They met under rather ___?___ circumstances at an auction of used camels.
6. With its fangs and twisted features, the mask was amazingly ___?___.
7. The customer service agent learned to phrase his sentences ___?___, to avoid making angry people even more upset.
8. She had her ___?___ and would not give in to peer pressure.

◆ Build Grammar Skills

PAST AND PAST PERFECT TENSES

The **past tense** of a verb, usually formed by adding -d or -ed to the present form, shows an action completed in the past. The **past perfect tense,** formed with *had* before the past participle, shows an action completed in the past before another action in the past.

Practice In your notebook, write the following sentences, underlining the verbs. Label each verb as past or past perfect.

1. When he opened his eyes ... sleep had given him new vigor.
2. He had achieved a doze when ... he heard ... the faint report of a pistol.
3. The softness of the earth had given him an idea. He stepped back from the quicksand ...

Build Your Portfolio

 Idea Bank

Writing

1. **Review** Write a review of "The Most Dangerous Game," summarizing the story and explaining why you liked or disliked it.

2. **Persuasive Essay** Prepare a persuasive essay either for or against hunting. Support your ideas with specific details.

3. **Movie Script** Select a scene from the story and write a movie script for it. Include detailed camera instructions and descriptions of the set as well as information on the characters' actions and dialogue. **[Media Link]**

Speaking and Listening

4. **Interview** With a partner, role-play an interview between Rainsford and a reporter. Ask questions that will get Rainsford to describe his experiences on Ship-Trap Island as fully as possible. **[Career Link]**

5. **Trial** With a group of classmates, put Rainsford on trial for killing General Zaroff. Decide who will play Rainsford, the judge, defense attorneys, and prosecutors. After each side presents its case, your classmates should decide whether Rainsford is guilty. **[Career Link]**

Projects

6. **Video Game Design** Imagine that you have been commissioned to design a video game based on this story. Write a cover sheet in which you describe the game and give it a name. Then present a series of sketches showing what the game will look like and how it will be played. **[Technology Link]**

7. **Technical Diagrams** Draw detailed, labeled diagrams of one or more of the traps Rainsford created. Your diagrams should show how the trap is constructed and how it works. **[Art Link]**

 Writing Mini-Lesson

Survival Manual

Rainsford triumphs because he has the knowledge he needs to survive. Put yourself in Rainsford's place and create a set of detailed instructions on how to survive a ruthless pursuer.

Writing Skills Focus:
Anticipate Readers' Questions

When writing any type of how-to instructions, you need to **anticipate readers' questions**. Think of questions readers are likely to have about your topic, then provide answers to these questions. For example, notice how Richard Connell anticipates the following questions in his description of a tiger trap: *How deep should the pit be? What is used to make the stakes? How are the stakes positioned in the pit?*

Model From the Story

The pit grew deeper; when it was above his shoulders, he climbed out and from some hard saplings cut stakes and sharpened them to a fine point. These stakes he planted in the bottom of the pit with the points sticking up.

Prewriting Review the story and note the techniques Rainsford uses. Consider what questions readers might have about the techniques and add details that would answer these questions. Then arrange your notes into a logical order that will be easy for readers to follow.

Drafting Using your notes, write a first draft of your survival manual. Ask questions you would expect from readers and add details to help answer these questions.

Revising Review your draft. Try to follow each of the instructions you've provided. For example, if you've described how to create a trap, try drawing the trap based on your instructions. Add any necessary details to make your instructions more clear.

Guide for Reading

Ernest Lawrence Thayer (1863–1940)

It's not surprising that "Casey at the Bat" reads like a sports story in verse. The poet, Ernest Lawrence Thayer, spent many years working as a newspaper reporter. Thayer began his reporting career as editor-in-chief of Harvard University's humor magazine, *The Lampoon*. He later worked at newspapers in both New York and California. "Casey at the Bat" was published in the *San Francisco Examiner* on June 3, 1888, under Thayer's pen name, Phin. The comedian De Wolf Hopper popularized the poem by reciting it as part of his act, and in 1953 the poem inspired an operetta called *The Mighty Casey*.

◆ Build Vocabulary

RELATED WORDS: FORMS OF *TUMULT*

Learning other forms of a word can help you expand your vocabulary. For example, you may already know that the adjective *tumultuous* means "wild and noisy." If so, when you come across the noun *tumult* in "Casey at the Bat," you'll be able to figure out that it means "a noisy commotion."

pallor
wreathed
writhing
tumult

WORD BANK

As you read "Casey at the Bat," you'll encounter the words on this list. Each word is defined on the page where it first appears. Preview the list before you read.

◆ Build Grammar Skills

PARTICIPLES

In his poem "Casey at the Bat," Ernest Lawrence Thayer captures the action of a baseball game by using **participles**—forms of verbs that act as adjectives. Participles fall into two groups: present participles and past participles. **Present participles** end in *-ing*. **Past participles** usually end in *-ed* but may also have irregular endings, such as *-t* or *-en*. Look at these examples from the poem:

present participle
Then when the *writhing* pitcher ground the ball into his hip,

past participle
Then from the *gladdened* multitude went up a joyous yell—

Casey at the Bat

◆ *Literature and Your Life*

CONNECT YOUR EXPERIENCE

Sporting events can really keep you on the edge of your seat! An athlete can break a world record or a losing team can charge to victory at the last minute. As you read this poem about a suspenseful baseball game, you may be reminded of nail-biting moments you've experienced while either watching or playing a sport.

Journal Writing Write a brief description of a suspenseful sporting event that you've either played in or witnessed.

THEMATIC FOCUS: IN SUSPENSE

The game of baseball can be filled with spine-tingling moments. No matter how skilled a player may be, or how important a game is, you never know just what will happen once the players take the field. Notice how this poem proves that point.

◆ Background for Understanding

SPORTS

Baseball is one of only a few sports in which there is no time clock. Unless a game is shortened by rain, it won't end until nine innings (or six or seven innings in some leagues) have been played and one team has come out on top. As a result, a team that's behind always has a chance to come back—even if they're behind by ten runs at the end of eight innings—as long as they keep getting base hits and avoid making the final out. "Casey at the Bat" captures the hopes of a team that's behind by two runs heading into the ninth inning. Notice how suspense builds as the game comes down to a final pitch.

◆ Literary Focus

CLIMAX AND ANTICLIMAX

The biggest moment of a story, or any type of narrative, is its **climax**. It is the turning point at which readers learn how the conflict, or central struggle in the story, will turn out. An **anticlimax** is similar to a climax because it also is the key event in the story. However, an anticlimax is always a letdown. It's the point at which you learn that the story will not turn out the way you'd expected.

◆ Reading Strategy

SUMMARIZING

If you want to describe a story or a poem to someone who has never read it, you'd probably do so by summarizing. When you **summarize**, you state briefly in your own words the main points and key details of the piece. This example shows one way to summarize the first stanza of the poem "Casey at the Bat":

Thayer's Version

It looked extremely rocky for the Mudville nine that day;

The score stood two to four, with but an inning left to play.

So, when Cooney died at second, and Burrows did the same, A pallor wreathed the features of the patrons of the game.

Summary

It is the last inning of a baseball game in which the Mudville team is losing by two runs. There are two outs against Mudville, and their fans are worried.

Casey at the Bat

Ernest Lawrence Thayer

It looked extremely rocky for the Mudville nine that day;
The score stood two to four, with but an inning left to play.
So, when Cooney died at second, and Burrows did the same,
A pallor wreathed the features of the patrons of the game.

5   A straggling few got up to go, leaving there the rest,
With that hope which springs eternal within the human breast.
For they thought: "If only Casey would get a whack at that,"
They'd put even money now, with Casey at the bat.

But Flynn preceded Casey, and likewise so did Blake,
10 And the former was a pudd'n, and the latter was a fake.
So on that stricken multitude a deathlike silence sat;
For there seemed but little chance of Casey's getting to the bat.

But Flynn let drive a "single," to the wonderment of all.
And the much-despised Blakey "tore the cover off the ball."
15 And when the dust had lifted, and they saw what had occurred,
There was Blakey safe at second, and Flynn a-huggin' third.

Then from the gladdened multitude went up a joyous yell—
It rumbled in the mountaintops, it rattled in the dell;[1]
It struck upon the hillside and rebounded on the flat;
20 For Casey, mighty Casey, was advancing to the bat.

---

1. dell (del) *n*.: Small, secluded valley.

There was ease in Casey's manner as he stepped into his place,
There was pride in Casey's bearing and a smile on Casey's face;
And when responding to the cheers he lightly doffed[2] his hat,
No stranger in the crowd could doubt 'twas Casey at the bat.

25 Ten thousand eyes were on him as he rubbed his hands with dirt,
Five thousand tongues applauded when he wiped them on his shirt;
Then when the <u>writhing</u> pitcher ground the ball into his hip,
Defiance glanced in Casey's eye, a sneer curled Casey's lip.

And now the leather-covered sphere came hurtling through the air,
30 And Casey stood a-watching it in haughty grandeur there.
Close by the sturdy batsman the ball unheeded sped;
"That ain't my style," said Casey. "Strike one," the umpire said.

◆ **Build Vocabulary**

pallor (pal´ ər) *n*.: Paleness
wreathed (rēthd) *v*.: Curled around
writhing (rīth´ iŋ) *v*.: Twisting; turning

2. **doffed** (däft) *v*.: Lifted.

Baseball Players Practicing, 1875, Thomas Eakins Museum of Art, Rhode Island School of Design

▲ **Critical Viewing** Compare and contrast the stance and uniform of the batter in the painting with that of players today. [**Compare and Contrast**]

From the benches, black with people, there went up a muffled roar,
Like the beating of the storm waves on the stern and distant shore.
35 "Kill him! kill the umpire!" shouted someone on the stand;
And it's likely they'd have killed him had not Casey raised his hand.

With a smile of Christian charity great Casey's visage[3] shone;
He stilled the rising tumult, he made the game go on;
He signaled to the pitcher, and once more the spheroid flew;
40 But Casey still ignored it, and the umpire said, "Strike two."

"Fraud!" cried the maddened thousands, and the echo answered "Fraud!"
But one scornful look from Casey and the audience was awed;
They saw his face grow stern and cold, they saw his muscles strain,
And they knew that Casey wouldn't let the ball go by again.

45 The sneer is gone from Casey's lips, his teeth are clenched in hate.
He pounds with cruel vengeance his bat upon the plate:
And now the pitcher holds the ball, and now he lets it go,
And now the air is shattered by the force of Casey's blow.

Oh, somewhere in this favored land the sun is shining bright,
50 The band is playing somewhere, and somewhere hearts are light:
And somewhere men are laughing, and somewhere children shout,
But there is no joy in Mudville: Mighty Casey has struck out.

---

3. **visage** (viz′ ij) *n.*: Face.

◆ **Build Vocabulary**

tumult (tōō′ məlt) *n.*: Noisy commotion

Guide for Responding

◆ *Literature and Your Life*

Reader's Response Did you expect the poem to end the way it did? Why or why not? What details made reading this poem a suspenseful experience?

Thematic Focus Think of a suspenseful sporting event in which your team lost and recall the reaction of the crowd. How did this situation compare with the situation described in "Casey at the Bat"?

☑ Check Your Comprehension

1. Explain how the crowd feels about Casey.
2. (a) What is Casey's attitude when he first comes to the plate? (b) How does his attitude change?
3. List three suspenseful points in the poem.
4. What is the outcome of Casey's turn at bat?

◆ Critical Thinking

INTERPRET

1. Describe the type of baseball player Casey is, citing examples from the poem. **[Analyze]**
2. How might Casey's attitude have affected his game? **[Draw Conclusions]**
3. Based on what you know about Casey, what do you think was his reaction after he struck out? **[Speculate]**

EVALUATE

4. Explain whether or not the poet is successful in building suspense in the poem. **[Analyze]**

Guide for Responding (continued)

◆ Reading Strategy

SUMMARIZING

Any time you describe the plot of a movie, television show, or novel to a friend, you're putting your **summarizing** skills to use. Summarize stanzas 4, 5, 8, 10, 12, and 13 (a summary of stanza 1 appears on page 35) of "Casey at the Bat." Include only the main ideas and the key details that support those ideas. Your summary should include enough information so that you could use it as the basis for a sports report about the game.

◆ Literary Focus

CLIMAX AND ANTICLIMAX

When you get to the point in a story or a narrative poem at which you learn how the conflict will be resolved, you've finally reached the **climax**. If the outcome is a downward turn of events, and one you had not expected, it is called an **anticlimax**.

1. Why is the climax the "high point" of a story?
2. Is the turning point of "Casey at the Bat" a climax or an anticlimax? Explain.

◆ Build Vocabulary

RELATED WORDS: FORMS OF *TUMULT*

On your paper, complete the following sentences with the appropriate form of the word *tumult*:

1. His supporters gave the senator a _____?_____ greeting following his reelection.
2. An explosion at the factory caused quite a _____?_____ downtown.

USING THE WORD BANK

For each numbered item, write a sentence that uses one word from the Word Bank.

1. Write the first sentence of a news article describing a noisy demonstration in the city.
2. Describe how a snake is moving along a tree branch in a rain forest.
3. Explain why you think your friend may not be feeling well today.
4. Tell about an old house that has ivy growing around its pillars.

◆ Build Grammar Skills

PARTICIPLES

Thayer vividly captures the actions of the players and the emotions of the audience through the use of carefully chosen **participles**—forms of verbs that act as adjectives. He uses both **present participles,** which end in *-ing,* and **past participles,** which usually end in -ed.

Practice Write these passages in your notebook. Identify the participle in each passage. Indicate whether it is a present or a past participle.

1. A straggling few got up to go, leaving there the rest,
2. So on that stricken multitude a deathlike sentence sat;
3. From the benches, black with people, there went up a muffled roar, Like the beating of the waves on the stern and distant shore.
4. He stilled the rising tumult, he made the game go on;
5. "Fraud!" cried the maddened thousands, and the echo answered "Fraud!"

Beyond Literature

Math Connection

Statistics in Sports Although you might not think of it, math plays an important role in baseball and in other sports. Statistics are kept on just about everything—from a baseball player's batting average during night games to the number of seconds a basketball player hangs in the air when performing a slam dunk. Not only do statistics help fans track how well their favorite players are performing, but they also help coaches and managers make key on-field decisions. For example, a baseball manager might check a player's batting average against a specific pitcher when deciding whether to pinch-hit for him or her. What types of statistics might have prompted the Mudville manager to pinch-hit for the Mighty Casey?

*B*uild *Y*our *P*ortfolio

 ## Idea Bank

Writing

1. Sports Headlines Brainstorm for a list of suspenseful sports moments. Then write a list of attention-grabbing sports headlines based on your list. **[Career Link]**

2. Sports How-to Write a step-by-step explanation of how to perform a sports-related activity. For example, you might tell how to throw a curve ball or how to execute a tennis serve. **[Physical Education Link]**

3. Résumé Research a baseball player. Then list his career highlights as if you were compiling information for a résumé—a summary of a person's job experience and education. **[Career Link]**

Speaking and Listening

4. Sports Interview Work with a partner to present a sports interview to the class. Have one person portray the interviewer and the other person portray a sports figure you admire. **[Career Link]**

5. Pep Talk What might the coach of the Mudville team say to boost the morale of his players? Compose a "pep talk" and present it to the class. **[Physical Education Link]**

Projects

6. Statistics Chart Create a chart comparing two different sets of baseball statistics. For example, you might compare the statistics of two different players or statistics from two different time periods. **[Math Link]**

7. Sports in Other Countries Research a sport that is very popular in another country and create a presentation based on your findings. **[Social Studies Link]**

 ## Writing Mini-Lesson

Sportscast

"The running back *blasted* through the defensive line." "She *spiked* the ball over the net." "The champs *annihilated* the challengers." The language of a good sportscast is vivid and lively. It captures the thrills and sometimes the disappointments of a sports event. Write a sportscast that really hooks your audience. You can base it on any sport you choose. The tip given here will help you.

Writing Skills Focus: Vivid Verbs

One of the keys to a good sportscast is the use of vivid verbs. **Vivid verbs** are action words with punch. They give life to your writing by making your descriptions precise and interesting. Notice how Ernest Lawrence Thayer uses vivid verbs to set the scene in "Casey at the Bat."

Model From the Poem

But Flynn *let drive* a "single," to the wonderment of all.

Prewriting Choose a topic by recalling a sports event you recently witnessed or in which you participated. As an alternative, you can make up an event. Then create a list of vivid verbs that apply to the sport you've chosen. For example, list ways a pitcher might throw a baseball or ways a batter might hit.

Drafting As you draft your sportscast, choose precise, descriptive verbs that are appropriate to your sport. For example, a figure skater probably would not career across the ice, but a hockey player might.

Revising Remember, your sportscast should make your audience feel as if they attended the event it describes. Look for places where you can liven up your descriptions by adding vivid verbs.

The mighty Casey is probably the most famous fictional slugger—a player who could build nervous excitement among the fans because of his ability to change the outcome of a game with a single swing of the bat. One of the greatest real-life sluggers of all time is Hank Aaron. Aaron, who played in the major leagues from 1954 to 1976, holds more batting records than any other player. His crowning achievement came when he hit his 715th home run, breaking the record held by the legendary Babe Ruth. In the following section from his autobiography, Aaron describes this achievement.

from I Had a Hammer

Hank Aaron

My father threw out the first ball, and then we took the field against the Dodgers. Their pitcher was Al Downing, a veteran lefthander whom I respected. Downing always had an idea of what he was doing when he was on the mound, and he usually pitched me outside with sliders and screwballs.[1] I crowded the plate against him to hit the outside pitch, but at the same time, I knew he would be trying to outthink me, which meant that I had to be patient and pick my spot. It didn't come in the second inning, when Downing walked me before I could take the bat off my shoulder. I scored when Dusty Baker doubled and Bill Buckner mishandled the ball in left field. Nobody seemed to care too much, but my run broke Willie Mays's National League record for runs scored—Willie had retired at the end of the 1973 season—and put me third all-time behind Ty Cobb and Ruth. I had always put great store in runs scored ever since Jackie Robinson pointed out that the purpose of coming up to the plate was to make it around the bases. The way I saw it, a run scored was just as important as one batted in. Apparently, though, Jackie and I were in the minority on that score.

I came up again in the fourth, with two outs and Darrell Evans on first base. The Dodgers were ahead 3–1, and I knew that Downing was not going to walk me and put the tying run on base. He was going to challenge me with everything he had—which was what it was going to take for me to hit my 715th home run. I knew all along that I wouldn't break the record against a rookie pitcher, because a rookie would be scared to come at me. It had to

---

1. **pitched me . . . screwballs:** Threw two types of pitches that cause the ball to move in an unnatural way. They are intended to confuse a batter and make the ball more difficult to hit.

be a pitcher with some confidence and nerve—a solid veteran like Downing.

Downing's first pitch was a change of pace that went into the dirt. The umpire, Satch Davidson, threw it out, and the first-base umpire, Frank Pulli, tossed Downing another one of the specially marked infrared balls. Downing rubbed it up and then threw his slider low and down the middle, which was not where he wanted it but which was fine with me. I hit it squarely, although not well enough that I knew it was gone. The ball shot out on a line over the shortstop, Bill Russell, who bent his knees as if he were going to jump up and catch it. That was one of the differences between Ruth and me: he made outfielders look up at the sky, and I made shortstops bend their knees.

I used to say that I never saw one of my home runs land, but when I see photographs or films of myself hitting home runs, I'm always looking out toward left field. I never realized I was doing it, though, and I still don't think I was watching to see the ball go over the fence. I think it was just a matter of following the ball with my eyes. From the time the pitcher gripped it, I was focused on the ball, and I didn't look away until it was time to run the bases. Anyway, I saw this one go out. And before it did, I saw Buckner run to the fence like he was going to catch it. During the pregame warm-ups, Buckner had practiced leaping against the fence, as if he planned to take the home run away from me, and I believe he was thinking about doing that as he ran back to the wall and turned. But the ball kept going. It surprised him, and it surprised me. I'm still not sure I hit that ball hard enough for it to go out. I don't know—maybe I did but I was so keyed up that I couldn't feel it. Anyway, something carried the ball into the bullpen, and about the time I got to first base I realized that I was the all-time home run king of baseball. Steve Garvey, the Dodgers' first baseman, shook my hand as I passed first, and Davey Lopes, the second baseman, stuck out his hand at second. I'm not sure if I ever shook with Lopes, though, because about that time a couple of college kids appeared out of nowhere and started running alongside me and pounding me on the back. I guess I was aware of them, because the clips show that I sort of nudged them away with my elbow, but I honestly don't remember them being there. I was in my own little world at the time. It was like I was running in a bubble and I could see all these people jumping up and down and waving their arms in slow motion. I remember that every base seemed crowded, like there were all these people I had to get through to make it to home plate. I just couldn't wait to get there. I was told I had a big smile on my face as I came around third. I purposely never smiled as I ran the bases after a home run, but I suppose I couldn't help it that time.

1. What would be your reaction to hitting a record-breaking home run? Compare your feelings with those Aaron describes.
2. How does Aaron feel about baseball? Support your answer.
3. Compare and contrast Aaron's personality with that of the mighty Casey.

◀ Critical Viewing Judging from the look on his face, how does Hank Aaron feel at this moment? [Infer]

*G*uide for Reading

Daphne du Maurier
(1907–1989)

You may already be familiar with Daphne du Maurier's work—without ever having opened one of her books.

Du Maurier's stories have inspired some of the most gripping movies ever made.

Among these is Alfred Hitchcock's film *The Birds*, based on the story of the same name.

A Family of Artists Du Maurier was born in London into a family of actors, artists, and writers. Her father was an actor and theater manager who specialized in playing criminals on the stage, and her grandfather was a novelist and artist who illustrated his own writings.

A Successful Career *The Loving Spirit* (1931) was du Maurier's first novel, which she wrote while secluded in a house in Cornwall on the southwest coast of England. The novel became a bestseller, propelling her into a life-long career as a writer. She followed with a series of romantic novels that were tinged with mystery and suspense: *Jamaica Inn* (1936), *Rebecca* (1938), and *Frenchman's Creek* (1941). Du Maurier also wrote numerous short stories and, in 1977, completed an autobiography, *Myself When Young*.

A Box Office Attraction Du Maurier's stories attracted the attention of film director Alfred Hitchcock, who specialized in suspenseful movies. In addition to *The Birds*, Hitchcock made two other films based on du Maurier's tales, including *Rebecca*, which won the Academy Award for Best Picture in 1940.

◆ Build Vocabulary

SUFFIXES: *-ful*

In "The Birds," the children are described as *fretful*. The word *fretful* contains the suffix *-ful*. The suffix *-ful* can mean "having the quality of," as in *forgetful*; "having the quantity that would fill," as in *handful*; or "full of," as in *fretful*. Therefore, the word *fretful* literally means "full of fret or worry." Thus, a person who is fretful, full of fret or worry, is irritable or discontented.

WORD BANK

Before you read, preview this list of words from the story.

> placid
> garish
> recounted
> sullen
> furtively
> imperative
> reconnaissance
> fretful

◆ Build Grammar Skills

COMPOUND SENTENCES

As Daphne du Maurier develops this story, she makes frequent use of compound sentences as a way to express a lot of detailed information. A **compound sentence** consists of two or more equally important, or coordinate, independent clauses joined by a coordinating conjunction—*and*, *but*, or *or*—or by a semicolon.

indep. clause
On December the third, the wind changed overnight,
indep. clause
and it was winter.

As you read "The Birds," notice the compound sentences and consider the effect they have on the telling of the story.

The Birds

◆ *Literature and Your Life*

CONNECT YOUR EXPERIENCE

You step outside and the sky is dark and threatening, with clouds closing in on you. Low rumbles of thunder are becoming louder by the second. You look at the threatening scene and an eerie feeling runs through you. Nature appears to be brooding, about to strike.

Writers have often been fascinated by nature's dark side. Sometimes—as du Maurier does in "The Birds"—they use fiction to ask questions about nature's moods.

THEMATIC FOCUS: IN SUSPENSE

One question that du Maurier explores in this suspenseful tale is, What happens when nature, whose moods are familiar to us, shows a darker side than has ever been seen before?

◆ Background for Understanding

SCIENCE

Use these silhouettes to help you picture the birds that appear in du Maurier's story. Try to imagine what it would be like to have thousands of these birds descend upon your town.

starling

crow

meadowlark

robin

Journal Writing Jot down three species of birds you commonly observe. Draw a silhouette of each bird and briefly describe it.

◆ Literary Focus

FORESHADOWING

As its name suggests, **foreshadowing** is the shadow of things to come—an author's use of clues to hint at future events. In "The Birds," for instance, du Maurier hints at danger to come when she writes, "The birds had been more restless than ever this fall of the year." Notice other examples of foreshadowing, details that seem disturbing or unusual.

◆ Reading Strategy

PREDICT

You can use foreshadowing to **predict** the outcome of a story before you actually read what happens. For example, by noticing small but troubling events, you can foresee much bigger troubles to come.

In reading "The Birds," base your predictions of future events on telltale details that some or all of the characters ignore. Jot down anything that seems disturbing, unusual, or out of place. Then apply an imaginary magnifying glass to these details. Ask yourself what would happen if this small trouble were multiplied many times. Use a graphic organizer like this one to help you record your details.

Unusual Detail	What Will Happen If It Intensifies

THE BIRDS

Daphne du Maurier

Attack of the Birds, 1994, Lev Tabenkin, Maya Polsky Gallery

▲ **Critical Viewing** Based on this painting, what do you think might happen in this story? **[Predict]**

n December the third the wind changed overnight and it was winter. Until then the autumn had been mellow, soft. The leaves had lingered on the trees, golden-red, and the hedgerows were still green. The earth was rich where the plow had turned it.

Nat Hocken, because of a wartime disability, had a pension and did not work full-time at the farm. He worked three days a week, and they gave him the lighter jobs: hedging, thatching, repairs to the farm buildings.

Although he was married, with children, his was a solitary disposition; he liked best to work alone. It pleased him when he was given a bank to build up, or a gate to mend at the far end of the peninsula, where the sea surrounded the farmland on either side. Then, at midday, he would pause and eat the pasty[1] that his wife had baked for him, and, sitting on the cliff's edge, watch the birds. Autumn was best for this, better than spring. In spring the birds flew inland, purposeful, intent; they knew where they were bound; the rhythm and ritual of their life brooked no delay. In autumn those that had not migrated overseas but remained to pass the winter were caught up in the same driving urge, but because migration was denied them followed a pattern of their own. Great flocks of them came to the peninsula, restless, uneasy, spending themselves in motion; now wheeling, circling in the sky, now settling to feed on the rich new-turned soil, but even when they fed it was as though they did so without hunger, without desire. Restlessness drove them to the skies again.

Black and white, jackdaw and gull, mingled in strange partnership, seeking some sort of liberation, never satisfied, never still. Flocks of starlings, rustling like silk, flew to fresh pasture, driven by the same necessity of movement, and the smaller birds, the finches and the larks, scattered from tree to hedge as if compelled.

Nat watched them, and he watched the sea birds too. Down in the bay they waited for the tide. They had more patience. Oyster catchers, redshank, sanderling, and curlew watched by the water's edge; as the slow sea sucked at the shore and then withdrew, leaving the strip of seaweed bare and the shingle churned, the sea birds raced and ran upon the beaches. Then that same impulse to flight seized upon them too. Crying, whistling, calling, they skimmed the placid sea and left the shore. Make haste, make speed, hurry and begone; yet where, and to what purpose? The restless urge of autumn, unsatisfying, sad, had put a spell upon them and they must flock, and wheel, and cry; they must spill themselves of motion before winter came.

"Perhaps," thought Nat, munching his pasty by the cliff's edge, "a message comes to the birds in autumn, like a warning. Winter is coming. Many of them perish. And like the people who, apprehensive of death before their time, drive themselves to work or folly, the birds do likewise."

The birds had been more restless than ever this fall of the year, the agitation more marked because the days were still. As the tractor traced its path up and down the western hills, the figure of the farmer silhouetted on the driving seat, the whole machine and the man upon it would be lost momentarily in the great cloud of wheeling, crying birds. There were many more than usual; Nat was sure of this.

> ◆ **Literary Focus**
> What might the birds' restlessness and large numbers foreshadow?

---

1. **pasty** (pas´ tē) *n*.: A meat pie.

◆ **Build Vocabulary**

placid (plas´ id) *adj*.: Tranquil; calm

Always, in autumn, they followed the plow, but not in great flocks like these, nor with such clamour.

Nat remarked upon it when hedging was finished for the day. "Yes," said the farmer, "there are more birds about than usual; I've noticed it too. And daring, some of them, taking no notice of the tractor. One or two gulls came so close to my head this afternoon I thought they'd knock my cap off! As it was, I could scarcely see what I was doing, when they were overhead and I had the sun in my eyes. I have a notion the weather will change. It will be a hard winter. That's why the birds are restless."

Nat, tramping home across the fields and down the lane to his cottage, saw the birds still flocking over the western hills, in the last glow of the sun. No wind, and the gray sea calm and full. Campion in bloom yet in the hedges, and the air mild. The farmer was right, though, and it was that night the weather turned. Nat's bedroom faced east. He woke just after two and heard the wind in the chimney. Not the storm and bluster of a sou' westerly gale, bringing the rain, but east wind, cold and dry. It sounded hollow in the chimney, and a loose slate rattled on the roof. Nat listened, and he could hear the sea roaring in the bay. Even the air in the small bedroom had turned chill: a draft came under the skirting of the door, blowing upon the bed. Nat drew the blanket round him, leaned closer to the back of his sleeping wife, and stayed wakeful, watchful, aware of misgiving without cause.

Then he heard the tapping on the window. There was no creeper on the cottage walls to break loose and scratch upon the pane. He listened, and the tapping continued until, irritated by the sound, Nat got out of bed and went to the window. He opened it, and as he did so something brushed his hand, jabbing at his knuckles, grazing the skin. Then he saw the flutter of the wings and it was gone, over the roof, behind the cottage.

It was a bird; what kind of bird he could not tell. The wind must have driven it to shelter on the sill.

He shut the window and went back to bed, but, feeling his knuckles wet, put his mouth to the scratch. The bird had drawn blood. Frightened, he supposed, and bewildered, the bird, seeking shelter, had stabbed at him in the darkness. Once more he settled himself to sleep.

Presently the tapping came again, this time more forceful, more insistent, and now his wife woke at the sound and, turning in the bed, said to him, "See to the window, Nat, it's rattling."

"I've already seen to it," he told her; "there's some bird there trying to get in. Can't you hear the wind? It's blowing from the east, driving the birds to shelter."

"Send them away," she said, "I can't sleep with that noise."

He went to the window for the second time, and now when he opened it there was not one bird upon the sill but half a dozen; they flew straight into his face, attacking him.

He shouted, striking out at them with his arms, scattering them; like the first one, they flew over the roof and disappeared. Quickly he let the window fall and latched it.

"Did you hear that?" he said. "They went for me. Tried to peck my eyes." He stood by the window, peering into the darkness, and could see nothing. His wife, heavy with sleep, murmured from the bed.

> Nat, tramping home across the fields and down the lane to his cottage, saw the birds still flocking over the western hills.

"I'm not making it up," he said, angry at her suggestion. "I tell you the birds were on the sill, trying to get into the room."

Suddenly a frightened cry came from the room across the passage where the children slept.

"It's Jill," said his wife, roused at the sound, sitting up in bed. "Go to her, see what's the matter."

Nat lit the candle, but when he opened the bedroom door to cross the passage the draft blew out the flame.

◆ **Reading Strategy**
Based on the detail of the frightened cry and other story details, predict what will happen in the children's room.

There came a second cry of terror, this time from both children, and stumbling into their room, he felt the beating of wings about him in the darkness. The window was wide open. Through it came the birds, hitting first the ceiling and the walls, then swerving in mid-flight, turning to the children in their beds.

"It's all right, I'm here," shouted Nat, and the children flung themselves, screaming, upon him, while in the darkness the birds rose and dived and came for him again.

"What is it, Nat, what's happened?" his wife called from the further bedroom, and swiftly he pushed the children through the door to the passage and shut it upon them, so that he was alone now in their bedroom with the birds.

He seized a blanket from the nearest bed and, using it as a weapon, flung it to right and left about him in the air. He felt the thud of bodies, heard the fluttering of wings, but they were not yet defeated, for again and again they returned to the assault, jabbing his hands, his head, the little stabbing beaks sharp as pointed forks. The blanket became a weapon of defense; he wound it about his head, and then in greater darkness beat at the birds with his bare hands. He dared not stumble to the door and open it, lest in doing so the birds should follow him.

How long he fought with them in the darkness he could not tell, but at last the beating of the wings about him lessened and then withdrew, and through the density of the blanket he was aware of light. He waited, listened; there was no sound except the fretful crying of one of the children from the bedroom beyond. The fluttering, the whirring of the wings had ceased.

He took the blanket from his head and stared about him. The cold gray morning light exposed the room. Dawn and the open window had called the living birds; the dead lay on the floor. Nat gazed at the little corpses, shocked and horrified. They were all small birds, none of any size; there must have been fifty of them lying there upon the floor. There were robins, finches, sparrows, blue tits, larks, and bramblings, birds that by nature's law kept to their own flock and their own territory, and now, joining one with another in their urge for battle, had destroyed themselves against the bedroom walls or in the strife had been destroyed by him. Some had lost feathers in the fight; others had blood, his blood, upon their beaks.

Sickened, Nat went to the window and stared out across his patch of garden to the fields.

It was bitter cold, and the ground had all the hard black look of frost. Not white frost, to shine in the morning sun, but the black frost that the east wind brings. The sea, fiercer now with the turning tide, white-capped and steep, broke harshly in the bay. Of the birds there was no sign. Not a sparrow chattered in the hedge beyond the garden gate, no early missel-thrush or blackbird pecked on the grass for worms. There was no sound at all but the east wind and the sea.

Nat shut the window and the door of the small bedroom, and went back across the

passage to his own. His wife sat up in bed, one child asleep beside her, the smaller in her arms, his face bandaged. The curtains were tightly drawn across the window, the candles lit. Her face looked garish in the yellow light. She shook her head for silence.

"He's sleeping now," she whispered, "but only just. Something must have cut him, there was blood at the corner of his eyes. Jill said it was the birds. She said she woke up, and the birds were in the room."

His wife looked up at Nat, searching his face for confirmation. She looked terrified, bewildered, and he did not want her to know that he was also shaken, dazed almost, by the events of the past few hours.

"There are birds in there," he said, "dead birds, nearly fifty of them. Robins, wrens, all the little birds from hereabouts. It's as though a madness seized them, with the east wind." He sat down on the bed beside his wife and held her hand. "It's the weather," he said, "it must be that, it's the hard weather. They aren't the birds, maybe, from here around. They've been driven down from upcountry."

"But, Nat," whispered his wife, "it's only this night that the weather turned. There's been no snow to drive them. And they can't be hungry yet. There's food for them out there in the fields."

"It's the weather," repeated Nat. "I tell you, it's the weather."

His face, too, was drawn and tired, like hers. They stared at one another for a while without speaking.

"I'll go downstairs and make a cup of tea," he said.

The sight of the kitchen reassured him. The cups and saucers, neatly stacked upon the dresser, the table and chairs, his wife's roll of knitting on her basket chair, the children's toys in a corner cupboard.

♦ **Build Vocabulary**
garish (gar´ ish) *adj.*: Too bright or gaudy

He knelt down, raked out the old embers, and relit the fire. The glowing sticks brought normality, the steaming kettle and the brown teapot comfort and security. He drank his tea, carried a cup up to his wife. Then he washed in the scullery,[2] and, putting on his boots, opened the back door.

The sky was hard and leaden, and the brown hills that had gleamed in the sun the day before looked dark and bare. The east wind, like a razor, stripped the trees, and the leaves, crackling and dry, shivered and scattered with the wind's blast. Nat stubbed the earth with his boot. It was frozen hard. He had never known a change so swift and sudden. Black winter had descended in a single night.

> ♦ Literary Focus
> What might this description of the sudden change in the weather foreshadow?

The children were awake now. Jill was chattering upstairs and young Johnny crying once again. Nat heard his wife's voice, soothing, comforting. Presently they came down. He had breakfast ready for them, and the routine of the day began.

"Did you drive away the birds?" asked Jill, restored to calm because of the kitchen fire, because of day, because of breakfast.

"Yes, they've all gone now," said Nat. "It was the east wind brought them in. They were frightened and lost, they wanted shelter."

"They tried to peck us," said Jill. "They went for Johnny's eyes."

"Fright made them do that," said Nat. "They didn't know where they were in the dark bedroom."

"I hope they won't come again," said Jill. "Perhaps if we put bread for them outside the window they will eat that and fly away."

She finished her breakfast and then went for her coat and hood, her schoolbooks and her satchel. Nat said nothing, but his wife

2. **scullery** (skul´ ər ē) *n.*: A room next to the kitchen where pots and pans are washed and stored.

looked at him across the table. A silent message passed between them.

"I'll walk with her to the bus," he said. "I don't go to the farm today."

And while the child was washing in the scullery he said to his wife, "Keep all the windows closed, and the doors too. Just to be on the safe side. I'll go to the farm. Find out if they heard anything in the night." Then he walked with his small daughter up the lane. She seemed to have forgotten her experience of the night before. She danced ahead of him, chasing the leaves, her face whipped with the cold and rosy under the pixie hood.

"Is it going to snow, Dad?" she said. "It's cold enough."

He glanced up at the bleak sky, felt the wind tear at his shoulders.

"No," he said, "it's not going to snow. This is a black winter, not a white one."

All the while he searched the hedgerows for the birds, glanced over the top of them to the fields beyond, looked to the small wood above the farm where the rooks and jackdaws gathered. He saw none.

The other children waited by the bus stop, muffled, hooded like Jill, the faces white and pinched with cold.

Jill ran to them, waving. "My dad says it won't snow," she called, "it's going to be a black winter."

She said nothing of the birds. She began to push and struggle with another little girl. The bus came ambling up the hill. Nat saw her on to it, then turned and walked back towards the farm. It was not his day for work, but he wanted to satisfy himself that all was well. Jim, the cowman, was clattering in the yard.

"Boss around?" asked Nat.

"Gone to market," said Jim. "It's Tuesday, isn't it?"

He clumped off round the corner of a shed. He had no time for Nat. Nat was said to be superior. Read books, and the like.

Nat had forgotten it was Tuesday. This showed how the events of the preceding night had shaken him. He went to the back door of the farmhouse and heard Mrs. Trigg singing in the kitchen, the wireless[3] making a background to her song.

"Are you there, missus?" called out Nat.

She came to the door, beaming, broad, a good-tempered woman.

"Hullo, Mr. Hocken," she said. "Can you tell me where this cold is coming from? Is it Russia? I've never seen such a change. And it's going on, the wireless says. Something to do with the Arctic Circle."

"We didn't turn on the wireless this morning," said Nat. "Fact is, we had trouble in the night."

"Kiddies poorly?"

"No . . ." He hardly knew how to explain it. Now, in daylight, the battle of the birds would sound absurd.

He tried to tell Mrs. Trigg what had happened, but he could see from her eyes that she thought his story was the result of a nightmare.

"Sure they were real birds," she said, smiling, "with proper feathers and all? Not the funny-shaped kind that the men see after closing hours on a Saturday night?"

"Mrs. Trigg," he said, "there are fifty dead birds, robins, wrens, and such, lying low on the floor of the children's bedroom. They went for me; they tried to go for young Johnny's eyes."

Mrs. Trigg stared at him doubtfully.

"Well there, now," she answered, "I suppose the weather brought them. Once in the bedroom, they wouldn't know where they were to. Foreign birds maybe, from that Arctic Circle."

"No," said Nat, "they were the birds you see about here every day."

"Funny thing," said Mrs. Trigg, "no explaining it, really. You ought to write up

---

3. **wireless** (wīr´ lis) *n.*: Radio.

and ask the *Guardian*. They'd have some answer for it. Well, I must be getting on."

She nodded, smiled, and went back into the kitchen.

Nat, dissatisfied, turned to the farm gate. Had it not been for those corpses on the bedroom floor, which he must now collect and bury somewhere, he would have considered the tale exaggeration too.

Jim was standing by the gate.

"Had any trouble with the birds?" asked Nat.

"Birds? What birds?"

"We got them up our place last night. Scores of them, came in the children's bedroom. Quite savage they were."

"Oh?" It took time for anything to penetrate Jim's head. "Never heard of birds acting savage," he said at length. "They get tame, like, sometimes. I've seen them come to the windows for crumbs."

"These birds last night weren't tame."

"No? Cold, maybe. Hungry. You put out some crumbs."

Jim was no more interested than Mrs. Trigg had been. It was, Nat thought, like air raids in the war. No one down this end of the country knew what the Plymouth folk had seen and suffered. You had to endure something yourself before it touched you. He walked back along the lane and crossed the stile to his cottage. He found his wife in the kitchen with young Johnny.

"See anyone?" she asked.

"Mrs. Trigg and Jim," he answered. "I don't think they believed me. Anyway, nothing wrong up there."

"You might take the birds away," she said. "I daren't go into the room to make the beds until you do. I'm scared."

▼ **Critical Viewing** Compare and contrast the mood of the painting with the mood of the story so far. **[Compare and Contrast]**

Landscape From a Dream, 1936-38, Paul Nash, Tate Gallery, London

"Nothing to scare you now," said Nat. "They're dead, aren't they?"

He went up with a sack and dropped the stiff bodies into it, one by one. Yes, there were fifty of them, all told. Just the ordinary, common birds of the hedgerow, nothing as large even as a thrush. It must have been fright that made them act the way they did. Blue tits, wrens—it was incredible to think of the power of their small beaks jabbing at his face and hands the night before. He took the sack out into the garden and was faced now with a fresh problem. The ground was too hard to dig. It was frozen solid, yet no snow had fallen, nothing had happened in the past hours but the coming of the east wind. It was unnatural, queer. The weather prophets must be right. The change was something connected with the Arctic Circle.

The wind seemed to cut him to the bone as he stood there uncertainly, holding the sack. He could see the white-capped seas breaking down under in the bay. He decided to take the birds to the shore and bury them.

When he reached the beach below the headland he could scarcely stand, the force of the east wind was so strong. It hurt to draw breath, and his bare hands were blue. Never had he known such cold, not in all the bad winters he could remember. It was low tide. He crunched his way over the shingle[4] to the softer sand and then, his back to the wind, ground a pit in the sand with his heel. He meant to drop the birds into it, but as he opened up the sack the force of the wind carried them, lifted them, as though in flight again, and they were blown away from him along the beach, tossed like feathers, spread and scattered, the bodies of the fifty frozen birds. There was something ugly in the sight. He did not

like it. The dead birds were swept away from him by the wind.

"The tide will take them when it turns," he said to himself.

He looked out to sea and watched the crested breakers, combing green. They rose stiffly, curled, and broke again, and because it was ebb tide the roar was distant, more remote, lacking the sound and thunder of the flood.

Then he saw them. The gulls. Out there, riding the seas.

What he had thought at first to be the whitecaps of the waves were gulls. Hundreds, thousands, tens of thousands . . . They rose and fell in the trough of the seas, heads to the wind, like a mighty fleet at anchor, waiting on the tide. To eastward, and to the west, the gulls were there. They stretched as far as his eye could reach, in close formation, line upon line. Had the sea been still they would have covered the bay like a white cloud, head to head, body packed to body. Only the east wind, whipping the sea to breakers, hid them from the shore.

◆ Literary Focus
What might this deceptively calm scene foreshadow?

Nat turned and, leaving the beach, climbed the steep path home. Someone should know of this. Someone should be told. Something was happening, because of the east wind and the weather, that he did not understand. He wondered if he should go to the call box by the bus stop and ring up the police. Yet what could they do? What could anyone do? Tens of thousands of gulls riding the sea there in the bay because of storm, because of hunger. The police would think him mad, or drunk, or take the statement from him with great calm. "Thank you. Yes, the matter has already been reported. The hard weather is driving the birds inland in great numbers." Nat looked about him. Still no sign of any other bird. Perhaps the cold had sent them all

---

4. **shingle** *n.*: Area of beach covered with water-worn gravel.

from upcountry? As he drew near to the cottage his wife came to meet him at the door. She called to him, excited. "Nat," she said, "it's on the wireless. They've just read out a special news bulletin. I've written it down."

"What's on the wireless?" he said.

"About the birds," she said. "It's not only here, it's everywhere. In London, all over the country. Something has happened to the birds."

Together they went into the kitchen. He read the piece of paper lying on the table.

"Statement from the Home Office at 11 A.M. today. Reports from all over the country are coming in hourly about the vast quantity of birds flocking above towns, villages, and outlying districts, causing obstruction and damage and even attacking individuals. It is thought that the Arctic airstream, at present covering the British Isles, is causing birds to migrate south in immense numbers, and that intense hunger may drive these birds to attack human beings. Householders are warned to see to their windows, doors, and chimneys, and to take reasonable precautions for the safety of their children. A further statement will be issued later."

> Householders are warned to see to their windows, doors, and chimneys, and to take reasonable precautions for the safety of their children.

A kind of excitement seized Nat; he looked at his wife in triumph.

"There you are," he said. "Let's hope they'll hear that at the farm. Mrs. Trigg will know it wasn't any story. It's true. All over the country. I've been telling myself all morning there's something wrong. And just now, down on the beach, I looked out to sea and there are gulls, thousands of them, tens of thousands—you couldn't put a pin between their heads—and they're all out there, riding on the sea, waiting."

"What are they waiting for, Nat?" she asked.

He stared at her, then looked down again at the piece of paper.

"I don't know," he said slowly. "It says here the birds are hungry."

He went over to the drawer where he kept his hammer and tools.

"What are you going to do, Nat?"

"See to the windows and the chimneys too, like they tell you."

"You think they would break in, with the windows shut? Those sparrows and robins and such? Why, how could they?"

He did not answer. He was not thinking of the robins and the sparrows. He was thinking of the gulls . . .

He went upstairs and worked there the rest of the morning, boarding the windows of the bedrooms, filling up the chimney bases. Good job it was his free day and he was not working at the farm. It reminded him of the old days, at the beginning of the war. He was not married then, and he had made all the black-out boards for his mother's house in Plymouth. Made the shelter too. Not that it had been of any use when the moment came. He wondered if they would take these precautions up at the farm. He doubted it. Too easygoing, Harry Trigg and his missus. Maybe they'd laugh at the whole thing. Go off to a dance or a whist drive.[5]

"Dinner's ready." She called him, from the kitchen.

"All right. Coming down."

He was pleased with his handiwork. The frames fitted nicely over the little panes and at the bases of the chimneys.

When dinner was over and his wife was washing up, Nat switched on the one

---

5. **whist drive** *n.*: A card game organized for a group.

o'clock news. The same announcement was repeated, the one which she had taken down during the morning, but the news bulletin enlarged upon it. "The flocks of birds have caused dislocation in all areas," read the announcer, "and in London the sky was so dense at ten o'clock this morning that it seemed as if the city was covered by a vast black cloud.

"The birds settled on rooftops, on window ledges, and on chimneys. The species included blackbird, thrush, the common house sparrow, and, as might be expected in the metropolis, a vast quantity of pigeons and starlings, and that frequenter of the London river, the black-headed gull. The sight has been so unusual that traffic came to a standstill in many thoroughfares, work was abandoned in shops and offices, and the streets and pavements were crowded with people standing about to watch the birds."

Various incidents were <u>recounted</u>, the suspected reason of cold and hunger stated again, and warnings to householders repeated. The announcer's voice was smooth and suave. Nat had the impression that this man, in particular, treated the whole business as he would an elaborate joke. There would be others like him, hundreds of them, who did not know what it was to struggle in darkness with a flock of birds. There would be parties tonight in London, like the ones they gave on election nights. People standing about, shouting and laughing . . . "Come and watch the birds!"

Nat switched off the wireless. He got up and started work on the kitchen windows. His wife watched him, young Johnny at her heels.

"What, boards for down here too?" she said. "Why, I'll have to light up before three o'clock. I see no call for boards down here."

"Better be sure than sorry," answered Nat. "I'm not going to take any chances."

"What they ought to do," she said, "is to call the Army out and shoot the birds. That would soon scare them off."

"Let them try," said Nat. "How'd they set about it?"

"They have the Army to the docks," she answered, "when the dockers strike. The soldiers go down and unload the ships."

"Yes," said Nat, "and the population of London is eight million or more. Think of all the buildings, all the flats and houses. Do you think they've enough soldiers to go around shooting birds from every roof?"

"I don't know. But something should be done. They ought to do something."

Nat thought to himself that "they" were no doubt considering the problem at that very moment, but whatever "they" decided to do in London and the big cities would not help the people here, three hundred miles away. Each householder must look after his own.

"How are we off for food?" he said.

"Now, Nat, whatever next?"

"Never mind. What have you got in the larder?"[6]

"It's shopping day tomorrow, you know that. I don't keep uncooked food hanging about, it goes off. Butcher doesn't call till the day after. But I can bring back something when I go in tomorrow."

Nat did not want to scare her. He thought it possible that she might not go to town tomorrow. He looked in the larder for himself, and in the cupboard where she kept her tins. They would do for a couple of days. Bread was low.

"What about the baker?"

"He comes tomorrow too."

He saw she had flour. If the baker did not call she had enough to bake one loaf.

"We'd be better off in the old days," he said, "when the women baked twice a week,

◆ **Build Vocabulary**

recounted (ri kount´ ed) *v.*: Told in detail; narrated

6. **larder** (lärd´ ər) *n.*: Place where food is kept; pantry.

The Birds ◆ 55

and had pilchards[7] salted, and there was food for a family to last a siege, if need be."

"I've tried the children with tinned fish, they don't like it," she said.

Nat went on hammering the boards across the kitchen windows. Candles. They were low in candles too. That must be another thing she meant to buy tomorrow. Well, it could not be helped. They must go early to bed tonight. That was, if . . .

He got up and went out of the back door and stood in the garden, looking down toward the sea. There had been no sun all day, and now, at barely three o'clock, a kind of darkness had already come, the sky <u>sullen</u>, heavy, colorless like salt. He could hear the vicious sea drumming on the rocks. He walked down the path, halfway to the beach. And then he stopped. He could see the tide had turned. The rock that had shown in midmorning was now covered, but it was not the sea that held his eyes. The gulls had risen. They were circling, hundreds of them, thousands of them, lifting their wings against the wind. It was the gulls that made the darkening of the sky. And they were silent. They made not a sound. They just went on soaring and circling, rising, falling, trying their strength against the wind.

Nat turned. He ran up the path, back to the cottage.

"I'm going for Jill," he said. "I'll wait for her at the bus stop."

"What's the matter?" asked his wife. "You've gone quite white."

"Keep Johnny inside," he said. "Keep the door shut. Light up now, and draw the curtains."

"It's only just gone three," she said.

"Never mind. Do what I tell you."

He looked inside the tool shed outside the back door. Nothing there of much use.

> ◆ **Literary Focus**
> What might the circling gulls foreshadow?

A spade was too heavy, and a fork no good. He took the hoe. It was the only possible tool, and light enough to carry.

He started walking up the lane to the bus stop, and now and again glanced back over his shoulder.

The gulls had risen higher now, their circles were broader, wider, they were spreading out in huge formation across the sky.

He hurried on; although he knew the bus would not come to the top of the hill before four o'clock he had to hurry. He passed no one on the way. He was glad of this. No time to stop and chatter.

At the top of the hill he waited. He was much too soon. There was half an hour still to go. The east wind came whipping across the fields from the higher ground. He stamped his feet and blew upon his hands. In the distance he could see the clay hills, white and clean, against the heavy pallor of the sky. Something black rose from behind them, like a smudge at first, then widening, becoming deeper, and the smudge became a cloud, and the cloud divided again into five other clouds, spreading north, east, south, and west, and they were not clouds at all; they were birds. He watched them travel across the sky, and as one section passed overhead, within two or three hundred feet of him, he knew, from their speed, they were bound inland, upcountry; they had no business with the people here on the peninsula. They were rooks, crows, jackdaws, magpies, jays, all birds that usually preyed upon the smaller species; but this afternoon they were bound on some other mission.

"They've been given the towns," thought Nat; "they know what they have to do. We don't matter so much here. The gulls will serve for us. The others go to the towns."

He went to the call box, stepped inside, and lifted the receiver. The exchange would do. They would pass the message on.

"I'm speaking from Highway," he said, "by the bus stop. I want to report large for-

---

7. **pilchards** (pil´ chərdz) *n*.: Small fish similar to sardines.

mations of birds traveling upcountry. The gulls are also forming in the bay."

"All right," answered the voice, laconic, weary.

"You'll be sure and pass this message on to the proper quarter?"

"Yes . . . yes . . ." Impatient now, fed-up. The buzzing note resumed.

"She's another," thought Nat, "she doesn't care. Maybe she's had to answer calls all day. She hopes to go to the pictures tonight. She'll squeeze some fellow's hand and point up at the sky and say 'Look at all them birds!' She doesn't care."

The bus came lumbering up the hill. Jill climbed out, and three or four other children. The bus went on towards the town.

"What's the hoe for, Dad?"

They crowded around him, laughing, pointing.

"I just brought it along," he said. "Come on now, let's get home. It's cold, no hanging about. Here, you. I'll watch you across the fields, see how fast you can run."

He was speaking to Jill's companions, who came from different families, living in the council houses.[8] A short cut would take them to the cottages.

"We want to play a bit in the lane," said one of them.

"No, you don't. You go off home or I'll tell your Mammy."

They whispered to one another, round-eyed, then scuttled off across the fields. Jill stared at her father, her mouth sullen.

"We always play in the lane," she said.

"Not tonight, you don't," he said. "Come on now, no dawdling."

He could see the gulls now, circling the fields, coming in toward the land. Still silent. Still no sound.

---

8. **council houses** *n.*: Housing units built by the government.

"Look, Dad, look over there, look at all the gulls."

"Yes. Hurry, now."

"Where are they flying to? Where are they going?"

"Upcountry, I dare say. Where it's warmer."

He seized her hand and dragged her after him along the lane.

"Don't go so fast. I can't keep up."

The gulls were copying the rooks and crows. They were spreading out in formation across the sky. They headed, in bands of thousands, to the four compass points.

"Dad, what is it? What are the gulls doing?"

They were not intent upon their flight, as the crows, as the jackdaws had been. They still circled overhead. Nor did they fly so high. It was as though they waited upon some signal. As though some decision had yet to be given. The order was not clear.

"Do you want me to carry you, Jill? Here, come pick-a-back."

This way he might put on speed; but he was wrong. Jill was heavy. She kept slipping. And was crying too. His sense of urgency, of fear, had communicated itself to the child.

"I wish the gulls would go away. I don't like them. They're coming closer to the lane."

He put her down again. He started running, swinging Jill after him. As they went past the farm turning he saw the farmer backing his car out of the garage. Nat called to him.

"Can you give us a lift?" he said.

"What's that?"

Mr. Trigg turned in the driving seat and stared at them. Then a smile came to his cheerful, rubicund face.

"It looks as though we're in for some fun," he said. "Have you seen the gulls? Jim

---

The Birds ◆ **57**

and I are going to take a crack at them. Everyone's gone bird-crazy, talking of nothing else. I hear you were troubled in the night. Want a gun?"

Nat shook his head.

The small car was packed. There was just room for Jill, if she crouched on top of petrol tins on the back seat.

"I don't want a gun," said Nat, "but I'd be obliged if you'd run Jill home. She's scared of the birds."

He spoke briefly. He did not want to talk in front of Jill.

"O.K.," said the farmer, "I'll take her home. Why don't you stop behind and join the shooting match? We'll make the feathers fly."

Jill climbed in, and turning the car, the driver sped up the lane. Nat followed after. Trigg must be crazy. What use was a gun against a sky of birds?

Now Nat was not responsible for Jill, he had time to look about him. The birds were circling still above the fields. Mostly herring gull, but the black-backed gull amongst them. Usually they kept apart. Now they were united. Some bond had brought them together. It was the black-backed gull that attacked the smaller birds, and even new-born lambs, so he'd heard. He'd never seen it done. He remembered this now, though, looking above him in the sky. They were coming in towards the farm. They were circling lower in the sky, and the black-backed gulls were to the front, the black-backed gulls were leading. The farm, then, was their target. They were making for the farm.

Nat increased his pace toward his own cottage. He saw the farmer's car turn and come back along the lane. It drew up beside him with a jerk.

"The kid has run inside," said the farmer. "Your wife was watching for her. Well, what do you make of it? They're saying in town the Russians have done it. The Russians have poisoned the birds."

"How could they do that?" asked Nat.

"Don't ask me. You know how stories get around. Will you join my shooting match?"

"No, I'll get along home. The wife will be worried else."

"My missus says if you could eat gull there'd be some sense in it," said Trigg. "We'd have roast gull, baked gull, and pickle 'em into the bargain. You wait until I let off a few barrels into the brutes. That'll scare 'em."

"Have you boarded your windows?" asked Nat.

"No. Lot of nonsense. They like to scare you on the wireless. I've had more to do today than to go round boarding up my windows."

"I'd board them now, if I were you."

"Garn. You're windy. Like to come to our place to sleep?"

"No, thanks all the same."

"All right. See you in the morning. Give you a gull breakfast."

The farmer grinned and turned his car to the farm entrance.

Nat hurried on. Past the little wood, past the old barn, and then across the stile to the remaining field.

As he jumped the stile he heard the whir of wings. A black-backed gull dived down at him from the sky, missed, swerved in flight, and rose to dive again. In a moment it was joined by others, six, seven, a dozen, black-backed and herring mixed. Nat dropped his hoe. The hoe was useless. Covering his head with his arms, he ran toward the cottage. They kept coming at him from the air, silent save for the beating wings. The terrible, fluttering wings. He could feel the blood on his hands, his wrists, his neck. Each stab of a swooping beak tore his flesh. If only he could keep them from his eyes. Nothing else mattered. He must keep them from his eyes. They had not learned yet how to cling to a shoulder, how to rip cloth-

> ◆ **Reading Strategy**
> What do you predict will happen to the farmer? Why?

ing, how to dive in mass upon the head, upon the body. But with each dive, with each attack, they became bolder. And they had no thought for themselves. When they dived low and missed, they crashed, bruised and broken, on the ground. As Nat ran he stumbled, kicking their spent bodies in front of him.

He found the door; he hammered upon it with his bleeding hands. Because of the boarded windows no light shone. Everything was dark.

"Let me in," he shouted, "it's Nat. Let me in."

He shouted loud to make himself heard above the whir of the gulls' wings.

Then he saw the gannet, poised for the dive, above him in the sky. The gulls circled, retired, soared, one after another, against the wind. Only the gannet remained. One single gannet above him in the sky. The wings folded suddenly to its body. It dropped like a stone. Nat screamed, and the door opened. He stumbled across the threshold, and his wife threw her weight against the door.

They heard the thud of the gannet as it fell.

His wife dressed his wounds. They were not deep. The backs of his hands had suffered most, and his wrists. Had he not worn a cap they would have reached his head. As to the gannet . . . the gannet could have split his skull.

The children were crying, of course. They had seen the blood on their father's hands.

"It's all right now," he told them. "I'm not hurt. Just a few scratches. You play with Johnny, Jill. Mammy will wash these cuts."

He half shut the door to the scullery so that they could not see. His wife was ashen. She began running water from the sink.

▼ Critical Viewing What do the scraggly tree and the scores of birds in the photograph convey about the setting of this story? [Infer]

"I saw them overhead," she whispered. "They began collecting just as Jill ran in with Mr. Trigg. I shut the door fast, and it jammed. That's why I couldn't open it at once when you came."

"Thank God they waited for me," he said. "Jill would have fallen at once. One bird alone would have done it."

Furtively, so as not to alarm the children, they whispered together as she bandaged his hands and the back of his neck.

"They're flying inland," he said, "thousands of them. Rooks, crows, all the bigger birds. I saw them from the bus stop. They're making for the towns."

"But what can they do, Nat?"

"They'll attack. Go for everyone out in the streets. Then they'll try the windows, the chimneys."

"Why don't the authorities do something? Why don't they get the Army, get machine guns, anything?"

"There's been no time. Nobody's prepared. We'll hear what they have to say on the six o'clock news."

Nat went back into the kitchen, followed by his wife. Johnny was playing quietly on the floor. Only Jill looked anxious.

"I can hear the birds," she said. "Listen, Dad."

Nat listened. Muffled sounds came from the windows, from the door. Wings brushing the surface, sliding, scraping, seeking a way of entry. The sound of many bodies, pressed together, shuffling on the sills. Now and again came a thud, a crash, as some bird dived and fell. "Some of them will kill themselves that way," he thought, "but not enough. Never enough."

"All right," he said aloud. "I've got boards over the windows, Jill. The birds can't get in."

He went and examined all the windows. His work had been thorough. Every gap was closed. He would make extra certain, however. He found wedges, pieces of old tin, strips of wood and metal, and fastened them at the sides to reinforce the boards. His hammering helped to deafen the sound of the birds, the shuffling, the tapping, and more ominous—he did not want his wife or the children to hear it—the splinter of cracked glass.

"Turn on the wireless," he said, "let's have the wireless."

This would drown the sound also. He went upstairs to the bedrooms and reinforced the windows there. Now he could hear the birds on the roof, the scraping of claws, a sliding, jostling sound.

He decided they must sleep in the kitchen, keep up the fire, bring down the mattresses, and lay them out on the floor. He was afraid of the bedroom chimneys. The boards he had placed at the chimney bases might give way. In the kitchen they would be safe because of the fire. He would have to make a joke of it. Pretend to the children they were playing at camp. If the worst happened, and the birds forced an entry down the bedroom chimneys, it would be hours, days perhaps, before they could break down the doors. The birds would be imprisoned in the bedrooms. They could do no harm there. Crowded together, they would stifle and die.

He began to bring the mattresses downstairs. At sight of them his wife's eyes widened in apprehension. She thought the birds had already broken in upstairs.

> Muffled sounds came from the windows, from the door. Wings brushing the surface, sliding, scraping, seeking a way of entry.

◆ Build Vocabulary

furtively (fur´ tiv lē) *adv.:* Stealthily, so as to avoid being heard

imperative (im per´ ə tiv) *adj.:* Absolutely necessary; urgent

"All right," he said cheerfully, "we'll all sleep together in the kitchen tonight. More cozy here by the fire. Then we shan't be worried by those silly old birds tapping at the windows."

He made the children help him rearrange the furniture, and he took the precaution of moving the dresser, with his wife's help, across the window. It fitted well. It was an added safeguard. The mattresses could now be laid, one beside the other, against the wall where the dresser had stood.

"We're safe enough now," he thought. "We're snug and tight, like an air-raid shelter. We can hold out. It's just the food that worries me. Food, and coal for the fire. We've enough for two or three days, not more. By that time . . ."

No use thinking ahead as far as that. And they'd be giving directions on the wireless. People would be told what to do. And now, in the midst of many problems, he realized that it was dance music only coming over the air. Not Children's Hour, as it should have been. He glanced at the dial. Yes, they were on the Home Service all right. Dance records. He switched to the Light program. He knew the reason. The usual programs had been abandoned. This only happened at exceptional times. Elections and such. He tried to remember if it had happened in the war, during the heavy raids on London. But of course. The B.B.C.[9] was not stationed in London during the war. The programs were broadcast from other, temporary quarters. "We're better off here," he thought; "we're better off here in the kitchen, with the windows and the doors boarded, than they are up in the towns. Thank God we're not in the towns."

At six o'clock the records ceased. The time signal was given. No matter if it scared the children, he must hear the news. There was a pause after the pips.[10] Then the an-

nouncer spoke. His voice was solemn, grave. Quite different from midday.

"This is London," he said. "A National Emergency was proclaimed at four o'clock this afternoon. Measures are being taken to safeguard the lives and property of the population, but it must be understood that these are not easy to effect immediately, owing to the unforeseen and unparalleled nature of the present crisis. Every householder must take precautions to his own building, and where several people live together, as in flats and apartments, they must unite to do the utmost they can to prevent entry. It is absolutely imperative that every individual stay indoors tonight and that no one at all remain on the streets, or roads, or anywhere withoutdoors.[11] The birds, in vast numbers, are attacking anyone on sight, and have already begun an assault upon buildings; but these, with due care, should be impenetrable. The population is asked to remain calm and not to panic. Owing to the exceptional nature of the emergency, there will be no further transmission from any broadcasting station until 7 A.M. tomorrow."

> ◆ *Literature and Your Life*
>
> Has a state of emergency ever been declared in your community because of a natural calamity, such as a blizzard or a hurricane?

They played the National Anthem. Nothing more happened. Nat switched off the set. He looked at his wife. She stared back at him.

"What's it mean?" said Jill. "What did the news say?"

"There won't be any more programs tonight," said Nat. "There's been a breakdown at the B.B.C."

"Is it the birds?" asked Jill. "Have the birds done it?"

---

9. **B.B.C.:** British Broadcasting Corporation.
10. **pips** *n.:* Beeping sounds that indicate the time.

11. **withoutdoors** *adv.:* Old-fashioned variation of outdoors.

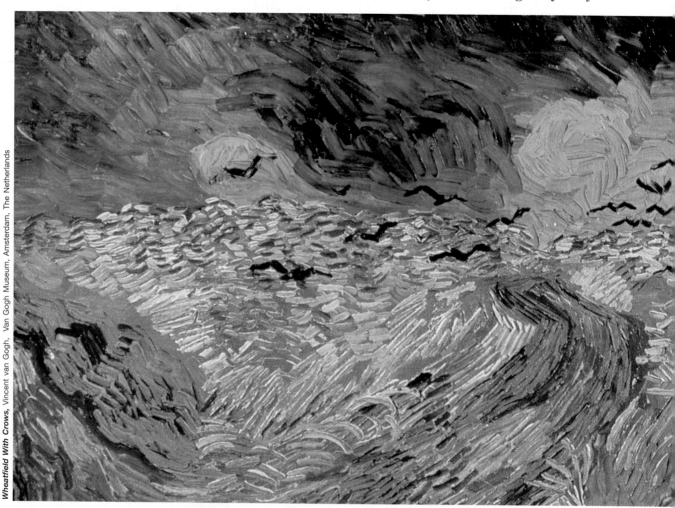

"No," said Nat, "it's just that everyone's very busy, and then of course they have to get rid of the birds, messing everything up, in the towns. Well, we can manage without the wireless for one evening."

"I wish we had a gramophone,"[12] said Jill, "that would be better than nothing."

She had her face turned to the dresser backed against the windows. Try as they did to ignore it, they were all aware of the shuffling, the stabbing, the persistent beating and sweeping of wings.

"We'll have supper early," suggested Nat, "something for a treat. Ask Mammy. Toasted cheese, eh? Something we all like?"

---

12. **gramophone** (gram´ ə fōn´) n.: Phonograph; record player.

He winked and nodded at his wife. He wanted the look of dread, of apprehension, to go from Jill's face.

He helped with the supper, whistling, singing, making as much clatter as he could, and it seemed to him that the shuffling and the tapping were not so intense as they had been at first. Presently he went up to the bedrooms and listened, and he no longer heard the jostling for place upon the roof.

"They've got reasoning powers," he thought; "they know it's hard to break in here. They'll try elsewhere. They won't waste their time with us."

Supper passed without incident, and then, when they were clearing away, they heard a new sound, droning, familiar, a sound they all knew and understood.

His wife looked up at him, her face alight. "It's planes," she said; "they're sending out planes after the birds. That's what I said they ought to do all along. That will get them. Isn't that gunfire? Can't you hear guns?"

It might be gunfire out at sea. Nat could not tell. Big naval guns might have an effect upon the gulls out at sea, but the gulls were inland now. The guns couldn't shell the shore because of the population.

"It's good, isn't it," said his wife, "to hear the planes?" And Jill, catching her enthusiasm, jumped up and down with Johnny. "The planes will get the birds. The planes will shoot them."

Just then they heard a crash about two miles distant, followed by a second, then a third. The droning became more distant, passed away out to sea.

"What was that?" asked his wife. "Were they dropping bombs on the birds?"

"I don't know," answered Nat. "I don't think so."

He did not want to tell her that the sound they had heard was the crashing of aircraft. It was, he had no doubt, a venture on the part of the authorities to send out <u>reconnaissance</u> forces, but they might have known the venture was suicidal. What could aircraft do against birds that flung themselves to death against propeller and fuselage, but hurtle to the ground themselves? This was being tried now, he supposed, over the whole country. And at a cost. Someone high up had lost his head.

"Where have the planes gone, Dad?" asked Jill.

"Back to base," he said. "Come on, now, time to tuck down for bed."

It kept his wife occupied, undressing the children before the fire, seeing to the bedding, one thing and another, while he went round the cottage again, making sure that nothing had worked loose. There was no further drone of aircraft, and the naval guns had ceased. "Waste of life and effort," Nat said to himself. "We can't destroy enough of them that way. Cost too heavy. There's always gas. Maybe they'll try spraying with gas, mustard gas. We'll be warned first, of course, if they do. There's one thing, the best brains of the country will be on to it tonight."

◆ **Build Vocabulary**

reconnaissance (ri kän′ ə səns) *adj.*: Exploratory in nature, as when examining or observing to seek information

◀ Critical Viewing Think of a name for this painting that describes the feeling it conveys. [Describe]

Somehow the thought reassured him. He had a picture of scientists, naturalists, technicians, and all those chaps they called the back-room boys, summoned to a council; they'd be working on the problem now. This was not a job for the government, for the chiefs of staff—they would merely carry out the orders of the scientists.

"They'll have to be ruthless," he thought. "Where the trouble's worst they'll have to risk more lives, if they use gas. All the livestock, too, and the soil—all contaminated. As long as everyone doesn't panic. That's the trouble. People panicking, losing their heads. The B.B.C. was right to warn us of that."

Upstairs in the bedrooms all was quiet. No further scraping and stabbing at the windows. A lull in battle. Forces regrouping. Wasn't that what they called it in the old wartime bulletins? The wind hadn't dropped, though. He could still hear it roaring in the chimneys. And the sea breaking down on the shore. Then he remembered the tide. The tide would be on the turn. Maybe the lull in battle was because of the tide. There was some law the birds obeyed, and it was all to do with the east wind and the tide.

He glanced at his watch. Nearly eight o'clock. It must have gone high water an hour ago. That explained the lull: the birds attacked with the flood tide. It might not work that way inland, upcountry, but it seemed as if it was so this way on the coast. He reckoned the time limit in his head. They had six hours to go without attack. When the tide turned again, around one-twenty in the morning, the birds would come back . . .

There were two things he could do. The first to rest, with his wife and the children, and all of them snatch what sleep they could, until the small hours. The second to go out, see how they were faring at the farm, see if the telephone was still working there, so that they might get news from the exchange.

He called softly to his wife, who had just settled the children. She came halfway up the stairs and he whispered to her.

"You're not to go," she said at once, "you're not to go and leave me alone with the children. I can't stand it."

Her voice rose hysterically. He hushed her, calmed her.

"All right," he said, "all right. I'll wait till morning. And we'll get the wireless bulletin then too, at seven. But in the morning, when the tide ebbs again, I'll try for the farm, and they may let us have bread and potatoes, and milk too."

His mind was busy again, planning against emergency. They would not have milked, of course, this evening. The cows would be standing by the gate, waiting in the yard, with the household inside, battened behind boards, as they were here at the cottage. That is, if they had time to take precautions. He thought of the farmer, Trigg, smiling at him from the car. There would have been no shooting party, not tonight.

The children were asleep. His wife, still clothed, was sitting on her mattress. She watched him, her eyes nervous.

"What are you going to do?" she whispered.

He shook his head for silence. Softly, stealthily, he opened the back door and looked outside.

It was pitch dark. The wind was blowing harder than ever, coming in steady gusts, icy, from the sea. He kicked at the step outside the door. It was heaped with birds. There were dead birds everywhere. Under the windows, against the walls. These were the suicides, the divers, the ones with broken necks. Wherever he looked he saw dead birds. No trace of the living. The living had flown seaward with the turn of the tide. The gulls would be riding the seas now, as they had done in the forenoon.

In the far distance, on the hill where the tractor had been two days before, something was burning. One of the aircraft that had crashed; the fire, fanned by the wind, had set light to a stack.

He looked at the bodies of the birds, and he had a notion that if he heaped them, one upon the other, on the windowsills they would make added protection for the next attack. Not much, perhaps, but something. The bodies would have to be clawed at, pecked, and dragged aside before the living birds could gain purchase on the sills and attack the panes. He set to work in the darkness. It was queer; he hated touching them. The bodies were still warm and bloody. The blood matted their feathers. He felt his stomach turn, but he went on with his work. He noticed grimly that every windowpane was shattered. Only the boards had kept the birds from breaking in. He stuffed the cracked panes with the bleeding bodies of the birds.

When he had finished he went back into the cottage. He barricaded the kitchen door, made it doubly secure. He took off his bandages, sticky with the birds' blood, not with his own cuts, and put on a fresh bandage.

His wife had made him cocoa and he drank it thirstily. He was very tired.

"All right," he said, smiling, "don't worry. We'll get through."

He lay down on his mattress and closed his eyes. He slept at once. He dreamt uneasily, because through his dreams there ran a thread of something forgotten. Some piece of work, neglected, that he should have done. Some precaution that he had known well but had not taken, and he could not put a name to it in his dreams. It was connected in some way with the burning aircraft and the stack upon the hill. He went on sleeping, though; he did not awake. It was his wife shaking his shoulder that awoke him finally.

"They've begun," she sobbed, "they've started this last hour. I can't listen to it any longer alone. There's something smelling bad too, something burning."

Then he remembered. He had forgotten to make up the fire. It was smoldering, nearly out. He got up swiftly and lit the lamp. The hammering had started at the windows and the doors, but it was not that he minded now. It was the smell of singed feathers. The smell filled the kitchen. He knew at once what it was. The birds were coming down the chimney, squeezing their way down to the kitchen range.

He got sticks and paper and put them on the embers, then reached for the can of paraffin.[13]

"Stand back," he shouted to his wife. "We've got to risk this."

He threw the paraffin onto the fire. The flame roared up the pipe, and down upon the fire fell the scorched, blackened bodies of the birds.

The children woke, crying. "What is it?" said Jill. "What's happened?"

Nat had no time to answer. He was raking the bodies from the chimney, clawing them out onto the floor. The flames still roared, and the danger of the chimney catching fire was one he had to take. The flames would send away the living birds from the chimney top. The lower joint was the difficulty, though. This was choked with the smoldering, helpless bodies of the birds caught by fire. He scarcely heeded the attack on the windows and the door: let them beat their wings, break their beaks, lose their lives, in the attempt to force an entry into his home. They would not break in. He thanked God he had one of the old cottages, with small windows, stout walls. Not like the new council houses. Heaven help them up the lane in the new council houses.

"Stop crying," he called to the children. "There's nothing to be afraid of, stop crying."

◆ Reading Strategy
What do you predict will happen next inside the house?

---

13. **paraffin** (par´ ə fin) *n.:* Kerosene.

He went on raking at the burning, smoldering bodies as they fell into the fire.

"This'll fetch them," he said to himself, "the draft and the flames together. We're all right, as long as the chimney doesn't catch. I ought to be shot for this. It's all my fault. Last thing, I should have made up the fire. I knew there was something."

Amid the scratching and tearing at the window boards came the sudden homely striking of the kitchen clock. Three A.M. A little more than four hours yet to go. He could not be sure of the exact time of high water. He reckoned it would not turn much before half-past seven, twenty to eight.

"Light up the Primus,"[14] he said to his wife. "Make us some tea, and the kids some cocoa. No use sitting around doing nothing."

That was the line. Keep her busy, and the children too. Move about, eat, drink; always best to be on the go.

He waited by the range. The flames were dying. But no more blackened bodies fell from the chimney. He thrust his poker up as far as it could go and found nothing. It was clear. The chimney was clear. He wiped the sweat from his forehead.

"Come on now, Jill," he said, "bring me some more sticks. We'll have a good fire going directly." She wouldn't come near him, though. She was staring at the heaped singed bodies of the birds.

"Never mind them," he said. "We'll put those in the passage when I've got the fire steady."

The danger of the chimney was over. It could not happen again, not if the fire was kept burning day and night.

"I'll have to get more fuel from the farm tomorrow," he thought. "This will never last. I'll manage, though. I can do all that with the ebb tide. It can be worked, fetching what we need, when the tide's turned. We've just got to adapt ourselves, that's all."

They drank tea and cocoa and ate slices of bread and Bovril.[15] Only half a loaf left, Nat noticed. Never mind though, they'd get by.

"Stop it," said young Johnny, pointing to the windows with his spoon, "stop it, you old birds."

"That's right," said Nat, smiling, "we don't want the old beggars, do we? Had enough of 'em."

They began to cheer when they heard the thud of the suicide birds.

"There's another, Dad," cried Jill, "he's done for."

"He's had it," said Nat. "There he goes, the blighter."

This was the way to face up to it. This was the spirit. If they could keep this up, hang on like this until seven, when the first news bulletin came through, they would not have done too badly.

"Give us a cigarette," he said to his wife. "A bit of a smoke will clear away the smell of the scorched feathers."

"There's only two left in the packet," she said. "I was going to buy you some from the Co-op."

"I'll have one," he said. "t'other will keep for a rainy day."

No sense trying to make the children rest. There was no rest to be got while the tapping and the scratching went on at the windows. He sat with one arm round his wife and the other round Jill, with Johnny on his mother's lap and the blankets heaped about them on the mattress.

"You can't help admiring the beggars," he said; "they've got persistence. You'd think they'd tire of the game, but not a bit of it."

Admiration was hard to sustain. The tapping went on and on and a new rasping note struck Nat's ear, as though a sharper beak than any hitherto had come to take over from its fellows. He tried to remember the names of birds; he tried to think which

---

14. **Primus** (prī′ məs) *n.*: Small, portable stove.

15. **Bovril** (bō′ vril) *n.*: Thick beef-flavored liquid used to make broth.

species would go for this particular job. It was not the tap of the woodpecker. That would be light and frequent. This was more serious, because if it continued long the wood would splinter as the glass had done. Then he remembered the hawks. Could the hawks have taken over from the gulls? Were there buzzards now upon the sills, using talons as well as beaks? Hawks, buzzards, kestrels, falcons—he had forgotten the birds of prey. He had forgotten the gripping power of the birds of prey. Three hours to go, and while they waited, the sound of the splintering wood, the talons tearing at the wood.

Nat looked about him, seeing what furniture he could destroy to fortify the door. The windows were safe because of the dresser. He was not certain of the door. He went upstairs, but when he reached the landing he paused and listened. There was a soft patter on the floor of the children's bedroom. The birds had broken through . . . He put his ear to the door. No mistake. He could hear the rustle of wings and the light patter as they searched the floor. The other bedroom was still clear. He went into it and began bringing out the furniture, to pile at the head of the stairs should the door of the children's bedroom go. It was a preparation. It might never be needed. He could not stack the furniture against the door, because it opened inward. The only possible thing was to have it at the top of the stairs.

"Come down. Nat, what are you doing?" called his wife.

"I won't be long," he shouted. "Just making everything shipshape up here."

He did not want her to come; he did not want her to hear the pattering of the feet in the children's bedroom, the brushing of those wings against the door.

At five-thirty he suggested breakfast, bacon and fried bread, if only to stop the growing look of panic in his wife's eyes and to calm the <u>fretful</u> children. She did not know about the birds upstairs. The bedroom, luckily, was not over the kitchen. Had it been so, she could not have failed to hear the sound of them up there, tapping the boards. And the silly, senseless thud of the suicide birds, the death and glory boys, who flew into the bedroom, smashing their heads against the walls. He knew them of old, the herring gulls. They had no brains. The blackbacks were different; they knew what they were doing. So did the buzzards, the hawks . . .

He found himself watching the clock, gazing at the hands that went so slowly round the dial. If his theory was not correct, if the attack did not cease with the turn of the tide, he knew they were beaten. They could not continue through the long day without air, without rest, without more fuel, without . . . His mind raced. He knew there were so many things they needed to withstand siege. They were not fully prepared. They were not ready. It might be that it would be safer in the towns after all. If he could get a message through on the farm telephone to his cousin, only a short journey by train upcountry, they might be able to hire a car. That would be quicker—hire a car between tides . . .

His wife's voice, calling his name, drove away the sudden, desperate desire for sleep.

"What is it? What now?" he said sharply.

"The wireless," said his wife. "I've been watching the clock. It's nearly seven."

"Don't twist the knob," he said, impatient for the first time. "It's on the Home where it is. They'll speak from the Home."

◆ **Build Vocabulary**

fretful (fret´ fəl) *adj.*: Irritable and discontented

There was a soft patter on the floor of the children's bedroom. The birds had broken through . . .

Over and Above #13, 1964, Clarence H. Carter

They waited. The kitchen clock struck seven. There was no sound. No chimes, no music. They waited until a quarter past, switching to the Light. The result was the same. No news bulletin came through.

"We've heard wrong," he said. "They won't be broadcasting until eight o'clock."

They left it switched on, and Nat thought of the battery, wondered how much power was left in it. It was generally recharged when his wife went shopping in the town. If the battery failed they would not hear the instructions.

▲ **Critical Viewing** What words would you use to describe the demeanor of this bird? **[Describe]**

"It's getting light," whispered his wife. "I can't see it, but I can feel it. And the birds aren't hammering so loud."

She was right. The rasping, tearing sound grew fainter every moment. So did the shuffling, the jostling for place upon the step, upon the sills. The tide was on the turn. By eight there was no sound at all. Only the wind. The children, lulled at last by the stillness, fell asleep. At half-past eight Nat switched the wireless off.

"What are you doing? We'll miss the news," said his wife.

"There isn't going to be any news," said Nat. "We've got to depend upon ourselves."

He went to the door and slowly pulled away the barricades. He drew the bolts and, kicking the bodies from the step outside the door, breathed the cold air. He had six working hours before him, and he knew he must reserve his strength for the right things, not waste it in any way. Food, and light, and fuel; these were the necessary things. If he could get them in sufficiency, they could endure another night.

He stepped into the garden, and as he did so he saw the living birds. The gulls had gone to ride the sea, as they had done before; they sought sea food, and the buoyancy of the tide, before they returned to the attack. Not so the land birds. They waited and watched. Nat saw them, on the hedgerows, on the soil, crowded in the trees, outside in the field, line upon line of birds, all still, doing nothing.

He went to the end of his small garden. The birds did not move. They went on watching him.

"I've got to get food," said Nat to himself. "I've got to go to the farm to find food."

He went back to the cottage. He saw to the windows and the doors. He went upstairs and opened the children's bedroom. It was empty, except for the dead birds on the floor. The living were out there, in the garden, in the fields. He went downstairs.

"I'm going to the farm," he said.

His wife clung to him. She had seen the living birds from the open door.

"Take us with you," she begged. "We can't stay here alone. I'd rather die than stay here alone."

He considered the matter. He nodded.

"Come on, then," he said. "Bring baskets, and Johnny's pram.[16] We can load up the pram."

They dressed against the biting wind, wore gloves and scarves. His wife put Johnny in the pram. Nat took Jill's hand.

"The birds," she whimpered, "they're all out there in the fields."

"They won't hurt us," he said, "not in the light."

They started walking across the field towards the stile, and the birds did not move. They waited, their heads turned to the wind.

When they reached the turning to the farm, Nat stopped and told his wife to wait in the shelter of the hedge with the two children.

"But I want to see Mrs. Trigg," she protested. "There are lots of things we can borrow if they went to market yesterday; not only bread, and . . ."

"Wait here," Nat interrupted. "I'll be back in a moment."

The cows were lowing, moving restlessly in the yard, and he could see a gap in the fence where the sheep had knocked their way through, to roam unchecked in the front garden before the farmhouse. No smoke came from the chimneys. He was filled with misgiving. He did not want his wife or the children to go down to the farm.

"Don't gib[17] now," said Nat, harshly, "do what I say."

She withdrew with the pram into the hedge, screening herself and the children from the wind.

He went down alone to the farm. He pushed his way through the herd of bellowing cows, which turned this way and that, distressed, their udders full. He saw the car standing by the gate, not put away in the garage. The windows of the farmhouse were smashed. There were many dead gulls lying in the yard and around the house. The living birds perched on the group of trees behind the farm and on the roof of the house. They were quite still. They watched him.

Jim's body lay in the yard . . . what was left of it. When the birds had finished, the

---

16. **pram** *n.*: Baby carriage.

17. **gib** (jib) *v.*: Hesitate.

cows had trampled him. His gun was beside him. The door of the house was shut and bolted, but as the windows were smashed it was easy to lift them and climb through. Trigg's body was close to the telephone. He must have been trying to get through to the exchange when the birds came for him. The receiver was hanging loose, the instrument torn from the wall. No sign of Mrs. Trigg. She would be upstairs. Was it any use going up? Sickened, Nat knew what he would find.

"Thank God," he said to himself, "there were no children."

◆ **Literary Focus**
Do you think the deaths of everyone at the farm foreshadow a similar fate for Nat and his family? Why or why not?

He forced himself to climb the stairs, but halfway he turned and descended again. He could see her legs protruding from the open bedroom door. Beside her were the bodies of the black-backed gulls, and an umbrella, broken.

"It's no use," thought Nat, "doing anything. I've only got five hours, less than that. The Triggs would understand. I must load up with what I can find."

He tramped back to his wife and children.

"I'm going to fill up the car with stuff," he said. "I'll put coal in it, and paraffin for the Primus. We'll take it home and return for a fresh load."

"What about the Triggs?" asked his wife.

"They must have gone to friends," he said.

"Shall I come and help you, then?"

"No; there's a mess down there. Cows and sheep all over the place. Wait, I'll get the car. You can sit in it."

Clumsily he backed the car out of the yard and into the lane. His wife and the children could not see Jim's body from there.

"Stay here," he said, "never mind the pram. The pram can be fetched later. I'm going to load the car."

Her eyes watched his all the time. He believed she understood, otherwise she would have suggested helping him to find the bread and groceries.

They made three journeys altogether, backwards and forwards between their cottage and the farm, before he was satisfied they had everything they needed. It was surprising, once he started thinking, how many things were necessary. Almost the most important of all was planking for the windows. He had to go round searching for timber. He wanted to renew the boards on all the windows at the cottage. Candles, paraffin, nails, tinned stuff; the list was endless. Besides all that, he milked three of the cows. The rest, poor brutes, would have to go on bellowing.

On the final journey he drove the car to the bus stop, got out, and went to the telephone box. He waited a few minutes, jangling the receiver. No good, though. The line was dead. He climbed on to a bank and looked over the countryside, but there was no sign of life at all, nothing in the fields but the waiting, watching birds. Some of them slept—he could see the beaks tucked into the feathers.

"You'd think they'd be feeding," he said to himself, "not just standing in that way."

Then he remembered. They were gorged with food. They had eaten their fill during the night. That was why they did not move this morning . . .

No smoke came from the chimneys of the council houses. He thought of the children who had run across the fields the night before.

"I should have known," he thought; "I ought to have taken them home with me."

He lifted his face to the sky. It was colorless and gray. The bare trees on the landscape looked bent and blackened by the east wind. The cold did not affect the living birds waiting out there in the fields.

"This is the time they ought to get them," said Nat; "they're a sitting target now. They must be doing this all over the country. Why don't our aircraft take off now and spray them with mustard gas? What are all our chaps doing? They must know, they must see for themselves."

He went back to the car and got into the driver's seat.

"Go quickly past that second gate," whispered his wife. "The postman's lying there. I don't want Jill to see."

He accelerated. The little Morris bumped and rattled along the lane. The children shrieked with laughter.

"Up-a-down, up-a-down," shouted young Johnny.

It was a quarter to one by the time they reached the cottage. Only an hour to go.

"Better have cold dinner," said Nat. "Hot up something for yourself and the children, some of that soup. I've no time to eat now. I've got to unload all this stuff."

He got everything inside the cottage. It could be sorted later. Give them all something to do during the long hours ahead. First he must see to the windows and the doors.

He went round the cottage methodically, testing every window, every door. He climbed on to the roof also, and fixed boards across every chimney, except the kitchen. The cold was so intense he could hardly bear it, but the job had to be done. Now and again he would look up, searching the sky for aircraft. None came. As he worked he cursed the inefficiency of the authorities.

"It's always the same," he muttered. "They always let us down. Muddle, muddle, from the start. No plan, no real organization. And we don't matter down here. That's what it is. The people upcountry have priority. They're using gas up there, no doubt, and all the aircraft. We've got to wait and take what comes."

He paused, his work on the bedroom chimney finished, and looked out to sea. Something was moving out there. Something gray and white amongst the breakers.

"Good old Navy," he said, "they never let us down. They're coming down-channel, they're turning in the bay."

He waited, straining his eyes, watering in the wind, towards the sea. He was wrong, though. It was not ships. The Navy was not there. The gulls were rising from the sea. The massed flocks in the fields, with ruffled feathers, rose in formation from the ground and, wing to wing, soared upwards to the sky.

◆ **Reading Strategy**
Predict what will happen next.

> The massed flocks in the fields, with ruffled feathers, rose in formation from the ground and, wing to wing, soared upwards to the sky.

The tide had turned again.

Nat climbed down the ladder and went inside the kitchen. The family were at dinner. It was a little after two. He bolted the door, put up the barricade, and lit the lamp.

"It's nighttime," said young Johnny.

His wife had switched on the wireless once again, but no sound came from it.

"I've been all round the dial," she said, "foreign stations, and that lot. I can't get anything."

"Maybe they have the same trouble," he said, "maybe it's the same right through Europe."

She poured out a plateful of the Triggs' soup, cut him a large slice of the Triggs' bread, and spread their dripping upon it.

They ate in silence. A piece of the dripping ran down young Johnny's chin and fell on to the table.

"Manners, Johnny," said Jill, "you should learn to wipe your mouth."

The tapping began at the windows, at the door. The rustling, the jostling, the pushing for position on the sills. The first thud of the suicide gulls upon the step.

"Won't America do something?" said his wife. "They've always been our allies, haven't they? Surely America will do something?"

Nat did not answer. The boards were strong against the windows, and on the chimneys too. The cottage was filled with stores, with fuel, with all they needed for the next few days. When he had finished dinner he would put the stuff away, stack it neatly, get everything shipshape, handy-like. His wife could help him, and the children too. They'd tire themselves out, between now and a quarter to nine, when the tide would ebb; then he'd tuck them down on their mattresses, see that they slept good and sound until three in the morning.

He had a new scheme for the windows, which was to fix barbed wire in front of the boards. He had brought a great roll of it from the farm. The nuisance was, he'd have to work at this in the dark, when the lull came between nine and three. Pity he had not thought of it before. Still, as long as the wife slept, and the kids, that was the main thing.

The smaller birds were at the window now. He recognized the light tap-tapping of their beaks and the soft brush of their wings. The hawks ignored the windows. They concentrated their attack upon the door. Nat listened to the tearing sound of splintering wood, and wondered how many million years of memory were stored in those little brains, behind the stabbing beaks, the piercing eyes, now giving them this instinct to destroy mankind with all the deft precision of machines.

"I'll smoke that last cigarette," he said to his wife. "Stupid of me, it was the one thing I forgot to bring back from the farm."

He reached for it, switched on the silent wireless. He threw the empty packet on the fire, and watched it burn.

Guide for Responding

◆ Literature and Your Life

Reader's Response Did you find this story exciting and suspenseful? Why or why not?

Thematic Focus Name at least two suspenseful situations from nature that you have either seen or heard about.

Group Activity The different types of birds in the story seem to have their own personalities and ways of behavior. With a small group, brainstorm for at least four personality traits of the gulls. Support each trait with an example of behavior from the story.

☑ Check Your Comprehension

1. According to the farmer, what was different about the birds this fall?
2. Why did a cry of terror come from the room in which the children slept?
3. Why did Nat ask the farmer to drive his daughter the rest of the way home after school?
4. What happened to the postman and the people who lived on the farm?
5. What preparations did Nat make just before the final attack of the birds was about to begin?

Guide for Responding (continued)

◆ Critical Thinking

INTERPRET

1. Why are the birds so destructive? [Analyze]
2. How do the successive announcements on the BBC help create a sense of suspense? [Analyze]
3. At a certain point, the BBC is no longer broadcasting. What does this imply about conditions in the cities of England? [Draw Conclusions]
4. In the end, will Nat and his family survive the attacks? Why or why not? [Speculate]
5. What makes the birds suddenly attack people and try to kill them? [Draw Conclusions]

APPLY

6. Do you think that an animal population could suddenly turn against people? Why? [Speculate]

EVALUATE

7. Do you think the inconclusive ending of this story is effective? Why or why not? [Evaluate]

◆ Reading Strategy

MAKE PREDICTIONS

As you read "The Birds," you made **predictions** based on story details. Now focus on the end of the story. The words "The tapping began at the windows" signal the beginning of yet another assault by the birds. Keeping in mind the story details up to this point, what do you think will happen? Why?

◆ Build Grammar Skills

COMPOUND SENTENCES

In "The Birds," du Maurier frequently uses **compound sentences**—sentences that consist of two or more independent clauses.

Practice Add a clause to each sentence to form a compound sentence.

Example: The sky was gray
Answer: The sky was gray, and the wind was howling.

1. The birds swooped down
2. The sky darkened
3. The radio was turned on
4. He had prepared for this moment
5. The tapping sound grew louder

◆ Literary Focus

FORESHADOWING

Daphne du Maurier uses **foreshadowing**—hinting at events to come—to build suspense and create a sense of impending doom.

1. How is Nat's sighting of masses of gulls riding the sea a foreshadowing of possible disaster?
2. How does the BBC announcement of a national emergency foreshadow tragic events?

◆ Build Vocabulary

USING THE SUFFIX -ful

The word *fretful* in "The Birds" contains the suffix -*ful*. Add the suffix -*ful* to these words. Tell their meaning.

1. sorrow   2. teaspoon   3. help

USING THE WORD BANK

On a separate sheet of paper, match the word from the Word Bank to its synonym.

1. placid   a. gloomy
2. garish   b. urgent
3. reconaissance   c. calm
4. sullen   d. exploratory
5. furtively   e. gaudy
6. imperative   f. stealthily

Beyond Literature

Media Connection

Alfred Hitchcock's *The Birds*
Imagine sitting in a dark movie theater watching flickering images of flocks of birds descending on an unsuspecting town. This was what it was like to watch Alfred Hitchcock's (1899–1980) classic tale of horror, *The Birds*, adapted from du Maurier's story. Released in 1963, Hitchcock's film is still regarded as one of the most terrifying movies ever made and has influenced many subsequent horror films. What do you think might have led Hitchcock to adapt du Maurier's story into a film?

Build Your Portfolio

Idea Bank

Writing

1. **The Final Outcome** Will Nat and his family survive the birds' attack? Write an ending to the story.

2. **Public Service Announcement** Write an announcement for broadcast on the BBC describing government measures—such as military actions—to stop attacks of the birds.

3. **Book vs. Movie** Watch a videotape of Alfred Hitchcock's 1963 film version of "The Birds." Then write an essay in which you compare and contrast the short story with the movie.

Speaking and Listening

4. **Panel Discussion** In "The Birds," people try to protect themselves from birds. In real life, birds often need protection from people. With a small group, hold a panel discussion in which you discuss ideas on what can be done to protect birds and their habitats. **[Science Link]**

5. **Scene** With a small group, review the scene in which Nat tries to convince Mr. Trigg to take precautions against the birds. Act out a continuation of the scene with additional dialogue in which Nat becomes more persuasive.

Projects

6. **Multimedia Presentation** Give a multimedia presentation on any four birds mentioned in the story. For each bird, research size, distinguishing features, natural habitat, and habits. Include photos or drawings and, if possible, include a recording of sounds made by each. **[Science Link]**

7. **A Picture of Flight** Draw or paint a picture of a bird in flight. Use an encyclopedia or other reference book to find a picture to serve as a model. **[Art Link]**

Writing Mini-Lesson

Bird's-Eye View of a Place

Imagine how different this story would be if it were told from a bird's-eye view! The action would be described from above, rather than below, and the perspective would be altered. Write a description of a familiar place as it would look to a bird overhead. Here are some tips to help you:

Writing Skills Focus: A Consistent Viewpoint

To make your bird's-eye view of a place clear, maintain a **consistent viewpoint.** As you write, remember that you are looking down on your scene. Wandering from this viewpoint will only confuse your readers.

Notice how du Maurier maintains the viewpoint of a person looking up in this passage.

Model From the Story

Then he saw the gannet, poised for the dive, above him in the sky. . . . Only the gannet remained. One single gannet above him in the sky.

Prewriting Choose a familiar place to describe. Then draw a rough sketch of the place as seen from above. Label the key details in the sketch. Your sketch will help you visualize the place from a bird's perspective.

Drafting Refer to your sketch as you draft your bird's-eye view. Include details that indicate a downward-looking perspective, and avoid making observations from a different point of view. For example, a bird in the sky would be able to see an entire basketball court at a glance. It wouldn't, however, be able to see the color of a person's eyes.

Revising Reread your bird's-eye view, checking for inconsistencies of viewpoint. Correct any passage that describes something from the ground up.

Writing Process Workshop

You observe things all the time: an action-packed basketball game, the passing of a thunderstorm, the results of a laboratory experiment. When you describe an event that you've watched over a period of time, you are writing an **observation.** By using vivid details, you can re-create the event and make your readers feel as if they are witnessing it themselves.

The following skills, introduced in this section's Writing Mini-Lessons, will help you write an observation of any event.

Writing Skills Focus

▶ **Use precise details** to create a vivid picture. For example, tell whether the liquid in a test tube is beet red or carrot red. (See p. 12.)

▶ **Anticipate readers' questions** by thinking about what they'll want to know and providing it. (See p. 33.)

▶ **Use vivid verbs** rather than general ones—like *hover* rather than *fly.* (See p. 40.)

▶ **Maintain a consistent perspective.** In observing a game, for example, don't shift from a spectator's vantage point to a player's. (See p. 74.)

Hank Aaron uses all these skills as he observes the events leading up to his record-breaking homer.

MODEL FROM LITERATURE

from *I Had a Hammer* by Hank Aaron

Downing's first pitch was a change of pace that went into the dirt. ① The umpire, Satch Davidson, threw it out, and the first-base umpire, Frank Pulli, tossed Downing another one of the specially marked infrared balls. Downing rubbed it up and then threw his slider low and down the middle, which was not where he wanted it ② but which was fine with me. . . . The ball shot out ③ on a line over the shortstop, Bill Russell, who bent his knees as if he were going to jump up and catch it. ④

① This precise detail about the first pitch helps create tension.

② Aaron answers a question readers might ask: Did Downing get the pitch where he wanted it?

③ *Shot out* is a more vivid verb than *traveled.*

④ Aaron describes the whole scene from a batter's vantage point.

Applying Language Skills: Using Vivid Verbs

A vivid verb describes an action more precisely than a general verb.

General Verb:
He <u>runs</u> down the highway.

Vivid Verb:
He <u>lopes</u> down the highway.

Notice how the vivid verb paints a picture of a man running with a long, swinging stride.

Practice On your paper, replace the general verb in each sentence with a more vivid one.

1. He [moves] across the basketball court.
2. She [walks] down the avenue.
3. The hawk [flies] on an updraft of warm air.

Writing Application As you draft your observation, use vivid verbs to describe actions. If you can't think of a vivid verb at the moment, mark the general verb you use and replace it when you revise your work.

Writer's Solution Connection
Writing Lab

To help you gather precise details for your observation, use the Sensory Word Bin Activities in the Writing Lab tutorial on Description.

Prewriting

Choose a Topic Come up with a topic by searching your memory for interesting events that you've recently witnessed. You can also choose one of the topic ideas listed here.

Topic Ideas

- The passing scene from a car or bus window
- A seasonal event or celebration
- A natural event, like a thunderstorm
- The behavior of a pet

Create a Chart of Vivid Verbs Across the top of your chart, jot down general verbs to describe your subject. Then, under each, list vivid verbs that convey the same idea. You can draw on these as you draft your observation.

General: Move	General: Fly
Lope	Glide
Stride	Soar

Develop Details by Anticipating Readers' Questions If you're observing a thunderstorm, think of questions readers might ask about it:

▶ Where did it take place?
▶ How long did it last?
▶ How close did the lightning strike?

Answer each question by listing details you might include in your observation.

Science Writing Tip In a scientific observation, you answer many questions with precise measurements rather than general terms: An object is 3.6 meters tall, not just "tall."

Drafting

Keep a Consistent Perspective Don't confuse readers by observing a sports event from the stands in one paragraph and from the field in the next. Avoid this kind of mix-up by reminding yourself of your vantage point each time you begin a new paragraph. Then, as you write your observation, picture what you're seeing *from* that location.

Mark Places to Use Precise Details Avoid pausing to fill in precise details. Just mark the place; you can go back and insert details like a player's name or uniform number later. Professional editors often use the abbreviation TC or TK, meaning that something is "to come."

Revising

Use a Checklist Go back to the Writing Skills Focus on the first page of the lesson and use the items as a checklist to evaluate and revise your observation.

▶ Have I used precise details?
  Fill in the details that you didn't have time to look up or remember as you drafted.

▶ Have I used vivid verbs rather than general verbs?
  Look for general verbs like move, fly, *and* go. *If possible, replace them with more vivid and specific verbs.*

▶ Have I anticipated and answered readers' questions?
  Have a peer reviewer read your observation and jot down his or her unanswered questions.

▶ Have I maintained a consistent viewpoint?
  Draw a crude picture of the scene you've observed, marking your vantage point with an X. In reviewing your observation, be sure that everything you described was viewed from position X.

REVISION MODEL

① crouched,
Suddenly the player by the net ~~bent down~~, then leaped
②The top of the net was six feet high, and she rose about two feet above it.
high to reach the ball. ~~She saw everyone below her.~~ ③

① The writer uses a more vivid verb.
② This sentence includes a precise detail and answers a question readers might have: How high did she jump?
③ The writer deletes a confusing shift in perspective.

Publishing

▶ **Classroom** Share details of your observations with classmates and identify types of jobs that require observational skills.

▶ **School Newspaper** Create an Observation Column for your school's newspaper.

▶ **Internet** Post your writing to a message board in a news group.

APPLYING LANGUAGE SKILLS: Using Adverbs

Adverbs modify adjectives, verbs, and other adverbs, and they can help answer readers' questions:

When?
              adv   v
The umpire *finally* misses a call.

Where?
                v   adv
The batter practices *here*
in the batting box.

How?
     v   adv
He grips the bat *wildly*.

To what extent?
                 adv   adj
The pitcher is *very* dedicated.
            adv   adv
That pitcher hardly *ever* loses.

Practice On your paper, fill in adverbs to answer questions.

1. The storm was supposed to arrive _____ in the evening. (When in the evening?)
2. A lightning bolt struck _____, felling a tree. (Where did it strike?)

Writing Application Review your observation and find questions that are unanswered. Then answer these questions for readers by using adverbs.

Writer's Solution Connection
Language Lab

For more practice with adverbs, complete the Language Lab Lesson on Problems with Modifiers.

Real-World Reading Workshop

Strategies for Success

When you read a work of literature or a reference work that's accompanied by maps, knowing how to read the map will enhance your understanding of the work. Knowing how to read a map is equally if not more important when you're visiting a new city or looking for a famous landmark. The type of map you'll use on such occasions is a street map, which often shows buildings, parks, and other landmarks, in addition to streets.

Identify Your Purpose Identify your purpose in looking at a street map. Are you looking for a specific landmark, a particular street, or do you want to know the general layout of a neighborhood? Do you want to get to a specific place from where you are? Knowing your purpose will help you focus on the part of the map that you need.

Get an Overview Once you've identified your purpose, determine whether the street map fits your needs. Does it show an entire city or just a section? Are all the streets shown on the map or only the major ones?

Then get familiar with the map. Which way is north on the map? Where do the names of the streets appear? How does the map indicate buildings or other landmarks?

Read the Map When you're in the city and you want to get from one place to another, start by finding your location on the map. You can then determine the direction you need to travel to get where you want to be.

Apply the Strategy

It's your first trip to our nation's capital. You want to plan a walking tour that includes the White House, Lincoln Memorial, National Aquarium, and Washington Monument.

1. Will this map suit your needs? Why or why not?
2. In what order will you visit the attractions? Why?
3. Approximately how many blocks will you walk to complete the tour?
4. Plan another walking tour for the next day. Write the directions and attractions in the order you will visit them.

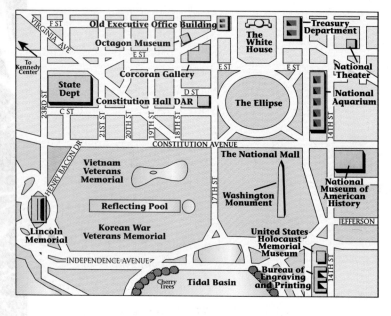

> ✔ Here are other situations in which a street map can be helpful:
> ▶ Meeting someone in an unfamiliar neighborhood
> ▶ Providing directions to your house
> ▶ Determining distances between places

PART 2 *It's a Mystery*

La Réponse Imprévue, René Magritte, Musées Royaux
des Beaux-Arts de Belgique, Bruxelles-Koninklijke
Musea voor Schone Kunsten van Belgie, Brussel

Guide for Reading

Sir Arthur Conan Doyle
(1859–1930)

The Englishman Sir Arthur Conan Doyle is known for creating the world's most famous fictional detective, Sherlock Holmes.

> *This larger-than-life character has outlived his creator and now outwits criminals in the movies.*

From Medicine to Mysteries

Perhaps it is no accident that the creator of the sharp-eyed, observant Holmes began his career as an eye doctor. In this profession, however, Doyle found little success and began writing stories to supplement his income. He probably modeled Sherlock Holmes, the hero of one of these stories, on a medical school professor who could diagnose a patient's illness from clues other doctors ignored.

The "Birth" of Sherlock Holmes

After several rejections from publishers, Doyle sold his first detective novel in 1887. In this novel, *A Study in Scarlet*, he introduces readers to the brilliant Holmes and to Holmes's devoted companion, Dr. John Watson. Perhaps remembering his own medical background, Doyle writes in the voice of Dr. Watson and pretends that the good doctor is telling the story.

The "Death" of Sherlock Holmes

Readers grew to love the odd detective who solved puzzling crimes. However, Doyle soon wearied of Holmes and killed off his own character in a story entitled "The Final Problem." The public would not stand for this outrage, however. Many readers wrote to Doyle, pleading with him to undo the death of Holmes. In the end, generous fees from publishers convinced Doyle to bring back the beloved detective. It seems as if he will never die again!

◆ Build Vocabulary

WORD ROOTS -*spec*-

In your Word Bank, you have the word *introspective*. This word is built on the root -*spec*-, which means "see" or "look." If you combine this root with *intro*, you have a word that means "looking inward." Therefore, an introspective person, like Sherlock Holmes, is one who looks within himself to find answers.

singular
avail
hoax
introspective
vex
conundrums
astuteness
formidable

WORD BANK

As you read "The Red-headed League," you will encounter the words on this list. Each word is defined on the page where it first appears. Preview the list before you read.

◆ Build Grammar Skills

COORDINATE ADJECTIVES

To describe Sherlock Holmes's many keen observations, Sir Arthur Conan Doyle uses numerous adjectives. Often, he uses more than one adjective before a noun, as in this example:

> I . . . found him deep in conversation with a *very stout, florid-faced, elderly* gentleman with *fiery red* hair.

Adjectives are **coordinate** if they each separately modify the noun; they are not coordinate if the final adjective is thought of as part of the noun.

Coordinate: *stout, florid-faced, elderly* gentleman

Not Coordinate: *fiery red* hair

The Red-headed League

◆ *Literature and Your Life*

CONNECT YOUR EXPERIENCE

A new student arrives in your school. Just a quick glance at him gives you clues to his personality: his clothes, shoes, and hairstyle; the way he carries himself; or any unusual habits, like cracking his knuckles. If you hear him speak, you get further clues about him.

This sizing up of people is part of the unpaid detective work of everyday life. As an amateur sleuth already, you'll want to read about the exploits of the world's greatest professional—Sherlock Holmes.

THEMATIC FOCUS: IT'S A MYSTERY

Notice the techniques that Holmes uses to solve the strange mystery of "The Red-headed League." How could you apply these techniques to mysteries that you encounter?

◆ Background for Understanding

LITERATURE

Sherlock Holmes, who is usually pictured wearing a cape and deerstalker cap, is recognizable throughout the world. He's even recognized by people who've never read a Sherlock Holmes mystery. New Holmes adventures continually appear in the form of television productions and movies. Even Commander Data, the android from *Star Trek: The Next Generation,* has spent fun-filled hours pretending to be Sherlock Holmes.

Journal Writing Think about the qualities of a successful detective. Jot down your ideas in your journal.

◆ Literary Focus

THE MYSTERY

A **mystery** is a story of suspense that usually contains the following elements: a crime, a crime-solver, a criminal, suspects, and key details such as clues, alibis, and characters' possible reasons for committing a crime. In most mysteries, the crime-solver, or detective, is the hero, and the reader "roots for" him or her.

◆ Reading Strategy

KEY DETAILS

Readers of mysteries try to solve the crime along with— or even before—the detective. You do this by noting **key details**, pieces of information having a bearing on the crime. These key details are often clues to solving the mystery.

The following passage from the story contains a key detail that helps Holmes to solve the mystery of "The Red-headed League":

> " . . . I have a small pawnbroker's business
> . . . I used to be able to keep two assistants, but now I only keep one; and I would have a job to pay him but that he is willing to come for half wages so as to learn the business."

From this passage, you might conclude that the assistant's willingness to work for "half wages" is suspicious. As you read this story, locate other key details and jot them down. Refer to your list as you attempt to solve the mystery.

The Red-headed League

Sir Arthur Conan Doyle

I had called upon my friend, Mr. Sherlock Holmes, one day in the autumn of last year and found him in deep conversation with a very stout, florid-faced, elderly gentleman with fiery red hair. With an apology for my intrusion, I was about to withdraw when Holmes pulled me abruptly into the room and closed the door behind me.

"You could not possibly have come at a better time, my dear Watson," he said cordially.

"I was afraid that you were engaged."

"So I am. Very much so."

"Then I can wait in the next room."

"Not at all. This gentleman, Mr. Wilson, has been my partner and helper in many of my most successful cases, and I have no doubt that he will be of the utmost use to me in yours also."

The stout gentleman half rose from his chair and gave a bob of greeting, with a quick little questioning glance from his small, fat-encircled eyes.

"Try the settee,"[1] said Holmes, relapsing into his armchair and putting his finger tips together, as was his custom when in judicial moods. "I know, my dear Watson, that you share my love of all that is bizarre and outside the conventions and humdrum routine of everyday life. You have shown your relish for it by the enthusiasm which has prompted you to chronicle, and, if you will excuse my saying so, somewhat to embellish so many of my own little adventures.

"Your cases have indeed been of the greatest interest to me," I observed.

---

1. settee (se tē´) *n*.: Small sofa.

"You will remember that I remarked the other day, just before we went into the very simple problem presented by Miss Mary Sutherland, that for strange effects and extraordinary combinations we must go to life itself, which is always far more daring than any effort of the imagination."

"A proposition which I took the liberty of doubting."

"You did, Doctor, but none the less you must come round to my view, for otherwise I shall keep on piling fact upon fact on you until your reason breaks down under them and acknowledges me to be right. Now, Mr. Jabez Wilson here has been good enough to call upon me this morning, and to begin a narrative which promises to be one of the most singular which I have listened to for some time. You have heard me remark that the strangest and most unique things are very often connected not with the larger but with the smaller crimes, and occasionally, indeed, where there is room for doubt whether any positive crime has been committed. As far as I have heard it is impossible for me to say whether the present case is an instance of crime or not, but the course of events is certainly among the most singular that I have ever listened to. Perhaps, Mr. Wilson, you would have the great kindness to recommence your narrative. I ask you not merely because my friend Dr. Watson has not heard the opening part but also because the peculiar nature of the story makes me anxious to have every possible detail from your lips. As a rule, when I have heard some slight indication of the course of events, I am able to guide myself by the thousands of other similar cases which occur to my memory. In the present instance I am forced to admit that the facts are, to the best of my belief, unique."

The portly client puffed out his chest with an appearance of some little pride and pulled a dirty and wrinkled newspaper from the inside pocket of his great coat. As he glanced down the advertisement column, with his head thrust forward and the paper flattened out upon his knee, I took a good look at the man and endeavored, after the fashion of my companion, to read the indications which might be presented by his dress or appearance.

I did not gain very much, however, by my inspection. Our visitor bore every mark of being an average commonplace British tradesman, obese, pompous, and slow. He wore rather baggy gray shepherd's check trousers, a not over-clean black frock coat, unbuttoned in the front, and a drab waistcoat with a heavy brassy Albert chain, and a square pierced bit of metal dangling down as an ornament. A frayed top hat and a faded brown overcoat with a wrinkled velvet collar lay upon a chair beside him. Altogether, look as I would, there was nothing remarkable about the man save his blazing red head, and the expression of extreme chagrin and discontent upon his features.

Sherlock Holmes's quick eye took in my occupation, and he shook his head with a smile as he noticed my questioning glances. "Beyond the obvious facts that he has at some time done manual labor, that he takes snuff,[2] that he is a Freemason,[3] that he has been in China, and that he has done a considerable amount of writing lately, I can deduce nothing else."

Mr. Jabez Wilson started up in his chair, with his forefinger upon the paper, but his eyes upon my companion.

"How, in the name of good fortune, did you know all that, Mr. Holmes?" he asked. "How did you know, for example, that I did manual labor? It's as true as gospel, for I began as a ship's carpenter."

"Your hands, my dear sir. Your right hand is quite a size larger than your left. You have

> ◆ *Literature and Your Life*
> Sherlock Holmes is able to figure out information about his client from his appearance. What sorts of clues can clothing give about a person?

2. **snuff:** Powdered tobacco.
3. **Freemason:** Member of a secret society.

worked with it, and the muscles are more developed."

"Well, the snuff, then, and the Freemasonry?"

"I won't insult your intelligence by telling you how I read that, especially as, rather against the strict rules of your order, you use an arc-and-compass breastpin."

"Ah, of course, I forgot that. But the writing?"

"What else can be indicated by that right cuff so very shiny for five inches, and the left one with the smooth patch near the elbow where you rest it upon the desk?"

"Well, but China?"

"The fish that you have tattooed immediately above your right wrist could only have been done in China. I have made a small study of tattoo marks and have even contributed to the literature of the subject. That trick of staining the fishes' scales of a delicate pink is quite peculiar to China. When, in addition, I see a Chinese coin hanging from your watch-chain, the matter becomes even more simple."

Mr. Jabez Wilson laughed heavily. "Well, I never!" said he. "I thought at first that you had done something clever, but I see that there was nothing in it, after all."

"I begin to think, Watson," said Holmes, "that I make a mistake in explaining. *'Omne ignotum pro magnifico,'*[4] you know, and my poor little reputation, such as it is, will suffer shipwreck if I am so candid. Can you not find the advertisement, Mr. Wilson?"

"Yes, I have got it now," he answered with his thick red finger planted halfway down the column. "Here it is. This is what began it all. You just read it for yourself, sir."

I took the paper from him and read as follows:

◆ Reading Strategy
One type of clue in a mystery is written evidence. What does this piece of evidence reveal?

To THE RED-HEADED LEAGUE:

On account of the bequest of the late Ezekiah Hopkins, of Lebanon, Pennsylvania, U. S A., there is now another vacancy open which entitles a member of the League to a salary of £4[5] a week for purely nominal services. All red-headed men who are sound in body and mind, and above the age of twenty-one years, are eligible. Apply in person on Monday, at eleven o'clock, to Duncan Ross, at the offices of the League, 7 Pope's Court, Fleet Street.

"What on earth does this mean?" I ejaculated after I had twice read over the extraordinary announcement.

Holmes chuckled and wriggled in his chair, as was his habit when in high spirits. "It is a little off the beaten track, isn't it?" said he. "And now, Mr. Wilson, off you go at scratch and tell us all about yourself, your household, and the effect which this advertisement had upon your fortunes. You will first make a note, Doctor, of the paper and the date."

"It is *The Morning Chronicle* of April 27, 1890. Just two months ago."

"Very good. Now, Mr. Wilson?"

---

5. **£4:** Four pounds in British money—a large amount at the time in which the story is set.

---

4. *Omne ignotum pro magnifico* (äm′ nā ig nō′ təm prō mag nē′ fē kō): Latin for "Whatever is unknown is magnified."

"Well, it is just as I have been telling you, Mr. Sherlock Holmes," said Jabez Wilson, mopping his forehead; "I have a small pawnbroker's business at Coburg Square, near the City. It's not a very large affair, and of late years it has not done more than just give me a living. I used to be able to keep two assistants, but now I only keep one; and I would have a job to pay him but that he is willing to come for half wages so as to learn the business."

"What is the name of this obliging youth?" asked Sherlock Holmes.

"His name is Vincent Spaulding, and he's not such a youth, either. It's hard to say his age. I should not wish a smarter assistant, Mr. Holmes; and I know very well that he could better himself and earn twice what I am able to give him. But, after all, if he is satisfied, why should I put ideas in his head?"

"Why, indeed? You seem most fortunate in having an employee who comes under the full market price. It is not a common experience among employers in this age. I don't know that your assistant is not as remarkable as your advertisement."

"Oh, he has his faults, too," said Mr. Wilson. "Never was such a fellow for photography. Snapping away with a camera when he ought to be improving his mind, and then diving down into the cellar like a rabbit into its hole to develop his pictures. That is his main fault, but on the whole he's a good worker. There's no vice in him."

"He is still with you, I presume?"

"Yes, sir. He and a girl of fourteen, who does a bit of simple cooking and keeps the place clean—that's all I have in the house, for I am a widower and never had any family. We live very quietly, sir, the three of us; and we keep a roof over our heads and pay our debts, if we do nothing more.

"The first thing that put us out was that advertisement. Spaulding, he came down into the office just this day eight weeks, with this very paper in his hand, and he says:

" 'I wish to the Lord, Mr. Wilson, that I was a red-headed man.'

" 'Why that?' I asks.

" 'Why,' says he, 'here's another vacancy on the League of the Red-headed Men. It's worth quite a little fortune to any man who gets it, and I understand that there are more vacancies than there are men, so that the trustees are at their wits' end what to do with the money. If my hair would only change color, here's a nice little crib all ready for me to step into.'

" 'Why, what is it, then?' I asked. You see, Mr. Holmes, I am a very stay-at-home man, and as my business came to me instead of my having to go to it, I was often weeks on end without putting my foot over the doormat. In that way I didn't know much of what was going on outside, and I was always glad of a bit of news.

" 'Have you never heard of the League of the Red-headed Men?' he asked with his eyes open.

" 'Never.'

" 'Why, I wonder at that, for you are eligible yourself for one of the vacancies.'

" 'And what are they worth?' I asked.

" 'Oh, merely a couple of hundred a year, but the work is slight, and it need not interfere very much with one's other occupations.'

"Well, you can easily think that that made me prick up my ears, for the business has not been over-good for some years, and an extra couple of hundred would have been very handy.

" 'Tell me all about it,' said I.

◆ *Literature and Your Life*

When something is "too good to be true," it usually is. What seems suspicious about this club?

" 'Well,' said he, showing me the advertisement, 'you can see for yourself that the League has a vacancy, and there is the address where you should apply for particulars. As far as I can make out, the League was founded by an American millionaire, Ezekiah Hopkins, who was very peculiar in his ways. He was himself red-headed, and he had a great sympathy for all red-headed men; so when he died it was found that he had left his enormous fortune in the hands of trustees, with instructions to apply the interest to the providing of easy berths to men whose hair is of that color. From all I hear it is splendid pay and very little to do.

" 'But,' said I, 'there would be millions of red-headed men who would apply.'

" 'Not so many as you might think,' he answered. 'You see it is really confined to Londoners, and to grown men. This American had started from London when he was young, and he wanted to do the old town a good turn. Then, again, I have heard it is no use your applying if your hair is light red, or dark red, or anything but real bright, blazing, fiery red. Now, if you cared to apply, Mr. Wilson, you would just walk in; but perhaps it would hardly be worth your while to put yourself out of the way for the sake of a few hundred pounds.'

"Now, it is a fact, gentlemen, as you may see for yourselves, that my hair is of a very full and rich tint, so that it seemed to me that if there was to be any competition in the matter I stood as good a chance as any man that I had ever met. Vincent Spaulding seemed to know so much about it that I thought he might prove useful so I just ordered him to put up the shutters for the day and to come right away with me. He was very willing to have a holiday,[6] so we shut the business up and started off for the address that was given us in the advertisement.

"I never hope to see such a sight as that again, Mr. Holmes. From north, south, east, and west every man who had a shade of red in his hair had tramped into the city to answer the advertisement. Fleet Street was choked with red-headed folk, and Pope's Court looked like a coster's orange barrow.[7] I should not have thought there were so many in the whole country as were brought together by that single advertisement. Every shade of color they were—straw, lemon, orange, brick, Irish-setter, liver, clay: but, as Spaulding said, there were not many who had the real vivid flame-colored tint. When I saw how many were waiting, I would have given it up in despair: but Spaulding would not hear of it. How he did it I could not imagine, but he pushed and pulled and butted until he got me through the crowd, and right up to the steps which led to the office. There was a double stream upon the stair, some going up in hope, and some coming back dejected: but we wedged in as well as we could and soon found ourselves in the office."

"Your experience has been a most entertaining one," remarked Holmes as his client paused and refreshed his memory with a huge pinch of snuff. "Pray continue your very interesting statement."

"There was nothing in the office but a couple of wooden chairs and a deal table, behind which sat a small man with a head that was even redder than mine. He said a few words to each candidate as he came up, and then he always managed to find some fault in them which would disqualify them. Getting a vacancy did

---

6. **holiday:** A day off from work; a vacation.
7. **coster's orange barrow:** Pushcart of a seller of oranges.

not seem to be such a very easy matter, after all. However, when our turn came the little man was much more favorable to me than to any of the others, and he closed the door as we entered, so that he might have a private word with us.

" 'This is Mr. Jabez Wilson,' said my assistant, 'and he is willing to fill a vacancy in the League.'

" 'And he is admirably suited for it,' the other answered. 'He has every requirement. I cannot recall when I have seen anything so fine.' He took a step backward, cocked his head on one side, and gazed at my hair until I felt quite bashful. Then suddenly he plunged forward, wrung my hand, and congratulated me warmly on my success.

"'It would be injustice to hesitate, said he. 'You will, however, I am sure, excuse me for taking an obvious precaution.' With that he seized my hair in both his hands, and tugged until I yelled with the pain. 'There is water in your eyes,' said he as he released me. 'I perceive that all is as it should be. But we have to be careful, for we have twice been deceived by wigs and once by paint. I could tell you tales of cobbler's wax which would disgust you with human nature.' He stepped over to the window and shouted through it at the top of his voice that the vacancy was filled. A groan of disappointment came up from below, and the folk all trooped away in different directions until there was not a red head to be seen except my own and that of the manager.

" 'My name,' said he, 'is Mr. Duncan Ross, and I am myself one of the pensioners upon the fund left by our noble benefactor. Are you a married man, Mr. Wilson? Have you a family?'

"I answered that I had not.

"His face fell immediately.

" 'Dear me!' he said gravely, 'that is very serious indeed! I am sorry to hear you say that. The fund was, of course, for the propagation and spread of the red-heads as well as for their maintenance. It is exceedingly unfortunate that you should be a bachelor.'

"My face lengthened at this, Mr. Holmes, for I thought that I was not to have the vacancy after all: but after thinking it over for a few minutes he said that it would be all right.

" 'In the case of another,' said he, 'the objection might be fatal, but we must stretch a point in favor of a man with such a head of hair as yours. When shall you be able to enter upon your new duties?

" 'Well, it is a little awkward, for I have a business already,' said I.

" 'Oh, never mind about that, Mr. Wilson!' said Vincent Spaulding. 'I should be able to look after that for you.'

" 'What would be the hours?' I asked.

" 'Ten to two.'

"Now a pawnbroker's business is mostly done of an evening, Mr. Holmes, especially Thursday and Friday evening, which is just before pay-day: so it would suit me very well to earn a little in the mornings. Besides, I knew that my assistant was a good man, and that he would see to anything that turned up.

" 'That would suit me very well,' said I. 'And the pay?'

" 'Is £4 a week.'

" 'And the work?'

" 'Is purely nominal.'

" 'What do you call purely nominal?'

" 'Well, you have to be in the office, or at least in the building, the whole time. If you leave, you forfeit your whole position forever. The will is very clear upon that point. You don't comply with the conditions if you budge from the office during that time.'

" 'It's only four hours a day, and I should not think of leaving,' said I.

" 'No excuse will <u>avail</u>,' said Mr. Duncan Ross: 'neither sickness nor business nor anything else. There you must stay, or you lose your billet.'[8]

" 'And the work?'

" 'Is to copy out the Encyclopedia Britannica. There is the first volume of it in that press. You must find your own ink, pens, and blotting-

---

8. **billet** (bil´ it) *n.*: Position; job.

◆ **Build Vocabulary**

avail (ə vāl´) *v.*: Be of help

paper, but we provide this table and chair. Will you be ready tomorrow?'

" 'Certainly,' I answered.

" 'Then, good-bye, Mr. Jabez Wilson, and let me congratulate you once more on the important position which you have been fortunate enough to gain.' He bowed me out of the room, and I went home with my assistant, hardly knowing what to say or do, I was so pleased at my own good fortune.

"Well, I thought over the matter all day, and by evening I was in low spirits again: for I had quite persuaded myself that the whole affair must be some great hoax or fraud, though what its object might be I could not imagine. It seemed altogether past belief that anyone could make such a will, or that they would pay such a sum for doing anything so simple as copying out the Encyclopedia Britannica. Vincent Spaulding did what he could to cheer me up, but by bedtime I had reasoned myself out of the whole thing. However, in the morning I determined to have a look at it anyhow, so I bought a penny bottle of ink, and with a quill-pen, and seven sheets of foolscap paper,[9] I started off for Pope's Court.

"Well, to my surprise and delight, everything was as right as possible. The table was set out ready for me, and Mr. Duncan Ross was there to see that I got fairly to work. He started me off upon the letter A, and then he left me; but he would drop in from time to time to see that all was right with me. At two o'clock he bade me good-day, complimented me upon the amount that I had written, and locked the door of the office after me.

"This went on day after day, Mr. Holmes, and on Saturday the manager came in and planked down four golden sovereigns for my week's work. It was the same next week, and the same the week after. Every morning I was there at ten, and every afternoon I left at two. By degrees Mr. Duncan Ross took to coming in only once of a morning, and then, after a time, he did not come in at all. Still, of course, I never dared to leave the room for an instant, for I was not sure when he might come, and the billet was such a good one, and suited me so well, that I would not risk the loss of it.

"Eight weeks passed away like this, and I had written about Abbots and Archery and Armor and Architecture and Attica, and hoped with diligence that I might get on to the B's before very long. It cost me something in foolscap, and I had pretty nearly filled a shelf with my writings. And then suddenly the whole business came to an end."

---

9. **foolscap paper:** Writing paper.

◆ **Build Vocabulary**

hoax (hōks) *n.:* Deceitful trick

"To an end?"

"Yes, sir. And no later than this morning. I went to my work as usual at ten o'clock, but the door was shut and locked, with a little square of cardboard hammered on to the middle of the panel with a tack. Here it is, and you can read for yourself."

He held up a piece of white cardboard about the size of a sheet of notepaper. It read in this fashion:

THE RED-HEADED LEAGUE
IS
DISSOLVED.
October 9, 1890.

Sherlock Holmes and I surveyed this curt announcement and the rueful face behind it, until the comical side of the affair so completely overtopped every other consideration that we both burst out into a roar of laughter.

"I cannot see that there is anything very funny," cried our client, flushing up to the roots of his flaming head. "If you can do nothing better than laugh at me, I can go elsewhere."

"No, no," cried Holmes, shoving him back into the chair from which he had half risen. "I really wouldn't miss your case for the world. It is most refreshingly unusual. But there is, if you will excuse my saying so, something just a little funny about it. Pray what steps did you take when you found the card upon the door?"

"I was staggered, sir. I did not know what to do. Then I called at the offices round, but none of them seemed to know anything about it. Finally, I went to the landlord, who is an accountant living on the ground floor, and I asked him if he could tell me what had become of the Red-headed League. He said that he had never heard of any such body. Then I asked him who Mr. Duncan Ross was. He answered that the name was new to him.

" 'Well,' said I, 'the gentleman at No. 4.'

" 'What, the red-headed man?'

" 'Yes.'

" 'Oh,' said he, 'his name was William Morris. He was a solicitor[10] and was using my

---

10. **solicitor:** Member of the legal profession.

room as a temporary convenience until his new premises were ready. He moved out yesterday.'

" 'Where could I find him?'

" 'Oh, at his new offices. He did tell me the address. Yes, 17 King Edward Street, near St. Paul's.'

"I started off, Mr. Holmes, but when I got to that address it was a manufactory of artificial kneecaps, and no one in it had ever heard of either Mr. William Morris or Mr. Duncan Ross."

"And what did you do then?" asked Holmes.

"I went home to Saxe-Coburg Square, and I took the advice of my assistant. But he could not help me in any way. He could only say that if I waited I should hear by post. But that was not quite good enough, Mr. Holmes. I did not wish to lose such a place without a struggle, so, as I had heard that you were good enough to give advice to poor folk who were in need of it, I came right away to you."

"And you did very wisely," said Holmes. "Your case is an exceedingly remarkable one, and I shall be happy to look into it. From what you have told me I think that it is possible that graver issues hang from it than might at first sight appear."

"Grave enough!" said Mr. Jabez Wilson. "Why, I have lost four pound a week."

"As far as you are personally concerned," remarked Holmes, "I do not see that you have any grievance against this extraordinary league. On the contrary, you are, as I understand, richer by some £30, to say nothing of the minute knowledge which you have gained on every subject which comes under the letter A. You have lost nothing by them."

"No, sir. But I want to find out about them, and who they are, and what their object was in playing this prank—if it was a prank—upon me. It was a pretty expensive joke for them, for it cost them two and thirty pounds."

"We shall endeavor to clear up these points for you. And, first, one or two questions, Mr.

◆ **Literary Focus**
At this point, another suspect enters the picture. What clues point toward this character as a suspect?

Wilson. This assistant of yours who first called your attention to the advertisement—how long had he been with you?"

"About a month then."

"How did he come?"

"In answer to an advertisement."

"Was he the only applicant?"

"No, I had a dozen."

"Why did you pick him?"

"Because he was handy and would come cheap."

"At half-wages, in fact."

"Yes."

"What is he like, this Vincent Spaulding?"

"Small, stout-built, very quick in his ways. no hair on his face, though he's not short of thirty. Has a white splash of acid upon his forehead."

Holmes sat up in his chair in considerable excitement. "I thought as much," said he. "Have you ever observed that his ears are pierced for earrings?"

"Yes, sir. He told me that a gypsy had done it for him when he was a lad."

"Hum!" said Holmes, sinking back in deep thought. "He is still with you?"

"Oh, yes, sir; I have only just left him."

"And has your business been attended to in your absence?"

"Nothing to complain of, sir. There's never very much to do of a morning."

"That will do, Mr. Wilson. I shall be happy to give you an opinion upon the subject in the course of a day or two. Today is Saturday, and I hope that by Monday we may come to a conclusion."

"Well, Watson," said Holmes when our visitor had left us, "what do you make of it all?"

"I make nothing of it," I answered frankly. "It is a most mysterious business."

"As a rule," said Holmes, "the more bizarre a thing is the less mysterious it proves to be. It is your commonplace, featureless crimes which are really puzzling, just as a commonplace face is the most difficult to identify. But I must be prompt over this matter."

"What are you going to do, then?" I asked.

"To smoke," he answered. "It is quite a three pipe problem, and I beg that you won't speak to me for fifty minutes." He curled himself up in his chair, with his thin knees drawn up to his hawk-like nose, and there he sat with his eyes closed and his black clay pipe thrusting out like the bill of some strange bird. I had come to the conclusion that he had dropped asleep, and indeed was nodding myself, when he suddenly sprang out of his chair with the gesture of a man who has made up his mind

and put his pipe down upon the mantelpiece.

"Sarasate[11] plays at the St. James's Hall this afternoon," he remarked. "What do you think, Watson? Could your patients spare you for a few hours?"

"I have nothing to do today. My practice is never very absorbing."

"Then put on your hat and come. I am going through the City first, and we can have some lunch on the way. I observe that there is a

---

11. Sarasate (sä rä sä´ tä): Spanish violinist and composer.

good deal of German music on the program, which is rather more to my taste than Italian or French. It is introspective, and I want to introspect. Come along!"

We traveled by the Underground as far as Aldersgate; and a short walk took us to Saxe-Coburg Square, the scene of the singular story which we had listened to in the morning. It was a poky, little, shabby-genteel place, where four lines of dingy two-storied brick houses looked out into a small railed-in enclosure, where a lawn of weedy grass and a few clumps of faded laurel bushes made a hard fight against a smoke-laden and uncongenial atmosphere. Three gilt balls and a brown board with "JABEZ WILSON" in white letters, upon a corner house, announced the place where our red-headed client carried on his business. Sherlock Holmes stopped in front of it with his head on one side and looked it all over, with his eyes shining brightly between puckered lids. Then he walked slowly up the street, and then down again to the corner, still looking keenly at the houses. Finally he returned to the pawnbroker's, and, having thumped vigorously upon the pavement with his stick two or three times, he went up to the door and knocked. It was instantly opened by a bright-looking, clean-shaven young fellow, who asked him to step in.

"Thank you," said Holmes, "I only wished to ask you how you would go from here to the Strand."

"Third right, fourth left," answered the assistant promptly, closing the door.

"Smart fellow, that," observed Holmes as we walked away. "He is, in my judgment, the fourth smartest man in London, and for daring I am not sure that he has not a claim to be third. I have known something of him before."

> ◆ **Reading Strategy**
>
> In this passage, Holmes is gathering key details that may be clues. See if you can identify those details.

◆ Build Vocabulary

introspective (in′ trə spek′ tiv) *adj.*: Causing one to look into one's own thoughts and feelings

"Evidently," said I, "Mr. Wilson's assistant counts for a good deal in this mystery of the Red-headed League. I am sure that you inquired your way merely in order that you might see him."

"Not him."

"What then?"

"The knees of his trousers."

"And what did you see?"

"What I expected to see."

"Why did you beat the pavement?"

"My dear doctor, this is a time for observation, not for talk. We are spies in an enemy's country. We know something of Saxe-Coburg Square. Let us now explore the parts which lie behind it."

The road in which we found ourselves as we turned round the corner from the retired Saxe-Coburg Square presented as great a contrast to it as the front of a picture does to the back. It was one of the main arteries which conveyed the traffic of the City to the north and west. The roadway was blocked with the immense stream of commerce flowing in a double tide inward and outward, while the footpaths were black with the hurrying swarm of pedestrians. It was difficult to realize as we looked at the line of fine shops and stately business premises that they really abutted on the other side upon the faded and stagnant square which we had just quitted.

"Let me see," said Holmes, standing at the corner and glancing along the line, "I should like just to remember the order of the houses here. It is a hobby of mine to have an exact knowledge of London. There is Mortimer's, the tobacconist, the little newspaper shop, the Coburg branch of the City and Suburban Bank, the Vegetarian Restaurant, and McFarlane's carriage-building depot. That carries us right on to the other block. And now, Doctor, we've done our work, so it's time we had some play. A sandwich and a cup of coffee, and then off to violin land, where all is sweetness and delicacy and harmony, and there are no red-headed clients to vex us with their conundrums."

My friend was an enthusiastic musician, being himself not only a very capable performer but a composer of no ordinary merit.

All the afternoon he sat in the stalls wrapped in the most perfect happiness, gently waving his long, thin fingers in time to the music, while his gently smiling face and his languid, dreamy eyes were as unlike those of Holmes, the sleuthhound, Holmes the relentless, keen-witted, ready-handed criminal agent, as it was possible to conceive. In his singular character the dual nature alternately asserted itself, and his extreme exactness and <u>astuteness</u> represented, as I have often thought, the reaction against the poetic and contemplative mood which occasionally predominated in him. The swing of his nature took him from extreme languor to devouring energy; and, as I knew well, he was never so truly <u>formidable</u> as when, for days on end, he had been lounging in his armchair amid his improvisations and his black-letter editions. Then it was that the lust of the chase would suddenly come upon him, and that his brilliant reasoning power would rise to the level of intuition, until those who were unacquainted with his methods would look askance at him as on a man whose knowledge was not that of other mortals. When I saw him that afternoon so enwrapped in the music at St. James's Hall I felt that an evil time might be coming upon those whom he had set himself to hunt down.

"You want to go home, no doubt, Doctor," he remarked as we emerged.

"Yes, it would be as well."

"And I have some business to do which will take some hours. This business at Coburg Square is serious."

"Why serious?"

"A considerable crime is in contemplation. I have every reason to believe that we shall be in time to stop it. But today being Saturday

rather complicates matters. I shall want your help tonight."

"At what time?"

"Ten will be early enough."

"I shall be at Baker Street at ten."

"Very well. And, I say, Doctor, there may be some little danger, so kindly put your army revolver in your pocket." He waved his hand, turned on his heel, and disappeared in an instant among the crowd.

I trust that I am not more dense than my neighbors, but I was always oppressed with a sense of my own stupidity in my dealings with Sherlock Holmes. Here I had heard what he had heard, I had seen what he had seen, and yet from his words it was evident that he saw clearly not only what had happened but what was about to happen, while to me the whole business was still confused and grotesque. As I drove home to my house in Kensington I thought over it all, from the extraordinary story

♦ **Build Vocabulary**

vex (veks) *v.*: Annoy

conundrums (kə nun´ drəmz) *n.*: Puzzling questions or problems

astuteness (ə sto͞ot´ nis) *n.*: Shrewdness

formidable (fôr´ mə də bəl) *adj.*: Awe-inspiring

of the red-headed copier of the Encyclopedia down to the visit to Saxe-Coburg Square, and the ominous words with which he had parted from me. What was this nocturnal expedition, and why should I go armed? Where were we going, and what were we to do? I had the hint from Holmes that this smooth-faced pawnbroker's assistant was a formidable man—a man who might play a deep game. I tried to puzzle it out, but gave it up in despair and set the matter aside until night should bring an explanation.

It was a quarter past nine when I started from home and made my way across the Park, and so through Oxford Street to Baker Street. Two hansoms[12] were standing at the door, and as I entered the passage I heard the sound of voices from above. On entering his room I found Holmes in animated conversation with two men, one of whom I recognized as Peter Jones, the official police agent, while the other was a long, thin, sadfaced man, with a very shiny hat and oppressively respectable frock coat.

"Ha! our party is complete," said Holmes, buttoning up his pea-jacket and taking his heavy hunting crop from the rack. "Watson, I think you know Mr. Jones, of Scotland Yard? Let me introduce you to Mr. Merryweather, who is to be our companion in tonight's adventure."

"We're hunting in couples again, Doctor, you see," said Jones in his consequential way. "Our friend here is a wonderful man for starting a chase. All he wants is an old dog to help him to do the running down."

"I hope a wild goose may not prove to be the end of our chase," observed Mr. Merryweather gloomily.

"You may place considerable confidence in Mr. Holmes, sir," said the police agent loftily.

"He has his own little methods, which are, if he won't mind my saying so, just a little too theoretical and fantastic, but he has the makings of a detective in him. It is not too much to say that once or twice, as in that business of the Sholto murder and the Agra treasure, he has been more nearly correct than the official force."

"Oh, if you say so, Mr. Jones, it is all right," said the stranger with deference. "Still, I confess that I miss my rubber.[13] It is the first Saturday night for seven-and-twenty years that I have not had my rubber."

---

12. **hansoms:** Two-wheeled covered carriages for two passengers.

13. **rubber:** Card games.

"I think you will find," said Sherlock Holmes, "that you will play for a higher stake tonight than you have ever done yet, and that the play will be more exciting. For you, Mr. Merryweather, the stake will be some £30,000: and for you, Jones, it will be the man upon whom you wish to lay your hands."

"John Clay, the murderer, thief, smasher, and forger. He's a young man, Mr. Merryweather, but he is at the head of his profession, and I would rather have my bracelets on him than on any criminal in London. He's a remarkable man, is young John Clay. His grandfather was a royal duke, and he himself has been to Eton[14] and Oxford.[15] His brain is as cunning as his fingers, and though we meet signs of him at every turn, we never know where to find the man himself. He'll crack a crib[16] in Scotland one week, and be raising money to build an orphanage in Cornwall the next. I've been on his track for years and have never set eyes on him yet."

"I hope that I may have the pleasure of introducing you tonight. I've had one or two little turns also with Mr. John Clay, and I agree with you that he is at the head of his profession. It is past ten, however, and quite time that we started. If you two will take the first hansom, Watson and I will follow in the second."

Sherlock Holmes was not very communicative during the long drive and lay back in the cab humming the tunes which he had heard in the afternoon. We rattled through an endless labyrinth of gas-lit streets until we emerged into Farrington Street.

"We are close there now," my friend remarked. "This fellow Merryweather is a bank director, and personally interested in the matter. I thought it as well to have Jones with us also. He is not a bad fellow, though an absolute imbecile in his profession. He has one positive virtue. He is as brave as a bulldog and as tenacious as a lobster if he gets his claws upon anyone. Here

---

14. **Eton:** Famous British secondary school for boys.
15. **Oxford:** Oldest university in Great Britain.
16. **crack a crib:** Break into and rob a house.

we are, and they are waiting for us."

We had reached the same crowded thoroughfare in which we had found ourselves in the morning. Our cabs were dismissed, and, following the guidance of Mr. Merryweather, we passed down a narrow passage and through a side door, which he opened for us. Within there was a small corridor, which ended in a very massive iron gate. This also was opened, and led down a flight of winding stone steps, which terminated at another formidable gate. Mr. Merryweather stopped to light a lantern, and then conducted us down a dark, earth-smelling passage, and so, after opening a third door, into a huge vault or cellar, which was piled all round with crates and massive boxes.

"You are not very vulnerable from above," Holmes remarked as he held up the lantern and gazed about him.

"Nor from below," said Mr. Merryweather, striking his stick upon the flags which lined the floor. "Why, dear me, it sounds quite hollow!" he remarked, looking up in surprise.

"I must really ask you to be a little more quiet!" said Holmes severely. "You have already imperiled the whole success of our expedition. Might I beg that you would have the goodness to sit down upon one of those boxes, and not to interfere?"

The solemn Mr. Merryweather perched himself upon a crate, with a very injured expression upon his face, while Holmes fell upon his knees upon the floor and, with the lantern and a magnifying lens, began to examine minutely the cracks between the stones. A few seconds sufficed to satisfy him, for he sprang to his feet again and put his glass in his pocket.

"We have at least an hour before us," he remarked, "for they can hardly take any steps until the good pawnbroker is safely in bed. Then they will not lose a minute, for the sooner they do their work the longer time they will have for their escape. We are at present, Doctor—as no doubt you have divined—in the cellar of the City branch of one of the principal London banks. Mr. Merryweather is the chairman of directors, and he will explain to you that there are reasons why the more daring criminals of London should take a considerable interest in this cellar at present."

"It is our French gold," whispered the director. "We have had several warnings that an attempt might be made upon it."

"Your French gold?"

"Yes. We had occasion some months ago to strengthen our resources and borrowed for that purpose 30,000 napoleons from the Bank of France. It has become known that we have never had occasion to unpack the money, and that it is still lying in our cellar. The crate upon which I sit contains 2,000 napoleons packed between layers of lead foil. Our reserve of bullion is much larger at present than is usually kept in a single branch office, and the directors have had misgivings upon the subject."

"Which were very well justified," observed Holmes.

"And now it is time that we arranged our little plans. I expect that within an hour matters will come to a head. In the meantime, Mr. Merryweather, we must put the screen over that dark lantern."

"And sit in the dark?"

"I am afraid so. I had brought a pack of cards in my pocket, and I thought that, as we were a *partie carrée*,[17] you might have your rubber after all. But I see that the enemy's preparations have gone so far that we cannot risk the presence of a light. And, first of all, we must choose our positions. These are daring men, and though we shall take them at a disadvantage, they may do us some harm unless we are careful. I shall stand behind this crate, and do you conceal yourselves behind those. Then, when I flash a light upon them, close in swiftly. If they fire, Watson, have no compunction about shooting them down."

I placed my revolver, cocked, upon the top of the wooden case behind which I crouched. Holmes shot the slide across the front of his lantern and left us in pitch darkness—such an absolute darkness as I have never before experienced. The smell of hot metal remained to assure us that the light was still there, ready to flash out at a moment's notice. To me, with my nerves worked up to a pitch of expectancy, there

---

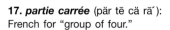

17. *partie carrée* (pär tē cä rä´): French for "group of four."

was something depressing and subduing in the sudden gloom, and in the cold dank air of the vault.

"They have but one retreat," whispered Holmes. "That is back through the house into Saxe-Coburg Square. I hope that you have done what I asked you, Jones?"

"I have an inspector and two officers waiting at the front door."

"Then we have stopped all the holes. And now we must be silent and wait."

What a time it seemed! From comparing notes afterwards it was but an hour and a quarter, yet it appeared to me that the night must have almost gone, and the dawn be breaking above us. My limbs were weary and stiff, for I feared to change my position; yet my nerves were worked up to the highest pitch of tension, and my hearing was so acute that I could not only hear the gentle breathing of my companions, but I could distinguish the deeper, heavier in-breath of the bulky Jones from the thin, sighing note of the bank director. From my position I could look over the case in the direction of the floor. Suddenly my eyes caught the glint of a light.

At first it was but a lurid spark upon the stone pavement. Then it lengthened out until it became a yellow line, and then, without any warning or sound, a gash seemed to open and a hand appeared; a white, almost womanly hand, which felt about in the center of the little area of light. For a minute or more the hand, with its writhing fingers, protruded out of the floor. Then it was withdrawn as suddenly as it appeared, and all was dark again save the single lurid spark which marked a chink between the stones.

Its disappearance, however, was but momentary. With a rending, tearing sound, one of the broad, white stones turned over upon its side and left a square, gaping hole, through which streamed the light of a lantern. Over the edge there peeped a clean-cut, boyish face, which looked keenly about it, and then, with a hand on either side of the aperture, drew itself shoulder-high and waist-high, until one knee rested upon the edge. In another instant he stood at the side of the hole and was hauling after him a companion, lithe and small like himself, with a pale face and a shock of very red hair.

"It's all clear," he whispered. "Have you the chisel and the bags? Great Scott! Jump, Archie, jump, and I'll swing for it."

Sherlock Holmes had sprung out and seized the intruder by the collar. The other dived down the hole, and I heard the sound of rending cloth as Jones clutched at his skirts. The light flashed upon the barrel of a revolver, but Holmes's hunting crop came down on the man's wrist, and the pistol clinked upon the stone floor.

"It's no use, John Clay," said Holmes blandly. "You have no chance at all."

"So I see," the other answered with the utmost coolness. "I fancy that my pal is all right, though I see you have got his coattails."

"There are three men waiting for him at the door," said Holmes.

"Oh, indeed! You seem to have done the thing very completely. I must compliment you."

"And I you," Holmes answered. "Your red-headed idea was very new and effective."

"You'll see your pal again presently," said Jones. "He's quicker at climbing down holes than I am. Just hold out while I fix the derbies."[18]

"I beg that you will not touch me with your filthy hands," remarked our prisoner as the handcuffs clattered upon his wrists. "You may not be aware that I have royal blood in my veins. Have the goodness, also, when you address me always to say 'sir' and 'please.'"

"All right," said Jones with a stare and a snigger. "Well, would you please, sir, march upstairs, where we can get a cab to carry your Highness to the police station?"

"That is better," said John Clay serenely. He made a sweeping bow to the three of us

◆ **Literary Focus**
At this point in the story, the suspense reaches its height. What story elements contribute to the building of suspense?

---

18. **derbies:** Handcuffs.

and walked quietly off in the custody of the detective.

"Really, Mr. Holmes," said Mr. Merryweather as we followed them from the cellar, "I do not know how the bank can thank you or repay you. There is no doubt that you have detected and defeated in the most complete manner one of the most determined attempts at bank robbery that have ever come within my experience."

"I have had one or two little scores of my own to settle with Mr. John Clay," said Holmes. "I have been at some small expense over this matter, which I shall expect the bank to refund, but beyond that I am amply repaid by having had an experience which is in many ways unique, and by hearing the very remarkable narrative of the Red-headed League."

"You see, Watson," he explained in the early hours of the morning as we sat over a glass of whisky and soda in Baker Street, "it was perfectly obvious from the first that the only possible object of this rather fantastic business of the advertisement of the League, and the copying of the Encyclopedia, must be to get this not over-bright pawnbroker out of the way for a number of hours every day. It was a curious way of managing it, but, really, it would be difficult to suggest a better. The method was no doubt suggested to Clay's ingenious mind by the color of his accomplice's hair. The £4 a week was a lure which must draw him, and what was it to them, who were playing for thousands? They put in the advertisement, one rogue has the temporary office, the other rogue incites the man to apply for it, and together

> ◆ **Literary Focus**
>
> Here, the solution to the mystery is revealed to Watson—and to the reader. Holmes explains the criminal's motivation and methods, and the story comes to a close.

they manage to secure his absence every morning in the week. From the time that I heard of the assistant having come for half wages, it was obvious to me that he had some strong motive for securing the situation."

"But how could you guess what the motive was?"

"Had there been women in the house, I should have suspected a mere vulgar intrigue. That, however, was out of the question. The man's business was a small one, and there was nothing in his house which could account for such elaborate preparations, and such an expenditure as they were at. It must, then, be something out of the house. What could it be? I thought of the assistant's fondness for photography, and his trick of vanishing into the cellar. The cellar! There was the end of this tangled clue. Then I made inquiries as to this mysterious assistant and found that I had to deal with one of the coolest and most daring criminals in London. He was doing something in the cellar—something which took many hours a day for months on end. What could it be, once more? I could think of nothing save that he was running a tunnel to some other building.

"So far I had got when we went to visit the scene of action. I surprised you by beating upon the pavement with my stick. I was ascertaining whether the cellar stretched out in front or behind. It was not in front. Then I rang the bell, and, as I hoped, the assistant answered it. We have had some skirmishes, but we had never set eyes upon each other before. I hardly looked at his face. His knees were what I wished to see. You must yourself have remarked how worn, wrinkled, and stained they were. They spoke of those hours of burrowing. The only remaining point was what they were burrowing for. I walked round the corner, saw that the City and Suburban Bank abutted on our friend's premises, and felt that I had solved my problem. When you drove home after the concert I called upon Scotland Yard and upon the chairman of the bank directors, with the result that you have seen."

"And how could you tell that they would make their attempt tonight?" I asked.

"Well, when they closed their League offices that was a sign that they cared no longer about Mr. Jabez Wilson's presence—in other words,

that they had completed their tunnel. But it was essential that they should use it soon, as it might be discovered, or the bullion might be removed. Saturday would suit them better than any other day, as it would give them two days for their escape. For all these reasons I expected them to come tonight."

"You reasoned it out beautifully," I exclaimed in unfeigned admiration. "It is so long a chain, and yet every link rings true."

"It saved me from ennui,"[19] he answered, yawning. "Alas ! I already feel it closing in upon me. My life is spent in one long effort to escape from the commonplaces of existence. These little problems help me to do so."

"And you are a benefactor of the race," said I.

He shrugged his shoulders. "Well, perhaps, after all, it is of some little use," he remarked. " *'L'homme c'est rien—l'oeuvre c'est tout,'*[20] as Gustave Flaubert wrote to George Sand."[21]

---

19. **ennui** (än´ wē): Boredom.
20. ***L'homme c'est rien—l'oeuvre c'est tout*** (lum sä rēn lʉvr sä tōō): French for "Man is nothing—the work is everything."
21. **Gustave Flaubert** (gōōs täv´ flō bār´) . . . **George Sand:** Notable French novelists of the nineteenth century.

Guide for Responding

◆ *Literature and Your Life*

Reader's Response What did you think of the solution to the mystery? Was it a satisfying ending to the story?

Thematic Focus When have you used your powers of observation to solve real-life mysteries?

Role Play With a partner, act out a scene that takes place between Holmes and Watson a year after the story ends. Have them reflect back on the highlights of the case.

☑ Check Your Comprehension

1. Why does Jabez Wilson come to see Sherlock Holmes?
2. As a member of the Red-headed League, what job is Wilson given?
3. Who does Holmes suspect is the master criminal?
4. Why do the criminals want Jabez Wilson out of the pawnbroker's shop?
5. What happens the night of the attempted burglary?

Guide for Responding (continued)

◆ Critical Thinking

INTERPRET

1. Why does Holmes find Jabez Wilson's story interesting? **[Infer]**
2. Why was the Red-headed League dissolved? **[Analyze]**
3. Which clues lead Holmes to visit Saxe-Coburg Square? **[Analyze]**
4. If Watson's portrait of Holmes is accurate, what is Holmes planning to do as the story ends? **[Speculate]**

EVALUATE

5. How would this story be different if it were told by Holmes rather than by Watson? Explain. **[Evaluate]**

EXTEND

6. Name three other professions in which Holmes's reasoning skills could be useful. Give reasons for your choices. **[Career Link]**

◆ Reading Strategy

KEY DETAILS

Finding **key details**—details that relate to the crime—helps you to participate in solving the mystery. Review the details you have noted, adding any you missed and indicating which ones seem most important.

1. Identify four clues to the mystery hidden in the story Wilson tells Holmes and Watson.
2. Explain how each of the four clues in Wilson's story suggests a solution to the mystery.

◆ Literary Focus

THE MYSTERY

Like most **mysteries**, "The Red-headed League" has a crime, a criminal, a crime-solver, clues, alibis, and characters' motives. In "The Red-headed League," however, there are few suspects, and solving the original crime leads Holmes to prevent a much bigger crime.

1. Identify the elements of the mystery within Jabez Wilson's story.
2. What clues point to Vincent Spaulding as the probable criminal?

◆ Build Vocabulary

USING THE ROOT -spec-

The following words contain the root -spec -. Knowing that the root means "look" or "see," match each word with its definition.

1. spectator   a. one who watches or observes
2. inspector   b. one who looks into
3. spectacle   c. strange or remarkable sight

USING THE WORD BANK

On your paper, write the following paragraph, filling in the blanks with words from the Word Bank:

I'm rather shy and ___?___, but my uncle has an extremely ___?___ personality. When confronted with ___?___, he has been known to shout, "Do not ___?___ me!" at no one in particular. His ___?___ is regarded by some as ___?___ and by some as an elaborate ___?___. Whenever I ask for help, however, he will ___?___ himself immediately.

◆ Build Grammar Skills

COORDINATE ADJECTIVES

Coordinate adjectives are adjectives of equal rank that separately modify the noun they precede.

To test whether adjectives are coordinate, switch their order. If the sentence still makes sense, the adjectives are probably coordinate.

Writing Application On your paper, write the following sentences. Supply adjectives to complete them. Separate coordinate adjectives with a comma.

1. The ___?___ ___?___ goblet was stolen.
2. The ___?___ ___?___ book contained a clue.
3. The detective once again had outwitted the ___?___ ___?___ villain.
4. The public was shocked that such a ___?___ ___?___ citizen had committed the crime.
5. The detective wore a ___?___ ___?___ coat.

Build Your Portfolio

Idea Bank

Writing

1. **Observation Journal** Choose an event, object, or person to observe. Observe your subject over a period of time and note what you see in your journal. **[Career Link]**

2. **Dramatic Scene** Write a scene that might have taken place between Spaulding and Wilson. Be sure to create dialogue that fits each character. **[Performing Arts Link]**

3. **Cause-and-Effect Essay** Reexamine the story and write an analysis of the crime in which you explain the cause-and-effect relationships of events.

Speaking and Listening

4. **Summary** Prepare a summary of the events leading up to the arrest of John Clay. Then, taking on the role of Sherlock Holmes, present your summary orally. **[Career Link]**

5. **Grilling the Suspect** With a partner, role-play an interrogation of Spaulding by Inspector Jones. Remember that Jones will want to know all the details about the crime, but Spaulding may not be willing to disclose them all. **[Career Link]**

Projects

6. **The Science of Detection** Choose one of these criminology topics: fingerprinting, lie detectors or bomb-detectors. Research the topic and write a brief report on your findings. **[Science Link; Career Link]**

7. **Planning the Heist** Draw a cross-sectional diagram of Saxe-Coburg Square. Present your diagram to the class and explain the details of John Clay's plan. **[Science Link]**

Writing Mini-Lesson

Detective Story

Sir Arthur Conan Doyle invented a detective whose personality and adventures are so real that readers still write to him at 221 Baker Street! Write a detective story that will appeal to today's readers. As you write, here's a clue that will help you.

Writing Skills Focus: Elaboration

Use **elaboration**—the development of ideas and details—to make your detective story, or any piece of writing, precise and complete. By elaborating, you can heighten suspense, as Doyle does in "The Red-headed League."

Model From the Story

I could distinguish the *deeper, heavier* in-breath of *the bulky* Jones from the *thin, sighing* note of the bank director.

Elaboration isn't something you do only in the drafting stage. You can gather details and ideas as you plan a story and insert them as you revise it.

Prewriting Mystery writers use these tricks to elaborate details *before* they write:
- Create brief biographies of characters, including information about their appearance and motives.
- Draw and fill in a sunburst diagram, putting the crime at the center and details about the suspects, the sleuth, and the setting on the lines radiating out from the center.

Drafting Begin your description with a few striking images that will capture the mood you want the set to convey. Refer to your sketch as you draft.

Revising Make a second sketch of your set based on the details provided in your draft. This will help you discover places where you may need to add precise details to complete the picture.

Guide for Reading

Walter de la Mare (1873–1956)

This Englishman's most famous poems, like "The Listeners," tell mysterious, incomplete stories. Perhaps de la Mare used his poetry to live a secret, mysterious life because his daytime jobs were so unmysterious. At the age of sixteen, for example, he began working in the statistics department of the Anglo-American Oil Company. Poems may have been his escape from numbers!

Not only did he write poems, but he also edited anthologies of poetry. These collections show that poetry is more than just famous poems by famous poets—it also includes folk songs, ballads, nursery rhymes, and children's chants.

Ishmael Reed (1938–)

He is as mysterious, various, and hilarious as his poem "Beware: Do Not Read This Poem." Born in Chattanooga, Tennessee, and raised in Buffalo, New York, he has worked as a hospital attendant, market researcher, newspaper manager, and clerk at an unemployment office. In addition to poetry collections like *Chattanooga* (1973), he has written satiric novels that make fun of American westerns, slave narratives, essays, plays, songs, and even operas.

Henriqueta Lisboa (1903–1985)

A Brazilian poet, Lisboa uses a few well-chosen words to create powerful poems. Her early lyrics deal with traditional poetic themes, while her later poems tell about the history of her region. In "Echo," she mysteriously magnifies the effect of a single image.

◆ Build Vocabulary

POETIC LICENSE AND VOCABULARY

The term **poetic license** refers to a poet's freedom to violate rules of word choice or spelling in order to create literary effects. Both Walter de la Mare and Ishmael Reed use poetic license. For example, de la Mare includes in his poem an old-fashioned form of the verb *spoke*—*spake*—and Reed fills his poem with misspellings and odd abbreviations.

WORD BANK

As you read these poems, you will encounter the words in this list. Each word is defined on the page where it first appears. Preview the list before you read.

| perplexed |
| thronging |
| legendary |
| strafing |

◆ Build Grammar Skills

PARALLELISM

All these poets create a sense of mystery by using **parallelism**, the repetition of grammatically similar words or groups of words. In "The Listeners," for example, de la Mare uses parallelism to describe separate actions that seem mysteriously connected.

These sentences are similar in their pattern of "And," subject, and verb— only the first one varies slightly by including the words *in the silence* between the subject and the verb.

And his <u>horse</u> in the silence <u>champed</u> the grasses . . .

And a <u>bird</u> <u>flew</u> up out of the turret . . .

And <u>he</u> <u>smote</u> upon the door again a second time . . .

The Listeners
Beware: Do Not Read This Poem ◆ Echo

◆ Literature and Your Life

CONNECT YOUR EXPERIENCE

A man knocks on a moonlit door. A parrot screams in a jungle. A woman disappears into a mirror. If you've ever seen a movie preview or a rock video, you know how images like these can convey a sense of mystery. They're strange. You're not sure how they connect, yet they seem to hint at an unknown story. These poems use images in the same way—to hint at mysteries and possibilities.

THEMATIC FOCUS: IT'S A MYSTERY

The mysteries that these poems suggest are not the kind that movie detectives wrap up in a matter of hours. Instead, they may cause you to ask: Does every mystery have a solution?

◆ Background for Understanding

FINE ART

Just as poets create mystery in lines of poetry, artists create mysterious images with lines they draw. Dutch artist M. C. Escher (1898–1970), for example, specialized in drawings that challenge the mind and delight the imagination. Look carefully at this Escher image.

Drawing Hands M.C.Escher/Cordon Art - Baarn - Holland. All rights reserved.

Journal Writing Briefly describe what you see in this drawing. Then tell why Escher's image is a mystery.

◆ Literary Focus

IMAGERY

Poets can't draw pictures with pens and brushes. However, they can use picture-painting words, called **imagery**, to help you experience their descriptions with all your senses—touch, taste, smell, and hearing, as well as sight. The poems in this section use imagery in a special way that gives you pictures of worlds that are haunted by mystery.

◆ Reading Strategy

USE YOUR SENSES

By **using your senses** when you read a poem, you use the poem's sensory language to create pictures in your mind. As you start to experience the poem in this way, you become more at home in its world and ready to understand its meaning.

Don't just read these mysterious poems as words on a page. Instead, read them as *experiences* by experiencing their images. In "The Listeners," for example, *hear* the exact sound of the "knocking on the moonlit door." Is it rapid or deliberate? *See* the way in which the moonlight falls on the door. Does it gleam on a brass doorknob? This trick will help you step through the words into the worlds of mystery they create.

his heart their strangeness,
ess answering his cry,
se moved, cropping the dark

starred and leafy sky;
ly smote on the door, even
d lifted his head:—
me, and no one answered,
my word,' he said.
st stir made the listeners,
ery word he spake[3]
hrough the shadowiness of
use
ne man left awake:
d his foot upon the stirrup
und of iron on stone,
silence surged softly backward,
plunging hoofs were gone.

oke.

Responding

◆ Critical Thinking

INTERPRET

1. How is this poem like a dream? **[Analyze]**
2. Why do you think de la Mare called the poem "The Listeners" rather than "The Traveler"? **[Infer]**
3. Would knowing more about the characters lessen the poem's mystery? Explain. **[Synthesize]**

APPLY

4. What's the difference between a puzzle and a mystery like the one presented in this poem? **[Distinguish]**

Beware:
Do Not Read This Poem

Ishmael Reed

tonite, *thriller* was
abt an ol woman, so vain she
surrounded her self w/
    many mirrors

5 It got so bad that finally she
locked herself indoors & her
whole life became the
    mirrors

one day the villagers broke
10 into her house, but she was too
swift for them. she disappeared
    into a mirror
each tenant who bought the house
after that lost a loved one to
15   the ol woman in the mirror:
    first a little girl
    then a young woman
    then the young woman/s husband
the hunger of this poem is <u>legendary</u>
20 it has taken in many victims
back off from this poem
it has drawn in yr feet
back off from this poem
it has drawn in yr legs
25 back off from this poem

it is a greedy mirror
you are into this poem. from
    the waist down
nobody can hear you can they?
30 this poem has had you up to here
    belch
this poem aint got no manners
you cant call out frm this poem
relax now & go w/ this poem
35 move & roll on to this poem

    do not resist this poem
    this poem has yr eyes
    this poem has his head
    this poem has his arms
40   this poem has his fingers
    this poem has his fingertips
this poem is the reader & the
    reader this poem

statistic: the us bureau of missing persons reports
45   that in 1968 over 100,000 people disappeared
    leaving no solid clues
        nor trace   only
a space   in the lives of their friends

♦ Build Vocabulary

legendary (lej´ ən der´ ē) *adj.*: Based on legends, or stories handed down for generations

Het Blind Huis, William Degouve de Nunques, State Museum, Kröller-Müller, Otterlo, The Netherlands

▲ **Critical Viewing** Does this painting convey the same feeling as "The Listeners"? Why or why not? **[Explain]**

Tropical Tree, 1990, Grimanesa Amoros, 75 x52", acrylic and mixed media on canvas, ©1997 Grimanesa Amoros/Licensed by VAGA, New York, NY

Echo

Henriqueta Lisboa

Translated by Hélcio Veiga Costa

Green parrot
let out a shrill scream.
Rock in sudden
anger, replied.

5   A great uproar
invaded the forest.
Thousands of parrots
screamed together
and rock echoed.

10   From all sides
strafing space
steely screams rained
and rained down.

Very piercing screams!

15   But no one died.

◆ **Build Vocabulary**

strafing (strāf´ ing) *adj.*: Attacking with machine-gun fire

Guide for Responding

◆ *Literature and Your Life*

Reader's Response Which poem did you find more mysterious? Why?

Thematic Focus When Reed describes you as disappearing into his poem, what does he suggest about the mystery of reading? What is strange about the echoes in Lisboa's poem?

☑ Check Your Comprehension

1. How is Reed's poem like "the ol woman in the mirror"?
2. What happens in the poem "Echo"?

◆ **Critical Thinking**

INTERPRET

1. How would you describe the speaker's tone of voice in Reed's poem? **[Infer]**
2. What message is the speaker trying to convey when he says, "this poem is the reader & the / reader this poem"? **[Interpret]**
3. How would "Echo" be different without the last line? **[Speculate]**

EXTEND

4. If you were setting these poems to music, what types of music would you choose? Explain. **[Music Link]**

x

Guide for Responding (continued)

◆ Reading Strategy

USE YOUR SENSES

You have entered new, mysterious worlds by **using your senses.** In "The Listeners," for example, you have stood on both sides of a "moonlit door," waiting with the Traveler and with the "phantom listeners" he addresses.

1. Why is sound as important as sight in experiencing the world of "The Listeners"?
2. In which of the other two poems do you *hear* a mystery? Explain.
3. (a) Which of the poems asks you to picture yourself? (b) Describe the picture or pictures of yourself that you see.

◆ Build Grammar Skills

PARALLELISM

Usually, parallelism suggests that the world is regular, rational, predictable. In these poems, however, the images that the parallel groups of words describe are startling and offbeat. The result is that the repetitions can throw you off balance and disturb—not reassure—you.

> **Parallelism** is the repeated use of specific grammatical forms.

In this passage from "Beware: Do Not Read This Poem," notice how two different grammatical forms are repeated in alternate lines.

> back off from this poem
>
> it has drawn in yr feet
>
> back off from this poem
>
> it has drawn in yr legs . . .

Practice Identify the parallelism in the following excerpts from the poems.

1. this poem has his head / this poem has his arms
2. And he felt in his heart their strangeness, / Their stillness answering his cry . . .
3. Stood listening in the quiet of the moonlight/
   To that voice from the world of men:/
   Stood thronging the faint moonbeams on the dark stair, . . .

Writing Application Write an eight-line poem describing something interesting you recently observed. Include at least two examples of parallelism.

◆ Literary Focus

IMAGERY

Poets use the picture-painting words called **imagery** to take you to mysterious places. The poems in this section use imagery in a special way that gives you pictures of worlds that are haunted by mystery.

1. Explain how the imagery in "The Listeners" helps you hear "silence" and see invisible "listeners."
2. Would you use sound effects, music, or both if you were making a short film based on "The Listeners"? Give reasons for your answer.
3. Ishmael Reed compares reading to disappearing into "a greedy mirror." How does the mirror imagery help you to experience the strangeness of reading?
4. Find two examples of imagery in "Echo" and show how they create a feeling of uncertainty.

◆ Build Vocabulary

POETIC LICENSE AND VOCABULARY IN POEMS

Poetic license is a poet's freedom to violate rules of vocabulary and grammar to create literary effects. Poets like Walter de la Mare and Ishmael Reed use old-fashioned words, symbols, and abbreviations for specific purposes.

1. What old-fashioned word does de la Mare include in lines 5–7?
2. Does his use of this word make the poem seem more mysterious? Why or why not?
3. Identify two examples of poetic license in line 34 of "Beware: Do Not Read This Poem."
4. How does Reed's use of poetic license in line 34 make his poem seem more unusual or strange?

USING THE WORD BANK

On your paper, rewrite the following paragraph and fill in the blanks with words from the Word Bank.

The detective entered the deserted house and stood in front of the mirror, ___?___ . Deep inside the mysterious glass, he could see the ___?___ parrots, a species that had never existed. Hundreds of them were ___?___ a forest clearing, ___?___ the trees with their steely cries.

*B*uild *Y*our *P*ortfolio

 ## Idea Bank

Writing

1. **Comic Strip** Create a comic strip about a mysterious poem that swallows people. **[Art Link]**

2. **TV Review** Write a summary of a television program about a real-life mystery that is difficult to solve. Include a brief thumbs-up or thumbs-down review of the program. **[Media Link]**

3. **Dramatic Scene** Write a dramatic scene that takes place "in the lone house" of "The Listeners" after the Traveler has galloped away. Use your scene to answer some of the questions left unanswered by the poem. **[Performing Arts Link]**

Speaking and Listening

4. **Oral Interpretation** With a partner, take turns reading aloud Ishmael Reed's "Beware: Do Not Read This Poem." Before you begin, ask yourself questions like: Should different parts of the poem be read louder or softer, at different speeds, or with different tones of voice?

5. **Storytelling** Make up and tell a story involving the Traveler and the Listeners from "The Listeners," the old woman from "Beware: Do Not Read This Poem," and the parrot from "Echo."

Projects

6. **Multimedia Presentation** "Echo" is set in Brazil's tropical rain forest. Give a multimedia presentation on this environment, taking the class on a magical mystery tour through its wonders. **[Science Link; Technology Link]**

7. **Art Exhibit** In a corner of your classroom, display some of the "impossible" scenes drawn by the Dutch artist M. C. Escher. Include a blank notebook with the exhibit and invite your classmates to fill it with comments. **[Art Link]**

 ## Writing Mini-Lesson

Movie Summary

"Beware: Do Not Read This Poem" begins like an answer to the question, What happened in the television program *Thriller*? A **summary** like Reed's briefly outlines important events and leaves out unimportant ones. Choose a movie you recently saw, and write a summary of it for a friend. It does not have to be in lines of poetry, but it should follow a clear timeline.

Writing Skills Focus: Sequence of Events

Show a clear **sequence of events**—the order in which things happen—when summarizing a movie, telling a story, or explaining a process. Notice how Reed uses words that show time to help readers understand the sequence of events in a television program.

Model From the Poem

first a little girl

then a young woman

then the young woman's husband . . .

Prewriting Draw a timeline like this one, including the key events of the movie in chronological order:

1.	2.	3.	4.	5.

Refer to the timeline as you draft and revise your summary.

Drafting Use words that show time to help readers understand the sequence of events. Examples: *first, before, after, finally, one day, then, meanwhile, at the same time, later.*

Revising Read your summary aloud to classmates and ask them whether they understand the order of events. If not, see where you can insert time words to clarify the sequence.

Guide for Reading

Keay Davidson (1953–   )

With every passing day, technology opens new doors to the world of science, and Keay Davidson loves the challenge of sharing these advances with readers. As a science reporter and the author of two books and many magazine articles, Davidson tracks the latest on everything from the space program to tornadoes.

Space Program Launches Reporter

While still in college, Davidson began work as a newspaper reporter. He held staff positions at three Georgia newspapers until moving to Florida in 1976 to take his first full-time reporting job. Davidson knew he'd found his true calling when, in 1979, he was assigned to cover science and the space program. In 1981, he moved to the West Coast to become a science reporter for the *Los Angeles Times*; then, in 1986, for the *San Francisco Examiner*.

Davidson doesn't limit his writing to newspapers, however; his articles have appeared in *National Geographic* and other magazines. He has co-authored a book, *Wrinkles in Time*, about new scientific theories on the origins of the universe.

In 1996, when the movie Twister *swept through theaters, Davidson introduced the science behind the special effects in* Twister: The Science of Tornadoes.

He also produced a special version of the book just for students.

Science: A Link Between Past and Present

Archaeology has always fascinated Davidson, who is drawn by its emotional impact. When an archaeological discovery alters our understanding of that history—as with the Caucasian mummies in this article—its impact can extend beyond science to change even the way we see ourselves.

◆ Build Vocabulary

SUFFIXES: *-ist*

Early in this article, you learn that a Chinese archaeologist is responsible for finding several mysterious mummies. *Archaeologist* is one of several words in the article that end in the suffix *-ist*, which means "one who practices." Knowing the meaning of *-ist*, you can then determine that an archaeologist is a person who practices archaeology, the scientific study of ancient peoples and cultures.

WORD BANK

As you read "Caucasian Mummies Mystify Chinese," you will encounter the words on this list. Each word is defined on the page where it first appears. Preview the list before you read. Notice other words that end in *-ist*.

dogmas
parched
archaeologist
imperialist
subjugation
reconcile

◆ Build Grammar Skills

ACTIVE AND PASSIVE VOICE

Lively writing, the kind that keeps you moving through a news article, usually features verbs in the active voice. A verb is in the **active voice** when the subject of the sentence performs the action. A verb is in the **passive voice** when the action is performed on the subject. When the performer of an action is not known or is not important, the writer uses the passive voice.

Active Voice: Wang Binghua <u>found</u> the first of more than 100 mummies . . .

Passive Voice: They <u>were buried</u> in simple graves, roughly 6 feet deep . . .

As you read "Caucasian Mummies Mystify Chinese," notice how Davidson uses both the active and passive voice.

Spine Tinglers

Caucasian Mummies Mystify Chinese

◆ *Literature and Your Life*

CONNECT YOUR EXPERIENCE

How were the Egyptian pyramids built? Why—and how—were towering slabs of rock arranged in circles at Stonehenge? These so-called unsolved mysteries—discoveries or events for which we have no easy explanation—are popular subjects for books, articles, and television programs. Think about why both fictional and true-life unexplained phenomena are so popular.

Journal Writing Write about a real-life unsolved mystery you've read about or seen on television. Why did it capture your interest?

THEMATIC FOCUS: IT'S A MYSTERY

How does modern science help us solve ancient mysteries?

◆ Background for Understanding

SOCIAL STUDIES

This article explores the importance of the discovery of more than one hundred mummies in China. Are you surprised to hear the word *mummy* in connection with a place other than ancient Egypt? In fact, mummies have been found all over the world, including Europe, Peru, and Mexico. While mummification was a ritual way of preserving the dead in some cultures, mummies also form naturally in certain environments. Because people were often buried with their clothing, jewelry, tools, and even food, mummies and their burial sites can tell us much about how ancient peoples lived.

◆ Literary Focus

NEWS ARTICLE

The purpose of a **news article**, such as "Caucasian Mummies Mystify Chinese" is to inform you—the reader—by answering six basic questions, known as the five W's and H: *who, what, when, where, why,* and *how*.

The article's opening sentences, called the lead, are written to capture your attention, summarize the main points of the story, and answer as many of the six questions as possible. Notice as you read that the reporter goes on to provide details in the form of facts, as well as expert opinions that add authority and interest to the article.

◆ Reading Strategy

MAIN IDEA

Whether you are researching magazine articles or simply scanning a news story for information, finding the main idea is an important reading skill. At first glance, the **main idea**—the most important point—of a piece of writing is not always obvious. In a well-written news article, the main idea is usually presented in the lead paragraph. The body of the article, however, may provide additional important details.

An easy way to focus on the main idea as you read is to look for answers to the six questions *who, what, when, where, why,* and *how*. As you read this article, jot down answers to these questions in a chart like this:

Who?	
What?	
When?	
Where?	
Why?	
How?	

Caucasian Mummies Mystify Chinese

Keay Davidson
from San Francisco Examiner

San Francisco—In dim light they appear to be sleeping, but they've been dead up to 4,000 years: more than 100 astoundingly well-preserved mummies unearthed in a Chinese desert, whose inexplicably blond hair and white skin could topple dogmas about early human history.

A former Stanford scientist is analyzing the mummies' DNA in hopes of answering haunting questions: Who are they? Where did they come from? And what on earth were these European-looking men, women and children doing in China's parched out-back 2,000 years before Jesus, when Europe was largely a dark forest? Sixteen years after the first mummies were found, the Chinese government has granted Western researchers their first close look at these faces from prehistory: a baby in colorful swaddling clothes; a 20-year-old girl with braided hair, found buried in a curled-up position with her hands by her chest, as if dozing; a man with a pigtail, scarlet-colored clothes and red, blue, and amber leg wrappings . . . .

The discovery—which could have far greater impact on our understanding of societal evolution than the lone, ancient "ice man" uncovered in the Alps in 1991—is described in an article by science writer Evan Hadingham in the April 1994 issue of *Discover* magazine. Based on the *Discover* article and *San Francisco Examiner* interviews with experts on genetics and Chinese history and culture, here's how the discoveries unfolded. In 1978 and 1979, Chinese archaeologist Wang Binghua found the first of what would prove to be more than 100 mummies in Xinjiang[1] Province. They had white skin, blond hair, long noses and skulls, and deep-set eyes—Caucasians,[2] perhaps from Northern Europe.

---

1. **Xinjiang** (zin jē ang´)
2. **Caucasian** (kô kā´ zhən) *adj.*: Belonging to one of the major geographical groups of human beings, including the native peoples of Europe, who are loosely called the *white race*, though their skin colors may vary.

◀ Critical Viewing What features of this mummy might help scientists to deduce facts about the man and his life? **[Deduce]**

Little Attention in the West

Only scanty press reports have reached the West, at least partly because of the region's isolation, Chinese bureaucratic inertia and the regime's suppression of foreign contacts, particularly after the Tiananmen Square massacre[3] of 1989.

Now the cloud of mystery is lifting thanks to an investigation organized by University of Pennsylvania China scholar Victor Mair, in collaboration with researchers in China, the United States and Italy. The collaboration required delicate negotiations with Chinese officials.

It would have been "absolutely unthinkable" for Chinese authorities to grant Westerners such access—including tissue samples from the mummies—only five years ago, Mair told *The Examiner.* "In the 1910s and 1920s, it was a game of the imperialist (Western) archaeologists to go in and take away important stuff—ancient manuscripts, artworks, paintings, statues . . . (Chinese officials are) very sensitive to that and they don't want to make the same situation recur," Mair said.

He also speculates that some Chinese officials may have initially hesitated to ballyhoo the find because they didn't know what to make of all those Caucasian faces. They date from a time when, according to regional histories and

---

3. **Tiananmen** (tyen´ an men´) **Square massacre:** The murder of approximately 3,000 pro-democracy demonstrators by Chinese soldiers in Beijing, the capital of China, on June 3, 1989.

◆ **Literary Focus**
Notice how sections of the article are introduced with subheads that function like abbreviated lead statements.

◆ **Build Vocabulary**
dogmas (dôg´ məz) *n.*: Firmly-held beliefs or doctrines

parched (pärcht) *adj.*: Dried up by heat

archaeologist (är´ kē äl´ ə jist) *n.*: Person who practices the scientific study of the remains of ancient ways of life

imperialist (im pir´ ē əl ist) *adj.*: Here, describing a person from a country that seeks to dominate weaker countries

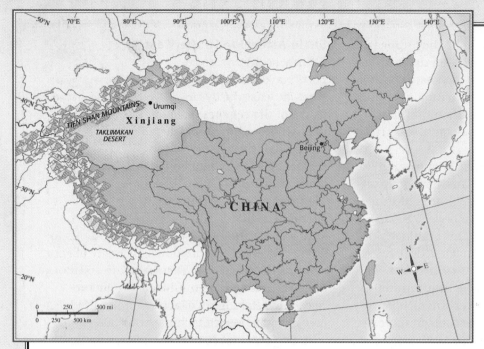

▲ **Critical Viewing** Find the Xinjiang province on the map. Based on its location, explain why Europeans might have settled in that particular part of China. [Draw Conclusions]

Francalacci's Stanford colleague, Luigi Luca Cavalli-Sforza, a population geneticist. "It's a very tricky type of analysis. Old DNA is generally very damaged.

"What I find most surprising of all is that these mummies were in such perfect condition," Cavalli-Sforza said. Their European-looking features are "sufficient, I think, to say these people came from Northern Europe. . . . My guess is that these (people) were kind of 'scouts' (who) were, most probably, traveling east and maybe settled there (in Xinjiang)." He believes thousands of mummies may yet be found.

national pride, China was advancing—developing writing and metal artifacts and wheeled vehicles—without help from foreign meddlers.

Bodies' Condition Excellent

The mummies were unearthed at scattered burial sites in an approximately 500-mile-wide region of northwest China, between the so-called Celestial (Tian Shan) Mountains and the Taklimakan[4] Desert. They range in age from 2000 B.C. to 300 B.C., based largely on radiocarbon dating.

Where do they come from? At the University of Sassari in Italy, anthropological geneticist[5] Paolo Francalacci—who worked at Stanford until recently—hopes to determine the mummies' likely place of origin by comparing their DNA, or genetic material, with modern DNA from different societies.

"It will take time before we know anything (from the DNA analysis)," cautions

Why has it taken so long for the news to get Western scholars' attention? While Western news media trumpeted the 5,000-year-old "ice man" found in the Austrian and Italian Alps, they have ignored the Chinese find—almost . . . .

Poor Chinese public relations could be partly to blame. Mair suspects that in the late 1970s, Chinese scholars were so startled by the Caucasian mummies that they weren't sure what to do with them.

"I think it flummoxed them when they found these Caucasian people out there . . . it's not what they expected," he said. "They didn't know how to put it into any of their schemes for history; it just didn't make sense to them . . . ."

◆ **Reading Strategy**
How does this question and those found elsewhere in the article help you gather information about the main idea?

---

4. **Taklimakan** (täk li mä kän)
5. **anthropological geneticist:** One who studies the historical development of human beings through the examination of their genes.

Nagging Questions

In 1987, Mair happened to be touring China when he entered a museum in Urumqi[6] that displayed mummies of a man, woman and child—a family, as it appeared. They had died 3,000 years earlier, "yet the bodies looked as if they were buried yesterday," he said.

What left him "thunderstruck," though, was their faces: They were Caucasians, apparently of European origin. "The questions kept nagging at me: Who were these people? How did they get out here at such an early date?"

The April 1994 issue of *Discover* includes a gallery of color photos of the corpses. They include a man with a painted image of the sun—a religious symbol?—on the temple of his head; the baby in swaddling clothes, its eyes covered with stones—a burial ritual?; a woman in a tall, peaked hat,. . . and a woman wearing a fur-lined coat, leather mittens and a two-pointed hat that, according to Chinese archaeologists, indicates she might have had *two husbands*—a possible result of a shortage of females. They were buried in simple graves, roughly 6 feet deep, with mats at the bottom. Some graves contain artifacts hinting that the living mourned the dead: For example, a baby was buried

---

6. **Urumqi** (ür üm chē)

with a sort of milk bottle fashioned from a sheep's udder.

"This is my favorite story in the seven years that I've edited *Discover* . . . because we were able to publish something monumental before anyone else," said the magazine's editor, Paul Hoffman.

Traditionally, Chinese historians insist that their society evolved on its own with little foreign input. That view has played well in modern China, which resents its past subjugation to foreign imperialists.

But Mair says the traditional view is hard to reconcile with the discovery of so many Caucasians who lived in what is now the westernmost edge of China, thousands of years before Marco Polo.[7] "The archaeological, linguistic, and textual evidence forces me to conclude that China has both significantly influenced and been influenced by other civilizations throughout history and, indeed, prehistory," Mair said. . . .

---

7. **Marco Polo** (1254–1324): Italian traveler and trader considered to be the first European to cross the length of Asia.

◆ Build Vocabulary

subjugation (sub´ jə gā´ shən) *n.*: Enslavement
reconcile (rek´ ən sīl´) *v.*: Bring into agreement

Guide for Responding

◆ *Literature and Your Life*

Reader's Response As you read about the Caucasian mummies and the questions they raise for historians, what questions of your own come to mind? What else would you like to know about these ancient people and the way they lived?

Thematic Focus After reading "Caucasian Mummies Mystify Chinese," do you agree that real-life mysteries can be just as intriguing as those created by storytellers? Why or why not?

Journal Writing The archaeologists who discovered the mummies and the scientists who are analyzing them both play important roles. Explain which you

would find more interesting—working in the field as an archaeologist or using science and technology in the lab—and why.

☑ Check Your Comprehension

1. What is remarkable about the mummies' appearance?
2. Where do experts think the people found in the Chinese desert originally came from?
3. (a) What year were the first mummies unearthed? (b) Was the article written at the time the mummies were discovered?
4. What kind of tests are scientists using to analyze the mummies?

Guide for Responding (continued)

◆ Critical Thinking

INTERPRET

1. How has the discovery of the mummies changed historians' view of early Chinese culture? **[Infer]**
2. Contrast news coverage of the discovery of the mummies with the news coverage of the "Ice Man." **[Compare and Contrast]**
3. Why might China have reacted as it did to the discovery of the mummies? **[Analyze]**

EVALUATE

4. Do you think the reporter clearly communicated why the discovery of the mummies is so important? Why or why not? **[Evaluate]**

APPLY

5. How will the tests that scientists are conducting help unlock the mystery surrounding the mummies? **[Apply]**

◆ Reading Strategy

MAIN IDEA

Noting the answers to *who, what, when, where, why,* and *how* as you read is a simple way to help identify the **main idea** of a piece of writing.

1. What is the action, or "news," described in the second sentence of the article, and *who* is performing it?
2. On *what* is this action being performed?
3. *Why* is this action being performed?
4. State the main idea of this article.

◆ Literary Focus

NEWS ARTICLE

Every **news article** is written to inform readers about the *who, what, when, where, why,* and *how* of a current event.

1. How does the article's lead grab your attention, and why does it make you want to read on?
2. The article includes quotations from an expert on China. How do these comments help you understand the news being reported?
3. Why doesn't the reporter include his own opinions about the mummies?
4. How might this story have been different had it been written as an encyclopedia article?

◆ Build Vocabulary

USING THE SUFFIX -ist

Write the following sentences on your paper and complete each with one of the following words:

a. archaeologists   **b.** geneticists   **c.** linguists

1. When the results of the DNA tests on the mummies are complete, _____?_____ will compare them with modern genetic material.
2. _____?_____ are trying to determine whether the ancient European settlers had any influence on the Chinese language.
3. The clothing and painted symbols found on the mummies are of special interest to _____?_____.

USING THE WORD BANK

Write the letter of the word that is the best synonym, or has the closest meaning, of the first word.

1. dogmas: (a) documents, (b) beliefs, (c) rumors
2. parched: (a) dried, (b). moist, (c) curved
3. archaeologist: (a) leader, (b) caretaker, (c) scientist
4. imperialist: (a) dominating, (b) wise, (c) proud
5. subjugation: (a)enslavement, (b) freedom, (c) celebration
6. reconcile: (a) reply, (b) settle, (c) begin

◆ Build Grammar Skills

ACTIVE AND PASSIVE VOICE

A verb is in the **active voice** when the subject of the sentence performs the action. A verb is in the **passive voice** when the action is performed on the subject.

Practice On your paper, rewrite the following sentences in the active voice. If a sentence cannot be rewritten in the active voice, give the reason.

1. Thousands of mummies may yet be found.
2. The excavation sites were visited by hundreds of archaeologists.
3. A mummified family was seen by Victor Mair while he was touring China.
4. A milk bottle had been given to the child.
5. The mummies' DNA was analyzed by a Stanford scientist.

Build Your Portfolio

Idea Bank

Writing

1. **Book Jacket** Write an exciting summary for the cover of a book about the discovery and significance of the Caucasian mummies. **[Career Link]**

2. **Short Story** Imagine how excited Wang Binghua must have been to discover the mummies. Write a short story about an archaeologist who makes a great find in another part of the world.

3. **Travel Brochure** Create a travel brochure promoting a tour of archaeological sites in China where mummies have been uncovered. Include illustrations and maps, as well as copy explaining the importance of the sites. If possible, use the Internet to gather information. **[Social Studies Link]**

Speaking and Listening

4. **Group Discussion** In a small group, discuss why ancient cultures might have preserved the dead or buried them with their belongings. What do these practices tell us? Make a list of at least three observations or conclusions. **[Social Studies Link]**

5. **Oral Presentation** As the first archaeologist to uncover the Caucasian mummies of China, you are invited to present your findings. Explain to your colleagues why your discovery is so important.

Projects

6. **Photo Essay** Refer to periodicals, including the April 1994 issue of *Discover,* to find illustrated articles about mummies. Photocopy the illustrations and write explanatory captions for each to create a photo essay. **[Art Link]**

7. **Costume Drawing** Based on the descriptions given in this article, draw the clothing worn by the Caucasian mummies, as you interpret it. **[Art Link]**

Writing Mini-Lesson

News Feature

"Caucasian Mummies Mystify Chinese" is a **news feature**. Though usually based at least indirectly on a news event, news features provide information of general value or interest, explore a human-interest angle of a news story, or describe a personality. Using a subject you find interesting—a hobby, sports hero, even a fashion trend—write a news feature.

Writing Skills Focus: Grabbing the Reader's Attention

Use a lively writing style with an opening that is a real **attention-grabber**. By opening your feature with a vivid or unexpected image or situation, you grab readers' attention and pull them in.

Model From the Article

In dim light they appear to be sleeping, but they've been dead up to 4,000 years . . .

While you may develop a great idea for an attention-grabber during the prewriting stage, you can continue to rework and refine it as you revise.

Prewriting If an attention-grabbing lead doesn't immediately spring to mind, review the five Ws and H questions and jot down answers for each. An answer may spark an idea for a strong opening. Alternatively, consider developing a particularly vivid or interesting image into an attention-grabbing lead.

Drafting Once you have pulled readers in with a strong attention-grabber, keep them interested with crisp, lively writing, and provide enough detail to give them a thorough understanding of your topic.

Revising Read your news feature as though you know nothing about the topic. Decide whether the lead interests you enough to read on. Make sure that, wherever possible, you use the active voice.

Writing Process Workshop

When you experience an exciting or frightening moment, you tend to remember it. For example, you may remember winning a big game or living through a dangerous weather event like this tornado. When you write about such an event, you are writing a **remembrance**. By giving a detailed, step-by-step account of the event, you help readers feel as if they are there sharing the memorable moment with you.

Re-create one of your most exciting or frightening experiences by writing a remembrance about it. The following skills, introduced in this section's Writing Mini-Lessons, will help you write your remembrance.

Writing Skills Focus

▶ **Grab readers' attention** immediately by starting with a striking description or gripping situation. An exciting opening always makes readers eager for more. (See p. 117.)

▶ **Offer elaboration** by providing vivid, colorful details that make your description precise and complete. (See p. 101.)

▶ **Provide a clear sequence of events.** Relate the details of your experience in order, so that readers are not confused about what happened first, next, and last. (See p. 109.)

In the following short piece, the author uses the above writing skills while describing a memorable encounter with a tornado.

WRITING MODEL

I've experienced some pretty bad weather, but last year's tornado was the first storm that ever struck fear in my heart.① First, the sky went from blue to black, and then the wind and rain began to whip furiously. ② I remember crouching at the window, staring in disbelief as our lawn furniture danced crazily through the air. ③

① The opening sentence grabs readers' attention.

② The author uses the words *first* and *then* to help show the order of events.

③ This colorful detail about the tornado makes it easy for readers to picture the scene clearly in their minds.

Prewriting

Choose a Topic To find a topic, think about the scariest or most exciting moments in your life. Choose the one moment you feel would interest readers the most. The following suggestions may help you.

Topic Ideas

- A crucial victory for me
- My brush with danger
- How I survived a storm
- My claim to fame

Elaborate a List of Details List as many details as you can that are related to the experience. Try to use colorful words and phrases to capture each detail. Look at these examples:

river flooded	helicopter rescue
piled sandbags	heavy rains
house floated away	sat on rooftop

Organize Events in Sequence Review your list. Think about the events that happened first, second, third, and so on. Number your notes accordingly. Don't be afraid to add new details that come to mind as you work.

3 river flooded	5 helicopter rescue
2 piled sandbags	1 heavy rains
6 house floated away	4 sat on rooftop

Drafting

Start With an Attention-Grabbing Beginning Begin your remembrance with remarkable details rather than dreary facts. Write something that will spark readers' curiosity about your experience. For example, you might dive right into the action, then go back and explain the events leading up to it; or you might begin with your reactions to the experience—for instance, "My heart beat wildy and I felt as if I'd explode!"

APPLYING LANGUAGE SKILLS: Using Precise Adjectives

As you're writing, use precise adjectives to enable readers to *see*, *hear*, *smell*, *feel*, and *taste* what you're describing. Look at this example:

General Adjective

I heard a <u>loud</u> noise.

Precise Adjective

I heard a <u>thunderous</u> noise.

Notice how the precise adjective helps you "hear" the noise better than the general adjective.

Practice On your paper, replace each italicized adjective with a more precise one.

1. We had a *bad* flood in our town.
2. The river did *big* damage to homes.
3. Workers made a *good* effort to help others.

Writing Application As you write your remembrance, use precise adjectives to describe people, places, and things. A thesaurus can help you find precise adjectives to replace general ones.

Writer's Solution Connection
Writing Lab

To help you find precise adjectives for your remembrance, use the Sensory Word Bins activity in the Writing Lab tutorial on Narration.

APPLYING LANGUAGE SKILLS: Avoiding Fragments and Run-on Sentences

A sentence fragment lacks a subject, a verb, or both and fails to express a complete thought.

Fragment: *Brave rescue workers.*

Correction: *Brave rescue workers saved the day.*

A run-on sentence has two or more main clauses incorrectly punctuated as a single sentence.

Run-on Sentence: *Rain fell, I waited.*

Correction: *Rain fell. I waited.*

Practice On your paper, correct these sentences.

1. The wet and weak house.
2. A rescue helicopter.
3. They lowered a ladder I climbed up.

Writing Application As you revise your remembrance, eliminate sentence fragments and run-on sentences.

Writer's Solution Connection
Language Lab

For more practice with sentence fragments and run-on sentences, complete the Language Lab activity on Fragments and Run-ons.

Use Time Words to Sequence Events As you describe events, include time words to help show the order in which things happen. Here are a few words you might use:

Examples of Time Words				
first	later	afterward	soon	last
next	then	suddenly	when	finally

Revising

Use a Checklist Turn back to the Writing Skills Focus on the first page of the lesson. Use the skills as a checklist while revising your writing, in order to improve it. If you can't answer yes to the following questions, revise your work as necessary.

▶ Have I grabbed the readers' attention?

▶ Have I elaborated my ideas by using vivid details?

▶ Have I made the sequence of events clear?

REVISION MODEL

① Rainwater crept up to my knees.
∧ There was lots of rain around me. I helped pile
② bulky canvas   ③ two days
∧ sandbags by the riverbank. The river flooded ∧. later

① The writer replaces the first sentence with a stronger attention-grabber.
② Additional details about the sandbags make it easier for readers to visualize them.
③ The author adds time words to make the sequence of events clearer.

Publishing

▶ **Classroom** Record your remembrance on tape. Set up a Listening Corner where classmates can listen to your story.

▶ **Library** Put your remembrance in a classroom book of memories and present it to the school or local library.

▶ **Other Classes** Visit other classes and share your remembrances orally. Answer questions listeners may have.

Real-World Reading Skills Workshop

Strategies for Success

You may sometimes flip through a magazine looking quickly at the pictures to see whether you want to read the articles. You may not have realized, however, that you can use photographs and illustrations to enhance your understanding of and appreciation for literature and other writing. Pictures often help to reinforce what is in the written text and sometimes even provide information that extends beyond the text.

Use Your Experiences When you look at a picture, you recall all of your past experiences and ideas about the subject you are observing. Often you can use this personal knowledge to help make new inferences, or draw conclusions, about what you see. For example, if you see a picture of someone in a specific car and you know the cost of the car, you might make inferences about the economic status of the person in the car. Be careful about jumping to conclusions, however. You won't know for certain whether the person in the picture owns the car, or has achieved a certain economic status, unless it is directly stated in the text or caption.

Use Visual Clues in Combination With Text

To get the most from illustrations and photographs, always read the text and captions. Ask yourself: How do the illustrations relate to the written text? What information do the visuals provide that isn't in the text? How do the captions help me understand the visuals?

Apply the Strategy

The picture on this page is from an article about computer programs in local schools. You can make inferences about the school's program simply by combining what you are told in the caption and shown in the picture.

1. What can you infer about the computer class based solely on the picture?
2. What do you know about the class based solely on the caption?
3. What information about the class is contained in both the caption and the picture?
4. Do the picture and the caption make you want to learn more about the computer class at this school? Explain your answer.

Students learn how to access the Internet in computer class.

✔ Here are other situations in which visual clues may provide additional information:

▶ Textbooks
▶ Magazine articles
▶ Computer applications
▶ Internet Web sites

Conducting telephone interviews is a great way to gather information for your writing or to learn more about a work of literature. Following are some tips to help you become a successful telephone interviewer.

Plan Your Questions As with a face-to-face interview, you need to be prepared when you interview someone over the phone. Before making the call, list the specific things you want to find out. It helps to research your topic first so you can ask appropriate questions.

Prepare for Responses Interviewers must be ready to record their information quickly. As you listen to a response, take brief notes on important information only. Jot down key words and phrases that will help you remember the entire answer later. Don't try to write out a response word for word, unless you plan to use it as a direct quote. If you miss part of an answer, politely ask the speaker to repeat it. If you plan to tape the interview, first notify the person of your intention.

Tips for Telephone Interviewing

✔ *To have a successful telephone interview, follow these suggestions:*

▶ Be polite. Begin and end the call by thanking the person for his or her time.
▶ Speak directly into the mouthpiece, slowly and clearly.
▶ Hold or prop the phone securely against your ear so you hear answers clearly.

Apply the Strategies

Find a partner and role-play the following situations. Conduct each interview with your backs to one another, so you cannot see your partner as you talk. Take notes on the answers you receive. Later, you can switch roles and perform the scene again.

1. Your favorite author is in town, staying at a nearby hotel. You call for an interview for a class report. What questions do you have about the writer's work and about his or her visit to your community?

2. A teacher in your school is out of town, receiving the "Teacher of the Year" award from the governor. You call the teacher for an interview for your school newspaper. What do you ask about the ceremony and the award?

3. You are in charge of buying uniforms for the school band or football team. However, you can order by catalog only. What questions will you ask the manufacturer over the phone about the uniforms?

Extended Reading Opportunities

A good spine tingler will keep you on the edge of your seat. Following are just a few possibilities for extending your exploration of spine-tingling situations.

Suggested Titles

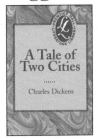

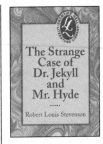

A Tale of Two Cities
Charles Dickens

This historical novel, set in London and Paris during the French Revolution, is filled with suspenseful plot twists such as false accusations, look-alike characters, and bitter people thirsting for revenge. At the center of it all is beautiful Lucy Manette—whose father wavers between sanity and madness after spending eighteen years in a French prison, and whose husband is later unjustly imprisoned and sentenced to die by the guillotine.

To Kill a Mockingbird
Harper Lee

This novel, set in the South in the early 1930's, is narrated by a strong-willed girl named Scout. Through Scout's narration, readers meet her older brother, Jem, and her beloved father, Atticus, a respected lawyer who defends an African American accused of attacking a white woman. Scout also recounts the chilling legend of Boo Radley, a neighborhood recluse, feared by all the children, who seems to be following Scout and her brother.

The Strange Case of Dr. Jekyll and Mr. Hyde
Robert Louis Stevenson

This is the story of a mild-mannered doctor who explores his dark side—with terrifying results. Fascinated with the idea of evil, the story's main character, Dr. Jekyll, develops a potion that changes him into the violent Mr. Hyde. Before long, however, Jekyll finds himself transforming into Hyde without the aid of the potion, leaving him, and terrified readers, to wonder which personality will finally win out.

Other Possibilities

Rebecca	Daphne du Maurier
Jurassic Park	Michael Crichton
The Adventures of Sherlock Holmes	Sir Arthur Conan Doyle
Buried in Ice: The Mystery of a Lost Arctic Expedition	Owen Beattie and John Geiger

Human Achievement, Tsing-Fang Chen, Lucia Gallery, NYC

UNIT 2

Challenges and Choices

An athlete challenges herself to be the best she can be. A powerful leader makes decisions that can affect an entire country. No matter who you are, life involves facing challenges and making choices. In these stories, poems, and essays, you'll see how people in many different situations deal with some of the challenges and choices life has to offer.

◆ 125

Guide for Reading

Carl Sandburg (1878–1967)

Imagine finding one subject so interesting that you could write six books on it. Carl Sandburg was so fascinated with the life and times of Abraham Lincoln that he wrote a six-volume biography of our sixteenth president.

Sandburg believed that the Civil War was our nation's most desperate crisis and Abraham Lincoln our greatest leader.

Sandburg's admiration for Lincoln inspired true dedication—all together, he spent eighteen years researching and writing the enormous biography. The finished work included *Abraham Lincoln: The Prairie Years*, in two volumes, and *Abraham Lincoln: The War Years*, in four volumes. Sandburg's many years of hard work won him a Pulitzer Prize, as well as recognition for having written what many people consider the greatest historical biography of the 1900's.

A Varied Life Carl August Sandburg was born on January 6, 1878, in Galesburg, Illinois. At the age of thirteen he left school, and for the next seven years he held a variety of odd jobs, including porter, scene changer, truck handler, dishwasher, potter, and itinerant farm worker. After the Spanish-American War broke out in 1898, Sandburg served briefly in the United States Army in Puerto Rico. This experience caused the strong antiwar feelings that Sandburg would hold throughout his life.

A Prize-Winning Writer After returning from Puerto Rico, Sandburg enrolled in Lombard College, where he discovered literature. In 1914, while working as a journalist, Sandburg published a group of poems in a literary journal and gained his first recognition as a poet. This was the beginning of a writing career that would earn him two Pulitzer Prizes—one for his Lincoln biography in 1940 and another for his *Complete Poems* in 1951.

◆ Build Vocabulary

SUFFIXES: -ic

Early in this selection, Sandburg describes Lincoln as being "clothed with despotic power." Notice that the word *despotic* contains the adjective-forming suffix *-ic*, which means "like" or "pertaining to." If you know that the noun *despot* means "absolute ruler," you can figure out that *despotic* power means "unlimited power," like that held by an absolute ruler.

WORD BANK

As you read the excerpt from "A Lincoln Preface," you will encounter the words on this list. Each word is defined on the page where it first appears. Preview the list before you read.

| despotic |
| chattel |
| cipher |
| slouching |
| censure |
| gaunt |
| droll |

◆ Build Grammar Skills

INDEPENDENT AND SUBORDINATE CLAUSES

A clause is a group of words that contains both a subject and a verb. An **independent clause,** or *main clause,* can stand by itself as a complete sentence. A **subordinate clause** has a subject and a verb but cannot stand alone. It must be linked to an independent clause in order to make sense. Look at the following example from "A Lincoln Preface." The independent clause is in boldface, and the subordinate clause is in italics.

S   V   S   V
Greeley is so rotten *that nothing can be done with him.*

Subordinate clauses are usually introduced by **subordinating conjunctions,** such as *because, when, before, if, since,* and *while,* or by **relative pronouns,** such as *that, which, who,* and *whom.*

from **A Lincoln Preface**

◆ *Literature and Your Life*

CONNECT YOUR EXPERIENCE

You may admire an athlete for her awesome ability and down-to-earth personality. You may look up to a relative for his kindness, strength, and humor. These people are heroes, and you appreciate them for their achievements or fine qualities. We are often inspired to pay tribute to our heroes in some way. Carl Sandburg, for example, wrote a six-volume biography of his hero, Abraham Lincoln.

Journal Writing Make a list of your heroes, jotting down the qualities that make each person heroic in your eyes. Think about ways in which you could pay tribute to the people on your list.

THEMATIC FOCUS: CHALLENGES AND CHOICES

Abraham Lincoln served as president during the bloodiest war in the history of the United States. Yet he faced the daily challenges and difficult choices of his presidency with compassion and humor, as you'll learn from this excerpt from his biography.

◆ Literary Focus

ANECDOTE

If you want to describe a friend's sense of humor to someone who doesn't know her, you might relate an anecdote about a time when your friend said or did something funny. An **anecdote** is a brief story about an interesting, amusing, or strange event. In the following portrait of Abraham Lincoln, Carl Sandburg uses anecdotes to give readers a sense of what Lincoln was like.

◆ Background for Understanding

HISTORY

Abraham Lincoln is remembered as one of our greatest presidents; yet at the time of his election in 1861, less than half the country supported him. One reason is that Lincoln was opposed to slavery—and many landowners in the southern United States still kept slaves. A month after his inauguration, eleven southern states had left the Union and declared themselves an independent Confederacy. Civil war broke out between the Union and the Confederacy.

Lincoln's background as a lawyer hardly prepared him to deal with a civil war, but he rose to the challenge and became the chief military strategist of the Union cause. Lincoln kept the Union states from splitting apart and eventually led them to victory in 1865. He had planned for the reconstruction of the southern states, but he was unable to complete those plans. Just six weeks after his second inauguration, Lincoln was assassinated by a supporter of the Confederacy, John Wilkes Booth.

Reading for Success

Interactive Reading Strategies

You wouldn't stand in front of a video game and just watch it like a movie. Video games are interactive—your choices and movements affect the way the game turns out. Reading is interactive, too. When you read, you get involved with the ideas, images, and information presented in the text. The more involved you are, the richer your understanding will be. When you read about familiar topics, your own experiences, ideas, and knowledge help bring meaning to the text. With difficult or unfamiliar topics, you may find it hard to interact with the text. Use these strategies to help you.

Set a purpose for reading.

Before you begin, decide *why* you're reading a piece. At times you may read purely for enjoyment, but often you read to learn something. For example, you might already know some facts about Abraham Lincoln, but the following selection may contain new information. Set a purpose to read for new information about Lincoln, then look for details in your reading that support this purpose.

Use your prior knowledge.

As you read, keep in mind what you already know about the subject—in this case, Lincoln. Use that knowledge to make connections with what the author is saying. You may find details in the text that confirm opinions you already have, as well as details that change your opinions.

Form a mental picture.

Use the author's words and descriptions to help you "see" a picture in your mind. This helps enhance your understanding and appreciation of the text.

Predict what will happen or what the author will say.

As you read, pause to ask yourself what might happen. You may base a prediction on your own experience in a similar situation. You might also base a prediction on information that has already been stated in the text. Continue to make predictions as you read.

Respond to the selection.

Think about what the author has said, and reflect on how you personally feel about the topic. Consider how you might take what you've learned from this work and use it in your own life.

As you read the excerpt from "A Lincoln Preface," look at the notes along the sides of the pages. The notes demonstrate how to apply these strategies to a work of literature.

from A Lincoln Preface

Carl Sandburg

> **Prior knowledge** about Lincoln's assassination will aid your understanding of this paragraph.

In the time of the April lilacs in the year 1865, a man in the City of Washington, D.C., trusted a guard to watch at a door, and the guard was careless, left the door, and the man was shot, lingered a night, passed away, was laid in a box, and carried north and west a thousand miles; bells sobbed; cities wore crepe;[1] people stood with hats off as the railroad burial car came past at midnight, dawn or noon.

During the four years of time before he gave up the ghost, this man was clothed with despotic power, commanding the most powerful armies till then assembled in modern warfare, enforcing drafts of soldiers, abolishing the right of habeus corpus,[2] directing politically and spiritually the wild, massive forces loosed in civil war.

> **Based on this paragraph, how might you predict** Lincoln will be portrayed later in the selection?

Four billion dollars' worth of property was taken from those who had been legal owners of it, confiscated, wiped out as by fire, at his instigation and executive direction; a class of chattel property recognized as lawful for two hundred years went to the scrap pile.

When the woman who wrote *Uncle Tom's Cabin*[3] came to see him in the White House, he greeted her, "So you're the little woman who wrote the book that made this great war," and as they seated themselves at a fireplace, "I do love an open fire: I always had one at home." As they were finishing their talk of the days of blood, he said, "I shan't last long after it's over."

An Illinois Congressman looked in on him as he had his face lathered for a shave in the White Houses

> **Picture** this scene; you get a sense of Lincoln as an everyday person.

and remarked, "If anybody had told me that in a great crisis like this the people were going out to a little one-horse town and pick out a one-horse lawyer for president, I wouldn't have believed it." The answer was, "Neither would I. But it was a time when a man with a policy would have been fatal to the country. I never had a policy. I have simply tried to do what seemed best each day, as each day came."

"I don't intend precisely to throw the Constitution overboard, but I will stick it in a hole if I can," he told a Cabinet officer. The enemy was violating the Constitution to destroy the Union, he argued, and therefore, "I will violate the Constitution, if necessary, to save the Union." He instructed a messenger to the Secretary of the Treasury, "Tell him not to bother himself about the Constitution. Say that I have that sacred instrument here at the White House, and I am guarding it with great care."

---

1. **crepe** (krāp) *n.*: Thin, black cloth worn to show mourning.
2. **habeus corpus** (hā bē əs kor´ pəs): Right of an imprisoned person to have a court hearing.
3. **woman . . . Cabin:** Harriet Beecher Stowe (1811–1896), whose novel stirred up opinion against slavery.

♦ **Build Vocabulary**

despotic (des pät´ ik) *adj.*: Like or in the manner of an absolute ruler or tyrant

chattel (chat´ əl) *n.*: A movable item of personal property

Lincoln Proclaiming Thanksgiving, Dean Cornwell, The Lincoln Museum, Fort Wayne, Indiana, a part of Lincoln National Corp.

▲ **Critical Viewing** What can you tell about Lincoln from this painting? [Infer]

When he was renominated, it was by the device of seating delegates from Tennessee, which gave enough added votes to seat favorable delegates from Kentucky, Missouri, Louisiana, Arkansas, and from one county in Florida. Until late in that campaign of 1864, he expected to lose the November election; military victories brought the tide his way; the vote was 2,200,000 for him and 1,800,000 against him. Among those who bitterly fought him politically, and accused him of blunders or crimes, were Franklin Pierce, a former president of the United States; Horatio Seymour, the Governor of New York;

This information helps you achieve your **purpose** of gaining new knowledge about Lincoln.

Samuel F. B. Morse, inventor of the telegraph; Cyrus H. McCormick, inventor of the farm reaper; General George B. McClellan, a Democrat who had commanded the Army of the Potomac; and the Chicago *Times*, a daily newspaper. In all its essential propositions the Southern Confederacy had the moral support of powerful, respectable elements throughout the North, probably more than a million votes believing in the justice of the cause of the South as compared with the North.

While propagandas raged, and the war winds howled, he sat in the White House, the Stubborn Man of History, writing that the Mississippi was one river and could not belong to two countries, that the plans for railroad connection from coast to coast must be pushed through and the Union Pacific[4] realized.

You can **predict**, based on this sentence, that Sandburg will now present contrasting sides of Lincoln's personality.

His life, mind and heart ran in contrasts. When his white kid gloves broke into tatters while shaking hands at a White House reception, he remarked, "This looks like a general bustification." When he talked with an Ohio friend one day during the 1864 campaign, he mentioned one public man, and murmured, "He's a thistle! I don't see why God lets him live." Of a devious Senator, he said, "He's too crooked to lie still!" And of a New York editor, "In early life in the West, we used to make our shoes last a great while with much mending, and sometimes, when far gone, we found the leather so rotten the stitches would not hold. Greeley is so rotten that nothing can be done with him. He is not truthful; the stitches all tear out." As

You might **respond** with surprise to Lincoln's harsh remarks.

he sat in the telegraph office of the War Department, reading cipher dispatches, and came to the words, Hosanna and Husband, he would chuckle, "Jeffy D.,"[5] and at the words, Hunter and Happy, "Bobby Lee."[6]

While the luck of war wavered and broke and came again, as generals failed and campaigns were lost, he held enough forces of the Union together to raise new armies and supply them, until generals were found who made war as victorious war has always been made, with terror, frightfulness, destruction, and valor and sacrifice past words of man to tell.

A slouching, gray-headed poet,[7] haunting the hospitals at Washington, characterized him as "the grandest figure on the crowded canvas of the

Footnotes are useful if you have no **prior knowledge** about a certain reference.

drama of the nineteenth century—a Hoosier Michael Angelo."[8]

His own speeches, letters, telegrams and official messages during that war form the most significant and enduring document from any one man on why the war began, why it went on, and the dangers beyond its end. He mentioned "the politicians," over and again "the politicians," with scorn and blame. As the platoons filed before him at a review of an army corps, he asked, "What is to become of these boys when the war is over?"

He was a chosen spokesman: yet there were times he was silent; nothing but silence could at those times have fitted a chosen spokesman; in the mixed shame and blame of the immense wrongs of two crashing civilizations, with nothing to say, he said nothing, slept not at all, and wept at those times in a way that made weeping appropriate, decent, majestic.

His hat was shot off as he rode alone one night in Washington; a son he loved died as he watched at the bed; his wife was accused of betraying information to the enemy, until denials from him were necessary; his best companion was a fine-hearted and brilliant son with a deformed palate and an impediment of speech; when a Pennsylvania Congressman told him the enemy had declared they would break into the city and hang him to a lamppost, he said he had considered "the violent preliminaries" to such a scene; on his left thumb was a scar where an ax had nearly chopped the thumb off when he was a boy; over one eye was a scar where he had been hit with a club in the hands of a man trying to steal the cargo off a Mississippi River flatboat; he threw a cashiered[9] officer out of his room in the White House, crying, "I can bear censure, but not insult. I never wish to see your face again."

---

8. Michael Angelo: Michelangelo (mik′ əl an′ jə lō), a famous Italian artist (1475–1564).

9. cashiered (ka shird′) v.: Dishonorably discharged.

◆ **Build Vocabulary**

cipher (sī′ fər) adj.: Code

slouching (slouch′ iŋ) adj.: Drooping

censure (sen′ shər) n.: Strong disapproval

---

4. Union Pacific: Railroad chartered by Congress in 1862 to form part of a transcontinental system.

5 "Jeffy D": Jefferson Davis (1808–1889) president of the Confederacy.

6. "Bobbie Lee": Robert E. Lee (1807–1870), commander in chief of the Confederate army.

7. slouching . . . poet: Walt Whitman (1819–1892).

The anecdotes in this paragraph help you to **picture** Lincoln as a complex and sometimes contradictory person.

As he shook hands with the correspondent of the London *Times*, he drawled, "Well, I guess the London *Times* is about the greatest power on earth—unless perhaps it is the Mississippi River." He rebuked with anger a woman who got on her knees to thank him for a pardon that saved her son from being shot at sunrise; and when an Iowa woman said she had journeyed out of her way to Washington just for a look at him, he grinned, "Well, in the matter of looking at one another, I have altogether the advantage."

He asked his Cabinet to vote on the high military command, and after the vote, told them the appointment had already been made; one Cabinet officer, who had been governor of Ohio, came away personally baffled and frustrated from an interview, to exclaim, to a private secretary, "That man is the most cunning person I ever saw in my life"; an Illinois lawyer who had been sent on errands carrying his political secrets, said, "He is a trimmer[10] and such a trimmer as the world has never seen."

He manipulated the admission of Nevada as a state in the Union, when her votes were needed for the Emancipation Proclamation,[11] saying, "It is easier to admit Nevada than to raise another million of soldiers." At the same time he went to the office of a former New York editor, who had become Assistant Secretary of War, and said the votes of three congressmen were wanted for the required three-quarters of votes in the House of Representatives, advising, "There are three that you can deal with better than anybody else . . . . Whatever promise you make to those men, I will perform it." And in the same week, he said to a Massachusetts politician that two votes were lacking, and, "Those two votes must be procured. I leave it to you to determine how it shall be done; but

remember that I am President of the United States and clothed with immense power, and I expect you to procure those votes." And while he was thus employing every last resource and device of practical politics to constitutionally abolish slavery, the abolitionist[12] Henry Ward Beecher attacked him with javelins of scorn and detestation in a series of editorials that brought from him the single comment, "Is thy servant a dog?"

When the King of Siam sent him a costly sword of exquisite embellishment, and two elephant tusks, along with letters and a photograph of the King, he acknowledged the gifts in a manner as lavish as the Orientals. Addressing the King of Siam as "Great and Good Friend," he wrote thanks for each of the gifts, including "also two elephant's tusks of length and magnitude, such as indicate they could have belonged only to an animal which was a native of Siam." After further thanks for the tokens received, he closed the letter to the King of Siam with strange grace and humor, saying, "I appreciate most highly your Majesty's tender of good offices in forwarding to this Government a stock from which a supply of elephants might be raised on our soil. . . . our political jurisdiction, however, does not reach a latitude so low as to favor the multiplication of the elephant, and steam on land as well as water has been our best agent of transportation . . . Meantime, wishing for your Majesty a long and happy life, and, for the generous and emulous people of Siam, the highest possible prosperity, I commend both to the blessing of Almighty God."

He sent hundreds of telegrams, "Suspend death sentence" or "Suspend execution" of So-and-So, who was to be shot at sunrise. The telegrams varied oddly at times, as in one, "If Thomas Samplogh, of the First Delaware Regiment, has been sentenced to death, and is not

If you have **prior knowledge** of Lincoln's nickname, "Honest Abe," you may **respond** with surprise that he sometimes bent the rules to accomplish his goals.

---

10. trimmer (trim′ ər) *n.*: Person who changes his opinion to suit the circumstances.
11. Emancipation Proclamation: Document issued by President Lincoln freeing the slaves in all territories still at war with the Union.

---

12. abolitionist (ab′ ə lish′ ən ist) *n.*: Person in favor of doing away with slavery in the United States.

yet executed, suspend and report the case to me." And another, "Is it Lieut. Samuel B. Davis whose death sentence is commuted? If not done, let it be done."

While the war drums beat, he liked best of all the stories told of him, one of two Quakeresses[13] heard talking in a railway car. "I think that Jefferson will succeed." "Why does thee think so?" "Because Jefferson is a praying man." "And so is Abraham a praying man." "Yes, but the Lord will think Abraham is joking."

An Indiana man at the White House heard him say, "Voorhees, don't it seem strange to you that I, who could never so much as cut off the head of a chicken, should be elected, or selected, into the midst of all this blood?"

A party of American citizens, standing in the ruins of the Forum in Rome, Italy, heard there the news of the first assassination of the first American dictator, and took it as a sign of the growing up and the aging of the civilization on the North American continent. Far out in Coles County, Illinois, a beautiful, gaunt old woman in a log cabin said, "I knowed he'd never come back."

Peculiersome Abe, N. C. Wyeth, The Free Library of Philadelphia

▲ Critical Viewing   What message does this painting convey about Lincoln? [Describe]

---

13. Quakeresses (kwāk´ ər es əz) n.: Female members of the religious group known as the Society of Friends, or Quakers.

◆ **Build Vocabulary**
gaunt (gônt) *adj.*: Thin and bony

Of men taking too fat profits out of the war, he said, "Where the carcass is there will the eagles be gathered together."

An enemy general, Longstreet, after the war, declared him to have been "the one matchless man in forty millions of people," while one of his private secretaries, Hay, declared his life to have been the most perfect in its relationships and adjustments since that of Christ.

Between the days in which he crawled as a baby on the dirt floor of a Kentucky cabin, and the time when he gave his final breath in Washington, he packed a rich life with work, thought, laughter, tears, hate, love.

With vast reservoirs of the comic and the droll, and notwithstanding a mastery of mirth and nonsense, he delivered a volume of addresses and letters of terrible and serious appeal, with import beyond his own day, shot through here and there with far, thin ironics, with paragraphs having raillery[14] of the quality of the Book of Job,[15] and echoes as subtle as the whispers of wind in prairie grass.

Perhaps no human clay pot has held more laughter and tears.

The facts and myths of his life are to be an American possession, shared widely over the world, for thousands of years, as the tradition of Knute or Alfred, Lao-tse or Diogenes, Pericles or Caesar,[16] are kept. This because he was not only a genius in the science of neighborly human relationships and an artist in the personal handling of life from day to day, but a strange friend and a friendly stranger to all forms of life that he met.

He lived fifty-six years of which fifty-two were lived in the West—the prairie years.

> Respond to Sandburg's appraisal of Lincoln as a great leader and a genius. In light of what you now know about Lincoln, do you agree with Sandburg?

---

16. **Knute** (knoot) **or Alfred, Lao-tse** (lou′ dzu′) **or Diogenes** (dī äj′ ə nēz), **Pericles** (per′ ə klēz) **or Caesar** (sē′ zər): Well-known thinkers and leaders from different eras and places.

---

14. **raillery** (rāl′ ər ē) *n.*: Good-natured teasing.
15. **Book of Job** (jōb): Book of the Old Testament in which a man named Job is tested by God.

◆ **Build Vocabulary**

droll (drōl) *adj.*: Comic and amusing in an odd way

Guide for Responding

◆ *Literature and Your Life*

Reader's Response Which anecdote about Abraham Lincoln revealed the most to you about his character?

Thematic Focus If you were to write a biography about someone who has faced many challenges and choices, who would it be?

Group Activity With a group, brainstorm for a list of people who have faced difficult challenges and made tough choices in their lives. Share your list with the class.

☑ Check Your Comprehension

1. To whom did Lincoln refer as "the little woman who wrote the book that made this great war"?
2. Why did Lincoln say he was willing to violate the Constitution?
3. According to Sandburg, Lincoln's favorite story about himself involves two Quaker women overheard talking. What does Lincoln's preference for this story reveal about his character?
4. Describe three personality traits that are revealed in Sandburg's portrait of Lincoln.

Guide for Responding (continued)

◆ Critical Thinking

INTERPRET

1. What was Lincoln's most important goal during the Civil War? **[Interpret]**
2. How did Lincoln use "practical politics" to end slavery? **[Connect]**
3. How does Sandburg show that Lincoln "packed a rich life with work, thought, laughter, tears, hate, love"? **[Distinguish]**
4. How does Sandburg's use of anecdotes personalize his portrait of Lincoln? **[Analyze]**
5. In what ways does Sandburg describe Lincoln as a complex man? **[Analyze]**

EVALUATE

6. Do you think Lincoln was justified in violating the Constitution? Why or why not? **[Make a Judgment; Support]**

EXTEND

7. How does this portrait of Lincoln compare with other biographical works you have read about great leaders? **[Literature Link]**

◆ Build Vocabulary

USING THE SUFFIX -ic

The suffix -ic means "like" or "pertaining to." Define each of these words, incorporating the definition of -ic into each answer.

1. problematic   4. artistic
2. dramatic   5. patriotic
3. poetic

USING THE WORD BANK

On your paper, write the letter of the word that is a synonym of the vocabulary word given.

1. despotic: (a) fearful, (b) lonely, (c) tyrannical
2. chattel: (a) idle talk, (b) personal property, (c) loud noise
3. cipher: (a) code, (b) quiet, (c) lazy
4. slouching: (a) stumbling, (b) drooping, (c) struggling
5. censure: (a) disapproval, (b) disappointment, (c) hardship
6. gaunt: (a) weak, (b) thin and bony, (c) clumsy
7. droll: (a) serious, (b) cruel, (c) comic

◆ Reading for Success

INTERACTIVE READING STRATEGIES

Review the reading strategies and the notes showing how to interact with the text. Then apply them to answer these questions.

1. Based on your prior knowledge of Lincoln, which anecdotes surprised you?
2. Which words or phrases in the first paragraph helped you to form a mental picture of what the author is describing?
3. Do you agree with Sandburg's opinion of Lincoln? Explain.

◆ Literary Focus

Anecdote

"A Lincoln Preface" contains many **anecdotes,** or brief stories, that reveal Lincoln's personality.

1. Describe three anecdotes Sandburg uses to reveal Lincoln's character.
2. What does each anecdote illustrate?

◆ Build Grammar Skills

INDEPENDENT CLAUSES AND SUBORDINATE CLAUSES

Writers use independent and subordinate clauses to achieve sentence variety and to show supporting or modifying ideas.

Practice On your paper, write *I* for *independent* or *S* for *subordinate* for each clause in italic type. Indicate the subordinating conjunction or relative pronoun in the subordinate clauses.

An **independent,** or main, **clause** can stand alone as a sentence. A **subordinate clause** must be linked to a main clause using a subordinating conjunction or a relative pronoun.

1. *When he was renominated,* it was by the device of seating delegates from Tennessee …
2. His hat shot off *as he rode alone one night in Washington* …
3. He rebuked with anger a woman *who got on her knees to thank him* …
4. He is not truthful; *the stitches all tear out.*

Build Your Portfolio

Idea Bank

Writing

1. **Gettysburg Address** According to legend, Lincoln drafted the Gettysburg Address on the back of an envelope. Find a copy of the Gettysburg Address. Then, on an envelope, jot down the key concepts and phrases that Lincoln may have written in a first draft of this address. **[Social Studies Link]**

2. **Newspaper Article** Write a brief news article describing the *who, what, where, when, why,* and *how* of Lincoln's death.

3. **Character Profile** Write a short profile of Lincoln, describing the traits, talents, and special skills that helped him succeed as president.

Speaking and Listening

4. **Dramatic Scene** With a partner or small group, enact one of the anecdotes Sandburg tells about Lincoln. **[Performing Arts Link]**

5. **Panel Discussion** Conduct a panel discussion on Lincoln's use of "practical politics" to end slavery with the passage of the Emancipation Proclamation. Panel members should prepare their remarks in advance. **[Social Studies Link]**

Projects

6. **Timeline** Create a timeline of the most significant events in Lincoln's life and presidency, including famous speeches and personal tragedies. **[Art Link; Social Studies Link]**

7. **Conflict Resolution** During a civil war, people are so close to issues that resolution is especially difficult. Choose a conflict in your school or community. Explain the conflict and the parties involved, and establish a step-by-step guide for resolving the conflict.

Writing Mini-Lesson

Anecdote

By using anecdotes that reveal Lincoln's personality, Carl Sandburg helps readers feel that they know Lincoln as a flesh-and-blood person and not simply as a shadowy figure from history. You, too, can use anecdotes to bring life to characters and events in your writing. The following tips will show you how.

Writing Skills Focus: Showing, Not Telling

How can you make the descriptions in your anecdote interesting and effective? One way is by **showing, not telling.** This means that you use details in your writing to get your point across, rather than state the obvious. For example, in the first paragraph of "A Lincoln Preface," Carl Sandburg wants to convey the grief people experienced when Lincoln died. Rather than say, "People were sad," Sandburg writes:

. . . bells sobbed; cities wore crepe; people stood with hats off . . .

Keep in mind the technique of showing, not telling, as you plan, draft, and revise your anecdote.

Prewriting Choose a person, place, or event to describe in an anecdote. Then decide on your main point—to illustrate someone's bravery, for example. Jot down details that will help make this point without having to state it directly.

Drafting Weave the details into an anecdote—a mini-story with a beginning, middle, and end. You may decide to add quotations to your anecdote, an effective method for showing, not telling.

Revising Show your anecdote to a friend and ask that person to describe its main point. If the point isn't clear, try to add details that are more specific. You might also want to add a title that conveys your point without stating it outright.

PART 1 *For the Good of All*

The Promise, Paulette Peters, Museum of American Folk Art

Guide for Reading

Martin Luther King, Jr. *(1929–1968)*

Dr. Martin Luther King, Jr., was one of the most dynamic civil rights leaders of the twentieth century. During the 1950's and 1960's, King organized nonviolent protests that helped to bring about equal rights for all Americans. His tireless efforts for civil rights inspired people of all races and earned King the 1964 Nobel Peace Prize.

Chief Dan George *(1899–1981)*

Chief Dan George had many careers, including actor and writer. Chief of the Squamish Band of Burrard Inlet in British Columbia, Canada, he was deeply concerned about developing mutual respect between Native Americans and other North Americans.

Rosa Parks *(1913–)*

In 1955, Rosa Parks was arrested for breaking an unjust law. This incident, described in *Rosa Parks: My Story*, sparked a boycott that led to the end of segregation on the Montgomery bus system. Park's courageous action marked the start of the civil rights movement.

Walt Whitman *(1819–1892)*

Walt Whitman, one of America's greatest poets, was a lover of democracy and a champion of the common individual. His expansive vision and spirit may be glimpsed in "I Hear America Singing."

◆ Build Vocabulary

WORD ROOTS: *-cred-*

Martin Luther King, Jr., expresses the dream that "this nation will rise up and live out the true meaning of its creed." The word *creed* comes from the root *-cred-*, which means "believe." Knowing the meaning of *-cred-* will help you determine that a creed is a statement of belief.

creed
oppression
oasis
exalted
prodigious
hamlet
complied
manhandled
determination
endurance

WORD BANK

As you read the selections, you will encounter the words on this list. Each word is defined on the page where it first appears. Preview the list before you read.

◆ Build Grammar Skills

USE OF *SHALL* AND *WILL*

Future time is expressed with **shall** or **will** and a main verb. At one time, the rule was that *shall* was used for the first person and *will* for the third person. Notice that Chief Dan George follows this rule:

First Person: I *shall* see our young braves ...

Third Person: They *will* be our new warriors ...

Now, however, that rule no longer applies. *Will* is always the appropriate helping verb to use to express future time. You can use *shall*, however, to express determination or formality, as in this statement from "I Have a Dream. . . .":

Determination: . . . all flesh *shall* see it.

I Have a Dream ◆ *from* Rosa Parks: My Story
There Is a Longing ◆ I Hear America Singing

◆ *Literature and Your Life*

CONNECT YOUR EXPERIENCE

Think of a time when you were inspired by someone's words—in a speech, a work of writing, or even a conversation. Why were you moved? Often, as in these selections, we find inspiration in the words of people who challenge us to be the best we can be.

THEMATIC FOCUS: FOR THE GOOD OF ALL

Accepting our differences . . . contributing to the good of all . . . striving for success. These challenges, and the choices they require us to make, are reflected in the following selections.

◆ Background for Understanding

HISTORY

Civil rights are freedoms that people are entitled to as members of a society. For example, the freedom of speech guaranteed by the United States Constitution is a civil right. Some Americans, including African Americans and members of other ethnic minorities, have not always enjoyed such civil rights and have had to struggle for equality. That struggle—marked by demonstrations, marches, and legal challenges—is known as the civil rights movement. The movement, which began in the 1950's and was led by figures such as Martin Luther King, Jr., and Rosa Parks, has led to the passage of new laws aimed at protecting the civil rights of everyone.

Journal Writing Jot down your thoughts about why it is dangerous for Americans to take civil rights for granted.

◆ Literary Focus

AUTHOR'S PURPOSE

An **author's purpose** is his or her reason for writing. For example, an author's purpose for writing a humorous story might be to entertain readers. Other purposes include persuading readers or explaining how to do something. As you read each selection, determine the author's purpose by asking yourself what the author wants to accomplish. Observe the techniques the author uses to achieve his or her purpose, then decide whether the author is successful.

◆ Reading Strategy

RESPOND

Whenever you read a work of literature, you **respond** to it. What you read might bring you joy or sadness, thrills or inspiration. There is always a response. You can't help but respond because you bring your own unique experiences and memories to everything you read. As you read a story, a speech, or a poem, something the author presents touches you and triggers an emotional response.

Each of these four selections evokes a bold image of what America is and what it might become. As you read them, ask yourself how they relate to you personally. What is it in your experience or memory that connects you to them? Your questioning may evoke an emotional response.

"I Have a Dream"

Martin Luther King, Jr.

. . . I say to you today, my friends, that in spite of the difficulties and frustrations of the moment I still have a dream. It is a dream deeply rooted in the American dream.

I have a dream that one day this nation will rise up and live out the true meaning of its creed: "We hold these truths to be self-evident; that all men are created equal."

I have a dream that one day on the red hills of Georgia the sons of former slaves and the sons of former slaveowners will be able to sit down together at the table of brotherhood.

I have a dream that one day even the state of Mississippi, a desert state sweltering with the heat of injustice and oppression, will be transformed into an oasis of freedom and justice.

I have a dream that my four little children will one day live in a nation where they will not be judged by the color of their skin but by the content of their character.

I have a dream today.

I have a dream that one day the state of Alabama, whose governor's lips are presently dripping with the words of interposition and nullification,[1] will be transformed into a situation where little black boys and black girls will be able to join hands with little white boys and white girls and walk together as sisters and brothers.

I have a dream today.

I have a dream that one day every valley shall be exalted, every hill and mountain shall be made low, the rough places will be made plains,

---

1. **Interposition** (in´ tər pə zish´ ən) **and nullification** (nul´ ə fi kā´ shən): Disputed doctrine that a state can reject federal laws considered to be violations of its rights.

◆ **Build Vocabulary**

creed (krēd) *n.*: Statement of belief

oppression (ə presh´ ən) *n.*: Keeping others down by the unjust use of power

oasis (ō ā´ sis) *n.*: Fertile place in the desert

exalted (eg zôlt´ əd) *v.*: Lifted up

◀ Critical Viewing What does this photograph tell you about the importance of Dr. King's message to those who heard his speech? **[Draw Conclusions]**

CONNECTIONS TO TODAY'S WORLD

Years after his death, Martin Luther King, Jr., continues to touch the lives of millions of people throughout the world. Politicians, writers, musicians—people from all walks of life—continue to promote King's message of equality and harmony. The following song by the popular Irish rock band U2 was written as a tribute to King and his message.

Pride
U2

One man come in the name of love
One man come and go
One man come, he to justify
One man to overthrow

Chorus:

In the name of love
What more in the name of love
In the name of love
What more in the name of love

One man caught on a barbed wire fence
One man he resist
One man washed on an empty beach
One man betrayed with a kiss

(Chorus)

Early morning, April four
Shot rings out in the Memphis sky
Free at last
They took your life
They could not take your pride

(Chorus)

1. What emotion does this song evoke? Explain.
2. What message does the song convey? Support your answer.
3. How does the song's message relate to King's message in "I Have a Dream"?

and the crooked places will be made straight, and the glory of the Lord shall be revealed, and all flesh shall see it together.[2]

This is our hope. This is the faith with which I return to the South. With this faith we will be able to transform the jangling discords of our nation into a beautiful symphony of brotherhood. With this faith we will be able to work together, to pray together, to struggle together, to go to jail together, to stand up for freedom together, knowing that we will be free one day.

This will be the day when all of God's children will be able to sing with new meaning "My country 'tis of thee, sweet land of liberty, of thee I sing. Land where my fathers died, land of the pilgrim's pride, from every mountainside, let freedom ring."

And if America is to be a great nation this must become true. So let freedom ring from the prodigious hilltops of New Hampshire. Let freedom ring from the mighty mountains of New York. Let freedom ring from the heightening

Alleghenies of Pennsylvania!

Let freedom ring from the snowcapped Rockies of Colorado!

Let freedom ring from the curvaceous peaks of California!

But not only that: let freedom ring from Stone Mountain of Georgia!

Let freedom ring from every hill and molehill of Mississippi. From every mountainside, let freedom ring.

When we let freedom ring, when we let it ring from every village and every hamlet, from every state and every city, we will be able to speed up that day when all of God's children, black men and white men, Jews and Gentiles, Protestants and Catholics, will be able to join hands and sing in the words of that old Negro spiritual, "Free at last! Free at last! Thank God almighty, we are free at last!"

---

2. **every valley . . . all flesh shall see it together:** Refers to a biblical passage (Isaiah 40: 4 and 5).

◆ **Build Vocabulary**

prodigious (prə dij´ əs) *adj.*: Wonderful; of great size

hamlet (ham´ lit) *n.*: Very small village

Guide for Responding

◆ *Literature and Your Life*

Reader's Response What kinds of feelings does Martin Luther King's speech stir in you?

Thematic Focus What does Martin Luther King challenge Americans to do?

Group Activity What can you do to foster tolerance and equality among students in your school? With a small group, brainstorm for practical ideas.

☑ **Check Your Comprehension**

1. In your own words, briefly state King's dream.
2. What are the roots, or sources, of this dream?
3. What will the hope of realizing his dream enable King to do?

◆ **Critical Thinking**

INTERPRET

1. Why does King mention the names of so many states in his speech? **[Infer]**
2. Explain the effect of repeating the phrase, "I have a dream." **[Analyze]**

EVALUATE

3. (a) To what degree do you think King's speech was persuasive? (b) What aspects of the speech made it so? **[Assess; Support]**

EXTEND

4. If you were to express King's dream in a drawing or painting, what images would you include? **[Art Link]**

from Rosa Parks: My Story

Rosa Parks (with Jim Haskins)

The Beginning, Artis Lane

▲ **Critical Viewing** How does this picture reflect the ideal of equal rights for all people? **[Analyze]**

When I got off from work that evening of December 1, I went to Court Square as usual to catch the Cleveland Avenue bus home. I didn't look to see who was driving when I got on, and by the time I recognized him, I had already paid my fare. It was the same driver who had put me off the bus back in 1943, twelve years earlier. He was still tall and heavy, with red, rough-looking skin. And he was still mean-looking. I didn't know if he had been on that route before—they switched the drivers around sometimes. I do know that most of the time if I saw him on a bus, I wouldn't get on it.

I saw a vacant seat in the middle section of the bus and took it. I didn't even question why there was a vacant seat even though there were quite a few people standing in the back. If I had thought about it at all, I would probably have figured maybe someone saw me get on and did not take the seat but left it vacant for me. There was a man sitting next to the window and two women across the aisle.

The next stop was the Empire Theater, and some whites got on. They filled up the white seats, and one man was left standing. The driver looked back and noticed the man standing. Then he looked back at us. He said, "Let me have those front seats," because they were the front seats of the black section. Didn't anybody move. We just sat right where we were, the four of us. Then he spoke a second time: "Y'all better make it light on yourselves and let me have those seats."

The man in the window seat next to me stood up, and I moved to let him pass by me, and then I looked across the aisle and saw that the two women were also standing. I moved over to the window seat. I could not see how standing up was going to "make it light" for me. The more we gave in and complied, the worse they treated us.

I thought back to the time when I used to sit up all night and didn't sleep, and my grandfather would have his gun right by the fireplace, or if he had his one-horse wagon going anywhere, he always had his gun in the back of the wagon. People always say that I didn't give up my seat because I was tired, but that isn't true. I was not tired physically, or no more tired than I usually was at the end of a working day. I was not old, although some people have an image of me as being old then. I was forty-two. No, the only tired I was, was tired of giving in.

The driver of the bus saw me still sitting there, and he asked was I going to stand up. I said, "No." He said, "Well, I'm going to have you arrested." Then I said, "You may do that." These were the only words we said to each other. I didn't even know his name, which was James Blake, until we were in court together. He got out of the bus and stayed outside for a few minutes, waiting for the police.

As I sat there, I tried not to think about what might happen. I knew that anything was possible. I could be manhandled or beaten. I could be arrested. People have asked me if it occurred to me then that I could be the test case the NAACP[1] had been looking for. I did not think about that at all. In fact if I had let myself think too deeply about what might happen to me, I might have gotten off the bus. But I chose to remain.

---

1. **NAACP:** *abbr.*: National Association for the Advancement of Colored People.

Beyond Literature

◆ Build Vocabulary

complied (kəm plīd´) *v.*: Carried out or fulfilled a request

manhandled (man´ han´ dəld) *v.*: Treated roughly

▲ **Critical Viewing** How has the artist combined Native American symbols with symbols of contemporary American society? What do you think was her purpose in doing so? **[Interpret]**

There Is a Longing . . .

Chief Dan George

There is a longing in the heart of my people
to reach out and grasp that which is
      needed
for our survival. There is a longing among
the young of my nation to secure for
      themselves
5 and their people the skills that will
provide them with a sense of worth and
purpose. They will be our new warriors.
Their training will be much longer and
more demanding than it was in olden days.
10 The long years of study will demand
more <u>determination</u>; separation from home
and family will demand <u>endurance</u>. But
      they
will emerge with their hand held forward,
not to receive welfare, but to grasp the
15 place in society that is rightly ours.

I am a chief, but my power to make war
is gone, and the only weapon left to me
is speech. It is only with tongue and speech
that I can fight my people's war.

20 Oh, Great Spirit![1] Give me back the courage
of the olden Chiefs. Let me wrestle with
my surroundings. Let me once again,
live in harmony with my environment.
Let me humbly accept this new culture
25 and through it rise up and go on. Like
the thunderbird[2] of old, I shall rise again
out of the sea; I shall grab the instruments
of the white man's success—his
education, his skills. With these new tools
30 I shall build my race into the proudest
segment of your society. I shall see our
young braves and our chiefs sitting in
the houses of law and government, ruling
and being ruled by the knowledge and
35 freedoms of *our* great land.

---

1. Great Spirit: For many Native Americans, the greatest power or god.
2. thunderbird: A powerful supernatural creature that was thought to produce thunder by flapping its wing and produce lightning by opening and closing its eyes. In the folklore of some Native American nations, the thunderbird is in constant warfare with the powers beneath the waters.

◆ **Build Vocabulary**

determination (dē tʉr′ mi nā′ shən) *n.:* Firm intention

endurance (en dʊr′ əns) *n.:* Ability to withstand hardship and stress and to carry on

I Hear America Singing

Walt Whitman

I hear America singing, the varied carols I hear,
Those of mechanics, each one singing his as it should be
    blithe and strong,
The carpenter singing his as he measures his plank or
    beam,
The mason singing his as he makes ready for work, or
    leaves off work,
5 The boatman singing what belongs to him in his boat, the
    deckhand singing on the steamboat deck,
The shoemaker singing as he sits on his bench, the hatter
    singing as he stands,
The wood-cutter's song, the ploughboy's on his way in the
    morning, or at noon intermission or at sundown,
The delicious singing of the mother, or of the young wife at
    work, or of the girl sewing or washing,
Each singing what belongs to him or her and to none else,
10 The day what belongs to the day—at night the party of
    young fellows, robust, friendly,
Singing with open mouths their strong melodious songs.

Guide for Responding

◆ Literature and Your Life

Reader's Response What personal feelings or experiences could you relate to the words of Rosa Parks, Chief Dan George, and Walt Whitman?

Thematic Focus In these selections, what challenges are faced by Rosa Parks, Native Americans, and American workers?

☑ Check Your Comprehension

1. What reason does Rosa Parks give for staying in her seat?
2. In "There Is a Longing," how will the speaker's people obtain a sense of worth and purpose?
3. What carols does the speaker hear in "I Hear America Singing"?

◆ Critical Thinking

INTERPRET
1. In "There Is a Longing," how do the "new warriors" the speaker wishes to see compare with the warriors of old? **[Compare and Contrast]**
2. Are the people really singing in "I Hear America Singing"? Explain. **[Interpret]**

EVALUATE
3. Why do you think that Rosa Parks's decision to remain seated on the bus was appropriate for a general civil rights test case? **[Make a Judgment]**
4. Has the speaker in "There Is a Longing" selected the best means for improving his people's lives? **[Assess]**
5. Would "I Hear America Singing" have been more or less effective if it had been written with a regular rhythm and rhyme scheme? **[Evaluate]**

APPLY
6. How do the ideas and issues in these three selections still hold true today? **[Synthesize]**

▲ **Critical Viewing** How does this painting capture the spirit of American workers celebrated in "I Hear America Singing"? **[Analyze]**

Guide for Responding (continued)

◆ Reading Strategy

RESPOND

As you read each of the selections, you may have **responded** to it emotionally by bringing your own unique experiences and memories to it. How do you feel about the works you've just read? Perhaps you felt joy or exhilaration, sadness or frustration. Take a moment to think about your responses to the selections in this group. For each piece you read, write down two or three lines or passages that moved you and explain the nature of your response.

◆ Literary Focus

AUTHOR'S PURPOSE

By focusing on content and style as you read, you can often discover an **author's purpose** and gain insight about a given work. For example, the persuasive style of Martin Luther King's "I Have a Dream" speech makes it clear that his purpose is to inspire others toward achieving his vision of America.

1. How does Martin Luther King use repetition to achieve his purpose?
2. What is the purpose of Rosa Parks's detailed description of her fateful bus ride?
3. Chief Dan George voices his appeal for his people's future. To whom is he speaking? Native Americans? Other Americans? Explain.

◆ Build Grammar Skills

USE OF *SHALL* AND *WILL*

Use **will** with a main verb to express future time.

Use **shall** to show formality or determination.

Writing Application In your notebook, write a sentence using *shall* or *will* to express each of the following situations.

1. A future outcome of Martin Luther King's speech
2. A statement by Rosa Parks showing her determination
3. A statement by a courtroom lawyer expressing his or her formal intention

◆ Build Vocabulary

USING THE WORD ROOT -*cred*-

The familiar words below contain the root -*cred*-, meaning "believe." On your paper, rewrite the following sentences, filling in the blank with an appropriate word from this list.

a. credit   **b.** incredible   **c.** credentials   **d.** credible

1. The members of the press were asked to show their _____?_____ as they entered the courtroom.
2. One reporter gave what she thought was a _____?_____ excuse for not having the proper identification.
3. However, the guard found it _____?_____ that a professional journalist would leave home without identification.
4. The reporter thought she should receive _____?_____ for originality.

USING THE WORD BANK

On a separate sheet of paper, write the word from the Word Bank that best completes each statement.

1. The opposite of *lowered* is _____?_____.
2. The society's _____?_____ was written in its bylaws.
3. A synonym for *mistreated* is _____?_____.
4. The _____?_____ has a population of only two hundred.
5. A synonym of *tremendous* is _____?_____.
6. Martin Luther King, Jr., never wavered in his _____?_____ to fight for equality.
7. The opposite of *protested* is _____?_____.
8. The opposite of *freedom* is _____?_____.
9. To experience freedom after slavery is like finding an _____?_____ in the desert.
10. It takes great _____?_____ to be a marathon runner.

Build Your Portfolio

 ## Idea Bank

Writing

1. **The American Dream** Martin Luther King states that his dream is rooted in the American dream. Write a paragraph in which you describe your own American dream.

2. **The Song of America** Walt Whitman hears America "singing" with diverse people. Write an essay in which you explain what makes you hear America singing. **[Social Studies Link]**

3. **Argument for the Defense** Write an opening argument—a statement presented in court with reasons for or against something—defending Parks's right to remain seated. **[Social Studies Link]**

Speaking and Listening

4. **Interview** Interview an adult to learn details about the people and issues that mark the current civil rights campaign. How do they differ from those of the past? **[Social Studies Link]**

5. **Radio News Report** Compose a radio news report in which you summarize what King says and explain his dream for America. **[Media Link]**

Projects

6. **America in Poetry** Present your own vision of America in an original poem. Then select recordings of appropriate music to accompany the reading of your poem. **[Music Link]**

7. **Multimedia Presentation** Create a multimedia presentation on an aspect of the American civil rights movement. Assemble appropriate photographs for your presentation, as well as video or audio recordings of civil rights speeches and events. **[Social Studies Link; Media Link]**

 ## Writing Mini-Lesson

Proposal for a School Speaker

Write a proposal to your principal, presenting a persuasive argument in favor of inviting a specific person to speak at a school assembly.

Writing Skills Focus: Benefits of Proposed Ideas

To give your proposal the best chance of being accepted, you must include the **benefits** such a speaker can provide the listeners. For example, notice the benefit Chief Dan George states will occur if Native Americans study hard.

Model From the Speech

. . . But they
will emerge with their hand held forward,
not to receive welfare, but to grasp the
place in society that is rightly ours.

Prewriting Draw a two-column chart like the one shown. In the column headed "Speaker," list different types of speakers you might want to invite (veterinarian, forest ranger). In the column headed "Benefits," list the benefits each speaker brings (advice on pets, how recycling helps the environment). Choose the speaker with the most benefits.

Speaker	Benefits

Drafting For the most effective proposal, present the benefits in order of importance—either from most to least important or vice versa. Offer support for each benefit you present.

Revising Have a classmate read your proposal, then ask him or her whether the benefits are easily understood. If not, rephrase them to make them more clear.

Guide for Reading

Ray Bradbury (1920–)

Years before space travel became a reality or computers became common household appliances, science-fiction writers were exploring the possibilities of technology and stretching the limits of readers' imaginations. One of the most celebrated science-fiction writers is Ray Bradbury. Bradbury has written numerous collections of stories and has won many awards, including the World Fantasy Award for lifetime achievement and the Grand Master Award from the Science Fiction Writers of America.

An astronaut has even named a lunar landmark Dandelion Crater, after Bradbury's autobiographical novel Dandelion Wine.

A Science-Fiction Writer's Beginnings

Bradbury was born in Waukegan, Illinois, and spent his boyhood along the western shores of Lake Michigan. At an early age, he developed a love of horror movies, fantasy cartoons, and suspenseful stories by writers such as Edgar Allan Poe.

In 1932, Bradbury's family moved to Tucson, Arizona. Bradbury wrote his first stories there in Tucson, banging out tales of space travel on a six-dollar typewriter, a Christmas gift from his parents. A year later, the family moved to Los Angeles, California, where Bradbury has resided ever since.

In high school, Bradbury pursued his passion for science fiction and fantasy by founding and editing a quarterly publication called *Futuria Fantasia*. By this time, he was already writing at least one story a week. This rapid and disciplined pace has continued: Every morning between 9 and 11, Bradbury sits down at his typewriter and drafts 2,000 to 3,000 words of manuscript.

◆ Build Vocabulary

WORD ROOTS: -clam-

In this story you'll encounter the word *acclaimed*, which contains -*claim*-, a variation of the root -*clam*-, meaning "call out" or "shout." Considering that the prefix *ac*- means "to" or "toward," you might guess that *acclaimed* means "called out toward." This is close to the actual definition, "greeted with loud applause or approval."

WORD BANK

portents
vile
ravenous
acclaimed
pandemonium
spurn

As you read "The Golden Kite, the Silver Wind," you will encounter the words on this list. Each word is defined on the page where it first appears. Preview the list before you read.

◆ Build Grammar Skills

ACTION VERBS AND LINKING VERBS

Verbs can be categorized as either action verbs or linking verbs. **Action verbs** express physical or mental actions. They tell you what the subject of the sentence does. **Linking verbs** express a state of being and connect the subject to a word or words that rename or describe the subject. The most common linking verb is some form of the verb *be* (*am, is, are, was, were*).

Following are examples of both an action verb and a linking verb from the story.

Action Verb: They both *sat* thinking.

Linking Verb: Life *was* full of symbols and omens.

The Golden Kite, the Silver Wind

◆ Literature and Your Life

CONNECT YOUR EXPERIENCE

Have you and a friend ever tried to outdo each other? Maybe your rivalry focused on who had the better CD collection or who could perform the most daring feat. The two of you may have become consumed by your rivalry, but most likely, no one else was hurt as a result of it. In this story, a rivalry becomes so intense that it leads to widespread suffering.

Journal Writing Write about a rivalry that caused suffering on both sides.

THEMATIC FOCUS: FOR THE GOOD OF ALL

This story shows how the choices people make can hurt both themselves and their rivals. How can people rise to the challenge of making choices that are for the good of all?

◆ Background for Understanding

HISTORY

"The Golden Kite, the Silver Wind" was written during the Cold War, a period of intense rivalry between the United States and the former Soviet Union. During this time, the two countries competed for position as the world's leading nation. Each action by one country—an alliance, the placement of a weapon, the launching of a satellite—was countered by a reaction from the other country.

Because both countries had huge arsenals of nuclear weapons, many people feared that the rivalry between the superpowers could escalate into a nuclear war with the potential of destroying all life on Earth. As you read, think about how the events in the story might relate to the situation between the United States and the Soviet Union at the time of the Cold War.

◆ Literary Focus

FABLE

A **fable** is a brief story, often with animals as characters, that teaches a lesson. The lesson, or moral, is sometimes directly stated in a single sentence at the end of the fable. Other times, the actions and choices of the characters guide you to the moral of the story. In this fable, the actions of two rival cities provide a lesson about the advantages of cooperation versus competition.

◆ Reading Strategy

PREDICT CONSEQUENCES OF ACTIONS

In this story, a Chinese village takes a series of actions that in turn sparks reactions from a rival village. As you read, try to **predict the consequences** of each action by considering events that have already occurred along with what you have learned about the characters and their motivations. Then read on to see whether you were correct.

A chart like the one shown might help you. Write down the events as they happen. Before you read further, predict the consequence of that event. You will see a pattern develop that will lead you to the moral of the story.

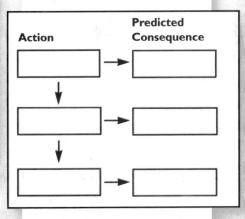

The Golden Kite, the Silver Wind

Ray Bradbury

▲ **Critical Viewing** This story describes the rivalry between two Mandarins. Why might two rulers become involved in a case of one-upmanship? [Speculate]

"In the shape of a *pig?*" cried the Mandarin.[1]

"In the shape of a pig," said the messenger, and departed.

"Oh, what an evil day in an evil year," cried the Mandarin. "The town of Kwan-Si, beyond the hill, was very small in my childhood. Now it has grown so large that at last they are building a wall."

"But why should a wall two miles away make my good father sad and angry all within the hour?" asked his daughter quietly.

"They build their wall," said the Mandarin, "in the shape of a pig! Do you see? Our own city wall is built in the shape of an orange. That pig will devour us, greedily!"

"Ah."

They both sat thinking.

Life was full of symbols and omens. Demons lurked everywhere, Death swam in the wetness of an eye, the turn of a gull's wing meant rain, a fan held *so*, the tilt of a roof, and, yes, even a city wall was of immense importance. Travelers and tourists, caravans, musicians, artists, coming upon these two towns, equally judging the <u>portents</u>, would say, "The city shaped like an orange? No! I will enter the city shaped like a pig and prosper, eating all, growing fat with good luck and prosperity!"

The Mandarin wept. "All is lost! These symbols and signs terrify. Our city will come on evil days."

"Then," said the daughter, "call in your stonemasons and temple builders. I will whisper from behind the silken screen and you will know the words."

The old man clapped his hands despairingly. "Ho, stonemasons!

Ho, builders of towns and palaces!"

The men who knew marble and granite and onyx and quartz came quickly. The Mandarin faced them most uneasily, himself waiting for a whisper from the silken screen behind his throne. At last the whisper came.

"I have called you here," said the whisper.

"I have called you here," said the Mandarin aloud, "because our city is shaped like an orange, and the <u>vile</u> city of Kwan-Si has this day shaped theirs like a <u>ravenous</u> pig—"

◆ Build Vocabulary

portents (pôr´ tentz) *n.*: Things that are thought to be signs of events to come; omens

vile (vīl) *adj.*: Evil; wicked

ravenous (rav´ ə nəs) *adj.*: Greedily hungry

---

1. **Mandarin** (man´ de rin): A high official of China; here, the ruling leader.

The Nymph of the Lo River, Attributed to Ku K'ai-chih, Freer Gallery of Art, Smithsonian Institution, Washington, D.C.

Here the stonemasons groaned and wept. Death rattled his cane in the outer courtyard. Poverty made a sound like a wet cough in the shadows of the room.

"And so," said the whisper, said the Mandarin, "you raisers of walls must go bearing trowels and rocks and change the shape of *our* city!"

The architects and masons gasped. The Mandarin himself gasped at what he had said. The whisper whispered. The Mandarin went on: "And you will change our walls into a club which may beat the pig and drive it off!"

The stonemasons rose up, shouting. Even the Mandarin, delighted at the words from his mouth, applauded, stood down from his throne. "Quick!" he cried. "To work!"

When his men had gone, smiling and bustling, the Mandarin turned with great love to the silken screen. "Daughter," he whispered, "I will embrace you." There was no reply. He stepped around the screen, and she was gone.

Such modesty, he thought. She has slipped away and left me with a triumph, as if it were mine.

The news spread through the city; the Mandarin was <u>acclaimed</u>. Everyone carried stone to the walls. Fireworks were set off and the demons of death and poverty did not linger, as all worked together. At the end of the month the wall had been changed. It was now a mighty bludgeon with which to drive pigs, boars, even lions, far away. The Mandarin slept like a happy fox every night.

"I would like to see the Mandarin of Kwan-Si when the news is learned. Such <u>pandemonium</u> and hysteria; he will likely throw himself from a mountain! A little more of that wine, oh Daughter-who-thinks-like-a-son."

But the pleasure was like a winter flower; it died swiftly. That very afternoon the messenger rushed into the courtroom. "Oh, Mandarin, disease, early sorrow, avalanches, grasshopper plagues, and poisoned well water!"

The Mandarin trembled.

"The town of Kwan-Si," said the messenger, "which was built like a pig and which animal we drove away by changing our walls to a mighty stick, has now turned triumph to winter ashes. They have built their city's walls like a great bonfire to burn our stick!"

The Mandarin's heart sickened within him, like an autumn fruit upon an ancient tree. "Oh, gods! Travelers will <u>spurn</u> us. Tradesmen, reading the symbols, will turn from the stick, so easily destroyed, to the fire, which conquers all!"

"No," said a whisper like a snowflake from behind the silken screen.

"No," said the startled Mandarin.

"Tell my stonemasons," said the whisper that was a falling drop of rain, "to build our walls in the shape of a shining lake."

The Mandarin said this aloud, his heart warmed.

"And with this lake of water," said the whisper and the old man, "we will quench the fire and put it out forever!"

The city turned out in joy to learn that once again they had been saved by the magnificent Emperor of ideas. They ran to the walls and built them nearer to this new vision, singing, not as loudly as before, of course, for they were tired, and not as quickly, for since it had taken a month to rebuild the wall the first time, they had had to neglect

◆ **Build Vocabulary**

acclaimed (ə klāmd´) *v.*: Greeted with loud applause or approval; hailed

pandemonium (pan´ də mōn´ nē əm) *n.*: Wild disorder, noise, or confusion

spurn (spʉrn) *v.*: Reject in a scornful way

business and crops and therefore were somewhat weaker and poorer.

There then followed a succession of horrible and wonderful days, one in another like a nest of frightened boxes.

"Oh, Emperor," cried the messenger, "Kwan-Si has rebuilt their walls to resemble a mouth with which to drink all our lake!"

"Then," said the Emperor, standing very close to his silken screen, "build our walls like a needle to sew up that mouth!"

"Emperor!" screamed the messenger. "They make their walls like a sword to break your needle!"

The Emperor held, trembling, to the silken screen. "Then shift the stones to form a scabbard to sheathe that sword!"[2]

"Mercy," wept the messenger the following morn, "they have worked all night and shaped their walls like lightning which will explode and destroy that sheath!"

Sickness spread in the city like a pack of evil dogs. Shops closed. The population, working now steadily for endless months upon the changing of the walls, resembled Death himself, clattering his white bones like musical instruments in the wind. Funerals began to appear in the streets, though it was the middle of summer, a time when all should be tending and harvesting. The Mandarin fell so ill that he had his bed drawn up by the silken screen and there he lay, miserably giving his architectural orders. The voice behind the screen was weak now, too, and faint, like the wind in the eaves.

◆ Literary Focus
What is the lesson to be learned from the actions of the two Mandarins?

"Kwan-Si is an eagle. Then our walls must be a net for that eagle. They are a sun to burn our net. Then we build a moon to eclipse their sun!"

Like a rusted machine, the city ground to a halt.

Rectangular box (detail), Avery Brundage Collection, Asian Art Museum of San Francisco

▲ Critical Viewing Based on this scene from an ancient Chinese box, make inferences about the setting and characters in this story. [Infer]

At last the whisper behind the screen cried out:

"In the name of the gods, send for Kwan-Si!"

Upon the last day of summer the Mandarin Kwan-Si, very ill and withered away, was carried into our Mandarin's courtroom by four starving footmen. The two mandarins were propped up, facing each other. Their breaths fluttered like winter winds in their mouths. A voice said:

"Let us put an end to this."

The old men nodded.

"This cannot go on," said the faint voice. "Our people do nothing but rebuild our cities to a different shape every day, every hour. They have no time to hunt, to fish, to love, to be good to their ancestors and their ancestors' children."

"This I admit," said the mandarins of

---

2. **scabbard** (skab´ ərd) **to sheathe** (shēth) **that sword!**: Case to hold the blade of the sword.

the towns of the Cage, the Moon, the Spear, the Fire, the Sword and this, that, and other things.

"Carry us into the sunlight," said the voice.

The old men were borne out under the sun and up a little hill. In the late summer breeze a few very thin children were flying dragon kites in all the colors of the sun, and frogs and grass, the color of the sea and the color of coins and wheat.

The first Mandarin's daughter stood by his bed.

"See," she said.

"Those are nothing but kites," said the two old men.

"But what is a kite on the ground?" she said. "It is nothing. What does it need to sustain it and make it beautiful and truly spiritual?"

"The wind, of course!" said the others.

"And what do the sky and the wind need to make *them* beautiful?"

"A kite, of course—many kites, to break the monotony, the sameness of the sky. Colored kites, flying!"

"So," said the Mandarin's daughter. "You, Kwan-Si, will make a last rebuilding of your town to resemble nothing more nor less than the wind. And we shall build like a golden kite. The wind will beautify the kite and carry it to wondrous heights. And

the kite will break the sameness of the wind's existence and give it purpose and meaning. One without the other is nothing. Together, all will be beauty and co-operation and a long and enduring life."

Whereupon the two mandarins were so overjoyed that they took their first nourishment in days, momentarily were given strength, embraced, and lavished praise upon each other, called the Mandarin's daughter a boy, a man, a stone pillar, a warrior, and a true and unforgettable son. Almost immediately they parted and hurried to their towns, calling out and singing, weakly but happily.

And so, in time, the towns became the Town of Golden Kite and the Town of the Silver Wind. And harvestings were harvested and business tended again, and the flesh returned, and disease ran off like a frightened jackal. And on every night of the year the inhabitants in the Town of the Kite could hear the good clear wind sustaining them. And those in the Town of the Wind could hear the kite singing, whispering, rising, and beautifying them.

"So be it," said the Mandarin in front of his silken screen.

◆ *Literature and Your Life*

Based on your own observations and experience, how does cooperation help those involved?

Guide for Responding

◆ *Literature and Your Life*

Reader's Response Do you think the Mandarin's daughter gave her father good advice? Explain.

Thematic Focus Are fables like "The Golden Kite, the Silver Wind" a good way of teaching people how to behave? Why or why not?

Journal Entry Describe a rivalry that you have been involved in or have observed. Discuss how the rivalry developed and how it was resolved.

☑ Check Your Comprehension

1. What event at the beginning of the story upsets and angers the Mandarin?
2. Why do the two cities continually rebuild their walls?
3. How is the rivalry between the two cities brought to an end?

Guide for Responding (continued)

◆ Critical Thinking

INTERPRET
1. Why does the Mandarin's daughter advise him from behind a screen? **[Analyze]**
2. What can you infer, or conclude, about the townspeople based on how they respond to the Mandarin's plans? **[Infer]**
3. Why did people have to get sick and even die before the Mandarins sought to bring an end to their rivalry? **[Draw Conclusions]**

EVALUATE
4. Should the townspeople have continued to follow the Mandarin's advice—even though doing so was resulting in disease and death? Why or why not? **[Make a Judgment]**

EXTEND
5. This story was written during the Cold War. (a) Why would the story have been especially appropriate for that time? (b) What countries or cultures from today's world could the two villages represent? Explain. **[Social Studies Link]**

◆ Reading Strategy

PREDICT CONSEQUENCES OF ACTIONS
As you read, you were probably able to **predict** the two towns' actions based on the pattern of events established early in the story.

1. What were the first hints that the rivalry between the two towns was going to have a disastrous outcome? Support your answer.
2. At what point in the story were you able to predict the outcome? Explain.

◆ Literary Focus

FABLE
Like other **fables,** "The Golden Kite, the Silver Wind" has a moral. Unlike most fables, however, this moral is not stated directly.

1. (a) What poor choices are made by the Mandarin's daughter and the Mandarin in this story? (b) What are the ultimate consequences of those choices?
2. Express the moral of the story in one sentence in your own words.

◆ Build Vocabulary

USING THE WORD ROOT -clam-
The following words contain -clam- or -claim-, a root meaning "call out" or "shout." Match each word with its definition.

1. exclaim   **a.** loud, noisy, and confused, like a loud outcry or uproar

2. proclamation   **b.** something that is announced officially

3. clamorous   **c.** to speak out suddenly, as in surprise or anger

USING THE WORD BANK
On your paper, write the following paragraph, filling in the blanks with words from the Word Bank or forms of those words.

The __?__ for the kingdom were not good. The crops had failed, lightning had struck the bell tower, and a dragon was causing __?__ across the countryside. Fierce and __?__ , the dragon terrified the peasants and devoured their livestock. "That __?__ dragon must be destroyed!" exclaimed the princess. __?__ offers of assistance, she rode off to fight the dragon. On her triumphant return home, the dragon-slaying princess was __?__ by her grateful people.

◆ Build Grammar Skills

ACTION VERBS AND LINKING VERBS
Action verbs express physical or mental actions. **Linking verbs** express a state of being.

Practice On your paper, write the following sentences. Identify the verbs and label each one as *action* or *linking*. Note that some sentences contain more than one verb.
1. Here the stone masons groaned and wept.
2. But the pleasure was like a winter flower; it died quickly.
3. One without the other is nothing.
4. The old man clapped his hands despairingly.
5. The towns became known as the Town of the Golden Kite and the Town of the Silver Wind.

Build Your Portfolio

 ## Idea Bank

Writing

1. **Fable** Write a fable that, like "The Golden Kite, the Silver Wind," teaches a lesson about conflict or cooperation.

2. **Persuasive Letter** Think about a specific conflict in today's world that you want to see resolved. Write a persuasive letter to the two sides urging them to end the conflict. Point out the negative consequences of the conflict and suggest a resolution that will benefit both sides.

3. **Science Report** Like a kite and the wind, many animals and plants exist together in a way that is helpful to both. Find out more about helpful relationships in nature. Then prepare a research report on one such relationship. **[Science Link]**

Speaking and Listening

4. **Dramatization** With a small group of classmates, develop and present a dramatic production of Bradbury's story.

5. **Improvisation** With a partner, act out the development and resolution of a conflict between two people. Do not discuss with each other ahead of time who the people are and what the conflict is. **[Performing Arts Link]**

Projects

6. **Good Advice** Collect morals from other fables, along with short sayings that convey useful advice. Assemble your collection into an illustrated booklet.

7. **Map** Create a map that illustrates some aspect of the Cold War. For example, you might show the alliances each side formed. If possible, use photographs, diagrams, and other media to help present your findings. **[Social Studies Link]**

 ## Writing Mini-Lesson

Public Service Ad Campaign

Create a series of advertisements that convey a message about the importance of resolving conflicts. Choose the medium—print, radio, television, and so on—through which the messages will be presented.

Writing Skills Focus: Use Appropriate Style for the Medium

When you whiz by a billboard on the highway, you don't have much time to read it. To work well, a billboard message must be short, eye-catching, and to the point. Other types of media lend themselves to other styles of communication. Dialogue, for example, works well in a radio ad. To make sure you get your message across, use an **appropriate style** for the medium.

Prewriting Brainstorm for a list of points you would like to make about conflicts and how to resolve them. For example, you might note how important it is for people to listen to one another to resolve conflicts. Review the list and choose the points you want to include in your campaign. Then identify the best way to convey these points through the medium you have chosen. For example, if you're preparing magazine ads, you'll need to find visuals to include.

Drafting Draft your ads, making sure that you follow the format appropriate to your medium. For example, if you're preparing print ads, you should write copy to accompany your visuals; if you're preparing television ads, create a brief script.

Revising Revise your campaign to make the best use of the medium you have chosen. If your ad is highly visual, for example, be sure that the verbs in your message work well with your images.

Writing Process Workshop

Abraham Lincoln and Martin Luther King, Jr., used their powers of persuasion to help our nation overcome tremendous challenges. Both are known for their rousing **persuasive speeches**—formal spoken presentations in which a speaker tries to convince an audience to act or think in a certain way. Follow in the footsteps of King and Lincoln by writing and presenting a persuasive speech on an issue that you believe is critical to today's generation.

The following skills, introduced in this section's Writing Mini-Lessons, will help you develop your speech.

Writing Skills Focus

▶ **Don't just tell listeners that they should accept your positions, show them why they should.** Provide anecdotes—brief stories—that illustrate why the cause for which you're arguing is right on target. (See p. 136.)

▶ **Mention the benefits of your ideas.** Tell listeners what they will gain by doing what you ask of them. (See p. 149.)

▶ **Use an appropriate style for your medium.** Take advantage of your personal contact with the audience. Write words that you can speak with emotion! (See p. 158.)

Martin Luther King, Jr., uses all these skills in the historic speech he delivered in Washington, D.C., in 1963.

MODEL FROM LITERATURE

from "I Have a Dream" by Martin Luther King, Jr.

When we let freedom ring, when we let it ring from every village and every hamlet, from every state and every city, ① we will be able to speed up that day when all of God's children, black men and white men, Jews and Gentiles, Protestants and Catholics, will be able to join hands and sing ② in the words of that old Negro spiritual, "Free at last! Free at last! Thank God almighty, we are free at last!" ③

① King adds to the impact of his speech by dramatizing, or showing, the situation that would occur if equal rights were to be realized.

② King explains how all people will benefit from equal rights.

③ By quoting a spiritual, King is able to let his speech "ring out" with emotion.

APPLYING LANGUAGE SKILLS: Active and Passive Voice

A verb in the active voice shows the subject doing an action. A verb in the passive voice shows the subject receiving an action.

Active Voice:

Workers <u>cut</u> the trees.

Passive Voice:

Trees <u>are cut</u> by workers.

Notice how the active voice makes writing more forceful and lively.

Practice Rewrite each sentence so the verb is in the active voice.

1. Medicinal plants are discovered by scientists in the rain forest.
2. Oxygen is produced by trees.
3. The rain forest can be saved by people who care.

Writing Application As you draft your speech, focus on using the active voice. Use the passive voice only when the performer of the action is unknown or unimportant.

Writer's Solution Connection Writing Lab

To help you come up with a topic, use the Inspirations in the Choosing a Topic section in the tutorial on Persuasion.

Prewriting

Choose a Topic Think of a current issue about which you have strong feelings and which you think is especially important. Then clarify your position on that issue. If no ideas come to mind, try one of these topics.

> ### Topic Ideas
> - Why people should recycle
> - Why the nation should have a third political party
> - Why education is important
> - Why teenagers should do volunteer work

Gather Evidence to Support Your Position Once you've chosen an issue and clarified your position on that issue, gather evidence—facts, statistics, and so on—that you can use to support your position. If possible, try to think of anecdotes—brief stories—that you can use to illustrate your position. For example, if you are arguing for the need to preserve the rain forest, you might tell the story of a particular species that could be wiped out. Most likely, you'll need to conduct research either in the library or on the Internet to help you pull together the facts, statistics, and anecdotes you'll need. You might use an organizer like this one as you gather support.

Facts	Statistics	Anecdotes
Rain forest that is cut down cannot be replaced in our lifetimes.	Rain forests used to cover about 20% of Earth's surface; today, cover about 7%.	Trip to rain forest in Brazil showed me the tremendous diversity in the rain forest.

Technology Tip To use the Internet to gather information, come up with a few key words related to your topic. Then use a search engine to find information related to the key words.

List the Benefits In addition to gathering evidence to support your position, list benefits that will result from the course of action you're proposing.

Drafting

Write in the Style of Your Medium As you write, remember that you will eventually deliver the speech aloud. Use powerful words and phrases that you can stress as you talk to your listeners face to face. Also think how you might use visual aids to help persuade your audience. Adapt your text so that it mentions your visual aids.

Use an Organization That Will Help Convince Your Audience As you draft your speech, present your evidence in an order that will hold the interest of your audience and leave a strong impression in their minds. You may want to use an order-of-importance organization, beginning with less important points and leading up to your strongest arguments.

Revising

Add Evidence to Strengthen Your Argument Read through your first draft, looking for places in which you can add evidence to bolster your argument. If you find that you have little evidence to support a key point, you may need to go back and conduct additional research to gather more evidence.

Practice Reading Your Speech Aloud Working either on your own or with classmates, read your speech aloud several times. Make sure that your speech flows seamlessly from one point to the next. If it doesn't, add transition words to make stronger connections. Also, look for places in which you can improve the way your speech sounds by replacing a word or restructuring a sentence.

Publishing

Present Your Speech Deliver your speech to your class, keeping the following points in mind:

▶ Use the volume and tone of your voice to emphasize key points and keep your audience engaged.
▶ Use hand gestures where appropriate to support what you're saying.
▶ Look at all of your listeners. Try to avoid focusing on just one or two people.

APPLYING LANGUAGE SKILLS: Using Parallel Structure

Using parallel structure—the repeated use of the same grammatical structure—is an excellent way to drive home your main points in a speech. Look at this example from Martin Luther King's speech:

Parallel Structure:
Let freedom ring from the prodigious hilltops of New Hampshire. Let freedom ring from the mighty mountains of New York.

Practice Write a passage using parallel structure that states these ideas.

Preserving the Rain Forest:

1. Saves endangered species
2. Protects native cultures
3. Helps prevent global warming

Writing Application Review your speech and find places where you can use parallel structure to emphasize a key point or strengthen the sound of your speech.

Writer's Solution Connection

Writing Lab

For more instruction on parallel structure and revision, work through the Revision section of the tutorial on Persuasion.

Radio, television, magazines, billboards—the world bombards you with advertisements. Advertisers try to persuade you to buy or do or believe something. Whether you hear, see, or read ads, you need to decide how you will respond to them.

Evaluate Persuasion First of all, it's important to recognize that the purpose of an advertisement is to persuade you. Keep this in mind as you evaluate the message of an ad. When you decide to respond to a persuasive message, you should do so thoughtfully, after you have evaluated the writer's message, not with just a "gut reaction."

Evaluate the Message To prepare to judge a persuasive message, first examine the writer's statements carefully. Evaluate them by answering questions like these:

▶ Are the statements true?
▶ Do the statements contain facts or are they statements of the writer's opinions?
▶ To what feelings or beliefs is the advertiser appealing?

Relate the Message to Your Life Once you've evaluated the writer's message, you will want to judge whether the message is in line with your situation or need. If you accept the ad's claims, you may choose to act in the way the advertiser wants.

Apply the Strategy

You're excited about your new pet. You're taking responsibility for your dog's care, so you want to make good decisions. You've seen many advertisements about pet food that make a variety of claims. Look at this one, and evaluate its message.

1. What is the writer's purpose? How do you know?
2. What evidence supports the writer's claim?
3. Does the writer's purpose match your purpose or need?
4. Should you buy K9 NutriFit based on this ad? Explain.

HOW TO PROVIDE PERFECT NUTRITIONAL BALANCE.

Now someone has taken the guesswork out of selecting the finest nutritional regimen for your best friend.

K9 NutriFit for puppies and dogs provides:
• all 36 essential canine nutrients
• the proper balance of fat content and calories
• today's best-selling canine nutrition management system

Discover the quality choice for today's dog. It's the difference between plain dog food and scientifically–balanced nutrition.

K9 NutriFit

K9 NutriFit for Puppies

Today's most popular canine nutrition system.

> ✔ Here are other situations in which it's important to evaluate advertising:
> ▶ Political campaigns
> ▶ Sales messages
> ▶ Information on packages

PART 2 *Putting Ourselves to the Test*

Hole in Sky, Monika Steinhoff

Guide for Reading

Robert Frost (1874–1963)

In January of 1961, when John F. Kennedy took the helm as president of the United States, he called on fellow New Englander Robert Frost—at the time probably America's most famous living poet—to recite two poems at the inauguration. Earlier in his career, Frost was not so well received in his native land. In 1912, unable to earn a living as a poet, he packed up his family and moved to England. After British editions of his poetry volumes *A Boy's Will* (1913) and *North of Boston* (1914) won praise on both sides of the Atlantic, Frost returned to the United States a celebrity. (See p. 412 for more on Robert Frost.)

Maya Angelou (1928–)

Three decades after Frost's appearance at the Kennedy inauguration, President-elect Bill Clinton invited fellow Arkansan Maya Angelou to perform a poem for his inaugural ceremonies. In both her poetry and her nonfiction, Angelou draws on her own experience, frequently exploring the problems of poverty, racism, and sexism. (For more information on Maya Angelou, see p. 244.)

Marge Piercy (1936–)

The young Marge Piercy seemed an unlikely future writer. Born into economic hardship in Detroit, Michigan, Piercy was the first person in her family to attend college. It took her more than ten years to win recognition as a writer, during which time six of her novels were rejected for publication. Now even better known as a poet, Piercy's *To be of use* (1973), and many other highly praised verse collections have been published.

◆ Build Vocabulary

SUFFIXES: -ly

The words *amicably* and *meticulously* end with the suffix *-ly*, which is often used to turn adjectives into adverbs of manner (adverbs that tell *how* or *in what manner*). If you know that the adjective *meticulous* means "very careful or thorough," you can figure out that *meticulously* must mean "in a very careful or thorough manner."

WORD BANK

As you read the three selections, you will encounter the words on this list. Each word is defined on the page where it first appears. Preview the list before you read.

diverged
amicably
meticulously
specters
ominous
unpalatable
dallying
submerged
harness

◆ Build Grammar Skills

COMMAS IN SERIES

A **comma** can make a big difference in the clarity of your writing. Separating three or more items in a series is one way that commas make writing clearer. Think about how the meaning of this sentence from "New Directions" would change if there were a comma after *meat*, or how confusing the meaning would be if there were no comma after *lard*:

> The next morning she left her house carrying the meat pies, lard, an iron brazier, and coals for a fire.

If the items in the series are already separated by conjunctions (such as *and* or *or*), commas are not necessary.

The Road Not Taken
New Directions ◆ To be of use

◆ *Literature and Your Life*

CONNECT YOUR EXPERIENCE

Each one of us makes choices every day. Some choices can make a major difference in your future. Will you pursue a certain career path? Will you challenge yourself to try something new? Choices like these are explored in the following selections, which often compare these choices to forks in the road of life.

Journal Writing What choices or decisions that young people make could change their lives forever? Jot down some important choices that people often make before they are thirty.

THEMATIC FOCUS: PUTTING OURSELVES TO THE TEST

In these three selections, decision making plays an important role. Do the speakers think things through carefully? Do they take the easy path? You decide as you read each selection.

◆ Background for Understanding

HISTORY

In the early twentieth century, job opportunities were limited for many Americans—particularly for African Americans like Annie Johnson, the central figure in Maya Angelou's "New Directions." At the time when this episode takes place, the most common occupation for African American women was domestic labor—cleaning, child care, and other household work. For women who were also raising families of their own, caring for someone else's household was an extra burden. That's probably why Annie Johnson struck off in a "new direction."

◆ Literary Focus

FIGURATIVE LANGUAGE

Figurative language is language that means more than it says literally. When Marge Piercy tells us she loves people who "jump into work head first/without dallying in the shallows," she is using figurative language. Piercy does not mean literally that the people she loves best are deep-sea divers. Rather, she is expressing her admiration for people who take on challenges courageously.

◆ Reading Strategy

GENERATE QUESTIONS

One way to get a better understanding of what you read is to create questions based on the text and then see if you can answer them. To **generate questions**, begin with the common question words *who, what, where, when, why,* and *how.* For example, consider the opening sentence of "New Directions":

> In 1903 the late Mrs. Annie Johnson of Arkansas found herself with two toddling sons, very little money, a slight ability to read and add simple numbers.

From that sentence alone, you could generate the following questions:
- When did these events happen?
- Where did they happen?
- To whom did they happen?
- What situation did she find herself in?

Read to find the answers to these questions. Continue to generate questions about this selection and answer them as you read. Do the same for the poems.

The Road Not Taken

Robert Frost

▲ **Critical Viewing** Compare and contrast the mood of this photograph with the mood of the poem. **[Compare and Cor**

Two roads diverged in a yellow wood,
And sorry I could not travel both
And be one traveler, long I stood
And looked down one as far as I could
5   To where it bent in the undergrowth;

Then took the other, as just as fair,
And having perhaps the better claim,
Because it was grassy and wanted
      wear;
Though as for that, the passing there
10   Had worn them really about the same,

And both that morning equally lay
In leaves no step had trodden black.
Oh, I kept the first for another day!
Yet knowing how way leads on to way,
15   I doubted if I should ever come back.

I shall be telling this with a sigh
Somewhere ages and ages hence:
Two roads diverged in a wood, and I—
I took the one less traveled by,
20   And that has made all the difference.

◆ Build Vocabulary

diverged (di vurjd´) *v.*: Branched out in different
directions.

Guide for Responding

◆ *Literature and Your Life*

Reader's Response Which of the speaker's
feelings or experiences seem most relevant to
your own life?

Thematic Response Think about the chal-
lenges and choices that the speaker faces.
Would you say he has put himself to a test?
Explain.

Journal Writing Describe a situation—real
or fictional—similar to the one faced by this
poem's speaker.

☑ Check Your Comprehension

1. (a) What two choices does the speaker
   face? (b) Which does he choose?
2. What is the speaker sorry he could not
   do?
3. What does he predict he will do in the
   future?

◆ Critical Thinking

INTERPRET

1. What sort of person does the speaker of
   this poem reveal himself to be? **[Classify]**
2. Assuming the speaker is the poet, to what
   decision in his life might the poem refer?
   Cite details to support your conclusion.
   [Infer; Support]
3. Why do you think the speaker expects to
   sigh when he recalls this incident in the future? **[Draw Conclusions]**

EVALUATE

4. Robert Frost once said that a poem "begins as a lump in the throat, a sense of
   wrong, a homesickness, a loneliness."
   Would you say that description applies in
   any way to this poem? Cite details to support your evaluation. **[Evaluate]**

APPLY

5. Do you think it is generally a good idea to
   choose a less traveled path in life? Explain
   your opinion. **[Hypothesize; Support]**

New Directions

❊ Maya Angelou ❊

In 1903 the late Mrs. Annie Johnson of Arkansas found herself with two toddling sons, very little money, a slight ability to read and add simple numbers. To this picture add a disastrous marriage and the burdensome fact that Mrs. Johnson was a Negro.

When she told her husband, Mr. William Johnson, of her dissatisfaction with their marriage, he conceded that he too found it to be less than he expected, and had been secretly hoping to leave and study religion. He added that he thought God was calling him not only to preach but to do so in Enid, Oklahoma. He did not tell her that he knew a minister in Enid with whom he could study and who had a friendly, unmarried daughter. They parted amicably, Annie keeping the one-room house and William taking most of the cash to carry himself to Oklahoma.

Annie, over six feet tall, big-boned, decided that she would not go to work as a domestic and leave her "precious babes" to anyone else's care. There was no possibility of being hired at the town's cotton gin or lumber mill, but maybe there was a way to make the two factories work for her. In her words, "I looked up the road I was going and back the way I come, and since I wasn't satisfied, I decided to step off the road and cut

me a new path." She told herself that she wasn't a fancy cook but that she could "mix groceries well enough to scare hungry away and from starving a man."

She made her plans meticulously and in secret. One early evening to see if she was ready, she placed stones in two five-gallon pails and carried them three miles to the cotton gin. She rested a little, and then, discarding some rocks, she walked in the darkness to the saw mill five miles farther along the dirt road. On her way back to her little house and her babies, she dumped the remaining rocks along the path.

That same night she worked into the early hours boiling chicken and frying ham. She made dough and filled the rolled-out pastry with meat. At last she went to sleep.

The next morning she left her house carrying the meat pies, lard, an iron brazier,[1] and coals for a fire. Just before lunch she

---

1. **iron brazier** (brā´ zhər): Pan for holding burning charcoal or coals as a heat source for cooking; a portable barbecue.

◆ Build Vocabulary

amicably (am´ i kə blē) *adv.*: Agreeably

meticulously (mə tik´ yōō ləs lē) *adv.*: Very carefully and precisely

Mill Hand's Lunch Bucket, 1978, Romare Bearden, From the Profile/Part 1; The Twenties series (Pittsburgh Memories). Collage on board, 13 3/4 x 18 1/8". ©1997 Romare Bearden Foundation/Licensed by VAGA, New York, NY

▲ Critical Viewing How does the artist use color, texture, and shape to create the overall mood of this collage? **[Analyze]**

appeared in an empty lot behind the cotton gin. As the dinner noon bell rang, she dropped the savors into boiling fat and the aroma rose and floated over to the workers who spilled out of the gin, covered with white lint, looking like specters.

Most workers had brought their lunches of pinto beans and biscuits or crackers, onions and cans of sardines, but they were tempted by the hot meat pies which Annie ladled out of the fat. She wrapped them in newspapers, which soaked up the grease, and offered them for sale at a nickel each. Although business was slow, those first days Annie was determined. She balanced her appearances between the two hours of activity.

So, on Monday if she offered hot fresh pies at the cotton gin and sold the remaining cooled-down pies at the lumber mill for three cents, then on Tuesday she went first to the lumber mill presenting fresh, just-cooked pies as the lumbermen covered in sawdust emerged from the mill.

For the next few years, on balmy spring days, blistering summer noons, and cold, wet, and wintry middays, Annie never disappointed her customers, who could count on seeing the tall, brown-skin woman bent over her brazier, carefully turning the meat pies. When she felt certain that the workers had become dependent on her, she built a stall between the two hives of industry and let the men run to her for their lunchtime provisions.

She had indeed stepped from the road which seemed to have been chosen for her and cut herself a brand-new path. In years that stall became a store where customers could buy cheese, meal, syrup, cookies, candy, writing tablets, pickles, canned goods, fresh fruit, soft drinks, coal, oil, and leather soles for worn-out shoes.

Each of us has the right and the responsibility to assess the roads which lie ahead, and those over which we have traveled, and if the future road looms ominous or unpromising, and the roads back uninviting, then we need to gather our resolve and, carrying only the necessary baggage, step off that road into another direction. If the new choice is also unpalatable, without embarrassment, we must be ready to change that as well.

◆ Build Vocabulary

specters (spek′ tərz) *n.*: Ghostly images; phantoms

ominous (äm′ ə nəs) *adj.*: Threatening; menacing

unpalatable (un pal′ it ə bəl) *adj.*: Distasteful; unpleasant

To be of use
Marge Piercy

The people I love the best
jump into work head first
without <u>dallying</u> in the shallows
and swim off with sure strokes almost out
    of sight.
5 They seem to become natives of that
    element,
the black sleek heads of seals
bouncing like half-<u>submerged</u> balls.

I love people who <u>harness</u> themselves, an
    ox to a heavy cart,
who pull like water buffalo, with massive
    patience,
10 who strain in the mud and the muck to
    move things forward,
who do what has to be done, again and
    again.
I want to be with people who submerge
in the task, who go into the fields to harvest
and work in a row and pass the bags along,
15 who are not parlor generals and field
    deserters
but move in a common rhythm
when the food must come in or the fire be
    put out.

The work of the
    world is common as mud.
Botched, it smears the hands, crumbles to
    dust.
20 But the thing worth doing well done
has a shape that satisfies, clean and
    evident.
Greek amphoras[1] for wine or oil,
Hopi[2] vases that held corn, are put in
    museums
but you know they were made to be used.
25 The pitcher cries for water to carry
and a person for work that is real.

---

1. **amphoras** (am´ fər əz) *n.*: Tall jars that have a narrow neck and base and two handles, used by the ancient Greeks and Romans.
2. **Hopi** (hō´ pē) *n.*: Pueblo tribe of Indians in northeastern Arizona.

◆ Build Vocabulary

dallying (dal´ ē iŋ) *v.*: Wasting time; loitering
submerged (səb mʉrjd´) *adj.*: Covered with something; underwater
harness (här´ nis) *v.*: Attach, as with straps for pulling or controlling

Guide for Responding

◆ *Literature and Your Life*

Reader's Response Would you rather meet Annie Johnson or the speaker of this poem? Explain.
Thematic Response How do Annie Johnson and the speaker of this poem feel about challenges?

☑ Check Your Comprehension

1. Why does Annie Johnson have to find a source of income?
2. How does she earn a living?
3. In the first stanza of the poem, what kind of people does the speaker say she loves best?

◆ Critical Thinking

INTERPRET
1. Why do you think Annie Johnson chose not to pursue a factory job or a job as a domestic? **[Infer]**
2. What does Johnson's achievement suggest about the human spirit in general? **[Draw Conclusions]**
3. What kinds of values do lines 12–18 of the poem stress? **[Analyze]**

APPLY
4. How important is it for a person to feel he or she is useful? Explain. **[Defend]**

Guide for Responding (continued)

◆ Literary Focus

FIGURATIVE LANGUAGE

The writers of these selections use **figurative language** to help us envision the decisive point in a person's life. For example, Frost and Angelou both use the image of a road or path to convey the idea of a career or way of life.

1. Compare Frost's "less traveled" road with the "new path" that Johnson carves for herself. What similar approaches to life do these images convey?
2. Contrast the way Frost's speaker approaches the two roads and the way the people in Piercy's opening stanza approach the water. What different approaches to life does the figurative language convey?

◆ Build Vocabulary

USING THE SUFFIX -*ly*

The suffix -*ly* is often used to turn adjectives into adverbs. Use the suffix -*ly* to turn each of the four adjectives into an adverb. List and define the newly created adverbs in your notebook. Also use each adverb in a sentence.

1. amicable: friendly
2. meticulous: very careful or thorough
3. ominous: menacing; threatening
4. unpalatable: unacceptable

USING THE WORD BANK

Copy these statements into your notebook, then indicate whether each is true or false.

1. If a stream of traffic *diverged*, it probably moved into different lanes or in different directions.
2. If you and your friend part *amicably*, you are most likely in a bad mood.
3. If you clean your room *meticulously*, it is messy.
4. Some children dress as *specters* on Halloween.
5. A smile is usually an *ominous* expression.
6. Most chefs try to cook *unpalatable* meals.
7. Window shoppers seem to enjoy *dallying*.
8. Deep-sea divers use air tanks when *submerged*.
9. In Alaska, some people *harness* dogs to a sled.

◆ Reading Strategy

GENERATE QUESTIONS

Asking and answering **questions** about a selection can help you remember its details and understand it better. Jot down two or three questions you asked yourself while reading each of these selections; then explain how they helped you with your reading.

◆ Build Grammar Skills

COMMAS IN A SERIES

When you list three or more items in a series, separate them with **commas** to make your meaning clear.

Practice Copy the following sentences into your notebook, adding or deleting commas where needed.

1. Mrs. Annie Johnson had little education less money, and two small sons to raise by herself.
2. She had no desire to work as a domestic or at the cotton gin or in the saw mill.
3. She decided to turn ham chicken dough and lard into meat pies to sell to the factory workers.
4. The workers enjoyed the meat pies along with their pinto beans, and crackers, and sardines.

Beyond Literature

Career Connection

Choosing a Career Choosing a career is one of the most important decisions you will ever make. How can you make the right career choice? Consider your values or goals, your interests, and your abilities. For example, do you value working with others or working alone? Are you interested in artistic activities or in working outdoors? Are you good at fixing a bicycle or at solving math problems? If you're unsure about what you do best, don't worry. You have lots of time to learn and even to change your mind. Take a moment right now to jot down some of your interests, listing what you like about each.

Build Your Portfolio

Idea Bank

Writing

1. Recipe Write a recipe that Annie Johnson could have used in her new business. The recipe could be for the meat pies described in the selection or for something else that Johnson might have sold. **[Home Economics Link]**

2. Dialogue Write a dialogue between the speaker of either poem and Annie Johnson. Consider what either speaker would be likely to say to Johnson and how Johnson might respond.

3. Job Description Write a one-page job description that you think could apply to one of the three selections. **[Career Link]**

Speaking and Listening

4. Job Interview Working with another student, role-play a job interview that might take place between Annie Johnson or the speaker of either poem and a potential employer. **[Career Link]**

5. Group Discussion Marge Piercy once said that she wanted her poems to be useful. Of the three selections, which do you find most "useful"? Share your ideas in a small-group discussion.

Projects

6. Docudrama Working in a small group, videotape an interview with a local businessperson, a teacher, or another professional to learn about the person's career. **[Career Link]**

7. Nutrition Report Would Annie Johnson's meals be popular with a health-conscious public today? Research the nutritional value and healthfulness of the ingredients in Johnson's meat pies, mentioned in the selection. Share your findings in an oral or written report. **[Health Link]**

Writing Mini-Lesson

Evaluation of Figurative Language

By using figurative language—such as the image of a road in Robert Frost's "The Road Not Taken"—writers hope to add clarity and color to their writing. Choose one of the selections and write an essay in which you evaluate the writer's use of figurative language.

> **Writing Skills Focus: Suitable Criteria for Effective Figurative Language**
>
> To help you evaluate the **effectiveness of figurative language**, answer the following questions:
> • Does the figurative language work for you or does it leave you confused?
> • What do you find interesting about the figurative language?
> • When making comparisons, does the writer avoid using clichés, or trite, overused expressions?
> • If the figurative language extends over several lines, does it remain logical and consistent?

Prewriting Choose a selection to evaluate, then list examples of figurative language in that selection. For each example, identify the basic comparison being stated or implied. Think about whether that comparison seems fresh and unusual.

Drafting State your reaction to the figurative language, then cite examples to support your reaction. Present the examples in some type of order— order of importance, for instance, or the order in which they appear in the work.

Revising Make sure you have offered enough examples to support all general statements about the selection. Check to see that your word choice is clear and precise and that your sentences flow logically and smoothly.

Guide for Reading

R. K. Narayan *(1906-   )*

If you could take all the swirling cultures, contradictions, and beauty of twentieth-century India and roll them up into one person, that person would probably resemble R. K. Narayan. In a career that has spanned more than sixty years, Narayan has written more than fifteen novels, as well as numerous collections of short stories, travel books, and essays. The sheer scope of his literary achievements has led at least one other writer to call him "the foremost Indian writer who writes in English."

A Novelist's Life Born in the major southern city of Madras, Narayan was one of nine children of a middle-class family. He attended Maharaja's College in the southern city of Mysore, but did not graduate until he was twenty-four. After briefly working as a teacher, he became a novelist. In 1935, he completed his first novel, *Swami and Friends.*

In his novels, legends, and short stories, Narayan skillfully combines traditional Western plots and themes with Indian subject matter to create works that are exotic yet accessible to Western readers. In 1958, Narayan was awarded the National Prize of the Indian Literary Academy, the nation's highest literary honor.

Universal Themes Most of Narayan's stories take place in the same fictional place, a town called Malgudi. While Malgudi is a distinctly southern Indian place, the tales that Narayan tells about it are universal. If you change the backdrop of any of Narayan's tales to a modern American town, you will find that the characters' struggles, plans, hopes, and dreams still apply. There is no aspect of the human experience about which Narayan has not written. It is this universal quality that makes his writing so special.

◆ Build Vocabulary

SUFFIXES: -ity

In this story, you will find the word *longevity* used by one of the characters. The suffix *-ity,* which means "state of" or "condition of," gives a clue to the meaning of the word *longevity.* You will recognize the base of the word is *long.* A way to define *longevity* would be "the *condition of* having a *long* life." In this story, one person appears to have a *longevity* of more than 500 years!

WORD BANK

sobriety
awry
literally
longevity
imperative
venture

As you read "Old Man of the Temple," you will encounter the words on this list. Each word is defined on the page where it first appears. Preview this list before you read and look for the words as they appear in the story.

◆ Build Grammar Skills

COMPOUND PREDICATES

In "Old Man of the Temple," R. K. Narayan uses compound predicates. A **compound predicate** consists of two or more verbs or verb phrases (a main verb plus a helping verb) that share the same subject. Compound predicates enable the writer to include a lot of action into a single sentence without having to repeat the subject.

$$\text{I took out my torch, got down, and walked}$$
$$\text{about, but could see no one.}$$

As you read "Old Man of the Temple," notice the author's frequent use of compound predicates to describe the many actions of his characters while still keeping the story moving briskly.

Old Man of the Temple

◆ *Literature and Your Life*

CONNECT YOUR EXPERIENCE

You see a shadow dart behind a tree on a cold autumn evening, but when you reach the tree and look, there is nothing there—what could it be? Although this story takes place in a far-off land, the narrator's experience is universal: He sees something and cannot believe his eyes. It is this element of the mysterious that makes reading ghost stories so much fun.

THEMATIC FOCUS: PUTTING OURSELVES TO THE TEST

How would you react if you were suddenly confronted with something that you could not explain? Would you face the challenge and try to solve the mystery or would you choose to avoid it?

◆ Background for Understanding

CULTURE

"Old Man of the Temple" takes place near Malgudi, a fictional town. Though it is a make-believe place, Malgudi could be any one of thousands of rural southern Indian towns. Imagine a place where all but the largest roads are unpaved. Through the morning mist, you can see cattle roaming along the dirt paths and farmers tilling the fields before the sun rises too high and the day becomes too hot to work. It is a place where the ruins of temples hundreds of years old decay amidst the creeping, cobralike tendrils of tropical vines.

Journal Writing Be a "ghost writer" and think up a ghost for a story. Describe it and tell why it appears as it does.

◆ Literary Focus

FANTASY

"Old Man of the Temple" is a **fantasy**—a work of fiction that includes characters, places, or events that could not reasonably exist or happen. We enjoy fantasy because it lets our imaginations run wild. When we read fantasy, we suspend our disbelief in the impossible in order to enjoy the tale. Fantasy must, however, contain some elements of real life, if only to give perspective to the fantastical elements.

◆ Reading Strategy

DISTINGUISH FANTASY FROM REALITY

As this story begins, a man and his driver are driving down a lonely rural road at night. That much can be established. Very soon, however, it becomes more and more difficult to **distinguish fantasy from reality**—to tell what is real and what is not.

As you read, it may help to jot down which elements of the story are real and which are fantastic. To organize your information, make a chart with two columns, labeled "Real" and "Fantastic." Write down the elements of the story in the appropriate column.

Real	Fantastic

Old Man of the Temple

R. K. Narayan

The Talkative Man said:

It was some years ago that this happened. I don't know if you can make anything of it. If you do, I shall be glad to hear what you have to say; but personally I don't understand it at all. It has always mystified me. Perhaps the driver was drunk; perhaps he wasn't.

I had engaged a taxi for going to Kumbum, which, as you may already know, is fifty miles from Malgudi.[1] I went there one morning and it was past nine in the evening when I finished my business and started back for the town. Doss,[2] the driver, was a young fellow of about twenty-five. He had often brought his car for me and I liked him. He was a well-behaved, obedient fellow, with a capacity to sit and wait at the wheel, which is really a rare quality in a taxi driver. He drove the car smoothly, seldom swore at passers-by, and exhibited perfect judgment, good sense, and sobriety; and so I preferred him to any other driver whenever I had to go out on business.

---

1. **Malgudi** (mäl g$\overline{oo}$′ dē): Fictional city about which Narayan often writes.
2. **Doss** (däs)

◆ **Build Vocabulary**

sobriety (sə brī′ ə tē) *n.*: Moderation, especially in the use of alcoholic beverages

---

◀ **Critical Viewing** The setting of this story—a fictional town in India—has elements of reality. Why might a writer include realistic details in a fantasy story? **[Speculate]**

It was about eleven when we passed the village Koopal,[3] which is on the way down. It was the dark half of the month and the surrounding country was swallowed up in the night. The village street was deserted. Everyone had gone to sleep; hardly any light was to be seen. The stars overhead sparkled brightly. Sitting in the back seat and listening to the continuous noise of the running wheels, I was half lulled into a drowse.

◆ Literary Focus
What realistic elements in this paragraph set the stage for the fantasy?

All of a sudden Doss swerved the car and shouted: "You old fool! Do you want to kill yourself?"

I was shaken out of my drowse and asked: "What is the matter?"

Doss stopped the car and said, "You see that old fellow, sir. He is trying to kill himself. I can't understand what he is up to."

I looked in the direction he pointed and asked, "Which old man?"

"There, there. He is coming towards us again. As soon as I saw him open that temple door and come out I had a feeling, somehow, that I must keep an eye on him."

I took out my torch, got down, and walked about, but could see no one. There was an old temple on the roadside. It was utterly in ruins; most portions of it were mere mounds of old brick; the walls were awry; the doors were shut to the main doorway, and brambles and thickets grew over and covered them. It was difficult to guess with the aid of the torch alone what temple it was and to what period it belonged.

"The doors are shut and sealed and don't look as if they had been opened for centuries now," I cried.

"No, sir," Doss said coming nearer. "I saw the old man open the doors and come out. He is standing there; shall we ask him to open them again if you want to go in and see?"

I said to Doss, "Let us be going. We are wasting our time here."

---

3. **Koopal** (kōō päl′)

We went back to the car. Doss sat in his seat, pressed the self-starter, and asked without turning his head, "Are you permitting this fellow to come with us, sir? He says he will get down at the next milestone."

"Which fellow?" I asked.

Doss indicated the space next to him.

"What is the matter with you, Doss? Have you had a drop of drink or something?"

"I have never tasted any drink in my life. sir," he said, and added, "Get down, old boy. Master says he can't take you."

"Are you talking to yourself?"

"After all, I think we needn't care for these unknown fellows on the road," he said.

"Doss," I pleaded. "Do you feel confident you can drive? If you feel dizzy don't drive."

"Thank you, sir," said Doss. "I would rather not start the car now. I am feeling a little out of sorts." I looked at him anxiously. He closed his eyes, his breathing became heavy and noisy, and gradually his head sank.

"Doss, Doss," I cried desperately. I got down, walked to the front seat, opened the door, and shook him vigorously. He opened his eyes, assumed a hunched-up position, and rubbed his eyes with his hands, which trembled like an old man's.

"Do you feel better?" I asked.

"Better! Better! Hi! Hi!" he said in a thin, piping voice.

"What has happened to your voice? You sound like someone else," I said.

"Nothing. My voice is as good as it was. When a man is eighty he is bound to feel a few changes coming on."

"You aren't eighty, surely," I said.

"Not a day less," he said. "Is nobody going to move this vehicle? If not, there is no sense in sitting here all day. I will get down and go back to my temple."

"I don't know how to drive," I said. "And

◆ **Build Vocabulary**

awry (ə rī′) adj.: Not straight

unless you do it, I don't see how it can move."

"Me!" exclaimed Doss. "These new chariots! God knows what they are drawn by, I never understand, though I could handle a pair of bullocks[4] in my time. May I ask a question?"

"Go on," I said.

"Where is everybody?"

"Who?"

"Lots of people I knew are not to be seen at all. All sorts of new fellows everywhere, and nobody seems to care. Not a soul comes near the temple. All sorts of people go about but not one who cares to stop and talk. Why doesn't the king ever come this way? He used to go this way at least once a year before."

"Which king?" I asked.

"Let me go, you idiot," said Doss, edging towards the door on which I was leaning. "You don't seem to know anything." He pushed me aside, and got down from the car. He stooped as if he had a big hump on his back, and hobbled along towards the temple. I followed him, hardly knowing what to do. He turned and snarled at me: "Go away, leave me alone. I have had enough of you."

"What has come over you, Doss?" I asked.

"Who is Doss, anyway? Doss, Doss, Doss. What an absurd name! Call me by my name or leave me alone. Don't follow me calling 'Doss, Doss.' "

4. **bullocks** (bōol′ əks) *n.:* Oxen; steer.

Leaf from a royal manuscript of the Shah-Jehan Nameh: A Procession in a Palace Courtyard, The Art Institute of Chicago

▲ **Critical Viewing** This painting shows a royal procession from the time of the old man's reminiscences. Point out details that illustrate the pageantry and lavishness associated with royalty in ancient India. **[Support]**

"What is your name?" I asked.

"Krishna Battar,[5] and if you mention my name people will know for a hundred miles around. I built a temple where there was only a cactus field before. I dug the earth, burnt every brick, and put them one upon another, all single-handed. And on the day the temple held up its tower over the surrounding country, what a crowd gathered! The king sent his chief minister . . ."

> ◆ Reading Strategy
> What clues in this paragraph help you distinguish what is real from what is not?

"Who was the king?"

"Where do you come from?" he asked.

"I belong to these parts certainly, but as far as I know there has been only a collector at the head of the district. I have never heard of any king."

"Hi! Hi! Hi!" he cackled, and his voice rang through the gloomy silent village. "Fancy never knowing the king! He will behead you if he hears it."

"What is his name?" I asked.

This tickled him so much that he sat down on the ground, literally unable to stand the joke any more. He laughed and coughed un-controllably.

"I am sorry to admit," I said, "that my parents have brought me up in such utter ignorance of worldly affairs that I don't know even my king. But won't you enlighten me? What is his name?"

"Vishnu Varma,[6] the emperor of emperors . . ."

I cast my mind up and down the range of my historical knowledge but there was no one by that name. Perhaps a local chief of pre-British days, I thought.

"What a king! He often visited my temple or sent his minister for the Annual Festival of the temple. But now nobody cares."

"People are becoming less godly nowadays," I said. There was silence for a moment. An idea occurred to me, I can't say why. "Listen to me," I said. "You ought not to be here any more."

"What do you mean?" he asked, drawing himself up, proudly.

"Don't feel hurt; I say you shouldn't be here any more because you are dead."

"Dead! Dead!" he said. "Don't talk nonsense. How can I be dead when you see me before you now? If I am dead how can I be saying this and that?"

"I don't know all that," I said. I argued and pointed out that according to his own story he was more than five hundred years old, and didn't he know that man's longevity was only a hundred? He constantly interrupted me, but considered deeply what I said.

He said: "It is like this . . . I was coming through the jungle one night after visiting my sister in the next village. I had on me some money and gold ornaments. A gang of robbers set upon me. I gave them as good a fight as any man could, but they were too many for me. They beat me down and knifed me; they took away all that I had on me and left thinking they had killed me. But soon I got up and tried to follow them. They were gone. And I returned to the temple and have been here since . . ."

I told him, "Krishna Battar, you are dead, absolutely dead. You must try and go away from here."

"What is to happen to the temple?" he asked.

"Others will look after it."

"Where am I to go? Where am I to go?"

"Have you no one who cares for you?" I asked.

"None except my wife. I loved her very much."

"You can go to her."

"Oh, no. She died four years ago . . ."

Four years! It was very puzzling. "Do you say four years back from now?" I asked.

◆ Build Vocabulary

literally (lit´ ər əl ē) adv.: Actually; in fact

longevity (län jev´ə tē) n.: The length or duration of a life

imperative (im per´ ə tiv) adj.: Absolutely necessary; urgent

venture (ven´ chər) n.: Chance

---

5. **Krishna Battar** (krish´ nə bə tar´
6. **Vishnu Varma** (vish´ n͞oo vär´ mə)

"Yes, four years ago from now." He was clearly without any sense of time.

So I asked, "Was she alive when you were attacked by thieves?"

"Certainly not. If she had been alive she would never have allowed me to go through the jungle after nightfall. She took very good care of me."

"See here," I said. "It is <u>imperative</u> you should go away from here. If she comes and calls you, will you go?"

"How can she when I tell you that she is dead?"

I thought for a moment. Presently I found myself saying, "Think of her, and only of her, for a while and see what happens. What was her name?"

"Seetha,[7] a wonderful girl . . ."

"Come on, think of her." He remained in deep thought for a while. He suddenly screamed, "Seetha is coming! Am I dreaming or what? I will go with her . . ." He stood up, very erect; he appeared to have lost all the humps and twists he had on his body. He drew himself up, made a dash forward, and fell down in a heap.

Doss lay on the rough ground. The only sign of life in him was his faint breathing. I shook him and called him. He would not open his eyes. I walked across and knocked on the door of the

___
7. **Seetha** (sē´ thə)

first cottage. I banged on the door violently.

Someone moaned inside, "Ah, it is come!"

Someone else whispered, "You just cover your ears and sleep. It will knock for a while and go away." I banged on the door and shouted who I was and where I came from.

I walked back to the car and sounded the horn. Then the door opened, and a whole family crowded out with lamps. "We thought it was the usual knocking and we wouldn't have opened if you hadn't spoken."

"When was this knocking first heard?" I asked.

"We can't say," said one. "The first time I heard it was when my grandfather was living; he used to say he had even seen it once or twice. It doesn't harm anyone, as far as I know. The only thing it does is bother the bullock carts passing the temple and knock on the doors at night . . ."

I said as a <u>venture</u>, "It is unlikely you will be troubled any more."

It proved correct. When I passed that way again months later I was told that the bullocks passing the temple after dusk never shied now and no knocking on the doors was heard at nights. So I felt that the old fellow had really gone away with his good wife.

◆ *Literature and Your Life*
What would you say to the family?

Guide for Responding

◆ *Literature and Your Life*

Reader's Response The narrator tells you, "I don't know if you can make anything of it. If you do, I shall be glad to hear what you have to say . . ." How would you answer him?

Thematic Focus Put yourself to the same test that the narrator faces. Would you have faced the challenge or would you have tried to avoid it?

Group Discussion A person's encounter with a ghost is a common scene in books and movies. Often these encounters are scary; sometimes they are quite funny; occasionally, they are both. As a group, come up with three examples of such scenes. Compare these scenes to the narrator's encounter with the ghost in "Old Man of the Temple."

☑ **Check Your Comprehension**

1. The narrator's trip seems to be going smoothly until something happens to Doss. Describe what happens.
2. What does the narrator say to cause the old man to think about his own situation?
3. How are peace and quiet finally restored?

Guide for Responding (continued)

◆ Critical Thinking

INTERPRET

1. Why does the narrator find Doss's words about the old man unbelievable? **[Analyze]**
2. How does the narrator react to Doss's transformation? **[Analyze]**
3. Why is the narrator suspicious of what the old man says? Give examples. **[Interpret]**
4. (a) Is the narrator the type of person who would be more likely to be ruled by his feelings or by reason? (b) Why? **[Infer]**
5. What purpose does the introduction of the family at the end of the story serve? **[Connect]**

EVALUATE

6. (a) Which elements of this story are uniquely Indian? (b) Which are universal? **[Classify]**

EXTEND

7. (a) How does this story compare with other fantasies you have read or seen on film? (b) Which elements of the plot or characters are similar? (c) Which are different? **[Compare and Contrast]**

◆ Reading Strategy

DISTINGUISH FANTASY FROM REALITY

"Old Man of the Temple" contains both **realistic and fantastic elements.** If you made a chart while reading, refer to it to answer these questions.

1. Name two elements that are fantastic.
2. (a) At what point does the plot become fantastical? (b) How do you know?

◆ Literary Focus

FANTASY

In "Old Man of the Temple," **fantasy**—in this instance, the narrator's encounter with a ghost–is essential to the plot of the story. This encounter is what the Talkative Man wants to tell us about; without it there is no story.

1. Why is this story a fantasy?
2. How does the inclusion of fantastic elements make the story appealing?
3. What realistic elements of the story make it believable?

◆ Build Vocabulary

USING THE SUFFIX -ity

Knowing that the suffix -ity means "the state or condition of being . . . ," write definitions for the following words:

1. brutality   3. generosity
2. severity   4. individuality

USING THE WORD BANK

On your paper, write the word whose meaning is closest to that of the first word.

1. sobriety: (a) sadness, (b) loneliness, (c) moderation
2. awry: (a) angry, (b) crooked, (c) clever
3. literally: (a) actually, (b) scholarly, (c) differently
4. longevity: (a) height, (b) endurance, (c) duration
5. imperative: (a) essential, (b) unnecessary, (c) ruler
6. venture: (a) game, (b) risk, (c) skill

◆ Build Grammar Skills

COMPOUND PREDICATES

Compound predicates enable a writer to describe the many actions of a single character without having to repeat the subject.

Practice On your paper, write the following sentences. Underline the compound predicate in each.

1. He stooped, wiped the beads of perspiration off his forehead, and hobbled along towards the temple.
2. He drove the car smoothly, seldom swore at passers-by, and exhibited perfect judgment.
3. I dug the earth, burnt every brick, and put them one upon another, all single-handed.

Writing Application On your paper, combine each group of sentences into a single sentence, using a compound predicate.

1. The old man came out of the temple. He looked in all directions. He began to walk.
2. I was sitting in the back seat of the car. I was listening to the hum of the motor. I dozed off.
3. I saw an old man run in front of the car. But I didn't see where he went.

Build Your Portfolio

Idea Bank

Writing

1. **Police Report** Imagine that you are a police officer who has been summoned to the scene by the family in the story. Write a brief description of the scene and each character's version of the events. **[Career Link]**

2. **Obituary** What kind of person do you think the old man was when he was alive? Using information in the story and information that you make up, write an obituary for the old man.

3. **Real Estate Advertisement** With a group of classmates, create a real-estate advertisement to sell the temple ruins. **[Career Link]**

Speaking and Listening

4. **Dramatic Reading** With a few classmates, give a dramatic reading of the story. Remember that for drama to be interesting, the characters must be brought to life—so don't hesitate to overact a little! **[Performing Arts Link]**

5. **Dramatic Monologue** Write a monologue in which the old man relates the elements of the story from his point of view. Deliver your monologue to the class. **[Performing Arts Link]**

Projects

6. **Cultural Map of India** Using an atlas, encyclopedia, or other reference books as guides, draw a map of India and locate areas of the major religions and languages on the map. **[Social Studies Link]**

7. **Report on Hinduism** Southern India, where this story takes place, is overwhelmingly Hindu. Write a brief research report on Hinduism and explain how Hinduism enriches your understanding of this story. **[Social Studies Link]**

Writing Mini-Lesson

Travel Brochure

India, the country in which this story takes place, is so diverse that a visitor could spend a year there and still see less than half of what there is to see. Choose a particular city, area, or attraction—either abroad or close to home—and write a travel brochure about that place.

Writing Skills Focus: Using a Persuasive Tone

Besides giving information, a successful brochure uses a **persuasive tone** to entice people to visit a particular place. Look at the following passage from a travel brochure on India:

Model

Be sure to visit the Taj Mahal, the world's most romantic and beautiful tomb. You'll see in it the love that an emperor bore for the wife he buried there. Also, you'll be amazed that this domed white marble building, 313 feet high, is so symmetrical that it doesn't seem large at all.

Phrases like *world's most romantic and beautiful tomb* and *you'll be amazed* create a persuasive tone by appealing to a tourist's desire for an unforgettable vacation experience.

Prewriting Decide on a place to write about and the features you'll describe. Gather appealing details that will persuade your audience to visit the place.

Drafting Many qualities can make the tone of your brochure persuasive. For instance, vivid sensory descriptions will appeal to people's imagination and a sense of humor will spark interest and a friendly, receptive attitude.

Revising Reread your draft. Would you be persuaded to visit the place? Can you make your tone more persuasive and your speaker even more likable?

Guide for Reading

Edith Hamilton (1867–1963)

Edith Hamilton's long journey on Earth began soon after the Civil War and ended in the Space Age. Her heart went on an even longer journey—back to the worlds of ancient Greece and Rome—to find messages that modern people could apply to their lives.

Educator of Young Women

Hamilton started out not as a writer, but as a groundbreaking educator. After graduating from Bryn Mawr College, she studied for a year in Europe, becoming the first woman to attend classes at the University of Munich, where she had to sit by herself on the lecture platform, separated from the male students. Shortly after completing her studies, she helped found the Bryn Mawr School in Baltimore, the first college preparatory school for women. As the school's headmistress, Hamilton taught a generation of young women the lesson she had learned: not to limit their goals simply because they were not men.

A Late-Blooming Writer

Although she made the Bryn Mawr School a success, Hamilton admitted later on that she had never really liked being headmistress. She left Bryn Mawr in 1922.

> *At an age when most people of her time would have considered retirement, Hamilton launched into what would become her true career.*

She began to write articles on the subject closest to her heart: ancient Greece. These pieces proved so popular that Hamilton was persuaded to turn them into a book, which was called *The Greek Way*, published in 1930. Her other books include *The Roman Way* (1932), *The Prophets of Israel* (1936), and *Mythology* (1942).

◆ Build Vocabulary

WORD ROOTS: -mort-

In this selection, you'll encounter the word *mortified*, which is based on the root -*mort*-, meaning "death."

By knowing the root, you might guess that the word *mortified* means to "feel dead." The actual meaning of the word is "deeply humiliated" or "wounded in self-respect."

WORD BANK

As you read "Perseus," you will encounter the words on this list. Each word is defined on the page where it first appears. Preview the list before you read, and look for the words as they appear in the story.

kindred
mortified
despair
wavering
revelry
deity
reconciled

◆ Build Grammar Skills

POSSESSIVE NOUNS

"Perseus" contains nouns in the **possessive case,** which shows ownership or kinship.

• The possessive case of singular nouns is formed by adding an apostrophe and -*s*:

    Athena's shield

• The possessive case of a singular proper noun ending in -*s* is formed by adding an apostrophe and an -*s*:

    Douglas's chart

• The possessive case of plural nouns ending in -*s* or -*es* is formed by adding an apostrophe:

    Terrible Sisters' island

• The possessive case of plural nouns that do not end in -*s* is formed by adding an apostrophe and an -*s*:

    fishermen's brothers

Perseus

◆ *Literature and Your Life*

CONNECT YOUR EXPERIENCE

Some people love to rise to difficult occasions, while others prefer to keep their lives on an even keel. Perseus, the main character in this selection, is the first sort of person—the type who thrives on grappling with thorny problems. Which sort are you?

THEMATIC FOCUS: PUTTING OURSELVES TO THE TEST

Perseus' passage from one peril to the next might make you wonder what you would do if you suddenly found yourself in his sandals, faced with the choice between taking on a highly dangerous mission or being viewed with scorn. What alternatives might you have in such a tight spot?

◆ Background for Understanding

CULTURE

"Perseus" takes place in a mythological world populated by Greek gods and goddesses. The cast of Greek gods you will meet in Perseus' story includes Zeus, the chief god, who fathered a number of human children; Athena, goddess of war and wisdom; and Hermes, the messenger god (whom you may know by his Roman name Mercury).

Journal Writing Perseus' world is full of mythic beauty and horror that go beyond normal human experience. Write a physical description of a fantastic creature of your own invention—either beautiful or monstrous (or both).

◆ Literary Focus

HERO IN A MYTH

Start with a brave young man who loves his mother. Add some sympathetic gods and a terrible monster. You now have the makings of a **hero in a myth**—a character who performs amazing feats in a tale involving supernatural beings and fantastic events. The hero in a myth is often aided by magical elements. Nevertheless, the hero must exhibit admirable qualities such as courage, loyalty, and fairness. As you read, think about how Perseus' good qualities make him worthy of the supernatural help he gets.

◆ Reading Strategy

PREDICT

"Perseus" begins with a prediction by an oracle (prophet) about a future event. When you read any work of literature, you too can **predict outcomes**—not by using supernatural powers, but by thinking about the world presented in the literature and about the logical consequences of the characters' actions. These factors help you narrow down many possible outcomes to the few most likely ones.

To help you predict outcomes in "Perseus," make a chart like this one.

Situation	Possible Outcome	Reasons for Prediction	Outcome

PERSEUS

Edith Hamilton

King Acrisius[1] of Argos had only one child, a daughter, Danaë.[2] She was beautiful above all the other women of the land, but this was small comfort to the King for not having a son. He journeyed to Delphi to ask the god if there was any hope that some day he would be the father of a boy. The priestess told him no, and added what was far worse: that his daughter would have a son who would kill him.

The only sure way to escape that fate was for the King to have Danaë instantly put to death—taking no chances, but seeing to it himself. This Acrisius would not do. His fatherly affection was not strong, as events proved, but his fear of the gods was. They visited with terrible punishment those who shed the blood of <u>kindred</u>. Acrisius did not dare slay his daughter. Instead, he had a house built all of bronze and sunk underground, but with part of the roof open to the sky so that light and air could come through. Here he shut her up and guarded her.

> So Danaë endured, the beautiful,
> To change the glad daylight for brass-
>   bound walls.
> And in that chamber secret as the
>   grave
> She lived a prisoner. Yet to her came
> Zeus in the golden rain.

◆ **Build Vocabulary**
kindred (kin′ drid) *n*.: Relatives

---

1. **King Acrisius** (a kris′ ē əs)
2. **Danaë** (dan′ ā ē)

Andromeda Liberated, Pierre Mignard. Louvre, Paris, France

As she sat there through the long days and hours with nothing to do, nothing to see except the clouds moving by overhead, a mysterious thing happened, a shower of gold fell from the sky and filled her chamber. How it was revealed to her that it was Zeus who had visited her in this shape we are not told, but she knew that the child she bore was his son.

For a time she kept his birth secret from her father, but it became increasingly difficult to do so in the narrow limits of that bronze house and finally one day the little boy—his name was Perseus—was discovered by his grandfather. "Your child!" Acrisius cried in great anger. "Who is his father?" But when Danaë answered proudly, "Zeus," he would not believe her. One thing only he was sure of, that the boy's life

◀ **Critical Viewing** The man with the sword is Perseus as an adult. Judging from this painting, how do you think others perceive him? Cite details in the artwork to support your answer. [**Draw Conclusions**]

was a terrible danger to his own. He was afraid to kill him for the same reason that had kept him from killing her, fear of Zeus and the Furies who pursue such murderers. But if he could not kill them outright, he could put them in the way of tolerably certain death. He had a great chest made, and the two placed in it. Then it was taken out to sea and cast into the water.

In that strange boat Danaë sat with her little son. The daylight faded and she was alone on the sea.

> When in the carven chest the winds and
>   waves
> Struck fear into her heart she put her
>   arms,
> Not without tears, round Perseus tenderly
> She said, "O son, what grief is mine.
> But you sleep softly, little child,
> Sunk deep in rest within your cheerless
>   home,
> Only a box, brass-bound. The night, this
>   darkness visible,
> The scudding waves so near to your soft
>   curls,
> The shrill voice of the wind, you do not
>   heed,
> Nestled in your red cloak, fair little face."

◆ Reading Strategy
Will Danaë and Perseus survive? On what do you base your prediction?

Through the night in the tossing chest she listened to the waters that seemed always about to wash over them. The dawn came, but with no comfort to her for she could not see it. Neither could she see that around them there were islands rising high above the sea, many islands. All she knew was that presently a wave seemed to lift them and carry them swiftly on and then, retreating, leave them on something solid and motionless. They had made land; they were safe from the sea, but they were still in the chest with no way to get out.

Fate willed it—or perhaps Zeus, who up to now had done little for his love and his child—that they should be discovered by a good man, a fisherman named Dictys. He came upon the great box and broke it open and took the pitiful cargo home to his wife who was as kind as he. They had no children and they cared for Danaë and Perseus as if they were their own. The two lived there many years, Danaë content to let her son follow the fisherman's humble trade, out of harm's way. But in the end more trouble came. Polydectes,[3] the ruler of the little island, was the brother of Dictys, but he was a cruel and ruthless man. He seems to have taken no notice of the mother and son for a long time, but at last Danaë attracted his attention. She was still radiantly beautiful even though Perseus by now was full grown, and Polydectes fell in love with her. He wanted her, but he did not want her son, and he set himself to think out a way of getting rid of him.

There were some fearsome monsters called Gorgons who lived on an island and were known far and wide because of their deadly power. Polydectes evidently talked to Perseus about them; he probably told him that he would rather have the head of one of them than anything else in the world. This seems practically certain from the plan he devised for killing Perseus. He announced that he was about to be married and he called his friends together for a celebration, including Perseus in the invitation. Each guest, as was customary, brought a gift for the bride-to-be, except Perseus alone. He had nothing he could give. He was young and proud and keenly <u>mortified</u>. He stood up before them all and did exactly what the King had hoped he would do, declared that he would give him a present better than any there. He would go off and kill Medusa and bring back her head as his gift. Nothing could have suited the King better. No one in his senses would have made such a proposal. Medusa was one of the Gorgons,

---

3. **Polydectes** (pol i dek´ tēz)

Museo Archeologico, Ferrara, Italy.

▲ **Critical Viewing** Do you think Zeus intervened to save Perseus and Danaë? Why or why not? [Speculate]

And they are three, the Gorgons, each with wings
And snaky hair, most horrible to mortals.
Whom no man shall behold and draw again
The breath of life,

for the reason that whoever looked at them were turned instantly into stone. It seemed that Perseus had been led by his angry pride into making an empty boast. No man unaided could kill Medusa.

But Perseus was saved from his folly. Two great gods were watching over him. He took ship as soon as he left the King's hall, not daring to see his mother first and tell her what he intended, and he sailed to Greece to learn where the three monsters were to be found. He went to Delphi, but all the priestess would say was to bid him seek the land where men eat not Demeter's golden grain, but only acorns. So he went to Dodona, in the land of oak trees, where the talking oaks were which declared Zeus's will and where the Selli lived who made their bread from acorns. They could tell him, however, no more than this, that he was under the protection of the gods. They did not know where the Gorgons lived.

When and how Hermes and Athena came to his help is not told in any story, but he must have known despair before they did so. At last, however, as he wandered on, he met a strange and beautiful person. We know what he looked like from many a poem, a young man with the first down upon his cheek when youth is loveliest, carrying, as no other young man ever did, a wand of gold with wings at one end, wearing a winged hat, too, and winged sandals. At sight of him hope must have entered Perseus' heart, for he would know that this could be none other than Hermes, the guide and the giver of good.

This radiant personage told him that before he attacked Medusa he must first be properly equipped, and that what he needed was in the possession of the nymphs of the North. To find the nymphs' abode, they must go to the Gray Women who alone could tell them the way. These women dwelt in a land where all was

◆ **Build Vocabulary**
mortified (môrt´ ə fīd´) *adj*.: Embarrassed
despair (di sper´) *n*.: Hopelessness

Critical Viewing ▶
In addition to his gifts
from the gods, what
does Perseus need to
slay Medusa?
[Draw Conclusions]

dim and shrouded in twilight. No ray of sun looked ever on that country, nor the moon by night. In that gray place the three women lived, all gray themselves and withered as in extreme old age. They were strange creatures, indeed, most of all because they had but one eye for the three, which it was their custom to take turns with, each removing it from her forehead when she had had it for a time and handing it to another.

All this Hermes told Perseus and then he unfolded his plan. He would himself guide Perseus to them. Once there Perseus must keep hidden until he saw one of them take the eye out of her forehead to pass it on. At that moment, when none of the three could see, he must rush forward and seize the eye and refuse to give it back until they told him how to reach the nymphs of the North.

He himself, Hermes said, would give him a sword to attack Medusa with—which could not be bent or broken by the Gorgon's scales, no matter how hard they were. This was a wonderful gift, no doubt, and yet of what use was a sword when the creature to be struck by it could turn the swordsman into stone before he was within striking distance? But another great deity was at hand to help. Pallas Athena stood beside Perseus. She took off the shield of polished bronze which covered her breast and held it out to him. "Look into this when you attack the Gorgon," she said. "You will be able to see her in it as in a mirror, and so avoid her deadly power."

Now, indeed, Perseus had good reason to hope. The journey to the twilight land was long, over the stream of Ocean and on to the very border of the black country where the Cimmerians dwell, but Hermes was his guide and he could not go astray. They found the Gray Women at last, looking in the wavering light like gray birds, for they had the shape of swans. But their heads were human and beneath their wings they had arms and hands. Perseus did just as Hermes had said, he held back until he saw one of them take the eye out of her forehead. Then before she could give it to her sister, he snatched it out of her hand. It was a moment or two before the three realized they had lost it. Each thought one of the others had it. But Perseus spoke out and told them he had taken it and that it would be theirs again only when they showed him how to find the nymphs of the North. They gave him full directions at once; they would have done anything to get their eye back. He returned it to them and went on the way they had pointed out to him. He was bound, although he did not know it, to the blessed country of the Hyperboreans,[4] at the back of the North Wind, of which it is said: "Neither by ship nor yet by land shall one find the wondrous road to the gathering place of the Hyperboreans." But Perseus had Hermes with him, so that the road lay open to him, and he received that host of happy people who are always banqueting and holding joyful revelry. They showed him great kindness: they welcomed him to their feast, and the maidens dancing to the sound of flute and lyre paused to get for him the gifts he sought. These were three: winged sandals, a magic wallet which would always become the right size for whatever was to be carried in it, and, most important of all, a cap which made the wearer invisible. With these and Athena's shield and Hermes' sword Perseus was ready for the Gorgons. Hermes knew where they lived, and leaving the happy land the two flew back across Ocean and over the sea to the Terrible Sisters' island.

By great good fortune they were all asleep when Perseus found them. In the mirror of the bright shield he could see them clearly, creatures with great wings and bodies covered with golden scales and hair a mass of twisting snakes. Athena was beside him now as well as Hermes. They told him which one was Medusa and that was important, for she alone of the three could be killed; the other two were immortal. Perseus on his winged sandals hovered above them, looking, however, only at the shield. Then he aimed a stroke down at Medusa's throat and Athena guided his hand. With a single sweep of his sword he cut through her neck and, his eyes still fixed on the shield with never a glance at her, he swooped low enough to seize the head. He dropped it into the wallet which closed around it. He had nothing to fear from it now. But the two other Gorgons had awakened and, horrified at the sight of their sister slain, tried to pursue the slayer. Perseus was safe; he had on the cap of darkness and they could not find him.

> So over the sea rich-haired Danaë's son,
> Perseus, on his winged sandals sped,
> Flying swift as thought.
> In a wallet of silver,
> A wonder to behold,
> He bore the head of the monster,
> While Hermes, the son of Maia,
> The messenger of Zeus,
> Kept ever at his side.

On his way back he came to Ethiopia and alighted there. By this time Hermes had left him. Perseus found, as Hercules was later to find, that a lovely maiden had been given up to be devoured by a horrible sea serpent. Her name was Andromeda and she was the daughter of a silly vain woman,

> That starred Ethiop queen who strove
> To set her beauty's praise above
> The sea-nymphs, and their power
> offended.

---

4. **Hyperboreans** (hī per bō′ rē anz)

◆ **Build Vocabulary**
wavering (wā′ vər iŋ) *adj.*: Flickering
revelry (rev′ əl rē) *n.*: Party

◆ **Literary Focus**
What heroic qualities does Perseus exhibit through these actions?

She had boasted that she was more beautiful than the daughters of Nereus, the Sea-god. An absolutely certain way in those days to draw down on one a wretched fate was to claim superiority in anything over any <u>deity</u>; nevertheless people were perpetually doing so. In this case the punishment for the arrogance the gods detested fell not on Queen Cassiopeia,[5] Andromeda's mother, but on her daughter. The Ethiopians were being devoured in numbers by the serpent; and, learning from the oracle that they could be freed from the pest only if Andromeda were offered up to it, they forced Cepheus,[6] her father, to consent. When Perseus arrived the maiden was on a rocky ledge by the sea, chained there to wait for the coming of the monster. Perseus saw her and on the instant loved her. He waited beside her until the great snake came for its prey; then he cut its head off just as he had the Gorgon's. The headless body dropped back into the water; Perseus took Andromeda to her parents and asked for her hand, which they gladly gave him.

With her he sailed back to the island and his mother, but in the house where he had lived so long he found no one. The fisherman Dictys' wife was long since dead, and the two others, Danaë and the man who had been like a father to Perseus, had had to fly and hide themselves from Polydectes, who was furious at Danaë's refusal to marry him. They had taken refuge in a temple, Perseus was told. He learned also that the King was holding a banquet in the

5. **Queen Cassiopeia** (kas´ ē ō pē´ ə)
6. **Cepheus** (sē fəs)

◀ **Critical Viewing** What does Perseus prove by killing the sea monster? **[Support]**

palace and all the men who favored him were gathered there. Perseus instantly saw his opportunity. He went straight to the palace and entered the hall. As he stood at the entrance, Athena's shining buckler on his breast, the silver wallet at his side, he drew the eyes of every man there. Then before any could look away he held up the Gorgon's head; and at the sight one and all, the cruel King and his servile courtiers, were turned into stone. There they sat, a row of statues, each, as it were, frozen stiff in the attitude he had struck when he first saw Perseus.

◆ **Reading Strategy**
How will the story end?

When the islanders knew themselves freed from the tyrant it was easy for Perseus to find Danaë and Dictys. He made Dictys king of the island, but he and his mother decided that they would go back with Andromeda to Greece and try to be <u>reconciled</u> to Acrisius, to see if the many years that had passed since he had put them in the chest had not softened him so that he would be glad to receive his daughter and grandson. When they reached Argos, however, they found that Acrisius had been driven away from the city, and where he was no one could say. It happened that soon after their arrival Perseus heard that the King of Larissa, in the North, was holding a great athletic contest, and he journeyed there to take part. In the discus-throwing when his turn came and he hurled the heavy missile, it swerved and fell among the spectators. Acrisius was there on a visit to the King, and the discus struck him. The blow was fatal and he died at once.

So Apollo's oracle was again proved true. If Perseus felt any grief, at least he knew that his grandfather had done his best to kill him and his mother. With his death their troubles came to an end. Perseus and Andromeda lived happily ever after. Their son, Electryon, was the grandfather of Hercules.

Medusa's head was given to Athena, who bore it always upon the aegis, Zeus's shield, which she carried for him.

◆ **Build Vocabulary**
deity (dē´ ə tē) *n.*: A god
reconciled (rek´ ən sīld) *adj.*: Became friends again

Guide for Responding

◆ Literature and Your Life

Reader's Response Which of Perseus' adventures would make the best action-adventure movie? Why?

Thematic Focus If you had been Perseus, would you have accepted King Polydectes' challenge to find a unique wedding present? Why or why not?

Group Discussion Perseus' grandfather, Acrisius, truly believed the prediction that his grandson would end up killing him. As a group, discuss what Acrisius could and should have done in response to this prediction: Was he at all justified in the actions he took? What alternatives did he have?

☑ Check Your Comprehension

1. (a) What prediction does the priestess make to Acrisius? (b) What two actions does Acrisius take to prevent the prophecy from coming true?
2. (a) Why does Perseus set out to kill Medusa? (b) What help does he receive from Hermes and Athena? (c) How does Perseus manage to kill Medusa?
3. How does Perseus eventually fulfill the priestess's prediction?

Guide for Responding (continued)

◆ Critical Thinking

INTERPRET

1. What is revealed about Acrisius' character through the actions he takes to escape fate? **[Infer]**
2. Why is it important that Perseus is Zeus's son? **[Infer]**
3. What might have led Athena and Hermes to help Perseus in his quest? **[Infer]**
4. What would have happened to Perseus if he had not received help from the gods? **[Predict]**
5. What does this myth suggest about people's ability to escape or control fate? Explain. **[Draw Conclusions]**

EVALUATE

6. Considering the actions he takes against Danaë and Perseus, does Acrisius deserve his fate? Why or why not? **[Make a Judgment]**

EXTEND

7. (a) What situations from other works of literature, movies, or real life can you recall in which someone tried to escape or control fate? (b) What were the outcomes? **[Literary Link]**

◆ Reading Strategy

PREDICT

An adventure-filled story like "Perseus" keeps you wondering what will happen next. If you made a **prediction** chart while reading, you might refer to it now to help you answer these questions:

1. What factors would allow you to predict that Perseus will succeed in his quest to kill Medusa?
2. The oracle's prophecy to Acrisius could have had several outcomes. (a) Why is Acrisius' death a logical outcome? (b) What aspects of his death could not have been predicted?

◆ Literary Focus

HERO IN A MYTH

The central character of "Perseus" is a good example of a **hero in a myth**, a character with admirable personality traits who performs amazing feats with the aid of supernatural elements.

What admirable personality traits does Perseus possess?

◆ Build Vocabulary

USING THE WORD ROOT -mort-

Knowing that the root *-mort-* means "dead," write definitions for the following words:

1. immortality
2. mortician
3. mortally
4. immortalize
5. mortuary

USING THE WORD BANK

On your paper, write the word whose meaning is closest to that of the first word:

1. deity: (a) goodness, (b) god, (c) generosity
2. mortified: (a) cleansed, (b) stiff, (c) humiliated
3. revelry: (a) party, (b) awakening, (c) disagreement
4. despair: (a) hopelessness, (b) ruin, (c) sacrifice
5. reconciled: (a) guessed, (b) became friends again, (c) forgotten
6. wavering: (a) greeting, (b) stumbling, (c) flickering
7. kindred: (a) relatives, (b) childhood, (c) hostility

◆ Build Grammar Skills

POSSESSIVE NOUNS

The **possessive case** of nouns indicates kinship and ownership. Determine whether each possessive noun is singular or plural and follow the appropriate rule to form the possessive case.

Practice In your notebook, write the following sentences. Use the correct form from the choices given in the parentheses:

1. The (oracles', oracle's) prophecy frightened Acrisius.
2. Perseus stole the Gray (Women's, Womens') eye.
3. Then he went to the (Gorgon's, Gorgons') island.
4. Looking at Medusa turned the (warriors, warriors') bodies into stone.
5. Perseus depended on the help of two (gods, gods').

Writing Application Write two or three paragraphs in which you summarize the key events of the myth of Perseus. Include at least five examples of nouns in the possessive case.

Build Your Portfolio

 ## Idea Bank

Writing

1. **Review** Write a brief review of "Perseus" to appear on an Internet Home Page. Citing details from the story, tell why people would or would not want to read the myth.

2. **Feature Article** Write a newspaper feature article on the life of Perseus. Decide the slant of your article: Is Perseus a brave, noble hero or merely a foolish young man with the great luck to have two gods on his side?

3. **Modern-Day Myth** Invent a modern-day "monster" and write a myth about a contemporary hero who destroys it. Include powerful helpers who come to the hero's aid.

Speaking and Listening

4. **Comic Skit** With a group of classmates, plan and perform a skit dramatizing the scene in which Perseus gets the eye from the three Gray Women. **[Performing Arts Link]**

5. **Trial** Imagine that Acrisius does not die, but he is brought to trial for his treatment of Danaë and Perseus. As a prosecuting attorney, present an opening argument to a jury of your classmates, accusing the king of intent to commit murder. **[Social Studies Link]**

Projects

6. **Mask** Using the medium of your choice, create a Medusa mask. Let your imagination fly; the only requirement is that you somehow suggest the snakes of Medusa's hair. **[Art Link]**

7. **Map** Draw a map showing Perseus' travels from the time of his birth until the end of the story. Illustrate your map with the various gods and monsters he meets. **[Art Link; Social Studies Link]**

 ## Writing Mini-Lesson

Speech of Introduction

Imagine that you have been selected to deliver a speech introducing Perseus at a large public gathering to celebrate his achievements. Your speech will tell your audience something of Perseus' background and will go on to praise and describe his deeds. You will end by introducing the great man himself, who will then speak to the audience you have warmed up for him.

Writing Skills Focus: Appealing to Your Audience

Of all the forms of writing, speeches pay the most attention to the **audience.** The audience is right there, breathing along with the speaker, taking in his or her words—nodding, frowning, laughing, crying, cheering. A successful speech-writer consciously appeals to the audience in various ways—for example, by arousing people's emotions, amusing them, making them think, or holding their attention with a gripping story.

Prewriting List the important facts of Perseus' life—the belief that he is a son of Zeus, his being cast to sea by his cruel grandfather, his devotion to his mother, his victory over Medusa, and so on. Then look over the list to choose events and details that will appeal to your audience or excite their admiration for Perseus.

Drafting As you write your speech, draw on the information in your list to appeal to your audience. Organize the information in time order or group the details into categories by focusing on each of Perseus' character traits and citing details from his life that relate to each trait.

Revising Reread your draft. Have you used the most appealing material from Perseus' story? Have you used too many pieces of information—should your speech be shorter? Have you left out anything that could win over the audience?

Guide for Reading

Yusef Komunyakaa *(1947–)*

He won the 1994 Pulitzer Prize for poetry for his book *Neon Vernacular: New and Selected Poems.* He grew up in Bogalusa, Louisiana, and earned the Bronze Star in Vietnam, serving as reporter and editor of the military newspaper *The Southern Cross.* One of his eight books of poetry is entitled *Dien Cai Dau,* which is Vietnamese for "crazy." He now teaches at Indiana University.

These are facts about the life of Yusef Komunyakaa (yōō´ sef kō mən ya´ kä). What you really need to know about him to understand his poem "Slam, Dunk, & Hook" is that he likes "connecting the abstract to the concrete. There's tension in that. I believe the reader or listener should be able to enter the poem as a participant." That's what Komunyakaa does in "Slam, Dunk, & Hook," which is about basketball, but also about life on city streets.

Lillian Morrison *(1917–)*

Lillian Morrison has worked as a librarian and has written and compiled many books. She has published seven books of her own poetry, including *Whistling the Morning In.* She has put together several anthologies of poems about sports (including one revolving around basketball and entitled, coincidentally, *Slam Dunk*), along with collections of riddles, playground chants, and autograph sayings.

Naomi Shihab Nye *(1952–)*

Naomi Shihab Nye spent her teenage years in Jerusalem and has since worked as a visiting writer at several institutions, including the University of Texas. Her books of poems have received such awards as the Pushcart Prize and recognition by the American Library Association. She says, "For me poetry has always been a way of paying attention to the world. . . ."

◆ Build Vocabulary

SPECIALIZED VOCABULARY: JARGON

"Slam, Dunk, & Hook" and "The Spearthrower" use **jargon**, special vocabulary used in a particular occupation, sport, or other well-defined activity. For instance, the term *feint* in "Slam, Dunk, & Hook" refers to a pretended move meant to take an opponent off guard. The term is much older than basketball, for it originally came from swordplay. Look for other examples of sports jargon as you read these two poems.

WORD BANK

Before you read, preview this list of words from the poems.

metaphysical
jibed
feint
surge

◆ Build Grammar Skills

PREPOSITIONAL PHRASES

Prepositional phrases are groups of words beginning with prepositions and ending with nouns or pronouns. The introductory preposition is a word like *on, between,* or *from* that shows relationships; the noun or pronoun in the phrase is called the object of the preposition. In this example from "Slam, Dunk, & Hook," *on* is the preposition and *sneakers* is the object of the preposition:

> Fast breaks. Lay ups. With Mercury's
> Insignia *on our sneakers,*

Prepositional phrases act either as adjectives to describe nouns and pronouns or as adverbs to describe verbs, adjectives, and other adverbs.

Slam, Dunk, & Hook
The Spearthrower ◆ Shoulders

◆ *Literature and Your Life*

CONNECT YOUR EXPERIENCE

These poems are about the exhilaration of pure physical action trained on an important goal. As you read, experience the sensations described and imagine what it means to spend every ounce of your strength for something you want with all your heart.

THEMATIC FOCUS: PUTTING OURSELVES TO THE TEST

These poems show people meeting physical challenges in sports contests and in everyday life. Do you excel when you're striving for a definite goal—and therefore risking failure—or do you perform better when the pressure is off?

Journal Writing Write three sentences describing your impressions of an athletic contest you saw recently. Try to make your readers see what you saw and hear what you heard.

◆ Background for Understanding

SPORTS

The title "The Spearthrower" refers not to the athlete who actually hurls the javelin but rather to the poet who sends her "signed song" of praise for women athletes into the "bullying dark" of athletic events formerly dominated by men. In associating the poet with the athlete, Morrison follows a tradition from ancient Greece, where poets sang songs honoring Olympic athletics.

The title "Slam, Dunk, & Hook" refers to various moves made by basketball players. A *slam-dunk* is a powerful leap in which a player's hands rise above the basket and push the ball through. A *hook shot* is a curving toss from under and to the side of the basket.

◆ Literary Focus

THEME IN POETRY

The surface of each of these poems vividly describes physical action, but underneath that surface is a **theme,** an idea about life that sits at the center of the poem. If the lines, images, and rhythms in the poem are its body, then the theme is its heart, its driving force.

In poetry, as in other literature, theme can be hinted at sideways or stated directly. In "The Spearthrower" and "Shoulders," the themes are stated directly. On the other hand, in "Slam, Dunk, & Hook," the theme is implied; there seems to be much more than a game at stake.

◆ Reading Strategy

FORM MENTAL IMAGES

A poet writes words that make your mind's eye see pictures. **Forming mental images** of a poem means turning the poet's words into pictures by applying your own experiences.

For example, when you see Komunyakaa's basketball players "poised in midair" like "storybook sea monsters," will you picture fearsome dragons with great wings or just long necks and sleepy eyes lifting out of the ocean?

When you read "Shoulders," how might you picture someone "stepping gently"? In light, tiptoeing steps or in heavy, slow steps?

When you form mental images as you read a poem, what you see will be based on your own experiences and imaginings—your life, your reading, your viewing, your dreams. In this way you collaborate with the poet; you find your way into the poem's world, and the poem finds its way into yours.

Slam, Dunk, & Hook

Yusef Komunyakaa

Fast breaks. Lay ups. With Mercury's[1]
Insignia[2] on our sneakers,
We outmaneuvered the footwork
Of bad angels. Nothing but a hot
5 Swish of strings like silk
Ten feet out. In the roundhouse[3]
Labyrinth[4] our bodies
Created, we could almost
Last forever, poised in midair
10 Like storybook sea monsters.
A high note hung there
A long second. Off
The rim. We'd corkscrew
Up & dunk balls that exploded
15 The skullcap of hope & good
Intention. Bug-eyed, lanky,
All hands & feet . . . sprung rhythm.
We were metaphysical when girls
Cheered on the sidelines.
20 Tangled up in a falling,
Muscles were a bright motor
Double-flashing to the metal hoop
Nailed to our oak.
When Sonny Boy's mama died

---

1. **Mercury's:** Mercury was the
   Roman god of travel.
2. **insignia** (in sig´ nē ə) *n.:* Emblems or
   badges; logos.
3. **roundhouse** *n.:* Area on the court beneath
   the basket.
4. **labyrinth** (lab´ ə rinth) *n.:* Maze.

25 He played nonstop all day, so hard
Our backboard splintered.
Glistening with sweat, we jibed
& rolled the ball off our
Fingertips. Trouble
30 Was there slapping a blackjack
Against an open palm.
Dribble, drive to the inside, feint,
& glide like a sparrow hawk.
Lay ups. Fast breaks.
35 We had moves we didn't know
We had. Our bodies spun
On swivels of bone & faith,
Through a lyric slipknot
Of joy, & we knew we were
40 Beautiful & dangerous.

◆ Build Vocabulary

metaphysical (met′ ə fiz′ i kəl) *adj.*: Spiritual; beyond the physical

jibed (jībd) *v.*: Stopped short and turned from side to side

feint (fānt) *v.*: Pretended move to catch the opponent off guard

Night Games, Ernie Barnes, The Company of Art, Los Angeles

▲ **Critical Viewing** Relate details in this painting to lines in the poem "Slam, Dunk, & Hook." [Connect]

The Spearthrower

Lillian Morrison

She walks alone
to the edge of the park
and throws into
the bullying dark
5   her javelin
of light,
her singing sign
her signed song
that the runner may run
10 far and long

her quick laps
on the curving track,
that the sprinter surge
and the hurdler leap,
15 that the vaulter soar,
clear the highest bar,
and the discus fly
as the great crowds cry
to their heroines
20 Come on!

◆ **Build Vocabulary**

surge (sʉrj)   *v.*: Increase suddenly; speed up

◀ **Critical Viewing** Based on the
young woman's expression,
what might her feelings be at
this moment? **[Infer]**

Shoulders

Naomi Shihab Nye

A man crosses the street in rain,
stepping gently, looking two times north
   and south,
because his son is asleep on his shoulder.

No car must splash him.
5 No car drive too near to his shadow.

This man carries the world's most sensitive
   cargo
but he's not marked.
Nowhere does his jacket say FRAGILE,
HANDLE WITH CARE.

10 His ear fills up with breathing.
He hears the hum of the boy's dream
deep inside him.

We're not going to be able
to live in the world
15 if we're not willing to do what he's doing
with one another.

The road will only be wide.
The rain will never stop falling.

Guide for Responding

◆ Literature and Your Life

Reader's Response Which images in these poems were clearest to you? Why?

Thematic Focus Do the subjects of these poems succeed in meeting their challenges? Explain.

☑ Check Your Comprehension

1. In "Slam, Dunk, & Hook," what did the players outmaneuver, according to lines 3–4?
2. What did Sonny Boy do when his mother died?
3. In "The Spearthrower," what specific athletic events are mentioned?
4. What do the great crowds cry, and to whom?
5. In "Shoulders," where are the father and child?
6. What does the father take care to prevent?

◆ Critical Thinking

INTERPRET

1. In "Slam, Dunk, & Hook," what does playing basketball help the neighborhood boys to do? **[Infer]**
2. Why might the basketball players be both "beautiful" and "dangerous"? **[Explain]**
3. In "The Spearthrower," what "signed song" does the poet throw? **[Explain]**
4. In "Shoulders," what is the double meaning of the poem's title? (Hint: Think of where the father is walking.) **[Interpret]**

EVALUATE

5. How well does Yusef Komunyakaa capture the actual feel of a basketball game? **[Assess]**

EXTEND

6. What sort of music would you choose to accompany each of these poems? **[Music Link]**

Guide for Responding (continued)

◆ Reading Strategy

FORM MENTAL IMAGES

Now that your mind has provided pictures to match the poets' words, you may find the poems sticking with you in a new way. In "Slam, Dunk, & Hook," for example, you may have pictured a worn, yellow backboard breaking in half from the intense pounding of a boy who had just lost his mother.

1. Which image in "Slam, Dunk, & Hook" creates the most vivid picture in your mind?
2. What picture does the poet create of herself in the opening lines of "The Spearthrower"?
3. The final image of "Shoulders" is a road. Describe what you see in your own words.

◆ Build Vocabulary

USING SPORTS JARGON

Jargon is special vocabulary used in the context of an occupation, sport, or other well-defined activity. Writing that uses too much jargon can be almost impossible to understand. However, when used well—in a limited way and for a clear purpose—certain kinds of jargon can add a contemporary liveliness to writing.

1. (a) What do the following terms mean: "Dribble," "drive to the inside," "Fast breaks"? (b) What impression of basketball do these words create?
2. Find five terms specific to track-and-field competition in "The Spearthrower."

USING THE WORD BANK

On your paper, rewrite the following paragraph and fill in the blanks with words from the Word Bank.

As we sat in the bleachers, we saw the center _____?_____ left, then pass the ball to the right, confusing the player guarding her. The player who caught the ball then ____?____, looking for a teammate closer to the basket. The moment was almost _____?_____, as she found an opening that allowed her to ___?___ past the guard and make her shot. Two points!

◆ Literary Focus

THEME IN POETRY

A poem uses sensory images, figurative language, sound devices, even its title, to communicate a **theme,** or central idea about life. Sometimes the theme in a poem is a familiar insight; at other times, it's a new idea. At still other times, the theme is more a feeling brought to the reader's attention.

1. The speaker in "Slam, Dunk, & Hook" says "We outmaneuvered the footwork/Of bad angels." What does that line suggest about the role of basketball in the street life of the neighborhood kids?
2. How does the "spearthrower" (that is, the poet who sings of women athletes) enable the runner to run and the discus to fly?
3. What idea about life is Nye expressing when she talks about the road always being wide and the rain always falling?

◆ Build Grammar Skills

PREPOSITIONAL PHRASES

All three poets use prepositional phrases to add details and complexity to descriptions.

Practice Use two or more prepositional phrases to add details to each of the following sentences:

1. André shot the basketball.
2. The ball rose and then hit the backboard.
3. Mala heard the starting gun and surged forward.
4. She crossed the finish line.
5. Her speed impressed her opponents.
6. The mother carried her child.
7. She walked slowly.
8. People moved to let her pass.

> **Prepositional phrases** are groups of words beginning with a preposition and ending with a noun or pronoun.

Build Your Portfolio

 Idea Bank

Writing

1. **Poem** Write a poem about your favorite individual or team sport. Your poem should create a vivid picture of the sport, particularly the way the players move. **[Physical Education Link]**

2. **Description** Take the three sentences you wrote in your journal describing a sports event and turn them into two paragraphs describing that event more fully.

3. **Story** Write a short story explaining how the father in "Shoulders" ended up walking along the busy highway in the rain carrying his sleeping child. Write from the father's point of view.

Speaking and Listening

4. **Oral Interpretation** With several other students perform an oral reading of "Slam, Dunk, & Hook." Plan who will read which section or line of the poem. If possible, memorize the poem and include actions. **[Performing Arts Link]**

5. **Sportscast** Choose one of the track-and-field events in "The Spearthrower" and do a sportscast describing the contest from start to finish. **[Performing Arts Link; Career Link]**

Projects

6. **Painting/Drawing** In your favorite visual medium, recreate the scene described in "Shoulders." Try to make your work convey a strong feeling. **[Art Link]**

7. **Multimedia Presentation** Give a multimedia presentation focusing on some aspect of women's athletic competitions: for example, a biography of one outstanding athlete or an exciting current topic. Include photographs and/or drawings, recordings, and videotapes if feasible.

 Writing Mini-Lesson

Sports Editorial

Write an editorial–a brief piece of writing that presents one side of an issue on a sports-related topic. For example, you might focus on a question such as: Do you think women's sports should get more media coverage? Would you like to see your city build a new sports arena?

Writing Skills Focus: Anticipation of Questions

To make sure your editorial persuades as many readers as possible, try to **anticipate questions** from readers who might disagree with you. Take a hard look at your opinion, and imagine how opponents might question it. Then, answer these questions as well as you can. For example, in writing an editorial arguing for increased funding of the school district's sports programs, you might anticipate such questions as: "Why should sports programs be funded when arts programs are cut back?" An answer might be: "Neither should be cut back. The district should propose a bond issue to raise money for its needs."

Prewriting Choose a sports-related issue and take a position. Then jot down questions and opposing viewpoints.

Drafting Write your editorial by stating the issue clearly and expressing your opinion reasonably. (Often, an editorial writer refers to himself or herself as "this writer.") Work in the questions you anticipated—and your answers.

Revising Show your editorial to several people. Try to find at least one reader who disagrees with you. Ask if your opinion sounds fair and if you have answered all objections effectively. If you hear a point that you should have raised, add it to your editorial.

Persuasive Essay

Writing Process Workshop

As the literature in this section reveals, writing can challenge us to look at things in new ways. One type of writing that can change the way we think is the **persuasive essay**. A persuasive essay is a short piece of writing that attempts to convince an audience to think or act in a certain way.

Develop a persuasive essay in which you convince readers to accept your position on an issue about which you care. The following skills, introduced in this section's Writing Mini-Lessons, will help you develop your persuasive essay.

Writing Skills Focus

▶ **Make effective use of figurative language**—language that means more than it says literally. (See p. 173.)

▶ **Appeal to your audience** by stirring their emotions, making them laugh, making them think, or keeping them in suspense. (See p. 195.)

▶ **Anticipate readers' questions.** Think about questions or objections that people may have to your arguments and try to address them. (See p. 203.)

▶ **Use a persuasive tone** in your writing in order to make people want to read on and to convince them to accept your point of view. (See p. 183.)

Maya Angelou uses all these skills as she argues for an individual's right to make his or her own choices in life.

MODEL FROM LITERATURE

from "New Directions" by Maya Angelou

① Angelou effectively uses the figurative image of a road to mean life.

② Words like *ominous* and *unpromising* appeal to readers' emotions.

③ Angelou persuades readers to "step off that road."

④ Angelou answers a question readers may ask: What if our new choice is also bad?

Each of us has the right and the responsibility to assess the roads which lie ahead, and those over which we have traveled, ① and if the future road looms ominous or unpromising, and the roads back uninviting, ② then we need to gather our resolve and, carrying only the necessary baggage, step off that road into another direction. ③ If the new choice is also unpalatable, without embarrassment, we must be ready to change that as well. ④

Prewriting

Choose a Topic Think of issues that are important to you. If nothing springs to mind, you may want to browse through magazines and newspapers to help spark ideas. Another option is to choose one of the following topics.

```
┌─────────────────────────────────────────────┐
│              Topic Ideas                      │
│  ■ Students should wear school uniforms.      │
│  ■ The country needs a female president.      │
│  ■ Paying taxes should be voluntary.          │
│  ■ Colleges should accept all applicants.     │
└─────────────────────────────────────────────┘
```

Anticipate Readers' Questions Once you've chosen your topic, decide on the position that you will present in your essay. Then list potential objections and questions about that position. For example, if your essay presents an argument in favor of all schools having computers, you might list these questions:

Sample Questions
 ▶ Who will pay for the computers?
 ▶ What if classrooms aren't big enough?
 ▶ What if all teachers can't teach the use of computers?

Gather Strong Evidence Using the questions and objections you listed as a starting point, gather evidence—facts, statistics, and reasons—to support your argument. This may require research, either in the library or on the Internet.

Plan Your Use of Figurative Language List examples of figurative language you might use in your essay. For example, you may come up with objects and events to compare to aspects of your topic. Look over the ideas you come up with, and evaluate the effectiveness of each one. Check off the examples that work best.

Example:
A computer is
 ▶ a ticket to the train ride of success
 ▶ a key to opening future's door
 ▶ like air that we need to breathe

Drafting

Appeal to Your Audience As you write, always keep your readers in mind. Use formal, respectful language, and address each concern you think your readers may have.

APPLYING LANGUAGE SKILLS: Avoiding Double Comparisons

A **double comparison** occurs when *more* and *-er* or *most* and *-est* are used with the same modifier.

Incorrect:
Computers are more better than typewriters.

Correct:
Computers are better than typewriters.

Practice Rewrite each sentence to avoid a double comparison.

1. Schools are the most best places for computers.
2. Work can be done more faster on a computer.
3. Students who use computers are more better prepared for future careers

Writing Application As you draft your persuasive essay, avoid using double comparisons.

Writer's Solution Connection
Language Lab

For additional instruction and practice in avoiding double comparisons, complete the Language Lab lesson on Forms of Comparisons.

APPLYING LANGUAGE SKILLS: Avoiding Faulty Logic

Never use poor reasoning in your arguments. For example, avoid making overgeneralizations—broad statements for which there are exceptions—and presenting questionable cause-and-effect sequences when one event is not clearly caused by another.

Practice Explain why each item is or is not an example of faulty logic.

1. People who don't have computers become failures for life.

2. In a few years, everyone will have a computer.

3. Computers make you smart.

Writing Application Review the arguments in your persuasive essay. Remove any faulty logic you find.

Writer's Solution Connection Writing Lab

To help you complete all stages of writing your persuasive essay, use the instruction and activities in the Tutorial on Persuasion.

Present Strong Support for Your Argument Use the evidence you've gathered to support each point you make. Your argument is only as strong as the support you offer.

Use a Persuasive Tone Carefully choose your words and phrases to make readers eager to agree with your views. When discussing computers, for example, you might mention the "lightning speed" and the "amazing accuracy" of the machines.

Revising

Hold a Peer Conference Share your draft with a classmate and get some feedback. Use the comments as guidelines for revising your essay. Ask your peer these questions:

▶ How effective is my figurative language?
▶ Have I anticipated all my readers' questions?
▶ How well have I appealed to my audience?
▶ How persuasive is the tone in my writing?

REVISION MODEL

① *one of the keys to the future*
Computers are very ~~important~~. They make it possible for ② *easy*

people all over the globe to communicate with one another in

③ *Not everyone has computer access today, but in just a few years virtually everyone will.*
an instant. People who haven't developed computer skills

④ *If you're one of those people, I urge you to turn on a computer and start developing your skills.*
will fall behind.

① The writer adds a figure of speech (figurative language) to capture the importance of computers.
② A simple change of wording makes this sentence even more persuasive.
③ The writer adds a sentence to address a possible objection.
④ The writer directly addresses a segment of his audience.

Publishing

▶ **Classroom** Invite classmates to read your persuasive essay. Encourage them to share their opinions.
▶ **Newspaper** Send your essay to your school or local newspaper as a Letter to the Editor.
▶ **Internet** Post your essay on a bulletin board or class Web site. See what responses you receive.

Real-World Reading Skills Workshop

Strategies for Success

A famous humorist once said, "All I know is what I read in the papers." The person really meant that you shouldn't believe something simply because it's in print. You have to challenge the text and decide whether or not the writer's statements are reliable.

Separate Facts From Opinions

Whenever you read a statement, first decide whether it is a provable fact or just a personal opinion. You can check a fact with a reliable source such as an encyclopedia or textbook. A personal opinion, on the other hand, only reflects someone's likes and dislikes, which can't be proved right or wrong. However, in an effective piece of writing, the writer will back up his or her opinions with facts. When you come across a writer's opinions, check to see whether they're supported by facts.

Consider the Writer's Background

Another consideration to keep in mind when evaluating a writer's opinions is the writer's background or level of expertise on the subject he or she is addressing. Ask yourself: What education or experience does the writer have that is related to the topic? What does the author gain if I accept the opinion?

Look for Faulty Reasoning

Another thing to look out for is writing that lacks logic. For example, a writer might ask you to believe something simply because everyone else does. Or an author may jump to conclusions without offering enough evidence. Whenever you read a statement, ask yourself, Does this make sense to me?

BILLY NEDER FOR CLASS PRESIDENT!!

Why should <u>you</u> vote for Billy Neder?

- He's a capable person who really understands what students need!

- He's had experience as class president three years in a row.

- He's good at math. So he'd make a great school leader!

- His father is our town mayor. Mayor Neder says, "Billy is your best candidate."

Apply the Strategy

Read the poster carefully. Then complete each item below.

1. Find an example of a provable fact. How could you go about proving it?
2. Find an example of a personal opinion. Is it a statement that you would challenge? Why?
3. Find an example of an expert opinion. How reliable do you feel it is? Why?
4. Find an example of faulty reasoning. Why doesn't the statement make sense?

✔ Here are other situations in which challenging the text is important:
- ▶ Reading a newspaper editorial
- ▶ Reading a scientific report
- ▶ Reading a government proposal

Speaking and Listening Workshop

How easily can you be persuaded to do something? Some people can be persuaded without much effort. But as a responsible listener, you should resist easy persuasion. You should evaluate *what* is said, not *how* it is said.

Listen for Loaded Language Loaded language can play on your emotions and trigger a response in you. For example:

"Don't be a <u>baby</u>! All the <u>really cool kids</u> are trying out for the team."

Ignore Empty Promises Listen carefully to the way certain statements are worded. You may find that certain words and phrases can trick you into believing things that aren't really true. For example:

"These sneakers are like having a new pair of feet! They <u>can</u> make you a fast runner! They're <u>something else</u>!"

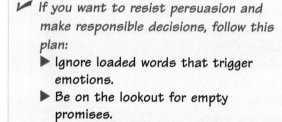

Tips for Resisting Persuasion

☑ *If you want to resist persuasion and make responsible decisions, follow this plan:*
  ▶ Ignore loaded words that trigger emotions.
  ▶ Be on the lookout for empty promises.
  ▶ Ask yourself, What is *really* being said?

Apply the Strategies

With a partner, role-play these situations. Work out a conversation that shows your attempts to resist persuasion.

1. A salesperson tries to persuade you to buy the most expensive sunglasses in the store. How does the salesperson use loaded words and make empty promises? What do you say to resist the persuasion?

2. A friend wants you to sign a petition supporting a cause with which you don't agree. What arguments does the friend give? What empty promises and loaded words are used? How do you answer?

Extended Reading Opportunities

The challenges that life brings and the choices we make in meeting those challenges have been the basis for many works of literature. Following are a few possibilities through which you can further explore challenges and choices.

Suggested Titles

The Old Man and the Sea
Ernest Hemingway

This novel tells of a man's heroic struggle with nature. The battle begins when the old fisherman Santiago hooks a giant marlin after going months without a catch. The old man puts up a fierce effort to conquer the huge and powerful fish, fighting exhaustion, hunger, injury, and even a pack of sharks. This story, told in Hemingway's lean, straightforward style, is a timeless tale of courage and adventure.

The Miracle Worker
William Gibson

This moving play is based on the true story of Helen Keller, who was left blind, deaf, and unable to speak following an illness when she was an infant. The title refers to Helen's teacher, Annie Sullivan, a young woman determined to meet the challenge of helping Helen to communicate. This play, Gibson's most famous, inspired an Academy Award-winning movie.

Rosa Parks: My Story
Rosa Parks with Jim Haskins

One of the pivotal moments of the American civil rights movement occurred on December 1, 1955, when Rosa Parks, an African American, chose not to give up her seat to a white rider on a bus in Montgomery, Alabama. Through this memoir, readers get a first-hand account of that dramatic event and its aftermath, as well as biographical information about one of the leaders of the civil rights movement.

Other Possibilities

Of Mice and Men	John Steinbeck
Lyddie	Katherine Paterson
Zlata's Diary: A Child's Life in Sarajevo	Zlata Filipovic
River Thunder	Will Hobbs

Thunderhead, 1933, Frederick Phillips, Atlas Galleries, Chicago, Illinois

Moments of Discovery

Any insight can be a moment of discovery—children learning about nature, a woman musing on past generations, a man realizing that certain human qualities go beyond culture. Whether big or small, the moments of discovery in these selections teach people something about themselves, others, and the world around them.

rederick Phillips '93

Guide for Reading

Barry Lopez (1945–)

If you have the slightest interest in nature, you're sure to be moved by the poetic nonfiction of Barry Lopez.

In his work, Lopez speaks for those that cannot speak for themselves—Santa Ana winds, wolves, herons, cottonwood trees, the majestic and forbidding Arctic.

Lopez has said, "I like to use the word *isumatug*. It's of eastern Arctic Eskimo dialect and refers to the storyteller, meaning 'the person who creates the atmosphere in which wisdom reveals itself.'" This notion of creating the right conditions so that others can discover the natural world for themselves is reflected in "Children in the Woods."

A Traveling Man Barry Lopez lived in a number of places when he was growing up. He was born in Port Chester, New York, but in 1948, his family moved to a suburb of Los Angeles. In 1955, his mother remarried, and her new husband adopted her sons and gave them his name. The following year, the family moved back to New York. Lopez spent three months traveling in Europe after he graduated from high school, then attended Notre Dame University in Indiana. By the time he graduated in 1966, he had traveled to every state except Hawaii, Alaska, and Oklahoma.

"Children in the Woods" is set in the Cascade Mountain forest that surrounds the house where Lopez and his wife have lived for more than twenty-five years. However, living in the same place has not prevented Lopez from exploring the world. He has journeyed to Alaska, the Galapagos Islands, Australia, Africa, the Antarctic, and the Arctic.

He observes: "Someone once asked me: 'What kind of writer are you?' and I said: 'I am a writer who travels. Some writers stay at home or inside a room. I am a writer who travels.'"

◆ Build Vocabulary

PREFIXES: *extra-*

In this essay, the author describes how he helped two children *extrapolate*, or draw conclusions, from a piece of bone they found. The word *extrapolate* contains the prefix *extra-*, which means "outside." When you extrapolate, you put facts and observations together to reach a conclusion that is outside the information you had when you first started.

WORD BANK

As you read "Children in the Woods," you will encounter the words on this list. Each word is defined on the page where it first appears. Preview the list before you read.

charged
acutely
elucidate
extrapolation
detritus
effervesce
myriad
insidious
ineffable

◆ Build Grammar Skills

FORMS OF ADJECTIVES

Most adjectives have a **basic**, or **positive**, form; a **comparative form** for comparing two items; and a **superlative form** for comparing more than two items. Almost all one-syllable adjectives and some two-syllable adjectives use *-er* to form the comparative and *-est* to form the superlative. Other adjectives use the words *more* and *most*, respectively, for the comparative and superlative forms. A few adjectives—*good, bad, little,* and *far,* for example—have irregular comparative and superlative forms.

This passage from the essay shows the use of two superlative adjectives:

The *quickest* door to open in the woods for a child is the one that leads to the *smallest* room ...

Children in the Woods

◆ *Literature and Your Life*

CONNECT YOUR EXPERIENCE

Some of your clearest ideas about how the world works may have come from observations and discoveries you made as a child. Mixing red and yellow paint to get orange, for example, might have shown you how colors are formed. In "Children in the Woods," Barry Lopez shares his thoughts on how to help children make the discoveries that enable them to understand their world.

THEMATIC FOCUS: MOMENTS OF DISCOVERY

Sometimes, without even trying, we stumble upon an experience that shows us how different aspects of the natural world all fit together. In this selection, children share such a moment of discovery while exploring in the woods.

Journal Writing In your journal, write about a time that a teacher, coach, or relative helped you discover something new about the world around you. How can you draw upon this experience to help young children learn for themselves about the world?

◆ Literary Focus

CENTRAL IDEA AND SUPPORT

Every essay has a **central idea**—a main point that the writer wants to make. In order to make this point, the writer uses **support**—ideas, facts, and details that back up the main idea. In this essay, Barry Lopez wants to make a point about the ways in which children learn about the natural world. As you read, look for the central idea and identify its support.

◆ Background for Understanding

SCIENCE

At one time, the emphasis in science was to describe the natural world as thoroughly as possible. During the early nineteenth century, descriptive science reached the height of its popularity. An educated man or woman was able to rattle off the names of dozens of different types of plants, animals, and rocks. Collecting and cataloging objects—birds' eggs, shells, butterflies, beetles, and orchids, to name a few—was a popular hobby.

Today, scientists still need to know the names of living things, but theories and explanations are now stressed in science. As Barry Lopez points out in his essay, names are not necessarily the best way for many of us to discover and appreciate the natural world.

Reading for Success

Strategies for Constructing Meaning

In order to understand a piece of writing fully, you must do more than simply comprehend the writer's words. You have to go a step further and put the words and ideas together in your own mind, so that they have meaning for you. Constructing meaning is particularly important when you are reading any kind of nonfiction—from short essays to lengthy textbooks. Use these strategies to help you construct meaning:

Make inferences.

Writers don't always tell you everything directly. You have to make inferences to arrive at ideas that writers suggest but don't say. You make an inference by considering the details that the writer includes or doesn't include. Think about what this choice of details tells you about the author's values or purpose in writing. Sometimes it's also helpful to "read between the lines." This means looking beyond the literal meaning of the words to obtain a full picture of what the author means.

Draw conclusions.

A conclusion is a general statement that you can make and explain by reasons, or support with details from the text. Making a series of inferences can lead you to draw a conclusion.

Interpret what you read.

Interpreting what you read, or explaining it in your own words, will help make the information your own. When you interpret, you also explain the importance of what the author is saying.

Identify relationships.

To fully understand the information presented to you, you need to examine the relationships between ideas and events. Writers might show these relationships among ideas in a text: sequence, or when events happen relative to one another; greater or lesser importance; and cause and effect.

Compare and contrast.

Compare and contrast ideas in the work with other ideas in the same work, or with ideas that are already familiar to you. For example, you might look for ways in which an experience described in an essay is similar to something you've done, or different from anything you've experienced or heard of.

As you read the following essay by Barry Lopez, look at the notes along the sides. These notes demonstrate how to apply these strategies to a work of literature.

Children in the Woods

Barry Lopez

When I was a child growing up in the San Fernando Valley in California, a trip into Los Angeles was special. The sensation of movement from a rural area into an urban one was sharp. On one of these charged occasions, walking down a sidewalk with my mother, I stopped suddenly, caught by a pattern of sunlight trapped in a spiraling imperfection in a windowpane. A stranger, an elderly woman in a cloth coat and a dark hat, spoke out spontaneously, saying how remarkable it is that children notice these things.

> **Compare and contrast** this experience with a similar one from your own childhood.

I have never forgotten the texture of this incident. Whenever I recall it I am moved not so much by any sense of my young self but by a sense of responsibility toward children, knowing

◀ **Critical Viewing** How might a child's discoveries during a walk in the woods be different from those of an adult? [Compare and Contrast]

◆ **Build Vocabulary**

charged (chärjd) *adj*.: Tensely expectant; intense

how <u>acutely</u> I was affected in that moment by that woman's words. The effect, for all I know, has lasted a lifetime.

Now, years later, I live in a rain forest in western Oregon, on the banks of a mountain river in relatively undisturbed country, surrounded by 150-foot-tall Douglas firs,[1] delicate deer-head orchids, and clearings where wild berries grow. White-footed mice and mule deer, mink and coyote move through here. My wife and I do not have children, but children we know, or children whose parents we are close to, are often here. They always want to go into the woods. And I wonder what to tell them.

In the beginning, years ago, I think I said too much. I spoke with an encyclopedic knowledge of the names of plants or the names of birds passing through in season. Gradually I came to say less. After a while the only words I spoke, beyond answering a question or calling attention quickly to the slight difference between a sprig of red cedar and a sprig of incense cedar,[2] were to <u>elucidate</u> single objects.

I remember once finding a fragment of a raccoon's jaw in an alder thicket. I sat down alongside the two children with me and encouraged them to find out who this was—with only the three teeth still intact in a piece of the animal's maxilla[3] to guide them. The teeth told by their shape and placement what this animal ate. By a kind of visual <u>extrapolation</u> its size became clear. There were other clues, immediately present, which told, with what I could add of climate and terrain, how this animal lived, how its broken jaw came to be lying here. Raccoon, they surmised. And tiny tooth marks along the bone's broken edge told of a mouse's hunger for calcium.

---

3. **maxilla** (mak sil´ ə) *n*.: Upper jaw.

▲ **Critical Viewing** Do you agree with the author that discoveries children make in nature can help them understand the world around them? **[Assess]**

◆ **Build Vocabulary**

acutely (ə kyo͞ot´ lē) *adv*.: Sharply

elucidate (i lo͞o´ sə dāt´) *v*.: Explain

extrapolation (ik strap´ ə lā´ shən) *n*.: Conclusions drawn by speculation on the basis of facts

---

1. **Douglas firs:** Tall evergreen trees of the pine family.
2. **sprig of red cedar . . . incense cedar:** Twigs from two types of trees of the pine family.

We set the jaw back and went on.

If I had known more about raccoons, finer points of osteology,[4] we might have guessed more: say, whether it was male or female. But what we deduced was all we needed. Hours later, the maxilla, lost behind us in the <u>detritus</u> of the forest floor, continued to <u>effervesce</u>. It was tied faintly to all else we spoke of that afternoon.

In speaking with children who might one day take a permanent interest in natural history—as writers, as scientists, as filmmakers, as anthropologists[5]—I have sensed that an extrapolation from a single fragment of the whole is the most invigorating experience I can share with them. I think children know that nearly anyone can learn the names of things; the impression made on them at this level is fleeting. What takes a lifetime to learn, they comprehend, is the existence and substance of <u>myriad</u> relationships: it is these relationships, not the things themselves, that ultimately hold the human imagination.

The brightest children, it has often struck me, are fascinated by metaphor—with what is shown in the set of relationships bearing on the raccoon, for example, to lie quite beyond the raccoon. In the end, you are trying to make clear to them that everything found at the edge of one's senses—the high note of the winter wren, the thick perfume of propo-lis that drifts downwind from spring willows, the brightness of wood chips scattered by beaver—that all this fits together. The indestructibility of these associations conveys a sense of permanence that nurtures the heart, that cripples one of the most <u>insidious</u> of human anxieties, the one that says, you do not belong here, you are unnecessary.

From this passage, you can **infer** that the author is concerned about people's relationships with nature.

Whenever I walk with a child, I think how much I have seen disappear in my own life. What will there be for this person when he is my age? If he senses something <u>ineffable</u> in the landscape, will I know enough to encourage it?—to somehow show him that, yes, when people talk about violent death, spiritual exhilaration, compassion, futility, final causes, they are drawing on forty thousand years of human meditation on *this*—as we embrace Douglas firs, or stand by a river across whose undulating back we skip stones, or dig out a camas bulb,[6] biting down into a taste so much wilder than last night's potatoes.

You might **interpret** this paragraph as: I want children to know that interaction with nature is at the core of much of human philosophy.

The most moving look I ever saw from a child in the woods was on a

---

4. **osteology** (äs´ tē äl´ ə jē) *n.*: Study of the structure and function of bones.
5. **anthropologists** (an´ thrə päl´ ə jists) *n.*: Specialists in the study of mankind, especially the cultures of mankind.

6. **camas** (kam´ əs) **bulbs:** Underground buds of a sweet and edible American plant.

◆ **Build Vocabulary**

detritus (di trīt´ əs) *n.*: Debris

effervesce (ef´ ər ves´) *v.*: To be lively

myriad (mir´ ē əd) *adj.*: Countless; innumerable

insidious (in sid´ ē əs) *adj.*: Treacherous in a sly, tricky way

ineffable (in ef´ ə bəl) *adj.*: Too overwhelming to be expressed in words

mud bar by the footprints of a heron.[7] We were on our knees, making handprints beside the footprints. You could feel the creek vibrating in the silt and sand. The sun beat down heavily on our hair. Our shoes were soaking wet. The look said: I did not know until now that I needed someone much older to confirm this, the feeling I have of life here. I can now grow older, knowing it need never be lost.

The quickest door to open in the woods for a child is the one that leads to the smallest room, by knowing the name each thing is called. The door that leads to the cathedral is marked by a hesitancy to speak at all, rather to encourage by example a sharpness of the senses. If one speaks it should only be to say, as well as one can, how wonderfully all this fits together, to indicate what a long, fierce peace can derive from this knowledge.

> By thinking about the author's experience with the activities that spark children's interest in nature, you might also **conclude** that it is better to emphasize discovery than to know the names of things.

---

7. **heron** (her´ ən): Wading bird with a long neck, long legs, and a long, tapered bill.

Beyond Literature

Career Connection

Careers in Nature Because the natural world provides so many opportunities for discovery, it's no wonder that many people choose careers that are linked to nature.

For example, zoologists study animals. Types of zoologists include ornithologists, who study birds; entomologists, who study insects; and ichthyologists, who study fish. Botanists study plants. Workers in related fields include foresters, who help manage forest resources, and agronomists, who work to increase crop production. Geologists study rocks, soils, and mountains. Meterologists study the atmosphere to understand changes in weather and climate. The list goes on and on, because careers in nature are almost as varied as nature itself.

ACTIVITY Use a reference book to find information about a specific career in nature. Jot down aspects of the career that appeal to you.

Guide for Responding

◆ Literature and Your Life

Reader's Response Would you like to explore the woods, beaches, or parks near your home with someone like Barry Lopez? Explain.

Thematic Focus How does "Children in the Woods" illustrate moments of discovery?

Journal Entry Describe a situation—real or imagined—where you helped another person discover something about the natural world.

☑ Check Your Comprehension

1. What happened to the author as a child in Los Angeles?
2. Where does the author live?
3. List three of the activities that took place on walks in the woods.
4. What, according to the author, is more important for children to know about nature than the names of plants and animals?

Guide for Responding (continued)

◆ Critical Thinking

INTERPRET
1. Why is the author concerned about what he tells children? **[Interpret]**
2. Why did the author change the way he told children about nature? **[Draw Conclusions]**
3. Why does the author use the method he does to teach children about nature? **[Infer]**
4. What do children gain from an understanding of relationships in nature? **[Analyze]**

APPLY
5. How could you apply Barry Lopez's ideas to teach art to children? **[Apply]**

EXTEND
6. How might an understanding of the relationships among the parts of a whole be useful in the following careers: auto mechanic, businessperson, wheat farmer, doctor? **[Career Link]**

◆ Reading for Success

STRATEGIES FOR CONSTRUCTING MEANING
Review the reading strategies and the notes showing how to construct meaning from what you read. Then apply the strategies to do the following:
1. For the paragraph that starts "In the beginning" on p. 216, compare and contrast the way Lopez dealt with children in the past with the way he deals with them now.
2. Explain how the children's inference about the raccoon bone is based on details they observed.
3. Draw inferences about the author's character from the paragraph beginning on p. 217 that starts: "The most moving look I ever saw. . . ."

◆ Literary Focus

CENTRAL IDEA AND SUPPORT
The **central idea** of this essay is the main point that Barry Lopez wants to convey.
1. State the central idea of "Children in the Woods" in your own words.
2. List three supports from the essay and explain how they illustrate the central idea.

◆ Build Vocabulary

USING THE PREFIX *extra-*
Use the meaning of the prefix *extra-* to explain the meaning of the following terms:
1. extraterrestrial (*terra* means "earth")
2. extraordinary

USING THE WORD BANK
On your paper, write the word from the Word Bank that answers each question.
1. What does a carbonated drink do when you open the can?
2. If you didn't understand a point someone made, what might you ask him or her to do?
3. What do scientists get when they use facts to help them draw conclusions?
4. What is the atmosphere at an awards ceremony a few seconds before the winner is announced?
5. What would you find scattered around a junkyard?
6. How might someone experience a bad headache?
7. How might you describe a disease that is deadly but very hard to detect?
8. How many stars are in the sky?
9. How could you describe a feeling so strong you can't put it into words?

◆ Build Grammar Skills

FORMS OF ADJECTIVES
Different **forms of an adjective** are used to describe one (positive), two (comparative), or more than two (superlative) things.

Practice On your paper, write the comparative and superlative forms of the following adjectives:
1. happy   2. exciting   3. tricky

Writing Application Write the following paragraph, filling each blank with the correct form of the listed adjective:

My cat has ___?___ (long) whiskers. In fact, she has the ___?___ (long) whiskers I've ever seen. She is ___?___ (outgoing) than most cats and is even ___?___ (friendly) than many dogs. I think she is the ___?___ (good) cat in the world.

Build Your Portfolio

 ## Idea Bank

Writing

1. **Poem** Write a poem about an important discovery about nature.

2. **Dialogue** Write a realistic dialogue between a curious child and a parent or teacher. In the dialogue, show how the adult guides the child to find an answer.

3. **Persuasive Essay** Drawing on Barry Lopez's ideas and your own, write a persuasive essay about teaching children about nature. You may choose to support techniques and ideas that are similar to Lopez's, or you might take a different approach.

Speaking and Listening

4. **Teaching Children** Select a topic that you are good at and that interests you. Keeping Barry Lopez's ideas in mind, decide how to teach young children about your topic. When you have finished preparing, teach your lesson to a child or small group of children. **[Career Link]**

5. **Dramatization** With a small group, dramatize one of the scenes from the essay. Add details and dialogue to help bring the scene to life.

Projects

6. **Relationship Map** Prepare a graphic organizer that shows the relationships among the living things that inhabit a nearby wood, park, or vacant lot. Embellish your graphic organizer with drawings or photographs. **[Science Link]**

7. **Rain-Forest Presentation** The woods that Barry Lopez describes are part of a temperate rain forest. Prepare a presentation on temperate rain forests. Include a world map that shows where temperate rain forests are located.
[Science Link]

 ## Writing Mini-Lesson

Field Guide

In "Children in the Woods," Barry Lopez vividly describes the woods around his home. You can also teach people about the wildlife you see each day by creating a field guide that focuses on five living things in or near your home. A field guide provides detailed descriptions of and information about particular types of wildlife or wildlife specific to a region.

Writing Skills Focus: Specific Examples

To help readers perceive important details, your field guide needs **specific examples.** A specific example, such as "a two-inch long gray centipede" is more useful and vivid than a vague example like "a bug." Notice how Lopez uses specific examples in this excerpt.

Model From the Essay

Now, years later, I live in a rain forest in western Oregon . . . surrounded by 150-foot-tall *Douglas firs*, delicate *deerhead orchids*, and clearings where wild berries grow. *White-footed mice* and *mule deer*, *mink* and *coyote* move through here.

Prewriting Brainstorm for a list of animals that live near your home. From your list, select the subjects for your field guide. Gather information about each animal.

Drafting Provide specific examples that show what the animals look like and how they behave. For example, if you are describing the feeding habits of rabbits, tell exactly which plants they eat.

Revising Have a classmate read your field guide and list questions that are left unanswered. Use the question to guide your revisions.

PART 1 *Finding Our Identity*

My Judy, Mabel Martin Davidson

Guide for Reading

Amy Tan (1952–   )

Like Waverly, the nine-year-old chess champion in this story, Amy Tan was something of a child prodigy, displaying literary promise at the ripe age of eight. Born in Oakland, California, she grew up in the San Francisco Bay area, the setting of her acclaimed first novel, *The Joy Luck Club*, from which "Rules of the Game" comes.

> *Tan has said that writing the novel helped her discover "how very Chinese" she was.*

A Chinese American Writer As a young woman, Tan supported herself as a technical writer, and she played the piano and wrote fiction for relaxation. Through writing, she discovered her own ethnic identity. Tan has said in interviews that she had tried to minimize her ethnicity when she was younger. All that changed when she began to write about the rich but painful intersection of two cultures in Chinese American women.

Cultural Tug of War In 1985, Tan wrote "Rules of the Game," which she later included in *The Joy Luck Club*, a novel that weaves together the stories of four Chinese mothers and their American-born daughters. *The Joy Luck Club* was made into a popular film, with Tan collaborating on the screenplay. Tan's later novels include *The Kitchen God's Wife* (1991) and *The Hundred Secret Senses* (1995).

◆ Build Vocabulary

WORD ORIGINS: WORDS FROM FRENCH

In this story the words *etiquette* ("proper behavior"), *souvenirs* ("reminders"), and *tournament* ("contest") all come from French. Many chess terms, as well, come from French. *Checkmate* is a French derivative of the Persian phrase *shah mat*, which means, literally, "The king is dead." *Pawn*, which refers to the lowliest chesspiece, comes from the French word *pion*, meaning "assistant." As you read "Rules of the Game," look for other words that might have come from French.

WORD BANK

Before you read, preview this list of words from the story.

pungent
benevolently
retort
prodigy
malodorous
concessions

◆ Build Grammar Skills

COMPLEX SENTENCES

To describe a tense relationship between two strong people, Amy Tan begins "Rules of the Game" with a complex sentence:

> I was six when my mother taught me the art of invisible strength.

A **complex sentence** is made up of one independent clause, which can stand by itself as a complete sentence (*I was six ...*), and at least one subordinate clause, which cannot stand by itself as a sentence (*... when my mother taught me the art of invisible strength*).

As you read "Rules of the Game," notice Amy Tan's use of complex sentences to show the highly charged tug of war between a mother and daughter.

Rules of the Game

◆ *Literature and Your Life*

CONNECT YOUR EXPERIENCE

In "Rules of the Game," a generational tug of war is complicated by a conflict between Chinese and American cultures. No matter what your cultural background, however, the battle of wills that takes place in this selection should be familiar to you.

THEMATIC FOCUS: FINDING OUR IDENTITY

In this story you get one point of view—that of the child seeking independence—but there is another side as well. How would you feel if you were a parent watching your child reject the values you have lived by?

Journal Writing In your journal, examine a cultural or generational conflict you know about.

◆ Background for Understanding

CULTURE

Chess, which plays a central role in Tan's story, is believed to have evolved from a game first played in India in the sixth century. It was known as *chaturanga,* a name that referred to the four divisions of an army of the period: elephants, horses, chariots, and foot soldiers. The game spread to Persia (the present Iran), and after conquering Persia in the seventh century, Arab invaders introduced chess to other lands around the Mediterranean Sea. During the Middle Ages, games of chess became part of courtship rituals between knights and ladies. Today, chess is played by people of all ages and cultural backgrounds around the world.

◆ Literary Focus

GENERATIONAL CONFLICT

Generational conflict exists when beliefs and values change from one generation to another. The "generation gap" becomes even wider, however, when parents have a cultural background that is different from the one in which they are raising their children. In "Rules of the Game," a Chinese mother and her American-born daughter, Waverly, are locked in a battle of wills.

◆ Reading Strategy

CONTRAST CHARACTERS

The first sentence of this story sets up the battle of wills that the story plays out. On one side, there is American-born Waverly, a young girl; on the other, her Chinese mother. Throughout the story, you will see these two characters engaged in conflict, with high stakes for each. In order to follow the story, you need to understand the way the writer is contrasting these two adversaries.

To fully explore the contrast between Waverly and Mrs. Jong, it may help you to develop a chart like the one shown. Use it to keep track of each character's traits, needs, and principal actions.

	Waverly	**Mrs. Jong**
Background	Born in the U.S.	Born in China
Significant Actions		
Significant Statements		
Personality Traits		
Hopes		

Rules
of the
Game

from
The Joy Luck Club
Amy Tan

I was six when my mother taught me the art of invisible strength. It was a strategy for winning arguments, respect from others, and eventually, though neither of us knew it at the time, chess games.

"Bite back your tongue," scolded my mother when I cried loudly, yanking her hand toward the store that sold bags of salted plums. At home, she said, "Wise guy, he not go against wind. In Chinese we say, Come from South, blow with wind—poom!—North will follow. Strongest wind cannot be seen."

The next week I bit back my tongue as we entered the store with the forbidden candies. When my mother finished her shopping, she quietly plucked a small bag of plums from the rack and put it on the counter with the rest of the items.

My mother imparted her daily truths so she could help my older brothers and me rise above our circumstances. We lived in San Francisco's Chinatown. Like most of the other Chinese children who played in the back alleys of restaurants and curio shops,[1] I didn't think we were poor. My bowl was always full, three five-course meals every day, beginning with a soup full of mysterious things I didn't want to know the names of.

We lived on Waverly Place, in a warm, clean, two-bedroom flat that sat above a small Chinese bakery specializing in steamed pastries and dim sum.[2] In the early morning, when the alley was still quiet, I could smell fragrant red beans as they were cooked down to a pasty sweetness. By daybreak, our flat was heavy with the odor of fried sesame balls and sweet curried chicken crescents. From my bed, I would listen as my father got ready for work, then locked the door behind him, one-two-three clicks.

At the end of our two-block alley was a small sandlot playground with swings and slides well-shined down the middle with use. The play area was bordered by wood-slat benches where old-country people sat cracking roasted watermelon seeds with their golden teeth and scattering the husks to an impatient gathering of gurgling pigeons. The best play-ground, however, was the dark alley itself. It was crammed with daily mysteries and adventures. My brothers and I would peer into the medicinal herb shop, watching old Li dole out onto a stiff sheet of white paper the right amount of insect shells, saffron-colored[3] seeds and <u>pungent</u> leaves for his ailing customers. It was said that he once cured a woman dying of an ancestral curse that had eluded the best of American doctors. Next to the pharmacy was a printer who specialized in gold-embossed wedding invitations and festive red banners.

Farther down the street was Ping Yuen Fish

---

1. curio (kyo͞or´ ē ō´) **shops:** Shops that sell unusual or rare items.
2. dim sum (dim´ tso͞om): Shells of dough filled with meat and vegetables and served as a light meal.
3. saffron-colored: Orange-yellow.

Market. The front window displayed a tank crowded with doomed fish and turtles struggling to gain footing on the slimy green-tiled sides. A hand-written sign informed tourists, "Within this store, is all for food, not for pet." Inside, the butchers with their bloodstained white smocks deftly gutted the fish while customers cried out their orders and shouted, "Give me your freshest," to which the butchers always protested, "All are freshest." On less crowded market days, we would inspect the crates of live frogs and crabs which we were warned not to poke, boxes of dried cuttlefish, and row upon row of iced prawns, squid, and slippery fish. The sanddabs made me shiver each time; their eyes lay on one flattened side and reminded me of my mother's story of a careless girl who ran into a crowded street and was crushed by a cab. "Was smash flat," reported my mother.

At the corner of the alley was Hong Sing's, a four-table cafe with a recessed stairwell in front that led to a door marked "Tradesmen." My brothers and I believed the bad people emerged from this door at night. Tourists never went to Hong Sing's, since the menu was printed only in Chinese. A Caucasian[4] man with a big camera once posed me and my playmates in front of the restaurant. He had us move to the side of the picture window so the photo would capture the roasted duck with its head dangling from a juice-covered rope. After he took the picture, I told him he should go into Hong Sing's and eat dinner. When he smiled and asked me what they served, I shouted, "Guts and duck's feet and octopus gizzards!" Then I ran off with my friends, shrieking with laughter as we scampered across the alley and hid in the entryway

grotto[5] of the China Gem Company, my heart pounded with hope that he would chase us.

My mother named me after the street that we lived on: Waverly Place Jong, my official name for important American documents. But my family called me Meimei,[6] "Little Sister," I was the youngest, the only daughter. Each morning before school, my mother would twist and yank on my thick black hair until she had formed two tightly wound pigtails. One day, as she struggled to weave a hard-toothed comb through my disobedient hair, I had a sly thought.

I asked her, "Ma, what is Chinese torture?" My mother shook her head. A bobby pin was wedged between her lips. She wetted her palm and smoothed the hair above my ear, then pushed the pin in so that it nicked sharply against my scalp.

"Who say this word?" she asked without a trace of knowing how wicked I was being. I shrugged my shoulders and said, "Some boy in my class said Chinese people do Chinese torture."

"Chinese people do many things," she said simply. "Chinese people do business, do medicine, do painting. Not lazy like American people. We do torture. Best torture."

My older brother Vincent was the one who actually got the chess set. We had gone to the annual Christmas party held at the First Chinese Baptist Church at the end of the alley. The missionary ladies had put together a Santa bag of gifts donated by members of another church. None of the gifts had names on them. There were separate sacks for boys and girls of different ages.

One of the Chinese parishioners had donned a Santa Claus costume and a stiff paper beard with cotton balls glued to it. I think the only children who thought he was the real thing were too young to know that Santa Claus

---

4. **Caucasian** (kô kā´ zhən) *adj.*: Person of European ancestry.

---

5. **entryway grotto** (grät´ ō) *n.*: The entryway resembled a cave.
6. **Meimei** (mā´ mā´)

was not Chinese. When my turn came up, the Santa man asked me how old I was. I thought it was a trick question; I was seven according to the American formula and eight by the Chinese calendar. I said I was born on March 17, 1951. That seemed to satisfy him. He then solemnly asked if I had been a very, very good girl this year and did I believe in Jesus Christ and obey my parents. I knew the only answer to that. I nodded back with equal solemnity.

Having watched the other children opening their gifts, I already knew that the big gifts were not necessarily the nicest ones. One girl my age got a large coloring book of biblical characters, while a less greedy girl who selected a small box received a glass vial of lavender toilet water. The sound of the box was also important. A ten-year-old boy had chosen a box that jangled when he shook it. It was a tin globe of the world with a slit for inserting money. He must have thought it was full of dimes and nickels, because when he saw that it had just ten pennies, his face fell with such undisguised disappointment that his mother slapped the side of his head and led him out of the church hall, apologizing to the crowd for her son who had such bad manners he couldn't appreciate such a fine gift.

As I peered into the sack, I quickly fingered the remaining presents, testing their weight, imagining what they contained. I chose a heavy, compact one that was wrapped in shiny silver foil and a red satin ribbon. It was a twelve-pack of Life Savers and I spent the rest of the party arranging and rearranging the candy tubes in the order of my favorites. My brother Winston chose wisely as well. His present turned out to be a box of intricate plastic parts; the instructions on the box proclaimed that when they were properly assembled he would have an authentic miniature replica of a World War II submarine.

Vincent got the chess set, which would have been a very decent present to get at a church Christmas party except it was obviously used and, as we discovered later, it was missing a black pawn and a white knight. My mother graciously thanked the unknown benefactor, saying, "Too good. Cost too much." At which point, an old lady with fine white, wispy hair nodded toward our family and said with a whistling whisper, "Merry, merry Christmas."

When we got home, my mother told Vincent to throw the chess set away. "She not want it. We not want it," she said, tossing her head stiffly to the side with a tight, proud smile. My brothers had deaf ears. They were already lining up the chess pieces and reading from the dog-eared instruction book.

◆ Reading Strategy
What do Mrs. Jong's statement and action regarding the chess set suggest about her sense of her own worth?

I watched Vincent and Winston play during Christmas week. The chess board seemed to hold elaborate secrets waiting to be untangled. The chessmen were more powerful than Old Li's magic herbs that cured ancestral curses. And my brothers wore such serious faces that I was sure something was at stake that was greater than avoiding the tradesmen's door to Hong Sing's.

"Let me! Let me!" I begged between games when one brother or the other would sit back with a deep sigh of relief and victory, the other annoyed, unable to let go of the outcome. Vincent at first refused to let me play, but when I offered my Life Savers as replacements for the buttons that filled in for the missing pieces, he relented. He chose the flavors: wild cherry for the black pawn and peppermint for the white knight. Winner could eat both. As our mother sprinkled flour and rolled out small doughy circles for the steamed dumplings that would be our dinner that night, Vincent explained the rules, pointing to each piece. "You have sixteen pieces and so do I. One king and queen, two bishops, two knights, two castles, and eight pawns. The pawns can only move forward one step, except on the first move. Then they can move two. But they can only take men by moving crossways like this, except in the beginning, when you can move ahead and take another pawn."

"Why?" I asked as I moved my pawn. "Why can't they move more steps?"

"Because they're pawns," he said.

"But why do they go crossways to take other men. Why aren't there any women and children?"

"Why is the sky blue? Why must you always ask stupid questions?" asked Vincent. "This is a game. These are the rules. I didn't make them up. See. Here. In the book." He jabbed a page with a pawn in his hand. "Pawn. P-A-W-N. Pawn. Read it yourself."

My mother patted the flour off her hands. "Let me see book," she said quietly. She scanned the pages quickly, not reading the foreign English symbols, seeming to search deliberately for nothing in particular.

"This American rules," she concluded at last. "Every time people come out from foreign country, must know rules. You not know, judge say, Too bad, go back. They not telling you why so you can use their way go forward. They say, Don't know why, you find out yourself. But they knowing all the time. Better you take it, find out why yourself." She tossed her head back with a satisfied smile.

I found out about all the whys later. I read the rules and looked up all the big words in a dictionary. I borrowed books from the Chinatown library. I studied each chess piece, trying to absorb the power each contained.

I learned about opening moves and why it's important to control the center early on; the shortest distance between two points is straight down the middle. I learned about the middle game and why tactics between two adversaries are like clashing ideas; the one who plays better has the clearest plans for both attacking and getting out of traps. I learned why it is essential in the endgame[7] to have foresight, a mathematical understanding of all possible moves, and patience; all weaknesses and advantages become evident to a strong adversary and are obscured to a tiring opponent. I discovered that

Chess Mates, 1992, Pamela Chin Lee, Courtesy of the artist

▲ Critical Viewing Based on details in the painting, who do you think is winning this chess game? Why? **[Support]**

for the whole game one must gather invisible strengths and see the endgame before the game begins.

I also found out why I should never reveal "why" to others. A little knowledge withheld is a great advantage one should store for future use. That is the power of chess. It is a game of secrets in which one must show and never tell.

I loved the secrets I found within the sixty-four black and white squares. I carefully drew a handmade chessboard and pinned it to the wall next to my bed, where at night I would stare for hours at imaginary battles. Soon I no longer lost any games or Life Savers, but I lost my adversaries. Winston and Vincent decided they were more interested in roaming the streets after school in their Hopalong Cassidy[8] cowboy hats.

---

7. **endgame** (end´ gām´): Final stage of a chess game in which each player has only a few pieces left on the board.

8. **Hopalong Cassidy:** Character in cowboy movies during the 1950's.

On a cold spring afternoon, while walking home from school, I detoured through the playground at the end of our alley. I saw a group of old men, two seated across a folding table playing a game of chess, others smoking pipes, eating peanuts, and watching. I ran home and grabbed Vincent's chess set, which was bound in a cardboard box with rubber bands. I also carefully selected two prized rolls of Life Savers. I came back to the park and approached a man who was observing the game.

"Want to play?" I asked him. His face widened with surprise and he grinned as he looked at the box under my arm.

"Little sister, been a long time since I play with dolls," he said, smiling benevolently. I quickly put the box down next to him on the bench and displayed my retort.

Lau Po, as he allowed me to call him, turned out to be a much better player than my brothers. I lost many games and many Life Savers. But over the weeks, with each diminishing roll of candies, I added new secrets. Lau Po gave me the names. The Double Attack from the East and West Shores. Throwing Stones on the Drowning Man. The Sudden Meeting of the Clan. The Surprise from the Sleeping Guard. The Humble Servant Who Kills the King. Sand in the Eyes of Advancing Forces. A Double Killing Without Blood.

There were also the fine points of chess etiquette. Keep captured men in neat rows, as well-tended prisoners. Never announce "Check" with vanity, lest someone with an unseen sword slit your throat. Never hurl pieces into the sandbox after you have lost a game, because then you must find them again, by yourself, after apologizing to all around you. By the end of the summer, Lau Po had taught me all he knew, and I had become a better chess player.

A small weekend crowd of Chinese people and tourists would gather as I played and defeated my opponents one by one. My mother would join the crowds during these outdoor exhibi-

tion games. She sat proudly on the bench, telling my admirers with proper Chinese humility, "Is luck."

A man who watched me play in the park suggested that my mother allow me to play in local chess tournaments. My mother smiled graciously, an answer that meant nothing. I desperately wanted to go, but I bit back my tongue. I knew she would not let me play among strangers. So as we walked home I said in a small voice that I didn't want to play in the local tournament. They would have American rules. If I lost, I would bring shame on my family.

"Is shame you fall down nobody push you," said my mother.

During my first tournament, my mother sat with me in the front row as I waited for my turn. I frequently bounced my

◆ Reading Strategy
Why does Waverly tell her mother she doesn't want to play in the tournament? What does her use of this strategy suggest about Waverly?

legs to unstick them from the cold metal seat of the folding chair. When my name was called, I leapt up. My mother unwrapped something in her lap. It was her chang, a small tablet of red jade which held the sun's fire. "Is luck," she whispered, and tucked it into my dress pocket. I turned to my opponent, a fifteen-year-old boy from Oakland. He looked at me, wrinkling his nose.

As I began to play, the boy disappeared, the color ran out of the room, and I saw only my white pieces and his black ones waiting on the other side. A light wind began blowing past my ears. It whispered secrets only I could hear.

"Blow from the South," it murmured. "The wind leaves no trail." I saw a clear path, the traps to avoid. The crowd rustled. "Shhh! Shhh!" said the corners of the room. The wind blew stronger. "Throw sand from the East to distract him." The knight came forward ready for the sacrifice. The wind hissed, louder and louder. "Blow, blow, blow. He cannot see. He is blind now. Make him lean away from the wind so he is easier to knock down."

"Check," I said, as the wind roared with

laughter. The wind died down to little puffs, my own breath.

My mother placed my first trophy next to a new plastic chess set that the neighborhood Tao society[9] had given to me. As she wiped each piece with a soft cloth, she said, "Next time win more, lose less."

"Ma, it's not how many pieces you lose," I said. "Sometimes you need to lose pieces to get ahead."

"Better to lose less, see if you really need."

At the next tournament, I won again, but it was my mother who wore the triumphant grin.

"Lost eight piece this time. Last time was eleven. What I tell you? Better off lose less!" I was annoyed, but I couldn't say anything.

I attended more tournaments, each one farther away from home. I won all games, in all divisions. The Chinese bakery downstairs from our flat displayed my growing collection of trophies in its window, amidst the dust-covered cakes that were never picked up. The day after I won an important regional tournament, the window encased a fresh sheet cake with whipped-cream frosting and red script saying, "Congratulations, Waverly Jong, Chinatown Chess Champion." Soon after that, a flower shop, headstone engraver, and funeral parlor offered to sponsor me in national tournaments. That's when my mother decided I no longer had to do the dishes. Winston and Vincent had to do my chores.

"Why does she get to play and we do all the work," complained Vincent.

"Is new American rules," said my mother. "Meimei play, squeeze all her brains out for win chess. You play, worth squeeze towel."

By my ninth birthday, I was a national chess champion. I was still some 429 points away from grand-master status, but I was touted as the Great American Hope, a child prodigy and a girl to boot. They ran a photo of me in Life magazine next to a quote in which Bobby Fischer[10] said, "There will never be a woman grand master." "Your move, Bobby," said the caption.

The day they took the magazine picture I wore neatly plaited braids clipped with plastic barrettes trimmed with rhinestones. I was playing in a large high school auditorium that echoed with phlegmy coughs and the squeaky rubber knobs of chair legs sliding across freshly waxed wooden floors. Seated across from me was an American man, about the same age as Lau Po, maybe fifty. I remember that his sweaty brow seemed to weep at my every move. He wore a dark, malodorous suit. One of his pockets was stuffed with a great white kerchief on which he wiped his palm before sweeping his hand over the chosen chess piece with great flourish.

In my crisp pink-and-white dress with scratchy lace at the neck, one of two my mother had sewn for these special occasions, I would clasp my hands under my chin, the delicate points of my elbows poised lightly on the table in the manner my mother had shown me for posing for the press. I would swing my patent leather shoes back and forth like an impatient child riding on a school bus. Then I would pause, suck in my lips, twirl my chosen piece in midair as if undecided, and then firmly plant it in its new threatening place, with a triumphant smile thrown back at my opponent for good measure.

I no longer played in the alley of Waverly Place. I never visited the playground where the pigeons and old men

---

9. **Tao** (dou) **society:** Group of people who believe in Taoism, a Chinese religion that stresses simplicity and unselfishness.

◆ **Build Vocabulary**

benevolently (bə nev′ ə lent lē) *adv.*: In a kind and well-meaning way

retort (ri tôrt′) *n.*: Sharp or clever reply

prodigy (präd′ ə jē) *n.*: Person who is amazingly talented or intelligent

malodorous (mal ō′ dər əs) adj.: Having a bad smell

10. **Bobby Fischer:** Born in 1943, this American chess prodigy attained the high rank of grand master in 1958.

gathered. I went to school, then directly home to learn new chess secrets, cleverly concealed advantages, more escape routes.

But I found it difficult to concentrate at home. My mother had a habit of standing over me while I plotted out my games. I think she thought of herself as my protective ally. Her lips would be sealed tight, and after each move I made, a soft "Hmmmmph" would escape from her nose.

"Ma, I can't practice when you stand there like that," I said one day. She retreated to the kitchen and made loud noises with the pots and pans. When the crashing stopped, I could see out of the corner of my eye that she was standing in the doorway. "Hmmmmph!" Only this one came out of her tight throat.

My parents made many concessions to allow me to practice. One time I complained that the bedroom I shared was so noisy that I couldn't think. Thereafter, my brothers slept in a bed in the living room facing the street. I said I couldn't finish my rice; my head didn't work right when my stomach was too full. I left the table with half-finished bowls and nobody complained. But there was one duty I couldn't avoid. I had to accompany my mother on Saturday market days when I had no tournament to play. My mother would proudly walk with me, visiting many shops, buying very little. "This my daughter Wave-ly Jong," she said to whoever looked her way.

One day, after we left a shop I said under my breath, "I wish you wouldn't do that, telling everybody I'm your daughter." My mother stopped walking. Crowds of people with heavy bags pushed past us on the sidewalk, bumping into first one shoulder, then another.

"Aiii-ya. So shame be with mother?" She grasped my hand even tighter as she glared at me.

I looked down. "It's not that, it's just so obvious. It's just so embarrassing."

"Embarrass you be my daughter?" Her voice was cracking with anger.

"That's not what I meant. That's not what I said."

"What you say?"

I knew it was a mistake to say anything more, but I heard my voice speaking. "Why do you have to use me to show off? If you want to show off, then why don't you learn to play chess." My mother's eyes turned into dangerous black slits. She had no words for me, just sharp silence.

I felt the wind rushing around my hot ears. I jerked my hand out of my mother's tight grasp and spun around, knocking into an old woman. Her bag of groceries spilled to the ground.

"Aii-ya! Stupid girl!" my mother and the woman cried. Oranges and tin cans careened down the sidewalk. As my mother stooped to help the old woman pick up the escaping food, I took off.

I raced down the street, dashing between people, not looking back as my mother screamed shrilly, "Meimei! Meimei!" I fled down an alley, past dark curtained shops and merchants washing the grime off their windows. I sped into the sunlight, into a large street crowded with tourists examining trinkets and souvenirs. I ducked into another dark alley, down another street, up another alley. I ran until it hurt and I realized I had nowhere to go, that I was not running from anything. The alleys contained no escape routes.

My breath came out like angry smoke. It was cold. I sat down on an upturned plastic pail next to a stack of empty boxes, cupping my chin with my hands, thinking hard. I imagined my mother, first walking briskly down one street or another looking for me, then giving up and returning home to await my arrival. After two hours, I stood up on creaking legs and slowly walked home.

◆ **Literary Focus**
What makes Waverly upset at her mother's behavior? Why is her mother's voice "cracking with anger"?

◆ **Build Vocabulary**

concessions (kən sesh′ ənz) n.: Things given or granted as privileges

The alley was quiet and I could see the yellow lights shining from our flat like two tiger's eyes in the night. I climbed the sixteen steps to the door, advancing quietly up each so as not to make any warning sounds. I turned the knob; the door was locked. I heard a chair moving, quick steps, the locks turning—click! click! click!—and then the door opened.

"About time you got home," said Vincent. "Boy, are you in trouble."

He slid back to the dinner table. On a platter were the remains of a large fish, its fleshy head still connected to bones swimming upstream in vain escape. Standing there waiting for my punishment, I heard my mother speak in a dry voice.

"We not concerning this girl. This girl not have concerning for us."

Nobody looked at me. Bone chopsticks[11] clinked against the insides of bowls being emptied into hungry mouths.

I walked into my room, closed the door, and lay down on my bed. The room was dark, the ceiling filled with shadows from the dinnertime lights of neighboring flats.

In my head, I saw a chessboard with sixty-four black and white squares. Opposite me was my opponent, two angry black slits. She wore a triumphant smile. "Strongest wind cannot be seen," she said.

Her black men advanced across the plane, slowly marching to each successive level as a single unit. My white pieces screamed as they scurried and fell off the board one by one. As her men drew closer to my edge, I felt myself growing light. I rose up into the air and flew out the window. Higher and higher, above the alley, over the tops of tiled roofs, where I was gathered up by the wind and pushed up toward the night sky until everything below me disappeared and I was alone.

I closed my eyes and pondered my next move.

---

11. **chopsticks** (chăp´ stiks´): Two small sticks of wood, bone, or ivory, held together in one hand and used as utensils for eating, cooking, and serving food.

Guide for Responding

◆ Literature and Your Life

Reader's Response The story ends without a final showdown. Who do you think will eventually win the "game"—Waverly or her mother? Why?

Thematic Focus Why do you think Waverly seems so angry with her mother?

Group Discussion As a group, consider games and sports that have complicated rules and strategies—for example, football, tennis, or Monopoly. Collaborate on a list of rules and strategies from various games that can be extended beyond the game to daily life—to the family, school, workplace, or political scene, for example.

☑ Check Your Comprehension

1. How does Waverly start playing chess?
2. Explain how she progresses from losing to her brothers at chess to being compared with Bobby Fischer in Life magazine.
3. Describe what happens between Waverly and Mrs. Jong at the market.
4. What happens when Waverly returns home after the incident at the market?
5. How does the story end?

Guide for Responding (continued)

◆ Critical Thinking

INTERPRET

1. How does Waverly show that she understands the use of strategy even before she starts playing chess? **[Analyze]**
2. Mrs. Jong gives Waverly rules of behavior in the form of Chinese sayings. (a) How does Waverly use these rules to win at chess? (b) How does she use them in her struggle with her mother? **[Connect]**
3. Why do you think Amy Tan called this story "Rules of the Game"? **[Connect]**

EVALUATE

4. Which elements of the struggle between Waverly and her mother are universal, and which are uniquely Chinese American? **[Assess]**

EXTEND

5. What other stories can you think of in which a child uses success in some activity to outgrow a parent? **[Literature Link]**

◆ Reading Strategy

CONTRAST CHARACTERS

"Rules of the Game" develops conflict between two strong characters who are both similar to and different from each other.

1. Why is Waverly in a better position than her mother to understand "American rules"?
2. What does Mrs. Jong want for her daughter that she doesn't have herself?
3. In what ways are Waverly and Mrs. Jong more alike than they admit?

◆ Literary Focus

GENERATIONAL CONFLICT

The cultural conflict in "Rules of the Game" heightens the **generational conflict** between a mother and her daughter.

1. What does Waverly resent about her mother's behavior when they are shopping together?
2. What might Mrs. Jong feel that her child does not yet understand?

◆ Build Vocabulary

Here are the original French words from which some of the English words in the story evolved. Write the English equivalent of each word, along with a sentence using the English word.

1. *reules*   2. *circonstances*   3. *solemnité*

USING THE WORD BANK

On your paper, write the word whose meaning is closest to that of the first word.

1. concessions: (a) things granted, (b) large meetings, (c) secrets
2. retort: (a) foolish deed, (b) clever reply, (c) old wisdom
3. malodorous: (a) evil-minded, (b) bad-smelling, (c) beautiful-sounding
4. prodigy: (a) young child, (b) large amount, (c) talented person
5. pungent: (a) sweet-tasting, (b) sharp-smelling, (c) witty
6. benevolently: (a) wealthily, (b) attractively, (c) in a kind way

◆ Build Grammar Skills

COMPLEX SENTENCES

In a complex sentence, the subordinate clause is usually introduced by a subordinating conjunction, such as *when, as,* or *because* or a relative pronoun such as *who, which,* or *that.*

> A **complex sentence** consists of one independent clause and at least one subordinate clause.

Practice On your paper write the following sentences from "Rules of the Game." Underline the independent clauses once and the subordinate clauses twice.

1. The next week I bit back my tongue as we entered the store with the forbidden candies.
2. When we got home, my mother told Vincent to throw the chess set away.
3. I came back to the park and approached a man who was observing the game.
4. As her men drew closer to my edge, I felt myself growing light.

Build Your Portfolio

Idea Bank

Writing

1. **Notes for a Magazine Article** Imagine that you are a journalist developing a feature article on chess prodigy Waverly Jong. Write notes about a visit to her home in Chinatown. Focus particularly on your impressions of Waverly and her mother. **[Career Link]**

2. **Letter** Write a letter from Mrs. Jong to her daughter expressing how she feels after the incident in the market.

3. **Extension** Write an extension of "Rules of the Game," telling what happens the following day in the Jong household.

Speaking and Listening

4. **Radio Commentary** Imagine that you are a radio announcer describing a national chess tournament in which Waverly Jong is a finalist. Set the scene for your listeners, focusing on Waverly and her opponent. **[Media Link]**

5. **Dialogue** With another classmate, create a dialogue between Waverly and her mother that takes place years after the events in this story, when Waverly is grown up.

Projects

6. **Chess Set** Design your own chess set. You can draw or paint your design or use modeling clay to sculpt your chess pieces. Label each figure. **[Art Link]**

7. **Game** Work with a partner to invent a game with its own rules, board, and pieces. Once you decide how your game is to be played, make a model of it with your partner. Then teach your game to your classmates and have a tournament.

Writing Mini-Lesson

Proposal to Change the Rules of a Game

Choose a sport or game with which you are familiar and think about how you might change the rules. Write a proposal meant to persuade some official body to adopt the rule change you suggest.

Writing Skills Focus: Clear and Logical Organization

Organize your proposal either subject by subject or feature by feature. In **subject by subject** organization, you discuss all the features of one subject (in this case, the current rules of your game, and where they are inadequate) and then the features of the other subject (in this case, the new rules you are proposing and how they would improve the game). If you organize **feature by feature,** you focus on each of the failings of the current rules and how your new rules would improve the situation in each case.

Prewriting Write down the rules you wish to change, and then list all their disadvantages. Next to each disadvantage, write how your new rules would correct the problem.

Drafting Decide how you want to organize your proposal. If you want to go subject by subject, present all the qualities of one subject first, then all the qualities of the next subject. If, on the other hand, you want to go feature by feature, discuss each aspect of your subjects in turn.

Use transitions such as *in contrast, instead of, on the one hand . . . on the other hand,* to highlight the differences between your two subjects.

Revising Reread your draft. Are the advantages of your new system over the old system clear? If you were an official of the sport or game, would you be persuaded to consider the ideas in the proposal?

Guide for Reading

Cynthia Rylant *(1954–)*

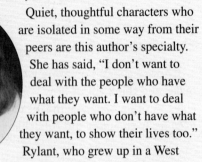

Quiet, thoughtful characters who are isolated in some way from their peers are this author's specialty. She has said, "I don't want to deal with the people who have what they want. I want to deal with people who don't have what they want, to show their lives too." Rylant, who grew up in a West Virginia mountain town, discovered a love of good writing in college English classes. She never thought about becoming a writer herself, however, until she took a job as a librarian and began reading lots of children's books.

Since publishing her first book, *When I Was Young in the Mountains*, in 1982, Rylant has produced a wide range of literary works—picture books, poetry, short stories, and novels. In 1993, her novel *Missing May* won the Newbery Award.

William Stafford *(1914– 1993)*

Reading a poem by William Stafford is like having a conversation with the poet. According to commentator Robert Bly, Stafford's poems are "spoken like a friend over coffee."

Stafford grew up in Kansas but spent his later years teaching and writing in Oregon. He didn't publish his first book, *West of Your City*, until he was forty-six. Throughout the remainder of his life, however, he produced a large volume of work. He wrote a poem every day and published numerous collections, including *Traveling in the Dark*, which won the National Book Award in 1962.

His writing earned Stafford the respect of important public figures. In fact, when Stafford died, the governor of Oregon called him "an Oregon treasure."

◆ Build Vocabulary

SUFFIXES: *-ment*

In "Checkouts," a girl admires a boy's dishevelment. Someone who is disheveled is untidy, and *dishevelment* refers to the condition of being untidy. The suffix *-ment* means "the state of or condition of." Added to a verb, it changes the verb into a noun. For example, adding *-ment* to the verb *disappoint* creates the noun *disappointment*.

WORD BANK

As you read these selections, you will encounter the words on this list. Each word is defined on the page where it first appears. Preview the list before you read.

intuition
reverie
shards
harried
brazen
dishevelment
perverse
articulate
lingered
demure

◆ Build Grammar Skills

PRONOUNS AND ANTECEDENTS

A **pronoun** takes the place of a noun in a sentence. Without pronouns, writers would have to repeat nouns, making long, unwieldy sentences. The noun that a pronoun replaces is the pronoun's **antecedent**. Every pronoun should have a clear antecedent. In this sentence, an arrow points from one pronoun to its antecedent.

Her parents wrote up the *list* and handed *it* to her.

At the beginning of "Checkouts," the author uses a pronoun that does not have an antecedent. As you read, think about why the author might have done so.

Checkouts ◆ Fifteen

◆ Literature and Your Life

CONNECT YOUR EXPERIENCE
You get on the school bus and sit alone instead of taking a seat next to someone you don't know. You can't go to a concert because you came down with a bad case of the flu. Missed opportunities for new adventures occur just about every day. In these two selections, young people experience lost opportunities for different reasons.

Journal Writing Write about a missed opportunity in your life. Imagine what might have happened if you had seized the opportunity.

THEMATIC FOCUS: FINDING OUR IDENTITY
In "Checkouts," a girl falls in love. In "Fifteen," a boy chances upon a riderless motorcycle. These opportunities for new experiences lead the two teenagers to discoveries about themselves.

◆ Background for Understanding

CULTURE
In "Checkouts," the main character is compared to "a Tibetan monk in solitary meditation." Tibet, once an independent nation north of the Himalaya Mountains, is now part of China. Its people are devout Buddhists. Buddhist monks live in seclusion, devoting their time to various spiritual pursuits, including meditation. Meditation involves clearing the mind of all thoughts to achieve a state of perfect calmness. In "Checkouts," the main character achieves this state by grocery shopping!

◆ Literary Focus

IRONY
Irony is a literary technique in which the outcome is different from what the reader or the characters expect or from what might logically be expected. For example, "Checkouts" follows a seemingly predictable story line about a budding relationship between a boy and a girl, but the outcome of this relationship turns out to be different from what readers might expect.

◆ Reading Strategy

RELATE TO PERSONAL EXPERIENCE
One of the great things about literature is that it allows you to travel to places you've never been and explore experiences you've never had. Even though you may never have had exactly the same experiences presented in a work, you will most likely have had some of the feelings that the characters experience, know people like the characters, or had experiences that are in some ways similar to those presented in the selection. As you read, look for these types of connections. Doing so will help you become more involved in what you read and help you to understand and appreciate the characters and events.

Checkouts

Cynthia Rylant

Her parents had moved her to Cincinnati, to a large house with beveled glass windows[1] and several porches and the *history* her mother liked to emphasize. You'll love the house, they said. You'll be lonely at first, they admitted, but you're so nice you'll make friends fast. And as an impulse tore at her to lie on the floor, to hold to their ankles and tell them she felt she was dying, to offer anything, anything at all, so they might allow her to finish growing up in the town of her childhood, they firmed their mouths and spoke from their chests and they said, It's decided.

They moved her to Cincinnati, where for a month she spent the greater part of every day in a room full of beveled glass windows, sifting through photographs of the life she'd lived and left behind. But it is difficult work, suffering, and in its own way a kind of art, and finally she didn't have the energy for it anymore, so she emerged from the beautiful house and fell in love with a bag boy at the supermarket. Of course, this didn't happen all at once, just like that, but in the sequence of things that's exactly the way it happened.

She liked to grocery shop. She loved it in the way some people love to drive long country roads, because doing it she could think and relax and wander. Her parents wrote up the list and handed it to her and off she went without complaint to perform what they regarded as a great sacrifice of her time and a sign that she was indeed a very nice girl. She had never told them how much she loved grocery shopping, only that she was "willing" to do it. She had an <u>intuition</u> which told her that her parents were not

---

1. **beveled** (bevʹ əld) **glass:** Glass having angled or slanted edges.

◆ Build Vocabulary

intuition (inʹ too wishʹ ən) *n.*: Knowledge of something without reasoning

▶ **Critical Viewing** The girl in this story relaxes by grocery shopping. How can performing everyday activities help a person to relax? **[Analyze]**

safe for sharing such strong, important facts about herself. Let them think they knew her.

Once inside the supermarket, her hands firmly around the handle of the cart, she would lapse into a kind of <u>reverie</u> and wheel toward the produce. Like a Tibetan monk in solitary meditation, she calmed to a point of deep, deep happiness; this feeling came to her, reliably, if strangely, only in the supermarket.

Then one day the bag boy dropped her jar of mayonnaise and that is how she fell in love.

He was nervous—first day on the job—and along had come this fascinating girl, standing in the checkout line with the unfocused stare one often sees in young children, her face turned enough away that he might take several full

◆ **Literary Focus**
Why is the description of how the girl fell in love ironic?

◆ **Build Vocabulary**

reverie (rev´ ər ē) *n.*: Dreamy thought of pleasant things

CONNECTIONS TO TODAY'S WORLD
Both Sides Now

Joni Mitchell

The girl in this story is intrigued by the fact that the bag boy contrasts sharply with the world in which she lives. As songwriter Joni Mitchell notes in this Grammy-winning song, the type of interest that Rylant's character takes can help lead a person toward a more complete view of the world.

Bows and flows of angel hair
And ice cream castles in the air
And feathered canyons everywhere
I've looked at clouds that way

5 But now they only block the sun
They rain and snow on everyone
So many things I could have done
But clouds got in my way

I've looked at clouds from both sides now
10 From up and down, and still somehow
It's clouds' illusions I recall
I really don't know clouds at all

Moons and Junes and Ferris wheels
The dizzy dancing way you feel
15 As every fairy tale comes real
I've looked at love that way

But now it's just another show
You leave them laughing when you go
And if you care don't let them know
20 Don't give yourself away

I've looked at love from both sides now
From give and take, and still somehow
It's love's illusions I recall
I really don't know love at all

25 Tears and fears and feeling proud
To say I love you, right out loud
Dreams and schemes and circus crowds
I've looked at life that way

But now old friends are acting strange
30 They shake their heads, they say I've changed
Something's lost, but something's gained
In living every day

I've looked at life from both sides now
From win and lose, and still somehow
35 It's life's illusions I recall
I really don't know life at all

1. What discovery does the speaker of this song make about herself?
2. How does the speaker's discovery relate to the experiences of Rylant's characters?
3. Have you ever experienced feelings like the ones expressed in this song? Explain.

looks at her as he packed sturdy bags full of food and the goods of modern life. She interested him because her hair was red and thick, and in it she had placed a huge orange bow, nearly the size of a small hat. That was enough to distract him, and when finally it was her groceries he was packing, she looked at him and smiled and he could respond only by busting her jar of mayonnaise on the floor, <u>shards</u> of glass and oozing cream decorating the area around his feet.

She loved him at exactly that moment, and if he'd known this perhaps he wouldn't have fallen into the brown depression he fell into, which lasted the rest of his shift. He believed he must have looked the jackass in her eyes, and he envied the sureness of everyone around him: the cocky cashier at the register, the grim and <u>harried</u> store manager, the bland butcher, and the <u>brazen</u> bag boys who smoked in the warehouse on their breaks. He wanted a second chance. Another chance to be confident and say witty things to her as he threw tin cans into her bags, persuading her to allow him to help her to her car so he might learn just a little about her, check out the floor of the car for signs of hobbies or fetishes and the bumpers for clues as to beliefs and loyalties.

But he busted her jar of mayonnaise and nothing else worked out for the rest of the day.

Strange, how attractive clumsiness can be. She left the supermarket with stars in her eyes, for she had loved the way his long nervous fingers moved from the conveyor belt to the bags, how deftly (until the mayonnaise) they had picked up her items and placed them in her bags. She had loved the way the hair kept falling into his eyes as he leaned over to grab a box or a tin. And the tattered brown shoes he wore with no socks. And the left side of his collar turned in rather than out.

The bag boy seemed a wonderful contrast to the perfectly beautiful house she had been forced to accept as her home, to the *history* she hated, to the loneliness she had become used to, and she couldn't wait to come back for more of his awkwardness and <u>dishevelment</u>.

Incredibly, it was another four weeks before they saw each other again. As fate would have

it, her visits to the supermarket never coincided with his schedule to bag. Each time she went to the store, her eyes scanned the checkouts at once, her heart in her mouth. And each hour he worked, the bag boy kept one eye on the door, watching for the red-haired girl with the big orange bow.

Yet in their disappointment these weeks there was a kind of ecstasy. It is reason enough to be alive, the hope you may see again some face which has meant something to you. The anticipation of meeting the bag boy eased the girl's painful transition into her new and jarring life in Cincinnati. It provided for her an anchor amid all that was impersonal and unfamiliar, and she spent less time on thoughts of what she had left behind as she concentrated on what might lie ahead. And for the boy, the long and often tedious hours at the supermarket which provided no challenge other than that of showing up the following workday . . . these hours became possibilities of mystery and romance for him as he watched the electric doors for the girl in the orange bow.

And when finally they did meet up again, neither offered a clue to the other that he, or she, had been the object of obsessive thought for weeks. She spotted him as soon as she came into the store, but she kept her eyes strictly in front of her as she pulled out a cart and wheeled it toward the produce. And he, too, knew the instant she came through the door—though the orange bow was gone, replaced by a small but bright yellow flower instead—and he never once turned his head in her direction but watched her from the corner of his vision as he tried to swallow back the fear in his throat.

It is odd how we sometimes deny ourselves

◆ Build Vocabulary

shards (shärdz) *n.*: Broken pieces

harried (har´ ēd) *adj.*: Worried

brazen (brā´ zən) *adj.*: Shamelessly bold

dishevelment (di shev´ əl ment) *n.*: A state of being untidy

the very pleasure we have longed for and which is finally within our reach. For some perverse reason she would not have been able to articulate, the girl did not bring her cart up to the bag boy's checkout when her shopping was done. And the bag boy let her leave the store, pretending no notice of her.

This is often the way of children, when they truly want a thing, to pretend that they don't. And then they grow angry when no one tried harder to give them this thing they so casually rejected, and they soon find themselves in a rage simply because they cannot say yes when they mean yes. Humans are very complicated.

◆ Build Vocabulary

perverse (pər vurs´) *adj.*: Contrary and willful

articulate (är tik´ yə lāt) *v.*: Express in words

lingered (liŋ´ gərd) *v.*: Stayed on, as if unwilling to leave

(And perhaps cats, who have been known to react in the same way, though the resulting rage can only be guessed at.)

The girl hated herself for not checking out at the boy's line, and the boy hated himself for not catching her eye and saying hello, and they most sincerely hated each other without having ever exchanged even two minutes of conversation.

Eventually—in fact, within the week—a kind and intelligent boy who lived very near her beautiful house asked the girl to a movie and she gave up her fancy for the bag boy at the supermarket. And the bag boy himself grew so bored with his job that he made a desperate search for something better and ended up in a bookstore where scores of fascinating girls lingered like honeybees about a hive. Some months later the bag boy and the girl with the orange bow again crossed paths, standing in line with their dates at a movie theater, and, glancing toward the other, each smiled slightly, then looked away, as strangers on public buses often do, when one is moving off the bus and the other is moving on.

Guide for Responding

◆ *Literature and Your Life*

Reader's Response Were you disappointed that the girl and boy did not get together? Explain.

Thematic Focus What does the girl learn about herself by falling in love with the bag boy?

Role Play With a partner, role-play a scene in the grocery store in which the girl and the boy actually speak to each other.

☑ Check Your Comprehension

1. What does the girl love about the bag boy?
2. What happens when the girl and the bag boy see each other for the second time?
3. Under what circumstances do the girl and the bag boy see each other for a third time?

◆ Critical Thinking

INTERPRET

1. What do you learn about the girl from her enjoyment of grocery shopping? **[Infer]**
2. How are the girl and the bag boy alike? **[Compare]**
3. What effect do their similarities have on the story? **[Analyze]**
4. How is their unacknowledged romance useful to both the girl and the boy? **[Analyze]**

EVALUATE

5. In a review of the book from which this story is taken, one critic said that in some stories Cynthia Rylant relies on telling rather than showing what her characters are like. Do you think this criticism applies to this story? Give examples to support your opinion. **[Evaluate]**

Fifteen
William Stafford

South of the Bridge on Seventeenth
I found back of the willows one summer
day a motorcycle with engine running
as it lay on its side, ticking over
5   slowly in the high grass. I was fifteen.

I admired all that pulsing gleam, the
shiny flanks, the <u>demure</u> headlights
fringed where it lay; I led it gently
to the road and stood with that
10 companion, ready and friendly, I was
    fifteen.

We could find the end of a road, meet
the sky out on Seventeenth. I thought
about
hills and, patting the handle, got back a

confident opinion. On the bridge we
    indulged
15 a forward feeling, a tremble. I was
    fifteen.

Thinking, back farther in the grass I found
the owner, just coming to, where he had
    flipped
over the rail. He had blood on his hand,
    was pale—
I helped him walk to his machine. He ran
    his hand
20 over it, called me a good man, roared away.

◆ **Build Vocabulary**

demure (di mur´) *adj.*: Shy or modest

Guide for Responding

◆ *Literature and Your Life*

Reader's Response What would you have done if you had been in the speaker's place? Why?

Thematic Focus What does the speaker discover about himself through this experience?

Journal Writing Write a brief description of a fantasy or adventure that you had at some point in your life.

☑ Check Your Comprehension

1. What does the speaker do when he first finds the motorcycle?
2. What does he imagine doing with the motorcycle?
3. What happened to the owner of the motorcycle?

◆ Critical Thinking

INTERPRET
1. What words in the poem make the motorcycle seem human? **[Analyze]**
2. What does the motorcycle represent to the speaker? **[Infer]**
3. How do the speaker's actions contrast with his fantasy? **[Compare and Contrast]**
4. What conclusions can you draw about the speaker's character based on his actions? Support your answer. **[Draw Conclusions]**

EVALUATE
5. Does the repetition of the sentence, "I was fifteen," enhance the poem or detract from it? Support your answer. **[Assess; Support]**

APPLY
6. In what way can fantasies like the one in this poem be useful? **[Generalize]**

Guide for Responding (continued)

◆ Reading Strategy

RELATE TO PERSONAL EXPERIENCE

The characters and events in these selections, and the feelings that the characters experience, may have called to mind people, feelings, and experiences from your own life.

1. What personal experiences do the events in "Fifteen" call to mind?
2. How do your memories of these experiences help you to appreciate the speaker's feelings and action?

◆ Build Vocabulary

USING THE SUFFIX *-ment*

The suffix *-ment*, which means "state of" or "condition of," can be added to a verb to create a noun. Add the suffix to each of the following words and use each new word in a sentence.

1. amuse   3. disappoint
2. enlighten   4. disillusion

USING THE WORD BANK

Substitute a word from the Word Bank for each italicized word or words. Write the words on your paper.

1. He was lost in a *daydream* of summer vacation.
2. The child's *untidiness* only added to her charm.
3. The captain took *willful* pleasure in changing his orders several times a day.
4. With a *shy* smile, she agreed to dance.
5. *A feeling beyond thought* told the mother that her child was safe.
6. The *broken piece* of pottery could be traced back five hundred years.
7. After the game, several players *stayed on* to discuss its outcome.
8. The *worried* doctor still had several patients to see.
9. The mayor tried to *express in words* her concern for the city.
10. The prisoners made a *bold* attempt to escape by digging a tunnel under the prison wall.

◆ Literary Focus

IRONY

In both these selections, the authors use **irony**—a discrepancy between what readers or characters expect and what actually happens—to capture the contradictory impulses and feelings of young people. In "Checkouts," for example, the girl and the bag boy are attracted to each other and yet they never act on those feelings.

1. What do you expect when the narrator says the girl fell in love?
2. What actually happens?
3. What point does this discrepancy between expectation and reality make?
4. In the fourth stanza of "Fifteen," the owner of the motorcycle calls the speaker "good man." In what way is this ironic?

◆ Build Grammar Skills

PRONOUNS AND ANTECEDENTS

A **pronoun** is a word that takes the place of a noun. The word that it replaces is its **antecedent**.
Practice On your paper, write each pronoun and its antecedent. Some sentences may have more than one pronoun.

1. The fifteen-year-old boy fell in love with the motorcycle as soon as he saw it.
2. As the boy admired the sleek machine, the open road seemed to beckon to him.
3. The boy lifted the motorcycle from the tall grass where it lay.
4. The boy took the owner by the hand and led him to the cycle.
5. The owner thanked the boy, then rode away from him.
6. Because the experience moved him, the boy will always remember it.

Writing Application Write a brief summary of "Checkouts" or "Fifteen." Use at least five pronouns. Underline each pronoun and draw a line to its antecedent.

Build Your Portfolio

 ## Idea Bank

Writing

1. **Classified Advertisement** Imagine that the owner of the motorcycle described in "Fifteen" wants to sell his motorcycle and buy a new one. Write a classified ad for him to place in a local newspaper. The ad must be brief but persuasive.

2. **Job Evaluation** Employers usually evaluate an employee's job performance on a yearly basis. Suppose you are the manager of the bag boy in "Checkouts." Write a paragraph about his performance on the job. **[Career Link]**

3. **Love Poem** Write a poem in which the girl in "Checkouts" expresses love for the bag boy.

Speaking and Listening

4. **Television News Report** Suppose a television news crew arrives at the scene of the motorcycle accident just as the man is about to ride off. The reporter interviews him and the boy. With two classmates, stage and present these interviews. **[Media Link]**

5. **Oral Story** Imagine you are the girl from "Checkouts" talking on the telephone to a friend in your old hometown. Tell the story of your infatuation with the bag boy.

Projects

6. **Audio Montage** Many popular songs tell the stories of failed romances. Put together an audio montage of three or four songs that tell stories similar to that of "Checkouts." **[Music Link]**

7. **Historic Homes** In "Checkouts," the girl's mother is pleased that the family has bought a house with "history." Prepare a report on a historic home in your community or in some place you have visited. **[Social Studies Link]**

 ## Writing Mini-Lesson

Scene From a Teen Soap Opera

Develop the script for a scene from a teen soap opera. You may choose a teen soap opera you have seen on television, you may use "Checkouts" as the basis of a soap opera, or you may make up an idea for a soap opera. The following will help you write a scene that appeals to teenage viewers.

Writing Skills Focus: Writing to Your Audience

To be successful, a teenage soap opera must appeal to its **audience**—teenage viewers. Think about the qualities that make successful soap operas popular among people your age. What are the characters like? What types of situations do the programs dramatize? Where do the programs take place? Use your answers to these questions to help you develop a scene that will grab the interest of a teenage audience.

Prewriting Come up with a situation and a set of characters that will interest your audience. Sketch out a rough plot for your scene, and jot down some key details about your characters.

Drafting Write a rough draft of your script. Include brief stage directions to describe the action and the characters' emotions. Keep your audience in mind as you write the dialogue. Ask yourself whether your characters speak and act in a way that will appeal to teenagers.

Revising Reading your draft aloud will let you hear whether the language sounds natural and whether viewers are getting all the information they need to understand what is happening. Rewrite language that doesn't sound natural. Add to the dialogue if you think the audience won't be able to follow what is happening.

Guide for Reading

Paul Laurence Dunbar
(1872–1906)

He didn't live to see his thirty-fifth birthday, but Paul Laurence Dunbar produced a tremendous outpouring of poetry and fiction during his brief lifetime. Born in Dayton, Ohio, the child of former slaves, Dunbar is widely recognized as the first African American poet of national stature.

Maya Angelou (1928–)

Born Marguerite Johnson in St. Louis, Missouri, Maya Angelou grew up in Arkansas and California. Her difficult childhood became the source for her extremely popular autobiography, *I Know Why the Caged Bird Sings*, which takes its title from Paul Laurence Dunbar's "Sympathy." (For more information on Maya Angelou, see p. 164.)

Emily Dickinson (1830–1886)

Emily Dickinson was born and lived most of her life in Amherst, Massachusetts. Outwardly her life was uneventful. The range and depth of her inner life, however, are suggested by the fact that she wrote at least 1,775 poems—each one compact with emotional power. She hid these poems in a bureau drawer, where they remained until after her death.

Charlayne Hunter-Gault
(1942–)

Born into a minister's family in South Carolina, Charlayne Hunter-Gault showed writing talent early in life and was accepted into several universities. However, encouraged by civil rights leaders to apply to the University of Georgia, she made history as one of the first African American students to enter an all-white institution.

◆ Build Vocabulary

LEVELS OF DICTION

Diction means word choice. You choose the words you use depending on your purpose, audience, and mood. The writers in this group use varying levels of diction. For example, Paul Laurence Dunbar, who uses **elevated**, or formal, **diction**, refers to a song as a "carol," whereas Maya Angelou uses the more down-to-earth "tune."

As you read the selections, decide what purpose seems to be served by each writer's level of diction.

keener
warp
epithets
effigies
disperse
imbued
perpetuated

WORD BANK

Before you read, preview this list of words from the selections.

◆ Build Grammar Skills

COMMONLY CONFUSED WORDS: *ACCEPT* AND *EXCEPT*

Accept is a verb that means "to receive" or "to agree to." **Except** can be a preposition or conjunction meaning "but" or a verb meaning "to leave out." Charlayne Hunter-Gault uses *except* as a conjunction meaning "but" in this sentence:

Ordinarily, there would not have been anything unusual about such a routine exercise, *except*, in this instance, the officials at the university had been fighting for two and a half years to keep me out.

Remember that *accept* and *except* are, in a loose sense, opposite in meaning. *Accept* means "to take **in**," and *except* means "to take **out.**"

Sympathy ◆ Caged Bird
We never know how high we are ◆ *from* In My Place

◆ *Literature and Your Life*

CONNECT YOUR EXPERIENCE
The writers in this group tell about the way a dream can drive our lives. The dream may be freedom or love or success; it may come true or it may not. If you've ever been driven by a dream, you'll be able to relate to the authors' messages—even if your experiences are very different from theirs.

Journal Writing Write about a dream you have and what it means to you.

THEMATIC FOCUS: FINDING OUR IDENTITY
As these writers suggest, a dream is part of your identity. It is something you grow toward; something that changes you. What happens when you are not allowed to reach for your dream?

◆ Background for Understanding

HISTORY
One important aspect of the civil rights movement of the late 1950's and 1960's was the change that it generated in the public schools and universities. Until the 1950's, southern public schools and universities were segregated; African American students did not attend the same schools as white students. This situation had been declared legal by the Supreme Court in the early twentieth century under the doctrine that such schools offered "separate but equal" education to all students. In the landmark *Brown* v. *Board of Education* decision of 1954, the Supreme Court overturned this doctrine and maintained that separate schools for different races could not offer equivalent education. In the early 1960's various African American students like Charlayne Hunter-Gault enrolled at formerly all-white institutions.

◆ Literary Focus

SYMBOL
A **symbol** is an object, person, or idea that represents something beyond itself. Authors may use symbols to make a point, create a mood, or reinforce a theme. Some symbols suggest universal meanings: For example, spring and dawn often symbolize new life and hope.

In this group of poems, Dunbar and Angelou both use caged and free birds to symbolize contrasting human circumstances.

◆ Reading Strategy

DRAW CONCLUSIONS
Whenever you **draw a conclusion,** you form an opinion about something based on evidence that you can identify. For example, in her poem "Caged Bird," Maya Angelou describes a free bird as one that "dares to claim the sky." This description is evidence that can lead you to the conclusion that to the speaker of this poem, freedom inspires strength and confidence.

Each of the works in this group invites you to draw a particular conclusion about the value of aspiring to something beyond your present circumstances. What evidence helps you draw this conclusion?

Sympathy

Paul Laurence Dunbar

I know what the caged bird feels, alas!
When the sun is bright on the upland slopes;
When the wind stirs, soft through the springing grass,
And the river flows like a stream of glass;
5   When the first bird sings and the first bud opes,
And the faint perfume from its chalice[1] steals—
I know what the caged bird feels!

I know why the caged bird beats his wing
Till its blood is red on the cruel bars;
10 For he must fly back to his perch and cling
When he fain[2] would be on the bough a-swing;
And a pain still throbs in the old, old scars
And they pulse again with a <u>keener</u> sting—
I know why he beats his wing!

15 I know why the caged bird sings, ah me,
When his wing is bruised and his bosom sore,—
When he beats his bars and he would be free;
It is not a carol of joy or glee,
But a prayer that he sends from his heart's deep core,
20 But a plea, that upward to Heaven he flings—
I know why the caged bird sings!

---

1. **chalice** (chal´ is) *n.*: Cup or goblet; here,
the cup-shaped part of a budding flower.
2. **fain** (fān) *adv.*: Gladly; eagerly.

◆ Build Vocabulary

keener (kēn´ ər) *adj.*: More clear; sharper

Caged Bird

Maya Angelou

A free bird leaps
on the back of the wind
and floats downstream
till the current ends
5   and dips his wing
in the orange sun rays
and dares to claim the sky.

But a bird that stalks
down his narrow cage
10 can seldom see through
his bars of rage
his wings are clipped and
his feet are tied
so he opens his throat to sing.

15 The caged bird sings
with a fearful trill
of things unknown
but longed for still
and his tune is heard
20 on the distant hill
for the caged bird
sings of freedom.

The free bird thinks of another breeze
and the trade winds soft through the sighing trees
25 and the fat worms waiting on a dawn-bright lawn
and he names the sky his own.

▲ Critical Viewing In
these poems, with which
bird does each poet
identify? How can you
tell? [Support]

We never know how high we are

Emily Dickinson

We never know how high we are
Till we are asked to rise
And then if we are true to plan
Our statures touch the skies—
The Heroism we recite
Would be a normal thing
Did not ourselves the Cubits[1] warp
For fear to be a King—

---

1. **Cubits** (kyoo´ bitz): Ancient measure of the length of the arm from the end of the middle finger to the elbow.

◆ **Build Vocabulary**

warp (wôrp) *v.*: Bend or twist out of shape; distort

Guide for Responding

◆ Literature and Your Life

Reader's Response What, if anything, has ever made you feel like a caged bird?

Thematic Focus What discovery does the speaker make in each poem?

Role Play With another student, create a dialogue between the caged bird and the free bird. Explore how they would feel toward each other and whether they would have any feelings in common.

☑ Check Your Comprehension

1. What does the caged bird want to do?
2. Of what does the free bird in Angelou's poem think?
3. According to Dickinson's poem, what happens when we are asked to rise to an occasion?

◆ Critical Thinking

INTERPRET
1. What might the cage represent in Dunbar's poem? **[Analyze]**
2. Compare and contrast the bird images used by Dunbar and Angelou. **[Compare and Contrast]**
3. Does Dickinson feel that people are capable of acting better than they do, or that they do not give themselves credit for the good things they actually accomplish? **[Distinguish]**

APPLY
4. Explain how a human being could be the equivalent of a caged bird or a free bird. **[Generalize]**

EXTEND
5. Is Dickinson more likely to see people as caged birds or free birds? **[Literature Link]**

from In My Place

Charlayne Hunter-Gault

On January 9, 1961, I walked onto the campus at the University of Georgia to begin registering for classes. Ordinarily, there would not have been anything unusual about such a routine exercise, except, in this instance, the officials at the university had been fighting for two and a half years to keep me out. I was not socially, intellectually, or morally undesirable. I was Black. And no Black student had ever been admitted to the University of Georgia in its 176-year history. Until the landmark *Brown* v. *Board of Education* decision that in 1954 declared separate but equal schools unconstitutional, the university was protected by law in its exclusion of people like me. In applying to the university, Hamilton Holmes and I were making one of the first major tests of the court's ruling in Georgia, and no one was sure just how hard it would be to challenge privilege. It would take us two and a half years of fighting our way through the system and the courts, but finally, with the help of the NAACP[1] Legal Defense and Educational Fund, Inc., and with the support of our family and friends, we won the right that should have been ours all along. With the ink barely dry on the court order of three days before, Hamilton Holmes and I walked onto the campus and into history.

We would be greeted by mobs of white students, who within forty-eight hours would hurl <u>epithets</u>, burn crosses and Black <u>effigies</u>, and finally stage a riot outside my dormitory while, nearby, state patrolmen ignored the call from university officials to come and intervene. Tear gas would <u>disperse</u> the crowd, but not before I got word in my dorm room, now strewn with glass from a rock through my window, that Hamilton

---

1. **NAACP** *abbr.*: National Association for the Advancement of Colored People.

◆ Build Vocabulary

epithets (ep´ ə thetz) *n.*: Abusive words or phrases; slurs

effigies (ef´ ə gēz) *n.*: Crude figures or dummies representing hated people or a group

disperse (dis pʉrs´) *v.*: Drive off or scatter in different directions

▲ **Critical Viewing** What character traits enable people to maintain their dignity in the face of discrimination? **[Analyze]**

and I were being suspended for our own safety. It might have been the end of the story but for the fact that the University of Georgia was now the lead case in a series of events that would become Georgia's entry into the Civil Rights Revolution. And we—like the legions of young Black students to follow in other arenas—were now <u>imbued</u> with an unshakable determination to take control of our destiny and force the South to abandon the wretched Jim Crow laws[2] it had <u>perpetuated</u> for generations to keep us in our place.

The newfound sense of mission that now motivated us evolved for me out of a natural desire to fulfill a dream I had nurtured from an early age. With a passion bordering on obsession, I wanted to be a journalist, a dream that would have been, if not unthinkable, at least undoable in the South of my early years. But no one ever told me not to dream, and when the time came to act on that dream, I would not let anything stand in the way of fulfilling it.

---

2. **Jim Crow laws:** Upholding or practicing discrimination against African Americans. Jim Crow was a derogatory name given to African Americans from the title of a nineteenth-century minstrel song.

◆ **Build Vocabulary**

imbued (im byo͞od´) *v.*: Inspired

perpetuated (pᵿr pech´ o͞o wāt id) *v.*: Caused to continue indefinitely; prolonged

---

Guide for Responding

◆ *Literature and Your Life*

Reader's Response If you had faced the obstacles Hunter-Gault did, would you have pursued your dream or given it up?

Thematic Focus What unfortunate discovery about people can you make from Hunter-Gault's difficulties during her early days at the University of Georgia?

☑ **Check Your Comprehension**

1. Why did the officials at the University of Georgia try to prevent Hunter-Gault from enrolling there?
2. How were Hunter-Gault and Hamilton Holmes treated by the other students at the university during their first two days?
3. Why did the author stay at the university, despite all the difficulties she faced?

◆ **Critical Thinking**

INTERPRET
1. What various reasons could account for the white students' violent reaction to Hunter-Gault's attempt to attend college with them? **[Analyze]**
2. What qualities did Hunter-Gault need in order to succeed in her mission? **[Draw Conclusions]**

APPLY
3. Hunter-Gault speaks of a "newfound sense of mission." How can a sense of pursuing a larger purpose, as well as her own personal goals, give someone strength? **[Relate]**

EXTEND
4. The author says, "No one ever told me not to dream." What might Paul Laurence Dunbar tell her about dreaming? **[Literature Link]**
5. Does Hunter-Gault's commitment to her dream fulfill Dickinson's idea of heroic behavior? **[Literature Link]**

Guide for Responding (continued)

◆ Reading Strategy

DRAW CONCLUSIONS

The poems and essay in this group of selections encourage you to **draw conclusions** about the value of dreaming in human life.

1. What conclusion can you draw from Dunbar's and Angelou's poems about how the dream of freedom affects the caged bird? What evidence led you to this conclusion?
2. What can you conclude from Dickinson's poem about who is responsible for a life falling short of its potential?
3. Hunter-Gault's pursuit of her dream led her to risk physical danger. What conclusion can you draw from this circumstance about her commitment to her dream?

◆ Build Vocabulary

USING LEVELS OF DICTION

Dunbar, Angelou, Dickinson, and Hunter-Gault all use different **levels of diction** to express their feelings about the importance of dreams and aspirations.

1. Find two examples of old-fashioned or elevated levels of diction in "Sympathy." What impression of the speaker do such words create in your mind?
2. Emily Dickinson is known for mixing levels of diction in her writing. Find one example of a simpler word choice and one example of a more elevated word choice in her poem.

USING THE WORD BANK

On your paper, write the word whose meaning is closest to that of the first word:

1. warp: (a) hit, (b) distort, (c) time
2. disperse: (a) scatter, (b) steal, (c) scold
3. perpetuated: (a) made happen, (b) prolonged, (c) honored
4. effigies: (a) speeches, (b) tombs, (c) dummies
5. keener: (a) sharper, (b) tastier, (c) better looking
6. imbued: (a) painted, (b) placed, (c) inspired
7. epithets: (a) books, (b) slurs, (c) legends

◆ Literary Focus

SYMBOL

A **symbol** is something that suggests a significance beyond its literal meaning. All writers, but particularly poets, use symbols to give their writing another dimension.

1. In "Sympathy," what might the bird's beating his wing on the cage bars symbolize in human life?
2. In "Caged Bird," the free bird "dares to claim the sky" and then "names the sky his own." Literally, this means the bird flies up, but what human experience might this action symbolize?
3. Dickinson says, "We never know how high we are / Till we are asked to rise." What might *height* and *rising* symbolize here?

◆ Build Grammar Skills

COMMONLY CONFUSED WORDS: *ACCEPT* AND *EXCEPT*

Accept is a verb that means "to receive" or "to agree to." *Except* can be a preposition or conjunction meaning "but" or a verb meaning "to leave out."

Practice On your paper, rewrite the following sentences, choosing the correct word to complete each:

1. Many white students could not (accept, except) Charlayne Hunter-Gault when she enrolled at the University of Georgia.
2. (Accept, Except) for her race, Hunter-Gault was not that different from many of the students attending the university.
3. No other student (accept, except) Hamilton Holmes knew how Hunter-Gault felt.
4. Pioneers like Hunter-Gault made it easier for the next generation to (accept, except) integration.
5. Formerly all-white schools like the University of Georgia were forced to (accept, except) African American students.

Build Your Portfolio

Idea Bank

Writing

1. Editorial Write an editorial for the student newspaper at the University of Georgia at the time of Charlayne Hunter-Gault's enrollment. Try to persuade the students at the university to change their behavior toward the new African American students. **[Media Link]**

2. Letter Write a letter from Dunbar to Angelou expressing his reaction to her poem. Is he flattered or angered that she borrowed symbols and images from his poem?

3. Dialogue Imagine that Emily Dickinson meets one of the African American writers in this group. Write a dialogue between them, discussing whether people are better or worse than they think they are.

Speaking and Listening

4. Choral Reading With other students, stage a choral reading of "Sympathy" and "Caged Bird." **[Performing Arts Link]**

5. Dramatic Monologue Imagine that you are the young Charlayne Hunter-Gault on the night before her first day at the University of Georgia. Prepare and perform a monologue expressing her feelings as she faces this crisis.

Projects

6. Multimedia Presentation Prepare a multimedia presentation on some facet of the civil rights movement. Include photographs, newspaper and magazine stories, audiotapes or videotapes in your presentation. **[Social Studies Link]**

7. Music Find or compose music that contrasts the songs of the caged bird and the free bird. Play or perform your music for the class. **[Music Link]**

Writing Mini-Lesson

Song Honoring a Hero

Charlayne Hunter-Goult was a hero to many of the people of her time. Think of a modern-day hero, and write words to a song celebrating this person. If you are musically inclined, you can set your words to music, or you can find an already existing melody and write appropriate words for it. In writing your song honoring a hero, the following may help you.

Writing Skills Focus: Clear and Consistent Purpose

If you define a **clear and consistent purpose,** your song of praise will be focused and effective. Following are a few of the purposes you might consider:

Possible Purposes:

- To entertain listeners with a great story
- To make listeners admire the hero
- To teach a lesson about life
- To praise an unsung everyday hero

Prewriting Decide on your purpose, then brainstorm for the qualities that make the hero admirable. Refer to your purpose as you accumulate information, to help you decide which qualities to emphasize in your song of praise.

Drafting Because you are writing a kind of poem, rather than a prose description, you will have to be more selective and use fewer words, which will have greater impact. Feel free to use figures of speech, such as similes, metaphors, and symbols.

Revising Read your song of praise out loud to see whether it is concise and flows smoothly. Make sure that your song accomplishes the purpose you set out to achieve.

Writing Process Workshop

Without even realizing it, we're always making comparisons. For example, as you read the selections in this section, you probably saw similarities and differences in the ways in which the characters addressed the theme of finding one's identity.

A **comparison-and-contrast essay** is a brief written exploration of the similarities and differences between two (or more) things. Using the skills listed below—which were introduced in this section's Writing Mini-Lessons—write a comparison-and-contrast essay on a topic that interests you.

Writing Skills Focus

▶ **Give specific examples** to show precisely how your two subjects are alike and different. (See p. 220.)

▶ **Use a clear and logical organization** to make it easy for readers to follow your comparison. (See p. 233.)

▶ **Keep your audience in mind.** Provide details to clarify any topics or terms they won't recognize. (See p. 243.)

▶ **Have a clear and consistent purpose** for writing. Make your purpose clear to your audience. (See p. 254.)

The poet Maya Angelou uses these skills as she compares and contrasts a free bird with a caged bird.

MODEL FROM LITERATURE

from "Caged Bird" by Maya Angelou

A free bird leaps
on the back of the wind
and floats downstream
till the current ends ①
and dips his wing
in the orange sun rays
and dares to claim the sky.

But a bird that stalks
down his narrow cage ②
can seldom see through
his bars of rage
his wings are clipped and
his feet are tied
so he opens his throat to sing. ③

① The poet gives specific examples of the free bird's actions, contrasting them with the caged bird's actions in the second verse.

② The poet organizes her details by describing each bird in a separate stanza.

③ Readers can sense Angelou's purpose: to compare and contrast freedom and slavery.

APPLYING LANGUAGE SKILLS: Clear Comparisons

When you write, always make clear exactly what you are comparing or contrasting.

Unclear:

Alaska is bigger than Texas.

Clear:

Alaska is bigger than Texas in area.

The phrase *in area* makes clear that the statement compares size, not population.

Practice On your paper, rewrite each sentence to make the comparison clear.

1. Photographs are easier than paintings.
2. Days are longer in the summer.
3. Air conditioners are more than fans.

Writing Application As you draft your comparison-and-contrast essay, use words that will show exactly what you are comparing and contrasting. If a statement is vague, add words that will clarify its meaning.

Writer's Solution Connection
Writing Lab

To help you gather and organize details for your essay, use the Venn Diagram activity in the tutorial on Exposition.

Prewriting

Brainstorm in a Small Group to Find a Topic With a small group of classmates, brainstorm to come up with possible topics. Start by looking at similarities and differences among the selections in this section. Then extend your discussion to topics such as actors, musicians, athletes, cities, television programs, and so on. First list the ideas your group comes up with, then choose the topic that you find most interesting.

Decide on Your Purpose After choosing a topic, decide on your reason for writing. It might be

▶ **To inform** readers about your two subjects.
▶ **To persuade** readers to accept a specific point of view related to the two subjects.
▶ **To entertain** your audience with humorous details.

Once you've decided on your purpose, gather details that will help you achieve your purpose.

Keep Your Audience in Mind Identify your audience. Then keep the answers to questions such as these in mind as you gather details and write your essay:

▶ How old are my readers?
▶ What type of language will appeal to them?
▶ What might they already know about my topic?
▶ What might they not know that I should explain?

Organize Your Details Before you begin writing, use a Venn diagram like this one to help organize your details. Write similarities in the space where the circles overlap, and note the differences in the outer sections of the circles.

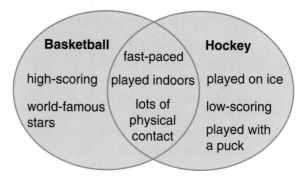

Drafting

Use a Clear and Logical Organization As you draft your essay, organize your details in a way that is easy to follow. For example, within each paragraph you might focus on similarities and differences in a single area or you might explore all of the similarities first, then explore all the differences.

Give Specific Examples Be specific about the ways in which your subjects are alike and different. For example, if you are comparing and contrasting a lion and a tiger, offer details such as the size and shape of each animal and how each moves.

Revising

Use a Checklist Go back to the Writing Skills Focus on the first page of the lesson and use the items as a checklist to evaluate and revise your comparison-and-contrast essay. Ask yourself the following questions and make revisions as necessary.

► Have I given specific examples?
► Have I used a clear and logical organization?
► Have I kept my audience in mind?
► Do I have a clear and consistent purpose?

REVISION MODEL

Basketball and hockey are both sports that are rising

① , but basketball is much more exciting.   ② fast-paced, end-to-end action.
in popularity. The two are filled with nonstop action.
③ In basketball, the action takes place on a hardwood floor; in hockey, it takes place on ice.
Hockey is played with a puck that moves so fast that

④ In contrast,
it's sometimes hard to see. Basketball is played with a

large ball that's easy to see—even when the players are

rushing down the court at breakneck speed.

① The writer adds a statement that clearly indicates his purpose—to argue that basketball is the more exciting sport.
② The writer adds more precise details.
③ The writer adds this sentence for those in his audience who may have little knowledge of either sport.
④ The writer adds a transition to make the essay easier to follow.

Publishing

Post Your Work on the Internet A great way to share your work is to post it on the Internet so that others interested in your topic can read it and respond to it. If you have little experience with the Internet, ask someone with computer expertise to help you.

APPLYING LANGUAGE SKILLS: Compound Sentences

A **compound sentence** consists of two or more independent clauses. You can create compound sentences by combining simple sentences.

Simple Sentences:
Bats are mammals. They can fly.

Compound Sentence:
Bats are mammals, and they can fly.

Practice On your paper, rewrite each pair of simple sentences as a compound sentence.

1. Bees are insects. Spiders are not.
2. Insects have wings. So do birds.
3. Bats see poorly. They hear very well.

Writing Application Review your comparison-and-contrast essay. Find places where you can join two simple sentences to make one compound sentence.

Writer's Solution Connection Language Lab

For more practice with compound sentences, complete the lesson on Varying Sentence Structure.

Real-World Reading Skills Workshop

Strategies for Success

Before you buy a product, it's wise to comparison-shop by checking out two or more competing brands. One way to do this is to read a consumer report— an evaluation of competing products written after the products were tested. Here's what to look for in your reading:

Consider the Source Most consumer reports are written by people who have no ties to any of the companies whose products they evaluate. Some reports, however, are written by people hired by a particular manufacturer. Naturally, their judgment may be biased. Always check the source of a report before deciding how reliable the findings are.

Answer Your Questions Before reading a report, think of questions you have about each brand. For example: How much does it cost? How long will it last? What are its benefits? What are its dangers? Then, as you read, look for the answer to each question. If you don't find all your answers, read another report on the same product.

Look at the Date Note the date that a report was written. A year-old report can be inaccurate today. Companies often make changes in their products. An item may now contain new ingredients or offer a different guarantee, for example. Always look for the most recent information.

SNEAKERS REPORT 6/27/93
from *Bounce Company Annual Report*

Dynamo Sneakers are the least expensive on the market. They retail for only $19.99, compared to $29.99 for Bounce Sneakers and $38.99 for Cushy Sneakers.

Of the three brands, Bounce was found to last longest for basketball use — the average life being 8 months. For walking only, both Bounce and Cushy had an average life of 12 months, compared to Dynamo's 7.

Cushy is the only sneaker of the three to offer an air-filled cushion under the arch of the foot. Both Dynamo and Bounce have plain rubber arch supports.

Last year, there were 54 complaints of foot injuries by Cushy users, compared to 38 for Dynamo.

Apply the Strategy

Imagine you want to buy sneakers. Use the consumer report to help you decide.

1. Do you feel the report is reliable? Why or why not?

2. What information about users' complaints is not given?

3. Which brand would you buy for basketball? Why?

4. Which brand would you buy for walking? Why?

5. Which brand do you feel offers the most benefits? Why?

> ✔ A consumer report can also be helpful if you are
> ► planning to start a business
> ► advertising a product
> ► inventing a new product

PART *2* # *Learning About Ourselves and Others*

Sunday School Boys (detail), 1990, Jonathan Green, Oil on canvas, 23" x 23", Courtesy of the artist

Learning About Ourselves and Others ◆ *259*

Guide for Reading

Saki (1870–1916)

Long before it became common for entertainers to be known by a single name, British writer H. H. Munro became famous using the memorable pen name Saki—a name most likely inspired by a character from Persian writer Omar Khayyam's series of poems *The Rubaiyat*.

> *Saki earned his popularity by writing humorous stories that poked fun at upper-class British society.*

Born in Burma, where his father was inspector general of the police force, Saki was sent at age two to live in England. He was raised in a strict household by two aunts. As a young adult, he returned to Burma to serve in the police force. Two years later, however, poor health forced him to return to England, where he began working as a journalist.

Beginnings as a Writer After serving as a foreign correspondent for *The Morning Post* in Russia and France, Saki settled in London. There he began writing short stories, and in 1904 he published a collection of short stories entitled *Reginald*, using his soon-to-be-famous pen name for the first time. He went on to write several more collections of stories and two novels, *The Unbearable Bassington* (1912) and *When William Came* (1913). His stories have carefully constructed plots that often feature a practical joke or a surprise ending. "The Interlopers" is one such story.

A Tragic End Unfortunately, Saki's career as a writer was a short one. When World War I broke out, he enlisted in the British army. Two years later, he was killed in France. In honor of his memory, the king issued a scroll that concludes with the words, "Let those who come after see to it that his name is not forgotten."

◆ Build Vocabulary

WORD ROOTS: *-dol-*

In "The Interlopers," you will come across the word *condolence*, which contains the root *-dol-*. Because *-dol-* means "pain," *condolence* literally means "a feeling of pain with another," or "an expression of sympathy for a grieving person."

precipitous
marauders
medley
condolence
languor
succor

WORD BANK

As you read the story, you will encounter the words on this list. Each word is defined on the page where it first appears. Preview the list before you read.

◆ Build Grammar Skills

COMMONLY CONFUSED WORDS: *BETWEEN* AND *AMONG*

Words with similar meanings can easily be confused. The prepositions **between** and **among** are two such words. When used correctly, *between* shows a relationship between two items at a time, and *among* shows a relationship among more than two items at a time. Note the following examples from "The Interlopers." The first example refers to two families; the second refers to many animals.

. . . similar scandals had embittered the relationships *between* the families for three generations.

. . . there was movement and unrest *among* the creatures that were wont to sleep through the dark hours.

The Interlopers

◆ *Literature and Your Life*

CONNECT YOUR EXPERIENCE

Everyone gets into arguments from time to time. Luckily, people can usually settle their differences and put past arguments behind them. Sometimes, however, a disagreement can last a lifetime. Such is the case with the two characters in "The Interlopers."

Journal Writing Jot down some negative consequences that can result from a long-standing dispute between two people.

THEMATIC FOCUS: LEARNING ABOUT OURSELVES AND OTHERS

Sometimes it takes a catastrophe to help people discover what's truly important in life. Such a moment of discovery takes place in "The Interlopers."

◆ Background for Understanding

SOCIAL STUDIES

Maybe you've heard of the Hatfields and the McCoys. These two families from Kentucky and West Virginia are famous for their bloody feud. A feud is a bitter, long-standing fight that often occurs between families. It usually begins with an insult or injury that the people involved feel must be avenged. The act of vengeance then prompts a response, resulting in a never-ending cycle. The brutality and drama of a feud can make a gripping story. That's why feuds often appear in literature. Shakespeare's *Romeo and Juliet* and Saki's "The Interlopers" are just two works of literature in which a feud is central to the plot.

◆ Literary Focus

CONFLICT

Most story plots are built around **conflict**, or struggle between opposing forces. An **external conflict** occurs between two or more characters, or between a character and the forces of nature. An **internal conflict** occurs within a character who possesses opposing ideas or feelings. The two characters in "The Interlopers" inherited an external conflict from their grandparents.

◆ Reading Strategy

IDENTIFY CAUSES AND EFFECTS

Conflicts usually have **causes**, or reasons. In "The Interlopers," two characters hate each other because of a land dispute that has been raging between their families for three generations. In this case, the cause is the land dispute, and the **effect**, or result, is the hatred between the two families.

Further causes and effects propel "The Interlopers" toward its surprising conclusion. Keep track of story events as you read by filling in a cause-and-effect chart like the one shown here.

Cause	Effect
Land dispute	Life-long feud

The
Interlopers

Saki

In a forest of mixed growth somewhere on the eastern spurs of the Carpathians,[1] a man stood one winter night watching and listening, as though he waited for some beast of the woods to come within the range of his vision, and, later, of his rifle. But the game for whose presence he kept so keen an outlook was none that figured in the sportsman's calendar as lawful and proper for the chase: Ulrich von Gradwitz[2] patrolled the dark forest in quest of a human enemy.

The forest lands of Gradwitz were of wide extent and well stocked with game; the narrow strip of <u>precipitous</u> woodland that lay on its outskirt was not remarkable for the game it harbored or the shooting it afforded, but it was the most jealously guarded of all its owner's territorial possessions. A famous lawsuit, in the days of his grandfather, had wrested it from the illegal possession of a neighboring family of petty landowners; the dispossessed party had never acquiesced in the judgment of the Courts, and a long series of poaching affrays[3] and similar scandals had embittered the relationships between the families for three generations. The neighbor feud had grown into a personal one since Ulrich had come to be head of his family; if there was a man in the world whom he detested and wished ill to it

---

1. **Carpathians** (kär pā′ thē ənz): Mountains in central Europe.
2. **Ulrich von Gradwitz** (ool′ rik fôn gräd′ vitz)
3. **poaching affrays** (pōch′ iŋ ə frāz′): Disputes about hunting on someone else's property.

◆ **Build Vocabulary**

precipitous (pri sip′ ə təs) *adj*.: Steep; sheer

marauders (mə rôd′ ərz) *n*.: Raiders; people who take goods by force

was Georg Znaeym,[4] the inheritor of the quarrel and the tireless game-snatcher and raider of the disputed border-forest. The feud might, perhaps, have died down or been compromised if the personal ill will of the two men had not stood in the way; as boys they had thirsted for one another's blood, as men each prayed that misfortune might fall on the other, and this wind-scourged winter night Ulrich had banded together his foresters to watch the dark forest, not in quest of four-footed quarry, but to keep a lookout for the prowling thieves whom he suspected of being afoot from across the land boundary. The roebuck[5] which usually kept in the sheltered hollows during a storm wind, were running like driven things tonight, and there was movement and unrest among the creatures that were wont to sleep through the dark hours. Assuredly there was a disturbing element in the forest, and Ulrich could guess the quarter from whence it came.

He strayed away by himself from the watchers whom he had placed in ambush on the crest of the hill, and wandered far down the steep slopes amid the wild tangle of undergrowth, peering through the tree trunks and listening through the whistling and skirling of the wind and the restless beating of the branches for sight or sound of the <u>marauders</u>. If only on this wild night, in this dark, lone spot, he might come across Georg Znaeym, man to man, with none to witness—that was the wish that was uppermost in his thoughts. And as he stepped round the trunk of a huge beech he came face to face with the man he sought.

The two enemies stood glaring at one another for a long silent moment. Each had a rifle in his hand, each had hate in his heart and murder uppermost in his mind. The chance had come to give full play to the passions of a lifetime. But a man who has been brought up under the code of a restraining civilization cannot easily nerve himself to shoot down his neighbor in cold blood and without word spoken, except for an offense against his hearth and honor. And before the moment of hesitation had given way to action a deed of Nature's own violence overwhelmed them both. A fierce shriek of the storm had been answered by a splitting crash over their heads, and ere they could leap aside a mass of falling beech tree had thundered down on them. Ulrich von Gradwitz found himself stretched on the ground, one arm numb beneath him and the other held almost as helplessly in a tight tangle of forked branches, while both legs were pinned beneath the fallen mass. His heavy shooting-boots had saved his feet from

---

4. **Georg Znaeym** (gā´ ôrg znä´ im)
5. **roebuck** (rō´ buk´) *n.*: Male deer.

being crushed to pieces, but if his fractures were not as serious as they might have been, at least it was evident that he could not move from his present position till someone came to release him. The descending twigs had slashed the skin of his face, and he had to wink away some drops of blood from his eyelashes before he could take in a general view of the disaster. At his side, so near that under ordinary circumstances he could almost have touched him, lay Georg Znaeym, alive and struggling, but obviously as helplessly pinioned down as himself. All round them lay a thick-strewn wreckage of splintered branches and broken twigs.

Relief at being alive and exasperation at his captive plight brought a strange medley of pious thank-offerings and sharp curses to Ulrich's lips. Georg, who was nearly blinded with the blood which trickled across his eyes, stopped his struggling for a moment to listen, and then gave a short, snarling laugh.

"So you're not killed, as you ought to be, but you're caught, anyway," he cried; "caught fast. Ho, what a jest, Ulrich von Gradwitz snared in his stolen forest. There's real justice for you!"

And he laughed again, mockingly and savagely.

"I'm caught in my own forest land," retorted Ulrich. "When my men come to release us you will wish, perhaps, that you were in a better plight than caught poaching on a neighbor's land, shame on you."

Georg was silent for a moment; then he answered quietly:

"Are you sure that your men will find much to release? I have men, too, in the forest tonight, close behind me, and *they* will be here first and do the releasing. When they drag me out from under these branches it won't

◆ **Reading Strategy**
Why do Georg and Ulrich tell each other about how their men will find them?

need much clumsiness on their part to roll this mass of trunk right over on the top of you. Your men will find you dead under a fallen beech tree. For form's sake I shall send my condolences to your family."

"It is a useful hint," said Ulrich fiercely. "My men had orders to follow in ten minutes' time, seven of which must have gone by already, and when they get me out—I will remember the hint. Only as you will have met your death poaching on my lands I don't think I can decently send any message of condolence to your family."

"Good," snarled Georg, "good. We fight this quarrel out to the death, you and I and our foresters, with no cursed interlopers to come between us. Death and damnation to you, Ulrich von Gradwitz."

◆ Build Vocabulary

medley (med′ lē) *n.:* Mixture of things not usually found together

condolence (kən dō′ ləns) *n.:* Expression of sympathy with a grieving person

languor (laŋ′ gər) *n.:* Lack of vigor; weakness

▼ **Critical Viewing** What kinds of encounters or incidents might occur in this setting? [Analyze]

"The same to you, Georg Znaeym, forest-thief, game-snatcher."

Both men spoke with the bitterness of possible defeat before them, for each knew that it might be long before his men would seek him out or find him; it was a bare matter of chance which party would arrive first on the scene.

Both had now given up the useless struggle to free themselves from the mass of wood that held them down; Ulrich limited his endeavors to an effort to bring his one partially free arm near enough to his outer coat pocket to draw out his wine flask. Even when he had accomplished that operation it was long before he could manage the unscrewing of the stopper or get any of the liquid down his throat. But what a heaven-sent draft it seemed! It was an open winter, and little snow had fallen as yet, hence the captives suffered less from the cold than might have been the case at that season of the year; nevertheless, the wine was warming and reviving to the wounded man, and he looked across with something like a throb of pity to where his enemy lay, just keeping the groans of pain and weariness from crossing his lips.

"Could you reach this flask if I threw it over to you?" asked Ulrich suddenly; "there is good wine in it, and one may as well be as comfortable as one can. Let us drink, even if tonight one of us dies."

"No, I can scarcely see anything; there is so much blood caked round my eyes," said Georg, "and in any case I don't drink wine with an enemy."

Ulrich was silent for a few minutes, and lay listening to the weary screeching of the wind. An idea was slowly forming and growing in his brain, an idea that gained strength every time that he looked across at the man who was fighting so grimly against pain and exhaustion. In the pain and languor that Ulrich himself was feeling the old fierce hatred seemed to be dying down.

"Neighbor," he said presently, "do as you please if your men come first. It was a fair compact. But as for me, I've changed my mind. If my men are the first to come you shall be the first to be helped, as though you were my guest. We have quarreled like devils all our lives over this stupid strip of forest, where the trees

◆ **Literary Focus**
What do you think motivates Ulrich's change of heart? Does this change reflect an internal or external conflict?

can't even stand upright in a breath of wind. Lying here tonight, thinking, I've come to think we've been rather fools; there are better things in life than getting the better of a boundary dispute. Neighbor, if you will help me to bury the old quarrel I— I will ask you to be my friend."

Georg Znaeym was silent for so long that Ulrich thought, perhaps, he had fainted with the pain of his injuries. Then he spoke slowly and in jerks.

"How the whole region would stare and gabble if we rode into the market square together. No one living can remember seeing a Znaeym and a von Gradwitz talking to one another in friendship. And what peace there would be among the forester folk if we ended our feud tonight. And if we choose to make peace among our people there is none other to interfere, no interlopers from outside . . . You would come and keep the Sylvester night beneath my roof, and I would come and feast on some high day at your castle . . . I would never fire a shot on your land, save when you invited me as a guest; and you should come and shoot with me down in the marshes where the wildfowl are. In all the countryside there are none that could hinder if we willed to make peace. I never thought to have wanted to do other than hate you all my life, but I think I have changed my mind about things too, this last half-hour. And you offered me your wine flask . . . Ulrich von Gradwitz, I will be your friend."

For a space both men were silent, turning over in their minds the wonderful changes that this dramatic reconciliation would bring about. In the cold, gloomy forest, with the wind tearing in fitful gusts through the naked branches and whistling round the tree trunks, they lay and waited for the help that would now bring release and succor to both parties. And each prayed a private prayer that his men might be the first to arrive, so that he might be

the first to show honorable attention to the enemy that had become a friend.

◆ **Reading Strategy**
How do both men feel about each other now? How do you think the story will end?

Presently, as the wind dropped for a moment, Ulrich broke silence.

"Let's shout for help," he said; "in this lull our voices may carry a little way."

"They won't carry far through the trees and undergrowth," said Georg, "but we can try. Together, then."

The two raised their voices in a prolonged hunting call.

"Together again," said Ulrich a few minutes later, after listening in vain for an answering halloo.

"I heard something that time, I think," said Ulrich.

"I heard nothing but the pestilential wind," said Georg hoarsely.

There was silence again for some minutes, and then Ulrich gave a joyful cry.

"I can see figures coming through the wood. They are following in the way I came down the hillside."

Both men raised their voices in as loud a shout as they could muster.

"They hear us! They've stopped. Now they see us. They're running down the hill toward us," cried Ulrich.

"How many of them are there?" asked Georg.

"I can't see distinctly," said Ulrich; "nine or ten."

"Then they are yours," said Georg; "I had only seven out with me."

"They are making all the speed they can, brave lads," said Ulrich gladly.

"Are they your men?" asked Georg. "Are they your men?" he repeated impatiently as Ulrich did not answer.

"No," said Ulrich with a laugh, the idiotic chattering laugh of a man unstrung with hideous fear.

"Who are they?" asked Georg quickly, straining his eyes to see what the other would gladly not have seen.

"Wolves."

◆ **Build Vocabulary**
succor (suk´ ər) *n.*: Aid; help; relief

Guide for Responding

◆ *Literature and Your Life*

Reader's Response With whom did you sympathize: Ulrich, Georg, neither, or both? Why?

Thematic Focus What did Ulrich and Georg discover about themselves and each other while they were trapped under the fallen tree?

Journal Entry When Ulrich and Georg finally ended their conflict, it was too late. List some benefits that might have been achieved by ending the conflict years earlier.

☑ Check Your Comprehension

1. What is Ulrich doing in the forest?
2. What has kept the feud between the families going for three generations?
3. Why don't Ulrich and Georg shoot each other when they meet in the forest?
4. How do the two men become trapped?

Guide for Responding *(continued)*

◆ Critical Thinking

INTERPRET

1. List ways in which Ulrich and Georg are alike, and ways in which they are different. **[Compare and Contrast]**
2. Why is Ulrich so angry at Georg for trespassing on a small and nearly worthless piece of land? **[Infer]**
3. Why doesn't Georg consider himself a poacher? **[Infer]**
4. Why do Ulrich and Georg end their feud when they find themselves trapped under the fallen tree? **[Infer]**
5. An interloper is someone who intrudes into the affairs of others. Give two interpretations of the story's title. **[Interpret]**

APPLY

6. Describe how the story might have continued if the two men had been rescued. **[Speculate]**

EXTEND

7. Disputes over land often occur among nations. What are some territorial disputes among nations in today's world? How might these disputes be resolved? **[Social Studies Link]**

◆ Build Grammar Skills

COMMONLY CONFUSED WORDS: *BETWEEN* AND *AMONG*

Between is used to show a relationship between two items at a time. *Among* is used to show a relationship among more than two items at a time.

Practice In your notebook, write the word that correctly completes each sentence.
1. Chris and I have only two dollars (between, among) us.
2. She stood (between, among) the other actors on stage.
3. He was the only child (between, among) a roomful of adults.
4. Let's keep this a secret (between, among) you and me.
5. There was a dispute (between, among) several of the people in the crowd.

◆ Literary Focus

CONFLICT

A **conflict** is a struggle between opposing forces. An **external conflict** pits characters against each other or against the forces of nature. An **internal conflict** pits a character against himself or herself.

Find an example of each of the following types of conflict in "The Interlopers" and explain the nature of the conflict.
1. A character in conflict with another character
2. A character in conflict with nature
3. A character in conflict with himself

◆ Reading Strategy

IDENTIFY CAUSES AND EFFECTS

Every conflict has both **causes** and **effects**. For example, the conflict between Ulrich's and Georg's grandfathers was caused by both men's desire for the same piece of land. One effect of this conflict is that Ulrich and Georg are now enemies. Identify two other causes and effects in the story.

◆ Build Vocabulary

USING THE WORD ROOT -*dol*-

The root -*dol*- means "pain." Read the definitions of the following words that contain -*dol*-. Then, on a separate sheet of paper, write a sentence that contains each word.
1. In*dol*ent means "avoiding the pain of work; lazy."
2. *Dol*eful means "full of sadness."

USING THE WORD BANK

In your notebook, write sentences as described below using one word from the Word Bank.
1. Write the lead sentence of a news article describing a robbery.
2. Describe the site of a rock-climbing expedition.
3. Tell what a group of rescue workers did for flood victims.
4. Write the first line of a letter to a friend who has lost an elderly family member.
5. Tell how you would feel after spending a week in bed with the flu.
6. Write the menu description for a special salad.

Build Your Portfolio

 ## Idea Bank

Writing

1. **Last Letter** Write a letter Ulrich or Georg might have written before the wolves closed in, telling how the members of both families should treat each other from now on.

2. **Happy Ending** Write a new ending for "The Interlopers" in which the two men are saved. Describe how the two former enemies announce their newly discovered friendship.

3. **Peaceful Speech** Imagine that you had been a friend of both Ulrich's and Georg's grandfathers when the feud began. Write a brief speech directed toward one of the two men in which you try to bring about a reconciliation.

Speaking and Listening

4. **Persuasive Argument** Form two groups of three students. One group will represent Ulrich and the other, Georg. Have each group present an argument including reasons why the person they represent is entitled to the disputed piece of land.

5. **Performance** Prepare a dramatic interpretation of the story to perform for the class.
[Performing Arts Link]

Projects

6. **Real-Estate Advertisement** Create a magazine advertisement announcing that the disputed piece of land is for sale. In your ad, describe the property, give a price, and tell whom a buyer should contact. **[Career Link]**

7. **Presentation on Wolves** Create a multimedia presentation on wolves that includes information on where they live, how they raise their young, how they form packs, and how they hunt. Include photos, drawings, film clips, or audio recordings in your presentation. **[Science Link; Art Link]**

 ## Writing Mini-Lesson

News Story

"Nature's own violence" spells doom for Ulrich and Georg when a huge tree crashes down upon them. Imagine that you are a reporter assigned to write a news story about the freak accident and its terrible aftermath. Keep the following in mind as you write.

> #### Writing Skills Focus: Elaboration for Understanding
>
> **Elaboration** is the development of ideas and details to make a piece of writing precise and complete. In a strong news story, the writer uses elaboration to answer the questions *who, what, when, where, why,* and *how.* Facts, statistics, sensory details, and quotations are types of elaboration that work well in news stories.

Prewriting Organize your story according to the three main parts of a news story:
1. The **headline** is the first thing a reader sees. Compose a short headline that grabs the reader's attention.
2. The **lead** is the first paragraph of a news story. Put your most important information here.
3. The **body** provides details on information presented in the lead. Elaborate most in this section.

Drafting Begin your news story with a striking statement about the accident that will capture your readers' attention. Then tell your story, following news-story organization. As you write, ask yourself what your readers will find interesting or what they'll need to know, and elaborate on those aspects of the story.

Revising Read your story aloud to a classmate and ask if any part of the story is unclear or requires further elaboration. Use the classmate's suggestions to guide you in making revisions.

Guide for Reading

James Michener (1907–1997)

This globe-trotting American writer began life as a foundling child in Doylestown, Pennsylvania. He was adopted by Mabel Michener and raised as a Quaker. After graduating from Swarthmore College, he worked as a book editor until he joined the navy during World War II. His experiences in the Pacific would set Michener on a new course after the war, when the editor stopped working on other people's manuscripts and started creating his own. Michener wrote eighteen related sketches called *Tales of the South Pacific* (1947), a work that won him a Pulitzer Prize. The book was soon adapted into a very popular musical by Richard Rodgers and Oscar Hammerstein; this play, *South Pacific,* was later turned into a film and has become an American classic.

Portraits of Lands and Cultures

This first work propelled Michener into a long and productive career as a portraitist of other lands and people. Two of his novels, *The Bridges at Toko-Ri* (1953) and *Sayonara* (1954), were set in Japan—both also were turned into films, as was his best-selling *Hawaii* (1959). Michener has also written about the Holy Land in *The Source* (1965), Spain in *Iberia* (1968), and South Africa in *The Covenant* (1980). He ranged ever farther afield in *Space,* a 1983 novel about the American space effort.

Michener also found inspiration close to home. *Centennial* (1974) covers centuries of life in Colorado, while *Chesapeake* (1978) does the same for Maryland's Eastern Shore region. In *Texas* (1985), Michener hardly left his own backyard, since he resided in Austin for many years.

◆ Build Vocabulary

WORD ROOTS: -vis-

In this selection, you will find the word *improvised* used twice to describe two very different things. What these improvised things have in common is that they are hastily put together, not planned ahead of time. Literally, *improvised* means "unforeseen"; the word is based on the Latin root -vis-, which means "see." In this case, it is preceded by the prefixes *im-* and *pro-,* which mean "not" and "before," respectively. Some other -vis- words you may know are *vision, invisible,* and *revise* (literally, "to see again").

improvised
laden
encompassed
impose
ingeniously

WORD BANK

Before you read, preview this list of words from the story. In your notebook, write the words you think you already know and their meanings.

◆ Build Grammar Skills

CORRECT USE OF *LIKE* AND *AS/AS IF*

Because he is telling a story that involves the passage of time as well as some complex human interactions, James Michener often uses subordinate clauses introduced by conjunctions. Take a look at one of his sentences, which includes a subordinate clause introduced by the conjunction *as:*

In time the rugs arrived, just *as Muhammed Zaqir had predicted they would.*

Notice that Michener does not write "...just *like* Muhammed Zaqir had predicted they would," because *like* is a preposition, not a conjunction, and must not be used to introduce clauses.

The Rug Merchant

◆ Literature and Your Life

CONNECT YOUR EXPERIENCE

Sometimes you make decisions and then find yourself unmaking them. You believe you have sized someone up, and then you discover that a bit more measuring tape is called for. That is what happens to someone in "The Rug Merchant."

Journal Writing How do you decide whether or not you like and trust someone? Write down the chief standards that you use to size up a new acquaintance as someone you would like to know.

THEMATIC FOCUS: LEARNING ABOUT OURSELVES AND OTHERS

Sometimes making discoveries about other people makes you see yourself in a new way too. Why do you think people are often reluctant to change their views about a person?

◆ Background for Understanding

CULTURE

People in central and western Asia invented carpets over a thousand years ago as coverings for earthen floors in dwellings and mosques. Most Oriental rugs are made of sheep's wool, but the finest are made of silk, which has a more supple texture than wool and can be made to produce glowing colors. Different designs are associated with different regions in Asia: Most have abstract or geometric patterns, although some include representational images—for example, people, plants, and animals.

◆ Literary Focus

CHARACTERIZATION IN ESSAYS

The setting is a hotel in the Middle East. A thin man, with a smile that never leaves his face, rides up on a camel, walks into a room, and throws dozens of beautiful rugs on the floor. These and many other details—what the man says, how he behaves, what other people say about him—will be added to his **characterization,** the act of creating and developing a character. Writers create and develop characters through **characterization.** What a character says, how he or she behaves, and what other people say about that character are all elements of characterization.

◆ Reading Strategy

MAKE INFERENCES ABOUT CHARACTERS

The rug merchant who walks into James Michener's room leaves his rugs and says, "No necessity to buy. I leave here. You study, you learn to like." His actions and words suggest either that he is hopelessly naive or that he has a sixth sense about who can be trusted. Michener uses such details to help you draw your own conclusions—**make inferences**—about what the character is like.

As you read, it may help to note any details that allow you to make inferences. To organize your information, make a chart like the one shown here.

Appearance (inference)	Words (inference)	Actions (inference)

The Rug Merchant

from *The World Is My Home: A Memoir*

James Michener

I once made a long trip over the Dasht-i-Margo, the desert in Afghanistan, to the ancient city of Herat,[1] where I lodged in a former mosque with earthen floors. I had been in my improvised quarters only a few minutes when a very thin, toothy man with longish black hair and a perpetual smile entered and started throwing onto the dirt floor twenty or thirty of the most enchantingly beautiful Persian rugs I had ever seen. Their designs were miraculous—intricate interweavings of Koranic symbols framed in geometric patterns that teased the eye—but their colors were also sheer delight: reds, yellows, greens and especially dark blues that were radiant.

They made my room a museum, one rug piled atop another, all peeking out at me, and when they were in place and the smiling man was satisfied with his handiwork—I supposed that this was a service of the so-called hotel—to my amazement he handed me a scrap of paper on which was written in pencil in English: "MUHAMMAD ZAQIR, RUG MERCHANT, HERAT."

Aware at last of how I had been trapped, I protested: "No! No! No rugs!" but without relaxing his smile the least bit he said in English: "No necessity to buy. I leave here. You study, you learn to like," and before I could protest further he was gone. I ran out to make him take back his rugs, for I wanted none of them, but he was already leading his laden camel away from the old mosque.

I assumed he had learned from the hotel manager that I was to be in Herat for five days, and it was obvious that he felt confident that within that period he could wear

---

1. **Herat** (he rät´)

◆ **Build Vocabulary**

improvised (im´ prə vīzd) *adj.*: Put together on the spur of the moment

laden (lād´ ən) *adj.*: Burdened

▲ **Critical Viewing** Do you think the carpet dealer is proud of his rugs? Explain. **[Deduce]**

me down and persuade me to buy a rug. He started on the evening of that first day; he came back after supper to sit with me in the shadowy light cast by a flickering lamp. He said: "Have you ever seen lovelier rugs? That one from my friend in Meshed. Those two from the dealer in Bukhara. This one from a place you know, maybe? Samarkand."

When I asked him how he was able to trade with such towns in the Soviet Union[2] he shrugged: "Borders? Out here we don't bother," and with a sweep of his hand that encompassed all the rugs he said: "Not one woven in Afghanistan," and I noted the compelling pronunciation he gave that name: Ahf-han-ee-stahn.

He sat for more than an hour with me that evening, and next day he was back before noon to start his serious bargaining: "Michener-sahib,[3] name German perhaps?" I told him it was more likely English, at which he laughed: "English, Afghans, many battles, English always win but next day you march back to India, nothing change." When I corrected him: "I'm not English," he said: "I know. Pennsylvania. Three, four, maybe five of your rugs look great your place Pennsylvania."

"But I don't need rugs there. I don't really want them."

"Would they not look fine Pennsylvania?" and as if the rugs were of little value, he kicked the top ones aside to reveal the glowing wonders of those below.

When he returned that second night he got down to even more serious business:

"The big white and gold one you like, six hundred dollars." On and on he went, and when it was clear that I had no interest whatever in the big ones, he subtly covered them over with the smaller six-by four-foot ones already in the room; then he ran out to his camel to fetch seven or eight of the size that I had in some unconscious way disclosed I might consider, and by the end of that session he knew that I was at least a possible purchaser of four or five of the handsome rugs.

"Ah, Michener-sahib, you have fine eye. That

---

2. **Soviet Union:** The Union of Soviet Socialist Republics consisted of fifteen republics strictly controlled by the country's central government until independence movements in 1991.
3. **Michener-sahib** (sä´ ib): Mr. Michener.

♦ **Build Vocabulary**

encompassed (en kum´ pəst) *v.*: Surrounded

one from China, silk and wool, look at those tiny knots." Then he gave me a lesson in rug making; he talked about the designs, the variation in knots, the wonderful compactness of the Chinese variety, the dazzling colors of the Samarkand. It was fascinating to hear him talk, and all the while he was wearing me down.

◆ **Literary Focus**
What do Zaqir's persistence and sales technique suggest about his understanding of people?

He was a persistent rascal, always watching till he saw me return to my mosque after work, then pouncing on me.

On the third day, as he sat drinking tea with me while our chairs were perched on his treasury of rugs, four and five deep at some places and covering the entire floor, he knocked down one after another of my objections: "You can't take them with you? No traveler can. I send them to you, camel here, ship Karachi, train New York, truck to your home Pennsylvania." Pasted onto the pages of his notebook were addresses of buyers from all parts of the world to whom he had shipped his rugs, and I noticed that they had gone out from Meshed in Iran, Mazar-e-Sharif in Afghanistan and Bukhara[4] in Russia; apparently he really moved about with his laden camel. But he also had, pasted close to the shipping address, letters from his customers proving that the rugs had finally reached their new owners. In our dealings he seemed to me an honest man.

On that third night, when it began to look as if I might escape without making a purchase even though I had shown an interest in six rugs, he hammered at me regarding payments: "Now, Michener-sahib, I can take American dollars, you know."

"I have no American dollars." Rapidly he ran through the currencies that he would accept, British, Indian, Iranian, Pakistani, Afghani, in that descending order, until I had to stop him with a truthful statement: "Muhammad, my friend, I have no money, none of any kind," and before the last word had been uttered he cried: "I take traveler's checks, American Express, Bank

---

4. **Bukhara** (bü kär´ ə)

America in California," and then I had to tell him the sad news: "Muhammad, friend. I have no traveler's checks. Left them all locked up in the American embassy in Kabul. Because there are robbers on the road to Meshed."

"I know. I know. But you are an honest man, Michener-sahib. I take your personal check."

When I said truthfully that I had none, he asked simply: "You like those six rugs?"

"Yes, you have made me appreciate them. I do."

With a sweeping gesture he gathered the six beauties, rolled them deftly into a bundle and thrust them into my arms: "You take them. Send me a check when you get to Pennsylvania."

"You would trust me?"

"You look honest. Don't I look honest?" And he picked up one of his larger rugs, a real beauty, and showed me the fine knots: "Bukhara. I got it there, could not pay. I send the money when I sell. Man in Bukhara trusts me. I trust you."

◆ **Reading Strategy**
What inference can you make about Zaqir based on his willingness to wait for payment for the rugs?

I said I could not <u>impose</u> on him in that way. Something might happen to me or I might prove to be a crook, and the discussion ended, except that as he left me he asked: "Michener, if you had the money, what rugs would you take with you?" and I said "None, but if you could ship them, I'd take those four," and he said: "Those four you shall have. I'll find a way."

Next day he was back in the mosque right after breakfast with an astonishing proposal: "Michener-sahib, I can let you have those four rugs, special price, four hundred fifty dollars." Before I could repeat my inability to pay, he said: "Bargain like this you never see again. Tell you what to do. You write me a check."

When I said, distressed at losing such a bargain: "But I really have no blank checks," he said: "You told me yesterday. I believe you.

But draw me one," and from his folder he produced a sheet of ordinary paper and a pencil. He showed me how to draw a copy of a blank check, bearing the name of the bank, address, amount, etc.—and for the first time in my life I actually drew a blank check, filled in the amount and signed it, whereupon Muhammad Zaqir placed it in his file, folded the four rugs I had bought, tied them with string and attached my name and address.

He piled the rugs onto his camel, and then mounted it to proceed on his way to Samarkand.

Back home in Pennsylvania I started to receive two different kinds of letters, perhaps fifteen of each. The following is a sample of the first category:

> I am a shipping agent in Istanbul and a freighter arrived here from Karachi bringing a large package, well wrapped, addressed to you in Pennsylvania. Upon receipt of your check for $19.50 American I will forward the package to you.

From Karachi, Istanbul, Trieste, Marseilles and heavens knows where else I received a steady flow of letters over a three-year period, and always the sum demanded was less than twenty dollars, so that I would say to myself: "Well, I've invested so much in it already, I may as well risk a little more." And off the check would go, with the rugs never getting any closer. Moreover, I was not at all sure that if they ever did reach me they would be my property, for my unusual check had never been submitted for payment, even though I had forewarned my local bank: "If it ever does arrive, pay it immediately, because it's a debt of honor."

The second group of letters explained the long delay:

> I am serving in Kabul as the Italian ambassador and was lately in Herat where a rug merchant showed me that remark-

able check you gave him for something like five hundred dollars. He asked me if I thought it would be paid if he forwarded it and I assured him that since you were a man of good reputation it would be. When I asked him why he had not submitted it sooner, he said: "Michener-sahib a good name. I show his check everybody like you, sell many rugs."

These letters came from French commercial travelers, English explorers, Indian merchants, almost anyone who might be expected to reach out-of-the-way Herat and take a room in that miserable old mosque.

In time the rugs arrived, just as Muhammad Zaqir had predicted they would, accompanied by so many shipping papers they were a museum in themselves. And after my improvised check had been used as an advertisement for nearly five years, it too came home to roost and was honored. Alas, shortly thereafter the rugs were stolen, but I remember them vividly and with longing. Especially do I remember the man who spent four days ingeniously persuading me to buy.

◆ **Build Vocabulary**

impose (im pōz´) v.: Put to some trouble

ingeniously (in jēn´ yəs lē) adv.: Cleverly

Beyond Literature

Media Connection

Michener and Hollywood "The Rug Merchant" comes from James Michener's autobiography, *The World Is My Home: A Memoir.* The book is well named, because Michener visited countless places all over the world. Many of Michener's visits have blossomed into books with titles a travel agent would love: *Tales of the South Pacific, Hawaii, Caravans, Chesapeake, Poland, Texas, Alaska,* and *Caribbean.* Because Michener's books often relate fascinating histories and describe exotic lands, Hollywood producers have snapped them up and turned them into screenplays for feature films and television movies. Films based on Michener's works include *The Bridges at Toko-Ri, Caravans, Hawaii, Return to Paradise, Sayonara,* and *South Pacific.* Television movies and series include *Centennial, Dynasty,* and *Space.* Incidentally, *Space* names one of the few places Michener never visited.

ACTIVITY Rent a video of a James Michener movie. Share your opinion of it with your classmates.

Guide for Responding

◆ **Literature and Your Life**

Reader's Response Would you have bought the rugs if you had been in James Michener's place? Why or why not?

Thematic Focus What did the rug merchant do that surprised you most?

Role Play With a partner, role play an interaction between a persuasive salesperson and a reluctant customer.

☑ **Check Your Comprehension**

1. List five offers the rug merchant made during his visit to Michener.
2. What did Michener learn from the rug merchant?
3. Michener didn't have any money with him. How did he pay for the rugs?
4. (a) How long did it take the rugs to reach Michener in Pennsylvania? (b) What had the rug merchant been doing during that time?

The Rug Merchant ◆ 277

Guide for Responding *(continued)*

◆ Critical Thinking

INTERPRET

1. Why do you think Michener continues his discussions with Zaqir even though he does not want to buy any rugs? **[Infer]**
2. Explain how Zaqir can strike Michener as both "an honest man" and "a rascal." **[Classify]**
3. What do you think Michener discovers about Zaqir in the course of their dealings? **[Infer]**
4. Why does Michener say that he will remember Zaqir? **[Draw Conclusions]**

APPLY

5. What does the essay suggest about the differences between Zaqir's culture and Michener's culture? **[Generalize]**

EXTEND

6. What could this essay teach someone about how to succeed as a salesperson? **[Career Link]**

◆ Reading Strategy

MAKE INFERENCES ABOUT CHARACTERS

By choosing a few crucial details, Michener shows us a great deal about a man he met only four times, but who continued to be part of his life for years to come.

1. What inference can you make about Zaqir's character based on his creation of the blank check?
2. What does Michener's willingness to pay the amounts demanded over the course of five years enable you to infer about his feelings for Zaqir?

◆ Literary Focus

CHARACTERIZATION IN ESSAYS

In "The Rug Merchant," James Michener weaves a portrait of an actual human being that is almost as vivid as any of his beautiful rugs.

1. State your single strongest impression of Zaqir and the actions or words that contribute to this impression.
2. Do you find Zaqir a believable, real-life human being or a fantastic but not convincing character? Explain.

◆ Build Vocabulary

USING THE WORD ROOT -vis-

Knowing that the Latin root -vis- means "see," write definitions for the following words.

1. visitation   2. invisibility   3. envision

USING THE WORD BANK

On your paper, write the word whose meaning is closest to that of the first word.

1. laden: (a) spoon, (b) burdened, (c) abandoned
2. improvised: (a) unplanned, (b) entertaining, (c) careful
3. encompassed: (a) directed, (b) ruled over, (c) included
4. ingeniously: (a) cleverly, (b) dishonestly, (c) stupidly
5. impose: (a) arrange, (b) bother, (c) stand

◆ Build Grammar Skills

CORRECT USE OF *LIKE* AND *AS/AS IF*

As can be used either as a preposition to introduce prepositional phrases or as a subordinating conjunction to introduce subordinate clauses. *Like* can be used as a preposition but not as a conjunction.

Used as Prepositions
Correct: It looks *like* spring.
My role *as* Hamlet was fun.

Used as Conjunctions
Correct: I did it just *as* you told me to do.

Incorrect: I did it just *like* you told me to.

Practice On your paper, rewrite each incorrect sentence correctly. If a sentence has no errors, write "correct."

1. He bent over the rugs just like a loving father bends over his child.
2. The rugs glowed like embers in a fireplace.
3. Zaqir returned, like Michener knew he would.
4. The rug merchant used the check as if it were cash.
5. Zaqir used the check like cash.

Build Your Portfolio

 Idea Bank

Writing

1. **Sales Catalog** Imagine that you are creating a sales catalog for Zaqir's rugs. Review the descriptions of the rugs in the essay, and then write a brief description of four different rugs, mentioning the patterns, colors, and type of weaving seen in each. **[Career Link]**

2. **Dramatic Scene** Based on one of Zaqir's visits to Michener, write a short dramatic scene that consists entirely of their conversation.

3. **Short Story** Imagine that Michener and Zaqir meet years later, after the rugs have come to Michener and been stolen. Write a story that sets forth the circumstances that bring them together again. What do they have to say to each other?

Speaking and Listening

4. **Conversation** Role-play a phone conversation between Michener and one of the many people who receive his rugs.

5. **Dramatic Monologue** Perform a dramatic monologue in the character of Zaqir, in which you express what Zaqir feels after he leaves Michener's hotel with the improvised check.

Projects

6. **Design a Rug** Design and draw a rug of your own. You may conduct research to get ideas for your rug or base your design on Michener's descriptions of Zaqir's rugs **[Art Link]**

7. **Report on Afghanistan** Assemble information about Afghanistan, including a map showing its location in Asia, facts about its land and people, photographs, and any objects you can find. **[Social Studies Link]**

 Writing Mini-Lesson

Letter of Complaint

Imagine a problem that might arise over the purchase of a rug or another household item. Suppose the item arrives damaged, or it is not the one you purchased. Write a letter of complaint attempting to address this problem. As you write, the following may help you.

Writing Skills Focus: Clear Explanation of the Problem

In order to succeed, a letter of complaint should contain a **clear explanation of the problem** at hand. The language should be direct and concise. If time or cause-effect relationships are involved, they should be clearly indicated.

Prewriting Make a list of all the important circumstances of the problem you are seeking to solve. Do not overload the letter with too much detail, but do provide enough information so that your reader knows what you expected to happen and how the result has fallen short. It may help you to list a chain of causes and effects in chronological order before you write. This will enable you to see whether you have your circumstances in clear order and whether you need more information.

Drafting State your problem clearly and firmly and include all the relevant information. Try to strike the right tone—emphasize the importance and justice of your complaint without insulting or irritating the reader. Finally, ask that a particular action (a refund or replacement, for example) be taken to resolve your problem.

Revising Reread your draft. Have you stated the problem as clearly and briefly as possible? Do you need to add any important details? Ask yourself how it would strike you, if you were on the receiving end of the letter. Look for ways to make your writing appeal to the reader and still do justice to your complaint.

Guide for Reading

Gladys Cardiff (1942–   )

According to Gladys Cardiff, "Combing" is one of the few poems she has written that did not require revision.

Born in Montana, where her Cherokee father and Irish/Welsh mother taught school on a Blackfoot reservation, Cardiff grew up in Seattle, Washington, and received a bachelor's degree and a master's degree in creative writing from the University of Washington.

Alice Walker (1944–   )

The youngest of eight children, this author thought she had been born into the wrong family because she always seemed to need more peace and quiet than the others. From the time she was eight, she kept a journal and wrote poems.

Walker was born in Eatonton, Georgia. As a child, she attended all-black schools and had many teachers who encouraged her love of reading and writing. Walker has written poetry, short stories, novels, and nonfiction. One of her best-known novels—*The Color Purple*—was made into an acclaimed motion picture.

E. E. Cummings (1894–1962)

Readers expect playful, lyrical, eccentric poems from this individualist New England poet. Born in Boston, Massachusetts, and nurtured in its rich literary tradition, Cummings graduated from Harvard University. Serving in Europe during World War I, Cummings was briefly imprisoned because his unusual printing in his letters home led the censors to believe he was a spy.

Wislawa Szymborska (1923–   )

"Question authority" might be the motto of this contemporary Polish poet. In "Astonishment," she uses the word *why* eight times. During World War II, when the Nazis closed Polish secondary schools and universities, Szymborska attended school illegally.

Today, the poet lives quietly in Poland, giving few interviews and letting her poetry speak for her. In 1996, she was awarded the Nobel Prize for Literature.

◆ Build Vocabulary

WORDS WITH MULTIPLE MEANINGS

Poets play with words, and words that have more than one meaning particularly lend themselves to play. For example, in "Women," Alice Walker uses the word *stout* to mean "sturdy," but it can also mean "courageous" or "heavyset"—definitions that could also work in the context of the poem.

WORD BANK

Before you read, preview this list of words from the poems.

intent
plaiting
stout
languid

◆ Build Grammar Skills

REFLEXIVE AND INTENSIVE PRONOUNS

A **reflexive pronoun** indicates that the subject is doing something to, for, or on behalf of itself:

For whatever we lose (like a you or a me)
it's always *ourselves* we find in the sea

Intensive pronouns draw attention to a person or thing and usually come right after the word. An intensive pronoun is not really needed in the sentence:

How they knew what we/ *Must* know/
Without knowing a page/ Of it/ *Themselves*.

Combing ◆ Women
◆ maggie and milly and molly and may ◆
Astonishment

◆ Literature and Your Life

CONNECT YOUR EXPERIENCE

Throughout our lives, we make discoveries that help us define and redefine who we are. Each of the poems that follows presents such a discovery. You may find that the discoveries or the poems' speakers lead you to personal discoveries of your own.

Journal Writing Start writing an entry about anything you like. Keep writing for five to ten minutes. Don't change the subject. Explore every idea you have about the subject. See if your exploration leads you to any personal discoveries.

THEMATIC FOCUS: LEARNING ABOUT OURSELVES AND OTHERS

These poems exemplify different ways of exploring one's identity—through family connections, nature, and an appreciation of the world around us. What are other ways of exploring identity?

◆ Background for Understanding

HISTORY

In "Women," the speaker expresses her admiration for the African American women of her mother's generation, who fought for the desegregation of public schools in the South. Until the mid-1950's, these schools were segregated, which means there were separate schools for white students and black students. In 1954, the United States Supreme Court ruled that separate schools for black students and white students created a system that was inherently unequal. Many southern states and local school districts forcibly resisted the federal government's attempts to integrate their schools.

◆ Literary Focus

MOMENT OF INSIGHT

Poets use specific images to explore ideas and feelings. As the poet writes, these specific images may lead to a **moment of insight**, a fresh new thought that arises from the poet's musings. Very specific details add up to a general insight into life, often expressed at the end of a poem.

◆ Reading Strategy

INTERPRET MEANING

The speakers of these poems describe moments of insight about life. You will be better prepared to understand the insight if you try to **interpret the meaning** behind the poets' words. Three practices will help you interpret the meaning of a poem. First, use sensory images—those you can see, hear, taste, touch, or smell—to form a picture in your mind of what is being described. Second, ask yourself why the poet has chosen these specific images. Third, connect what is being said to your own experience.

Combing

Gladys Cardiff

Woman Combing Girl's Hair (detail), Malcolm T. Liepke

▲ **Critical Viewing** What words would you use to describe the mood of the painting? Would you use the same words to describe the mood of the poem? [**Describe; Compare**]

Bending, I bow my head
And lay my hand upon
Her hair, combing, and think
How women do this for
5 Each other. My daughter's hair
Curls against the comb,
Wet and fragrant—orange
Parings. Her face, downcast,
Is quiet for one so young.

10 I take her place. Beneath
My mother's hands I feel
The braids drawn up tight
As a piano wire and singing,
Vinegar-rinsed. Sitting
15 Before the oven I hear
The orange coils tick
The early hour before school.

She combed her grandmother
Mathilda's hair using
20 A comb made out of bone.
Mathilda rocked her oak wood
Chair, her face downcast,
Intent on tearing rags
In strips to braid a cotton
25 Rug from bits of orange
And brown. A simple act,

Preparing hair. Something
Women do for each other,
Plaiting the generations.

Women

Alice Walker

They were women then
My mama's generation
Husky of voice—<u>Stout</u> of
Step
5 With fists as well as
Hands
How they battered down
Doors
And ironed
10 Starched white
Shirts
How they led
Armies
Headragged Generals
15 Across mined
Fields

Booby-trapped
Ditches
To discover books
20 Desks
A place for us
How they knew what we
Must know
Without knowing a page
25 Of it
Themselves.

◆ **Build Vocabulary**

Stout (stout) *adj.*: Sturdy; forceful

The **Quiltmakers**, Paul Goodnight, Color Circle Art Publishing, Inc.

▲ **Critical Viewing** Draw conclusions about the artist's attitude toward these women. Is it similar to the one expressed by Alice Walker? [**Draw Conclusions**]

maggie
and milly
and molly
and may

E. E. Cummings

maggie and milly and molly and may
went down to the beach (to play one day)

and maggie discovered a shell that sang
so sweetly she couldn't remember her
troubles, and

5   milly befriended a stranded star
whose rays five languid fingers were;

and molly was chased by a horrible thing
which raced sideways while blowing
bubbles: and

may came home with a smooth round stone
10   as small as a world and as large as alone.

For whatever we lose (like a you or a me)
it's always ourselves we find in the sea

◆ **Build Vocabulary**

languid (laŋ´ gwid) *adj.*: Drooping; weak

Astonishment

Wisława Szymborska
Translated by Grażyna Drabik, Austin Flint, and Sharon Olds

Why as one person, and one only?
Why this one, not another? And why here?
On Tuesday? At home, not in a nest?
Why in skin, not scales? With a face, not a
    leaf?
5 And why do I come, I myself, only once?
On this earth? Near a small star?
After many epochs[1] of absence?
Instead of always, and as all?
As all insects, and all horizons?

10 And why right now? Why bone and
    blood?
Myself as myself with myself? Why—
not nearby or a hundred miles away,
not yesterday or a hundred years ago—
do I sit and stare into a dark corner,
15 just as it looks up, suddenly raising its
    head,
this growling thing that is called a dog?

---

1. **epochs** (ep´ əks) *n*.: Periods or spans of time.

Guide for Responding

◆ Literature and Your Life

Reader's Response Which poem did you like best? Why?

Thematic Focus What do the speakers of these poems discover about themselves and others?

☑ Check Your Comprehension

1. How many generations of her family does the speaker of "Combing" mention?
2. As a child, how did the speaker wear her hair?
3. Name two things the women described in "Women" did.
4. What did these women know?
5. Why did maggie, milly, molly, and may go to the beach?
6. According to the speaker, what do we always find in the sea?
7. What is the speaker of "Astonishment" doing as she thinks her thoughts?

◆ Critical Thinking

INTERPRET

1. What is the effect of the repetition of the color orange in "Combing"? **[Analyze]**
2. What words in Walker's poem convey the power of the women? **[Interpret]**
3. According to Cummings' poem, what kinds of things can you find out about yourself at the sea? **[Infer]**
4. What does the speaker of "Astonishment" find astonishing? **[Infer]**

APPLY

5. Compare the mothers in "Women" with at least two other mothers you have read about. **[Compare and Contrast]**

EXTEND

6. How does the poet use her knowledge of science to make her point in "Astonishment"? **[Science Link]**

Guide for Responding (continued)

◆ Reading Strategy

To truly appreciate these poems, you had to go beyond the literal meaning of the words and **interpret** the poet's deeper **meaning**. To do so, you may have used sensory images to form a picture in your mind, asked yourself questions about the poet's decisions, or related the poem to your own experience.

1. (a) What images did you have in your mind while reading "Combing"? (b) How did they add to your understanding of the poem?
2. Describe your thinking as you read "Women."
3. In "maggie and milly and molly and may," why did the poet tell what each girl found at the beach?
4. (a) What strategy or strategies did you use to help you interpret meaning while reading "Astonishment"? (b) How helpful was the strategy?

◆ Literary Focus

MOMENT OF INSIGHT

Poets sometimes write to discover what they think. The point at which it becomes clear just what the poet is thinking is the **moment of insight**. In "Combing," for example, a woman combing her daughter's hair is reminded of her own mother and the times when she used to comb hair. Then she has a moment of insight: Combing hair is something the women in her family have always done for one another. It connects various generations. The reader is prepared for this moment of insight by everything the poet has written up to that point.

1. What moment of insight do you experience along with the speaker in Alice Walker's poem "Women"?
2. What words does E. E. Cummings use to express the moment of insight in "maggie and milly and molly and may"?
3. How is the moment of insight set off structurally in "Combing"?
4. Which moment of insight meant the most to you? Explain why.
5. Which moment of insight came as the greatest surprise to you? Explain why.

◆ Build Vocabulary

WORDS WITH MULTIPLE MEANINGS

Give two definitions of the italicized word in each sentence and explain how the multiple meanings of the word add to the meaning of the sentence.
1. The king sent his *stoutest* soldiers into battle.
2. The sharp-tongued talk-show host offered some *fresh* opinions on the subject.

USING THE WORD BANK

Write the word from the Word Bank that is an antonym for each of the following words.
1. sturdy
2. unbraiding
3. distracted
4. weak

◆ Build Grammar Skills

REFLEXIVE AND INTENSIVE PRONOUNS

myself	ourselves
yourself	yourselves
herself, himself, itself	themselves

The words in the box can be either **reflexive** or **intensive pronouns**. When the subject of a sentence performs an action to, for, or on behalf of the pronoun, it is a reflexive pronoun—it *reflects* back to the subject. When the pronoun is used to emphasize a noun or another pronoun, it is intensive—it makes the noun or pronoun more *intense*.

Practice On your paper, write the reflexive or intensive pronoun and label it correctly.
1. The speaker describes herself in the act of combing her daughter's hair.
2. The mothers understood what kind of education their children needed even though they themselves had had little schooling.
3. Take E. E. Cummings's advice and look for yourself in the sea.
4. In "Astonishment," the speaker asks herself many questions.

Writing Application Write two sentences—one in which you use *myself* as an intensive pronoun and one in which you use *myself* as a reflexive pronoun.

Build Your Portfolio

 ## Idea Bank

Writing

1. **Postcard** Imagine that you have taken a trip to the seashore. Write a postcard to a friend describing one thing you experienced at the shore and telling why it was significant to you.

2. **Poem** Write a poem in which the speaker is one of the women described in "Women." What moment of insight about her child might she have? **[Social Studies Link]**

3. **Dialogue** Suppose that the speaker of "Combing" and the speaker of "Astonishment" were to meet. Write a dialogue in which the two talk about the search for identity.

Speaking and Listening

4. **Oral Interpretation** With two classmates, prepare an oral reading of "Combing." Work together to get the right speed and inflection for the whole poem. **[Performing Arts Link]**

5. **Television Interview** With a partner, prepare an interview for a television documentary about the civil rights movement. **[Media Link; Social Studies Link]**

Projects

6. **Multimedia Presentation** Create a multimedia presentation about the sea. Choose a specific part of the world to portray, and conduct research to discover what kind of plant and animal life you would find there. **[Science Link]**

7. **Photo Essay** Prepare a photo essay of mothers and daughters. Try to include mothers and daughters of all ages and backgrounds. Write captions that reflect your response to each photo. **[Art Link]**

 ## Writing Mini-Lesson

Journal Entry

Poetry is one way of exploring ideas and feelings. Another way is through journal writing. Write a journal entry in which you describe an experience that led you to a moment of insight. Keep the following point in mind as you develop your journal entry.

Writing Skills Focus: Elaboration to Add Emotional Depth

Among the most common pieces of advice given to aspiring writers is, "Show, don't tell." In your journal entry, include details that will help readers *feel* what you are describing. If you were scared, for example, you might describe sweaty palms or trembling hands. If you were happy, you might describe your light heart or the bounce in your step.

Prewriting Start by jotting down experiences that led you to important discoveries. Then choose one of these experiences as your topic. Next, note the details of that experience. Finally, arrange your details in the order in which they occurred.

Drafting Using your notes as a starting point, recount the experience. Include the details that give emotional depth to your description. Spell out the moment of insight near the end of your journal entry.

Revising Read over your journal entry, crossing out any details that do not specifically lead to the moment of insight. Notice whether there are places where you might use intensive pronouns to emphasize your main idea.

Writing Process Workshop

Any time you read a newspaper or watch the news on television, you're probably bombarded with information about all the problems that exist in our world. When an individual takes the time to focus on a particular problem, however, he or she can usually come up with one or more solutions. A great way to present a solution to a problem is in a **problem-and-solution essay**—a brief piece of writing that clearly identifies a problem, proposes a solution, and outlines the details of that solution.

Put your problem-solving skills to the test by writing a problem-and-solution essay on an issue that you feel is important. The following skills, introduced in this section's Writing Mini-Lessons, will help you develop your essay.

Writing Skills Focus

▶ **Explain the problem clearly** Make sure readers understand what the problem is and why it exists. (See p. 279.)

▶ **Elaborate for understanding** by providing details that answer the *who? what? when? where? why?* and *how?* questions. (See p. 269.)

▶ **Elaborate to add emotional depth** Provide details that will engage your readers and stimulate their emotions by helping them sense or feel the situation. (See p. 287.)

Saki uses all these skills as he describes a problem that two characters face in his story "The Interlopers."

① The writer explains the problem that the characters face: a tree has fallen on them.

② The writer uses words and phrases such as *numb* and *tight tangle* that add emotional depth and allow readers to "feel" the problem that has occurred.

③ The writer elaborates with more details about the character's legs to explain why the problem exists.

MODEL FROM LITERATURE

from "The Interlopers" by Saki

A fierce shriek of the storm had been answered by a splitting crash over their heads, and ere they could leap aside a mass of falling beech tree had thundered down on them. ① Ulrich von Gradwitz found himself stretched on the ground, one arm numb beneath him and the other held almost helplessly in a tight tangle of forked branches, ② while both legs were pinned beneath the fallen mass. ③

Prewriting

Choose a Topic Create a list of problems that face your school, your community, our nation, or the entire world. Go over your list, and jot down possible solutions to each problem you've identified. Review your problems and solutions and choose a topic based on the following criteria:

Criteria for Choosing a Topic

- The problem should be one that your audience will find important.
- The problem should be one about which you have strong feelings.
- Your solution should be a creative one.

Outline the Problem Clearly Once you've chosen your topic, use a sunburst organizer like this one to point out various aspects of the problem, along with possible causes of the problem.

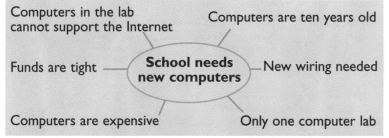

Computers in the lab cannot support the Internet

Computers are ten years old

Funds are tight

School needs new computers

New wiring needed

Computers are expensive

Only one computer lab

Elaborate Details for Understanding Gather additional details about the problem and begin to explore possible solutions by asking *who? what? when? where? why?* and *how?* questions about it.

- ▶ Why, exactly, does the problem exist?
- ▶ When and where does the problem exist?
- ▶ Who or what is causing the problem?
- ▶ Who or what can solve the problem?
- ▶ How, exactly, can the problem be solved?
- ▶ Why is your solution a strong one?

Drafting

Explain the Problem and Solution Clearly In your opening paragraph, explain the exact nature of the problem and identify possible causes. Use your prewriting notes to help you. Then, in a series of additional paragraphs, provide a step-by-step explanation of your solution to the problem.

Use coordinating and subordinating conjunctions to show the relationships among your ideas.

A **coordinating conjunction** joins two clauses, each of which can stand by itself.

The park needs fixing, <u>and</u> we can do it.

A **subordinating conjunction** introduces a clause that describes another part of the sentence.

The park can be fixed <u>if</u> we raise enough money.

Practice Provide a coordinating or subordinating conjunction to complete each item.

1. The park is dangerous, ___ we can make it safe.
2. We can buy new swings ___ a bake sale is held.
3. Let's all pitch in, ___ the problem will be solved.

Writing Application As you draft, use coordinating or subordinating conjunctions to connect your ideas.

Writer's Solution Connection
Writing Lab

To help you outline the steps of your solution, use the Chain of Events activity in the tutorial on Exposition.

APPLYING LANGUAGE SKILLS:
Adverb Clauses

Adverb clauses are subordinate clauses that modify a verb, adjective, adverb, or verbal by telling *where, when, in what manner, to what extent, under what condition,* or *why.*

Examples:

Why: We need to raise money because the swings are old.

When: We can buy new swings after money is raised.

Practice Add an adverb clause to answer each question in parentheses.

1. We need a new seesaw _____. (*Why?*)
2. We can install the new seesaw _____. (*When?*)
3. Our kids need a better park _____. (*Why?*)
4. We can make the park safer _____. (*When?*)

Writing Application Review your problem-and-solution essay. See where you can add adverb clauses to answer the question *Why? When?* or *Where?*

Elaborate to Add Emotional Depth As you write, offer details to help readers understand the seriousness or urgency of the problem. Help your audience see that the problem must be dealt with immediately. Then offer details to convince readers that your solution will indeed work.

Revising

Use a Peer Reviewer Have a peer review your essay and answer the following questions.

▶ Does the essay clearly explain the problem and its causes in the first paragraph? How could the explanation of the problem be improved?
▶ Does the essay present a clear, detailed explanation of the solution? What, if any, details should be added or deleted?
▶ Does the essay convey the importance of the problem? If not, what can be done to make the essay more convincing?

Use your classmate's responses to these questions to help you revise. If any of the classmate's comments were unclear, be sure to ask for clarification.

REVISION MODEL

① playground is in serious need of repair.

② The landing area beneath the slides is strewn with gravel. The seesaw is about to fall apart.

The Oak Street Park is in bad shape. Swings are broken

③ Children may easily be hurt on them.

and splintered.

① The writer explains the problem more clearly.
② The writer adds details to help readers better understand the problem.
③ The writer adds this statement to stress the importance of the problem.

Publishing

Publish Your Essay in a School or Local Newspaper If you have a creative solution to an important problem, share it. If your essay focuses on a school issue, see if you can get the essay published in the school newspaper. If it focuses on a local or national issue, try one of your local newspapers.

Real-World Reading Skills Workshop

Strategies for Success

Suppose you need information on a specific topic, such as the planet Mars. You have a general science book that covers many topics: plants, animals, the solar system, and so on. How can you find the specific information you seek? Follow this strategy:

Check the Table of Contents In the front of the book, skim the chapter titles for a reference to your specific topic. The table of contents might indicate a more general topic that is related to your topic. For example, a science book might have a chapter entitled "Our Solar System."

Check the Index Many books have an index at the back. This alphabetical listing of topics is much more detailed than a table of contents. Look for your topic. If you can't find it, look for it listed under another heading in the index.

Use Subheads and Captions Within a chapter itself, scan the pages for subheads and picture captions that refer to your topic. Also, look for key words that may be boldfaced or italicized in the text.

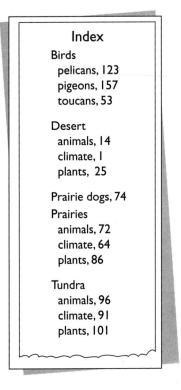

Index

Birds
pelicans, 123
pigeons, 157
toucans, 53

Desert
animals, 14
climate, 1
plants, 25

Prairie dogs, 74
Prairies
animals, 72
climate, 64
plants, 86

Tundra
animals, 96
climate, 91
plants, 101

Apply the Strategy

Use the table of contents and the index to answer these questions.

1. Which chapter would probably have information on an oasis? Which page?

2. Which chapter would probably have information on the North Pole? Which page?

3. Which chapter would probably have information on prairie dogs? Which page?

4. Which chapter would probably have information on toucans? Which page?

Our World

Contents

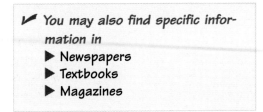

✔ *You may also find specific information in*
  ▶ Newspapers
  ▶ Textbooks
  ▶ Magazines

Speaking and Listening Workshop

You probably don't realize it, but there are many situations in which you conduct business—even at this stage of your life. Returning a defective product to the store, ordering an item that is out of stock, requesting information about a product you are interested in buying, and recruiting customers for a service you offer—such as babysitting or lawn mowing—are all forms of conducting business. In all these instances, there are guidelines you can follow that will help you get the best results.

Be Polite Whether you are making a complaint, requesting information, or offering a service, be polite and respectful. People will be more inclined to listen to what you have to say and to respond favorably.

Be Specific State your needs clearly. If you are returning a product, do you want an exchange, a refund, or a different item? If you are offering a service, what are your hours and fees?

Tips for Conducting Business

✔ If you want to conduct business in a successful way, follow these strategies:
▶ Be polite and respectful
▶ Be specific about your complaint
▶ Be precise about what you want or what you are offering

Apply the Strategies

With a partner, role-play these situations. Work out a conversation in which you conduct business in the best possible way. Later, switch roles with your partner.

1. You are returning a sweater that is too big for you. The sweater was a gift, so you don't have a receipt.
2. You want to buy a CD that is out of stock at your local record store.
3. You are interested in doing yard work and are available every Saturday and every other Sunday.

Extended Reading Opportunities

Stories in which characters make discoveries about themselves and the world around them have always been popular with readers. Following are just a few possibilities that explore characters' moments of discovery.

Suggested Titles

Great Expectations
Charles Dickens

Set in nineteenth-century England, this classic novel traces the passage of a boy called Pip into adulthood. Along the way, he encounters many memorable characters, including a pair of escaped convicts, a wealthy old woman who hasn't left her house since being jilted on her wedding day, and a beautiful young girl who captures his heart. Through a series of adventures, Pip makes many discoveries about himself, the people close to him, and the society in which he lives.

When the Legends Die
Hal Borland

This is the story of a young man who discovers his identity and cultural heritage as he struggles with the challenges of nature. After his father kills another brave, Thomas Black Bull and his parents flee the Ute reservation in southwestern Colorado to live in the wilderness. There they follow the old ways of Native Americans— hunting, fishing, and fighting for survival. Life is good until Thomas's parents die and he is left on his own.

The House on Mango Street
Sandra Cisneros

This book, a mixture of poetry and prose, tells the story of Esperanza Cordero, a young girl living in Chicago. Through her neighbors on Mango Street, Esperanza makes many discoveries about life as she explores questions such as: Should a girl get married or pursue her education? How does writing help people express their ideas and solve their problems? Why is growing up so confusing?

Other Possibilities

I Heard the Owl Call My Name	Margaret Craven
China Boy	Gus Lee
Sisters/Hermanas	Gary Paulsen

Scientist's Hobby: Failure #18 of the Anti-Gravity Pack, 1992, Bruce Widdows, Courtesy of George Adams Gallery, New York

The Lighter Side

What's so funny? It might be an animal trainer teaching 5,000 flies how to "act." It might be a tongue-in-cheek reminiscence by a famous comedian. It might be an outlandish poem told in "nonsense" language. Check out these stories, essays, poems, and more. You're sure to find something to make you smile.

Guide for Reading

James Thurber (1894–1961)

When you read some of James Thurber's work, you may find yourself asking, "Is this fiction or nonfiction?"

In both his writing and his cartoonlike drawings, Thurber liked to blur the line between the real and the not-so-real.

Many of his essays, for example, are composed of little stories, and his memoirs contain obvious fiction.

There's no question, however, that "The Secret Life of Walter Mitty" is pure fiction. This amusing fantasy became an instant classic when it first appeared in 1939. It was reprinted by *Reader's Digest* and was also made into a popular movie.

A Lifetime of Writing

A native of Columbus, Ohio, James Thurber began his writing career as a reporter for the *Columbus Evening Dispatch*. It was through his later work on *The New Yorker* magazine, however, that he became well known as a humorous writer and cartoonist.

During his lifetime, Thurber wrote more than twenty volumes of plays, stories, essays, fables, reminiscences, and verse. Even after losing his vision in the early 1940's, he continued to write until his death in 1961. Thurber received honorary degrees from Williams College and Yale University and, in 1960, won the Antoinette Perry award for the theatrical review *A Thurber Carnival*.

◆ Build Vocabulary

WORD ROOTS: *-scrut-*

At one point in "The Secret Life of Walter Mitty," Thurber describes the main character as being "inscrutable." You can figure out the meaning of *inscrutable* if you know the meaning of the word root from which it is derived. *Inscrutable* comes from the word root *-scrut-*, which means "to search or examine." *Inscrutable* literally means "not able to be searched or examined," or "not easily understood."

rakishly
hurtling
distraught
haggard
insolent
insinuatingly
cur
cannonading
derisive
inscrutable

WORD BANK

Before you read, preview this list of words from the story.

◆ Build Grammar Skills

PRONOUN AND ANTECEDENT AGREEMENT

You will notice that the pronouns Thurber uses agree with their **antecedents**—the words they replace—in gender (masculine, feminine, or neuter) and number (singular or plural). Notice the pronouns in this example:

Walter Mitty reached in a pocket and brought out the gloves. *He* put *them* on.

The pronoun *he*—masculine and singular— agrees with its antecedent, *Walter Mitty*, which is masculine and singular. The pronoun *them*, plural and neuter, agrees with its antecedent, *gloves*, which is plural and neuter.

The Secret Life of Walter Mitty

◆ *Literature and Your Life*

CONNECT YOUR EXPERIENCE

You're relaxing on a park bench on a warm summer day. Suddenly, you're someone else—a movie star accepting an award or a basketball superstar slam-dunking the winning basket. Then, you're you again; you were daydreaming. "The Secret Life of Walter Mitty" is about a man whose frequent, adventurous daydreams will amuse and entertain you.

Journal Writing Can daydreaming ever help a person achieve his or her goals? Explore your answer to this question in a journal entry.

THEMATIC FOCUS: THE LIGHTER SIDE

A very tall man folds himself into a compact car. A tiny girl is pulled along by a huge dog on a leash. The contrasts in situations like these can make you smile. Contrast plays an important part in "The Secret Life of Walter Mitty," where the differences between Walter Mitty's real life and his secret life provide some amusing moments.

◆ Background for Understanding

SCIENCE

The human mind works both logically and randomly. As the psychologist William James noted around the turn of the century, a person's thoughts often form an unorganized and seemingly unconnected series of insights, memories, and reflections. A single incident, for example, can stimulate an almost endless flow of thoughts. In "The Secret Life of Walter Mitty," the title character's thoughts often jump back and forth between his fantastic imaginings and the realities of his life.

◆ Literary Focus

POINT OF VIEW

Point of view is the perspective from which a story is told. "The Secret Life of Walter Mitty" is not told by Walter Mitty himself, but it is told in such a way that you the reader know his thoughts and feelings. This is called the **limited third person** point of view. The words *third person* indicate that the narrator is "outside" of the story, and the word *limited* means that the narrator reveals the thoughts and feelings of only one character. By telling the story from the point of view of one character, the author encourages you to sympathize with this character. You know what this character thinks and feels in a way you never can with people in real life.

The Man With Three Masks, John Rush, Courtesy of the artist

Reading for Success

Interactive Reading Strategies

To get the most out of many things in life, you have to get involved. This rule is as true in reading as it is in playing sports or visiting new places. By interacting with what you read, you'll read more effectively. You'll better understand and remember what you read. Use these strategies to interact with what you're reading.

Set a purpose for your reading.

You might read a short story for enjoyment, or read a biography to learn about a noteworthy individual. Giving yourself a purpose focuses your thoughts. For example, for "The Secret Life of Walter Mitty," your purpose might be to find out what is Walter Mitty's "secret life."

Ask questions.

As you read, question what's going on in the story or article. For example, ask *why* a character behaves as he does or *what* caused an event to happen. Then search the text for answers as you read on.

Read between the lines.

Authors don't always state everything directly; sometimes they just suggest ideas. When you "read between the lines," you look beyond the words to find out what else the author means.

Clarify.

If you come to a passage you don't understand, pause to clarify the meaning of what you're reading. You may have to read back or ahead to figure out an unclear situation, or you may have to go outside the text to find out what something means.

Expect the unexpected.

From many years of reading, you've come to expect stories to develop in a certain way. However, sometimes authors will play with your expectations. Be prepared.

As you read "The Secret Life of Walter Mitty," look at the notes along the sides. The notes demonstrate how to apply these strategies to your reading.

The Secret Life of Walter Mitty

James Thurber

"We're going through!" The Commander's voice was like thin ice breaking. He wore his full-dress uniform, with the heavily braided white cap pulled down rakishly over one cold gray eye. "We can't make it, sir. It's spoiling for a hurricane, if you ask me." "I'm not asking you, Lieutenant Berg," said the Commander. "Throw on the power lights! Rev her up to 8,500! We're going through!" The pounding of the cylinders increased: ta-pocketa-pocketa-pocketa-*pocketa-pocketa*. The Commander stared at the ice forming on the pilot window. He walked over and twisted a row of complicated dials. "Switch on No. 8 auxiliary!" he shouted. "Switch on No. 8 auxiliary!" repeated Lieutenant Berg. "Full strength in No. 3 turret!" shouted the Commander. "Full strength in No. 3 turret!" The crew, bending to their various tasks in the huge, hurtling eight-engined Navy hydroplane,[1]

looked at each other and grinned. "The Old Man'll get us through," they said to one another. "The Old Man ain't afraid of Hell!". . .

"Not so fast! You're driving too fast!" said Mrs. Mitty. "What are you driving so fast for?"

> This abrupt shift in the action is a reminder to **expect the unexpected.**

"Hmm?" said Walter Mitty. He looked at his wife, in the seat beside him, with shocked astonishment. She seemed grossly unfamiliar, like a strange woman who had yelled at him in a crowd. "You were up to fifty-five," she said. "You know I don't like to go more than forty. You were up to fifty-five." Walter Mitty drove on toward Waterbury in silence, the roaring of the SN202 through the worst storm in twenty years of Navy flying fading in the remote, intimate airways of his mind. "You're tensed up again," said Mrs. Mitty. "It's one of your days. I wish you'd let Dr. Renshaw look you over."

> This paragraph **clarifies** what was happening in the opening paragraph of the story—Walter Mitty was daydreaming.

Walter Mitty stopped the car in front of the building where his wife went to have her hair done. "Remember to get those overshoes while I'm having my

---

1. **hydroplane** (hī′ drə plān) *n.*: Seaplane.

◆ Build Vocabulary

rakishly (rāk′ ish lē) *adv.*: With a careless, casual look; dashing

hurtling (hʉrt′ liŋ) *adj.*: Moving swiftly and with great force

▲ **Critical Viewing** Analyze the significance of the mask in this painting. Why does the man hold one mask up to his face and have other masks nearby? **[Analyze]**

brought out the gloves. He put them on, but after she had turned and gone into the building and he had driven on to a red light, he took them off again. "Pick it up, brother!" snapped a cop as the light changed, and Mitty hastily pulled on his gloves and lurched ahead. He drove around the streets aimlessly for a time, and then he drove past the hospital on his way to the parking lot.

. . . "It's the millionaire banker, Wellington McMillan," said the pretty nurse. "Yes?" said Walter Mitty, removing his gloves slowly. "Who has the case?" "Dr. Renshaw and Dr. Benbow, but there are two specialists here, Dr. Remington from New York and Mr. Pritchard-Mitford from London. He flew over." A door opened down a long, cool corridor and Dr. Renshaw came out. He looked distraught and haggard. "Hello, Mitty," he said. "We're having the devil's own time with McMillan, the millionaire banker and close personal friend of Roosevelt. Obstreosis of the ductal tract.[2] Wish you'd take a look at him." "Glad to," said Mitty.

In the operating room there were whispered introductions: "Dr. Remington, Dr. Mitty. Mr. Pritchard-Mitford, Dr. Mitty." "I've read your book on streptothricosis,"

hair done," she said. "I don't need overshoes," said Mitty. She put her mirror back into her bag. "We've been all through that," she said, getting out of the car. "You're not a young man any longer." He raced the engine a little. "Why don't you wear your gloves? Have you lost your gloves?" Walter Mitty reached in a pocket and

> By **reading between the lines,** you can infer that Mrs. Mitty thinks her husband is helpless.

> This paragraph, like the first, provides details to meet your **purpose**—to find out what Walter Mitty's secret life is.

---

2. **obstreosis of the ductal tract:** Thurber has invented this and other medical terms.

said Pritchard-Mitford, shaking hands. "A brilliant performance, sir." "Thank you," said Walter Mitty. "Didn't know you were in the States, Mitty," grumbled Remington. "Coals to Newcastle,[3] bringing Mitford and me up here for tertiary." "You are very kind," said Mitty. A huge, complicated machine, connected to the operating table, with many tubes and wires, began at this moment to go pocketa-pocketa-pocketa. "The new anesthetizer is giving way!" shouted an intern. "There is no one in the East who knows how to fix it!" "Quiet, man!" said Mitty, in a low, cool voice. He sprang to the machine, which was now going pocketa-pocketa-queep-pocketa-queep. He began fingering delicately a row of glistening dials. "Give me a fountain pen!" he snapped. Someone handed him a fountain pen. He pulled a faulty piston out of the machine and inserted the pen in its place. "That will hold for ten minutes," he said. "Get on with the operation." A nurse hurried over and whispered to Renshaw, and Mitty saw the man turn pale. "Coreopsis has set in," said Renshaw nervously. "If you would take over, Mitty?" Mitty looked at him and at the craven figure of Benbow, who drank, and at the grave, uncertain faces of the two great specialists. "If you wish," he said. They slipped a white gown on him; he adjusted a mask and drew on thin gloves; nurses handed him shining . . .

"Back it up, Mac! Look out for that Buick!" Walter Mitty jammed on the brakes. "Wrong lane, Mac," said the parking-lot attendant, looking at Mitty closely. "Gee. Yeh," muttered Mitty. He began cautiously to back out of the lane marked "Exit Only." "Leave her sit there," said the attendant. "I'll put her away." Mitty got out of the car. "Hey, better leave the key." "Oh," said Mitty, handing the man the ignition key. The attendant vaulted into the car, backed it up with insolent skill, and put it where it belonged.

> This paragraph might prompt the **question**, "Why is Walter Mitty treated this way in his real life?"

They're so cocky, thought Walter Mitty, walking along Main Street; they think they know everything. Once he had tried to take his chains off, outside New Milford, and he had got them wound around the axles. A man had had to come out in a wrecking car and unwind them, a young, grinning garageman. Since then Mrs. Mitty always made him drive to a garage to have the chains taken off. The next time, he thought, I'll wear my right arm in a sling; they won't grin at me then. I'll have my right arm in a sling and they'll see I couldn't possibly take the chains off myself. He kicked at the slush on the sidewalk. "Overshoes," he said to himself, and he began looking for a shoe store.

When he came out into the street again, with the overshoes in a box under his arm, Walter Mitty began to wonder what the other thing was his wife had told him to get. She had told him, twice, before they set out from their house for Waterbury. In a way he hated these weekly trips to town—he was always getting something wrong.

◆ Build Vocabulary

distraught (di strôt´) *adj*.: Extremely troubled; confused; distracted

haggard (hag´ ərd) *adj*.: Having a wild, worn look, as from sleeplessness

insolent (in´ sə lənt) *adj*.: Boldly disrespectful in speech or behavior

---

3. **coals to Newcastle:** The proverb "bringing coals to Newcastle" means bringing things to a place unnecessarily—Newcastle, England, was a coal center and so did not need coal brought to it.

Kleenex, he thought, Squibb's, razor blades? No. Toothpaste, toothbrush, bicarbonate, carborundum, initiative and referendum?[4] He gave it up. But she would remember it. "Where's the what's-its-name?" she would ask. "Don't tell me you forgot the what's-its-name." A newsboy went by shouting something about the Waterbury trial.

. . . "Perhaps this will refresh your memory." The District Attorney suddenly thrust a heavy automatic at the quiet figure on the witness stand. "Have you ever seen this before?" Walter Mitty took the gun and examined it expertly. "This is my Webley-Vickers 50.80," he said calmly. An excited buzz ran around the courtroom. The Judge rapped for order. "You are a crack shot with any sort of firearms, I believe?" said the District Attorney, <u>insinuatingly</u>. "Objection!" shouted Mitty's attorney. "We have shown that the defendant could not have fired the shot. We have shown that he wore his right arm in a sling on the night of the fourteenth of July." Walter Mitty raised his hand briefly and the bickering attorneys were stilled. "With any known make of gun," he said evenly, "I could have killed Gregory Fitzhurst at three hundred feet *with my left hand*." Pandemonium broke loose in the courtroom. A woman's scream rose above the bedlam and suddenly a lovely, dark-haired girl was in Walter Mitty's arms. The District Attorney struck at her savagely. Without rising from his chair, Mitty let the man have it on the point of the chin. "You miserable <u>cur</u>!" . . .

"Puppy biscuit," said Walter Mitty. He stopped walking and the buildings of Waterbury rose up out of the misty courtroom and surrounded

> When you **clarify** that cur means "a mean, ugly dog," you can appreciate the humor here.

him again. A woman who was passing laughed. "He said 'Puppy biscuit,'" she said to her companion. "That man said 'Puppy biscuit' to himself." Walter Mitty hurried on. He went into an

---

4. **carborundum** (kär′ bə run′ dəm), **initiative** (i nish′ ē ə tiv) **and referendum** (ref′ ə ren′ dəm): Thurber is purposely making a nonsense list; carborundum is a hard substance used for scraping, initiative is the right of citizens to introduce ideas for laws, and referendum is the right of citizens to vote on laws.

A. & P., not the first one he came to but a smaller one farther up the street. "I want some biscuit for small, young dogs," he said to the clerk. "Any special brand, sir?" The greatest pistol shot in the world thought a moment. "It says 'Puppies Bark for It' on the box," said Walter Mitty.

His wife would be through at the hairdresser's in fifteen minutes, Mitty saw in looking at his watch, unless they had trouble drying it; sometimes they had trouble drying it. She didn't like to get to the hotel first; she would want him to be there waiting for her as usual. He found a big leather chair in the lobby, facing a window, and he put the overshoes and the puppy biscuit on the floor beside it. He picked up an old copy of *Liberty* and sank down into the chair. "Can Germany Conquer the World Through the Air?" Walter Mitty looked at the pictures of bombing planes and of ruined streets.

. . . "The <u>cannonading</u> has got the wind up in young Raleigh,[5] sir," said the sergeant. Captain Mitty looked up at him through tousled hair. "Get him to bed," he said wearily. "With the others. I'll fly alone." "But you can't, sir," said the sergeant anxiously. "It takes two men to handle that bomber and the Archies[6] are pounding hell out of the air. Von Richtman's circus[7] is between here and Saulier." "Somebody's got to get that ammunition dump," said Mitty. "I'm going over. Spot of brandy?" He poured a drink for the

> Look at the footnote to **clarify** the meaning of "Von Richtman's circus."

---

5. **has got the wind up in young Raleigh:** Has made young Raleigh nervous.
6. **Archies:** Slang term for antiaircraft guns.
7. **Von Richtman's circus:** German airplane squadron.

◆ Build Vocabulary

insinuatingly (in sin′ yoo āt′ iŋ lē) *adv.*: Hinting or suggesting indirectly; implying

cur (kʉr) *n.*: Mean, contemptible person; mean, ugly dog

cannonading (kan′ ən ād′ iŋ) *n.*: Continuous firing of artillery

New Orleans Fantasy (detail), Max Papart, Nahan Galleries, New York

▲ **Critical Viewing** Describe a situation that might make Walter Mitty daydream about being a circus performer. **[Hypothesize]**

sergeant and one for himself. War thundered and whined around the dugout and battered at the door. There was a rending of wood and splinters flew through the room. "A bit of a near thing," said Captain Mitty carelessly. "The box barrage is closing in," said the sergeant. "We only live once, Sergeant," said Mitty, with his faint, fleeting smile. "Or do we?" He poured another brandy and tossed it off. "I never see a man could hold his brandy like you, sir," said the sergeant. "Begging your pardon, sir." Captain Mitty stood up and strapped on his huge Webley-Vickers automatic. "It's forty kilometers through hell, sir," said the sergeant. Mitty finished one last brandy. "After all," he said softly, "what isn't?" The pounding of the cannon increased; there was the rat-tat-tatting of machine guns, and from somewhere came the menacing pocketa-pocketa-pocketa of the new flame-throwers. Walter Mitty walked to the door of the dugout humming "Auprès de Ma Blonde."[8] He turned and waved to the sergeant. "Cheerio!" he said . . . .

Something struck his shoulder. "I've been looking all over this hotel for you," said Mrs. Mitty. "Why do you have to hide in this old chair? How did you expect me to find you?" "Things close in," said Walter Mitty vaguely. "What?" Mrs. Mitty said. "Did you get the what's-its-name? The puppy biscuit? What's in that box?" "Overshoes," said Mitty. "Couldn't you have put them on in the store?" "I was thinking," said Walter Mitty. "Does it ever occur to you that I am sometimes thinking?" She looked at him. "I'm going to take your temperature when I get you home," she said.

They went out through the revolving doors that made a faintly <u>derisive</u> whistling sound when you pushed them. It was two blocks to the parking lot. At the drugstore on the corner she said, "Wait here for me. I forgot something. I won't be a minute." She was more than a minute. Walter Mitty lighted a cigarette. It began to rain, rain with sleet in it. He stood up against the wall of the drugstore, smoking. . . . He put his shoulders back and his heels together. "To hell with the handkerchief," said Walter Mitty scornfully. He took one last drag on his cigarette and snapped it away. Then, with that faint, fleeting smile playing about his lips, he faced the firing squad; erect and motionless, proud and disdainful, Walter Mitty the Undefeated, <u>inscrutable</u> to the last.

> By now, you've met your **purpose**. You not only know what Walter Mitty's secret life is, but you know why he lives it.

---

8. **"Auprès de Ma Blonde"** (ō pre′ də mä blôn′ d): "Next to My Blonde," a popular French song.

◆ **Build Vocabulary**

derisive (di rī′ siv) *adj.*: Showing contempt or ridicule

inscrutable (in skrōōt′ ə bəl) *adj.*: That which cannot be easily understood; baffling; mysterious

Guide for Responding

◆ Literature and Your Life

Reader's Response Do you feel sorry for Walter Mitty? Why or why not?

Thematic Focus Why is the contrast between Walter Mitty's real life and his daydreams humorous?

Journal Entry Some of the brief instances of Walter Mitty's real life are funny. Briefly describe a few of Mitty's more humorous moments between daydreams.

☑ Check Your Comprehension

1. How is Walter Mitty jarred out of his first daydream?
2. Describe each of the five characters Mitty daydreams himself to be.
3. What triggers Mitty's second, third, and fourth daydreams, and how is he pulled out of each one?

Guide for Responding (continued)

◆ Critical Thinking

INTERPRET

1. Compare and contrast Mitty in real life with Mitty in his daydreams. **[Compare and Contrast]**
2. Explain the significant difference between the way people treat Mitty in real life and the way they treat him in his daydreams. **[Draw Conclusions]**
3. How does Mrs. Mitty's personality trigger Mitty's last daydream? **[Infer]**
4. In what way is Mitty's last daydream an apt comment on his fate in real life? **[Draw Conclusions]**

EVALUATE

5. Thurber reveals Walter Mitty's personality by presenting two sides of Mitty—his real-life experiences and his daydreams. Why is this method effective? **[Assess]**

APPLY

6. Mark Twain wrote, "The secret source of humor is not joy but sorrow." How do humor and sorrow go hand in hand? **[Apply]**

◆ Reading for Success

INTERACTIVE READING STRATEGIES

Review the reading strategies and the notes showing how to interact with a text. Then apply them to answer the following questions.

1. What is Walter Mitty's secret life?
2. Reading between the lines, what conclusions can you draw about Walter Mitty's relationship with his wife?
3. Why does Walter Mitty spend so much time day-dreaming?

◆ Literary Focus

POINT OF VIEW

James Thurber presents "The Secret Life of Walter Mitty" from a limited **third-person point of view**, taking us inside the mind of Walter Mitty.

1. How do you feel about Walter Mitty as a result of seeing the world through his eyes?
2. How would the story have been different if Mrs. Mitty had told it?

◆ Build Vocabulary

USING THE WORD ROOT *-scrut-*

The word root *-scrut-* means "to search or examine." Define each of these words. Incorporate the definition of *-scrut-* into each answer.

1. scrutiny (*n.*)   3. inscrutably (*adv.*)
2. scrutinize (*v.*)   4. inscrutability (*n.*)

USING THE WORD BANK

In your notebook, write the letter of the word that is closest in meaning to each word from the Word Bank.

1. rakishly: (a) carelessly casual, (b) fiendishly, (c) raggedly
2. hurtling: (a) slowing, (b) injuring, (c) speeding
3. distraught: (a) defeated, (b) troubled, (c) extended
4. haggard: (a) exhausted, (b) lively, (c) unhappy
5. insolent: (a) strong, (b) sleepless, (c) disrespectful
6. insinuatingly: (a) nervously, (b) indirectly, (c) sternly
7. cur: (a) gentleman, (b) scoundrel, (c) lawyer
8. cannonading: (a) photographing, (b) proclaiming, (c) bombarding
9. derisive: (a) kind, (b) ill, (c) insulting
10. inscrutable: (a) baffling, (b) cruel, (c) painful

◆ Build Grammar Skills

PRONOUN AND ANTECEDENT AGREEMENT

A pronoun must **agree** with its **antecedent** in gender and number.

Practice Write the following sentences in your notebook. Circle each pronoun and draw an arrow to its antecedent. Then label each pronoun as singular or plural; masculine, feminine, or neuter.

1. "Hmm?" said Walter Mitty. He looked at his wife . . . with shocked astonishment. She seemed grossly unfamiliar.
2. The crew, bending to their various tasks, looked at each other and grinned.
3. ". . . The defendant could not have fired the shot. . . He wore his right arm in a sling on the night of the fourteenth of July."

Build Your Portfolio

 ## Idea Bank

Writing

1. **One More Daydream** Make up another day-dream for Walter Mitty that is true to Mitty's personality.

2. **Written Recommendation** Should Walter Mitty stop daydreaming and take control of his life or should he keep daydreaming to add some happiness to his days? Write a recommendation in which you suggest to Walter Mitty what he should do.

3. **Diary Entry** Write a diary entry about a day with Walter Mitty from Mrs. Mitty's point of view. In Mrs. Mitty's own voice, tell how she feels when her husband seems preoccupied.

Speaking and Listening

4. **Performance** With a group of classmates, act out one of Walter Mitty's daydreams. Rehearse the scene by reading the parts aloud until they seem natural. **[Performing Arts Link]**

5. **Panel Discussion** Are daydreams of little consequence, or might they lead the daydreamer to a possible future career or to an idea for a fantastic new invention? With a small group of classmates, hold a panel discussion on the value of daydreams.

Projects

6. **Daydream Illustrations** James Thurber drew illustrations for many of his written works. Draw an illustration for each of Walter Mitty's five daydreams. Write titles for your illustrations and display them in class. **[Art Link]**

7. **Report on Dreaming** Prepare a written report on the latest scientific facts and theories about dreaming. **[Science Link]**

 ## Writing Mini-Lesson

Character Profile

Walter Mitty imagines himself as a variety of fearless characters who take bold action. Imagine a character who does great things, like discovering the cure for a disease or breaking an Olympic record. Write a character profile that clearly describes that character.

Writing Skills Focus: Main Impression

Your character profile should convey a **main impression** of the character. Is this person incredibly brilliant? If so, include details to show his or her brilliance and avoid details that do not relate to it. Notice how Thurber conveys the main impression of a bold and decisive "Commander" Mitty.

Model From the Story

"We can't make it, sir. It's spoiling for a hurricane, if you ask me." "I'm not asking you, Lieutenant Berg," said the Commander. "Throw on the power lights! Rev her up to 8,500! We're going through!"

Prewriting To create a main impression, decide upon the chief character trait you want to convey. Then jot down details that support the trait. These might include physical description, actions, achievements, spoken words, ideas, thoughts, and feelings.

Drafting Decide on the most effective order for presenting your details. For example, you might use this order: (1) Physical Description, (2) Thoughts and Feelings, (3) Words and Actions. Write your draft, elaborating on those details.

Revising Show your character profile to a classmate and ask that person to describe the chief character trait. If the trait isn't clear, provide additional details that support the trait and eliminate those that don't.

PART 1 *Everyday Humor*

Man Prepared to Jump/Fly, Fred Hilliard, Stock Illustration Source, Inc.

Guide for Reading

Anton Chekhov (1860–1904)

Life was hard for the majority of people who lived in Russia in the 1800's. Until 1861, most Russians were serfs—people bound to the service of a small group of wealthy land-owning nobles. The serfs had few rights and were forced to work long hours in the fields for little money. Those who challenged Russia's rigid social structure were dealt with harshly, often being sent into icy exile in Siberia.

Anton Chekhov vividly captured the harsh realities of nineteenth-century Russian life in his writing.

A Physician and Writer The grandson of a serf who had purchased his freedom, Chekhov grew up in a small Russian coastal town. He later moved to Moscow, where he attended medical school. While studying medicine, he began writing humorous sketches and short stories for publication in various newspapers. After Chekhov graduated from medical school, writing became his major focus, though he practiced medicine on a part-time basis throughout his life.

Accomplishments as a Writer

Chekhov wrote more than 1,000 short stories during his lifetime. He also wrote several critically acclaimed plays, including *The Seagull* (1896), *Uncle Vanya* (1899), and *The Three Sisters* (1901). Although he did not become famous outside of Russia until after his death, he is now regarded as one of the finest playwrights and short-story writers the world has ever produced.

◆ Build Vocabulary

WORD ROOTS: -nym-

In "The Inspector-General" you will find the word *anonymous*, which contains the word root -nym-, meaning "name." *Anonymous* literally means "without a *name*" or "with no known or acknowledged name." What other words can you think of that contain the root -nym-?

WORD BANK

incognito
anonymous
trundle
valet
buffet

As you read "The Inspector-General," you will encounter the words on this list. Each word is defined on the page where it first appears. Preview the list before you read.

◆ Build Grammar Skills

DOUBLE NEGATIVES

People don't always speak in grammatically correct sentences. It's not surprising, then, that the dialogue in Chekhov's play includes sentences with grammatical errors. For example, the driver of a horse cart uses a pair of double negatives when describing the habits of the inspector-general:

[He] *Don't* want *no one* to see him, *don't* want *no one* to know who he is.

A **double negative** is the use of two negative words when only one is correct. This example can be corrected by changing each *no one* to *anyone*.

◆ *Literature and Your Life*

CONNECT YOUR EXPERIENCE

Sometimes people hide their identities or pretend to be someone else. Maybe they are trying to impress someone or are playing a practical joke. Often their charade doesn't have the effect they've planned. The results can be embarrassing, even humorous. "The Inspector-General" captures such a situation.

THEMATIC FOCUS: EVERYDAY HUMOR

Although the character in Chekhov's play feels humiliated when his charade backfires, the situation is humorous because he seems to be getting what he deserves.

Journal Writing Jot down your memories of humorous movies or television programs you have seen involving failed schemes of unlikeable characters.

◆ Background for Understanding

HISTORY

From the 1500's until the Marxist revolution of 1917, Russia was ruled by czars—iron-fisted emperors who held tight control over virtually every aspect of Russian life. To keep a close eye on local officials throughout Russia's vast landscape, the czars employed people in the position of inspector-general. The inspectors-general were charged with observing how local schools, courts, hospitals, and so on were functioning. Because of people's resentment of the czar's absolute authority, the inspectors-general were often unpopular among the public.

◆ Literary Focus

IRONY

When a literary work such as Chekhov's takes a surprising turn, it creates **irony**—a contrast between an expected outcome and an actual outcome. Several kinds of irony are used in literature. In **verbal irony** a word or phrase is used to suggest the opposite of its usual meaning. In **dramatic irony** there is a contradiction between what a character thinks and what the reader knows is true. In **irony of situation**, an event occurs that directly contradicts the expectations of the characters or of the reader. Writers often use irony to create humor.

◆ Reading Strategy

READ BETWEEN THE LINES

Writers often withhold key pieces of information to keep readers guessing or make them uncertain about the outcome of a work. For example, a writer might not immediately reveal a character's identity. Instead, it is left up to the reader to piece together the character's identity based on what the character says or does, or details of his or her appearance. When you use information that the writer does provide to draw conclusions about missing details, you are **reading between the lines.**

In "The Inspector-General," a traveler begins asking his driver questions about the inspector-general. Chekhov doesn't say why he is asking these questions, but you can come up with the answer by reading between the lines. Pay close attention to the types of questions the traveler asks, and note the details of his behavior. What do these details reveal about the traveler's motives?

The Inspector-General

Anton Chekhov

❧

The curtain goes up to reveal falling snow and a cart facing away from us. Enter the STORYTELLER, who begins to read the story. Meanwhile, the TRAVELER enters. He is a middle-aged man of urban appearance, wearing dark glasses and a long overcoat with its collar turned up. He is carrying a small traveling bag. He climbs into the cart and sits facing us.

STORYTELLER [*The Inspector-General*]. In deepest incognito, first by express train, then along back roads, Pyotr Pavlovich Posudin[1] was hastening toward the little town of N____, to which he had been summoned by an anonymous letter. "I'll take them by surprise," he thought to himself. "I'll come down on them like a thunderbolt out of the blue. I can just

---

1. **Pyotr Pavlovich Posudin** (pyō′ tr pāv lō′ vich pō sū′ dən)

◆ Build Vocabulary

incognito (in käg′ ni tō′) *n.*: A disguised condition

anonymous (ə nän′ ə məs) *adj.*: Without a known or acknowledged name

trundle (trun′ dəl) *v.*: To roll along; to rotate

---

imagine their faces when they hear who I am." *[Enter the DRIVER, a peasant, who climbs onto the cart, so that he is sitting with his back to us, and the cart begins to trundle slowly away from us.]* And when he thought to himself for long enough, he fell into conversation with the driver of the cart. What did he talk about? About himself, of course. *[Exit the STORYTELLER.]*

TRAVELER. I gather you've got a new inspector-general in these parts.

DRIVER. True enough.

TRAVELER. Know anything about him? *[The DRIVER turns and looks at the TRAVELER, who turns his coat collar up a little higher.]*

DRIVER. Know anything about him? Of course we do! We know everything about all of them up there! Every last little clerk—we know the color of his hair and the size of his boots! *[He turns back to the front, and the TRAVELER permits himself a slight smile.]*

TRAVELER. So, what do you reckon? any good, is he? *[The DRIVER turns around.]*

DRIVER. Oh, yes, he's a good one, this one.

TRAVELER. Really?

DRIVER. Did one good thing straight off.

TRAVELER. What was that?

DRIVER. He got rid of the last one. Holy terror he was! Hear him coming five miles off! Let's say he's going to this little town. Somewhere like we're going, say. He'd let all the world

Valmondois Sous la Neige, Maurice de Vlaminck

know about it a month before. So now he's on his way, say, and it's like thunder and lightning coming down the road. And when he gets where he's going, he has a good sleep. He has a good eat and drink, and then he starts. Stamps his feet, shouts his head off. Then he has another good sleep, and off he goes.

TRAVELER. But the new one's not like that?

DRIVER. Oh, no. The new one goes everywhere on the quiet. Creeps around like a cat. Don't want no one to see him, don't want no one to know who he is. Say he's going into this town down the road here. Someone there sent him a letter on the sly, let's say. "Things going on here you should know about." Something of that kind. Well, now, he creeps out of his office, so none of them up there see him go. He hops on a train just like

▲ Critical Viewing What might life be like in a setting such as this one? [Speculate]

anyone else, just like you or me. When he gets off, he don't go jumping into a cab or nothing fancy. Oh, no. He wraps himself up from head to toe so you can't see his face, and he wheezes away like an old dog so no one can recognize his voice.

◆ Literary Focus
Why is this description of the new inspector-general ironic?

TRAVELER. Wheezes? That's not wheezing! That's the way he talks! So I gather.

DRIVER. Oh, is it? But the tales they tell about him. You'd laugh till you burst your tripes![2]

TRAVELER [sourly]. I'm sure I would.

DRIVER. He drinks, mind!

TRAVELER *[startled].* Drinks?

DRIVER. Oh, like a hole in the ground. Famous for it.

TRAVELER. He's never touched a drop! I mean, from what I've heard.

DRIVER. Oh, not in public, no. Goes to some great ball—"No thank you, not for me." Oh, no, he puts it away at home! Wakes up in the morning, rubs his eyes, and the first thing he does, he shouts, "Vodka!" So in runs his <u>valet</u> with a glass. Fixed himself up a tube behind his desk, he has. Leans down, takes a pull on it, no one the wiser.

TRAVELER *[offended].* How do you know all this, may I ask?

DRIVER. Can't hide it from the servants, can you? The valet and the coachman have got tongues in their heads. Then again, he's on the road, say, going about his business, and he keeps the bottle in his little bag. *[The* TRAVELER *discreetly pushes the traveling bag out of the* DRIVER'S *sight.]* And his housekeeper . . .

TRAVELER. What about her?

DRIVER. Runs circles around him, she does, like a fox round his tail. She's the one who wears the trousers.[3] The people aren't half so frightened of him as they are of her.

TRAVELER. But at least he's good at his job, you say?

DRIVER. Oh, he's a blessing from heaven, I'll grant him that.

TRAVELER. Very cunning, you were saying.

---

2. **tripes** (trīps) *n.*: Parts of the stomach, usually of an ox or a sheep.
3. **wears the trousers:** Has the greatest authority; is really in charge.

◆ Build Vocabulary

valet (val´ it) *n.*: A man's personal servant who takes care of the man's clothes

White Night, Edvard Munch, National Gallery, Oslo

▲ **Critical Viewing** How well does the mood of this painting match the mood of this play? **[Connect]**

DRIVER. Oh, he creeps around, all right.

TRAVELER. And then he pounces, yes? I should think some people must get the surprise of their life, mustn't they?

DRIVER. No, no. Let's be fair, now. Give him his due. He don't make no trouble.

TRAVELER. No. I mean, if no one knows he's coming . . .

DRIVER. Oh, that's what *he* thinks, but *we* all know.

TRAVELER. You know?

DRIVER. Oh, some gentleman gets off the train at the station back there with his greatcoat up to his eyebrows and says, "No, I don't want a cab, thank you. Just an ordinary horse and cart for me." Well, we'd put two and two together, wouldn't we? Say it was you, now, creeping along down the road here. The lads would be down there in a cab by now! By the time you got there, the whole town would be as regular as clockwork! And you'd think to yourself, "Oh, look at that! As clean as a whistle! And they don't know I was coming!" No, that's why he's such a blessing after the other one. This one believes it.

TRAVELER. Oh, I see.

DRIVER. What, you thought we didn't know him? Why, we've got the electric telegraph these days! Take today, now. I'm going past the station back there this morning, and the fellow who runs the buffet comes out like a bolt of lightning. Arms full of baskets and bottles. "Where are you off to?" I say. "Doing drinks and refreshments for the inspector-general!" he says, and he jumps into a carriage and goes flying down the road to here. So there's the inspector-general, all muffled up like a roll of carpet, going secretly along in a cart somewhere, and when he gets there, nothing to be seen but vodka and cold salmon!

TRAVELER. [shouts]. Turn around!

DRIVER [to the horse]. Whoa, boy! Whoa! [To the TRAVELER.] Oh, so what's this, then? Don't want to go running into the inspector-general, is

that it? [The TRAVELER gestures impatiently for the DRIVER to turn the cart around. DRIVER to the horse.] Back we go, then, boy. Home we go. [He turns the cart around and the TRAVELER takes a swig from his traveling bag.] Though if I know the old devil, he's like as not turned around and gone home again himself. [Blackout.]

◆ **Reading Strategy**

What has the traveler figured out by reading (actually, *listening*) between the lines?

◆ **Build Vocabulary**

buffet (bə fā´) *n.*: Restaurant with a counter or table where refreshments are served

Guide for Responding

◆ Literature and Your Life

Reader's Response Do you feel any sympathy for the inspector-general? Why or why not?

Thematic Focus Why does the conversation between the traveler and the driver become more and more humorous as it continues?

☑ Check Your Comprehension

1. What is the subject of the entire conversation between the traveler and the driver?
2. According to the driver, how does everyone know that the inspector-general has arrived?
3. At the end of the play, what does the traveler order the driver to do?

Guide for Responding *(continued)*

◆ Critical Thinking

INTERPRET
1. Why does the traveler question the driver about the inspector-general? **[Infer]**
2. How would you characterize the inspector-general based on the driver's description of him? Support your answer. **[Analyze]**
3. In what ways are the old and new inspectors-general alike? In what ways are they different? **[Compare and Contrast]**

EVALUATE
4. Who do you think is the wiser person, the traveler or the driver? Why? **[Make a Judgment]**

EXTEND
5. Based on this play, what lessons can be learned about how to perform effectively in a job as an inspector-general? **[Career Link]**

◆ Reading Strategy

READ BETWEEN THE LINES
In "The Inspector-General," Chekhov withholds a key piece of information: the traveler's identity. By **reading between the lines**—piecing together key details—you can figure out that the the traveler is in fact the inspector-general.
1. When did you first realize that the traveler was the inspector-general?
2. What details led you to this conclusion?
3. What evidence is there that the driver is aware of the traveler's identity?
4. Do you think the driver was aware of the traveler's identity from the beginning? Explain.

◆ Literary Focus

IRONY
The fact that the driver is aware of the traveler's identity is an example of **irony**, a contrast between an expected outcome and an actual outcome.
1. Why is the driver's remark that the inspector-general is "a good one" an example of verbal irony?
2. Why are the results of the traveler's attempts to hide his identity an example of irony of situation?

◆ Build Vocabulary

USING THE WORD ROOT -*nym*-
The word root -*nym*- means "name." Using the clues in parentheses, define each word.
1. pseudonym   3. synonym
   (*pseudo-* = "false")   (*syn-* = "together")
2. antonym
   (*ant-* = "opposite")

USING THE WORD BANK
In your notebook, complete each sentence with a word from the Word Bank.
1. The heavy trucks slowly ___?___ along the bumpy road.
2. An ___?___ donor gave $10,000 to the hospital fund.
3. The ___?___ pressed the pants of the hotel guest.
4. The ___?___ featured delicious main courses and desserts.
5. Traveling ___?___, the spy checked into the motel under a false name.

◆ Build Grammar Skills

DOUBLE NEGATIVES
A **double negative** is the use of two negative words when only one is correct. Double negatives are not acceptable in standard written English.

Practice In your notebook, rewrite each sentence, correcting any double negatives.
1. At first, the traveler thinks that nobody knows nothing about him.
2. He doesn't think that no one can figure out who he is.
3. There's not nothing particularly special about the friendly driver.
4. The fellow who runs the buffet isn't doing nothing but getting ready for the inspector-general.
5. In the end, the traveler doesn't say nothing but "Turn around!"

Writing Application Sometimes double negatives are used in dialogue to capture the way certain people actually speak. Write a brief passage of dialogue between two characters who occasionally use double negatives. Then write out how you'd correct each double negative.

Build Your Portfolio

 Idea Bank

Writing

1. **Advice Column** Write an advice column directed toward the inspector-general, providing advice on how he can improve his job performance. **[Career Link]**

2. **Letter to the Czar** Assume the role of the inspector-general and write a letter to the czar explaining why you did not follow through with your planned inspection.

3. **Dialogue** Imagine that the Russian czar has summoned the inspector-general to explain why he did not complete his inspection. Create a dialogue that might take place on such an occasion.

Speaking and Listening

4. **Speech to Town Officials** Putting yourself in the role of the inspector-general, deliver a speech to town officials on a subject of community interest. **[Community Link]**

5. **Performance** With a partner, read aloud the parts of the driver and the traveler, paying close attention to the tone of voice and style of delivery that seem to work best for both characters. **[Performing Arts Link]**

Projects

6. **Report on Russian Life** Conduct research to learn about what life was like in Russia during the hundreds of years when czars ruled. Present your findings to the class. **[Social Studies Link]**

7. **Multimedia Report** Identify examples of irony in movies or television programs. Then put together a multimedia presentation in which you show these examples and explain their effect. **[Media Link]**

 Writing Mini-Lesson

Ad for a New Inspector-General

Pretend that you're the Russian czar, and have just fired the inspector-general for failing to inspect the town. Write a newspaper ad to find a new inspector-general.

Writing Skills Focus: Necessary Background

In any piece of writing, it's essential to provide readers with **background information** they'll need. In a story, for example, readers need background information on the characters and setting. Make sure your ad contains all necessary background so that potential job candidates have enough information to decide whether or not to apply for the job.

Prewriting A newspaper ad for a job contains the following four types of information. Jot down notes on the information you will include for each.

1. **Job Description** Gives the job title and explains the duties of the job.
2. **Applicant Qualifications** Tells what experience and educational background are necessary.
3. **Job Benefits** Gives the salary and other rewards.
4. **Contact Information** Indicates whom to contact for a job interview.

Drafting Refer to your notes as you draft your ad. Devote a short paragraph to each of the four types of information. To attract qualified job applicants, begin your ad with an attention-grabbing first sentence, such as "Do you love to travel to exciting places?"

Revising Have a classmate read your ad to see whether any of the information is unclear or insufficient. If problems exist, add more background information where needed.

Guide for Reading

Bill Cosby (1937–   )

One of the most popular and influential entertainers in the United States, Bill Cosby has been breaking new ground for decades and making people laugh while doing it. The son of a navy cook and a domestic worker, Cosby grew up in the housing projects of Philadelphia. He left high school to join the navy but soon regretted that choice and eventually earned his high-school diploma through a correspondence course. He cut short his studies at Temple University to pursue stand-up comedy in the coffeehouses of Philadelphia in the early 1960's. His career as a comedian soon went national.

In 1965, he became the first African American performer to star in a prime-time television drama when he played the role of tennis coach and undercover agent Alexander Scott in the action series *I Spy*, a role for which he won an Emmy award. Cosby's greatest success came with his extremely popular television situation comedy, *The Cosby Show*, which ran from 1984 to 1992. Cosby has written a number of books, including *The Wit and Wisdom of Fat Albert, Fatherhood, Time Flies,* and *Childhood*.

Ralph Helfer (1937–   )

One of the leading animal trainers in the world, Ralph Helfer has persuaded animals to do what directors want them to do in more than 5,000 movies and television programs. In his book *The Beauty of the Beasts*, Helfer explains that his work as a stuntman and wild-animal trainer has led to his being "clawed by lions, attacked by bears, bitten by poisonous snakes, and nearly suffocated by pythons." Helfer and his trained animals have won 18 PATSY awards for the best animal performances on the screen. He is the founder of Marineworld/Africa USA.

◆ Build Vocabulary

SPECIALIZED VOCABULARY: SPORTS JARGON

Jargon refers to special language that comes from a particular activity, such as a profession, sport, or art. Much of the fun of reading "Go Deep to the Sewer" comes from Bill Cosby's inventive use of sports jargon, beginning with the title. "Go deep to ..." is an expression that refers to the far edges of the playing field. For example, in football the expression "goes deep" refers to a wide receiver going out for a long pass.

lateral
yearned
decoy
interpretation
skeptical

WORD BANK

Before you read, preview this list of words from the selections.

◆ Build Grammar Skills

ADJECTIVE CLAUSES

Writers use adjective clauses to add key descriptive details to a sentence. An **adjective clause** is a subordinate clause (a group of words that contains a subject and a verb but cannot stand on its own) that modifies a noun or pronoun in another clause. Look at Cosby's first sentence:

> The essence of childhood, of course, is play,
> adjective clause 1—modifies *play*
> *which my friends and I did endlessly on streets*
> adjective clause 2—modifies *streets*
> *that we reluctantly shared with traffic.*

Adjective clauses are introduced by the relative pronouns *who, whom, whose, which,* and *that* and the subordinating conjunctions *where, when,* and *why.*

◆ *Literature and Your Life*

CONNECT YOUR EXPERIENCE

Life gives some people lemons, and they make lemonade. Life gives other people lemons, and they make big meringue pies to toss so that others will laugh. Maybe you are one of those lucky individuals who can find something funny in most experiences—even difficult ones. These two selections focus on the lighter side of personal experiences.

THEMATIC FOCUS: EVERYDAY HUMOR

Think about how these humorous memoirs might inspire you to see the lighter side of some of your own experiences.

Journal Writing Jot down a list of entertaining tales from your life.

◆ Background for Understanding

PERFORMING ARTS

Ralph Helfer originally used a method of animal training that involved making the animal fear the trainer, often by punishing misbehavior. After following this method for years and being injured and threatened by the animals he was trying to train, Helfer decided to develop a new system, which he called "affection training." The trainer who practices affection training wins the animal's confidence and loyalty rather than its fear by displaying love, patience, and understanding. Helfer says, "Instead of dealing with my animals physically, I deal with them emotionally." He argues that animals trained through fear remain dangerous to work with and explains that he has not been injured by an animal since he began to use the affection-training method.

◆ Literary Focus

HUMOROUS REMEMBRANCE

A **humorous remembrance** is a memoir that looks at the past through glasses that, if not exactly rose-colored, have great comic eyebrows attached. Such a remembrance communicates what is funny about the writer's past experience, as in "Fly Away," or finds something funny in an experience that may have had its painful moments, as in "Go Deep to the Sewer."

◆ Reading Strategy

RECOGNIZE SITUATIONAL HUMOR

You read something that makes you laugh. Why? Sometimes you get the verbal humor—funny-sounding words or clever puns, or you respond to a character with a wacky attitude toward life. Sometimes you **recognize situational humor:** You see what is laughable about a particular set of circumstances. Much of the humor in "Go Deep to the Sewer" and "Fly Away" is situational, arising from actions that take place in wildly inappropriate settings or with unusual props. As you read these memoirs, look for each humorous situation and note what makes each one comic. Use a graphic organizer such as the one shown to capture your observations.

What Is Being Done?	Who Is Doing it?
Where?	Using What?

Go Deep to the Sewer

Bill Cosby

The essence of childhood, of course, is play, which my friends and I did endlessly on streets that we reluctantly shared with traffic. As a daring receiver in touch football, I spent many happy years running up and down those asphalt fields, hoping that a football would hit me before a Chevrolet did.

My mother was often a nervous fan who watched me from her window.

"Bill, don't get run over!" she would cry in a moving concern for me.

"Do you see me getting run over?" I would cleverly reply.

And if I ever *had* been run over, my mother had a seat for it that a scalper[1] would have prized.

Because the narrow fields of those football games allowed almost no <u>lateral</u> movement, an end run was possible only if a car pulled out and blocked for you. And so I worked on my pass-catching, for I knew I had little chance of ever living my dream: taking a handoff and sweeping to glory along the curb, dancing over the dog dung like Red Grange.

The quarterback held this position not because he was the best

---

◀ **Critical Viewing** How does this painting help you picture the setting and the characters in Cosby's essay? **[Connect]**

1. scalper (skalp´ ər) *n.*: Person who buys tickets and sells them later at higher than regular prices.

◆ **Build Vocabulary**

lateral (lat´ ər əl) *adj.*: Sideways

passer but because he knew how to drop to one knee in the huddle and diagram plays with trash.

"Okay, Shorty," Junior Barnes would say, "this is you: the orange peel."

"I don' wanna be the orange peel," Shorty replied. "The orange peel is Albert. I'm the gum."

"But let's make 'em *think* he's the orange peel," I said, "an' let 'em think Albert's the manhole."

"Okay, Shorty," said Junior, "you go out ten steps an' then cut left behind the black Oldsmobile."

"I'll sorta go *in* it first to shake my man," said Shorty, "an' then, when he don' know where I am, you can hit me at the fender."

"Cool. An' Arnie, you go down to the corner of Locust an' fake takin' the bus. An' Cos, you do a zig out to the bakery. See if you can shake your man before you hit the rolls."

"Suppose I start a fly pattern to the bakery an' then do a zig out to the trash can," I said.

"No, they'll be expecting that."

I spent most of my boyhood trying to catch passes with the easy grace of my heroes at Temple;[2] but easy grace was too hard for me. Because I was short and thin, my hands were too small to catch a football with arms extended on the run. Instead, I had to stagger backwards and smother the ball in my chest. How I <u>yearned</u> to grab the ball in my hands while <u>striding</u> smoothly ahead, rather than receiving it like someone who was catching a load of wet wash. Often, after a pass had bounced off my hands, I returned to the quarterback and glumly said, "Jeeze, Junior, I don' know what

happened." He, of course, knew what had happened: he had thrown the ball to someone who should have been catching it with a butterfly net.

◆ **Literary Focus**
What view of his childhood is Cosby presenting here?

Each of these street games began with a quick review of the rules: two-hand touch, either three or four downs, always goal-to-go, forward passing from anywhere, and no touchdowns called back because of traffic in motion. If a receiver caught a ball near an oncoming car while the defender was running for his life, the receiver had guts, and possibly a long excuse from school.

I will never forget one particular play from those days when I was trying so hard to prove my manhood between the manholes. In the huddle, as Junior, our permanent quarterback, dropped to one knee to arrange the garbage offensively, I said, "Hey, Junior, make me a <u>decoy</u> on this one."

Pretending to catch the ball was what I did best.

"What's a decoy?" he said.

"Well, it's—"

"I ain't got time to learn. Okay, Eddie, you're the Dr Pepper cap an' you go deep toward New Jersey."

"An' I'll fool around short," I said.

"No, Cos, you fake goin' deep an' then buttonhook at the DeSoto. An' Harold, you do a zig out between 'em. *Somebody* get free."

Moments later, the ball was snapped to him and I started sprinting down the field with my defender, Jody, who was matching me stride for stride. Wondering if I would be

---

2. **Temple:** Temple University in Philadelphia, Pennsylvania.

◀ **Critical Viewing** Compare and contrast the details in this photograph with those in Cosby's essay. [Compare]

◆ **Build Vocabulary**
yearned (yūrnd) *v.*: Longed for; desired
decoy (dē´ koi) *n.*: Person used to lure others into a trap

able to get free for a pass sometime within the next hour, I stopped at the corner and began sprinting back to Junior, whose arm had been cocked for about fifteen seconds, as if he'd been posing for a trophy. Since Eddie and Harold also were covered, and since running from scrimmage was impossible on that narrow field, I felt that this might be touch football's first eternal play: Junior still standing there long after Eddie, Harold, and I had dropped to the ground, his arm still cocked as he tried to find some way to pass to himself.

But unlimited time was what we had and it was almost enough for us. Often we played in the street until the light began to fade and the ball became a blur in the dusk. If there is one memory of my childhood that will never disappear, it is a bunch of boys straining to find a flying football in the growing darkness of a summer night.

There were, of course, a couple of streetlamps on our field, but they were useful only if your pattern took you right up to one of them to make your catch. The rest of the field was lost in the night; and what an adventure it was to refuse to surrender to that night, to hear the quarterback cry "Ball!" and then stagger around in a kind of gridiron blindman's buff.

"Hey, you guys, dontcha think we should call the game?" said Harold one summer evening.

"Why do a stupid thing like that?" Junior replied.

"'Cause I can't see the ball."

"Harold, that don't make you special. Nobody can see the ball. But y' *know* it's up there."

And we continued to stagger around as night fell on Philadelphia and we kept looking for a football that could have been seen only on radar screens.

One day last year in a gym, I heard a boy say to his father, "Dad, what's a Spal*deen?*"

This shocking question left me depressed, for it is one thing not to know the location of the White House or the country that gave its name to Swiss cheese, but when a boy doesn't know what a Spal*deen* is, our educational system has failed. For those of you ignorant of basic American history, a Spal*deen* was a pink rubber ball with more bounce than can be imagined today. Baseball fans talk about the lively ball, but a lively baseball is a sinking stone compared to a Spal*deen,* which could be dropped from your eye level and bounce back there again, if you wanted to do something boring with it. And when you connected with a Spal*deen* in stickball, you put a pink rocket in orbit, perhaps even over the house at the corner and into another neighborhood, where it might gently bop somebody's mother sitting on a stoop.

I love to remember all the street games that we could play with a Spal*deen.* First, of course, was stickball, an organized version of which is also popular and known as baseball. The playing field was the same rectangle that we used for football: it was the first rectangular diamond. And for this game, we had outfield walls in which people happened to live and we had bases that lacked a certain uniformity: home and second were manhole covers, and first and third were the fenders of parked cars.

◆ Reading Strategy
What makes the lack of uniformity in the bases humorous?

One summer morning, this offbeat infield caused a memorable <u>interpretation</u> of the official stickball rules. Junior hit a two-sewer shot and was running toward what should have been third when third suddenly drove away in first. While the bewildered Junior tried to arrive safely in what had become a twilight zone, Eddie took my throw from center field and tagged him out.

"I'm not out!" cried Junior in outrage. "I'm right here on third!"

And he did have a point, but so did

Eddie, who replied, not without a certain logic of his own, "But third ain't *there* anymore."

In those games, our first base was as mobile as our third; and it was a floating first that set off another lively division of opinion on the day that Fat Albert hit a drive over the spot from which first base had just driven away, leaving us without a good part of the right field foul line. The hit would have been at least a double for anyone with movable legs, but Albert's destination was first, where the play might have been close had the right fielder hit the cut-off man instead of a postman.

"Foul ball!" cried Junior, taking a guess that happened to be in his favor.

"You're out of your mind, Junior!" cried Albert, an observation that often was true, no matter what Junior was doing. "It went right over the fender!"

"What fender?"

"If that car comes back, you'll *see* it's got a fender," said Albert, our automotive authority.

However, no matter how many pieces of our field drove away, nothing could ever take away the sweetness of having your stick connect with a Spal*deen* in a magnificent *whoppp* and drive it so high and far that it bounced off a window with a view of New Jersey and then caromed back to the street, where Eddie would have fielded it like Carl Furillo[3] had he not backed into a coal shute.

---

3. **Carl Furillo** (kärl fər il´ ō): Baseball player for the Brooklyn Dodgers in the 1950's.

◆ **Build Vocabulary**

interpretation (in tʉr´ prə tā´ shən) *n.*: Explanation

Guide for Responding

◆ *Literature and Your Life*

Reader's Response Would you enjoy playing stickball and football under the circumstances Bill Cosby describes? Why or why not?

Thematic Focus If you were telling someone about this selection, which part would you single out as the funniest?

☑ Check Your Comprehension

1. What obstacles did Cosby and his friends face when they played their games?
2. What did Junior the quarterback use to diagram plays for his team?
3. What did the young Bill Cosby dream of doing?
4. Why does Eddie insist that Junior is out after his "two-sewer shot"?

◆ Critical Thinking

INTERPRET

1. Why do you think the boys kept playing football long past daylight? **[Infer]**
2. What does their ability to deal with unusual obstacles in playing their games suggest about the boys' attitude toward life? **[Draw Conclusions]**
3. How do you think Bill Cosby really felt as a boy about the fact that he couldn't catch passes the way he wanted to? **[Analyze]**
4. (a) What does Cosby mean when he says "The essence of childhood, of course, is play, ..."? (b) Do you agree with him? **[Make a Judgment]**

EXTEND

5. What life skills do you think Cosby and his playmates developed in playing football and stickball on the streets of Philadelphia? **[Career Link]**

Fly Away

Ralph Helfer

"I need 5,000 trained flies. Can you do it? Yes or no!" The voice at the other end of the phone was insistent.

"Well, I . . ."

"Of course you can't, Helfer. *Nobody* can. Look, I told the director I'd make a couple of calls. So, now I have. The answer is obviously NO!"

"I *can* do it," I said, fitting my sentence neatly in between my caller's constant jabber, "but I'll need a couple of days."

The voice on the phone was silent a moment. Then: "You're kidding."

"No, really. Two days, and I'll be ready. What do they have to do?"

"There's this artificial, dead-looking 'thing' lying on the ground in the forest. The director wants thousands of flies to be crawling on it without flying away."

"Okay," I said. "Consider it done."

"No, wait. Then, he wants them *all* to fly away, on command—but not before."

"Okay, no problem," I said. "Two days."

"Wait. Did you hear what I said? They can't leave until he says okay. How are you going to keep them there, let alone have them fly away when he wants them to??"

"I'll stick each of their 20,000 legs in glue! Look, don't worry. Call me later, and I'll give you the figure. 'Bye."

Sometimes affection training was not the only answer. One could not "pet" a fly or earn its respect. I knew I would have to resort to the laws of nature for the answer to this one. I'd had the opportunity to work with various insects in the past. But *5,000!* I hoped I hadn't bitten off more than I could chew.

I went to work, first converting an old box in which we'd been keeping crickets (we raised them to feed to the tarantulas). The box was about three feet high by two feet square. Patching up a few holes, I scrubbed it clean, fixed a crooked door, and set it inside the snake room.

The next day I visited a good friend of mine, Professor Jonathan Ziller, an entomologist and researcher. His work area consisted of twenty to thirty lab-type cages made of fine-mesh wire. Each contained a different species of insect. Over a cup of coffee, I told him of my needs. We walked over to a cage that was being heated by a

special infrared lamp. Inside I could see massive swarms of maggots—fly larvae, ready to be hatched into their next stage. As I stood there, the professor calculated the exact time when they would become flies. As his watch struck the "birthing" time, thousands of flies left their maggot bodies and were suddenly airborne, buzzing about the cage.

We both agreed that these flies, an unusually large type that resembled the horsefly, would be perfect. An added plus was the fact that they were all hybrid, incapable of breeding. Hence, in releasing them I would not be running the risk of upsetting the natural balance of the environment.

The professor gave me a batch of fly larvae, which he'd calculated would hatch on the morning of the shoot, along with a vial of a special, harmless tranquilizer in a gas capsule. The gas would be released when the tip of the cigarette-sized plastic tube was broken. With the vial set inside the fly box, all the flies could be put to sleep within seconds. Once the gas had dissipated in a matter of moments, the flies would awaken. The tranquilizer was, of course, harmless to people. A handshake later, I was off, gently carrying my brood with me.

On the morning of the shoot, all the flies hatched right on schedule. I loaded up and headed for the studio location. When I arrived, I was greeted by a crew of disbelievers with tongue-in-cheek attitudes. Bets and jokes were being made in every direction, all in good-natured fun.

The director, a big, friendly sort, came

◆ **Reading Strategy**
Why are the workers on the movie set making jokes? Do you think they expect Helfer to succeed in making 5,000 flies do what he wants?

over to me with a suspicious look in his eyes. "Is it true?"

"What?"

"That you can put 5,000 flies on something and they'll crawl around, but you can guarantee they won't fly right off?"

"It's true."

"Then when I tell you to let them go, they'll all fly away immediately?"

"Give or take a few."

"A few what?"

"Flies that won't fly away."

"If you pull this off, I'll double your fee," he said in disbelief.

"Ready whenever you are," I said, and headed for my fly house.

The camera was set. The "dead thing" turned out to be a special-effects monster baby that had supposedly died a while back and was now to be swarming with flies. Somebody was to walk by, and the flies would then have to fly away.

Everything was ready.

The skeptical assistant director yelled for the "fly man." One of my trainers and I carried the fly house over and set it near the camera. The loud buzzing of an enormous number of flies was obvious. Sheets of heavy paper prevented anyone from seeing into the box.

"Now, Ralph, I'll roll the camera whenever you say—okay?" asked the director.

"Sure, but everything has to be ready. I've only got 10,042 flies—just enough for two shots."

His look told me he wasn't sure whether I was putting him on or not.

"10,042—really!" he mumbled, and walked over to the camera.

◆ **Build Vocabulary**

skeptical (skep′ ti kəl) *adj.*: Doubting; questioning

▲ **Critical Viewing** After reading the selection, what other challenges can you think of that might be faced by people in the film industry who work with animals? **[Speculate]**

With everything set, I opened the small door of the fly house. Hiding the gas capsule in the palm of my hand and reaching inside, I broke it open, closed the door, and waited for fifteen seconds. To everybody's amazement, the buzzing stopped. Next, I opened the door and scooped out three or four handfuls of flies. I shook them out as one would when counting a pound of peanuts. Putting the little sleeping flies all over the "body," I began to dramatically count the last few: "Five-thousand twenty, five-thousand twenty-one, five-thousand

twenty-one . . . that makes it half!"

I told everyone to hold still, then I gave the flies a verbal cue: "Okay guys—Jack, Bill, Mary—come on, up and at 'em!"

Slowly the flies started to awaken, then move around. In a few moments the whole mass of them was swarming all over the "thing," but they were still too drowsy to fly, as my professor friend had told me they would be.

"Okay, roll!" yelled the director. The camera rolled on the fly swarm, and I shot a look at the crew. They appeared to be in

shock. Then, having gotten enough footage, the director shouted, "Okay, Ralph, *now!*"

My great moment.

"Okay, group," I said to the flies. "Get ready: on the count of three, all of you take off."

◆ **Literary Focus**
How does Helfer signal here that the high point of his narrative is approaching?

The crew, absolutely bug-eyed (forgive the pun), was hypnotized.

"One," I counted. They looked from the flies to me.

"Two."

"Three!" I yelled, clapping my hands and stamping my foot at the same time. Five thousand twenty-one flies flew up, up, around and around. The camera hummed, until the director, rousing himself from his amazed state, said, "Cut!"

The entire crew was silent for a moment, and then they burst into applause and delighted laughter.

"You did it, you really did it!" said the director, slapping me heartily on the back. "I'm not even going to ask you how. I don't even want to know. But if I ever need a trained *anything,* you're the man I'll call!"

Straight-faced, I said, "Well, actually, I've recently trained 432 flies to form a chorus line on my arm, and on cue they all kick a leg at the same time."

The director, poker-faced, looked straight at me. "Which one?" he asked.

"Which one what?"

"Which leg?"

"The left one, of course!"

We all broke up laughing and headed home.

Guide for Responding

◆ *Literature and Your Life*

Reader's Response What surprised you the most about Helfer's achievement?

Thematic Focus What, if any, humorous experiences does this selection bring to mind? Why?

Group Discussion As the use of computer-generated images in movies grows more realistic, "live" effects like the one Helfer describes are becoming rare. With a group of classmates, discuss what has been gained and lost with the increasing use of computers to create special effects in movies and television.

☑ Check Your Comprehension

1. What was Helfer asked to do?
2. What plan did he develop?
3. What happened at the shoot?
4. How did the director and crew react?

◆ Critical Thinking

INTERPRET

1. Why do you think Helfer kept the tranquilizer capsule hidden at the shoot? **[Infer]**
2. What does the way Helfer planned and executed the effect suggest about his skills as an animal trainer? **[Draw Conclusions]**
3. Why does Helfer pretend to count out the number of flies? **[Analyze]**
4. How do you think Helfer feels about his achievement? **[Infer]**

EVALUATE

5. Should Helfer have revealed his secret to the director? Why or why not? **[Make a Judgment]**

EXTEND

6. From what Helfer tells about his work, what skills do you think being an animal trainer requires? **[Career Link]**

Guide for Responding (continued)

◆ Reading Strategy

RECOGNIZE SITUATIONAL HUMOR

Both selections build their effects around **situational humor**—circumstances that combine actions, people, and settings in funny, and often improbable, ways.

1. In Cosby's memoir, what makes Junior's diagramming plays in trash funnier than if he had used a chalkboard?
2. What is amusing about the way Cosby describes his attempts at catching passes?
3. What details provide the humor in Cosby's description of playing ball after dusk?
4. What is funny about the bases Cosby describes in the boys' stickball game?
5. What makes the pinpoint perfection of Helfer's flies funnier than the antics of trained seals would be?
6. Helfer pretends to count the sleeping flies. Why is this funny?
7. How does the audience reaction to Helfer's achievement add to the humor of the situation?

◆ Build Vocabulary

USING SPORTS JARGON

In his memoir Bill Cosby uses **jargon**—the special language from a particular activity—for comic effect. He takes terms from baseball and football and combines them with features of street life to create some memorable phrases.

Find three examples of Cosby's playful use of sports jargon in "Go Deep to the Sewer." Define each example.

Explain how each of the following examples of sports jargon might be used in everyday speech.

1. slam dunk   3. punt
2. on deck

USING THE WORD BANK

On your paper write the word whose meaning is closest to that of the first word.

1. skeptical: (a) questioning, (b) vague, (c) angry
2. yearned: (a) stretched, (b) longed, (c) remembered
3. decoy: (a) charming, (b) lure, (c) rot
4. lateral: (a) exact, (b) one-sided, (c) sideways

◆ Literary Focus

HUMOROUS REMEMBRANCE

A **humorous remembrance** focuses on the lighter side of an event from the writer's past.

1. What serious elements enter into Cosby's humorous remembrance?
2. What overall impression of his work does Helfer communicate in his remembrance?
3. Cosby's remembrance strings together a series of experiences that make up his memory of childhood play. Helfer's memoir focuses on one particularly remarkable job experience. Which piece do you find more appealing, and why?

◆ Build Grammar Skills

ADJECTIVE CLAUSES

Adjective clauses enable writers to add information—facts, details, comments, and so on— to describe more fully a person, place, thing, or event in their writing.

> An **adjective clause** is a subordinate clause that modifies a noun or pronoun.

Practice On your paper, write the following sentences from the selections. Draw one line under the adjective clause in each, and draw an arrow to the noun or pronoun that the clause modifies.

1. My mother was often a nervous fan who watched me from her window.
2. We walked over to a cage that was being heated by a special infrared lamp.
3. I love to remember all the street games that we could play with a Spal*deen*.
4. I went to work, first converting an old box in which we'd been keeping crickets ...
5. I will never forget one particular play from those days when I was trying so hard to prove my manhood between the manholes.

Writing Application Write a paragraph describing a humorous experience from your childhood. Use at least three adjective clauses in your paragraph.

Build Your Portfolio

 ## Idea Bank

Writing

1. **Sports Report** Think of a sport with which you are familiar. Then imagine the sport being played in an inappropriate area with comic possibilities—for example, volleyball in your school cafeteria. Write a "serious" sports report describing such a game.

2. **Résumé** Imagine that you are an animal trainer, and create a résumé for yourself listing and briefly describing your education or training and your job experiences. **[Career Link]**

3. **Dramatic Scene** Write a dramatic scene based on one of the selections. Create dialogue and stage directions actors could use to perform the scene. **[Performing Arts Link]**

Speaking and Listening

4. **Stand-up Comic Monologue** Bill Cosby's memoir first began as part of his stand-up comedy routine. Take an incident or situation in your own life that has comic potential, and write a two-minute monologue emphasizing the funny aspects of that experience.

5. **Interview** With another student, role-play a television interview with Ralph Helfer, discussing some of his more entertaining experiences training animals. **[Media Link]**

Projects

6. **Research Report** Do some research on current methods of training animals, and report your findings to the class.

7. **Multimedia Biography** Prepare a multimedia biography of Bill Cosby. Include photographs as well as video or audio recordings.

 ## Writing Mini-Lesson

Humorous Personal Narrative

Choose a memorable experience and write a **humorous narrative** about it. Try to start off on the right note, catching your readers' attention and making them smile in anticipation of your story. The following may help you get your narrative rolling.

Writing Skills Focus: Strong Introduction

As both Bill Cosby and Ralph Helfer show you, the first few sentences of a humorous personal narrative set the tone for the whole story. Writing a **strong introduction** will win over your readers and make them want to smile with you. You can try a number of strategies for writing a strong introduction. For example, Ralph Helfer plunges right into his story with some dialogue:

Model From the Story

"I need 5,000 trained flies. Can you do it? Yes or no!" The voice at the other end of the phone was insistent.

Prewriting Think of the funniest and most memorable aspects of the incident you've chosen. Jot down the details that come to mind. Then list some ways in which you might exaggerate these details.

Drafting Decide on your strategy for writing a strong introduction: whether you want to try writing dialogue, stating your main idea, posing a question to your readers, flashing back from the outcome of the incident, or offering a piece of advice. Then relate your experience, following basic chronological order, making sure to include the funniest details and actions you can remember.

Revising Reread your draft. Have you included amusing details and actions? Is the opening likely to capture your readers' attention? Will your introduction make them want to read further?

Guide for Reading

Patricia Volk (1943–   )

Patricia Volk's quirky sense of humor can be seen in her short stories, novels, and articles. Volk's amusing tone is also a key element in her written advertisements, many of which have won awards. The selection you're about to read is a feature article, not an advertisement, but it may influence how you think, just as an ad does.

> *Don't be surprised if "An Entomological Study of Apartment 4A" makes you want to purchase a can of bug spray.*

Beginnings as a Writer Initially, Volk's focus was on the visual arts, rather than on writing. She worked as an art director at several advertising agencies, as well as magazines such as *Seventeen* and *Harper's Bazaar*. Within a few years, however, her passion for writing began to reveal itself, and in 1988, she became a full-time writer.

Writing Reveals the Writer

Volk's experiences and background are reflected in her writing. You can see her artistic training in the vivid descriptions and delightful details that are sprinkled throughout her work. In addition, her keen appreciation for the everyday humor of modern urban life reflects the fact that she has spent almost all of her life in New York City.

◆ Build Vocabulary

PREFIXES: *micro-*

In this article, Patricia Volk describes bugs as "microcosms." The word *microcosm* contains the prefix *micro-*, which means "small." Because *-cosm-* means "world" or "universe," *microcosm* literally means "little world." By referring to bugs as *microcosms*, Volk means that they are like miniature versions of the world. By examining such miniature versions, you can gain an understanding of the larger world.

WORD BANK

microcosms
metaphors
poignant
malevolence
immortalized

As you read "An Entomological Study of Apartment 4A," you will encounter the words on this list. Each word is defined on the page where it first appears. Preview the list before you read.

◆ Build Grammar Skills

PARTICIPIAL PHRASES

A **participial phrase** consists of a participle—a verb form that acts as an adjective to modify a noun or pronoun—and the words that complete or modify its meaning. In this sentence from "An Entomological Study of Apartment 4A," the italicized words, beginning with the past participle *stacked*, make up a participial phrase that modifies *hall*:

Sorkin greets me in a hall *stacked six feet high with drawers of Pyraustinae, a moth.*

Participial phrases enable writers to include additional descriptions. As you read the article, keep an eye out for participial phrases.

An Entomological Study of Apartment 4A

◆ Literature and Your Life

CONNECT YOUR EXPERIENCE

Often, we're fascinated by creatures that repel us. Even if you can't bear to look at that many-legged thing that just scurried under the stove, you still want to know what it is. This natural curiosity inspired Patricia Volk to collect the bugs she found in her apartment and take them to an expert for identification. This article is the result of her adventures.

Journal Writing By making light of the problem of having bugs in her apartment, Patricia Volk was able to learn new and interesting things about these unwelcome guests. In your journal, examine how a different approach to a problem—perhaps a less serious approach—can lead to a rewarding solution.

THEMATIC FOCUS: EVERYDAY HUMOR

Patricia Volk's approach to the bugs in her city apartment gives us a lighter look at an everyday annoyance.

◆ Background for Understanding

SCIENCE

In everyday speech, the words *bug* and *insect* are used to refer to many different types of animals. In science, however, referring to a spider as a *bug* or an *insect* is highly inaccurate. In fact, it's worse than calling a cat a *dog*. Insects are six-legged animals such as ants, bees, butterflies, fleas, grasshoppers, beetles, termites, and cockroaches. Insects also include true bugs, which, as Volk points out in her article, "have a modified beaklike mouth." Spiders, mites, and ticks—all of which have eight legs—are not insects.

◆ Literary Focus

FEATURE ARTICLE

The purpose of a **feature article**, such as "An Entomological Study of Apartment 4A," is to entertain readers or to provide information on a subject of interest. Feature articles, which appear in newspapers or magazines, are often human-interest stories, which means that they focus on some interesting aspect of a person or group of individuals. These articles are designed to interest readers in a subject and to evoke an emotional response to the subjects' achievements, problems, or ideas.

◆ Reading Strategy

SET A PURPOSE FOR READING

As a feature article, "An Entomological Study of Apartment 4A" is full of useful and interesting material. To get the most out of what you read, **set a purpose** for reading before you begin and then read to achieve your purpose. For example, if your purpose is to gather information for an extra-credit science report, you might focus on obtaining useful facts. If your primary purpose is to amuse yourself, you might look for a funny event or fascinating fact that you could share with others.

To help you set and achieve a purpose for reading this article, make a table similar to the one that follows. As you read, fill in the table with notes about the article that fulfill your purpose.

My Purpose	Items That Will Help Me Achieve My Purpose	Details That Achieve My Purpose

An Entomological Study of Apartment 4A

Patricia Volk

Louis Sorkin has a prominent forehead, gently rounded abdomen and powerful bandy legs. During the day, he can be found in the entomology department of the American Museum of Natural History. Sorkin, a senior scientific assistant, has agreed to identify the insects that have been calling my home home since we asked Fred, the building pest control operator, to stop spraying.

"God bless you," Fred used to say at the door, as if we might be seeing each other for the last time.

"What's in this stuff, anyway?" I said to him one day. Malathion, a controversial pesticide, was on the list.

Normally I admire bugs, which happens to be the scientific name for insects that have a modified beaklike mouth. As a child, I collected them in glass cigar tubes my father brought home from his restaurant. Bugs are <u>microcosms</u> and microcosms are <u>metaphors</u>. But something was eating grooves in my favorite brown hat. A black crawly thing with more legs than the Rockettes had staked out the north bedroom wall. There was a fauna in the freezer and a bug as shiny as patent leather had moved into the water gauge of our electric coffee maker. Darkest of all, there were definite signs of wildlife in the back-room closet a former tenant had jury-rigged into a shower. Whatever it was, it was big.

What I'm hoping Louis N. Sorkin will tell me is what eats what and whether biological warfare is an apartment possibility. California used Australian ladybugs to get rid of cottony-cushion scale. The Mormons lucked out when sea gulls saved them from the locusts. Could my pests have natural enemies on the food chain, something besides the Tokay gecko that barks at night and looks like a Tokay gecko?

◆ Build Vocabulary

microcosms (mī krə käz´ əms) *n.:* Little worlds
metaphors (met´ə fôrz´) *n.:* Figures of speech in which things are spoken of as if they were something else

Sorkin greets me in a hall stacked six feet high with drawers of Pyraustinae, a moth. We scuttle into a room crammed with journals, papers and boxes of stoppered vials. On the wall, a sign reads, "Feeling Lousy?" Sorkin's desk is littered with dental tools, mail, baby food jars and mugs with spoons—roach heaven.

I hand him my hat. He tweezes something off the brim and puts it under his microscope.

"This is a shed skin of one of the dermestid beetles in the larval stage," he says. "I think this one is the Anthrenus species. They've been grazing along it here . . . here . . . they like wool. In New York City, they live under the parquet[1] floor. Hair is a very good food source for them."

"What do they eat on hair?"

"The hair itself. It's protein."

I empty two shopping bags filled with takeout containers and hand over the freezer specimen.

It turns out that it's an immature German cockroach, which means, Sorkin says, it could have been found anywhere. Of my 21 specimens, 11 are German cockroaches. This comes as a big surprise because some look like black dots, some are pear-shaped with pale dorsal banding and some look like greasy pecan shells. Sorkin explains that roaches have a three-stage metamorphosis, going from egg to wingless nymph to adult. During the nymph stage, they molt up to seven times.

"German cockroaches are called Belgian cockroaches in Germany," Sorkin says, scratching his arm. I scratch mine too. "They're also called steam-bugs, shiners and Yankee settlers."

---

1. **parquet** (pär kā´) **floor:** Wooden floor in which the pieces of wood fit together to form a pattern.

He studies a bug I found in my colander under the grapes.

"Oh! Otiorhynchus ovatus! A strawberry root weevil. It's an outdoor weevil that sometimes comes into homes as it migrates."

"How would it get into a fourth-floor apartment?"

"They crawl."

"Would it eat my roaches?"

"It would starve."

I show him an arachnid that has spun a web in its container. Maybe it eats strawberry root weevils.

"This is a jumping spider. Normally it would be outside."

Sorkin peers into the container with the north-wall stalker.

"A house centipede!" His mustache twitches. "This is a neat animal! Chilopoda have their front legs modified to inject venom. They're predators. They live on roaches and spiders and probably other centipedes."

Bingo! A natural roach enemy. "So if I introduce more Chilopods, they'll get rid of the roaches?"

"Not completely. You'd have to isolate your apartment. If you could keep them from gaining access through cracks and wall voids and holes around pipes and the door to the hallway, yeah, you could have a really insect-free zone."

The phone rings. It rings all day. Louis Sorkin is the 911 of insect emergencies. If you open your safe and bugs fly in your face or you need to know whether New Mexican centipedes produce cyanide, Sorkin's your man.

He studies two flies I found on the bathroom windowsill. There's no masking his disgust.

"These are a little moldy or fungus-y. They look like houseflies, Musca domestica."

He checks a dust ball from under our bed for dust mites, which spend their days with their mouths open, waiting for scales to drop from our skin.

"Can't see much here."

"Is it true that there are things that live on our eyelids?"

"There are two species of certain follicle mites around the nose and forehead."

"What's the reason for us to have them?"

"They're just there. Demidex folliculorum. They feed on the material in the hair follicles and usually don't cause any trouble whatsoever. Hold your skin tight like this"—Sorkin pulls his forehead to the side with four fingers—"and push it with a 3-by-5 card and look at what you pushed on a slide, you might even find them."

I try it, but even with magnification of 200, nothing shows up. Maybe moisturizer kills them.

Sorkin checks sweepings from the backroom closet shower.

"This is an American cockroach. You also have the shed skin of what looks like another Anthrenus species and an Odd beetle. The reason it has that name is because the male and female don't look alike. So you've got three different things in here."

On deck is my strangest bug. It suspends itself in liquid, like a peanut in pudding.

"Oh yeah." Sorkin recognizes it instantly. "This is a tortoise beetle. When they're alive they're sometimes gold-colored."

"How did it get in the apartment?"

"Flew."

Sorkin helps me load the containers back into the shopping bag. I head home thinking about the high drama that goes on behind the kitchen pegboard and wondering about the strawberry root weevil. What compelled it to climb four stories to a place where it would find nothing to eat? A strawberry root weevil entering an apartment is a suicidal gesture . . . .

The next morning, while I'm getting coffee, a juvenile roach heads for the food processor. Although I can do 3.8 m.p.h. on the treadmill and the fastest roach in the world can only go 2.9, I'm no match for it. In the sink, there's a mature female that looks like she's carrying a purse. She died with her egg case stuck in her. Before Sorkin, I never would have found this poignant. Sipping coffee, I gaze at the ceiling. That's when it hits me: I've neglected my prime bug habitat.

Back at the museum, Sorkin rotates a new container with hundreds of insects and insect fragments I've retrieved from our glass ceiling fixture.

"There's . . . a hover fly . . . a spotted cucumber beetle . . . staphylinid beetles . . . a carabid stink beetle . . . ichneumon wasps . . . leaf hoppers . . . a ladybird beetle . . . a fungus beetle . . . a silverfish . . . mirid plant bugs . . . a chironomid midge . . . drugstore beetles . . . and . . . more dermestids. All these insects are attracted to light and they fly in. Then they die and the dermestids eat them."

"How do the dermestids know they're in there?"

"They smell them."

◆ **Literary Focus**
How does this passage add human interest to the article?

◆ **Build Vocabulary**

poignant (poin´ yənt) *adj.*: Drawing forth compassion; moving

malevolence (mə lev´ ə ləns) *n.*: Bad or evil feelings or intentions

CONNECTIONS TO TODAY'S WORLD

A poem might make you smile and a story can set you chuckling, but a cartoon can really crack you up—especially if it's a cartoon by Gary Larson. In his popular cartoons from *The Far Side*, Larson has poked fun at humans, animals, birds, and even bugs.

"Shoot! Drain's clogged. ... Man, I hate to think what might be down there."

"Think about it, Ed. ... The class Insecta contains 26 orders, almost 1,000 families, and over 750,000 described species — but I can't shake the feeling we're all just a bunch of bugs."

1. Do you think these cartoons are funny? Point out specific details to support your answer.
2. In what ways do these cartoons poke fun at the way people perceive nature? How does this technique make the cartoons funny?

I ask Sorkin about my most surprising insect encounter:

"One night, I was making guacamole and when I put in the chili powder it started to move. How could insects live on something so hot?"

"Oh, cigarette beetles are very common in dried pepper. They do quite well. Some insects feed on insecticide."

I follow Sorkin to another room. He points to a heap of black molts from his tarantula (they would make terrific earmuffs), then lifts the lid off a plastic tray. There it is, ready to pounce, a furry ball of malevolence. Sorkin shows me a jar of preserved insects saved at the 100th anniversary dinner of the New York Entomological Society. There's a cerambycid larva as big as a parsnip, giant meal worms and a black thing the size of a small hamburger.

"This is a belostomadid, or true water bug, from Thailand. The body has a Gorgonzola cheese flavor."

Sorkin's personal favorite is grubs over easy.

"Tastes like bacon," he says.

"Are bugs kosher?"[2]

---

2. **kosher** (kō′ shər) *adj.*: Fit to eat according to Jewish dietary laws.

"Uh, well, yes and no. There are references in the Bible that say six species of locust are kosher, but there's some discussion that people were really referring to locust *beans*."

Sorkin is encyclopedic. Sorkin can answer anything. Talking to Sorkin is like playing "Stump the Stars": No, a roach cannot live on the glue of one postage stamp for a year. Even though we find them that way, insects don't always die on their backs. (Their legs bend in or they twitch and fall over.) There is no such thing as a *hen*-roach. It would not destroy the balance of nature if all pest species were eliminated from apartments, since that's not their natural habitat anyway. Roaches probably got into Biosphere 2 on packaging, same as we import them from the supermarket. After you've finished the bananas, fruit flies go back outside. Centipedes don't have a hundred legs. They have one pair per body segment, and 20 to 30 segments is normal. New insects are being discovered all the time. Recently Sorkin was <u>immortalized</u> by a parasitic moth mite, *Charletonia sorkini*.

◆ **Reading Strategy**
What purpose can you achieve by learning these odd and interesting facts?

"Can you look at a bite and tell what did it?"

"Sometimes," Sorkin says. "Bedbugs bite in a line. Fleas," he taps his sock, "usually bite at ground level."

I show him the back of my neck.

"None of your samples did that."

I thank Sorkin for his help. While my problem hasn't been solved, at least I know more about it. And I don't have cereal mites, black carpet beetles, termites, bedbugs, furniture carpet beetles, Trogoderma beetles, fleas and Anthrenus carpet beetles. Head lice, now that the kids are out of elementary school, are a thing of the past. If many of my insects come in with fresh air, what's the alternative? When you think about it, living close to nature, even on a tiny scale, is a privilege in a city.

When greeting, insects antennate, tapping each other with their antennae to check out who they're dealing with. Sorkin and I nod goodbye and shake hands, a Homo sapiens-specific ritual.

◆ **Build Vocabulary**

immortalized (i môr´ tə līzd) *v.:* Given lasting fame

Guide for Responding

◆ Literature and Your Life

Reader's Response What was the most interesting thing you learned from this article?

Thematic Focus How can maintaining a light attitude help people cope with problems or annoyances?

Journal Entry Explore your thoughts and feelings about pests and pest control.

☑ Check Your Comprehension

1. Why did the author have bugs in her apartment?
2. What reason does the author give for visiting the entomologist?
3. (a) What do most of the bugs in the first batch turn out to be? (b) Why does this surprise the author?
4. Where does the author find her "prime bug habitat"?

Guide for Responding (continued)

◆ Critical Thinking

INTERPRET
1. Describe the author's initial attitude toward bugs using evidence from the article to support your description. **[Support]**
2. Does the author learn what she had hoped from the entomologist? Explain. **[Draw Conclusions]**
3. What is the significance of the fact that the author finds a dead cockroach "poignant"? **[Interpret]**
4. How is the author's attitude toward bugs changed by what she learns? **[Infer]**
5. How does the author demonstrate her change in attitude? **[Analyze]**

EVALUATE
6. Were the author's visits to the entomologist worthwhile? Explain. **[Make a Judgment]**

APPLY
7. "Humor has more to do with a way of looking at a situation than with what's actually going on. Some of the funniest stories center on serious problems, awkward situations, or everyday annoyances." Do you agree with this statement? Support your opinion. **[Generalize]**

◆ Reading Strategy

SET A PURPOSE FOR READING
Reading with a **purpose** makes it easier to identify and remember important information.
1. What was your purpose for reading?
2. Why did you select this particular purpose?
3. Identify three pieces of information from the article that helped you achieve your purpose.

◆ Literary Focus

FEATURE ARTICLE
A **feature article** takes an entertaining look at a subject about which people want to know.
1. How well does "An Entomological Study of Apartment 4A" fit the definition of a feature article?
2. What characteristics of a human-interest story are seen in the article?

◆ Build Vocabulary

USING THE PREFIX *micro-*
On your paper, briefly describe how the prefix *micro-* can help you understand the following words.

1. microwave
2. microscope
3. microcomputer
4. microbiologist

USING THE WORD BANK
On your paper, write the following sentences. Then fill in the blanks with a form of the most appropriate word from the Word Bank.
1. In poems and stories, a road is often a ____?____ for life.
2. The wicked villain planned to blow up the city out of sheer ____?____ .
3. Philosophers have said that people are ____?____ of nature; by understanding people, you can understand nature.
4. The hero's adventures were ____?____ in song and story.
5. The ____?____ plot had us all sniffling by the end of the movie.

◆ Build Grammar Skills

PARTICIPIAL PHRASES
A **participle** is a verb form that is used as an adjective to modify an noun or pronoun. A **participial phrase** consists of the participle plus the words that complete or modify its meaning.

Practice On your paper, write the following sentences from the article. Underline the participial phrase and circle the noun or pronoun it modifies. Then draw an arrow to connect the participial phrase to the word it modifies. All the participial phrases in these sentences begin with past participles.
1. We scuttle into a room crammed with journals, papers and boxes of stoppered vials.
2. I empty two shopping bags filled with takeout containers and hand over the freezer specimen.
3. It was an article jam-packed with fascinating facts.
4. Sorkin shows me a jar of preserved insects saved at the 100th anniversary dinner of the New York Entomological Society.

Build Your Portfolio

 ## Idea Bank

Writing

1. **Animal Organizer** In the article, Volk mentions many different types of animals. Prepare a chart that sorts the animals into the following categories: "Insects," "Arachnids," "Chilopods," and "Other." Write a descriptive paragraph for each category. **[Science Link]**

2. **Bug Story** Write a humorous story about a real or imagined incident that involves insects or spiders.

3. **Public Relations Campaign** Patricia Volk's article deals with a misunderstood and underappreciated form of life—the bug. Select a different creature that has a "bad reputation." Write a plan for improving that creature's image.

Speaking and Listening

4. **Oral Report** Prepare and present an oral report on common house and garden pests in your area. Use visual aids to enhance your report.

5. **Dialogue** Write a humorous dialogue between Patricia Volk and one or more of the bugs in her apartment. Practice your dialogue with a partner, then perform it for the class. **[Performing Arts Link]**

Projects

6. **Insect Survey** Take a census of the insects in your home or in a small outdoor area. Report your finding in the form of a bar graph or pie chart. **[Math Link]**

7. **Pet Arthropod** Prepare an illustrated manual that explains how to take care of an arthropod pet, such as a caterpillar, spider, praying mantis, cricket, or ant colony. **[Science Link; Art Link]**

 ## Writing Mini-Lesson

Letter to an Expert

Imagine that you want to ask entomologist Louis Sorkin to identify and provide information about an interesting insect that you found. Write a letter in which you request information from the insect expert.

Writing Skills Focus: Level of Formality

When writing a letter, it is important to use the right **level of formality**. A letter to a stranger may seem rude if it is too informal; a letter to a friend may seem cold or awkward if it is too formal. When in doubt, err on the side of formality. It is better to be considered a little too proper than to be considered impolite.

Tips for Your Letter

- Include your address and the date.
- Address the recipient with the appropriate title and last name.
- Get to the point quickly.
- Avoid slang.
- Be polite—say "thank you."
- End with a formal closing, such as *Sincerely* or *Very truly yours*.

Prewriting List insects that you've found inside or outside of your home. Choose one that interests you. Then jot down the questions that you would like to ask about it.

Drafting In the body of your letter, identify who you are, tell why you're interested in the insect, then ask the questions you have. Be straightforward and use the appropriate level of formality.

Revising Make sure that your letter contains a heading, inside address, salutation, body, closing, and signature. If you are not certain about the standard form of a business letter, consult a grammar book.

Writing Process Workshop

Letter to an Author

As you read the selections in this section, questions may have come to mind that you'd like to ask one or more of the authors. Maybe you'd like to learn more about Bill Cosby's childhood or ask Ralph Helfer about how he learned so much about flies. Choose an author in this section or in another part of the book whose work captured your interest. Then write a letter to that author praising his or her work, offering constructive criticism, or asking questions. Don't be surprised if you get a reply—many authors answer letters from their readers.

The following skills, introduced in this section's Writing Mini-Lessons, will help you write a letter to an author.

Writing Skills Focus

▶ **Start with a strong introduction.** Grab the author's attention and interest in your opening sentence. (See p. 329.)

▶ **Give necessary background information** in your letter. Tell the author a little about yourself. Also, don't forget to identify the work that you read. (See p. 315.)

▶ **Offer your main impression** of the author's work. Explain why you liked or disliked it. (See p. 306.)

▶ **Maintain a level of formality.** Be polite and always show respect. Don't use slang in your letter. (See p. 338.)

Notice how the writer uses these skills in this model.

WRITING MODEL

Dear Mr. Helfer:

  If my handwriting is shaky, it's because I'm still laughing after reading your story "Fly Away." ① It was the funniest thing I've ever read! I think you have a tremendous sense of humor ② ③. . . .

  I'm a high-school freshman who loves teaching his dog to do tricks. ④ Would you be interested in a partner after I finish school?

                    Sincerely,
                    Daryl Drew

① The writer tries to capture the author's interest with an amusing opening line.

② Notice that although the writer uses a personal tone, he avoids using slang.

③ The writer makes it clear that his main impression of the author's work is favorable.

④ The writer gives some useful background information about himself.

Applying Language Skills: Avoiding Run-on Sentences

A **run-on sentence** joins two or more sentences together incorrectly.

Incorrect:

I liked your book, it made me laugh.

Correct:

I liked your book. It made me laugh.

A run-on sentence can be corrected by breaking it into smaller sentences. You can also rewrite it as a compound sentence by adding a comma and a coordinating conjunction such as *and, but,* or *or.*

Practice On your paper, correct each run-on sentence.

1. The characters were unusual, they behaved strangely.
2. The story, it was different and fresh, was great.
3. The ending was clever, I was fooled, so were my friends.

Writer's Solution Connection
Writing Lab

To help you follow the proper format, draft your letter in the Letter Shell in the tutorial on Response to Literature.

Prewriting

Choose an Author Look over the table of contents of this book and recall which selections you've read. Choose a selection by a living author that sparked an especially strong reaction in you.

Jot Down Your Reactions Once you've chosen a selection, jot down your reactions to it. Note what you liked most, what you liked least, and why.

Make a List of Questions Continue gathering your thoughts by coming up with as many questions as you can about the selection.

Examples of Questions

1. Who inspired the main character?
2. How does the story relate to your experience?
3. How did you come up with the idea for the story?

Plan Your Background Information Once you've collected your ideas about the selection, think about the background information you'd like to provide about yourself. For example, you might mention:

▶ Your age or grade level
▶ Your personal interests
▶ When and where you read the author's work
▶ Other works you've read by the same author

Drafting

Create a Strong Beginning Authors are likely to get hundreds—even thousands—of letters from readers. As a result, it's important that the first sentence of your letter grabs the author's interest and curiosity. Don't start by simply giving your name or asking a general question such as, "How are you?" Instead, try one of these approaches:

Approaches to Beginning a Letter

▶ Start with a strong statement about how much you liked the work.
▶ Start by describing the lasting impact the work has had on you.
▶ Immediately connect the work to an important personal experience.
▶ Use a humorous opening to grab the author's interest.

Use an appropriate level of formality and the appropriate format Remember that you're writing a letter to an established author. Avoid using slang and jargon that you might use in a letter to one of your friends. In addition, be sure to follow appropriate letter format.

Offer Your Main Impression Don't make the author wonder whether or not you liked his or her work. State your feelings clearly and directly.

Revising

Strengthen Your Main Impression Revise your letter, looking for places where you can strengthen your main impression by replacing a vague adjective with a more specific one or by adding details.

Add Background About Yourself A letter to an author is an excellent way for an author to get to know readers. Add details about your interests and experiences that in some way relate to the work.

REVISION MODEL

Dear Mr. Cosby:

① I've always enjoyed watching your program on television, but
∧I never knew you were a talented writer until I read your

essay "Go Deep to the Sewer." I could relate to the characters
② because my friends and I used to play football in a parking lot when
  I was younger.
in the essay.∧ I thought your descriptions of the rules of the

                              hilarious
games you played were ③ funny. . . .
                              ∧

① The writer strengthens the opening sentence.
② The writer clarifies this statement by adding personal background.
③ The writer replaces "funny" with a more precise adjective.

Publishing

Send Your Letter The best way for your letter to reach the author is for you to send it to the author's publisher or agent. You can find information and addresses in the acknowledgements section of this book.

Use E-Mail Instead of sending your letter through the mail, you may want to use e-mail. Browse the Internet to see whether there is a Web site through which you can reach the author. If not, direct your e-mail to the publisher or agent.

APPLYING LANGUAGE SKILLS: Avoiding Misplaced Modifiers

A **misplaced modifier** modifies the wrong word in a sentence.

Incorrect:
At age ten, you were my favorite author.

Correct:
You were my favorite author when I was ten.

Practice On your paper, rewrite each sentence to eliminate a misplaced modifier.

1. The story is based on the author's personal experiences, which made me laugh out loud.
2. I wrote a story on a computer with a surprise ending.
3. Soaring gracefully above the treetops, I watched the hawk disappear from view.

Writing Application Check your letter carefully for misplaced modifiers. If you find any, revise your sentences.

Writer's Solution Connection Language Lab

For additional instruction and practice, complete the lesson on Misplaced Modifiers.

Real-World Reading Skills Workshop

Strategies for Success

This book is filled with brief literary works—short stories, articles, essays, poems. Most of the selections can be read in one sitting. A novel, a full-length play, or an in-depth work of nonfiction, on the other hand, is more likely to be read over an extended period of time. In addition, extended works are likely to involve many more characters, settings, and events than shorter works do. As a result, you should approach reading longer works somewhat differently from shorter works.

Plan Your Reading An extended work may take several days or even weeks to complete. Before you start, plan your times for reading. Set goals for how much you want to read at each sitting. Try to read every day if possible. Don't let too much time elapse between readings, or you may forget important details that you read earlier.

Notice Changes That Occur In a brief work of literature, there is usually not enough time for major changes to take place. In a longer work, on the other hand, many things may change as time goes on. As you read, ask yourself questions such as: *How much time passes from one chapter to the next? What new settings are introduced? How do the main characters change by the end of the work?*

Appreciate Details A short-story writer or a poet does not have much time or space for elaborate detail. A novelist or a biographer does, however. As you read, take time to enjoy descriptive passages about a setting or character. Do not "race over" those parts in order to get to the plot.

Lord of the Flies

William Golding

Apply the Strategy

Use the chapter listings for the first half of the novel *Lord of the Flies* to answer these questions.

1. Approximately how many pages per day will you have to read in order to complete the first five chapters of *Lord of the Flies* in three days?

2. Which two chapters might you plan to read on the same day?

3. What is the setting of the book? How can you tell?

✔ Here are several situations in which you may apply the skills for reading a novel:
▶ Reading a novel for a school assignment
▶ Reading a novel for summer pleasure
▶ Reading a nonfiction book while working on a paper

PART 2 *Out of the Ordinary*

Spotted Dogs on Tree, © Dave Cutler, Stock Illustration Source, Inc.

Guide for Reading

T. S. Eliot *(1888–1965)*

T. S. Eliot's collection of humorous poems, *Old Possum's Book of Practical Cats* (1939), was the inspiration for *Cats!*—one of the most popular musicals of all time. The work was something of a departure for Eliot, better known as a serious poet. Though born in the United States, Eliot settled in England while still a young man, working as a teacher and bank clerk. He first won literary attention with his poetry collection *Prufrock, and Other Observations*, published in 1917. Eliot went on to become one of the world's leading poets, winning the Nobel Prize for Literature in 1948.

Victor Hernández Cruz *(1949–   )*

A native of Puerto Rico, Victor Hernández Cruz emigrated to New York City with his family while still a boy. As a poet, Cruz pioneered a style called Nuyorican, a combination of English and Spanish dotted with slang that became popular among New York poets of Puerto Rican descent. He is also known for powerful oral readings that twice saw him crowned World Heavyweight Poetry Champion in Taos, New Mexico.

Lewis Carroll *(1832–1898)*

Charles Lutwidge Dodgson was a professor of mathematics, an ordained deacon in the Church of England, and a talented early photographer. Yet today he is best remembered for two children's books he wrote under the pen name of Lewis Carroll: *Alice's Adventures in Wonderland* (1865) and its sequel, *Through the Looking-Glass* (1871). Both feature a young girl named Alice whose curiosity leads her into amazing fantasy worlds. Huge bestsellers from almost the moment they first appeared, the *Alice* books have been the basis of numerous stage plays, television adaptations, and live and animated movies.

◆ Build Vocabulary

WORD ORIGINS: PORTMANTEAU WORDS

"Jabberwocky" contains many invented words, including some formed by blending two words into one—like *chortled*, which combines *chuckled* and *snort*. Such words are now known as **portmanteau words**, a term Carroll himself coined from the once-popular luggage item called a portmanteau, in which two booklike compartments closed into one traveling case.

bafflement
levitation
feline
depravity
larder
suavity
projectiles
chortled

WORD BANK

Before you read, preview this list of words from the poems.

◆ Build Grammar Skills

PARTS OF SPEECH DETERMINED BY FUNCTION

Though "Jabberwocky" is filled with made-up words, you can usually tell their **part of speech** from their **function.** Consider the opening:

'Twas brillig, and the slithy toves

Did gyre and gimble in the wabe;

You can tell that *toves* and *wabe* are nouns because they follow *the*, and it is clear that they name something. You can also tell that *gyre* and *gimble* must be verbs because they come after the helping verb *did* and indicate actions that the toves performed. *Slithy* must be an adjective because it describes *toves* and has a common adjective ending, *-y*.

Macavity: The Mystery Cat
◆ Problems With Hurricanes ◆
Jabberwocky

◆ *Literature and Your Life*

CONNECT YOUR EXPERIENCE

If you search your memory, you can most likely recall amusing nursery rhymes and songs that made you laugh when you were a young child. However, children's verses aren't the only types of poems that can be funny. Through the clever use of language and the depiction of amusing characters and events, poems such as the ones you're about to read can make you laugh out loud.

Journal Writing Recall humorous verses that you read as a child and describe what made them funny.

THEMATIC FOCUS: OUT OF THE ORDINARY

In these poems, out-of-the-ordinary events and language help to achieve humor. Identify the details that make the poems funny.

◆ Background for Understanding

LITERATURE

Alice encounters a creature called a Jabberwock in the first chapter of *Through the Looking-Glass*. She cannot understand it, so the character Humpty Dumpty explains some of its words, including these:

brillig: four o'clock in the afternoon, the time when you begin broiling things for dinner

toves: creatures that are something like badgers, something like lizards, and something like corkscrews

gyre: to go round and round like a gyroscope

gimble: to make holes like a gimlet (a hand tool that bores holes)

wabe: the grass plot around a sundial

borogoves: thin, shabby-looking birds with feathers sticking out all around, something like a live mop

mome: having lost the way home

raths: something like green pigs

◆ Literary Focus

HUMOROUS DICTION

A writer's **diction**, or word choice, can help achieve humor. For example, writers may invent unusual words, intentionally use the wrong word, or use formal or informal English in inappropriate situations. They also use slang expressions that readers will find humorous or overuse jargon, the specialized vocabulary of a particular field or profession. As you read the next three poems, think about how each writer's word choice contributes to the humor.

◆ Reading Strategy

CONTRAST THE SERIOUS AND THE RIDICULOUS

One way in which these poems achieve humor is by combining the **serious** with the **ridiculous**. Consider, for example, these lines from "Problems With Hurricanes":

> How would your family
> feel if they had to tell
> The generations that you
> got killed by a flying
> Banana.

Death is serious indeed, but a flying banana is just plain silly, and the combination of the two details brings a chuckle to most readers.

As you read, contrast the serious and ridiculous details in each of the three poems. You might list the details on a chart like the one shown.

Serious Details	Ridiculous Details
death family feelings future generations	flying banana

Macavity:
The Mystery
Cat

T. S. Eliot

Illustration from *Old Possum's Book of Practical Cats,* Edward Gorey

◀ **Critical Viewing** Judging from this illustration, what do you think is the spirit of the poem? **[Infer]**

Macavity's a Mystery Cat: he's called the Hidden Paw—
For he's the master criminal who can defy the Law.
He's the bafflement of Scotland Yard,[1] the Flying Squad's[2] despair;
For when they reach the scene of crime—*Macavity's not there!*

5   Macavity, Macavity, there's no one like Macavity,
He's broken every human law, he breaks the law of gravity.
His powers of levitation would make a fakir[3] stare,
And when you reach the scene of crime—*Macavity's not there!*
You may seek him in the basement, you may look up in the air—
10   But I tell you once and once again, *Macavity's not there!*

Macavity's a ginger cat, he's very tall and thin;
You would know him if you saw him, for his eyes are sunken in.
His brow is deeply lined with thought, his head is highly domed;
His coat is dusty from neglect, his whiskers are uncombed.
15   He sways his head from side to side, with movements like a snake;
And when you think he's half asleep, he's always wide awake.

Macavity, Macavity, there's no one like Macavity,
For he's a fiend in feline shape, a monster of depravity.
You may meet him in a by-street, you may see him in the square—
20   But when a crime's discovered, then *Macavity's not there!*

He's outwardly respectable. (They say he cheats at cards.)
And his footprints are not found in any file of Scotland Yard's.
And when the larder's looted, or the jewel-case is rifled,
Or when the milk is missing, or another Peke's[4] been stifled,
25   Or the greenhouse glass is broken, and the trellis past repair—
Ay, there's the wonder of the thing! *Macavity's not there!*

---

1. **Scotland Yard:** London police.
2. **Flying Squad:** Criminal-investigation department.
3. **fakir** (fə kir´) *n.*: Muslim or Hindu beggar who claims to perform miracles.
4. **Peke:** Short for Pekingese, a small dog with long, silky hair and a pug nose.

◆ Build Vocabulary

bafflement (baf´ əl mənt) *n.*: Puzzlement; bewilderment

levitation (lev i tā´ shən) *n.*: The illusion of keeping a heavy body in the air without visible support

feline (fē´ lin) *adj.*: Catlike

depravity (dē prav´ ə tē) *n.*: Crookedness; corruption

larder (lärd´ ər) *n.*: Place where food is kept; pantry

Illustration from *Old Possum's Book of Practical Cats*, Edward Gorey

▲ **Critical Viewing** How do you think the three men feel at this moment? [Speculate]

And when the Foreign Office⁵ find a Treaty's gone astray,
Or the Admiralty⁶ lose some plans and drawings by the way,
There may be a scrap of paper in the hall or on the stair—
30   But it's useless to investigate—*Macavity's not there!*
And when the loss has been disclosed, the Secret Service say:
"It *must* have been Macavity!"—but he's a mile away.
You'll be sure to find him resting, or a-licking of his thumbs,
Or engaged in doing complicated long-division sums.

35   Macavity, Macavity, there's no one like Macavity,
There never was a Cat of such deceitfulness and suavity.
He always has an alibi, and one or two to spare:
At whatever time the deed took place—MACAVITY WASN'T THERE!
And they say that all the Cats whose wicked deeds are widely known
40   (I might mention Mungojerrie, I might mention Griddlebone)
Are nothing more than agents for the Cat who all the time
Just controls their operations: the Napoleon of Crime!⁷

---

5. **Foreign Office:** British equivalent of the U.S. Department of State.
6. **Admiralty:** British government department in charge of naval affairs.
7. **the Napoleon of Crime:** A criminal mastermind; an emperor of crime—just as Napoleon Bonaparte (1769–1821) was a masterful military strategist who had himself crowned emperor.

◆ **Build Vocabulary**

suavity (swä′ və tē) *n.*: Quality of being socially smooth

Guide for Responding

◆ *Literature and Your Life*

Reader's Response Did you find this poem amusing? Why or why not?

Thematic Focus What out-of-the-ordinary aspects of Macavity's personality and behavior contribute to this poem's humor?

Journal Writing In a poem or paragraph, describe a pet or another animal that you find mysterious.

☑ **Check Your Comprehension**

1. Briefly describe Macavity's appearance.
2. Give four examples of Macavity's misdeeds.
3. Why are the police unable to charge Macavity?

◆ **Critical Thinking**

INTERPRET
1. Cite details to show that the tone of this poem is humorous. **[Support]**
2. Why do you think Eliot keeps repeating the line "Macavity's not there"? **[Analyze]**
3. How might the *cavity* part of the name *Macavity* be related to the cat's unusual behavior? **[Analyze]**

APPLY
4. What qualities of cats might have prompted Eliot to associate them with criminal activities? **[Speculate]**

Problems With Hurricanes

Victor Hernández Cruz

A campesino[1] looked at the air
And told me:
With hurricanes it's not the wind
or the noise or the water.
5   I'll tell you he said:
it's the mangoes, avocados
Green plantains[2] and bananas
flying into town like projectiles.

How would your family
10   feel if they had to tell
The generations that you
got killed by a flying
Banana.

---

1. **campesino** (käm´ pe sē nô) *n.*: Spanish term for a simple farmer or another person who lives in a rural area.
2. **plantains** (plan´ tins) *n.*: Starchy tropical fruits that resemble bananas.

Death by drowning has honor
15   If the wind picked you up
and slammed you
Against a mountain boulder
This would not carry shame
But
20   to suffer a mango smashing
Your skull
or a plantain hitting your
Temple at 70 miles per hour
is the ultimate disgrace.

25   The campesino takes off his hat—
As a sign of respect
toward the fury of the wind
And says:
Don't worry about the noise
30   Don't worry about the water
Don't worry about the wind—
If you are going out
beware of mangoes
And all such beautiful
35   sweet things.

◆ **Build Vocabulary**

projectiles (prə jek′ tilz) *n*.: Objects that are
hurled through the air

JABBERWOCKY

Lewis Carroll

The Jabberwock, 1872, John Tenniel

'Twas brillig, and the slithy toves
    Did gyre and gimble in the wabe;
All mimsy were the borogoves,
    And the mome raths outgrabe.

5 "Beware the Jabberwock, my son!
    The jaws that bite, the claws that
      catch!
Beware the Jubjub bird, and shun
    The frumious Bandersnatch!"

He took his vorpal sword in hand:
10   Long time the manxome foe he
      sought—
So rested he by the Tumtum tree,
    And stood awhile in thought.

And as in uffish thought he stood,
    The Jabberwock, with eyes of
      flame,
15 Came whiffling through the tulgey
      wood,
    And burbled as it came!

▲ **Critical Viewing** How does the monster in this picture compare with the Jabberwock you imagine as you read the poem? **[Compare and Contrast]**

One, two! One, two! And through and
 through
    The vorpal blade went snicker-snack!
He left it dead, and with its head
20   He went galumphing back.

"And hast thou slain the Jabberwock?
    Come to my arms, my beamish boy!
O frabjous day! Callooh! Callay!"
    He chortled in his joy.

25 'Twas brillig, and the slithy toves
        Did gyre and gimble in the wabe;
All mimsy were the borogoves,
        And the mome raths outgrabe.

◆ Build Vocabulary

chortled (chōrt´ əld) v.: Made a jolly, chuckling
sound

Guide for Responding

◆ Literature and Your Life

Reader's Response What amusing mental
images did these poems bring to mind?

Thematic Response What out-of-the-ordinary language or events contribute to the humor
in these poems?

Journal Writing (a) Describe a life-threatening
weather condition. Your description may be serious
or humorous. (b) Try rewriting "Jabberwocky" with
familiar words to see whether it is still funny.

✓ Check Your Comprehension

1. In "Hurricanes," according to the *campesino*,
   what makes hurricanes worse than drowning
   or being picked up by the wind and slammed
   into a mountain?
2. (a) What does the *campesino* conclude you
   need not worry about during a hurricane?
   (b) What does he say you should beware of?
3. State in your own words the warning given in
   the second stanza of "Jabberwocky."
4. What key events occur in lines 9–20 of
   "Jabberwocky"?

◆ Critical Thinking

INTERPRET

1. In the *campesino*'s view, what seems to be the
   difference between a noble and a shameful
   hurricane death? **[Distinguish]**
2. How would you describe the tone of "Hurricanes"? Cite details to support your response.
   [Analyze; Support]
3. How would you describe the overall mood, or
   atmosphere, of "Jabberwocky"? Cite details to
   support your answer. **[Analyze; Support]**
4. What, if anything, might "Jabberwocky" be poking fun at? Explain. **[Infer]**

EVALUATE

5. One critic said that "Jabberwocky," despite its
   odd language, tells a story like many legends of
   knights and dragons. Do you agree? Why or
   why not? **[Assess]**

EXTEND

6. What do *you* think is the most dangerous thing
   about a hurricane? **[Science Link]**

Guide for Responding (continued)

◆ Reading Strategy

CONTRAST THE SERIOUS AND THE RIDICULOUS

In all three poems, a combination of **serious** and **ridiculous** details is used to create humor.

1. Sum up what is most serious and most ridiculous in each of the three poems.
2. Of the three, which poem do you think is the most serious? Why?
3. Using details from one or more of the poems as examples, explain why combining serious and ridiculous details creates humor.

◆ Literary Focus

HUMOROUS DICTION

In all three poems, **diction**, or word choice, helps achieve humor. In "Jabberwocky," readers delight in the silly sounds of invented words like *galumphing*. In "Macavity," there is a humorous contrast between the formal diction of the speaker and the actual identity of Macavity and the nature of his activities. In "Problems With Hurricanes," there are humorous contrasts between serious phrases like "ultimate disgrace" and unexpected phrases like "flying banana."

1. Find at least three words and phrases in "Macavity" that seem typical of mystery or crime fiction. How do these contribute to the humor?
2. Does diction play an equally strong role in creating the humor in all three poems? Explain.

Beyond Literature

Science Connection

Hurricanes The campesino in "The Problem With Hurricanes" says "Don't worry about the water,/Don't worry about the wind," but that is exactly what you should worry about when a hurricane approaches. The winds of a hurricane swirl at 75 miles per hour or more. As a hurricane approaches land, strong winds and heavy rains form huge ocean waves called storm surges that can cause severe flooding. Most hurricane activity occurs along the Gulf of Mexico and the Atlantic coast. What kinds of storms do you get in your area?

◆ Build Vocabulary

USING PORTMANTEAU WORDS

Chortled, combining *chuckle* and *snort*, is still widely used today. It is one of the best known **portmanteau words**—invented words formed by blending two words into one—used in "Jabberwocky."

1. Complete the origins of these portmanteau words coined for "Jabberwocky":
   a. *mimsy* = miserable + ?
   b. *burbled* = gurgled + ?
2. Use a dictionary, if necessary, to explain the origins of these portmanteau words: (a) smog, (b) brunch, (c) motel.

USING THE WORD BANK

In your notebook, complete each sentence with a word from the Word Bank.

1. The magician seemed to perform ___?___, for it looked like her assistant was floating in air.
2. Bullets and darts are types of ___?___.
3. Lions and tigers are part of the ___?___ family.
4. The poem was written in invented language, to the ___?___ of many readers.
5. Store the food in the ___?___.
6. The sinner had engaged in many forms of ___?___.
7. Jack, ___?___ with glee and mischief as he hid in the corner, observed the outcome of his practical joke.
8. Cary Grant was an actor of great sophistication and ___?___.

◆ Build Grammar Skills

PART OF SPEECH FROM FUNCTION

Though you cannot be sure of the meanings of the invented words in "Jabberwocky," you can usually figure out the part of speech of each word from its function.

Practice In your notebook, indicate the part of speech of each numbered word below. Also, explain why you think the word is that part of speech.

And as in (1) *uffish* thought he stood,
The (2) *Jabberwock*, with eyes of flame,
Came (3) *whiffling* through the (4) *tulgey* wood,
And (5) *burbled* as it came!

Build Your Portfolio

 Idea Bank

Writing

1. **Wanted Poster** Create a wanted poster for Macavity, in which you list his crimes and describe his appearance and habits. **[Art Link]**

2. **News Report** Write a newspaper article reporting the events of any one of the poems. If you choose "Jabberwocky," clarify unfamiliar words.

3. **Rewrite for Another Setting** Rewrite "Jabberwocky" or "Macavity" with a more contemporary American setting or "Problems With Hurricanes" with a new setting.

Speaking and Listening

4. **Choral Reading** Working in a small group, prepare a choral reading of one of the poems. You might alternate reading stanzas or certain groups of lines, and you might read certain lines or parts as a group. **[Performing Arts Link]**

5. **Oral Report** Using science books or other factual sources, research the properties of looking-glasses, or mirrors; the behavior of cats; or the causes and effects of hurricanes. Present your findings in an oral report. **[Science Link]**

Projects

6. **Glossary** Working with a classmate, create an alphabetical glossary that defines and illustrates the use of each invented word in "Jabberwocky."

7. **Farm Report** Find out more about weather conditions and foods grown in Puerto Rico. Present your findings in a report that might appear in a farmers' magazine. Try to include information maps, charts, photographs, and other visuals. **[Social Studies Link; Science Link]**

 Writing Mini-Lesson

Fantastic Poem

All three poems are unusual, to say the least. In fact, they might qualify as **fantasy**—writing that knowingly breaks the rules of reality. Write your own out-of-this-world poem about a fantastic creature or event.

Writing Skills Focus: Precise Details

When you write about something unfamiliar to readers, you need to provide **precise details** so that your readers understand what you're talking about. Look at this example:

Vague: It had a big bump on its face.

More Precise: It had a bulbous pimple on its snout.

Most Precise: It had a bulbous purple pimple on a green snout as long as an alligator's.

Include precise details in your poem to help readers picture what you're describing.

Prewriting List precise details that you might use to describe the out-of-this-world creature or event. Choose details that you think will help you achieve an overall mood—humorous, eerie, or the like. If you plan to write a poem with a rhyme scheme, compile a list of rhyming words.

Drafting Write either a free-verse poem—one without regular rhythm or rhyme scheme—or one with a regular rhythm and rhyme scheme. Create an image of the creature, using precise details that contribute to your overall mood.

Revising Read your poem aloud to be sure you have achieved your desired effect. Check to see whether you have used precise details that convey the appearance or character of the out-of-this-world creature or the fantastic nature of the event.

Guide for Reading

Harold Courlander (1908–)

Harold Courlander has had a long, distinguished career as a builder of bridges between different cultures. "I have always had a special interest in using fiction and nonfiction narration to bridge communications between other cultures and our own," he has said.

Courlander has studied and written about numerous cultures—African, West Indian, Native American, and African American. His long list of publications includes a number of folk-tale collections as well as books on the literature and music of other cultures. The settings for his novels range from eighteenth-century Africa to rural Mississippi to the Hopi people before the arrival of the Europeans. In addition, Courlander has compiled and edited several albums of folk music from recordings he made in his research in the field. Regarding folk tales, Courlander has said, "Folk tales as such have no special meaning for me unless they convey human values, philosophical outlook, cultural heritage . . . ."

George Herzog (1901–1984)

Born in Budapest, Hungary, George Herzog pioneered in the field of ethnomusicology, which is the study of music for its cultural values and social significance. During his long career, Herzog founded programs of ethnomusicological studies at various American universities. He also taught courses in linguistics and cultural anthropology—the study of the customs of different ethnic groups—and introduced American students to the study of folk music as an academic discipline. Herzog published numerous books on folk music, including the music of Native American and West African cultures.

◆ Build Vocabulary

PREFIXES: re-

In this story, the word *refrain* uses the prefix *re-*, which means "back" or "again." *Refrain* puts the prefix *re-* together with the root *-frain-*, based on the Latin word *frenere*, which means "to curb." So the word *refrain* means "to hold oneself back."

You already know many words that start with the prefix *re-*: *return, renew, reflect, redo, rethink, rewrite, review,* and *revise,* to name just a few. See if you can add more words to this list. Keep your eyes open; there is one more *re-* word in the story.

WORD BANK

ford
refrain
scowling

As you read "Talk," you will encounter the words on this list. Each word is defined on the page where it first appears. Preview the list before you read.

◆ Build Grammar Skills

ADVERB CLAUSES

"Talk" tells an action-packed story at a galloping pace, due in part to the use of adverb clauses to help describe what is going on. An **adverb clause** is a subordinate clause that modifies a verb, an adjective, or an adverb in another clause. Adverb clauses clarify actions in other clauses by telling *where, when, why, how, to what extent,* or *under what conditions* the actions occur. Adverb clauses are introduced by conjunctions, such as *when, where, because, since, if, as,* and *why.* For example:

The man *became* angry, *because his dog had never talked before, . . .*

In this example, *because* introduces an adverb clause that explains why the man became angry.

◆ *Literature and Your Life*

CONNECT YOUR EXPERIENCE

Your breakfast muffin somersaults out of your hands and lands jam-side-down on the floor. Then your jacket wrestles with you and wins. They may be called "inanimate objects," but too often they seem to have mischievous little minds of their own. You'd love to yell at them, but you'd feel silly talking to things that can't talk back. "Talk" is an African folk tale that whimsically nudges this idea a step further into "What if?" territory.

THEMATIC FOCUS: OUT OF THE ORDINARY

This funny folk tale makes light of human beings' sense of superiority to the rest of the things on this planet. How would you react if you discovered that your possessions had minds of their own?

◆ Background for Understanding

GEOGRAPHY

"Talk" is set on the west coast of Africa, in the country now known as the Republic of Ghana, whose capital is Accra. Many of the story's details reflect the everyday reality of life there. The first character in the story is a "country man" (more than 65 percent of the population in Ghana is rural) who sets out to dig yams, one of the staples of the diet of rural Ghanaians. This country man owns a cow. Among the other characters in the story are a fisherman and a weaver, common occupations in Ghana, a country known for its beautiful hand-woven cloths. A river figures prominently in "Talk"—more than half of Ghana's landmass is occupied by the Volta River basin, which is filled with streams, marshes, and lagoons.

◆ Literary Focus

HUMOROUS FOLK TALE

A **folk tale** is an anonymous story passed down by word of mouth from one generation to the next. Whether they are heroic or humorous, folk tales express the beliefs and values of the cultures that create them. Folk tales typically present simple characters and far-fetched situations. Meant to entertain and to instruct, such stories often use humor or exaggeration to appeal to their audiences.

◆ Reading Strategy

RECOGNIZE ILLOGICAL SITUATIONS

A cartoon coyote races over a cliff edge and treads thin air for a few seconds before the gravity of his situation sinks in. You know that this could not possibly happen in real life. You automatically check each new event you see or hear against your experience of life and your understanding of the laws of nature. This checking-out process enables you to **recognize illogical situations** when you see them—like the coyote running on empty air or the first bit of chat in "Talk."

Illogical situations can make a work of fantasy more fantastic and entertaining. On the other hand, illogical situations can distract you from a story that otherwise seems to be realistic. Keep track of the illogical situations you come across in "Talk" by jotting down what happens each time; why it is illogical; and what, if anything, each illogical situation adds to the story.

Situation	Why Illogical	Adds What to Story?

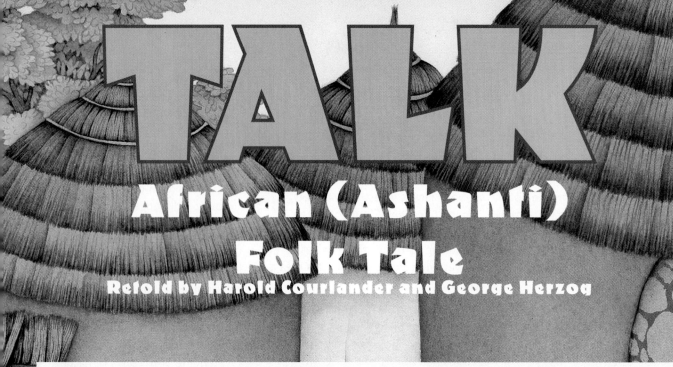

TALK

African (Ashanti) Folk Tale

Retold by Harold Courlander and George Herzog

Once, not far from the city of Accra on the Gulf of Guinea, a country man went out to his garden to dig up some yams to take to market. While he was digging, one of the yams said to him, "Well, at last you're here. You never weeded me, but now you come around with your digging stick. Go away and leave me alone!"

The farmer turned around and looked at his cow in amazement. The cow was chewing her cud and looking at him.

"Did you say something?" he asked.

The cow kept on chewing and said nothing, but the man's dog spoke up. "It wasn't the cow who spoke to you," the dog said. "It was the yam. The yam says leave him alone."

The man became angry, because his dog had never talked before, and he didn't like his tone besides. So he took his knife and cut a branch from a palm tree to whip his dog. Just then the palm tree said, "Put that branch down!"

The man was getting very upset about the way things were going, and he started to throw the palm branch away, but the palm branch said, "Man, put me down softly!"

He put the branch down gently on a stone, and the stone said, "Hey, take that thing off me!"

This was enough, and the frightened farmer started to run for his village. On the way he met a fisherman going the other way with a fish trap on his head.

"What's the hurry?" the fisherman asked.

"My yam said, 'Leave me alone!' Then the dog said, 'Listen to what the yam says!' When I went to whip the dog with a palm branch the tree said, 'Put that branch down!' Then the palm branch said, 'Do it softly!' Then the stone said, 'Take that thing off me!'"

"Is that all?" the man with the fish trap asked. "Is that so frightening?"

"Well," the man's fish trap said, "did he take it off the stone?"

"Wah!" the fisherman shouted. He threw the fish trap on the ground and began to run with the farmer, and on the trail they met a weaver with a bundle of cloth on his head.

"Where are you going in such a rush?" he asked them.

"My yam said, 'Leave me alone!'" the farmer said. "The dog said, 'Listen to what the yam says!' The tree said, 'Put that branch down!' The branch said, 'Do it softly!' And the stone said, 'Take that thing off me!'"

"And then," the fisherman continued, "the fish trap said, 'Did he take it off?'"

"That's nothing to get excited about," the weaver said. "No reason at all."

"Oh, yes it is," his bundle of cloth said. "If it happened to you you'd run too!"

"Wah!" the weaver shouted. He threw his bundle on the trail and started running with the other men.

They came panting to the ford in the river and found a man bathing. "Are you chasing a gazelle?" he asked them.

The first man said breathlessly, "My yam talked at me, and it said, 'Leave me alone!' And my dog said, 'Listen to your yam!' And when I cut myself a branch the tree said, 'Put that branch down!' And the branch said, 'Do it softly!' And the stone said, "Take that thing off me!' "

The fisherman panted. "And my trap said, 'Did he?' "

The weaver wheezed. "And my bundle of cloth said, 'You'd run too!' "

"Is that why you're running?" the man in the river asked.

"Well, wouldn't you run if you were in their position?" the river said.

The man jumped out of the water and began to run with the others. They ran down the main street of the village to the house of the chief. The chief's servant brought his stool out, and he came and sat on it to listen to their complaints. The men began to recite their troubles.

"I went out to my garden to dig yams," the farmer said, waving his arms. "Then everything began to talk! My yam said, 'Leave me alone!' My dog said, 'Pay attention to your yam!' The tree said, 'Put that branch down!' The branch said, 'Do it softly!' And the stone said, 'Take it off me!' "

"And my fish trap said, 'Well, did he take it off?' " the fisherman said.

"And my cloth said, 'You'd run too!' " the weaver said.

"And the river said the same," the bather said hoarsely, his eyes bulging.

The chief listened to them patiently, but he couldn't refrain from scowling. "Now this is really a wild story," he said at last. "You'd better all go back to your work before I punish you for disturbing the peace."

So the men went away, and the chief shook his head and mumbled to himself, "Nonsense like that upsets the community."

"Fantastic, isn't it?" his stool said. "Imagine, a talking yam!"

◆ **Build Vocabulary**

ford (förd) *n.*: Shallow place in a river that can be crossed

refrain (ri frān´) *v.*: To hold back

scowling (skou´ iŋ): Contracting the eyebrows and frowning to show displeasure

---

Guide for Responding

◆ Literature and Your Life

Reader's Response Which situation in "Talk" struck you as the funniest? Why?

Thematic Focus "Talk" comes to us from western Africa. Does its humor span the gap between two different cultures? Do you think most Americans would find "Talk" funny? Why or why not?

Group Activity As a group, come up with three stories or movies in which objects or animals talk to human beings. (You might think of other folk tales,

fairy tales, or fantasies.) Compare them with what happens in "Talk." Are the objects in other stories meant to be funny? How do people react when the objects start to speak?

☑ Check Your Comprehension

1. What happens when the country man goes out to dig up some yams to take to market?
2. What upsets each man who joins the country man?
3. (a) What does the chief say to them? (b) Who gets the last word?

Guide for Responding (continued)

◆ Critical Thinking

INTERPRET

1. (a) Why is the fisherman so calm when the farmer tells his crazy story? (b) Why does he get so upset when his fish trap speaks to him? **[Analyze]**
2. What reason might the objects and animals have for speaking all of a sudden? **[Deduce]**
3. Why would the report of objects and animals speaking upset the whole community? **[Infer]**
4. What aspects of human nature does the story hold up to ridicule? **[Draw Conclusions]**

APPLY

5. What do you think the chief should have said to the men who came rushing in to him? **[Modify]**
6. What might the chief say when his stool talks back to him? **[Hypothesize]**

EXTEND

7. The plot of "Talk" develops by repeating variations on an incident several times. Identify one other story that uses repetition as noticeably as "Talk" does. Which repetition do you like better? **[Literature Link]**

◆ Build Vocabulary

USING THE PREFIX re-

Knowing that the prefix re- means "back" or "again," write definitions for the following words.

1. regenerate   3. recreation
2. renovation   4. refresh

USING THE WORD BANK

On your paper, write the word whose meaning is most nearly *opposite* that of the first word.

1. scowling: (a) frowning, (b) smiling, (c) resting
2. ford: (a) icy canal, (b) shallow underwater spot, (c) deep underwater spot
3. refrain: (a) continue, (b) stop, (c) begin

◆ Reading Strategy

RECOGNIZE ILLOGICAL SITUATIONS

"Talk" builds a series of **illogical situations**. If you made a chart while reading the story, refer to it to answer these questions.

1. What is illogical about what happens to each man in "Talk"?
2. Does the use of illogical situations grow funnier or less funny as the story goes on?
3. Is the chief's reaction to the men logical or illogical? Explain.

◆ Literary Focus

HUMOROUS FOLK TALE

"Talk" is a **humorous folk tale** that uses simple characters and a far-fetched situation to make a point about human nature.

1. How are the characters in "Talk" different from characters in other stories in this book?
2. What image of its culture does the folk tale seem to project?

◆ Build Grammar Skills

ADVERB CLAUSES

Adverb clauses allow writers to explain *when, where, how*, and *why* events happen.

> An **adverb clause** is a subordinate clause that modifies a verb, an adjective, or an adverb.

Practice On your paper, write the following sentences. Underline the adverb clauses in each and indicate what it tells about the word it modifies.

1. While the country man was digging, one of his yams began to talk to him.
2. Wouldn't you run if you were in their position?
3. When I went to whip the dog, the tree told me to put the branch down.
4. You had better all go back to work before I punish you for disturbing the peace.
5. Wherever the first man ran, he found talking objects.

Build Your Portfolio

Idea Bank

Writing

1. **Sequel** Imagine what several of the characters in "Talk" do next and write a sequel to this story.

2. **News Report** Prepare a news report describing what happens in "Talk" from the point of view of the nonhumans. **[Media Link]**

3. **Humorous Folk Tale** Think of your school as a community, with its own culture, customs, and values. Write a humorous folk tale set in your school using simple characters and a far-fetched situation.

Speaking and Listening

4. **Dramatic Reading** Work with other students to give a dramatic reading of the story. Exercise your creativity in bringing the nonhuman characters to life. **[Performing Arts Link]**

5. **Interview** Imagine that a famous television interviewer or talk show host is conducting an interview with one of the nonhuman characters in "Talk." With another student, role-play this situation. **[Media Link]**

Projects

6. **Storyboard** Create a storyboard for a cartoon of "Talk." First decide on the events you think should be shown. Then draw a series of pictures illlustrating these situations, with a caption under each. **[Art Link]**

7. **Multimedia Report** "Talk" is set in West Africa, near the Gulf of Guinea. Prepare a report about this region. Include as much multimedia material as you can find—a map; photographs of people, land, and art; tapes of voices and music; and actual art objects and cloths, if you can find them.

Writing Mini-Lesson

Book-Jacket Blurb

A **book-jacket blurb** is a combination summary and advertisement, telling potential readers enough about a book to whet their interest without giving away the whole story—all in about 300 words or less. Choose a novel or nonfiction book that you have read recently and write a book-jacket blurb to entice readers to buy it.

Writing Skills Focus: Clear and Consistent Purpose

If you define a **clear and consistent purpose** for yourself each time you write, your writing will stay on course and be focused, clear, and forceful. Make a list of possible writing purposes, and then choose the one that seems most effective.

Possible Purposes:
- to amuse readers
- to arouse curiosity
- to appeal to a sense of adventure
- to inform

Prewriting Once you have decided on your purpose, determine which aspects of your book you want to emphasize in the blurb. For example, if you want to amuse your readers, think about some of the funniest moments in the book. Make a list of the examples you want to include.

Drafting Again, think of your purpose as you write. If you want to amuse your readers, be as funny as the book is. If you quote directly from the book, be sure your quotation is accurate.

Revising Pretend that you are a reader who knows nothing about the book, and decide what impression you would get from this blurb. If necessary, rewrite your blurb until you have struck the note you want.

Guide for Reading

Shirley Jackson (1919–1965)

As a writer, Shirley Jackson seems to wear two hats. On one hand, she writes warmhearted portraits of family life. On the other, she is a master of horror fiction. Jackson brings her comic eye to both forms, capturing the humor of family life and adding a touch of humor to her tales of horror by grounding her eerie happenings in everyday events.

Jackson's stories are like an ordinary scene in someone's living room — until you realize that all the furniture is slightly askew.

The Stormy Road to Fame Born in San Francisco, Jackson spent most of her adult life in the East.

She first won attention with her short story "The Lottery," which appeared in 1948 in the eminent literary magazine *The New Yorker*. This eerie tale of a bizarre and deadly small-town New England lottery provoked more reader reaction than anything the magazine had ever published before.

More Horrors Throughout her writing career Jackson continued to produce gripping horror novels—like *The Bird's Nest* (1954), about a woman with multiple personalities; and *The Sundial* (1958), about a group of people who believe the end of the world is near. In 1959 came one of Jackson's best-known works, *The Haunting of Hill House*, in which psychic researchers try to find out if an eerie mansion is really haunted. The novel was the basis of the popular 1963 film *The Haunting*.

◆ Build Vocabulary

RELATED WORDS: FORMS OF *OMEN*

Even though they are spelled slightly differently, *omen* and *ominously* are related words. An *omen* is "a sign or event that foretells the future." Such signs can be positive or negative, but *ominously* focuses only on the negative: It means "in a way that seems to foretell future doom or evil; in a dark, threatening way."

irradiated
loitered
endeavoring
ominously
buffeted
insatiable
omen
impertinent

WORD BANK

As you read the story, you will encounter the words on this list. Each word is defined on the page where it first appears. Preview the list before you read.

◆ Build Grammar Skills

CAPITALIZATION OF PROPER NOUNS

A **proper noun** names a specific person, place, or thing and begins with a capital letter. If the proper noun is a title consisting of more than one word, the first word, the last word, and all other important words begin with a capital letter.

Person: Shirley Jackson, Mr. John Philip Johnson
Place: Vermont, San Francisco
Thing: *The Haunting of Hill House* (book title)

You'll find that Shirley Jackson uses proper nouns to refer to details of the setting of her story. Notice that all the key words in these proper nouns are capitalized.

One Ordinary Day, With Peanuts

◆ *Literature and Your Life*

CONNECT YOUR EXPERIENCE

Have you ever felt as if there just weren't enough hours in a day? People often criticize the pace of modern life, complaining that they find it too hectic. As you will see, several of the characters in Shirley Jackson's story are experiencing a frenzied day.

Journal Writing In your notebook, briefly describe a hectic day in your own life or someone else's. Try to capture the nervous energy, nerve-racking tension, or humor of such a day.

THEMATIC FOCUS: OUT OF THE ORDINARY

In Jackson's story, eeriness combines with humor to turn a hectic "ordinary day" into an out-of-the-ordinary experience. As you read, try to separate what is ordinary from what is out of the ordinary. Also, think about what the story may be saying about modern life.

◆ Background for Understanding

GEOGRAPHY AND CULTURE

Though Jackson never specifically names the city in which her tale is set, the details she gives in passing—"Coney Island," for example, and "the Bronx Zoo"—all indicate a New York City setting. New York was America's most populous city when Jackson was alive, and it remains so today. More than 7 million people live in the five boroughs that officially make up the city: Manhattan, Brooklyn, the Bronx, Queens, and Staten Island. On a typical workday, a few million more travel in from the suburbs—most of them to work on the island borough of Manhattan, the best-known part of New York City and the part people usually mean when they say "New York, New York."

◆ Literary Focus

SURPRISE ENDING

Many short stories end with a memorable or humorous twist. A **surprise ending** is an unexpected twist at the close of a story. Though the ending surprises readers, it must still be acceptable to them and not seem as if it comes completely out of the blue. The writer makes a surprise ending acceptable by hinting at it earlier in the story, without giving the surprise away. As you read Jackson's story, see whether you can predict the ending.

◆ Reading Strategy

QUESTION CHARACTERS' ACTIONS

Jackson's story focuses on the actions of Mr. John Philip Johnson. The title suggests that his actions are ordinary, but the reader must decide whether that is really the case.

One way to do so is to **question the character's actions**; that is, to ask and answer questions about those actions. For example, you might ask yourself the following questions at different points in the story:

- What motives, or reasons, might the character have for this action?
- What behavior on the part of other characters may have led to this action?
- Does the action seem consistent with the character's personality, past behavior, and/or remarks? Why or why not?

One Ordinary Day, With Peanuts

SHIRLEY JACKSON

Mr. John Philip Johnson shut his front door behind him and came down his front steps into the bright morning with a feeling that all was well with the world on this best of all days, and wasn't the sun warm and good, and didn't his shoes feel comfortable after the resoling, and he knew that he had undoubtedly chosen the precise very tie which belonged with the day and the sun and his comfortable feet, and, after all, wasn't the world just a wonderful place? In spite of the fact that he was a small man, and the tie was perhaps a shade vivid, Mr. Johnson irradiated this feeling of well-being as he came down the steps and onto the dirty sidewalk, and he smiled at people who passed him, and some of them even smiled back. He stopped at the newsstand on the corner and bought his paper, saying "*Good* morning" with real conviction to the man who sold him the paper and the two or three other people who were lucky enough to be buying papers when Mr. Johnson skipped up. He remembered to fill his pockets with candy and peanuts, and then he set out to get himself uptown. He stopped in a flower shop and bought a carnation for his buttonhole, and stopped almost immediately afterward to give the carnation to a small child in a carriage, who looked at him dumbly, and then smiled, and Mr. Johnson smiled, and the child's mother looked at Mr. Johnson for a minute and then smiled too.

When he had gone several blocks uptown, Mr. Johnson cut across the avenue and went along a side street, chosen at random; he did not follow the same route every morning, but preferred to pursue his eventful way in wide detours, more like a puppy than a man intent upon business. It happened this morning that halfway down the block a moving van was parked, and the furniture from an

◆ Build Vocabulary

irradiated (ir rā′ dē āt′ id) *v.*: Gave out; radiated

upstairs apartment stood half on the sidewalk, half on the steps, while an amused group of people loitered, examining the scratches on the tables and the worn spots on the chairs, and a harassed woman, trying to watch a young child and the movers and the furniture all at the same time, gave the clear impression of endeavoring to shelter her private life from the people staring at her belongings. Mr. Johnson stopped, and for a moment joined the crowd, and then he came forward and, touching his hat civilly, said, "Perhaps I can keep an eye on your little boy for you?"

The woman turned and glared at him distrustfully, and Mr. Johnson added hastily, "We'll sit right here on the steps." He beckoned to the little boy, who hesitated and then responded agreeably to Mr. Johnson's genial smile. Mr. Johnson brought out a handful of peanuts from his pocket and sat on the steps with the boy, who at first refused the peanuts on the grounds that his mother did not allow him to accept food from strangers; Mr. Johnson said that probably his mother had not intended peanuts to be included, since elephants at the circus ate them, and the boy considered, and then agreed solemnly. They sat on the steps cracking peanuts in a comradely fashion, and Mr. Johnson said, "So you're moving?"

"Yep," said the boy.

"Where you going?"

"Vermont."

"Nice place. Plenty of snow there. Maple sugar, too; you like maple sugar?"

"Sure."

"Plenty of maple sugar in Vermont. You going to live on a farm?"

"Going to live with Grandpa."

"Grandpa like peanuts?"

"Sure."

"Ought to take him some," said Mr. Johnson, reaching into his pocket. "Just you and Mommy going?"

"Yep."

"Tell you what," Mr. Johnson said. "You take some peanuts to eat on the train."

The boy's mother, after glancing at them frequently, had seemingly decided that Mr. Johnson was trustworthy, because she had devoted herself wholeheartedly to seeing that the movers did not—what movers rarely do, but every housewife believes they will—crack a leg from her good table, or set a kitchen chair down on a lamp. Most of the furniture was loaded by now, and she was deep in that nervous stage when she knew there was something she had forgotten to pack—hidden away in the back of a closet somewhere, or left at a neighbor's and forgotten, or on a clothesline—and was trying to remember under stress what it was.

"This all, lady?" the chief mover said, completing her dismay.

Uncertainly, she nodded.

"Want to go on the truck with the furniture, sonny?" the mover asked the boy, and laughed. The boy laughed too and said to Mr. Johnson, "I guess I'll have a good time at Vermont."

"Fine time," said Mr. Johnson, and stood up. "Have one more peanut before you go," he said to the boy.

The boy's mother said to Mr. Johnson, "Thank you so much; it was a great help to me."

"Nothing at all," said Mr. Johnson gallantly. "Where in Vermont are you going?"

The mother looked at the little boy accusingly, as though he had given away a secret of some importance, and said unwillingly, "Greenwich."

"Lovely town," said Mr. Johnson. He took out a card, and wrote a name on the back. "Very good friend of mine lives in Greenwich," he said. "Call on him for anything you need. His wife makes the best doughnuts in town," he added soberly to the little boy.

"Swell," said the little boy.

"Goodbye," said Mr. Johnson.

He went on, stepping happily with his new-shod feet, feeling the warm sun on his back and on the top of his head. Halfway down the block he met a stray dog and fed him a peanut.

At the corner, where another wide avenue

faced him, Mr. Johnson decided to go on uptown again. Moving with comparative laziness, he was passed on either side by people hurrying and frowning, and people brushed past him going the other way, clattering along to get somewhere quickly. Mr. Johnson stopped on every corner and waited patiently for the light to change, and he stepped out of the way of anyone who seemed to be in any particular hurry, but one young lady came too fast for him, and crashed wildly into him when he stooped to pat a kitten which had run out onto the sidewalk from an apartment house and was now unable to get back through the rushing feet.

"Excuse me," said the young lady, trying frantically to pick up Mr. Johnson and hurry on at the same time, "terribly sorry."

The kitten, regardless now of danger, raced back to its home. "Perfectly all right," said Mr. Johnson, adjusting himself carefully. "You seem to be in a hurry."

"Of course I'm in a hurry," said the young lady. "I'm late."

She was extremely cross and the frown between her eyes seemed well on its way to becoming permanent. She had obviously awakened late, because she had not spent any extra time in making herself look pretty, and her dress was plain and unadorned with collar or brooch, and her lipstick was noticeably crooked. She tried to brush past Mr. Johnson, but, risking her suspicious displeasure, he took her arm and said, "Please wait."

"Look," she said ominously, "I ran into you and your lawyer can see my lawyer and I will gladly pay all damages and all inconveniences suffered therefrom but please this minute let me go because *I am late.*"

"Late for what?" said Mr. Johnson; he tried his winning smile on her but it did no more than keep her, he suspected, from knocking him down again.

"Late for work," she said between her teeth. "Late for my employment. I have a job and if I am late I lose exactly so much an hour and I cannot really afford what your pleasant conversation is costing me, be it *ever* so pleasant."

"I'll pay for it," said Mr. Johnson. Now these were magic words, not necessarily because they were true, or because she seriously expected Mr. Johnson to pay for anything, but because Mr. Johnson's flat statement, obviously innocent of irony, could not be, coming from Mr. Johnson, anything but the statement of a responsible and truthful and respectable man.

"What *do* you mean?" she asked.

"I said that since I am obviously responsible for your being late I shall certainly pay for it."

"Don't be silly," she said, and for the first time the frown disappeared. "*I* wouldn't expect you to pay for anything—a few minutes ago I was offering to pay *you.* Anyway," she added, almost smiling, "it *was* my fault."

"What happens if you don't go to work?"

She stared. "I don't get paid."

"Precisely," said Mr. Johnson.

"What do you mean, precisely? If I don't show up at the office exactly twenty minutes ago I lose a dollar and twenty cents an hour, or two cents a minute or. . ." She thought. ". . . Almost a dime for the time I've spent talking to you."

Mr. Johnson laughed, and finally she laughed, too. "You're late already," he pointed out. "Will you give me another four cents worth?"

"I don't understand why."

"You'll see," Mr. Johnson promised. He led her over to the side of the walk, next to the buildings, and said, "Stand here," and went out into the rush of people going both ways. Selecting and considering, as one who must make a choice involving perhaps whole years of lives, he estimated the people going by. Once he almost moved, and then at the last minute thought better of it and drew back. Finally, from half a block away, he saw what he wanted, and moved out into the center of the traffic to intercept a young man, who was hurrying, and dressed as though he had awakened late, and frowning.

"Oof," said the young man, because Mr.

◆ **Reading Strategy**
Why might Mr. Johnson offer to pay for the young woman's time?

◆ **Build Vocabulary**

ominously (äm´ ə nəs lē) *adv.*: In a threatening way

Johnson had thought of no better way to intercept anyone than the one the young woman had unwittingly used upon him. "Where do you think you're going?" the young man demanded from the sidewalk.

"I want to speak to you," said Mr. Johnson ominously.

The young man got up nervously, dusting himself and eyeing Mr. Johnson. "What for?" he said. "What'd *I* do?"

"That's what bothers me most about people nowadays," Mr. Johnson complained broadly to the people passing. "No matter whether they've done anything or not, they always figure someone's after them. About what you're going to do," he told the young man.

"Listen," said the young man, trying to brush past him, "I'm late, and I don't have any time to listen. Here's a dime, now get going."

"Thank you," said Mr. Johnson, pocketing the dime. "Look," he said, "what happens if you stop running?"

"I'm late," said the young man, still trying to get past Mr. Johnson, who was unexpectedly clinging.

"How much you make an hour?" Mr. Johnson demanded.

"A communist, are you?" said the young man. "Now will you please let me—"

"No," said Mr. Johnson insistently, "*how* much?"

"Dollar fifty," said the young man. "And *now* will you—"

"You like adventure?"

The young man stared, and, staring, found himself caught and held by Mr. Johnson's genial smile; he almost smiled back and then repressed it and made an effort to tear away. "I got to *hurry,*" he said.

"Mystery? Like surprises? Unusual and exciting events?"

"You selling something?"

▶ Critical Viewing This scene is filled with anonymous people moving about. What might Mr. Johnson think about these people? [Speculate]

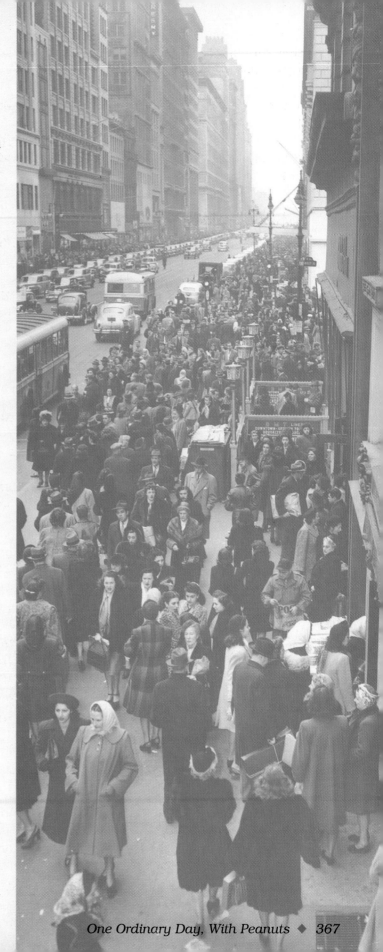

▲ **Critical Viewing** Based upon this photograph, what can you infer about the setting of this story? [Infer]

"Sure," said Mr. Johnson. "You want to take a chance?"

The young man hesitated, looking longingly up the avenue toward what might have been his destination and then, when Mr. Johnson said, "I'll pay for it," with his own peculiar convincing emphasis, turned and said, "Well, okay. But I got to *see* it first, what I'm buying."

Mr. Johnson, breathing hard, led the young man over to the side where the girl was standing; she had been watching with interest Mr. Johnson's capture of the young man and now, smiling timidly, she looked at Mr. Johnson as though prepared to be surprised at nothing.

Mr. Johnson reached into his pocket and took out his wallet. "Here," he said, and handed a bill to the girl. "This about equals your day's pay."

"But no," she said, surprised in spite of herself. "I mean, I *couldn't*."

"Please do not interrupt," Mr. Johnson told her. "And *here*," he said to the young man, "this will take care of *you*." The young man accepted the bill dazedly, but said, "Probably counterfeit," to the young woman out of the side of his mouth. "Now," Mr. Johnson went on, disregarding the young man, "what is your name, miss?"

"Kent," she said helplessly. "Mildred Kent."

"Fine," said Mr. Johnson. "And you, sir?"

"Arthur Adams," said the young man stiffly.

"Splendid," said Mr. Johnson. "Now, Miss Kent, I would like you to meet Mr. Adams. Mr. Adams, Miss Kent."

Miss Kent stared, wet her lips nervously, made a gesture as though she might run, and said, "How do you do?"

Mr. Adams straightened his shoulders,

scowled at Mr. Johnson, made a gesture as though he might run, and said, "How do you do?"

"Now *this*," said Mr. Johnson, taking several bills from his wallet, "should be enough for the day for both of you. I would suggest, perhaps, Coney Island[1]—although I personally am not fond of the place—or perhaps a nice lunch somewhere, and dancing, or a matinee,[2] or even a movie, although take care to choose a really *good* one; there are *so* many bad movies these days. "You might," he said, struck with an inspiration, "visit the Bronx Zoo, or the Planetarium.[3] Anywhere, as a matter of fact," he concluded, "that you would like to go. Have a nice time."

As he started to move away, Arthur Adams, breaking from his dumbfounded stare, said, "But see here, mister, you *can't* do this. Why—how do you know—I mean, *we* don't even know—I mean, how do you know we won't just take the money and not do what you said?"

"You've taken the money," Mr. Johnson said. "You don't have to follow any of my suggestions. You may know something you prefer to do—perhaps a museum, or something."

"But suppose I just run away with it and leave her here?"

"I know you won't," said Mr. Johnson gently, "because you remembered to ask *me* that. Goodbye," he added, and went on.

As he stepped up the street, conscious of the sun on his head and his good shoes, he heard from somewhere behind him the young man saying, "Look, you know you don't *have* to if you don't want to," and the girl saying, "But unless *you* don't want to. . ." Mr. Johnson smiled to himself and then thought that he had better hurry along; when he wanted to he could move very quickly, and before the young woman had gotten around to saying, "Well, *I* will if *you* will," Mr. Johnson was several blocks away and had already stopped twice, once to

1. **Coney Island:** Famous beach area and amusement park in Brooklyn, one of the five boroughs of New York City.
2. **matinee:** Here, an afternoon performance of an on- or off-Broadway show.
3. **Planetarium:** The Hayden Planetarium, adjoining the American Museum of Natural History in New York City.

help a lady lift several large packages into a taxi and once to hand a peanut to a seagull. By this time he was in an area of large stores and many more people and he was <u>buffeted</u> constantly from either side by people hurrying and cross and late and sullen. Once he offered a peanut to a man who asked him for a dime, and once he offered a peanut to a bus driver who had stopped his bus at an intersection and had opened the window next to his seat and put out his head as though longing for fresh air and the comparative quiet of the traffic. The man wanting a dime took the peanut because Mr. Johnson had wrapped a dollar bill around it, but the bus driver took the peanut and asked ironically, "You want a transfer, Jack?"

On a busy corner Mr. Johnson encountered two young people—for one minute he thought they might be Mildred Kent and Arthur Adams—who were eagerly scanning a newspaper, their backs pressed against a storefront to avoid the people passing, their heads bent together. Mr. Johnson, whose curiosity was <u>insatiable</u>, leaned onto the storefront next to them and peeked over the man's shoulder; they were scanning the "Apartments Vacant" columns.

Mr. Johnson remembered the street where the woman and her little boy were going to Vermont and he tapped the man on the shoulder and said amiably, "Try down on West Seventeen. About the middle of the block, people moved out this morning."

"Say, what do you—" said the man, and then, seeing Mr. Johnson clearly, "Well thanks. Where did you say?"

"West Seventeen," said Mr. Johnson. "About the middle of the block." He smiled again and said, "Good luck."

"Thanks," said the man.

"Thanks," said the girl, as they moved off.

"Goodbye," said Mr. Johnson.

He lunched alone in a pleasant restaurant,

◆ **Build Vocabulary**

buffeted (buf´ it ed) *v.*: Jostled; knocked about

insatiable (in sā´ shə bəl) *adj.*: Unable to be satisfied

where the food was rich, and only Mr. Johnson's excellent digestion could encompass two of their whipped-cream-and-chocolate-and-rum-cake pastries for dessert. He had three cups of coffee, tipped the waiter largely, and went out into the street again into the wonderful sunlight, his shoes still comfortable and fresh on his feet. Outside he found a beggar staring into the windows of the restaurant he had left and, carefully looking through the money in his pocket, Mr. Johnson approached the beggar and pressed some coins and a couple of bills into his hand. "It's the price of the veal cutlet lunch plus tip," said Mr. Johnson. "Goodbye."

After his lunch he rested; he walked into the nearest park and fed peanuts to the pigeons. It was late afternoon by the time he was ready to start back downtown, and he had refereed two checker games and watched a small boy and girl whose mother had fallen asleep and awakened with surprise and fear which turned to amusement when she saw Mr. Johnson. He had given away almost all of his candy, and had fed all the rest of his peanuts to the pigeons, and it was time to go home. Although the late afternoon sun was pleasant, and his shoes were still entirely comfortable, he decided to take a taxi downtown.

He had a difficult time catching a taxi, because he gave up the first three or four empty ones to people who seemed to need them more; finally, however, he stood alone on the corner and—almost like netting a frisky fish—he hailed desperately until he succeeded in catching a cab which had been proceeding with haste uptown and seemed to draw in towards Mr. Johnson against its own will.

"Mister," the cab driver said as Mr. Johnson climbed in, "I figured you was an <u>omen</u>, like. I wasn't going to pick you up at all."

"Kind of you," said Mr. Johnson ambiguously.

"If I'd of let you go it would of cost me ten bucks," said the driver.

"Really?" said Mr. Johnson.

"Yeah," said the driver. "Guy just got out of the cab, he turned around and give me ten bucks, said take this and bet it in a hurry on a horse named Vulcan,[4] right away."

"Vulcan?" said Mr. Johnson, horrified. "A fire sign[5] on a Wednesday?"

"What?" said the driver. "Anyway, I said to myself if I got no fare between here and there I'd bet the ten, but if anyone looked like they needed the cab I'd take it as an omen and I'd take the ten home to the wife."

"You were very right," said Mr. Johnson heartily. "This is Wednesday, you would have lost your money. Monday, yes, or even Saturday. But never never never a fire sign on a Wednesday. Sunday would have been good, now."

"Vulcan don't run on Sunday," said the driver.

"You wait till another day," said Mr. Johnson. "Down this street, please, driver. I'll get off on the next corner."

"He *told* me Vulcan, though," said the driver.

"I'll tell you," said Mr. Johnson, hesitating with the door of the cab half open. "You take that ten dollars and I'll give you another ten dollars to go with it, and you go right ahead and bet that money on any Thursday on any horse that has a name indicating. . . let me see, Thursday . . . well, grain. Or any growing food."

◆ Reading Strategy
Do the actions in this paragraph seem consistent with Mr. Johnson's personality, past behavior, and remarks?

"Grain?" said the driver. "You mean a horse named, like, Wheat or something?"

"Certainly," said Mr. Johnson. "Or, as a matter of fact, to make it even easier, any horse whose name includes the letters C, R, L. Perfectly simple."

"Tall corn?" said the driver, a light in his eye. "You mean a horse named, like, Tall Corn?"

"Absolutely," said Mr. Johnson. "Here's your money."

"Tall Corn," said the driver. "Thank *you*, mister."

"Goodbye," said Mr. Johnson.

---

4. **Vulcan:** Also the name of the Roman god of fire.
5. **fire sign:** Term borrowed from astrology but referring here to Vulcan.

He was on his own corner and went straight up to his apartment. He let himself in and called "Hello?" and Mrs. Johnson answered from the kitchen, "Hello, dear, aren't you early?"

"Took a taxi home," Mr. Johnson said. "I remembered the cheesecake, too. What's for dinner?"

Mrs. Johnson came out of the kitchen and kissed him; she was a comfortable woman, and smiling as Mr. Johnson smiled. "Hard day?" she asked.

"Not very," said Mr. Johnson, hanging his coat in the closet. "How about you?"

"So-so," she said. She stood in the kitchen doorway while he settled into his easy chair and took off his good shoes and took out the paper he had bought that morning. "Here and there," she said.

"I didn't do so badly," Mr. Johnson said. "Couple young people."

"Fine," she said. "I had a little nap this afternoon, took it easy most of the day. Went into a department store this morning and accused the woman next to me of

◆ Literary Focus
What is surprising about these details?

shoplifting, and had the store detective pick her up. Sent three dogs to the pound—*you* know, the usual thing. Oh, and listen," she added, remembering.

"What?" asked Mr. Johnson.

"Well," she said, "I got onto a bus and asked the driver for a transfer, and when he helped someone else first I said that he was impertinent, and quarreled with him. And then I said why wasn't he in the army, and I said it loud enough for everyone to hear, and I took his number and I turned in a complaint. Probably got him fired."

"Fine," said Mr. Johnson. "But you do look tired. Want to change over tomorrow?"

"I *would* like to," she said. "I could do with a change."

"Right," said Mr. Johnson. "What's for dinner?"

"Veal cutlet."

"Had it for lunch," said Mr. Johnson.

◆ **Build Vocabulary**

omen (ō′ mən) *n.*: Sign foretelling a future event, either good or evil

impertinent (im pʉrt′ ən ənt) *adj.*: Rude; impolite

Guide for Responding

◆ Literature and Your Life

Reader's Response Were you surprised by the story's ending? Why or why not?

Thematic Response Think about the humor that the story contains. In what way is the humor achieved by what is out of the ordinary in the story?

Journal Entry Jot down some details from an ordinary day in your life that turned out not to be so ordinary.

☑ Check Your Comprehension

1. What does Mr. John Philip Johnson do for the woman who is moving to Vermont?
2. What does Mr. Johnson do for Mr. Adams and Miss Kent?
3. What does Mr. Johnson keep in his pocket and hand out to various people he meets?
4. According to what she tells her husband when he gets home, how did Mrs. Johnson spend her day?
5. What do the couple decide they will do on the next day?

Guide for Responding (continued)

◆ Critical Thinking

INTERPRET

1. (a) In what ways is Mr. Johnson's day ordinary, as the title suggests? (b) In what ways is his day out of the ordinary? **[Compare and Contrast]**
2. What does Mr. Johnson help the people he meets to appreciate? **[Connect]**
3. At the story's end, what do we discover about Mr. and Mrs. Johnson? **[Infer]**
4. What is unusual about the attitudes of Mr. and Mrs. Johnson? **[Draw Conclusions]**

APPLY

5. At what aspects of modern life does this story poke fun? **[Generalize]**

EXTEND

6. How might someone avoid the job problems that Miss Kent and Mr. Adams seem to have? **[Career Link]**

◆ Reading Strategy

QUESTION CHARACTERS' ACTIONS

The surprising revelations at the end of Jackson's story make us rethink the motives for Mr. Johnson's earlier actions.

1. What seemed to motivate Mr. Johnson's behavior toward others as he traveled around New York?
2. What does the decision to "change roles" with his wife suggest about his motives?

◆ Literary Focus

SURPRISE ENDING

Much of the humor and charm in Jackson's story comes from the **surprise ending**—the events that go against the readers' expectations.

1. Considering Mr. Johnson's behavior throughout the story, why does the ending come as a surprise?
2. Look back at the story. What hints point to the unexpected ending?
3. What might the ending suggest about human experience and the factors that control it?

◆ Build Vocabulary

USING RELATED WORDS

For each item below, determine the meaning of each word in italics. Use the meaning of the related word to help you.

1. *irradiated*—related word: radiant
2. *new-shod*—related word: shoe
3. *planetarium*—related word: planet
4. *insatiable*—related word: satisfy

USING THE WORD BANK

Choose the letter of the word that is most nearly the same in meaning as the first word *as it is used in the story.*

1. irradiated: (a) darkened, (b) glowed, (c) frozen
2. loitered: (a) dirtied, (b) delivered, (c) lingered
3. endeavoring: (a) trying, (b) asking, (c) preparing
4. ominously: (a) threateningly, (b) brightly, (c) loudly
5. buffeted: (a) cooked, (b) shined, (c) shoved
6. insatiable: (a) unquenchable, (b) indefinite, (c) odd
7. omen: (a) stamp, (b) signal, (c) cause
8. impertinent: (a) impatient, (b) unrelated, (c) impolite

◆ Build Grammar Skills

PROPER NOUNS

When you use proper nouns, be careful to use correct capitalization.

Practice Copy these sentences into your notebook, and correct the errors in capitalization.

1. Shirley Jackson was married to Critic and Author Stanley edgar Hyman.
2. The Family lived in north Bennington, Vermont.
3. Some of Jackson's short Fiction appeared in the collection *the Lottery and other stories.*
4. In one of jackson's stories a Man named mr. Johnson hands out peanuts in New York city.
5. He also helps a woman on west Seventeenth street.

Writing Application Write a paragraph about a big city or another place you have visited. Include at least ten proper nouns. Then exchange papers with a classmate, identify the proper nouns in his or her paragraph, and check to see that your classmate has used capitalization correctly.

Build Your Portfolio

Idea Bank

Writing

1. **Classified Ad** Write the classified ad for the apartment on West Seventeenth Street that the woman and little boy vacated in moving to Vermont. **[Journalism Link]**

2. **Diary Entry** Imagine that you are one of the people who met *Mrs.* Johnson on this not-so-ordinary day. Write a diary entry describing your feelings before and after the encounter.

3. **Job Description** Write a job description for Miss Kent or Mr. Adams. Include relevant details from the story. **[Career Link]**

Speaking and Listening

4. **Dramatic Scene** Working with a classmate, write and perform the conversation that might take place between Miss Kent and Mr. Adams as they go off to enjoy themselves. **[Performing Arts Link]**

5. **Retold Story** Retell this tale orally as if it were a bedtime story. Make appropriate changes for an audience of one or more fairly young children.

Projects

6. **Map** Create a map of New York City that shows all the real places the story mentions—Coney Island, the Bronx Zoo, the [Hayden] Planetarium, and so on. Also show a likely route for Mr. Johnson's travels on the day of the story. **[Social Studies Link]**

7. **Economic Report** Based on the information in the story, calculate the daily and weekly salaries of Miss Kent and Mr. Adams. Assume that each works eight hours a day and forty hours a week. **[Math Link; Social Studies Link]**

Writing Mini-Lesson

Summary

Would you say Mr. Johnson's day is as ordinary as he says it is? Which incidents would you include in a summary of his day? Remember, a **summary** is an account that provides only the most important details. Write a summary of an out-of-the-ordinary day—*Mrs.* Johnson's, perhaps, or someone else's.

Writing Skills Focus: Following Criteria

Here are some guidelines, or a set of **criteria**, for writing an effective summary:

- Include only the most important events, characters, and other details.
- Recount events in chronological order.
- Use transitions like *next, meanwhile, later,* and *at the same time* to make the order of the events clear.

Prewriting Start by choosing whose day you'll summarize. It can be Mrs. Johnson, a real person you know, yourself, or a character you make up. Fill out an hour-by-hour schedule showing all the events of the person's unusual day. Then decide which are important enough to include in a summary.

Drafting Recount the events of the day in chronological order. Use transitions to make the order of events clear.

Revising Be sure you have included all the important events, characters, and other details and omitted unimportant ones. Also make sure that your sentences flow smoothly, with clear transitions showing the order of events. Check to see that your word choice is clear and precise and that your writing is free from spelling, grammar, capitalization, and other mechanical errors.

Writing Process Workshop

When you're deciding whether or not to see a new movie, you probably look at television or newspaper reviews of the movie to see what the critics think. A movie review is one type of **critical evaluation**—a written or spoken examination of what is and is not effective in a literary work, television program, or movie. Most often, a critical evaluation includes a brief summary of the work and makes a recommendation to readers or viewers.

Try your hand at writing a critical evaluation of one of the selections in this section. The following skills, introduced in this section's Writing Mini-Lessons, will help you.

Writing Skills Focus

▶ **Have a clear and consistent purpose** for writing. Keep your purpose in mind as you develop and write your evaluation. (See p. 361.)

▶ **Follow the criteria** for writing a critical evaluation: Explain what you did and did not like about the piece, support your points, summarize key events in the selection, and make a recommendation. (See p. 373.)

▶ **Offer precise details** about the work so that readers understand exactly what you are saying. (See p. 355.)

In the following model, the writer applies all the above skills in a critical evaluation of Shirley Jackson's "One Ordinary Day, With Peanuts."

---

① The writer includes a summary of the story.

② This passage gives an indication of the writer's purpose.

③ The writer provides specific details to support her opinion of the story.

WRITING MODEL

In Shirley Jackson's short story "One Ordinary Day, With Peanuts," a man spends his day helping strangers. ① First, he shares peanuts with a boy about to move to Vermont . . .

Jackson's story is quite entertaining ② because of the carefree nature of its main character and its clever surprise ending. ③

Prewriting

Choose a Topic To which selection in this section did you have the strongest reaction? That selection will make the best topic for a critical evaluation. If necessary, scan the Table of Contents or flip through the book to spark your memory.

Clarify Your Opinion Once you've chosen your selection, collect your thoughts about it. Create a chart like this one, listing what you liked about the selection and what you didn't like about it.

What I Liked	What I Didn't Like

Identify Your Purpose Look over your list of likes and dislikes. Decide whether you will or will not recommend the work to readers.

Follow the Criteria Begin by jotting down a brief summary of the selection. After summarizing the story events, go back and check off those that are most important. Cross out those that you feel are minor. Then number the most important events according to the order in which they occurred in the story. After listing your opinions, jot down details from the story that will help support each opinion.

Drafting

Follow the Criteria Using the details you've gathered, begin drafting your evaluation. Start with a paragraph that reveals your overall opinion of the selection. Follow with a brief summary of the key details. Then elaborate on your opinion of the work. End with a recommendation to readers.

Offer Precise Details It's not enough to simply say that you found a story humorous, you must back up your opinions. Explain *why* you found the story humorous, and cite specific examples of details that contribute to the humor.

APPLYING LANGUAGE SKILLS: Direct Quotations

In your evaluation, include **direct quotations**, word-for-word passages taken directly from the selection. Place quotation marks before and after each quotation you use. If you quote a passage of ten lines or longer, indent the entire passage and set it off from the text that introduces it and follows it up.

Practice In your notebook, add quotation marks before and after each direct quotation.

1. William Least Heat Moon writes, Nameless, Tennessee, was a town of maybe ninety people if you pushed it . . .
2. The old people I remember from my childhood were strong in their beliefs, recalls Rudolfo Anaya.

Writing Application As you draft your critical evaluation, make sure that you use the necessary punctuation marks when using a direct quotation.

Writer's Solution Connection
Writing Lab

Use the Evaluation Word Bin activity in the tutorial on Response to Literature to help you come up with words to express your opinions.

APPLYING LANGUAGE SKILLS: Degree of Comparison

Use the **comparative degree** when comparing two things and the **superlative degree** when comparing three or more things.

Comparative:
Carroll's poem is <u>funnier</u> than Eliot's.

Superlative:
Jackson's story is the <u>funniest</u> piece of all.

Practice On your paper, write the correct form of each word in brackets.

1. "Macavity" is a [long] poem than "Jabberwocky."
2. "Talk" is the [good] folk tale I ever read.
3. Jackson is the [clever] author of them all.
4. The ending was [strange] than I thought it would be.

Writing Application Review your critical evaluation. Check to be sure you used the correct degrees of comparison in your writing.

Writer's Solution Connection
Language Lab

For more instruction and practice, complete the lesson on Forms of Comparison.

Use Strong Evaluative Modifiers Present your opinions as forcefully and clearly as possible by using precise adjectives to either praise or criticize the work. Look at these examples:

Mild Praise	High Praise	Mild Disapproval	Strong Disapproval
readable	stimulating	slow moving	painfully boring
factual	honest	inconsistent	biased

Revising

Use a Checklist Use the following checklist to help you revise your critical evaluation.

▶ Have you clearly expressed your opinion of the work?
▶ What can you do to strengthen your support for your opinion?
▶ Have you summarized the selection in a way that will enable readers to follow what you're talking about?

Use a Model Look at the revisions made in this paragraph from a review of *The Miracle Worker*, written by Susana Seaton, a student at Long Beach High School in Long Beach, Mississippi. Notice that Susana deletes a redundant passage and clarifies the last sentence by replacing a weak phrase with a strong adjective.

REVISION MODEL

I recently saw a movie version of William Gibson's play *The Miracle Worker*. This is a story of Helen Keller. The movie was very effective—the acting was terrific, and the final scene of the "miracle" at the water pump brought tears to my eyes, ~~and the movie was not maudlin and very emotional.~~

insignificant.

Helen Keller's problems made my own troubles seem less ~~than what they are.~~

Publishing

Create a Class Publication With some classmates, create a class magazine of literary reviews.

Real-World Reading Skills Workshop

Strategies for Success

Whenever you read, try to determine the author's purpose in writing. Doing so will help you to respond more critically to the work. For example, if you know that an author's purpose is to persuade, you won't want to accept everything that the writer says at face value. In order to persuade, a writer may leave out certain facts and choose others that will spark the reader's emotions.

Ask yourself the following questions to determine a writer's purpose. Note that sometimes a piece of writing may have more than one purpose. For instance, an article that provides information may also advance a certain point of view.

Does the writer want to inform me?
Many times, a writer's goal is to educate readers by sharing information on a topic. For example, the purpose of an encyclopedia article is to give you facts about a subject. A news report is meant to inform you about a recent event.

Does the writer wish to persuade me?
Sometimes writers want to convince readers to agree with their opinion on an issue. A newspaper editorial is an example of writing that tries to persuade. Writers might even urge readers to take some kind of action. For example, a campaign speech urges people to vote for a particular candidate.

Does the writer want to entertain me?
In some cases, a writer's only purpose is to amuse you. A humorous novel or a joke book is meant to make you laugh. A horror story aims to give you a good scare, which is another way of entertaining you.

Apply the Strategy

A newspaper contains many kinds of writing with different purposes. Read the description of each newspaper feature below. Explain whether the purpose of each is most likely to *inform, persuade,* or *entertain.* Then point out any additional purposes that each may have.

1. Front-page news article on a war that has broken out overseas
2. Comic strips and cartoons
3. Letter to the editor that explains the need for a new traffic light in town
4. Humorous column about the annoyances of spring cleaning
5. Weather forecast
6. Advertisement for a sale on shoes

✔ Here are situations in which judging a writer's purpose can be helpful:
▶ Reading a pamphlet you've been handed on the street
▶ Browsing through a magazine for an article to read
▶ Looking in the library for a good book

Speaking and Listening Workshop

You speak with more than just your mouth—the rest of your body sends out messages, too. People are influenced by the way you sit, stand, and look as you speak. Your "body language" is an important part of communicating with others.

Posture Counts When you talk on the phone with friends, you might be lying on your bed or slumped in a chair. But in a formal face-to-face conversation, you can't be so casual. It is important to sit or stand straight as you speak. Otherwise, the other person may feel that you lack respect or aren't really interested in the conversation.

Maintain Eye Contact In a face-to-face conversation, it is always important to maintain good eye contact. Looking away can annoy or confuse the other person. Your body language may make you appear to be more interested in something else you see.

Tips for Using Good Body Language

✔ *If you want to make a good impression when speaking in a formal situation, follow these suggestions:*

- ▶ Stand or sit up straight. Don't slouch or hunch over as you speak and listen.
- ▶ Maintain good eye contact. Don't look away from the person with whom you are speaking.
- ▶ Wear a smile. A friendly face helps to ensure a friendly conversation.

Apply the Strategies

With a partner, role-play these situations. Use good body language as you speak and listen. Later, switch roles and perform each situation again.

1. You are being interviewed for a summer job—perhaps as a camp worker, a baby sitter, or a sales clerk.
2. The town mayor is honoring you for being an outstanding citizen. You are asked to say a few words after being presented with an award.
3. You meet a new student in the school cafeteria. During lunch, you tell the student about school, your town, and your interests.

Extended Reading Opportunities

Everyone can use a laugh now and then. Following are just a few possibilities for extending your exploration of the lighter side.

Suggested Titles

The Prince and the Pauper
Mark Twain

In this social satire, set in sixteenth-century England, a young prince and a London street beggar exchange identities. Twain uses both understatement and exaggeration to describe the confusing events that follow. The amusing twists and turns of the plot ultimately reveal a deeper message—that it is wrong to judge people by their outward appearances, and that anyone can be a king.

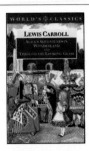

Alice's Adventures in Wonderland
Lewis Carroll

In this fanciful story, a young girl falls down a rabbit hole and finds herself in a strange country where nothing seems to make sense. At times she grows huge as a giant; at other times she shrinks to the size of a mouse. Along the way, Alice meets an assortment of extraordinary characters, including a talking rabbit, a sleepy doormouse, and a grinning Cheshire cat. More than just a children's story, this book uses satire and symbolism to poke fun at society.

Childhood
Bill Cosby

In this entertaining book, funnyman Bill Cosby shares humorous reminiscences from his own childhood. He recalls getting scolded for his bad manners, acting up in school, suffering through crushes on girls, and playing sports on the streets of Philadelphia. Each tale is told in the sidesplitting style that has secured for Cosby his place as one of the country's best-loved comedians.

Other Possibilities

The Little Prince   Antoine de St. Exupery
The Pigman and Me   Paul Zindel
She Loves You: A Curious Tale   Elaine Segal
  Concerning a Miraculous Intervention

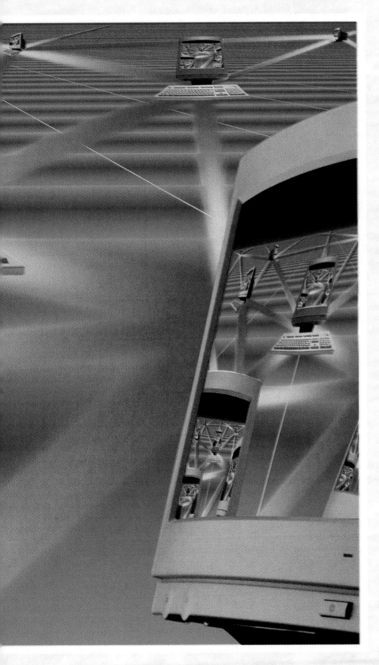

Visions of the Future

People have always tried to imagine the future. Some have worried that today's human carelessness will produce the problems of tomorrow. Others have looked toward the future with hope and optimism. Still others have imagined inventions and developments beyond our wildest dreams. As you read these selections, ask yourself how each writer's vision compares with your own.

Guide for Reading

Bill Gates *(1955–)*

With a fortune of $23.9 billion as of January 1997, Bill Gates is "the richest man in the world, and maybe the smartest," according to *Newsweek* magazine. This world-famous businessman is the chief executive officer and co-founder of Microsoft Corporation, the world's largest computer software company.

A Computer Genius Gates's fascination with computers began in the eighth grade. He and his friend Paul Allen taught themselves the computer language BASIC and began writing programs. One of Gates's early programs created schedules for students—it even contained extra instructions that ensured Gates a spot as one of the few boys in a class full of girls. In high school, Gates spent the summers working as a computer programmer. He and Paul Allen also invented a way to use a new microprocessor chip to analyze and graph traffic data.

Envisioning the Future Although Gates and Allen's Traf-O-Data machine was not a huge success, they continued to believe in the importance of microprocessors. The two teenagers realized something that computer manufacturers did not: Microprocessors would improve rapidly and could become the "brains" of small, powerful computers.

In 1975, Gates and Allen wrote the first version of BASIC for a microcomputer. By doing so, they made it possible for other programs to be written. The two friends soon started their own company, which has grown into a corporation with more than 21,000 employees and $8 billion a year in sales.

Looking Forward Gates's ability to envision a future with inexpensive computing power enabled him to build a software empire. In his book *The Road Ahead*, Gates examines the future of computer technology.

◆ Build Vocabulary

WORD ROOTS: *-simul-*

In this excerpt from *The Road Ahead*, Bill Gates describes a television program from his childhood during which a man spun ten plates simultaneously on the noses of ten dogs. The word *simultaneous* contains the word root *-simul-*, which means "same." Thus, events that are simultaneous happen at the same time. What other words can you think of that contain the root *-simul-*?

simultaneously
capacious
precursors
infrared
parlance

WORD BANK

As you read *The Road Ahead,* you will encounter the words on this list. Each word is defined on the page where it first appears. Preview this list before you read.

◆ Build Grammar Skills

PRONOUN AGREEMENT WITH INDEFINITE PRONOUN ANTECEDENTS

A **pronoun** must agree in number (singular or plural) and gender with its antecedent, the word to which it refers. When the antecedent is a singular indefinite pronoun—a word like *anyone* or *someone*—a writer must use gender-neutral pronouns. In this example *his or her*, which is gender-neutral and singular, refers to the indefinite singular antecedent *anyone*.

> The message could be . . . read later by *anyone*, at *his* or *her* convenience.

It would be incorrect to use the word *their* in place of *his or her* in the above sentence. Because *their* is plural, it would not agree with the singular antecedent.

from The Road Ahead

◆ *Literature and Your Life*

CONNECT YOUR EXPERIENCE

Technology changes at an astounding pace. Computers that seem cutting-edge when new don't have enough processing power, memory, or features a few years later. A video game that once impressed you may now seem slow and unexciting. In this essay, Bill Gates takes you on a tour of the technological innovations that will replace today's groundbreaking technology.

THEMATIC FOCUS: VISIONS OF THE FUTURE

Having a vision of the future has helped Bill Gates achieve tremendous success. As you read this selection, you may be inspired to begin developing your own vision of the future that might one day help you establish a successful career.

Journal Writing In your journal, speculate about the kinds of technology that will exist twenty years in the future. How will this technology affect your life?

◆ Background for Understanding

TECHNOLOGY

The Internet consists of tens of thousands of computer networks that are connected to one another via telephone lines and that follow an agreed-upon set of rules for communication. These networks belong to commercial organizations, educational institutions, governmental agencies, or not-for-profit organizations. (This is why Internet addresses contain the suffixes *.com, .edu, .gov,* or *.org.*)

Through the Internet, people can access "pages" of information. These pages may include text, graphics, sounds, programs, and "links" to other pages. In *The Road Ahead,* Bill Gates envisions a new Internet service—the delivery of high-quality video programming when the customer wants it.

◆ Literary Focus

EXPOSITORY WRITING

The Road Ahead is an example of **expository writing**, writing that informs or explains something by presenting information. Expository writing usually contains details, examples, and facts conveyed in an informative tone. A newspaper article on a current event, a chapter in a history book, an entry in an encyclopedia—all these are examples of expository writing. As you read this essay, notice how the author uses facts to share information and to support his opinions. Use a graphic organizer like this one to note each of Gate's opinions and to list the facts he uses to back it up.

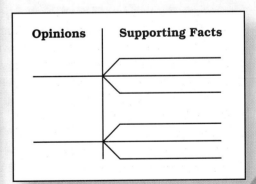

Opinions	Supporting Facts

Reading for Success

Strategies for Reading Critically

When you read a work that presents an individual's perspective or ideas on a subject, it is a good idea to read the work critically. When you read critically, you examine and question the writer's ideas, especially in light of his or her purpose. You also evaluate the information the writer includes (or doesn't include) as support, and you form a judgment about the content and quality of the work. Here are specific strategies that will help you read critically.

Distinguish fact from opinion.

A fact is a statement that can be proven true by consulting a reliable source, such as an encyclopedia or an unbiased expert. An opinion, on the other hand, is a belief that is based on a writer's attitudes or values. Some written works contain both fact and opinion. However, it's always important to be able to tell the two apart.

Recognize an author's purpose or bias.

▶ The author's purpose is his or her reason for writing—to inform, entertain, or persuade, for example. Sometimes an author has more than one purpose. In *The Road Ahead*, for example, Bill Gates both informs and entertains his readers.

▶ Bias is a strong feeling for or against something. A writer's bias is influenced by his or her experience. For example, Bill Gates's involvement in his software company influences his attitude about technology. Be aware of factors that might bias a writer's opinion.

Evaluate the writer's point and message.

Evaluating involves making a critical judgment. To do so, first ask yourself whether the writer's opinions are supported by facts. Then decide whether the writer's conclusions are logical and well thought out. Finally, determine whether the writer's background or experience qualifies him or her to write on that subject.

Judge the writer's work.

To apply your critical judgment to the work as a whole, ask yourself questions like these:

▶ Do the statements follow logically?
▶ Is the material clearly organized?
▶ Are the writer's points interesting and well-supported?
▶ Did the piece hold my interest throughout my reading?

As you read the following essay by Bill Gates, look at the notes along the sides. These notes demonstrate how to apply these strategies to a work of literature.

from The Road Ahead

Bill Gates

When I was a kid, *The Ed Sullivan Show* came on at eight o'clock on Sunday nights. Most Americans with television sets tried to be at home to watch it because that might be the only time and place to see the Beatles, Elvis Presley, the Temptations, or that guy who could spin ten plates <u>simultaneously</u> on the noses of ten dogs. But if you were driving back from your grandparents' house or on a Cub Scout camping trip, too bad. Not being at home on Sunday at eight meant that you also missed out on the Monday morning talk about Sunday night's show.

> This passage reveals the author's **bias** toward forms of communication that do not require people to adjust their schedules.

Conventional television allows us to decide what we watch but not when we watch it. The technical term for this sort of broadcasting is "synchronous."[1] Viewers have to synchronize their schedules with the time of a broadcast that's sent to everybody at the same time. That's how I watched *The Ed Sullivan Show* thirty years ago, and it's how most of us will watch the news tonight.

> Because this explanation of *synchronous communications* is factual and clear, you might **judge** this passage as being effective.

In the early 1980's the videocassette recorder gave us more flexibility. If you cared enough about a program to fuss with timers and tapes in advance, you could watch it whenever you liked. You could claim from the broadcasters the freedom and luxury to serve as your own program scheduler—and millions of people do. When you tape a television show, or when you let your answering machine take an incoming message so that you don't have to pick up the phone, you're converting synchronous communications into a more convenient form: "asynchronous" communications.

It's human nature to find ways to convert synchronous communications into asynchronous forms. Before the invention of writing 5,000 years ago, the only form of communication was the spoken word and the listener had to be in the presence of the speaker or miss his message. Once the message could be written, it could be stored and read later by anybody, at his or her convenience. I'm writing these words at home on a summer evening, but I have no idea where or when you'll read them. One of the benefits the communications revolution will bring to all of us is more control over our schedules.

> Although the date for the invention of writing is a **fact**, the author's statement about human nature is an **opinion**.

Once a form of communication is asynchronous, you also get an increase in the variety of selection possibilities. Even people who rarely

---

1. **synchronous** (siŋ´ krə nəs) *adj.*: Happening at the same time; simultaneous.

◆ **Build Vocabulary**

simultaneously (sī´ məl tā´ nē əs lē) *adv.*: At the same time

commercial radio, which had been bringing electronic entertainment into homes for twenty years. But no broadcast medium we have right now is comparable to the communications media we'll have once the Internet evolves to the point at which it has the broadband capacity[2] necessary to carry high-quality video.

> You might **judge** this passage unfavorably because the author does not provide facts to support his statements.

Because consumers already understand the value of movies and are used to paying to watch them, video-on-demand is an obvious development. There won't be any intermediary VCR. You'll simply select what you want from countless available programs.

No one knows when residential broadband networks capable of supporting video-on-demand will be available in the United States and other developed countries, let alone in developing countries. Many corporate networks already have enough bandwidth,[3] but even in the U.S. most homes will have to make do for some time—maybe more than a decade—with narrowband and midband access. Fortunately, these lower-capacity bandwidths work fine for many Internet-based services such as games, electronic mail, and banking. For the next few years, interactivity in homes will be limited to these kinds of services, which will be delivered to personal computers and other information appliances.

> The **author's purpose** in this passage is to explain why the most sophisticated Internet applications will not be available to most residences for a while.

Even after broadband residential networks

▲ **Critical Viewing** Illustrations help you tell what a piece of expository writing is about. How well does this picture capture the spirit of the essay? **[Evaluate]**

record television programs routinely rent movies from the thousands of choices available at local video rental stores for just a few dollars each. The home viewer can spend any evening with Elvis, the Beatles—or Greta Garbo.

Television has been around for fewer than sixty years, but in that time it has become a major influence in the life of almost everyone in the developed nations. In some ways, though, television was just an enhancement of

---

2. broadband capacity *n.*: Ability to transmit a huge amount of electronic information quickly.
3. bandwidth *n.*: Amount of electronic information that can be transmitted in a given amount of time; capacity.

have become common, television shows will continue to be broadcast as they are today, for synchronous consumption. But after they air, these shows—as well as thousands of movies and virtually all other kinds of video—will also be available whenever you want to view them. If a new episode of *Seinfeld* is on at 9:00 P.M. on Thursday night, you'll also be able to see it at 9:13 P.M., 9:45 P.M., or 11:00 A.M. on Saturday. And there will be thousands of other choices. Your request for a specific movie or TV show episode will register, and the bits[4] will be routed to you across the network. It will feel as if there's no intermediary machinery between you and the object of your interest. You'll indicate what you want, and presto! you'll get it.

Movies, TV shows, and other kinds of digital information will be stored on "servers," which are computers with <u>capacious</u> disks. Servers will provide information for use anywhere on the network, just as they do for today's Internet. If you ask to see a particular movie, check a fact, or retrieve your electronic mail, your request will be routed by switches to the server or servers storing that information. You won't know whether the movie, TV show, query response, or e-mail that arrives at your house is stored on a server down the road or on the other side of the country, and it won't matter to you.

The digitized data will be retrieved from the server and routed by switches back to your television, personal computer, or telephone—your "information appliance." These digital devices

will succeed for the same reason their analog <u>precursors</u> did—they'll make some aspect of life easier. Unlike the dedicated word processors[5] that brought the first microprocessors to many offices, most of these information appliances will be general-purpose, programmable computers connected to the network.

Even if a show is being broadcast live, you'll

---

5. **dedicated word processors** *n.*: Machines that can be used only for word processing. Unlike personal computers, dedicated machines perform only one function.

◆ Build Vocabulary

capacious (kə pā´ shəs) *adj.*: Able to hold much; roomy

precursors (pri kʉr´ sərz) *n.*: Things that prepare the way for what will follow

▲ **Critical Viewing** Computers and the Internet are now a part of everyday life. How do Gates's predictions about future technologies relate to your own experiences? **[Apply]**

---

4. **bits** *n.*: Units of electronic information.

be able to use your <u>infrared</u> remote control to start it, stop it, or go to any earlier part of the program, at any time. If somebody comes to the door, you'll be able to pause the program for as long as you like. You'll be in absolute control—except, of course, you won't be able to forward past part of a live show as it's taking place.

Most viewers can appreciate the benefits of video-on-demand and will welcome the convenience it gives them. Once the costs to build a broadband network are low enough, video-on-demand has the potential to be what in computer <u>parlance</u> is called a "killer application," or just "killer app"—a use of technology so attractive to consumers that it fuels market forces and makes the underlying invention on which it depends all but indispensable.

> This passage, with its use of business terms like *market forces* and *money-making essentials*, suggests that part of the **author's purpose** for writing is to attract investors to his company and its Internet projects.

Killer applications change technological advances from curiosities into moneymaking essentials.

◆ Build Vocabulary

parlance (pär′ ləns) *n.:* Style of speaking or writing; language

infrared (in′ frə red′) *adj.:* Of light waves that lie just beyond the red end of the visible spectrum

Beyond Literature

Career Connection

Careers in Technology Technological advances are responsible for many of today's career opportunities. For example, technology used in the construction industry creates the need for bulldozer operators and electricians. Ambulance drivers, X-ray technicians, and surgeons are all part of the health field. Many technological job opportunities—such as machinists, tool-and-die makers, engineering technicians, and chemists—are part of the manufacturing sector. Transportation careers include bus drivers, railroad-switch tenders, air-traffic controllers, airplane pilots, and astronauts. Of course, people who can use, service, or design computers are essential to most fields of work. What kinds of technological careers interest you?

Guide for Responding

◆ Literature and Your Life

Reader's Response What do you think about an Internet video service like the one Gates describes?

Thematic Focus How is *The Road Ahead* an example of a vision of the future?

Group Activity With a partner, develop and perform a skit in which a teenager in the year 2025 teaches a grandparent how to use the new video-on-demand technology.

☑ Check Your Comprehension

1. What kinds of technology allow for asynchronous communication?
2. How will video-on-demand work?
3. What sort of interactive Internet services are possible with narrowband or midband access?
4. List three reasons why Gates thinks video-on-demand will be a huge success.

Guide for Responding (continued)

◆ Critical Thinking

INTERPRET

1. Why is Gates well qualified to write this essay? **[Infer]**
2. Why does Gates start the essay with a description of *The Ed Sullivan Show?* **[Connect]**
3. According to Gates, how will video delivery in the future differ from video delivery now? **[Compare and Contrast]**
4. Why will video delivery over the Internet be a significant development? **[Draw Conclusions]**

APPLY

5. How might the advances that Gates predicts directly affect your life in the future? **[Predict]**

EXTEND

6. What technological development has had the greatest impact on society during your lifetime? Support your answer. **[Technology Link]**

◆ Reading for Success

STRATEGIES FOR READING CRITICALLY

Review the reading strategies and the notes showing how to read critically. Then apply the strategies to answer the following questions.

1. What is your judgment of *The Road Ahead?* Support your opinion with details from the essay.
2. *The Road Ahead,* from which this essay is taken, presents autobiographical anecdotes and ideas about the future of computer technology. What might a fan of Bill Gates say is the purpose of this book? What might a critic say?

◆ Literary Focus

EXPOSITORY WRITING

Expository writing gives information, discusses ideas, or explains a process. Sometimes the writer includes personal details that make the essay more interesting.

1. What is the main idea of Gates's essay?
2. Identify three facts that support the main idea.
3. How does Gates give the essay a personal flavor?

◆ Build Vocabulary

USING THE WORD ROOT *-simul-*

The word root *-simul-* means "same." Using this information, match the following words with their definitions.

1. simulcast
2. simulation

  a. nearly, but not exactly, the same
  b. broadcast at the same time on radio and television

USING THE WORD BANK

On your paper, rewrite the following sentences, replacing the italicized words with the appropriate word from the Word Bank or with a phrase that includes one of the words.

1. The expert hiker could pack an amazing amount of gear in her *large and roomy* backpack.
2. The two runners reached the finish line *at the same time.*
3. In the British *manner of speaking and writing,* an apartment is a "flat" and a truck is a "lorry."
4. In the restaurant's kitchen, *special lamps that emitted heat rays* kept the food warm.
5. Vinyl records and reel-to-reel tapes were the *things that came before and prepared the way for* compact discs and cassette tapes.

◆ Build Grammar Skills

PRONOUN AGREEMENT
WITH INDEFINITE PRONOUN ANTECEDENTS

Pronouns must agree with their **antecedents** in number and gender. For example, a pronoun that refers to a singular indefinite pronoun should be singular and gender-neutral.

Writing Application On your paper, write corrected versions of the following sentences.

1. Everyone must find the answer for themselves.
2. Did anyone remember to bring their textbook?
3. Each student did his best.
4. Someone left their coat in the closet.
5. Anybody can get on the Internet if they have the right program.

Build Your Portfolio

 ## Idea Bank

Writing

1. **Interview Questions** Make a list of the top ten questions you would like to ask Bill Gates about his career or about the future of technology. **[Career Link]**

2. **Description of the Future** Technology may make life in the future very different from the way it is today. Write a description of how you imagine a typical day in the future.

3. **Business Proposal** Write a proposal to Microsoft or another large company about a new Internet service of your own creation. Describe the service and explain the advantages to the company in developing and offering it. **[Career Link]**

Speaking and Listening

4. **Role Play** Assume the role of Bill Gates and present your ideas about Internet video delivery to an audience of your classmates. Conclude your presentation with a brief question-and-answer session. **[Performing Arts Link]**

5. **Oral Report** In *The Road Ahead*, Bill Gates tells about something he knows very well. Now it's your turn. Prepare and deliver an oral report or demonstration on a topic you know well.

Projects

6. **Multimedia Presentation** Prepare a multimedia presentation about the Internet. If possible, include demonstrations of electronic mail and Web browsing. Prepare a handout with a list of your favorite Web sites. **[Technology Link]**

7. **Advertising Campaign** Put together an advertising campaign for Internet Video Delivery that convinces people to use this new service.

 ## Writing Mini-Lesson

Letter for a Time Capsule

Like Bill Gates, you can make predictions about the future. Write a letter for a time capsule that will be sealed until the year 2020. Offer predictions about technology or politics, or present your hopes for your own future. Here's a tip to help you write your letter.

Writing Skills Focus: Clear Beginning, Middle, and End

In a letter, the **beginning** usually introduces the writer's purpose, the **middle** includes most of the information and ideas, and the **end** wraps up the letter with a summary or conclusion.

Model

To Myself in the Year 2020:

By now, you may have forgotten this letter, which contains your wishes at age fifteen.

I hope you went to college, majored in computer science, and now have an exciting, well-paying job developing virtual-reality games. I also hope you live in a peaceful world where pollution and crime are no longer major problems.

Most of all, I hope you've kept your sense of humor!

Prewriting List your ideas on separate note cards. Try different ways of organizing your ideas.

Drafting Write your letter, using your organized note cards as a guide. Make sure you write a beginning, middle, and end to your letter.

Revising Revise your letter so that your structure is clear. Add details to make your ideas clearer.

Part 1 Fantastic Ideas

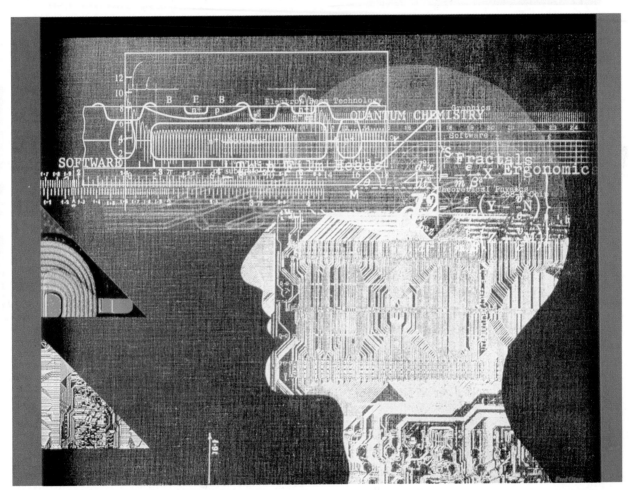

Profile on Microchip, Fred Otnes, Stock Illustration Source, Inc.

Guide for Reading

Isaac Asimov *(1920–1992)*

When asked what he would do if a doctor gave him six months to live, Isaac Asimov replied, "Type faster." One noteworthy fact about this writer is the amazing amount of material he produced. During his last thirty years, he wrote a book about every six weeks.

Child Prodigy Asimov came to the United States from Russia when he was three years old. By the time he entered first grade, he had already taught himself to read. Realizing that his parents could not read English, he had asked the neighborhood children to tell him the sound of each letter of the alphabet. Then he began sounding out words himself. As a child, Asimov spent most of his time in his parents' candy store reading library books and pulp magazines (printed on cheap pulp paper, these magazines contained sensational stories of crime and love).

The Young Storyteller Growing up, Asimov wished for permanent reading material. Books had to be returned to the library, and magazines returned to the racks to be sold. At age eleven, Asimov decided to write his own books, which would make up his personal library.

Literary Achievements During his life, Isaac Asimov wrote more than 470 books on a wide variety of subjects, including science, history, Shakespeare, and the Bible, but he is best known as a writer of science fiction.

Isaac Asimov is considered one of the "founding fathers" of science fiction.

His most famous works include *I Robot, The Foundation Trilogy, Fantastic Voyage* (which was made into a movie), and short stories like "Nightfall" and "The Machine That Won the War."

◆ Build Vocabulary

PREFIXES: *circum-*

The word *circumvent* in this story begins with the prefix *circum-*, which means "around." Once you know this prefix, you can determine that *circumvent* refers to getting around something. It actually means "to go around; to avoid."

WORD BANK

erratic
grisly
imperturbable
oracle
surcease
subsidiary
circumvent

As you read "The Machine That Won the War," you will encounter the words on this list. Each word is defined on the page where it first appears. Preview this list before you read.

◆ Build Grammar Skills

CONTRACTIONS

A **contraction** is a shortened form of a word in which an apostrophe replaces the missing letter or letters. Contractions help a writer say things in a shorter, less formal way. Contractions can be used to make the character's words sound like everyday speech, as in these examples from "The Machine That Won the War."

He said, "*I'll* (I will) miss it after a grisly fashion."

And now *we're* (we are) alive and *it's* (it is) the Denebians who are shattered and destroyed.

The Machine That Won the War

◆ *Literature and Your Life*

CONNECT YOUR EXPERIENCE

Your everyday life is more dependent on computers than you may think. Computers track purchases in stores, banking transactions, and library records. Sometimes, as in this story, computers are used for important military applications.

THEMATIC FOCUS: FANTASTIC IDEAS

In this futuristic story, a computer is used to defend Earth against invaders from another solar system. As you read, think about this: If you had to make an important decision, would you rely on a computer for help?

◆ Background for Understanding

TECHNOLOGY

The small, personal computers you are familiar with had not yet been invented when Isaac Asimov wrote this story. Instead, computers were big, cumbersome machines like the ENIAC shown here. Solving problems on such computers required the setting of thousands of cables and switches by hand. Other early computers were called UNIVAC, EDVAC, MANIAC, and BINAC. Perhaps Asimov was thinking of these machines when he named the computer in "The Machine That Won the War." The name he uses is Multivac.

◆ Literary Focus

SCIENCE FICTION

This story is **science fiction**, a form of literature in which the writer creates settings, characters, and situations that are not found in reality. The setting might be an altered present, an alternative past, or a possible future. All these changes to time or reality are based on real science, but the writer makes free use of imagination. As you read, notice details that tell you this story is set in the future.

Journal Writing Choose a science-fiction movie, television series, or book that you like. List details—such as characters, vehicles, and machines—that are not found in reality.

◆ Reading Strategy

IDENTIFY RELEVANT DETAILS

At the beginning of the story, a character says, "It's hard to remember when we weren't at war with Deneb, and it seems against nature now to be at peace and to look at the stars without anxiety." This mention of the stars is a **relevant,** or important, **detail** that causes you to realize that the war was not between countries on Earth, and you realize that the story is set in the future. Throughout the story, Asimov uses such details to describe this future world. Look at this example:

> We hadn't reached the point where manned vessels had had to take over and where interstellar warps could swallow up a planet clean, if aimed correctly.

Even though you don't know what an interstellar warp is, you know that it's dangerous if it can "swallow up a planet clean." Recognizing relevant details like this will help you understand and appreciate the story.

The Machine That Won the War

Isaac Asimov

The celebration had a long way to go and even in the silent depths of Multivac's underground chambers, it hung in the air.

If nothing else, there was the mere fact of isolation and silence. For the first time in a decade, technicians were not scurrying about the vitals of the giant computer, the soft lights did not wink out their erratic patterns, the flow of information in and out had halted.

It would not be halted long, of course, for the needs of peace would be pressing. Yet now, for a day, perhaps for a week, even Multivac might celebrate the great time, and rest.

Lamar Swift took off the military cap he was wearing and looked down the long and empty main corridor of the enormous computer. He sat down rather wearily in one of the technician's swing-stools, and his uniform, in which he had never been comfortable, took on a heavy and wrinkled appearance.

He said, "I'll miss it all after a grisly fashion. It's hard to remember when we weren't at war with Deneb, and it seems against nature now to be at peace and to look at the stars without anxiety."

The two men with the Executive Director of the Solar Federation were both younger than Swift. Neither was as gray. Neither looked quite as tired.

John Henderson, thin-lipped and finding it hard to control the relief he felt in the midst of triumph, said, "They're destroyed! They're destroyed! It's what I keep saying to myself over and over and I still can't believe it. We all talked so much, over so many years, about the menace hanging over Earth and all its worlds, over every human being, and all the time it was true, every word of it. And now we're alive and it's the Denebians who are shattered and destroyed. They'll be no menace now, ever again."

"Thanks to Multivac," said Swift, with a quiet glance at the imperturbable Jablonsky, who through all the war had been Chief Interpreter of science's oracle. "Right, Max?"

Jablonsky shrugged. He said, "Well, that's what *they* say." His broad thumb moved in the direction of his right

◆ Build Vocabulary

erratic (er at′ ik) *adj*.: Irregular; random

grisly (griz′ lē) *adj*.: Horrifying; gruesome

imperturbable (im′ pər tur′ bə bəl) *adj*.: Unable to be excited or disturbed

oracle (ō′ rə kəl) *n*.: Source of knowledge or wise counsel

shoulder, aiming upward.

"Jealous, Max?"

"Because they're shouting for Multivac? Because Multivac is the big hero of mankind in this war?" Jablonsky's craggy face took on an air of suitable contempt. "What's that to me? Let Multivac be the machine that won the war, if it pleases them."

Henderson looked at the other two out of the corners of his eyes. In this short interlude that the three had instinctively sought out in the one peaceful corner of a metropolis gone mad; in this entr'acte[1] between the dangers of war and the difficulties of peace; when, for one moment, they might all find surcease; he was conscious only of his weight of guilt.

Suddenly, it was as though that weight were too great to be borne longer. It had to be thrown off, along with the war; now!

Henderson said, "Multivac had nothing to do with victory. It's just a machine."

"A big one," said Swift.

"Then just a big machine. No better than the data fed it." For a moment, he stopped, suddenly unnerved at what he was saying.

Jablonsky looked at him. "You should know. You supplied the data. Or is it just that you're taking the credit?"

"*No*," said Henderson angrily. "There is no credit. What do you know of the data Multivac had to use: predigested from a hundred subsidiary computers here on Earth, on the Moon, on Mars, even on Titan. With Titan always delayed and always feeling that its figures would introduce an unexpected bias."

"It would drive anyone mad," said Swift, with gentle sympathy.

Henderson shook his head. "It wasn't just that. I admit that eight years ago when I replaced Lepont as Chief Programmer, I was nervous. But there was an exhilaration about things in those days. The war was still long range; an adventure without real danger. We hadn't reached the point where manned vessels had had to take over and where interstellar warps could swallow up a

planet clean, if aimed correctly. But then, when the real difficulties began—"

Angrily—he could finally permit anger—he said, "You know nothing about it."

"Well," said Swift. "Tell us. The war is over. We've won."

"Yes." Henderson nodded his head. He had to remember that. Earth had won, so all had been for the best. "Well, the data became meaningless."

"Meaningless? You mean that literally?" said Jablonsky.

"Literally. What would you expect? The trouble with you two was that you weren't out in the thick of it. You never left Multivac, Max, and you, Mr. Director, never left the Mansion except on state visits where you saw exactly what they wanted you to see."

"I was not as unaware of that," said Swift, "as you may have thought."

"Do you know," said Henderson, "to what extent data concerning our production capacity, our resource potential, our trained manpower—everything of importance to the war effort, in fact—had become unreliable and untrustworthy during the last half of the war? Group leaders, both civilian and military, were intent on projecting their own improved image, so to speak, so they obscured the bad and magnified the good. Whatever the machines might do, the men who programmed them and interpreted the results had their own skins to think of and competitors to stab. There was no way of stopping that. I tried, and failed."

"Of course," said Swift, in quiet consolation. "I can see that you would."

"Yet I presume you provided Multivac with data in your programming?" Jablonsky said. "You said nothing to us about unreliability."

"How could I tell you? And if I did, how

◆ Build Vocabulary

surcease (sur sēs´) *n.*: An end

subsidiary (səb sid´ ē er´ ē) *adj.*: Secondary; supporting

---

1. **entr'acte** (än trakt´) *n.*: Interval.

▲ **Critical Viewing** In this story, a machine becomes a hero. Compare and contrast Multivac with other computers or machines in literature or in film. **[Compare and Contrast; Extend]**

could you afford to believe me?" demanded Henderson, savagely. "Our entire war effort was geared to Multivac. It was the one great weapon on our side, for the Denebians had nothing like it. What else kept up morale in the face of doom but the assurance that Multivac would always predict and <u>circumvent</u> any Denebian move, and would always direct and prevent the circumvention of our moves? Great Space, after our Spy-warp was blasted out of hyperspace we lacked any reliable Denebian data to feed Multivac and we didn't dare make *that* public."

"True enough," said Swift.

"Well, then," said Henderson, "if I told you the data was unreliable, what could you have done but replace me and refuse to believe me? I couldn't allow that."

"What did you do?" said Jablonsky.

"Since the war is won, I'll tell you what I did. I corrected the data."

"How?" asked Swift.

"Intuition, I presume. I juggled them till they looked right. At first, I hardly dared. I changed a bit here and there to correct what were obvious impossibilities. When the sky didn't collapse about us, I got braver. Toward the end, I scarcely cared. I just wrote out the necessary data as it was needed. I even had the Multivac Annex prepare data for me according to a private programming pattern I had devised for the purpose."

"Random figures?" said Jablonsky.

"Not at all. I introduced a number of necessary biases."

Jablonsky smiled, quite unexpectedly, his dark eyes sparkling behind the crinkling of the lower lids. "Three times a report was brought to me about unauthorized uses of the Annex, and I let it go each time. If it had mattered, I would have followed it up and spotted you, John, and found out what you were doing. But, of course, nothing about Multivac mattered in those days, so you got away with it."

"What do you mean, nothing mattered?" asked Henderson, suspiciously.

"Nothing did. I suppose if I had told you this at the time, it would have spared you your agony, but then if you had told me what you were doing, it would have spared me mine. What made you think Multivac was in working order, whatever the data you supplied it?"

"Not in working order?" said Swift.

"Not really. Not reliably. After all, where were my technicians in the last years of the war? I'll tell you, they were feeding computers on a thousand different space devices. They were gone! I had to make do with kids I couldn't trust and veterans who were out-of-date. Besides, do you think I could trust the solid-state components coming out of Cryogenics[2] in the last years? Cryogenics wasn't any better placed as far as personnel was concerned than I was. To me, it didn't matter whether the data being supplied Multivac were reliable or not. The results weren't reliable. That much I knew."

"What did you do?" asked Henderson.

"I did what you did, John. I introduced the bugger factor. I adjusted matters in accordance with intuition—and that's how the machine won the war."

Swift leaned back in the chair and stretched his legs out before him. "Such revelations. It turns out then that the material handed me to guide me in my decision-making capacity was a man-made interpretation of man-made data. Isn't that right?"

"It looks so," said Jablonsky.

"Then I perceive I was correct in not placing too much reliance upon it," said

---

2. **Cryogenics** (krī′ ō jen′ iks): Here, a department concerned with the science of low-temperature phenomena.

Swift.

"You didn't?" Jablonsky, despite what he had just said, managed to look professionally insulted.

"I'm afraid I didn't. Multivac might seem to say, Strike here, not there; do this, not that; wait, don't act. But I could never be certain that what Multivac seemed to say, it really did say; or what it really said, it really meant. I could never be certain."

"But the final report was always plain enough, sir," said Jablonsky.

"To those who did not have to make the decision, perhaps. Not to me. The horror of the responsibility of such decisions was unbearable and not even Multivac was sufficient to remove the weight. But the point is I was justified in doubting and there is tremendous relief in that."

Caught up in the conspiracy of mutual confession, Jablonsky put titles aside. "What was it you did then, Lamar? After all, you did make decisions. How?"

"Well, it's time to be getting back perhaps, but—I'll tell you first. Why not? I did make use of a computer, Max, but an older one than Multivac, much older."

He groped in his own pocket and brought out a scattering of small change; old-fashioned coins dating to the first years before the metal shortage had brought into being a credit system tied to a computer-complex.

◆ Reading Strategy
Is this detail about the money of the future believable? Why or why not?

Swift smiled rather sheepishly. "I still need these to make money seem substantial to me. An old man finds it hard to abandon the habits of youth." He dropped the coins, one by one, back into his pocket.

He held the last coin between his fingers, staring absently at it. "Multivac is not the first computer, friends, nor the best-known, nor the one that can most efficiently lift the load of decision from the shoulders of the executive. A machine *did* win the war, John; at least a very simple computing device did; one that I used every time I had a particularly hard decision to make."

With a faint smile of reminiscence. he flipped the coin he held. It glinted in the air as it spun and came down in Swift's outstretched palm. His hand closed over it and brought it down on the back of his left hand. His right hand remained in place, hiding the coin.

"Heads or tails, gentlemen?" said Swift.

Guide for Responding

◆ Literature and Your Life

Reader's Response What was your opinion of Multivac as you read the story?

Thematic Focus Name one way Asimov's vision of the future matches what you know about the present.

Group Activity With two or three classmates, write and act out a scene in which a computer plays a role. Set your scene at least twenty years in the future.

☑ Check Your Comprehension

1. What is the reason for the celebration at the opening of the story? Why is Multivac seen as a hero?
2. What does each man reveal about his wartime activities?
3. What is the primitive computing device that Swift used?

Guide for Responding (continued)

◆ Critical Thinking

INTERPRET
1. Why do the three men decide to make their confessions? **[Infer]**
2. Compare and contrast the jobs of the three men. **[Compare and Contrast]**
3. Suppose that Henderson and Jablonsky had been able to do their jobs properly. Would the outcome of the war have been different? **[Deduce]**
4. In what way was Multivac responsible for winning the war? **[Draw Conclusions]**

APPLY
5. How do the activities of humans, rather than machines, affect Henderson's decisions? **[Apply]**

EXTEND
6. Computers can solve many—but not all—problems. Explain the difference in these types of problems. **[Technology Link]**

◆ Reading Strategy

IDENTIFY RELEVANT DETAILS
Now that you have identified **relevant,** or important, **details,** you may find that you have a clearer idea of Asimov's vision of the future.
1. Asimov's future world includes a vastly expanded space program in which computers play important roles. Find a detail that proves this.
2. In Asimov's future world, people have many of the same faults and failings that they have now. Identify two details that show this.
3. What detail does Asimov use to show how the monetary system in his future world is different from the way it is now?

◆ Literary Focus

SCIENCE FICTION
The fact that this story takes place in the future and that it contains ideas that have some basis in science, indicates that it is **science fiction**.
1. Find two details that tell you the story takes place in the future.
2. Name three elements in the story that are based on scientific ideas.

◆ Build Vocabulary

USING THE PREFIX *circum-*
The prefix *circum-* means "around." Define each of these words. Incorporate the definition of *circum-* into each answer.
1. circumnavigate
2. circumference
3. circumstance
4. circumscribe

USING THE WORD BANK
In your notebook, write the letter of the word that means about the same as the first word.
1. erratic: (a) slow, (b) random, (c) rapid
2. grisly: (a) private, (b) oily, (c) horrifying
3. imperturbable: (a) unexcitable, (b) increasing, (c) unhappy
4. oracle: (a) wise person, (b) loyal pet, (c) generous host
5. surcease: (a) a beginning, (b) an overabundance, (c) an end
6. subsidiary: (a) foremost, (b) subsiding, (c) secondary
7. circumvent: (a) avoid, (b) encourage, (c) reward

◆ Build Grammar Skills

CONTRACTIONS
When you use a **contraction,** write it as one word, putting an apostrophe in place of the missing letters.

Practice In your notebook, write each italicized pair of words as a contraction.
1. Multivac *would not* be quiet for long.
2. They *could not* remember when they *were not* at war.
3. Henderson exclaimed, "*They are* finally destroyed!"
4. Swift said, "*I am* afraid I *did not* use the data."
5. "*It is* time to start celebrating," said Swift.
6. Henderson and Jablonsky *will not* believe Swift's answer.

Build Your Portfolio

 ## Idea Bank

Writing

1. **Diary Entry** Write a diary entry for any one of the characters for any day during the war. Look back at the story to refresh your memory about the problems each man faced during the war.

2. **Newspaper Story** Write a newspaper story about the end of the war. Include answers to the five W's (*who? what? when? where? why?*) in your story. **[Media Link]**

3. **Title Memo** Imagine that you are an assistant to Isaac Asimov. Write Asimov a memo explaining why you think the story's title is good or suggesting another title and explaining why you think it's better. Include reasons that relate to the story. **[Career Link]**

Speaking and Listening

4. **Discussion of a Concept** The characters relied on intuition to adjust the data fed to Multivac. With a small group, discuss the role of intuition in any decision. Present a summary of your group's findings to the class.

5. **Performance** With three other students, act out a scene from the story. You may wish to write a script first, and then rehearse before performing your scene for the class. **[Performing Arts Link]**

Projects

6. **Poster** With a partner, discuss and then create a poster advertising the movie version of this story. **[Art Link]**

7. **History of Computers** Investigate the history of computers. Prepare an oral report for the class. Include visual aids, such as drawings, photographs, and magazine ads. **[Technology Link]**

 ## Writing Mini-Lesson

Directions for Operating a Simple Machine

Asimov does not say how Multivac works, but you can assume that the directions for operating it would have been clearly written. Write your own directions for operating a simple machine, such as a microwave, a VCR, or a hair dryer.

Writing Skills Focus: Clear Explanation of Procedures

To be useful, directions must provide a **clear explanation of a procedure**. Organization is a key feature of helpful directions. Notice how a boldfaced heading and numbered list help clarify steps in this example.

Recording an Outgoing Message
1. Enter your three-digit code.
2. After four beeps, press 4.
3. Wait one second, then record your announcement.
4. Press 4 to end recording.

In certain types of directions, a clearly labeled illustration is also helpful.

Prewriting Before writing directions for using a machine, you should go through the steps yourself. Go through the process mentally or, better yet, use the machine. Write down and number each step.

Drafting Write directions based on your notes. Use precise language and directional words such as *up, down, left*, and *right*. Organize your directions by using headings and numbered or bulleted lists. For extra clarity, sketch the machine and label its parts.

Revising Put yourself in the place of someone who has never seen the machine before. Reread your directions, asking yourself if you've left out any steps. Revise as necessary for clarity.

CONNECTIONS TO TODAY'S WORLD

Thematic Connection

FANTASTIC IDEAS

Years before the first astronaut ventured into space, science-fiction writers were transporting readers to distant planets and introducing technological wonders that seemed possible only in the imagination. Amazingly, many of the events, settings, and inventions that science-fiction pioneers such as H. G. Wells and Jules Verne brought to life in their stories and novels have become a reality only decades later. At the same time, science-fiction has continually grown in popularity and has extended beyond literature to movies and television. Contemporary writers such as Isaac Asimov and Arthur C. Clarke have continued to stretch the boundaries of readers' imaginations, exploring such possibilities as permanent space stations and colonies on other planets. Meanwhile, millions of viewers have flocked to theaters to see *Star Wars* and other movies in which human heroes battle alien creatures far into the future and deep in space.

Of all the science-fiction stories to be presented either in print or on film, the *Star Trek* series may be the most popular. The original *Star Trek* television series that first aired in 1968 has been adapted into several successful movies and has inspired a variety of spinoff series, including *Star Trek: The Next Generation*. The selection that follows is a portion of a script from the television series *Star Trek: The Next Generation*. Like the science-fiction stories in this section, the episode is set in space in the future. As you read, try to imagine which, if any, of the fantastic devices described in the selection—such as a transporter that can "beam" a person from one place to another in a matter of seconds—will someday become a reality.

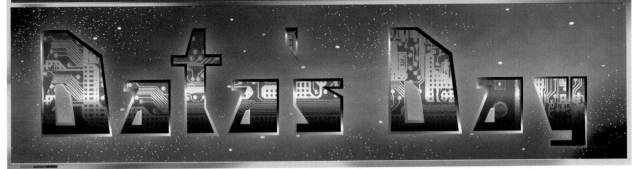

STAR TREK: THE NEXT GENERATION

Story by **Harold Apter**

Teleplay by **Harold Apter and Ronald D. Moore**

In this episode, the crew of the starship Enterprise makes contact with one of the ships of their fiercest enemies, the Romulans, the warlike inhabitants of a distant planet. At the beginning of this segment, Vulcan Ambassador T'Pel of the Federation (an alliance of planets that includes Earth) is about to be beamed aboard the Romulan ship for a negotiation session. Her mission is to negotiate with the enemy Romulans to restore full diplomatic relations between the Federation and the Romulan Empire.

[*The image of* MENDAK, *a Romulan Admiral, comes on the screen. His attitude is neutral . . . a shrewd negotiator careful not to give anything away.*]

CAST

PICARD, Captain of the *USS Enterprise*
RIKER, First Officer
DATA, an android
BEVERLY, Dr. Crusher, Ship's Doctor
GEORDI, Engineering Officer
WORF, Security Officer
O'BRIEN, Transporter Operator
T'PEL, Vulcan Ambassador
MENDAK, A Romulan Admiral

ABBREVIATIONS

EXT.: Exterior
INT.: Interior
V.O.: Voice-over
O.S.: Offscreen

MENDAK: I am Admiral Mendak.

T'PEL: There is no established protocol for a meeting of this nature. The logical course is for me to transport aboard your ship and begin the negotiations.

MENDAK: [*noncommittal*] Yes . . . [*looks at* PICARD] Captain, I note your defensive systems have been activated.

[PICARD *glances at* WORF *and receives a quick nod in return.*]

PICARD: As are yours, Admiral.

MENDAK: [*smiles*] It was not meant as an accusation . . . [*to* T'PEL] Indeed, I salute your show of strength. Ambassador, we are honored by your presence. You may transport aboard at your convenience.

T'PEL: The honor is mine.

[*The view screen returns to*

a shot of the Romulan ship. T'PEL *turns to* PICARD . . . *more than a trace of arrogance in her attitude.*]

T'PEL: Instruct your Transporter room to stand-by. I will beam to their ship without further delay.

[PICARD *is reluctant . . . he makes one last attempt.*]

PICARD: [*quiet*] Ambassador, I must once again urge you to reconsider. The Enterprise can accommodate a Romulan delegation without sacrificing security or—

T'PEL: [*withering*] Captain Picard, I find your arguments illogical. Please carry out my instructions.

[*She exits to Turbolift.* RIKER *and* PICARD *exchange a look of exasperation with the Ambassador.*]

PICARD: [*to com*] Bridge to Transporter Room Three.

O'BRIEN'S COM VOICE: O'Brien here.

PICARD: Prepare to beam Ambassador T'Pel to the Romulan ship.

O'BRIEN'S COM VOICE: Aye, sir.

PICARD: [*to* WORF] Maintain a lock on her signal once she's aboard their vessel. At the first sign of trouble I want to be able to bring her back.

WORF: Understood.

[*As* WORF *reads his console.*]

WORF: Transporter activated . . .

[WORF *reacts with alarm at something on the console just as* O'BRIEN*'s voice comes over the com . . .*]

WORF: Captain—!

O'BRIEN'S COM VOICE: Transporter emergency!

I'm losing her signal!

WORF: Boosting power to autosequencers.

DATA: Engaging computer override.

RIKER: [*to com, urgent*] O'Brien, what's happening down there?

O'BRIEN'S COM VOICE: I'm losing the pattern . . . trying to re-establish . . .

[*An ominous silence . . . everyone on the Bridge waits for a long, tense beat . . .*]

O'BRIEN'S COM VOICE: [*defeated*] I'm sorry, sir . . . I wasn't able to retrieve the signal . . . the Ambassador's dead.

[*On* PICARD*'s reaction . . .*]

FADE OUT.

The Enterprise crew searches for the reasons for the transporter accident, but find nothing wrong with the equipment. When informed of T'Pel's death, Admiral Mendak, captain of the Romulan Warbird *Devoras*, accuses Captain Picard of staging the accident to prevent the negotiations. He accuses the Federation of not being serious about the peace process.

INT. SICKBAY

[DATA *enters.* BEVERLY *is working at a lab table with a large scanning/analysis device with a single computer screen and keypad built into it.*]

DATA: I wish to examine the remains of Ambassador T'Pel found on the Transporter pad.

BEVERLY: I'm working on my report right now.

DATA: Have you compared the genetic code with the Ambassador's last recorded Transporter ID trace?

▲ Critical Viewing Looking at this photograph, what can you infer about the crew of the *USS Enterprise*? [**Infer**]

BEVERLY: No . . . that's not part of the standard procedure. Why?

DATA: [*hesitates*] I could be pursuing an untamed ornithoid without cause.

[*She looks at him blankly for a moment.*]

BEVERLY: A wild goose chase?

[DATA *nods.*]

BEVERLY: Okay . . . Let's see what happens . . . Computer, access Transporter ID trace of Ambassador T'Pel.

[*Transporter information comes up on the terminal screen.*]

RETURN TO SCENE—INTERCUT[1] AS NEEDED

BEVERLY: All right . . . there's the genetic record of the Ambassador when she beamed aboard the Enterprise.

[BEVERLY *takes a small disk containing some organic material and sets it into a slot in the machine. She begins to work the console and now genetic information from the material comes up on the other side of the screen.* BEVERLY *begins to run both sets of information through a test . . . the information on both sides should be virtually identical.*]

---

1. **intercut:** Interrupt a scene by inserting a new shot.

▲ **Critical Viewing** This picture of Data shows a face with a blank—though perhaps slightly pleasant—stare. Why is this expression an appropriate one for Data? [**Draw Conclusions**]

BEVERLY: Now, the breakdown of the organic material found on the Transporter pad should be identical. [*beat as she reads screen*] Mitochondrial structure fits all general parameters . . . no change in the nucleotide bases . . .

[*The test stops and the two screens highlight sections of the genetic code that are different.*]

BEVERLY: [*frowns*] There's a slight discrepancy in the base pair sequence.

[*She runs another test . . . the screens then stop on another section of code that's different.*]

BEVERLY: [*to* DATA] Chemically, these are identical . . . however, the organic sample from the Transporter is showing numerous single-bit errors . . . like replicated material.

DATA: Can you postulate an explanation for the discrepancy?

BEVERLY: I'd say the DNA was either mutated by the Transporter during the rematerialization process . . .

DATA: [*he expected this*] A supposition not supported by the Transporter records.

BEVERLY: Or these aren't the remains of the Ambassador.

[*On their reactions . . .*]

FADE OUT.

FADE IN:

INT. READY ROOM

[DATA, GEORDI, RIKER and PICARD.]

DATA: [*to* PICARD] The only abnormality found during my investigation was a temporary increase in the matter to energy signal ratio. This fluctuation was well within operating parameters and would normally not invite further consideration. However, due to the circumstances, I decided to investigate the possibility that a *second* Transporter signal had caused the fluctuation. Although this was highly improbable, it was the only remaining theory.

RIKER: A second transporter signal? From where?

DATA: From the Devoras.

GEORDI: Romulan transporters operate on similar subspace frequencies to our own. With minor adjustments they could be made to simulate our own transporter carrier wave.

PICARD: So they beamed the Ambassador off our own pad.

DATA: While simultaneously a small amount of genetically similar material was left in the Ambassador's place.

RIKER: To make us believe she died as a result of the "malfunction."

DATA: Yes, sir.

Although the safest course of action would be to contact Starfleet for instructions, Picard decides to confront the Romulans. Enterprise's crew sets a course to intercept the Devoras and prepares for battle. Closing in, the Enterprise hails the Devoras and opens up a communications channel.

ON VIEWSCREEN—INTERCUT AS NEEDED

[MENDAK's *image appears.*]

MENDAK: Captain Picard, you agreed to leave the Neutral Zone without—

PICARD: [*firm*] Admiral Mendak, you are holding our Ambassador captive.

[*A wisp of a smile plays about* MENDAK's *lips . . . he seems to enjoy this a little.*]

MENDAK: I can assure you . . . there is no one being held captive aboard this ship.

PICARD: We know about the Transporter "malfunction" and that you are holding Ambassador T'Pel.

[MENDAK *waits for a beat . . . then nods to someone o.s.*]

WORF: Captain, Romulan Warbird decloaking to starboard!

EXT. SPACE—THE ENTERPRISE & ROMULANS

[*Another Romulan ship decloaks and now two Romulans are facing the Enterprise.*]

INT. MAIN BRIDGE

[*As before. Intercut with Viewscreen.*]

MENDAK: I suggest you leave . . . now.

[PICARD *will not be moved.*]

PICARD: It is my responsibility to protect the lives of Federation citizens. I will not permit this abduction to succeed.

[MENDAK *isn't taking him seriously yet.*]

MENDAK: Captain, you're not going to start an incident which might—-

PICARD: [*final*] I am prepared to take whatever action is necessary to obtain the Ambassador's return.

[MENDAK *takes* PICARD's *measure for a moment.* MENDAK *finally sees that* PICARD *means business.*]

MENDAK: Fortunately . . . I'm not ready to start a war today . . .

[MENDAK *gestures to someone o.s. and Ambassador* T'PEL *moves into view, wearing a Romulan uniform. There are shocked reactions around the Bridge.*]

RIKER: T'Pel?

T'PEL: Sub-Commander Selok, actually.

[*It's all clear to* PICARD *now.*]

PICARD: A spy.

MENDAK: A patriot, Captain . . . she has

▲ **Critical Viewing** The *USS Enterprise* explores the outer reaches of space at warp speed. Do you think that such a technologically advanced ship will ever be built? Why or why not? **[Predict]**

performed her service to the Empire with distinction.

T'PEL/SELOK: [*smiles*] Thank you for your . . . help, Captain.

MENDAK: You can see now that we are not holding one of your citizens . . . and we thank you for returning our sister to us. [*voice hardens*] But my patience has limits . . . the game is over. I expect you to leave peacefully. Now.

[*The transmission ends.*]

WORF: Sir, long-range scanners show three more Romulan ships moving into this sector.

[PICARD *takes that in . . . looks at* RIKER.]

RIKER: [*quiet*] Some days you get the bear, some days the bear gets you.

[PICARD *sees the only rational course of action.*]

PICARD: Reverse course . . . take us back to Federation territory, warp six. Engage.

EXT. SPACE – THE ENTERPRISE & ROMULANS

[*The Enterprise turns and moves away.*]

INT. MAIN BRIDGE

[*As before . . . push in on* DATA.]

DATA [V.O.]: Captain Picard once drew an analogy between life and a chess game . . . he said that the loss of a single piece does not concede the game itself.

[DATA *glances over his shoulder at the others on the Bridge. People are returning to normal business. The Red Alert indicators turn off.*]

Guide for Responding

◆ *Literature and Your Life*

Reader's Response After reading this script, would you like to see the episode? Why or why not?

Thematic Focus Do you believe that the types of events and technological wonders depicted in this episode might become a reality? Why or why not?

☑ Check Your Comprehension

1. What happens when Ambassador T'Pel attempts to beam aboard the Romulan ship?
2. What important discovery does Data make?
3. What is T'Pel's true identity?

◆ Critical Thinking

INTERPRET

1. Based on their actions in this selection, how would you characterize the Romulans? Support your answer. **[Analyze]**
2. How does the Romulans' behavior contrast with that of the *Enterprise* crew? Support your answer. **[Compare and Contrast]**
3. What details and events in this selection help to build suspense or interest in the outcome? Explain. **[Support]**
4. Why is the ending surprising? **[Analyze]**

EXTEND

5. How might this episode be different if it had been written as a short story, rather than in the form of a television script? **[Literature Link]**

Thematic Connection

FANTASTIC IDEAS

Like the science-fiction stories in this section, this episode from *Star Trek: The Next Generation*, presents a vision of the future in which humans inhabit space colonies and travel effortlessly from planet to planet.

1. Compare and contrast the details of the setting of this episode with those of one of the science-fiction stories in this section. What are the similarities? What are the differences?
2. What is it about science-fiction television programs, movies, and stories that attracts audiences? Support your answer.

Idea Bank

Writing

1. **Television Listing** Write a brief summary of this episode to appear as a listing in a television guide. Describe the events in a way that will entice viewers to watch the program.

2. **Description of a Future Invention** This episode is filled with technological wonders, such as transporters that can "beam" people from one spaceship to another. Use your imagination to dream up some other technological wonder that might be invented in the distant future. Then write a detailed description of this invention.

Speaking and Listening

3. **Dramatic Performance** With a group of classmates, assume the roles of the various characters in this episode and act it out for your classmates. Try to deliver your lines in a way that fits the characters and captures their emotions. **[Performing Arts Link]**

Projects

4. **Internet Research** The Internet is filled with Web sites that feature information about *Star Trek*. Do some exploring to see what you can learn about this amazingly popular series. Share your findings with your classmates. **[Technology Link]**

$\mathcal{G}$uide for Reading

Robert Frost *(1874–1963)*

The title of his poem "Fire and Ice" could well describe two different views of this poet. Witty and warm to some, he appeared cold and biting to others. All agreed, however, that Frost put poetry first in his life. The result was a large body of work that made him the most popular American poet of his time. Frost won four Pulitzer Prizes. (See page 164 for more on Robert Frost.)

Sara Teasdale *(1884–1933)*

Sara Teasdale's poetry—much of it on the subject of love—was rooted in her own experience. Because of difficulties with her personal relationships, Teasdale had a sad life, and she often expressed her sadness through poetry. She once commented that "poems are written because of a state of emotional irritation" and that the poem "free[s] the poet from an emotional burden."

Richard Brautigan *(1935–1984)*

With the 1967 publication of his novel *Trout Fishing in America*, this writer became a chief spokesperson of the hippie generation. Ironically, Brautigan was actually a product of the beat generation that preceded the hippies by more than a decade. Nevertheless, in his writing Brautigan was definitely a free spirit.

Edwin Muir *(1887–1959)*

A prolific writer who produced many volumes of poetry and several novels, Edwin Muir had visions of the future that were rooted in his past. He spent his first fourteen years on a farm in the Orkney Islands north of the Scottish mainland, and much of his imagery comes from this place.

◆ Build Vocabulary

SUFFIXES: *-ous*

Sara Teasdale describes "wild plum trees in tremulous white." The word *tremulous* is related to the word *tremble*. The suffix *-ous* means "full of" or "characterized by." Added to the base form of a word, it becomes an adjective. So *tremulous* means "characterized by trembling" or "quivering."

WORD BANK

As you read these poems, you will encounter the words on this list. Each word is defined on the page where it first appears. Preview the list before you read.

perish
suffice
tremulous
covenant
confounds
steeds
archaic

◆ Build Grammar Skills

COMMONLY CONFUSED WORDS: *LIE* AND *LAY*

In "The Horses," Edwin Muir describes unused objects using two different but related verbs:

The tractors <u>lie</u> about our fields.
. . . ploughs, long <u>laid</u> aside.

The verb *lie* means "to be in a reclining position." It is never followed by a direct object. The verb *lay* means "to place" or "to put down." It may be followed by a direct object. Confusion sometimes occurs because the past tense of *lie* is *lay*. Become familiar with the principal parts:

lie, lying, lay, (has) lain
lay, laying, laid, (has) laid

Fire and Ice ◆ All Watched Over by Machines of Loving Grace ◆ There Will Come Soft Rains ◆ The Horses

◆ *Literature and Your Life*

CONNECT YOUR EXPERIENCE

Is the world heading toward a gloomy destruction or a golden age of harmony? You may have seen movies or read books about future worlds with very different views of the future. Some are frightening; some are enticing; some are thought-provoking. As you'll discover in the following selections, poets, also, have used their craft to explore visions of the future.

Journal Writing Write about a story you have read or a movie you have seen about a future world. Describe your feelings about this world.

THEMATIC FOCUS: FANTASTIC IDEAS

These poems present fantastic ideas that may prompt you to think about the direction in which our world is moving.

◆ Background for Understanding

HISTORY

In "There Will Come Soft Rains," Sara Teasdale mentions "the war," but she does not specify which war. The poet and her husband both opposed World War I (1914–1918), even though their position was not a popular one.

World War I, called the Great War at the time, was the first war fought with machine guns, which could spit out 600 to 700 bullets per minute. The war pitted Germany against France, England, and Russia. When soldiers left their trenches to charge the enemy, they could be sure that large numbers of them would be brutally cut down by machine-gun fire. The impersonality of this type of warfare horrified many.

◆ Literary Focus

ALLITERATION

Alliteration is the repetition of a consonant sound at the beginning of a word. Poets use alliteration to emphasize certain words, and to create sounds and musical effects. The first two lines of "Fire and Ice" begin, "Some say." The repetition of the s sound creates the effect of whispering and adds a sense of slyness to the poem.

◆ Reading Strategy

RECOGNIZE A POET'S PURPOSE

These poems are like wake-up calls. Each poet's purpose is to call attention to a situation or an attitude that the poet finds troubling or worthy of thought. Learning to recognize a poet's purpose will help you better understand a poem.

One thing that will help you **recognize a poet's purpose** is to look for the meaning behind the words. Notice if a word seems startling, surprising, or jarring. Ask yourself, "Why has the poet chosen that word?" The answer may lead you to the poet's purpose. Using a graphic organizer like this one, note each word or detail that jars you or sparks your emotions. Next to each word, jot down its effect.

Key Words		Effects
_____	→	_____
_____	→	_____
_____	→	_____

Fire
and
Ice

Robert Frost

Some say the world will end in fire,
Some say in ice.
From what I've tasted of desire
I hold with those who favor fire.
5 But if it had to <u>perish</u> twice,
I think I know enough of hate
To say that for destruction ice
Is also great
And would <u>suffice</u>.

▲ **Critical Viewing** Aside from desire and hate, what other human conditions can you associate with fire and ice? **[Apply]**

◆ **Build Vocabulary**

perish (per´ ish) *v.*: Die

suffice (sə fīs´) *v.*: To be enough

All Watched Over by Machines of Loving Grace

Richard Brautigan

I like to think (and
the sooner the better!)
of a cybernetic[1] meadow
where mammals and computers
5   live together in mutually
programming harmony
like pure water
touching clear sky.

I like to think
    (right now, please!)
10 of a cybernetic forest
filled with pines and electronics

where deer stroll peacefully
past computers
as if they were flowers
15   with spinning blossoms.
I like to think
    (it has to be!)
of a cybernetic ecology
where we are free of our labors
and joined back to nature,
20   returned to our mammal
brothers and sisters,
and all watched over
by machines of loving grace.

---

1. **cybernetic** (sĭ bər net´ ik) *adj.:*
Having to do with computers.

Guide for Responding

◆ Literature and Your Life

Reader's Response How do the views of these two poets compare with your own views of the future? Explain.

Thematic Focus How do these poets connect a vision of the future with the past?

☑ Check Your Comprehension

1. What is the subject of "Fire and Ice"?
2. What two things does the speaker of "All Watched Over by Machines of Loving Grace" want to see living in harmony?

◆ Critical Thinking

INTERPRET

1. How might the "fire" of desire bring an end to the world? **[Speculate]**
2. In what way is ice a fitting metaphor for hatred? **[Interpret]**
3. Why does Brautigan say "machines of loving grace" to describe computers? **[Infer]**

APPLY

4. Compare your own experiences with computers with Brautigan's vision of the future. **[Relate]**

"There Will Come Soft Rains"

(War Time)

Sara Teasdale

There will come soft rains and the smell of the ground,
And swallows circling with their shimmering sound;

And frogs in the pools singing at night,
And wild plum-trees in <u>tremulous</u> white;

5   Robins will wear their feathery fire
Whistling their whims on a low fence-wire;

And not one will know of the war, not one
Will care at last when it is done.

Not one would mind, neither bird nor tree
10   If mankind perished utterly;

And Spring herself, when she woke at dawn,
Would scarcely know that we were gone.

◆ **Build Vocabulary**
tremulous (trem´ yə ləs) *adj.*: Quivering

The Horses

Edwin Muir

Barely a twelvemonth after
The seven days war that put the world to sleep,
Late in the evening the strange horses came.
By then we had made our <u>covenant</u> with silence,
5   But in the first few days it was so still
We listened to our breathing and were afraid.
On the second day
The radios failed; we turned the knobs; no answer.
On the third day a warship passed us, heading north,
10   Dead bodies piled on the deck. On the sixth day
A plane plunged over us into the sea. Thereafter
Nothing. The radios dumb;
And still they stand in corners of our kitchens,
And stand, perhaps, turned on, in a million rooms
15   All over the world. But now if they should speak,
If on a sudden they should speak again,
If on the stroke of noon a voice should speak,
We would not listen, we would not let it bring
That old bad world that swallowed its children quick
20   At one great gulp. We would not have it again.
Sometimes we think of the nations lying asleep,
Curled blindly in impenetrable sorrow,
And then the thought <u>confounds</u> us with its strangeness.

The tractors lie about our fields; at evening
25   They look like dank sea-monsters couched and waiting.
We leave them where they are and let them rust:
'They'll moulder away and be like other loam.'[1]
We make our oxen drag our rusty ploughs,
Long laid aside. We have gone back
30   Far past our fathers' land.
                And then, that evening

---

1. **loam** (lōm) *n.*: Dark, rich soil.

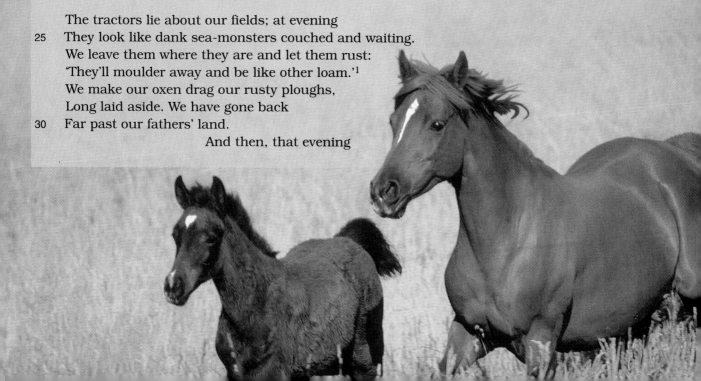

Late in the summer the strange horses came.
We heard a distant tapping on the road,
A deepening drumming; it stopped, went on again

35　And at the corner changed to hollow thunder.
We saw the heads
Like a wild wave charging and were afraid.
We had sold our horses in our fathers' time
To buy new tractors. Now they were strange to us

40　As fabulous <u>steeds</u> set on an ancient shield
Or illustrations in a book of knights.
We did not dare go near them. Yet they waited,
Stubborn and shy, as if they had been sent
By an old command to find our whereabouts

45　And that long-lost <u>archaic</u> companionship.
In the first moment we had never a thought
That they were creatures to be owned and used.
Among them were some half-a-dozen colts
Dropped in some wilderness of the broken world,

50　Yet new as if they had come from their own Eden.[2]
Since then they have pulled our ploughs and borne
　　our loads,
But that free servitude still can pierce our hearts.
Our life is changed; their coming our beginning.

2.　**Eden:** In the Bible, the garden where life began with Adam and Eve; paradise.

◆ **Build Vocabulary**

steeds (stēdz) *n.*: Horses

archaic (är kā´ ik) *adj.*: Seldom-used; old-fashioned

Guide for Responding

◆ Literature and Your Life

Reader's Response　What do *you* think nature's attitude toward humans is? Explain.

Thematic Focus　What kind of future do these poems envision?

☑ **Check Your Comprehension**

1. According to "There Will Come Soft Rains," how does nature feel about humans?
2. In "The Horses," what has happened to the world?

◆ Critical Thinking

INTERPRET

1. What is the theme of "There Will Come Soft Rains"? **[Interpret]**
2. In "The Horses," in what way are the horses associated with rebirth and renewal? **[Associate]**
3. What role will the horses serve in the future? Support you answer. **[Speculate]**

APPLY

4. How might "There Will Come Soft Rains" be different if it had been written in the age of nuclear weapons? **[Connect]**

Guide for Responding (continued)

◆ Reading Strategy

RECOGNIZE THE POETS' PURPOSE

All these poems have a similar purpose: The poets want to warn readers to consider the possible impact of present events and developments on the future. You can **recognize the poets' purposes** by looking carefully at their choice of words and details. For example, Edwin Muir contrasts images of total devastation with images of the primitive beauty of horses to lead readers to think about the negative effects and destructive potential of technology.

1. "There Will Come Soft Rains" describes the world after a devastating war. Why doesn't the poet describe war itself?
2. What do you think is Teasdale's purpose? Why?
3. In "All Watched Over by Machines of Loving Grace," how does the phrase "cybernetic meadow" help you recognize the poet's purpose?

◆ Build Grammar Skills

COMMONLY CONFUSED WORDS: LIE AND LAY

Study the use of *lie* and *lay* in the following sentences.

- **Lie:** I always *lie* on my side to get to sleep.
  She *lay* awake for hours worrying.
  The cows *have lain* under that tree all day.
- **Lay:** *Lay* your clothes on the bed.
  Workers *laid* our new carpet yesterday.
  I *have laid* the baby in the cradle.

Practice On your paper, write the correct form of the verb for each sentence.

1. In "Fire and Ice," the poet (lies, lays) out two different scenarios of the end of the world.
2. In "All Watched Over by Machines of Loving Grace," the poet pictures deer strolling by computers that (lie, lay) in the grass.
3. In "There Will Come Soft Rains," the reader can almost picture frogs singing their songs on logs (lying, laying) in a pond.
4. In "The Horses," dead bodies (lay, laid) on the deck of a ship.

◆ Literary Focus

ALLITERATION

Poets may use **alliteration**—the repetition of consonant sounds at the beginning of words—to help create a mood by emphasizing certain sounds. For example, in the first stanza of "There Will Come Soft Rains," the s sound seems to whisper, emphasizing the peaceful nature of the scene.

1. What other alliteration creates a peaceful sound in "There Will Come Soft Rains"?
2. What feeling does "feathery fire" create?
3. Find two examples of alliteration in "Fire and Ice" and explain their effect.

◆ Build Vocabulary

USING THE SUFFIX -ous

Make an adjective out of each of these words by adding the suffix -ous, meaning "full of" or "characterized by." Then, in your notebook, complete each sentence by adding one of the new words.

    a. peril **b.** courage **c.** mischief **d.** clamor

1. The mayor made a ____?____ decision to take an unpopular stand.
2. The ____?____ kittens unwound a whole ball of yarn.
3. After a ____?____ voyage, the passengers gave thanks for reaching land safely.
4. The ____?____ crowd forcefully demanded an end to the unjust policy.

USING THE WORD BANK

On your paper, write the letter of the correct synonym for each first word.

1. covenant: (a) church, (b) argument, (c) agreement
2. suffice: (a) be helpful, (b) be enough, (c) be wrong
3. steeds: (a) rewards, (b) cattle, (c) horses
4. confounds: (a) irritates, (b) surprises, (c) confuses
5. tremulous: (a) quivering, (b) huge, (c) emotional
6. archaic: (a) curved, (b) simple, (c) old-fashioned

Build Your Portfolio

 ## Idea Bank

Writing

1. Diary Entry Poet Richard Brautigan envisions a future when computers can improve people's lives. Write a diary entry for a day—in the present or future—that is enriched by computers.

2. Poem Write a poem of your own that expresses a vision of the future. Your vision can be either one that people should strive for or one that should be avoided.

3. Short Story Write a short story based on "The Horses" that takes the speaker twenty years into the future. Show what has happened to the relationship between horses and humans.

Speaking and Listening

4. Panel Discussion With a group, hold a panel discussion with a moderator and several people with different points of view. Debate the question: Computers—hope of the future or scourge of the present? **[Technology Link]**

5. Oral Interpretation Prepare a dramatic reading of "Fire and Ice." Work on using tone of voice and facial expressions to emphasize meaning. **[Performing Arts Link]**

Projects

6. Bumper Stickers Design a bumper sticker with an anti-war slogan based on the ideas in "There Will Come Soft Rains." **[Art Link]**

7. Job Expo With a group, research jobs related to the computer profession. Present your findings in a Job Expo for your class. Write short blurbs describing several kinds of jobs. Draw pictures or cut photos from magazines to illustrate the jobs. Group members can be available at the Job Expo to answer questions. **[Career Link]**

 ## Writing Mini-Lesson

Poem to a Future Generation

These poems make readers think about the present by describing the future. In "There Will Come Soft Rains," for example, the poet emphasizes the destructiveness of war by imagining a future in which all humans have been destroyed. Write a short poem that does the opposite by describing one or more good qualities of today's world for people living in the future.

Writing Skills Focus: Brevity and Clarity

In your poem, strive for **brevity** and **clarity.** Brevity means stating your thoughts in as few words as possible. Clarity means making sure those words create clear images.

For example, "Fire and Ice" is only nine lines long, but it conveys a powerful message. That's because Frost focused his poem on two clear one-word images—fire and ice—that are easy to picture and that stir up many associations in readers' minds.

Prewriting Start by deciding on the message that you'd like to convey. Then brainstorm to create a list of images from the present that will help you convey your message. Try to come up with images that are clear and brief and will spark an association in your readers' minds.

Drafting Put your images together in a way that will give a clear picture of the present to the future generation. Use as few words as possible to present each image.

Revising Have a classmate read your poem and underline any words that do not create a clear picture or do not seem necessary. Revise your poem to eliminate these words.

Writing Process Workshop

Process Explanation

If you've ever tried to program a VCR or bake a cake, you know how important it can be to have a clear, easy-to-follow explanation of how to perform a process. Think of a process that you know well—for example, how to throw a baseball or how to log onto the Internet. Then write a clear explanation of that process that will help readers to perform the process even if they have no prior knowledge of your topic.

The following skills, introduced in this section's Writing Mini-Lessons, will help you write your **process explanation**.

Writing Skills Focus

▶ **Provide a clear beginning, middle, and end** to your writing. Identify the process you are explaining, give all the necessary information, and make the end result clear. (See p. 390.)

▶ **Explain all procedures clearly.** Present the steps of the process in the order in which they occur. Also, avoid leaving out important details of any of the steps. (See p. 401.)

▶ **Be brief and precise** in your writing. Don't add unnecessary information. (See p. 418.)

Bill Gates uses all these skills as he explains how computer servers will help people in the future.

MODEL FROM LITERATURE

from *The Road Ahead* by Bill Gates

Movies, TV shows, and other kinds of digital information will be stored on "servers," which are computers with capacious disks. ① If you ask to see a particular movie, check a fact, or retrieve your electronic mail, your request will be routed by switches to the server or servers storing that information. ② The digitalized data will be retrieved from the server and routed by switches back to your television, personal computer, or telephone. ③

① Gates begins by explaining what a server is and then goes on to explain how it works.

② The author offers a clear explanation of how a server operates.

③ Gates's process explanation is clear and to the point.

Applying Language Skills: Using Transitions to Indicate Time

A **transition** is a word or phrase that introduces the next part of your writing. Some transitions show time order. For example:

I can underline on my computer. First I highlight the words. Then I hit the underline key.

Notice how the transitions make the process easier to understand.

Practice Add a transition to each sentence to make the time order clearer.

1. ___ I turn on my printer.

2. ___ I press the *print* key on the computer.

3. ___ I retrieve the pages after they are printed.

Writing Application As you draft your process explanation, use transition words that show time order. Try to vary the words you use as you write.

Writer's Solution Connection
Writing Lab

Use the Transition Word Bin activity in the tutorial on Exposition to help you connect the steps in the process.

Prewriting

Choose a Topic Make a list of activities that you know well. The activities can range from simple day-to-day tasks, such as tying a shoelace, to more complex processes, such as setting up a new computer. Review your list and choose the topic that most interests you.

Identify Your Audience Identify the people for whom you're writing by considering who would want to learn about the process you're explaining. For example, if you're explaining how to tie a shoe, you'd most likely want to target your writing toward young children.

Plan Your Beginning, Middle, and End Create an outline that lays out the steps of the process in the order in which they should be performed. List the details of each step. Use the following format for your outline:

I. Beginning: What process will you explain?
II. Middle: What are the steps?
  A. First step
    1. Detail
    2. Detail
  B. Second step
  C. Third step
III. End: How will you conclude your explanation?

Plan a Clear Explanation Consider using time words—such as *first, next, later, after,* and *last*—to help show the order of steps in your process. Also, consider how an illustration or diagram might help readers understand the process better.

Drafting

Use a Clear Organization Following your outline, write a draft of your process explanation. Be careful to present all the steps in the order in which they occur.

Make Your Writing Clear and Brief As you write, assume that readers know little or nothing about your topic. Write your explanation in easy-to-understand terms. Avoid using specialized vocabulary that readers might not know. In addition, be careful not to confuse readers by giving more information than is necessary. Don't stray from your original topic or purpose for writing.

Add a Diagram You may want to consider including one or more diagrams to illustrate what you're describing. If so, you'll probably want to refer to your diagram or diagrams in your text.

Revising

Test Out Your Writing on a Classmate The best way to see whether your process explanation is effective is to have a classmate read it and try to perform the activity based on your explanation alone. For example, if you're explaining how to make a peanut butter and jelly sandwich, have the classmate take a loaf of bread, a jar of peanut butter, and a jar of jelly, and make a sandwich following your directions. The classmate should avoid using any prior knowledge he or she has of the process.

Watch closely as the classmate performs the task. Notice any steps that are left out or any wording that causes confusion. Then make appropriate revisions.

Use a Model Look at this Writing Model to help you make additional revisions. Notice that with a few small changes, the writer makes the explanation much clearer.

REVISION MODEL

① computer ② First

It is easy to use a spell checker. Press the *spell* key.

② then

The computer highlights words it doesn't recognize

or know. ③

① The writer adds a word to make the beginning clearer.
② The writer adds time-order words to make the steps clearer.
③ The writer takes out words that are unnecessary.

Publishing

Create a Class How-to Book Work with your classmates to create a book of process explanations. Gather all the papers you and your classmates have written. Arrange them in an order that makes sense. Create a table of contents and a cover. Then reproduce enough copies for the entire class.

APPLYING LANGUAGE SKILLS: Eliminating Unnecessary Words

As you revise, take out words that repeat what has already been said. Look at this example.

Incorrect:
Computers help and aid us.

Correct:
Computers help us.

Practice Rewrite each sentence after eliminating unnecessary words.

1. Read and look at the computer menu.
2. Choose or select the file you wish to retrieve.
3. Look at the computer screen, review what you've written, and think about it.

Writing Application Review your process explanation to find any words that are unnecessary. Remove the words before making a final copy of your work.

Writer's Solution Connection Language Lab

For additional practice, complete the lesson on Eliminating Unnecessary Words.

Real-World Reading Skills Workshop

Strategies for Success

Whether you're in school taking a test or at home using a brand-new appliance, you can't begin until you read the directions. You need to review the directions carefully so you'll succeed at the task that faces you. Follow these tips:

Read Slowly Enough to Notice Each Word If you're about to take a test, you may be eager to get started. If you read the directions too quickly, however, you may answer questions the wrong way. Take the reading time you need so every word registers.

Notice the Order of Steps Directions often are given in more than one sentence. There may be several steps for you to follow. Before you do anything else, read all the directions through once. Then go back and reread any parts you do not understand clearly. If there is someone who can clarify the meaning, ask that person for help.

Look at Helpful Drawings or Diagrams New appliances, such as a VCR or an answering machine, usually come with diagrams as part of the directions. Study the drawings carefully. Match up the pieces or the features illustrated in the diagrams with the actual pieces or features.

How to Record Your Outgoing Message

1. Hold down the ANNOUNCE button for 2 seconds until you hear a beep.

2. Speak in a normal voice about 12 inches from the machine. Ask callers to leave their name, phone number, and message.

3. Press the STOP button when you finish your message. The machine will beep once.

4. Press the ANNOUNCE button to hear your outgoing message. If you wish to replace it with another recorded message, repeat steps 1 through 3.

Apply the Strategy

Did the manufacturer provide clear directions? Read the directions for recording an outgoing message. Then answer these questions.

1. What is the first thing you must do to record an outgoing message?
2. How far away from the machine should you stand while speaking?
3. What do you do after you finish recording your message?
4. At which two times will the machine beep?
5. How do you record a new message?

✔ *Here are other situations in which reading directions is important:*
  ▶ *Operating the alarm on a clock radio*
  ▶ *Using a cookbook to prepare a meal*
  ▶ *Taking a test in school*
  ▶ *Using a new computer*

PART 2 *Reaching for Tomorrow*

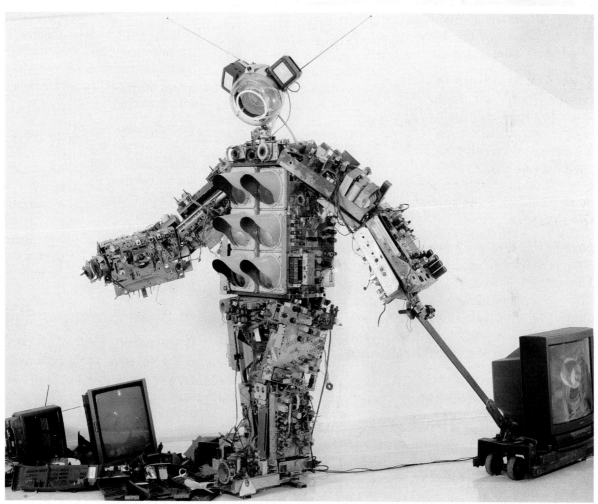

SYS Cop, 1994, Nam June Palk, Carl Solway Gallery

Reaching for Tomorrow ◆ 423

Guide for Reading

Arthur C. Clarke (1917–)

For more than fifty years, Arthur C. Clarke has been turning out exceptional works of fiction and nonfiction. Born in Somerset, England, he wrote his first science-fiction stories while in the air force during World War II. Of more than fifty works, Clarke's most famous is his collaboration with film director Stanley Kubrick on the screenplay for *2001: A Space Odyssey.* Equally distinguished is Clarke's nonfiction. In a 1945 essay, he predicted the development of communications satellites long before they were a reality.

Rachel Carson (1907–1964)

Rachel Carson enrolled in the Pennsylvania College for Women to study writing. A lifelong love of science and nature, however, caused her to change her field of study to marine biology. She was later able to pursue both fields by writing eloquently about nature.

Carson's widely praised book *The Sea Around Us* came out of her years as a biologist and editor at the United States Fish and Wildlife Service. Her most significant work, however, was *Silent Spring,* a chilling and well-documented warning about the dangers of pesticides. Before her book, few people understood the dangers of pollution or the interconnectedness of all life.

Bryan Woolley (1937–)

Born in Texas, Bryan Woolley has been a teacher, a journalist, and a novelist. His novel *November 22,* about the events in Dallas on the day President John F. Kennedy was assassinated, was praised by *Texas Monthly* as an outstanding book about Texas. In 1979, the author wrote "To the Residents of A.D. 2029," about his concerns for the present and his hopes for the future.

◆ Build Vocabulary

WORD ROOTS: -ann-

In "If I Forget Thee, Oh Earth . . . ," you will come across the word *perennial.* It builds on the root -ann-, which comes from *annum,* the Latin word for "year." In *perennial,* the *a* has been changed to *e* because of the addition of the prefix *per-. Perennial* means "through the years." Perennial flowers blossom year after year, whereas annual flowers blossom for only one year, then die.

WORD BANK

As you read the selections, you will encounter the words on this list. Each word is defined on the page where it first appears. Preview the list before you read.

purged
pyre
perennial
blight
moribund
postulated
beleaguered
schism

◆ Build Grammar Skills

CORRELATIVE CONJUNCTIONS

Correlative conjunctions are pairs of conjunctions used to link words of equal rank. In "To the Residents of A.D. 2029," the line "As long as we *both* as a race *and* as a crowd of individuals" contains the correlative conjunctions *both . . . and*, which link the words *race* and *crowd*.

> **Common Correlative Conjunctions**
> both . . . and
> either . . . or
> neither . . . nor
> not only . . . but / but also
> whether . . . or

"If I Forget Thee, Oh Earth . . ."
◆ from Silent Spring ◆
To the Residents of A.D. 2029

◆ Literature and Your Life

CONNECT YOUR EXPERIENCE

Perhaps you are aware of local dangers to the environment and of individuals or groups that are seeking to correct them. In these readings, the authors encourage readers to think about environmental problems and their solutions.

Journal Writing In your journal, list what you consider to be environmental dangers and number them from most to least threatening.

THEMATIC FOCUS: REACHING FOR TOMORROW

These selections encourage you to reach for tomorrow by looking at present-day problems. As you read, you may find yourself wondering: What can I do to prevent future environmental tragedies?

◆ Background for Understanding

SCIENCE

Recent concerns about the atmosphere revolve around the ozone layer, which shields the Earth from 95 to 99 percent of the sun's harmful ultraviolet rays. Since the mid-1970's, some scientists have been concerned about a breakdown in the ozone layer caused by the use of CFCs found in aerosol sprays and refrigerants. Environmental scientists are closely monitoring the thinning ozone layer.

◆ Literary Focus

EXHORTATION

An **exhortation** is an urgent appeal or warning. In "If I Forget Thee, Oh Earth . . .," Arthur C. Clarke—without actually stating it in words—is urging readers to pay attention to problems on Earth before the planet becomes unlivable.

An exhortation may be fiction or nonfiction. The warning may be stated or implied. To be effective, however, exhortation must be presented in a way that readers will hear it.

◆ Reading Strategy

DISTINGUISH BETWEEN FACT AND OPINION

In his essay, Bryan Woolley states, "Parts of our land are overcrowded, parts neglected, parts abused, parts destroyed." He also says, "Our present disrespect for the natural world is our most serious stupidity to date." Only the first statement is a fact. The second is an opinion. It may be based on fact, but the author has drawn a conclusion that may or may not be justified.

When you read, it is important to **distinguish between fact and opinion.** Facts can be tested for accuracy. Opinions cannot. You must decide whether there is sufficient evidence to support the opinion before deciding whether or not you agree with it.

Make a chart like the one shown. As you read, record at least one fact and one opinion from each selection.

Selection	Fact	Opinion

"If I Forget Thee, Oh Earth..."

Arthur C. Clarke

When Marvin was ten years old, his father took him through the long, echoing corridors that led up through Administration and Power, until at last they came to the uppermost levels of all and were among the swiftly growing vegetation of the Farmlands. Marvin liked it here: it was fun watching the great, slender plants creeping with almost visible eagerness toward the sunlight as it filtered down through the plastic domes to meet them. The smell of life was everywhere, awakening inexpressible longings in his heart: no longer was he breathing the dry, cool air of the residential levels, purged of all smells but the faint tang of ozone.[1] He wished he could stay here for a little while, but Father would not let him. They went onward until they had reached the entrance to the Observatory, which he had never visited: but they did not stop, and Marvin knew with a sense of rising excitement that there could be only one goal left. For the first time in his life, he was going Outside.

There were a dozen of the surface vehicles, with their wide balloon tires and pressurized cabins, in the great servicing chamber. His father must have been expected, for they were led at once to the little scout car waiting by the huge circular door of the airlock. Tense with expectancy,

1. **ozone** (ōʹ zōn) *n.*: Form of oxygen with a sharp odor.

◆ **Build Vocabulary**

purged (pʉrjd) *v.*: Cleansed; emptied

Marvin settled himself down in the cramped cabin while his father started the motor and checked the controls. The inner door of the lock slid open and then closed behind them: he heard the roar of the great air pumps fade slowly away as the pressure dropped to zero. Then the "Vacuum" sign flashed on, the outer door parted, and before Marvin lay the land which he had never yet entered.

He had seen it in photographs, of course: he had watched it imaged on television screens a hundred times. But now it was lying all around him, burning beneath the fierce sun that crawled so slowly across the jet-black sky. He stared into the west, away from the blinding splendor of the sun—and there were the stars, as he had been told but had never quite believed. He gazed at them for a long time, marveling that anything could be so bright and yet so tiny. They were intense unscintillating points, and suddenly he remembered a rhyme he had once read in one of his father's books:

Twinkle, twinkle, little star,
How I wonder what you are.

Well, *he* knew what the stars were. Whoever asked that question must have been very stupid. And what did they mean by "twinkle"? You could see at a glance that all the stars shone with the same steady, unwavering light. He abandoned the puzzle and turned his attention to the landscape around him.

They were racing across a level plain at almost a hundred miles an hour, the great balloon tires sending up little spurts of dust behind them. There was no sign of

---

◄ Critical Viewing From the moon, Earth looks like a big blue-and-white marble. How do photographs like this one convey the preciousness and fragility of our home planet? **[Analyze]**

the Colony: in the few minutes while he had been gazing at the stars, its domes and radio towers had fallen below the horizon. Yet there were other indications of man's presence, for about a mile ahead Marvin could see the curiously shaped structures clustering round the head of a mine. Now and then a puff of vapor would emerge from a squat smokestack and would instantly disperse.

They were past the mine in a moment: Father was driving with a reckless and exhilarating skill as if—it was a strange thought to come into a child's mind—he were trying to escape from something. In a few minutes they had reached the edge of the plateau on which the Colony had been built. The ground fell sharply away beneath them in a dizzying slope whose lower stretches were lost in shadow. Ahead, as far as the eye could reach, was a jumbled wasteland of craters, mountain ranges, and ravines. The crests of the mountains, catching the low sun, burned like islands of fire in a sea of darkness: and above them the stars still shone as steadfastly as ever.

There could be no way forward—yet there was. Marvin clenched his fists as the car edged over the slope and started the long descent. Then he saw the barely visible track leading down the mountainside, and relaxed a little. Other men, it seemed, had gone this way before.

Night fell with a shocking abruptness as they crossed the shadow line and the sun dropped below the crest of the plateau. The twin searchlights sprang into life, casting blue-white bands on the rocks ahead, so that there was scarcely need to check their speed. For hours they drove through valleys and past the foot of mountains whose peaks seemed to comb the stars, and sometimes they emerged for a moment into the sunlight as they climbed over higher ground.

And now on the right was a wrinkled, dusty plain, and on the left, its ramparts and terraces rising mile after mile into the sky, was a wall of mountains that marched into the distance until its peaks sank from sight below the rim of the world. There was no sign that men had ever explored this land, but once they passed the skeleton of a crashed rocket, and beside it a stone cairn[2] surmounted by a metal cross.

It seemed to Marvin that the mountains stretched on forever: but at last, many hours later, the range ended in a towering, precipitous headland[3] that rose steeply from a cluster of little hills. They drove down into a shallow valley that curved in a great arc toward the far side of the mountains: and as they did so, Marvin slowly realized that something very strange was happening in the land ahead.

The sun was now low behind the hills on the right: the valley before them should be in total darkness. Yet it was awash with a cold white radiance that came spilling over the crags beneath which they were driving. Then, suddenly, they were out in the open plain, and the source of the light lay before them in all its glory.

It was very quiet in the little cabin now that the motors had stopped. The only sound was the faint whisper of the oxygen feed and an occasional metallic crepitation as the outer walls of the vehicle radiated away their heat. For no warmth at all came from the great silver crescent that floated low above the far horizon and flooded all this land with pearly light. It was so brilliant that minutes passed before Marvin could accept its challenge and look steadfastly into its glare, but at last he could discern the outlines of continents, the hazy border of the atmosphere, and the white islands of cloud. And even at this distance, he could see the glitter of sunlight on the polar ice.

It was beautiful, and it called to his heart across the abyss of space. There in that shining crescent were all the wonders that he had never known—the hues of sunset skies, the moaning of the sea on pebbled shores, the patter of falling rain, the unhurried benison of snow. These and a thousand others should have been his rightful heritage, but he knew them only from the books and ancient records, and the thought filled him with the anguish of exile.

Why could they not return? It seemed so peaceful beneath those lines of marching cloud. Then Marvin, his eyes no longer blinded by the glare, saw that the portion of the disk that should have been in darkness was gleaming faintly with an evil phosphorescence:[4] and he remembered. He was looking upon the funeral pyre of a world—upon the radioactive aftermath of Armageddon.[5] Across a quarter of a million miles of space, the glow of dying atoms was still visible, a perennial reminder of the ruinous past. It would be centuries yet before that deadly glow died from the rocks and life could return again to fill that silent, empty world.

And now Father began to speak, telling Marvin the story which until this moment had meant no more to him than the fairy

2. **cairn** (kern) n.: Pile of stones left as a monument.
3. **precipitous headland** (prē sip′ ə təs hed′ land): Steep cliff.
4. **phosphorescence** (fäs′ fə res′ əns) n.: Emission of light resulting from exposure to radiation.
5. **Armageddon** (är′ mə ged′ ən) n.: In the Bible, the place where the final battle between good and evil is to be fought.

◆ **Literary Focus**
What warning is implied in this description of the Earth?

◆ **Build Vocabulary**

pyre (pīr) n.: Pile of wood on which a body is burned at a funeral

perennial (pə ren′ ē əl) adj.: Lasting through the year or for a long time

tales he had once been told. There were many things he could not understand: it was impossible for him to picture the glowing, multicolored pattern of life on the planet he had never seen. Nor could he comprehend the forces that had destroyed it in the end, leaving the Colony, preserved by its isolation, as the sole survivor. Yet he could share the agony of those final days, when the Colony had learned at last that never again would the supply ships come flaming down through the stars with gifts from home. One by one the radio stations had ceased to call: on the shadowed globe the lights of the cities had dimmed and died, and they were alone at last, as no men had ever been alone before, carrying in their hands the future of the race.

Then had followed the years of despair, and the long-drawn battle for survival in their fierce and hostile world. That battle had been won, though barely: this little oasis of life was safe against the worst that Nature could do. But unless there was a goal, a future toward which it could work, the Colony would lose the will to live, and

◆ Reading Strategy
Is the statement about the Colony's need for a goal a fact or an opinion?

neither machines nor skill nor science could save it then.

So, at last, Marvin understood the purpose of this pilgrimage. He would never walk beside the rivers of that lost and legendary world, or listen to the thunder raging above its softly rounded hills. Yet one day—how far ahead?—his children's children would return to claim their heritage. The winds and the rains would scour the poisons from the burning lands and carry them to the sea, and in the depths of the sea they would waste their venom until they could harm no living things. Then the great ships that were still waiting here on the silent, dusty plains could lift once more into space, along the road that led to home.

That was the dream: and one day, Marvin knew with a sudden flash of insight, he would pass it on to his own son, here at this same spot with the mountains behind him and the silver light from the sky streaming into his face.

He did not look back as they began the homeward journey. He could not bear to see the cold glory of the crescent Earth fade from the rocks around him, as he went to rejoin his people in their long exile.

Guide for Responding

◆ Literature and Your Life

Reader's Response Could you endure the kind of life Marvin has with only the hope that some distant descendants could return to Earth?

Thematic Focus In what way was "reaching for tomorrow" an important part of this story?

☑ Check Your Comprehension

1. What two things does Marvin experience for the first time in his life?
2. How did the Colony survive the nuclear holocaust on Earth?

◆ Critical Thinking

INTERPRET
1. (a) Where is the Colony located? (b) What evidence supports your conclusion? **[Infer]**
2. How does the choice of this setting make the story more realistic? **[Analyze]**

EVALUATE
3. Does this story succeed as a warning about the future? **[Assess]**

EXTEND
4. What changes or additions to the story might turn it into a good science-fiction movie? **[Performing Arts Link]**

from Silent Spring

Rachel Carson

▲ **Critical Viewing** Spring blossoms adorn the land-scape with beautiful colors and forms. What does the spring represent to you? **[Relate]**

There was once a town in the heart of America where all life seemed to live in harmony with its surroundings. The town lay in the midst of a checkerboard of prosperous farms, with fields of grain and hill-sides of orchards where, in spring, white clouds of bloom drifted above the green fields. In autumn, oak and maple and birch set up a blaze of color that flamed and flickered across a backdrop of pines. Then foxes barked in the

▲ Critical Viewing: The aerial spraying of crops kills pests. However, this practice also has harmful side effects. What do you think these might be? [Hypothesize]

hills and deer silently crossed the fields, half hidden in the mists of the fall mornings.

Along the roads, laurel, viburnum and alder, great ferns and wildflowers delighted the traveler's eye through much of the year. Even in winter the roadsides were places of beauty, where countless birds came to feed on the berries and on the seed heads of the dried weeds rising above the snow. The countryside was, in fact, famous for the abundance and variety of its bird life, and when the flood of migrants was pouring through in spring and fall people traveled from great distances to observe them. Others came to fish the streams, which flowed clear and cold out of the hills and contained shady pools where trout lay. So it had been from the days many years ago when the first settlers raised their houses, sank their wells, and built their barns.

Then a strange blight crept over the area and everything began to change. Some evil spell had settled on the community: mysterious maladies swept the flocks of chickens; the cattle and sheep sickened and died. Everywhere was a shadow of death. The farmers spoke of much

◆ Build Vocabulary

blight (blīt) *n.:* Something that destroys or prevents growth

illness among their families. In the town the doctors had become more and more puzzled by new kinds of sickness appearing among their patients. There had been several sudden and unexplained deaths, not only among adults but even among children, who would be stricken suddenly while at play and die within a few hours.

There was a strange stillness. The birds, for example—where had they gone? Many people spoke of them, puzzled and disturbed. The feeding stations in the backyards were deserted. The few birds seen anywhere were <u>moribund</u>; they trembled violently and could not fly. It was a spring without voices. On the mornings that had once throbbed with the dawn chorus of robins, catbirds, doves, jays, wrens, and scores of other bird voices there was now no sound; only silence lay over the fields and woods and marsh.

On the farms the hens brooded, but no chicks hatched. The farmers complained that they were unable to raise any pigs—the litters were small and the young survived only a few days. The apple trees were coming into bloom but no bees droned among the blossoms, so there was no pollination and there would be no fruit.

The roadsides, once so attractive, were now lined with browned and withered vegetation as though swept by fire. These, too, were silent, deserted by all living things. Even the streams were now lifeless. Anglers no longer visited them, for all the fish had died.

In the gutters under the eaves and between the shingles of the roofs, a white granular powder still showed a few patches; some weeks before it had fallen like snow upon the roofs and the lawns, the fields and streams.

No witchcraft, no enemy action had silenced the rebirth of new life in this stricken world. The people had done it themselves.

This town does not actually exist, but it might easily have a thousand counterparts in America or elsewhere in the world. I know of no community that has experienced all the misfortunes I describe. Yet every one of these disasters has actually happened somewhere, and many real communities have already suffered a substantial number of them. A grim specter has crept upon us almost unnoticed, and this imagined tragedy may easily become a stark reality we all shall know.

◆ **Literary Focus**
What words heighten the impact of the warning at the end of this paragraph?

Guide for Responding

◆ *Literature and Your Life*

Reader's Response Is Carson's technique of describing environmental problems in a fictional town effective? Explain.

Thematic Focus For what kind of tomorrow does Rachel Carson want readers to reach?

☑ Check Your Comprehension

1. Name two symptoms of the environmental problem Rachel Carson describes.
2. According to Carson, who had caused the problem?

◆ Critical Thinking

INTERPRET
1. Rachel Carson describes sickness in three main categories of living things. What are they? **[Classify]**
2. What point does she make by dealing with all three categories? **[Draw Conclusions]**

EVALUATE
3. Is Rachel Carson's exhortation made more or less effective by the composite picture she paints? Explain. **[Make a Judgment]**

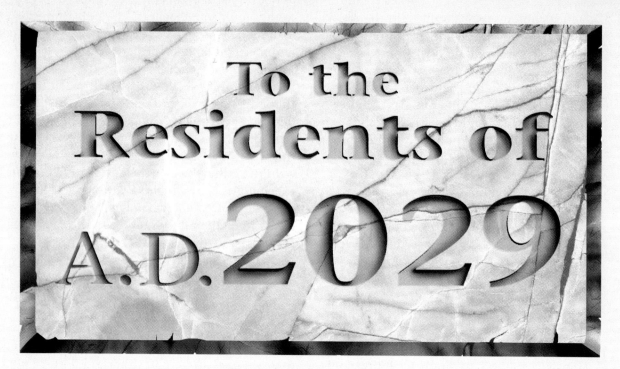

To the Residents of A.D. 2029

Bryan Woolley

Every writer's secret dream has been fulfilled for me. I know, as surely as anyone can know such things, that my works will be read fifty years from now. Well, one work, anyway.

This is because Collin County is about to dedicate a new courthouse and jail in McKinney, and somewhere in the vicinity of that structure the Collin County Historical Commission is going to bury a time capsule that will be opened in A.D. 2029, assuming that somebody's still around then, and that he can read. And I've been asked to contribute something to the capsule, probably because Mrs. Elisabeth Pink—the lady responsible for its contents—and I knew each other slightly long ago, in an era that by 2029 will be known as Prehistory. My contribution, Mrs. Pink's letter says, "could be either on our current status or what you think the future will hold."

I wish I could report to the future that our current status is hunky-dory, that we live in the Golden Age of something or other. Until recently it was possible for Americans to believe that. There's no doubt that in the twentieth century, at least, the people of the United States have enjoyed the highest standard of living that the world has known up to this point in history. We've had so much of everything, in fact, that we've thought our supplies of the essentials of life—land, food, air, water, fuel— would last forever, and we've been wasteful. Sometimes we've even been wasteful of human life itself.

Lately, though, a sense of decline has set in. We've begun to realize that we're in trouble. We've poured so much filth into our water that much of it is undrinkable, and no life can live in it. Even the life of the ocean, the great mother of us all, is threatened. Scientists say the last wisp of pure, natural air in the continental United States was absorbed into our generally polluted atmosphere over Flagstaff, Arizona, several years ago. Parts of our land are overcrowded, parts neglected, parts abused, parts destroyed. We continue to depend on unrenewable

▲ Critical Viewing Pollution damages the water, air, and land. What can be done to prevent pollution? [Discuss]

resources—petroleum; natural gas, and coal—for most of the fuel that heats and cools our homes; runs our industry, agriculture, and business; and propels our transportation. We've suddenly discovered that those resources are disappearing forever. Without usable land, air, water, and fuel, food production would be impossible, of course. In addition, the United States and the Soviet Union are at this moment trying to make treaties that we hope will keep us from destroying all life and the possibility of life if we decide to destroy each other before the fuel runs out.

So I would classify the current status that Mrs. Pink mentions as shaky, which makes the outlook for the future—even so near a future as A.D. 2029—uncertain.

An uncertain future is no new thing, of course. The future has always existed only in the imagination, a realm of hope and dread with which we can do little more than play games. But the games sometimes become serious. The Europeans postulated another land across the ocean for centuries and then came and found it. Jules Verne traveled under the sea and to the moon in his mind many years before we could make the machines to catch up with him. If, as we say, Necessity is the mother of Invention, then Desire is the father of Possibility.

Because of man's amazing record of making his dreams come true, I refuse to be pessimistic about the future, despite the frightening aspects of the present. As long as we—both as a race and as a crowd of individuals—retain our capacity for dreaming, we also keep the possibility of doing. And when doing becomes necessary, we invent a means to do so. Especially when we're in danger, as we are now.

Some of our present dangers surely will be around in 2029, for they're part of being human. We're too far from solving poverty, disease, and probably even war to be done with them in another half-century. Collin County probably will still need its courts and its jail—maybe more courts and a newer, stronger jail.

◆ **Literary Focus**
Why is the appeal to us "as a race and as a crowd of individuals" effective?

But if my generation and my sons' generation do what we must to prolong the possibility of survival and the likelihood of this being read, most of the problems about which I'm worrying may seem quaint. If so, they'll be replaced by others that will seem as serious to those who gather to open the time capsule as mine do to me. Golden Ages exist only in retrospect, never for those who are trying to cope with them.

So for the beleaguered residents of 2029 I wish four things:

—A deeper understanding of history, to better avoid repeating the errors of the past, for if each generation keeps on inventing its own mistakes, some of the old ones will have to be thrown out.

—A healing of the schism between man and

The Light Touches All and Forgets-Me-Not, from "Painterly Photography" by Elizabeth Murray

▲ **Critical Viewing:** How can respect for wildflowers and other parts of nature improve the quality of human life? **[Speculate]**

the rest of nature. Our present disrespect for the natural world is our most serious stupidity to date. We must realize that man can't long outlive the other living creatures.

—A wider and more profound appreciation of beauty. Music, poetry, pictures, and stories feed the soul as surely as wheat and meat and rice feed the body, and the soul of America is malnourished.

—A sense of humor. If man ever stops laughing at himself, he can no longer endure life, nor will he have reason to.

◆ **Build Vocabulary**

postulated (päs´ chə lāt´ ed) *v.*: Claimed

beleaguered (bi lē´ gərd) *adj.*: Worried; tormented

schism (siz´ əm) *n.*: Split or division

Guide for Responding

◆ *Literature and Your Life*

Reader's Response Do you take a pessimistic or an optimistic view of the future? Why?

Thematic Focus What gives the author hope for tomorrow?

Group Activity In a small group, discuss the four things the author wishes for the future. Draw up a group list of four wishes for the future.

☑ **Check Your Comprehension**

1. Why is the author guaranteed an audience in fifty years?
2. Name two environmental problems mentioned by the author.
3. According to the author, what makes the future uncertain?

◆ **Critical Thinking**

INTERPRET

1. Identify at least two pessimistic signs for the future that Bryan Woolley mentions in his essay. **[Analyze]**
2. What specific evidence does he mention to support his statement that human beings have a record of making dreams come true? **[Support]**

EVALUATE

3. Does the author present a convincing argument for an optimistic view of the future? Explain. **[Assess]**

EXTEND

4. If society were to take the author's warning seriously, what would be three good career choices for the future? **[Career Link]**

Guide for Responding (continued)

◆ Reading Strategy

DISTINGUISH BETWEEN FACT AND OPINION

In these selections, the authors use both facts and opinions to try to persuade readers to adopt a certain outlook on environmental issues. Before deciding whether or not you agree with the outlook, you must **distinguish between fact and opinion.** A **fact** is a statement that can be proved true or false. An **opinion** is an expression of someone's belief. It cannot be proved true or false. If you made a chart, use it to answer these questions.

1. What is one fact mentioned in the chapter from "Silent Spring"?
2. What is one opinion expressed in that chapter?
3. (a) What facts support this opinion? (b) Do you agree with this opinion? Explain.
4. Identify two facts and two opinions in Bryan Woolley's essay, and explain what makes each a fact or an opinion.

◆ Literary Focus

EXHORTATION

In these selections, each author has written an **exhortation**—an urgent appeal or warning—to get you to think about problems that could cause the end of life on Earth as you know it. In "If I Forget Thee, Oh Earth . . . ," the warning is implied in a work of fiction. In nonfiction, the warning may be stated or it may be implied by the facts and ideas the author chooses to emphasize.

1. How does Arthur C. Clarke make his science-fiction story believable enough for you to take it seriously as an exhortation?
2. Rachel Carson creates a fictional place to show many examples of the dangers of pesticides. What effect does this have on her warning?
3. (a) What argument for an optimistic outlook does Bryan Woolley use in his exhortation? (b) What is the effect of his positive outlook?

◆ Build Vocabulary

USING THE WORD ROOT -ann-

In "If I Forget Thee, Oh Earth . . . ," the glow of dying atoms emanating from Earth is a *perennial* reminder of the mistakes of the past. *Perennial* comes from the Latin root -*ann*-, meaning "year." Use your knowledge of prefixes and suffixes to write the correct definition of each word.

1. annually   3. centennial
2. biannual   4. semiannual

USING THE WORD BANK

On your paper, rewrite these sentences, filling in each blank with a word from the Word Bank.

1. The ____?____ politician pleaded with his colleagues to revive the ____?____ bill he had proposed.
2. Brown spots on the shrubs warned of a ____?____ in the ____?____ garden.
3. The holy man had been cremated on a ____?____.
4. The police ____?____ that the burglar would return.
5. The leader of the ____?____ wished that she had ____?____ all opposition from her group.

◆ Build Grammar Skills

CORRELATIVE CONJUNCTIONS

Correlative conjunctions are pairs of conjunctions used to link words of equal rank. Common correlative conjunctions include *both . . . and, not only . . . but/but also, either . . . or, neither . . . nor, whether . . . or.*

Writing Application Combine each pair of sentences into one sentence by using correlative conjunctions.

1. Endangered species include animals. Endangered species also include plants.
2. The parents did not conserve electricity. The children did not conserve electricity.
3. Cut down on fuel consumption. If you don't, be prepared to pay higher fuel prices.
4. Nuclear weapons kill directly. They also kill indirectly.

Build Your Portfolio

 Idea Bank

Writing

1. **Bumper Sticker Slogan** Create an original bumper sticker to promote an environmental cause that you support. Remember to get your idea across in as few words as possible.

2. **Memo** As a descendant of Marvin in "If I Forget Thee, Oh Earth . . . ," you have just returned from an advance exploration of Earth. Write a memo explaining what members of the Colony need to do to prepare for a return.

3. **Poem** Rachel Carson extols the beauties of the natural world. Write a poem that does the same. Focus on an aspect of nature you enjoy.

Speaking and Listening

4. **Speech** Prepare a speech about an environmental issue that concerns you. Think about what effect you want to have on your audience, and choose and organize information that will help you achieve that effect. **[Science Link]**

5. **Storytelling** Imagine you are one of the Colonists in "If I Forget Thee, Oh Earth. . . ." Tell your child a story about growing up on Earth, especially as it contrasts with life in the Colony.

Projects

6. **Poster** Create a poster contrasting the image Rachel Carson describes at the beginning of *Silent Spring* with an image that represents the second scene she describes. Include a title or a slogan that sums up the message of your poster. **[Art Link]**

7. **Time Capsule** Prepare a time capsule with several items from the present that would represent your era accurately to someone opening the capsule in fifty years. **[Social Studies Link]**

 Writing Mini-Lesson

Environmental Report

Rachel Carson's book *Silent Spring* had an enormous impact on the way many people viewed pest control, in large part due to its well-documented facts. Prepare your own report on an environmental issue. Be sure to include enough pertinent facts to support your main idea.

Writing Skills Focus: Elaboration to Prove a Point

Your report will be more convincing if you **elaborate** with facts and statistics **to prove your point.** Notice how Rachel Carson elaborates on her general statement, "Everywhere was a shadow of death."

> The farmers spoke of much illness among their families. In the town the doctors had become more and more puzzled by new kinds of sickness appearing among their patients.

Gather the facts and statistics you will use before you start writing. When revising, be sure every general statement is supported by facts.

Prewriting Choose an environmental issue on which to focus your report. Then collect facts and statistics, either firsthand or from reference books. Use note cards to record each fact and its source. Put your note cards in an order that makes sense to you and prepare an outline from the cards.

Drafting Write a strong introduction, body, and conclusion for your environmental report. As you write, back up each of your statements with facts.

Revising Have a classmate read your draft and point out areas where a lack of facts or statistics weakens your main point. If necessary, conduct additional research to support your statements.

Guide for Reading

Shu Ting *(1952–   )*

Shu Ting uses poetry to express her personal feelings—even though the Communist government of China has condemned such expression as anti-communist.

Shu Ting began writing poetry in 1979. Her works were well received. While still in her twenties, Shu Ting gained nationwide fame as a poet. During the 1980's, she became known as one of the "Misty Poets" of China. The term derives from a government literary critic's appraisal of an anti-communist poem by poet Gu Chen as "misty." The writings of the Misty Poets have fueled—and continue to fuel —a ceaseless struggle for democracy in China. The poem "Gifts," with Shu Ting's characteristic gentle touch and concern for others, bears a personal message for the future.

Nelson Mandela *(1918–   )*

Considered a living testament to the strength of the human spirit, Nelson Mandela emerged from a twenty–seven-year prison term to become the first black president of South Africa.

Mandela was born in a country whose white government maintained a strict policy of apartheid, or legal discrimination against blacks. In 1944, Mandela began protesting apartheid. Twenty years later, after several arrests, he was sentenced to life in prison for acts of sabotage.

Mandela remained in prison until 1990. After his release, he continued to fight for equal rights for all South Africans. In 1991, apartheid was finally abolished and, in 1993, Mandela and South African president F. W. de Klerk shared the Nobel Peace Prize. The next year Mandela was elected president. "Glory and Hope" is his inaugural address.

◆ Build Vocabulary

SUFFIXES: *-logy*

In "Glory and Hope," Nelson Mandela speaks of an *ideology*. If you know that the suffix *-logy* means "the study, science, or theory of," you can figure out that *ideology* means "the study of ideas," or, more specifically, "the ideas on which a political, economic, or social system is based."

pinions
hieroglyphics
confer
pernicious
ideology
chasms
covenant
inalienable

WORD BANK

As you read the selections, you will encounter the words on this list. Each word is defined on the page where it first appears. Preview the list before you read.

◆ Build Grammar Skills

SUBJECT AND VERB AGREEMENT

Verbs must **agree** in number (singular or plural) with their subjects. In this example from "Glory and Hope," notice how verb endings change to match a singular or a plural subject.

...the grass turns (singular) green and the

flowers bloom (plural).

In the example, the singular verb *turns* agrees with the singular subject *grass*, and the plural verb *bloom* agrees with the plural subject *flowers*.

Gifts ◆ Glory and Hope

◆ *Literature and Your Life*

CONNECT YOUR EXPERIENCE

A television newscast shows angry demonstrators chanting for freedom in a distant land. As you watch, you may not feel that what you're seeing affects you personally. Yet as these selections show, freedom is a concern shared by all people throughout the world.

THEMATIC FOCUS: REACHING FOR TOMORROW

Will people of all races and nationalities learn to respect each other and enjoy freedom in the future? These selections convey hope for a peaceful future.

Journal Writing List three things you can do today to help achieve freedom and peace for tomorrow.

◆ Background for Understanding

CULTURE

Apartheid, which means "apartness" in the Afrikaans language, is the policy of segregation and discrimination that was once practiced against nonwhites by the South African government. Under apartheid, housing, education, and transportation were segregated by law.

Apartheid became law in South Africa in 1948. Opposition to the policy grew—both inside and outside the country. In 1986, the governments of many nations, including the United States, reduced trade with South Africa in order to help end apartheid. The policy was finally abolished in 1991.

◆ Literary Focus

TONE

Tone is the attitude a writer takes toward an audience or subject. The tone of a literary work might be formal, informal, playful, or serious. The author's word choice is a key to understanding the tone of a piece. As you read, notice each writer's choice of words. How do the words contribute to the tone of each piece?

◆ Reading Strategy

EVALUATE THE WRITER'S MESSAGE

A writer's message is the idea that he or she wants to communicate. In his inaugural address, for example, Nelson Mandela has a message of hope for the people of South Africa.

You **evaluate a writer's message** by first identifying the message and then judging whether the message is valid, clearly reasoned out, and well-supported. You can evaluate a message without necessarily agreeing or disagreeing with it.

As you read these selections, first identify the message in each. Then evaluate each writer's message.

Gifts

Shu Ting

My dream is the dream of a pond
Not just to mirror the sky
But to let the willows and ferns
Suck me dry.
5   I'll climb from the roots to the veins,
And when leaves wither and fade
I will refuse to mourn
Because I was dying to live.

My joy is the joy of sunlight.
10   In a moment of creation
I will leave shining words
In the pupils of children's eyes
Igniting golden flames.
Whenever seedlings sprout
15   I shall sing a song of green.
I'm so simple I'm profound!

My grief is the grief of birds.
The Spring will understand:
Flying from hardship and failure
20   To a future of warmth and light.
There my blood-stained pinions
Will scratch hieroglyphics
On every human heart
For every year to come.

25   Because all that I am
Has been a gift from earth.

▲ **Critical Viewing** Relate this photograph to the first stanza of the poem.
What image from nature could illustrate
your "dream"? [Connect]

◆ **Build Vocabulary**

pinions (pin´ yənz) *n.*: The last bony sections of a
bird's wings

hieroglyphics (hī ər ō´ glif´ iks) *n.*: Pictures or symbols that represent words or ideas

Glory and Hope

by Nelson Mandela

Your majesties, your royal highnesses, distinguished guests, comrades and friends: Today, all of us do, by our presence here, and by our celebrations in other parts of our country and the world, <u>confer</u> glory and hope to newborn liberty.

Out of the experience of an extraordinary human disaster that lasted too long must be born a society of which all humanity will be proud.

Our daily deeds as ordinary South Africans must produce an actual South African reality that will reinforce humanity's belief in justice, strengthen its confidence in the nobility of the human soul and sustain all our hopes for a glorious life for all.

All this we owe both to ourselves and to the peoples of the world who are so well represented here today.

To my compatriots, I have no hesitation in saying that each one of us is as intimately attached to the soil of this beautiful country as are the famous jacaranda trees of Pretoria and the mimosa trees of the bushveld.[1]

Each time one of us touches the soil of this land, we feel a sense of personal renewal. The national mood changes as the seasons change.

We are moved by a sense of joy and exhilaration when the grass turns green and the flowers bloom.

That spiritual and physical oneness we

◆ Build Vocabulary

confer (kən fʉr´) v.: To give

---

1. **bushveld** (bʊʊsh´ velt) n.: Southern African grassland with abundant shrubs and thorny vegetation.

all share with this common homeland explains the depth of the pain we all carried in our hearts as we saw our country tear itself apart in terrible conflict, and as we saw it spurned, outlawed and isolated by the peoples of the world, precisely because it has become the universal base of the <u>pernicious ideology</u> and practice of racism and racial oppression.

We, the people of South Africa, feel fulfilled that humanity has taken us back into its bosom, that we, who were outlaws not so long ago, have today been given the rare privilege to be host to the nations of the world on our own soil.

We thank all our distinguished international guests for having come to take possession with the people of our country of what is, after all, a common victory for justice, for peace, for human dignity.

We trust that you will continue to stand by us as we tackle the challenges of building

peace, prosperity, nonsexism, nonracialism and democracy.

We deeply appreciate the role that the masses of our people and their democratic, religious, women, youth, business, traditional and other leaders have played to bring about this conclusion. Not least among them is my Second Deputy President, the Honorable F. W. de Klerk.

We would also like to pay tribute to our security forces, in all their ranks, for the distinguished role they have played in securing our first democratic elections and the transition to democracy, from bloodthirsty forces which still refuse to see the light.

The time for the healing of the wounds has come.

The moment to bridge the <u>chasms</u> that divide us has come.

The time to build is upon us.

We have, at last, achieved our political emancipation. We pledge ourselves to liberate all our people from the continuing bondage of poverty, deprivation, suffering, gender and other discrimination.

We succeeded to take our last steps to freedom in conditions of relative peace. We commit ourselves to the construction of a complete, just and lasting peace.

▼ **Critical Viewing** Cities marked with a star are national capitals. Why do you suppose South Africa has three national capitals? **[Speculate]**

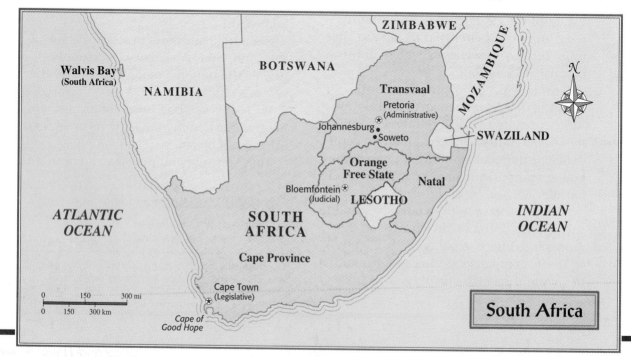

South Africa

We have triumphed in the effort to implant hope in the breasts of the millions of our people. We enter into a <u>covenant</u> that we shall build the society in which all South Africans, both black and white, will be able to walk tall, without any fear in their hearts, assured of their <u>inalienable</u> right to human dignity—a rainbow nation at peace with itself and the world.

As a token of its commitment to the renewal of our country, the new Interim Government of National Unity will, as a matter of urgency, address the issue of amnesty for various categories of our people who are currently serving terms of imprisonment.

We dedicate this day to all the heroes and heroines in this country and the rest of the world who sacrificed in many ways and surrendered their lives so that we could be free.

Their dreams have become reality. Freedom is their reward.

We are both humbled and elevated by the honor and privilege that you, the people of South Africa, have bestowed on us, as the first President of a united, democratic, nonracial and nonsexist South Africa, to lead our country out of the valley of darkness.

We understand it still that there is no easy road to freedom.

We know it well that none of us acting alone can achieve success.

We must therefore act together as a united people, for national reconciliation, for nation building, for the birth of a new world.

Let there be justice for all.

Let there be peace for all.

Let there be work, bread, water and salt for all.

Let each know that for each the body, the mind and the soul have been freed to fulfill themselves.

Never, never and never again shall it be that this beautiful land will again experience the oppression of one by another and suffer the indignity of being the skunk of the world.

The sun shall never set on so glorious a human achievement!

Let freedom reign. God bless Africa!

◆ Build Vocabulary

pernicious (pər nish´ əs) *adj.*: Destructive

ideology (ī dē äl´ ə jē) *n.*: Ideas on which a political, economic, or social system is based

chasms (kaz´ əmz) *n.*: Deep cracks in the Earth's surface; narrow gorges

covenant (kuv´ ə nənt) *n.*: Agreement or contract

inalienable (in āl´ yən ə bəl) *adj.*: Not able to be taken away or transferred

Guide for Responding

◆ *Literature and Your Life*

Reader's Response What do you admire most about the messages in the poem and speech?

Thematic Focus What kind of future do Mandela and Shu Ting see for their people?

☑ Check Your Comprehension

1. In "Gifts," how does the poet describe her dream, her joy, and her grief?
2. According to Mandela, what is "newborn" in South Africa?
3. What does Mandela say is the "inalienable right" of all people?

◆ Critical Thinking

INTERPRET

1. In "Gifts," what are the seedlings that sprout from the poet's words? **[Draw Conclusions]**
2. Citing examples, describe what life was like in the old South Africa. **[Support]**
3. Describe the new South Africa that Mandela envisions. **[Draw Conclusions]**

APPLY

4. What ideas expressed in Mandela's speech are especially important for safeguarding the human rights of all people throughout today's world? Explain. **[Generalize]**

Guide for Responding (continued)

◆ Reading Strategy

EVALUATE THE WRITER'S MESSAGE

You **evaluate** a writer's message by examining his or her reasoning and support and by judging the validity of the message.

1. What is Nelson Mandela's message?
2. How does he support his message?
3. Evaluate Shu Ting's message in "Gifts."

◆ Literary Focus

TONE

The **tone**, or writer's attitude toward his or her audience and subject, is quite different in each of these selections. That difference is not merely because one is a speech and the other a poem. An additional difference is the intended audience for each selection.

1. What is the tone of each selection?
2. What words, phrases, or passages does each writer use to convey the tone?
3. Is the tone appropriate for each piece? Explain.

Beyond Literature

History Connection

Today's South Africa The ending of apartheid in 1991 began a new era of freedom and equality in South Africa. South African schools began to admit students of all races. Health care ceased to be provided on a racial basis. Imports and exports began to flow freely into and out of the nation, and once again, South African athletes were permitted to participate in international sporting events. Despite problems such as a high unemployment rate and the unequal distribution of certain services, many South Africans are now optimistic about the future.

Activity Use the Internet or the library to find more information about South Africa today.

◆ Build Vocabulary

USING THE SUFFIX -*logy*

Remembering that the suffix -*logy* means "the study, science, or theory of," write definitions for the following words:

1. zoology
2. sociology
3. biology

USING THE WORD BANK

On a separate sheet of paper, write the word or words from the Word Bank that complete each statement.

1. To give is to ____?____.
2. ____?____ rights cannot be taken away.
3. A destructive system of ideas is a ____?____ ____?____.
4. A solemn agreement is a ____?____.
5. ____?____ are sections of birds' wings.
6. ____?____ are picture writings.
7. Beautiful ____?____ are gorgeous gorges.

◆ Build Grammar Skills

SUBJECT AND VERB AGREEMENT

A **verb** form should always **agree** with its **subject** in number.

Practice In your notebook, rewrite each sentence, correcting any errors in subject-verb agreement.

1. Words of freedom comes from the lips of Nelson Mandela.
2. Shu Ting, one of the Misty Poets, write of personal feelings.
3. People throughout South Africa listens to Mandela's speech.
4. Shu Ting, like other poets, want to leave a message for future generations.
5. All people who believe in freedom rejoices in the transformation of South Africa.

Build Your Portfolio

 ## Idea Bank

Writing

1. **Letter to Nelson Mandela** Write a letter to Nelson Mandela in which you share which parts of his speech you found most inspiring. **[Social Studies Link]**

2. **Futuristic Essay** Write an essay in which you present your vision of human rights in the future. **[Social Studies Link]**

3. **Radio News Report** Write a radio news report about Mandela's speech. Include a brief summary, as well as background material on Mandela. **[Career Link]**

Speaking and Listening

4. **Oral Interpretation** With a small group, read aloud "Glory and Hope," with each group member reading a section of the speech. **[Performing Arts Link]**

5. **Panel Discussion** Hold a panel discussion on the kind of world you would like to leave to future generations. Discuss important issues such as human rights and the environment. **[Social Studies Link]**

Projects

6. **Multimedia Presentation** Give a multimedia presentation on South Africa. Discuss the geography, climate, and history of the nation. If possible, provide relevant photos or audio and video recordings. **[Social Studies Link; Media Link]**

7. **Poster** Design a poster that expresses in words and pictures the concept of a better world in the future. **[Art Link]**

 ## Writing Mini-Lesson

Speech for a Historic Figure

In his speech "Glory and Hope," Nelson Mandela presents a memorable message on the future of South Africa. Choose another historic figure from the past or present, and write a speech for that person.

Writing Skills Focus: Transitions to Show Importance

Present a clear and easy-to-follow speech by using **transitions to show importance**. Transitions—such as *first, more importantly, better, best,* and *least*—show a clear relationship among ideas. Notice how Nelson Mandela uses the transition "not least" to indicate the important role of an individual.

Model From the Speech

We deeply appreciate the role . . . leaders have played. . . . Not least among them is my Second Deputy President, the Honorable F. W. de Klerk.

Prewriting After choosing the historic figure, determine the purpose of your speech. For example, if you're writing a speech for a scientist, the purpose might be to explain a new scientific discovery.

Drafting Organize your ideas using transitions to show the relative importance of each. You can arrange your ideas from least important to most important or do the reverse.

Revising Read your speech aloud and listen to how it sounds. If your ideas are not logically organized, rearrange them using transitions to show importance.

Writing Process Workshop

When you write an **essay for a test,** the pressure is on. You have a limited amount of time to collect and organize your ideas, and to communicate them in an essay. This lesson will help you develop the skills you need to write successful test essays. The following, which were introduced in this section's Writing Mini-Lessons, are just two of the skills that will help you to write successful test essays.

Writing Skills Focus

▶ **Elaborate to prove a point** by offering facts, examples, and statistics. Give as much solid support as possible for your main ideas. (See p. 439.)

▶ **Use transitions to show importance** among your ideas. Use words such as *first, more importantly, better, best,* and *least* to show how important one idea is in relation to another. (See p. 447.)

In the following brief essay for a test, the writer uses the above skills to answer this question: *What does author Rachel Carson fear about the future of our environment?*

① The writer gives specific examples to support his opening statement that Rachel Carson has many concerns about the environment.

② The writer uses the transitions *first, equally tragic,* and *even worse* to show the relative importance of his ideas and examples.

MODEL

Rachel Carson expresses many concerns about the future of our environment. Mainly, she fears that our world will become polluted with toxic fallout that will poison our air, land, and water. As a result, vegetation will go from green to brown and wither away. Also, living things will contract strange new illnesses. ① First, farm animals—such as chickens, sheep, and cattle—will die. Equally tragic, fish and birds will also die. Even worse, Carson worries that many humans will die from mysterious diseases. ②

Prewriting

Choose a Topic Usually on an essay test, the topic is assigned to you. Sometimes, however, you may be given several topics from which to choose. Choose one of the following topics related to the selections in this unit.

Topic Choices

1. Compare and contrast the message that Rachel Carson conveys in *Silent Spring* with Bryan Woolley's message in "To the Residents of A.D. 2029." Support your points with details from both selections.
2. Explain what lessons other nations can learn from Nelson Mandela's speech.
3. Explain the ways in which the experiences of immigrants on Earth are similar to those of the characters in Arthur C. Clarke's story.

Plan Your Time Imagine that you have twenty minutes to complete your essay. Quickly plan out your time. Allow a few minutes to gather and organize your thoughts, a chunk of time to draft your essay, and a few minutes to make quick revisions.

Plan the Points You Will Elaborate Make a list of the main ideas you will introduce in your essay. Under each main idea, note the supporting details you will offer.

Main idea	Main idea
Supporting detail	Supporting detail
Supporting detail	Supporting detail
Supporting detail	Supporting detail

Drafting

Include an Introduction, a Body, and a Conclusion Draft your essay in ten to fifteen minutes. Begin with an introduction that sums up your main points. Then write one paragraph for each point. Provide two or three details from the appropriate selection or selections to support each point. End with a conclusion that either sums up your ideas or raises an additional point for readers to keep in mind.

APPLYING LANGUAGE SKILLS: Commonly Confused Words

As you write, be sure to use accurate words, not similar-sounding words that mean something else.

Incorrect:
We must be ready to except the future.

Correct:
We must be ready to accept the future.

Practice Write each sentence with its correct word.

1. Computers have a great (affect/effect) on us.
2. (Besides/Beside) being used for work, they can be used for play.
3. Have no (allusions/illusions) about the power of computers.

Writing Application As you draft your essay, be as careful as possible about choosing correct words.

Writer's Solution Connection
Writing Lab

To learn more about writing essays for tests, see the instruction and activities on essay tests in the tutorial on Practical and Technical Writing.

APPLYING LANGUAGE SKILLS: Varying Sentence Length and Structure

Length: As you write, alternate long sentences with short sentences.

Some people say computers rule us whether we're awake or asleep. They're right.

Structure: Start some sentences with a noun or pronoun. Start others with a phrase or transition.

Computers are great now. In the future, they'll be even greater.

Practice Rewrite this passage to establish better sentence variety.

We have a computer at home. We also have computers in school. I enjoy using computers. I know how to play many computer games. I also know a variety of programs.

Writing Application Varying sentence length and structure will add to the effectiveness of any test essay. Try to establish variety as you write, because you may not have time to make revisions later.

Writer's Solution Connection
Language Lab

For additional practice, complete the lesson on Varying Sentence Structure.

Use Transitions to Show Importance As you draft your essay, introduce new ideas and details with transition words that show relative importance. You may either place your most important ideas first or save them for last. Your transitions will tell readers the importance of each idea or detail.

Revising

Allow Time for Revisions Because you're pressured for time, it's tempting to skip the revision stage when writing a test essay. Doing so is a mistake, however. When drafting your essay, you may leave out important words or details that you won't notice unless you read over your writing. Allow a few minutes to review your writing quickly. Focus on the following points:

▶ Be sure that your main points are clear.
If your main points are not evident, or if they are not clearly worded, go back and rephrase them.

▶ Look for any missing details.
If you haven't included at least two or three details to support each main point, add new details.

▶ Correct errors in grammar and spelling.
Your teacher will have a more favorable response to your essay if it is free of such errors.

Publishing

▶ **Share Your Work** A successful test essay demonstrates how much you've learned about an area of study. Others may also benefit from your efforts. You may want to share your essay with people close to you—friends or family members.

Real-World Reading Skills Workshop

Strategies for Success

Whenever you read a passage, it's important to look at each word. Some words are more important than others, however. Those words are **key words.** Without them, the meaning of the entire passage would be lost. Follow these tips for recognizing key words in your reading:

Find the Subject and Verb A sentence cannot be complete without a subject and a verb. The subject names whom or what the sentence is about. The verb tells what the subject does. In the sentence *The telephone rang loudly,* the key words are *telephone* (subject) and *rang* (verb). Focusing on these two words will help you to understand the essence of the sentence.

Look for Instruction Words When you read directions, as on a test, the key words include verbs that give commands. (The subject *you,* which does not appear, is understood.) For example, read these directions: *Print your name and then sign it directly below.* The two command verbs are *print* and *sign.* Without those key words, you wouldn't know what to do.

Look for Signal Words Writers often use signal words that indicate the importance of ideas (*most importantly,* for example) or explain the relationships among ideas (*in contrast, after, as a result,* and so on). These words are crucial to recognize because they help you to follow the writer's main points.

Test Directions

1. Do nothing until you read through these directions completely.

2. Print your full name in the upper left corner of your paper, last name first.

3. Print today's date in the upper right corner.

4. Fold your paper vertically down the middle.

5. Unfold the paper and number your paper from 1 to 10.

6. Ignore directions 2 to 5 above and put down your pen.

Apply the Strategy

Read the test directions on the paper. Then answer these questions.

1. What are the key verbs in directions 1 to 6?
2. Can you find any key subjects in the test directions? If so, what are they?
3. What are the key descriptive words in directions 1 to 6? What nouns or verbs do they describe?
4. If you took this test, would you do any writing or folding? Why?

✔ Here are some other situations in which recognizing key words can be helpful:
► Reading a contract you plan to sign
► Reading a science or social studies textbook
► Reading an instruction manual
► Reading an encyclopedia article

Speaking and Listening Workshop

Following Oral Directions

In the course of a day, you probably hear many kinds of directions. Your teachers may explain how to do a homework assignment. Your parents may describe a household chore for you to do. It's important that you listen closely to the directions so that you'll be able to do the job correctly.

Listen for Important Words Once a student stayed up all night writing an essay for class. Imagine his surprise the next day when the teacher said, "I didn't ask you to *write* an essay. I told you to *read* one!"

When directions are spoken, pay careful attention to the verbs, or command words. What verbs do you find in these directions?

Please collect the dirty dishes that are on the table. Scrape off any food into the garbage container, and then place the dishes in the dishwasher. Then sweep and mop the floor.

When directions are spoken, also listen closely for the nouns. Look again at the directions above. What nouns do you find?

Tips for Following Oral Directions

✔ *If you want to succeed at following oral directions, heed these helpful hints:*

▶ Listen carefully to the speaker's words. Try to pick out the key verbs and nouns.

▶ Don't do anything to distract your listening, such as gazing out a window.

▶ Keep your eyes on the speaker. He or she may use gestures to emphasize certain words.

▶ Repeat the directions to yourself before following them. Ask questions if necessary.

Apply the Strategies

With a partner, role-play these situations. After your partner gives you the directions, see how well you can carry them out.

1. Your gym teacher tells you a series of exercises to follow to help you keep physically fit.
2. Your acting coach describes a scene in which you play a certain type of character in a particular situation.
3. An airline flight attendant gives you instructions on what to do in case of an emergency landing.
4. The neighbor who has hired you as a baby sitter gives you instructions for taking care of the children.

Extended Reading Opportunities

People have always tried to imagine what life might be like in the future. Following are just a few possibilities through which you can explore visions of the future.

Suggested Titles

Farenheit 451
Ray Bradbury

This book is set in a time when firemen *start* fires—fires that burn books. Guy Montag is a fireman who enjoys his job and never thinks of questioning the system. Then he meets a teenage girl who tells him of a time when people were not afraid to think for themselves. Suddenly Montag realizes that he can no longer blindly accept the laws of his society.

The Time Machine
H. G. Wells

In this classic science-fiction tale, written more than one hundred years ago, H. G. Wells provides a grim view of the future. The story focuses on an inventor who travels into the future in a time machine he has built. On his travels, he views the progressive destruction of society and even life itself, eventually witnessing a time when giant crabs are the only surviving life form, and the sun and the Earth are dying.

Dragonsong
Anne McCaffrey

Set in the imaginary world of Pern, *Dragonsong* tells the story of Menolly, a young musician. When the laws of her society prevent Menolly from developing her musical talents, she wanders away from her home and discovers a group of rare and enchanting fire lizards. Menolly's relationship with the fire lizards and her unshakeable love for her music are the basis of this fantasy story.

Other Possibilities

Star Crossing: How to Get Around in the Universe	Judith Herbst
A Man on the Moon: The Voyages of the Apollo Astronauts	Andrew Chaikin
River Rats	Caroline Stevermer

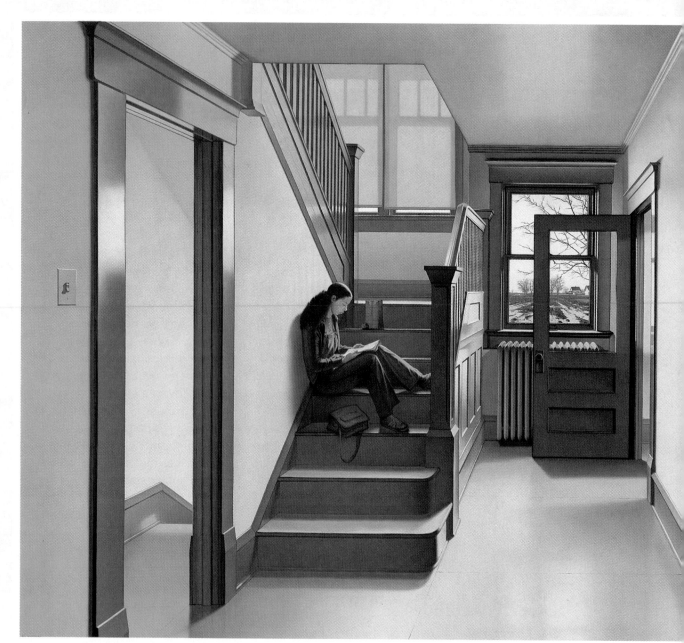

Reading, 1973, Billy Morrow Jackson, Wichita Art Museum, Wichita, Kansas

Short Stories

A short story is a brief visit to an imaginary world. This world could be nineteenth-century Paris, the American Southwest, or the swamp country of South Carolina. Wherever you travel, you will meet fictional characters who deal with problems that are surprisingly real: for example, how to win someone's love or how to treat a younger brother. As you live through these problems with the characters, you may gain insights into your own life and into the world around you.

Guide for Reading

O. Henry (1862–1910)

William Sydney Porter, alias O. Henry, began his writing career under difficult circumstances: He was serving time in prison. Little in Porter's early life indicates that he was destined to become one of America's greatest short-story writers.

Wandering Toward Writing

Born in Greensboro, North Carolina, Porter dropped out of school at the age of sixteen to work at his uncle's drugstore. In 1882, he left to seek his fortune in Texas. He worked at a ranch, then at a general land office, and later at the First National Bank in Austin. By the time of his marriage in 1887, he had started writing sketches, some of which were published. Encouraged by this success, Porter started a humorous weekly in 1894. This venture failed, but Porter was firmly set on a writing career. He moved to Houston, where he worked for the *Houston Post* as a reporter, columnist, and cartoonist.

From Convict to Toast of the Town

In February 1896, Porter was indicted for embezzling bank funds. Although he had a chance of being pardoned, Porter chose to flee to Honduras. He returned to Texas when he learned his wife was dying. After her death, he was arrested, convicted, and sent to prison in Ohio. While serving his sentence, which was shortened to three years and three months for good behavior, Porter began writing short stories about life in the southwestern United States and Central America, drawing upon his experiences in Texas and Honduras. These stories were extremely popular with magazine readers. When he was released from prison, W. S. Porter became O. Henry.

O. Henry moved to New York City in 1902, and soon was writing stories at a rapid rate. For many of these stories, including "The Gift of the Magi," O. Henry drew upon his experiences and observations to depict the lives, loves, and losses of everyday people in New York City.

◆ Build Vocabulary

PREFIXES: *de-*

In "The Gift of the Magi," you will encounter the word *depreciate*, which means "to reduce in value." This word is derived from a Latin word meaning "price" and contains the prefix *de-*, which in this case means "down." When something depreciates, its price goes down.

The prefix *de-* has several other meanings. In addition to "down," it can also mean "away from," as in the word *deviate,* or "undo," as in *defrost.* As you read the story, look for other words that contain this versatile prefix.

instigates
depreciate
cascade
chaste
meretricious
ravages
discreet

WORD BANK

Before you read, preview this list of words from the story.

◆ Build Grammar Skills

SENTENCE FRAGMENTS

A **sentence fragment** is an incomplete sentence written as a sentence. Fragments lack a subject, a verb, or both, or don't express a complete thought. Avoid fragments in formal writing. However, in pieces of creative writing, sentence fragments can be used intentionally to add emphasis, to create the illusion of people talking to themselves, or to capture in dialogue how people actually speak. This story begins with the following fragment.

One dollar and eighty-seven cents.

The fragment lacks both a subject (in this case, *she*) and a verb (in this case, *had*). To make this a complete sentence, you would add the words *she* and *had* to form this sentence: She had one dollar and eighty-seven cents.

The Gift of the Magi

◆ *Literature and Your Life*

CONNECT YOUR EXPERIENCE

Quivering with excitement, you tear off the wrapping paper on your birthday gift. You open the box—and your spirits sink. Your gift is a lopsided sweater, made by an inexperienced knitter in your least favorite color. Hiding your disappointment, you thank the giver enthusiastically. After all, it's the thought that counts.

Gifts are sometimes less appropriate or more meaningful than they first appear. In this story, a husband and wife discover the unexpected problems and joys of giving gifts.

THEMATIC FOCUS: WORKING TOWARD A GOAL

As this story shows, a person may strive toward a goal with the best of intentions, only to find that his or her effort was misdirected. How can people redirect their efforts in such a situation?

Journal Writing In your journal, describe an incident—real or imagined—in which someone tried to do something nice but had his or her plans go awry. Explain what, if anything, the person did to fix problems resulting from his or her actions.

◆ Background for Understanding

ECONOMICS

When you read a story that was written more than ten years ago, you will find that prices or amounts of money seem ridiculously low. This is because the United States has experienced inflation over the years. Inflation is a continual increase in most or all major prices throughout an economy. Although the causes of inflation are hotly debated, the effects are clear: The purchasing power of a unit of currency goes down. In the story, which was written at the beginning of the twentieth century, $32 is a month's rent for Della and Jim. Today, $32 would not even pay for a night in an inexpensive motel.

◆ Literary Focus

PLOT

The events in a story make up its **plot,** which is traditionally divided into five parts: *exposition, rising action, climax, falling action*, and *resolution*. The exposition provides background information and sets the scene for the conflict—a struggle between opposing people or forces that drives the action of the story. The introduction of the conflict marks the beginning of the rising action, in which the conflict intensifies until it reaches the high point, or climax, of the story. After the climax, the action falls to a resolution. The resolution shows how the situation turns out and ties up loose ends.

As you read the story, jot down events associated with the different parts of the plot on a diagram like this one.

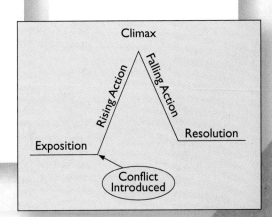

Reading for Success

Strategies for Reading Fiction

Fiction, which includes novels and short stories, is literature of the imagination. The characters and events are made up by the author. Fiction can be strongly based on real people and events or may be wildly inventive. The following strategies will help you get more out of the fiction you read.

Predict.

As the events of the story unfold, try to figure out what will happen next. Look for hints in the story that suggest things to come. As you read on, you will see if your predictions are correct.

Identify with the characters and the situation.

Although characters in fiction aren't real people, they do have thoughts and feelings like we do. Try to identify with characters by putting yourself in their situation and thinking about how you'd respond.

Picture the action in your mind.

When you use your imagination and the details the author provides, a story will reel out in your mind like a movie. With practice, you will find that reading a story can be better than watching a movie—the casting is always exactly to your taste, and there are no limits on the costumes, scenery, or special effects.

Question.

Stories are more interesting when you ask questions about characters and events. Why does a character act in a certain way? What does something really mean? As you read, look for the answers to your questions.

Make inferences.

Writers do not tell you everything directly. To truly appreciate the characters and the situation, you need to "read between the lines" and look beyond what the words state to what they imply. For example, you can make inferences about a character's personality based on his or her actions.

Draw conclusions.

Try to piece together the details and the inferences you make to draw conclusions about a story's theme—the author's central message about life or human nature. You may also draw conclusions about what you think of the author or whether you like a particular type of story.

As you read the following short story, notice the notes along the side. The notes demonstrate how to apply these strategies to your reading.

The Gift of the Magi

O. Henry

One dollar and eighty-seven cents. That was all. And sixty cents of it was in pennies. Pennies saved one and two at a time by bulldozing the grocer and the vegetable man and the butcher until one's cheeks burned with the silent imputation of parsimony[1] that such close dealing implied. Three times Della counted it. One dollar and eighty-seven cents. And the next day would be Christmas.

> To **identify** with Della's problem, recall a time you worked very hard to accomplish something but fell short of your goal.

There was clearly nothing to do but flop down on the shabby little couch and howl. So Della did it. Which instigates the moral reflection that life is made up of sobs, sniffles, and smiles, with sniffles predominating.

While the mistress of the home is gradually subsiding from the first stage to the second, take a look at the home. A furnished flat[2] at $8 per week. It

> The narrative voice in the story is mocking, condescending, and opinionated. **Question** why the author chose to tell the story in this way.

◆ **Build Vocabulary**

instigates (in´ stə gāts´) *v*.: Urges on; stirs up

---

1. **silent imputation** (im pyōō tā´ shən) **of parsimony** (pär´ sə mō´ nē): Silent accusation of stinginess.
2. **flat** (flat) *n*.: Apartment.

did not exactly beggar description,[3] but it certainly had that word on the lookout for the mendicancy squad.[4]

In the vestibule below was a letter-box into which no letter would go, and an electric button from which no mortal finger could coax a ring. Also appertaining thereunto was a card bearing the name "Mr. James Dillingham Young."

The "Dillingham" had been flung to the breeze during a former period of prosperity when its possessor was being paid $30 per week. Now, when the income was shrunk to $20, the letters of "Dillingham" looked blurred, as though they were thinking seriously of contracting to a modest and unassuming D. But whenever Mr. James Dillingham Young came home and reached his flat above he was called "Jim" and greatly hugged by Mrs. James Dillingham Young, already introduced to you as Della.

> From the description of Jim's name, you can **infer** that Jim's loss of income has taken its toll on his self-confidence.

Which is all very good.

Della finished her cry and attended to her cheeks with the powder rag. She stood by the window and looked out dully at a gray cat walking a gray fence in a gray backyard. Tomorrow would be Christmas Day, and she had only $1.87 with which to buy Jim a present. She had been saving every penny she could for months, with this result. Twenty dollars a week doesn't go far. Expenses had been greater than she had calculated. They always are. Only $1.87 to buy a present for Jim. Her Jim. Many a happy hour she had spent planning for something nice for him. Something fine and rare and sterling—

---

3. **beggar description:** Resist description.
4. **mendicancy** (men' di ken' se) **squad:** Police who arrested beggars.

◆ **Build Vocabulary**

depreciate (di prē' shē āt) v.: Reduce in value
cascade (kas kād') n.: Waterfall

something just a little bit near to being worthy of the honor of being owned by Jim.

There was a pier glass[5] between the windows of the room. Perhaps you have seen a pier glass in an $8 flat. A very thin and very agile person may, by observing his reflection in a rapid sequence of longitudinal strips, obtain a fairly accurate conception of his looks. Della, being slender, had mastered the art.

Suddenly she whirled from the window and stood before the glass. Her eyes were shining brilliantly, but her face had lost its color within twenty seconds. Rapidly she pulled down her hair and let it fall to its full length.

> Ask yourself why Della is acting in this way. What is she thinking?

Now, there were two possessions of the James Dillingham Youngs in which they both took a mighty pride. One was Jim's gold watch that had been his father's and his grandfather's. The other was Della's hair. Had the Queen of Sheba[6] lived in the flat across the airshaft, Della would have let her hair hang out the window some day to dry just to depreciate Her Majesty's jewels and gifts. Had King Solomon been the janitor, with all his treasures piled up in the basement, Jim would have pulled out his watch every time he passed, just to see him pluck at his beard from envy.

So now Della's beautiful hair fell about her rippling and shining like a cascade of brown waters. It reached below her knee and made itself almost a garment for her. And then she did it up again nervously and quickly. Once she faltered for a minute and stood still while a tear or two splashed on the worn red carpet.

On went her old brown jacket; on went her

> By **reading between the lines,** you can tell that Della loves and honors her husband. The qualities that Della wants in a gift for Jim reflect her regard for him.

---

5. **pier** (pir) **glass:** Tall mirror.
6. **Queen of Sheba:** In the Bible, the beautiful queen who visited King Solomon to test his wisdom.

Hairdresser's Window, 1907, John Sloan, Wadsworth Atheneum, Hartford, Connecticut

old brown hat. With a whirl of skirts and with the brilliant sparkle still in her eyes, she fluttered out the door and down the stairs to the street.

Where she stopped the sign read: "Mme. Sofronie. Hair Goods of All Kinds." One flight up

▲ **Critical Viewing** How do you think Della felt as she approached Madame Sofronie's shop? **[Analyze]**

Della ran, and collected herself, panting. Madame, large, too white, chilly, hardly looked the "Sofronie."

"Will you buy my hair?" asked Della.

"I buy hair," said Madame. "Take yer hat off and let's have a sight at the looks of it."

Down rippled the brown cascade.

"Twenty dollars," said Madame, lifting the mass with a practiced hand.

"Give it to me quick," said Della.

Oh, and the next two hours tripped by on rosy wings. Forget the hashed metaphor. She was ransacking the stores for Jim's present.

She found it at last. It surely had been made for Jim and no one else. There was no other like it in any of the stores, and she had turned all of them inside out. It was a platinum fob chain[7] simple and chaste in design, properly proclaiming its value by substance alone and not by meretricious ornamentation—as all good things should do. It was even worthy of The Watch. As soon as she saw it she knew that it must be Jim's. It was like him. Quietness and value—the description applied to both. Twenty-one dollars they took from her for it, and she hurried home with the 87 cents. With that chain on his watch Jim might be properly anxious about the time in any company. Grand as the watch was he sometimes looked at it on the sly on account of the old leather strap that he used in place of a chain.

When Della reached home her intoxication gave way a little to prudence and reason. She got out her curling irons and lighted the gas and went to work repairing the ravages made by generosity added to love. Which is always a tremendous task, dear friends—a mammoth task.

Within forty minutes her head was covered with tiny, close-lying curls that made her look wonderfully like a truant schoolboy. She looked at her reflection in the mirror long, carefully, and critically.

"If Jim doesn't kill me," she said to herself, "before he takes a second look at me, he'll say I look like a Coney Island[8] chorus girl. But what could I do—oh! what could I do with a dollar and eighty-seven cents?"

At 7 o'clock the coffee was made and the frying-pan was on the back of the stove hot and ready to cook the chops.

Jim was never late. Della doubled the fob chain in her hand and sat on the corner

> Put yourself in Della's place by remembering a time when you did something considerate for someone you cared about.

> From the way Della thinks about her husband in this passage and earlier in the story, you can **conclude** that she is loving, proud, and anxious to please him.

Carved Tortoiseshell Comb, mid 19th century, England or France, Cooper–Hewitt National Design Museum

---

▲ Critical Viewing How do you think Della might have felt about an elaborate, expensive comb like this one? [Connect]

◆ Build Vocabulary

chaste (chāst) *adj.*: Pure or clean in style; not ornate

meretricious (mer´ ə trish´ əs) *adj.*: Attractive in a cheap, flashy way

ravages (rav´ ij iz) *n.*: Ruins; devastating damages

---

7. **fob** (fäb) **chain:** Small chain connecting a watch to its pocket.

8. **Coney Island:** Beach and amusement park in Brooklyn, New York

of the table near the door that he always entered. Then she heard his step on the stair away down on the first flight, and she turned white for just a moment. She had a habit of saying little silent prayers about the simplest everyday things, and now she whispered: "Please God, make him think I am still pretty."

The door opened and Jim stepped in and closed it. He looked thin and very serious. Poor fellow, he was only twenty-two—and to be burdened with a family! He needed a new overcoat and he was without gloves.

Jim stopped inside the door, as immovable as a setter at the scent of quail. His eyes were fixed upon Della, and there was an expression in them that she could not read, and it terrified her. It was not anger, nor surprise, nor disapproval, nor horror, nor any of the sentiments that she had been prepared for. He simply stared at her fixedly with that peculiar expression on his face.

Della wriggled off the table and went for him.

"Jim, darling," she cried, "don't look at me that way. I had my hair cut off and sold it because I couldn't have lived through Christmas without giving you a present. It'll grow out again—you won't mind, will you? I just had to do it. My hair grows awfully fast. Say 'Merry Christmas!' Jim, and let's be happy. You don't know what a nice—what a beautiful, nice gift I've got for you."

"You've cut off your hair?" asked Jim, laboriously, as if he had not arrived at that patent fact yet even after the hardest mental labor.

"Cut it off and sold it," said Della. "Don't you like me just as well, anyhow? I'm me without my hair, ain't I?"

Jim looked about the room curiously.

"You say your hair is gone?" he said, with an air almost of idiocy.

"You needn't look for it," said Della. "It's sold, I tell you—sold and gone, too. It's Christmas Eve, boy. Be good to me, for it went for you. Maybe the hairs of my head were numbered," she went on with a sudden serious sweetness, "but nobody could ever count my love for you. Shall I put the chops on, Jim?"

Out of his trance Jim seemed quickly to wake. He enfolded his Della. For ten seconds let us regard with <u>discreet</u> scrutiny some inconsequential object in the other direction. Eight dollars a week or a million a year—what is the difference? A mathematician or a wit would give you the wrong answer. The Magi brought valuable gifts, but that was not among them. This dark assertion will be illuminated later on.

Jim drew a package from his overcoat pocket and threw it upon the table.

"Don't make any mistake, Dell," he said, "about me. I don't think there's anything in the way of a haircut or a shave or a shampoo that could make me like my girl any less. But if you'll unwrap that package you may see why you had me going a while at first."

White fingers and nimble tore at the string and paper. And then an ecstatic scream of joy; and then, alas! a quick feminine change to hysterical tears and wails, necessitating the immediate employment of all the comforting powers of the lord of the flat.

For there lay The Combs—the set of combs, side and back, that Della had worshipped for

---

You can **infer** that Della is impractical—Jim obviously needs a warm coat and gloves. You may also **conclude** from these details and others earlier in the story that Della and Jim are struggling financially.

Ask yourself **questions** about what Jim thinks about Della's new hairstyle, then **predict** how he is going to behave.

Picture the conversation between Della and Jim as a scene from a movie. Imagine how Jim's stunned surprise makes him move and speak. Envision Della trying to hide her anxiety by speaking too fast and too cheerfully.

In response to Jim's mysterious statement, you might ask the question: What is in the package?

◆ **Build Vocabulary**

discreet (dis krēt´) *adj.*: Tactful; respectful

long in a Broadway window. Beautiful combs, pure tortoise shell, with jeweled rims—just the shade to wear in the beautiful vanished hair. They were expensive combs, she knew, and her heart had simply craved and yearned over them without the least hope of possession. And now, they were hers, but the tresses that should have adorned the coveted adornments were gone.

From Della's reaction, you can **infer** that she is devastated that she cannot use the combs but is grateful for Jim's thoughtfulness.

But she hugged them to her bosom, and at length she was able to look up with dim eyes and a smile and say: "My hair grows so fast, Jim!"

And then Della leaped up like a little singed cat and cried, "Oh, oh!"

Jim had not yet seen his beautiful present. She held it out to him eagerly upon her open palm. The dull precious metal seemed to flash with a reflection of her bright and ardent spirit.

"Isn't it a dandy, Jim? I hunted all over town to find it. You'll have to look at the time a hundred times a day now. Give me your watch. I want to see how it looks on it."

Instead of obeying, Jim tumbled down on the couch and put his hands under the back of his head and smiled.

"Dell," said he, "let's put our Christmas presents away and keep 'em a while. They're too nice to use just at present. I sold the watch to get the money to buy your combs. And now suppose you put the chops on."

The Magi, as you know, were wise men—wonderfully wise men—who brought gifts to the Babe in the manger. They invented the art of giving Christmas presents. Being wise, their gifts were no doubt wise ones, possibly bearing the privilege of exchange in case of duplication. And here I have lamely related to you the uneventful chronicle of two foolish children in a flat who most unwisely sacrificed for each other the greatest treasures of their house. But in a last word to the wise of these days let it be said that of all who give gifts these two were the wisest. Of all who give and receive gifts, such as they are wisest. Everywhere they are wisest. They are the magi.

To **identify** with the situation, in which both "perfect" presents turn out to be useless, recall how you felt in a situation in which what you expected and what actually happened were very different.

Guide for Responding

◆ *Literature and Your Life*

Reader's Response If you were Jim or Della, how would you feel about the gift you received?

Thematic Focus Is giving a special gift a worthy goal? Explain your answer.

Journal Writing In the story, Della and Jim sell their most prized possessions to buy the "perfect" gift for each other. Think of a person to whom you would like to give a special gift. In your journal, describe the gift you would like to give and explain why the gift would be perfect for the recipient.

☑ Check Your Comprehension

1. What is the setting of the story?
2. At the beginning of the story, what possessions do Jim and Della prize the most?
3. What does Della do to get money for Jim's present?
4. What does Jim do to get money for Della's present?
5. Why is Jim particularly sorry that Della cut her hair?
6. Why does Jim react as he does when he sees Della's gift to him?

Guide for Responding (continued)

◆ Critical Thinking

INTERPRET

1. How do Della and Jim feel toward each other? Give evidence from the story to support your answer. **[Support]**

2. Why does the author describe Della and Jim as "two foolish children in a flat who most unwisely sacrificed for each other the greatest treasures of their house"? **[Infer]**

3. What does the author mean by "Of all who give and receive gifts, such as they are wisest. . . . They are the magi." **[Interpret]**

4. In your own words, state the central message of "The Gift of the Magi." **[Draw Conclusions]**

EVALUATE

5. Did Della and Jim do the right thing? Explain. **[Make a Judgment]**

APPLY

6. In your opinion, is it possible to be foolish and wise at the same time? Why or why not? **[Generalize]**

7. If you were either Jim or Della, how would you feel about the gift you received? **[Apply]**

◆ Build Vocabulary

USING THE PREFIX: *de-*

The prefix *de-* means "down," "away from," or "undo." Define each of the following words, incorporating the definition of *de-* into each answer.

1. demerit

2. delegate

3. deform

USING THE WORD BANK

In your notebook, write the word from the Word Bank that most closely matches the meaning of the words below.

1. waterfall	4. gaudy	6. cheapen
2. pure	5. damage	7. provoke
3. tactful		

◆ Reading for Success

STRATEGIES FOR READING FICTION

Apply the reading strategies and notes showing how to read fiction to answer these questions.

1. What can you conclude about Jim and Della from the descriptions in the second through fifth paragraphs of the story?

2. What can you infer about Della's mood from the following sentence: "She stood by the window and looked out dully at a gray cat walking a gray fence in a gray backyard"?

3. How might the information in the paragraph on p. 460 starting "Now there were two possessions . . ." have helped you predict the ending?

◆ Literary Focus

PLOT

The **plot** of a story is a series of related events. It usually begins with an *exposition*. Then the *conflict* is introduced. The action intensifies during the *rising action*. The *climax*, or high point of the story, is followed by the *falling action*, which leads to the *resolution* and the tying up of loose ends.

1. What happens during the story's exposition?

2. What is the conflict in the story?

3. At what point is the climax reached?

4. How is the conflict resolved?

◆ Build Grammar Skills

SENTENCE FRAGMENTS

A **sentence fragment** lacks a subject, a verb, or both, or doesn't express a complete thought. Sentence fragments are not acceptable in formal writing except when used for special effect.

Practice In your notebook, list five sentence fragments from the story.

Writing Application Rewrite the following paragraph, correcting the sentence fragments.

Birthday party tomorrow. Have to get a gift. Fast. But what? A T-shirt? Which is always what people get when they don't know what to buy. Boring. Stuffed animal? Nah. Too dumb. CD? Might work!

Build Your Portfolio

 Idea Bank

Writing

1. Letter of Appreciation Write a letter of appreciation to someone whose thoughtfulness you regard as a treasured gift.

2. Sequel Even though the central conflict is resolved at the end of this story, readers may still wonder what happens next. Write a sequel that tells what happened to Della, Jim, the combs, and the watch.

3. Surprise Ending Write a story of your own with a surprise ending. Keep in mind that a good surprise ending is unexpected but not completely off-the-wall.

Speaking and Listening

4. Play With a small group of classmates, act out the story of "The Gift of the Magi." You may use the existing stage version of the story, which you can find in a library, or create a version of your own. **[Performing Arts Link]**

5. Monologue Assume the role of either Della or Jim and retell "The Gift of the Magi." Practice and revise your retelling until it is convincing, then perform your monologue for an audience. **[Performing Arts Link]**

Projects

6. Comic Book Create a comic-book version of "The Gift of the Magi." Illustrate all important plot events in the story. **[Art Link]**

7. Multicultural Gifts With a small group of classmates, find out about a gift-giving occasion in a culture other than your own. Share your findings in a multimedia report. **[Social Studies Link; Technology Link]**

 Writing Mini-Lesson

Thank-You Letter

When people give you a gift or do something thoughtful for you, it's good manners to thank them. Think of a special gift that you received. Then write a thank-you letter expressing your appreciation.

Writing Skills Focus: Elaboration to Make Writing Personal

Make your thank-you letter more meaningful by **elaborating to make your writing personal.** Include details explaining *why* you like a gift and why it is meaningful to you. Share news regarding the gift and people of interest to the giver in your letter.

Model

Dear Abuelo,

I just love the snorkeling equipment you sent me for my birthday. When I saw the purge valve on the snorkel, I had to laugh. I must've made a real impression on you two summers ago when I tried to clear my old-fashioned snorkel and ended up inhaling what felt like half the bay.

I'm *really* looking forward to using my new equipment when we visit you and Abuela in December. Thanks to you, I won't have to surface every 30 seconds and pour out the water in my snorkel!

Prewriting Make a list of the reasons you like the gift, and think of other news you want to share.

Drafting As you write your letter, include personal details, such as features of the gift that particularly impress you, the way the gift makes you feel, and news about family and friends.

Revising Rework your letter, adding extra details and personal touches.

Plot, Character, and Point of View

In a Village Near Paris, 1909, Lyonel Feininger, The
University of Iowa Museum of Art, ©1997 Artists Rights
Society (ARS), New York, VG Bild Kinst, Bonn

Guide for Reading

Joan Aiken (1924–)

Unexplained mysteries, weird noises in the night, and eerie occurrences are all things you're likely to find in a Joan Aiken story. Aiken, the daughter of poet Conrad Aiken and sister of two other writers, was born in England.

> *During her childhood, the family lived in a creepy old house, an experience that helped to foster Aiken's fascination with mystery and the unexplained.*

An Early Start Aiken began writing when she was five years old and published her first story at age sixteen. "Writing," she has said, "is just the family trade." After working as a features editor for a magazine, a copywriter for a large London advertising agency, and with the United Nations in London, Aiken decided to devote herself exclusively to writing. The result has been an immense output of novels, poems, plays, and stories.

Words of Wit In addition to her interest in the mysterious, Aiken is also known for her wit. Many of her stories are humorous and imaginative, as are the titles of her books. Her first collection of short stories, for example, was called *All You Ever Wanted*. It was followed by another volume entitled *More Than You Bargained For.*

Like many writers, Aiken sometimes uses personal experiences in her stories. "Sonata for Harp and Bicycle" takes place in London, where Aiken has a home. The main character, Jason, is an advertising copywriter, a job that Aiken once held. As you read, you'll see evidence of Aiken's wit, as well as her flair for telling a spooky tale.

◆ Build Vocabulary

WORD ORIGINS: WORDS FROM MYTHS

Myths are fictional tales that explain the actions of gods or the causes of natural phenomena. Many English words come from myths. For example, the word *tantalizingly*, which appears in "Sonata for Harp and Bicycle," comes from the name Tantalus, a king in Greek mythology. He enraged the gods and was punished by being able to see but never reach water and food. Thus, *tantalizingly* means "done in a teasing manner by promising something and then withholding it."

encroaching
tantalizingly
furtive
menacing
reciprocate
ardent
gossamer
preposterous
engendered
improbably

WORD BANK

Before you read, preview this list of words from the story.

◆ Build Grammar Skills

COMMAS BEFORE INTERROGATIVE ELEMENTS

One use of the **comma** is to indicate a pause before a short **interrogative element**—a word or group of words that poses a question—at the end of a sentence. Notice how a comma sets off the question in each of these examples from "Sonata for Harp and Bicycle."

> . . . but there is the liberty of the individual to be considered, *don't you think?*

> You wouldn't be much loss, *would you?*

As you read the selection, look for other examples of sentences with final interrogative elements set off by commas.

Sonata for Harp and Bicycle

◆ Literature and Your Life

CONNECT YOUR EXPERIENCE

Someone starts behaving in a strange, unpredictable way. Something disappears without explanation. Real-life mysteries happen all the time. Some people may ignore the mystery. Others might wonder about it but not try to solve it. Certain people, however, will always try to solve a mystery—even if there's danger involved.

Journal Writing In your journal, explore your answer to this question: Why do people love a mystery?

THEMATIC FOCUS: WORKING TOWARD A GOAL

In this story, a young copywriter stumbles into a mysterious situation and feels compelled to get to the bottom of it—even though others advise him against it.

◆ Background for Understanding

MUSIC

A sonata (sə nät´ ə), derived from the Italian word *suonare*, "to sound," is a musical composition for one or two instruments. Sonatas composed after 1750 contain several movements, or parts, and are written for a keyboard instrument alone or for another solo instrument (a flute, for example) and a piano.

The movements of a sonata are related to one another thematically. In a typical sonata, the first movement is lively, the second is slow, and the optional third movement is graceful and lively.

◆ Literary Focus

RISING ACTION AND CLIMAX

The most exciting part of a story is the **rising action**—the part that makes you want to keep reading. The rising action is the portion of the plot that builds to the **climax**—or high point of interest. In "Sonata for Harp and Bicycle," the rising action includes a complicated and puzzling mystery that fuels suspense.

◆ Reading Strategy

PREDICT

To **predict** is to guess what will happen based upon what you already know. As you read "Sonata for Harp and Bicycle," make predictions by looking for examples of *foreshadowing*—clues about future events that the author provides.

For example, the first sentence of the story, in which a new employee is told that "no one is allowed to remain in the building after five o'clock" is a clue. It might lead you to guess that something unusual or dangerous occurs in the building after five o'clock. While you read "Sonata for Harp and Bicycle," stay one step ahead of the plot by continually updating and revising your predictions.

Use a chart like this to help you. In one column, record clues you find. Jot down a prediction beside each clue. Then note what actually happens.

Clue	Prediction	What Actually Happens

Sonata for Harp and Bicycle

Joan Aiken

"No one is allowed to remain in the building after five o'clock," Mr. Manaby told his new assistant, showing him into the little room that was like the inside of a parcel.

"Why not?"

"Directorial policy," said Mr. Manaby. But that was not the real reason.

Gaunt and sooty, Grimes Buildings lurched up the side of a hill toward Clerkenwell.[1] Every little office within its dim and crumbling exterior owned one tiny crumb of light—such was the proud boast of the architect—but toward evening the crumbs were collected as by an immense vacuum cleaner, absorbed and demolished, yielding to an uncontrollable mass of dark that came tumbling in through windows and doors to take their place. Darkness infested the building like a flight of bats returning willingly to roost.

"Wash hands, please. Wash hands, please," the intercom began to bawl in the passages at a quarter to five. Without much need of prompting, the staff hustled like lemmings along the corridors to green- and blue-tiled washrooms that mocked with an illustration of cheerfulness the encroaching dusk.

"All papers into cases, please," the voice warned, five minutes later. "Look at your desks, ladies and gentlemen. Any documents left lying about? Kindly put them away. Desks must be left clear and tidy. Drawers must be shut."

A multitudinous shuffling, a rustling as of innumerable bluebottle flies might have been heard by the attentive ear after this injunction,

---

1. **Clerkenwell:** District of London.

◆ **Build Vocabulary**

encroaching (en krōch´ iŋ) *adj.*: Intruding in a gradual or sneaking way

◀ **Critical Viewing** As the moon rises over nighttime London, centuries of history seem to blend together and coexist. How might this setting have inspired this story, in which events separated by fifty years unexpectedly converge? **[Speculate]**

as the employees of Moreton Wold and Company thrust their papers into cases, hurried letters and invoices into drawers, clipped statistical abstracts together and slammed them into filing cabinets, dropped discarded copy into wastepaper baskets. Two minutes later, and not a desk throughout Grimes Buildings bore more than its customary coating of dust.

"Hats and coats on, please. Hats and coats on, please. Did you bring an umbrella? Have you left any shopping on the floor?" At three minutes to five the homegoing throng was in the lifts[2] and on the stairs; a clattering, staccato-voiced flood darkened momentarily the great double doors of the building, and then as the first faint notes of St. Paul's[3] came echoing faintly on the frosty air, to be picked up near at hand by the louder chimes of St. Biddulph's-on-the-Wall, the entire premises of Moreton Wold stood empty.

"But why is it?" Jason Ashgrove, the new copywriter, asked his secretary one day. "Why are the staff herded out so fast? Not that I'm against it, mind you; I think it's an admirable idea in many ways, but there is the liberty of the individual to be considered, don't you think?"

"Hush!" Miss Golden, the secretary, gazed at him with large and terrified eyes. "You mustn't ask that sort of question. When you are taken onto the Established Staff you'll be told. Not before."

"But I want to know now," Jason said in discontent. "Do you know?"

"Yes, I do," Miss Golden answered <u>tantalizingly</u>. "Come on, or we shan't have finished the Oat Crisp layout by a quarter to." And she stared firmly down at the copy in front of her, lips folded, candyfloss hair falling over her face, lashes hiding eyes like peridots,[4] a girl with a secret.

---

2. **lifts** (lifts) *n.*: British term for elevators.
3. **St. Paul's:** Famous church in London.
4. **peridots** (per′ ə däts′) *n.*: Yellowish-green gems.

◆ Build Vocabulary

tantalizingly (tan′ tə līz′ iŋ glē) *adv.*: In a teasing or tormenting way

Jason was annoyed. He rapped out a couple of rude and witty rhymes which Miss Golden let pass in a withering silence.

"What do you want for your birthday, Miss Golden? Sherry? Fudge? Bubble bath?"

"I want to go away with a clear conscience about Oat Crisps," Miss Golden retorted. It was not true; what she chiefly wanted was Mr. Jason Ashgrove, but he had not realized this yet.

◆ **Reading Strategy**
Do you think the relationship between Miss Golden and Jason will grow into a loving one?

"Come on, don't tease! I'm sure you haven't been on the Established Staff all that long," he coaxed her. "What happens when one is taken on, anyway? Does the Managing Director have us up for a confidential chat? Or are we given a little book called *The Awful Secret of Grimes Buildings*?"

Miss Golden wasn't telling. She opened her drawer and took out a white towel and a cake of rosy soap.

"Wash hands, please! Wash hands, please!"

Jason was frustrated. "You'll be sorry," he said. "I shall do something desperate."

"Oh no, you mustn't!" Her eyes were large with fright. She ran from the room and was back within a couple of moments, still drying her hands.

"If I took you out for a coffee, couldn't you give me just a tiny hint?"

▼ **Critical Viewing** Londoners are accustomed to the sound of Big Ben, the bell in the Clock Tower of the Houses of Parliament, pictured here. This story also mentions the chimes of St. Paul's and St. Biddulph's-on-the-Wall. Why might a city build so many public timepieces? **[Deduce]**

Side by side Miss Golden and Mr. Ashgrove ran along the green-floored passages, battled down the white marble stairs among the hundred other employees from the tenth floor, the nine hundred from the floors below.

He saw her lips move as she said something, but in the clatter of two thousand feet the words were lost.

◆ Reading Strategy
This paragraph contains clues to what will happen later in the story.

"—fire escape," he heard, as they came into the momentary hush of the carpeted entrance hall. And "—it's to do with a bicycle. A bicycle and a harp."

"I don't understand."

Now they were in the street, chilly with the winter dusk smells of celery on carts, of swept-up leaves heaped in faraway parks, and cold layers of dew sinking among the withered evening primroses in the bombed areas. London lay about them wreathed in twilit mystery and fading against the barred and smoky sky. Like a ninth wave the sound of traffic overtook and swallowed them.

"Please tell me!"

But, shaking her head, she stepped onto a scarlet homebound bus and was borne away from him.

Jason stood undecided on the pavement, with the crowds dividing around him as around the pier of a bridge. He scratched his head, looked about him for guidance.

An ambulance clanged, a taxi hooted, a drill stuttered, a siren wailed on the river, a door slammed, a brake squealed, and close beside his ear a bicycle bell tinkled its tiny warning.

A bicycle, she had said. A bicycle and a harp.

Jason turned and stared at Grimes Buildings.

Somewhere, he knew, there was a back way in, a service entrance. He walked slowly past the main doors, with their tubs of snowy chrysanthemums, and up Glass Street. A tiny <u>furtive</u> wedge of darkness beckoned him, a snicket, a hacket, an alley carved into the thickness of the building. It was so narrow that at any moment, it seemed, the overtopping

walls would come together and squeeze it out of existence.

Walking as softly as an Indian, Jason passed through it, slid by a file of dustbins,[5] and found the foot of the fire escape. Iron treads rose into the mist, like an illustration to a Gothic[6] fairy tale.

He began to climb.

When he had mounted to the ninth story he paused for breath. It was a lonely place. The lighting consisted of a dim bulb at the foot of every flight. A well of gloom sank beneath him. The cold fingers of the wind nagged and fluttered at the tails of his jacket, and he pulled the string of the fire door and edged inside.

Grimes Buildings were triangular, with the street forming the base of the triangle, and the fire escape the point. Jason could see two long passages coming toward him, meeting at an acute angle where he stood. He started down the left-hand one, tiptoeing in the cavelike silence. Nowhere was there any sound, except for the faraway drip of a tap. No night watchman would stay in the building; none was needed. Burglars gave the place a wide berth.

Jason opened a door at random; then another. Offices lay everywhere about him, empty and forbidding. Some held lipstick-stained tissues, spilled powder, and orange peels; others were still foggy with cigarette smoke. Here was a Director's suite of rooms—a desk like half an acre of frozen lake, inch-thick carpet, roses, and the smell of cigars. Here was a conference room with scattered squares of doodled blotting paper. All equally empty.

He was not sure when he first began to notice the bell. Telephone, he thought at first, and then he remembered that all the outside lines were disconnected at five. And this bell, anyway, had not the regularity of a telephone's double ring: there was a tinkle, and then silence; a long ring, and then silence; a whole volley of rings together, and then silence.

Jason stood listening, and fear knocked against his ribs and shortened his breath. He

---

5. **dustbins:** British term for garbage cans.
6. **Gothic:** Mysterious.

▲ **Critical Viewing** Like fog, the mood of a story may blur the boundaries between reality and fantasy. How does the mood of this story make it difficult to tell where reality ends and fantasy begins? **[Distinguish]**

knew that he must move or be paralyzed by it. He ran up a flight of stairs and found himself with two more endless green corridors beckoning him like a pair of dividers.

Another sound now: a waft of ice-thin notes, riffling up an arpeggio[7] like a flurry of snowflakes. Far away down the passage it

echoed. Jason ran in pursuit, but as he ran the music receded. He circled the building, but it always outdistanced him, and when he came back to the stairs he heard it fading away to the story below.

He hesitated, and as he did so heard again the bell; the bicycle bell. It was approaching him fast, bearing down on him, urgent, <u>menacing</u>. He could hear the pedals, almost see the shimmer of an invisible wheel. Absurdly, he was

---

7. **arpeggio** (är pej′ ō) *n.*: Notes of a chord played one after the other instead of together.

◆ **Build Vocabulary**

furtive (fʉr′ tiv) *adj.*: Preventing observation; sneaky

menacing (men′ is iŋ) *v.*: Threatening

reminded of the insistent clamor of an ice-cream vendor, summoning children on a sultry Sunday afternoon.

There was a little fireman's alcove beside him, with buckets and pumps. He hurled himself into it. The bell stopped beside him, and then there was a moment while his heart tried to shake itself loose in his chest. He was looking into two eyes carved out of expressionless air; he was held by two hands knotted together out of the width of dark.

"Daisy, Daisy?" came the whisper. "Is that you, Daisy? Have you come to give me your answer?"

Jason tried to speak, but no words came.

"It's not Daisy! Who are you?" The sibilants[8] were full of threat. "You can't stay here. This is private property."

He was thrust along the corridor. It was like being pushed by a whirlwind—the fire door opened ahead of him without a touch, and he was on the openwork platform, clutching the slender railing. Still the hands would not let him go.

"How about it?" the whisper mocked him. "How about jumping? It's an easy death compared with some."

Jason looked down into the smoky void. The darkness nodded to him like a familiar.[9]

"You wouldn't be much loss, would you? What have you got to live for?"

Miss Golden, Jason thought. She would miss me. And the syllables Berenice Golden lingered in the air like a chime. Drawing on some unknown deposit of courage he shook himself loose from the holding hands and ran down the fire escape without looking back.

Next morning when Miss Golden, crisp, fragrant, and punctual, shut the door of Room 492 behind her, she stopped short of the hat-pegs with a horrified gasp.

---

8. **sibilants** (sib´ əl əntz) *n.*: Hissing sounds.
9. **a familiar**: A spirit.

"Mr. Ashgrove, your hair!"

"It makes me look more distinguished, don't you think?" he said.

It had indeed this effect, for his impeccable dark cut had turned to a stippled silver which might have been envied by many a diplomat.

"How did it happen? You've not—" her voice sank to a whisper—"*you've not been in Grimes Buildings after dark?*"

"Miss Golden—Berenice," he said earnestly. "Who was Daisy? Plainly you know. Tell me the story."

"Did you see him?" she asked faintly.

"Him?"

"William Heron—The Wailing Watchman. Oh," she exclaimed in terror, "I can see you did. Then you are doomed—doomed!"

"If I'm doomed," said Jason, "let's have coffee, and you tell me the story quickly."

"It all happened over fifty years ago," said Berenice, as she spooned out coffee powder with distracted extravagance. "Heron was the night watchman in this building, patrolling the corridors from dusk to dawn every night on his bicycle. He fell in love with a Miss Bell who taught the harp. She rented a room—this room—and gave lessons in it. She began to reciprocate his love, and they used to share a picnic supper every night at eleven, and she'd stay on a while to keep him company. It was an idyll,[10] among the fire buckets and the furnace pipes.

"On Halloween he had summoned up the courage to propose to her. The day before he had told her he was going to ask her a very important question, and he came to the Buildings with a huge bunch of roses and a bottle of wine. But Miss Bell never turned up.

"The explanation was simple. Miss Bell, of course, had been losing a lot of sleep through her nocturnal romance, and so she used to take a nap in her music room between seven and ten, to save going home. In order to make

---

10. **idyll** (ī´ dəl) *n.*: Romantic scene, usually in the country.

sure that she would wake up, she persuaded her father, a distant relative of Graham Bell,[11] to attach an alarm-waking fixture to her telephone which called her every night at ten. She was too modest and shy to let Heron know that she spent those hours in the building, and to give him the pleasure of waking her himself.

"Alas! On this important evening the line failed, and she never woke up. The telephone was in its infancy at that time, you must remember.

---

11. **Graham Bell:** Alexander Graham Bell (1847–1922), the inventor of the telephone.

"Heron waited and waited. At last, mad with grief and jealousy, having called her home and discovered that she was not there, he concluded that she had betrayed him; he ran to the fire escape, and cast himself off it, holding the roses and the bottle of wine.

"Daisy did not long survive him but pined away soon after. Since that day their ghosts

---

▼ **Critical Viewing** After the other workers have fled, Berenice and Jason remain behind to change the ending of the ghosts' story. Do you think they will succeed in their mission? **[Predict]**

Office at Night, 1940, Edward Hopper, Walker Art Center, Minneapolis, Minnesota

have haunted Grimes Buildings, he vainly patrolling the corridors on his bicycle, she playing her harp in the room she rented. *But they never meet.* And anyone who meets the ghost of William Heron will himself, within five days, leap down from the same fatal fire escape."

She gazed at him with tragic eyes.

"In that case we must lose no time," said Jason, and he enveloped her in an embrace as prompt as it was <u>ardent.</u> Looking down at the <u>gossamer</u> hair sprayed across his pin-stripe, he added, "Just the same it is a <u>preposterous</u> situation. Firstly, I have no intention of jumping off the fire escape—" here, however, he repressed a shudder as he remembered the cold, clutching hands of the evening before— "and secondly, I find it quite nonsensical that those two inefficient ghosts have spent fifty years in this building without coming across each other. We must remedy the matter, Berenice. We must not begrudge our new-found happiness to others."

He gave her another kiss so impassioned that the electric typewriter against which they were leaning began chattering to itself in a frenzy of enthusiasm.

"This very evening," he went on, looking at his watch, "we will put matters right for that unhappy couple and then, if I really have only five more days to live, which I don't for one moment believe, we will proceed to spend them together, my bewitching Berenice, in the most advantageous manner possible."

She nodded, spellbound.

"Can you work a switchboard?" he added. She nodded again. "My love, you are perfection itself. Meet me in the switchboard room then,

at ten this evening. I would say, have dinner with me, but I shall need to make one or two purchases and see an old R.A.F.[12] friend. You will be safe from Heron's curse in the switchboard room if he always keeps to the corridors."

"I would rather meet him and die with you," she murmured.

"My angel, I hope that won't be necessary. Now," he said, sighing, "I suppose we should get down to our day's work."

Strangely enough the copy they wrote that day, although <u>engendered</u> from such agitated minds, sold more packets of Oat Crisps than any other advertising matter before or since.

That evening when Jason entered Grimes Buildings he was carrying two bottles of wine, two bunches of red roses, and a large canvas-covered bundle. Miss Golden, who had concealed herself in the switchboard room before the offices closed for the night, eyed these things with surprise.

"Now," said Jason, after he had greeted her, "I want you first to ring our own extension."

"No one will reply, surely?"

"I think she will reply."

Sure enough, when Berenice rang Extension 170 a faint, sleepy voice, distant and yet clear, whispered, "Hullo?"

"Is that Miss Bell?"

"Yes."

Berenice went a little pale. Her eyes sought Jason's and, prompted by him, she said formally, "Switchboard here, Miss Bell. Your ten o'clock call."

"Thank you," the faint voice said. There was a click and the line went blank.

"Excellent," Jason remarked. He unfastened his package and slipped its straps over his shoulders. "Now plug into the intercom."

Berenice did so, and then said, loudly and clearly, "Attention. Night watchman on duty, please. Night watchman on duty. You have an urgent summons to Room 492. You have an urgent summons to Room 492." The intercom echoed and reverberated through the empty

---

12. **R.A.F.:** Royal Air Force.

corridors, then coughed itself to silence.

"Now we must run. You take the roses, sweetheart, and I'll carry the bottles."

Together they raced up eight flights of stairs and along the passages to Room 492. As they neared the door a burst of music met them— harp music swelling out, sweet and triumphant. Jason took a bunch of roses from Berenice, opened the door a little way, and gently deposited them, with a bottle, inside the door. As he closed it again Berenice said breathlessly, "Did you see anyone?"

"No," he said. "The room was too full of music." She saw that his eyes were shining.

They stood hand in hand, reluctant to move away, waiting for they hardly knew what. Suddenly the door opened again. Neither Berenice nor Jason, afterward, would speak of what they saw but each was left with a memory, bright as the picture on a Salvador Dali[13] calendar, of a bicycle bearing on its saddle a harp, a bottle of

_____

13. **Salvador Dali** (sal´ və dôr´ dä´ lē): Modern artist (1904–1989) famous for his unusual pictures.

wine, and a bouquet of red roses, sweeping improbably down the corridor and far, far away.

◆ **Literary Focus**
The story has reached its climax. Describe what is happening.

"We can go now," Jason said.

He led Berenice to the fire door, tucking the bottle of Médoc in his jacket pocket. A black wind from the north whistled beneath them as they stood on the openwork platform, looking down.

"We don't want our evening to be spoiled by the thought of a curse hanging over us," he said, "so this is the practical thing to do. Hang onto the roses." And holding his love firmly, Jason pulled the rip cord of his R.A.F. friend's parachute and leaped off the fire escape.

A bridal shower of rose petals adorned the descent of Miss Golden, who was possibly the only girl to be kissed in midair in the district of Clerkenwell at ten minutes to midnight on Halloween.

Guide for Responding

◆ Literature and Your Life

Reader's Response If you were in Jason's place, would you try to solve the mystery of the Grimes Buildings? Why or why not?

Thematic Focus What is Jason's goal? Does he accomplish it?

Group Discussion With a group, discuss mysteries you've heard about or experienced. Were any of the mysteries ever solved?

☑ Check Your Comprehension

1. Why does Jason first sneak into the Grimes Buildings after five P.M.?
2. How do the bicycle, the fire escape, and the harp relate to the buildings' secret?
3. What is Jason's plan for helping Daisy Bell and William Heron?
4. How does Jason avoid the fate that awaits anyone who sees Heron's ghost?

Guide for Responding *(continued)*

◆ Critical Thinking

INTERPRET

1. Why don't the Grimes Buildings need a night watchman? **[Speculate]**
2. Why does Berenice Golden agree to meet Jason in the Grimes Buildings after dark? **[Infer]**
3. In what way does love beget, or lead to, love in this story? **[Draw Conclusions]**

APPLY

4. What lesson do the circumstances of William Heron's death teach about the process of making decisions? **[Generalize]**
5. How do the events of this story support the saying that "love conquers all"? **[Apply]**

EVALUATE

6. Explain, using examples from the story, why the title "Sonata for Harp and Bicycle" is appropriate for this selection. **[Evaluate]**

◆ Reading Strategy

PREDICT

When you make **predictions,** you piece together clues in the text to try to guess what will happen next. What event in Aiken's story does each of these excerpts help you predict?

1. "... close beside his ear a bicycle bell tinkled its tiny warning."
2. "Daisy, Daisy?" came the whisper. "Is that you, Daisy? Have you come to give me your answer?"
3. Miss Golden, Jason thought. She would miss me. And the syllables Berenice Golden lingered in the air like a chime.

◆ Literary Focus

RISING ACTION AND CLIMAX

In a literary work, the events that build up to the **climax**—or high point of the story—are called the **rising action**.

1. At what point in the story does the rising action begin? Explain.
2. What is the climax of the story? Support your answer.

◆ Build Vocabulary

USING WORDS FROM MYTHS

Use the clues below to match each word with the letter of its definition.

CLUES FROM GREEK MYTHOLOGY

Echo: nymph who pines away until only her voice remains
Hercules: son of Zeus, known for his strength
Narcissus: beautiful youth in love with his reflection
Titan: one of a race of giant deities

1. echo_____?_____		a. powerful or courageous
2. herculean_____?_____		b. of great size
3. narcissism_____?_____		c. repetition of a sound
4. titanic_____?_____		d. self-love

USING THE WORD BANK

Copy each word from the Word Bank; then write the letter of its synonym.

1. encroaching		a. passionate	
2. tantalizingly		b. frightening	
3. furtive		c. created	
4. menacing		d. delicate	
5. reciprocate		e. teasingly	
6. ardent		f. unlikely	
7. gossamer		g. secretive	
8. preposterous		h. intruding	
9. engendered		i. nonsensical	
10. improbably		j. return	

◆ Build Grammar Skills

COMMAS BEFORE INTERROGATIVE ELEMENTS

A **comma** is used to set off a short **interrogative element** (a word or group of words that poses a question) at the end of a sentence.

Practice On a sheet of paper, rewrite the following sentences, adding commas where needed.

1. The story was suspenseful wasn't it?
2. You like tales of the supernatural don't you?
3. You know another good story by Joan Aiken do you?
4. What's it about anyway?
5. You'd love to see the movie wouldn't you?

Build Your Portfolio

Idea Bank

Writing

1. **Memo** Imagine you're designing the sets for a stage production of "Sonata for Harp and Bicycle." Write a memo to the producer describing your ideas for the sets.

2. **Continuation** Write a continuation of the story in which you tell what happens next to Jason and Berenice.

3. **Evaluation** Joan Aiken has said, "A flat or unsatisfactory ending is the worst sin a writer can commit." Evaluate how well Aiken followed her own advice, citing examples from the story.

Speaking and Listening

4. **Talk-Show Interview** Develop and perform a talk-show interview featuring Berenice, Jason, the two ghosts, and the host of the program. Plan the interview so that the two pairs of guests tell what happened at the Grimes Buildings from their own perspectives. **[Media Link]**

5. **Debate** Choose a real-life mystery that has been a subject of controversy—for example, the question of whether there is life on other planets. With a group of classmates, stage a debate that explores the two sides of the controversy.

Projects

6. **Mystery Timeline** Research a famous real-life mystery and create a timeline that outlines the facts and details of the mystery. Present the timeline to the class. **[Social Studies Link]**

7. **Illustration** The Grimes Buildings featured a "dim and crumbling exterior" and, every evening, "darkness infested the building." Create a painting or illustration that captures this eerie scene. **[Art Link]**

Writing Mini-Lesson

Newspaper Report on a Strange Occurrence

Using your imagination or drawing from real-life stories you've heard, think of a strange or mysterious occurrence that would capture people's interest. Then write a newspaper story that provides a detailed account of the occurrence.

Writing Skills Focus: Dramatic Effects

Dramatic effects are story elements designed to create excitement and suspense. These might include an opening statement that heightens curiosity, a surprise ending, or a bizarre setting, as in this model:

Model From the Story

It was a lonely place. The lighting consisted of a dim bulb at the foot of every flight. A well of gloom sank beneath him. The cold fingers of the wind nagged and fluttered at the tails of his jacket.

Prewriting Start by creating a timeline that outlines the main details leading up to and following the occurrence. Look over your timeline and determine the events and details that will have the strongest dramatic impact on your audience. Feature these in your report.

Drafting Start your report with a dramatic opening statement that will grab your audience's attention. For example, you might begin with the outcome of events, then go back and explain the events leading up to it. Also, try to come up with an ending that will leave your readers thinking.

Revising Have a classmate read your report and make suggestions for what you can do to make it more engaging. How can you improve the beginning? What gripping details can you add?

Guide for Reading

James Hurst (1922–)

James Hurst is no stranger to either the quiet beauty of a coastal swamp or the deadly fury of a hurricane.

Like the main character of this story, Hurst grew up on a farm in coastal North Carolina, a region known for both its tranquil landscapes and its violent storms.

A Man of Many Talents Hurst has done a lot more than write. He studied chemical engineering at North Carolina State College, served in the army during World War II, studied opera at New York's prestigious Juilliard School of Music, and eventually took a job in a New York bank. Hurst's career at the bank lasted for thirty-four years.

Career as a Writer While working at the bank, Hurst devoted his evenings to writing and published short stories in a variety of small magazines. Published in *The Atlantic* magazine in 1960, "The Scarlet Ibis" is by far Hurst's most popular and successful story.

About the Story One of the qualities that makes "The Scarlet Ibis" such a powerful story is Hurst's use of symbols—objects, people, or ideas that have an underlying meaning. The story's central symbol is a scarlet ibis, a type of bird rarely seen in the United States. When asked why he chose the ibis, Hurst wrote, "The ancient Egyptians worshipped the ibis because they believed it destroyed the crocodiles. . . . I wanted the bird to represent [the character of] Doodle [the younger brother of the story's narrator]— not Doodle's physical self, but his spirit." As you read the story, think about the ways in which the ibis symbolizes Doodle's spirit.

◆ Build Vocabulary

IRREGULAR PLURALS: -x to -ces

This selection contains the word *vortex*, which often refers to the center of a situation. The word has an unusual plural: *vortices*. To form the plural, you must change the *e* to *i* and the *-x* to *-ces*. Words that form the plural in this way—for example, *appendix* and *index*—often have two acceptable plurals. This is true of the plural of *vortex*, which can be written as either *vortices* or *vortexes*.

imminent
iridescent
vortex
infallibility
entrails
precariously
evanesced

WORD BANK

The words in this list are from this story. Before you read, jot down the definition of any words you recognize. Then check to see whether you're right.

◆ Build Grammar Skills

INFINITIVES AND INFINITIVE PHRASES

The story contains many **infinitives**—verb forms that come after the word *to* and act as nouns, adjectives, or adverbs. Infinitives are often part of an **infinitive phrase,** which is an infinitive with modifiers, complements, or a subject, all acting together as a single part of speech. Look at these examples:

Infinitive as a Noun: the grindstone begins *to turn* . . .

Infinitive Phrase as a Noun: its song seems *to die up in the leaves* . . .

Infinitive Phrases as Adjectives and Modifying Someone: I wanted more than anything else someone *to race to Horsehead Landing*, someone *to box with,* and someone *to perch with in the top fork of the great pine* . . .

The Scarlet Ibis

◆ *Literature and Your Life*

CONNECT YOUR EXPERIENCE

Relationships can be very complicated. Sometimes your best pal can also be your biggest pain in the neck. This type of two-sided relationship often occurs among brothers and sisters. The narrator of this story has a range of conflicting feelings toward his younger brother. Although his brother is his closest companion, the narrator is embarrassed by him and places tremendous demands on him.

THEMATIC FOCUS: FACING CONFLICTS

As you read this story, you'll discover what happens as the narrator tries to work through his conflicting feelings toward his brother.

◆ Background for Understanding

SCIENCE

Found mostly in the tropics of South America, the scarlet ibis is a wading bird with long legs, a long, slender neck, and a wingspan of more than three feet. Bright scarlet in color with black-tipped wings, the scarlet ibis is strikingly beautiful.

These exquisite birds rarely appear in the United States except in Florida. As a result, the discovery of a scarlet ibis in this story's setting, a cotton farm in coastal North Carolina, is an unexpected and dramatic sight.

Journal Writing Jot down how you think you would react if a scarlet ibis or some other type of rare bird suddenly landed in your backyard or on your block. Would you find any special meaning in the event?

◆ Literary Focus

POINT OF VIEW

The **point of view** is the vantage point from which a story is told. Almost all stories are told either from a **third-person point of view**, in which the narrator does not participate in the action, or from a **first-person point of view**, in which the narrator is one of the characters and refers to himself or herself as "I." "The Scarlet Ibis" is told from a first-person point of view. By using the first-person point of view, Hurst makes readers feel as if they are a part of the action and enables them to experience firsthand how the events make the narrator feel.

◆ Reading Strategy

IDENTIFY WITH A CHARACTER

Authors who write in the first person invite you to walk through the story in the shoes of one of the characters. To take advantage of this opportunity, try to **identify with the character** by putting yourself in the character's place and thinking about how you would respond if you experienced the situations and events that the character experiences.

As you read "The Scarlet Ibis," use a chart like the one shown to help you identify with the story's narrator. List key events from the story in one column and record the narrator's reaction to each event. Then note what you might have said, done, or thought in a similar situation.

Story Event	How the Narrator Reacted	How I Might Have Reacted

The Scarlet Ibis

James Hurst

It was in the clove of seasons, summer was dead but autumn had not yet been born, that the ibis lit in the bleeding tree. The flower garden was stained with rotting brown magnolia petals and ironweeds grew rank amid the purple phlox. The five o'clocks by the chimney still marked time, but the oriole nest in the elm was untenanted and rocked back and forth like an empty cradle. The last graveyard flowers were blooming, and their smell drifted across the cotton field and through every room of our house, speaking softly the names of our dead.

It's strange that all this is still so clear to me, now that the summer has long since fled and time has had its way. A grindstone stands where the bleeding tree stood, just outside the kitchen door, and now if an oriole sings in the elm, its song seems to die up in the leaves, a silvery dust. The flower garden is prim, the house a gleaming white, and the pale fence across the yard stands straight and spruce. But sometimes (like right now), as I sit in the cool, green-draped parlor, the grindstone begins to turn, and time with all its changes is ground away—and I remember Doodle.

Doodle was just about the craziest brother a boy ever had. Of course, he wasn't a crazy crazy like old Miss Leedie, who was in love with President Wilson and wrote him a letter every day, but was a nice crazy, like someone you meet in your dreams. He was born when I was six and was, from the outset, a disappointment. He seemed all head, with a tiny body which was red and shriveled like an old man's. Everybody thought he was going to die—everybody except Aunt Nicey, who had delivered him. She said he would live because he was born in a caul[1] and cauls were made from Jesus' nightgown. Daddy had Mr. Heath, the carpenter, build a little mahogany coffin for him. But he didn't die, and when he was three months old Mama and Daddy decided they might as well name him. They named him William Armstrong, which was like tying a big tail on a small kite. Such a name sounds good only on a tombstone.

I thought myself pretty smart at many things, like holding my breath, running, jumping, or climbing the vines in Old Woman Swamp, and I wanted more than anything else someone to race to Horsehead Landing, someone to box with, and someone to perch with in the top fork of the great pine behind the barn, where across the fields and swamps you could see the sea. I wanted a brother. But Mama, crying, told me that even if William Armstrong lived, he would never do these things with me. He might not, she sobbed, even be "all there." He might, as long as he lived, lie on the rubber sheet in the center of the bed in the front bedroom where the white marquisette curtains billowed out in the afternoon sea breeze, rustling like palmetto fronds.[2]

It was bad enough having an invalid brother, but having one who possibly was not all there was unbearable, so I began to make plans to kill him by smothering him with a pillow. However, one afternoon as I watched him, my head poked between the iron posts of the foot of the bed, he looked straight at me and grinned. I skipped through the rooms, down the echoing halls, shouting, "Mama, he smiled. He's all there! He's all there!" and he was.

When he was two, if you laid him on his stomach, he began to try to move himself, straining terribly. The doctor said that with his weak heart this strain would probably kill him, but it didn't. Trembling, he'd push himself up, turning first red, then a soft purple, and finally collapse back onto the bed like an old worn-out doll. I can still see Mama watching him, her hand pressed tight across her mouth, her eyes wide and unblinking. But he learned to crawl (it was his third winter), and we brought him out of the front bedroom, putting him on the rug before the fireplace. For the first time he became one of us.

As long as he lay all the time in bed, we called him William Armstrong, even though it was formal and sounded as if we were referring to one of our ancestors, but with his creeping around on the deerskin rug and beginning to talk, something had to be done about his name. It was I who renamed him. When he crawled, he crawled backwards, as if he were in reverse and couldn't change gears. If you called him, he'd turn around as if he were going in the other direction, then he'd back right up to you to be picked up. Crawling backward made him look like a doodle-bug, so I began to call him Doodle, and in time even Mama and Daddy thought it was a better name than William Armstrong. Only Aunt Nicey disagreed. She said caul babies should be treated with special respect since they might turn out to be saints. Renaming my brother was perhaps the kindest thing I ever did for him, because nobody expects much from someone called Doodle.

---

1. **caul:** (kôl) *n*.: Membrane enclosing a baby at birth.
2. **palmetto fronds:** Palm leaves.

Although Doodle learned to crawl, he showed no signs of walking, but he wasn't idle. He talked so much that we all quit listening to what he said. It was about this time that Daddy built him a go-cart and I had to pull him around. At first I just paraded him up and down the piazza, but then he started crying to be taken out into the yard and it ended up by my having to lug him wherever I went. If I so much as picked up my cap, he'd start crying to go with me and Mama would call from wherever she was, "Take Doodle with you."

He was a burden in many ways. The doctor had said that he mustn't get too excited, too hot, too cold, or too tired and that he must always be treated gently. A long list of don'ts went with him, all of which I ignored once we got out of the house. To discourage his coming with me, I'd run with him across the ends of the cotton rows and careen him around corners on two wheels. Sometimes I accidentally turned him over, but he never told Mama. His skin was very sensitive, and he had to wear a big straw hat whenever he went out. When the going got rough and he had to cling to the sides of the go-cart, the hat slipped all the way down over his ears. He was a sight. Finally, I could see I was licked. Doodle was my brother and he was going to cling to me forever, no matter what I did, so I dragged him across the burning cotton field to share with him the only beauty I knew, Old Woman Swamp. I pulled the go-cart through the saw-tooth fern, down into the green dimness where the palmetto fronds whispered by the stream. I lifted him out and set him down in the soft rubber grass beside a tall pine. His eyes were round with wonder as he gazed about him, and his little hands began to stroke the rubber grass. Then he began to cry.

"For heaven's sake, what's the matter?" I asked, annoyed.

◆ *Literature and Your Life*

How would you feel if you had to take a brother like Doodle everywhere you went?

"It's so pretty," he said. "So pretty, pretty, pretty."

After that day Doodle and I often went down into Old Woman Swamp. I would gather wildflowers, wild violets, honeysuckle, yellow jasmine, snakeflowers, and water lilies, and with wire grass we'd weave them into necklaces and crowns. We'd bedeck ourselves with our handiwork and loll about thus beautified, beyond the touch of the everyday world. Then when the slanted rays of the sun burned orange in the tops of the pines, we'd drop our jewels into the stream and watch them float away toward the sea.

There is within me (and with sadness I have watched it in others) a knot of cruelty borne by the stream of love, much as our blood sometimes bears the seed of our destruction, and at times I was mean to Doodle. One day I took him up to the barn loft and showed him his casket, telling him how we all had believed he would die. It was covered with a film of Paris green[3] sprinkled to kill the rats, and screech owls had built a nest inside it.

Doodle studied the mahogany box for a long time, then said, "It's not mine."

"It is," I said. "And before I'll help you down from the loft, you're going to have to touch it."

"I won't touch it," he said sullenly.

"Then I'll leave you here by yourself," I threatened, and made as if I were going down.

Doodle was frightened of being left. "Don't go leave me, Brother," he cried, and he leaned toward the coffin. His hand, trembling, reached out, and when he touched the casket he screamed. A screech owl flapped out of the box into our faces, scaring us and covering us with Paris green. Doodle was paralyzed, so I put him on my shoulder and carried him down the ladder, and even when we were outside in the bright sunshine, he clung to me, crying, "Don't leave me. Don't leave me."

---

3. **Paris green:** Poisonous green powder.

Two Boys in a Punt, N. C. Wyeth, Courtesy of Dr. and Mrs. William A. Morton, Jr.

▲ Critical Viewing Doodle and his brother spend many hours
exploring Old Woman Swamp. What can you tell about the brothers'
relationship from this illustration and the details in the story? [Infer]

When Doodle was five years old, I was embarrassed at having a brother of that age who couldn't walk, so I set out to teach him. We were down in Old Woman Swamp and it was spring and the sick-sweet smell of bay flowers hung everywhere like a mournful song. "I'm going to teach you to walk, Doodle," I said.

He was sitting comfortably on the soft grass, leaning back against the pine. "Why?" he asked.

I hadn't expected such an answer. "So I won't have to haul you around all the time."

"I can't walk, Brother," he said.

"Who says so?" I demanded.

"Mama, the doctor–everybody."

"Oh, you can walk," I said, and I took him by the arms and stood him up. He collapsed onto the grass like a half-empty flour sack. It was as if he had no bones in his little legs.

"Don't hurt me, Brother," he warned.

"Shut up. I'm not going to hurt you. I'm going to teach you to walk." I heaved him up again, and again he collapsed.

This time he did not lift his face up out of the rubber grass. "I just can't do it. Let's make honeysuckle wreaths."

"Oh yes you can, Doodle," I said. "All you got to do is try. Now come on," and I hauled him up once more.

It seemed so hopeless from the beginning that it's a miracle I didn't give up. But all of us must have something or someone to be proud of, and Doodle had become mine. I did not know then that pride is a wonderful, terrible thing, a seed that bears two vines, life and death. Every day that summer we went to the pine beside the stream of Old Woman Swamp, and I put him on his feet at least a hundred times each afternoon. Occasionally I too became discouraged because it didn't seem as if he was trying, and I would say, "Doodle, don't you *want* to learn to walk?"

He'd nod his head, and I'd say, "Well, if you don't keep trying, you'll never learn." Then I'd paint for him a picture of us as old men, white-haired, him with a long white beard and me still pulling him around in the go-cart. This never failed to make him try again.

Finally one day, after many weeks of practicing, he stood alone for a few seconds. When he fell, I grabbed him in my arms and hugged him, our laughter pealing through the swamp like a ringing bell. Now we knew it could be done. Hope no longer hid in the dark palmetto thicket but perched like a cardinal in the lacy toothbrush tree, brilliantly visible. "Yes, yes," I cried, and he cried it too, and the grass beneath us was soft and the smell of the swamp was sweet.

With success so <u>imminent</u>, we decided not to tell anyone until he could actually walk. Each day, barring rain, we sneaked into Old Woman Swamp, and by cotton-picking time Doodle was ready to show what he could do. He still wasn't able to walk far, but we could wait no longer. Keeping a nice secret is very hard to do, like holding your breath. We chose to reveal all on October eighth, Doodle's sixth birthday, and for weeks ahead we mooned around the house, promising everybody a most spectacular surprise. Aunt Nicey said that, after so much talk, if we produced anything less tremendous than the Resurrection,[4] she was going to be disappointed.

At breakfast on our chosen day, when Mama, Daddy, and Aunt Nicey were in the dining room, I brought Doodle to the door in the go-cart just as usual and had them turn their backs, making them cross their hearts and hope to die if they peeked. I helped Doodle up, and when he was standing alone I let them look. There wasn't a sound as Doodle walked slowly across the room and sat down at his place at the table. Then Mama began to cry and ran over to him, hugging him and kissing him. Daddy hugged him too, so I went to Aunt Nicey, who was thanks praying in the doorway, and began to waltz her around. We danced together quite well until she came down on my big toe with her brogans, hurting me so badly I thought I was crippled for life.

Doodle told them it was I who had taught him

---

4. the Resurrection: (res´ e rek´ shen): The rising of Jesus Christ from the dead after his death and burial.

to walk, so everyone wanted to hug me, and I began to cry.

"What are you crying for?" asked Daddy, but I couldn't answer. They did not know that I did it for myself; that pride, whose slave I was, spoke to me louder than all their voices, and that Doodle walked only because I was ashamed of having a crippled brother.

Within a few months Doodle had learned to walk well and his go-cart was put up in the barn loft (it's still there) beside his little mahogany coffin. Now, when we roamed off together, resting often, we never turned back until our destination had been reached, and to help pass the time, we took up lying. From the beginning Doodle was a terrible liar and he got me in the habit. Had anyone stopped to listen to us, we would have been sent off to Dix Hill.

My lies were scary, involved, and usually pointless, but Doodle's were twice as crazy. People in his stories all had wings and flew wherever they wanted to go. His favorite lie was about a boy named Peter who had a pet peacock with a ten-foot tail. Peter wore a golden robe that glittered so brightly that when he walked through the sunflowers they turned away from the sun to face him. When Peter was ready to go to sleep, the peacock spread his magnificent tail, enfolding the boy gently like a closing go-to-sleep flower, burying him in the gloriously iridescent, rustling vortex. Yes, I must admit it. Doodle could beat me lying.

Doodle and I spent lots of time thinking about our future. We decided that when we were grown we'd live in Old Woman Swamp and pick dog-tongue for a living. Beside the stream, he planned, we'd build us a house of whispering leaves and the swamp birds would be our chickens. All day long (when we weren't gathering dog-tongue) we'd swing through the cypresses on the rope vines, and if it rained we'd huddle beneath an umbrella tree and play stickfrog. Mama and Daddy could come and live with us if they wanted to. He even came up with the idea that he could marry Mama and I could marry

Daddy. Of course, I was old enough to know this wouldn't work out, but the picture he painted was so beautiful and serene that all I could do was whisper Yes, yes.

Once I had succeeded in teaching Doodle to walk, I began to believe in my own infallibility and I prepared a terrific development program for him, unknown to Mama and Daddy, of course. I would teach him to run, to swim, to climb trees, and to fight. He, too, now believed in my infallibility, so we set the deadline for these accomplishments less than a year away, when, it had been decided, Doodle could start to school.

◆ **Reading Strategy**
The narrator becomes even more determined to help Doodle after his success with walking. Would you have felt the same way? Why or why not?

That winter we didn't make much progress, for I was in school and Doodle suffered from one bad cold after another. But when spring came, rich and warm, we raised our sights again. Success lay at the end of summer like a pot of gold, and our campaign got off to a good start. On hot days, Doodle and I went down to Horsehead Landing and I gave him swimming lessons or showed him how to row a boat. Sometimes we descended into the cool greenness of Old Woman Swamp and climbed the rope vines or boxed scientifically beneath the pine where he had learned to walk. Promise hung about us like the leaves, and wherever we looked, ferns unfurled and birds broke into song.

That summer, the summer of 1918, was blighted. In May and June there was no rain

◆ **Build Vocabulary**

imminent (im′ ə nent) adj.: Likely to happen soon

iridescent (ir′ ə des′ ənt) adj.: Having shifting, rainbowlike colors

vortex (vôr′ teks) n.: Center of a situation, which draws in all that surrounds it

infallibility (in fal′ ə bil′ ə tē) n.: Condition of being unable to fail

Scarlet Ibis, John James Audubon, New-York Historical Society

▲ Critical Viewing Like its relative—the sacred ibis of Egypt—the scarlet ibis lives in swampy areas and uses its long bill to probe in mud and shallow water for food. How would you react if this exotic bird showed up in *your* back yard? [Relate]

uniformly so that the tassels touched the ground. Doodle and I followed Daddy out into the cotton field, where he stood, shoulders sagging, surveying the ruin. When his chin sank down onto his chest, we were frightened, and Doodle slipped his hand into mine. Suddenly Daddy straightened his shoulders, raised a giant knuckly fist, and with a voice that seemed to rumble out of the earth itself began cursing heaven, hell, the weather, and the Republican Party. Doodle and I, prodding each other and giggling, went back to the house, knowing that everything would be all right.

And during that summer, strange names were heard through the house: Chateau Thierry, Amiens, Soissons, and in her blessing at the supper table, Mama once said, "And bless the Pearsons, whose boy Joe was lost at Belleau Wood."[5]

So we came to that clove of seasons. School was only a few weeks away, and Doodle was far behind schedule. He could barely clear the ground when climbing up the rope vines and his swimming was certainly not passable. We decided to double our efforts, to make that last drive and reach our pot of gold. I made him swim until he turned blue and row until he couldn't lift an oar. Wherever we went, I purposely walked fast, and although he kept up, his face turned red and his eyes became glazed. Once, he could go no further, so he collapsed on the ground and began to cry.

"Aw, come on, Doodle," I urged. "You can do it. Do you want to be different from everybody else when you start school?"

◆ Literary Focus
What more do you learn about the narrator through his words and actions toward Doodle?

and the crops withered, curled up, then died under the thirsty sun. One morning in July a hurricane came out of the east, tipping over the oaks in the yard and splitting the limbs of the elm trees. That afternoon it roared back out of the west, blew the fallen oaks around, snapping their roots and tearing them out of the earth like a hawk at the <u>entrails</u> of a chicken. Cotton bolls were wrenched from the stalks and lay like green walnuts in the valleys between the rows, while the cornfield leaned over

5. **Château Thierry:** (sha to tye re'), **Amiens** (a myan'), **Soissons** (swä sôn'), . . . **Belleau** (belo') **Wood:** Places in France where battles were fought during World War I.

"Does it make any difference?"

"It certainly does," I said. "Now, come on," and I helped him up.

As we slipped through dog days, Doodle began to look feverish, and Mama felt his forehead, asking him if he felt ill. At night he didn't sleep well, and sometimes he had nightmares, crying out until I touched him and said, "Wake up, Doodle. Wake up."

It was Saturday noon, just a few days before school was to start. I should have already admitted defeat, but my pride wouldn't let me. The excitement of our program had now been gone for weeks, but still we kept on with a tired doggedness. It was too late to turn back, for we had both wandered too far into a net of expectations and had left no crumbs behind.

Daddy, Mama, Doodle, and I were seated at the dining-room table having lunch. It was a hot day, with all the windows and doors open in case a breeze should come. In the kitchen Aunt Nicey was humming softly. After a long silence, Daddy spoke. "It's so calm, I wouldn't be surprised if we had a storm this afternoon."

"I haven't heard a rain frog," said Mama, who believed in signs, as she served the bread around the table.

"I did," declared Doodle. "Down in the swamp."

"He didn't," I said contrarily.

"You did, eh?" said Daddy, ignoring my denial.

"I certainly did," Doodle reiterated, scowling at me over the top of his iced-tea glass, and we were quiet again.

Suddenly, from out in the yard, came a strange croaking noise. Doodle stopped eating, with a piece of bread poised ready for his mouth, his eyes popped round like two blue buttons. "What's that?" he whispered.

I jumped up, knocking over my chair, and had reached the door when Mama called, "Pick up the chair, sit down again, and say excuse me."

By the time I had done this, Doodle had excused himself and had slipped out into the yard. He was looking up into the bleeding tree. "It's a great big red bird!" he called.

The bird croaked loudly again, and Mama and Daddy came out into the yard. We shaded our eyes with our hands against the hazy glare of the sun and peered up through the still leaves. On the topmost branch a bird the size of a chicken, with scarlet feathers and long legs, was perched <u>precariously</u>. Its wings hung down loosely, and as we watched, a feather dropped away and floated slowly down through the green leaves.

"It's not even frightened of us," Mama said.

"It looks tired," Daddy added. "Or maybe sick."

Doodle's hands were clasped at his throat, and I had never seen him stand still so long. "What is it?" he asked.

Daddy shook his head. "I don't know, maybe it's—"

At that moment the bird began to flutter, but the wings were uncoordinated, and amid much flapping and a spray of flying feathers, it tumbled down, bumping through the limbs of the bleeding tree and landing at our feet with a thud. Its long, graceful neck jerked twice into an S, then straightened out, and the bird was still. A white veil came over the eyes and the long white beak unhinged. Its legs were crossed and its clawlike feet were delicately curved at rest. Even death did not mar its grace, for it lay on the earth like a broken vase of red flowers, and we stood around it, awed by its exotic beauty.

"It's dead," Mama said.

"What is it?" Doodle repeated.

"Go bring me the bird book," said Daddy.

I ran into the house and brought back the bird book. As we watched, Daddy thumbed through its pages. "It's a scarlet ibis," he said, pointing to a picture. "It lives in the tropics—South America to Florida. A storm must have brought it here."

♦ **Build Vocabulary**

entrails (en′ trālz) *n.*: Internal organs, specifically intestines

precariously (prē ker′ ē əs lē) *adv.*: Insecurely

Sadly, we all looked back at the bird. A scarlet ibis! How many miles it had traveled to die like this, in *our* yard, beneath the bleeding tree.

"Let's finish lunch," Mama said, nudging us back toward the dining room.

"I'm not hungry," said Doodle, and he knelt down beside the ibis.

"We've got peach cobbler for dessert," Mama tempted from the doorway.

Doodle remained kneeling. "I'm going to bury him."

"Don't you dare touch him," Mama warned. "There's no telling what disease he might have had."

"All right," said Doodle. "I won't."

Daddy, Mama, and I went back to the dining-room table, but we watched Doodle through the open door. He took out a piece of string from his pocket and, without touching the ibis, looped one end around its neck. Slowly, while singing softly "Shall We Gather at the River," he carried the bird around to the front yard and dug a hole in the flower garden, next to the petunia bed. Now we were watching him through the front window, but he didn't know it. His awkwardness at digging the hole with a shovel whose handle was twice as long as he was made us laugh, and we covered our mouths with our hands so he wouldn't hear.

◆ **Reading Strategy**
With whose response toward the ibis do you most strongly identify? Why?

When Doodle came into the dining room, he found us seriously eating our cobbler. He was pale and lingered just inside the screen door. "Did you get the scarlet ibis buried?" asked Daddy.

Doodle didn't speak but nodded his head.

"Go wash your hands, and then you can have some peach cobbler," said Mama.

"I'm not hungry," he said.

"Dead birds is bad luck," said Aunt Nicey, poking her head from the kitchen door. "Specially *red* dead birds!"

As soon as I had finished eating, Doodle and I hurried off to Horsehead Landing. Time was short, and Doodle still had a long way to go if he was going to keep up with the other boys when he started school. The sun, gilded with the yellow cast of autumn, still burned fiercely, but the dark green woods through which we passed were shady and cool. When we reached the landing, Doodle said he was too tired to swim, so we got into a skiff and floated down the creek with the tide. Far off in the marsh a rail was scolding, and over on the beach locusts were singing in the myrtle trees. Doodle did not speak and kept his head turned away, letting one hand trail limply in the water.

After we had drifted a long way, I put the oars in place and made Doodle row back against the tide. Black clouds began to gather in the southwest, and he kept watching them, trying to pull the oars a little faster. When we reached Horsehead Landing, lightning was playing across half the sky and thunder roared out, hiding even the sound of the sea. The sun disappeared and darkness descended, almost like night. Flocks of marsh crows flew by, heading inland to their roosting trees, and two egrets, squawking, arose from the oyster-rock shallows and careened away.

Doodle was both tired and frightened, and when he stepped from the skiff he collapsed onto the mud, sending an armada of fiddler crabs rustling off into the marsh grass. I helped him up, and as he wiped the mud off his trousers, he smiled at me ashamedly. He had failed and we both knew it, so we started back home, racing the storm. We never spoke (What are the words that can solder cracked pride?), but I knew he was watching me, watching for a sign of mercy. The lightning was near now, and from fear he walked so close behind me he kept stepping on my heels. The faster I walked, the faster he walked, so I began to run. The rain was coming, roaring through the pines, and then, like a bursting Roman candle, a gum tree ahead of us was shattered by a bolt of lightning. When the deafening peal of thunder had

died, and in the moment before the rain arrived, I heard Doodle, who had fallen behind,
cry out, "Brother, Brother, don't leave me!
Don't leave me!"

The knowledge that Doodle's and my plans
had come to naught was bitter, and that streak
of cruelty within me awakened. I ran as fast as
I could, leaving him far behind with a wall of
rain dividing us. The drops stung my face like
nettles, and the wind flared the wet glistening
leaves of the bordering trees. Soon I could hear
his voice no more.

I hadn't run too far before I became tired,
and the flood of childish spite evanesced as
well. I stopped and waited for Doodle. The
sound of rain was everywhere, but the wind
had died and it fell straight down in parallel
paths like ropes hanging from the sky. As I
waited, I peered through the downpour, but no
one came. Finally I went back and found him
huddled beneath a red nightshade bush beside
the road. He was sitting on the ground, his face
buried in his arms, which were resting on his
drawn-up knees. "Let's go, Doodle," I said.

He didn't answer, so I placed my hand on his
forehead and lifted his head. Limply, he fell
backwards onto the earth. He had been bleeding from the mouth, and his neck and the front
of his shirt were stained a brilliant red.

"Doodle! Doodle!" I cried, shaking him, but
there was no answer but the ropy rain. He lay
very awkwardly, with his head thrown far back,
making his vermilion neck appear unusually
long and slim. His little legs, bent sharply at
the knees, had never before seemed so fragile,
so thin.

I began to weep, and the tear-blurred vision
in red before me looked very familiar. "Doodle!"
I screamed above the pounding storm and
threw my body to the earth above his. For a
long long time, it seemed forever, I lay there
crying, sheltering my fallen scarlet ibis from
the heresy[6] of rain.

---

6. **heresy** (her′ e se): Idea opposed to the beliefs of a
religion or philosophy.

Guide for Responding

◆ Literature and Your Life

Reader's Response How did the end of the
story make you feel? Why?

Thematic Focus How else might the narrator
have resolved his conflicting feelings about Doodle?

☑ Check Your Comprehension

1. How does Doodle disappoint his brother?
2. What motivates the narrator to teach Doodle to walk?
3. What other plans does he make for Doodle?
4. Summarize the circumstances leading to
   Doodle's death.

Beyond Literature

Science Connection

Sea Birds The scarlet ibis is only one of a
myriad of types of sea birds found in North
America. Birds of the Pacific coast include the
black oystercatcher and the western gull.
Birds of the Atlantic coast include the
American oystercatcher and the common
tern. In winter, the southern coasts are home
to certain varieties of ducks, geese, and other
birds that nest in the Arctic during the summer. Some birds, such as the great blue heron,
usually live in inland waters but sometimes
nest near the ocean in order to hunt for fish
along the coasts. What birds live in your area?
Do any of them live near water?

◆ Build Vocabulary

evanesced (ev ə nest′) v.: Faded away

Guide for Responding (continued)

◆ Critical Thinking

INTERPRET

1. (a) What is Doodle's attitude toward his brother? (b) How would you describe the narrator's attitude toward Doodle? **[Analyze]**
2. Why does the narrator set such demanding goals for Doodle? **[Infer]**
3. In what ways does Doodle show that he has his own unique personality? **[Support]**
4. How is Doodle like the scarlet ibis? **[Compare]**
5. How does the appearance of the scarlet ibis hint at the outcome of the story? **[Analyze]**

EVALUATE

6. Do you think that the narrator is to blame for Doodle's death? Why or why not? **[Make a Judgment]**

APPLY

7. The story opens with the narrator, now an adult, remembering events from long ago. How does the passage of time change people and their feelings about past events? **[Apply]**

◆ Reading Strategy

IDENTIFY WITH A CHARACTER

To fully appreciate the narrator's experiences, try to put yourself in his place and think about what you would have done and how you would have felt.
1. If you were in the narrator's place, how do you think you might have treated Doodle? Why?
2. What can you learn from the narrator's experiences that you can apply to your relationships?

◆ Literary Focus

POINT OF VIEW

Point of view is the vantage point from which a story is told. This story is told from a first-person point of view—the narrator is one of the characters.
1. How does Hurst's use of the first-person point of view make you feel like part of the story?
2. What is the effect of having the narrator look back at the events years after they happened?
3. How might the story be different if it were told from the mother's or the father's point of view?

◆ Build Vocabulary

USING IRREGULAR PLURALS

Remembering that some words become plural by changing -x to -ces, change the following words from singular to plural. Use a dictionary to help you.
1. index   2. appendix   3. apex   4. matrix

USING THE WORD BANK

On your paper, write the word from the Word Bank that best completes each sentence.
1. Several of Liam's friends were swept into the _____?_____ of his tragedy.
2. We admired the _____?_____ skin of the trout.
3. We credited Ms. Chang, who never seemed to make a mistake, with _____?_____.
4. The headlights revealed the _____?_____ of a dead animal on the highway.
5. Our memories of the house _____?_____ over time.
6. The darkening sky told us that a storm was _____?_____.

◆ Build Grammar Skills

INFINITIVES AND INFINITIVE PHRASES

An **infinitive** is the form of the verb that comes after the word *to* and acts as a noun, adjective, or adverb. An infinitive that appears with modifiers, a complement, or a subject is called an **infinitive phrase.** When you write, be careful not to create a split infinitive, which results when you insert an adverb between the word *to* and the verb.

Incorrect: He began *to rapidly break away from the pack.*

Correct: He rapidly began *to break away from the pack.*

Practice Identify the infinitives and infinitive phrases in each item and tell how they function.
1. He began to try to move himself.
2. Doodle wanted to follow his brother everywhere.
3. Doodle still had a long way to go if he was going to keep up with his older brother.

Writing Application In your notebook, rewrite the following sentences to eliminate split infinitives.
1. I began to affectionately call him Doodle.
2. His hands began to steadily stroke the grass.
3. People thought he was going to soon die.

Build Your Portfolio

 ## Idea Bank

Writing

1. **Journal Entry** Put yourself in the place of the narrator. How would you have felt on the night of Doodle's death? Write a journal entry describing your feelings about your brother's death.

2. **Essay About a Symbol** Write a brief essay explaining how the scarlet ibis serves as the story's central symbol. (A symbol is an object, person, or idea that has an underlying meaning.) Support your ideas with details from the story.

3. **Analysis of the Theme** In a brief paper, analyze the story's theme. Tell the lessons the story teaches that readers can apply to their lives. Use details from the story for support.

Speaking and Listening

4. **Eulogy** Prepare and deliver a eulogy—a speech in honor of someone who has died—that the narrator might have presented at Doodle's funeral. **[Performing Arts Link]**

5. **Skit** Imagine that the narrator didn't tell his mother about the actual events of Doodle's death until years later. With a partner, act out the conversation that could have taken place when the narrator made this revelation.

Projects

6. **Travel Brochure** The story's setting—coastal North Carolina—is an area of striking natural beauty. Gather information, along with maps and photographs, of the region. Use the materials you gather to create a travel brochure to attract tourists. **[Career Link]**

7. **Map** Create a map of the story's setting. Base your map on the details Hurst provides. Label the spots where key events in the story take place.

 ## Writing Mini-Lesson

Character Sketch

Create a character sketch of the narrator or his brother, Doodle, based on what you learn from the story. In your sketch, present the key personality traits of the character you chose. Use the following tips to help you present each personality trait.

Writing Skills Focus: Elaborate by Providing Details

As you develop your character sketch, elaborate on your main points by providing details to support each point and further explanations to deepen the reader's understanding. For example, rather than just saying that Doodle was physically challenged, explain the physical limitations he had. Where possible, quote brief passages from the story that point out these limitations. In addition, extend the reader's understanding of Doodle's physical limitations by pointing out how they affected his personality.

Prewriting Choose which character you will focus on and review the story to gather details about that character. Based on his actions in the story, try to draw as many conclusions as you can about his personality. Take notes on the main points you want to make about your character.

Drafting Begin with an introduction that makes a few generalizations about the character. Then elaborate on each generalization in a paragraph in which you cite details and events from the story for support.

Revising Look over your character sketch to make sure that you have provided enough information to support and explain each of the generalizations you made. If necessary, further elaborate on one or more of the character's traits.

Guide for Reading

Toni Cade Bambara
(1939–1995)

This writer's interest in her African American heritage comes through clearly in her writing, which often centers on the emerging identity of the black woman. She has said, "I write because I really think I've got hold of something, that if I share it, might save somebody else some time, might lift someone's spirits, or might enable someone to see more clearly." Bambara's cultural identity is even evident in her name. She adopted the name Bambara after finding the word on a sketchbook of her great-grandmother's. It is the name of an African tribe known for its textiles.

Bambara wrote two collections of short stories—*Gorilla, My Love*, where "Blues Ain't No Mockin Bird" first appeared, and *The Sea Birds Are Still Alive*—as well as a novel, *The Salt Eaters*.

Isabel Allende *(1942–)*

Recalling her early years, Isabel Allende has said, "I had a very lonely life when I was a child but very interesting—only adults around me . . . a very extravagant family." Allende grew up in Chile, where she lived with her grandparents. Her uncle was the former Chilean president Salvador Allende. In 1973, Salvador Allende's government was overthrown by General Augusto Pinochet—a ruthless dictator whose brutality toward his people attracted worldwide attention and led to his removal from power. Isabel Allende fled to Venezuela, where she lived in exile for a time before moving to California.

Allende's first novel, *The House of the Spirits,* was inspired by her extravagant family. Two of its main characters, Esteban and Clara, are based on her grandparents. Allende's other books include *Of Love and Shadows, Eva Luna, The Stories of Eva Luna, The Infinite Plan,* and *Paula.*

◆ Build Vocabulary

PREFIXES: *dis-*

Some words in these stories begin with the prefix *dis-*, which means "opposite." Knowing this, you can figure out the meaning of *dishonest, disappear, discover,* and other words with this prefix.

WORD BANK

lassoed
formality
pallid
vanquished
fetid
impassive
disconsolately
unrequited

As you read these stories, you will encounter the words on this list. Each word is defined on the page where it first appears. Preview the list before you read.

◆ Build Grammar Skills

POSSESSIVE NOUNS

In these stories, you will see many **possessive nouns**—nouns that show ownership, belonging, or another close relationship. The chart shows how to form possessive nouns.

Rules for Possessive Forms of Nouns	Examples
To form the possessive of singular nouns, add an apostrophe and s.	• our neighbor's yard • a pirate's mustache
To form the possessive of plural nouns that end in s, just add an apostrophe.	• the twins' bicycle • the folks' bed
To form the possessive of plural nouns that do not end in s, add an apostrophe and s.	• people's groceries

Blues Ain't No Mockin Bird
◆ Uncle Marcos ◆

◆ *Literature and Your Life*

CONNECT YOUR EXPERIENCE

Certain people from our childhoods become etched in our memories forever. It may be because of their unique personality traits or the lessons they taught us. In these stories, you'll meet two memorable characters who have left an indelible impression on the stories' narrators.

Journal Writing Write a brief description of a memorable person from your childhood.

THEMATIC FOCUS: APPRECIATING OTHERS

The narrators of these stories show great admiration for the characters they portray. Others in the stories do not share this attitude. Why do people have different perspectives toward others?

◆ Background for Understanding

LANGUAGE

"Blues Ain't No Mockin Bird" is written in dialect—a way of speaking that is common to people in a particular region or group. Dialect affects pronunciation, word choice, and sentence structure. You'll notice, for example, that the characters in Bambara's story don't pronounce the *g* on the ends of *-ing* words. Bambara's use of dialect makes her story sound informal and intimate, as if it were being related orally.

LITERATURE

Imagine a world in which people can rise up and float in the air, it can rain continuously for years, and a person can be born with the tail of a pig. These fantastic details capture how a group of writers—mostly from Latin America—stretch the boundaries of reality in their works. The authors, who include Isabel Allende, practice a style of writing known as "magical realism," in which fantastic details are blended with realistic ones to stretch the boundaries of readers' imaginations.

◆ Literary Focus

DIRECT AND INDIRECT CHARACTERIZATION

If you say that your friend is loyal, you're using **direct characterization.** If you tell a story that demonstrates your friend's loyalty without stating it directly, you're using **indirect characterization.** Allende and Bambara don't just say their characters are interesting or eccentric; they show you through the characters' own words and actions and through the way other characters respond to them.

◆ Reading Strategy

MAKE INFERENCES ABOUT CHARACTERS

In "Blues Ain't No Mockin Bird," Granny and Granddaddy Cain have a confrontation with photographers who are filming a documentary. When one photographer asks, "Mind if we shoot a bit around here?" Granny replies, "I do indeed." Based on what she says, you can **make an inference**—a reasonable conclusion based on the details the author provides—that she values her privacy and that she will not be pushed around.

In "Uncle Marcos," Clara remembers the time her uncle serenaded a woman with a barrel organ, accompanied by a parrot. From this, you can infer that Uncle Marcos is romantic and unpredictable.

When you read, look deeper than the actual words on the page and ask yourself what the author is implying about the characters as he or she describes their words and actions.

Blues Ain't No Mockin Bird

Toni Cade Bambara

Sharecropper, Elizabeth Catlett, Courtesy Evan Tibbs Collection

The puddle had frozen over, and me and Cathy went stompin in it. The twins from next door, Tyrone and Terry, were swingin so high out of sight we forgot we were waitin our turn on the tire. Cathy jumped up and came down hard on her heels and started tap-dancin. And the frozen patch splinterin every which way underneath kinda spooky. "Looks like a plastic spider web," she said. "A sort of weird spider, I guess, with many mental problems." But really it looked like the crystal paperweight Granny kept in the parlor. She was on the back porch, Granny was, making the cakes drunk. The old ladle dripping rum into the Christmas tins, like it used to drip maple syrup into the pails when we lived in the Judson's woods, like it poured cider into the vats when we were on the Cooper place, like it used to scoop butter-milk and soft cheese when we lived at the dairy.

"Go tell that man we ain't a bunch of trees."

"Ma'am?"

"I said to tell that man to get away from here with that camera." Me and Cathy look over toward the meadow where the men with the station wagon'd been roamin around all mornin. The tall man with a huge camera <u>lassoed</u> to his shoul-der was buzzin our way.

"They're makin movie pictures," yelled Tyrone, stiffenin his legs and twistin so

the tire'd come down slow so they could see.

"They're makin movie pictures," sang out Terry.

"That boy don't never have anything original to say," say Cathy grown-up.

By the time the man with the camera had cut across our neighbor's yard, the twins were out of the trees swingin low and Granny was onto the steps, the screen door bammin soft and scratchy against her palms. "We thought we'd get a shot or two of the house and everything and then—"

"Good mornin," Granny cut him off. And smiled that smile.

"Good mornin," he said, head all down the way Bingo does when you yell at him about the bones on the kitchen floor. "Nice place you got here, aunty. We thought we'd take a—"

"Did you?" said Granny with her eye-brows. Cathy pulled up her socks and giggled.

"Nice things here," said the man, buzzin his camera over the yard. The pecan barrels, the sled, me and Cathy, the flowers, the printed stones along the driveway, the trees, the twins, the tool-shed.

"I don't know about the thing, the it, and the stuff," said Granny, still talkin with her eyebrows. "Just people here is what I tend to consider."

Camera man stopped buzzin. Cathy giggled into her collar.

◀ **Critical Viewing** As you read, compare Granny with the woman in the illustration. [**Compare and Contrast**]

◆ **Build Vocabulary**

lassoed (las´ ōd) *adj.*: Wrapped around

"Mornin, ladies," a new man said. He had come up behind us when we weren't lookin. "And gents," discoverin the twins givin him a nasty look. "We're filmin for the county," he said with a smile. "Mind if we shoot a bit around here?"

"I do indeed," said Granny with no smile. Smilin man was smiling up a storm. So was Cathy. But he didn't seem to have another word to say, so he and the camera man backed on out the yard, but you could hear the camera buzzin still. "Suppose you just shut that machine off," said Granny real low through her teeth, and took a step down off the porch and then another.

"Now, aunty," Camera said, pointin the thing straight at her.

"Your mama and I are not related."

Smilin man got his notebook out and a chewed-up pencil.

"Listen," he said movin back into our yard, "we'd like to have a statement from you . . . for the film. We're filmin for the county, see. Part of the food stamp campaign. You know about the food stamps?"

Granny said nuthin.

"Maybe there's somethin you want to say for the film. I see you grow your own vegetables," he smiled real nice. "If more folks did that, see, there'd be no need—"

Granny wasn't sayin nuthin. So they backed on out, buzzin at our clothesline and the twins' bicycles, then back on down to the meadow. The twins were danglin in the tire, lookin at Granny. Me and Cathy were waitin, too, cause Granny always got somethin to say. She teaches steady with no let-up. "I was on this bridge one time," she started off. "Was a crowd cause this man was goin to jump, you understand. And a minister was there and the police and some other folks. His woman was there, too."

◆ **Literary Focus**

How does Bambara use indirect characterization to tell you how Granny feels about having the photographers on her property?

"What was they doin?" asked Tyrone.

"Tryin to talk him out of it was what they was doin. The minister talkin about how it was a mortal sin, suicide. His woman takin bites out of her own hand and not even knowin it, so nervous and cryin and talkin fast."

"So what happened?" asked Tyrone.

"So here comes . . . this person . . . with a camera, takin pictures of the man and the minister and the woman. Takin pictures of the man in his misery about to jump, cause life so bad and people been messin with him so bad. This person takin up the whole roll of film practically. But savin a few, of course."

"Of course," said Cathy, hatin the person. Me standin there wonderin how Cathy knew it was "of course" when I didn't and it was *my* grandmother.

After a while Tyrone say, "Did he jump?"

"Yeh, did he jump?" say Terry all eager. And Granny just stared at the twins till their faces swallow up the eager and they don't even care any more about the man jumpin. Then she goes back onto the porch and lets the screen door go for itself. I'm lookin to Cathy to finish the story cause she knows Granny's whole story before me even. Like she knew how come we move so much and Cathy ain't but a third cousin we picked up on the way last Thanksgivin visitin. But she knew it was on account of people drivin Granny crazy till she'd get up in the night and start packin. Mumblin and packin and wakin everybody up sayin, "Let's get on away from here before I kill me somebody." Like people wouldn't pay her for things like they said they would. Or Mr. Judson bringin us boxes of old clothes and raggedy magazines. Or Mrs. Cooper comin in our kitchen and touchin everything and sayin how clean it all was. Granny goin crazy, and Granddaddy Cain pullin her off the people, sayin, "Now, now, Cora." But next day loadin up the truck, with rocks all in his jaw, madder than Granny in the first place.

"I read a story once," said Cathy soundin like Granny teacher. "About this lady Goldilocks who barged into a house that wasn't even hers. And not invited, you understand. Messed over the people's groceries and broke up the people's furniture. Had the nerve to sleep in the folks' bed."

"Then what happened?" asked Tyrone. "What they do, the folks, when they come in to all this mess?"

"Did they make her pay for it?" asked Terry, makin a fist. "I'd've made her pay me."

I didn't even ask. I could see Cathy actress was very likely to just walk away and leave us in mystery about this story which I heard was about some bears.

"Did they throw her out?" asked Tyrone, like his father sounds when he's bein extra nasty-plus to the washin-machine man.

"Woulda," said Terry. "I woulda gone upside her head with my fist and—"

"You woulda done whatcha always do—go cry to Mama, you big baby," said Tyrone. So naturally Terry starts hittin on Tyrone, and next thing you know they tumblin out the tire and rollin on the ground. But Granny didn't say a thing or send the twins home or step out on the steps to tell us about how we can't afford to be fightin amongst ourselves. She didn't say nuthin. So I get into the tire to take my turn. And I could see her leanin up against the pantry table, staring at the cakes she was puttin up for the Christmas sale, mumblin real low and grumpy and holdin her forehead like it wanted to fall off and mess up the rum cakes.

Behind me I hear before I can see Grand daddy Cain comin through the woods in his field boots. Then I twist around to see the shiny black oilskin cuttin through what little left there was of yellows, reds, and oranges. His great white head not quite round cause of this bloody thing high on his shoulder, like he was wearin a cap on sideways. He takes the shortcut through the pecan grove, and the sound of twigs snapping overhead and underfoot travels clear and cold all the way up to us. And here comes Smilin and Camera up behind him like they was goin to do somethin. Folks like to go for him sometimes. Cathy say it's because he's so tall and quiet and like a king. And people just can't stand it. But Smilin and Camera don't hit him in the head or nuthin. They just buzz on him as he stalks by with the chicken hawk slung over his shoulder, squawkin, drippin red down the back of the oilskin. He passes the porch and stops a second for Granny to see he's caught the hawk at last, but she's just starin and mumblin, and not at the hawk. So he nails the bird to the toolshed door, the hammerin crackin through the eardrums. And the bird flappin himself to death and droolin down the door to paint the gravel in the driveway red, then brown, then black. And the two men movin up on tiptoe like they was invisible or we were blind, one.

"Get them persons out of my flower bed, Mister Cain," say Granny moanin real low like at a funeral.

"How come your grandmother calls her husband 'Mister Cain' all the time?" Tyrone whispers all loud and noisy and from the city and don't know no better. Like his mama, Miss Myrtle, tell us never mind the formality as if we had no better breeding than to call her Myrtle, plain. And then this awful thing—a giant hawk—come wailin up over the meadow, flyin low and tilted and screamin, zigzaggin through the pecan grove, breakin branches and hollerin, snappin past the clothesline, flyin every which way, flyin into things reckless with crazy.

◆ **Build Vocabulary**

formality (fôr mal′ ə tē) *n.*: Established rules or customs

"He's come to claim his mate," say Cathy fast, and ducks down. We all fall quick and flat into the gravel driveway, stones scrapin my face. I squinch my eyes open again at the hawk on the door, tryin to fly up out of her death like it was just a sack flown into by mistake. Her body holdin her there on that nail, though. The mate beatin the air overhead and clutchin for hair, for heads, for landin space.

The camera man duckin and bendin and runnin and fallin, jigglin the camera and scared. And Smilin jumpin up and down swipin at the huge bird, tryin to bring the hawk down with just his raggedy ole cap. Granddaddy Cain straight up and silent, watchin the circles of the hawk, then aimin the hammer off his wrist. The giant bird fallin, silent and slow. Then here comes Camera and Smilin all big and bad now that the awful screechin thing is on its back and broken, here they come. And Granddaddy Cain looks up at them like it was the first time noticin, but not payin them too much mind cause he's listenin, we all listenin, to that low groanin music comin from the porch. And we figure any minute, somethin in my back tells me any minute now, Granny gonna bust through that screen with somethin in her hand and murder on her mind. So Granddaddy say above the buzzin, but quiet, "Good day, gentlemen." Just like that. Like he'd invited them in to play cards and they'd stayed too long and all the sandwiches were gone and Reverend Webb was droppin by and it was time to go.

They didn't know what to do. But like Cathy say, folks can't stand Granddaddy tall and silent and like a king. They can't neither. The smile the men smilin is pullin the mouth back and showin the teeth. Lookin like the wolf man, both of them. Then Granddaddy holds his hand out—this huge hand I used to sit in when I was a baby and he'd carry me through the house to my mother like I was a gift

on a tray. Like he used to on the trains. They called the other men just waiters. But they spoke of Granddaddy separate and said, The Waiter. And said he had engines in his feet and motors in his hands and couldn't no train throw him off and couldn't nobody turn him round. They were big enough for motors, his hands were. He held that one hand out all still and it gettin to be not at all a hand but a person in itself.

"He wants you to hand him the camera," Smilin whispers to Camera, tiltin his head to talk secret like they was in the jungle or somethin and come upon a native that don't speak the language. The men start untyin the straps, and they put the camera into that great hand speckled with the hawk's blood all black and crackly now. And the hand don't even drop with the weight, just the fingers move, curl up around the machine. But Granddaddy lookin straight at the men. They lookin at each other and everywhere but at Granddaddy's face.

"We filmin for the county, see," say Smilin. "We puttin together a movie for the food stamp program . . . filmin all around these parts. Uhh, filmin for the county."

"Can I have my camera back?" say the tall man with no machine on his shoulder, but still keepin it high like the camera was still there or needed to be. "Please, sir."

Then Granddaddy's other hand flies up like a sudden and gentle bird, slaps down fast on top of the camera and lifts off half like it was a calabash[1] cut for sharing.

"Hey," Camera jumps forward. He gathers up the parts into his chest and everything unrollin and fallin all over. "Whatcha tryin to do? You'll ruin the film." He looks down into his chest of metal reels and things like he's protectin a kitten from the cold.

---

1. **calabash** (kal´ ə bash) *n.*: Large gourdlike fruit.

"You standin in the misses' flower bed," say Granddaddy. "This is our own place."

The two men look at him, then at each other, then back at the mess in the camera man's chest, and they just back off. One sayin over and over all the way down to the meadow, "Watch it, Bruno. Keep ya fingers off the film." Then Granddaddy picks up the hammer and jams it into the oilskin pocket, scrapes his boots, and goes into the house. And you can hear the squish of his boots headin through the house. And you can see the funny shadow

◆ Reading Strategy
What do you think is going through the men's minds as they back off?

he throws from the parlor window onto the ground by the string-bean patch. The hammer draggin the pocket of the oilskin out so Granddaddy looked even wider. Granny was hummin now—high not low and grumbly. And she was doin the cakes again, you could smell the molasses from the rum.

"There's this story I'm goin to write one day," say Cathy dreamer. "About the proper use of the hammer."

"Can I be in it?" Tyrone say with his hand up like it was a matter of first come, first served.

"Perhaps," say Cathy, climbin onto the tire to pump us up. "If you there and ready."

Guide for Responding

◆ Literature and Your Life

Reader's Response What character from the story would you most like to meet? Why?

Thematic Focus If you were a character in the story, how would your perspective of the filmmakers compare with Granny's?

Journal Entry In your journal, jot down whether or not you think that the filmmakers had the right to film the Cains. Support your opinion.

☑ Check Your Comprehension

1. Why are the photographers filming in the area?
2. How does Granny react toward the pair of photographers?
3. What story does Cathy tell?
4. What does Granny ask Granddaddy to do?
5. Describe Granddaddy's behavior toward the photographers.

◆ Critical Thinking

INTERPRET
1. What is the cameraman's attitude toward the Cain family? **[Infer]**
2. (a) What is the main point of Granny's story about the man who attempted suicide? (b) How does the story help explain Granny's behavior? **[Draw Conclusion]**
3. (a) What does the killing of the hawk's mate reveal about Granddaddy? (b) How does Granddaddy's action prepare you for what he does later in the story? **[Analyze]**
4. How do the two hawks resemble Granny and Granddaddy?
5. What do you think is the story's theme, or central message? Support your answer. **[Infer]**

EVALUATE
6. Is Grandaddy's treatment of the photographers justified? Explain. **[Make a Judgment]**

EXTEND
7. If you were to pursue a career as a reporter or photographer, what could you learn from this story that you could apply to your work? **[Career Link]**

Uncle Marcos

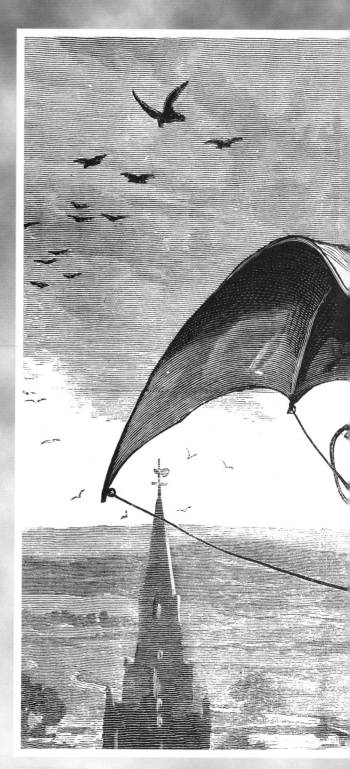

. . . It had been two years since Clara had last seen her Uncle Marcos, but she remembered him very well. His was the only perfectly clear image she retained from her whole childhood, and in order to describe him she did not need to consult the daguerreotype[1] in the drawing room that showed him dressed as an explorer leaning on an old-fashioned double-barreled rifle with his right foot on the neck of a Malaysian tiger, the same triumphant position in which she had seen the Virgin standing between plaster clouds and <u>pallid</u> angels at the main altar, one foot on the <u>vanquished</u> devil. All Clara had to do to see her uncle was close her eyes and there he was, weather-beaten and thin, with a pirate's mustache through which his strange, sharklike smile peered out at her. It seemed impossible that he could be inside that long black box that was lying in the middle of the courtyard.

---

1. **daguerreotype** (də ger´ ō tīp´) *n.*: Early type of photograph.

◆ **Build Vocabulary**

pallid (pal´ id) *adj.*: Pale

vanquished (vaŋ´ kwisht) *adj.*: Defeated

▶ Critical Viewing In this story, a man tries to build a flying machine. What character traits might you find in someone who attempts such a feat? [Speculate]

from
The House of the Spirits
Isabel Allende

Each time Uncle Marcos had visited his sister Nivea's home, he had stayed for several months, to the immense joy of his nieces and nephews, particularly Clara, causing a storm in which the sharp lines of domestic order blurred. The house became a clutter of trunks, of animals in jars of formaldehyde,[2] of Indian lances and sailor's bundles. In every part of the house people kept tripping over his equipment, and all sorts of unfamiliar animals appeared that had traveled from remote lands only to meet their death beneath Nana's irate broom in the farthest corners of the house. Uncle Marcos's manners were those of a cannibal, as Severo put it. He spent the whole night making incomprehensible movements in the drawing room; later they turned out to be exercises designed to perfect the mind's control over the body and to improve digestion. He performed alchemy[3] experiments in the kitchen, filling the house with <u>fetid</u> smoke and ruining pots and pans with solid substances that stuck to their bottoms and were impossible to remove. While the rest of the household tried to sleep, he dragged his suitcases up and down the halls, practiced making strange, high-pitched sounds on savage instruments, and taught Spanish to a parrot whose native language was an Amazonic dialect. During the day, he slept in a hammock that he had strung between two columns in the hall, wearing only a loincloth that put Severo in a terrible mood but that Nivea forgave because Marcos had convinced her that it was the same costume in which Jesus of Nazareth had preached. Clara remembered perfectly, even though she had been only a tiny child, the first time her Uncle Marcos came to the house after one of his voyages. He settled in as if he planned to stay forever. After a short time, bored with having to appear at ladies' gatherings where the mistress of the house played the piano, with playing cards, and with dodging all his relatives' pressures to pull himself together and take a job as a clerk in Severo del Valle's law practice, he bought a barrel organ and took to the streets with the hope of seducing his Cousin Antonieta and entertaining the public in the bargain. The machine was just a rusty box with wheels, but he painted it with seafaring designs and gave it a fake ship's smokestack. It ended up looking like a coal stove. The organ played either a military march or a waltz, and in between turns of the handle the parrot, who had managed to learn Spanish although he had not lost his foreign accent, would draw a crowd with his piercing shrieks. He also plucked slips of paper from a box with his beak, by way of selling fortunes to the curious. The little pink, green, and blue papers were so clever that they always divulged the exact secret wishes of the customers. Besides fortunes there were little balls of sawdust to amuse the children. The idea of the organ was a last desperate attempt to win the hand of Cousin Antonieta after more conventional means of courting her had failed. Marcos thought no woman in her right mind could remain <u>impassive</u> before a barrel-organ serenade. He stood beneath her window one evening and played his military march and his waltz just as she was taking tea with a group of female friends. Antonieta did not realize the music was meant for her until the parrot called her by her full name, at which point she appeared in the window. Her reaction was not what her suitor had hoped for. Her friends offered to spread the news to every salon[4] in the city, and the next day people thronged the downtown streets hoping to see Severo del Valle's brother-in-law playing the organ and selling little sawdust balls with a motheaten parrot, for the sheer pleasure of proving that even in the best of families there could be good reason for embarrassment. In the face of this stain to the family reputation, Marcos was forced to give up organ grinding and resort to less conspicuous ways of winning over

---

4. **salon** (sə län´) *n.*: Regular gathering of distinguished guests that meets in a private home.

---

2. **formaldehyde** (fôr mal´ də hīd´) *n.*: Solution used as a preservative.
3. **alchemy** (al´ kə mē) *adj.*: Early form of chemistry, with philosophic and magical associations.

◆ **Build Vocabulary**

fetid (fet´ id) *adj.*: Rancid; rank; smelly
impassive (im pas´ iv) *adj.*: Showing no emotion

his Cousin Antonieta, but he did not renounce his goal. In any case, he did not succeed, because from one day to the next the young lady married a diplomat who was twenty years her senior; he took her to live in a tropical country whose name no one could recall, except that it suggested negritude,[5] bananas, and palm trees, where she managed to recover from the memory of that suitor who had ruined her seventeenth year with his military march and his waltz. Marcos sank into a deep depression that lasted two or three days, at the end of which he announced that he would never marry and that he was embarking on a trip around the world.

♦ Literary Focus
What does the fact that Uncle Marcos's "deep depression" lasted only a few days tell you about his character?

He sold his organ to a blind man and left the parrot to Clara, but Nana secretly poisoned it with an overdose of cod-liver oil, because no one could stand its lusty glance, its fleas, and its harsh, tuneless hawking of paper fortunes and sawdust balls.

That was Marcos's longest trip. He returned with a shipment of enormous boxes that were piled in the far courtyard, between the chicken coop and the woodshed, until the winter was over. At the first signs of spring he had them transferred to the parade grounds, a huge park where people would gather to watch the soldiers file by on Independence Day, with the goosestep they had learned from the Prussians. When the crates were opened, they were found to contain loose bits of wood, metal, and painted cloth. Marcos spent two weeks assembling the contents according to an instruction manual written in English, which he was able to decipher thanks to his invincible imagination and a small dictionary. When the job was finished, it turned out to be a bird of prehistoric dimensions, with the face of a furious eagle, wings that moved, and a propeller on its back. It caused an uproar. The families of the oligarchy[6] forgot all about the barrel organ, and Marcos became the star attraction of the season. People took Sunday outings to see the bird; souvenir vendors and strolling photographers made a fortune. Nonetheless, the public's interest quickly waned. But then Marcos announced that as soon as the weather cleared he planned to take off in his bird and cross the mountain range. The news spread, making this the most talked-about event of the year. The contraption lay with its stomach on terra firma,[7] heavy and sluggish and looking more like a wounded duck than like one of those newfangled airplanes they were starting to produce in the United States. There was nothing in its appearance to suggest that it could move, much less take flight across the snowy peaks. Journalists and the curious flocked to see it. Marcos smiled his immutable[8] smile before the avalanche of questions and posed for photographers without offering the least technical or scientific explanation of how he hoped to carry out his plan. People came from the provinces to see the sight. Forty years later his greatnephew Nicolás, whom Marcos did not live to see, unearthed the desire to fly that had always existed in the men of his lineage. Nicolás was interested in doing it for commercial reasons, in a gigantic hot-air sausage on which would be printed an advertisement for carbonated drinks. But when Marcos announced his plane trip, no one believed that his contraption could be put to any practical use. The appointed day dawned full of clouds, but so many people had turned out that Marcos did not want to disappoint them. He showed up punctually at the appointed spot and did not once look up at the sky, which was growing darker and darker with thick gray clouds. The astonished crowd filled all the nearby streets, perching on rooftops and the balconies of the nearest houses and squeezing into the park. No political gathering managed to attract so many people until half a century later, when the first Marxist candidate attempted, through strictly democratic channels, to become President. Clara would remember this holiday as long as she lived. People dressed in their spring best, thereby getting a

---

5. **negritude** (neg´ rə tood´) *n*.: Blacks and their cultural heritage.
6. **oligarchy** (äl´ i gär´ kē) *n*.: Government ruled by a few.

7. **terra firma** (ter´ a fur´ ma) *n*.: Firm earth; solid ground.
8. **immutable** (im myoot´ ə bəl) *adj*.: Never changing.

step ahead of the official opening of the season, the men in white linen suits and the ladies in the Italian straw hats that were all the rage that year. Groups of elementary-school children paraded with their teachers, clutching flowers for the hero. Marcos accepted their bouquets and joked that they might as well hold on to them and wait for him to crash, so they could take them directly to his funeral. The bishop himself, accompanied by two incense bearers, appeared to bless the bird without having been asked, and the police band played happy, unpretentious music that pleased everyone. The police, on horseback and carrying lances, had trouble keeping the crowds far enough away from the center of the park, where Marcos waited dressed in mechanic's overalls, with huge racer's goggles and an explorer's helmet. He was also equipped with a compass, a telescope, and several strange maps that he had traced himself based on various theories of Leonardo da Vinci and on the polar knowledge of the Incas.[9] Against all logic, on the second try the bird lifted off without mishap and with a certain elegance, accompanied by the creaking of its skeleton and the roar of its motor. It rose flapping its wings and disappeared into the clouds, to a send-off of applause, whistlings, handkerchiefs, drumrolls, and the sprinkling of holy water. All that remained on earth were the comments of the amazed crowd below and a multitude of experts, who attempted to provide a reasonable explanation of the miracle. Clara continued to stare at the sky long after her uncle had become invisible. She thought she saw him ten minutes later, but it was only a migrating sparrow. After three days the initial euphoria that had accompanied the first airplane flight in the country died down and no one gave the episode another thought, except for Clara, who continued to peer at the horizon.

After a week with no word from the flying uncle, people began to speculate that he had gone so high that he had disappeared into outer space, and the ignorant suggested he would reach the moon. With a mixture of sadness and relief, Severo decided that his brother-in-law and his machine must have fallen into some hidden crevice of the cordillera,[10] where they would never be found. Nivea wept <u>disconsolately</u> and lit candles to San Antonio, patron of lost objects. Severo opposed the idea of having masses said, because he did not believe in them as a way of getting into heaven, much less of returning to earth, and he maintained that masses and religious vows, like the selling of indulgences, images, and scapulars,[11] were a dishonest business. Because of his attitude, Nivea and Nana had the children say the rosary,[12] behind their father's back for nine days. Meanwhile, groups of volunteer explorers and mountain climbers tirelessly searched peaks and passes, combing every accessible stretch of land until they finally returned in triumph to hand the family the mortal remains of the deceased in a sealed black coffin. The intrepid traveler was laid to rest in a grandiose funeral. His death made him a hero and his name was on the front page of all the papers for several days. The same multitude that had gathered to see him off the day he flew away in his bird paraded past his coffin. The entire family wept as befit the occasion, except for Clara, who continued to watch the sky with the patience of an astronomer. One week after he had been buried, Uncle Marcos, a bright smile playing behind his pirate's

◆ **Reading Strategy**
What inference can you make about what Clara believes concerning her uncle and his fate?

---

9. **Leonardo da Vinci** (le ə när´ do də vin´ che) . . . **Incas:** Leonardo da Vinci (1452–1519) was an Italian painter, sculptor, architect, and scientist. The Incas were Native Americans who dominated ancient Peru until the Spanish conquest.

10. **cordillera** (kor´ dil yer´ə) *n.*: System or chain of mountains.
11. **indulgences, images, and scapulars** (skap´ yə lərz): Indulgences are pardons for sins, images are pictures or sculptures of religious figures, and scapulars are garments worn by Roman Catholics as tokens of religious devotion.
12. **say the rosary:** Use a set of beads to say prayers.

◆ **Build Vocabulary**

disconsolately (dis kän´ sə lit lē) *adv.*: Unhappily

mustache, appeared in person in the doorway of Nivea and Severo del Valle's house. Thanks to the surreptitious[13] prayers of the women and children, as he himself admitted, he was alive and well and in full possession of his faculties, including his sense of humor. Despite the noble lineage of his aerial maps, the flight had been a failure. He had lost his airplane and had to return on foot, but he had not broken any bones and his adventurous spirit was intact. This confirmed the family's eternal devotion to San Antonio, but was not taken as a warning by future generations, who also tried to fly, although by different means. Legally, however, Marcos was a corpse. Severo del Valle was obliged to use all his legal ingenuity to bring his brother-in-law back to life and the full rights of citizenship. When the coffin was pried open in the presence of the appropriate authorities, it was found to contain a bag of sand. This discovery ruined the reputation, up till then untarnished, of the volunteer explorers and mountain climbers, who from that day on were considered little better than a pack of bandits.

Marcos's heroic resurrection made everyone forget about his barrel-organ phase. Once again he was a sought-after guest in all the city's salons and, at least for a while, his name was cleared. Marcos stayed in his sister's house for several months. One night he left without saying goodbye, leaving behind his trunks, his books, his weapons, his boots, and all his belongings. Severo, and even Nivea herself, breathed a sigh of relief. His visit had gone on too long. But Clara was so upset that she spent a week walking in her sleep and sucking her thumb. The little girl, who was only seven at the time, had learned to read from her uncle's storybooks and been closer to him than any other member of the family because of her prophesying powers. Marcos maintained that his niece's gift could be a source of income and a good opportunity for him to cultivate his own clairvoyance.[14] He believed that all human beings possessed this ability, particularly his own family, and that if it did not function well it was simply due to a lack of training. He bought a crystal ball in the Persian bazaar, insisting that it had magic powers and was from the East (although it was later found to be part of a buoy from a fishing boat), set it down on a background of black velvet, and announced that he could tell people's fortunes, cure the evil eye, and improve the quality of dreams, all for the modest sum of five centavos.[15] His first customers were the maids from around the neighborhood. One of them had been accused of stealing, because her employer had misplaced a valuable ring. The crystal ball revealed the exact location of the object in question: it had rolled beneath a wardrobe. The next

---

15. centavos (sen ta′ vos) *n*.: Brazilian currency equal to I/100 of a cruzeiro.

▼ **Critical Viewing** This sketch of a helicopter by Italian artist and inventor Leonardo da Vinci predates the first working helicopters by about 450 years. What do you think Uncle Marcos would have thought of Leonardo da Vinci? **[Speculate]**

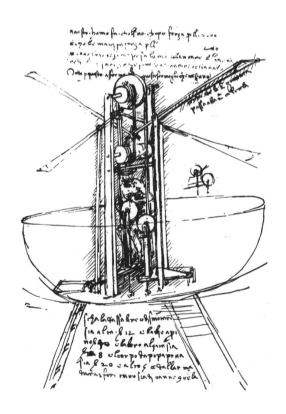

---

13. surreptitious (sur′ əp tish′ əs) *adj*.: Secretive.
14. clairvoyance (kler voi′ əns) *n*.: Ability to perceive things that are not in sight or can't be seen.

day there was a line outside the front door of the house. There were coachmen, storekeepers, and milkmen; later a few municipal employees and distinguished ladies made a discreet appearance, slinking along the side walls of the house to keep from being recognized. The customers were received by Nana, who ushered them into the waiting room and collected their fees. This task kept her busy throughout the day and demanded so much of her time that the family began to complain that all there ever was for dinner was old string beans and jellied quince.[16] Marcos decorated the carriage house with some frayed curtains that had once belonged in the drawing room but that neglect and age had turned to dusty rags. There he and Clara received the customers. The two divines wore tunics "color of the men of light," as Marcos called the color yellow. Nana had dyed them with saffron powder, boiling them in pots usually reserved for rice and pasta. In addition to his tunic, Marcos wore a turban around his head and an Egyptian amulet around his neck. He had grown a beard and let his hair grow long and he was thinner than ever before. Marcos and Clara were utterly convincing, especially because the child had no need to look into the crystal ball to guess what her clients wanted to hear. She would whisper in her Uncle Marcos's ear, and he in turn would transmit the message to the client, along with any improvisations of his own that he thought pertinent. Thus their fame spread, because all those who arrived sad and bedraggled at the consulting room left filled with hope. Unrequited lovers were told how to win over indifferent hearts, and the poor left with foolproof tips on how to place their money at the dog tracks. Business grew so prosperous that the waiting room was always packed with people, and Nana began to suffer dizzy spells from being on her feet so many hours a day. This time Severo had no need to intervene to put a stop to his brother-in-law's venture, for both Marcos and

◆ Reading Strategy
What can you infer about the motives of the ladies who didn't want to be recognized?

Clara, realizing that their unerring guesses could alter the fate of their clients, who always followed their advice to the letter, became frightened and decided that this was a job for swindlers. They abandoned their carriage-house oracle and split the profits, even though the only one who had cared about the material side of things had been Nana.

Of all the del Valle children, Clara was the one with the greatest interest in and stamina for her uncle's stories. She could repeat each and every one of them. She knew by heart words from several dialects of the Indians, was acquainted with their customs, and could describe the exact way in which they pierced their lips and earlobes with wooden shafts, their initiation rites, the names of the most poisonous snakes, and the appropriate antidotes for each. Her uncle was so eloquent that the child could feel in her own skin the burning sting of snakebites, see reptiles slide across the carpet between the legs of the jacaranda[17] room divider, and hear the shrieks of macaws behind the drawing-room drapes. She did not hesitate as she recalled Lope de Aguirre's search for El Dorado,[18] or the unpronounceable names of the flora and fauna her extraordinary uncle had seen; she knew about the lamas who take salt tea with yak lard and she could give detailed descriptions of the opulent women of Tahiti, the rice fields of China, or the white prairies of the North, where the eternal ice kills animals and men who lose their way, turning them to stone in seconds. Marcos had various travel journals in which he recorded his excursions and impressions, as well as a collection of maps and books of stories and fairy tales that he kept in the trunks he stored in the junk room at the far end of the third courtyard.

---

16. **quince** (kwins): Golden or greenish-yellow hard apple-shaped fruit.

17. **jacaranda** (jak´ a ran´ da): Type of tropical American tree.
18. **Lope de Aguirre's** (lo´ pā *the* ə gir´ es) . . .
El Dorado: Lope de Aguirre was a Spanish adventurer (1510–1561) in colonial South America who searched for a legendary country called El Dorado, which was supposedly rich in gold.

◆ **Build Vocabulary**

unrequited (un ri kwīt´ id) *adj.*: Not returned; not reciprocated

From there they were hauled out to inhabit the dreams of his descendants, until they were mistakenly burned half a century later on an infamous pyre.

Now Marcos had returned from his last journey in a coffin. He had died of a mysterious African plague that had turned him as yellow and wrinkled as a piece of parchment. When he realized he was ill, he set out for home with the hope that his sister's ministrations and Dr. Cuevas's knowledge would restore his health and youth, but he was unable to withstand the sixty days on ship and died at the latitude of Guayaquil,[19] ravaged by fever and hallucinating about musky women and hidden treasure. The captain of the ship, an Englishman by the name of Longfellow, was about to throw him overboard wrapped in a flag, but Marcos, despite his savage appearance and his delirium, had made so many friends on board and seduced so many women that the passengers prevented him from doing so, and Longfellow was obliged to store the body side by side with the vegetables of the Chinese cook, to preserve it from the heat and mosquitoes of the tropics until the ship's carpenter had time to improvise a coffin. At El Callao[20] they obtained a more appropriate container, and several days later the captain, furious at all the troubles this passenger had caused the shipping company and himself personally, unloaded him without a backward glance, surprised that not a soul was there to receive the body or cover the expenses he had incurred. Later he learned that the post office in these latitudes was not as reliable as that of far-off England, and that all his telegrams had vaporized en route. Fortunately for Longfellow, a customs lawyer who was a friend of the del Valle family appeared and offered to take charge, placing Marcos and all his paraphernalia in a freight car, which he shipped to the capital to the only known address of the deceased: his sister's house. . . .

---

19. **Guayaquil** (gwĭ ä kēl´): Seaport in western Ecuador.

20. **El Callao** (kə yä´ ō): Seaport in western Peru.

Guide for Responding

◆ *Literature and Your Life*

Reader's Response Which adventure would you most like to share with Uncle Marcos? Why?

Thematic Focus If you were a character in this story, how would you feel about Uncle Marcos?

Journal Writing Jot down your memories of an eccentric person you've encountered. What made the person eccentric? What sort of impression did the person make upon you?

☑ Check Your Comprehension

1. What four words could you use to describe Uncle Marcos?
2. Why was it easy for the townspeople to believe that Uncle Marcos had died in a plane crash?
3. How did Uncle Marcos and Clara tell fortunes?

◆ Critical Thinking

INTERPRET

1. What is each character's attitude toward Uncle Marcos? **[Interpret]**
2. How do the other characters' attitudes toward Uncle Marcos differ from Clara's? **[Compare and Contrast]**
3. Severo says: "Uncle Marcos's manners were those of a cannibal." What evidence from this story refutes Severo's claim? **[Support]**
4. What does Cousin Antonieta think of Uncle Marcos's method of courtship? **[Infer]**

EXTEND

5. What kind of job do you think Uncle Marcos would be good at? Explain. **[Career Link]**

APPLY

6. What lessons can be learned from Uncle Marcos and his approach to life? **[Apply]**

CONNECTIONS TO TODAY'S WORLD

The spirit of Uncle Marcos is alive and well! Just about every day, people come up with new inventions with the potential to change how we live. One organization that drives many of the important inventions that are made is NASA. The sketch below shows a proposal for a new type of satellite that would collect information about the sun's rays.

1. What important information is captured in this sketch?
2. In what ways might the person or people who came up with this idea be similar to Uncle Marcos?

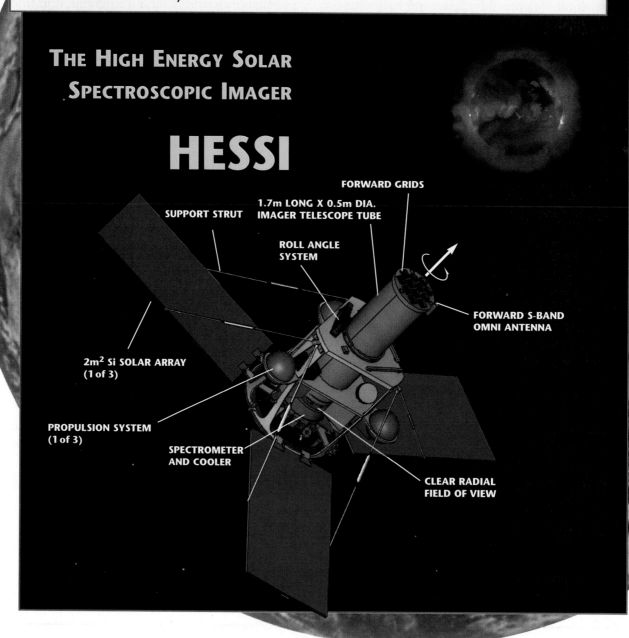

THE HIGH ENERGY SOLAR SPECTROSCOPIC IMAGER

HESSI

SUPPORT STRUT

1.7m LONG X 0.5m DIA. IMAGER TELESCOPE TUBE

FORWARD GRIDS

ROLL ANGLE SYSTEM

FORWARD S-BAND OMNI ANTENNA

2m² Si SOLAR ARRAY (1 of 3)

PROPULSION SYSTEM (1 of 3)

SPECTROMETER AND COOLER

CLEAR RADIAL FIELD OF VIEW

Guide for Responding (continued)

◆ Reading Strategy

MAKE INFERENCES ABOUT CHARACTERS
Based on the characters' actions in this story, you can **make inferences,** or draw conclusions, about their personalities.

1. How does the photographer in "Blues Ain't No Mockin Bird" feel about the people he is filming? Support your answer.
2. In "Uncle Marcos," what details might lead you to infer that Marcos enjoys having an audience for his adventures?
3. What evidence supports the inference that Clara is an unusual child?

◆ Literary Focus

DIRECT AND INDIRECT CHARACTERIZATION
Characterization refers to a writer's revelations of a character's personality traits. In **direct characterization,** a writer simply states a fact about a character. In **indirect characterization,** a writer implies facts about a character by showing you what the character says or does and how other characters react to him or her. Notice Bambara's use of indirect characterization in this passage:

> "Nice things here," said the man, buzzin his camera over the yard. The pecan barrels, the sled, me and Cathy, the flowers, the printed stones along the driveway, the trees, the twins, the toolshed.

The man's actions show that he thinks the people have about the same importance as the things. You can infer that the man is insensitive and rude. If Bambara had simply said, "The man was insensitive and rude," she would have been using direct characterization.

1. Find an example of indirect characterization for two of the characters in each story.
2. For each example, rewrite it as direct characterization.
3. Which method do you think is more effective: indirect characterization or direct characterization? Explain your answer.

◆ Build Vocabulary

USING THE PREFIX dis-
In your notebook, write each sentence, completing it with a word that uses the prefix dis- with the italicized word.

1. The twins *agreed* to let Cathy and the narrator swing in the tire, but they ____?____ about when.
2. Granny demanded *respect*, but the cameraman treated her with ____?____.
3. Uncle Marcos exercised with *graceful* movements, but sometimes his behavior seemed ____?____ to Severo.
4. Uncle Marcos wanted only to *please* Cousin Antonieta, but he managed to ____?____ her instead.

USING THE WORD BANK
In your notebook, write the letter of the word or words closest in meaning to the first word.

1. lassoed: (a) loosened, (b) raced toward, (c) wrapped around
2. formality: (a) established customs, (b) casual attitude, (c) honesty
3. vanquished: (a) disappeared, (b) defeated, (c) cleaned
4. fetid: (a) fresh, (b) sweet, (c) smelly
5. impassive: (a) emotionless, (b) excited, (c) fair
6. disconsolately: (a) slowly, (b) unhappily, (c) quickly
7. unrequited: (a) not returned, (b) unreasonable, (c) not quiet

◆ Build Grammar Skills

POSSESSIVE NOUNS
Possessive nouns show ownership, belonging, or another close relationship. Review the chart on p. 496 to see how to form possessive nouns.

Practice In your notebook, change each underlined phrase into the correct possessive form.

1. the picture *of Uncle Marcos*: ____?____ picture
2. the curiosity *of the townspeople*: the ____?____ curiosity
3. the rudeness *of the cameraman*: the ____?____ rudeness
4. the argument *of the twins*: the ____?____ argument
5. the dignity *of Granddaddy Cain*: ____?____ dignity

Build Your Portfolio

 ## Idea Bank

Writing

1. **Letter** Suppose you were there the day Uncle Marcos took off in his airplane. Write a letter to a friend describing the event and what you thought of it.

2. **Character Sketch** What type of person do you think Clara became as an adult? Use your imagination to create a character sketch describing what Clara is like as an adult.

3. **Persuasive Essay** Write a persuasive essay that answers this question: Do the news media have the right to intrude in people's lives in order to get a story?

Speaking and Listening

4. **Debate** Sometimes imaginative and adventurous people like Uncle Marcos are seen as irresponsible. With three classmates, debate whether colorful characters make an important contribution to family life and to society. Two people in your group will take the pro side, and two will take the con side. **[Social Studies Link]**

5. **Monologue** Put yourself in the place of the cameraman in "Blues Ain't No Mockin Bird." Explain to your boss what happened to your camera. **[Career Link]**

Projects

6. **Illustrated Report** Bambara's title refers to a type of music called the blues. Research this type of music and gather photographs, illustrations, and recordings, if possible. Present your findings to the class. **[Music Link]**

7. **Illustration** Illustrate a scene from one of the stories using your favorite art medium. Add a caption and display your work in class. **[Art Link]**

 ## Writing Mini-Lesson

Magazine Feature

These stories feature amazing characters, brought to life through vivid details. Picture an amazing person you know or have read about and write a magazine feature about that person.

Writing Skills Focus: Main Impression

As you write, focus your magazine feature on a **main impression**—in this case, what makes the person truly amazing. Include details that support the main impression and avoid details that do not support it. In this example, Isabel Allende includes only those details that show Uncle Marcos is unusual.

Model From the Story

While the rest of the household tried to sleep, he dragged his suitcases up and down the halls, practiced making strange, high-pitched sounds on savage instruments, and taught Spanish to a parrot whose native language was an Amazonic dialect.

Prewriting Decide on your main impression and list details that support it. Consider these categories: physical appearance, personality traits, activities, talents, and goals.

Drafting Using your prewriting notes, write about your amazing person. For each characteristic you mention, give an example that shows how the person exhibits that characteristic. Look through magazines for models of feature articles to help you write your own feature.

Revising Give your feature to a peer for review. See if your reviewer can accurately state the main impression. If not, look for places where greater detail or clearer description is needed. Discard any details that do not contribute to the main impression.

Writing Process Workshop

Personal Narrative

Like the writers in this unit, we all have tales to tell. In fact, if you look back on your own life so far, you're likely to find many events and experiences that would make great stories. Bring one of these experiences to life by writing a **personal narrative**—a true story about a memorable experience or event from your life. Include your personal feelings about the event you're describing to enable your readers to connect with your narrative. The following skills, introduced in this section's Writing Mini-Lessons, will help you write your personal narrative.

Writing Skills Focus

▶ **Elaborate to make your writing personal** by providing details that capture how the experience affected you. (See p. 466.)

▶ **Provide vivid details** to help readers picture the people, setting, and events in your narrative. (See p. 495.)

▶ **Give a main impression** of the experience and its impact on you. (See p. 514.)

▶ **Create dramatic effects**, such as a suspenseful beginning or a surprise ending. (See p. 481.)

Author James Hurst uses several of these skills in this passage from "The Scarlet Ibis."

MODEL FROM LITERATURE

from "The Scarlet Ibis" by James Hurst

It was bad enough having an invalid brother, but having one who possibly was not all there was unbearable, so I began to make plans to kill him by smothering him with a pillow. ① However, one afternoon as I watched him, my head poked between the iron posts of the foot of the bed, he looked straight at me and grinned. ② I skipped through the rooms, down the echoing halls, shouting, "Mama, he smiled. He's all there! He's all there!" and he was. ③

① Details about the narrator's feelings provide vivid insights into his personality.

② The writer introduces a dramatic twist that grabs the reader's interest.

③ The events are described through vivid details that create a picture in the reader's mind.

APPLYING LANGUAGE SKILLS: Active and Passive Voice

A verb in the **active voice** shows the subject performing an action. A verb in the **passive voice** shows the subject receiving an action.

Active Voice:
I <u>chased</u> the thief.

Passive Voice:
The thief <u>was chased</u> by me.

Notice how the active voice makes writing more forceful and lively.

Practice Rewrite each sentence so that the verb is in the active voice.

1. The chase was joined by the police.
2. The wallet was dropped by the thief.
3. I was excited by this sudden surprise.

Writing Application As you draft your personal narrative, write most of your sentences using the active voice. Use the passive voice only when the performer of the action is unknown or unimportant.

Writer's Solution Connection
Writing Lab

To help you choose a topic, use the Sunburst Diagram activity in the Choosing a Topic section in the tutorial on Narration.

Prewriting

Choose a Topic Choose a memorable experience from your life on which to base your personal narrative. If no ideas come to mind, try the following suggestions.

- Look through your journal or scrapbook.
- Ask a family member to recall interesting moments from your life.
- Think about some of your "firsts"—your first pet, first trip, or first day in a new school, for example.

Plan Your Story Details Once you've chosen your topic, write detailed notes that answer the following questions: *Who* else was involved in the experience or event? *Where* and *when* did it take place? *What* happened first, next, and last? *Why* was the experience memorable? *How* did the experience make me feel?

Consider Your Purpose The purpose of most narratives is to entertain, but narratives can have other purposes as well. Decide what effect you want your narrative to have on your readers. Here are some tips for achieving different purposes.

To amuse:	• Use exaggeration
	• Emphasize the absurdity or silliness of a situation
To teach a lesson:	• Show clear causes and effects
	• Use precise language
To frighten:	• Create dark, eerie settings
	• Use suspenseful language

Drafting

Use Elaboration to Make Your Writing Personal As you draft your narrative, offer enough details so that readers can connect in a personal way with your narrative. Make them feel as if only you—and no other writer—could have told this particular story. Remember to share your personal feelings about the narrative's events.

Create Dramatic Effects Look for ways to make your narrative as interesting or exciting as possible. For example, you might begin with details that will grab readers' interest and arouse their curiosity. Later, add details that will heighten their curiosity. Even if your narrative doesn't have a surprise ending, make the ending one that readers will find memorable.

Revising

Use a Checklist Go back to the Writing Skills Focus on the first page of this lesson, and use the items as a checklist to evaluate and revise your personal narrative. Ask yourself:

▶ Are my characters, setting, and events detailed enough?
Have one or more peers read your narrative. If they have questions about the content, add clarifying details.

▶ Is my writing personal enough?
Consider details you can add to make your narrative sound more like you.

▶ Have I given a main impression?
Find those places where you have expressed your feelings about your experience. Decide whether you need to elaborate on those feelings.

▶ Does my work contain dramatic elements?
Discuss with a peer whether your narrative is exciting. Add details that will further heighten readers' interest.

REVISION MODEL

Below is a revised paragraph from a personal narrative by Kileen Cheng, a student at Westwood High School in Round Rock, Texas. Notice that Kileen adds a sentence to increase suspense and to make a smoother transition into the story. She also replaces a vague word with one that is precise and adds details about the setting to help explain why the room had a relaxing effect on her.

Minutes later, we were on our way to the hospital. *After what seemed like an eternity, we finally arrived.* My mom and I easily found his room. I hesitantly opened the door and *crept* ~~went~~ inside. The room was rather small, with a low ceiling, and *was crowded with* ~~had lots of~~ flowers of all different colors, shapes, and sizes. *The flowers added a warm glow and a feeling of home. The fresh fragrance* They helped me relax, and the whole atmosphere made me forget momentarily about life's complications.

Publishing

▶ **Personal Drama** Together with classmates, act out a staged version of your narrative.

▶ **Magazine** Submit your personal narrative to a magazine that publishes true stories.

APPLYING LANGUAGE SKILLS: Using Pronouns

In a personal narrative, you often use the **pronouns** *I, me, my,* and *mine.*

I ran home quickly.

The dog chased Bob and me.

It bit my pants.

The dog wasn't mine.

Notice the pronoun form used in each sentence.

Practice On your paper, choose the correct pronoun to complete each sentence.

1. There was a loud noise on (my, mine) block.
2. (Me, I) ran outside to see what it was.
3. A neighbor called to my sister and (I, me).
4. A friend of (my, mine) came over to help.

Writing Application As you revise your personal narrative, check to see whether you have used the correct pronouns in your sentences. If you find any errors, correct them before making your final copy.

Writer's Solution Connection
Writing Lab

For more instruction on pronouns and revision, work through the Revision section of the tutorial on Narration.

Strategies for Success

Recognizing the main ideas in a short story can help you to appreciate that story more. In the same way, spotting the main ideas in a nonfiction article will help you to better understand the article and enjoy it more.

Check the Lead Sentence In an article, each paragraph may contain its own main idea, which is often stated in the lead sentence—or first sentence—of the paragraph. As you read the rest of the paragraph, you'll find details to support the main idea.

Look at the End of the Article The end of an article sometimes summarizes the main ideas that were discussed previously. When you read an article, study the last paragraph carefully. Do you find earlier ideas being repeated? If so, they probably are main ideas.

Draw Your Own Conclusion Sometimes in an article, a main idea is not stated directly. Instead, you must make inferences about the main idea based on details that are provided. If you can't find a main idea in any sentence, ask yourself: What is the point of the paragraph? To what do all the details lead? Your answer will be the main idea.

Apply the Strategy

How well can you recognize main ideas? Read the article entitled "How Our Government Works." Then see if you can answer these questions.

1. What is the main idea of the first paragraph? Which sentence states the idea?
2. Is the main idea stated directly in the second paragraph? If so, where?
3. What is the main idea of the third paragraph? Is it stated directly?
4. Does the article summarize its main ideas? If so, where?

How Our Government Works

Our government has three branches, and each is affected by the other two. The legislative branch makes our laws. This branch includes the Senate and House of Representatives.

The executive branch exists to see that our laws are carried out. This branch is headed by the President.

The judicial branch interprets and explains our laws. This branch is made up of all our judges, including the Supreme Court. We need all three branches — the legislative, executive, and judicial — in order for our society to function.

✔ Here are other situations in which recognizing main ideas can be helpful:
▶ Reading a news story in the newspaper
▶ Reading a scientific research paper
▶ Reading a biographical sketch
▶ Reading an information sheet about a club

PART 2 Setting and Theme

Opened Door, Rose Weinstock

Guide for Reading

Leslie Marmon Silko
(1948–   )

Storytelling has been an important part of Leslie Marmon Silko's life practically from the day she was born. Raised on the Laguna Pueblo reservation in New Mexico, she grew up listening to tribal stories told by her great-grandmother and great-aunts. Drawing upon elements from the traditional tales she heard as a child, Silko has forged a successful career as a writer.

In her stories, novels, and poems, Silko explores what life is like for Native Americans in today's world. Many of her works, including "The Man Who Sends Rain Clouds," capture the contrast between traditional values and beliefs and the elements of modern-day life.

Mark Twain *(1835–1910)*

Born Samuel Langhorne Clemens, this great American humorist grew up in the river town of Hannibal, Missouri. Though Twain traveled and lived all over the United States, it is the great Mississippi River that runs through the heart of his life and work.

As a young man, he learned the trade of the riverboat pilot and took his pen name from a sounding cry used on Mississippi steamboats: 'By the mark—twain,' which means the water is two fathoms deep. Although Twain worked as a printer, prospector, reporter, editor, and lecturer, writing was his true calling. He was the best-known and most successful author of his generation. Some of his most popular works include *Tom Sawyer*, *The Adventures of Huckleberry Finn*, and *Life on the Mississippi*.

◆ Build Vocabulary

SUFFIXES: -ous

Prodigious. Deleterious. Ominous. Judicious. These words have two things in common: They all appear in "The Invalid's Story," and they all are many-syllabled words ending with the suffix *-ous*, which means "full of." For instance, *prodigious* combines *prodigy*, meaning "a marvel or wonder," with *-ous*; *prodigious* means "wonderful" or "amazing." In Twain's story, the word *prodigious* refers to a mistake. Fortunately for the reader, this prodigious mistake leads to a humorous story.

cloister
pagans
perverse
prodigious
deleterious
ominous
judicious
placidly
desultory

Word Bank

Before you read, preview this list of words from the stories.

◆ Build Grammar Skills

PUNCTUATING DIALOGUE

Both of these stories rely heavily on **dialogue**—conversation involving at least two speakers. Follow these rules for punctuating the dialogue:

- Use quotation marks before and after a speaker's exact words.
- Begin a new paragraph each time the speaker changes.
- Use commas to separate quotations from words that identify the speaker—no matter where those words appear in the sentence. The comma always appears before the quotation marks.
- When a paragraph ends while a character is still speaking, quotation marks do not appear at the end of that paragraph. However, they do appear at the beginning of the new paragraph.

The Man to Send Rain Clouds
◆ The Invalid's Story ◆

◆ *Literature and Your Life*

CONNECT YOUR EXPERIENCE

At some time, everyone has to deal with the loss of a loved one. People cope with this in different ways. They may try to preserve the loved one's memory, or they may look to fulfill the person's last wishes. These stories present two very different sets of circumstances surrounding a person's death and others' responses to it.

THEMATIC FOCUS: FACING CONFLICTS

As these stories reveal, dealing with death can involve working out difficult and sometimes unexpected issues and situations.

◆ Background for Understanding

CULTURE

"The Man to Send Rain Clouds" explores the traditions of the Pueblo Indians. The Pueblos have lived in the southwestern United States for nearly 3,000 years. They first came into contact with Europeans when the Spanish arrived in the 1500's. During the twentieth century, the Pueblos have incorporated many aspects of the industrial world into their lives. Nevertheless, they have tried to maintain their ancient traditions and beliefs—including the view that if they keep themselves in harmony with the natural world, nature will give them what they need, such as sufficient rainfall for their crops. The Pueblos' balancing of modern ways with their own customs and views provides the central conflict in Silko's story.

Journal Writing Jot down what you know about the Pueblo people and other Native American cultures.

◆ Literary Focus

SETTING

In each of these stories, events grow out of the **setting**—the place and time of the action. In some stories, the setting simply provides a backdrop for the actions and characters. In other stories—including these—the setting shapes the characters' actions.

In addition to time and place, a story's setting includes the **cultural background** against which the action takes place: the customs, ideas, values, and beliefs of the society in which it occurs. The cultural background for "The Man to Send Rain Clouds" consists of the customs and beliefs of the Pueblo people.

◆ Reading Strategy

USE YOUR SENSES

A dry wintry desert waiting for rain. A stifling boxcar with a smelly package. The setting of each story gives your senses a real workout. As you read each one, **use your senses** to picture the setting and the characters in your mind.

Draw from your own experiences to see, hear, smell, taste, or feel what each author describes. For example, when Twain describes a piece of cheese with an overpowering odor, search your memory to recall when you've smelled especially pungent cheese, and try to re-create the sensation in your mind.

Use a graphic organizer like this one to help you record key details appealing to each sense.

Sights	Sounds	Smells	Tastes	Physical Sensations

The Man to Send Rain Clouds

Leslie Marmon Silko

They found him under a big cottonwood tree. His Levi jacket and pants were faded light blue so that he had been easy to find. The big cottonwood tree stood apart from a small grove of winterbare cottonwoods which grew in the wide, sandy arroyo. He had been dead for a day or more, and the sheep had wandered and scattered up and down the arroyo. Leon and his brother-in-law, Ken, gathered the sheep and left them in the pen at the sheep camp before they returned to the cottonwood tree. Leon waited under the tree while Ken drove the truck through the deep sand to the edge of the arroyo. He squinted up at the sun and unzipped his jacket—it sure was hot for this time of year. But high and northwest the blue mountains were still in snow. Ken came sliding down the low, crumbling bank about fifty yards down, and he was bringing the red blanket.

Before they wrapped the old man, Leon took a piece of string out of his pocket and tied a small gray feather in the old man's long white hair. Ken gave him the paint. Across the brown wrinkled forehead he drew a streak of white and along the high cheekbones he drew a strip of blue paint. He paused and watched Ken throw pinches of corn meal and pollen into the wind that fluttered the small gray feather. Then Leon painted with yellow under the old man's broad nose, and finally, when he had painted green across the chin, he smiled.

"Send us rain clouds, Grandfather." They laid the bundle in the back of the pickup and covered it with a heavy tarp before they started back to the pueblo.

They turned off the highway onto the sandy pueblo road. Not long after they passed the store and post office they saw Father Paul's car coming toward them. When he recognized their faces he slowed his car and waved for them to stop. The young priest rolled down the car window.

"Did you find old Teofilo?" he asked loudly.

Leon stopped the truck. "Good morning, Father. We were just out to the sheep camp. Everything is O.K. now."

"Thank God for that. Teofilo is a very old man. You really shouldn't allow him to stay at the sheep camp alone."

"No, he won't do that any more now."

"Well, I'm glad you understand. I hope I'll be seeing you at Mass[1] this week—we missed you last Sunday. See if you can get old Teofilo to come with you." The priest smiled and waved at them as they drove away.

Louise and Teresa were waiting. The table was set for lunch, and the coffee was boiling on the black iron stove. Leon looked at Louise and then at Teresa.

"We found him under a cottonwood tree in the big arroyo near sheep camp. I guess he sat down to rest in the shade and never got up again." Leon walked toward the old man's bed. The red plaid shawl had been shaken and spread carefully over the bed, and a new brown flannel shirt and pair of stiff new Levi's were arranged neatly beside the pillow. Louise held the screen door open while Leon and Ken

---

1. **Mass** (mas): Church service celebrated by Roman Catholics.

Feast Day, San Juan Pueblo, 1921, William Penhallow Henderson, National Museum of American Art, Smithsonian Institution

▲ **Critical Viewing** In this tale of the Southwest, Native American customs clash with and then harmonize with customs brought by Spanish and Mexican missionaries. How do the ideas in the painting and the story connect with your own experience of old ways and new ways? **[Relate]**

carried in the red blanket. He looked small and shriveled, and after they dressed him in the new shirt and pants he seemed more shrunken.

It was noontime now because the church bells rang the Angelus.[2] They ate the beans with hot bread, and nobody said anything until after Teresa poured the coffee.

Ken stood up and put on his jacket. "I'll see about the gravediggers. Only the top layer of soil is frozen. I think it can be ready before dark."

Leon nodded his head and finished his coffee. After Ken had been gone for a while, the neighbors and clanspeople came quietly to embrace Teofilo's family and to leave food on the

table because the gravediggers would come to eat when they were finished.

The sky in the west was full of pale yellow light. Louise stood outside with her hands in the pockets of Leon's green army jacket that was too big for her. The funeral was over, and the old men had taken their candles and medicine bags[3] and were gone. She waited until the body was laid into the pickup before she said anything to Leon. She touched his arm, and he noticed that her hands were still dusty from the corn meal that she had sprinkled around the old man. When she spoke, Leon could not hear her.

---

2. **Angelus** (an´ ja ləs): Bell rung at morning, noon, and evening to announce a prayer.

3. **medicine bags:** Bags containing objects that were thought to have special powers.

"What did you say? I didn't hear you."

"I said that I had been thinking about something."

"About what?"

◆ **Literary Focus**
What two different elements in the cultural setting does this request suggest?

"About the priest sprinkling holy water for Grandpa. So he won't be thirsty."

Leon stared at the new moccasins that Teofilo had made for the ceremonial dances in the summer. They were nearly hidden by the red blanket. It was getting colder, and the wind pushed gray dust down the narrow pueblo road. The sun was approaching the long mesa where it disappeared during the winter. Louise stood there shivering and watching his face. Then he zipped up his jacket and opened the truck door. "I'll see if he's there."

Ken stopped the pickup at the church, and Leon got out: and then Ken drove down the hill to the graveyard where people were waiting. Leon knocked at the old carved door with its symbols of the Lamb.[4] While he waited he looked up at the twin bells from the king of Spain with the last sunlight pouring around them in their tower.

The priest opened the door and smiled when he saw who it was. "Come in! What brings you here this evening?"

The priest walked toward the kitchen, and Leon stood with his cap in his hand, playing with the earflaps and examining the living room—the brown sofa, the green armchair, and the brass lamp that hung down from the ceiling by links of chain. The priest dragged a chair out of the kitchen and offered it to Leon.

"No thank you, Father. I only came to ask you if you would bring your holy water to the graveyard."

The priest turned away from Leon and looked out the window at the patio full of shadows and the dining-room windows of the nuns' cloister across the patio. The curtains were heavy, and the light from within faintly penetrated; it was impossible to see the nuns inside eating supper. "Why didn't you tell me he was dead? I could have brought the Last Rites[5] anyway."

Leon smiled. "It wasn't necessary, Father."

The priest stared down at his scuffed brown loafers and the worn hem of his cassock. "For a Christian burial it was necessary."

His voice was distant, and Leon thought that his blue eyes looked tired.

"It's O.K. Father, we just want him to have plenty of water."

The priest sank down into the green chair and picked up a glossy missionary magazine. He turned the colored pages full of lepers and pagans without looking at them.

"You know I can't do that, Leon. There should have been the Last Rites and a funeral Mass at the very least."

Leon put on his green cap and pulled the flaps down over his ears. "It's getting late, Father. I've got to go."

When Leon opened the door Father Paul stood up and said, "Wait." He left the room and came back wearing a long brown overcoat. He followed Leon out the door and across the dim churchyard to the adobe steps in front of the church. They both stooped to fit through the low adobe entrance. And when they started down the hill to the graveyard only half of the sun was visible above the mesa.

The priest approached the grave slowly, wondering how they had managed to dig into the frozen ground; and then he remembered that this was New Mexico, and saw the pile of cold loose sand beside the hole. The people stood close to each other with little clouds of steam puffing from their faces. The priest looked at

---

4. **the Lamb:** Jesus Christ, as the sacrificial Lamb of God.

5. **the Last Rites:** Religious ceremony for a dying person or for someone who has just died.

◆ **Build Vocabulary**

cloister (klois´ tər) *n*.: Place devoted to religious seclusion

pagans (pā´ gənz) *n*.: People who are not Christians, Muslims, or Jews

perverse (pər vʉrs´) *adj*.: Continuing in a stubborn way to do what is wrong or harmful; improper; wicked

them and saw a pile of jackets, gloves, and scarves in the yellow, dry tumbleweeds that grew in the graveyard. He looked at the red blanket, not sure that Teofilo was so small, wondering if it wasn't some <u>perverse</u> Indian trick—something they did in March to ensure a good harvest—wondering if maybe old Teofilo was actually at sheep camp corraling the sheep for the night. But there he was, facing into a cold dry wind and squinting at the last sunlight, ready to bury a red wool blanket while the faces of his parishioners were in shadow with the last warmth of the sun on their backs.

His fingers were stiff, and it took him a long time to twist the lid off the holy water. Drops of water fell on the red blanket and soaked into dark icy spots. He sprinkled the grave and the water disappeared almost before it touched the dim, cold sand; it reminded him of something—he tried to remember what it was, because he thought if he could remember he might understand this. He sprinkled more water; he shook the container until it was empty, and the water fell through the light from sundown like August rain that fell while the sun was still shining, almost evaporating before it touched the wilted squash flowers.

The wind pulled at the priest's brown Franciscan robe[6] and swirled away the corn meal and pollen that had been sprinkled on the blanket. They lowered the bundle into the ground, and they didn't bother to untie the stiff pieces of new rope that were tied around the ends of the blanket. The sun was gone, and over on the highway the eastbound lane was full of headlights. The priest walked away slowly. Leon watched him climb the hill, and when he had disappeared within the tall, thick walls, Leon turned to look up at the high blue mountains in the deep snow that reflected a faint red light from the west. He felt good because it was finished, and he was happy about the sprinkling of the holy water; now the old man could send them big thunderclouds for sure.

---

6. **Franciscan** (fran sis´ kən) **robe:** Robe worn by a member of the Franciscan religious order, founded in 1209 by Saint Francis of Assisi.

Guide for Responding

◆ Literature and Your Life

Reader's Response Were you surprised by the various characters' reactions in the story? Explain your answer.

Thematic Focus What lesson can be taken away from this story about working out differences in cultural beliefs?

☑ Check Your Comprehension

1. What do Leon and Ken find at the opening of the story?
2. What happens when the men meet Father Paul?
3. Why does Leon ask the priest for holy water?
4. How does Father Paul respond to Leon's request at first?
5. What happens at the end of the story?

◆ Critical Thinking

INTERPRET

1. Why doesn't Leon tell Father Paul about Teofilo's death at first? **[Analyze]**
2. Why is Father Paul upset about the burial ceremony? **[Analyze]**
3. What insight into the Pueblo people does Father Paul gain during the ceremony? **[Infer]**
4. What do Leon's final thoughts suggest about his views of death? **[Draw Conclusions]**
5. What does this story reveal about the contrasts between Pueblo and Christian beliefs? **[Compare and Contrast]**

EXTEND

6. (a) Describe another situation that you know about in which two cultures have clashed.
   (b) What can be done to resolve such conflicts? **[Social Studies Link]**

THE
Invalid's Story

Mark Twain

I seem sixty and married, but these effects are due to my condition and sufferings, for I am a bachelor, and only forty-one. It will be hard for you to believe that I, who am now but a shadow, was a hale, hearty man two short years ago—a man of iron, a very athlete!—yet such is the simple truth. But stranger still than this fact is the way in which I lost my health. I lost it through helping to take care of a box of guns on a two-hundred-mile railway journey one winter's night. It is the actual truth, and I will tell you about it.

I belong in Cleveland, Ohio. One winter's night, two years ago, I reached home just after dark, in a driving snowstorm, and the first thing I heard when I entered the house was that my dearest boyhood friend and schoolmate, John B. Hackett, had died the day before, and that his last utterance had been a desire that I would take his remains home to his poor old father and mother in Wisconsin. I was greatly shocked and grieved, but there was no time to waste in emotions; I must start at once. I took the card, marked "Deacon Levi Hackett, Bethlehem, Wisconsin," and hurried off through the whistling storm to the railway station. Arrived there I found the long white-pine box which had been described to me; I fastened the card to it with some tacks, saw it put safely aboard the express car, and then ran into the eating room to provide myself with a sandwich and some cigars. When I returned, presently, there was my coffin-box *back again*, apparently, and a young fellow examining around it, with a card in his hands, and some tacks and a hammer! I was astonished and puzzled. He began to nail on his card, and I rushed out to the express car, in a good deal of a state of mind, to ask for an explanation. But no—there was my box, all right, in the express car; it hadn't been disturbed. [The fact is that without my suspecting it a <u>prodigious</u> mistake had been made. I was carrying off a box of *guns* which that young fellow had come to the station to ship to a rifle company in Peoria, Illinois, and *he* had got my corpse.] Just then the conductor sang out "All aboard," and I jumped into the express car and got a comfortable seat on a bale of buckets. The expressman was there, hard at work—a plain man of fifty, with a simple, honest, good-natured face, and a breezy, practical heartiness in his general style. As the train moved off a stranger skipped into the car and set a package of peculiarly mature and capable Limburger cheese[1] on one end of my coffin-box—I mean my box of guns. That is to say, I know *now* that it was Limburger cheese, but at that time I never had heard of the article in my life, and of course was wholly ignorant of its character. Well, we sped through the wild night, the bitter storm raged on, a cheerless misery stole over me, my heart went down, down, down! The old expressman made

◆ Build Vocabulary

prodigious (prə dij′ əs) *adj.*: Enormous

deleterious (del′ ə tir′ ē əs) *adj.*: Injurious; harmful to health or well-being

---

1. **Limburger cheese:** Cheese with a strong odor.

a brisk remark or two about the tempest and the arctic weather, slammed his sliding doors to, and bolted them, closed his window down tight, and then went bustling around, here and there and yonder, setting things to rights, and all the time contentedly humming "Sweet By and By" in a low tone, and flatting a good deal.

◆ **Reading Strategy**
What senses can you use to experience this description? How can an "odor" be "searching"?

Presently I began to detect a most evil and searching odor stealing about on the frozen air. This depressed my spirits still more, because of course I attributed it to my poor departed friend. There was something infinitely saddening about his calling himself to my remembrance in this dumb, pathetic way, so it was hard to keep the tears back. Moreover, it

▼ **Critical Viewing**   Examine this painting of a railway station in 1874. How difficult do you think it was to get from one place to another at this time in history? What details in the painting support your ideas? **[Support]**

distressed me on account of the old expressman, who, I was afraid, might notice it. However, he went humming tranquilly on, and gave no sign; and for this I was grateful. Grateful, yes, but still uneasy; and soon I began to feel more and more uneasy every minute, for every minute that went by that odor thickened up the more, and got to be more and more gamy and hard to stand. Presently, having got things arranged to his satisfaction, the expressman got some wood and made up a tremendous fire in his stove. This distressed me more than I can tell, for I could not but feel that it was a mistake. I was sure that the effect would be deleterious upon my poor departed friend. Thompson—the expressman's name was Thompson, as I found out in the course of the night—now went poking around his car, stopping up whatever stray cracks he could find, remarking that it didn't make any difference what kind of a night it was outside, he calculated to make us comfortable, anyway. I said nothing, but I believed he was not choosing the right way. Meantime he was humming to himself just as before; and meantime, too, the

Sacramento Railroad Station, 1874, William Hahn, The Fine Arts Museum of San Francisco

stove was getting hotter and hotter, and the place closer and closer. I felt myself growing pale and qualmish,[2] but grieved in silence and said nothing. Soon I noticed that the "Sweet By and By" was gradually fading out; next it ceased altogether, and there was an <u>ominous</u> stillness. After a few moments Thompson said—

"Pfew! I reckon it ain't no cinnamon 't I've loaded up thish-year stove with!"

He gasped once or twice, then moved toward the cof—gun-box, stood over that Limburger cheese part of a moment, then came back and sat down near me, looking a good deal impressed. After a contemplative pause, he said, indicating the box with a gesture—

"Friend of yourn?"

"Yes," I said with a sigh.

"He's pretty ripe, *ain't* he!"

Nothing further was said for perhaps a couple of minutes, each being busy with his own thoughts; then Thompson said, in a low awed voice—

"Sometimes it's uncertain whether they're really gone or not—*seem* gone, you know—body warm, joints limber—and so, although you *think* they're gone, you don't really know. I've had cases in my car. It's perfectly awful, becuz *you* don't know what minute they'll rise up and look at you!" Then, after a pause, and slightly lifting his elbow toward the box,—"But *he* ain't in no trance! No, sir, I go bail for *him*!"

We sat some time, in meditative silence, listening to the wind and the roar of the train; then Thompson said, with a good deal of feeling:

"Well-a-well, we've all got to go, they ain't no getting around it. Man that is born of woman is of few days and far between, as Scriptur'[3] says. Yes, you look at it any way you want to, it's awful solemn and cur'us: they ain't *nobody* can get around it; *all's* got to go—just *everybody*, as you may say. One day you're hearty and strong"—here he scrambled to his feet and broke a pane and stretched his nose out at it a

American Express Train, Currier & Ives

moment or two, then sat down again while I struggled up and thrust my nose out at the same place, and this we kept on doing every now and then—"and next day he's cut down like the grass, and the places which knowed him then knows him no more forever, as Scriptur' says. Yes'ndeedy, it's awful solemn and cur'us; but we've all got to go, one time or another; they ain't no getting around it."

There was another long pause; then—

"What did he die of?"

---

2. qualmish (kwäm' ish) *adj.*: Slightly ill.
3. Scriptur': Scripture, the Bible.

◆ **Build Vocabulary**

ominous (äm' ə nəs) *adj.*: Threatening

judicious (jōō dish' əs) *adj.*: Showing good judgment

placidly (plas' id lē) *adv.*: Calmly; quietly

desultory (des' əl tôr' ē) *adj.*: Random

▲ **Critical Viewing** Imagine yourself on a train like the one in "The Invalid's Story." Predict what you might see, hear, feel, and smell on such a journey. [Predict]

I said I didn't know.

"How long has he ben dead?"

It seemed judicious to enlarge the facts to fit the probabilities; so I said:

"Two or three days."

But it did no good: for Thompson received it with an injured look which plainly said. "Two or three *years*, you mean." Then he went right along, placidly ignoring my statement, and gave his views at considerable length upon the unwisdom of putting off burials too long. Then he lounged off toward the box, stood a moment, then came back on a sharp trot and visited the broken pane, observing:

"'Twould 'a' ben a durn sight better, all around, if they'd started him along last summer."

Thompson sat down and buried his face in his red silk handkerchief, and began to slowly sway and rock his body like one who is doing his best to endure the almost unendurable. By this time the fragrance—if you may call it fragrance—was just about suffocating, as near as you can come at it. Thompson's face was turning gray: I knew mine hadn't any color left in it. By and by Thompson rested his forehead in his left hand, with his elbow on his knee, and sort of waved his red handkerchief toward the box with his other hand, and said:

◆ **Literary Focus**
What kind of atmosphere do the details in this paragraph create?

"I've carried a many a one of 'em—some of 'em considerable overdue, too—but, lordy, he just lays over 'em all!—and does it *easy*. Cap, they was heliotrope[4] to *him*!"

This recognition of my poor friend gratified me, in spite of the sad circumstances, because it had so much the sound of a compliment.

Pretty soon it was plain that something had got to be done. I suggested cigars. Thompson thought it was a good idea. He said:

"Likely it'll modify him some."

We puffed gingerly along for a while, and tried hard to imagine that things were improved. But it wasn't any use. Before very long, and without any consultation, both cigars were quietly dropped from our nerveless fingers at the same moment. Thompson said, with a sigh:

"No, Cap, it don't modify him worth a cent. Fact is, it makes him worse, becuz it appears to stir up his ambition. What do you reckon we better do, now?"

I was not able to suggest anything: indeed, I had to be swallowing and swallowing all the time, and did not like to trust myself to speak. Thompson fell to maundering,[5] in a desultory and low-spirited way, about the miserable

---

4. **heliotrope** (hē′ lē ə trōp′) *n*.: Sweet-smelling plant.
5. **maundering** (môn′ dər iŋ) *v*.: Talking in an unconnected way.

experiences of this night: and he got to referring to my poor friend by various titles—sometimes military ones, sometimes civil ones; and I
noticed that as fast as my poor friend's effectiveness grew, Thompson promoted him accordingly—gave him a bigger title. Finally he
said:

"I've got an idea. Suppos'n' we buckle down
to it and give the Colonel a bit of a shove toward t'other end of the car?—about ten foot,
say. He wouldn't have so much influence, then,
don't you reckon?"

I said it was a good scheme. So we took in a
good fresh breath at the broken pane, calculat-
ing to hold it till we got through: then we went
there and bent over that deadly cheese and
took a grip on the box. Thompson nodded "All
ready," and then we threw ourselves forward
with all our might: but Thompson slipped, and
slumped down with his nose on the cheese,
and his breath got loose. He gagged and
gasped, and floundered up and made a break
for the door, pawing the air and saying
hoarsely, "Don't hender me!—gimme the road!
I'm a-dying; gimme the road!" Out on the cold
platform I sat down and held his head awhile,
and he revived. Presently he said:

"Do you reckon we started the Gen'rul any?"
I said no: we hadn't budged him.

"Well, then, that idea's up the flume. We got
to think up something else. He's suited wher'
he is, I reckon; and if that's the way he feels
about it, and has made up his mind that he
don't wish to be disturbed, you bet he's a-going
to have his own way in the business. Yes, better leave him right wher' he is, long as he wants
it so; becuz he holds all the trumps, don't you
know, and so it stands to reason that the man
that lays out to alter his plans for him is going
to get left."

But we couldn't stay out there in that mad
storm; we should have frozen to death. So we
went in again and shut the door, and began to
suffer once more and take turns at the break in
the window. By and by, as we were starting
away from a station where we had stopped a
moment Thompson pranced in cheerily, and
exclaimed:

"We're all right, now! I reckon we've got the
Commodore this time. I judge I've got the stuff
here that'll take the tuck out of him."

It was carbolic acid. He had a carboy[6] of it.
He sprinkled it all around everywhere; in fact
he drenched everything with it, rifle-box,
cheese and all. Then we sat down, feeling pretty
hopeful. But it wasn't for long. You see the two
perfumes began to mix, and then—well, pretty
soon we made a break for the door; and out
there Thompson swabbed his face with his
bandanna and said in a kind of disheartened
way:

"It ain't no use. We can't buck agin *him*. He
just utilizes everything we put up to modify him
with, and gives it his own flavor and plays it
back on us. Why. Cap, don't you know, it's as
much as a hundred times worse in there now
than it was when he first got a-going. I never
did see one of 'em warm up to his work so, and
take such a dumnation interest in it. No, sir, I
never did, as long as I've ben on the road: and
I've carried a many a one of 'em, as I was telling
you."

We went in again after we were frozen pretty
stiff; but my, we couldn't *stay* in, now. So we
just waltzed back and forth, freezing, and
thawing, and stifling, by turns. In about an
hour we stopped at another station; and as we
left it Thompson came in with a bag, and said—

"Cap, I'm a-going to chance him once more—
just this once; and if we don't fetch him this
time, the thing for us to do, is to just throw up
the sponge and withdraw from the canvass.[7]
That's the way *I* put it up."

He had brought a lot of chicken feathers,
and dried apples, and leaf tobacco, and rags,
and old shoes, and sulphur, and asafetida,[8]
and one thing or another: and he piled them on
a breadth of sheet iron in the middle of the
floor, and set fire to them.

When they got well started. I couldn't see,

---

6. **carboy** (kär´ boi´) *n*.: Large glass bottle enclosed in
basketwork to prevent it from breaking.
7. **withdraw from the canvass** (kan´ vəs): Give up the
attempt.
8. **asafetida** (as´ ə fet´ ə də) *n*.: Bad-smelling substance
from certain plants, used as medicine.

myself, how even the corpse could stand it. All that went before was just simply poetry to that smell—but mind you, the original smell stood up out of it just as sublime as ever—fact is, these other smells just seemed to give it a better hold: and my, how rich it was! I didn't make these reflections there—there wasn't time—made them on the platform. And breaking for the platform, Thompson got suffocated and fell: and before I got him dragged out, which I did by the collar, I was mighty near gone myself. When we revived, Thompson said dejectedly:

"We got to stay out here, Cap. We got to do it. They ain't no other way. The Governor wants to travel alone, and he's fixed so he can outvote us."

And presently he added:

"And don't you know, we're *pisoned*. It's *our* last trip, you can make up your mind to it. Typhoid fever is what's going to come of this. I feel it a-coming right now. Yes, sir, we're elected, just as sure as you're born.

We were taken from the platform an hour later, frozen and insensible, at the next station, and I went straight off into a virulent fever, and never knew anything again for three weeks. I found out, then, that I had spent that awful night with a harmless box of rifles and a lot of innocent cheese; but the news was too late to save *me*; imagination had done its work, and my health was permanently shattered; neither Bermuda nor any other land can ever bring it back to me. This is my last trip; I am on my way home to die.

Guide for Responding

◆ Literature and Your Life

Reader's Response Did you find the story entertaining? Why or why not?

Thematic Focus What conflict do the narrator and Thompson face in this story?

Journal Writing Explain why you did or did not find this story humorous.

☑ Check Your Comprehension

1. What is the purpose of the narrator's journey?
2. Describe the mistake the narrator makes at the station. How does he complicate the mistake?
3. What makes the narrator and Thompson so uncomfortable?
4. What steps do they take to correct this problem?
5. What happens to the narrator in the end?

◆ Critical Thinking

INTERPRET

1. (a) Contrast what the narrator and Thompson believe to be true with what is really true.
   (b) How does this contrast contribute to the story's humor? **[Compare and Contrast]**
2. Thompson's description of the corpse's powerful odor makes it sound as if the corpse is deliberately trying to smell bad. How does this attitude add to the story's humor? **[Analyze]**
3. How would the characters' experience have been different if they'd known the source of the odor? **[Speculate]**
4. (a) Find at least three places in the story where the narrator exaggerates details. (b) How does the use of exaggeration contribute to the story's humor? **[Analyze]**

APPLY

5. How would the story be different if it were set in today's world? **[Connect]**

EXTEND

6. Would this story make a good movie? Why or why not? **[Media Link]**

Guide for Responding (continued)

◆ Literary Focus

SETTING

In both these stories, **setting**—the time, place, and culture in which the story unfolds—strongly influences the action. In fact, if you took the stories out of their settings, the central conflict in each would disappear, the characters would have no reason to behave as they do, and the story would evaporate altogether.

1. In "The Man to Send Rain Clouds," what aspects of the Native American culture affect the action, and how?
2. Why is the desert setting important in the action?
3. In "The Invalid's Story," describe the physical environment in which the narrator and Thompson sit.
4. What factors in this environment drive the action of the story?

◆ Build Vocabulary

USING THE SUFFIX *-ous*

Add the suffix *-ous*, meaning "full of," to each of the following words to create a new word. Define each new word.

1. melody + *-ous* =
2. prestige + *-ous* =
3. riot + *-ous* =

USING THE WORD BANK

On your paper, write the word or words closest in meaning to that of the first word.

1. deleterious: (a) delaying, (b) tasty, (c) harmful
2. cloister: (a) religious retreat, (b) group, (c) injury
3. judicious: (a) legal, (b) prudent, (c) imaginative
4. desultory: (a) romantic, (b) evil, (c) random
5. placidly: (a) quietly, (b) coldly, (c) politely
6. pagans: (a) aliens, (b) villains, (c) nonbelievers
7. ominous: (a) threatening, (b) dishonest, (c) dark
8. prodigious: (a) inventive, (b) enormous, (c) joyous
9. perverse: (a) untidy, (b) persisting in error, (c) on the other side

◆ Reading Strategy

USE YOUR SENSES

Each of these stories is filled with images, or word pictures, that appeal to various senses and help you picture in your mind the setting, the characters, and the events.

1. In "The Man to Send Rain Clouds," which two senses would you say Silko appeals to most? Support your answer.
2. List two images that especially stand out in Silko's story. Explain your answer.
3. While most stories use images of sight, sound, and sensation, "The Invalid's Story" is one of the few stories to play almost exclusively to the sense of smell. Find two images in the story that most vividly capture the smell of the cheese. Explain why each image is effective.

◆ Build Grammar Skills

PUNCTUATING DIALOGUE

When you **punctuate dialogue**, signal a change in speaker with a new paragraph and a new set of quotation marks.

When you write dialogue, being careful to use correct punctuation will help your readers keep track of who is saying what and when.

Practice On your paper, rewrite the following exchange of dialogue, adding correct punctuation.

Thompson shook his head. Cap, how long ago did you say the General left this vale of tears for a better place? Just a few days ago. Well I'm impressed—the General seems to have got himself a jim-dandy head start in the smelling business. He is a real go-getter, he is. Mr. Thompson, I'm afraid I don't find this very funny. Neither do I, Cap.

Writing Application Recall a conversation that you had in the past few days. Then re-create the conversation in writing. Follow the rules for punctuating dialogue.

Build Your Portfolio

 ## Idea Bank

Writing

1. **Suggestion Letter** Assume the role of the narrator in "The Invalid's Story," and write to the railroad company encouraging changes in their baggage-handling policies.

2. **Essay** Write a brief essay in which you explain what Silko's story reveals about Pueblo culture. Support your points with details from the story. You might point out, for example, what the story suggests about the Pueblo attitude toward nature.

3. **Research** Conduct research to learn more about either Pueblo culture or about railroad travel during the late 1800's. Present your findings in a written report. **[Social Studies Link]**

Speaking and Listening

4. **Dramatic Reading** With another classmate, prepare and deliver a dramatic reading of "The Invalid's Story." Use body language to emphasize the characters' misery.

5. **Persuasive Speech** "The Man to Send Rain Clouds" captures how the Pueblos have preserved their cultural heritage. Prepare and deliver a persuasive speech about why it is important for people to preserve their cultural heritages.

Projects

6. **Map** Create a map charting the route of the train in Twain's story. Include labels showing where events from the story might have occurred. **[Social Studies Link]**

7. **Diagram** Centuries ago, the Pueblos developed a sophisticated system for irrigating their land. Through research, find out about this system, and create a diagram illustrating how it works. **[Science Link]**

 ## Writing Mini-Lesson

Eulogy

When someone dies, one way of dealing with your sense of loss is to express your feelings for the person in a formal speech called a eulogy. Write a eulogy in memory of a relative, someone else you knew well, or perhaps a public figure. As you write, the following may help you.

Writing Skills Focus: Tone

Tone refers to the attitude a writer projects toward his or her subject. The tone of a piece of writing can be sarcastic or respectful, affectionate or angry. When you write, think about the attitude you want to communicate toward your subject, and find words that express that attitude. Look at this passage from "The Man to Send Rain Clouds."

> Leon turned to look up at the high blue mountains in the deep snow that reflected a faint red light from the west. He felt good because it was finished, and he was happy about the sprinkling of the holy water; now the old man could send them big thunderclouds for sure.

Notice that this description of Teofilo's burial has a peaceful, hopeful tone.

Prewriting Make a list of words to describe the person you are honoring that create the tone you want to project. Use your imagination to come up with incidents from the character's life that support your attitude toward him or her.

Drafting Begin your eulogy with a statement that sums up the attitude you wish to convey. Follow with details that support the statement.

Revising Review your draft, eliminating any language that strikes a wrong note and adding details that will strengthen the tone.

Guide for Reading

Guy de Maupassant
(1850–1893)

Perhaps the best-known short-story writer in the world, Guy de Maupassant is known for his realistic stories that capture the surprising and sometimes unfortunate twists and turns of life. In "The Necklace," a middle-class woman's dreams of becoming part of the social elite suddenly turn into a nightmare.

Maupassant was raised in northern France. As a young man, he served in the Franco-Prussian War, gathering experiences that would later appear in some of his stories. When the war ended, he took a job as a government clerk and devoted his spare time to writing. Maupassant became the literary apprentice of the well-known writer Gustave Flaubert, who introduced him to other illustrious writers of the day. Although Maupassant became quite successful and wealthy, his later years were shadowed by ill health and depression.

Tomás Rivera (1935–1984)

Born in Crystal City, Texas, Tomás Rivera soon joined what he called the "migrant labor stream" that travels throughout the farmlands of the United States. Faced with the challenge of alternating schooling with work in the fields, Rivera pursued his education tirelessly. His persistence paid off, as he eventually earned a Ph.D. in Spanish Literature.

Rivera's concern for the education of minorities led him to a career as an educator, limiting the time he could devote to his writing. Nevertheless, he has become one of the most renowned Mexican American authors in the United States. His work most often focuses on the experiences of migrant farm workers, as in "The Harvest." Why do you think writers like Rivera so often focus their work on subjects closely tied to their experiences?

◆ Build Vocabulary

WORD ROOTS: -ject-

Have you ever dreaded an *injection* or *rejected* an offer? These words are formed from the root *-ject-*, which means "to throw." In "The Necklace," you'll encounter the word *dejection*. Given the fact that the prefix *de-* means "down," the root *-ject-* means "to throw," and the suffix *-tion* means "the state of being," what do you think *dejection* means? See how the meaning you come up with fits the word's context in the story.

déclassé
rueful
resplendent
disheveled
profoundly
harrowed
astutely

WORD BANK

As you read these stories, you will encounter the words on this list. Each word is defined on the page where it first appears. Preview the list before you read.

◆ Build Grammar Skills

PARTICIPIAL PHRASES

A **participial phrase** is a participle (a form of a verb that acts as an adjective) accompanied by its modifiers and complement. The entire phrase acts as an adjective, modifying a noun or pronoun. By using participial phrases, writers can pack a sentence with precise details. Look at this example from "The Necklace":

> She washed the dishes, *wearing down her pink nails on greasy casseroles and the bottoms of saucepans.*

The italicized words make up the entire participial phrase, which modifies the subject *She*. The participle in this phrase is *wearing*.

The Necklace ◆ The Harvest

◆ *Literature and Your Life*

CONNECT YOUR EXPERIENCE

Think of a time when a simple or surprising discovery had a lasting impact on your life. Both of these stories capture the lasting impact of a character's discovery. Watch for the moment of discovery, and think about how the discovery changes each character's world.

Journal Writing Jot down your memories of an important discovery that had a lasting impact on your life.

THEMATIC FOCUS: LEARNING ABOUT OURSELVES AND OTHERS

As these two stories illustrate, some discoveries are pleasant and enriching, while others can be very unpleasant. Consider how we can learn from both types of discoveries.

◆ Background for Understanding

CULTURE

Tomás Rivera and the characters in "The Harvest" share an identity with close to one million migrant workers throughout the United States. Migrant workers move from region to region, harvesting and processing crops. Often, they are poorly paid, and they sometimes cannot qualify for unemployment compensation and disability insurance. Many migrant workers are children, and their periodic uprooting makes it difficult for them to obtain an education. Tomás Rivera faced this obstacle, and his concern with the migrant workers with whom he grew up is reflected in both his writing and his work as an educator.

◆ Literary Focus

THEME

The **theme** of a literary work is the insight about life that it communicates. Sometimes the theme of a work is stated directly. More often, however, the theme is conveyed indirectly through the experiences of the characters, through the events and setting of the work, or through the use of literary devices, such as irony and symbols. For example, if a story shows a character finding that he has more in common with someone than expected, the story's theme might be an insight about the feelings that all people share.

◆ Reading Strategy

DRAW CONCLUSIONS

In determining the theme of most stories, you usually need to **draw conclusions**— to piece together details in the story and make decisions about the underlying meaning of these details. For example, if a story depicts a character who makes a tough decision, you might piece together what you know about the character to draw conclusions about why he made his decision. As you read these stories, use the details that the authors provide to draw conclusions about why the characters act as they do. Then try to draw conclusions about how the characters' actions might relate to the themes of the stories. You might use a chart like the one shown.

Character's Actions	Related Character Traits	Reasons for the Actions	What This Suggests About Theme

The Necklace

Guy de Maupassant

She was one of those pretty, charming young women who are born, as if by an error of Fate, into a petty official's family. She had no dowry,[1] no hopes, not the slightest chance of being appreciated, understood, loved, and married by a rich and distinguished man; so she slipped into marriage with a minor civil servant at the Ministry of Education.

Unable to afford jewelry, she dressed simply: but she was as wretched as a déclassé, for women have neither caste nor breeding—in them beauty, grace, and charm replace pride of birth. Innate refinement, instinctive elegance, and suppleness of wit give them their place on the only scale that counts, and these qualities make humble girls the peers of the grandest ladies.

She suffered constantly, feeling that all the attributes of a gracious life, every luxury, should rightly have been hers. The poverty of her rooms—the shabby walls, the worn furniture, the ugly upholstery—caused her pain. All these things that another woman of her class would not even have noticed, tormented her and made her angry. The very sight of the little Breton girl who cleaned for her awoke rueful thoughts and the wildest dreams in her mind. She dreamt of thick carpeted reception rooms with Oriental hangings, lighted by tall, bronze torches, and with two huge footmen in knee breeches made drowsy by the heat from the stove, asleep in the wide armchairs. She dreamt of great drawing rooms upholstered in old silks, with fragile little tables holding priceless knickknacks, and of enchanting little sitting rooms redolent of perfume, designed for tea-time chats with intimate friends—famous, sought-after men whose attentions all women longed for.

When she sat down to dinner at her round table with its three-day-old cloth, and watched her husband opposite her lift the lid of the soup tureen and exclaim, delighted: "Ah, a good home-made beef stew! There's nothing better . . ." she would visualize elegant dinners with gleaming silver amid tapestried walls peopled by knights and ladies and exotic birds in a fairy forest; she would think of exquisite dishes served on gorgeous china, and of gallantries whispered and received with sphinx-like smiles[2] while eating the pink flesh of trout or wings of grouse.

She had no proper wardrobe, no jewels, nothing. And those were the only things that she loved—she felt she was made for them. She would have so loved to charm, to be envied, to be admired and sought after.

---

1. **dowry** (dou´ rē) n.: Property that a woman brought to her husband at marriage.

2. **gallantries whispered and received with sphinx** (sfiŋks)-**like smiles**: Flirtatious compliments whispered and received with mysterious smiles.

She had a rich friend, a schoolmate from the convent she had attended, but she didn't like to visit her because it always made her so miserable when she got home again. She would weep for whole days at a time from sorrow, regret, despair, and distress.

Then one evening her husband arrived home looking triumphant and waving a large envelope.

"There," he said, "there's something for you."

She tore it open eagerly and took out a printed card which said:

"The Minister of Education and Madame Georges Ramponneau[3] request the pleasure of the company of M. and Mme. Loisel[4] at an evening reception at the Ministry on Monday, January 18th."

Instead of being delighted, as her husband had hoped, she tossed the invitation on the table and muttered, annoyed:

"What do you expect me to do with that?"

"Why, I thought you'd be pleased, dear. You never go out and this would be an occasion for you, a great one! I had a lot of trouble getting it. Everyone wants an invitation; they're in great demand and there are only a few reserved for the employees. All the officials will be there."

She looked at him, irritated, and said impatiently:

"I haven't a thing to wear. How could I go?"

It had never even occurred to him. He stammered:

"But what about the dress you wear to the theater? I think it's lovely. . . ."

He fell silent, amazed and bewildered to see that his wife was crying. Two big tears escaped from the corners of her eyes and rolled slowly toward the corners of her mouth. He mumbled:

"What is it? What is it?"

But, with great effort, she had overcome her misery; and now she answered him calmly, wiping her tear-damp cheeks:

"It's nothing. It's just that I have no evening dress and so I can't go to the party. Give the invitation to one of your colleagues whose wife will be better dressed than I would be."

He was overcome. He said:

"Listen, Mathilde,[5] how much would an evening dress cost—a suitable one that you could wear again on other occasions, something very simple?"

She thought for several seconds, making her calculations and at the same time estimating how much she could ask for without eliciting an immediate refusal and an exclamation of horror from this economical government clerk.

At last, not too sure of herself, she said:

"It's hard to say exactly but I think I could manage with four hundred francs."

He went a little pale, for that was exactly the amount he had put aside to buy a rifle so that he could go hunting the following summer near Nanterre, with a few friends who went shooting larks around there on Sundays.

However, he said:

"Well, all right, then. I'll give you four hundred francs. But try to get something really nice."

As the day of the ball drew closer, Madame Loisel seemed depressed, disturbed, worried—despite the fact that her dress was ready. One evening her husband said:

"What's the matter? You've really been very strange these last few days."

And she answered:

"I hate not having a single jewel, not one stone, to wear. I shall look so dowdy.[6] I'd almost rather

---

◆ **Reading Strategy**
What conclusion can you draw about Madame Loisel on the basis of her reaction to this invitation?

---

3. **Madame Georges Ramponneau** (ma dam´ zhôrzh ram pə nō´)
4. **Loisel** (lwa zel´)

---

5. **Mathilde** (ma tēld´)
6. **dowdy** (dou´dē) adj.: Shabby.

◆ **Build Vocabulary**

déclassé (dā´ klä sā´) adj.: Lowered in social status

rueful (r\overline{oo}´ fəl) adj.: Feeling sorrow or regret

---

not go to the party."

He suggested:

"You can wear some fresh flowers. It's considered very chic[7] at this time of year. For ten francs you can get two or three beautiful roses."

That didn't satisfy her at all.

"No . . . there's nothing more humiliating than to look poverty-stricken among a lot of rich women."

Then her husband exclaimed:

"Wait—you silly thing! Why don't you go and see Madame Forestier[8] and ask her to lend you some jewelry. You certainly know her well enough for that, don't you think?"

She let out a joyful cry.

"You're right. It never occurred to me."

The next day she went to see her friend and related her tale of woe.

Madame Forestier went to her mirrored wardrobe, took out a big jewel case, brought it to Madame Loisel, opened it, and said:

"Take your pick, my dear."

Her eyes wandered from some bracelets to a pearl necklace, then to a gold Venetian cross set with stones, of very fine workmanship. She tried on the jewelry before the mirror, hesitating, unable to bring herself to take them off, to give them back. And she kept asking:

"Do you have anything else, by chance?"

"Why yes. Here, look for yourself. I don't know which ones you'll like."

All at once, in a box lined with black satin, she came upon a superb diamond necklace, and her heart started beating with overwhelming desire. Her hands trembled as she picked it up. She fastened it around her neck over her high-necked dress and stood there gazing at herself ecstatically.

Hesitantly, filled with terrible anguish, she asked:

"Could you lend me this one—just this and nothing else?"

"Yes, of course."

She threw her arms around her friend's neck, kissed her ardently, and fled with her treasure.

The day of the party arrived. Madame Loisel was a great success. She was the prettiest woman there—resplendent graceful, beaming, and deliriously happy. All the men looked at her, asked who she was, tried to get themselves introduced to her. All the minister's aides wanted to waltz with her. The minister himself noticed her.

She danced enraptured—carried away, intoxicated with pleasure, forgetting everything in this triumph of her beauty and the glory of her success, floating in a cloud of happiness formed by all this homage, all this admiration, all the desires she had stirred up—by this victory so complete and so sweet to the heart of a woman.

When she left the party, it was almost four in the morning. Her husband had been sleeping since midnight in a small, deserted sitting room, with three other gentlemen whose wives were having a wonderful time.

He brought her wraps so that they could leave and put them around her shoulders—the plain wraps from her everyday life whose shabbiness jarred with the elegance of her evening dress. She felt this and wanted to escape quickly so that the other women, who were enveloping themselves in their rich furs, wouldn't see her.

Loisel held her back.

"Wait a minute. You'll catch cold out there. I'm going to call a cab."

But she wouldn't listen to him and went hastily downstairs. Outside in the street, there was no cab to be found; they set out to look for one, calling to the drivers they saw passing in the distance.

They walked toward the Seine,[9] shivering and miserable. Finally, on the embankment, they found one of those ancient nocturnal broughams[10] which are only to be seen in Paris at night, as if they were ashamed to show their shabbiness in daylight.

It took them to their door in the Rue des Martyrs, and they went sadly upstairs to their apartment. For her, it was all over. And he was

◆ **Literary Focus**

What insight about life is suggested by the contrast between Madame Loisel's beautiful dress and the "plain wraps of her everyday life"?

---

7. **chic** (shēk) *adj.*: Fashionable.
8. **Forestier** (fô rə styā´)

9. **Seine** (sān): River flowing through Paris.
10. **broughams** (brōōms) *n.*: Horse-drawn carriages.

▲**Critical Viewing** Imagine Mathilde trying on piece after piece of her wealthy friend's jewelry. What can you tell about her personality from this behavior? **[Infer]**

thinking that he had to be at the Ministry by ten.

She took off her wraps before the mirror so that she could see herself in all her glory once more. Then she cried out. The necklace was gone; there was nothing around her neck.

Her husband, already half undressed, asked: "What's the matter?"

She turned toward him in a frenzy:

"The . . . the . . . necklace—it's gone."

He got up, thunderstruck.

"What did you say? . . . What! . . . Impossible!"

And they searched the folds of her dress, the folds of her wrap, the pockets, everywhere. They didn't find it.

◆ **Build Vocabulary**

resplendent (ri splen´ dənt) *adj*: Shining brightly

He asked:

"Are you sure you still had it when we left the ball?"

"Yes. I remember touching it in the hallway of the Ministry."

"But if you had lost it in the street, we would have heard it fall. It must be in the cab."

"Yes, most likely. Do you remember the number?"

"No. What about you—did you notice it?"

"No."

They looked at each other in utter dejection. Finally Loisel got dressed again.

"I'm going to retrace the whole distance we covered on foot," he said, "and see if I can't find it."

And he left the house. She remained in her evening dress, too weak to go to bed, sitting crushed on a chair, lifeless and blank.

Her husband returned at about seven o'-clock. He had found nothing.

He went to the police station, to the newspapers to offer a reward, to the offices of the cab companies—in a word, wherever there seemed to be the slightest hope of tracing it.

She spent the whole day waiting, in a state of utter hopelessness before such an appalling catastrophe.

Loisel returned in the evening, his face lined and pale; he had learned nothing.

"You must write to your friend," he said, "and tell her that you've broken the clasp of the necklace and that you're getting it mended. That'll give us time to decide what to do."

She wrote the letter at his dictation.

By the end of the week, they had lost all hope.

Loisel, who had aged five years, declared: "We'll have to replace the necklace."

The next day they took the case in which it had been kept and went to the jeweler whose name appeared inside it. He looked through his ledgers:

"I didn't sell this necklace, madame. I only supplied the case."

Then they went from one jeweler to the next, trying to find a necklace like the other, racking their memories, both of them sick with worry and distress.

In a fashionable shop near the Palais Royal,

they found a diamond necklace which they decided was exactly like the other. It was worth 40,000 francs. They could have it for 36,000 francs.

They asked the jeweler to hold it for them for three days, and they stipulated that he should take it back for 34,000 francs if the other necklace was found before the end of February.

Loisel possessed 18,000 francs left him by his father. He would borrow the rest.

He borrowed, asking a thousand francs from one man, five hundred from another, a hundred here, fifty there. He signed promissory notes,[11] borrowed at exorbitant rates, dealt with usurers and the entire race of moneylenders. He compromised his whole career, gave his signature even when he wasn't sure he would be able to honor it, and horrified by the anxieties with which his future would be filled, by the black misery about to descend upon him, by the prospect of physical privation and moral suffering, went to get the new necklace, placing on the jeweler's counter 36,000 francs.

When Madame Loisel went to return the necklace, Madame Forestier said in a faintly waspish tone:

"You could have brought it back a little sooner! I might have needed it."

She didn't open the case as her friend had feared she might. If she had noticed the substitution, what would she have thought? What would she have said? Mightn't she have taken Madame Loisel for a thief?

Madame Loisel came to know the awful life of the poverty-stricken. However, she resigned herself to it with unexpected fortitude. The crushing debt had to be paid. She would pay it. They dismissed the maid; they moved into an attic under the roof.

She came to know all the heavy household chores, the loathsome work of the kitchen. She washed the dishes, wearing down her pink nails on greasy casseroles and the bottoms of saucepans. She did the laundry, washing shirts and dishcloths which she hung on a line to dry; she took the garbage down to the street every morning, and carried water upstairs, stopping at every floor to get her breath. Dressed like a working-class woman, she went to the fruit store, the grocer, and the butcher with her basket on her arm, bargaining, outraged, contesting each sou[12] of her pitiful funds.

Every month some notes had to be honored and more time requested on others.

Her husband worked in the evenings, putting a shopkeeper's ledgers in order, and often at night as well, doing copying at twenty-five centimes a page.

And it went on like that for ten years.

After ten years, they had made good on everything, including the usurious rates and the compound interest.

Madame Loisel looked old now. She had become the sort of strong woman, hard and coarse, that one finds in poor families. Disheveled, her skirts askew, with reddened hands, she spoke in a loud voice, slopping water over the floors as she washed them. But sometimes, when her husband was at the office, she would sit down by the window and muse over that party long ago when she had been so beautiful, the belle of the ball.

How would things have turned out if she hadn't lost that necklace? Who could tell? How strange and fickle life is! How little it takes to make or break you!

Then one Sunday when she was strolling along the Champs Elysées[13] to forget

◆ **Literary Focus**
What insight about the effect of hardship on one's character does this description of Madame Loisel suggest?

---

12. sou (sōō) *n*.: Former French coin, worth very little; the centime (sän tēm′), mentioned later, was also of little value.

13. Champs Elysées (shän zā lē zā′): Fashionable street in Paris.

◆ **Build Vocabulary**

disheveled (di shev′ əld) *adj*.: Disarranged and untidy

profoundly (prō found′ lē) *adj*.: Deeply and intensely

---

11. promissory (präm′ i sôr′ ē) **notes**: Written promises to pay back borrowed money.

the week's chores for a while, she suddenly caught sight of a woman taking a child for a walk. It was Madame Forestier, still young, still beautiful, still charming.

Madame Loisel started to tremble. Should she speak to her? Yes, certainly she should. And now that she had paid everything back, why shouldn't she tell her the whole story?

She went up to her.

"Hello, Jeanne."

The other didn't recognize her and was surprised that this plainly dressed woman should speak to her so familiarly. She murmured:

"But . . . madame! . . . I'm sure . . . You must be mistaken."

"No, I'm not. I am Mathilde Loisel."

Her friend gave a little cry.

"Oh! Oh, my poor Mathilde, how you've changed!"

"Yes, I've been through some pretty hard times since I last saw you and I've had plenty of trouble—and all because of you!"

"Because of me? What do you mean?"

"You remember the diamond necklace you lent me to wear to the party at the Ministry?"

"Yes. What about it?"

"Well, I lost it."

"What are you talking about? You returned it to me."

"What I gave back to you was another one just like it. And it took us ten years to pay for it. You can imagine it wasn't easy for us, since we were quite poor . . . Anyway, I'm glad it's over and done with."

Madame Forestier stopped short.

"You say you bought a diamond necklace to replace that other one?"

"Yes. You didn't even notice then? They really were exactly alike."

And she smiled, full of a proud, simple joy.

Madame Forestier, profoundly moved, took Mathilde's hands in her own.

"Oh, my poor, poor Mathilde! Mine was false. It was worth five hundred francs at the most!"

Guide for Responding

◆ Literature and Your Life

Reader's Response Do you feel sorry for Madame Loisel? Why or why not?

Thematic Focus Do you think Madame Loisel discovered anything about herself as a result of her ordeal? Explain.

Journal Writing Write about what you would have done if you were in Madame Loisel's place.

☑ Check Your Comprehension

1. What explanation does Madame Loisel give for being upset about the special invitation?
2. What happens to spoil Madame Loisel's triumph at the party?
3. What happens to Madame Loisel in the ten years she works to pay off the cost of the necklace?

◆ Critical Thinking

INTERPRET

1. Do you think the author wants us to sympathize with Madame Loisel's unhappiness at the beginning of the story? Why or why not? **[Infer]**
2. How are the things that Madame Loisel values different from what her husband values? **[Compare and Contrast]**
3. (a) How does Madame Loisel change during the course of the story? (b) What causes her to change? **[Analyze]**
4. What symbolic meaning does the necklace have for Madame Loisel? **[Interpret]**
5. In what way is the ending of the story ironic, or surprising? **[Interpret]**

EXTEND

6. What does the story show you about life in middle-class French society in the late nineteenth century? **[Social Studies Link]**

The Harvest

Tomás Rivera

The end of September and the beginning of October. That was the best time of the year. First, because it was a sign that the work was coming to an end and that the return to Texas would start. Also, because there was something in the air that the folks created, an aura of peace and death. The earth also shared that feeling. The cold came more frequently, the frosts that killed by night, in the morning covered the earth in whiteness. It seemed that all was coming to an end. The folks felt that all was coming to rest. Everyone took to thinking more. And they talked more about the trip back to Texas, about the harvests, if it had gone well or bad for them, if they would return or not to the same place next year. Some began to take long walks around the grove. It seemed like in these last days of work there was a wake over the earth. It made you think.

That's why it wasn't very surprising to see Don Trine take a walk by himself through the grove and to walk along the fields every afternoon. This was at the beginning, but when some youngsters asked him if they could tag along, he even got angry. He told them he didn't want anybody sticking behind him.

"Why would he want to be all by hisself, anyway?"

"To heck with him: it's his business."

"But, you notice, it never fails. Every time, why, sometimes I don't even think he eats supper, he takes his walk. Don't you think that's a bit strange?"

"Well, I reckon. But you saw how he got real mad when we told him we'd go along with him. It wasn't anything to make a fuss over. This ain't his land. We can go wherever we take a liking to. He can't tell us what to do."

"That's why I wonder, why'd he want to walk by hisself?"

And that's how all the rumors about Don Trine's walks got started. The folks couldn't figure out why or what he got out of taking off by himself every afternoon. When he would leave,

Farmworker de Califas, Tony Ortega, Courtesy of the artist

and somebody would spy on him, somehow or other he would catch on, then take a little walk, turn around and head right back to his chicken coop. The fact of the matter is that everybody began to say he was hiding the money he had earned that year or that he had found some buried treasure and every day, little by little, he was bringing it back to his coop. Then they began to say that when he was young he had run around with a gang in Mexico and that he always carried around a lot of money with him. They said, too, that even if it was real hot, he carried a belt full of money beneath his undershirt. Practically all the speculation centered on the idea that he had money.

"Let's see, who's he got to take care of? He's an old bachelor. He ain't never married or had a family. So, with him working so many years . . . Don't you think he's bound to have money? And then, what's that man spend his money on? The only thing he buys is his bit of food every Saturday. Once in a while, a beer, but that's all."
"Yeah, he's gotta have a pile of money, for sure. But, you think he's going to bury it around here?"
"Who said he's burying anything? Look, he always goes for his food on Saturday. Let's check close where he goes this week, and on Saturday, when he's on his errand, we'll see what he's hiding. Whadda you say?"
"Good'nuff. Let's hope he doesn't catch on to us."
That week the youngsters closely watched

◆ **Build Vocabulary**

harrowed (har´ ōd) v.: Broken up and leveled by a harrow, a frame with spikes or disks, drawn by a horse or tractor

---

◄ **Critical Viewing** The bright colors in this painting capture the heat of the day and the energetic labors of the farm workers in the fields. Does this image capture the setting of the story as you imagine it? **[Evaluate]**

Don Trine's walks. They noticed that he would disappear into the grove, then come out on the north side, cross the road then cross the field until he got to the irrigation ditch. There he dropped from sight for a while, then he reappeared in the west field. It was there where he would disappear and linger the most. They noticed also that, so as to throw people off his track, he would take a different route, but he always spent more time around the ditch that crossed the west field. They decided to investigate the ditch and that field the following Saturday.

◆ **Reading Strategy**
What conclusion would you draw about Don Trine from his mysterious behavior?

When that day arrived, the boys were filled with anticipation. The truck had scarcely left and they were on their way to the west field. The truck had not yet disappeared and they had already crossed the grove. What they found they almost expected. There was nothing in the ditch, but in the field that had been <u>harrowed</u> after pulling the potatoes they found a number of holes.

"You notice all the holes here? The harrow didn't make these. Look, here's some foot prints, and notice that the holes are at least a foot deep. You can stick your arm in them up to your elbow. No animal makes these kind of holes. Whadda you think?"
"Well, it's bound to be Don Trine. But, what's he hiding? Why's he making so many holes? You think the landowner knows what he's up to?"
"Naw, man. Why, look, you can't see them from the road. You gotta come in a ways to notice they're here. What's he making them for? What's he using them for? And, look, they're all about the same width. Whadda you think?"
"Well, you got me. Maybe we'll know if we hide in the ditch and see what he does when he comes here."
"Look, here's a coffee can. I bet you this is what he digs with."

Campesino, 1976, Daniel DeSiga, Wight Art Gallery, University of California, Los Angeles

▲ **Critical Viewing** What does this painting tell you about the lives of Don Trine and the other migrant farm workers in "The Harvest"? **[Infer]**

"I think you're right."

The boys had to wait until late the following Monday to discover the reason for the holes. But the word had spread around so that everybody already knew that Don Trine had a bunch of holes in that field. They tried not to let on but the allusions they made to the holes while they were out in the fields during the day were very obvious. Everybody thought there had to be a big explanation. So, the youngsters spied more carefully and <u>astutely</u>.

That afternoon they managed to fool Don Trine and saw what he was doing. They saw, and as they had suspected, Don Trine used the coffee can to dig a hole. Every so often, he would measure with his arm the depth of the hole. When it went up to his elbow, he stuck in his left arm, then filled dirt in around it with his right hand, all the way up to the elbow.

◆ **Build Vocabulary**

astutely (ə stoot′ lē) *adv.*: Cleverly or cunningly

Then he stayed like that for some time. He seemed very satisfied and even tried to light a cigarette with one hand. Not being able to, he just let it hang from his lips. Then he dug another hole and repeated the process. The boys could not understand why he did this. That was what puzzled them the most. They had believed that, with finding out what it was he did, they would understand everything. But it didn't turn out that way at all. The boys brought the news to the rest of the folks in the grove and nobody there understood either. In reality, when they found out that the holes didn't have anything to do with money, they thought Don Trine was crazy and even lost interest in the whole matter. But not everybody.

The next day one of the boys who discovered what Don Trine had been up to went by himself to a field. There he went through the same procedure that he had witnessed the day before. What he experienced and what he never forgot was feeling the earth move, feeling the earth grasp his fingers and even caressing them. He also felt the warmth of the earth. He sensed he was inside someone. Then he understood what Don Trine was doing. He was not crazy, he simply liked to feel the earth when it was sleeping.

That's why the boy kept going to the field every afternoon, until one night a hard freeze came on so that he could no longer dig any

holes in the ground. The earth was fast asleep. Then he thought of next year, in October at harvest time, when once again he could repeat what Don Trine did. It was like when someone died. You always blamed yourself for not loving him more before he died.

Guide for Responding

◆ *Literature and Your Life*

Reader's Response What do you think of Don Trine? Why?

Thematic Focus Were you surprised by the boys' discovery? Explain.

☑ Check Your Comprehension

1. What does Don Trine do every afternoon that arouses the curiosity of his fellow workers?
2. What do the people think he is doing?
3. What does the boy discover about Don Trine's behavior?

◆ Critical Thinking

INTERPRET

1. How does the opening paragraph foreshadow, or hint at, the ending of the story? **[Apply]**
2. What do the boys' speculations about Don Trine reveal about them? **[Infer]**
3. What does the one boy's ability to understand Don Trine suggest about the boy? **[Infer]**
4. What is the meaning of the last two sentences? **[Interpret]**

APPLY

5. What can we learn from this story to help us avoid misunderstanding people's actions? **[Apply]**

Guide for Responding (continued)

◆ Reading Strategy

DRAW CONCLUSIONS

By piecing together what you know about the characters in these stories, you can **draw conclusions** about the reasons for their actions. You can then use your understanding of their behavior to draw broader conclusions about human nature.

1. What conclusion can you draw about Madame Loisel from her response to the invitation her husband brings home?
2. Many of the characters in "The Necklace" place a high value on material goods. What conclusion can you draw about such values on the basis of this story? Explain.
3. What conclusion can you draw about human nature from the fact that most of the workers are satisfied with speculating about Don Trine's afternoon walk, as opposed to trying to understand it?
4. What conclusion can you draw about the importance of nature to the human spirit from the ending of Rivera's story?

◆ Literary Focus

THEME

Both these stories convey important **themes,** or general insights, related to human values. In both stories, the themes are conveyed indirectly through the characters' comments and actions.

1. Toward the end of "The Necklace," Madame Loisel thinks, "How strange and fickle life is! How little it takes to make or break you!" What does this statement suggest about the complexity of life?
2. Considering Madame Loisel's feelings at the beginning of the story, along with the events that occur in the aftermath of the ball and the surprising twist that occurs at the end, what would you say is the theme of "The Necklace"? Support your answer.
3. Using the last two paragraphs as a clue, what do you think is the theme of "The Harvest"? Support your answer.

◆ Build Vocabulary

USING THE WORD ROOT -ject-

Complete each sentence with one of the words containing the root -ject-, which means "to throw."

    a. trajectory   **b.** eject   **c.** projectile

1. When his engines went out, the pilot had to ___?___.
2. Based on its ___?___, the players could tell the ball would miss the basket.
3. Without regard for people's safety, he hurled a ___?___ into the crowd.

USING THE WORD BANK

On your paper, write the word that comes closest in meaning to the first word.

1. astutely: (a) cleverly, (b) grandly, (c) thriftily
2. resplendent: (a) beautiful, (b) wealthy, (c) sturdy
3. profoundly: (a) slowly, (b) deeply, (c) quietly
4. déclassé: (a) decorated, (b) lowered in social status, (c) tardy
5. harrowed: (a) mad, (b) frightened, (c) plowed
6. rueful: (a) amused, (b) sweet, (c) regretting
7. disheveled: (a) attractive, (b) messy, (c) rusty

◆ Build Grammar Skills

PARTICIPIAL PHRASES

In both stories, the writers use **participial phrases**—groups of words consisting of a participle modified by an adverb or adverb phrase or accompanied by a complement—to pack sentences with details about the characters and their actions.

Practice Identify the participial phrases and the words they modify in the following sentences.

1. Dancing all night, Madame Loisel forgot her cares.
2. At home she looked for the necklace, reaching desperately through her clothing.
3. Don Trine's walks were a mystery confounding all the workers.
4. The boy, sifting the soil through his fingers, suddenly understood what Don Trine felt.

Build Your Portfolio

 Idea Bank

Writing

1. **Character Sketch** Write a character sketch of Monsieur Loisel, based on his actions and the comments of the narrator in "The Necklace."

2. **Different Point of View** By the end of "The Harvest," you have a clear sense of Don Trine's character and motivations. Rewrite the story using Trine as your first-person narrator.

3. **Essay About the Use of Irony** Irony, the contrast between an expected outcome and an actual outcome or between appearance and reality, plays a key role in "The Necklace." Review the story, looking for examples of irony. Then write an essay in which you discuss the role of irony in the story. Use passages from the story to support your points.

Speaking and Listening

4. **Improvisation** With another student, improvise a conversation between Madame Loisel and her husband after she returns from meeting her old friend ten years later.

5. **Debate** With a group of classmates, stage a debate on the issue of whether or not Madame Loisel deserved her fate.

Projects

6. **Illustration** Illustrate one of the scenes from "The Necklace," using any medium you like. Share your illustration with the class. **[Art Link]**

7. **Music** Find Mexican music to accompany a reading of "The Harvest." Share your music with the class, and explain why you chose it. **[Music Link]**

 Writing Mini-Lesson

Scene for a Television Drama

Drama began thousands of years ago as stories were acted out around the campfire. Today we continue to watch stories being acted out around a cool, electronic campfire—the television. Imagine one of the stories you have read so far turned into a television drama. What would the final, climactic scenes of the drama be like?

Writing Skills Focus: Climax and Resolution

Every story—whether told as narrative or acted out as drama—reaches a high point of interest called a **climax**. The climax is the point at which the audience's tension and involvement peak. The climax usually takes the form of a confrontation between the main character and someone else or an action sequence involving the main character doing something like winning a race, surviving an earthquake, facing down a hostile crowd. Following the climax, the **resolution** shows how the drama's central conflict will be resolved.

Prewriting Choose one of the stories you have read in this book and write its climax and resolution as a scene for a television drama. Note the actions that you believe make up the climax and resolution of this story.

Drafting Turn the narration of the story's climax and resolution into dialogue (conversation) and stage directions. Review dramatic format (you might look at the plays in this book). Include instructions to the camera person, indicating close-ups and wide shots.

Revising After you have written your scene for a television drama, ask a friend to read it to see if it makes sense. Read it over yourself, and make any changes needed to clarify or enliven the action.

Writing Process Workshop

As you've learned from this section, a **short story** can be suspenseful, touching, or amusing. Its action can occur at any time or in any place. The story might be narrated by one of the characters or it might be told by a narrator who is an outside observer.

Despite all these differences, short stories do share some common elements. All short stories are fictional, or made-up, narratives. In most short stories, the main character faces a conflict, or problem, that is resolved by the end of the story. Write a short story that includes these elements.

The following skills, introduced in this section's Writing Mini-Lessons, will help you.

Writing Skills Focus

▶ **Write in a tone that reflects the attitude of the characters** in your story. The tone might be sarcastic, respectful, or angry, for example. (See p. 533.)

▶ **Provide a climax and resolution** for your story. The climax is the high point of interest or suspense. The resolution is the end of the story, where readers learn how the characters' conflict is finally resolved. (See p. 547.)

Toni Cade Bambara uses these skills in this climactic scene from "Blues Ain't No Mockin Bird."

① This is the climax, the most highly charged moment in the story.

② The matter-of-fact tone shared by the narrator and Granddaddy heightens the intensity of this scene by providing a contrast.

MODEL FROM LITERATURE

from "Blues Ain't No Mockin Bird" by Toni Cade Bambara

Then Granddaddy's other hand flies up like a sudden and gentle bird, slaps down fast on top of the camera and lifts off half like it was a calabash cut for sharing. ①

"Hey," Camera jumps forward. He gathers up the parts into his chest and everything unrollin and fallin all over. "Whatcha tryin to do? You'll ruin the film." He looks down into his chest of metal reels and things like he's protectin a kitten from the cold.

"You standin in the misses' flower bed," ② says Granddaddy. "This is our own place."

Prewriting

Choose an Idea Come up with a story idea by wondering, What if? For example, What if aliens invaded Earth? or What if people could become invisible? You can also choose one of the topic ideas listed here.

Story Ideas

- A man loses his memory while traveling
- Three families volunteer to colonize a distant planet
- Two best friends have a terrible fight
- A teenager travels back in time

Plan the Tone of Your Story Think about your story's characters, and ask yourself how those characters feel about themselves, about the other characters in the story, and about the problems they face. Make notes on your characters' attitudes. Are they happy? Bitter? Respectful? Rude? Sincere? Sarcastic? Then think how you might express that tone in your writing.

Plot the Climax and Resolution Before you begin to write, you must know what conflict your characters will face. Ask yourself:

▶ How will the characters struggle with their problem?
▶ How might their problem worsen?
▶ What will ultimately happen?

Your answers will allow you to plan the climax and resolution of your story.

Drafting

Choose a Point of View Choose the point of view from which you will tell your story. You can use a first-person point of view, in which the narrator is a character in the story; a third-person limited point of view, in which the narrator does not participate in the action and can see into the mind of only one character; or a third-person omniscient point of view, in which the narrator does not take part in the story and can see into the minds of all the characters. The point of view from which a story is told can have great impact.

APPLYING LANGUAGE SKILLS: Subject and Verb Agreement With Collective Nouns

A **collective noun** names a group. It may be singular, where the group acts as a single unit, or plural, where the group acts as separate parts. Singular collective nouns take a singular verb. Plural collective nouns take a plural verb.

Singular: *The class is on a field trip.*

Plural: *The class are writing their stories.*

Practice Write each sentence, using the verb that agrees with the collective noun.

1. The crowd (has, have) stayed together.
2. The group (is, are) now spreading out.
3. The army (is, are) charging as a single unit.
4. The crowd (has, have) run to their homes.

Writing Application Review your story draft to make sure that any collective nouns you have used agree with their verbs. If not, correct the verb.

Include a Climax and Resolution Toward the end of your story, give a vivid description of the climax—the moment when the excitement and drama reach their highest point. Then provide a resolution that tells how everything turns out.

Revising

Use a Checklist Review the Writing Skills Focus on the first page of this lesson, and use the items as a checklist to evaluate and revise your short story. Ask yourself:

▶ Does my writing have a distinct tone?
Have one or more peers review your draft. Ask them to identify the tone of your writing. If they do not identify the tone you intended, consider how you might add, change, or remove details to achieve your desired tone.

▶ Does my story have a clear climax and resolution?
Have your peers identify the highest emotional point of your story. Then have them describe how the conflict turns out. If they are unsure of what your climax or resolution is, consider ways to make it clearer.

Work With a Peer Reviewer After reviewing your own work, have a peer make additional suggestions for revising your story. Have your peer reviewer keep these questions in mind:

1. How are the characters introduced, and how well are they developed? What makes them believable? How can they be improved?
2. How entertaining is the story? How can it be made more entertaining?
3. How clearly is the main conflict presented? How can it be made clearer?
4. How realistic is the dialogue? How can it be improved?

Publishing

Present Your Narrative to a Live Audience Reading your narrative aloud to a group is a great way to share it with others. Take time to practice beforehand—either alone in front of the mirror or with another person. Then, when presenting your narrative, read slowly and clearly and make eye contact with your audience. Vary the volume and tone of your voice for emphasis, and when you read dialogue, try to take on the personalities of the different characters.

Real-World Reading Skills Workshop

Strategies for Success

A short story is not meant to be objective, so it's acceptable for a story writer to reveal a specific opinion through his or her writing. Other types of writing, however, *are* meant to be objective. Yet writers sometimes have a bias—a leaning toward a specific position. How can you recognize bias while reading?

Look for Loaded Words Loaded words are used to trigger a positive or a negative emotion in you. For example, politicians who cut budgets might call themselves "thrifty." In contrast, they might call opponents who increase funding for certain projects "reckless spenders." Look for vocabulary that unfairly creates bias.

Watch Out for Stereotyping
Stereotypes label all members of a group with the same qualities, ignoring the individual differences among them. For example, the argument that "all politicians are crooks" is stereotyping and creates bias.

Beware of Slanted Arguments A slanted argument promotes only one side of an issue and intentionally omits facts that go against that side. For example, a politician might urge you to vote for him because he showed up for work one hundred days in a row—but he might not tell you that he missed eighty days during the year.

> ✔ Here are other situations in which to watch for bias in your reading:
> ▶ A letter to the editor of a newspaper
> ▶ A petition that is being circulated
> ▶ A copy of a campaign speech
> ▶ A newspaper ad asking for your support

Vote NO for Rec Center

The teenagers in our town are asking for a new recreation center. I say we vote NO on their demand. First, teens are noisy and blast their boom boxes way too loudly. Where are the type of mature youths that we used to be? Last year, more than fifty of our teens were arrested for creating disturbances. Few of these irresponsible troublemakers have any regard for neatness or responsibility. They don't deserve a new rec center.

Apply the Strategy

Read the newspaper editorial. Then answer the questions that follow.

1. What loaded vocabulary appears in the article? Which words create a positive emotion? Which words create a negative emotion?

2. What examples of stereotyping do you find in the editorial? How does each example create bias?

3. What slanted arguments can you detect in the article? For each argument, what facts may the writer have left out in order not to hurt his case?

Speaking and Listening Workshop

Oral Storytelling

Long before people recorded stories in written form, they shared them orally. Whenever you share a story aloud with friends, you are carrying on a tradition that originated several centuries ago. Here are some tips to help you become a skilled storyteller.

Know Your Story Well Before you tell a story, read it to yourself several times or go over the details in your mind. Know all the characters and story events. If the story is long or complicated, jot down some notes to help you remember key details.

Speak With Emotion As you tell your story, be enthusiastic. Be as excited about the story as you want your audience to be. When there is dialogue between characters, try to give each speaker a distinct voice. Speak clearly and slowly so that listeners will understand you.

Use Your Body Good storytellers don't use their voices alone. They use their entire bodies. Before speaking, plan gestures or motions to make with your arms, legs, or head. Practice until these movements look natural. Animated movements will help make your story come alive.

Tips for Oral Storytelling

✔ *If you want to be an effective story-teller, follow these strategies:*
- ▶ *Look directly at your audience.*
- ▶ *Speak clearly and with emotion.*
- ▶ *Use your body to act out the story.*

Apply the Strategies

Be a storyteller in each situation below. Take the time necessary to prepare before sharing your story with classmates.

1. You are a cave dweller who has just had an exciting encounter. It might have been with an animal, such as a bear or lion, or with some other danger, like fire. Share your experience with your cave family.

2. You are a candidate for the neighborhood Liar's Club. To become a member, you must tell a whopping tall tale filled with impossible characters and events. Spin the most outrageous story you can imagine.

3. You are a clown hired to entertain at a children's birthday party. You have been asked to tell a familiar tale, such as "The Three Little Pigs" or "Hansel and Gretel." Retell the story, pretending your audience is a group of young children.

Extended Reading Opportunities

For ages, people have created stories in an attempt to understand and share their experiences. Great writers from many different time periods and cultures have penned short stories. Following are just a few possibilities for extending your exploration of short stories.

Suggested Titles

The Short Stories of Isaac Bashevis Singer
Isaac Bashevis Singer

Singer—a Yiddish novelist, short-story writer, critic, and journalist—was born in Poland and emigrated to the United States in 1935 to pursue a career as a writer. In Singer's realistic stories, the forces of good and evil often collide. The forty-seven stories in this collection show the great compassion in Singer's writing, as well as his skillful blending of Jewish culture with other world cultures.

The Joy Luck Club
Amy Tan

This book tells the stories of four Chinese mothers and their American-born daughters. Each chapter focuses on one woman's story—a mother growing up in China long ago or a daughter living in modern-day San Francisco. Combined into a novel, these interwoven stories explore the difficulties that can result when two cultures meet head-on, as well as the fierce love that mothers and daughters share, no matter what their backgrounds.

21 Great Stories
Abraham H. Lass and Norma L. Tasman, editors

This collection features the work of twenty masterful storytellers. Within this volume, you'll find a wide range of styles. Stories by James Thurber and Mark Twain will amuse you. A mystery by Sir Arthur Conan Doyle will stump you. Two tales of terror by Edgar Allan Poe will chill you. Other great writers represented in this book include Ray Bradbury, Guy de Maupassant, Jack London, John Steinbeck, and James Joyce.

Other Possibilities

Across the Sea of Stars   Arthur C. Clarke, editor
Alfred Hitchcock's Ghostly Gallery   Alfred Hitchcock, editor
Cat Encounters: A Cat Lover's Anthology   Seon Manley and
                                                Lewis Gogo, editors

Street Reflections, 1988, Robert Vickery, oil on canvas, 16 x 20 inches, signed lower
left: "Robert Vickery '88" ©1997 Robert Vickery/Licensed by VAGA, New York, NY

Nonfiction

If fiction takes you on imaginative flights of fancy, nonfiction brings you back down to Earth. Nonfiction includes true stories about real people, places, and experiences. It also includes practical writing that informs you about something and persuasive writing that urges you to think or act in a certain way. On the following pages, you'll find many different types of nonfiction—from a reflective essay to a diary entry to a transcript of a radio news feature. Although all are different, each one in some way reflects real life.

$\mathcal{G}$uide for Reading

Sally Ride (1951–)

She might have become a professional tennis player, a science teacher, or a writer. What Sally Ride chose to be, however, was an astronaut.

Reaching for the Stars Ride's determination, competitive spirit, and academic excellence have enabled her to achieve her goals and to serve as a role model for others. Although best known for her scholarly pursuits, she is also a talented athlete. As a youngster, she ranked eighteenth nationally on the junior tennis circuit.

In 1973, Ride received degrees in English literature and physics from Stanford University. She then went on to earn graduate degrees from Stanford. In 1978, she read about NASA's call for astronauts in the Stanford University newspaper. She was one of more than 8,000 candidates to apply to the space program. Twenty-nine men and six women were accepted—including Sally Ride.

In June 1983, Sally Ride became the first American woman in space.

Ride was preparing for her third space mission when the space shuttle *Challenger* exploded shortly after liftoff in January 1986, killing all seven crew members. The accident put a temporary halt to shuttle missions, and as a result Ride didn't return to space. She did, however, play a key role on the Presidential Commission investigating the accident.

After NASA In 1987, Ride retired from NASA. Since then, she has worked as a science teacher and a writer. She is currently a professor of physics at the University of California at San Diego and Director of the California Space Institute, and is the author of several books on space.

◆ Build Vocabulary

WORD ROOTS: -nov-

In this essay, Sally Ride describes how seeing the Earth from space led her to "assume the role of a novice geologist." The word *novice* contains the word root -nov-, which means "new." A novice is someone who is new to an activity. In this case, Ride, who is a physicist, is a beginner at the science of geology. What other words can you think of in which the word root -nov- appears?

articulate
surreal
ominous
novice
muted
eddies
subtle
eerie
diffused
extrapolating

WORD BANK

As you read this essay, you will encounter the words on this list. Pair up with a classmate, and work together to write definitions for as many of the words as you can. As you read, check to see if you're right.

◆ Build Grammar Skills

CORRECT USE OF ITS AND IT'S

Although they are pronounced the same way, the posessive pronoun *its* and the contraction *it's* mean very different things. *Its*, which means "belonging to it," does not contain an apostrophe. The contraction *it's* (short for "it is") does contain an apostrophe. To avoid confusing the two words, substitute the words *it is* into the sentence. If the resulting sentence is correct, the contraction *it's* is the correct choice. Look at these examples from Ride's essay:

It's (it is) more than 22,000 miles lower . . .

In *its* light, we see ghostly clouds . . .

As you read the essay, pay attention to the way *its* and *it's* are used.

Single Room, Earth View

◆ *Literature and Your Life*

CONNECT YOUR EXPERIENCE

At street level, a city can be a confusing place. An orange-and-white barricade blocks the street for no apparent reason. You take a shortcut through a park—and find yourself lost in an unexpected spot.

From the viewing deck of a tall building, you can see the layout of the city. With your new perspective you understand things that baffled you before. You can see that the barricade protects a parade route, and that the path through the park bends in an odd way.

In this essay, you will experience what it's like to look down on the entire Earth, as Sally Ride describes her view from space.

THEMATIC FOCUS: OBSERVATIONS

How can observing places and situations from different perspectives give you a better understanding of the world around us?

Journal Writing Record your memories of a time when you looked at something from a new perspective.

◆ Background for Understanding

HISTORY

During her training as an astronaut, Sally Ride was a member of the support crew for the second and third space shuttle flights. Her turn to fly came on June 18, 1983, when she served as a flight engineer and mission specialist aboard the shuttle *Challenger*—the same shuttle that would explode shortly after liftoff three years later. Ride was the first American woman in space. Interestingly, her historic mission took place twenty years and two days after Soviet cosmonaut Valentina Tereshkova became the first woman in space.

◆ Literary Focus

OBSERVATION

In an **observation,** a writer describes an event he or she saw firsthand and watched over an extended period of time. The writer includes a lot of details and chooses vivid, precise words to re-create the event for the reader. Observations often focus on scientific phenomena, such as the behavior of a wild animal or the outcome of a laboratory experiment. In this essay, astronaut Sally Ride, a trained scientist, relays her observations of Earth's surface from the space shuttle. As you read, note the systematic, precise way in which she describes what she observed.

Reading for Success

Strategies for Reading Nonfiction

Nonfiction is writing about real life. A work of nonfiction may describe real people, places, events, objects, or ideas. Nonfiction includes biographies, autobiographies, and essays. Although works of nonfiction vary in topic, type, and purpose, they all share one key characteristic: They all are true. However, this does not mean that you should accept all of the writer's ideas. You need to judge the facts for yourself and form your own opinions. Use these strategies to help you get the most out of the nonfiction you read.

Recognize the author's purpose.

▶ Consider the details that the writer includes or fails to include. Think about what this tells you about the author's beliefs and purpose in writing.

▶ Based on what you discover about the author's purpose, decide whether you should accept the writer's ideas wholeheartedly—or whether you should be skeptical.

Identify the author's main points.

Ask yourself what the author wants you to learn or think as a result of reading his or her work of nonfiction. These main points are the most important ideas in the work.

Identify the evidence for the author's main points.

Each point the author makes must be supported by evidence. Evaluate the facts the author uses to back up his or her points. Ask yourself whether the writer offers enough facts to support each point thoroughly. Also look at the type of evidence the writer presents. Is it convincing?

Recognize patterns of organization.

▶ A work of nonfiction should be organized so that the main points and supporting evidence are easy for readers to follow.

▶ Transition words, such as *next, compared to*, or *most important,* will clue you into the type of organization the writer is using.

Vary your reading rate.

▶ Read quickly if you are reviewing familiar material, scanning for a particular idea, or just want the gist of a work of nonfiction.

▶ Read slowly and carefully if it is important that you fully understand the material. At times, you will even want to go back and reread key passages.

As you read the essay by Sally Ride, notice the notes along the side. The notes demonstrate how to apply these strategies to your reading.

Single Room, Earth View

Sally Ride

Everyone I've met has a glittering, if vague, mental image of space travel. And naturally enough, people want to hear about it from an astronaut: "How did it feel . . . ?" "What did it look like . . . ?" "Were you scared?" Sometimes, the questions come from reporters, their pens poised and their tape recorders silently reeling in the words; sometimes, it's wide-eyed, ten-year-old girls who want answers. I find a way to answer all of them, but it's not easy.

> From these details, you can guess that Ride's **purpose** is to describe what space travel is like.

Imagine trying to describe an airplane ride to someone who has never flown. An <u>articulate</u> traveler could describe the sights but would find it much harder to explain the difference in perspective provided by the new view from a greater distance, along with the feelings, impressions, and insights that go with the new perspective. And the difference is enormous: Spaceflight moves the traveler another giant step farther away. Eight and one-half thunderous minutes after launch, an astronaut is orbiting high above the Earth, suddenly able to watch typhoons form, volcanoes smolder, and meteors streak through the atmosphere below.

> Here, Ride states a **main point**: Spaceflight gives the viewer a new perspective, as well as new feelings, impressions, and insights.

While flying over the Hawaiian Islands, several astronauts have marveled that the islands look just as they do on a map. When people first hear that, they wonder what should be so surprising about Hawaii looking the way it does in the atlas. Yet, to the astronauts it is an absolutely startling sensation: The islands really do look as if that part of the world has been carpeted with a big page torn out of Rand-McNally,[1] and all we can do is try to convey the <u>surreal</u> quality of that scene.

> The astronauts' surprised reaction to seeing Hawaii is **evidence** that backs up the idea that spaceflight results in new feelings.

In orbit, racing along at five miles per second, the space shuttle circles the Earth once every 90 minutes. I found that at this speed, unless I kept my nose pressed to the window, it was almost impossible to keep track of where we were at any given moment—the world below simply changes too fast. If I turned my concentration away for too long, even just to change film in a camera, I could miss an entire land mass. It's embarrassing to float up to a window, glance outside, and then have to ask a crewmate, "What continent is this?"

We could see smoke rising from fires that dotted the entire east coast of Africa, and in the same orbit only moments later, ice floes jostling for position in the Antarctic. We could see the Ganges River dumping its murky, sediment-laden water into the Indian Ocean and watch

---

1. **Rand-McNally:** Publishers of atlases.

◆ **Build Vocabulary**

articulate (är tik′ yə lit) *adj.*: Expressing oneself clearly and easily

surreal (sə rē′ əl) *adj.*: Strange

<u>ominous</u> hurricane clouds expanding and rising like biscuits in the oven of the Caribbean.

Mountain ranges, volcanoes, and river deltas appeared in salt-and-flour relief, all leading me to assume the role of a <u>novice</u> geologist. In such moments, it was easy to imagine the dynamic upheavals that created jutting mountain ranges and the internal wrenchings that created rifts and seas. I also became an instant believer in plate tectonics;[2] India really is crashing into Asia, and Saudi Arabia and Egypt really are pulling apart, making the Red Sea wider. Even though their respective motion is really no more than mere inches a year, the view from overhead makes theory come alive.

Spectacular as the view is from 200 miles up, the Earth is not the awe-inspiring "blue marble" made famous by the photos from the moon. From space shuttle height, we can't see the en-

▲ **Critical Viewing** What do you imagine it would be like to be aboard this shuttle? [Speculate]

tire globe at a glance, but we can look down the entire boot of Italy, or up the East Coast of the United States from Cape Hatteras to Cape Cod. The panoramic view inspires an appreciation for the scale of some of nature's phenomena. One day, as I scanned the sandy expanse of Northern Africa, I couldn't find any of the familiar land-

marks—colorful outcroppings of rock in Chad, irrigated patches of the Sahara. Then I realized they were obscured by a huge dust storm, a cloud of sand that enveloped the continent from Morocco to the Sudan.

Since the space shuttle flies fairly low (at least by orbital standards; it's more than 22,000 miles lower than a typical TV satellite), we can make out both natural and manmade features in surprising detail. Familiar geographical features like San Francisco Bay, Long Island, and Lake Michigan are easy to recognize, as are many cities, bridges, and airports. The Great Wall of China is *not* the only manmade object visible from space.

The signatures of civilization are usually seen in straight lines (bridges or runways) or sharp delineations (abrupt transitions from desert to irrigated land, as in California's Imperial Valley). A modern city like New York doesn't leap from the canvas of its surroundings, but its straight piers and concrete runways catch the eye—and around them, the city materializes. I found Salina, Kansas (and pleased my in-laws, who live there) by spotting its long runway amid the wheat fields near the city. Over Florida, I could see the launch pad where we had begun our trip, and the landing strip, where we would eventually land.

Some of civilization's more unfortunate effects on the environment are also evident from orbit. Oil slicks glisten on the surface of the Persian

---

2. **plate tectonics:** Theory that the Earth's surface consists of plates whose constant motion explains continental drift, mountain building, large earthquakes, and so forth.

◆ **Build Vocabulary**

ominous (äm′ ə nəs) *adj.*: Threatening

novice (näv′ is) *adj.*: Beginner

muted (myo͞ot′ əd) *adj.*: Weaker; less intense

eddies (ed′ ēz) *n.*: Circular currents

subtle (sut′ əl) *adj.*: Not obvious

eerie (ir′ ē) *adj.*: Mysterious

diffused (di fyo͞ozd′) *v.*: Spread out

Ride states the **main point** of this paragraph in the first sentence, then gives evidence for the point by describing pollution that can be observed from the space shuttle.

Gulf, patches of pollution-damaged trees dot the forests of central Europe. Some cities look out of focus, and their colors muted, when viewed through a pollutant haze. Not surprisingly, the effects are more noticeable now than they were a decade ago. An astronaut who has flown in both Skylab and the space shuttle reported that the horizon didn't seem quite as sharp, or the colors quite as bright, in 1983 as they had in 1973.

Of course, informal observations by individual astronauts are one thing, but more precise measurements are continually being made from space: The space shuttle has carried infrared film to document damage to citrus trees in Florida and in rain forests along the Amazon. It has carried even more sophisticated sensors in the payload bay. Here is one example: sensors used to measure atmospheric carbon monoxide levels, allowing scientists to study the environmental effects of city emissions and land-clearing fires.

Most of the Earth's surface is covered with water, and at first glance it all looks the same: blue. But with the right lighting conditions and a couple of orbits of practice, it's possible to make out the intricate patterns in the oceans—eddies and spirals become visible because of the subtle differences in water color or reflectivity.

If your purpose for reading this essay is to learn how a view from space benefits science on Earth, you would slow down your **reading rate** to make sure you understood how space observations enable oceanographers to see the "big picture."

Observations and photographs by astronauts have contributed significantly to the understanding of ocean dynamics, and some of the more intriguing discoveries prompted the National Aeronautics and Space Administration to fly an oceanographic observer for the express purpose of studying the ocean from orbit. Scientists' understanding of the energy balance in the oceans has increased significantly as a result of the discoveries of circular and spiral eddies tens of kilometers in diameter, of standing waves hundreds of kilometers long, and of spiral eddies that sometimes trail into one another for thousands of kilometers. If a scientist wants to study features on this scale, it's much easier from an orbiting vehicle than from the vantage point of a boat.

Believe it or not, an astronaut can also see the wakes of large ships and the contrails[3] of airplanes. The sun angle has to be just right, but when the lighting conditions are perfect, you can follow otherwise invisible oil tankers on the Persian Gulf and trace major shipping lanes through the Mediterranean Sea. Similarly, when atmospheric conditions allow contrail formation, the thousand-mile-long condensation trails let astronauts trace the major air routes across the northern Pacific Ocean.

Part of every orbit takes us to the dark side of the planet. In space, night is very, very black—but that doesn't mean there's nothing to look at. The lights of cities sparkle; on nights when there was no moon, it was difficult for me to tell the Earth from the sky—the twinkling lights could be stars or they could be small cities. On one nighttime pass from Cuba to Nova Scotia, the entire East Coast of the United States appeared in twinkling outline.

By providing vivid details about seeing cities and rivers at night, Ride achieves her **purpose** of describing what space travel is like.

When the moon is full, it casts an eerie light on the Earth. In its light, we see ghostly clouds and bright reflections on the water. One night, the Mississippi River flashed into view, and because of our viewing angle and orbital path, the reflected moonlight seemed to flow downstream—as if Huck Finn[4] had tied a candle to his raft.

Of all the sights from orbit, the most spectacular may be the magnificent displays of lightning that ignite the clouds at night. On Earth, we see lightning from below the clouds; in orbit, we see it from above. Bolts of lightning are diffused by

---

3. **contrails** (kän′ trāls′) *n.*: White trails of condensed water vapor that sometimes form in the wake of aircraft.
4. **Huck Finn:** Hero of Mark Twain's novel *The Adventures of Huckleberry Finn.*

the clouds into bursting balls of light. Sometimes, when a storm extends hundreds of miles, it looks like a transcontinental brigade is tossing fireworks from cloud to cloud.

As the shuttle races the sun around the Earth, we pass from day to night and back again during a single orbit—hurtling into darkness, then bursting into daylight. The sun's appearance unleashes spectacular blue and orange bands along the horizon, a clockwork miracle that astronauts witness every 90 minutes. But, I really can't describe a sunrise in orbit. The drama set against the black backdrop of space and the magic of the materializing colors can't be captured in an astronomer's equations or an astronaut's photographs.

I once heard someone (not an astronaut)

> The **pattern of organization** Ride uses is organizing by type. She simply groups related facts and ideas. This type of organization lends itself to an observation or a description in which all points are equally important.

suggest that it's possible to imagine what spaceflight is like by simply <u>extrapolating</u> from the sensations you experience on an airplane. All you have to do, he said, is mentally raise the airplane 200 miles, mentally eliminate the air noise and the turbulence, and you get an accurate mental picture of a trip in the space shuttle.

Not true. And while it's natural to try to liken spaceflight to familiar experiences, it can't be brought "down to Earth"—not in the final sense. The environment is different, the perspective is different. Part of the fascination with space travel is the element of the unknown—the conviction that it's different from earthbound experiences. And it is.

◆ **Build Vocabulary**

extrapolating (ek strap´ ə lāt´ iŋ) *v.*: Arriving at a conclusion by making inferences based on known facts

---

Guide for Responding

◆ *Literature and Your Life*

Reader's Response Would you like to be an astronaut like Sally Ride? Why or why not?

Thematic Focus How do spaceflights give us a better appreciation for the world around us?

Group Activity Brainstorm for a list of reasons why going on a spaceflight would be interesting to you. Then, as a group, come to a consensus on a "top three" list.

☑ **Check Your Comprehension**

1. How does the view of Earth from the space shuttle differ from the view of Earth from the moon?
2. What does Ride regard as the most spectacular sight from orbit?
3. Name three natural features that Ride saw from orbit.
4. Identify three examples that she observed of humans' effect on the environment.

Beyond Literature

History Connection

The Challenger Tragedy On January 28, 1986, a six-person crew lifted off at Cape Canaveral, Florida, and thundered toward space aboard the space shuttle *Challenger*. Suddenly, disaster struck. Just 73 seconds into the flight, the *Challenger* broke up in a huge fireball, killing all on board. All future shuttle missions were canceled while a special commission determined the cause of the accident. The culprit turned out to be a faulty O ring, one of a series of circular rubber rings that seal the joints between sections of the shuttle's solid-fuel rocket boosters. After the O rings were redesigned, space shuttles once again zoomed into space. The first flight was that of the shuttle *Discovery*, on September 29, 1988. Do you think space travel is worth the risks involved? Why or why not?

Guide for Responding (continued)

◆ Critical Thinking

INTERPRET

1. According to Ride, how is riding on the space shuttle different from riding on an airplane? **[Compare and Contrast]**
2. Why did Ride find it easier to imagine geological forces from space? **[Interpret]**
3. An astronaut reported that colors did not seem as bright in 1983 as in 1973. What does this suggest? **[Infer]**
4. How does space travel help us understand conditions on Earth? **[Draw Conclusions]**

EVALUATE

5. Is the title of the essay appropriate? Explain. **[Make a Judgment]**

APPLY

6. How have Ride's descriptions of the Earth affected your thoughts about our planet? **[Relate]**

◆ Reading for Success

STRATEGIES FOR READING NONFICTION

Review the reading strategies and notes showing how to read nonfiction. Then apply those strategies to answer the following questions.

1. What is the author's purpose in writing this essay?
2. What are the author's main points?
3. How does the author support these main points?

◆ Literary Focus

OBSERVATION

In an **observation**, a writer carefully notes the facts and events that he or she witnesses firsthand, and describes them vividly so that readers feel as if they had experienced the event themselves. In "Single Room, Earth View," Sally Ride shares her observations of traveling in the space shuttle.

1. How does Ride show her talent for observation in finding civilization's "signatures"?
2. How does she prove herself to be a careful observer of Earth's oceans?
3. How does she use comparisons to everyday phenomena to help readers follow her observations?

◆ Build Vocabulary

USING THE WORD ROOT -nov-

The word root -*nov*- means "new." In your notebook, write a definition that incorporates the word *new* for each term.

1. novel (*adj.*)   2. innovate (*v.*)   3. renovate (*v.*)

USING THE WORD BANK

In your notebook, fill in the blanks with words in the Word Bank or forms of those words.

Normally ___?___, the scientist felt like a tongue-tied ___?___ speaker. The low, ___?___ murmuring of her audience sounded frightening and ___?___. She turned on the overhead projector, and the smell of burning dust, ___?___ but unmistakable, ___?___ through the air. "I know this seems ___?___," she said, putting on the first slide. "However, what we can ___?___ from the evidence is clear. The odd, ___?___ patterns of ___?___ and whirlpools on Planet X are signs of intelligent life. We are not alone."

◆ Build Grammar Skills

CORRECT USE OF *ITS* AND *IT'S*

Its is a possessive pronoun that means "belonging to it." *Its* does not have an apostrophe. *It's* is a contraction of *it is*. *It's* has an apostophe to show where a letter has been removed to create the contraction.

When in doubt about whether to use *its* or *it's*, substitute the phrase *it is* into the sentence. If the meaning of the sentence remains the same, *it's* is correct. If the sentence stops making sense or its meaning changes, *its* is correct.

Practice In your notebook, write each of these sentences. Choose *its* or *it's* to complete each one.

1. ___?___ exciting to fly on the space shuttle.
2. Earth reveals ___?___ features to the astonauts.
3. Sometimes ___?___ difficult to identify what you see.
4. At times, pollution rears ___?___ ugly head.
5. After seeing Earth from space, ___?___ clear that people have a powerful effect on ___?___ land and oceans.

Build Your Portfolio

 ## Idea Bank

Writing

1. **Description From Above** Write a description of a familiar place as it would appear to someone looking down from above.

2. **Eyewitness Report** In any job, you will need to describe incidents you observe—such as a meeting or someone else's job performance. Practice this skill by writing an eyewitness report about something you saw this week. **[Career Link]**

3. **Persuasive Essay** Write a persuasive essay arguing for public support for the space program. Back up your points with facts, vivid descriptions, and statistics. **[Science Link]**

Speaking and Listening

4. **Interview** With three classmates, assume the roles of three astronauts and the journalist who is interviewing them. Prepare questions and answers before conducting the interview.

5. **Description Feedback** Thoroughly describe something you observed to a partner, then have your partner restate your description in his or her own words. Discuss any differences in understanding. Then switch roles.

Projects

6. **Game** Create a board game in which the object is to travel through space to Pluto and back to Earth. Include obstacles that players must avoid to achieve success. **[Science Link]**

7. **Space Exploration Report** Prepare a report on one aspect of space exploration, such as women astronauts or the space shuttle. If possible, use NASA's World Wide Web site to obtain information and illustrations for your report. **[Science Link; Technology Link]**

 ## Writing Mini-Lesson

Observation From Space

Imagine that you are an astronaut in space. Perhaps you are orbiting the Earth on the space shuttle or planting a flag on the surface of Mars. Write an observation that will capture the minds and imaginations of readers on Earth.

Writing Skills Focus: Vivid Adjectives

To make your experiences come alive for your readers, use **vivid adjectives** to paint a picture in words. For example, if something is colorful, tell what colors it is. If the weather is hot, tell whether it is *scorching, steamy,* or *searing.*

Look at how Ride uses vivid adjectives to describe the Earth from space.

Model From the Essay

We could see the Ganges River dumping its *murky, sediment-laden* water into the Indian Ocean and watch *ominous* hurricane clouds expanding and rising like biscuits in the oven of the Caribbean.

Prewriting Make a sketch of what you'll describe in your observation. Annotate your drawing with details about different objects and events.

Drafting To make sure you get down all your ideas, write your first draft without stopping to change what you've written. Concentrate on getting across what you perceive through your five senses.

Revising Look for places where you can add vivid adjectives to enliven your description. For example, you might change the phrase "the surface of the moon" to "the gray, rocky, utterly desolate surface of the moon."

PART 1 *Essays and Personal Accounts*

Discussion, Milton Avery, Mount Holyoke College Art Museum, South Hadley, Massachusetts

Guide for Reading

Isaac Bashevis Singer *(1904 – 1991)*

I. B. Singer once said that he believed that "life itself is a story." This belief is reflected in his many short stories, novels, and nonfiction pieces that capture the lessons of everyday life. Born in Poland, Singer moved to New York City in 1935 and later became an American citizen. Writing in Yiddish, the language of some Eastern European Jews and their descendants, Singer established himself as one of the most popular and respected writers of this century, earning the Nobel Prize for Literature in 1978.

Lorraine Hansberry *(1930 – 1965)*

Lorraine Hansberry was born and raised in Chicago, Illinois. After high school, she studied art for two years before moving to New York City. While working at several jobs, she wrote *A Raisin in the Sun*, which, in 1959, became the first play by an African American woman to be produced on Broadway. "On Summer" is from *To Be Young, Gifted, and Black*, a collection of her writings that was published after her death.

Rudolfo Anaya *(1937–)*

Rudolfo Anaya was born in Pastura, New Mexico, and his writing reflects his Mexican American heritage. Anaya says, "For those of us who listen to the Earth, and to the old legends and the myths of the people, the whispers of the blood draw us to our past." It is the past that concerns Anaya in much of his writing. His first novel, *Bless Me, Ultima* (1972), won national acclaim for its moving depiction of the culture and history of New Mexico. Anaya has also published *The Heart of Aztlan* (1976) and *Tortuga* (1979), as well as many stories and articles. His essay "A Celebration of Grandfathers" reflects on the "old ones" he remembers from his childhood.

◆ Build Vocabulary

PREFIXES: *fore-*

"The Washwoman" contains the word *forebears,* which means "ancestors"—or, more loosely, "relatives who came before us." The prefix *fore-,* meaning "before" or "occurring earlier," can help you piece together the meaning of this word and others that contain the prefix.

| forebears |
| rancor |
| obstinacy |
| pious |
| aloofness |
| perplexes |
| permeate |
| epiphany |

WORD BANK

Before you read, preview this list of words from the selections.

◆ Build Grammar Skills

COMMONLY CONFUSED WORDS: *AFFECT* AND *EFFECT*

When Hansberry writes that cancer was an enemy with "shape and effect and source," she uses a word that is frequently misused: *effect.* Most often, as in this sentence, *effect* is a noun meaning "the result." *Effect* can also be a verb meaning "to bring about" or "to cause." *Affect* is always a verb meaning "to influence." Look at these examples:

> verb
> How will reading these essays *affect* you emotionally?

> noun
> And she would drop dark hints to the *effect* that she was not certain of her own children.

> verb
> Can an essay *effect* change?

The Washwoman ◆ On Summer
◆ A Celebration of Grandfathers ◆

◆ *Literature and Your Life*

CONNECT YOUR EXPERIENCE

These authors journey deep into their past to find people who gave them gifts that weren't in boxes or tied with bows. What are some special gifts in your life that didn't come in packages? Who gave them to you, and what did you do with them?

Journal Writing Jot down notes about the best gifts you have received and the best gifts you can ever hope to give.

THEMATIC FOCUS: APPRECIATING OTHERS

Sometimes the most special gift we can receive is a new way of viewing ourselves and the world around us. In these essays, the authors write about important people in their lives who helped them find new ways of looking at life.

◆ Background for Understanding

HISTORY

"The Washwoman" takes place in the early twentieth century prior to World War I in what is now Poland. At the time, Poland did not exist as an independent nation. Instead, it was divided into three sections ruled by Russia, Austria-Hungary, and Germany. The population consisted largely of members of the working class, who worked long hours in the fields in order to earn enough to survive. Because Poland had long been known for its religious tolerance, the population included a sizeable number of Jewish people who had settled there centuries earlier. Most of the Jews spoke Yiddish and maintained their own cultural traditions.

◆ Literary Focus

ESSAY

An **essay** is a short piece of nonfiction in which a writer expresses a personal view of a topic. There are different types of essays. "The Washwoman" is an example of a **narrative essay,** which tells a story. "On Summer" is a **persuasive essay,** which tries to convince readers to accept a position or take a course of action. In this case, Hansberry tries to convince readers to appreciate summer. "A Celebration of Grandfathers" is a **reflective essay**—a type of essay in which a writer reflects on his or her feelings about a topic of personal importance.

◆ Reading Strategy

IDENTIFY THE AUTHOR'S ATTITUDE

In any type of essay, the **author's attitude** toward his or her subject colors the presentation of information. For example, when describing a person he or she deeply respects, a writer will use descriptive words that convey this respect and include details that will help readers understand and share the respect for the subject.

As you read these essays, use a sunburst diagram like the one shown to help you identify the authors' attitudes toward their subjects. On the lines surrounding the center, jot down words and details that hint at the writer's attitude toward the subject. When you've finished, review the details you've listed and decide what they suggest about the writer's attitude. Write a statement of that attitude in the center of the diagram.

Author's Attitude:

The Washwoman

Isaac Bashevis Singer

The Oldest Inhabitant, 1876, Julian Alden Weir, Butler Institute of American Art, Youngstown, Ohio

Our home had little contact with Gentiles.[1] The only Gentile in the building was the janitor. Fridays he would come for a tip, his "Friday money." He remained standing at the door, took off his hat, and my mother gave him six groschen.[2]

Besides the janitor there were also the Gentile washwomen who came to the house to fetch our laundry. My story is about one of these.

She was a small woman, old and wrinkled. When she started washing for us, she was already past seventy. Most Jewish women of her age were sickly, weak, broken in body. All the old women in our street had bent backs and leaned on sticks when they walked. But this washwoman, small and thin as she was, possessed a strength that came from generations of peasant <u>forebears</u>. Mother would count out to her a bundle of laundry that had accumulated over several weeks. She would lift the unwieldy pack, load it on her narrow shoulders, and carry it the long way home. She lived on Krochmalna Street too, but at the other end, near the Wola section. It must have been a walk of an hour and a half.

She would bring the laundry back about two weeks later. My mother had never been

---

1. **Gentiles:** Any persons not Jewish; here, specifically Christians.
2. **groschen** (grō′ shən): Austrian cent or penny.

◀ **Critical Viewing** Based on her clothing and her expression, what do you imagine this woman is like? Why? **[Infer]**

so pleased with any washwoman. Every piece of linen sparkled like polished silver. Every piece was neatly ironed. Yet she charged no more than the others. She was a real find. Mother always had her money ready, because it was too far for the old woman to come a second time.

Laundering was not easy in those days. The old woman had no faucet where she lived but had to bring in the water from a pump. For the linens to come out so clean, they had to be scrubbed thoroughly in a washtub, rinsed with washing soda, soaked, boiled in an enormous pot, starched, then ironed. Every piece was handled ten times or more. And the drying! It could not be done outside because thieves would steal the laundry. The wrung-out wash had to be carried up to the attic and hung on clotheslines. In the winter it would become as brittle as glass and almost break when touched. And there was always a to-do with other housewives and washwomen who wanted the attic clothesline for their own use. Only God knows all the old woman had to endure each time she did a wash!

She could have begged at the church door or entered a home for the penniless and aged. But there was in her a certain pride and love of labor with which many Gentiles have been blessed. The old woman did not want to become a burden, and so she bore her burden.

My mother spoke a little Polish, and the old woman would talk with her about many things. She was especially fond of me and used to say I looked like Jesus. She repeated this every time she came, and Mother would frown and whisper to herself, her lips barely moving, "May her words be scattered in the wilderness."

The woman had a son who was rich. I no longer remember what sort of business he had. He was ashamed of his mother, the washwoman, and never came to see her. Nor did he ever give her a groschen. The old woman told this without <u>rancor</u>. One day the son was married. It seemed that he had made a good match. The wedding took place in a church. The son had not invited the old mother to his wedding, but she went to the church and waited at the steps to see her son lead the "young lady" to the altar.

The story of the faithless son left a deep impression on my mother. She talked about it for weeks and months. It was an affront not only to the old woman but to the entire institution of motherhood. Mother would argue, "Nu, does it pay to make sacrifices for children? The mother uses up her last strength, and he does not even know the meaning of loyalty."

And she would drop dark hints to the effect that she was not certain of her own children: Who knows what they would do some day? This, however, did not prevent her from dedicating her life to us. If there was any delicacy in the house, she would put it aside for the children and invent all sorts of excuses and reasons why she herself did not want to taste it. She knew charms that went back to ancient times, and she used expressions she had inherited from generations of devoted mothers and grandmothers. If one of the children complained of a pain, she would say, "May I be your ransom and may you outlive my bones!" Or she would say, "May I be the atonement for the least of your fingernails." When we ate she used to say, "Health and marrow in your bones!" The day before the new moon she gave us a kind of candy that was said to prevent parasitic worms. If one of us had something in his eye, Mother would lick the eye clean with her tongue. She also fed us rock candy against coughs, and from time to time she would take us to be blessed against the evil eye. This did not prevent her from studying *The Duties of the*

◆ **Build Vocabulary**

forebears (fôr′ bers) *n*.: Ancestors

rancor (raŋ′ kər) *n*.: Deep spite or bitter hate

Heart, The Book of the Covenant, and other serious philosophic works.

But to return to the washwoman. That winter was a harsh one. The streets were in the grip of a bitter cold. No matter how much we heated our stove, the windows were covered with frostwork and decorated with icicles. The newspapers reported that people were dying of the cold. Coal became dear. The winter had become so severe that parents stopped sending children to cheder,[3] and even the Polish schools were closed.

On one such day the washwoman, now nearly eighty years old, came to our house. A good deal of laundry had accumulated during the past weeks. Mother gave her a pot of tea to warm herself, as well as some bread. The old woman sat on a kitchen chair trembling and shaking, and warmed her hands against the teapot. Her fingers were gnarled from work, and perhaps from arthritis too. Her fingernails were strangely white. These hands spoke of the stubbornness of mankind, of the will to work not only as one's strength permits but beyond the limits of one's power. Mother counted and wrote down the list: men's undershirts, women's vests, long-legged drawers, bloomers, petticoats, shifts, featherbed covers, pillowcases, sheets, and the men's fringed garments. Yes, the Gentile woman washed these holy garments as well.

The bundle was big, bigger than usual. When the woman placed it on her shoulders, it covered her completely. At first she swayed, as though she were about to fall under the load. But an inner <u>obstinacy</u> seemed to call out: No, you may not fall. A donkey may permit himself to fall under his burden, but not a human being, the crown of creation.

It was fearful to watch the old woman staggering out with the enormous pack, out into the frost, where the snow was dry as salt and the air was filled with dusty white whirlwinds, like goblins dancing in the cold. Would the old woman ever reach Wola?

She disappeared, and Mother sighed and prayed for her.

Usually the woman brought back the wash after two or, at the most, three weeks. But three weeks passed, then four and five, and nothing was heard of the old woman. We remained without linens. The cold had become even more intense. The telephone wires were now as thick as ropes. The branches of the trees looked like glass. So much snow had fallen that the streets had become uneven, and sleds were able to glide down many streets as on the slopes of a hill. Kindhearted people lit fires in the streets for vagrants[4] to warm themselves and roast potatoes in, if they had any to roast.

For us the washwoman's absence was a catastrophe. We needed the laundry. We did not even know the woman's address. It seemed certain that she had collapsed, died. Mother declared she had had a premonition, as the old woman left our house that last time, that we would never see our things again. She found some old torn shirts and washed and mended them. We mourned, both for the laundry and for the old, toil-worn woman who had grown close to us through the years she had served us so faithfully.

More than two months passed. The frost had subsided, and then a new frost had come, a new wave of cold. One evening, while Mother was sitting near the kerosene lamp mending a shirt, the door opened and a small puff of steam, followed by a gigantic bundle, entered. Under the bundle tottered the old woman, her face as white as a linen sheet. A few wisps of white hair straggled out from beneath her shawl. Mother uttered a half-choked cry. It was as though a corpse had entered the room. I ran toward the old woman and helped her unload her pack. She was even thinner now, more bent. Her face had become more gaunt, and her head shook from side to side as though she were saying no. She could not utter a clear word, but mumbled something with her sunken mouth and pale lips.

After the old woman had recovered somewhat, she told us that she had been ill, very ill.

---

3. **cheder** (khā′ dər) *n.*: Religious school.

4. **vagrants** (vā′ grәntz) *n.*: People who wander from place to place, especially those without regular jobs.

Just what her illness was, I cannot remember. She had been so sick that someone had called a doctor, and the doctor had sent for a priest. Someone had informed the son, and he had contributed money for a coffin and for the funeral. But the Almighty had not yet wanted to take this pain-racked soul to Himself. She began to feel better, she became well, and as soon as she was able to stand on her feet once more, she resumed her washing. Not just ours, but the wash of several other families too.

"I could not rest easy in my bed because of the wash," the old woman explained. "The wash would not let me die."

"With the help of God you will live to be a hundred and twenty," said my mother, as a benediction.

"God forbid! What good would such a long life be? The work becomes harder and harder . . . my strength is leaving me . . . I do not want to be a burden on anyone!" The old woman muttered and crossed herself, and raised her eyes toward heaven.

◆ **Build Vocabulary**

obstinacy (äb´ stə nə sē) *n.*: Stubbornness
pious (pī ´ əs) *adj.*: Showing religious devotion

Fortunately there was some money in the house and Mother counted out what she owed. I had a strange feeling: the coins in the old woman's washed-out hands seemed to become as worn and clean and pious as she herself was. She blew on the coins and tied them in a kerchief. Then she left, promising to return in a few weeks for a new load of wash.

But she never came back. The wash she had returned was her last effort on this earth. She had been driven by an indomitable will to return the property to its rightful owners, to fulfill the task she had undertaken.

And now at last her body, which had long been no more than a shard[5] supported only by the force of honesty and duty, had fallen. Her soul passed into those spheres where all holy souls meet, regardless of the roles they played on this earth, in whatever tongue, of whatever creed. I cannot imagine paradise without this Gentile washwoman. I cannot even conceive of a world where there is no recompense for such effort.

---

5. **shard** (shärd) *n.*: Fragment or broken piece.

Guide for Responding

◆ *Literature and Your Life*

Reader's Response Whom do you know who seems to give so much and ask so little?

Thematic Focus How does looking back on people from your past make it easier to concentrate on their strengths rather than their flaws?

☑ Check Your Comprehension

1. Explain the relationship of the washwoman to Singer's family.
2. Retell the events of the last few months of the washwoman's life.

◆ **Critical Thinking**

INTERPRET
1. What values does the washwoman represent? **[Analyze]**
2. In what ways is the washwoman like the author's mother? **[Compare and Contrast]**
3. This washwoman is more than just a washwoman to Singer. What greater significance does she have to him? **[Make a Judgment]**

EXTEND
4. How might the washwoman's life be different if she lived in Poland in the year 2000? How might it be the same? **[Social Studies Link]**

On Summer

Lorraine Hansberry

It has taken me a good number of years to come to any measure of respect for summer. I was, being May-born, literally an "infant of the spring" and, during the later childhood years, tended, for some reason or other, to rather worship the cold aloofness of winter. The adolescence, admittedly lingering still, brought the traditional passionate commitment to melancholy autumn—and all that. For the longest kind of time I simply thought that *summer* was a mistake.

In fact, my earliest memory of anything at all is of waking up in a darkened room where I had been put to bed for a nap on a summer's afternoon, and feeling very, very hot. I acutely disliked the feeling then and retained the bias for years. It had originally been a matter of the heat but, over the years, I came actively to associate displeasure with most of the usually celebrated natural features and social by-products of the season: the too-grainy texture of sand; the too-cold coldness of the various waters we constantly try to escape into, and the icky-perspiry feeling of bathing caps.

It also seemed to me, esthetically[1] speaking, that nature had got inexcusably carried away on the summer question and let the whole thing get to be rather much. By duration alone, for instance, a summer's day seemed maddeningly excessive; an utter overstatement. Except for those few hours at either end of it, objects always appeared in too sharp a relief against backgrounds; shadows too pronounced and light too blinding. It always gave me the feeling of walking around in a motion picture which had been too artsily-craftsily exposed. Sound also had a way of coming to the ear without that muting influence, marvelously common to winter, across patios or beaches or through the woods. I suppose I found it too stark and yet too intimate a season.

My childhood Southside[2] summers were the ordinary city kind, full of the street games which the other rememberers have turned into fine ballets these days and rhymes that anticipated what some people insist on calling modern poetry:

Oh, Mary Mack, Mack, Mack
With the silver buttons, buttons, buttons
All down her back, back, back
She asked her mother, mother, mother
For fifteen cents, cents, cents
To see the elephant, elephant, elephant
Jump the fence, fence, fence
Well, he jumped so high, high, high
'Til he touched the sky, sky, sky
And he didn't come back, back, back
'Til the Fourth of Ju-ly, ly, ly!

---

1. **esthetically** (es thet′ ik lē) *adv.*: Artistically.

2. **Southside:** Section of Chicago, Illinois.

Don Nemesio, 1977, Esperanza Martinez

▲ **Critical Viewing** In this essay, Rudolfo Anaya celebrates the wisdom and experience of his grandfather and of the other elders of the community in which he grew up. What lessons can you learn from your grandparents and other older members of your own community? **[Generalize]**

so that a new generation would know what they had known, so the string of life would not be broken.

Today we would say that the old abuelitos lived authentic lives.

Newcomers to New Mexico often say that time seems to move slowly here. I think they mean they have come in contact with the inner strength of the people, a strength so solid it causes time itself to pause. Think of it. Think of the high, northern New Mexico villages, or the lonely ranches on the open llano.[7] Think of the Indian pueblo[8] which lies as solid as rock in the face of time. Remember the old people whose eyes seem like windows that peer into a distant past that makes absurdity of our

7. **llano** (yä′ nō): Plain.
8. **pueblo** (pweb′ lō): Village or town.

contemporary world. That is what one feels when one encounters the old ones and their land, a pausing of time.

We have all felt time stand still. We have all been in the presence of power, the knowledge of the old ones, the majestic peace of a mountain stream or an aspen grove or red buttes rising into blue sky. We have all felt the light of dusk <u>permeate</u> the earth and cause time to pause in its flow.

I felt this when first touched by the spirit of Ultima, the old *curandera*[9] who appears in my first novel, *Bless Me, Ultima.* This is how the young Antonio describes what he feels:

When she came the beauty of the llano unfolded before my eyes, and the

9. **curandera** (kōō rän dä′ rä): Medicine woman.

◆ **Build Vocabulary**

perplexes (pər′ pleks′ iz) *v.:* Confuses or makes hard to understand

permeate (pʉr′ mē āt) *v.:* Spread or flow throughout

gurgling waters of the river sang to the hum of the turning earth. The magical time of childhood stood still, and the pulse of the living earth pressed its mystery into my living blood. She took my hand, and the silent, magic powers she possessed made beauty from the raw, sun-baked llano, the green river valley, and the blue bowl which was the white sun's home. My bare feet felt the throbbing earth, and my body trembled with excitement. Time stood still . . .

At other times, in other places, when I have been privileged to be with the old ones, to learn, I have felt this inner reserve of strength upon which they draw. I have been held motionless and speechless by the power of curanderas. I have felt the same power when I hunted with Cruz, high on the Taos[10] mountain, where it was more than the incredible beauty of the mountain bathed in morning light, more than the shining of the quivering aspen, but a connection with life, as if a shining strand of light connected the particular and the cosmic. That feeling is an epiphany of time, a standing still of time.

◆ **Literary Focus**
How does Anaya use personal experience to help him reflect on his feelings about the strength and power of the old ones?

But not all of our old ones are curanderos or hunters on the mountain. My grandfather was a plain man, a farmer from Puerto de Luna[11] on the Pecos River. He was probably a descendent of those people who spilled over the mountain from Taos, following the Pecos River in search of farmland. There in that river valley he settled and raised a large family.

Bearded and walrus-mustached, he stood five feet tall, but to me as a child he was a giant. I remember him most for his silence. In the summers my parents sent me to live with him on his farm, for I was to learn the ways of a farmer. My uncles also lived in that valley, the valley called Puerto de Luna, there where only the flow of the river and the whispering of the wind marked time. For me it was a magical place.

I remember once, while out hoeing the fields, I came upon an anthill and before I knew it I was badly bitten. After he had covered my welts with the cool mud from the irrigation ditch, my grandfather calmly said: "Know where you stand." That is the way he spoke, in short phrases, to the point.

One very dry summer, the river dried to a trickle, there was no water for the fields. The young plants withered and died. In my sadness and with the impulses of youth I said, "I wish it would rain!" My grandfather touched me, looked up in the sky and whispered, "Pray for rain." In his language there was a difference. He felt connected to the cycles that brought the rain or kept it from us. His prayer was a meaningful action, because he was a participant with the forces that filled our world, he was not a bystander.

A young man died at the village one summer. A very tragic death. He was dragged by his horse. When he was found I cried, for the boy was my friend. I did not understand why death had come to one so young. My grandfather took me aside and said: "Think of the death of the trees and the fields in the fall. The leaves fall, and everything rests, as if dead. But they bloom again in the spring. Death is only this small transformation in life."

These are the things I remember, these fleeting images, few words.

I remember him driving his horse-drawn wagon into Santa Rosa in the fall when he brought his harvest produce to sell in the town. What a tower of strength seemed to come in that small man huddled on the seat of the giant wagon. One click of his tongue and the horses obeyed, stopped or turned as he wished. He never raised his whip. How unlike today when so much teaching is done with loud words and threatening hands.

◆ **Build Vocabulary**

epiphany (ē pif′ ə nē) *n.:* Moment of sudden understanding

---

10. **Taos** (tä′ ōs)
11. **Puerto de Luna** (pwer′ tō dä lōō′ nə): Port of the Moon, the name of a town.

▲ **Critical Viewing** How well does this photograph fit the essay? Explain. **[Evaluate]**

Evenings were spent mainly on the back porches where screen doors slammed in the darkness with those really very special summertime sounds. And, sometimes, when Chicago nights got too steamy, the whole family got into the car and went to the park and slept out in the open on blankets. Those were, of course, the best times of all because the grownups were invariably reminded of having been children in rural parts of the country and told the best stories then. And it was also cool and sweet to be on the grass and there was usually the scent of freshly cut lemons or melons in the air. And Daddy would lie on his back, as fathers must, and explain about how men thought the stars above us came to be and how far away they were. I never did learn to believe that anything could be as far away as *that*. Especially the stars.

My mother first took us south to visit her Tennessee birthplace one summer when I was seven or eight, I think. I woke up on the back seat of the car while we were still driving through some place called Kentucky and my mother was pointing out to the beautiful hills on both sides of the highway and telling my brothers and my sister about how her father had run away and hidden from his master in those very hills when he was a little boy. She said that his mother had wandered among the wooded slopes in the moonlight and left food for him in secret places. They were very beautiful hills and I looked out at them for miles and miles after that wondering who and what a master might be.

I remember being startled when I first saw my grandmother rocking away on her porch. All my life I had heard that she was a great beauty and no one had ever remarked that

◆ **Build Vocabulary**

aloofness (ə lo͞of′ nəs) *n.:* State of being distant, removed, or uninvolved

▲ **Critical Viewing** How does this photograph of the Maine coast add to the descriptions in the essay? **[Connect]**

they meant a half century before. The woman that I met was as wrinkled as a prune and could hardly hear and barely see and always seemed to be thinking of other times. But she could still rock and talk and even make wonderful cupcakes which were like cornbread, only sweet. She was captivated by automobiles and, even though it was well into the Thirties,[3] I don't think she had ever been in one before we came down and took her driving. She was a little afraid of them and could not seem to negotiate the windows, but she loved driving. She died the next summer and that is all that I remember about her, except that she was born in slavery and had memories of it and they didn't sound anything like *Gone With the Wind*.[4]

Like everyone else, I have spent whole or bits of summers in many different kinds of places since then: camps and resorts in the Middle West and New York State; on an island; in a tiny Mexican village; Cape Cod, perched atop the Truro bluffs at Longnook Beach that Millay[5] wrote about; or simply strolling the streets of Provincetown[6] before the hours when the parties begin.

And, lastly, I do not think that I will forget days spent, a few summers ago, at a beautiful lodge built right into the rocky cliffs of a bay on the Maine coast. We met a woman there who had lived a purposeful and courageous life and who was then dying of cancer. She had, characteristically, just written a book and taken up painting. She had also been of radical viewpoint all her life; one of those people who energetically believe that the world *can* be changed for the better and spend their lives trying to do just that. And that was the way she thought of cancer; she absolutely refused to award it the stature of tragedy, a devastating instance of the brooding doom and inexplicability[7] of the absurdity of human destiny, etc., etc. The kind of characterization given, lately, as we all know, to far less formidable foes in life than cancer.

But for this remarkable woman it was a matter of nature in imperfection, implying, as always, work for man to do. It was an *enemy*, but a palpable one with shape and effect and

---

3. Thirties: The 1930's.
4. *Gone With the Wind*: Novel set in the South during the Civil War period.

5. Millay: Edna St. Vincent Millay (1892–1950), American poet.
6. Provincetown: Resort town at the northern tip of Cape Cod, Massachusetts.
7. inexplicability (in eks´ pli kə bil´ ə tē) *n*.: Condition that cannot be explained.

source; and if it existed, it could be destroyed. She saluted it accordingly, without despondency, but with a lively, beautiful and delightfully ribald anger. There was one thing, she felt, which would prove equal to its relentless ravages and that was the genius of man. Not his mysticism, but man with tubes and slides and the stubborn human notion that the stars are very much within our reach.

The last time I saw her she was sitting surrounded by her paintings with her manuscript laid out for me to read, because, she said, she wanted to know what a *young person* would think of her thinking; one must always keep up with what *young people* thought about things because, after all, they were *change*.

Every now and then her jaw set in anger as we spoke of things people should be angry about. And then, for relief, she would look out at the lovely bay at a mellow sunset settling on the water. Her face softened with love of all that beauty and, watching her, I wished with all my power what I knew that she was wishing: that she might live to see at least one more *summer*. Through her eyes I finally gained the sense of what it might mean; more than the coming autumn with its pretentious melancholy; more than an austere and silent winter which must shut dying

◆ Reading Strategy
How does Hansberry's attitude toward summer change?

people in for precious months; more even than the frivolous spring, too full of too many false promises, would be the gift of another summer with its stark and intimate assertion of neither birth nor death but life at the apex; with the gentlest nights and, above all, the longest days.

I heard later that she did live to see another summer. And I have retained my respect for the noblest of the seasons.

Guide for Responding

◆ Literature and Your Life

Reader's Response How do Hansberry's ideas about summer compare with your own?

Thematic Focus How do Hansberry's experiences cause her to change her way of thinking about summer?

Journal Writing List associations you have with each season of the year. Include places and events that have a special significance during each season.

☑ Check Your Comprehension

1. What did Hansberry dislike about summer before she met the woman in Maine?
2. Describe some of Hansberry's memories of childhood summers.
3. Tell why meeting the woman in Maine had such a lasting effect on Hansberry.

◆ Critical Thinking

INTERPRET

1. Why does Hansberry include the section about her grandmother? **[Draw Conclusions]**
2. Why does Hansberry refer to summer as "the noblest of seasons"? **[Infer]**
3. Is this essay about summer, or is it really about something else? Explain your answer. **[Identify]**

EVALUATE

4. (a) How does Hansberry appeal to your emotions in this essay? (b) How does this emotional appeal make the essay more effective? **[Evaluate]**

EXTEND

5. For each season of the year, list three or four destinations around the globe that might persuade a person that that particular season was "the noblest of seasons." Then explain why the geography and climate of one particular season in one particular place are uplifting to the human spirit. **[Social Studies Link]**

A Celebration of Grandfathers

Rudolfo A. Anaya

"Buenos días le de Dios, abuelo."[1] God give you a good day, grandfather. This is how I was taught as a child to greet my grandfather, or any grown person. It was a greeting of respect, a cultural value to be passed on from generation to generation, this respect for the old ones.

The old people I remember from my childhood were strong in their beliefs, and as we lived daily with them we learned a wise path of life to follow. They had something important to share with the young, and when they spoke the young listened. These old abuelos and abuelitas[2] had worked the earth all their lives, and so they knew the value of nurturing, they knew the sensitivity of the earth. The daily struggle called for cooperation, and so every person contributed to the social fabric, and each person was respected for his contribution.

◆ **Reading Strategy**
How do the facts about the author's past help you understand his attitude toward his subject?

The old ones had looked deep into the web that connects all animate and inanimate forms of life, and they recognized the great design of the creation.

These *ancianos*[3] from the cultures of the Rio Grande, living side by side, sharing, growing together, they knew the rhythms and cycles of time, from the preparation of the earth in the spring to the digging of the acequias[4] that brought the water to the dance of harvest in the fall. They shared good times and hard times. They helped each other through the epidemics and the personal tragedies, and they shared what little they had when the hot winds burned the land and no rain came. They learned that to survive one had to share in the process of life.

Hard workers all, they tilled the earth and farmed, ran the herds and spun wool, and carved their saints and their kachinas[5] from cottonwood late in the winter nights. All worked with a deep faith which perplexes the modern mind.

Their faith shone in their eyes; it was in the strength of their grip, in the creases time wove into their faces. When they spoke, they spoke plainly and with few words, and they meant what they said. When they prayed, they went straight to the source of life. When there were good times, they knew how to dance in celebration and how to prepare the foods of the fiestas.[6] All this they passed on to the young,

---

1. **Buenos días le de Dios, abuelo** (bweˊ nôs dēˊ äs lā dā dēˊ ōs ä bwäˊ lō)
2. **abuelitas** (a bwā lēˊ täs): Grandmothers.
3. **ancianos** (än cē äˊ nōs): Old people; ancestors.

4. **acequias** (ä sāˊ kē əs): Irrigation ditches.
5. **kachinas** (kə chēˊ nəz): Small wooden dolls, representing the spirit of an ancestor or a god.
6. **fiestas** (fē esˊ təz): Celebrations; feasts.

Don Nemesio, 1977, Esperanza Martinez

▲ **Critical Viewing** In this essay, Rudolfo Anaya celebrates the wisdom and experience of his grandfather and of the other elders of the community in which he grew up. What lessons can you learn from your grandparents and other older members of your own community? **[Generalize]**

so that a new generation would know what they had known, so the string of life would not be broken.

Today we would say that the old abuelitos lived authentic lives.

Newcomers to New Mexico often say that time seems to move slowly here. I think they mean they have come in contact with the inner strength of the people, a strength so solid it causes time itself to pause. Think of it. Think of the high, northern New Mexico villages, or the lonely ranches on the open llano.[7] Think of the Indian pueblo[8] which lies as solid as rock in the face of time. Remember the old people whose eyes seem like windows that peer into a distant past that makes absurdity of our

7. **llano** (yä´ nō): Plain.
8. **pueblo** (pweb´ lō): Village or town.

contemporary world. That is what one feels when one encounters the old ones and their land, a pausing of time.

We have all felt time stand still. We have all been in the presence of power, the knowledge of the old ones, the majestic peace of a mountain stream or an aspen grove or red buttes rising into blue sky. We have all felt the light of dusk <u>permeate</u> the earth and cause time to pause in its flow.

I felt this when first touched by the spirit of Ultima, the old *curandera*[9] who appears in my first novel, *Bless Me, Ultima*. This is how the young Antonio describes what he feels:

> When she came the beauty of the llano unfolded before my eyes, and the

9. **curandera** (kōō rän dä´ rä): Medicine woman.

◆ **Build Vocabulary**

perplexes (pər´ pleks´ iz) v.: Confuses or makes hard to understand

permeate (pʉr´ mē āt) v.: Spread or flow throughout

gurgling waters of the river sang to the hum of the turning earth. The magical time of childhood stood still, and the pulse of the living earth pressed its mystery into my living blood. She took my hand, and the silent, magic powers she possessed made beauty from the raw, sun-baked llano, the green river valley, and the blue bowl which was the white sun's home. My bare feet felt the throbbing earth, and my body trembled with excitement. Time stood still . . .

At other times, in other places, when I have been privileged to be with the old ones, to learn, I have felt this inner reserve of strength upon which they draw. I have been held motionless and speechless by the power of curanderas. I have felt the same power when I hunted with Cruz, high on the Taos[10] mountain, where it was more than the incredible beauty of the mountain bathed in morning light, more than the shining of the quivering aspen, but a connection with life, as if a shining strand of light connected the particular and the cosmic. That feeling is an epiphany of time, a standing still of time.

◆ Literary Focus
How does Anaya use personal experience to help him reflect on his feelings about the strength and power of the old ones?

But not all of our old ones are curanderos or hunters on the mountain. My grandfather was a plain man, a farmer from Puerto de Luna[11] on the Pecos River. He was probably a descendent of those people who spilled over the mountain from Taos, following the Pecos River in search of farmland. There in that river valley he settled and raised a large family.

Bearded and walrus-mustached, he stood five feet tall, but to me as a child he was a giant. I remember him most for his silence. In the summers my parents sent me to live with him on his farm, for I was to learn the ways of a farmer. My uncles also lived in that valley, the valley called Puerto de Luna, there where

only the flow of the river and the whispering of the wind marked time. For me it was a magical place.

I remember once, while out hoeing the fields. I came upon an anthill and before I knew it I was badly bitten. After he had covered my welts with the cool mud from the irrigation ditch, my grandfather calmly said: "Know where you stand." That is the way he spoke, in short phrases, to the point.

One very dry summer, the river dried to a trickle, there was no water for the fields. The young plants withered and died. In my sadness and with the impulses of youth I said, "I wish it would rain!" My grandfather touched me, looked up in the sky and whispered, "Pray for rain." In his language there was a difference. He felt connected to the cycles that brought the rain or kept it from us. His prayer was a meaningful action, because he was a participant with the forces that filled our world, he was not a bystander.

A young man died at the village one summer. A very tragic death. He was dragged by his horse. When he was found I cried, for the boy was my friend. I did not understand why death had come to one so young. My grandfather took me aside and said: "Think of the death of the trees and the fields in the fall. The leaves fall, and everything rests, as if dead. But they bloom again in the spring. Death is only this small transformation in life."

These are the things I remember, these fleeting images, few words.

I remember him driving his horse-drawn wagon into Santa Rosa in the fall when he brought his harvest produce to sell in the town. What a tower of strength seemed to come in that small man huddled on the seat of the giant wagon. One click of his tongue and the horses obeyed, stopped or turned as he wished. He never raised his whip. How unlike today when so much teaching is done with loud words and threatening hands.

◆ Build Vocabulary

epiphany (ē pif´ ə nē) n.: Moment of sudden understanding

---

10. **Taos** (tä´ ōs)
11. **Puerto de Luna** (pwer´ tō dä lōō´ nə): Port of the Moon, the name of a town.

El Lenador, 1934, Tom Lea, Museum of Fine Arts, Museum of New Mexico

◀ **Critical Viewing** How does the elderly farmer in this painting compare with the image you have of the author's grandfather? **[Compare and Contrast]**

I would run to greet the wagon, and the wagon would stop. "Buenos días le de Dios, abuelo," I would say. This was the prescribed greeting of esteem and respect. Only after the greeting was given could we approach these venerable old people. "Buenos días le de Dios, mi hijo,"[12] he would answer and smile, and then I could jump up on the wagon and sit at his side. Then I, too, became a king as I rode next to the old man who smelled of earth and sweat and the other deep aromas from the orchards and fields of Puerto de Luna.

We were all sons and daughters to him. But today the sons and daughters are breaking with the past, putting aside los abuelitos. The old values are threatened, and threatened most

where it comes to these relationships with the old people. If we don't take the time to watch and feel the years of their final transformation, a part of our humanity will be lessened.

I grew up speaking Spanish, and oh! how difficult it was to learn English. Sometimes I would give up and cry out that I couldn't learn. Then he would say, "Ten paciencia."[13] Have patience. *Paciencia*, a word with the strength of centuries, a word that said that someday we would overcome. *Paciencia*, how soothing a word coming from this old man who could still sling hundred-pound bags over his shoulder, chop wood for hours on end, and hitch up his own horses and ride to town and back in one day.

---

12. mi hijo (mē ē′ hō): My son.

13. Ten paciencia (ten pä sē en′ sē ä)

"You have to learn the language of the Americanos,"[14] he said. "Me, I will live my last days in my valley. You will live in a new time, the time of the gringos."[15]

A new time did come, a new time is here. How will we form it so it is fruitful? We need to know where we stand. We need to speak softly and respect others, and to share what we have. We need to pray not for material gain, but for rain for the fields, for the sun to nurture growth, for nights in which we can sleep in peace, and for a harvest in which everyone can share. Simple lessons from a simple man. These lessons he learned from his past which was deep and strong as the currents of the river of life, a life which could be stronger than death.

He was a man; he died. Not in his valley, but nevertheless cared for by his sons and daughters and flocks of grandchildren. At the end, I would enter his room which carried the smell of medications and Vicks, the faint pungent odor of urine, and cigarette smoke. Gone were the aroma of the fields, the strength of his young manhood. Gone also was his patience in the face of crippling old age. Small things bothered him; he shouted or turned sour when his expectations were not met. It was because he could not care for himself, because he was returning to that state of childhood, and all those wishes and desires were now wrapped in a crumbling old body.

"Ten paciencia," I once said to him, and he smiled. "I didn't know I would grow this old," he said. "Now, I can't even roll my own cigarettes." I rolled a cigarette for him, placed it in his mouth and lit it. I asked him why he smoked, the doctor had said it was bad for him. "I like to see the smoke rise," he said. He would smoke and doze, and his quilt was spotted with little burns where the cigarettes dropped. One of us had to sit and watch to make sure a fire didn't start.

I would sit and look at him and remember what was said of him when he was a young man. He could mount a wild horse and break it, and he could ride as far as any man. He could dance all night at a dance, then work the acequia the following day. He helped neighbors, they helped him. He married, raised children. Small legends, the kind that make up everyman's life.

He was 94 when he died. Family, neighbors, and friends gathered; they all agreed he had led a rich life. I remembered the last years, the years he spent in bed. And as I remember now, I am reminded that it is too easy to romanticize old age. Sometimes we forget the pain of the transformation into old age, we forget the natural breaking down of the body. Not all go gentle into the last years, some go crying and cursing, forgetting the names of those they loved the most, withdrawing into an internal anguish few of us can know. May we be granted the patience and care to deal with our ancianos.

For some time we haven't looked at these changes and needs of the old ones. The American image created by the mass media is an image of youth, not of old age. It is the beautiful and the young who are praised in this society. If analyzed carefully, we see that same damaging thought has crept into the way society views the old. In response to the old, the mass media have just created old people who act like the young. It is only the healthy, pink-cheeked, outgoing, older persons we are shown in the media. And they are always selling something, as if an entire generation of old people were salesmen in their lives. Commercials show very lively old men, who must always be in excellent health according to the new myth, selling insurance policies or real estate as they are out golfing; older women selling coffee or toilet paper to those just married. That image does not illustrate the real life of the old ones.

Real life takes into account the natural cycle of growth and change. My grandfather pointed to the leaves falling from the tree. So time brings with its transformation the often painful, wearing-down process. Vision blurs, health wanes; even the act of walking carries with it the painful reminder of the autumn of life. But this process is something to be faced, not something to be hidden away by false images. Yes, the old can be young at heart, but

---

14. **Americanos** (ä mer′ ē kä′ nōs): Americans.
15. **gringos** (griŋ′ gōs): Foreigners; North Americans.

in their own way, with their own dignity. They do not have to copy the always young image of the Hollywood star.

My grandfather wanted to return to his valley to die. But by then the families of the valley had left in search of a better future. It is only now that there seems to be a return to the valley, a revival. The new generation seeks its roots, that value of love for the land moves us to return to the place where our ancianos formed the culture.

I returned to Puerto de Luna last summer, to join the community in a celebration of the founding of the church. I drove by my grandfather's home, my uncles' ranches, the neglected adobe[16] washing down into the earth from whence it came. And I wondered, how might the values of my grandfather's generation live in our own? What can we retain to see us through these hard times? I was to become a farmer, and I became a writer. As I plow and plant my words, do I nurture as my grandfather did in his fields and orchards? The answers are not simple.

"They don't make men like that anymore," is a phrase we hear when one does honor to a man. I am glad I knew my grandfather. I am glad there are still times when I can see him in my dreams, hear him in my reverie. Sometimes I think I catch a whiff of that earthy aroma that was his smell, just as in lonely times sometimes I catch the fragrance of Ultima's herbs. Then I smile. How strong these people were to leave such a lasting impression.

So, as I would greet my abuelo long ago, it would help us all to greet the old ones we know with this kind and respectful greeting: "Buenos días le de Dios."

◆ Reading Strategy
Sum up the author's attitude toward the "old ones."

---

16. adobe (ä dō′ bē): Sun-dried clay brick.

Guide for Responding

◆ Literature and Your Life

Reader's Response How do the "old ones" in Anaya's life compare with the "old ones" in your own life?

Thematic Focus What perspective does Anaya offer on how old people should be treated as they age and as they die?

Group Activity Make a list of recommendations for the way younger people might greet, respect, or help care for older people in their homes and neighborhoods.

☑ Check Your Comprehension

1. What are some of the qualities Anaya remembers about old people from his childhood?
2. What does Anaya remember about his own grandfather?
3. How does the "new time" in which Anaya lives differ from the time of his grandfather?

◆ Critical Thinking

INTERPRET

1. How does the world of the old ones compare with the modern world? **[Compare and Contrast]**
2. How do the author's values differ from those of his grandfather? How are his values the same? **[Compare and Contrast]**
3. Why do you think the essay ends with the very same words with which it begins? **[Analyze]**

APPLY

4. What do the grandfathers that Anaya celebrates have in common with Singer's washwoman or Singer's mother? **[Synthesize]**

EXTEND

5. Explain how geography and history helped shape the values of the old ones. **[Social Studies Link]**

Guide for Responding (continued)

◆ Reading Strategy

IDENTIFY THE AUTHOR'S ATTITUDE

In all three essays, the **author's attitude** toward the subject comes through clearly in the choice of words and details. For example, Rudolfo Anaya shows his admiration and respect for the older generation when he describes the older generation's strength in its beliefs and tells about how the younger people would listen carefully whenever older people spoke.

1. What three adjectives do you think Singer might select to describe his attitude toward the washwoman? Support your answers with details from the essay.
2. What is Hansberry's attitude toward summer? How can you tell?
3. Anaya's attitude comes from his heritage and his own experience. Do you think he could convince others who do not have the same background to adopt his attitude? Why or why not?

◆ Literary Focus

ESSAY

An **essay** is a short piece of nonfiction in which a writer expresses a personal view of a topic. These selections illustrate three different types of essays: narrative essays, which tell a story; persuasive essays, which try to convince readers to accept a position or take a course of action; and reflective essays—essays in which a writer reflects on his or her feelings about a topic of personal importance.

1. In addition to entertaining readers, narrative essays often make important points about life. What points does I. B. Singer make through his story about the washwoman?
2. In a persuasive essay, the writer presents facts, reasons, anecdotes, and other types of information in an attempt to sway the reader's opinion. What are some of the facts and reasons that Lorraine Hansberry presents to persuade you to accept her opinion about summer?
3. Why is "A Celebration of Grandfathers" a good example of a reflective essay? Support your answer with details from the selection.

◆ Build Vocabulary

USING THE PREFIX *fore-*

Complete the following analogies using these words: *foreground, foresee, forethought,* which all contain the prefix *fore-*, meaning "occurring earlier."

1. *Ahead* is to *behind* as ____?____ is to *background*.
2. *Reflection* is to the *past* as ____?____ is to the *future*.
3. *To anticipate* is to ____?____ as *to find* is to *discover*.

USING THE WORD BANK

On your paper, write the word from the Word Bank that best matches each clue.

1. a synonym for *confuses*
2. a three-syllable word that describes an uninvolved state
3. long-ago relatives of your relatives
4. the opposite of peace and harmony
5. the end to a state of confusion
6. a quality of donkeys
7. people with this quality may be found in a mosque, church, or temple
8. the word you might use in describing an inescapable odor

◆ Build Grammar Skills

COMMONLY CONFUSED WORDS: *AFFECT* AND *EFFECT*

These essays are about people and experiences that **affected,** or influenced, the authors deeply. One **effect,** or result, of these experiences was the essay each wrote. As these sentences illustrate, *affect* is a verb meaning "to influence," while *effect* is often a noun meaning "the result." *Effect* can also be a verb meaning "to bring about" or "to accomplish."

Practice Revise the following sentences, correcting any errors in the use of *affect* and *effect*.

1. The documentary effected Sean emotionally.
2. It was about the affects of the Great Depression.
3. There were many statements to the affect that Hoover was to blame.
4. Sean thought it was unfair to blame the affects of the Depression on President Hoover.
5. Sean did, however, know how negatively the Depression had effected his great-grandparents.

Build Your Portfolio

 Idea Bank

Writing

1. **Summary** Write a brief essay summarizing the key points of one of these essays. Start with a paragraph in which you sum up the overall message and introduce the key points. Then write a paragraph about each of the main points.

2. **Reflective Essay** Write a reflective essay about a subject of personal importance to you. For example, you might write about why a specific person has influenced you, or you might reflect on a single experience that had a powerful impact.

3. **Essay About Themes** Each of these essays has a theme, or central message, that we can apply to our own lives. Write an essay in which you explain the lessons that you learned from the three selections. Cite details to support your points.

Speaking and Listening

4. **Interview** Interview an older person whom you know and admire. Find out key details about the person's life and important lessons that he or she has learned. Share your findings with the class. **[Community Link]**

5. **Persuasive Speech** Prepare and present a persuasive speech on the importance of respecting and learning from older generations. Use details from Anaya's and Singer's essays for support.

Projects

6. **Collage** Create a collage in which you use a collection of images to pay tribute to older generations. **[Art Link]**

7. **Medley of Songs** Find a series of songs connected to the themes of the three essays. Play them for the class, and explain how each one relates to one of the essays. **[Music Link]**

 Writing Mini-Lesson

Proposal for a Celebration

Choose your favorite season of the year and think of the perfect way to celebrate it in your community. Then put together a formal proposal that you could present to the local government, outlining a series of festivities that could be held to commemorate this special season. Keep the following tip in mind as you develop your proposal:

Writing Skills Focus: Clear Explanation of Cause and Effect

To create a successful proposal, you need to outline the **causes and effects** of each activity you suggest. In fact, you should probably start by explaining what caused you to make your proposal—what it is about the season that makes it worth celebrating. Then clearly state the reasons for each activity you suggest and indicate the positive effects of that activity. For example, you might suggest a fishing contest to celebrate spring, because it would help build an appreciation of the beauty of the environment in which you live.

Prewriting Start by deciding on a season. Then brainstorm to come up with a list of activities that would capture the spirit of that season.

Drafting Propose the celebration in full detail. Tell when each event will happen, where it will take place, and who is likely to take part. As you do so, explain cause-and-effect relationships, and use cause-and-effect signal words such as *because, why, for, therefore, so, result,* and *effect.*

Revising Share your draft with a classmate. Ask him or her to decide whether each cause-and-effect relationship is clearly stated. Then discuss whether or not he or she found the proposal convincing. If not, encourage him or her to make suggestions on how you can improve it.

Guide for Reading

Lady Bird Johnson (1912–)

On one of the most tragic days in American history, November 22, 1963, Lady Bird Johnson became First Lady of the United States. President John F. Kennedy had just been killed by an assassin in Dallas, Texas. On board *Air Force One*, the President's airplane, Vice President Lyndon Baines Johnson took the oath of office to become the thirty-sixth President of the United States. On his left stood Kennedy's widow, Jackie, her clothing still spattered with her husband's blood. On his right stood his wife, Lady Bird Johnson.

Texas-born Claudia Alta Taylor received her nickname at age two, when a nurse said she was as pretty as a lady bird. In 1934, she married Lyndon Johnson, then a congressional secretary. Throughout Lyndon Johnson's political career, Lady Bird was a most valued advisor and campaigner.

John McPhee (1931–)

Nonfiction writer John McPhee has found success in writing about topics that fascinate him. One such subject is sports. After graduating from Princeton University, McPhee worked at *Time* magazine, and then at *The New Yorker*. McPhee has written many books and essays. In *Levels of the Game* (1969), an account of the 1968 U.S. Open Tennis Championships, McPhee reveals his admiration for Arthur Ashe.

Joan Didion (1934–)

Joan Didion is descended from a long line of pioneers. Her great-great-grandmother went west in a covered wagon in 1846. As a young woman, Didion won a writing contest sponsored by *Vogue* magazine. Eventually she became an editor there. Her reputation in the literary world, however, is based on her novels and essays. The essay "Georgia O'Keeffe" pays tribute to an artist who herself displayed a strong pioneer spirit.

◆ **Build Vocabulary**

WORD ROOTS: -sent-/-sens-

In "Georgia O'Keeffe," Joan Didion refers to a sentimental appreciation of art. The word *sentimental* contains the root *-sent-* (sometimes spelled *-sens-*), which means "feeling or perceiving." The root is an important clue to the meaning of the word, which is "having excessive feelings or emotions."

tumultuous
implications
poignant
legacy
enigma
condescending
sentimental
genesis
rancor
immutable

WORD BANK

Before you read, preview this list of words from the selections.

◆ **Build Grammar Skills**

APPOSITIVES AND APPOSITIVE PHRASES

Look at the following passages from Lady Bird Johnson's diary. What purpose is served by words in italics?

> . . . our Secret Service man, *Rufus Youngblood*, vaulted over the front seat . . .

> . . . Kenny O'Donnell, *the President's top aide*, . . .

In both cases, the italicized words help to identify the people Johnson mentions. The first example features an **appositive**—a noun or pronoun placed near another noun or pronoun to identify, rename, or explain it. The second contains an **appositive phrase**—an appositive accompanied by other words that modify it. As you read these selections, notice how the writers use appositives.

◆ *from* A White House Diary ◆
Arthur Ashe Remembered ◆ Georgia O'Keeffe

◆ *Literature and Your Life*

CONNECT YOUR EXPERIENCE

Through the media, we have many opportunities to see and hear famous people. Seldom, however, do we find out what famous people are truly like. In the following selections, you'll have a rare chance to see the private sides of three famous Americans.

THEMATIC FOCUS: LEARNING ABOUT OURSELVES AND OTHERS

As the selections illustrate, the good times, the hard work, and—perhaps most of all—the tragedies of life can lead to discoveries about what really matters in life.

◆ Background for Understanding

HISTORY

Any American old enough to remember the day President John F. Kennedy was assassinated—November 22, 1963—will never forget it. At the moment that radio and television commentators reported the news of the fatal shooting, the United States came to a halt. A shocked nation stayed glued to television sets to get the details of the unfolding story. People wept openly in their homes and in the streets. President Kennedy had been a young, vibrant, and popular leader, who had fostered a sense of optimism about the future. With his assassination, this optimism was shattered. A stunned nation shared the feelings of newly sworn-in President Lyndon Johnson when he said, "This is a sad time for all people. We have suffered a loss that cannot be weighed. For me, it is a deep personal tragedy."

Journal Writing List a few local or world events of your lifetime that caused people either joy or sorrow.

◆ Literary Focus

BIOGRAPHICAL AND AUTOBIOGRAPHICAL WRITING

Biographical writing is a form of nonfiction in which a writer tells the story of another person's life. **Autobiographical** writing is a form of nonfiction in which a person tells about his or her own life. The entry from *A White House Diary* is an autobiographical account. As the diary reveals, autobiographical writing shows events from the author's perspective and lets you share the author's thoughts and feelings. In a piece of biographical writing, on the other hand, you are presented with a writer's view of a subject's life and do not have direct access to the subject's thoughts and feelings.

◆ Reading Strategy

FIND THE WRITER'S MAIN POINTS AND SUPPORT

A key to understanding and enjoying any literary work is the ability to **find the writer's main points** and the details—facts, events, quotations, and more—that support those points. Sometimes writers will directly state the main points in the opening paragraph. Other times, however, writers depend on the cumulative effect of their writing to communicate their message.

To find the main ideas of these selections, look closely at each paragraph to determine the main idea it conveys. A paragraph's main idea may be stated in a single sentence, or you may have to draw a conclusion about its main idea from the supporting information it presents. For example, if a paragraph in a biography describes an incident in which the subject risked her life to save someone, you might conclude that the paragraph's main point relates to the subject's bravery and selflessness. Once you've finished reading, try to piece together the key ideas of the individual paragraphs to determine the main points of the work as a whole.

from *A White House Diary*

Lady Bird Johnson

DALLAS, FRIDAY, NOVEMBER 22, 1963

It all began so beautifully. After a drizzle in the morning, the sun came out bright and clear. We were driving into Dallas. In the lead car were President and Mrs. Kennedy, John and Nellie Connally,[1] a Secret Service car full of men, and then our car with Lyndon and me and Senator Ralph Yarborough.

The streets were lined with people—lots and lots of people—the children all smiling, placards, confetti, people waving from windows. One last happy moment I had was looking up and seeing Mary Griffith leaning out of a window waving at me. (Mary for many years had been in charge of altering the clothes which I purchased at Neiman-Marcus.)

Then, almost at the edge of town, on our way to the Trade Mart for the Presidential luncheon, we were rounding a curve, going down a hill, and suddenly there was a sharp, loud report. It sounded like a shot. The sound seemed to me to come from a building on the right above my shoulder. A moment passed, and then two more shots rang out in rapid succession. There had been such a gala air about the day that I thought the noise must come from firecrackers—part of the celebration. Then the Secret Service[2] men were suddenly down in the lead car. Over the car radio system, I heard "Let's get out of here!" and our Secret Service man, Rufus Youngblood,

▲ **Critical Viewing** What do the people's facial expressions reveal about their feelings in the aftermath of President Kennedy's assassination? **[Infer]**

vaulted over the front seat on top of Lyndon, threw him to the floor, and said, "Get down."

Senator Yarborough and I ducked our heads. The car accelerated terrifically—faster and faster. Then, suddenly, the brakes were put on so hard that I wondered if we were going to make it as we wheeled left and went around the corner. We pulled up to a building. I looked up and saw a sign, "HOSPITAL." Only then did I believe that this might be what it was. Senator Yarborough kept saying in an excited voice, "Have they shot the President? Have they shot the President?" I said something like, "No, it can't be."

As we ground to a halt—we were still the third car—Secret Service men began to pull, lead,

---

1. John and Nellie Connally: John Connally, then Governor of Texas, and his wife, Nellie.
2. Secret Service: Division of the U.S. Treasury Department, responsible for protecting the President.

▲ **Critical Viewing** What does this photograph reveal about the mood in the moments leading up to the assassination? [Infer]

guide, and hustle us out. I cast one last look over my shoulder and saw in the President's car a bundle of pink, just like a drift of blossoms, lying on the back seat. It was Mrs. Kennedy lying over the President's body.

The Secret Service men rushed us to the right, then to the left, and then onward into a quiet room in the hospital—a very small room. It was lined with white sheets, I believe.

People came and went—Kenny O'Donnell, the President's top aide, Congressman Homer Thornberry, Congressman Jack Brooks. Always there was Rufe right there and other Secret Service agents—Emory Roberts, Jerry Kivett, Lem Johns, and Woody Taylor. People spoke of how widespread this might be. There was talk about where we would go—to the plane, to our house, back to Washington.

Through it all Lyndon was remarkably calm and quiet. He suggested that the Presidential plane ought to be moved to another part of the field. He spoke of going back out to the plane in unmarked black cars. Every face that came in,

you searched for the answer. I think the face I kept seeing the answer on was the face of Kenny O'Donnell, who loved President Kennedy so much.

It was Lyndon who spoke of it first, although I knew I would not leave without doing it. He said, "You had better try to see Jackie and Nellie." We didn't know what had happened to John.

I asked the Secret Service if I could be taken to them. They began to lead me up one corridor and down another. Suddenly I found myself face to face with Jackie in a small hallway. I believe it was right outside the operating room. You always think of someone like her as being insulated, protected. She was quite alone. I don't think I ever saw anyone so much alone in my life. I went up to her, put my arms around her, and said something to her. I'm sure it was something like "God, help us all," because my feelings for her were too <u>tumultuous</u> to put into words.

And then I went to see Nellie. There it was different, because Nellie and I have gone through so many things together since 1938. I hugged her tight and we both cried and I said, "Nellie, John's going to be all right." And Nellie said, "Yes, John's going to be all right." Among her many other fine qualities, she is also strong.

I turned and went back to the small white room where Lyndon was. Mac Kilduff, the President's press man on this trip, and Kenny O'Donnell were coming and going. I think it was from Kenny's face that I first knew the truth and from Kenny's voice that I first heard the words "The President is dead." Mr. Kilduff entered and said to Lyndon, "Mr. President."

It was decided that we would go immediately to the airport. Hurried plans were made about how we should get to the cars and who was to ride in which car. Our departure from the hospital and approach to the cars was one of the swiftest walks I have ever made.

We got in. Lyndon told the agents to stop the sirens. We drove along as fast as we could. I

◆ **Build Vocabulary**

tumultuous (tōō mul′ chōō əs) *adj.:* Greatly disturbed

looked up at a building and there, already, was a flag at half-mast. I think that was when the enormity of what had happened first struck me.

When we got to the field, we entered *Air Force One*[3] for the first time. There was a TV set on and the commentator was saying, "Lyndon B. Johnson, now President of the United States." The news commentator was saying the President had been shot with a 30-30 rifle. The police had a suspect. They were not sure he was the assassin.

On the plane, all the shades were lowered. We heard that we were going to wait for Mrs. Kennedy and the coffin. There was a telephone call to Washington—I believe to the Attorney General.[4] It was decided that Lyndon should be sworn in here as quickly as possible, because of national and world implications, and because we did not know how widespread this was as to intended victims. Judge Sarah Hughes, a Federal Judge in Dallas—and I am glad it was she—was called and asked to come in a hurry to administer the oath.

Mrs. Kennedy had arrived by this time, as had the coffin. There, in the very narrow confines of the plane—with Jackie standing by Lyndon, her hair falling in her face but very composed, with me beside him, Judge Hughes in front of him, and a cluster of Secret Service people, staff, and Congressmen we had known for a long time around him—Lyndon took the oath of office.

It's odd the little things that come to your mind at times of utmost stress, the flashes of deep compassion you feel for people who are really not at the center of the tragedy. I heard a Secret Service man say in the most desolate voice—and I hurt for him: "We never lost a President in the Service." Then, Police Chief Curry of Dallas came on the plane and said, "Mrs. Kennedy, believe me, we did everything we possibly could." That must have been an agonizing moment for him.

We all sat around the plane. The casket was in the corridor. I went in the small private room to see Mrs. Kennedy, and though it was a very hard thing to do, she made it as easy as possible. She said things like, "Oh, Lady Bird, we've liked you two so much. . . . Oh, what if I had not been there. I'm so glad I was there."

I looked at her. Mrs. Kennedy's dress was stained with blood. One leg was almost entirely covered with it and her right glove was caked, it was caked with blood—her husband's blood. Somehow that was one of the most poignant sights—that immaculate woman exquisitely dressed, and caked in blood.

I asked her if I couldn't get someone in to help her change and she said, "Oh, no. Perhaps later I'll ask Mary Gallagher but not right now." And then with almost an element of fierceness—if a person that gentle, that dignified, can be said to have such a quality—she said, "I want them to see what they have done to Jack."

I tried to express how we felt. I said, "Oh, Mrs. Kennedy, you know we never even wanted to be Vice President and now, dear God, it's come to this." I would have done anything to help her, but there was nothing I could do, so rather quickly I left and went back to the main part of the airplane where everyone was seated.

The flight to Washington was silent, each sitting with his own thoughts. One of mine was a recollection of what I had said about Lyndon a long time ago—he's a good man in a tight spot. I remembered one little thing he had said in that hospital room—"Tell the children to get a Secret Service man with them."

Finally we got to Washington, with a cluster of people waiting and many bright lights. The casket went off first, then Mrs. Kennedy, and then we followed. The family had come to join her. Lyndon made a very simple, very brief, and, I think, strong statement to the people there. Only about four sentences. We got in helicopters, dropped him off at the White House, and I came home in a car with Liz Carpenter.[5]

---

5. **Liz Carpenter:** Mrs. Johnson's press secretary.

◆ Build Vocabulary

implications (im′ pli kā′ shənz) *n*.: Suggestions or indirect indications

poignant (poin′ yənt) *adj*.: Drawing forth pity or compassion; moving

---

3. **Air Force One:** Name of the airplane officially assigned to transport the president of the United States.
4. **Attorney General:** Chief law officer of the nation, head of the U.S. Department of Justice.

▲ **Critical Viewing** This photograph shows Lyndon Johnson beginning to assume his duties as president. Based on the details in the photo, how do you think he felt at that time? Why? **[Analyze]**

Beyond Literature

History Connection

Lyndon Johnson and the Vietnam War On March 31, 1968, President Johnson announced that he would not seek reelection. More than any other factor, his decision resulted from his support of the Vietnam War and the criticism that followed. During his presidency, the United States became more and more deeply involved in the war. When he took office, there were only about 16,300 American military advisors in Vietnam. By 1968, the United States had more than 500,000 troops there, and Americans were bitterly divided over the war.

Activity With a group, conduct research to learn more about the Vietnam War and the protests that resulted from it. Share your findings with the class.

Guide for Responding

◆ *Literature and Your Life*

Reader's Response What do you admire most about Lady Bird Johnson? Why?

Thematic Focus What do you think Lady Bird Johnson discovers about life during the ordeal of the Kennedy assassination?

☑ Check Your Comprehension

1. What does Lady Bird Johnson hear over the car radio system immediately after the shots are fired?
2. What is the "bundle of pink" that Lady Bird Johnson sees lying on the back seat of the president's car?
3. Where does Lyndon Johnson take the oath of office for president of the United States?
4. When she enters the private room on the presidential airplane to speak with Mrs. Kennedy, what sight moves Lady Bird Johnson most?

◆ Critical Thinking

INTERPRET

1. Lady Bird Johnson says of Mrs. Kennedy at the hospital, "I don't think I ever saw anyone so much alone in my life." In what ways is Mrs. Kennedy alone? **[Deduce]**
2. Mrs. Kennedy does not change her bloodstained clothing. In what way is wearing the clothing a tribute to her husband? **[Interpret]**
3. With frightful suddenness, the assassination drastically changes the lives of Lady Bird Johnson and Lyndon Johnson. Cite examples from the diary entry that indicate they are up to the tasks before them. **[Support]**

EXTEND

4. Why is this diary an especially valuable source for people, such as historians and teachers, who are interested in the Kennedy assassination or the Lyndon Johnson presidency? **[Social Studies Link]**

Arthur Ashe
Remembered

John McPhee

He once described his life as "a succession of fortunate circumstances." He was in his twenties then. More than half of his life was behind him. His memory of his mother was confined to a single image: in a blue corduroy bathrobe she stood in a doorway looking out on the courts and playing fields surrounding their house, which stood in the center of a Richmond playground. Weakened by illness, she was taken to a hospital that day, and died at the age of twenty-seven. He was six.

It was to be his tragedy, as the world knows, that he would leave his own child when she was six, that his life would be trapped in a medical irony as a result of early heart disease, and death would come to him prematurely, as it had to his mother.

His mother was tall, with long soft hair and a face that was gentle and thin. She read a lot. She read a lot to him. His father said of her, "She was just like Arthur Junior. She never argued. She was quiet, easygoing, kindhearted."

If by legacy her son never argued, he was also schooled, instructed, coached not to argue, and as he moved alone into alien country he fashioned not-arguing into an enigma and turned the enigma into a weapon. When things got tough (as I noted in these pages twenty-four years ago), he had control. Even in very tight moments, other players thought he was toying with them. They

▲ **Critical Viewing** In 1975, Arthur Ashe won the men's singles championship at Wimbledon. What do you think is going through his mind as he displays his trophy? [Speculate]

rarely knew what he was thinking. They could not tell if he was angry. It was maddening, sometimes, to play against him. Never less

than candid, he said that what he liked best about himself on a tennis court was his demeanor: "What it is is controlled cool, in a way. Always have the situation under control, even if losing. Never betray an inward sense of defeat."

◆ Reading Strategy
What is the writer's main point in this paragraph?

And of course he never did—not in the height of his athletic power, not in the statesmanship of the years that followed, and not in the endgame of his existence. If you wished to choose a single image, you would see him standing there in his twenties, his lithe body a braid of cables, his energy without apparent limit, in a court situation indescribably bad, and all he does is put his index finger on the bridge of his glasses and push them back up the bridge of his nose. In the shadow of disaster, he hits out. Faced with a choice between a conservative, percentage return or a one-in-ten flat-out blast, he chooses the blast. In a signature manner, he extends his left arm to point upward at lobs as they fall toward him. His overheads, in fire bursts, put them away. His backhand is, if anything, stronger than his forehand, and his shots from either side for the most part are

explosions. In motions graceful and decisive, though, and with reactions as fast as the imagination, he is a master of drop shots, of cat-and-mouse, of miscellaneous dinks and chips and (riskiest of all) the crosscourt half-volley. Other tennis players might be wondering who in his right mind would attempt something like that, but that is how Ashe plays the game: at the tensest moment, he goes for the all but impossible. He is predictably unpredictable. He is unreadable. His ballistic serves move in odd patterns and come off the court in unexpected ways. Behind his impassive face— behind the enigmatic glasses, the lifted chin, the first-mate-on-the-bridge look—there seems to be, even from this distance, a smile.

◆ Literary Focus
The writer of this remembrance has balanced the tragic and the joyful aspects of Arthur Ashe's life. What are those two aspects?

◆ Build Vocabulary

legacy (leg´ ə sē) *n.*: Anything handed down from an ancestor

enigma (i nig´ mə) *n.*: Puzzling or baffling matter; riddle.

Guide for Responding

◆ Literature and Your Life

Reader's Response After reading this selection, what are your feelings about Arthur Ashe? Why?

Thematic Focus What does Arthur Ashe discover are the advantages of "controlled cool" during a tennis match?

☑ Check Your Comprehension

1. In what ways is Arthur Ashe like his mother?
2. How does Ashe use the traits he inherited from his mother to his advantage when playing tennis?
3. What does Arthur Ashe do in a disastrous situation in a tennis match?
4. What does Arthur Ashe never betray in tennis or in life?

◆ Critical Thinking

INTERPRET

1. What later proved to be tragically ironic, or surprising, about Arthur Ashe's early statement that his life is "a succession of fortunate circumstances"? **[Connect]**
2. What does Ashe's ability never to betray an inward sense of defeat say about his character? **[Draw Conclusions]**
3. Use examples to show how the writer uses the way Arthur Ashe played tennis to illustrate how Ashe lived life. **[Support]**

APPLY

4. How can one aspect of Ashe's approach to tennis—going for the difficult shot when in trouble—be applied as an approach to life? **[Apply]**

Georgia O'Keeffe

Joan Didion

"Where I was born and where and how I have lived is unimportant," Georgia O'Keeffe told us in the book of paintings and words published in her ninetieth year on earth. She seemed to be advising us to forget the beautiful face in the Stieglitz[1] photographs. She appeared to be dismissing the rather condescending romance that had attached to her by then, the romance of extreme good looks and advanced age and deliberate isolation. "It is what I have done with where I have been that should be of interest." I recall an August afternoon in Chicago in 1973 when I took my daughter, then seven, to see what Georgia O'Keeffe had done with where she had been. One of the vast O'Keeffe "Sky Above Clouds" canvases floated over the back stairs in the Chicago Art Institute that day, dominating what seemed to be several stories of empty light, and my daughter looked at it once, ran to the landing, and kept on looking. "Who drew it," she whispered after a while. I told her. "I need to talk to her," she said finally.

My daughter was making, that day in Chicago, an entirely unconscious but quite basic assumption about people and the work they do. She was assuming that the glory she saw in the work reflected a glory in its maker, that the painting was the painter as the poem is the poet, that every choice one made alone—every word chosen or rejected, every brush stroke laid or not laid down—betrayed one's character. *Style is character.* It seemed to me that afternoon that I had rarely seen so instinctive an application of this familiar principle, and I recall being pleased not only that my daughter responded to style as character but that it was Georgia O'Keeffe's particular style to which she responded: this was a hard woman who had imposed her 192 square feet of clouds on Chicago.

"Hardness" has not been in our century a quality much admired in women, nor in the past twenty years has it even been in official favor for men. When hardness surfaces in the very old we tend to transform it into "crustiness" or eccentricity, some tonic pepperiness to be indulged at a distance. On the evidence of her work and what she has said about it, Georgia O'Keeffe is neither "crusty" nor eccentric. She is simply hard, a straight shooter, a woman clean of received wisdom and open to what she sees. This is a woman who could early on dismiss most of her contemporaries as "dreamy," and would later single out one she liked as "a very poor painter." (And then add, apparently by way of softening the judgment: "I guess he wasn't a painter at all. He had no courage and I believe that to create one's own world in any of the arts takes courage.") This is a woman who in 1939 could advise her admirers that they were missing her point, that their appreciation of her famous flowers was merely sentimental. "When I paint a red hill," she observed coolly in the catalogue for an exhibition that year, "you say it is too bad that I don't always paint flowers. A flower touches almost everyone's heart. A red hill doesn't touch everyone's heart." This is a woman who could describe the genesis of one of her most well-known paintings—the "Cow's

---

1.   **Stieglitz** (stēg´ lits): Alfred Stieglitz (1864–1946); U.S. photographer and husband of Georgia O'Keeffe.

Skull: Red, White and Blue" owned by the Metropolitan[2] —as an act of quite deliberate and derisive orneriness. "I thought of the city men I had been seeing in the East," she wrote. "They talked so often of writing the Great American Novel—the Great American Play—the Great American Poetry. . . . So as I was painting my cow's head on blue I thought to myself, 'I'll make it an American painting. They will not think it great with the red stripes down the sides—Red White and Blue—but they will notice it.'"

The city men. The men. They. The words crop up again and again as this astonishingly aggressive woman tells us what was on her mind when she was making her astonishingly aggressive paintings. It was those city men

2. **Metropolitan:** Metropolitan Museum of Art in New York City.

▲ **Critical Viewing** Georgia O'Keeffe is famous for her paintings of flowers. Notice how the white trumpet flower in this painting fills the canvas with bold lines and shapes. What can you guess about the personality of the artist from her work? **[Deduce]**

who stood accused of sentimentalizing her flowers: "I made you take time to look at what I saw and when you took time to really notice my flower you hung all your associations with flowers on my flower and you write

◆ **Build Vocabulary**

condescending (kän′ di sen′ diŋ) *adj.*: Characterized by looking down on someone

sentimental (sen′ tə ment′ əl) *adj.*: Excessively or foolishly emotional

genesis (jen′ ə sis) *n.*: Birth; origin; beginning

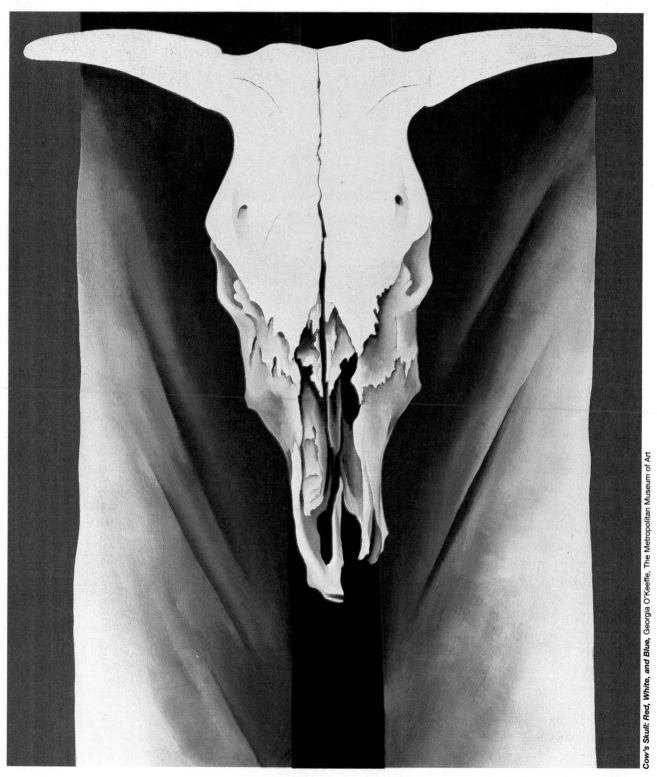

Cow's Skull: Red, White, and Blue, Georgia O'Keeffe, The Metropolitan Museum of Art

▲ **Critical Viewing** Why do you think that some critics—especially men who felt that women should adopt attitudes and behaviors traditionally thought of as feminine—found O'Keeffe's work inappropriate, disturbing, and even threatening? **[Hypothesize]**

about my flower as if I think and see what you think and see—and I don't." *And I don't.* Imagine those words spoken, and the sound you hear is *don't tread on me.*[3] "The men" believed it impossible to paint New York, so Georgia O'Keeffe painted New York. "The men" didn't think much of her bright color, so she made it brighter. The men yearned toward Europe so she went to Texas, and then New Mexico. The men talked about Cézanne,[4] "long involved remarks about the 'plastic quality' of his form and color," and took one another's long involved remarks, in the view of this angelic rattlesnake in their midst, altogether too seriously. "I can paint one of those dismal-colored paintings like the men," the woman who regarded herself always as an outsider remembers thinking one day in 1922, and she did: a painting of a shed "all low-toned and dreary with the tree beside the door." She called this act of <u>rancor</u> "The Shanty" and hung it in her next show. "The men seemed to approve of it," she reported fifty-four years later, her contempt undimmed. "They seemed to think that maybe I was beginning to paint. That was my only low-toned dismal-colored painting."

◆ **Literary Focus**
What does this paragraph reveal about O'Keeffe?

Some women fight and others do not. Like so many successful guerrillas in the war between the sexes, Georgia O'Keeffe seems to have been equipped early with an <u>immutable</u> sense of who she was and a fairly clear understanding that she would be required to prove it. On the surface her upbringing was conventional. She was a child on the Wisconsin prairie who played with china dolls and painted watercolors with cloudy skies because sunlight was too hard to paint and, with her brother and sisters, listened every night to her mother read stories of the Wild West, of Texas, of Kit Carson and Billy the Kid. She told adults that she wanted to be an artist and was embarrassed when they asked what kind of artist she wanted to be: she had no idea "what kind." She had no idea what artists did. She had never seen a picture that interested her, other than a pen-and-ink Maid of Athens in one of her mother's books, some Mother Goose illustrations printed on cloth, a tablet cover that showed a little girl with pink roses, and the painting of Arabs on horseback that hung in her grandmother's parlor. At thirteen, in a Dominican convent, she was mortified when the sister corrected her drawing. At Chatham Episcopal Institute in Virginia she painted lilacs and sneaked time alone to walk out to where she could see the line of the Blue Ridge Mountains on the horizon. At the Art Institute in Chicago she was shocked by the presence of live models and wanted to abandon anatomy lessons. At the Art Students League in New York one of her fellow students advised her that, since he would be a great painter and she would end up teaching painting in a girls' school, any work of hers was less important than modeling for him. Another painted over her work to show her how the Impressionists did trees. She had not before heard how the Impressionists did trees and she did not much care.

◆ **Reading Strategy**
What kind of support does Didion use in this paragraph to indicate that O'Keeffe had "an immutable sense of who she was"?

---

3. **Don't tread on me:** Motto of the first official American flag to be flown by a naval vessel, on December 3, 1775.
4. **Cézanne** (sē zän´): Paul Cézanne (1836–1906), French Impressionist and Postimpressionist painter.

◆ **Build Vocabulary**
rancor (raŋ´ kər) *n.*: Hatred; spite
immutable (im´ myo͞ot´ ə bəl) *adj.*: Never changing

At twenty-four she left all these opinions behind and went for the first time to live in Texas, where there were no trees to paint and no one to tell her how not to paint them. In Texas there was only the horizon she craved. In Texas she had her sister Claudia with her for a while, and in the late afternoons they would walk away from town and toward the horizon and watch the evening star come out. "That evening star fascinated me," she wrote. "It was in some way very exciting to me. My sister had a gun, and as we walked she would throw bottles into the air and shoot as many as she could before they hit the ground. I had nothing but to walk into nowhere and the wide sunset space with the star. Ten watercolors were made from that star." In a way one's interest is compelled as much by the sister Claudia with the gun as by the painter Georgia with the star, but only the painter left us this shining record. Ten watercolors were made from that star.

Guide for Responding

◆ Literature and Your Life

Reader's Response Which of O'Keeffe's qualities do you admire most? Why?

Thematic Focus Through her contact with "the city men," what does O'Keeffe discover about how she herself wants to paint?

Journal Writing In your journal, discuss your reactions to the examples of O'Keeffe's works included in these pages. Also explore your thoughts about what you learn about her as a person in this selection.

☑ Check Your Comprehension

1. Where does O'Keeffe spend her early childhood?
2. What signs of her character does O'Keeffe show while growing up?
3. How does O'Keeffe assert herself among the male artists whom she knows?
4. To what place does O'Keeffe move and find what she craves?

◆ Critical Thinking

INTERPRET

1. What is meant by "hardness," a key character trait attributed to O'Keeffe? Give examples from the text. **[Interpret]**
2. What do the ways in which O'Keeffe responds to suggestions that she paint differently tell you about her character? **[Draw Conclusions]**
3. What do you think O'Keeffe finds attractive about Texas? **[Infer]**
4. Explain what Didion means by saying O'Keeffe had "an immutable sense of who she was." **[Interpret]**
5. Explain how the words "Style is character" are appropriate for Georgia O'Keeffe. Cite evidence from the text. **[Draw Conclusions]**

APPLY

6. O'Keeffe says "that to create one's own world in any of the arts takes courage." What does she mean by that statement? **[Synthesize]**

EVALUATE

7. What qualities of O'Keeffe's paintings make them "aggressive paintings"? **[Criticize]**

Guide for Responding (continued)

◆ Reading Strategy

FIND THE WRITER'S MAIN POINTS AND SUPPORT

Recognizing a writer's **main points** and **supporting evidence** is essential to understanding and enjoying a literary work. Look back at the selections and write two examples of support that the writer uses for each of the following main points. Then list two other main points that each writer made.

1. Mrs. Kennedy made Lady Bird Johnson's visit on the plane as easy as possible.
2. Not arguing proved to be a potent weapon for Arthur Ashe on the tennis court.
3. Georgia O'Keeffe was a hard, straight shooter.

◆ Build Grammar Skills

APPOSITIVES AND APPOSITIVE PHRASES

Appositives and appositive phrases, which are often set off by commas, can be used to combine two short sentences into a single sentence.

An **appositive** is a noun or pronoun placed near another noun or pronoun to provide more information about it. An **appositive phrase** contains other words that modify the appositive.

Practice On a sheet of paper, combine each pair of sentences by changing one sentence into an appositive phrase.

1. Lady Bird Johnson kept a diary. She was the First Lady of the United States.
2. In Dallas, the sun was shining. Dallas is a large city in Texas.
3. Rufus Youngblood yelled, "Get down!" He was a secret service agent.
4. One region inspired artist Georgia O'Keeffe. It was the desert of the Southwest.

◆ Literary Focus

BIOGRAPHICAL AND AUTOBIOGRAPHICAL WRITING

Biographical and autobiographical writing both present a detailed portrait of a single person's life. "Arthur Ashe Remembered" and "Georgia O'Keeffe" are examples of **biographical writing,** which tells about the life of a person other than the writer. *A White House Diary* is an example of **autobiographical writing,** in which the writer tells about his or her own life.

1. Cite at least two details from *A White House Diary* that reveal the compassion of Lady Bird Johnson.
2. What does "Arthur Ashe Remembered" reveal about what Ashe was like as a person?
3. In what ways was Georgia O'Keeffe a "loner"?
4. Using these selections as examples, explain how the view of the subject presented in autobiographical writing is different from that in biographical writing.

◆ Build Vocabulary

USING THE WORD ROOT -sent-/-sens-

The word root *-sent-*, sometimes spelled *-sens-*, means "feeling or perceiving." Match each *"-sent-"* word with its definition. Use the part-of-speech labels as clues.

1. sensitize   a. (*adv.*) with an acute response or feeling
2. sensitively   b. (*v.*) to cause to respond or feel acutely
3. sentimentality   c. (*n.*) condition of being excessively emotional

USING THE WORD BANK

Match each word pair with its meaning.

1. poignant genesis   a. emotional riddle
2. tumultuous implications   b. unchangable inheritance
3. immutable legacy   c. patronizing hatred
4. sentimental enigma   d. turbulent indications
5. condescending rancor   e. moving beginning

Build Your Portfolio

 ## Idea Bank

Writing

1. **Letter of Condolence** Imagine you were alive at the time of President Kennedy's assassination. Write a letter to his widow expressing your sympathy and describing the late President's importance to the nation. **[Social Studies Link]**

2. **How-to Essay** Arthur Ashe excelled in the sport of tennis. Write a how-to essay in which you explain how to play a sport, a video game, or a board game at which you excel. Be sure to include a description of any required equipment.

3. **Essay** The subjects of these selections were all strong role models. Write a short essay in which you discuss what you can learn from the three subjects that you can apply to your own life.

Speaking and Listening

4. **News Report** Develop and present to the class a radio news report on the assassination of President Kennedy. **[Social Studies Link]**

5. **Speech** Present a speech on the advantages of practicing Arthur Ashe's "controlled cool" in daily life. Discuss how calm discussions can help settle differences. **[Social Studies Link]**

Projects

6. **Internet Exploration** Use the Internet to gather additional information about the subject of one of these selections. Present your findings to the class in an informal oral report. **[Social Studies Link; Media Link]**

7. **Museum Exhibit** Find reproductions of several of Georgia O'Keeffe's paintings. Write informational captions for each painting. Put the reproductions and the captions together to create an exhibit of O'Keeffe's work. **[Fine Art Link]**

 ## Writing Mini-Lesson

Awards Speech

You are an official at an awards ceremony for an influential person, such as Lady Bird Johnson, Arthur Ashe, or Georgia O'Keeffe. Write a speech that introduces the award winner. To make your speech easy to follow, be sure it is coherent.

Writing Skills Focus: Coherence

A piece of writing has **coherence** when each idea flows logically out of the previous ideas. The first step in achieving coherence is to make sure that all your key points fit together and to arrange them in an order that makes sense. Then use transition words, such as *then* and *next*, to highlight the relationships among ideas. You can also repeat key words to establish clear connections among sentences or paragraphs. Notice how John McPhee links the content of one paragraph to the next by repeating an idea.

Model From the Selection

. . . She *never argued*. She was quiet, easygoing, kindhearted.

If by legacy her son *never argued*, he was also . . . .

Prewriting Select an influential person whom you admire. Then jot down the main points you'd like to make about that person.

Drafting Begin your speech with an attention-grabbing opening, such as an amusing anecdote. Then, present your main points in a logical order. You might organize them in either chronological order or order of importance.

Revising Read your speech and ask a classmate to suggest places where you can rearrange ideas or add transitions to make your speech clearer.

Writing Process Workshop

Cause-and-Effect Essay

In "Single Room, Earth View," astronaut Sally Ride recounts viewing pollution-damaged trees from the vantage point of her orbit around Earth. In this passage, Ride is describing a cause—pollution—and its effect—damaged trees. A type of writing that explores the reasons that a particular event or situation occurred is the **cause-and-effect essay**. Write your own cause-and-effect essay on a topic of your choice. The following skills, introduced in this section's Writing Mini-Lessons, will help you write a cause-and-effect essay.

Writing Skills Focus

▶ **Use vivid adjectives** to create a clear and lively picture for readers to "see" in their minds. (See p. 564.)

▶ **Give clear explanations** of the cause and the effects. Be sure to offer reasons for the results you describe. (See p. 583.)

▶ **Create coherence** by arranging your ideas and details in a logical order. (See p. 598.)

Sally Ride uses all these skills as she explains civilization's negative effects on our environment.

MODEL FROM LITERATURE

from *Single Room, Earth View* by Sally Ride

Some of civilization's more unfortunate effects on the environment are also evident from orbit. ① Oil slicks glisten on the surface of the Persian Gulf, patches of pollution-damaged trees dot the forests of central Europe. Some cities look out of focus, and their colors muted, when viewed through a pollutant haze. ② Not surprisingly, the effects are more noticeable now than they were a decade ago. ③

① Ride begins by clearly stating the cause: civilization. She is now ready to explain the effects.

② Ride uses vivid adjectives, such as <u>pollution-damaged</u>, <u>muted</u>, and <u>pollutant</u>.

③ The essay has coherence because the ideas flow logically and the order of details makes sense.

APPLYING LANGUAGE SKILLS: Coordinating and Subordinating Conjunctions

A **coordinating conjunction** joins words or phrases:

A bridge went up, _and_ more people moved to town.

A **subordinating conjunction** introduces an adverb clause:

After a bridge went up, more people moved to town.

Use the type of conjunction that best expresses your idea.

Practice Join each pair of sentences using a coordinating or subordinating conjunction.

1. The population grew. The high school expanded.
2. Our town grew. Other towns did not.
3. A new factory opened. More jobs were created.

Writing Application As you draft your essay, use coordinating or subordinating conjunctions to join sentences. In each case, use the type that works best for you.

Writer's Solution Connection
Writing Lab

To help you come up with a topic, use the Inspirations in the Choosing a Topic section in the tutorial on Exposition.

Prewriting

Choose a Topic Choose a topic that interests you, such as changes that have occurred in your neighborhood, the impact of a new government policy, or the effects of a recent world event. Many topics may require you to do some research.

Outline Causes and Effects To help identify clearly the causes and effects you'll present in your essay, use a cluster diagram like the one shown here. Write an effect in the center circle, then write the causes in clusters around the effect.

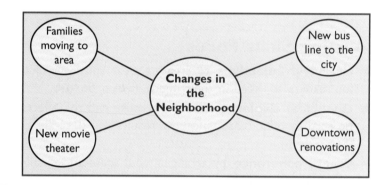

List Vivid Adjectives List adjectives you might use in your essay. Start with a general adjective, and then list vivid adjectives that will make your descriptions more precise and colorful.

General Adjective: big
Vivid Adjectives: enormous, gigantic, gargantuan

Organize Your Details Coherently Choose the best organization for your cause-and-effect essay. You might want to use chronological order, in which you arrange details according to when in time they occurred, or order of importance organization, in which you list details from most to least important (or from least to most important). Whatever organization you choose, jot down your main details on separate note cards, then arrange the cards in the proper order.

Drafting

Write a Strong Introduction Begin with an introductory paragraph that captures readers' interest, highlights the importance of your topic, and touches on the main points you'll make.

Use Transitions to Show Relationships As you draft, use transition words and phrases, such as _because of_ and _as a result_, to clearly indicate the causes and effects you're describing.

Revising

Use a Checklist Go back to the Writing Skills Focus on the first page of the lesson, and use the items as a checklist to evaluate and revise your cause-and-effect essay.

▶ Have I used vivid adjectives rather than general ones?
   Look over your draft, and identify all the adjectives. If any seem too general, replace them with more specific, lively ones.

▶ Have I clearly explained each cause and effect?
   Have a peer review your essay and jot down points he or she does not understand. Then find a way to explain those ideas more clearly.

▶ Does my essay have coherence?
   Reread your draft to check how smoothly the ideas flow. Is there a way to rearrange your details to improve your presentation?

REVISION MODEL

① were invented,   ② booming
After elevators, many small towns grew to big cities.

③
Before the age of elevators, the U.S. was a country made

up mainly of small towns.

① The writer explains the cause more clearly.
② The writer uses a more vivid adjective.
③ The writer rearranges details to make his ideas more coherent.

Work With a Peer Reviewer After revising your own work, have a classmate review your essay, looking for any missing details and any places where you can add transitions to make relationships clearer.

Publishing

▶ **Classroom** Share your cause-and-effect essay with your classmates.

▶ **Internet** Post your essay on an electronic bulletin board. Consult with an experienced Internet user if you're unsure about how to publish on-line.

APPLYING LANGUAGE SKILLS: Avoiding Shifts in Tense

As you write, don't shift from past tense to present tense or from present tense to past tense.

Incorrect: The bridge went up, so the town grows.

Correct: The bridge went up, so the town grew.

Practice On your paper, rewrite the sentences so that the verb tense does not shift.

1. If one business does well, another did well, too.
2. Because more drivers came here, roads are paved.
3. After a town expands, it needed more services.
4. As elevators were installed, buildings grow.

Writing Application As you revise your essay, check for shifts in the verb tense. If shifts occur, make the necessary changes.

Writer's Solution Connection
Writing Lab

For more instruction on proofreading and revision, work through the Revision section of the tutorial on Exposition.

Strategies for Success

There may be times when you need to get information from a chart. You might have to check the times on a bus schedule, for example, or find a chemical element on the periodic table. Charts are also included in many nonfiction articles. Get the most from charts by learning how to read them correctly.

Study the Chart When you first look at a chart, note how it is organized. The information usually appears in columns. Notice how each column is labeled. Do the columns run vertically? Horizontally? Both ways? What does each column show?

Know What You Want to Find A chart may offer more information than you need. In order to read it successfully, you must know exactly what you want to find. For example, a bus schedule might list departure and arrival times for many stations. Do you want to know when a bus will leave or when it will arrive? Which station do you need?

Read the Small Print Some charts contain special symbols that indicate footnotes at the bottom of the chart. Read the footnotes carefully. They may help clarify information on the chart.

Apply the Strategy

Use the calorie chart to answer these questions. Remember to study the chart carefully before answering.

1. What is the calorie allowance for a 14-year-old boy? For a 14-year-old girl?
2. What is the difference in calorie allowance for males and females more than 51 years old?
3. Which age ranges show the same weights for males? For females?
4. What happens to the recommended calorie allowance as a person grows older?

RECOMMENDED DAILY CALORIE ALLOWANCES*

	Age	Average Weight**	Calories
Males	11–14	99	2,700
	15–18	145	2,800
	19–22	154	2,900
	23–50	154	2,700
	51+	154	2,400
Females	11–14	101	2,200
	15–18	120	2,100
	19–22	120	2,100
	23–50	120	2,000
	51+	120	1,800

* for normally active people in temperate climates
** in pounds

✔ Here are other situations in which reading a chart is helpful:
- ▶ Finding the mileage between two cities
- ▶ Finding the populations of each of the fifty states
- ▶ Learning about former presidents
- ▶ Discovering the nutritional values of foods

PART 2

Visual Essays and Workplace Writing

Busy Office Flowchart, Celia Johnson/Stock Illustration Source, Inc.

Guide for Reading

Scott McCloud (1960–   )

Like many of us, Scott McCloud had a childhood passion for comics. For McCloud, however, this passion wasn't a passing phase.

McCloud has developed his passion for comics into a successful career.

Beginnings Scott McCloud originally came from Massachusetts and now lives in California. He started drawing comics at the age of twelve and, after graduating with high honors from Syracuse University in 1982, he plunged into what quickly became a very successful career as a cartoonist. His award-winning comic book series *Zot!,* published when he was just twenty-five, uses robots and teleportation machines to tell the story of a teenager seeking the "Doorway at the Edge of the Universe." This work was followed by *Destroy!* which parodies superhero comics.

Explaining His Art Having established himself as a successful comic book writer, McCloud went on to produce a book, *Understanding Comics: The Invisible Art,* in which he combines words and pictures to explain how comics work, how they affect readers, the different forms they can take, and, above all, why he loves them and has made them his life's work. The book has won wide critical acclaim. Garry Trudeau, the creator of *Doonesbury,* said that McCloud's book "shows us how the mind processes [comics] . . . and how words combine with pictures to work their singular magic."

◆ Build Vocabulary

WORD ROOTS: *-stat-*

In his visual essay, Scott McCloud uses the word *static* (see p. 612) to describe each frame of a comic strip. The word *static* contains the Latin root *-stat-,* which means "to stand." Knowing this root, you could easily guess that *static* refers to something that stands unchanging. What other words can you think of that contain the root *-stat-?*

WORD BANK

As you read the comic, you will encounter the words on this list. Note the definitions so that you'll be familiar with the words when you come to them.

> **obsessed** (əb sest´) *adj.:* Greatly preoccupied with (p. 607)
> **aesthetic** (es thet´ ik) *adj.:* Relating to the appreciation of beauty (p. 609)
> **arbitrary** (är´ bə trer´ ē) *adj.:* Not fixed by rules but left to one's judgment (p. 612)

◆ Build Grammar Skills

PUNCTUATION OF INTRODUCTORY WORDS

Because Scott McCloud's selection takes the form of a comic strip, the reader must leapfrog from each individual frame (box containing a picture and words) to the next. To make the hops and landings smoother, McCloud uses **introductory words and phrases** at the beginning of many of the frames. Look at these examples:

Frame 5: *Soon,* I was hooked.
Frame 6: *In less than a year,* I became totally obsessed with comics!

As these examples illustrate, a comma is placed after an introductory word or phrase to set it off from the rest of a sentence. Look for other examples of introductory words and phrases as you read the selection.

Understanding Comics

◆ *Literature and Your Life*

CONNECT YOUR EXPERIENCE

What comes to mind when you think of comics? If you're like most people, you probably think of superheroes, humorous animal characters, or amusing people with exaggerated facial features. As you read this selection, however, you'll discover that comics have a much broader definition than you might expect.

Journal Writing Jot down your definition of the term *comics*. Refer to your definition again after you read McCloud's essay.

THEMATIC FOCUS: OUT OF THE ORDINARY

When people need a laugh, they often turn to the comic section of a newspaper. What is it that makes comics humorous? Is it the out-of-the-ordinary characters and situations? The words? The images? Or a combination?

◆ Background for Understanding

HUMANITIES

Comic strips began appearing in American newspapers in the late 1800's. One of the early strips, which featured a character called the Yellow Kid and was published in a New York newspaper, became so popular that the sales of the newspaper increased. As a result, other papers began to run comic strips to boost their own circulation.

Comic books were first introduced in the 1930's. One of the most popular early comic book series, *Superman,* first appeared in 1938 and has remained popular to this day. In recent years, comic books have begun addressing more sophisticated themes and the popularity of comic books has increased dramatically among adults.

◆ Literary Focus

VISUAL ESSAY

If someone read this selection aloud to you, you might get the gist of its ideas, but you would miss out on the author's unique approach, not to mention the fun of seeing the work on the page. That's because the selection is a **visual essay,** an exploration of a topic that conveys its ideas through visual elements as well as language. Like a standard essay, a visual essay presents an author's views of a single topic. Unlike other essays, however, much of the meaning in a visual essay is conveyed through illustrations or photographs.

◆ Reading Strategy

USE VISUALS AS A KEY TO MEANING

Visual essays, newspaper and magazine articles, manuals —much of the nonfiction that we read today is accompanied by illustrations or photographs. When you read these types of pieces, you can **use the visuals as a key to meaning** by looking carefully at each illustration or photograph and thinking about how it reinforces or adds to what is presented in the written text. In the following piece by Scott McCloud, you'll discover that the visuals play as important a role in conveying meaning as the words do. Some of the pictures add humor to apparently straightforward statements. Other pictures add details that it would take a great number of words to present. In still other cases, the pictures signal flashbacks in time or the presentation of a fantasy.

As you read, think about how each of the pictures reinforces or extends the words that McCloud presents.

Guide for Reading ◆ 605

excerpt from

UNDERSTANDING COMICS

Scott McCloud

HI, I'M *SCOTT McCLOUD.*

JANUARY

WHEN I WAS A *LITTLE KID* I KNEW *EXACTLY* WHAT COMICS WERE.

COMICS WERE THOSE *BRIGHT, COLORFUL MAGAZINES* FILLED WITH *BAD ART, STUPID STORIES* AND *GUYS IN TIGHTS.*

© and ™ 1994 Scott McCloud

I READ *REAL* BOOKS, NATURALLY. I WAS MUCH TOO *OLD* FOR COMICS!

BUT WHEN I WAS IN *8th GRADE,* A FRIEND OF MINE (WHO WAS A LOT *SMARTER* THAN I WAS) CONVINCED ME TO GIVE COMICS ANOTHER LOOK AND LENT ME HIS COLLECTION.

SOON, I WAS *HOOKED!*

THE REALLY *OLD* X-MEN BY STAN & JACK

IN LESS THAN A *YEAR,* I BECAME *TOTALLY OBSESSED* WITH COMICS! I DECIDED TO BECOME A *COMICS ARTIST* IN *10th GRADE* AND BEGAN TO *PRACTICE, PRACTICE, PRACTICE!*

I FELT THAT THERE WAS SOMETHING *LURKING* IN COMICS... SOMETHING THAT HAD *NEVER BEEN DONE.*

SOME KIND OF *HIDDEN POWER!*

BUT WHENEVER I TRIED TO *EXPLAIN* MY FEELING, I FAILED *MISERABLY.*

COMIC BOOKS?! HA! HA! HA!

BUT IT-- BUT IT'S-- BUH...

SURE, I REALIZED THAT COMIC BOOKS WERE USUALLY *CRUDE, POORLY-DRAWN, SEMILITERATE, CHEAP, DISPOSABLE KIDDIE FARE--*

--BUT--

THEY DON'T *HAVE* TO BE!

THE *PROBLEM* WAS THAT FOR *MOST PEOPLE,* THAT WAS WHAT *"COMIC BOOK" MEANT!*

DON'T GIMME THAT *COMIC BOOK* TALK, BARNEY!

IF PEOPLE FAILED TO *UNDERSTAND* COMICS, IT WAS BECAUSE THEY DEFINED WHAT COMICS COULD BE *TOO NARROWLY!*

A *PROPER DEFINITION,* IF WE COULD *FIND* ONE, MIGHT GIVE *LIE* TO THE STEREOTYPES--

--AND SHOW THAT THE *POTENTIAL* OF COMICS IS *LIMITLESS* AND *EXCITING!*

THIS IS WHERE OUR JOURNEY *BEGINS.*

THE WORLD OF COMICS IS A *HUGE* AND *VARIED* ONE. OUR DEFINITION MUST ENCOMPASS ALL THESE TYPES--

--WHILE NOT BEING *SO* BROAD AS TO INCLUDE ANYTHING WHICH IS CLEARLY *NOT* COMICS.

"COMICS" IS THE WORD WORTH DEFINING, AS IT REFERS TO THE MEDIUM *ITSELF,* NOT A SPECIFIC *OBJECT* AS *"COMIC BOOK"* OR *"COMIC STRIP"* DO.

WE CAN ALL VISUALIZE *A* COMIC.

GENERIC GUY ™

BUT WHAT--

--IS--

--COMICS?

MASTER COMICS ARTIST *WILL EISNER* USES THE TERM *SEQUENTIAL ART* WHEN DESCRIBING COMICS.

TAKEN *INDIVIDUALLY,* THE PICTURES BELOW ARE MERELY *THAT-- PICTURES.*

HOWEVER, WHEN PART OF A *SEQUENCE,* EVEN A SEQUENCE OF ONLY *TWO,* THE ART OF THE *IMAGE* IS *TRANSFORMED* INTO SOMETHING *MORE: THE ART OF COMICS!*

NOTICE THAT THIS DEFINITION IS STRICTLY *NEUTRAL* ON MATTERS OF *STYLE, QUALITY* OR *SUBJECT MATTER.*

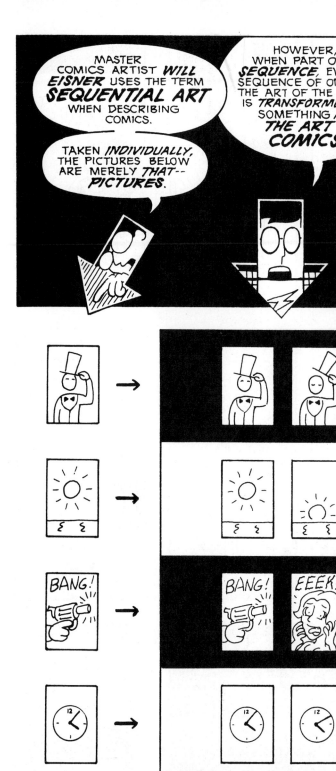

BANG!

EEEK!

MUCH HAS ALREADY BEEN WRITTEN ON THE VARIOUS *SCHOOLS* OF COMIC ART; ON *PARTICULAR ARTISTS, PARTICULAR TITLES, PARTICULAR TRENDS...*

BUT TO *DEFINE* COMICS, WE MUST FIRST DO A LITTLE *AESTHETIC SURGERY* AND SEPARATE *FORM* FROM *CONTENT!*

THE ARTFORM--THE *MEDIUM*--KNOWN AS COMICS IS A *VESSEL* WHICH CAN HOLD ANY *NUMBER* OF *IDEAS* AND *IMAGES*.

THE *"CONTENT"* OF THOSE IMAGES AND IDEAS IS, OF COURSE, UP TO *CREATORS,* AND WE ALL HAVE DIFFERENT *TASTES.*

=GLUG=
=GLUG=

PTUI!!!

=GAAK=
=WHEEEEZ=
=KAF! KAF!=
GLUGH-GGH...

=ahem=

THE *TRICK* IS TO NEVER MISTAKE THE *MESSAGE*--

--FOR THE *MESSENGER.*

AT ONE TIME OR ANOTHER VIRTUALLY *ALL* THE GREAT MEDIA HAVE RECEIVED *CRITICAL EXAMINATION,* IN AND OF *THEMSELVES.*

BUT FOR *COMICS,* THIS ATTENTION HAS BEEN *RARE.* *

LET'S SEE IF WE CAN HELP *RECTIFY* THE SITUATION.

© and ™ 1994 Scott McCloud

The complete **Understanding Comics** is 215 pages in 9 chapters and examines all aspects of comics. The above excerpt is from Chapter One.

Guide for Responding

◆ *Literature and Your Life*

Reader's Response Did you enjoy this selection? Why or why not?

Thematic Focus What did you find most humorous about the selection? Why?

Journal Writing Look back at the definition of comics you wrote before you read the selection. Note whether or not the selection has in any way changed your definition.

☑ Check Your Comprehension

1. When and how did McCloud become hooked on comics?
2. Why does McCloud feel that people have failed to understand comics?
3. How does McCloud ultimately define comics?

Guide for Responding (continued)

◆ Critical Thinking

INTERPRET

1. Why do you think people tend to have a narrow definition of comics? **[Infer]**
2. What does McCloud mean by the terms *message* and *messenger* when he says, "Never mistake the message for the messenger"? **[Analyze]**
3. McCloud's final definition of "comics" does not include anything about being humorous or entertaining the reader. Do you accept his definition? Why or why not? **[Make a Judgment]**
4. What do you think the "hidden power" of comics might be? **[Speculate]**

EVALUATE

5. Do you think McCloud is justified in comparing comics to art forms such as film, music, and theater? Why or why not? **[Make a Judgment]**

APPLY

6. What activities do you enjoy that you would define differently or more broadly than other people might? Explain. **[Apply]**

◆ Reading Strategy

USE VISUALS AS A KEY TO MEANING

To fully understand and appreciate McCloud's piece, it is important to **use the visuals as a key to the meaning** by considering how the illustrations reinforce and enhance the words.

1. Find three places in which the illustrations add humor to text that is straightforward and serious. Explain each example.
2. Find two illustrations that add meaning to McCloud's definition of a comic. Explain.

◆ Literary Focus

VISUAL ESSAY

McCloud's piece is a **visual essay**—a piece of nonfiction in which a writer combines words and visuals to communicate his or her ideas on a topic.

1. What is the main idea of this piece? How do both the visuals and images convey this idea?
2. Why would the selection lose its impact if either the words or the visuals were eliminated?

◆ Build Vocabulary

USING THE WORD ROOT -stat-

Each of the following words contains the root -stat-, which means "to stand." Write a definition of each word. Incorporate the meaning of the root in your definition.

1. statue   2. stationary (*adj.*)   3. statistics

USING THE WORD BANK

In your notebook, write the word(s) whose meaning is closest to that of the first word.

1. obsessed: (a) feverish, (b) filled the thoughts of, (c) did not interest
2. arbitrary: (a) changeable, (b) legal, (c) mediocre
3. aesthetic: (a) painless, (b) artistic, (c) romantic

◆ Build Grammar Skills

PUNCTUATION OF INTRODUCTORY WORDS

Introductory words and phrases—such as *then*, *as a result*, and *in contrast*—help readers to follow a piece of writing by showing how sentences and paragraphs relate to one another. Commas appear after introductory words or phrases to set them off from the rest of a sentence.

Practice Add punctuation as needed to the following sentences.

1. Of course I didn't appreciate the range of ideas that comic books could express.
2. Anyway I finally realized that I could say anything in a comic book.
3. All right so why have I bothered to define comics at such length?
4. Hey show some respect for the art of comics.
5. As comic strips became increasingly popular more newpapers began to publish them.

Writing Application Write a paragraph describing a memorable experience you've had recently. Begin each sentence with an introductory word or phrase followed by a comma.

Build Your Portfolio

 ## Idea Bank

Writing

1. **Letter to the Author** Write a letter to Scott McCloud responding to his ideas about comics. Tell whether you agree or disagree with his definition of comics and why.

2. **Definition** Write a brief definition of a hobby or other activity that you enjoy. Point out any ways in which your definition is different from definitions others might offer.

3. **Essay on Humor** Write a short essay about McCloud's use of humor in *Understanding Comics*. Discuss his use of visuals and other techniques, and explain how he uses humor both to entertain and to inform.

Speaking and Listening

4. **Skit** Many comic strips recently have been made into movies. With a group, plan and act out a scene from a movie based on one of your favorite comics. **[Performing Arts Link]**

5. **Panel Discussion** Hold a television-style panel discussion in which you and a group of classmates discuss whether comics can be an effective way of addressing serious issues, such as social problems and political developments.

Projects

6. **Comic Strip** Create a comic strip of your own using comics from the newspaper as models. **[Art Link]**

7. **Internet Research Report** Browse the Internet to learn more about the history of comics or about one of today's popular comic strips. Share your findings with the class. If possible, download or print visuals to use in your presentation. **[Technology Link]**

 ## Writing Mini-Lesson

Visual Essay

Think of an activity that especially interests you—your favorite sport, for example. Then develop an essay in which you combine words and visuals—photographs, charts, illustrations, and so on—to communicate what this activity means to you. Keep the following in mind:

Writing Skills Focus: Knowledge Level of Audience

When you write about a topic that you know well, you should recognize that your audience may not have as much knowledge of your topic as you do. For this reason, it's important to identify your **audience** and determine their **knowledge level** of your subject. If you're writing for people who share your knowledge of the subject, you can use specialized terms that a less knowledgeable audience wouldn't recognize, and you can leave out basic details. If, on the other hand, you're writing for an audience unfamiliar with your topic, you'll need to include basic details and define each term you introduce.

Prewriting Start by listing the reasons why you're interested in the activity you chose. Then gather visuals that you can use to illustrate these reasons. For example, if you appreciate the gracefulness of basketball players, you might find photographs that capture this quality. Next, decide on your audience, and determine how well they know your topic.

Drafting Assemble the visuals you've gathered into a logical order. Then write a short passage to accompany each one. As you write, keep the knowledge level of your audience in mind. Be sure to define any terms they wouldn't recognize.

Revising Review your visual essay. Does it clearly communicate what the activity means to you? What details can you add to make it clearer?

Guide for Reading

Alex Chadwick (1947–)

As you read Alex Chadwick's interview with pilot Linda Finch, notice the references to sound effects, such as an airplane engine starting, wheels turning, and a propeller whirring. Chadwick's work as a correspondent for National Public Radio for over twenty years has been marked by his use of such sounds to anchor his stories in reality.

Before becoming a radio correspondent, Chadwick earned a degree in communications from American University in Washington, D.C., and worked in Maine as both a radio reporter and a commercial fisherman. His accomplishments in radio include his essays and features on the critically acclaimed radio programs *Morning Edition* and *All Things Considered*. He also co-hosted the Public Broadcasting Service television series *Childhood* in 1991.

Steve Gietschier (1948–)

Steve Gietschier holds the game of basketball dear to his heart: His experiences coaching his daughter's team led him to seek out the assignment of reviewing *In These Girls, Hope Is a Muscle*, author Madeleine Blais's gripping account of a high-school girls' basketball team's championship season.

Born in New York City, Gietschier earned a bachelor's degree from Georgetown University in Washington, D.C., and a doctorate from Ohio State University. Since 1986, he has been the Director of Historical Records at *The Sporting News* in St. Louis, Missouri, the newspaper that originally published his review of Madeleine Blais's book.

◆ Build Vocabulary

WORD ROOTS: -dyna-

aerodynamics
hydraulic
pursue
improbable
derides
legacy
riveting
ruminative
adept
compelling

When you want to find a word with power packed into it, look for one that includes the root *-dyna-*. This root comes from the Greek word *dynamikos*, which means "power" or "strength." In describing a vintage airplane, Alex Chadwick uses the word *aerodynamics*. If the prefix *aero-* means "of the air," what might *aerodynamics* mean?

WORD BANK

As you read these selections, you will encounter the words on this list. Each word is defined on the page where it first appears. Preview the list before you read.

◆ Build Grammar Skills

HYPHENS

These selections contain a variety of examples of **hyphens**—punctuation marks used to connect two or more words that function as a single word. Notice the use of hyphens in this sentence:

> Alex Chadwick interviews Linda Finch, a *forty-six-year-old* grandmother who traced Amelia Earhart's *round-the-world* flight in a plane with *nine-cylinder, air-cooled* engines.

The hyphens used in this sentence form compound modifiers. Hyphens are not used in compound modifiers that include words ending in *-ly* (*badly damaged*, for example) or with compound proper adjectives (*New England* cooking, for instance). Hyphens are used, however, in many compound nouns, such as *mother-in-law*.

◆ Earhart Redux ◆
In These Girls, Hope Is a Muscle

◆ *Literature and Your Life*

CONNECT YOUR EXPERIENCE

A woman decides to fly around the Earth in an antique airplane because another woman disappeared on a similar flight in a similar plane sixty years ago. A girls' basketball team struggles to win the state championship that slipped through their fingers the previous year. Sometimes a failure can be the most powerful incentive for a new victory. If you've ever wanted something, lost it, and wanted it even more, you'll know the truth at the heart of these true stories.

THEMATIC FOCUS: WORKING TOWARD A GOAL

These selections tell about real women who are defined by the challenges they take on. What do you think it is like to live your life focused almost entirely on a single goal?

◆ Background for Understanding

HISTORY

Born in 1897, Amelia Earhart became interested in aviation in her twenties. In 1932, she became the first woman to fly solo across the Atlantic Ocean. In May 1937, she began an attempt to fly around the world, accompanied only by a navigator. After having flown three quarters of the way around the globe, they disappeared on July 1, near New Guinea. Earhart's final message reported empty fuel tanks. Although a wide-ranging search was made, her plane was never found. Sixty years later, in May 1997, Linda Finch successfully re-created Earhart's flight around the Earth in a similar aircraft.

Journal Writing Write about a time when you achieved a goal after trying and failing several times.

◆ Literary Focus

WORKPLACE WRITING

You don't have to be a novelist or a poet to write for a living. Writing is an important part of a wide range of occupations—television reporting, advertising, police work, even automechanics. Any writing that is done as part of a person's job responsibilities is called **workplace writing.** Following are three examples of workplace writing: a radio interview; a review of a book; and book-jacket copy created by a publisher. What qualities do the pieces share?

◆ Reading Strategy

DETERMINE THE AUTHOR'S PURPOSE

Workplace writing is shaped most of all by its **purpose**—the goal the writer sets out to achieve. On a basic level, the purpose of workplace writing is usually quite easy to see. For example, one of the pieces you are about to read is a radio interview, and you know without even reading it that the interview will present inside information straight from the interviewee's mouth. However, when you actually read the interview, you'll need to look a little further: What *particular* purposes is this interviewer trying to achieve? Does he want to create suspense? Is his goal to make you admire his subject? You can determine the writer's purpose from clues within the interview: what he asks about, how he describes the subject, how he begins and ends the interview.

As you read these three pieces, look for words and details that provide clues to each author's purpose.

Earhart Redux

Alex Chadwick

Date: March 17, 1997

BOB EDWARDS, HOST: This is *Morning Edition.* I'm Bob Edwards.

In Oakland, California, this morning, pilot Linda Finch takes off on an adventure that actually started 60 years ago. On this day in 1937, Amelia Earhart began her attempt to become the first person to fly around the world at the equator. She failed.

Her plane disappeared over the Pacific Ocean, but in that, she achieved a measure of immortality.

In the latest National Geographic Radio Expedition, NPR's[1] Alex Chadwick reports Linda Finch hopes to finish what Amelia Earhart began.

SOUNDS OF MACHINERY

ALEX CHADWICK, NPR REPORTER: The door to the hangar is bigger than any big theater movie screen. And it's opening slowly and improbably, folding outward on a horizontal midline and upward from the bottom. And there is Linda Finch's amazing airplane: 1930's <u>aerodynamics</u>, like an artifact from an old movie, or a dream.

LINDA FINCH, PILOT: The aircraft is very rare. There were only fifteen manufactured initially in the twenties and thirties, and there are only two left in the world.

CHADWICK: Ms. Finch is pretty rare herself. A 46-year-old grandmother who owns several nursing homes in Texas, and a pilot who restores and flies vintage fighters. Even so, replicating Amelia Earhart's flight is difficult. And though she doesn't like to say so, a little risky.

SOUNDS OF DOORS OPENING AND CLOSING

FINCH: We'll be flying in an aircraft that is the exact same model Amelia flew. And we'll be following the same route that she flew around the world.

---

1. **NPR's:** National Public Radio's.

CHADWICK: Well, I'm sure some people hearing about this flight would say, what is the point of setting off in an aircraft that's already failed in this once? I mean, it's dangerous. Maybe recklessly dangerous.

FINCH: Well, I have a lot of advantages that Amelia didn't have. We will have modern navigation, communication, and flight instruments that she just didn't have available at the time. The flight, I believe, needs to be done in the right airplane, to be historically correct, to generate the excitement in order to communicate our message.

I started learning about Amelia and really feel like I came to know her. And although I think that flying was definitely a part of her being, that she really flew to get the recognition to convince people that they could do what they wanted. Especially women in the 1930's. That people weren't limited to small lives. That they could have their dreams.

CHADWICK: Amelia Earhart was an aviation pioneer, daring and determined. The second flyer after Lindbergh[2] to solo across the Atlantic. Fourteen others had died trying to repeat his flight, and Amelia nearly did when a crucial instrument failed in bad weather.

Here's that earlier flyer after her Atlantic flight, when President Hoover presented her with a gold medal from the National Geographic Society.

AMELIA EARHART, PILOT: I came down until I could see the flight path blinking in the darkness. If it had been a smooth sea, I might have come too far. Whether I was 50 feet off the water or 150, I do not know, without my altimeter. I was too close, however.

CHADWICK: The plane that Amelia used on her round-the-world attempt, the Lockheed Electra 10-E, is 38.5 feet long, with a 55-foot wingspan. The tail angles back on a small, solid rubber rear wheel. The nose tilts upwards toward the sky. She glows like a polished aluminum athlete, broad-shouldered. Beautiful as a swan dive.

SOUND OF AIRPLANE ENGINE

She carries two nine-cylinder radial Pratt and Whitney Wasp engines. These are the first air-cooled engines developed. At 650 pounds, they produced more than 400 horsepower when they were introduced in 1926, and that was an extraordinary weight-power ratio for the time.

Linda Finch's plane has later, more powerful versions of that engine, as did Amelia Earhart's. Except for new navigation and communication gear, their planes are identical.

FINCH: The aircraft was in boxes and pieces and parts. And one of the things that I discovered was that prior to World War II, there were no parts manuals. You get just a big box of pieces, and it's like a jigsaw puzzle, you have to figure out how to put it together.

CHADWICK: She describes the Electra as graceful and slow in flight. Almost peaceful. Amelia did all her flying, but carried a navigator co-pilot. And so will Linda. The cockpit is a narrow, confined space, barely enough room for twin controls. And the enormous, banquet-sized steering wheels.

SOUND OF WHEELS TURNING

What do these wheels feel like? They look like they came out of 1940's British sports cars or something.

FINCH: Exactly, and the wood is so worn. We actually had some new ones we could have put in. But I like these because they're worn and they've been in the airplane, obviously, since it was new.

CHADWICK: So, this is all human-powered controls for turning things and making the airplane fly?

FINCH: Absolutely. People are very surprised that there is just a thin cable and actually you move the cable. Everyone always says, does it have hydraulic controls? Absolutely not.

CHADWICK: These things here, these switches and hand controls. Those are original on the plane. This is what Amelia Earhart flew.

FINCH: Exactly. There are many things, the controls, throttle, and the propeller and mixture controls, the fuel selector gauges, the magneto

◆ Build Vocabulary

aerodynamics (er´ ō dī nam´ iks) *n.*: Branch of mechanics dealing with the forces exerted by air or other gases in motion

hydraulic (hī drô´ lik) *adj.*: Operated by the movement and pressure of liquid

---

2. **Lindbergh:** Charles Lindbergh (1902–1974) made the first solo nonstop flight across the Atlantic Ocean on May 20–21, 1927.

switches, the gear indicator. All of the things that have to do with the airplane mechanically are in fact the same as Amelia's.

CHADWICK: The plane was in the airport in Memphis, en route for tests elsewhere. Linda and navigator Bob Fodge had refilled the main battery the evening before, and something had gone wrong. Overnight it leaked acid, eating away at a small panel of the undercarriage. They had to remove it.

The technology is 60 and 70 years old. Linda Finch knows how it works. Why it works. Why it's reliable. But she is attempting to fly around the world in an airplane where the rivets all show. And the cockpit windows slide open, and little accidents cause the flawless aluminum skin to weaken and decay.

The navigation electronics are as good as you could get. She has an on-board satellite link to the Internet. Schools can check her progress hourly. But the actual airplane is decades older than Linda Finch herself. And on many portions of this flight, she's going to have to overload that plane with fuel in order to cross open water.

What does your daughter think? What does your family think, when you are setting off to re-create a flight that Amelia Earhart did not survive?

FINCH: Well, my daughter is very supportive and excited and pleased, and is real involved in the project. On the other hand, she's a worrier. So, she always worries.

And she's most happy that we'll actually be sending the airplane's position back on the Internet every hour. So, I think she'll be watching that quite closely to see where we are.

CHADWICK: Oakland; across the country to Miami; then San Juan, Puerto Rico; Cumana, Venezuela; Paramari, Vos Serena; down to Natale in Brazil, and across to Africa. Dakkar, Injamana, Khartoum. It'll be hot over the desert. Karachi, Calcutta, Rangoon. In a couple of months, she'll get to Lahe, New Guinea, the last place that Amelia Earhart was ever seen.

Here's Amelia, after flying the Atlantic.

EARHART: I hope that the flight has meant something to women in aviation. If it has, I shall feel it justified. But I can't claim anything else.

CHADWICK: And here is Linda Finch. In a tan wool gabardine flight suit, strains showing in her face a little from the work and the stress, but mostly looking eager to go finish that great adventure.

FINCH: Well, I don't know what happened to Amelia Earhart, and neither does anyone else, certainly. When I'm reading a book about Amelia and I get to the last communications that they heard from her, that's really where I stop reading. Because I just think it doesn't matter. What does matter is what Amelia did with her life, and that's really the focus of our project.

SOUND OF AN AIRPLANE PROPELLER

CHADWICK: Pilot Linda Finch, who sets out today to fly around the world in a Lockheed Electra 10-E, the plane Amelia Earhart flew.

For Radio Expeditions, this is Alex Chadwick reporting.

Guide for Responding

◆ *Literature and Your Life*

Reader's Response Do you admire Linda Finch for undertaking her adventure? Explain.

Thematic Focus Finch's up-to-date communications and navigation technology were far advanced over Amelia Earhart's. Do you think this 1990's technology detracts from Finch's achievement?

☑ **Check Your Comprehension**

Summarize what you've just learned about Linda Finch.

◆ **Critical Thinking**

INTERPRET

1. (a) How does the interviewer, Alex Chadwick, seem to feel about Finch and her mission? (b) How can you tell? **[Analyze]**

2. What effect does Chadwick create by including the voice of Amelia Earhart several times in his interview with Linda Finch? **[Speculate]**

EVALUATE

3. What details add to the suspense about the outcome of Finch's endeavor? **[Evaluate]**

In These Girls, Hope Is a Muscle

Book Review by Steve Gietschier

If you have not yet had the opportunity to give your heart to a women's high school basketball team or to feel the passion of women's athletics in general, reading this book may be the start of something big. Although its poetic title alone could win an award, the text is even better: beautifully written, heartfelt, gently humorous but most important, forthright in its insistence that women as well as men should be able to <u>pursue</u> genuine excellence through sports.

Blais explains how <u>improbable</u> it is to find a championship basketball team of either gender, John Calipari's Massachusetts' squad[1] excluded, in Amherst, Mass., a town she <u>derides</u> as "probably the only place in the United States where men can wear berets and not get beaten up." Amherst, she says, "is, for the most part, smoke free, nuclear free and eager to free Tibet."[2] It is the proud home of Bread & Circus, the self-proclaimed world's largest health food store. More significantly, Amherst is, in Blais' view, "an achingly democratic sort of place in which tryouts for Little League, with their inevitable rejections, have caused people to suggest that more teams should be created so that no one is left out."

Far from an athlete herself, Blais nevertheless was still able to find unfolding within Amherst's "self-absorbed loftiness" the glistening struggle for superb competitors, the Lady Hurricanes of Amherst Regional High School. Picking up their story with the final game of the 1991–92 season,

---

1. **John Calipari's Massachusetts' squad:** Coach of an excellent basketball team at University of Massachusetts.
2. **to free Tibet:** Once a semi-independent state, Tibet has been part of China since the 1950's.

◆ Build Vocabulary

pursue (pər sōō′) *v.*: Seek

improbable (im präb′ ə bəl) *adj.*: Unlikely to happen

derides (di rīdz′) *v.*: Ridicules

▲ **Critical Viewing** What does this player's facial expression suggest about what's going on in her mind? [Infer]

Blais followed their efforts throughout 1992–93, an epic campaign dedicated to overcoming a long legacy of being good, but just not good enough.

On the surface, then, this book is a simple tale of a singular basketball season, following in the footsteps of "Friday Night Lights" and "Fall River Dreams" (reviewed in TSN, January 23, 1995). Readers looking for no more than a good story can chart the season game by game and turn one page after another in anticipation of the next victory.

But there is so much more here to savor and absorb. The young women who give themselves so completely to their team's quest are extraordinary each in her own way. Burdened with the pains of adolescence, the duties that high school imposes and, in some cases, the tough circumstances of families rent asunder,[3] they learn from one another how to dig deep to find the resources they need to reach their goal.

In the process, they journey in so many ways to places Amherst women have never gone before, proving to themselves, their families, their town and all who will look with open eyes that women's sports can be an astoundingly fulfilling and moving experience.

---

3. **rent** (rent) **asunder** (ə sun´ dər): Torn apart.

◆ **Build Vocabulary**

legacy (leg´ ə sē) *n.:* Anything handed down from an ancestor

▲ **Critical Viewing** How does this picture capture the team's emotions? [Analyze]

Book-Jacket Copy for

In These Girls,

Advance praise for *In These Girls, Hope Is a Muscle:*

This book is the product of a perfect marriage. The subject is timely and fascinating, and Madeleine Blais is a first-rate reporter and writer.   —Tracy Kidder

Blais's narrative gift has produced a touching, exciting book about a subject largely ignored until now, namely women athletes. Her story of a year in the life of a high school basketball team and its hometown goes far beyond the obvious to illuminate how people really feel, how things really work.   —Anne Bernays

Begun as an article that appeared in the *New York Times Magazine, In These Girls, Hope Is a Muscle* offers a riveting close-up of the girls on a high school basketball team whose passion for the sport is rivaled only by their loyalty to one another. Reminiscent of John McPhee's *A Sense of Where You Are* and H. G. Bissinger's *Friday Night Lights*, Pulitzer Prize-winning journalist Madeleine Blais's book takes the reader through a singular season in the history of the Lady Hurricanes of Amherst, Massachusetts.

For years they had been known as a finesse team, talented and hardworking players who in the end lacked that final hardscrabble ingredient that would take them over the top to the state championship. They seemed doomed to mirror the college town they represented: kindly, ruminative, at times ineffectual; more adept at quoting Emily Dickinson[1] and singing nature songs than going to the basket.

One season, all that changed. Madeleine Blais takes us from tryouts to practices

---

1. **Emily Dickinson:** (1830–1886), poet who was born and lived most of her life in Amherst, Massachusetts.

Hope Is a Muscle Madeleine Blais

during the regular season, up through the final championship game against the mighty Hillies from Haverhill. The result is an astoundingly moving narrative that captures the complexities of girls' experiences in high school, in sports, and in our society. As their coach says, unlike training boys—whose arrogance and confidence often have to be eroded before a team can pull together—working with girls is all constructive. The way to build a girls' team is to build each player's self-confidence. During the course of this season we see the Amherst Lady Hurricanes in their fierce, funny, sister-hood-is-powerful quest for excellence.

As Blais reports, "This is just one team in one season. It alone cannot change the discrimination against girls and their bodies throughout history." But it is a compelling, funny, and touching literary exploration of one group of girls' fight for success and, perhaps

most of all, respect. *In These Girls, Hope Is a Muscle* is both a dramatization of the success of the women's movement and a testimony to all the changes that have yet to come.

Madeleine Blais worked at the *Miami Herald* for eight years. A collection of her work, *The Heart Is an Instrument: Portraits in Journalism*, was published by the University of Massachusetts Press in 1992. Now a resident of Amherst, she has been on the faculty at the University of Massachusetts for six years.

◆ Build Vocabulary

riveting (riv´ it in) *adj.:* Firmly holding attention

ruminative (rōō´ mə nə təv) *adj.:* Meditative

adept (ə dept´) *adj.:* Highly skilled; expert

compelling (kəm pel´ in) *adj.:* Forceful

Guide for Responding

◆ Literature and Your Life

Reader's Response Does reading the book-jacket blurb and the review of *In These Girls, Hope Is a Muscle* make you want to read the book itself? Explain.

Thematic Focus Most of the challenges you have read about in the stories and poems in this book involve individuals. In what ways is a challenge different when it involves a group of people, like a basketball team?

☑ Check Your Comprehension

1. Who are the Lady Hurricanes, and what did they accomplish?
2. According to the book-jacket blurb, how is working with a team of girls different from training boys to work as a team?
3. According to the book review, what do the girls prove about women's sports?

◆ Critical Thinking

INTERPRET

1. Why do you think Steve Gietschier likes the book *In These Girls, Hope Is a Muscle*? **[Infer]**
2. The commentary in the book-jacket blurb closely echoes the author's writing in the book itself. Sum up the author's main idea and her attitude toward her subject. **[Summarize]**
3. Both the book-jacket blurb and the review are positive descriptions of *In These Girls, Hope Is a Muscle*. What differences can you see between the two pieces? **[Contrast]**

EVALUATE

4. What does the title *In These Girls, Hope Is a Muscle* mean, and why might the reviewer call this title "poetic"? **[Criticize]**

Guide for Responding (continued)

◆ Reading Strategy

DETERMINE AUTHOR'S PURPOSE

In each of these selections, the author has a general **purpose**, or reason for writing, and one or more specific purposes.

1. The general purpose of Chadwick's interview with Linda Finch is to present inside information about Finch's upcoming adventure. One of his more specific purposes is to convey a specific impression of Finch. What is that impression? Support your answer.

2. The general purpose of the book-jacket blurb for *In These Girls, Hope Is a Muscle* is to convey information about the book. Based on the words and details the writer includes, what other purpose do you think the blurb serves? Explain.

◆ Build Vocabulary

USING THE WORD ROOT *-dyna-*

These words contain the root *-dyna-*, which means "power" or "strength." Look up each word in a dictionary. Then write your own definition in which you incorporate the meaning of the root *-dyna-*.

1. dynasty   2. hydrodynamic   3. thermodynamic

USING THE WORD BANK

In your notebook, write the word whose meaning is closest to that of the first word.

1. hydraulic: (a) strong, (b) powered by liquid, (c) old-fashioned
2. pursue: (a) chase, (b) quarrel with, (c) refer to
3. aerodynamics: (a) air movement, (b) flight, (c) piloting skill
4. riveting: (a) difficult, (b) beautiful, (c) gripping
5. improbable: (a) unlikely, (b) impossible, (c) odd
6. compelling: (a) unwilling, (b) noisy, (c) fascinating
7. adept: (a) clumsy, (b) skillful, (c) modified
8. ruminative: (a) intellectual, (b) wealthy, (c) spoiled
9. legacy: (a) burden, (b) victory, (c) heritage
10. derides: (a) belittles, (b) ignores, (c) notices

◆ Literary Focus

WORKPLACE WRITING

Both of these selections are examples of **workplace writing**—writing that is performed as part of a person's job.

1. Why is it important for a radio journalist to be a good writer?
2. What is the role of writing in putting together an interview?
3. What qualities do you think make a successful interview? Support your answer.
4. Do you think that Chadwick's interview is effective? Why or why not?
5. What are the most important characteristics of a book-jacket blurb? Why?
6. Do you think that the blurb for *In These Girls, Hope Is a Muscle* is effective? Why or why not?
7. What other occupations can you think of in which writing is important?

◆ Build Grammar Skills

HYPHENS

A **hyphen** is a punctuation mark used to connect two or more words that function as a single word. Often hyphens are used to form compound modifiers, such as *quick-witted* or *slow-paced*. Hyphens are also used in many compound nouns. Hyphens *are not* used in compound modifiers that include words ending in *-ly* or with compound proper adjectives.

Practice On your paper, write the following sentences, adding hyphens where necessary.
1. Many planes once used air cooled engines.
2. The old fashioned aircraft had twin engines.
3. Finch's clear headed, calm, collected attitude impressed the interviewer.
4. Recently invented navigation technology helped Finch succeed.
5. Finch's round the world flight took several weeks.
6. Finch exhibited great self confidence in attempting her flight.

Build Your Portfolio

Idea Bank

Writing

1. **Book-Jacket Blurb** Choose a book you like, and write a book-jacket blurb that makes the book appealing to readers. Decide on your target audience, and play up the features of the book that would appeal to this audience.

2. **Sports Article** Using your imagination to come up with the details, create a sports article describing the game in which the Lady Hurricanes won the state championship.

3. **Review** Choose a television or radio program that you either like or dislike very much, and write a review expressing your opinion. Support your points with examples from the program.

Speaking and Listening

4. **Book Chat** Another way in which publishers promote books is through reviews on radio programs. With classmates, stage a book chat in which you review a book that you've read recently.

5. **Dramatization** Work with classmates to perform Alex Chadwick's interview. You will need a male reader to play Chadwick, a female reader to play Finch, at least one person to create the sound effects, and a director to coordinate everyone's efforts. **[Performing Arts Link]**

Projects

6. **Research Project** Research one aspect of the role of women in aviation—for example, women who have flown in spacecraft or who piloted planes during the Persian Gulf War. Present your information as an oral report with visual displays.

7. **Commemorative Stamp** Design a commemorative stamp honoring women in sports. **[Art Link]**

Writing Mini-Lesson

Radio Feature Story

Imagine that you are a radio correspondent like Alex Chadwick. Choose a current event or issue that interests you. Then prepare and present a radio program that informs listeners about the event or issue. Use this tip to help you develop your story:

Writing Skills Focus: Use of Sources

A radio feature story is only as good as the research on which it's based. To make your feature story as thorough and convincing as possible, gather information about your topic from a variety of **sources**, such as newspapers, magazines, nonfiction books, and Internet sites. If your topic relates to a local issue or event, you may even want to conduct interviews to get a firsthand view from people who have direct involvement with your topic.

Prewriting Start by determining the best sources from which to gather information about your topic. If you're dealing with a topic that's very current, your best bet is probably newspaper and magazine articles. In addition, you'll probably have some luck using key words to browse the Internet for information. Finally, you may want to contact government agencies or other local organizations to locate people you might interview.

Drafting Use the information you've gathered to create a script for your feature. Try to begin with attention-grabbing information. Then present your information in an order that fits your topic. For example, if you're describing an event, you may want to present details in chronological order.

Revising Read your script aloud to yourself. Focus on what it says as well as how it sounds. Where necessary, add information and replace words with ones that are more lively. Finally, record your feature and share it with the class.

CONNECTIONS TO TODAY'S WORLD
Internet Web Site

With the Internet explosion of the last several years, it's now possible to get information on virtually any topic with a just a few clicks of a mouse. Unlike most printed information, which doesn't change over time, the information delivered through the Internet is interactive and ever-changing. Web pages are updated regularly, and people who visit them can choose their own pathways through the information. Following are some samples from a Web site on Edgar Allan Poe. Notice that the site includes both text and images.

Edgar Allan Poe

Biographical Pages

INDEX	Short summary of Poe's life
1) Edgar's mother Eliza	2) Edgar's Childhood
3) Edgar's Teens	4) The Army and the Death of Fanny Allan
5) Al Aaraaf and West Point	6) Poems by Edgar A. Poe, Maria Clemm and Henry Poe
7) The Saturday Visitor Contest & The Death of John Allan	8) The Messenger and Marriage to Virginia Clemm
9) Break with the Messenger and the Blank Period	10) Usher and Rue Morgue
11) Virginia's Health and Tales of Ratiocination	

Edgar Allan Poe, son of actress Eliza Poe and actor David Poe, Jr., born January 19, 1809, was mostly known for his poems and short tales and his literary criticism. He has been given credit for inventing the detective story, and his psychological thrillers have been influences for many writers worldwide.

Edgar and his brother and sister were orphaned before Edgar's third birthday, and Edgar was taken in to the home of John and Fanny Allan in Richmond, Virginia. The Allans lived in England for five years (1815–1820), where Edgar also attended school. In 1826, he entered the University of Virginia. Although a good student, he was forced to gambling since John Allan did not provide well enough. Allan refused to pay Edgar's debts and Edgar had to leave the university after only one year.

In 1827, Edgar published his first book, *Tamerlane and Other Poems,* anonymously under the signature "A Bostonian." The poems were heavily influenced by Byron and showed a youthful attitude.

Later, in 1827, Edgar enlisted in the army under the name Edgar A. Perry, where his quarrels with John Allan continued. Edgar did well in the army, but in 1829 he left and decided to apply for a cadetship at West Point.

- Images
- Some Poe Trivia
- Rabies?!
- Listen to the Raven
- Some of my own poems!

Credits

Images Related to Poe and these Pages

1. Based on these samples, what types of things can you learn about Poe from the Web site?

2. How is the Web site different from a book about Poe?

3. What advantages does the Internet have over books?

4. What are some of the advantages of books versus the Internet?

Writing Process Workshop

Have you heard people talk about the "information super-highway"? They're referring to the vast amounts of information available to you instantly on computers. Of course, you can also find information in books, newspapers, magazines, and other printed sources, including this book. Make your own contribution to the "information age" by writing an **informational report** that provides an in-depth set of facts on a topic that interests you.

The following skills, introduced in this section's Writing Mini-Lessons, will help you write an informational report.

Writing Skills Focus

▶ **Identify your audience's knowledge level of your topic.** Consider what your readers may or may not already know about the topic you are presenting. Their level of knowledge will affect how much information you include. (See p. 615.)

▶ **Use a variety of sources** when gathering information for your report. In addition to books, newspapers, and maga- zines, you might use pictures, the Internet, or personal inter- views, for example. (See p. 625.)

Scott McCloud uses both these skills as he shares information about comics.

① The writer considers his audience's knowledge and assumes they have all seen a comic before.

② The source of the writer's quote might be a book, a magazine article, or an interview with Will Eisner himself.

③ The writer uses pic- tures as an additional source for gathering information.

MODEL FROM LITERATURE

from *Understanding Comics* by Scott McCloud

"Comics" is the word worth defining, as it refers to the medium itself, not a specific object as "comic book" or "comic strip" do. We can all visualize a comic. ① But what is comics? Master comics artist Will Eisner uses the term sequential art when describing comics. ② Taken individually, the pictures below are merely that—pictures. However, when part of a sequence, even a sequence of only two, the art of the image is transformed into something more: the art of comics. ③

Prewriting

Choose a Topic Think about a topic that especially interests you or about which you have an in-depth knowledge. You can also choose one of the topic ideas listed here:

```
┌─────────────────────────────────────────────┐
│                Topic Ideas                   │
│  ■ Today's music or music performers         │
│  ■ A widely watched spectator sport          │
│  ■ An important year in history              │
│  ■ A popular political leader                │
└─────────────────────────────────────────────┘
```

Consider Your Audience's Knowledge On your paper, make brief notes on the age and background of your readers. Then make a two-column list. In one column, jot down facts your audience may already know about your subject. In the other column, jot down information they may not know.

Readers' Age: What They Know	Readers' Background: What They Don't Know

Plan and Find Your Sources Make a list of facts, statistics, and quotations you will need for your report. Next to each one, note a possible source. Look for those sources in the library, or request an interview with an expert who can provide you with information.

Technology Tip The Internet is a great source of information. If you aren't sure how to use the Internet, ask a teacher, librarian, or experienced Internet user for help.

Drafting

Develop a Clear Organization Plan Using the information you've gathered, begin drafting your report. Start with a paragraph that introduces your subject and your main points. Follow with a series of paragraphs, each focusing on a single point or aspect of your subject. Make sure that each body paragraph has a topic sentence and several supporting sentences. End with a conclusion that sums up your main points.

APPLYING LANGUAGE SKILLS: Adjective Clauses

An **adjective clause** is a group of words with a subject and a verb that work together to modify a noun. You can sometimes combine information by using an adjective clause.

Without an Adjective Clause:
We drink water. The water is filtered at a plant.

With an Adjective Clause:
The water that we drink is filtered at a plant.

Practice On your paper, combine each pair of sentences by using an adjective clause.

1. Inspectors check the water. They go to the plant daily.
2. They carry a special instrument. It measures chlorine levels.

Writing Application As you draft your report, try to identify places where you can combine information into one sentence by using an adjective clause.

Writer's Solution Connection
Writing Lab

For tips on interviewing an expert, work through the Prewriting section of the tutorial on Exposition.

APPLYING LANGUAGE SKILLS: Appositives and Appositive Phrases

An **appositive** is a noun or pronoun that identifies or explains a previous noun or pronoun:

Our mayor, Sara Leeds, has served for six years.

An appositive phrase is an appositive plus modifiers:

The mayor, our highest official, will run again.

Practice On your paper, combine each pair of sentences into a single sentence by using an appositive or an appositive phrase.

1. The water inspector is Mr. Jones. He writes a report each month.
2. His report goes to the Health Department. It's an office run by the state.

Writing Application As you revise your report, see whether there are places where you can combine information by using appositives and appositive phrases.

Writer's Solution Connection
Writing Lab

For help in revising, use the revision checks for transitions and language variety in the tutorial on Expositon.

Consider Your Audience's Level of Knowledge As you write, always keep your readers in mind. Don't try to impress them with information beyond their level of understanding. Use formal vocabulary, not slang, but remain "reader friendly" as you present your facts.

Science Writing Tip When writing about a science topic, provide definitions for words or terms that your audience may not know.

Revising

Have a Peer Review Your Work Ask a classmate to read your informational report and then answer the following questions:

▶ Is the main idea clear? How can it be made more specific?
▶ Does the report include facts, statistics, and quotations that support the main ideas?
▶ Is the information clear and easy to understand?
▶ Are all unfamiliar terms defined?

REVISION MODEL

Americans speak in different dialects. ①, or forms of language. New Yorkers call soft ② My Arkansas aunt, on the other hand, says "soda pop." drinks "soda." In Ohio, soft drinks are referred to as "pop."

① The writer defines a term her audience may not know.
② The writer adds information she obtained from a new source: an interview.

Publishing

▶ **Classroom** Present your report to the class as a special television or radio broadcast.
▶ **Magazine** Send a copy of your report to a magazine that publishes informational articles.
▶ **Internet** Post your report on the Internet.

Real-World Reading Skills Workshop

Strategies for Success

As you know, speed limits are not always the same. A car riding on a highway may be allowed to go 55 miles per hour. Near a hospital or school, the speed limit might be only 15 miles per hour. The speed at which you read can also vary. You need to adjust your reading rate depending on the situation.

What Are You Reading? You do many types of reading. You might look at the comics in a newspaper, or you may read a scientific report in a medical journal. Adjust your reading rate according to the type of material before you. The more serious the selection, the more slowly you should read it.

Why Are You Reading? You may read for many different reasons. You might study a chapter in your social studies textbook to prepare for a test. You may read an article in a music magazine purely for relaxation or fun. Your reading rate is determined partly by your purpose for reading. The more serious the purpose, the more slowly you should read.

When and Where Are You Reading? Your reading rate also depends on the time and place where you read. For a timed test in school, you need to read faster than for pleasure reading at home during the weekend. Know how much time you have to complete your reading, and adjust your rate accordingly.

Apply the Strategy

Consider different types of reading materials. Then answer these questions:

1. List two types of reading material you would read slowly.

2. List two types of reading material you would read quickly.

3. Describe the reading rate you would use in the following situations:

   ▶ Reading an encyclopedia article about London, looking for information for a report on the Houses of Parliament

   ▶ Reading an instruction manual on how to install a new computer program

   ▶ Scanning the television listings for a program to watch

✔ *Here are other situations in which you need to adjust your reading rate:*

   ▶ *Reviewing notes the night before a test*

   ▶ *Browsing through a store catalog*

   ▶ *Reading a friendly letter or a business letter*

Speaking and Listening Workshop

Giving an Oral Presentation

The most successful news reporters know how to present the news effectively. They speak in a way that holds viewers' interest so they don't tune out. You, too, can make successful oral presentations by following these guidelines:

Speak in a Strong, Clear Voice When you speak before a group, your words will be wasted if no one can hear them. Use a strong, confident tone of voice, and speak clearly. Don't speak too quickly, or listeners won't understand what you're saying.

Make Eye Contact As you speak, try to look at the audience as much as possible. Even if you're using notes, pause from time to time to look up. Avoid gazing at the walls or window, which will distract your listeners.

Use Your Body Effectively As you speak, practice good posture. Don't hunch over or fidget nervously with your hands or fingers. However, use body motions where it will help your presentation. For example, you might point to a visual aid or use a gesture to stress a particular idea.

Tips for Giving an Oral Presentation

✔ To give an effective oral presentation to a small or a large group, follow these strategies:
- ▶ Be loud and clear; don't mumble or slur your words.
- ▶ Maintain good eye contact.
- ▶ Stand straight; move your body naturally.

Apply the Strategies

Practice giving an oral presentation in each of the following situations. After each presentation, invite audience members to offer feedback.

1. You have applied for a job. As part of your interview, the company president and vice president ask you to make a brief presentation to them, telling why you'd like the job.

2. You have been chosen to represent your school in a statewide speaking contest. You are supposed to speak about your school and its curriculum to a group of ten judges.

3. You are a television newscaster who is broadcasting a report on an event that occurred recently in your neighborhood or town.

Extended Reading Opportunities

True stories—such as histories, biographies, and articles that provide information or express the writer's opinion—can help us to understand our world. Following are just a few possibilities through which you can explore the many types of nonfiction.

Suggested Titles

Today's Nonfiction

This collection includes a variety of contemporary nonfiction by some of today's most important writers. In *Today's Nonfiction,* you will encounter biographies and personal accounts, essays, and feature articles on a wide range of interesting and relevant topics.

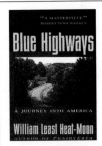

Blue Highways: A Journey Into America
William Least Heat Moon

William Least Heat Moon lives and writes in Columbia, Missouri. His best-selling book *Blue Highways: A Journey Into America* is an account of his 14,000-mile journey through the back roads of the United States in a converted van named "Ghost Dancing." Readers who go along for the ride will enjoy Least Heat Moon's sensitive descriptions of the people and places he encounters on his travels.

All Things Bright and Beautiful
James Herriott

This book is just one in a series of best-selling autobiographical works by a veterinarian living in Yorkshire, England. Through the many humorous and heartwarming anecdotes in these pages, Herriott shares his love for life, humanity, and, of course, the many animals in his care.

Other Possibilities

The Negro Leagues: The Story of Black Baseball	Jacob Margolies
Into a Strange Land: Unaccompanied Refugee Youth in America	Brent Ashbranner and Melissa Ashbranner
On Board the Titanic	Shelley Tanaka

The Sheridan Theatre, 1937, Edward Hopper, Collection of the Newark Museum

Drama

When you read a play, you're likely to get completely swept up in the experience. This is because reading a play exercises your imagination. All the action unfolds through dialogue, so you, the reader, must infer each character's thoughts and feelings. In addition to dialogue, stage directions also help you picture the ways that characters speak and move.

Following are a teleplay by acclaimed playwright Horton Foote and a classic tragedy by William Shakespeare. As you read each one, use the dialogue, stage directions, and your own imagination to help you "see" the performance in your mind.

Reading for Success

Strategies for Reading Drama

One of the earliest literary forms, drama dates back to prehistoric times when people reenacted scenes of exciting moments of a hunt or acted out their fears and hopes in religious rites. In modern drama, people continue to act out the struggles and triumphs of life.

While plays share many elements with prose, fiction, and poetry, the greatest difference is that drama is designed to be performed on a stage before an audience. The story is told mostly through dialogue and action. The stage directions indicate when and how the actors move and sometimes suggest sound and lighting effects. It is the doing or acting quality that makes drama unique in literature. Although people frequently read and enjoy a drama's text, you must always keep in mind that it was written to be performed.

When you read a drama, apply the following strategies to interact with the text:

Envision the action.

Reading a drama without envisioning the action is like watching a movie with your eyes shut. Your understanding and appreciation of the drama will be enriched if you use the stage directions and other details to help you form mental pictures of the action. How do the actors move? What tones of voice do they use?

Predict.

As you read a drama, make predictions about what you think will happen. Look for hints in the dialogue or action that seem to suggest a certain outcome. As you read on, you will see whether your predictions are correct.

Question.

Note the questions that come to mind as you read. For example, why do the characters act as they do? What causes events to happen? Why does the writer include certain information? Look for answers to your questions as you read.

Be aware of the historical context.

When does the action of the drama occur? What are the conditions of the times? If the drama takes place in a setting from the past or in a foreign city, you may have to consider that customs and accepted conduct may be different from your experiences.

Summarize.

Dramas are often broken into acts or scenes. These natural breaks give you an opportunity to review the action. What is the conflict? What is happening toward its resolution? Put the characters' actions and words together as you summarize.

You will be a more effective reader of drama if you use these strategies. You will be better able to understand the conflict and resolution of a play and apply your understanding to your own world.

PART 1 *Today's Drama*

Balcony at the Alhambra, 1911, Spencer Gore, York City Art Gallery, England

Guide for Reading

Horton Foote (1916–)

The computer was not around when Horton Foote started writing plays over fifty years ago, so he used a pen. Today, he still uses a pen. He says, "The whole process of writing is a life force for me. I love the theater, you see. I love actors. I love directors, I love stagehands. I love the whole process."

From Actor to Writer After high school, Foote left his hometown of Wharton, Texas, to go to acting school—first in California and then in New York. While in New York, he formed friendships with fellow actors and, together, they formed an off-Broadway theater company. He began writing plays at that time, and since then, writing has been the focus of his career.

During the 1950's and early 1960's, Foote wrote scripts for live television in what is called television's "golden age." One of his first teleplays, *The Trip to Bountiful*, was later made into an award-winning film.

> *Foote is best known as a screenwriter whose characters are everyday people with everyday problems.*

A World of His Own Many of Foote's plays are set in the fictional town of Harrison, Texas. Foote bases this town on his own hometown, and his characters on people he has known. He says that his plays are often concerned "with defining what home is and where home is and how we get to home."

Some recurring themes in Foote's plays are human shortcomings, family issues, and the relationships between generations. *The Dancers*, which comes from a 1956 collection of television plays called *Harrison, Texas*, reflects these themes.

◆ Build Vocabulary

HOMOGRAPHS

In "The Dancers," a daughter tries to console her mother, who has been crying. *Console* is a homograph—a word that has two or more meanings but is always spelled the same. In this case, *console* is a verb pronounced "kun *sohl*" and meaning "to comfort." Console can also be a noun, pronounced "*kon* sohl" and meaning "a television cabinet that is made to stand on the floor." The only way to tell the proper meaning and pronunciation of a homograph is to look at the context in which it appears.

| genteel |
| mortified |
| defiance |
| console |

WORD BANK

Before you read, preview this list of words from the play.

◆ Build Grammar Skills

LINKING VERBS AND PREDICATE ADJECTIVES

A **linking verb** connects a subject to a word later in the sentence. Verbs used most often as linking verbs are forms of *be* and verbs associated with the five senses (look, sound, smell, feel, and taste), as well as a few other verbs (such as *appear, seem, become*). When the word later in the sentence describes the subject, it is a **predicate adjective**. When it renames the subject, it is a predicate noun.

Do not make the mistake of using an adverb instead of a predicate adjective after a linking verb.

Correct: Inez felt foolish.

Incorrect: Inez felt foolishly.

The Dancers

◆ *Literature and Your Life*

CONNECT YOUR EXPERIENCE

Like everyone, you probably experience times when your social life doesn't go smoothly. You might go to a party where you don't know anyone, or mistakenly make plans with two different people for the same evening. As you read this play, notice how the characters respond to awkward situations like these.

Journal Writing Jot down different ways of declining and accepting a social invitation.

THEMATIC FOCUS: FACING CONFLICTS

In "The Dancers," the characters face some common interpersonal problems: conflicts between mother and daughter, friends and acquaintances. As you read, think about similar problems you've faced. How do the characters' actions remind you of your own?

◆ Background for Understanding

CULTURE

In the 1950's, when "The Dancers" is set, people danced differently from the way they do now. Partners held each other, and their movements were synchronized and predetermined, depending on the type of dance. It was not uncommon for children to take dance lessons, in which they learned how to do ballroom dances such as the Waltz, the Foxtrot, and the Cha-Cha.

◆ Literary Focus

STAGING

The way a play is brought to life on the stage is called **staging.** Staging includes the sets, lighting, sound effects, costumes, and the way the actors move and deliver their lines. Staging is based on the stage directions the playwright includes in a drama. These directions, which are bracketed and italicized, describe sets, props, lighting, sound effects, and the appearance, personalities, and movements of the characters. The director, designers, actors, and other people working on the play adapt and interpret stage directions to determine how the play is staged. When you read a play, you use the dialogue, stage directions, and your imagination to stage the play in your mind's eye.

◆ Reading Strategy

ENVISION THE ACTION

Plays are meant to be performed, so it is important to **envision the action.** As you read, form a picture in your mind. Use the stage directions provided by the author to help you do so. Look at this example:

> [HORACE *is smiling over the compliments, half wanting to believe what they say, but then not so sure. He is dancing with her around the room as the lights fade.*]

By carefully reading this description and drawing from your own experiences, you can picture Horace's face as he dances with his sister. The details in the description reveal that although Horace is smiling, he is feeling uncertain. Based on your experiences, you can picture how Horace might look with a tentative smile on his face.

As you read, use a graphic organizer like this one to note details of the setting and of characters' physical appearances. Recording such details will be an additional aid in picturing the action.

Details of Characters			Details of Setting
Horace			

The Dancers

Horton Foote

CHARACTERS

WAITRESS in the local drugstore[1]

EMILY CREWS, a popular seventeen year old

ELIZABETH CREWS, Emily's mother

HORACE, a sensitive eighteen year old

INEZ STANLEY, Horace's older sister

HERMAN STANLEY, Inez's husband

MARY CATHERINE DAVIS, a plainer girl of Emily's age

VELMA MORRISON, another young girl

TOM DAVIS, Mary Catherine's father

MRS. DAVIS, Mary Catherine's mother

1. **drugstore:** At the time the play is set, drugstores commonly offered counter service for the purchase of light meals, snacks, beverages, and ice cream.

[*Scene:* The stage is divided into four acting areas: *downstage left is the living room of* INEZ *and* HERMAN STANLEY. *Downstage right is part of a small-town drugstore. Upstage right is the living room of* ELIZABETH CREWS. *Upstage left, the yard and living room of* MARY CATHERINE DAVIS. *Since the action should flow continuously from one area to the other, only the barest amount of furnishings should be used to suggest what each area represents. The lights are brought up on the drugstore, downstage right.* WAITRESS *is there.* INEZ STANLEY *comes into the drugstore. She stands for a moment thinking. The* WAITRESS *goes over to her.*]

WAITRESS. Can I help you?

INEZ. Yes, you can if I can think of what I came in here for. Just gone completely out of my mind. I've been running around all day. You see, I'm expecting some company tonight. My brother Horace. He's coming on a visit.

[ELIZABETH CREWS *and her daughter* EMILY *come into the drugstore.* EMILY *is about seventeen and very pretty. This afternoon, however, it is evident that she is unhappy.*]

Hey . . .

ELIZABETH. We've just been by your house.

INEZ. You have? Hello, Emily.

EMILY. Hello.

ELIZABETH. We made some divinity[2] and took it over for Horace.

INEZ. Well, that's so sweet of you.

ELIZABETH. What time is he coming in?

INEZ. Six thirty.

ELIZABETH. Are you meeting him?

INEZ. No—Herman. I've got to cook supper. Can I buy you all a drink?

ELIZABETH. No, we have to get Emily over to the beauty parlor.

INEZ. What are you wearing tonight, Emily?

ELIZABETH. She's wearing that sweet little net[3] I got her the end of last summer. She's never worn it to a dance here.

INEZ. I don't think I've ever seen it. I'll bet it looks beautiful on her. I'm gonna make Horace bring you by the house so I can see you before the dance.

WAITRESS. Excuse me. . . .

INEZ. Yes?

WAITRESS. Have you thought of what you wanted yet? I thought I could be getting it for you.

INEZ. That's sweet, honey . . . but I haven't thought of what I wanted yet. [*To* ELIZABETH *and* EMILY.] I feel so foolish. I came in here for something, and I can't remember what.

WAITRESS. Cosmetics?

INEZ. No . . . you go on. I'll think and call you.

WAITRESS. All right. [*She goes.*]

INEZ. Emily, I think it's so sweet of you to go to the dance with Horace. I know he's going to be thrilled when I tell him.

ELIZABETH. Well, you're thrilled too, aren't you, Emily?

EMILY. Yes, ma'am.

ELIZABETH. I told Emily she'd thank me some day for not permitting her to sit home and miss all the fun.

EMILY. Mama, it's five to four. My appointment is at four o'clock.

ELIZABETH. Well, you go on in the car.

EMILY. How are you gonna get home?

ELIZABETH. I'll get home. Don't worry about me.

EMILY. OK. [*She starts out.*]

---

2. **divinity:** Soft, creamy candy made of sugar, egg whites, corn syrup, flavoring, and nuts.

3. **sweet little net:** Dress made of delicate, lacy fabric.

INEZ. 'Bye, Emily.

EMILY. 'Bye.

[*She goes on out.*]

ELIZABETH. Does Horace have a car for tonight?

INEZ. Oh, yes. He's taking Herman's.

ELIZABETH. I just wondered. I wanted to offer ours if he didn't have one.

INEZ. That's very sweet—but we're giving him our car every night for the two weeks of his visit. Oh—I know what I'm after. Flowers. I have to order Emily's corsage for Horace. I came in here to use the telephone to call you to find out what color Emily's dress was going to be.

ELIZABETH. Blue.

INEZ. My favorite color. Walk me over to the florist.

ELIZABETH. All right.

[*They go out as the lights fade. The lights are brought up downstage left on the living room of* INEZ STANLEY. HERMAN STANLEY *and his brother-in-law,* HORACE, come in. HERMAN *is carrying* HORACE's *suitcase.* HERMAN *is in his middle thirties.* HORACE *is eighteen, thin, sensitive, but a likable boy.*]

HERMAN. Inez. Inez. We're here.

[*He puts the bag down in the living room.* INEZ *comes running in from stage right.*]

INEZ. You're early.

HERMAN. The bus was five minutes ahead of time.

INEZ. Is that so? Why, I never heard of that. [*She kisses her brother.*] Hello, honey.

HORACE. Hello, sis.

INEZ. You look fine.

HORACE. Thank you.

INEZ. You haven't put on a bit of weight though.

HORACE. Haven't I?

INEZ. Not a bit. I'm just going to stuff food down you and put some weight on you while you're here. How's your appetite?

HORACE. Oh, it's real good. I eat all the time.

INEZ. Then why don't you put on some weight?

HORACE. I don't know. I guess I'm just the skinny type.

INEZ. How are the folks?

HORACE. Fine.

INEZ. Mother over her cold?

HORACE. Yes, she is.

INEZ. Dad's fine?

HORACE. Just fine.

INEZ. Oh, Herman, did you ask him?

HERMAN. Ask him what?

INEZ. Ask him what? About his tux.

HERMAN. No, I didn't. . . .

INEZ. Honestly, Herman. Here we have him a date with the prettiest and most popular girl in Harrison and Herman says ask him what. You did bring it, didn't you, Bubber?

HORACE. Bring what?

INEZ. Your tux.

HORACE. Oh, sure.

INEZ. Well, guess who I've got you a date with. Aren't your curious?

HORACE. Uh. Huh.

INEZ. Well, guess . . .

[*A pause. He thinks.*]

HORACE. I don't know.

INEZ. Well, just try guessing. . . .

HORACE. Well . . . uh . . . [*He is a little embarrassed. He stands trying to think. No names come to him.*] I don't know.

INEZ. Emily Crews. Now isn't she a pretty girl?

HORACE. Yes. She is.

INEZ. And the most popular girl in this town. You know her mother is a very close friend of mine and she called me day before yesterday and she said I hear Horace is coming to town and I said yes you were and she said that the boy Emily is going with is in summer school and couldn't get away this week-end and Emily said she wouldn't go to the dance at all but her mother said that she had insisted and wondered if you'd take her. . . .

HORACE. Her mother said. Does Emily want me to take her?

INEZ. That isn't the point, Bubber. The point is that her mother doesn't approve of the boy Emily is in love with and she likes you. . . .

HORACE. Who likes me?

INEZ. Emily's mother. And she thinks you would make a very nice couple.

HORACE. Oh. [*A pause.*] But what does Emily think?

▲ **Critical Viewing** During the 1950's, the neighborhood drugstore was a place to hear local gossip and get something to eat, as well as a place to obtain medicine, soap, and other necessities. Why do you think several scenes in "The Dancers" take place in the drugstore? [Hypothesize]

INEZ. Emily doesn't know what to think, honey. I'm trying to explain that to you. She's in love.

HORACE. Where am I supposed to take her to?

INEZ. The dance.

HORACE. But, Inez, I don't dance well enough. . . . I don't like to go to dances . . . yet.

INEZ. Oh, Horace. Mother wrote me you were learning.

HORACE. Well . . . I am learning. But I don't dance well enough yet.

INEZ. Horace, you just make me sick. The trouble with you is that you have no confidence in yourself. I bet you can dance.

HORACE. No, I can't. . . .

INEZ. Now let's see. [INEZ *goes to the radio and turns it on. She comes back to him.*] Now, come on. Show me what you've learned. . . .

HORACE. Aw, sis. . . .

HERMAN. Inez. Why don't you let the boy alone?

INEZ. Now you keep out of this, Herman Stanley. He's my brother and he's a stick. He's missing all the fun in life and I'm not going to have him a stick. I've sat up nights thinking of social engagements to keep him busy every minute of these next two weeks—I've got three dances scheduled for him. So he can*not* dance. Now come on, dance with me. . . . [*He takes her by the arm awkwardly. He begins to lead her around the room.*] Now, that's fine. That's just fine. Isn't that fine, Herman?

HERMAN. Uh. Huh.

INEZ. You see all you need is confidence. And I want you to promise me you'll talk plenty when you're with the girl, not just sit there in silence and only answer when you're asked a question. . . . Now promise me.

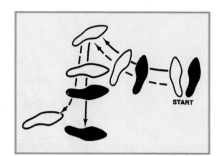

HORACE. I promise.

INEZ. Fine. Why, I think he dances real well. Don't you, Herman?

HERMAN. Yes, I do. Just fine, Inez.

INEZ. Just a lovely dancer, all he needs is confidence. He is very light on his feet. And he has a fine sense of rhythm—why, brother, you're a born dancer—

[HORACE *is smiling over the compliments, half wanting to believe what they say, but then not so sure. He is dancing with her around the room as the lights fade. They are brought up on the area upstage right.* EMILY CREWS *is in her living room. She has on her dressing gown.*[4] *She is crying.* ELIZABETH, *her mother, comes in from upstage right.*]

ELIZABETH. Emily.

EMILY. Yes, ma'am.

ELIZABETH. Do you know what time it is?

EMILY. Yes, ma'am.

ELIZABETH. Then why in the world aren't you dressed?

EMILY. Because I don't feel good.

ELIZABETH. Emily. . . .

EMILY. I don't feel good. . . . [*She begins to cry.*] Oh, Mother, I don't want to go to the dance tonight. Please, ma'am, don't make me. I'll do anything in this world for you if you promise me. . .

ELIZABETH. Emily. This is all settled. You are going to that dance. Do you understand me? You are going to that dance. That sweet, nice brother of Inez Stanley's will be here any minute. . . .

---

4. **dressing gown:** Loose robe.

◆ *Literature and Your Life*

Have you ever received a compliment that you suspected wasn't really true? How did it make you feel?

EMILY. Sweet, nice brother. He's a goon. That's what he is. A regular goon. A bore and a goon. . . .

ELIZABETH. Emily. . . .

EMILY. That's all he is. Just sits and doesn't talk. Can't dance. I'm not going to any dance or any place else with him and that's final.

[*She runs out stage right.*]

ELIZABETH. Emily . . . Emily . . . You get ready this minute. . . . [*The doorbell rings. Yelling.*] Emily . . . Emily . . . Horace is here. I want you down those stairs in five minutes . . . dressed.

[*She goes out stage left and comes back in followed by* HORACE, *all dressed up. He has a corsage box in his hand.*]

Hello, Horace.

HORACE. Good evening.

ELIZABETH. Sit down, won't you, Horace? Emily is a little late getting dressed. You know how girls are.

HORACE. Yes, ma'am.

[*He sits down. He seems a little awkward and shy.*]

ELIZABETH. Can I get you something to drink, Horace?

HORACE. No, ma'am.

[*A pause.* ELIZABETH *is obviously very nervous about whether* EMILY *will behave or not.*]

ELIZABETH. Are you sure I can't get you a Coca-Cola or something?

HORACE. No. Thank you.

ELIZABETH. How's your family?

HORACE. Just fine, thank you.

ELIZABETH. I bet your sister was glad to see you.

HORACE. Yes, she was.

ELIZABETH. How's your family? Oh, I guess I

asked you that, didn't I?

HORACE. Yes, you did.

[ELIZABETH *keeps glancing off stage right, praying that* EMILY *will put in an appearance.*]

ELIZABETH. I understand you've become quite an accomplished dancer. . . .

HORACE. Oh . . . well . . . I. . . .

ELIZABETH. Inez tells me you do all the new steps.

HORACE. Well—I. . . .

ELIZABETH. Excuse me. Let me see what is keeping that girl.

[*She goes running off stage right.* HORACE *gets up. He seems very nervous. He begins to practice his dancing. He seems more un-sure of himself and awkward. . . . We can hear* ELIZABETH *offstage knocking on* EMILY's *door. At first* HORACE *isn't conscious of the knocking or the ensuing conversation and goes on practicing his dancing. When he first becomes conscious of what's to follow he tries to pay no attention. Then gradually he moves over to the far stage-left side of the stage. The first thing we hear is* ELIZA-BETH's *genteel tapping at* EMILY's *door. Then she begins to call, softly at first, then louder and louder.*]

Emily. Emily. Emily Crews. Emily Carter Crews . . . [*The pounding offstage is getting louder and louder.*] Emily. I can hear you in there. Now open that door.

EMILY. [*Screaming back.*] I won't. I told you I won't.

ELIZABETH. Emily Carter Crews. You open that door immediately.

EMILY. I won't.

ELIZABETH. I'm calling your father from

◆ **Build Vocabulary**

genteel (jen tēl´) *adj*.: Refined; polite

▲ **Critical Viewing** What does this photograph reveal about life in the 1950's? **[Infer]**

downtown if you don't open that door right this very minute.

EMILY. I don't care. I won't come out.

ELIZABETH. Then I'll call him. [*She comes running in from right stage.* HORACE *quickly gets back to his chair and sits.*] Excuse me, Horace.

[*She crosses through the room and goes out upstage right.* HORACE *seems very ill at ease. He looks at the box of flowers. He is very warm. He begins to fan himself.* ELIZABETH *comes back in the room from upstage right. She is very nervous. But she tries to hide her nervousness in an overly social manner.* ELIZABETH *has decided to tell a fib.*]

Horace, I am so sorry to have to ruin your evening, but my little girl isn't feeling well. She has a headache and a slight temperature and I've just called the doctor and he says he thinks it's very advisable that she stay in this evening. She's upstairs insisting she go, but I do feel under the circumstances I had just

better keep her in. I hope you understand.

HORACE. Oh, yes ma'am. I do understand.

ELIZABETH. How long do you plan to visit us, Horace?

HORACE. Two weeks.

ELIZABETH. That's nice. [*They start walking off-stage left.*] Please call Emily tomorrow and ask her out again. She'll just be heartbroken if you don't.

HORACE. Yes, ma'am. Good night.

ELIZABETH. Good night, Horace. [HORACE *goes out.* ELIZABETH *calls out after him.*] Can you see, Horace? [*In the distance we hear* HORACE *answer.*]

HORACE. Yes, ma'am.

ELIZABETH. Now you be sure and call us tomorrow. You hear? [*She stands waiting for a moment. Then she walks back across stage to upstage right, screaming at the top of her voice.*] Emily Carter Crews. You have <u>mortified</u> me. You have mortified me to death. I have, for your information, called your father and he is interrupting his work and is coming home this very minute and he says to tell you that you are not to be allowed to leave this house again for two solid weeks. Is that perfectly clear?

[*She is screaming as she goes out upstage right. The lights are brought down. They are brought up immediately downstage right on the drugstore. It is half an hour later.* HORACE *comes in. He seats himself at the counter. He still has the box of flowers. The drugstore is deserted. A* WAITRESS *is up near the front with her arms on the counter. She keeps glancing at a clock.* HORACE *is examining a menu.*]

◆ **Build Vocabulary**

mortified (môr′ tə fīd) *v*.: Humiliated

defiance (di fī′ əns) *n*.: Open resistance

HORACE. Can I have a chicken salad sandwich?

WAITRESS. We're all out of that.

HORACE. Oh.

[*He goes back to reading the menu.*]

WAITRESS. If it's all the same to you, I'd rather not make a sandwich. I'm closing my doors in ten minutes.

HORACE. Oh. Well, what would you like to make?

WAITRESS. Any kind of ice cream or soft drinks. [*She looks up at the ice cream menu.*] Coffee is all gone.

HORACE. How about a chocolate ice cream soda?

WAITRESS. OK. Coming up. [*She starts to mix the soda. She talks as she works.*] Going to the dance?

HORACE. No.

WAITRESS. The way you're all dressed up I thought for sure you were going.

HORACE. No. I was, but I changed my mind.

[MARY CATHERINE DAVIS *comes in the drugstore from downstage right. Somehow in her young head she has gotten the idea that she is a plain girl and in* defiance *for the pain of that fact she does everything she can to make herself look plainer.*]

◆ **Reading Strategy**
What do you think Mary Catherine does to make herself look plainer?

WAITRESS. Hello, Mary Catherine. Been to the movies?

MARY CATHERINE. Yes, I have.

[*The* WAITRESS *puts the drink down in front of* HORACE. *He begins to drink.*]

WAITRESS. What'll you have, Mary Catherine?

MARY CATHERINE. Vanilla ice cream.

WAITRESS. OK. [*She gets the ice cream. She talks as she does so.*] There weren't many at the picture show tonight, I bet. I can always tell by whether we have a crowd in here or not after the first show. I guess everybody is at the dance.

MARY CATHERINE. I could have gone, but I didn't want to. I didn't want to miss the picture show. Emily Crews didn't go. Leo couldn't get home from summer school and she said she was refusing to go. Her mother made a date for her with some boy from out of town without consulting her and she was furious about it. I talked to her this afternoon. She said she didn't know yet how she would get out of it, but she would. She said she had some rights. Her mother doesn't approve of Leo and that's a shame because they are practically engaged.

WAITRESS. I think Emily is a very cute girl, don't you?

MARY CATHERINE. Oh, yes. I think she's darling.

[HORACE *has finished his drink and is embarrassed by their talk. He is trying to get the* WAITRESS*'s attention but doesn't quite know how. He finally calls to the* WAITRESS.]

◆ **Literary Focus:**
What do you think Horace might be doing to get the waitress's attention?

HORACE. Miss. . .

WAITRESS. Yes?

HORACE. How much do I owe you?

WAITRESS. Twenty cents.

HORACE. Thank you.

[*He reaches in his pocket for the money.*]

WAITRESS. Emily has beautiful clothes, doesn't she?

MARY CATHERINE. Oh, yes. She does.

WAITRESS. Her folks are rich?

MARY CATHERINE. She has the prettiest things. But she's not a bit stuck up. . . .

[*He holds the money out to the* WAITRESS.]

HORACE. Here you are.

WAITRESS. Thank you. [*She takes the money and rings it up in the cash register.* HORACE *goes on out.* WAITRESS *shakes her head as he goes.*] There's a goofy nut if I ever saw one. He's got flowers under his arm. He's wearing a tux and yet he's not going to the dance. Who is he?

MARY CATHERINE. I don't know. I never saw him before.

[*The* WAITRESS *walks to the edge of the area and looks out. She comes back shaking her head. She sits on the stool beside* MARY CATHERINE.]

WAITRESS. [*While laughing and shaking her head.*] I ought to call the Sheriff and have him locked up. Do you know what he's doing?

MARY CATHERINE. No. What?

WAITRESS. Standing on the corner. Dancing back and forth. He's holding his arm up like he's got a girl and everything. Wouldn't it kill you? [*Goes to the front and looks out.*] See him?

MARY CATHERINE. No. He's stopped.

WAITRESS. What's he doing?

MARY CATHERINE. Just standing there. Looking kind of lost.

[MARY CATHERINE *comes back to the counter. She starts eating her ice cream again.*]

WAITRESS. Well—it takes all kinds.

MARY CATHERINE. I guess so.

[*She goes back to eating her ice cream. The lights are brought down. The lights are brought up on the area downstage left. The living room of the* STANLEYS. INEZ *is there reading a book.* HERMAN *comes in.*]

HERMAN. Hi, hon.

INEZ. Hello. . . .

HERMAN. What's the matter with you? You look down in the dumps.

INEZ. No, I'm just disgusted.

HERMAN. What are you disgusted about?

INEZ. Horace. I had everything planned so beautifully for him and then that silly Emily has to go and hurt his feelings.

HERMAN. Well, honey, that was pretty raw, the trick she pulled.

INEZ. I know. But he's a fool to let that get him down. He should have just gone to the dance by himself and proved her wrong. . . . Why like I told him. Show her up. Rush a different girl every night. Be charming. Make yourself popular. But it's like trying to talk to

---

▼ **Critical Viewing** Look at the way these teenagers are dancing, and notice how they are dressed. How do the teens in this photo compare with teenagers today? [**Compare and Contrast**]

a stone wall. He refused to go out any more. He says he's going home tomorrow.

HERMAN. Where is he now?

INEZ. Gone to the movies.

HERMAN. Well, honey. I hate to say it, but in a way it serves you right. I've told you a thousand times if I've told you once. Leave the boy alone. He'll be all right. Only don't push him. You and your mother have pushed the boy and pushed him and pushed him.

INEZ. And I'm going to keep on pushing him. I let him off tonight because his feelings were hurt, but tomorrow I'm going to have a long talk with him.

HERMAN. Inez. Leave the boy alone.

INEZ. I won't leave him alone. He is my brother and I'm going to see that he learns to have a good time.

HERMAN. Inez. . . .

INEZ. Now you just let me handle this, Herman. He's starting to college next year and it's a most important time in his life. He had no fun in high school. . . .

HERMAN. Now. He must have had some fun. . . .

INEZ. Not like other people. And he's not going through four years of college like a hermit with his nose stuck in some old book. . . . [*She jumps up.*] I'll never forgive Elizabeth for letting Emily behave this way. And I told her so. I said Elizabeth Crews, I am very upset. . . .

[*She is angrily walking up and down as the lights fade. They are brought up downstage right on the drugstore area. The* WAITRESS *is there alone.* MARY CATHERINE *comes in from downstage right.*]

WAITRESS. Did you go to the movies again tonight?

MARY CATHERINE. Uh-huh. Lila, do you remember when I was telling you about Emily's date and how she wouldn't go out with him because he was such a bore?

WAITRESS. Uh. . . .

MARY CATHERINE. Oh, I just feel awful. That was the boy sitting in here. . . .

WAITRESS. Last night . . . ?

MARY CATHERINE. Yes. I went riding with Emily and some of the girls this afternoon and we passed by his sister's house and there sat the boy.

WAITRESS. Sh . . . sh. . . . [*She has seen* HORACE *come into the area from downstage right. He comes to the counter. He seems very silent. He picks up a menu.*] Back again tonight?

HORACE. Uh-huh.

WAITRESS. What'll you have?

HORACE. A cup of coffee. . . .

WAITRESS. All out. We don't serve coffee after eight unless we happen to have some left over from suppertime. . . .

HORACE. Thanks. [*He gets up.*]

WAITRESS. Nothing else?

HORACE. No, thanks.

[*He goes over to the magazine rack. He picks up a magazine and starts looking through it.* EMILY CREWS *comes in from downstage right. She doesn't see* HORACE. *She goes right over to* MARY CATHERINE.]

EMILY. Leora and I were riding around the square and we saw you sitting here. . . .

[MARY CATHERINE *points to* HORACE. *She turns around and sees him.* EMILY *looks a little embarrassed. He happens to glance up and sees her.*]

HORACE. Hello, Emily.

EMILY. Hello, Horace. . . . Do you know Mary Catherine Davis?

HORACE. No. How do you do.

MARY CATHERINE. How do you do.

EMILY. I feel awfully bad about last night, Horace. My mother says you know I wasn't really sick. I just wanted to tell you that it had nothing to do with you, Horace. It was a battle between me and my mother. Mary Catherine can tell you. I promised the boy I go with not to go with any other boys. . . .

HORACE. Oh, that's all right, I understand.

EMILY. You see, we've gone steady for two years. All the other boys in town understand it and their feelings are not a bit hurt if I turn them down. Are they, Mary Catherine?

MARY CATHERINE. No.

EMILY. Mary Catherine is my best friend and she can tell you I'm not stuck up. And I would have gone, anyway, except I was so mad at my mother. . . .

MARY CATHERINE. Emily is not stuck up a bit. Emily used to date all the boys before she began going with Leo steadily. Didn't you, Emily?

EMILY. Uh-huh. How long are you going to be here, Horace?

HORACE. Well, I haven't decided, Emily.

EMILY. Well, I hope you're not still hurt with me.

HORACE. No, I'm not, Emily.

EMILY. Well, I'm glad for that. Mary Catherine, can you come with us?

MARY CATHERINE. No, I can't, Emily. Velma came in after the first show started and I promised to wait here for her and we'd walk home together.

EMILY. Come on. We can ride around and watch for her.

MARY CATHERINE. No, I don't dare. You know how sensitive Velma is. If she looked in here and saw I wasn't sitting at this counter she'd go right home and not speak to me again for two or three months.

EMILY. Velma's too sensitive. You shouldn't indulge her in it.

MARY CATHERINE. I'm willing to grant you that. But you all are going off to college next year and Velma and I are the only ones that are going to be left here and I can't afford to get her mad at me.

EMILY. OK. I'll watch out for you and if we're still riding around when Velma gets out, we'll pick you up.

MARY CATHERINE. Fine. . . .

EMILY. 'Bye. . . .

MARY CATHERINE. 'Bye. . . .

EMILY. 'Bye, Horace.

HORACE. Good-bye, Emily.

[*She goes downstage right.*]

MARY CATHERINE. She's a lovely girl. She was my closest friend until this year. Now we're still good friends, but we're not as close as we were. We had a long talk about it last week. I told her I understood. She and Eloise Dayton just naturally have a little more in common now. They're both going steady and they're going to the same college. *A pause.* They're going to Sophie Newcomb.[5] Are you going to college?

HORACE. Uh-huh.

MARY CATHERINE. You are? What college?

HORACE. The university. . . .

MARY CATHERINE. Oh. I know lots of people there. [*A pause.*] I had a long talk with Emily about my not getting to go. She said she thought it was wonderful that I wasn't showing any bitterness about it. [*A pause.*] I'm getting a job next week so I can save up enough money to go into Houston to business school. I'll probably work in Houston some day. If I don't get too lonely. Velma Morrison's oldest sister went into Houston and got herself a job but she almost died from loneliness. She's back here now working at the courthouse. Oh, well . . . I don't think I'll get lonely. I think a change of scenery would be good for me.

[VELMA MORRISON *comes in downstage right. She is about the same age as* MARY CATHERINE. *She is filled with excitement.*]

VELMA. Mary Catherine, you're going to be furious with me. But Stanley Sewell came in right after you left and he said he'd never forgive me if I didn't go riding with him. . . . I said I had to ask you first. As I had asked you to wait particularly for me and that I knew you were very sensitive.

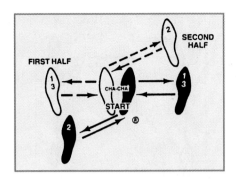

MARY CATHERINE. I'm very sensitive. You're very sensitive. . . . I have never in my life stopped speaking to you over anything.

[*A car horn is heard off stage.*]

VELMA. Will you forgive me if I go?

MARY CATHERINE. Oh, sure.

[VELMA *goes running out.*]

VELMA. Thank you.

[*She disappears out the door.*]

MARY CATHERINE. I'm not nearly as close to Velma as I am to Emily. I think Emily's beautiful, don't you?

HORACE. Yes. She's very pretty.

MARY CATHERINE. Well, Lila's going to kill us if we don't stop holding her up. Which way do you go?

HORACE. Home.

MARY CATHERINE. I go that way, too. We can walk together.

HORACE. OK. [*They go out of the area.*]

MARY CATHERINE. Good night, Lila.

WAITRESS. Good night.

[*They continue walking out downstage left as the lights fade. The lights are brought up on the living room of the* CREWS's *house.* ELIZABETH CREWS *is there, crying.* EMILY *comes in.*]

EMILY. Mother, what is it? Has something happened to Daddy?

ELIZABETH. No. He's in bed asleep.

EMILY. Then what is it?

ELIZABETH. Inez blessed me out and stopped speaking to me over last night. She says we've ruined the boy's whole vacation. You've broken his heart, given him all kinds of complexes and he's going home tomorrow. . . .

---

5. **Sophie Newcomb:** H. Sophie Newcomb College for Women in New Orleans, Louisiana.

EMILY. But I saw him at the drugstore tonight and I had a long talk with him and he said he understood. . . .

ELIZABETH. But Inez doesn't understand. She says she'll never forgive either of us again.

[*She starts to cry.*]

EMILY. Oh, Mother. I'm sorry. . . .

ELIZABETH. Emily. if you'll do me one favor. I promise you I'll never ask another thing of you again as long as I live. And I will never nag you about going out with Leo again as long as I live. . . .

EMILY. What is the favor, Mother?

ELIZABETH. Let that boy take you to the dance day after tomorrow. . . .

EMILY. Now, Mother. . . .

ELIZABETH. Emily. I get down on my knees to you. Do me this one favor. . . . [*A pause.*] Emily. . . . Emily. . . . [*She is crying again.*]

EMILY. Now, Mother, please. Don't cry. I'll think about it. I'll call Leo and see what he says. But please don't cry like this. . . . Mother . . . Mother.

[*She is trying to <u>console</u> her as the lights fade. The lights are brought up on upstage left. It is* MARY CATHERINE*'s yard and living room. Music can be heard in the distance.* HORACE *and* MARY CATHERINE *come walking in downstage left, go up the center of the stage until they reach the upstage area.*]

MARY CATHERINE. Well, this is where I live.

HORACE. In that house there?

MARY CATHERINE. Uh-huh. [*A pause.*]

HORACE. Where is that music coming from?

MARY CATHERINE. The Flats. . . .

◆ **Build Vocabulary**

console (kən sōl') *v.*: Comfort

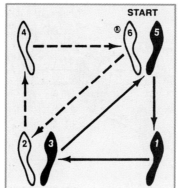

HORACE. What's the Flats?

MARY CATHERINE. I don't know what it is. That's just what they call it. It's nothing but a bunch of barbecue restaurants and beer joints down there and they call it the Flats. There used to be a creek running down there that they called Willow Creek but it's all dry now. My father says when he was a boy, every time the river flooded, Willow Creek would fill up. The river doesn't overflow any more since they took the raft[6] out of it. I like to come out here at night and listen to the music. Do you like to dance . . . ?

HORACE. Well . . . I . . . .

MARY CATHERINE. I love to dance.

HORACE. Well . . . I don't dance too well.

MARY CATHERINE. There's nothing to it but confidence.

HORACE. That's what my sister says. . . .

MARY CATHERINE. I didn't learn for the longest kind of time for lack of confidence and then Emily gave me a long lecture about it and I got confidence and went ahead and learned. Would you like to come in for a while?

HORACE. Well . . . if it's all right with you. . . .

MARY CATHERINE. I'd be glad to have you.

HORACE. Thank you.

[*They go into the area.* MARY CATHERINE*'s father,* TOM DAVIS, *is seated there in his undershirt. He works in a garage.*]

MARY CATHERINE. Hello, Daddy.

TOM. Hello, baby.

MARY CATHERINE. Daddy, this is Horace.

TOM. Hello, son.

HORACE. Howdy do, sir.

---

6. **raft:** Natural dam formed by debris, leaves, and trees.

[*They shake hands.*]

MARY CATHERINE. Horace is Mrs. Inez Stanley's brother. He's here on a visit.

TOM. That's nice. Where's your home, son?

HORACE. Flatonia.

TOM. Oh, I see. Well, are you young people going to visit for a while?

MARY CATHERINE. Yes, sir.

TOM. Well, I'll leave you then. Good night.

MARY CATHERINE. Good night, Daddy.

HORACE. Good night, sir. [*He goes out upstage left.*] What does your father do?

MARY CATHERINE. He works in a garage. He's a mechanic. What does your father do?

HORACE. He's a judge.

MARY CATHERINE. My father worries so because he can't afford to send me to college. My mother told him that was all foolishness. That I'd rather go to business school anyway.

HORACE. Had you rather go to business school?

MARY CATHERINE. I don't know. [*A pause.*] Not really. But I'd never tell him that. When I was in the seventh grade I thought I would die if I couldn't get there, but then when I was in the ninth, Mother talked to me one day and told me Daddy wasn't sleeping at nights for fear I'd be disappointed if he couldn't send me, so I told him the next night I decided I'd rather go to business school. He seemed relieved. [*A pause.*]

HORACE. Mary Catherine. I . . . uh . . . heard you say a while ago that you didn't dance because you lacked confidence and uh . . . then I heard you say you talked it over with Emily and she told you what was wrong and you got the confidence and you went ahead . . .

MARY CATHERINE. That's right. . . .

HORACE. Well . . . It may sound silly and all to you . . . seeing I'm about to start my first year of college . . . but I'd like to ask you a question. . . .

MARY CATHERINE. What is it, Horace?

HORACE. How do you get confidence?

MARY CATHERINE. Well, you just get it. Someone points it out to you that you lack it and then you get it. . . .

HORACE. Oh, is that how it's done?

MARY CATHERINE. That's how I did it.

HORACE. You see I lack confidence. And I . . . sure would like to get it. . . .

MARY CATHERINE. In what way do you lack confidence, Horace . . . ?

HORACE. Oh, in all kinds of ways. [*A pause.*] I'm not much of a mixer.[7] . . .

MARY CATHERINE. I think you're just mixing fine tonight.

HORACE. I know. That's what's giving me a little encouragement. You're the first girl I've ever really been able to talk to. I mean this way. . . .

MARY CATHERINE. Am I, Horace. . . ?

HORACE. Yes.

MARY CATHERINE. Well, I feel in some ways that's quite a compliment.

HORACE. Well, you should feel that way. [*A pause.*] Mary Catherine. . . .

MARY CATHERINE. Yes, Horace?

HORACE. I had about decided to go back home tomorrow or the next day, but I understand there's another dance at the end of the week. . . .

MARY CATHERINE. Uh-huh. Day after tomorrow.

HORACE. Well . . . I . . . don't know if you have a date or not . . . but if you don't have . . . I feel if I could take you . . . I would gain the confidence to go. . . . I mean . . .

---

7. **a mixer:** Someone who socializes easily.

MARY CATHERINE. Well, Horace. . . . You see. . .

HORACE. I know I'd gain the confidence. My sister is a swell dancer and she'll let me practice with her every living minute until it's time for the dance. Of course I don't know if I could learn to jitterbug by then or rumba or do anything fancy, you understand, but I know I could learn the fox trot and I can waltz a little now. . . .

MARY CATHERINE. I'm sure you could.

HORACE. Well, will you go with me?

MARY CATHERINE. Yes, Horace. I'd love to. . . .

HORACE. Oh, thank you, Mary Catherine. I'll just practice night and day. I can't tell you how grateful Inez is going to be to you. . . . Mary Catherine, if we played the radio softly could we dance now?

MARY CATHERINE. Why certainly, Horace.

HORACE. You understand I'll make mistakes. . .

MARY CATHERINE. I understand. . . .

[*She turns the radio on very softly.*]

HORACE. All right.

MARY CATHERINE. Yes. . . .

[*He approaches her very cautiously and takes her in his arms. He begins awkwardly to dance.* MARY CATHERINE *is very pleased and happy.*]

Why, you're doing fine, Horace. Just fine.

HORACE. Thank you, Mary Catherine. Thank you.

[*They continue dancing.* HORACE *is very pleased with himself although he is still dancing quite awkwardly. The lights fade. The lights are brought up on the area downstage left. It is early next morning.* INEZ *is there reading.* HORACE *comes in*

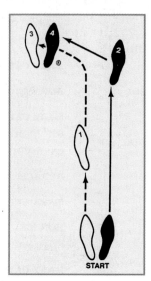

whistling. He seems brimming over with happiness.]

INEZ. What are you so happy about?

HORACE. I'm just happy.

INEZ. Wait until you hear my news and you'll be happier.

HORACE. Is that so?

INEZ. Miss Emily has seen the light.

HORACE. What?

INEZ. She has succumbed.

HORACE. What do you mean?

INEZ. She has crawled on her knees.

HORACE. She's crawled on her knees? I don't get it. . . .

INEZ. She has eaten dirt.

HORACE. Sister, what's all this about?

INEZ. Last night around ten o'clock she called in the meekest kind of voice possible and said, Inez, I've called up to apologize to you. I have apologized to Horace in the drugstore. Did she?

HORACE. Uh. Huh.

INEZ. And now I want to apologize to you and to tell you how sorry I am I behaved so badly. . . .

HORACE. Well. Isn't that nice of her, Inez?

INEZ. Wait a minute. You haven't heard the whole thing. And then her highness added, tell Horace if he would like to invite me to the dance to call me and I'd be glad to accept. And furthermore, Elizabeth called this morning and said they were leaving

---

▶ **Critical Viewing** Do you think Horace would have a better time at the dance with Mary Catherine or with Emily? Why? [Speculate]

for Houston to buy her the most expensive evening dress in sight. Just to impress you with.

HORACE. Oh. . . . [*He sits down on a chair.*]

INEZ. Brother. What is the matter with you? Now are you gonna start worrying about this dancin' business all over again? You are the biggest fool sometimes. We've got today and tomorrow to practice.

HORACE. Inez. . . .

INEZ. Yes?

HORACE. I already have a date with someone tomorrow. . . .

INEZ. You do?

HORACE. Yes. I met a girl last night at the drugstore and I asked her.

INEZ. What girl did you ask?

HORACE. Mary Catherine Davis. . . .

INEZ. Well, you've got to get right out of it. You've got to call her up and explain what just happened.

HORACE. But, Inez. . . .

INEZ. You've got to do it, Horace. They told me they are spending all kinds of money for that dress. I practically had to threaten Elizabeth with never speaking to her again to bring this all about. Why, she will never forgive me now if I turn around and tell her you can't go. . . . Horace. Don't look that way. I can't help it. For my sake, for your sister's sake you've got to get out of this date with Mary Catherine Davis. . . . Tell her . . . tell her . . . anything. . . .

HORACE. OK. [*A pause. He starts out.*] What can I say?

INEZ. I don't know, Horace. [*A pause.*] Say . . .

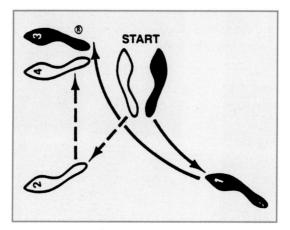

well just tell her the truth. That's the best thing. Tell her that Emily's mother is your sister's best friend and that Emily's mother has taken her into Houston to buy her a very expensive dress. . . .

HORACE. What if Mary Catherine has bought a dress . . . ?

INEZ. Well, she can't have bought an expensive dress. . . .

HORACE. Why not?

INEZ. Because her people can't afford it. Honey, you'll be the envy of every young man in Harrison, bringing Emily Crews to the dance. . . . Why, everybody will wonder just what it is you have. . . .

HORACE. I'm not going to do it.

INEZ. Horace. . . .

HORACE. I don't want to take Emily. I want to take Mary Catherine and that's just what I'm going to do.

INEZ. Horace. . . .

HORACE. My mind is made up. Once and for all. . . .

INEZ. Then what am I gonna do? [*She starts to cry.*] Who's gonna speak to Elizabeth? She'll bless me out putting her to all this trouble. Making her spend all this money and time. . . . [*She is crying loudly now.*] Horace. You just can't do this to me. You just simply can't. . . .

HORACE. I can't help it. I'm not taking Emily Crews—

INEZ. Horace. . . .

HORACE. I am not taking Emily Crews.

[*He is firm. She is crying as the lights fade. The lights are brought up on the upstage left area.* MARY CATHERINE'S FATHER *is seated there.*]

He is in his undershirt. In the distance dance music can be heard. MRS. DAVIS *comes in from stage left.*]

MRS. DAVIS. Don't you think you'd better put your shirt on, Tom? Mary Catherine's date will be here any minute.

TOM. What time is it?

MRS. DAVIS. Nine o'clock.

TOM. The dance has already started. I can hear the music from here.

MRS. DAVIS. I know. But you know young people, they'd die before they'd be the first to a dance. Put your shirt on, Tom.

TOM. OK.

MRS. DAVIS. As soon as her date arrives we'll go.

TOM. OK.

[MARY CATHERINE *comes in from stage left. She has on an evening dress and she looks very pretty.*]

MRS. DAVIS. Why, Mary Catherine. You look lovely. Doesn't she look lovely, Tom?

TOM. Yes, she does.

MRS. DAVIS. Turn around, honey, and let me see you from the back. [*She does so.*] Just as pretty as you can be, Mary Catherine.

MARY CATHERINE. Thank you.

[HORACE *comes in from downstage left in his tux with a corsage box. He walks up the center of the stage to the upstage left area.*]

That's Horace. [*She goes to the corner of the area.*] Hello, Horace.

HORACE. Hello, Mary Catherine.

MARY CATHERINE. You've met my mother and father.

HORACE. Yes. I have. I met your father the other night and your mother yesterday afternoon.

MRS. DAVIS. Hello, Horace.

TOM. Hello, son.

MRS. DAVIS. Well, we were just going. You all have a good time tonight.

HORACE. Thank you.

MRS. DAVIS. Come on, Tom.

TOM. All right. Good night and have a nice time.

MARY CATHERINE. Thank you, Daddy. [*They go out stage left.* HORACE *hands her the corsage box. She takes it and opens it.*] Oh, thank you, Horace. Thank you so much. [*She takes the flowers out.*] They're just lovely. Will you pin them on for me?

HORACE. I'll try. [*He takes the corsage and the pin. He begins to pin it on.*] Will about here be all right?

MARY CATHERINE. Just fine. [*He pins the corsage on.*] Emily told me about the mix-up between your sister and her mother. I appreciate your going ahead and taking me anyway. If you had wanted to get out of it I would have understood. Emily and I are very good friends . . . and. . . .

HORACE. I didn't want to get out of it, Mary Catherine. I wanted to take you.

MARY CATHERINE. I'm glad you didn't want to get out of it. Emily offered to let me wear her new dress. But I had already bought one of my own.

HORACE. It's very pretty, Mary Catherine.

MARY CATHERINE. Thank you. [*A pause.*] Well, the dance has started. I can hear the music. Can't you?

HORACE. Yes.

MARY CATHERINE. Well, we'd better get going. . . .

HORACE. All right. [*They start out.*] Mary Catherine. I hope you don't think this is silly, but could we practice just once more. . . .

MARY CATHERINE. Certainly we could. . . .

[*They start to dance.* HORACE *has improved although he is no Fred Astaire. They are dancing around and suddenly* HORACE *breaks away.*]

HORACE. Mary Catherine. I'm not good enough yet. I can't go. I'm sorry. Please let's just stay here.

MARY CATHERINE. No, Horace. We have to go.

HORACE. Please, Mary Catherine. . . .

MARY CATHERINE. I know just how you feel, Horace, but we have to go. [*A pause.*] I haven't told you the whole truth, Horace. This is my first dance, too. . . .

HORACE. It is?

MARY CATHERINE. Yes. I've been afraid to go. Afraid I wouldn't be popular. The last two dances I was asked to go and I said no.

HORACE. Then why did you accept when I asked you?

MARY CATHERINE. I don't know. I asked myself that afterwards. I guess because you gave me a kind of confidence. [*A pause. They dance again.*] You gave me confidence and I gave you confidence. What's the sense of getting confidence, Horace, if you're not going to use it?

[*A pause. They continue dancing.*]

HORACE. That's a pretty piece.

MARY CATHERINE. Yes, it is.

[*A pause. They dance again.* HORACE *stops.*]

HORACE. I'm ready to go if you are, Mary Catherine.

MARY CATHERINE. I'm ready. [*They start out.*] Scared?

HORACE. A little.

MARY CATHERINE. So am I. But let's go.

HORACE. OK.

[*They continue out the area down the center of the stage and off downstage right as the music from the dance is heard.*]

Beyond Literature

Humanities Connection

Dance Fads Through the years, dance fads have come and gone, requiring the learning of many new dances. Among the earliest dances to sweep America in the twentieth century were the Tango, the Hesitation Waltz, the Bunny Hop, the Turkey Trot, and the Charleston. Decades later, Chubby Checker's 1960 hit record "The Twist" ushered in the new dance of the same title. Soon additional new dances swept the nation. Spurred on by hit songs, these dances included the Hucklebuck, the Pony, the Hully-Gully, the Mashed Potato, the Frug, the Watusi, the Limbo, and the Monkey.

Activity What dances do you know how to do? Form a small group of students and teach each other some popular dances.

Guide for Responding

◆ *Literature and Your Life*

Reader's Response What did you admire about Horace? Why?

Thematic Focus Compare the ways in which Emily and Horace react when asked to do something they don't want to do.

☑ Check Your Comprehension

1. Why is Inez so determined that Horace will have a social life?
2. Why does Emily refuse to go to the dance with Horace?
3. How does Horace meet Mary Catherine?
4. Why does Inez want Horace to break his date with Mary Catherine? Give two reasons.

Guide for Responding (continued)

◆ Critical Thinking

INTERPRET
1. What types of people are Elizabeth and Inez? Use evidence from the play to support your answer. **[Support]**
2. How does Horace demonstrate that he is a sensitive and considerate person? **[Analyze]**
3. In what ways are Horace and Mary Catherine well suited to be friends? **[Infer]**

EVALUATE
4. Is Emily's behavior on the first night justified? Explain. **[Make a Judgment]**

APPLY
5. (a) Name one insight about human relationships that you gained from this play. (b) How can this insight be applied to your own life? **[Apply]**

◆ Reading Strategy

ENVISION THE ACTION
By carefully reading stage directions and drawing from your own experiences about how people and places look, you can **envision the action** of the play—viewing it in your mind just as you would on the stage.
1. Stage directions in the opening scene tell you that it is evident that Emily is unhappy. How do Emily's face, posture, and actions show this?
2. Picture the scene in which Mary Catherine tells the waitress about the date Emily Crews wanted to break. How does Horace act as he sits at the counter? What is the waitress doing as she listens?
3. Describe Mary Catherine's living room.

◆ Literary Focus

STAGING
The way a play is presented is called **staging.** Horton Foote's short, simple stage directions give theater groups or readers a great deal of freedom in staging "The Dancers."
1. Select two examples of stage directions in "The Dancers" that leave most of the specifics up to the imagination.
2. Explain in detail how you would stage the place, action, or event described in your examples.

◆ Build Vocabulary

USING HOMOGRAPHS
Choose the correct homograph for each italicized word. In your notebook, write its letter.
a. converse (kən vʉrs´): to talk
b. converse (kän´ vʉrs): the opposite
c. buffet (bə fā´): a counter for refreshments
d. buffet (buf´ it): to strike repeatedly
e. contract (kən trakt´): to get, as a disease
f. contract (kän´ trakt): a binding agreement

1. First go from right to left; then do the *converse.*
2. They usually *converse* for an hour after dinner.
3. Did Paul *contract* pneumonia?
4. The partners signed a *contract.*
5. The winds continued to *buffet* the little ship.
6. We arranged the food on the *buffet.*

USING THE WORD BANK
In your notebook, write the letter of the word that means the opposite of the first word.
1. genteel: (a) gentle, (b) refined, (c) impolite
2. mortified: (a) honored, (b) humiliated, (c) loved
3. defiance: (a) resistance, (b) anger, (c) cooperation
4. console: (a) cause grief, (b) ease grief, (c) table

◆ Build Grammar Skills

LINKING VERBS AND PREDICATE ADJECTIVES
A **linking verb** connects a subject with a word later in the sentence. When the later word describes the subject, it is called a **predicate adjective.** Avoid mistakenly using an adverb where a predicate adjective is needed.

Practice Copy each sentence in your notebook. Circle each linking verb and predicate adjective. Correct any sentence in which an adverb is mistakenly used by replacing the adverb with a predicate adjective.
1. At the end of the evening, John was angry.
2. When George asked her out, Donna was happily.
3. Juana looked beautifully in her gown.
4. Rick is uncertain whether he'll go to the dance.
5. Wanda felt sadly about how things turned out.

Build Your Portfolio

 ## Idea Bank

Writing

1. Diary Entry Write a diary entry that Horace might have written about the first day of his visit. Have Horace explain how he felt about what happened.

2. Casting Notes Which actors do you think would be best for the movie roles of Horace, Emily, and Mary Catherine? Write a short paper in which you make suggestions and give a reason for each choice.

3. News Report Suppose you were at the dance that Horace and Mary Catherine attended. Envision what that dance might have been like. Write an article for the school paper describing the dance. **[Media Link]**

Speaking and Listening

4. Musical Accompaniment Put together a musical soundtrack for a movie version of "The Dancers." Play your choices for the class. **[Music Link]**

5. Counseling With a partner, role-play the following situation. One of you is a family counselor, and the other is Elizabeth. Elizabeth describes the problems she has with Emily. The counselor explains Elizabeth's choices. **[Career Link]**

Projects

6. Dance Demonstration With a partner, learn one type of ballroom dance and demonstrate it for the class. **[Performing Arts Link]**

7. Costume Designs Imagine that you are the costume designer for a film version of the play. Draw costumes for Horace and Mary Catherine for the dance they attend. **[Art Link]**

 ## Writing Mini-Lesson

Script

Horton Foote is known for his ability to create characters who speak and act like people in real life. Try your hand at writing a realistic scene in which one character invites another character to go out.

> **Writing Skills Focus:
> Realistic Dialogue**
>
> Use **realistic dialogue** to make your characters believable. Keep in mind that people often don't speak in complete sentences. In addition, they sometimes pause in between thoughts. People are also likely to use contractions and may even commit grammatical errors. Look at this example from the play. Notice that Horace pauses between thoughts.
>
> #### Model From the Play
>
> HORACE. Well . . . I . . . don't know if you have a date or not . . . but if you don't have . . . I feel if I could take you . . . I would gain the confidence to go . . . I mean . . .

Prewriting Think of a situation in which one character extends an invitation to another character. Then decide on the personalities of the characters. Are they confident? Are they nervous? Do they use slang? Jot down notes about each character and the ways in which they speak.

Drafting Put yourself in the place of each character as you write the dialogue. Use words that show what the character is thinking and feeling.

Revising Read your script aloud. Does it sound realistic? Can you tell the difference between the characters by the way they speak? If not, change the dialogue until it sounds true to life.

Writing Process Workshop

Dramatic Scene

William Shakespeare once wrote, "All the world's a stage." What he meant was that everyone's life—including yours—is filled with some type of drama. In literature, a drama is a story told through dialogue that is meant to be performed by actors. In most dramas, there is a central conflict, or problem, that the characters must try to solve.

Write your own **dramatic scene** in which a character faces or works out some type of problem. The following skills will help you.

Writing Skills Focus

▶ **Use realistic dialogue.** Even though the characters are imaginary, have them speak the same way that people in real life would speak. Readers will then identify with the characters and care more about them. (See p. 660.)

▶ **Use stage directions** to help readers envision the action. Stage directions convey your ideas about sets, props, and sound effects. They also tell how characters act, move, and speak.

Playwright Horton Foote uses realistic dialogue in this dramatic scene between a mother and her daughter who refuses to come out of her room to meet her date for a dance.

MODEL FROM LITERATURE

from *The Dancers* by Horton Foote

ELIZABETH. Emily. I can hear you in there. Now open that door.

EMILY. [*Screaming back.*] I won't. I told you I won't. ①

ELIZABETH. Emily Carter Crews. You open that door immediately. ②

EMILY. I won't.

ELIZABETH. I'm calling your father from downtown if you don't open that door this very minute. ③

EMILY. I don't care. I won't come out.

ELIZABETH. Then I'll call him.

① Emily angrily repeats her words, just as people often do in real life.

② Elizabeth addresses her child by her full name, as a parent might do to show anger.

③ Elizabeth resorts to a threat that is sometimes heard in real-life families.

APPLYING LANGUAGE SKILLS: Sentence Fragments

A **fragment** is an incomplete sentence punctuated as a sentence. In formal writing, fragments are not acceptable. They can, however, be used in dialogue to capture the way people actually speak. Notice the variety of end marks that can be used.

TED. Do you mind if . . .

KIM. Whatever. But if you—

TED. If I what?

KIM. Oh, please!

Practice On your paper, add punctuation to this dialogue:

AL. It's just that

SUE. Cat got your tongue

AL. Why do you always

SUE. Interrupt

Writing Application As you draft your dramatic scene, use punctuation for fragments in the dialogue. Choose the punctuation that would best show actors how to deliver the dialogue.

Writer's Solution Connection
Writing Lab

For help on choosing an audience for your dramatic scene, use the Audience Profile in the Prewriting section of the tutorial on Creative Writing.

Prewriting

Choose an Idea Find an idea for your dramatic scene by recalling a challenging problem you once faced or witnessed. You can also make up a problem. If you like, choose one of the topic ideas listed here.

Topic Ideas

- Two students argue in the school cafeteria
- A teenager meets a favorite celebrity
- One family member plays a practical joke on another
- A sales clerk has difficulty with a customer

Develop Your Characters Before you can write dialogue for a character, you must know who that character is. For each character in your scene, answer these questions:

- ▶ What is the person's name?
- ▶ How old is the person?
- ▶ What does the person look like?
- ▶ Where is the person from? Where does the person live now?
- ▶ What kind of education does the person have?
- ▶ What job does the person have?

Think About the Dialogue Once you have defined your characters, consider how they think and behave. Answer these questions:

- ▶ How does the character feel about himself or herself? About other people?
- ▶ Is the person shy? Polite? Loud? Rude? Caring? Callous?
- ▶ What other character traits does the person possess?

Based on your answers, imagine how each character might speak to someone else in a dramatic situation.

Drafting

Write Realistic Dialogue As you write, always keep in mind who your characters are. Make their words sound believable. Try to hear the conversation in your mind as you write. Write their lines so that readers will exclaim, "Yes, I know someone who would say the same thing!"

Style Tip Formal prose requires you to write in complete sentences, but playwriting allows you more freedom. Characters may speak in incomplete sentences, with pauses, or in slang if it makes the dialogue sound realistic.

Use Stage Directions As you draft your dramatic scene, include stage directions that will communicate your specific ideas about sets, props, and sound effects. Through stage directions, you can also describe the appearance, speaking style, and movements of any of the characters. Refer to the plays in this section to see how playwrights use stage directions.

Revising

Use a Checklist Go back to the Writing Skills Focus on the first page of this lesson to evaluate and revise your dramatic scene.

▶ Have I used realistic dialogue?
   Reread your dialogue aloud with a classmate. Listen to the way it sounds. If any part of a character's conversation sounds unnatural, consider how you may rewrite it to make it sound more realistic.

▶ Does the dialogue remain consistent?
   Listen again to the way your characters speak throughout the scene. Decide whether each character's personality remains the same from beginning to end. If any dialogue doesn't reflect the speaker's basic character traits, change it to make the manner of speech consistent.

REVISION MODEL

① Hey,
ERIC. ~~Excuse me,~~ Sharon! Wait up. We gotta talk.

② Like
SHARON. [*Sarcastically.*] Yeah, right. ⌃ I really want to!

① The writer uses a word more consistent with the rest of the character's speech.
② The writer adds an expression often heard in real-life conversations.

Publishing

Stage Your Scene Mount a production of your scene for the class. Working with other students, gather costumes, props, and musical accompaniment or sound effects. Perform the scene live, or videotape the scene to share with other students.

APPLYING LANGUAGE SKILLS: Brackets and Parentheses

In a dramatic scene, stage directions appear either in **brackets** or in **parentheses.**

MEG. [*Whispering.*] Are you asleep?

MEG. (*Whispering.*) Are you asleep?

Be consistent when writing stage directions. Use brackets only or parentheses only. Do not alternate between the two.

Practice Use either brackets or parentheses to set off the stage directions.

BOB. Whirling around. You scared me!

MEG. I'm sorry. She laughs. You looked so funny.

Writing Application Review your dramatic scene to find where you used stage directions. If they aren't in brackets or parentheses, or if your usage isn't consistent, make revisions.

Writer's Solution Connection
Writing Lab

To help you revise your scene, use the instruction and activities in the Revision section of the tutorial on Creative Writing.

Real-World Reading Skills Workshop

Strategies for Success

Sometimes in a newspaper or magazine, you'll find an editorial, which expresses the writer's personal opinion on an issue. Analyze the writer's position before deciding whether or not you agree with it.

Identify the Opinion Before you can accept or reject an opinion, you need to know what the opinion is. Usually in an editorial, the writer states his or her opinion near the beginning. Words such as *think, believe, personally, should, best,* and *worst* can signal that an opinion is being expressed.

Identify Supporting Details Once you have determined the writer's opinion, analyze how the writer supports the opinion. Types of support may include facts, examples, and details. If the writer offers facts, judge them for their reliability. This may require checking the facts yourself. Reject an opinion that is supported only by other opinions.

Look at Both Sides Remember that there are always two sides to an issue. Responsible writers will address both sides, explaining why they feel their point of view is the more acceptable one. Beware of writers who purposely omit facts that might hurt their case or who fail to answer their critics' concerns.

Apply the Strategy

Read the editorial "The World's Worst Baby Sitter." Then analyze the writer's position by answering these questions.

1. What is the writer's opinion about television? Where in the article is it stated?

2. What facts, examples, and details does the writer give to support that opinion?

3. How reliable do you feel the writer's facts are? Where might you check them for accuracy?

4. How much does the writer say about the positive side of watching television? What arguments do you feel he or she avoids that opponents might raise?

5. Do you ultimately agree or disagree with the writer? Why?

The World's Worst Baby Sitter

The average American child today watches entirely too much television. Recent studies show that on average, a child between the ages of six and seventeen views four and a half hours of television per day. That's more than thirty hours per week! In other words, every week children spend more than one full day watching television!

Television is ruining the minds of our youth. Before television, families actually carried on a conversation together. Today, parents use television as a convenient baby sitter, but there is a large price to pay for that in the long run. Children don't receive the mental stimulation they need. They become zombies who learn only to look, not think.

✔ Here are other situations in which analyzing a position is helpful:
► Reading a political candidate's speech
► Reading a letter to the editor
► Reading a fund-raising advertisement
► Reading a petition you are asked to sign

PART 2 *History and Traditions*

Interior of the Theater of San Carlo in Naples, (detail), 19th C. Musee Conde, Chantilly, France, Giraudon/Art Resource, NY

the Shakespearean theater

Romeo and Juliet

Of all the love stories ever written, that of Romeo and Juliet is the most famous. To many people, Shakespeare's tragic lovers represent the essence of romantic love. When Shakespeare wrote *The Tragedy of Romeo and Juliet*, he was a young man, and the play is a young man's play about young love.

THE THEATER IN SHAKESPEARE'S DAY

Romeo and Juliet, like most of Shakespeare's plays, was produced in a public theater. Public theaters were built around roofless courtyards without artificial light. Performances, therefore, were given only during daylight hours. Surrounding the courtyard were three levels of galleries with benches where wealthier playgoers sat. Less wealthy spectators, called groundlings, stood and watched a play from the courtyard, which was called the pit.

Most of Shakespeare's plays were performed in the Globe theater. No one is certain exactly what the Globe looked like, though Shakespeare tells us it was round or octagonal. We know that it was open to the sky and held between 2,500 and 3,000 people. Scholars disagree about its actual dimensions and size. The discovery of its foundation in 1990 was exciting because the eventual excavation will reveal clues about the plays, actors, and the audience. The tiny part of the foundation initially uncovered yielded a great number of hazelnut shells. Hazelnuts were Elizabethan popcorn; people munched on them all during the performance.

The stage was a platform that extended into the pit. Actors entered and left the stage from doors located behind the platform. The portion of the galleries behind and above the stage was used primarily as dressing and storage rooms. The second-level gallery right above the stage, however, was used as an upper stage. It would have been here that the famous balcony scene in *Romeo and Juliet* was enacted.

There was no scenery in the theaters of Shakespeare's day. Settings were indicated by references in the dialogue. As a result, one scene could follow another in rapid succession. The actors wore elaborate clothing. It was, in fact, typical Elizabethan clothing, not costuming. Thus, the plays produced in Shakespeare's day were fast-paced, colorful productions. Usually a play lasted two hours.

One other difference between Shakespeare's theater and today's is that acting companies in the sixteenth century were made up only of men and boys. Women did not perform on the stage. This was not considered proper for a woman. Boys of eleven, twelve, or thirteen—before their voices changed—performed the female roles, and no one in the audience thought it the least bit odd, because they were accustomed to it.

THE GLOBE TODAY

Building a replica of Shakespeare's Globe was the dream of American actor Sam Wanamaker. After long years of fund-raising and construction, the theater opened to its first full season on June 8, 1997, with a production of *Henry V*. Like the earlier Globe, this one is made of wood, with a thatched roof and lime plaster covering the walls. The stage and the galleries are covered, but the "bear pit," where the modern-day groundlings stand, is open to the skies, exposing the spectators to the weather.

The story of Romeo and Juliet is retold in *West Side Story,* a musical set in New York City. Tony, a founding member of an Anglo gang, and Maria, sister of the leader of a rival Puerto Rican gang, meet at a dance. Maria's brother, angry to see his sister dancing with an Anglo, sends her home. Tony finds where Maria lives and joins her on the fire escape outside her window. In a scene that mirrors the balcony scene in Romeo and Juliet, they sing of their love for each other.

from West Side Story

MARIA
. . . Tonight, tonight,
It all began tonight,
I saw you and the world went away.
Tonight, tonight,
There's only you tonight,
What you are, what you do, what you
    say.

TONY
Today, all day I had a feeling
A miracle would happen—
I know now I was right.
For here you are
And what was just a world is a star
Tonight!

BOTH
Tonight, tonight
The world is full of light,
With suns and moons all over the
    place,
Tonight, tonight,
The world is wild and bright,
Going mad, shooting sparks into
    space.
Today the world was just an address,
A place for me to live in,
No better than all right,
But here you are
And what was just a world is a star
    Tonight!

1. How can love change a person's perception of the world?

2. In *Romeo and Juliet,* the lovers come from feuding families; in *West Side Story,* rival gangs. What other types of circumstances create a setting for a tragic love story? What might be done to work out these situations to create happy endings?

Guide for Reading

William Shakespeare
(1564–1616)

William Shakespeare is widely regarded as the greatest writer in English Literature.

Almost 400 years after Shakespeare's death, his 37 plays continue to be read widely and produced frequently throughout the world. They have as powerful an impact on audiences today as when they were first staged.

Stage Celebrity Not much is known about Shakespeare's early life. We do know, however, that by 1594 Shakespeare had developed a reputation as an actor, had written several plays, and had become the principal playwright of the Lord Chamberlain's Men, a successful London theater company. In 1599, the company built the famous Globe theater, where most of Shakespeare's plays were performed. When James I became king in 1603, following Queen Elizabeth I's death, he took control of the Lord Chamberlain's Men and renamed the company The King's Men. He continued in that role until 1610, when he retired to Stratford-on-Avon.

When Were They Written? Because Shakespeare wrote his plays to be performed, not published, no one knows exactly when each play was written. However, scholars have charted periods in Shakespeare's development as a playwright. During his early years, he wrote a number of comedies, several histories, and two tragedies. *Romeo and Juliet*—inspiration for the musical *West Side Story,* ballets, songs, stories, and movies—was written around 1595. Just before, and at the turn of the seventeenth century, Shakespeare wrote several of his finest romantic comedies (*As You Like It, Twelfth Night,* and *Much Ado About Nothing*). During the first decade of the seventeenth century, Shakespeare created his greatest tragedies (*Hamlet, Othello, King Lear,*

Macbeth, Antony and Cleopatra, and *Coriolanus*). Finally, toward the end of his life, Shakespeare wrote several plays referred to as romances or tragicomedies.

Shakespeare's Impact on English No other individual has played a more significant role in shaping the English language than Shakespeare. In addition to introducing many new words into the language, Shakespeare penned hundreds of memorable lines that are familiar to millions of people throughout the world—even people who have never read one of Shakespeare's plays. Following are just a few of his most famous lines. See how many you recognize.

From *Hamlet:*
To be, or not to be: that is the question:
Whether 'tis nobler in the mind to suffer
The slings and arrows of outrageous fortune,
Or take arms against a sea of troubles, . . .

From *Romeo and Juliet:*
What's in a name? That which we call a rose
By any other name would smell as sweet.

. . . parting is such sweet sorrow, . . .

From *Macbeth:*
Fair is foul, and foul is fair.

From *Julius Caesar:*
Friends, Romans, countrymen, lend me your ears;
I come to bury Caesar, not to praise him.

From *As You Like It:*
All the world's a stage,
And all the men and women merely players . . .

From *Richard the Third:*
A horse, a horse! My kingdom for a horse!

From *Twelfth Night:*
If music be the food of love, play on . . .

Guide for Reading

◆ *Literature and Your Life*

CONNECT YOUR EXPERIENCE

The world is filled with rivalries—among countries, families, schools, groups of friends. Sometimes rivalries can become so fierce that the members of one group will refuse to associate with their rivals. In the most extreme instances, rivalries can even erupt into violence. This is the case in Shakespeare's play, which captures a long-standing feud between two families in Renaissance Italy.

THEMATIC FOCUS: FACING CONFLICTS

As you read about the conflict between the rival families in this play, you'll probably find yourself wondering what might have caused the conflict and what could have been done to resolve it.

Journal Writing Describe a rivalry with which you are familiar, then jot down your thoughts about what might be done to put an end to the rivalry.

◆ Background for Understanding

LITERATURE

The story of star-crossed lovers from feuding families was told and retold many times before Shakespeare first produced this play. Shakespeare's play is based on *The Tragicall Historye of Romeus and Juliet* by Arthur Brooke, which was published in 1562. Brooke's 3,000-line poem has a highly moral tone: disobedience, as well as fate, leads to the deaths of the two lovers. Brooke's poem, in turn, was based on a French version of the story, written in 1559. The earliest version of the story that sets the action in Verona was written around 1530.

LANGUAGE

As you read, most of the unfamiliar words you will encounter are explained in footnotes. The following, however, appear so frequently that learning them now will make your reading of the play easier.

◆ Reading Strategy

USE TEXT AIDS

While watching reruns of old sitcoms from the 1970's, you may be amazed and amused by the clothes people wear and the language they use. The way people speak in casual conversation has changed noticeably in thirty years, and it has changed even more since Shakespeare's time, over 400 years ago. As a result, much of the language in Shakespeare's play, and in other early works of literature, will probably be unfamiliar to you. To make sure that you understand the dialogue, it is crucial that you **use the text aids**—the numbered explanations of Shakespeare's language that appear beside the text. Each time you come across a footnoted term, read the corresponding explanation to ensure that you grasp the meaning of the passage.

against: for; in preparation for	**happy:** fortunate
alack: alas (an exclamation of sorrow)	**hence:** away; from here
an, and: if	**hie:** hurry
anon: soon	**hither:** here
aye: yes	**marry:** indeed
but: only; except	**whence:** where
e'en: even	**wilt:** will
e'er: ever	**withal:** in addition; notwithstanding
haply: perhaps	**would:** wish

The Tragedy of Romeo and Juliet

◆ Literary Focus

CHARACTER

Characters are the people or animals who take part in a literary work. **Round characters** have many personality traits, like real people. **Flat characters**, on the other hand, are one-dimensional, embodying only a single trait. Shakespeare's plays often include flat characters who provide comic relief.

In a play, the personalities of characters are revealed largely through their interactions with other characters, who often possess contrasting traits. Such characters, who highlight or bring out the personality traits of another character in a play, are called **dramatic foils.** For example, In Act I of *Romeo and Juliet*, Benvolio, who tries to quiet a group of brawling servants, is a dramatic foil to Tybalt, a character with a fiery, hot temper. As you read, use a graphic organizer like this one to note each character's personality traits. Look for characters who have contrasting traits. This will help you identify dramatic foils.

Character	Personality Traits

◆ Build Vocabulary

PREFIXES: TRANS-

In the first act of *The Tragedy of Romeo and Juliet*, Romeo, on discovering that his own sadness is making his sympathetic friend Benvolio unhappy, speaks of "love's transgression." The word *transgression* includes the prefix *trans-*, which means "through" or "across." Notice how the prefix contributes to the overall meaning of the word *transgression:* "the act of going across a boundary of right behavior." What other words can you think of that contain the prefix *trans-* and what do they mean?

WORD BANK

Before you read, preview this list of words from the selection.

pernicious
augmenting
grievance
transgression
heretics

◆ Build Grammar Skills

PUNCTUATING WORDS OF DIRECT ADDRESS

In a play, most of what the audience learns about the characters—even the characters' names—is revealed through dialogue. As a result, you'll find that the characters often use words of direct address, interrupters that clearly indicate to whom a character is speaking. Commas are used to set off the words of direct address from the other words in a sentence. Look at these examples:

You, *Capulet*, shall go
along with me; . . .

My *noble uncle*, do you
know the cause?

the tragedy of
Romeo

PROLOGUE

Scene: *Verona; Mantua*

[*Enter* CHORUS]

CHORUS. Two households, both alike in dignity.[1]
    In fair Verona, where we lay our scene,
From ancient grudge break to new mutiny.[2]
    Where civil blood makes civil hands unclean.[3]

5 From forth the fatal loins of these two foes
    A pair of star-crossed[4] lovers take their life;
Whose misadventured piteous overthrows[5]
    Doth with their death bury their parents' strife.
The fearful passage of their death-marked love,

10 And the continuance of their parents' rage,
Which, but[6] their children's end, naught could remove,
    Is now the two hours' traffic[7] of our stage;
The which if you with patient ears attend,
What here shall miss, our toil shall strive to mend.[8]

                      [*Exit.*]

---

1. dignity: High social rank.
2. mutiny: Violence.
3. Where . . . unclean: In which the blood of citizens stains citizens' hands.
4. star-crossed: Ill-fated by the unfavorable positions of the stars.
5. Whose . . . overthrows: Whose unfortunate, sorrowful destruction.
6. but: Except.
7. two hours' traffic: Two hours' business.
8. What . . . mend: What is not clear in this prologue we actors shall try to clarify in the course of the play.

CHARACTERS

CHORUS
ESCALUS, Prince of Verona
PARIS, a young count, kinsman to the Prince
MONTAGUE
CAPULET
AN OLD MAN, of the Capulet family
ROMEO, son to Montague
MERCUTIO, kinsman to the Prince and friend to Romeo
BENVOLIO, nephew to Montague and friend to Romeo
TYBALT, nephew to Lady Capulet
FRIAR LAWRENCE, Franciscan
FRIAR JOHN, Franciscan
BALTHASAR, servant to Romeo
SAMPSON, servant to Capulet
GREGORY, servant to Capulet
PETER, servant to Juliet's nurse
ABRAM, servant to Montague
AN APOTHECARY
THREE MUSICIANS
AN OFFICER
LADY MONTAGUE, wife to Montague
LADY CAPULET, wife to Capulet
JULIET, daughter to Capulet
NURSE TO JULIET
CITIZENS OF VERONA, Gentlemen and Gentlewomen of both houses, Maskers, Torchbearers, Pages, Guards, Watchmen, Servants, and Attendants

and Juliet
WILLIAM SHAKESPEARE

Act 1

Scene i. *Verona. A public place.*

[*Enter* SAMPSON *and* GREGORY, *with swords and bucklers,*[1] *of the house of Capulet.*]

SAMPSON. Gregory, on my word, we'll not carry coals.[2]

GREGORY. No, for then we should be colliers.[3]

SAMPSON. I mean, an we be in choler, we'll draw.[4]

GREGORY. Ay, while you live, draw your neck out of collar.[5]

5 **SAMPSON.** I strike quickly, being moved.

GREGORY. But thou art not quickly moved to strike.

SAMPSON. A dog of the house of Montague moves me.

GREGORY. To move is to stir, and to be valiant is to stand.
Therefore, if thou art moved, thou run'st away.

10 **SAMPSON.** A dog of that house shall move me to stand. I
will take the wall[6] of any man or maid of Montague's.

GREGORY. That shows thee a weak slave; for the weakest
goes to the wall.

SAMPSON. 'Tis true; and therefore women, being the weaker
15 vessels, are ever thrust to the wall. Therefore I will push
Montague's men from the wall and thrust his maids to the wall.

GREGORY. The quarrel is between our masters and us their men.

SAMPSON. 'Tis all one. I will show myself a tyrant. When I have
fought with the men, I will be civil with the maids—I will cut
20 off their heads.

GREGORY. The heads of the maids?

SAMPSON. Ay, the heads of the maids or their maidenheads.
Take it in what sense thou wilt.

GREGORY. They must take it in sense that feel it.

25 **SAMPSON.** Me they shall feel while I am able to stand;
and 'tis known I am a pretty piece of flesh.

GREGORY. 'Tis well thou art not fish; if thou hadst, thou hadst been
Poor John. Draw thy tool![7] Here comes two of the house of Montagues.

[*Enter two other Servingmen,* ABRAM *and* BALTHASAR.]

1. **bucklers:** Small shields.

2. **carry coals:** Endure insults.
3. **colliers:** Sellers of coal.

4. **an . . . draw:** If we are angered, we'll draw our swords.
5. **collar:** The hangman's noose.

◆ **Reading Strategy**
Restate each line, substituting the words in the footnotes.

6. **take the wall:** Assert superiority by walking nearest the houses and therefore farthest from the gutter.

◆ **Literary Focus**
What does this conversation reveal about the Capulets and the Montagues?

7. **tool:** Weapon.

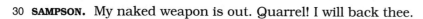

30 **SAMPSON.** My naked weapon is out. Quarrel! I will back thee.

GREGORY. How? Turn thy back and run?

SAMPSON. Fear me not.

GREGORY. No, marry. I fear thee!

SAMPSON. Let us take the law of our sides;[8] let them begin.

35 **GREGORY.** I will frown as I pass by, and let them take it as they list.[9]

SAMPSON. Nay, as they dare. I will bite my thumb[10] at them, which is disgrace to them if they bear it.

ABRAM. Do you bite your thumb at us, sir?

SAMPSON. I do bite my thumb, sir.

40 **ABRAM.** Do you bite your thumb at us, sir?

SAMPSON. [*Aside to* GREGORY] Is the law of our side if I say ay?

GREGORY. [*Aside to* SAMPSON] No.

SAMPSON. No, sir, I do not bite my thumb at you, sir; but I bite my thumb, sir.

45 **GREGORY.** Do you quarrel, sir?

ABRAM. Quarrel, sir? No, sir.

SAMPSON. But if you do, sir, I am for you. I serve as good a man as you.

ABRAM. No better.

SAMPSON. Well, sir.

[*Enter* BENVOLIO.]

50 **GREGORY.** Say "better." Here comes one of my master's kinsmen.

SAMPSON. Yes, better, sir.

ABRAM. You lie.

SAMPSON. Draw, if you be men. Gregory, remember thy swashing[11] blow.   [They fight.]

55 **BENVOLIO.** Part, fools!
    Put up your swords. You know not what you do.

[*Enter* TYBALT.]

TYBALT. What art thou drawn among these heartless hinds?[12]
    Turn thee, Benvolio; look upon thy death.

BENVOLIO. I do but keep the peace. Put up thy sword,

8. **take . . . sides:** Make sure the law is on our side.
9. **list:** Please.

10. **bite . . . thumb:** Make an insulting gesture.

11. **swashing:** Hard downward swordstroke.

12. **heartless hinds:** Cowardly servants. Hind also meant "a female deer."

60 Or manage it to part these men with me.

TYBALT. What, drawn, and talk of peace? I hate the word
    As I hate hell, all Montagues, and thee.
    Have at thee, coward!   [*They fight.*]

[*Enter an* OFFICER, *and three or four Citizens with clubs or partisans.*[13]]

OFFICER. Clubs, bills,[14] and partisans! Strike! Beat them down!
65 Down with the Capulets! Down with the Montagues!

[*Enter old* CAPULET *in his gown, and his* WIFE.]

CAPULET. What noise is this? Give me my long sword, ho!

LADY CAPULET. A crutch, a crutch! Why call you for a sword?

CAPULET. My sword, I say! Old Montague is come
    And flourishes his blade in spite[15] of me.

[*Enter old* MONTAGUE *and his* WIFE.]

70 MONTAGUE. Thou villain Capulet!—Hold me not; let me go.

LADY MONTAGUE. Thou shalt not stir one foot to seek a foe.

[*Enter* PRINCE ESCALUS, *with his Train.*[16]]

PRINCE. Rebellious subjects, enemies to peace,
    Profaners[17] of this neighbor-stained steel–
    Will they not hear? What, ho! You men, you beasts,
75 That quench the fire of your pernicious rage
    With purple fountains issuing from your veins!
    On pain of torture, from those bloody hands
    Throw your mistempered[18] weapons to the ground
    And hear the sentence of your moved prince.
80 Three civil brawls, bred of an airy word
    By thee, old Capulet, and Montague,
    Have thrice disturbed the quiet of our streets
    And made Verona's ancient citizens
    Cast by their grave beseeming ornaments[19]
85 To wield old partisans, in hands as old,
    Cank'red with peace, to part your cank'red hate.[20]
    If ever you disturb our streets again,
    Your lives shall pay the forfeit of the peace.
    For this time all the rest depart away.
90 You, Capulet, shall go along with me;
    And, Montague, come you this afternoon,
    To know our farther pleasure in this case,
    To old Freetown, our common judgment place.
    Once more, on pain of death, all men depart.

◆ **Literary Focus**
What can you tell about the character traits of Benvolio and Tybalt from their brief conversation?

13. partisans: Spearlike weapons with broad blades.
14. bills: Weapons consisting of hook-shaped blades with long handles.

15. spite: Defiance.

16. Train: Attendants.

17. Profaners: Those who show disrespect or contempt.

18. mistempered: Hardened for a wrong purpose; bad-tempered.

19. Cast . . . ornaments: Put aside their dignified and appropriate clothing.
20. Cank'red . . . hate: Rusted from lack of use, to put an end to your malignant feuding.

[*Exit all but* MONTAGUE, *his* WIFE, *and* BENVOLIO.]

95 **MONTAGUE.** Who set this ancient quarrel new abroach?[21]
Speak, nephew, were you by when it began?

BENVOLIO. Here were the servants of your adversary
And yours, close fighting ere I did approach.
I drew to part them. In the instant came
100 The fiery Tybalt, with his sword prepared;
Which, as he breathed defiance to my ears,
He swung about his head and cut the winds,
Who, nothing hurt withal, hissed him in scorn.
While we were interchanging thrusts and blows,
105 Came more and more, and fought on part and part,[22]
Till the Prince came, who parted either part.

LADY MONTAGUE. O, where is Romeo? Saw you him today?
Right glad I am he was not at this fray.

BENVOLIO. Madam, an hour before the worshiped sun
110 Peered forth the golden window of the East,
A troubled mind drave me to walk abroad:
Where, underneath the grove of sycamore
That westward rooteth from this city side,
So early walking did I see your son.
115 Towards him I made, but he was ware[23] of me
And stole into the covert[24] of the wood.
I, measuring his affections[25] by my own,
Which then most sought where most might not be found,[26]
Being one too many by my weary self,
120 Pursued my humor not pursuing his,[27]
And gladly shunned who gladly fled from me.

MONTAGUE. Many a morning hath he there been seen,
With tears augmenting the fresh morning's dew,
Adding to clouds more clouds with his deep sighs;
125 But all so soon as the all-cheering sun
Should in the farthest East begin to draw
The shady curtains from Aurora's[28] bed,
Away from light steals home my heavy[29] son
And private in his chamber pens himself,
130 Shuts up his windows, locks fair daylight out,
And makes himself an artificial night.
Black and portentous[30] must this humor prove
Unless good counsel may the cause remove.

BENVOLIO. My noble uncle, do you know the cause?

---

21. Who . . . abroach?: Who reopened this old fight?

22. on . . . part: On one side and the other.

◆ **Reading Strategy**
How would Benvolio describe his spotting of Romeo in contemporary English?

23. ware: Aware; wary.
24. covert: Hidden place.
25. measuring . . . affections: Judging his feelings.
26. Which . . . found: Which wanted to be where there was no one else.
27. pursued . . . his: Followed my own mind by not following after Romeo.

28. Aurora: Goddess of the dawn.
29. heavy: Sad, moody.
30. portentous: Promising bad fortune.

◆ **Build Vocabulary**
pernicious (pər nish´ əs) *adj.*: Causing great injury or ruin

augmenting (ôg ment´ iŋ) *v.*: Increasing; enlarging

135 **MONTAGUE.** I neither know it nor can learn of him.

BENVOLIO. Have you importuned[31] him by any means?

MONTAGUE. Both by myself and many other friends;
But he, his own affections' counselor,
Is to himself—I will not say how true—
140 But to himself so secret and so close,
So far from sounding[32] and discovery,
As is the bud bit with an envious worm
Ere he can spread his sweet leaves to the air
Or dedicate his beauty to the sun.
145 Could we but learn from whence his sorrows grow,
We would as willingly give cure as know.

[*Enter* ROMEO.]

BENVOLIO. See, where he comes. So please you step aside;
I'll know his <u>grievance</u>, or be much denied.

MONTAGUE. I would thou wert so happy by thy stay
150 To hear true shrift.[33] Come, madam, let's away.

[*Exit* MONTAGUE *and* WIFE.]

BENVOLIO. Good morrow, cousin.

ROMEO.   Is the day so young?

BENVOLIO. But new struck nine.

ROMEO.   Ay me! Sad hours seem long.
Was that my father that went hence so fast?

BENVOLIO. It was. What sadness lengthens Romeo's hours?

155 **ROMEO.** Not having that which having makes them short.

BENVOLIO. In love?

ROMEO. Out—

BENVOLIO. Of love?

ROMEO. Out of her favor where I am in love.

160 **BENVOLIO.** Alas that love, so gentle in his view,[34]
Should be so tyrannous and rough in proof![35]

ROMEO. Alas that love, whose view is muffled still,[36]
Should without eyes see pathways to his will!
Where shall we dine? O me! What fray was here?
165 Yet tell me not, for I have heard it all.
Here's much to do with hate, but more with love.[37]
Why then, O brawling love, O loving hate,

31. **importuned:**
Questioned deeply.

32. **sounding:**
Understanding.

33. **I . . . shrift:** I hope you
are lucky enough to hear
him confess the truth.

♦ *Literature
and Your Life*
How does Romeo's
moody behavior
compare with that
of teens you know
who are having
problems with their
girlfriend or
boyfriend?

34. **view:** Appearance.
35. **in proof:** When
experienced.
36. **whose . . . still:** Cupid
is traditionally represented
as blindfolded.
37. **but . . . love:** Loyalty
to family and love of
fighting. In the following
lines, Romeo speaks of
love as a series of
contradictions—a union
of opposites.

◆ **Build Vocabulary**

grievance (grē′ vəns) *n.:*
Injustice; complaint

transgression (trans gresh′
ən) *n.:* Wrongdoing; sin

▲ **Critical Viewing** In this scene, Benvolio coaxes Romeo into explaining why he's been so moody lately. How does what Benvolio says and does compare with the way you would find out what's troubling a friend? **[Compare and Contrast]**

O anything, of nothing first created!
O heavy lightness, serious vanity,
170 Misshapen chaos of well-seeming forms,
Feather of lead, bright smoke, cold fire, sick health,
Still-waking sleep, that is not what it is!
This love feel I, that feel no love in this.
Dost thou not laugh?

BENVOLIO.   No, coz,[38] I rather weep.

ROMEO. Good heart, at what?

175 **BENVOLIO.**   At thy good heart's oppression.

ROMEO. Why, such is love's <u>transgression</u>.
Griefs of mine own lie heavy in my breast,
Which thou wilt propagate, to have it prest
With more of thine.[39] This love that thou hast shown
180 Doth add more grief to too much of mine own.
Love is a smoke made with the fume of sighs;
Being purged, a fire sparkling in lovers' eyes;
Being vexed, a sea nourished with loving tears.
What is it else? A madness most discreet,[40]
185 A choking gall,[41] and a preserving sweet.
Farewell, my coz.

BENVOLIO.   Soft![42] I will go along.
And if you leave me so, you do me wrong.

ROMEO. Tut! I have lost myself; I am not here;

38. coz: Cousin.

39. Which . . . thine: Which griefs you will increase by adding your own sorrow to them.

40. discreet: Intelligently sensitive.
41. gall: A bitter liquid.

42. Soft!: Hold on a minute.

This is not Romeo, he's some other where.

190 **BENVOLIO.** Tell me in sadness,[43] who is that you love?

ROMEO. What, shall I groan and tell thee?

BENVOLIO.   Groan? Why, no;
But sadly tell me who.

ROMEO. Bid a sick man in sadness make his will.
Ah, word ill urged to one that is so ill!
195 In sadness, cousin, I do love a woman.

BENVOLIO. I aimed so near when I supposed you loved.

ROMEO. A right good markman. And she's fair I love.

BENVOLIO. A right fair mark, fair coz, is soonest hit.

ROMEO. Well, in that hit you miss. She'll not be hit
200 With Cupid's arrow. She hath Dian's wit,[44]
And, in strong proof[45] of chastity well armed,
From Love's weak childish bow she lives uncharmed.
She will not stay[46] the siege of loving terms,
Nor bide th' encounter of assailing eyes,
205 Nor ope her lap to saint-seducing gold.
O, she is rich in beauty; only poor
That, when she dies, with beauty dies her store.[47]

BENVOLIO. Then she hath sworn that she will still live chaste?

ROMEO. She hath, and in that sparing make huge waste;
210 For beauty, starved with her severity,
Cuts beauty off from all posterity.[48]
She is too fair, too wise, wisely too fair
To merit bliss by making me despair.[49]
She hath forsworn to[50] love, and in that vow
215 Do I live dead that live to tell it now.

BENVOLIO. Be ruled by me; forget to think of her.

ROMEO. O, teach me how I should forget to think!

BENVOLIO. By giving liberty unto thine eyes.
Examine other beauties.

ROMEO.   'Tis the way
220 To call hers, exquisite, in question more.[51]
These happy masks that kiss fair ladies' brows,
Being black puts us in mind they hide the fair.
He that is strucken blind cannot forget
The precious treasure of his eyesight lost.

43. in sadness: Seriously.

44. Dian's wit: The mind of Diana, goddess of chastity.
45. proof: Armor.

46. stay: Endure; put up with.

47. That . . . store: In that her beauty will die with her if she does not marry and have children.

48. in . . . posterity: By denying herself love and marriage, she wastes her beauty, which will not live on in future generations.
49. She . . . despair: She is being too good—she'll earn happiness in heaven by dooming me to live without her love.
50. forsworn to: Sworn not to.

51. 'Tis . . . more: That way will only make her beauty more strongly present in my mind.

225 Show me a mistress that is passing fair:
What doth her beauty serve but as a note
Where I may read who passed that passing fair?[52]
Farewell. Thou canst not teach me to forget.

BENVOLIO. I'll pay that doctrine, or else die in debt.[53]   [*Exit.*]

52. who . . . fair: Who surpassed in beauty that very beautiful woman.
53. I'll . . . debt: I'll teach you to forget, or else die trying.

Scene ii. *A street.*

[*Enter* CAPULET, COUNTY PARIS, *and the* CLOWN, *his servant.*]

CAPULET. But Montague is bound as well as I,
In penalty alike; and 'tis not hard, I think,
For men so old as we to keep the peace.

PARIS. Of honorable reckoning[1] are you both,
5   And pity 'tis you lived at odds so long.
But now, my lord, what say you to my suit?

CAPULET. But saying o'er what I have said before:
My child is yet a stranger in the world,
She hath not seen the change of fourteen years;
10   Let two more summers wither in their pride
Ere we may think her ripe to be a bride.

PARIS. Younger than she are happy mothers made.

CAPULET. And too soon marred are those so early made.
Earth hath swallowed all my hopes[2] but she;
15   She is the hopeful lady of my earth.[3]
But woo her, gentle Paris, get her heart;
My will to her consent is but a part.
An she agree, within her scope of choice
Lies my consent and fair according voice,[4]
20   This night I hold an old accustomed feast,
Whereto I have invited many a guest,
Such as I love; and you among the store,
One more, most welcome, makes my number more.
At my poor house look to behold this night
25   Earth-treading stars[5] that make dark heaven light.
Such comfort as do lusty young men feel
When well-appareled April on the heel
Of limping Winter treads, even such delight
Among fresh fennel buds shall you this night
30   Inherit at my house. Hear all, all see,
And like her most whose merit most shall be;
Which, on more view of many, mine, being one,

1. reckoning: Reputation.

◆ Literary Focus
What can you tell about Lord Capulet's character traits based on his talk with Paris?

2. hopes: Children.
3. She . . . earth: My hopes for the future rest in her; she will inherit all that is mine.

4. and . . . voice: If she agrees, I will consent to and agree with her choice.

5. Earth-treading stars: Young ladies.

May stand in number, though in reck'ning none.[6]
Come, go with me. [*To* SERVANT, *giving him a paper*]
  Go, sirrah, trudge about
35 Through fair Verona; find those persons out
Whose names are written there, and to them say
My house and welcome on their pleasure stay.[7]   [*Exit with* PARIS.]

SERVANT. Find them out whose names are written here? It is written
that the shoemaker should meddle with his yard and the tailor with
40 his last, the fisher with his pencil and the painter with his nets;[8] but
I am sent to find those persons whose names are here writ, and can
never find what names the writing person hath here writ. I must to
the learned. In good time![9]

[*Enter* BENVOLIO *and* ROMEO.]

BENVOLIO. Tut, man, one fire burns out another's burning;
45   One pain is less'ned by another's anguish;
Turn giddy, and be holp by backward turning;[10]
    One desperate grief cures with another's languish.
Take thou some new infection to thy eye,
And the rank poison of the old will die.

50 **ROMEO.** Your plantain leaf[11] is excellent for that.

BENVOLIO. For what, I pray thee?

ROMEO. For your broken shin.

BENVOLIO. Why, Romeo, art thou mad?

ROMEO. Not mad, but bound more than a madman is;
Shut up in prison, kept without my food,
55 Whipped and tormented and—God-den,[12] good fellow.

SERVANT. God gi' go-den. I pray, sir, can you read?

ROMEO. Ay, mine own fortune in my misery.

SERVANT. Perhaps you have learned it without book.
But, I pray, can you read anything you see?

60 **ROMEO.** Ay, if I know the letters and the language.

SERVANT. Ye say honestly. Rest you merry.[13]

ROMEO. Stay, fellow; I can read. [*He reads the letter.*]
"Signior Martino and his wife and daughters;
County Anselm and his beauteous sisters;
65 The lady widow of Vitruvio;
Signior Placentio and his lovely nieces;
Mercutio and his brother Valentine;

6. Which . . . none: If you look at all the young girls, you may see her as merely one among many, and not worth special admiration.

7. stay: Await.

8. shoemaker . . . nets: The servant is confusing workers and their tools. He intends to say that people should stick with what they know.

9. In good time!: Just in time! The servant has seen Benvolio and Romeo, who can read.

10. Turn . . . turning: If you're dizzy from turning one way, turn the other way.

11. plantain leaf: Leaf used to stop bleeding.

12. God-den: Good afternoon; good evening.

13. Rest you merry: May God keep you happy—a way of saying farewell.

Mine uncle Capulet, his wife and daughters;
My fair niece Rosaline; Livia;
70 Signior Valentio and his cousin Tybalt;
Lucio and the lively Helena."
A fair assembly. Whither should they come?

SERVANT. Up.

ROMEO. Whither? To supper?

75 **SERVANT.** To our house.

ROMEO. Whose house?

SERVANT. My master's.

ROMEO. Indeed I should have asked you that before.

SERVANT. Now I'll tell you without asking. My master is the great
80 rich Capulet; and if you be not of the house of Montagues, I pray
come and crush a cup of wine. Rest you merry.   [*Exit.*]

BENVOLIO. At this same ancient[14] feast of Capulet's
Sups the fair Rosaline whom thou so loves;
With all the admirèd beauties of Verona.
85 Go thither, and with unattainted[15] eye
Compare her face with some that I shall show,
And I will make thee think thy swan a crow.

ROMEO. When the devout religion of mine eye
Maintains such falsehood, then turn tears to fires:
90 And these, who, often drowned, could never die,
Transparent <u>heretics</u>, be burnt for liars![16]
One fairer than my love? The all-seeing sun
Ne'er saw her match since first the world begun.

BENVOLIO. Tut! you saw her fair, none else being by,
95 Herself poised with herself in either eye;[17]
But in that crystal scales[18] let there be weighed
Your lady's love against some other maid
That I will show you shining at this feast,
And she shall scant show well that now seems best.

100 **ROMEO.** I'll go along, no such sight to be shown,
But to rejoice in splendor of mine own.[19]   [*Exit.*]

14. **ancient:** Long-established; traditional.

15. **unattainted:** Unprejudiced.

◆ **Reading Strategy**
How does the text aid help you understand Romeo's assertion in lines 90–95?

16. **When . . . liars!:** When I see Rosaline as just a plain-looking girl, may my tears turn to fire and burn my eyes out!

17. **Herself . . . eye:** Rosaline compared with no one else.
18. **crystal scales:** Your eyes.

19. **mine own:** My own love, Rosaline.

◆ **Build Vocabulary**
heretics (her´ ə tiks) *n.:* Those who hold to a belief opposed to the established teachings of a church

Scene iii. *A room in* CAPULET'*s house.*

[*Enter* CAPULET'S WIFE, *and* NURSE.]

LADY CAPULET. Nurse, where's my daughter? Call her forth to me.

NURSE. Now, by my maidenhead at twelve year old,
I bade her come. What, lamb! What, ladybird!
God forbid, where's this girl? What, Juliet!

[*Enter* JULIET.]

JULIET. How now? Who calls?

NURSE.   Your mother.

5 **JULIET.**   Madam, I am here
What is your will?

LADY CAPULET. This is the matter—Nurse, give leave[1] awhile;
We must talk in secret. Nurse, come back again.
I have rememb'red me; thou's hear our counsel.[2]
10 Thou knowest my daughter's of a pretty age.

NURSE. Faith, I can tell her age unto an hour.

LADY CAPULET. She's not fourteen.

NURSE.   I'll lay fourteen of my teeth—
And yet, to my teen[3] be it spoken, I have but four—
She's not fourteen. How long is it now
To Lammastide?[4]

15 **LADY CAPULET.**   A fortnight and odd days.[5]

NURSE. Even or odd, of all days in the year,
Come Lammas Eve at night shall she be fourteen.
Susan and she (God rest all Christian souls!)
Were of an age.[6] Well, Susan is with God;
20 She was too good for me. But, as I said,
On Lammas Eve at night shall she be fourteen;
That shall she, marry; I remember it well.
'Tis since the earthquake now eleven years.
And she was weaned (I never shall forget it),
25 Of all the days of the year, upon that day;
For I had then laid wormwood to my dug,
Sitting in the sun under the dove house wall.
My lord and you were then at Mantua.
Nay, I do bear a brain. But, as I said,
30 When it did taste the wormwood on the nipple
Of my dug and felt it bitter, pretty fool,

1. **give leave:** Leave us alone.
2. **thou's . . . counsel:** You shall hear our conference.

3. **teen:** Sorrow.

4. **Lammastide:** August 1, a holiday celebrating the summer harvest.
5. **A fortnight and odd days:** Two weeks plus a few days.

6. **Susan . . . age:** Susan, the Nurse's child, and Juliet were the same age.

▲ **Critical Viewing** What do this picture and the conversation among Juliet, her nurse, and her mother tell you about their relationship and personalities? **[Infer]**

To see it tetchy and fall out with the dug!
Shake, quoth the dovehouse! 'Twas no need, I trow,
To bid me trudge.
35 And since that time it is eleven years,
For then she could stand high-lone; nay, by th' rood,
She could have run and waddled all about;
For even the day before, she broke her brow;
And then my husband (God be with his soul!
40 'A was a merry man) took up the child.
"Yea," quoth he, "dost thou fall upon thy face?
Thou wilt fall backward when thou hast more wit;
Wilt thou not, Jule?" and, by my holidam,
The pretty wretch left crying and said, "Ay."
45 To see now how a jest shall come about!
I warrant, and I should live a thousand years,
I never should forget it. "Wilt thou not, Jule?" quoth he,
And, pretty fool, it stinted and said, "Ay."

LADY CAPULET. Enough of this. I pray thee hold thy peace.

50 **NURSE.** Yes, madam. Yet I cannot choose but laugh
To think it should leave crying and say, "Ay."

And yet, I warrant, it had upon it brow
A bump as big as a young cock'rel's stone;
A perilous knock; and it cried bitterly.
55 "Yea," quoth my husband, "fall'st upon thy face?
Thou wilt fall backward when thou comest to age,
Wilt thou not, Jule?" It stinted and said, "Ay."

JULIET. And stint thou too, I pray thee, nurse, say I.

NURSE. Peace, I have done. God mark thee to His grace!
60 Thou wast the prettiest babe that e'er I nursed.
And I might live to see thee married once,
I have my wish.

LADY CAPULET. Marry, that "marry" is the very theme
I came to talk of. Tell me, daughter Juliet,
65 How stands your dispositions to be married?

JULIET. It is an honor that I dream not of.

NURSE. An honor? Were not I thine only nurse,
I would say thou hadst sucked wisdom from thy teat.

LADY CAPULET. Well, think of marriage now. Younger than you,
70 Here in Verona, ladies of esteem,
Are made already mothers. By my count,
I was your mother much upon these years
That you are now a maid.[7] Thus then in brief;
The valiant Paris seeks you for his love.

75 **NURSE.** A man, young lady! Lady, such a man
As all the world—why, he's a man of wax.[8]

LADY CAPULET. Verona's summer hath not such a flower.

NURSE. Nay, he's a flower, in faith—a very flower.

LADY CAPULET. What say you? Can you love the gentleman?
80 This night you shall behold him at our feast.
Read o'er the volume of young Paris' face,
And find delight writ there with beauty's pen;
Examine every married lineament,
And see how one another lends content;[9]
85 And what obscured in this fair volume lies
Find written in the margent[10] of his eyes.
This precious book of love, this unbound lover,
To beautify him only lacks a cover.[11]
The fish lives in the sea, and 'tis much pride
90 For fair without the fair within to hide.
That book in many's eyes doth share the glory,

♦ **Literary Focus**
What can you tell about the nurse's personality from her unrefined expressions and tales, and from Lady Capulet's and Juliet's reactions?

7. **I . . . maid:** I was your mother when I was as old as you are now.

8. **he's . . . wax:** He's a model of a man.

♦ **Reading Strategy**
Why is note 8 essential?

9. **Examine . . . content:** Examine every harmonious feature of his face, and see how each one enhances every other. Throughout this speech, Lady Capulet compares Paris to a book.
10. **margent:** margin. Paris's eyes are compared to the margin of a book, where whatever is not clear in the text (the rest of his face) can be explained by notes.
11. **cover:** Metaphor for wife.

That in gold clasps locks in the golden story;
So shall you share all that he doth possess,
By having him making yourself no less.

95 **NURSE.** No less? Nay, bigger! Women grow by men.

LADY CAPULET. Speak briefly, can you like of Paris' love?

JULIET. I'll look to like, if looking liking move;[12]
But no more deep will I endart mine eye
Than your consent gives strength to make it fly.[13]

[*Enter* SERVINGMAN.]

100 **SERVINGMAN.** Madam, the guests are come, supper served up, you
called, my young lady asked for, the nurse cursed in the pantry,
and everything in extremity. I must hence to wait. I beseech you
follow straight.   [*Exit.*]

LADY CAPULET. We follow thee. Juliet, the County stays.[14]

105 **NURSE.** Go, girl, seek happy nights to happy days.   [*Exit.*]

Scene iv. *A street*

[*Enter* ROMEO, MERCUTIO, BENVOLIO, *with five or six other* MASKERS; TORCHBEARERS.]

ROMEO. What, shall this speech[1] be spoke for our excuse?
Or shall we on without apology?

BENVOLIO. The date is out of such prolixity.[2]
We'll have no Cupid hoodwinked with a scarf,
5 Bearing a Tartar's painted bow of lath,
Scaring the ladies like a crowkeeper,
Nor no without-book prologue, faintly spoke
After the prompter, for our entrance;
But, let them measure us by what they will,
10 We'll measure them a measure and be gone.

ROMEO. Give me a torch. I am not for this ambling.
Being but heavy,[3] I will bear the light.

MERCUTIO. Nay, gentle Romeo, we must have you dance.

ROMEO. Not I, believe me. You have dancing shoes
15 With nimble soles; I have a soul of lead
So stakes me to the ground I cannot move.

MERCUTIO. You are a lover. Borrow Cupid's wings
And soar with them above a common bound.

12. I'll . . . move: If looking favorably at someone leads to liking him, I'll look at Paris in a way that will lead to liking him.
13. But . . . fly: But I won't look harder than you want me to.

◆ *Literature and Your Life*
Relate Juliet's reaction to times when you've been asked to perform a chore you don't want to do.

14. the County stays: The Count, Paris, is waiting.

1. this speech: Romeo asks whether he and his companions, being uninvited guests, should follow custom by announcing their arrival in a speech.
2. The . . . prolixity: Such wordiness is outdated. In the following lines, Benvolio says, in sum: "Let's forget about announcing our entrance with a show. The other guests can look over as they see fit. We'll dance a while, then leave."
3. heavy: Weighed down with sadness.

ROMEO. I am too sore enpiercèd with his shaft
20   To soar with his light feathers; and so bound
    I cannot bound a pitch above dull woe.
    Under love's heavy burden do I sink.

MERCUTIO. And, to sink in it, should you burden love—
    Too great oppression for a tender thing.

25 **ROMEO.** Is love a tender thing? It is too rough,
    Too rude, too boist'rous, and it pricks like thorn.

MERCUTIO. If love be rough with you, be rough with love.
    Prick love for pricking, and you beat love down.
    Give me a case to put my visage⁴ in.
30   A visor for a visor!⁵ What care I
    What curious eye doth quote deformities?⁶
    Here are the beetle brows shall blush for me.

BENVOLIO. Come, knock and enter; and no sooner in
    But every man betake him to his legs.⁷

35 **ROMEO.** A torch for me! Let wantons light of heart
    Tickle the senseless rushes⁸ with their heels;
    For I am proverbed with a grandsire phrase,⁹
    I'll be a candleholder and look on;
    The game was ne'er so fair, and I am done.¹⁰

40 **MERCUTIO.** Tut! Dun's the mouse, the constable's own word!¹¹
    If thou art Dun,¹² we'll draw thee from the mire
    Of this sir-reverence love, wherein thou stickest
    Up to the ears. Come, we burn daylight, ho!

ROMEO. Nay, that's not so.

MERCUTIO.   I mean, sir, in delay
45   We waste our lights in vain, like lights by day.
    Take our good meaning, for our judgment sits
    Five times in that ere once in our five wits.¹³

ROMEO. And we mean well in going to this masque,
    But 'tis no wit to go.

MERCUTIO.   Why, may one ask?

ROMEO. I dreamt a dream tonight.

50 **MERCUTIO.**   And so did I.

ROMEO. Well, what was yours?

MERCUTIO.   That dreamers often lie.

ROMEO. In bed asleep, while they do dream things true.

---

4. **visage:** Mask.
5. **A visor . . . visor!:** A mask for a mask—which is what my real face is like!
6. **quote deformities:** Notice my ugly features.
7. **betake . . . legs:** Start dancing.
8. **Let . . . rushes:** Let fun-loving people dance on the floor coverings.
9. **proverbed . . . phrase:** Directed by an old saying.
10. **The game . . . done:** No matter how much enjoyment may be had, I won't have any.
11. **Dun's . . . word!:** Lie low like a mouse—that's what a constable waiting to make an arrest might say.
12. **Dun:** Proverbial name for a horse.

13. **Take . . . wits:** Understand my intended meaning. That shows more intelligence than merely following what your senses perceive.

◆ **Literary Focus**
What can you tell about Mercutio's personality from his jokes and fanciful stories? In what way is he a foil for the sulky Romeo?

▲ **Critical Viewing** Their way lit by torchbearers, Romeo and his friends prepare to invite themselves to Capulet's feast. What do these uninvited guests need to do to attend the feast? [Infer]

MERCUTIO. O, then I see Queen Mab[14] hath been with you.
   She is the fairies' midwife, and she comes
55 In shape no bigger than an agate stone
   On the forefinger of an alderman,
   Drawn with a team of little atomies[15]
   Over men's noses as they lie asleep;
   Her wagon spokes made of long spinners'[16] legs,
60 The cover, of the wings of grasshoppers;
   Her traces, of the smallest spider web;
   Her collars, of the moonshine's wat'ry beams;
   Her whip, of cricket's bone; the lash, of film;[17]
   Her wagoner, a small gray-coated gnat,
65 Not half so big as a round little worm
   Pricked from the lazy finger of a maid;
   Her chariot is an empty hazelnut,
   Made by the joiner squirrel or old grub,[18]
   Time out o' mind the fairies' coachmakers.
70 And in this state she gallops night by night
   Through lovers' brains, and then they dream of love;
   On courtiers' knees, that dream on curtsies straight;
   O'er lawyers' fingers, who straight dream on fees;
   O'er ladies' lips, who straight on kisses dream,
75 Which oft the angry Mab with blisters plagues,

14. **Queen Mab:** The queen of fairyland.

15. **atomies:** Creatures.

16. **spinners:** Spiders.

17. **film:** Spider's thread.

18. **old grub:** An insect that bores holes in nuts.

Because their breath with sweetmeats[19] tainted are.
Sometimes she gallops o'er a courtier's nose,
And then dreams he of smelling out a suit;[20]
And sometime comes she with a tithe pig's[21] tail
80 Tickling a parson's nose as 'a lies asleep,
Then he dreams of another benefice.[22]
Sometime she driveth o'er a soldier's neck,
And then dream he of cutting foreign throats,
Of breaches, ambuscadoes,[23] Spanish blades,
85 Of healths[24] five fathom deep; and then anon
Drums in his ear, at which he starts and wakes,
And being thus frighted, swears a prayer or two
And sleeps again. This is that very Mab
That plats[25] the manes of horses in the night
90 And bakes the elflocks[26] in foul sluttish hairs,
Which once untangled much misfortune bodes.
This is the hag, when maids lie on their backs,
That presses them and learns them first to bear,
Making them women of good carriage.[27]
This is she—

95 **ROMEO.**   Peace, peace, Mercutio, peace!
Thou talk'st of nothing.

MERCUTIO.   True, I talk of dreams;
Which are the children of an idle brain,
Begot of nothing but vain fantasy;
Which is as thin of substance as the air,
100 And more inconstant than the wind, who woos
Even now the frozen bosom of the North
And, being angered, puffs away from thence,
Turning his side to the dew-dropping South.

BENVOLIO. This wind you talk of blows us from ourselves.
105 Supper is done, and we shall come too late.

ROMEO. I fear, too early; for my mind misgives
Some consequence yet hanging in the stars
Shall bitterly begin his fearful date
With this night's revels and expire the term
110 Of a despisèd life, closed in my breast,
By some vile forfeit of untimely death.[28]
But he that hath the steerage of my course
Direct my sail! On, lusty gentlemen!

BENVOLIO. Strike, drum.
                    [*They march about the stage, and retire to one side.*]

19. **sweetmeats:** Candy.

20. **smelling . . . suit:** Finding someone who has a petition (suit) for the king and who will pay the courtier to gain the king's favor for the petition.
21. **tithe pig:** A pig donated to a parson.
22. **benefice:** A church appointment that included a guaranteed income.
23. **ambuscadoes:** Ambushes.
24. **healths:** Toasts ("To your health!").
25. **plats:** Tangles.
26. **elflocks:** Tangled hair.

27. **carriage:** Posture.

28. **my mind . . . death:** My mind is fearful that some future event, fated by the stars, shall start to run its course tonight and cut my life short.

Scene v. *A hall in* CAPULET'*s house.*

[SERVINGMEN *come forth with napkins.*]

    FIRST SERVINGMAN. Where's Potpan, that he helps not to
      take away? He shift a trencher![1] He scrape a trencher!

    SECOND SERVINGMAN. When good manners shall lie all in one or two
      men's hands, and they unwashed too, 'tis a foul thing.

5 **FIRST SERVINGMAN.** Away with the join-stools, remove the
      court cupboard, look to the plate. Good thou, save me a
      piece of marchpane,[2] and, as thou loves me, let the porter
      let in Susan Grindstone and Nell. Anthony, and Potpan!

    SECOND SERVINGMAN. Ay, boy, ready.

10 **FIRST SERVINGMAN.** You are looked for and called for,
      asked for and sought for, in the great chamber.

    THIRD SERVINGMAN. We cannot be here and there too.
      Cheerly, boys! Be brisk awhile, and the longer liver
      take all.   [*Exit.*]

[*Enter* CAPULET, *his* WIFE, JULIET, TYBALT, NURSE, *and all the*
GUESTS *and* GENTLEWOMEN *to the* MASKERS.]

15 **CAPULET.** Welcome, gentlemen! Ladies that have their toes
      Unplagued with corns will walk a bout[3] with you.
      Ah, my mistresses, which of you all
      Will now deny to dance? She that makes dainty,[4]
      She I'll swear hath corns. Am I come near ye now?
20 Welcome, gentlemen! I have seen the day
      That I have worn a visor and could tell
      A whispering tale in a fair lady's ear,
      Such as would please. 'Tis gone, 'tis gone, 'tis gone.
      You are welcome, gentlemen! Come, musicians, play.
                          [*Music plays, and they dance.*]
25 A hall,[5] a hall! Give room! And foot it, girls.
      More light, you knaves, and turn the tables up,
      And quench the fire; the room is grown too hot.
      Ah, sirrah, this unlooked-for sport comes well.
      Nay, sit; nay, sit, good cousin Capulet;
30 For you and I are past our dancing days.
      How long is't now since last yourself and I
      Were in a mask?

    SECOND CAPULET. By'r Lady, thirty years.

    CAPULET. What, man? 'Tis not so much, 'tis not so much;

1. trencher: Wooden platter.

2. marchpane: Marzipan, a confection made of sugar and almonds.
3. walk a bout: Dance a turn.
4. makes dainty: Hesitates, acts shy.
5. A hall: Clear the floor, make room for dancing.

▲ **Critical Viewing** What can you tell about Romeo's personality from his words and behavior regarding Rosaline? **[Draw Conclusions]**

35	'Tis since the nuptial of Lucentio,	
	Come Pentecost as quickly as it will,	
	Some five-and-twenty years, and then we masked.	

SECOND CAPULET. 'Tis more, 'tis more. His son is elder, sir;
His son is thirty.

CAPULET.   Will you tell me that?
40   His son was but a ward[6] two years ago.

6. **ward:** Minor.

ROMEO. [*To a* SERVINGMAN] What lady's that which doth enrich the hand
Of yonder knight?

SERVINGMAN.   I know not, sir.

ROMEO. O, she doth teach the torches to burn bright!
It seems she hangs upon the cheek of night
45   As a rich jewel in an Ethiop's ear—
Beauty too rich for use, for earth too dear!
So shows a snowy dove trooping with crows
As yonder lady o'er her fellows shows.
The measure done, I'll watch her place of stand
50   And, touching hers, make blessèd my rude hand.
Did my heart love till now? Forswear[7] it, sight!
For I ne'er saw true beauty till this night.

7. **Forswear:** Deny.

TYBALT. This, by his voice, should be a Montague.
Fetch me my rapier, boy. What! Dares the slave
55   Come hither, covered with an antic face,[8]
To fleer[9] and scorn at our solemnity?
Now, by the stock and honor of my kin,
To strike him dead I hold it not a sin.

8. **antic face:** Strange, fantastic mask.
9. **fleer:** Mock.

CAPULET. Why, how now, kinsman? Wherefore storm you so?

60 **TYBALT.** Uncle, this is a Montague, our foe,
A villain, that is hither come in spite
To scorn at our solemnity this night.

CAPULET. Young Romeo is it?

TYBALT.   'Tis he, that villain Romeo.

CAPULET. Content thee, gentle coz,[10] let him alone.
65   'A bears him like a portly gentleman,[11]
And, to say truth, Verona brags of him
To be a virtuous and well-governed youth.
I would not for the wealth of all this town
Here in my house do him disparagement.[12]
70   Therefore be patient; take no note of him.
It is my will, the which if thou respect,

10. **coz:** Here coz is used as a term of address for a relative.
11. **'A . . . gentleman:** He behaves like a dignified gentleman.
12. **disparagement:** Insult.

Show a fair presence and put off these frowns,
An ill-beseeming semblance[13] for a feast.

TYBALT. It fits when such a villain is a guest.
I'll not endure him.

75 **CAPULET.**   He shall be endured.
What, goodman[14] boy! I say he shall. Go to![15]
Am I the master here, or you? Go to!
You'll not endure him, God shall mend my soul![16]
You'll make a mutiny among my guests!
80 You will set cock-a-hoop.[17] You'll be the man!

TYBALT. Why, uncle, 'tis a shame.

CAPULET.   Go to, go to!
You are a saucy boy. Is't so, indeed?
This trick may chance to scathe you.[18] I know what.
You must contrary me! Marry, 'tis time–
85 Well said, my hearts!—You are a princox[19]—go!
Be quiet, or—more light, more light!—For shame!
I'll make you quiet. What!—Cheerly, my hearts!

TYBALT. Patience perforce with willful choler meeting[20]
Makes my flesh tremble in their different greeting.
90 I will withdraw; but this intrusion shall,
Now seeming sweet, convert to bitt'rest gall.   *[Exit.]*

ROMEO. If I profane with my unworthiest hand
This holy shrine,[21] the gentle sin is this:
My lips, two blushing pilgrims, ready stand
95 To smooth that rough touch with a tender kiss.

JULIET. Good pilgrim, you do wrong your hand too much,
Which mannerly devotion shows in this;
For saints have hands that pilgrims' hands do touch
And palm to palm is holy palmers'[22] kiss.

100 **ROMEO.** Have not saints lips, and holy palmers too?

JULIET. Ay, pilgrim, lips that they must use in prayer.

ROMEO. O, then, dear saint, let lips do what hands do!
They pray; grant thou, lest faith turn to despair.

JULIET. Saints do not move,[23] though grant for prayers' sake.

105 **ROMEO.** Then move not while my prayer's effect I take.
Thus from my lips, by thine my sin is purged.   *[Kisses her.]*

JULIET. Then have my lips the sin that they have took.

13. ill-beseeming semblance: Inappropriate appearance.
14. goodman: Term of address for someone below the rank of gentleman.
15. Go to!: Expression of angry impatience.
16. God . . . soul!: Expression of impatience, equivalent to, "God save me!"
17. You will set cock-a-hoop: You want to swagger like a barnyard rooster.

18. This . . . you: This trait of yours may turn to hurt you.
19. princox: Rude youngster; wise guy.

20. Patience . . . meeting: Enforced self-control mixing with strong anger.

21. shrine: Juliet's hand.

22. palmers: Pilgrims who at one time carried palm branches from the Holy Land.

◆ Literary Focus
What character traits do Romeo and Juliet reveal in the words they say to each other?

23. move: Initiate involvement in earthly affairs.

ROMEO. Sin from my lips? O trespass sweetly urged![24]
    Give me my sin again.   [*Kisses her.*]

JULIET.   You kiss by th' book.[25]

110   **NURSE.** Madam, your mother craves a word with you.

ROMEO. What is her mother?

NURSE.   Marry, bachelor,
    Her mother is the lady of the house,
    And a good lady, and a wise and virtuous.
    I nursed her daughter that you talked withal.
115   I tell you, he that can lay hold of her
    Shall have the chinks.[26]

ROMEO.   Is she a Capulet?
    O dear account! My life is my foe's debt.[27]

BENVOLIO. Away, be gone; the sport is at the best.

ROMEO. Ay, so I fear; the more is my unrest.

120   **CAPULET.** Nay, gentlemen, prepare not to be gone;
    We have a trifling foolish banquet towards.[28]
    Is it e'en so?[29] Why then, I thank you all.
    I thank you, honest gentlemen. Good night.
    More torches here! Come on then; let's to bed.
125   Ah, sirrah, by my fay,[30] it waxes late;
    I'll to my rest.
    [*Exit all but* JULIET *and* NURSE.]

24. O . . . urged!: Romeo is saying, in substance, that he is happy. Juliet calls his kiss a sin, for now he can take it back—by another kiss.
25. by th' book: As if you were following a manual of courtly love.

26. chinks: Cash.
27. My life . . . debt: since Juliet is a Capulet, Romeo's life is at the mercy of the enemies of his family.

28. towards: Being prepared.
29. Is . . . so?: Is it the case that you really must leave?
30. fay: Faith.

▼ **Critical Viewing** What does Romeo and Juliet's formal, stylized conversation reveal about the time and culture in which the story takes place? **[Infer]**

JULIET. Come hither, nurse. What is yond gentleman?

NURSE. The son and heir of old Tiberio.

JULIET. What's he that now is going out of door?

130 **NURSE.** Marry, that, I think, be young Petruchio.

JULIET. What's he that follows here, that would not dance?

NURSE. I know not.

JULIET. Go ask his name—If he is married,
My grave is like to be my wedding bed.

135 **NURSE.** His name is Romeo, and a Montague,
The only son of your great enemy.

JULIET. My only love, sprung from my only hate!
Too early seen unknown, and known too late!
Prodigious³¹ birth of love it is to me
140 That I must love a loathèd enemy.

31. Prodigious: Monstrous; foretelling misfortune.

NURSE. What's this? What's this?

JULIET.   A rhyme I learnt even now.
Of one I danced withal. [*One calls within,* "Juliet."]

NURSE.   Anon, anon!
Come, let's away; the strangers all are gone.   [*Exit.*]

Guide for Responding

◆ Literature and Your Life

Reader's Response If you were Romeo and Juliet, would you pursue a relationship? Explain.

Thematic Focus What are some signs that the Capulet-Montague feud might be worked out peacefully? What are some obstacles to achieving this goal?

☑ Check Your Comprehension

1. How does Romeo's attitude change during the course of this act?
2. What possible threats to Romeo's and Juliet's love already exist in Act I?

◆ Critical Thinking

INTERPRET

1. Compare and contrast the personalities of Romeo and Juliet in Act I. **[Compare and Contrast]**
2. How does Juliet's comment when she sends her nurse to find out Romeo's name echo back to the Prologue? **[Connect]**
3. How does Shakespeare generate suspense in the first act? **[Support]**

EXTEND

4. Based on the Prologue and other hints provided in the first act, what do you think will happen as the plot unfolds? Why? **[Predict]**

Guide for Responding (continued)

◆ Reading Strategy

USE TEXT AIDS

Using **text aids**—the explanations of words and passages appearing in the margins—makes it easier to understand the English of Shakespeare's day.

1. Rewrite Capulet's scolding of Tybalt in Scene iv, lines 77–89, substituting the words in the text aids for the annotated words in the play.
2. Using your answer to question 1, express Capulet's meaning in your own words.

◆ Build Grammar Skills

PUNCTUATING WORDS OF DIRECT ADDRESS

When **words of direct address** appear in the middle of a sentence, they are preceded and followed by commas; when used at the beginning of a sentence, they are followed by a comma; and when used at the end, they are preceded by a comma.

Practice On a sheet of paper, correct the following sentences of dialogue from *The Tragedy of Romeo and Juliet*.

1. Nurse where's my daughter?
2. Good morrow cousin.
3. Turn thee Benvolio; look upon thy death.
4. My noble uncle do you know the cause?
5. I thank you honest gentlemen.

◆ Literary Focus

CHARACTER

Shakespeare's play includes a variety of memorable **characters**—people who take part in the action of a literary work.

1. Gregory and Sampson are both **flat characters** —characters with one dimension—who appear only in the first scene. What personality trait do they embody and what purpose do they serve in the play?
2. Romeo, Mercutio, and Benvolio are all **round characters**—characters with many personality traits. List the character traits of each one.
3. A **dramatic foil** is a character whose personality traits contrast with and highlight those of another character. In what ways are Benvolio and Mercutio dramatic foils for Romeo?

◆ Build Vocabulary

USING THE PREFIX *trans-*

The prefix *trans-* means "through" or "across." Define each of these words. Incorporate the definition of *trans-* into each answer.

1. transcontinental   **3.** translate   **5.** transform
2. transport   **4.** transplant

USING THE WORD BANK

Write the letter of the word that is the best synonym of the first word.

1. pernicious: (a) harmful, (b) courageous, (c) helpful
2. augmenting: (a) propelling, (b) increasing, (c) decreasing
3. grievance: (a) confusion, (b) praise, (c) complaint
4. transgression: (a) crime, (b) deed, (c) travel
5. heretics: (a) believers, (b) learners, (c) dissenters

Idea Bank

Writing

1. **Advice Column** Write a letter from Romeo or Juliet to an advice columnist in which he or she asks what to do about falling in love with the wrong person. Then write the advice columnist's response. **[Career Link]**

2. **Character Analysis** Choose one of the main characters introduced in the first act. Then write a short essay in which you analyze this character's personality traits.

Speaking and Listening

3. **Reading** Select a scene from Act I to perform with the appropriate number of classmates. Practice reading your lines aloud so that you can deliver them meaningfully. Pay attention to other people's lines so that you can respond to what they say with feeling. After you have practiced several times, perform your reading for the class. **[Performing Arts Link]**

Guide for Reading, Act II

◆ Review and Anticipate

In Act I, you learned of a bitter, long-standing feud between two families, the Montagues and the Capulets. You were also introduced to the play's title characters, who meet at a feast at the Capulets' house. Having immediately fallen in love, Romeo and Juliet discover that they come from opposing sides of the Capulet-Montague feud.

Based on what you've learned about the personalities of Romeo and Juliet, how do you expect them to respond to their love for each other? Will they pursue their love? Will they reveal their love to their families? How do you think their families will react?

◆ Literary Focus

BLANK VERSE

Blank verse is unrhymed verse written in iambic pentameter, or ten-syllable lines in which every second syllable is stressed. For example, when Romeo sees Juliet appear at her window, he exclaims,

> Bŭt sóft! Whăt líght thrŏugh yóndĕr wíndŏw bréaks?
> Ĭt ĭs thĕ eást, ănd Júlĭĕt ĭs thĕ sún!

Much of *Romeo and Juliet* is written in blank verse. This formal meter is well suited to serious subjects and has been used in many of the greatest poems and verse dramas in English. In Shakespeare's plays, important or aristocratic characters typically speak in blank verse. Minor or comic characters most often do not speak in verse.

Lines in iambic pentameter can also be rhymed. This gives extra emphasis to the words a character speaks. In addition, a sense of completeness or finality is created when two successive lines rhyme, forming a rhymed couplet. Because of this, the exits of major characters and the ends of scenes are often marked by a rhymed couplet.

◆ Build Grammar Skills

LOGICAL COMPARISONS

Shakespeare frequently uses memorable, striking comparisons in his plays. Look at the following example, which compares the name *rose* to all other flower names.

> That which we call a rose / By any other name would smell as sweet.

Whenever one member of a group is compared to other members—as in this example—the word *other* or *else* must be included to create a **logical comparison.** You'll notice that if the word *other* were omitted from the previous passage, the name *rose* would be illogically compared with itself as well as with all other names.

◆ Reading Strategy

READING BLANK VERSE

Blank verse can be a little distracting if you are not used to it. Like a really good song, blank verse can get you so absorbed in admiring the skill needed to produce it that you miss the meaning. To get the most meaning out of blank verse, keep in mind that thoughts or phrases do not necessarily end with the end of the line. Whether you read the words aloud or to yourself, read blank verse in sentences, pausing where the punctuation indicates and not necessarily at the end of every line.

◆ Build Vocabulary

PREFIXES: *inter-*

In Act II, you'll encounter the word *intercession,* which includes the prefix *inter-,* meaning "between" or "among." The word *intercession* refers to the act of going between two people or groups involved in a dispute in an effort to resolve the dispute. What other words can you think of that contain the prefix *inter-?*

WORD BANK

Before you read, preview this list of words.

cunning
procure
vile
predominant
intercession
sallow
waverer
lamentable
unwieldy

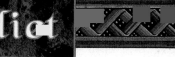

Act II

Prologue

[*Enter* CHORUS.]

> **CHORUS.** Now old desire[1] doth in his deathbed lie,
>   And young affection gapes to be his heir;[2]
> That fair[3] for which love groaned for and would die,
>   With tender Juliet matched, is now not fair.
> 5   Now Romeo is beloved and loves again,
>   Alike bewitchèd[4] by the charm of looks;
> But to his foe supposed he must complain,[5]
>   And she steal love's sweet bait from fearful hooks.
> Being held a foe, he may not have access
> 10   To breathe such vows as lovers use to swear,
> And she as much in love, her means much less
>   To meet her new belovèd anywhere;
> But passion lends them power, time means to meet,
>   Temp'ring extremities with extreme sweet.[6]

[*Exit.*]

1. **old desire:** Romeo's love for Rosaline.
2. **young . . . heir:** Romeo's new love for Juliet is eager to replace his love for Rosaline.
3. **fair:** Beautiful woman (Rosaline).
4. **Alike bewitched:** Both Romeo and Juliet are enchanted.
5. **complain:** Address his words of love.
6. **Temp'ring . . . sweet:** Easing their difficulties with great delights.

Scene i. *Near* CAPULET'S *orchard.*

[*Enter* ROMEO *alone.*]

> **ROMEO.** Can I go forward when my heart is here?
> Turn back, dull earth,[1] and find thy center[2] out.

[*Enter* BENVOLIO *with* MERCUTIO. ROMEO *retires.*]

> **BENVOLIO.** Romeo! My cousin Romeo! Romeo!

> **MERCUTIO.**   He is wise.
>   And, on my life, hath stol'n him home to bed.

> 5 **BENVOLIO.** He ran this way and leapt this orchard wall.
>   Call, good Mercutio.

> **MERCUTIO.**   Nay, I'll conjure[3] too.
>   Romeo! Humors! Madman! Passion! Lover!
>   Appear thou in the likeness of a sigh;
>   Speak but one rhyme, and I am satisfied!
> 10   Cry but "Ay me!" pronounce but "love" and "dove";
>   Speak to my gossip[4] Venus one fair word,
>   One nickname for her purblind son and heir,
>   Young Abraham Cupid, he that shot so true

1. **dull earth:** Lifeless body.
2. **center:** Heart, or possibly soul (Juliet).

3. **conjure:** Recite a spell to make Romeo appear.

4. **gossip:** Merry old lady.

When King Cophetua loved the beggar maid!
15 He heareth not, he stirreth not, he moveth not;
The ape is dead,[5] and I must conjure him.
I conjure thee by Rosaline's bright eyes,
By her high forehead and her scarlet lip,
By her fine foot, straight leg, and quivering thigh,
20 And the demesnes that there adjacent lie,
That in thy likeness thou appear to us!

BENVOLIO. And if he hear thee, thou wilt anger him.

MERCUTIO. This cannot anger him. 'Twould anger him
To raise a spirit in his mistress' circle
25 Of some strange nature, letting it there stand
Till she had laid it and conjured it down.
That were some spite; my invocation
Is fair and honest; in his mistress' name,
I conjure only but to raise up him.

30 **BENVOLIO.** Come, he hath hid himself among these trees
To be consorted[6] with the humorous[7] night.
Blind is his love and best befits the dark.

MERCUTIO. If love be blind, love cannot hit the mark.
Now will he sit under a medlar tree
35 And wish his mistress were that kind of fruit
As maids call medlars[8] when they laugh alone.
O, Romeo, that she were, O that she were
An open *et cetera*, thou a pop'rin pear!
Romeo, good night. I'll to my truckle bed;[9]
40 This field bed is too cold for me to sleep.
Come, shall we go?

BENVOLIO.   Go then, for 'tis in vain
To seek him here that means not to be found.

[*Exit with others.*]

Scene ii. CAPULET'S *orchard.*

ROMEO. [*Coming forward*] He jests at scars that never felt a wound.

[*Enters* JULIET *at a window.*]

But soft! What light through yonder window breaks?
It is the East, and Juliet is the sun!
Arise, fair sun, and kill the envious moon,
5 Who is already sick and pale with grief
That thou her maid art far more fair than she.
Be not her maid, since she is envious.

5. The ape is dead:
Romeo, like a trained monkey, seems to be playing.

6. consorted: Associated.
7. humorous: Humid; moody, like a lover.

8. medlars: Applelike fruits.

9. truckle bed: Trundlebed, placed under a larger bed when not in use.

◆ **Literary Focus**
What effect does Shakespeare achieve by breaking up a rhymed couplet into two separate scenes?

Her vestal livery[1] is but sick and green,
And none but fools do wear it. Cast it off.

10 It is my lady! O, it is my love!
O, that she knew she were!
She speaks, yet she says nothing. What of that?
Her eye discourses; I will answer it.
I am too bold; 'tis not to me she speaks.

15 Two of the fairest stars in all the heaven,
Having some business, do entreat her eyes
To twinkle in their spheres[2] till they return.
What if her eyes were there, they in her head?
The brightness of her cheek would shame those stars

20 As daylight doth a lamp; her eyes in heaven
Would through the airy region stream so bright
That birds would sing and think it were not night.
See how she leans her cheek upon that hand,
O, that I were a glove upon that hand,
That I might touch that cheek!

JULIET.   Ay me!

25 **ROMEO.**   She speaks.
O, speak again, bright angel, for thou art
As glorious to this night, being o'er my head,
As is a wingèd messenger of heaven
Unto the white-upturnèd wond'ring eyes

30 Of mortals that fall back to gaze on him
When he bestrides the lazy puffing clouds
And sails upon the bosom of the air.

JULIET. O Romeo, Romeo! Wherefore art thou Romeo?[3]
Deny thy father and refuse thy name;

35 Or, if thou wilt not, be but sworn my love,
And I'll no longer be a Capulet.

ROMEO. [*Aside*] Shall I hear more, or shall I speak at this?

JULIET. 'Tis but thy name that is my enemy.
Thou art thyself, though not[4] a Montague.

40 What's Montague? It is nor hand, nor foot,
Nor arm, nor face. O, be some other name
Belonging to a man.
What's in a name? That which we call a rose
By any other name would smell as sweet.

45 So Romeo would, were he not Romeo called,
Retain that dear perfection which he owes[5]
Without that title. Romeo, doff[6] thy name;

---

1. **livery:** Clothing or costume worn by a servant.

2. **spheres:** Orbits.

◆ **Reading Strategy**
How does reading Romeo's speech in complete sentences help you grasp its meaning?

3. **Wherefore . . . Romeo?** Why are you Romeo—a Montague?

4. **though not:** Even if you were not.

5. **owes:** Owns; possesses.
6. **doff:** Remove.

And for thy name, which is no part of thee,
Take all myself.

ROMEO.   I take thee at thy word.
50   Call me but love, and I'll be new baptized;
Henceforth I never will be Romeo.

JULIET. What man art thou, thus bescreened in night,
So stumblest on my counsel?[7]

ROMEO.   By a name
I know not how to tell thee who I am.
55   My name, dear saint, is hateful to myself
Because it is an enemy to thee.
Had I it written, I would tear the word.

JULIET. My ears have yet not drunk a hundred words
Of thy tongue's uttering, yet I know the sound.
60   Art thou not Romeo, and a Montague?

ROMEO. Neither, fair maid, if either thee dislike.

JULIET. How camest thou hither, tell me, and wherefore?
The orchard walls are high and hard to climb,
And the place death, considering who thou art,
65   If any of my kinsmen find thee here.

ROMEO. With love's light wings did I o'erperch[8] these walls;
For stony limits cannot hold love out,
And what love can do, that dares love attempt.
Therefore thy kinsmen are no stop to me.

70   **JULIET.** If they do see thee, they will murder thee.

ROMEO. Alack, there lies more peril in thine eye
Than twenty of their swords! Look thou but sweet,
And I am proof[9] against their enmity.

JULIET. I would not for the world they saw thee here.

75   **ROMEO.** I have night's cloak to hide me from their eyes;
And but[10] thou love me, let them find me here.
My life were better ended by their hate
Than death prorogued,[11] wanting of thy love.

JULIET. By whose direction found'st thou out this place?

80   **ROMEO.** By love, that first did prompt me to inquire.
He lent me counsel, and I lent him eyes.
I am no pilot; yet, wert thou as far
As that vast shore washed with the farthest sea,
I should adventure[12] for such merchandise.

◄ Critical Viewing
When Romeo enters the Capulets' orchard, he overhears Juliet talking to herself. What do Juliet's musings to herself and her later conversation with Romeo reveal about her character? [Draw Conclusions]

85 **JULIET.** Thou knowest the mask of night is on my face;
Else would a maiden blush bepaint my cheek
For that which thou hast heard me speak tonight.
Fain would I dwell on form¹³—fain, fain deny
What I have spoke; but farewell compliment!¹⁴
90 Dost thou love me? I know thou wilt say "Ay";
And I will take thy word. Yet, if thou swear'st,
Thou mayst prove false. At lovers' perjuries,
They say Jove laughs. O gentle Romeo,
If thou dost love, pronounce it faithfully.
95 Or if thou thinkest I am too quickly won,
I'll frown and be perverse¹⁵ and say thee nay,
So thou wilt woo; but else, not for the world.
In truth, fair Montague, I am too fond,¹⁶
And therefore thou mayst think my havior light;¹⁷
100 But trust me, gentleman, I'll prove more true
Than those that have more <u>cunning</u> to be strange.¹⁸
I should have been more strange, I must confess,
But that thou overheard'st, ere I was ware,
My truelove passion. Therefore pardon me,
105 And not impute this yielding to light love,
Which the dark night hath so discoveréd.¹⁹

    ROMEO. Lady, by yonder blessèd moon I vow,

13. **Fain . . . form:** Eagerly would I follow convention (by acting reserved).
14. **compliment:** Conventional behavior.

15. **be perverse:** Act contrary to my true feelings.

16. **fond:** Affectionate.

17. **my havior light:** My behavior immodest or unserious.
18. **strange:** Distant and cold.
19. **discoveréd:** Revealed.

◆ **Build Vocabulary**
cunning (kun´ iŋ) *n.*: Cleverness; slyness

That tips with silver all these fruit-tree tops—

JULIET. O, swear not by the moon, th' inconstant moon,
110   That monthly changes in her circle orb,
      Lest that thy love prove likewise variable.

ROMEO. What shall I swear by?

JULIET.   Do not swear at all;
      Or if thou wilt, swear by thy gracious self,
115   Which is the god of my idolatry,
      And I'll believe thee.

      ROMEO.   If my heart's dear love—

JULIET. Well, do not swear. Although I joy in thee,
      I have no joy of this contract[20] tonight.
      It is too rash, too unadvised, too sudden;
      Too like the lightning, which doth cease to be
120   Ere one can say it lightens. Sweet, good night!
      This bud of love, by summer's ripening breath,
      May prove a beauteous flow'r when next we meet.
      Good night, good night! As sweet repose and rest
      Come to thy heart as that within my breast!

125 **ROMEO.** O, wilt thou leave me so unsatisfied?

JULIET. What satisfaction canst thou have tonight?

ROMEO. Th' exchange of thy love's faithful vow for mine.

JULIET. I gave thee mine before thou didst request it;
      And yet I would it were to give again.

130 **ROMEO.** Wouldst thou withdraw it? For what purpose, love?

JULIET. But to be frank[21] and give it thee again.
      And yet I wish but for the thing I have.
      My bounty[22] is as boundless as the sea,
      My love as deep; the more I give to thee,
135   The more I have, for both are infinite,
      I hear some noise within. Dear love, adieu!

[NURSE *calls within.*]

      Anon, good nurse! Sweet Montague, be true.
      Stay but a little, I will come again.   [*Exit.*]

      ROMEO. O blessèd, blessèd night! I am afeard,
140   Being in night, all this is but a dream,
      Too flattering-sweet to be substantial.[23]

              [*Enter* JULIET *again.*]

◆ **Reading Strategy**
How would you rephrase in standard English what Romeo and Juliet are saying to each other?

20. **contract:** Betrothal.

21. **frank:** Generous.

22. **bounty:** What I have to give.

23. **substantial:** Real.

JULIET. Three words, dear Romeo, and good night indeed.
If that thy bent[24] of love be honorable,
Thy purpose marriage, send me word tomorrow,
145   By one that I'll procure to come to thee,
Where and what time thou wilt perform the rite;
And all my fortunes at thy foot I'll lay
And follow thee my lord throughout the world.

NURSE. [*Within*] Madam!

JULIET. I come anon.—But if thou meanest not well,
150   I do beseech thee—

NURSE.   [*Within*] Madam!

JULIET.   By and by[25] I come.—
To cease thy strife[26] and leave me to my grief.
Tomorrow will I send.

ROMEO.   So thrive my soul—

JULIET. A thousand times good night!   [*Exit.*]

155 **ROMEO.** A thousand times the worse, to want thy light!
Love goes toward love as schoolboys from their books;
But love from love, toward school with heavy looks.

[*Enter* JULIET *again.*]

JULIET. Hist! Romeo, hist! O for a falc'ner's voice
To lure this tassel gentle[27] back again!
160   Bondage is hoarse[28] and may not speak aloud,
Else would I tear the cave where Echo[29] lies
And make her airy tongue more hoarse than mine
With repetition of "My Romeo!"

ROMEO. It is my soul that calls upon my name.
165   How silver-sweet sound lovers' tongues by night,
Like softest music to attending ears!

JULIET. Romeo!

ROMEO.   My sweet?

JULIET.   What o'clock tomorrow
Shall I send to thee?

ROMEO.   By the hour of nine.

JULIET. I will not fail. 'Tis twenty year till then.
170   I have forgot why I did call thee back.

ROMEO. Let me stand here till thou remember it.

24. **bent:** Purpose;
intention.

25. **By and by:** At once.
26. **strife:** Efforts.

27. **tassel gentle:** Male
falcon.
28. **Bondage is hoarse:**
Being bound in by my
family restricts my speech.
29. **Echo:** In classical
mythology, the nymph Echo,
unable to win the love of
Narcissus, wasted away in
a cave until nothing was left
of her but her voice.

◆ **Reading Strategy**
Notice that Juliet's
question (ll.167–168),
although broken into
two lines, is actually
a single sentence.

◆ **Build Vocabulary**
procure (prō kyoor') *v.*:
Get; obtain

JULIET. I shall forget, to have thee still stand there,
    Rememb'ring how I love thy company.

ROMEO. And I'll stay, to have thee still forget,
175   Forgetting any other home but this.

JULIET. 'Tis almost morning. I would have thee gone—
    And yet no farther than a wanton's[30] bird,
    That lets it hop a little from his hand,
    Like a poor prisoner in his twisted gyves,[31]
180   And with a silken thread plucks it back again,
    So loving-jealous of his liberty.

ROMEO. I would I were thy bird.

JULIET.   Sweet, so would I.
    Yet I should kill thee with much cherishing.
    Good night, good night! Parting is such sweet sorrow
185   That I shall say good night till it be morrow. [*Exit.*]

ROMEO. Sleep dwell upon thine eyes, peace in thy breast!
    Would I were sleep and peace, so sweet to rest!
    Hence will I to my ghostly friar's[32] close cell,[33]
    His help to crave and my dear hap[34] to tell.   [*Exit.*]

Scene iii. FRIAR LAWRENCE'S *cell.*

[*Enter* FRIAR LAWRENCE *alone, with a basket.*]

FRIAR. The gray-eyed morn smiles on the frowning night,
    Check'ring the eastern clouds with streaks of light;
    And fleckèd[1] darkness like a drunkard reels
    From forth day's path and Titan's burning wheels.[2]
5   Now, ere the sun advance his burning eye
    The day to cheer and night's dank dew to dry,
    I must upfill this osier cage[3] of ours
    With baleful[4] weeds and precious-juicèd flowers.
    The earth that's nature's mother is her tomb.
10   What is her burying grave, that is her womb;
    And from her womb children of divers kind[5]
    We sucking on her natural bosom find,
    Many for many virtues excellent,
    None but for some, and yet all different.
15   O, mickle[6] is the powerful grace[7] that lies
    In plants, herbs, stones, and their true qualities;
    For naught so <u>vile</u> that on the earth doth live
    But to the earth some special good doth give;
    Nor aught so good but, strained[8] from that fair use,

---

30. wanton's: Spoiled, playful child's.

31. gyves (jīvz): Chains.

32. ghostly friar's: Spiritual father's.
33. close cell: Small room.
34. dear hap: Good fortune.

1. fleckèd: Spotted.

2. Titan's burning wheels: Wheels of the sun god's chariot.

3. osier cage: Willow basket.
4. baleful: Poisonous.

5. divers kind: Different kinds.
6. mickle: Great.
7. grace: Divine power.
8. strained: Turned away.

◆ **Build Vocabulary**

vile (vīl) *adj.:* Worthless; cheap; low

20   Revolts from true birth,[9] stumbling on abuse.
      Virtue itself turns vice, being misapplied,
      And vice sometime by action dignified.

[*Enter* ROMEO.]

      Within the infant rind[10] of this weak flower
      Poison hath residence and medicine power;[11]
25   For this, being smelt, with that part cheers each part;[12]
      Being tasted, stays all senses with the heart.[13]
      Two such opposèd kings encamp them still[14]
      In man as well as herbs—grace and rude will;
      And where the worser is <u>predominant</u>,
30   Full soon the canker[15] death eats up that plant.

      ROMEO. Good morrow, father.

      FRIAR.   *Benedicite!*[16]
      What early tongue so sweet saluteth me?
      Young son, it argues a distemperèd head[17]
      So soon to bid good morrow to thy bed.
35   Care keeps his watch in every old man's eye,
      And where care lodges, sleep will never lie;
      But where unbruisèd youth with unstuffed[18] brain
      Doth couch his limbs, there golden sleep doth reign,
      Therefore thy earliness doth me assure
40   Thou art uproused with some distemp'rature;[19]
      Or if not so, then here I hit it right—
      Our Romeo hath not been in bed tonight.

      ROMEO. That last is true. The sweeter rest was mine.

      FRIAR. God pardon sin! Wast thou with Rosaline?

45   **ROMEO.** With Rosaline, my ghostly father? No.
      I have forgot that name and that name's woe.

      FRIAR. That's my good son! But where hast thou been then?

      ROMEO. I'll tell thee ere thou ask it me again.
      I have been feasting with mine enemy,
50   Where on a sudden one hath wounded me
      That's by me wounded. Both our remedies
      Within thy help and holy physic[20] lies.
      I bear no hatred, blessèd man, for, lo,
      My <u>intercession</u> likewise steads my foe.[21]

55   **FRIAR.** Be plain, good son, and homely in thy drift.[22]
      Riddling confession finds but riddling shrift.[23]

      ROMEO. Then plainly know my heart's dear love is set

---

9. Revolts . . . birth: Conflicts with its real purpose.

10. infant rind: Tender skin.

11. and medicine power: And medicinal quality has power.

12. with . . . part: With that quality—odor—revives each part of the body.

13. stays . . . heart: Kills (stops the working of the five senses along with the heart).

14. still: Always.

15. canker: A destructive caterpillar.

16. *Benedicite!*: God bless you!

17. distemperèd head: Troubled mind.

18. unstuffed: Not filled with cares.

19. distemp'rature: Illness.

20. physic (fiz′ ik): Medicine.

21. My . . . foe: My plea also helps my enemy (Juliet, a Capulet).

22. and . . . drift: And simple in your speech.

23. Riddling . . . shrift: A confusing confession will get you uncertain forgiveness. The Friar means that unless Romeo speaks clearly, he will not get clear and direct advice.

◆ **Build Vocabulary**

predominant (prē däm′ ə nənt) *adj.*: Having dominating influence over others

intercession (in′ tər sesh′ ən) *n.*: The act of pleading on behalf of another

On the fair daughter of rich Capulet;
As mine on hers, so hers is set on mine,
60 And all combined, save[24] what thou must combine
By holy marriage. When and where and how
We met, we wooed, and made exchange of vow,
I'll tell thee as we pass; but this I pray,
That thou consent to marry us today.

65 **FRIAR.** Holy Saint Francis! What a change is here!
Is Rosaline, that thou didst love so dear,
So soon forsaken? Young men's love then lies
Not truly in their hearts, but in their eyes.
Jesu Maria! What a deal of brine[25]
70 Hath washed thy <u>sallow</u> cheeks for Rosaline!
How much salt water thrown away in waste
To season love, that of it doth not taste!
The sun not yet thy sighs from heaven clears,
Thy old groans ring yet in mine ancient ears.
75 Lo, here upon thy cheek the stain doth sit
Of an old tear that is not washed off yet.
If e'er thou wast thyself, and these woes thine,
Thou and these woes were all for Rosaline.
And art thou changed? Pronounce this sentence then:
80 Women may fall[26] when there's no strength[27] in men.

ROMEO. Thou chidst me oft for loving Rosaline.

FRIAR. For doting,[28] not for loving, pupil mine.

ROMEO. And badst[29] me bury love.

FRIAR.   Not in a grave
To lay one in, another out to have.

85 **ROMEO.** I pray thee chide me not. Her I love now
Doth grace[30] for grace and love for love allow.[31]
The other did not so.

FRIAR.   O, she knew well
Thy love did read by rote, that could not spell.[32]
But come, young <u>waverer</u>, come go with me.
90 In one respect I'll thy assistant be;
For this alliance may so happy prove
To turn your households' rancor[33] to pure love.

ROMEO. O, let us hence! I stand on[34] sudden haste.

FRIAR. Wisely and slow. They stumble that run fast.   [*Exit.*]

24. **And . . . save:** And we
are united in every way,
except for (save).

25. **brine:** Salt water
(tears).

◆ **Literary Focus**
Which syllables are
stressed and which
are unstressed in
Friar Lawrence's
speech ?

26. **fall:** Be weak or
inconstant.
27. **strength:** Constancy;
stability.
28. **doting:** Being
infatuated.
29. **badst:** Urged.
30. **grace:** Favor.
31. **allow:** Give.
32. **Thy . . . spell:** Your
love was someone who
recites words from memory
with no understanding of
them.
33. **rancor:** Hatred.
34. **stand on:** Insist on.

◆ **Build Vocabulary**
sallow (sal′ ō) *adj.:* Of a
sickly, pale-yellowish
complexion

waverer (wā′ vər ər) *n.:*
One who changes or is
unsteady

Scene iv. *A street.*

[*Enter* BENVOLIO *and* MERCUTIO.]

    MERCUTIO. Where the devil should this Romeo be?
      Came he not home tonight?

    BENVOLIO. Not to his father's. I spoke with his man.

    MERCUTIO. Why, that same pale hardhearted wench, that Rosaline,
5   Torments him so that he will sure run mad.

    BENVOLIO. Tybalt, the kinsman to old Capulet,
      Hath sent a letter to his father's house.

    MERCUTIO. A challenge, on my life.

    BENVOLIO. Romeo will answer it.

10   **MERCUTIO.** Any man that can write may answer a letter.

    BENVOLIO. Nay, he will answer the letter's master, how he dares, being
      dared.

    MERCUTIO. Alas, poor Romeo, he is already dead: stabbed
      with a white wench's black eye; run through the ear
15   with a love song; the very pin of his heart cleft with the
      blind bow-boy's butt-shaft;[1] and is he a man to encounter Tybalt?

    BENVOLIO. Why, what is Tybalt?

    MERCUTIO. More than Prince of Cats.[2] O, he's the coura-
      geous captain of compliments.[3] He fights as you sing
20   pricksong [4]—keeps time, distance, and proportion; he
      rests his minim rests,[5] one, two, and the third in your
      bosom! The very butcher of a silk button,[6] a duelist, a
      duelist! A gentleman of the very first house,[7] of the first
      and second cause.[8] Ah, the immortal *passado!* The
25   *punto reverso!* The hay![9]

    BENVOLIO. The what?

    MERCUTIO. The pox of such antic, lisping, affecting fantas-
      ticoes—these new tuners of accent![10] By Jesu, a very
      good blade! A very tall man! A very good whore! Why,
30   is not this a <u>lamentable</u> thing, grandsir, that we
      should be thus afflicted with these strange flies, these
      fashionmongers, these pardon-me's,[11] who stand so
      much on the new form that they cannot sit at ease on
      the old bench? O, their bones, their bones!

[*Enter* ROMEO.]

1. **pin . . . butt-shaft:**
Center of his heart pierced
by Cupid's blunt arrow.
2. **Prince of Cats:** Tybalt,
or a variation of it, is the
name of the cat in medieval
stories of Reynard the Fox.
3. **captain of
compliments:** Master of
formal behavior.
4. **as you sing pricksong:**
That is to say, with
attention to precision and
correctness.
5. **rests . . . rests:**
Observes all formalities.
6. **button:** An exact spot
on his opponent's shirt.
7. **first house:** Finest
school of fencing.
8. **the first and second
cause:** Reasons that would
cause a gentleman to
challenge another to a duel.
9. ***passado!* . . . *punto
reverso!* . . . hay!:** Lunge. . .
backhanded stroke . . .
home thrust.
10. **The pox . . . accent:**
May the plague strike these
absurd characters with their
phony manners—these men
who speak in weird,
newfangled ways!
11. **these pardon-me's:**
These men who are always
saying "Pardon me"
(adopting ridiculous
manners).

◆ **Build Vocabulary**

lamentable (lam´ ən tə
bəl) *adj.:* Distressing; sad

▲ **Critical Viewing** How is the rowdy behavior of the young Montagues typical of a group of teenaged friends? [Generalize]

◆ **Literary Focus**
Most of *Romeo and Juliet* is written in blank verse, which gives the character's words a formal, elegant feel. Why do you think that the conversation between Romeo and his friends is not in blank verse?

35 **BENVOLIO.** Here comes Romeo! Here comes Romeo!

MERCUTIO. Without his roe, like a dried herring.[12] O flesh, flesh, how art thou fishified! Now is he for the numbers[13] that Petrarch flowed in. Laura,[14] to his lady, was a kitchen wench (marry, she had a better love to be-

40 rhyme her), Dido a dowdy, Cleopatra a gypsy, Helen and Hero hildings and harlots, Thisbe a gray eye or so, but not to the purpose. Signior Romeo, *bon jour!* There's a French salutation to your French slop. You gave us the counterfeit fairly last night.

45 **ROMEO.** Good morrow to you both. What counterfeit did I give you?

MERCUTIO. The slip,[15] sir, the slip. Can you not conceive?

ROMEO. Pardon, good Mercutio. My business was great, and in such a case as mine a man may strain courtesy.

50 **MERCUTIO.** That's as much as to say, such a case as yours constrains a man to bow in the hams.[16]

ROMEO. Meaning, to curtsy.

MERCUTIO. Thou hast most kindly hit it.

ROMEO. A most courteous exposition.

12. **Without . . . herring:** Worn out.
13. **numbers:** Verses of love poems.
14. **Laura:** Laura and the other ladies mentioned are all notable figures of European love literature. Mercutio is saying that Romeo thinks that none of them compare with Rosaline.
15. **slip:** Escape. *Slip* is also a term for counterfeit coin.
16. **hams:** Hips.

55 **MERCUTIO.** Nay, I am the very pink of courtesy.

ROMEO. Pink for flower.

MERCUTIO. Right.

ROMEO. Why, then is my pump[17] well-flowered.

MERCUTIO. Sure wit, follow me this jest now till thou hast
60 worn out thy pump, that, when the single sole of it is
worn, the jest may remain, after the wearing, solely
singular.[18]

ROMEO. O single-soled jest, solely singular for the singleness![19]

65 **MERCUTIO.** Come between us, good Benvolio! My wits faints.

ROMEO. Swits and spurs, swits and spurs; or I'll cry a
match.[20]

MERCUTIO. Nay, if our wits run the wild-goose chase, I
am done; for thou hast more of the wild goose in one of
70 thy wits than, I am sure, I have in my whole five. Was I
with you there for the goose?

ROMEO. Thou wast never with me for anything when thou
wast not there for the goose.

MERCUTIO. I will bite thee by the ear for that jest.

75 **ROMEO.** Nay, good goose, bite not!

MERCUTIO. Thy wit is a very bitter sweeting;[21] it is a most sharp sauce.

ROMEO. And is it not, then, well served in to a sweet
goose?

MERCUTIO. O, here's a wit of cheveril,[22] that stretches from an inch
80 narrow to an ell broad!

ROMEO. I stretch it out for that word "broad," which added
to the goose, proves thee far and wide a broad goose.

MERCUTIO. Why, is not this better now than groaning for
love? Now art thou sociable, now art thou Romeo; now
art thou what thou art, by art as well as by nature. For
85 this driveling love is like a great natural[23] that runs
lolling[24] up and down to hide his bauble[25] in a hole.

BENVOLIO. Stop there, stop there!

MERCUTIO. Thou desirest me to stop in my tale against the hair.[26]

90 **BENVOLIO.** Thou wouldst else have made thy tale large.

17. pump: Shoe.

18. when . . . singular:
The jest will outwear the
shoe and will then be all
alone.
19. O . . . singleness!: O
thin joke, unique for only
one thing—weakness!

20. Swits . . . match: Drive
your wit harder to beat me
or else I'll claim victory in
this match of word play.

21. sweeting: A kind of
apple.

22. cheveril: Easily
stretched kid leather.

23. natural: Idiot.
24. lolling: With
tongue hanging out.
25. bauble: Toy.

26. the hair: Natural
inclination.

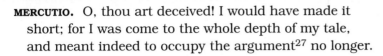

MERCUTIO. O, thou art deceived! I would have made it
short; for I was come to the whole depth of my tale,
and meant indeed to occupy the argument[27] no longer.

ROMEO. Here's goodly gear![28]

[*Enter* NURSE *and her Man,* PETER.]

95   A sail, a sail!

MERCUTIO. Two, two! A shirt and a smock.[29]

NURSE. Peter!

PETER. Anon.

NURSE. My fan, Peter.

100 **MERCUTIO.** Good Peter, to hide her face; for her fan's the
fairer face.

NURSE. God ye good morrow, gentlemen.

MERCUTIO. God ye good-den, fair gentlewoman.

NURSE. Is it good-den?

105 **MERCUTIO.** 'Tis no less, I tell ye; for the bawdy hand of the
dial is now upon the prick of noon.

NURSE. Out upon you! What a man are you!

ROMEO. One, gentlewoman, that God hath made, himself to mar.

NURSE. By my troth, it is well said. "For himself to mar,"
110 quoth 'a? Gentlemen, can any of you tell me where I
may find the young Romeo?

ROMEO. I can tell you; but young Romeo will be older
when you have found him than he was when you sought
him. I am the youngest of that name, for fault[30] of a
115 worse.

NURSE. You say well.

MERCUTIO. Yea, is the worst well? Very well took,[31] i' faith! Wisely,
wisely.

NURSE. If you be he, sir, I desire some confidence[32] with you.

120 **BENVOLIO.** She will endite him to some supper.

MERCUTIO. A bawd, a bawd, a bawd! So ho!

ROMEO. What hast thou found?

MERCUTIO. No hare, sir; unless a hare, sir, in a lenten pie,

27. occupy the argument:
Talk about the matter.
28. goodly gear: Good
stuff for joking (Romeo sees
the Nurse approaching).

29. A shirt and a smock:
A man and a woman.

30. fault: Lack.

31. took: Understood.

32. confidence: The Nurse
means conference.

that is something stale and hoar ere it be spent.

[*He walks by them and sings.*]

125   An old hare hoar,
       And an old hare hoar,
       Is very good meat in Lent;
       But a hare that is hoar
       Is too much for a score
130   When it hoars ere it be spent.

Romeo, will you come to your father's? We'll to dinner thither.

ROMEO. I will follow you.

MERCUTIO. Farewell, ancient lady. Farewell, [*singing*]
"Lady, lady, lady."[33]   [*Exit* MERCUTIO, BENVOLIO.]

135 **NURSE.** I pray you, sir, what saucy merchant was this that
    was so full of his ropery?[34]

ROMEO. A gentleman, nurse, that loves to hear himself talk
    and will speak more in a minute than he will stand to
    in a month.

140 **NURSE.** And 'a[35] speak anything against me, I'll take him
    down, and 'a were lustier than he is, and twenty such
    Jacks; and if I cannot, I'll find those that shall. Scurvy
    knave! I am none of his flirt-gills;[36] I am none of his
    skainsmates.[37] And thou must stand by too, and suffer
145 every knave to use me at his pleasure!

PETER. I saw no man use you at his pleasure. If I had, my
    weapon should quickly have been out, I warrant you. I
    dare draw as soon as another man, if I see occasion in
    a good quarrel, and the law on my side.

150 **NURSE.** Now, afore God, I am so vexed that every part about
    me quivers. Scurvy knave! Pray you, sir, a word; and,
    as I told you, my young lady bid me inquire you out.
    What she bid me say, I will keep to myself; but first let
    me tell ye, if ye should lead her in a fool's paradise, as
155 they say, it were a very gross kind of behavior, as they
    say; for the gentlewoman is young; and therefore, if
    you should deal double with her, truly it were an ill
    thing to be off'red to any gentlewoman, and very
    weak[38] dealing.

160 **ROMEO.** Nurse, commend[39] me to thy lady and mistress.
    I protest unto thee—

33. **"Lady . . . lady":** Line from an old ballad, "Chaste Susanna."

34. **ropery:** The Nurse means roguery, the talk and conduct of a rascal.

35. **'a:** He.

36. **flirt-gills:** Common girls.
37. **skainsmates:** Criminals; cutthroats.

◆ Literary Focus
Why didn't Shakespeare have the Nurse speak in blank verse?

38. **weak:** Unmanly.
39. **commend:** Convey my respect and best wishes.

NURSE. Good heart, and i' faith I will tell her as much.
Lord, Lord, she will be a joyful woman.

ROMEO. What wilt thou tell her, nurse? Thou dost not
165 mark me.

NURSE. I will tell her, sir, that you do protest, which, as I
take it, is a gentlemanlike offer.

ROMEO. Bid her devise
Some means to come to shrift[40] this afternoon;
170 And there she shall at Friar Lawrence' cell
Be shrived and married. Here is for thy pains.

NURSE. No, truly, sir; not a penny.

ROMEO. Go to! I say you shall.

NURSE. This afternoon, sir? Well, she shall be there.

175 **ROMEO.** And stay, good nurse, behind the abbey wall.
Within this hour my man shall be with thee
And bring thee cords made like a tackled stair.[41]
Which to the high topgallant[42] of my joy
Must be my convoy[43] in the secret night.
180 Farewell. Be trusty, and I'll quit[44] thy pains.
Farewell. Commend me to thy mistress.

NURSE. Now God in heaven bless thee! Hark you, sir.

ROMEO. What say'st thou, my dear nurse?

NURSE. Is your man secret? Did you ne'er hear say,
185 Two may keep counsel, putting one away?[45]

ROMEO. Warrant thee my man's as true as steel.

NURSE. Well, sir, my mistress is the sweetest lady. Lord,
Lord! When 'twas a little prating[46] thing—O, there is a
nobleman in town, one Paris, that would fain lay knife
190 aboard;[47] but she, good soul, had as lieve[48] see a toad,
a very toad, as see him. I anger her sometimes, and tell
her that Paris is the properer man; but I'll warrant
you, when I say so, she looks as pale as any clout[49]
in the versal world.[50] Doth not rosemary and Romeo be-
195 gin both with a letter?

ROMEO. Ay, nurse; what of that? Both with an *R*.

NURSE. Ah, mocker! That's the dog's name.[51] *R* is for the—
No; I know it begins with some other letter; and she
hath the prettiest sententious[52] of it, of you and rosemary,

40. **shrift:** Confession.

41. **tackled stair:** Rope
ladder.
42. **topgallant:** Summit.
43. **convoy:** Conveyance.
44. **quit:** Reward; pay you
back for.

45. **Two . . . away:** Two
can keep a secret if one is
ignorant, or out of the way.

46. **prating:** Babbling.

47. **fain . . . aboard:**
Eagerly seize Juliet for
himself.
48. **had as lieve:** Would as
willingly.
49. **clout:** Cloth.
50. **versal world:** Universe.

51. **dog's name:** *R* sounds
like a growl.
52. **sententious:** The Nurse
means *sentences*—clever,
wise sayings.

200   that it would do you good to hear it.

ROMEO. Commend me to thy lady.

NURSE. Ay, a thousand times. [*Exit* ROMEO.] Peter!

PETER. Anon.

NURSE. Before, and apace.[53]   [*Exit, after* PETER.]

Scene v. CAPULET'S *orchard.*

[*Enter* JULIET.]

    JULIET. The clock struck nine when I did send the nurse;
        In half an hour she promised to return.
        Perchance she cannot meet him. That's not so.
        O, she is lame! Love's heralds should be thoughts,
5   Which ten times faster glides than the sun's beams
        Driving back shadows over low'ring[1] hills.
        Therefore do nimble-pinioned doves draw Love,[2]
        And therefore hath the wind-swift Cupid wings.
        Now is the sun upon the highmost hill
10   Of this day's journey, and from nine till twelve
        Is three long hours; yet she is not come.
        Had she affections and warm youthful blood,
        She would be as swift in motion as a ball;
        My words would bandy her[3] to my sweet love,
15   And his to me.
        But old folks, many feign[4] as they were dead—
        Unwieldy, slow, heavy and pale as lead.

[*Enter* NURSE *and* PETER.]

    O God, she comes! O honey nurse, what news?
    Hast thou met with him? Send thy man away.

20 **NURSE.** Peter, stay at the gate.   [*Exit* PETER.]

    JULIET. Now, good sweet nurse—O Lord, why lookest thou
        sad?
        Though news be sad, yet tell them merrily;
        If good, thou shamest the music of sweet news
        By playing it to me with so sour a face.

25 **NURSE.** I am aweary, give me leave[5] awhile.
        Fie, how my bones ache! What a jaunce[6] have I!

    JULIET. I would thou hadst my bones, and I thy news.
        Nay, come, I pray thee speak. Good, good nurse, speak.

53. Before, and apace: Go ahead of me, and quickly.

> ◆ *Literature and Your Life*
> How does this passage capture how time drags when you're waiting for something to happen?

1. low'ring: Darkening.

2. Therefore . . . Love: Therefore, doves with quick wings pull the chariot of Venus, goddess of love.

3. bandy her: Send her rapidly.

4. feign: Act.

5. give me leave: Excuse me; give me a moment's rest.
6. jaunce: Rough trip.

◆ **Build Vocabulary**
unwieldy (un wēl´ dē) *adj.*: Awkward; clumsy

NURSE. Jesu, what haste? Can you not stay a while?
30   Do you not see that I am out of breath?

JULIET. How art thou out of breath when thou hast breath
    To say to me that thou art out of breath?
    The excuse that thou dost make in this delay
    Is longer than the tale thou dost excuse.
    Is thy news good or bad? Answer to that.
35   Say either, and I'll stay the circumstance.[7]
    Let me be satisfied, is't good or bad?

NURSE. Well, you have made a simple[8] choice; you know
    not how to choose a man. Romeo? No, not he. Though
    his face be better than any man's, yet his leg excels all
40   men's; and for a hand and a foot, and a body, though
    they be not to be talked on, yet they are past compare.
    He is not the flower of courtesy, but, I'll warrant him,
    as gentle as a lamb. Go thy ways, wench; serve God.
    What, have you dined at home?

45   **JULIET.** No, no. But all this I did know before.
    What says he of our marriage? What of that?

NURSE. Lord, how my head aches! What a head have I!
    It beats as it would fall in twenty pieces.
    My back a[9] t'other side—ah, my back, my back!
50   Beshrew[10] your heart for sending me about
    To catch my death with jauncing up and down!

JULIET. I' faith, I am sorry that thou art not well.
    Sweet, sweet, sweet nurse, tell me, what says my love?

NURSE. Your love says, like an honest gentleman, and a
55   courteous, and a kind, and a handsome, and, I warrant,
    a virtuous—Where is your mother?

JULIET. Where is my mother? why, she is within.
    Where should she be? How oddly thou repliest!
    "Your love says, like an honest gentleman,
    'Where is your mother?' "

60 **NURSE.**   O God's Lady dear!
    Are you so hot?[11] Marry come up, I trow.[12]
    Is this the poultice[13] for my aching bones?
    Henceforward do your messages yourself.

JULIET. Here's such a coil![14] Come, what says Romeo?

7. **stay the circumstance:** Wait for the details.

8. **simple:** Foolish; simpleminded.

9. **a:** On.
10. **Beshrew:** Shame on.

11. **hot:** Impatient; hot-tempered.
12. **Marry . . . trow:** Indeed, cool down, I say.
13. **poultice:** Remedy.
14. **coil:** Disturbance.

65 **NURSE.** Have you got leave to go to shrift today?

JULIET. I have.

NURSE. Then hie you hence to Friar Lawrence' cell;
There stays a husband to make you a wife.
Now comes the wanton[15] blood up in your cheeks:
70 They'll be in scarlet straight at any news.
Hie you to church: I must another way,
To fetch a ladder, by the which your love
Must climb a bird's nest soon when it is dark.
I am the drudge, and toil in your delight:
75 But you shall bear the burden soon at night.
Go; I'll to dinner; hie you to the cell.

JULIET. Hie to high fortune! Honest nurse, farewell. [*Exit.*]

Scene vi. FRIAR LAWRENCE'S *cell.*

[*Enter* FRIAR LAWRENCE *and* ROMEO.]

FRIAR. So smile the heavens upon this holy act
That afterhours with sorrow chide us not![1]

ROMEO. Amen, amen! But come what sorrow can,
It cannot countervail[2] the exchange of joy
5 That one short minute gives me in her sight.
Do thou but close our hands with holy words,
Then love-devouring death do what he dare—
It is enough I may but call her mine.

FRIAR. These violent delights have violent ends
10 And in their triumph die, like fire and powder,[3]
Which, as they kiss, consume. The sweetest honey
Is loathsome in his own deliciousness
And in the taste confounds[4] the appetite.
Therefore love moderately: long love doth so;
15 Too swift arrives as tardy as too slow.

[*Enter* JULIET.]

Here comes the lady. O, so light a foot
Will ne'er wear out the everlasting flint.[5]
A lover may bestride the gossamers[6]
That idles in the wanton summer air,
20 And yet not fall; so light is vanity.[7]

JULIET. Good even to my ghostly confessor.

FRIAR. Romeo shall thank thee, daughter, for us both.

15. **wanton:** Excited.

♦ **Literary Focus**
Why does Juliet's last line rhyme with the Nurse's last line?

1. **That . . . not!:** That the future does not punish us with sorrow.

2. **countervail:** Equal.

3. **powder:** Gunpowder.

4. **confounds:** Destroys.

5. **flint:** Stone.

6. **gossamers:** Spider webs.

7. **vanity:** Foolish things that cannot last.

JULIET. As much to him,[8] else is his thanks too much.

ROMEO. Ah, Juliet, if the measure of thy joy
25 Be heaped like mine, and that thy skill be more
To blazon it,[9] then sweeten with thy breath

8. **As . . . him:** The same greeting to him.

9. **and . . . it:** And if you are better able to proclaim it.

◆ **Reading Strategy**
Although Romeo's words are in blank verse, the ideas he expresses do not end at the line breaks. How can you read these lines to grasp most effectively their meaning as well as their poetry?

◀ Critical Viewing
What do Romeo and Juliet's words and actions reveal about their feelings for each other? [Interpret]

This neighbor air, and let rich music's tongue
Unfold the imagined happiness that both
Receive in either by this dear encounter.

30 **JULIET.** Conceit, more rich in matter than in words,
Brags of his substance, not of ornament.[10]
They are but beggars that can count their worth;
But my true love is grown to such excess
I cannot sum up sum of half my wealth.

35 **FRIAR.** Come, come with me, and we will make short work;
For, by your leaves, you shall not stay alone
Till Holy Church incorporate two in one.   [*Exit.*]

10. **Conceit . . .
ornament:** Understanding
does not need to be
dressed up in words.

Guide for Responding

◆ Literature and Your Life

Reader's Response Do you think Friar Lawrence is right in agreeing to marry Romeo and Juliet? Explain.

Thematic Focus What can Romeo and Juliet do to overcome the obstacles that stand in the way of their happiness?

Journal Entry In Scene ii, Juliet says "'Tis twenty year till then," meaning that it will seem like a very long time until the following morning, when she can send a messenger to Romeo. Describe an incident, real or imaginary, in which time seemed to drag too slowly or fly too quickly.

☑ Check Your Comprehension

1. Why does Juliet cry out in Scene ii, "O Romeo, Romeo, Romeo! Wherefore (Why) art thou Romeo?"
2. What doubts and fears does Juliet express even as she realizes that Romeo loves her?
3. What weakness in Romeo's character does Friar Lawrence point out before agreeing to assist the lovers in their plan to wed? How does Romeo defend himself?
4. Why does Friar Lawrence finally agree to marry Romeo and Juliet? Why does the Nurse help them carry out their plan?

◆ Critical Thinking

INTERPRET

1. Explain the role that darkness plays in helping Romeo and Juliet learn of their love for each other. **[Support]**
2. Describe Juliet's feelings in Scene v as she waits for the Nurse and then as she waits for the Nurse to reveal Romeo's message. **[Interpret]**
3. Aside from wanting Romeo and Juliet to be happy, what other motives does Friar Lawrence have for marrying the couple? **[Compare and Contrast]**
4. Although the events of Act II are joyful ones, Shakespeare foreshadows, or hints at, more sinister events that will occur later. Find at least two examples of foreshadowing and explain each example. **[Support]**
5. Are the feelings that Romeo and Juliet have for each other true love or infatuation? Explain. **[Draw Conclusions]**

EVALUATE

6. Why do you think the love scene in Capulet's garden is the most famous in all of literature? **[Assess]**

APPLY

7. Juliet is thirteen years old and Romeo not much older. In what way is their love typical of adolescence, and in what way is it not? **[Relate]**

Guide for Responding (continued)

◆ Literary Focus

BLANK VERSE

Blank verse is unrhymed iambic pentameter—ten-syllable lines in which every second syllable is stressed. Poets and playwrights like Shakespeare often depart from the normal pattern to avoid monotony, to imitate the rhythms of real speech, or to vary the "music" of the verse.

On a separate piece of paper, indicate the pattern of unaccented and accented syllables in Scene ii, lines 43–51. Use the ˘ mark for an unaccented syllable and the ´ mark for an accented one. This is how the first line should look:

Whăt's ín ă náme? Thăt whích wĕ cáll ă róse

◆ Reading Strategy

READING BLANK VERSE

When you **read blank verse**, there's no need to be intimidated by the way the verse appears on the page. Simply read the words as if they were normal speech, without worrying about line breaks or the singsong rhythm of iambic pentameter.

To help you practice focusing on the meaning of the lines in a Shakespeare play, do the following.

1. Copy lines 1 through 8 of Juliet's speech at the beginning of Scene v as a single double-spaced paragraph. Read your paragraph aloud. Then mark your paragraph to indicate where it is natural to take a breath or pause.
2. Rewrite the paragraph in your own words.

◆ Build Grammar Skills

LOGICAL COMPARISONS

Include the word *other* or *else* when comparing one member of a group with the other members.

Writing Application Rewrite each sentence or passage, correcting any illogical comparisons.
1. Romeo is more open-minded than the Montagues.
2. Juliet appears as does the sun, brighter than any object in the heavens.
3. Juliet's eyes are twinkling stars, fairer than any stars in the universe.
4. "...Though his face be better than any man's."

◆ Build Vocabulary

USING THE PREFIX *inter-*

Match each word on the left with its meaning on the right.
1. international   a. between or among states
2. interpersonal   b. between planets
3. interstate   c. between or among nations
4. interplanetary   d. between persons

USING THE WORD BANK

Match each expression on the left with its meaning on the right. (Some expressions contain two vocabulary words.)
1. lamentable intercession   a. low slyness
2. to procure quickly   b. dominating hue
3. vile cunning   c. sickly skin tone
4. predominant color   d. awkward tool
5. sallow complexion   e. sad pleading
6. unwieldy implement   f. cowardly fluctuator
7. spineless waverer   g. to obtain fast

Idea Bank

Writing

1. **Poem in Iambic Pentameter** Create a poem that consists of at least eight lines in iambic pentameter. Your poem may be in blank verse, consist of rhymed couplets, or follow some other rhyme scheme.

2. **Adaptation** Adapt Shakespeare's famous balcony scene to another time and place in history, such as ancient Greece, medieval Japan, or the United States during the Civil War. Change the language and setting, but retain the underlying meaning of the dialogue.

Speaking and Listening

3. **Persuasion** Romeo persuades the Friar to perform his marriage to Juliet. Practice your powers of persuasion by role-playing a situation of your choice with a partner. Obtain feedback from your partner. Then switch roles.

Guide for Reading, Act III

◆ Review and Anticipate

You'll recall that in Act II, Romeo and Juliet express their love for each other and enlist the aid of Juliet's nurse and Friar Lawrence to arrange a secret marriage ceremony. As the act closes, the young couple are about to be married. Before performing the ceremony, however, Friar Lawrence warns Romeo: "These violent delights have violent ends...." What does he mean? How might this statement hint at events that will occur in Act III and the others that follow?

◆ Literary Focus

SOLILOQUY, ASIDE, AND MONOLOGUE

A **soliloquy** is a speech in which a character, alone on stage, expresses his or her thoughts to the audience. An **aside** is a remark made to the audience, unheard by the other characters. There are two differences between these devices. First, a soliloquy is usually lengthy; an aside is brief. Second, a soliloquy is usually spoken when no other characters are present; an aside is delivered with other characters present but unable to hear. Both devices, however, let the audience know what a character is really thinking or feeling.

Similar to a soliloquy is a **monologue**, which is a lengthy speech. Unlike a soliloquy, however, a monologue is addressed to other characters, not to the audience.

◆ Build Grammar Skills

COMMONLY CONFUSED WORDS: WHO AND WHOM

You'll find that Act III is filled with examples of the pronouns *who* and *whom*. Notice that the pronoun *who* is used when the pronoun is the subject of the verb or is a predicate nominative (a noun or pronoun that renames or explains the subject of a sentence). The pronoun *whom* is used when the pronoun receives the action of the verb or when it is the object of a preposition (as in "With *whom* are you speaking?"). Look at these examples:

> subject
> ...*who* began this bloody fray?

> direct object
> Tybalt, ..., *whom* Romeo's hand did slay.

Sometimes it's helpful to reword a sentence to determine whether *who* or *whom* is correct. For example, rewording the second example—"... Romeo's hand did slay *whom*"—makes it clear that the pronoun receives the action of the verb.

◆ Reading Strategy

PARAPHRASE

Because Shakespeare writes in long passages of blank verse and uses unfamiliar language, his plays can be difficult to understand. One way to make sure you don't miss the meaning of key passages is to **paraphrase**—to identify key ideas and words and express them in your own words. Example:

Shakespeare's version

This gentleman, the Prince's near ally / My very friend, hath got his mortal hurt / In my behalf ...

Paraphrased

My good friend, a close relative of the prince, has been fatally wounded defending me ...

◆ Build Vocabulary

WORDS FROM MYTHS

In this act, the word *martial*, meaning "military" or "warlike," is used to describe a sword fight. The word *martial* is one of many English words that come from mythology, ancient stories that seek to explain natural phenomena. The word is derived from the Roman god of war, Mars.

gallant
fray
martial
exile
eloquence
fickle

WORD BANK

Before you read, preview this list of words.

Scene i. *A public place.*

[*Enter* MERCUTIO, BENVOLIO, *and* MEN.]

    BENVOLIO. I pray thee, good Mercutio, let's retire.
    The day is hot, the Capels are abroad,
    And, if we meet, we shall not 'scape a brawl,
    For now, these hot days, is the mad blood stirring.

5 **MERCUTIO.** Thou art like one of these fellows that, when he enters
    the confines of a tavern, claps me his sword upon the table and
    says, "God send me no need of thee!" and by the operation of
    the second cup draws him on the drawer,[1] when indeed there is
    no need.

10 **BENVOLIO.** Am I like such a fellow?

    MERCUTIO. Come, come, thou art as hot a Jack in thy mood as any in
    Italy; and as soon moved to be moody, and as soon moody to be
    moved.[2]

    BENVOLIO. And what to?

15 **MERCUTIO.** Nay, and there were two such, we should have none
    shortly, for one would kill the other. Thou! Why, thou wilt quarrel
    with a man that hath a hair more or a hair less in his beard than
    thou hast. Thou wilt quarrel with a man for cracking nuts, having
    no other reason but because thou hast hazel eyes. What eye but
20 such an eye would spy out such a quarrel? Thy head is as full of
    quarrels as an egg is full of meat; and yet thy head hath been
    beaten as addle[3] as an egg for quarreling. Thou hast quarreled
    with a man for coughing in the street, because he hath wakened
    thy dog that hath lain asleep in the sun. Didst thou not fall out
25 with a tailor for wearing his new doublet[4] before Easter? With an-
    other for tying his new shoes with old riband?[5] And yet thou wilt
    tutor me from quarreling![6]

    BENVOLIO. And I were so apt to quarrel as thou art, any man should
    buy the fee simple[7] of my life for an hour and a quarter.[8]

30 **MERCUTIO.** The fee simple? O simple![9]

[*Enter* TYBALT, PETRUCHIO, *and* OTHERS.]

◆ **Reading Strategy**
How would you restate Benvolio's comments in your own words?

---

1. **and . . . drawer:** And by the effect of the second drink, draws his sword against the waiter.

2. **and . . . moved:** And as quickly stirred to anger as you are eager to be so stirred.

3. **addle:** Scrambled; crazy.

4. **doublet:** Jacket.
5. **riband:** Ribbon.
6. **tutor . . . quarreling:** Instruct me not to quarrel.
7. **fee simple:** Complete possession.
8. **an hour and a quarter:** Length of time that a man with Mercutio's fondness for quarreling may be expected to live.
9. **O simple!:** O stupid!

BENVOLIO. By my head, here comes the Capulets.

MERCUTIO. By my heel I care not.

TYBALT. Follow me close, for I will speak to them.
35 Gentlemen, good-den. A word with one of you.

MERCUTIO. And but one word with one of us? Couple it with something; make it a word and a blow.

TYBALT. You shall find me apt enough to that, sir, and you will give me occasion.[10]

40 **MERCUTIO.** Could you not take some occasion without giving?

TYBALT. Mercutio, thou consortest[11] with Romeo.

MERCUTIO. Consort?[12] What, dost thou make us minstrels? And thou make minstrels of us, look to
45 hear nothing but discords.[13] Here's my fiddlestick; here's that shall make you dance. Zounds,[14] consort!

BENVOLIO. We talk here in the public haunt of men.
Either withdraw unto some private place,
Or reason coldly of your grievances,
50 Or else depart. Here all eyes gaze on us.

MERCUTIO. Men's eyes were made to look, and let them gaze.
I will not budge for no man's pleasure, I.

[*Enter* ROMEO.]

TYBALT. Well, peace be with you, sir. Here comes my man.[15]

MERCUTIO. But I'll be hanged, sir, if he wear your livery.[16]
55 Marry, go before to field,[17] he'll be your follower!
Your worship in that sense may call him man.

TYBALT. Romeo, the love I bear thee can afford
No better term than this: thou art a villain.[18]

ROMEO. Tybalt, the reason that I have to love thee
60 Doth much excuse the appertaining[19] rage
To such a greeting. Villain am I none.
Therefore farewell. I see thou knowest me not.

TYBALT. Boy, this shall not excuse the injuries
That thou hast done me; therefore turn and draw.

65 **ROMEO.** I do protest I never injured thee,
But love thee better than thou canst devise[20]
Till thou shalt know the reason of my love;

10. **occasion:** Cause; reason.

11. **consortest:** Associate with.
12. **Consort:** Associate with; consort also meant a group of musicians.
13. **discords:** Harsh sounds.
14. **Zounds:** Exclamation of surprise or anger ("By God's wounds").

15. **man:** The man I'm looking for; "man" also meant "manservant."
16. **livery:** Servant's uniform.
17. **field:** Dueling place.

18. **villain:** Low, vulgar person.

19. **appertaining:** Appropriate.

20. **devise:** Understand; imagine.

And so, good Capulet, which name I tender[21]
As dearly as mine own, be satisfied.

70 **MERCUTIO.** O calm, dishonorable, vile submission!
Alla stoccata[22] carries it away.   [*Draws.*]
Tybalt, you ratcatcher, will you walk?

TYBALT. What wouldst thou have with me?

MERCUTIO. Good King of Cats, nothing but one of your nine lives.
75 That I mean to make bold withal,[23] and, as you shall use me hereafter, dry-beat[24] the rest of the eight. Will you pluck your sword
out of his pilcher[25] by the ears? Make haste, lest mine be about
your ears ere it be out.

TYBALT. I am for you.   [*Draws.*]

80 **ROMEO.** Gentle Mercutio, put thy rapier up.

MERCUTIO. Come, sir, your *passado*!   [*They fight.*]

ROMEO. Draw, Benvolio; beat down their weapons.
Gentlemen, for shame! Forbear this outrage!
Tybalt, Mercutio, the Prince expressly hath
85 Forbid this bandying in Verona streets.
Hold, Tybalt! Good Mercutio!

[TYBALT *under* ROMEO'S *arms thrusts* MERCUTIO *in, and flies.*]

MERCUTIO.   I am hurt.
A plague a[26] both houses! I am sped.[27]
Is he gone and hath nothing?

BENVOLIO.   What, art thou hurt?

MERCUTIO. Ay, ay, a scratch, a scratch. Marry, 'tis enough.
90 Where is my page? Go, villain, fetch a surgeon.

[*Exit* PAGE.]

ROMEO. Courage, man. The hurt cannot be much.

MERCUTIO. No, 'tis not so deep as a well, nor so wide as a church
door; but 'tis enough, 'twill serve. Ask for me tomorrow, and you
shall find me a grave man. I am peppered,[28] I warrant, for this
95 world. A plague a both your houses! Zounds, a dog, a rat, a mouse,
a cat, to scratch a man to death! A braggart, a rogue, a villain,
that fights by the book of arithmetic![29] Why the devil came you
between us? I was hurt under your arm.

ROMEO. I thought all for the best.

100 **MERCUTIO.** Help me into some house, Benvolio,

21. **tender:** Value.

22. *Alla stoccata:* At the
thrust—an Italian fencing
term that Mercutio uses as
a nickname for Tybalt.

23. **make bold withal:**
Make bold with; take.
24. **dry-beat:** Thrash.
25. **pilcher:** Scabbard.

26. **a:** On.
27. **sped:** Wounded; done
for.

28. **peppered:** Finished off.

29. **by . . . arithmetic:** By
formal rules.

Or I shall faint. A plague a both your houses!
They have made worms' meat of me. I have it,[30]
And soundly too. Your houses!

30. **I have it:** I've got my deathblow

[*Exit* MERCUTIO *and* BENVOLIO.]

ROMEO. This gentleman, the Prince's near ally,[31]
105 My very friend, hath got his mortal hurt
In my behalf—my reputation stained
With Tybalt's slander—Tybalt, that an hour
Hath been my cousin. O sweet Juliet,
Thy beauty hath made me effeminate
110 And in my temper soft'ned valor's steel!

31. **ally:** Relative.

[*Enter* BENVOLIO.]

BENVOLIO. O Romeo, Romeo, brave Mercutio is dead!
That <u>gallant</u> spirit hath aspired[32] the clouds,
Which too untimely here did scorn the earth.

32. **aspired:** Climbed to.

ROMEO. This day's black fate on moe[33] days doth depend;[34]
115 This but begins the woe others must end.

33. **moe:** More.
34. **depend:** Hang over.

[*Enter* TYBALT.]

BENVOLIO. Here comes the furious Tybalt back again.

ROMEO. Alive in triumph, and Mercutio slain?
Away to heaven respective lenity,[35]
And fire-eyed fury be my conduct[36] now!
120 Now, Tybalt, take the "villain" back again
That late thou gavest me; for Mercutio's soul
Is but a little way above our heads,
Staying for thine to keep him company.
Either thou or I, or both, must go with him.

35. **respective lenity:** Thoughtful mercy.
36. **conduct:** Guide.

125 **TYBALT.** Thou, wretched boy, that didst consort him here,
Shalt with him hence.

ROMEO.   This shall determine that.

[*They fight.* TYBALT *falls.*]

BENVOLIO. Romeo, away, be gone!
The citizens are up, and Tybalt slain.
Stand not amazed. The Prince will doom thee death
130 If thou art taken. Hence, be gone, away!

37. **fool:** Plaything.

ROMEO. I am fortune's fool![37]

BENVOLIO.   Why dost thou stay?

◆ **Build Vocabulary**

gallant (gal´ ənt) *adj.*: Brave and noble

[*Exit* ROMEO.]

◀ **Critical Viewing** Because Romeo refuses to fight with Tybalt, Mercutio decides it is up to him to defend Romeo's honor. Mercutio's death goads Romeo into dueling with Tybalt. What do you think of Romeo's actions? Are they justifiable? Are they right? [**Make a Judgment**]

[*Enter* CITIZENS.]

    CITIZEN. Which way ran he that killed Mercutio?
      Tybalt, that murderer, which way ran he?

    BENVOLIO. There lies that Tybalt.

    CITIZEN.   Up, sir, go with me.
135 I charge thee in the Prince's name obey.

[*Enter* PRINCE, OLD MONTAGUE, CAPULET, *their* WIVES, *and all.*]

    PRINCE. Where are the vile beginners of this <u>fray</u>?

    BENVOLIO. O noble Prince, I can discover³⁸ all
      The unlucky manage³⁹ of this fatal brawl.
      There lies the man, slain by young Romeo,
140 That slew thy kinsman, brave Mercutio.

    LADY CAPULET. Tybalt, my cousin! O my brother's child!
      O Prince! O cousin! Husband! Oh, the blood is spilled
      Of my dear kinsman! Prince, as thou art true,
      For blood of ours shed blood of Montague.
145 O cousin, cousin!

    PRINCE. Benvolio, who began this bloody fray?

    BENVOLIO. Tybalt, here slain, whom Romeo's hand
      did slay.
      Romeo, that spoke him fair, bid him bethink
150 How nice⁴⁰ the quarrel was, and urged withal
      Your high displeasure. All this—utterèd
      With gentle breath, calm look, knees humbly bowed—

38. **discover:** Reveal.
39. **manage:** Course.

◆ **Literary Focus**
Is Benvolio's speech a soliloquy, aside, or monologue? Explain.

40. **nice:** Trivial.

◆ **Build Vocabulary**
fray (frā) *n.:* Noisy fight

Could not take truce with the unruly spleen[41]
Of Tybalt deaf to peace, but that he tilts[42]
155 With piercing steel at bold Mercutio's breast;
Who, all as hot, turns deadly point to point,
And, with a <u>martial</u> scorn, with one hand beats
Cold death aside and with the other sends
It back to Tybalt, whose dexterity
160 Retorts it. Romeo he cries aloud,
"Hold, friends! Friends, part!" and swifter than his tongue,
His agile arm beats down their fatal points,
And 'twixt them rushes; underneath whose arm
An envious[43] thrust from Tybalt hit the life
165 Of stout Mercutio, and then Tybalt fled;
But by and by comes back to Romeo,
Who had but newly entertained[44] revenge,
And to't they go like lightning; for, ere I
Could draw to part them, was stout Tybalt slain;
170 And, as he fell, did Romeo turn and fly.
This is the truth, or let Benvolio die.

LADY CAPULET. He is a kinsman to the Montague;
Affection makes him false, he speaks not true.
Some twenty of them fought in this black strife,
175 And all those twenty could but kill one life.
I beg for justice, which thou, Prince, must give.
Romeo slew Tybalt; Romeo must not live.

PRINCE. Romeo slew him; he slew Mercutio.
Who now the price of his dear blood doth owe?

180 MONTAGUE. Not Romeo, Prince; he was Mercutio's friend;
His fault concludes but what the law should end,
The life of Tybalt.[45]

PRINCE.   And for that offense
Immediately we do <u>exile</u> him hence.
I have an interest in your hate's proceeding.
185 My blood[46] for your rude brawls doth lie a-bleeding;
But I'll amerce[47] you with so strong a fine
That you shall all repent the loss of mine.
I will be deaf to pleading and excuses;
Nor tears nor prayers shall purchase out abuses.
190 Therefore use none. Let Romeo hence in haste,
Else, when he is found, that hour is his last.
Bear hence this body and attend our will.[48]
Mercy but murders, pardoning those that kill.

[*Exit with others.*]

41. **spleen:** Angry nature.
42. **tilts:** Thrusts.

43. **envious:** Full of hatred.

44. **entertained:** Considered.

45. **His fault . . . Tybalt:** By killing Tybalt, he did what the law would have done.
46. **My blood:** Mercutio was related to the Prince.
47. **amerce:** Punish.
48. **attend our will:** Await my decision.

◆ Build Vocabulary

martial (mär´ shəl) *adj.*: Military

exile (eg´ zīl) *v.*: Banish

Scene ii. CAPULET'S *orchard.*

[*Enter* JULIET *alone.*]

     JULIET. Gallop apace, you fiery-footed steeds,[1]
       Towards Phoebus' lodging![2] Such a wagoner
       As Phaëton[3] would whip you to the west
       And bring in cloudy night immediately.
5   Spread thy close curtain, love-performing night,
       That runaways' eyes may wink,[4] and Romeo
       Leap to these arms untalked of and unseen.
       Lovers can see to do their amorous rites,
       And by their own beauties; or, if love be blind,
10   It best agrees with night. Come, civil night,
       Thou sober-suited matron all in black,
       And learn me how to lose a winning match,
       Played for a pair of stainless maidenhoods.
       Hood my unmanned blood, bating in my cheeks,[5]
15   With thy black mantle till strange[6] love grow bold,
       Think true love acted simple modesty,
       Come, night; come, Romeo; come, thou day in night;
       For thou wilt lie upon the wings of night
       Whiter than new snow upon a raven's back.
20   Come, gentle night; come, loving, black-browed night;
       Give me my Romeo; and when I shall die,
       Take him and cut him out in little stars,
       And he will make the face of heaven so fine
       That all the world will be in love with night
25   And pay no worship to the garish sun
       O, I have bought the mansion of a love,
       But not possessed it; and though I am sold,
       Not yet enjoyed. So tedious is this day
       As is the night before some festival
30   To an impatient child that hath new robes
       And may not wear them. O, here comes my nurse,

[*Enter* NURSE, *with cords.*]

       And she brings news; and every tongue that speaks
       But Romeo's name speaks heavenly <u>eloquence</u>.
       Now, nurse, what news? What hast thou there, the cords
       That Romeo did thee fetch?

35 **NURSE.**   Ay, ay, the cords.

     JULIET. Ay me! What news? Why dost thou wring thy hands?

     NURSE. Ah, weraday![7] He's dead, he's dead, he's dead!

1. **fiery-footed steeds:** Horses of the sun god, Phoebus.
2. **Phoebus' lodging:** Below the horizon.
3. **Phaëton:** Phoebus' son, who tried to drive his father's horses but was unable to control them.
4. **That runaways' eyes may wink:** So that the eyes of busybodies may not see.

5. **Hood . . . cheeks:** Hide the untamed blood that makes me blush.
6. **strange:** Unfamiliar.

◆ **Literary Focus**
Should Juliet's speech be classified as a soliloquy, aside, or monologue? Why?

7. **Ah, weraday!:** Alas!

◆ **Build Vocabulary**
eloquence (el´ ə kwəns) *n.*: Speech that is vivid, forceful, graceful, and persuasive

We are undone, lady, we are undone!
Alack the day! He's gone, he's killed, he's dead!

JULIET. Can heaven be so envious?

40 **NURSE.**   Romeo can,
Though heaven cannot. O Romeo, Romeo!
Who ever would have thought it? Romeo!

JULIET. What devil art thou that dost torment me thus?
This torture should be roared in dismal hell.
45 Hath Romeo slain himself? Say thou but "Ay,"
And that bare vowel "I" shall poison more
Than the death-darting eye of cockatrice.[8]
I am not I, if there be such an "Ay,"[9]
Or those eyes' shot[10] that makes thee answer "Ay."
50 If he be slain, say "Ay"; or if not, "No."
Brief sounds determine of my weal or woe.

NURSE. I saw the wound, I saw it with mine eyes,
(God save the mark![11]) here on his manly breast.
A piteous corse,[12] a bloody piteous corse;
55 Pale, pale as ashes, all bedaubed in blood,
All in gore-blood. I sounded[13] at the sight.

JULIET. O, break, my heart! Poor bankrout,[14] break at once!
To prison, eyes; ne'er look on liberty!
Vile earth, to earth resign;[15] end motion here,
60 And thou and Romeo press one heavy bier![16]

NURSE. O Tybalt, Tybalt, the best friend I had!
O courteous Tybalt! Honest gentleman!
That ever I should live to see thee dead!

JULIET. What storm is this that blows so contrary?[17]
65 Is Romeo slaught'red, and is Tybalt dead?
My dearest cousin, and my dearer lord?
Then, dreadful trumpet, sound the general doom![18]
For who is living, if those two are gone?

NURSE. Tybalt is gone, and Romeo banishèd;
70 Romeo that killed him, he is banishèd.

JULIET. O God! Did Romeo's hand shed Tybalt's blood?

NURSE. It did, it did! Alas the day, it did!

JULIET. O serpent heart, hid with a flow'ring face!
Did ever dragon keep so fair a cave?
75 Beautiful tyrant! Fiend angelical!

8. **cockatrice:** Serpent that, in fables, could kill with its glance.
9. **"Ay":** Yes.
10. **eyes' shot:** The Nurse's glance.

11. **God save the mark!:** May God save us from evil!
12. **corse:** Corpse.

13. **sounded:** Swooned; fainted.
14. **bankrout:** Bankrupt.

15. **Vile . . . resign:** Let my body return to the earth.
16. **bier:** Platform on which a corpse is displayed before burial.

17. **contrary:** In opposite directions.

18. **dreadful . . . doom:** Let the trumpet that announces doomsday be sounded.

Dove-feathered raven! Wolvish-ravening lamb!
Despisèd substance of divinest show!
Just opposite to what thou justly seem'st—
A damnèd saint, an honorable villain!
80 O nature, what hadst thou to do in hell
When thou didst bower the spirit of a fiend
In mortal paradise of such sweet flesh?
Was ever book containing such vile matter
So fairly bound? O, that deceit should dwell
In such a gorgeous palace!

85 **NURSE.**   There's no trust,
No faith, no honesty in men; all perjured,
All forsworn,[19] all naught, all dissemblers.[20]
Ah, where's my man? Give me some *aqua vitae*.[21]
These griefs, these woes, these sorrows make me old.
Shame come to Romeo!

90 **JULIET.**   Blistered be thy tongue
For such a wish! He was not born to shame.
Upon his brow shame is ashamed to sit;
For 'tis a throne where honor may be crowned
Sole monarch of the universal earth.
95 O, what a beast was I to chide at him!

NURSE. Will you speak well of him that killed your cousin?

JULIET. Shall I speak ill of him that is my husband?
Ah, poor my lord, what tongue shall smooth thy name
When I, thy three-hours wife, have mangled it?
100 But wherefore, villain, didst thou kill my cousin?
That villain cousin would have killed my husband.
Back, foolish tears, back to your native spring!
Your tributary[22] drops belong to woe,
Which you, mistaking, offer up to joy.
105 My husband lives, that Tybalt would have slain;
And Tybalt's dead, that would have slain my husband.
All this is comfort; wherefore weep I then?
Some word there was, worser than Tybalt's death,
That murd'red me. I would forget it fain;
110 But O, it presses to my memory
Like damnèd guilty deeds to sinners' minds!
"Tybalt is dead, and Romeo—banishèd."
That "banishèd," that one word "banishèd,"
Hath slain ten thousand Tybalts. Tybalt's death
115 Was woe enough, if it had ended there;

19. forsworn: Are liars.
20. dissemblers:
Hypocrites.
21. *aqua vitae*: Brandy.

◆ **Reading Strategy**
How would Juliet
express these
thoughts in contem-
porary language?

22. tributary: In tribute.

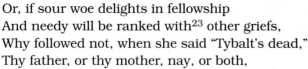

Or, if sour woe delights in fellowship
And needly will be ranked with[23] other griefs,
Why followed not, when she said "Tybalt's dead,"
Thy father, or thy mother, nay, or both,
120   Which modern[24] lamentation might have moved?
But with a rearward[25] following Tybalt's death,
"Romeo is banishèd"—to speak that word
Is father, mother, Tybalt, Romeo, Juliet,
All slain, all dead. "Romeo is banishèd"—
125   There is no end, no limit, measure bound,
In that word's death; no words can that woe sound.
Where is my father and my mother, nurse?

NURSE. Weeping and wailing over Tybalt's corse.
Will you go to them? I will bring you thither.

130 **JULIET.** Wash they his wounds with tears? Mine shall be spent,
When theirs are dry, for Romeo's banishment.
Take up those cords. Poor ropes, you are beguiled,
Both you and I, for Romeo is exiled.
He made you for a highway to my bed;
135   But I, a maid, die maiden-widowèd.
Come, cords; come, nurse. I'll to my wedding bed;
And death, not Romeo, take my maidenhead!

NURSE. Hie to your chamber. I'll find Romeo
To comfort you. I wot[26] well where he is.
140   Hark ye, your Romeo will be here at night.
I'll to him; he is hid at Lawrence' cell.

JULIET. O, find him! Give this ring to my true knight
And bid him come to take his last farewell.

                                       [Exit with NURSE.*]*

Scene iii. FRIAR LAWRENCE'S *cell.*

[Enter FRIAR LAWRENCE.*]*

FRIAR. Romeo, come forth, thou fearful man.
Affliction is enamored of thy parts.[1]
And thou art wedded to calamity.

[Enter Romeo.]

ROMEO. Father, what news? What is the Prince's doom?[2]
5   What sorrow craves acquaintance at my hand
That I yet know not?

FRIAR.   Too familiar

23. **needly . . . with:** Must be accompanied by.

24. **modern:** Ordinary.
25. **rearward:** Follow up: literally, a rear guard.

26. **wot:** know.

1. **Affliction . . . parts:** Misery is in love with your attractive qualities.

2. **doom:** Final decision.

Is my dear son with such sour company.
I bring thee tidings of the Prince's doom.

ROMEO. What less than doomsday³ is the Prince's doom?

10 **FRIAR.** A gentler judgment vanished⁴ from his lips—
Not body's death, but body's banishment.

ROMEO. Ha, banishment? Be merciful, say "death";
For exile hath more terror in his look,
Much more than death. Do not say "banishment."

15 **FRIAR.** Here from Verona art thou banishèd.
Be patient, for the world is broad and wide.

ROMEO. There is no world without⁵ Verona walls,
But purgatory, torture, hell itself.
Hence banishèd is banished from the world,
20 And world's exile is death. Then "banishèd"
Is death mistermed. Calling death "banishèd,"
Thou cut'st my head off with a golden ax
And smilest upon the stroke that murders me.

FRIAR. O deadly sin! O rude unthankfulness!
25 Thy fault our law calls death;⁶ but the kind Prince,
Taking thy part, hath rushed⁷ aside the law,
And turned that black word "death" to "banishment."
This is dear mercy, and thou seest it not.

ROMEO. 'Tis torture, and not mercy. Heaven is here,
30 Where Juliet lives; and every cat and dog
And little mouse, every unworthy thing,
Live here in heaven and may look on her;
But Romeo may not. More validity,⁸
More honorable state, more courtship lives
35 In carrion flies than Romeo. They may seize
On the white wonder of dear Juliet's hand
And steal immortal blessing from her lips,
Who, even in pure and vestal modesty,
Still blush, as thinking their own kisses sin;
40 But Romeo may not, he is banishèd.
Flies may do this but I from this must fly;
They are freemen, but I am banishèd.
And sayest thou yet that exile is not death?
Hadst thou no poison mixed, no sharp-ground knife,
45 No sudden mean⁹ of death, though ne'er so mean,¹⁰
But "banishèd" to kill me—"banishèd"?
O friar, the damned use that word in hell;

3. **doomsday:** My death.

4. **vanished:** Escaped; came forth.

5. **without:** Outside.

6. **Thy fault . . . death:** For what you did our law demands the death penalty.
7. **rushed:** Pushed.

8. **validity:** Value.

◆ **Literary Focus**
What characteristics of a monologue are present in Romeo's lament?

9. **mean:** Method.
10. **mean:** Humiliating.

▲ **Critical Viewing** Friar Lawrence explains that the Prince has decided to be merciful: Instead of being put to death for killing Tybalt, Romeo is to be banished. Why does Romeo react so badly to this news? **[Analyze]**

Howling attends it! How hast thou the heart,
Being a divine, a ghostly confessor,
50   A sin-absolver, and my friend professed,
To mangle me with that word "banishèd"?

FRIAR. Thou fond mad man, hear me a little speak.

ROMEO. O, thou wilt speak again of banishment.

FRIAR. I'll give thee armor to keep off that word;
55   Adversity's sweet milk, philosophy,
To comfort thee, though thou art banishèd.

ROMEO. Yet "banished"? Hang up philosophy!
Unless philosophy can make a Juliet,
Displant a town, reverse a prince's doom,
60   It helps not, it prevails not. Talk no more.

FRIAR. O, then I see that madmen have no ears.

ROMEO. How should they, when that wise men have no eyes?

FRIAR. Let me dispute[11] with thee of thy estate.[12]

ROMEO. Thou canst not speak of that thou dost not feel.
65   Wert thou as young as I, Juliet thy love,
An hour but married, Tybalt murderèd,
Doting like me, and like me banishèd,
Then mightst thou speak, then mightst thou tear thy hair,
And fall upon the ground, as I do now,

11. **dispute:** Discuss.
12. **estate:** Condition; situation.

70   Taking the measure of an unmade grave.

[*Enter* NURSE *and knock.*]

FRIAR. Arise, one knocks. Good Romeo, hide thyself.

ROMEO. Not I; unless the breath of heartsick groans
        Mistlike infold me from the search of eyes. [*Knock.*]

FRIAR. Hark, how they knock! Who's there? Romeo, arise;
75   Thou wilt be taken.—Stay awhile!—Stand up; [*Knock.*]
        Run to my study.—By and by![13]—God's will,
        What simpleness[14] is this.—I come, I come! [*Knock.*]
        Who knocks so hard? Whence come you? What's your will?

[*Enter* NURSE.]

NURSE. Let me come in, and you shall know my errand.
        I come from Lady Juliet.

80 **FRIAR.**   Welcome then.

NURSE. O holy friar, O, tell me, holy friar,
        Where is my lady's lord, where's Romeo?

FRIAR. There on the ground, with his own tears made drunk.

NURSE. O, he is even in my mistress' case,
85   Just in her case! O woeful sympathy!
        Piteous predicament! Even so lies she,
        Blubb'ring and weeping, weeping and blubb'ring.
        Stand up, stand up! Stand, and you be a man.
        For Juliet's sake, for her sake, rise and stand!
90   Why should you fall into so deep an O?[15]

ROMEO. [*Rises.*] Nurse—

NURSE. Ah sir, ah sir! Death's the end of all.

ROMEO. Spakest thou of Juliet? How is it with her?
        Doth not she think me an old murderer,
95   Now I have stained the childhood of our joy
        With blood removed but little from her own?
        Where is she? And how doth she? And what says
        My concealed lady[16] to our canceled love?

NURSE. O, she says nothing, sir, but weeps and weeps;
100   And now falls on her bed, and then starts up,
        And Tybalt calls; and then on Romeo cries,
        And then down falls again.

ROMEO.   As if that name,

◆ **Reading Strategy**
How would you paraphrase Friar Lawrence's words if the scene were set in modern times?

13. **By and by!:** In a minute! (said to the person knocking).
14. **simpleness:** Silly behavior (Romeo does not move).

15. **O:** Cry of grief.

16. **concealed lady:** Secret bride.

Shot from the deadly level[17] of a gun,
Did murder her; as that name's cursèd hand
105   Murdered her kinsman. O, tell me, friar, tell me,
In what vile part of this anatomy
Doth my name lodge? Tell me, that I may sack[18]
The hateful mansion.

17. **level:** Aim.

18. **sack:** Plunder.

[*He offers to stab himself, and* NURSE *snatches the dagger away.*]

FRIAR.   Hold thy desperate hand.
Art thou a man? Thy form cries out thou art;
110   Thy tears are womanish, thy wild acts denote
The unreasonable fury of a beast.
Unseemly[19] woman in a seeming man!
And ill-beseeming beast in seeming both![20]
Thou hast amazed me. By my holy order,
115   I thought thy disposition better tempered.
Hast thou slain Tybalt? Wilt thou slay thyself?
And slay thy lady that in thy life lives,
By doing damnéd hate upon thyself?
Why railest thou on thy birth, the heaven, and earth?
120   Since birth and heaven and earth, all three do meet
In thee at once; which thou at once wouldst lose.
Fie, fie, thou shamest thy shape, thy love, thy wit,[21]
Which, like a usurer,[22] abound'st in all,
And usest none in that true use indeed
125   Which should bedeck[23] thy shape, thy love, thy wit.
Thy noble shape is but a form of wax,
Digressing from the valor of a man;
Thy dear love sworn but hollow prejury,
Killing that love which thou hast vowed to cherish;
130   Thy wit, that ornament to shape and love,
Misshapen in the conduct[24] of them both,
Like powder in a skilless soldier's flask,[25]
Is set afire by thine own ignorance,
And thou dismemb'red with thine own defense.[26]
135   What, rouse thee, man! Thy Juliet is alive,
For whose dear sake thou wast but lately dead.[27]
There art thou happy.[28] Tybalt would kill thee,
But thou slewest Tybalt. There art thou happy.
The law, that threat'ned death, becomes thy friend
140   And turns it into exile. There art thou happy.
A pack of blessings light upon thy back;
Happiness courts thee in her best array;
But, like a misbehaved and sullen wench,[29]

19. **Unseemly:** Inappropriate (because unnatural).
20. **And . . . both!:** That is, Romeo inappropriately has lost his human nature because he seems like a man and woman combined.

21. **wit:** Mind; intellect.
22. **Which, like a usurer:** Who, like a rich money-lender.
23. **bedeck:** Do honor to.

24. **conduct:** Management.
25. **flask:** Powder flask.

26. **And thou . . . defense:** The friar is saying that Romeo's mind, which is now irrational, is destroying rather than aiding him.
27. **but lately dead:** Only recently declaring yourself dead.
28. **happy:** Fortunate.

29. **wench:** Low, common girl.

Thou puts up[30] thy fortune and thy love.
145 Take heed, take heed, for such die miserable.
Go get thee to thy love, as was decreed,
Ascend her chamber, hence and comfort her.
But look thou stay not till the watch be set,[31]
For then thou canst not pass to Mantua,
150 Where thou shalt live till we can find a time
To blaze[32] your marriage, reconcile your friends,
Beg pardon of the Prince, and call thee back
With twenty hundred thousand times more joy
Than thou went'st forth in lamentation.
155 Go before, nurse. Commend me to thy lady,
And bid her hasten all the house to bed,
Which heavy sorrow makes them apt unto.[33]
Romeo is coming.

NURSE. O Lord, I could have stayed here all the night
160 To hear good counsel. O, what learning is!
My lord, I'll tell my lady you will come.

ROMEO. Do so, and bid my sweet prepare to chide.[34]

[NURSE *offers to go in and turns again.*]

NURSE. Here, sir, a ring she bid me give you, sir.
Hie you, make haste, for it grows very late. [*Exit.*]

165 **ROMEO.** How well my comfort is revived by this!

FRIAR. Go hence; good night; and here stands all your state:[35]
Either be gone before the watch be set,
Or by the break of day disguised from hence.
Sojourn[36] in Mantua. I'll find out your man,
170 And he shall signify[37] from time to time
Every good hap to you that chances here.
Give me thy hand. 'Tis late. Farewell; good night.

ROMEO. But that a joy past joy calls out on me,
It were a grief so brief to part with thee.
175 Farewell. [*Exit.*]

Scene iv. *A room in* CAPULET's *house.*

[*Enter old* CAPULET, *his* WIFE, *and* PARIS.]

CAPULET. Things have fall'n out, sir, so unluckily
That we have had no time to move[1] our daughter.
Look you, she loved her kinsman Tybalt dearly,
And so did I. Well, we were born to die.

---

30. **puts up:** Pouts over.

31. **watch be set:** Watchmen go on duty.

32. **blaze:** Announce publicly.

33. **apt unto:** Likely to do.

34. **chide:** Rebuke me (for slaying Tybalt).

35. **here . . . state:** This is your situation.

36. **Sojourn:** Remain.
37. **signify:** Let you know.

1. **move:** Discuss your proposal with.

5   'Tis very late; she'll not come down tonight.
       I promise you, but for your company,
       I would have been abed an hour ago.

    PARIS. These times of woe afford no times to woo.
       Madam, good night. Commend me to your daughter.

10 **LADY.** I will, and know her mind early tomorrow;
       Tonight she's mewed up to her heaviness.[2]

    CAPULET. Sir, Paris, I will make a desperate tender[3]
       Of my child's love. I think she will be ruled
       In all respects by me; nay more, I doubt it not.
15   Wife, go you to her ere you go to bed;
       Acquaint her here of my son[4] Paris' love
       And bid her (mark you me?) on Wednesday next—
       But soft! What day is this?

    PARIS.   Monday, my lord.

    CAPULET. Monday! Ha, ha! Well, Wednesday is too soon.
20   A[5] Thursday let it be—a Thursday, tell her,
       She shall be married to this noble earl.
       Will you be ready? Do you like this haste?
       We'll keep no great ado[6]—a friend or two;
       For hark you, Tybalt being slain so late,
25   It may be thought we held him carelessly,[7]
       Being our kinsman, if we revel much.
       Therefore we'll have some half a dozen friends,
       And there an end. But what say you to Thursday?

    PARIS. My lord, I would that Thursday were tomorrow.

30 **CAPULET.** Well, get you gone. A Thursday be it then.
       Go you to Juliet ere you go to bed;
       Prepare her, wife, against[8] this wedding day.
       Farewell, my lord.—Light to my chamber, ho!
       Afore me,[9] it is so very late
35   That we may call it early by and by.
       Good night.   [*Exit.*]

Scene v. CAPULET'S *orchard.*

[*Enter* ROMEO *and* JULIET *aloft.*]

    JULIET. Wilt thou be gone? It is not yet near day.
       It was the nightingale, and not the lark,[1]
       That pierced the fearful hollow of thine ear.
       Nightly she sings on yond pomegranate tree.

2. mewed . . . heaviness:
Locked up with her sorrow.
3. desperate tender: Risky
offer.

4. son: Son-in-law.

5. A: On.

6. We'll . . . ado: We won't
make a great fuss.

7. held him carelessly: Did
not respect him enough.

8. against: For.

9. Afore me: Indeed (a
mild oath).

1. nightingale . . . lark:
The nightingale was associated with the night, the lark
with dawn.

5   Believe me, love, it was the nightingale.

ROMEO. It was the lark, the herald of the morn;
No nightingale. Look, love, what envious streaks
Do lace the severing[2] clouds in yonder East.
Night's candles[3] are burnt out, and jocund day
10   Stands tiptoe on the misty mountaintops.
I must be gone and live, or stay and die.

JULIET. Yond light is not daylight; I know it, I.
It is some meteor that the sun exhales[4]
To be to thee this night a torchbearer
15   And light thee on thy way to Mantua.
Therefore stay yet; thou need'st not to be gone.

ROMEO. Let me be ta'en, let me be put to death.
I am content, so thou wilt have it so.
I'll say yon gray is not the morning's eye,
20   'Tis but the pale reflex of Cynthia's brow;[5]
Nor that is not the lark whose notes do beat
The vaulty heaven so high above our heads.
I have more care to stay than will to go.
Come, death, and welcome! Juliet wills it so.
25   How is't, my soul? Let's talk; it is not day.

JULIET. It is, it is! Hie hence, be gone, away!
It is the lark that sings so out of tune,
Straining harsh discords and unpleasing sharps.[6]
Some say the lark makes sweet division;[7]
30   This doth not so, for she divideth us.
Some say the lark and loathèd toad change eyes;[8]
O, now I would they had changed voices too,
Since arm from arm that voice doth us affray,[9]
Hunting thee hence with hunt's-up[10] to the day.
35   O, now be gone! More light and light it grows.

ROMEO. More light and light—more dark and dark our woes.

[*Enter* NURSE.]

NURSE. Madam!

JULIET. Nurse?

NURSE. Your lady mother is coming to your chamber.
40   The day is broke; be wary, look about.   [*Exit.*]

JULIET. Then, window, let day in, and let life out.

ROMEO. Farewell, farewell! One kiss, and I'll descend. [*He goeth down.*]

---

2. **severing:** Parting.
3. **Night's candles:** Stars.

4. **exhales:** Sends out.

5. **reflex . . . brow:** Reflection of the moon (Cynthia was a name for the moon goddess).

6. **sharps:** Shrill high notes.
7. **division:** Melody.

8. **change eyes:** Exchange eyes (because the lark has a beautiful body with ugly eyes and the toad has an ugly body with beautiful eyes).
9. **affray:** Frighten.
10. **hunt's-up:** Morning song for hunters.

◆ **Reading Strategy**
How might you translate Romeo and Juliet's conversation into plain contemporary English?

JULIET. Art thou gone so, love-lord, ay husband-friend?
I must hear from thee every day in the hour,
45 For in a minute there are many days.
O, by this count I shall be much in years[11]
Ere I again behold my Romeo!

ROMEO. Farewell!
I will omit no opportunity
50 That may convey my greetings, love, to thee.

JULIET. O, think'st thou we shall ever meet again?

ROMEO. I doubt it not; and all these woes shall serve
For sweet discourses[12] in our times to come.

JULIET. O God, I have an ill-divining[13] soul!
55 Methinks I see thee, now thou art so low,
As one dead in the bottom of a tomb.
Either my eyesight fails, or thou lookest pale.

ROMEO. And trust me, love, in my eye so do you.
Dry sorrow drinks our blood.[14] Adieu, adieu!   [*Exit.*]

60 **JULIET.** O Fortune, Fortune! All men call thee <u>fickle</u>.
If thou art fickle, what dost thou[15] with him
That is renowned for faith? Be fickle, Fortune,
For then I hope thou wilt not keep him long
But send him back.

[*Enter* MOTHER.]

65 **LADY CAPULET.** Ho, daughter! Are you up?

JULIET. Who is't that calls? It is my lady mother.
Is she not down so late,[16] or up so early?
What unaccustomed cause procures her hither?[17]

LADY CAPULET. Why, how now, Juliet?

JULIET.   Madam, I am not well.

70 **LADY CAPULET.** Evermore weeping for your cousin's death?
What, wilt thou wash him from his grave with tears?
And if thou couldst, thou couldst not make him live.
Therefore have done. Some grief shows much of love;
But much of grief shows still some want of wit.

75 **JULIET.** Yet let me weep for such a feeling[18] loss.

LADY CAPULET. So shall you feel the loss, but not the friend
Which you weep for.

11. **much in years:** Much older.

12. **discourses:** Conversations.
13. **ill-divining:** Predicting evil.

14. **Dry sorrow . . . blood:** It was once believed that sorrow drained away the blood.
15. **dost thou:** Do you have to do.

16. **Is she . . . late:** Has she stayed up so late?
17. **What . . . hither?:** What unusual reason brings her here?

18. **feeling:** Deeply felt.

◆ **Build Vocabulary**
fickle (fik´əl) *adj.:* Changeable

JULIET. Feeling so the loss,
I cannot choose but ever weep the friend.

LADY CAPULET. Well, girl, thou weep'st not so much for his death
80   As that the villain lives which slaughtered him.

JULIET. What villain, madam?

LADY CAPULET. That same villain Romeo.

JULIET. [*Aside*] Villain and he be many miles asunder.[19]—
God pardon him! I do, with all my heart;
And yet no man like he doth grieve my heart.

85 **LADY CAPULET.** That is because the traitor murderer lives.

JULIET. Ay, madam, from the reach of these my
    hands.
Would none but I might venge my cousin's death!

LADY CAPULET. We will have vengeance for it, fear thou not.
Then weep no more. I'll send to one in Mantua,
90   Where that same banished runagate[20] doth live,
Shall give him such an unaccustomed dram[21]
That he shall soon keep Tybalt company;
And then I hope thou wilt be satisfied.

JULIET. Indeed I never shall be satisfied
95   With Romeo till I behold him—dead[22]—
Is my poor heart so for a kinsman vexed.
Madam, if you could find out but a man
To bear a poison, I would temper[23] it;
That Romeo should, upon receipt thereof,
100   Soon sleep in quiet. O, how my heart abhors
To hear him named and cannot come to him,
To wreak[24] the love I bore my cousin
Upon his body that hath slaughtered him!

LADY CAPULET. Find thou the means, and I'll find such a man.
105   But now I'll tell thee joyful tidings, girl.

JULIET. And joy comes well in such a needy time.
What are they, beseech your ladyship?

LADY CAPULET. Well, well, thou hast a careful[25] father, child;
One who, to put thee from thy heaviness,
110   Hath sorted out[26] a sudden day of joy
That thou expects not nor I looked not for.

JULIET. Madam, in happy time![27] What day is that?

◆ **Literary Focus**
What characteristics of an aside do you see in Juliet's words in lines 82–84?

19. **asunder:** Apart.

20. **runagate:** Renegade; runaway.
21. **unaccustomed dram:** Unexpected dose of poison.

22. **dead:** Juliet is deliberately ambiguous here. Her mother thinks *dead* refers to Romeo. But Juliet is using the word with the following line, in reference to her heart.
23. **temper:** Mix; weaken.

24. **wreak** (reek): Avenge; express.

25. **careful:** Considerate.

26. **sorted out:** Selected.

27. **in happy time:** Just in time.

LADY CAPULET. Marry, my child, early next Thursday morn
  The gallant, young, and noble gentleman,
115 The County Paris, at Saint Peter's Church,
  Shall happily make thee there a joyful bride.

JULIET. Now by Saint Peter's Church, and Peter too,
  He shall not make me there a joyful bride!
  I wonder at this haste, that I must wed
120 Ere he that should be husband comes to woo.
  I pray you tell my lord and father, madam,
  I will not marry yet; and when I do, I swear
  It shall be Romeo, whom you know I hate,
  Rather than Paris. These are news indeed!

◀ Critical Viewing
Juliet pleads with her parents to change their minds about marrying her to Paris. Why do her parents think their plan is a good one? What does Juliet know that makes their plan a bad one? **[Analyze]**

125 **LADY CAPULET.** Here comes your father. Tell him so yourself,
And see how he will take it at your hands.

[*Enter* CAPULET *and* NURSE.]

CAPULET. When the sun sets the earth doth drizzle dew,
But for the sunset of my brother's son
It rains downright.
130 How now? A conduit,[28] girl? What, still in tears?
Evermore show'ring? In one little body
Thou counterfeits a bark,[29] a sea, a wind:
For still thy eyes, which I may call the sea,
Do ebb and flow with tears; the bark thy body is,
135 Sailing in this salt flood; the winds, thy sighs,
Who, raging with thy tears and they with them,
Without a sudden calm will overset
Thy tempest-tossèd body. How now, wife?
Have you delivered to her our decree?

140 **LADY CAPULET.** Ay, sir; but she will none, she gives you thanks.[30]
I would the fool were married to her grave!

CAPULET. Soft! Take me with you,[31] take me with you, wife.
How? Will she none? Doth she not give us thanks?
Is she not proud?[32] Doth she not count her blest,
145 Unworthy as she is, that we have wrought[33]
So worthy a gentleman to be her bride?

JULIET. Not proud you have, but thankful that you have.
Proud can I never be of what I hate,
But thankful even for hate that is meant love.

150 **CAPULET.** How, how, how, how, chopped-logic?[34] What is this?
"Proud"—and "I thank you"—and "I thank you not"—
And yet "not proud"? Mistress minion[35] you,
Thank me no thankings, nor proud me no prouds,
But fettle[36] your fine joints 'gainst Thursday next
155 To go with Paris to Saint Peter's Church,
Or I will drag thee on a hurdle[37] thither.
Out, you greensickness carrion![38] Out, you baggage![39]
You tallow-face![40]

LADY CAPULET.   Fie, fie! What, are you mad?

JULIET. Good father, I beseech you on my knees,
160 Hear me with patience but to speak a word.

CAPULET. Hang thee, young baggage! Disobedient wretch!
I tell thee what—get thee to church a Thursday

28. **conduit:** Water pipe.

29. **bark:** Boat.

30. **she . . . thanks:** She'll have nothing to do with it, thank you.
31. **Soft! Take . . . you:** Wait a minute. Let me understand you.
32. **proud:** Pleased.
33. **wrought:** Arranged.

34. **chopped-logic:** Contradictory, unsound thought and speech.
35. **Mistress minion:** Miss Uppity.
36. **fettle:** Prepare.

37. **hurdle:** Sled on which prisoners were taken to their execution.
38. **greensickness carrion:** Anemic lump of flesh.
39. **baggage:** Naughty girl.
40. **tallow-face:** Wax-pale face.

Or never after look me in the face.
Speak not, reply not, do not answer me!
165 My fingers itch. Wife, we scarce thought us blest
That God had lent us but this only child;
But now I see this one is one too much,
And that we have a curse in having her.
Out on her, hilding![41]

NURSE.   God in heaven bless her!
170 You are to blame, my lord, to rate[42] her so.

CAPULET. And why, my Lady Wisdom? Hold your tongue,
Good Prudence. Smatter with your gossips, go![43]

NURSE. I speak no treason.

CAPULET.   O, God-i-god-en!

NURSE. May not one speak?

CAPULET.   Peace, you mumbling fool!
175 Utter your gravity[44] o'er a gossip's bowl,
For here we need it not.

LADY CAPULET.   You are too hot.

CAPULET. God's bread![45] It makes me mad.
Day, night; hour, tide, time; work, play;
Alone, in company; still my care hath been
180 To have her matched; and having now provided
A gentleman of noble parentage,
Of fair demesnes,[46] youthful, and nobly trained,
Stuffed, as they say, with honorable parts,[47]
Proportioned as one's thought would wish a man—
185 And then to have a wretched puling[48] fool,
A whining mammet,[49] in her fortune's tender,[50]
To answer "I'll not wed, I cannot love;
I am too young, I pray you pardon me"!
But, and you will not wed, I'll pardon you!
190 Graze where you will, you shall not house with me.
Look to't, think on't; I do not use to jest.
Thursday is near; lay hand on heart, advise:[51]
And you be mine, I'll give you to my friend;
And you be not, hang, beg, starve, die in the streets,
195 For, by my soul, I'll ne'er acknowledge thee,
Nor what is mine shall never do thee good.
Trust to't. Bethink you. I'll not be forsworn.[52]   [*Exit.*]

JULIET. Is there no pity sitting in the clouds

---

41. **hilding:** Worthless person.

42. **rate:** Scold; berate.

43. **Smatter . . . go!:** Go chatter with the other old women.

44. **gravity:** Wisdom.

45. **God's bread!:** By the holy Eucharist!

46. **demesnes:** Property.
47. **part:** Qualities.

48. **puling:** Whining.
49. **mammet:** Doll.
50. **tender:** When good fortune is offered her.

51. **advise:** Consider.

52. **forsworn:** Made to violate my promise.

That sees into the bottom of my grief?
200 O sweet my mother, cast me not away!
Delay this marriage for a month, a week;
Or if you do not, make the bridal bed
In that dim monument where Tybalt lies.

LADY CAPULET. Talk not to me, for I'll not speak a word.
205 Do as thou wilt, for I have done with thee.   [*Exit.*]

JULIET. O God!—O nurse, how shall this be prevented?
My husband is on earth, my faith in heaven.[53]
How shall that faith return again to earth
Unless that husband send it me from heaven
210 By leaving earth?[54] Comfort me, counsel me.
Alack, alack, that heaven should practice stratagems[55]
Upon so soft a subject as myself!
What say'st thou? Hast thou not a word of joy?
Some comfort, nurse.

NURSE.   Faith, here it is.
215 Romeo is banished; and all the world to nothing[56]
That he dares ne'er come back to challenge[57] you;
Or if he do, it needs must be by stealth.
Then, since the case so stands as now it doth,
I think it best you married with the County.
220 O, he's a lovely gentleman!
Romeo's a dishclout to him.[58] An eagle, madam,
Hath not so green, so quick, so fair an eye
As Paris hath. Beshrew my very heart,
I think you are happy in this second match,
225 For it excels your first; or if it did not,
Your first is dead—or 'twere as good he were
As living here and you no use of him.

JULIET. Speak'st thou from thy heart?

NURSE. And from my soul too; else beshrew them both.

230 **JULIET.** Amen!

NURSE. What?

JULIET. Well, thou hast comforted me marvelous much.
Go in; and tell my lady I am gone,
Having displeased my father, to Lawrence' cell,
235 To make confession and to be absolved.[59]

NURSE. Marry, I will; and this is wisely done.   [*Exit.*]

JULIET. Ancient damnation![60] O most wicked fiend!

---

53. my faith in heaven: My marriage vow is recorded in heaven.

54. leaving earth: Dying.

55. stratagems: Tricks; plots.

56. all . . . nothing: The odds are overwhelming.

57. challenge: Claim.

58. a dishclout to him: A dishcloth compared with him.

59. absolved: Receive forgiveness for my sins.

60. Ancient damnation!: Old devil.

Is it more sin to wish me thus forsworn,
Or to dispraise my lord with that same tongue
240 Which she hath praised him with above compare
So many thousand times? Go, counselor!
Thou and my bosom henceforth shall be twain.[61]
I'll to the friar to know his remedy.
If all else fail, myself have power to die.

[*Exit.*]

Guide for Responding

◆ Literature and Your Life

Reader's Response What would you do if you were in Romeo's or Juliet's situation?

Thematic Focus Why is it that when people make an effort to work out a conflict it sometimes makes matters worse?

✓ Check Your Comprehension

1. Trace the sequence of events that begins with Tybalt's insult to Romeo and ends with Tybalt's death and Romeo's banishment.

2. Describe the clashing emotions Juliet feels when the Nurse reports Tybalt's death and Romeo's banishment.

3. In his long speech to Romeo, Friar Lawrence mentions three things for which Romeo should consider himself fortunate. What are they?

4. What decision concerning Paris and Juliet does Lord Capulet make in Scene iv? Describe Juliet's reaction to this plan.

5. What advice does the Nurse give Juliet at the end of Act III? Describe Juliet's reaction to this advice.

◆ Critical Thinking

INTERPRET

1. What does Romeo mean when he says, after killing Tybalt, "I am fortune's fool!"? **[Interpret]**

2. Why didn't Escalus sentence Romeo to death, in keeping with his speech in Act I? **[Draw Conclusions]**

3. As Romeo and Juliet are about to part, how do they differ in their views of the future? **[Compare and Contrast]**

4. Explain why you think Romeo and Juliet's troubles do or do not result primarily from fate. Support your answer with details from the play. **[Support]**

EVALUATE

5. How should Romeo have acted in Scene I? Support your answer. **[Criticize]**

EXTEND

6. Up to this point, the Nurse has acted as a counselor for Juliet. What qualities should a counselor have? **[Career Link]**

Guide for Responding (continued)

◆ Literary Focus

SOLILOQUY, ASIDE, AND MONOLOGUE

A **soliloquy** is a speech in which a character, alone on stage, speaks directly to the audience. An **aside** is a brief remark to the audience, uttered while other characters are nearby but unable to hear. A **monologue** is a lengthy speech addressed to other characters, rather than to the audience.

1. What thoughts and feelings does Juliet reveal in her soliloquy that opens Scene ii?
2. When Lady Capulet, in Scene v, refers to Romeo as a villain, Juliet utters the aside "Villain and he be many miles asunder." In your own words, what is Juliet saying? Why is it important that the audience, but not Lady Capulet, hear this remark?
3. Reread Friar Lawrence's monologue in Scene iii beginning "Hold thy desperate hand." What criticisms is he addressing to Romeo?

◆ Build Vocabulary

USING WORDS FROM MYTHOLOGY

Use the clues that follow to help you complete these sentences with the words provided.

a. nemesis **b.** mercurial **c.** odyssey

1. The mood of a ___?___ person can change quickly.
2. An ___?___ is a very long journey.
3. A ___?___ is a person who punishes.

MYTHOLOGICAL CLUES

Nemesis: Greek goddess of vengeance
Mercury: Swift Roman messenger to the gods
Odyssey: Ancient Greek epic about the wanderings of Odysseus

USING THE WORD BANK

Write the letter of the word that is the best synonym of the first word.

1. gallant: (a) enchanting, (b) courageous, (c) cowardly
2. fray: (a) brawl, (b) condition, (c) truce
3. martial: (a) financial, (b) deputy, (c) warlike
4. exile: (a) expel, (b) travel, (c) arrive
5. eloquence: (a) beauty, (b) expressiveness, (c) value
6. fickle: (a) fruitful, (b) erratic, (c) constant

◆ Reading Strategy

PARAPHRASE

Paraphrasing involves identifying key ideas and restating them in your own words.

1. Paraphrase lines 29 through 51 of scene iii.
2. Extend your paraphrasing skills by choosing a paragraph that you've written and restating it in language that Shakespeare might have used.

◆ Build Grammar Skills

COMMONLY CONFUSED WORDS: *WHO* AND *WHOM*

The pronoun *who* is used when the pronoun is the subject of the verb or is a predicate nominative. The pronoun *whom* is used when the pronoun receives the action of the verb or when it is the object of a preposition.

Practice On a sheet of paper, complete the following sentences by adding *who* or *whom*.

1. ___?___ began the argument that resulted in two deaths and Romeo's banishment?
2. Romeo, ___?___ has good intentions, tries to separate the combatants.
3. Romeo is a person to ___?___ banishment seems worse than death.
4. Juliet states that Romeo is the man ___?___ she will marry.

Idea Bank

Writing

1. **Editorial** Imagine that you're the editor of the Verona newspaper. Write an editorial on whether the Prince's response to Tybalt's death was appropriate. Support your argument with details from Acts I through III.
2. **Soliloquy** Write a brief soliloquy, either in prose or in blank verse, that Juliet might deliver just before meeting with the Friar.

Speaking and Listening

3. **Debate** Form two teams to debate the following issue: Is Romeo a victim of fate or of his own character?

Guide for Reading, Act IV

◆ Review and Anticipate

Romeo and Juliet are married for only a few hours when disaster strikes. Mercutio is killed by Tybalt in a duel meant for Romeo; enraged by Mercutio's death, Romeo fights with Tybalt and kills him. As a result, Romeo is banished forever from Verona. To make matters worse, Juliet's parents are determined to marry her to Paris. What do you think is going to happen to Romeo and Juliet? What, if anything, can they do to preserve their relationship?

◆ Reading Strategy

PREDICT

Dramatic irony, which occurs when the audience knows more about a situation than a character does, keeps the audience guessing about what will happen next. Will a character find out what the audience knows, and, if so, how will this happen and how will he or she react? What will happen if the character doesn't get the necessary information? As you continue reading, **predict**—make educated guesses—about what will happen next. Base your predictions on what you know about the characters' personalities and the information available to each of them. Also look for places where the author foreshadows, or hints at, future events. Jot down your predictions in a chart like this one.

Prediction	Actual Outcome

◆ Build Grammar Skills

PARALLEL STRUCTURE

To emphasize how a character thinks or feels, Shakespeare often uses **parallel structure**, or the expression of similar ideas in similar grammatical forms. For example, in Act IV, Juliet expresses to Friar Lawrence the magnitude of her contempt at the thought of marrying Paris by voicing a string of commands, each beginning with the words *bid me,* followed by a verb.

> O, bid me leap . . . /From off the battlements of any tower . . .
> . . . or bid me lurk / Where serpents are . . .
> Or bid me go into a new-made grave . . .

◆ Literary Focus

DRAMATIC IRONY

Dramatic irony is a contradiction between what a character thinks or says and what the audience or reader knows to be true. For example, in Act III, Scene iv, Lord Capulet decides that the way to ensure Juliet's future happiness is to have her wed Paris. He does not know what you know—that Juliet is already married. Such dramatic irony adds suspense and involves us emotionally in the action. It can even make us want to step into the world of the play and give the characters a correct understanding of the situation they are in.

◆ Build Vocabulary

SUFFIXES: *-ward*

In Act IV, Lord Capulet says that he is happy because his once *wayward* daughter is again obedient. The word *wayward* contains the suffix *-ward,* meaning "in a direction." Based on your knowledge of this suffix, you might guess that the definition of the word is "in the direction of a specific route." This is close to the actual definition: "insistent upon having one's own way."

WORD BANK

Before you read, preview these words.

pensive
vial
enjoined
wayward
dismal
loathsome
pilgrimage

ct IV

Scene i. FRIAR LAWRENCE'S *cell.*

[*Enter* FRIAR LAWRENCE *and* COUNTY PARIS.]

    FRIAR. On Thursday, sir? The time is very short.

    PARIS. My father[1] Capulet will have it so,
    And I am nothing slow to slack his haste.[2]

    FRIAR. You say you do not know the lady's mind.
5   Uneven is the course;[3] I like it not.

    PARIS. Immoderately she weeps for Tybalt's death,
    And therefore have I little talked of love;
    For Venus smiles not in a house of tears.
    Now, sir, her father counts it dangerous
10   That she do give her sorrow so much sway,
    And in his wisdom hastes our marriage
    To stop the inundation[4] of her tears,
    Which, too much minded[5] by herself alone,
    May be put from her by society.
15   Now do you know the reason of this haste.

    FRIAR. [*Aside*] I would I knew not why it should be slowed.—
    Look, sir, here comes the lady toward my cell.

[*Enters* JULIET.]

    PARIS. Happily met, my lady and my wife!

    JULIET. That may be, sir, when I may be a wife.

20 **PARIS.** That "may be" must be, love, on Thursday next.

    JULIET. What must be shall be.

    FRIAR.   That's a certain text.[6]

    PARIS. Come you to make confession to this father?

    JULIET. To answer that, I should confess to you.

    PARIS. Do not deny to him that you love me.

25 **JULIET.** I will confess to you that I love him.

    PARIS. So will ye, I am sure, that you love me.

1. father: Future father-in-law.
2. I . . . haste: I won't slow him down by being slow myself.
3. Uneven . . . course: Irregular is the plan.

4. inundation: Flood.
5. minded: Thought about.

6. That's . . . text: That's a certain truth.

JULIET. If I do so, it will be of more price,[7]
Being spoke behind your back, than to your face.

PARIS. Poor soul, thy face is much abused with tears.

30 **JULIET.** The tears have got small victory by that,
For it was bad enough before their spite.[8]

PARIS. Thou wrong'st it more than tears with that report.

JULIET. That is no slander, sir, which is a truth;
And what I spake, I spake it to my face.

35 **PARIS.** Thy face is mine, and thou hast sland'red it.

JULIET. It may be so, for it is not mine own.
Are you at leisure, holy father, now,
Or shall I come to you at evening mass?

FRIAR. My leisure serves me, <u>pensive</u> daughter, now.
40   My lord, we must entreat the time alone.[9]

PARIS. God shield[10] I should disturb devotion!
Juliet, on Thursday early will I rouse ye.
Till then, adieu, and keep this holy kiss.   [*Exit.*]

JULIET. O, shut the door, and when thou hast done so,
45   Come weep with me—past hope, past care, past help!

FRIAR. O Juliet, I already know thy grief;
It strains me past the compass of my wits.[11]
I hear thou must, and nothing may prorogue[12] it,
On Thursday next be married to this County.

50 **JULIET.** Tell me not, friar, that thou hearest of this,
Unless thou tell me how I may prevent it.
If in thy wisdom thou canst give no help,
Do thou but call my resolution wise
And with this knife I'll help it presently.[13]
55   God joined my heart and Romeo's, thou our hands;
And ere this hand, by thee to Romeo's sealed,
Shall be the label to another deed,[14]
Or my true heart with treacherous revolt
Turn to another, this shall slay them both.
60   Therefore, out of thy long-experienced time,
Give me some present counsel; or, behold,
'Twixt my extremes and me[15] this bloody knife
Shall play the umpire, arbitrating[16] that
Which the commission of thy years and art
65   Could to no issue of true honor bring.[17]

Be not so long to speak. I long to die
If what thou speak'st speak not of remedy.

FRIAR. Hold, daughter. I do spy a kind of hope,
Which craves[18] as desperate an execution
70　As that is desperate which we would prevent
　　If, rather than to marry County Paris,
　　Thou hast the strength of will to slay thyself,
　　Then is it likely thou wilt undertake
　　A thing like death to chide away this shame,
75　That cop'st with death himself to scape from it;[19]
　　And, if thou darest, I'll give thee remedy.

JULIET. O, bid me leap, rather than marry Paris.
　　From off the battlements of any tower,
　　Or walk in thievish ways,[20] or bid me lurk
80　Where serpents are; chain me with roaring bears,
　　Or hide me nightly in a charnel house,[21]
　　O'ercovered quite with dead men's rattling bones,
　　With reeky[22] shanks and yellow chapless[23] skulls;
　　Or bid me go into a new-made grave
85　And hide me with a dead man in his shroud—
　　Things that, to hear them told, have made me tremble—
　　And I will do it without fear or doubt,
　　To live an unstained wife to my sweet love.

FRIAR. Hold, then. Go home, be merry, give consent
90　To marry Paris. Wednesday is tomorrow.
　　Tomorrow night look that thou lie alone;
　　Let not the nurse lie with thee in thy chamber.
　　Take thou this <u>vial</u>, being then in bed,
　　And this distilling liquor drink thou off;
95　When presently through all thy veins shall run
　　A cold and drowsy humor;[24] for no pulse
　　Shall keep his native[25] progress, but surcease;[26]
　　No warmth, no breath, shall testify thou livest;
　　The roses in thy lips and cheeks shall fade
100　To wanny ashes,[27] thy eyes' windows[28] fall
　　Like death when he shuts up the day of life;
　　Each part, deprived of supple government,[29]
　　Shall, stiff and stark and cold, appear like death;
　　And in this borrowed likeness of shrunk death
105　Thou shalt continue two-and-forty hours,
　　And then awake as from a pleasant sleep.
　　Now, when the bridegroom in the morning comes
　　To rouse thee from thy bed, there art thou dead.

18. **craves:** Requires.

19. **That cop'st . . . it:** That bargains with death itself to escape from it.

20. **thievish ways:** Roads where criminals lurk.

21. **charnel house:** Vault for bones removed from graves to be reused.
22. **reeky:** Foul-smelling.
23. **chapless:** Jawless.

24. **humor:** Fluid; liquid.
25. **native:** Natural.
26. **surcease:** Stop.
27. **wanny ashes:** To the color of pale ashes.
28. **eyes' windows:** Eyelids.
29. **supple government:** Ability for maintaining motion.

◆ **Build Vocabulary**

vial (vī′ əl) *n*.: Small bottle containing medicine or other liquids

Then, as the manner of our country is,
110 In thy best robes uncovered on the bier[30]
Thou shalt be borne to that same ancient vault
Where all the kindred of the Capulets lie.
In the meantime, against[31] thou shalt awake,
Shall Romeo by my letters know our drift;[32]
115 And hither shall he come; and he and I
Will watch thy waking, and that very night
Shall Romeo bear thee hence to Mantua.
And this shall free thee from this present shame,
If no inconstant toy[33] nor womanish fear
120 Abate thy valor[34] in the acting it.

JULIET. Give me, give me! O, tell not me of fear!

FRIAR. Hold! Get you gone, be strong and prosperous
In this resolve. I'll send a friar with speed
To Mantua, with my letters to thy lord.

125 **JULIET.** Love give me strength, and strength shall help afford.
Farewell, dear father.   [*Exit with* FRIAR.]

Scene ii. *Hall in* CAPULET'S *house.*

[*Enter* FATHER CAPULET, MOTHER, NURSE *and* SERVINGMEN *two or three.*]

CAPULET. So many guests invite as here are writ.   [*Exit a* SERVINGMAN.]
Sirrah, go hire me twenty cunning[1] cooks.

SERVINGMAN. You shall have none ill, sir; for I'll try[2] if they can lick
their fingers.

5 **CAPULET.** How canst thou try them so?

SERVINGMAN. Marry, sir, 'tis an ill cook that cannot lick his own fingers[3]
Therefore he that cannot lick his fingers goes not with me.

CAPULET. Go, begone.   [*Exit* SERVINGMAN.]
We shall be much unfurnished[4] for this time.
10 What, is my daughter gone to Friar Lawrence?

NURSE. Ay, forsooth.[5]

CAPULET. Well, he may chance to do some good on her.
A peevish self-willed harlotry it is.[6]

[*Enter* JULIET.]

NURSE. See where she comes from shrift with merry look.

15 **CAPULET.** How now, my headstrong? Where have you been gadding?

30. uncovered on the bier: Displayed on the funeral platform.

31. against: Before.
32. drift: Purpose; plan.

33. inconstant toy: Passing whim.
34. Abate thy valor: Lessen your courage.

1. cunning: Skillful.

2. try: Test.

3. 'tis . . . fingers: It's a bad cook that won't taste his own cooking.
4. unfurnished: Unprepared.
5. forsooth: In truth.
6. A peevish . . . it is: It is the ill-tempered, selfish behavior of a woman without good breeding.

◆ **Build Vocabulary**

enjoined (en joind´) *v.*: Ordered

wayward (wā´ wərd) *adj.*: Insistent upon having one's own way; headstrong

JULIET. Where I have learnt me to repent the sin
Of disobedient opposition
To you and your behests,[7] and am <u>enjoined</u>
By holy Lawrence to fall prostrate[8] here
20   To beg your pardon. Pardon, I beseech you!
Henceforward I am ever ruled by you.

CAPULET. Send for the County. Go tell him of this.
I'll have this knot knit up tomorrow morning.

JULIET. I met the youthful lord at Lawrence' cell
25   And gave him what becomèd[9] love I might,
Not stepping o'er the bounds of modesty.

CAPULET. Why, I am glad on't. This is well. Stand up.
This is as't should be. Let me see the County.
Ay, marry, go, I say, and fetch him hither.
30   Now, afore God, this reverend holy friar,
All our whole city is much bound[10] to him.

JULIET. Nurse, will you go with me into my closet[11]
To help me sort such needful ornaments[12]
As you think fit to furnish me tomorrow?

35 **LADY CAPULET.** No, not till Thursday. There is time enough.

CAPULET. Go, nurse, go with her. We'll to church tomorrow.

                                          [*Exit* JULIET *and* NURSE.]

LADY CAPULET. We shall be short in our provision.[13]
'Tis now near night.

CAPULET.   Tush, I will stir about,
And all things shall be well, I warrant thee, wife.
40   Go thou to Juliet, help to deck up her.[14]
I'll not to bed tonight; let me alone.
I'll play the housewife for this once. What, ho![15]
They are all forth; well, I will walk myself
To County Paris, to prepare up him
45   Against tomorrow. My heart is wondrous light,
Since this same <u>wayward</u> girl is so reclaimed.

                                        [*Exit with* MOTHER.]

Scene iii. JULIET'S *chamber.*

[*Enter* JULIET *and* NURSE.]

JULIET. Ay, those attires are best; but, gentle nurse,
I pray thee leave me to myself tonight;
For I have need of many orisons[1]

---

7. behests: Requests.
8. fall prostrate: Lie face down in humble submission.

9. becomèd: Suitable; proper.

10. bound: Indebted.

11. closet: Private room.
12. ornaments: Clothes.

13. short . . . provision: Lacking time for preparation.

14. deck up her: Dress her; get her ready.

15. What, ho!: Capulet is calling for his servants.

◆ **Literary Focus**
What is ironic about Lord Capulet's relief and joy?

1. orisons: Prayers.

To move the heavens to smile upon my state,[2]

5 Which, well thou knowest, is cross[3] and full of sin.

[*Enter* MOTHER.]

LADY CAPULET. What are you busy, ho? Need you my help?

JULIET. No, madam; we have culled[4] such necessaries
As are behoveful[5] for our state tomorrow.
So please you, let me now be left alone,

10 And let the nurse this night sit up with you:
For I am sure you have your hands full all
In this so sudden business.

LADY CAPULET.   Good night.
Get thee to bed, and rest: for thou hast need.

[*Exit* MOTHER *and* NURSE.]

JULIET. Farewell! God knows when we shall meet again.

15 I have a faint cold fear thrills through my veins
That almost freezes up the heat of life.
I'll call them back again to comfort me.
Nurse!—What should she do here?
My dismal scene I needs must act alone.

20 Come, vial.
What if this mixture do not work at all?
Shall I be married then tomorrow morning?
No, no! This shall forbid it. Lie thou there.

[*Lays down a dagger.*]

What if it be a poison which the friar

25 Subtly hath minist'red[6] to have me dead,
Lest in this marriage he should be dishonored
Because he married me before to Romeo?
I fear it is; and yet methinks it should not,
For he hath still been tried[7] a holy man.

30 How if, when I am laid into the tomb,
I wake before the time that Romeo
Come to redeem me? There's a fearful point!
Shall I not then be stifled in the vault,
To whose foul mouth no healthsome air breathes in,

35 And there die strangled ere my Romeo comes?
Or, if I live, is it not very like
The horrible conceit[8] of death and night,
Together with the terror of the place—
As in a vault, an ancient receptacle

40 Where for this many hundred years the bones
Of all my buried ancestors are packed;

2. **state:** Condition.

3. **cross:** Selfish; disobedient.

4. **culled:** Chosen.

5. **behoveful:** Desirable; appropriate.

◆ **Reading Strategy**
What do you predict will happen to Juliet? Do you think that everything will turn out as she and the Friar planned?

6. **minist'red:** Given me.

7. **tried:** Proved.

8. **conceit:** Idea; thought.

◆ **Build Vocabulary**
dismal (diz´ məl) *adj.*: Causing gloom or misery

◄ **Critical Viewing** Juliet decides to take Friar Lawrence's potion despite her fears and misgivings. Do you think her decision is courageous. Why or why not? **[Evaluate]**

Where bloody Tybalt, yet but green in earth,⁹
Lies fest'ring in his shroud; where, as they say,
At some hours in the night spirits resort—
45 Alack, alack, is it not like¹⁰ that I,
So early waking—what with <u>loathsome</u> smells,
And shrieks like mandrakes¹¹ torn out of the earth,
That living mortals, hearing them, run mad—
O, if I wake, shall I not be distraught,¹²
50 Environèd¹³ with all these hideous fears,
And madly play with my forefathers' joints,
And pluck the mangled Tybalt from his shroud,
And, in this rage, with some great kinsman's bone
As with a club dash out my desp'rate brains?
55 O, look! Methinks I see my cousin's ghost
Seeking out Romeo, that did spit his body
Upon a rapier's point. Stay, Tybalt, stay!
Romeo, Romeo, Romeo, I drink to thee.

[*She falls upon her bed within the curtains.*]

9. **green in earth:** Newly entombed.

10. **like:** Likely.

11. **mandrakes:** Plants with forked roots that resemble human legs. The mandrake was believed to shriek when uprooted and cause the hearer to go mad.
12. **distraught:** Insane.
13. **Environèd:** Surrounded.

Scene iv. *Hall in* CAPULET's *house.*

[*Enter* LADY OF THE HOUSE *and* NURSE.]

LADY CAPULET. Hold, take these keys and fetch more spices, nurse.

NURSE. They call for dates and quinces¹ in the pastry.²

[*Enter old* CAPULET.]

CAPULET. Come, stir, stir, stir! The second cock hath crowed,
5   The curfew bell hath rung, 'tis three o'clock.
Look to the baked meats, good Angelica;³
Spare not for cost.

NURSE.   Go, you cotquean,⁴ go,
Get you to bed! Faith, you'll be sick tomorrow
For this night's watching.⁵

1. **quinces:** Golden apple-shaped fruit.
2. **pastry:** Baking room.
3. **Angelica:** This is probably the Nurse's name.
4. **cotquean** (kät´ kwēn): Man who does housework.
5. **watching:** Staying awake.

◆ **Build Vocabulary**

loathsome (lōth´ səm) *adj.*: Disgusting

CAPULET. No, not a whit. What, I have watched ere now
10 All night for lesser cause, and ne'er been sick.

LADY CAPULET. Ay, you have been a mouse hunt[6] in your time;
But I will watch you from such watching now.

[*Exit* LADY *and* NURSE.]

CAPULET. A jealous hood,[7] a jealous hood!

[*Enter three or four* FELLOWS *with spits and logs and baskets.*]
                          Now, fellow,
What is there?

15 **FIRST FELLOW.** Things for the cook, sir; but I know not what.

CAPULET. Make haste, make haste.   [*Exit* FIRST FELLOW.]
Sirrah, fetch drier logs.
Call Peter; he will show thee where they are.

SECOND FELLOW. I have a head, sir, that will find out logs
20 And never trouble Peter for the matter.

CAPULET. Mass,[8] and well said; a merry whoreson, ha!
Thou shalt be loggerhead.[9]   [*Exit* SECOND FELLOW, *with the others.*]
Good faith, 'tis day.
The County will be here with music straight,
For so he said he would.   [*Play music.*]
25   I hear him near.
Nurse! Wife! What, ho! What, nurse, I say!

[*Enter* NURSE.]
Go waken Juliet; go and trim her up.
I'll go and chat with Paris. Hie, make haste,
Make haste! The bridegroom he is come already:
30 Make haste, I say.   [*Exit.*]

Scene v. JULIET'S *chamber.*

NURSE. Mistress! What, mistress! Juliet! Fast,[1] I warrant her, she.
Why, lamb! Why, lady! Fie, you slugabed.[2]
Why, love, I say! Madam; Sweetheart! Why, bride!
What, not a word? You take your pennyworths now;
5 Sleep for a week; for the next night, I warrant,
The County Paris hath set up his rest
That you shall rest but little. God forgive me!
Marry, and amen. How sound is she asleep!
I needs must wake her. Madam, madam, madam!
10 Ay, let the County take you in your bed;
He'll fright you up, i' faith. Will it not be?

6. **mouse hunt:** Woman chaser.

7. **jealous hood:** Jealousy.

◆ **Literary Focus**
How is the bustle and excitement in the Capulet household an example of dramatic irony?

8. **Mass:** By the Mass (an oath).
9. **loggerhead:** Blockhead.

1. **Fast:** Fast asleep.
2. **slugabed:** Sleepy head.

I needs must wake her. Madam, madam, madam!

[*Draws aside the curtains.*]

What, dressed, and in your clothes, and down again?[3]

3. **down again:** Back in bed.

I must needs wake you. Lady! Lady! Lady!

15 Alas, alas! Help, help! My lady's dead!
O weraday that ever I was born!
Some *aqua vitae*, ho! My lord! My lady!

[*Enter* MOTHER.]

LADY CAPULET. What noise is here?

NURSE.   O lamentable day!

LADY CAPULET. What is the matter?

NURSE.   Look, look! O heavy day!

20 **LADY CAPULET.** O me, O me! My child, my only life!
Revive, look up, or I will die with thee!
Help, help! Call help.

[*Enter* FATHER.]

CAPULET. For shame, bring Juliet forth; her lord is come.

NURSE. She's dead, deceased; she's dead, alack the day!

LADY CAPULET. Alack the day, she's dead, she's dead, she's dead!

25 **CAPULET.** Ha! Let me see her. Out alas! She's cold,
Her blood is settled, and her joints are stiff;
Life and these lips have long been separated.
Death lies on her like an untimely frost
30 Upon the sweetest flower of all the field.

NURSE. O lamentable day!

LADY CAPULET.   O woeful time!

CAPULET. Death, that hath ta'en her hence to make me wail,
Ties up my tongue and will not let me speak.

[*Enter* FRIAR LAWRENCE *and the* COUNTY PARIS, *with* MUSICIANS.]

FRIAR. Come, is the bride ready to go to church?

35 **CAPULET.** Ready to go, but never to return.
O son, the night before thy wedding day
Hath Death lain with thy wife. There she lies,
Flower as she was, deflowerèd by him.
Death is my son-in-law, Death is my heir;
40 My daughter he hath wedded. I will die
And leave him all. Life, living, all is Death's.

PARIS. Have I thought, love, to see this morning's face,
And doth it give me such a sight as this?

LADY CAPULET. Accursed, unhappy, wretched, hateful day!
45 Most miserable hour that e'er time saw
In lasting labor of his pilgrimage!
But one, poor one, one poor and loving child,
But one thing to rejoice and solace⁴ in,
And cruel Death hath catched it from my sight.

50 **NURSE.** O woe! O woeful, woeful, woeful day!
Most lamentable day, most woeful day
That ever ever I did yet behold!
O day, O day, O day! O hateful day!
Never was seen so black a day as this.
55 O woeful day! O woeful day!

PARIS. Beguiled,⁵ divorcèd, wrongèd, spited, slain!
Most detestable Death, by thee beguiled,
By cruel, cruel thee quite overthrown.
O love! O life!—not life, but love in death!

60 **CAPULET.** Despised, distressèd, hated, martyred, killed!
Uncomfortable⁶ time, why cam'st thou now
To murder, murder our solemnity?⁷
O child, O child! My soul, and not my child!
Dead art thou—alack, my child is dead,
65 And with my child my joys are burièd!

FRIAR. Peace, ho, for shame! Confusion's cure lives not
In these confusions.⁸ Heaven and yourself
Had part in this fair maid—now heaven hath all,
And all the better is it for the maid.
70 Your part in her you could not keep from death,
But heaven keeps his part in eternal life.
The most you sought was her promotion,
For 'twas your heaven she should be advanced;
And weep ye now, seeing she is advanced
75 Above the clouds, as high as heaven itself?
O, in this love, you love your child so ill
That you run mad, seeing that she is well.⁹
She's not well married that lives married long,
But she's best married that dies married young.
80 Dry up your tears and stick your rosemary¹⁰
On this fair corse, and, as the custom is,
And in her best array bear her to church:
For though fond nature¹¹ bids us all lament,

4. **solace:** Find comfort.

5. **Beguiled:** Cheated.

6. **Uncomfortable:** Painful, upsetting.
7. **solemnity:** Solemn rites.

8. **Confusion's . . . confusions:** The remedy for this calamity is not to be found in these outcries.

9. **well:** Blessed in heaven.
10. **rosemary:** An evergreen signifying love and remembrance.
11. **fond nature:** Mistake-prone human nature.

◆ **Build Vocabulary**

pilgrimage (pil′ grəm ij) *n.:* Long journey

Yet nature's tears are reason's merriment.[12]

85   CAPULET.   All things that we ordainèd festival[13]
Turn from their office to black funeral—
Our instruments to melancholy bells,
Our wedding cheer to a sad burial feast;
Our solemn hymns to sullen dirges[14] change;
90   Our bridal flowers serve for a buried corse;
And all things change them to the contrary.

FRIAR.   Sir, go you in; and, madam, go with him;
And go, Sir Paris. Everyone prepare
To follow this fair corse unto her grave.
95   The heavens do low'r[15] upon you for some ill;
Move them no more by crossing their high will.
[*Exit, casting rosemary on her and shutting the curtains.
The* NURSE *and* MUSICIANS *remain.*]

FIRST MUSICIAN.   Faith, we may put up our pipes and be gone.

NURSE.   Honest good fellows, ah, put up, put up!
For well you know this is a pitiful case.[16]   [*Exit*]

100   FIRST MUSICIAN.   Ay, by my troth, the case may be amended.

[*Enter* PETER.]

PETER.   Musicians, O, musicians, "Heart's ease," "Heart's ease"! O, and
you will have me live, play "Heart's ease."

FIRST MUSICIAN.   Why "Heart's ease"?

PETER.   O, musicians, because my heart itself plays "My heart is full."
105   O, play me some merry dump[17] to comfort me.

FIRST MUSICIAN.   Not a dump we! 'Tis no time to play now.

PETER.   You will not then?

FIRST MUSICIAN.   No.

PETER.   I will then give it you soundly.

110   FIRST MUSICIAN.   What will you give us?

PETER.   No money, on my faith, but the gleek.[18] I will give you[19] the
minstrel.[20]

FIRST MUSICIAN.   Then will I give you the serving-creature.

PETER.   Then will I lay the serving-creature's dagger on your pate.
115   I will carry no crotchets.[21] I'll *re* you, I'll *fa* you. Do you note me?

FIRST MUSICIAN.   And you *re* us and *fa* us, you note us.

SECOND MUSICIAN.   Pray you put up your dagger, and put out your wit.

12. **Yet . . . merriment:**
While human nature causes
us to weep for Juliet,
reason should cause us to
be happy (since she is in
heaven).
13. **ordainèd festival:**
Planned to be part of a
celebration.
14. **dirges:** Funeral hymns.

◆ **Literary Focus**
What is ironic about
Friar Lawrence say-
ing in line 84 that
"nature's tears are
reason's merriment"?

15. **low'r:** Frown.

16. **case:** Situation;
instrument case.

17. **dump:** Sad tune.

18. **gleek:** Scornful speech.
19. **give you:** Call you.
20. **minstrel:** A
contemptuous term (as
opposed to *musician*).

21. **crotchets:** Whim;
quarter notes.

Then have at you with my wit!

120 **PETER.** I will dry-beat you with an iron wit, and put up my iron
dagger. Answer me like men.

"When griping grief the heart doth wound,
  And doleful dumps the mind oppress,
    Then music with her silver sound"—

125 Why "silver sound"? Why "music with her silver sound"? What say
you, Simon Catling?

FIRST MUSICIAN. Marry, sir, because silver hath a sweet sound.

PETER. Pretty! What say you, Hugh Rebeck?

130 **SECOND MUSICIAN.** I say "silver sound" because musicians sound for
silver.

PETER. Pretty too! What say you, James Soundpost?

135 **THIRD MUSICIAN.** Faith, I know not what to say.

PETER. O, I cry you mercy,[22] you are the singer. I will say for you. It is
"music with her silver sound" because musicians have no gold for
sounding.

> 22. **cry you mercy:** Beg
> your pardon.

"Then music with her silver sound
With speedy help doth lend redress."   [*Exit.*]

FIRST MUSICIAN. What a pestilent knave is this same!

140 **SECOND MUSICIAN.** Hang him, Jack! Come, we'll in here, tarry for the
mourners, and stay dinner.

[*Exit with others.*]

Guide for Responding

◆ Literature and Your Life

Reader's Response Should Romeo and Juliet have
followed Friar Lawrence's advice? Why or why not?

Thematic Focus When is it better to work
things out through a direct confrontation? When is it
better to use indirect means?

☑ Check Your Comprehension

1. Describe Friar Lawrence's plan for Juliet.
2. What three fears rise up in Juliet just before she
   drinks the potion?

◆ Critical Thinking

INTERPRET

1. What does Juliet's soliloquy in Scene iii reveal
   about her personality? **[Interpret]**
2. How has Juliet's character developed since the
   start of the play? Support your answer. **[Draw
   Conclusions]**
3. Do you think Paris is worthy of Juliet? Explain.
   [Analyze]

EVALUATE

4. Evaluate Friar Lawrence's plan. What do you anticipate might go wrong with it? **[Assess]**

Guide for Responding (continued)

◆ Literary Focus

DRAMATIC IRONY

Dramatic irony is a contradiction between what a character thinks, says, or does and what the audience or reader knows to be true. Because the audience has knowledge that the characters do not, it can foresee events to come even as the characters rush blindly toward their fate.

1. How is Juliet's meeting with Paris in Friar Lawrence's cell an example of dramatic irony?
2. Review Scene iv, in which Capulet is preparing for Juliet's wedding to Paris. What makes this scene an example of dramatic irony?
3. Find at least one other example of dramatic irony in the first four acts. Explain the example.

◆ Build Grammar Skills

PARALLEL STRUCTURE

Shakespeare often uses **parallel structures**—such as strings of similarly constructed sentences or phrases—to emphasize similar ideas.

Writing Application Rewrite the following to include a series of questions with parallel structures.

> Just before she drinks the Friar's potion, Juliet is tormented by questions. She asks herself what will happen if the mixture does not work. Voicing her worst fears, Juliet wonders whether the potion is poison. In agony, she finds herself contemplating what might happen if she wakes before Romeo arrives.

◆ Reading Strategy

PREDICT

You can **predict**—or make educated guesses about—the direction of future events in a literary work by considering what you know about the characters and thinking about how they'd be most likely to respond to their situations. You can also use **foreshadowing**—clues about events yet to occur—to help you in making predictions.

1. Find at least three examples of foreshadowing in the first four acts and explain how each example can help you predict future events.
2. What do you predict will happen in the final act?

◆ Build Vocabulary

USING THE SUFFIX *-ward*

Knowing that the suffix *-ward* means "in a direction," match each word on the left with its meaning.

1. forward   **a.** in the direction of the sky
2. skyward   **b.** toward or on the outside
3. outward   **c.** in the direction of the front; ahead

USING THE WORD BANK

Complete each analogy with a word from the Word Bank.

1. ____?____ is to *gloomy* as *bright* is to *glistening*
2. ____?____ is to *commanded* as *requested* is to *asked*
3. *exhausted* is to *rested* as *beautiful* is to ____?____
4. *long* is to ____?____ as *destructive* is to *tornado*
5. *sedan* is to *car* as ____?____ is to *container*
6. *day* is to *night* as *obedient* is to ____?____
7. ____?____ is to *thoughtful* as *leaping* is to *jumping*

Idea Bank

Writing

1. **Love Letter** Create a love letter that Juliet might have written for Romeo to read if she were never to awaken. For a challenge, try using language similar to that spoken by Juliet in the play.

2. **Your Own Ending** If you were to write your own ending for the play, what would it be? Write a narrative of events that would occur in your version of Act V. Make sure that your version develops naturally out of the events in Acts I through IV.

Speaking and Listening

3. **Renaissance Music Presentation** Collect examples of the kind of music that would have been played by the musicians in Scene v. Using the recordings you collect, along with facts you obtain through library research, prepare and deliver an informal oral presentation on Renaissance music. **[Social Studies Link; Music Link]**

Guide for Reading, Act V

◆ Review and Anticipate

You'll recall that in Act IV, Juliet escapes her unwanted marriage to Paris by taking a potion that puts her into a deathlike sleep for forty-two hours. Believing that she is dead, her family plans a funeral in place of her wedding. Having instructed Juliet to take the potion as part of a scheme to save her marriage to Romeo, Friar Lawrence sends a fellow friar to Mantua to tell Romeo about the plan of the ruse and to bring him back to rescue Juliet from her family tomb. What do you think might go wrong with Friar Lawrence's scheme?

◆ Literary Focus

TRAGEDY

A **tragedy** is a drama in which the central character meets with disaster or great misfortune. In the great tragedies of the past, including Shakespeare's, the central character's downfall is usually the result of fate, a serious character flaw, or a combination of the two. Other causes, however, may also be involved. Though flawed, the tragic hero or heroine is usually of noble stature and basically good. The downfall, therefore, always seems worse than what the character deserves. Yet a great tragedy is not depressing. It uplifts the audience by showing the greatness of spirit of which people are capable.

◆ Build Grammar Skills

SUBJECT AND VERB AGREEMENT IN INVERTED SENTENCES

Shakespeare's characters often use sentences with an **inverted word order**—sentences in which the verb comes before the subject. For example, Friar Lawrence uses a sentence with inverted word order in Act V when he asks, "What says Romeo?" When using inverted sentences such as this one, it is easy to make errors in **subject and verb agreement**. However, you can easily check to make sure that the subject agrees with its verb in number by changing the word order of the sentence so that the subject comes before the verb. Notice that if you change the order of the previous example to "Romeo says what?" you can clearly see that both the subject and the verb are singular.

◆ Reading Strategy

IDENTIFY CAUSES AND EFFECTS

A **cause** is an action, event, or situation that produces a result. An **effect** is the result produced by a cause. One way to understand a play or other kind of story is to analyze the chain of causes and effects that advances the plot. To do this, you need to notice how one event causes another event—its effect—and how that event in turn has its own effect.

Juliet takes the Friar's potion → Juliet falls into a deathlike sleep → Everyone thinks Juliet is dead → _____ → _____ → _____

◆ Build Vocabulary

PREFIXES: *ambi-*

Toward the end of the fifth act of *The Tragedy of Romeo and Juliet*, the Prince speaks of clearing up ambiguities. The word *ambiguities* contains the prefix *ambi-*, which means "both." Notice how the meaning of the prefix contributes to the overall meaning of the word: "statements or events that have two or more possible meanings."

WORD BANK

Before you read, preview this list of words.

remnants
penury
haughty
sepulcher
ambiguities
scourge

Romeo and Juliet

Act V

Scene i. *Mantua. A street.*

[*Enter* ROMEO.]

   ROMEO. If I may trust the flattering truth of sleep,[1]
     My dreams presage[2] some joyful news at hand.
     My bosom's lord[3] sits lightly in his throne,
     And all this day an unaccustomed spirit
5   Lifts me above the ground with cheerful thoughts.
     I dreamt my lady came and found me dead
     (Strange dream that gives a dead man leave to think!)
     And breathed such life with kisses in my lips
     That I revived and was an emperor.
10 Ah me! How sweet is love itself possessed,
     When but love's shadows[4] are so rich in joy!

[*Enter* ROMEO'S MAN, BALTHASAR, *booted.*]

     News from Verona! How now, Balthasar?
     Dost thou not bring me letters from the friar?
     How doth my lady? Is my father well?
15 How fares my Juliet? That I ask again,
     For nothing can be ill if she be well.

   MAN. Then she is well, and nothing can be ill.
     Her body sleeps in Capels' monument,[5]
     And her immortal part with angels lives.
20 I saw her laid low in her kindred's vault
     And presently took post[6] to tell it you.
     O, pardon me for bringing these ill news,
     Since you did leave it for my office,[7] sir.

   ROMEO. Is it e'en so? Then I defy you, stars!
25 Thou knowest my lodging. Get me ink and paper
     And hire post horses. I will hence tonight.

   MAN. I do beseech you, sir, have patience.
     Your looks are pale and wild and do import
     Some misadventure.[8]

   ROMEO.   Tush, thou art deceived.
30 Leave me and do the thing I bid thee do.
     Hast thou no letters to me from the friar?

1. flattering . . . sleep: Pleasing illusions of dreams.
2. presage: Foretell.
3. bosom's lord: Heart.

4. shadows: Dreams; unreal images.

5. Capels' monument: The Capulets' burial vault.

6. presently took post: Immediately set out on horseback.
7. office: Duty.

8. import/Some misadventure: Suggest some misfortune.

MAN. No, my good lord.

ROMEO.   No matter. Get thee gone.
And hire those horses. I'll be with thee straight.

Well, Juliet, I will lie with thee tonight.   [*Exit* BALTHASAR.]
35 Let's see for means. O mischief, thou art swift
To enter in the thoughts of desperate men!
I do remember an apothecary,[9]
And hereabouts 'a dwells, which late I noted
In tatt'red weeds, with overwhelming brows,
40 Culling of simples.[10] Meager were his looks,
Sharp misery had worn him to the bones;
And in his needy shop a tortoise hung,
An alligator stuffed, and other skins
Of ill-shaped fishes; and about his shelves
45 A beggarly account[11] of empty boxes,
Green earthen pots, bladders, and musty seeds,
Remnants of packthread, and old cakes of roses[12]
Were thinly scatterèd, to make up a show.
Noting this penury, to myself I said,
50 "And if a man did need a poison now
Whose sale is present death in Mantua,
Here lives a caitiff[13] wretch would sell it him."
O, this same thought did but forerun my need,
And this same needy man must sell it me.
55 As I remember, this should be the house.
Being holiday, the beggar's shop is shut.
What, ho! Apothecary!

[*Enter* APOTHECARY.]

APOTHECARY.   Who calls so loud?

ROMEO. Come hither, man. I see that thou art poor.
Hold, there is forty ducats.[14] Let me have
60 A dram of poison, such soon-speeding gear[15]
As will disperse itself through all the veins
That the life-weary taker may fall dead,
And that the trunk[16] may be discharged of breath
As violently as hasty powder fired
65 Doth hurry from the fatal cannon's womb.

APOTHECARY. Such mortal drugs I have; but Mantua's law
Is death to any he that utters[17] them.

ROMEO. Art thou so bare and full of wretchedness
And fearest to die? Famine is in thy cheeks,

◆ **Literary Focus**
How does the exchange between Romeo and the man suggest the role of fate in bringing about the tragedy?

9. **apothecary:** One who prepares and sells drugs and medicines.

10. **In tatt'red . . . simples:** In torn clothing, with overhanging eyebrows, sorting out herbs.

11. **beggarly account:** Small number.

12. **cakes of roses:** Pressed rose petals (used for perfume).

13. **caitiff:** Miserable.

14. **ducats:** Gold coins.
15. **soon-speeding gear:** Fast-working stuff.

16. **trunk:** Body.
17. **utters:** Sells.

◆ **Build Vocabulary**
remnants (rem´ nənts) *n.:* Remaining persons or things
penury (pen´ yə rē) *n.:* Extreme poverty

70　Need and oppression starveth in thy eyes.
Contempt and beggary hangs upon thy back:
The world is not thy friend, nor the world's law;
The world affords no law to make thee rich;
Then be not poor, but break it and take this.

75　**APOTHECARY.**　My poverty but not my will consents.

ROMEO.　I pay thy poverty and not thy will.

APOTHECARY.　Put this in any liquid thing you will
And drink it off, and if you had the strength
Of twenty men, it would dispatch you straight.

80　**ROMEO.**　There is thy gold—worse poison to men's souls,
Doing more murder in this loathsome world,
Than these poor compounds[18] that thou mayst not sell.
I sell thee poison; thou hast sold me none.
Farewell. Buy food and get thyself in flesh.
85　Come, cordial[19] and not poison, go with me
To Juliet's grave; for there must I use thee.　　　　[*Exit.*]

18. compounds: Mixtures.

19. cordial: Health-giving drink.

Scene ii. FRIAR LAWRENCE'S *cell.*

[*Enter* FRIAR JOHN *to* FRIAR LAWRENCE.]

JOHN.　Holy Franciscan friar, brother, ho!

[*Enter* FRIAR LAWRENCE.]

LAWRENCE.　This same should be the voice of Friar John.
Welcome from Mantua. What says Romeo?
Or, if his mind be writ, give me his letter.

5　**JOHN.**　Going to find a barefoot brother out,
One of our order, to associate[1] me
Here in this city visiting the sick,
And finding him, the searchers[2] of the town,
Suspecting that we both were in a house
10　Where the infectious pestilence did reign,
Sealed up the doors, and would not let us forth,
So that my speed to Mantua there was stayed.

LAWRENCE.　Who bare my letter, then, to Romeo?

JOHN.　I could not send it—here it is again—
15　Nor get a messenger to bring it thee,
So fearful were they of infection.

LAWRENCE.　Unhappy fortune! By my brotherhood,

1. associate: Accompany.

2. searchers: Health officers who search for victims of the plague.

◆ **Reading Strategy**
What do you think will be the effects of the failure of Friar John to deliver the letter to Romeo?

The letter was not nice,[3] but full of charge,
Of dear import;[4] and the neglecting it
20 May do much danger. Friar John, go hence,
Get me an iron crow and bring it straight
Unto my cell.

    JOHN.   Brother, I'll go and bring it thee.   [*Exit.*]

    LAWRENCE. Now must I to the monument alone.
    Within this three hours will fair Juliet wake.
25 She will beshrew[5] me much that Romeo
    Hath had no notice of these accidents;[6]
    But I will write again to Mantua,
    And keep her at my cell till Romeo come—
    Poor living corse, closed in a dead man's tomb!   [*Exit.*]

Scene iii. *A churchyard; in it a monument belonging to the* CAPULETS

[*Enter* PARIS *and his* PAGE *with flowers and sweet water.*]

    PARIS. Give me thy torch, boy. Hence, and stand aloof.[1]
    Yet put it out, for I would not be seen.
    Under yond yew trees lay thee all along,[2]
    Holding thy ear close to the hollow ground.
5   So shall no foot upon the churchyard tread
    (Being loose, unfirm, with digging up of graves)
    But thou shalt hear it. Whistle then to me,
    As signal that thou hearest something approach.
    Give me those flowers. Do as I bid thee, go.

10 **PAGE.** [*Aside*] I am almost afraid to stand alone
    Here in the churchyard; yet I will adventure.[3]   [*Retires.*]

    PARIS. Sweet flower, with flowers thy bridal bed I strew
    (O woe! thy canopy is dust and stones)
    Which with sweet[4] water nightly I will dew;
15 Or, wanting that, with tears distilled by moans.
    The obsequies[5] that I for thee will keep
    Nightly shall be to strew thy grave and weep.

                                    [*Whistle* BOY.]

    The boy gives warning something doth approach.
    What cursèd foot wanders this way tonight
20 To cross[6] my obsequies and true love's rite?
    What, with a torch? Muffle me, night, awhile.   [*Retires.*]

[*Enter* ROMEO, *and* BALTHASAR *with a torch, a mattock, and a crow of iron.*]

    ROMEO. Give me that mattock and the wrenching iron.

3. **nice:** Trivial.

4. **full of charge, Of dear import:** Urgent and important.

5. **beshrew:** Blame.

6. **accidents:** Happenings.

1. **aloof:** Apart.

2. **lay . . . along:** Lie down flat.

3. **adventure:** Chance it.

4. **sweet:** Perfumed.

5. **obsequies:** Memorial ceremonies.

6. **cross:** Interrupt.

Hold, take this letter. Early in the morning
See thou deliver it to my lord and father.
25 Give me the light. Upon thy life I charge thee,
Whate'er thou hearest or seest, stand all aloof
And do not interrupt me in my course.
Why I descend into this bed of death
Is partly to behold my lady's face,
30 But chiefly to take thence from her dead finger
A precious ring—a ring that I must use
In dear employment.[7] Therefore hence, be gone.
But if thou, jealous,[8] dost return to pry
In what I farther shall intend to do,
35 By heaven, I will tear thee joint by joint
And strew this hungry churchyard with thy limbs.
The time and my intents are savage-wild,
More fierce and more inexorable[9] far
Than empty[10] tigers or the roaring sea.

40 **BALTHASAR.** I will be gone, sir, and not trouble ye.

ROMEO. So shalt thou show me friendship. Take thou that.
Live, and be prosperous; and farewell, good fellow.

7. dear employment:
Important business.
8. jealous: Curious.

9. inexorable:
Uncontrollable.
10. empty: Hungry.

▲ Critical Viewing What is Romeo thinking and feeling as he
enters the Capulets' tomb? [Interpret]

BALTHASAR. [*Aside*] For all this same, I'll hide me hereabout.
His looks I fear, and his intents I doubt.   [*Retires.*]

45 **ROMEO.** Thou detestable maw,[11] thou womb of death,
Gorged with the dearest morsel of the earth,
Thus I enforce thy rotten jaws to open,
And in despite[12] I'll cram thee with more food.

[ROMEO *opens the tomb.*]

PARIS. This is that banished haughty Montague
50 That murd'red my love's cousin—with which grief
It is supposed the fair creature died—
And here is come to do some villainous shame
To the dead bodies. I will apprehend[13] him.
Stop thy unhallowèd toil, vile Montague!
55 Can vengeance be pursued further than death?
Condemnèd villain, I do apprehend thee.
Obey, and go with me; for thou must die.

ROMEO. I must indeed; and therefore came I hither.
Good gentle youth, tempt not a desp'rate man.
60 Fly hence and leave me. Think upon these gone;
Let them affright thee. I beseech thee, youth,
Put not another sin upon my head
By urging me to fury. O, be gone!
By heaven, I love thee better than myself,
65 For I come hither armed against myself.
Stay not, be gone. Live, and hereafter say
A madman's mercy bid thee run away.

PARIS. I do defy thy conjurations.[14]
And apprehend thee for a felon[15] here.

70 **ROMEO.** Wilt thou provoke me? Then have at thee, boy!

[*They fight.*]

PAGE. O Lord, they fight! I will go call the watch.

[*Exit.* PARIS *falls.*]

PARIS. O, I am slain! If thou be merciful,
Open the tomb, lay me with Juliet.   [*Dies.*]

ROMEO. In faith, I will. Let me peruse[16] this face.
75 Mercutio's kinsman, noble County Paris!
What said my man when my betossèd[17] soul
Did not attend[18] him as we rode? I think
He told me Paris should have married Juliet.
Said he not so, or did I dream it so?

11. **maw:** Stomach.

12. **despite:** Scorn.

◆ **Literary Focus**
Why is Romeo's intention to feed himself to the tomb especially tragic?

13. **apprehend:** Seize; arrest.

14. **conjurations:** Solemn appeals.
15. **felon:** Criminal.

16. **peruse:** Look over.
17. **betossèd:** Upset.
18. **attend:** Give attention to.

◆ **Build Vocabulary**
haughty (hôt´ē) *adj.*: Arrogant

▲ **Critical Viewing** In the tomb, Romeo pulls back the shroud to reveal what he thinks is Juliet's dead body. What clues about her appearance should have led him to realize she was still alive? **[Support]**

80 Or am I mad, hearing him talk of Juliet,
To think it was so? O, give me thy hand,
One writ with me in sour misfortune's book!
I'll bury thee in a triumphant grave.
A grave? O, no, a lanthorn,[19] slaught'red youth,
85 For here lies Juliet, and her beauty makes
This vault a feasting presence[20] full of light.
Death, lie thou there, by a dead man interred.

                                                   [Lays him in the tomb.]

How oft when men are at the point of death
Have they been merry! Which their keepers[21] call
90 A lightning before death. O, how may I
Call this a lightning? O my love, my wife!
Death, that hath sucked the honey of thy breath,
Hath had no power yet upon thy beauty.
Thou art not conquered. Beauty's ensign[22] yet
95 Is crimson in thy lips and in thy cheeks,
And death's pale flag is not advanced there.

19. lanthorn: Windowed structure on top of a room to admit light; also, a lantern.
20. feasting presence: Chamber fit for a celebration.

21. keepers: Jailers.

22. ensign: Banner.

Tybalt, liest thou there in thy bloody sheet?
O, what more favor can I do to thee
Than with that hand that cut thy youth in twain

100 To sunder²³ his that was thine enemy?
Forgive me, cousin!, Ah, dear Juliet,
Why art thou yet so fair? Shall I believe
That unsubstantial Death is amorous,²⁴
And that the lean abhorrèd monster keeps

105 Thee here in dark to be his paramour?
For fear of that I still will stay with thee
And never from this pallet²⁵ of dim night
Depart again. Here, here will I remain
With worms that are thy chambermaids. O, here

110 Will I set up my everlasting rest
And shake the yoke of inauspicious²⁶ stars
From this world-wearied flesh. Eyes, look your last!
Arms, take your last embrace! And, lips, O you
The doors of breath, seal with a righteous kiss

115 A dateless²⁷ bargain to engrossing²⁸ death!
Come, bitter conduct;²⁹ come, unsavory guide!
Thou desperate pilot,³⁰ now at once run on
The dashing rocks thy seasick weary bark!
Here's to my love! [*Drinks.*] O true apothecary!

120 Thy drugs are quick. Thus with a kiss I die.   [*Falls.*]

[*Enter* FRIAR LAWRENCE, *with lanthorn, crow, and spade.*]

FRIAR. Saint Francis be my speed!³¹ How oft tonight
Have my old feet stumbled³² at graves! Who's there?

BALTHASAR. Here's one, a friend, and one that knows you well.

FRIAR. Bliss be upon you! Tell me, good my friend,

125 What torch is yond that vainly lends his light
To grubs³³ and eyeless skulls? As I discern,
It burneth in the Capels' monument.

BALTHASAR. It doth so, holy sir; and there's my master,
One that you love.

FRIAR.   Who is it?

130 **BALTHASAR.**   Romeo.

FRIAR. How long hath he been there?

BALTHASAR.   Full half an hour.

FRIAR. Go with me to the vault.

◆ Literary Focus
What is tragically
ironic in Romeo's
observations about
Juliet?

23. **sunder:** Cut off.
24. **amorous:** Full of love.

25. **pallet:** Bed.

26. **inauspicious:** Promising misfortune.

27. **dateless:** Eternal.
28. **engrossing:** All-encompassing.
29. **conduct:** Guide (poison).
30. **pilot:** Captain (Romeo himself).

31. **speed:** Help.
32. **stumbled:** Stumbling was thought to be a bad omen.

33. **grubs:** Worms.

◆ Reading Strategy
How is Friar
Lawrence's late
arrival another exam-
ple of chance con-
tributing to this
tragedy?

BALTHASAR.   I dare not, sir.
My master knows not but I am gone hence,
And fearfully did menace me with death
If I did stay to look on his intents.

135 **FRIAR.** Stay then; I'll go alone. Fear comes upon me.
O, much I fear some ill unthrifty[34] thing.

BALTHASAR. As I did sleep under this yew tree here,
I dreamt my master and another fought,
And that my master slew him.

FRIAR.   Romeo!
140 Alack, alack, what blood is this which stains
The stony entrance of this sepulcher?
What mean these masterless[35] and gory swords
To lie discolored by this place of peace?

Romeo! O, pale! Who else? What, Paris too?
145 And steeped in blood? Ah, what an unkind[36] hour
Is guilty of this lamentable chance!
The lady stirs.

JULIET. O comfortable[37] friar! Where is my lord?
I do remember well where I should be,
150 And there I am. Where is my Romeo?

FRIAR. I hear some noise. Lady, come from that nest
Of death, contagion, and unnatural sleep.
A greater power than we can contradict
Hath thwarted our intents. Come, come away.
155 Thy husband in thy bosom there lies dead;
And Paris too. Come, I'll dispose of thee
Among a sisterhood of holy nuns.
Stay not to question, for the watch is coming.
Come, go, good Juliet. I dare no longer stay.

160 **JULIET.** Go, get thee hence, for I will not away.
What's here? A cup, closed in my truelove's hand?
Poison, I see, hath been his timeless[38] end.
O churl![39] Drunk all, and left no friendly drop
To help me after? I will kiss thy lips.
165 Haply some poison yet doth hang on them
To make me die with a restorative.[40]
Thy lips are warm!

CHIEF WATCHMAN. [*Within*] Lead, boy. Which way?

---

34. unthrifty: Unlucky.

35. masterless: Discarded (without masters).

[Enters the tomb.]

36. unkind: Unnatural.

[JULIET rises.]

37. comfortable: Comforting.

[Exit FRIAR.]

38. timeless: Untimely; too soon.
39. churl: Rude fellow.

[Kisses him.] **40. restorative:** Medicine.

◆ **Build Vocabulary**
sepulcher (sep´ əl kər) *n.:* Tomb

JULIET. Yea, noise? Then I'll be brief. O happy[41] dagger!

[*Snatches* ROMEO'S *dagger.*]

This is thy sheath; there rust, and let me die.

[*She stabs herself and falls.*]

[*Enter* PARIS' *boy and watch.*]

170   **BOY.** This is the place. There, where the torch doth burn.

    CHIEF WATCHMAN. The ground is bloody. Search about the churchyard.
      Go, some of you; whoe'er you find attach.[42]

[*Exit some of the* WATCH.]

      Pitiful sight! Here lies the County slain;
      And Juliet bleeding, warm, and newly dead,
175   Who here hath lain this two days burièd.
      Go, tell the Prince; run to the Capulets;
      Raise up the Montagues; some others search.

[*Exit others of the* WATCH.]

      We see the ground whereon these woes do lie,
      But the true ground[43] of all these piteous woes
180   We cannot without circumstance descry.[44]

[*Enter some of the* WATCH, *with* ROMEO'S MAN, BALTHASAR.]

    SECOND WATCHMAN. Here's Romeo's man. We found him in
      the churchyard.

    CHIEF WATCHMAN. Hold him in safety till the Prince come hither.

[*Enter* FRIAR LAWRENCE *and another* WATCHMAN.]

    THIRD WATCHMAN. Here is a friar that trembles, sighs and weeps.
      We took this mattock and this spade from him
185   As he was coming from this churchyard's side.

    CHIEF WATCHMAN. A great suspicion! Stay the friar too.

[*Enter the* PRINCE *and* ATTENDANTS.]

    PRINCE. What misadventure is so early up,
      That calls our person from our morning rest?

[*Enter* CAPULET *and his* WIFE *with others.*]

    CAPULET. What should it be, that is so shrieked abroad?

190   **LADY CAPULET.** O, the people in the street cry "Romeo,"
      Some "Juliet," and some "Paris"; and all run
      With open outcry toward our monument.

    PRINCE. What fear is this which startles in your ears?

    CHIEF WATCHMAN. Sovereign, here lies the County Paris slain;

---

41. happy: Convenient; opportune.

42. attach: Arrest.

43. ground: Cause.

44. without circumstance descry: See clearly without details.

◆ **Reading Strategy**
How might the outcome have been different if the characters had come to the churchyard in a different order?

195 And Romeo dead; and Juliet, dead before,
Warm and new killed.

PRINCE. Search, seek, and know how this foul murder comes.

CHIEF WATCHMAN. Here is a friar, and slaughtered Romeo's man,
With instruments upon them fit to open
200 These dead men's tombs.

CAPULET. O heavens! O wife, look how our daughter bleeds!
This dagger hath mista'en, for, lo, his house[45]
Is empty on the back of Montague,
And it missheathèd in my daughter's bosom!

205 LADY CAPULET. O me, this sight of death is as a bell
That warns my old age to a sepulcher.

[*Enter* MONTAGUE *and others.*]

PRINCE. Come, Montague; for thou art early up
To see thy son and heir more early down.

MONTAGUE. Alas, my liege,[46] my wife is dead tonight!
210 Grief of my son's exile hath stopped her breath.
What further woe conspires against mine age?

PRINCE. Look, and thou shalt see.

MONTAGUE. O thou untaught! What manners is in this,
To press before thy father to a grave?

215 PRINCE. Seal up the mouth of outrage[47] for a while,
Till we can clear these <u>ambiguities</u>
And know their spring, their head, their true descent;
And then will I be general of your woes[48]
And lead you even to death. Meantime forbear,
220 And let mischance be slave to patience.[49]
Bring forth the parties of suspicion.

FRIAR. I am the greatest, able to do least,
Yet most suspected, as the time and place
Doth make against me, of this direful[50] murder;
225 And here I stand, both to impeach and purge[51]
Myself condemnèd and myself excused.

PRINCE. Then say at once what thou dost know in this.

FRIAR. I will be brief, for my short date of breath[52]
230 Is not so long as is a tedious tale.
Romeo, there dead, was husband to that Juliet;
And she, there dead, that's Romeo's faithful wife.

45. house: Sheath.

46. liege (lēj): Lord.

47. mouth of outrage:
Violent cries.

48. general . . . woes:
Leader in your sorrow.

49. let . . . patience: Be
patient in the face of
misfortune.

50. direful: Terrible.
51. impeach and purge:
Accuse and declare
blameless.
52. date of breath: Term of
life.

◆ **Build Vocabulary**
ambiguities (am′ bə gyōō′ ə
tēz) *n.:* Statements or events
whose meanings are unclear

▲ **Critical Viewing** The chain of events in the play leads to the deaths of Juliet, Romeo, Paris, Tybalt, and Mercutio. How might some or all of this bloodshed have been prevented? **[Analyze]**

I married them; and their stol'n marriage day
Was Tybalt's doomsday, whose untimely death
Banished the new-made bridegroom from this city;
For whom, and not for Tybalt, Juliet pined.

235

You, to remove that siege of grief from her,
Betrothed and would have married her perforce
To County Paris. Then comes she to me
And with wild looks bid me devise some mean

240

To rid her from this second marriage,
Or in my cell there would she kill herself.
Then gave I her (so tutored by my art)

A sleeping potion; which so took effect
As I intended, for it wrought on her
245   The form of death. Meantime I writ to Romeo
That he should hither come as[53] this dire night
To help to take her from her borrowed grave,
Being the time the potion's force should cease,
But he which bore my letter, Friar John,
250   Was stayed by accident, and yesternight
Returned my letter back. Then all alone
At the prefixèd hour of her waking
Came I to take her from her kindred's vault;
Meaning to keep her closely[54] at my cell
255   Till I conveniently could send to Romeo.
But when I came, some minute ere the time
Of her awakening, here untimely lay
The noble Paris and true Romeo dead.
She wakes; and I entreated her come forth
260   And bear this work of heaven with patience;
But then a noise did scare me from the tomb,
And she, too desperate, would not go with me,
But, as it seems, did violence on herself.
All this I know, and to the marriage
265   Her nurse is privy;[55] and if aught in this
Miscarried by my fault, let my old life
Be sacrificed some hour before his time
Unto the rigor[56] of severest law.

      PRINCE.   We still have known thee for a holy man.
270   Where's Romeo's man? What can he say to this?

      BALTHASAR.   I brought my master news of Juliet's death;
And then in post he came from Mantua
To this same place, to this same monument.
275   This letter he early bid me give his father,
And threat'ned me with death, going in the vault,
If I departed not and left him there.

      PRINCE.   Give me the letter. I will look on it.
Where is the County's page that raised the watch?
280   Sirrah, what made your master[57] in this place?

      BOY.   He came with flowers to strew his lady's grave;
And bid me stand aloof, and so I did.
Anon comes one with light to ope the tomb;
And by and by my master drew on him;
And then I ran away to call the watch.

◆ **Reading Strategy**
What could Friar
Lawrence have done
differently that might
have prevented the
tragedy from
happening?

53. as: On.

54. closely: Hidden;
secretly.

55. privy: Secretly informed
about.

56. rigor: Strictness.

57. made your master:
Was your master doing.

285 **PRINCE.** This letter doth make good the friar's words,
Their course of love, the tidings of her death;
And here he writes that he did buy a poison
Of a poor pothecary and therewithal
Came to this vault to die and lie with Juliet.
290 Where be these enemies? Capulet, Montague.
See what a <u>scourge</u> is laid upon your hate,
That heaven finds means to kill your joys with love.
And I, for winking at[58] your discords too,
Have lost a brace[59] of kinsmen. All are punished.

295 **CAPULET.** O brother Montague, give me thy hand.
This is my daughter's jointure,[60] for no more
Can I demand.

MONTAGUE.   But I can give thee more;
For I will raise her statue in pure gold,
That whiles Verona by that name is known,
300 There shall no figure at such rate[61] be set
As that of true and faithful Juliet.

CAPULET. As rich shall Romeo's by his lady's lie—
Poor sacrifices of our enmity![62]

PRINCE. A glooming[63] peace this morning with it brings.
305 The sun for sorrow will not show his head.

58. **winking at:** Closing my eyes to.
59. **brace:** Pair (Mercutio and Paris).

60. **jointure:** Wedding gift; marriage settlement.

61. **rate:** Value.
62. **enmity:** Hostility.
63. **glooming:** Cloudy; gloomy.

◆ **Build Vocabulary**

scourge (skŭrj) *n.:* Whip or other instrument for inflicting punishment

Beyond Literature

Media Connection

Shakespeare Comes to Hollywood If William Shakespeare were alive today, he would be making a fortune collecting residuals for *The Tragedy of Romeo and Juliet.* Residuals are fees collected by performers and writers for each rerun of filmed or taped material. Since the dawning of the motion-picture industry, many of Shakespeare's plays have been made into movies. Hollywood producers and directors realize that Shakespeare's plays combine dramatic situations with universal themes, a combination that translates into success at the box office. The movies based upon Shakespearean plays include *Romeo and Juliet, Macbeth, Othello, Hamlet, Henry V, Richard III, Kiss Me Kate* (based upon The *Taming of the Shrew*), *Julius Caesar, King Lear,* and *Antony and Cleopatra.* In the case of some of the plays, such as *Hamlet* and *King Lear,* several film versions have been made. In addition, the stars of Shakespearean movies comprise some of the world's finest actors. A partial list includes Laurence Olivier, Charlton Heston, Kathryn Grayson, John Gielgud, Deborah Kerr, James Mason, Marlon Brando, Diana Rigg, Orson Welles, Richard Chamberlain, Paul Scofield, and Lynn Redgrave. What specific elements and qualities of *The Tragedy of Romeo and Juliet* have made it a candidate for a great motion picture?

Go hence, to have more talk of these sad things;
  Some shall be pardoned, and some punishèd;
For never was a story of more woe
Than this of Juliet and her Romeo.

[Exit all.]

Guide for Responding

◆ Literature and Your Life

Reader's Response Were you in any way surprised by the way in which this play ends? Why or why not?

Thematic Focus Why do you think that a tragedy or a disaster often has to occur before rival groups make the effort to work out their conflicts?

Group Activity Suppose that you could have stepped into the action of the play for exactly one minute. In a small group, discuss when you would have stepped in and what you would have said or done.

☑ Check Your Comprehension

1. At the start of Scene i, why is Romeo happy and expecting joyful news?
2. Why does the Friar go to Juliet's tomb?
3. What causes Paris and Romeo to fight?
4. How do Romeo and Juliet die?
5. How does the relationship of the feuding families change at the end of the play?

◆ Critical Thinking

INTERPRET

1. Why isn't it surprising that Friar Lawrence's scheme fails? Base your answer both on your own experience and on events from the play. **[Analyze]**
2. (a) Hearing Balthasar's report of Juliet's death (Scene i), Romeo exclaims, "Then I defy you, stars!" What might he mean by this? (b) How are his words consistent with what you know of his character? **[Connect]**
3. (a) In what ways is chance to blame for the deaths of Romeo and Juliet? (b) In what ways are Romeo and Juliet to blame for their deaths? (c) In what ways are their families to blame? **[Analyze]**
4. What lessons can be learned from Shakespeare's play about the destructive effects of hatred? Support your answer. **[Draw Conclusions]**

EVALUATE

5. Was it necessary for Romeo and Juliet to die for the feud between the Montagues and Capulets to end? Explain. **[Assess]**

APPLY

6. Explain how the lesson that the play teaches could be applied to a specific situation in today's world. **[Apply]**

Guide for Responding (continued)

◆ Literary Focus

TRAGEDY

A **tragedy** is a drama in which the central character or characters suffer disaster or great misfortune. In many tragedies, the downfall results from fate, a serious character flaw, or a combination of the two. Other contributing causes may be present as well. The theme of a tragedy is the central idea or insight about life that explains why the downfall occurred.

1. What character traits of the lovers may have led to their destruction?
2. What events reveal the tragic influence of fate or chance?
3. What other causes or conditions are important to the way events turn out?
4. Using your answers to the preceding questions, write a one-sentence statement of the theme, or central message, of *Romeo and Juliet*. You might put your sentence in a form like the following: "The theme of the play is that ____?____ leads to the destruction of ____?____."

◆ Build Grammar Skills

SUBJECT AND VERB AGREEMENT IN INVERTED SENTENCES

To determine whether the verb of an **inverted sentence**—one in which the verb precedes the subject—should be singular or plural, rearrange the sentence so that the subject comes before the verb.

Practice Write the form of the verb in parentheses that correctly completes each sentence.

1. Through the churchyard (walks, walk) the watchman.
2. Where (is, are) Romeo and Juliet?
3. Upon ghastly sights (stumbles, stumble) the watchman.
4. Silent and still (is, are) the couple.
5. Into deepest sorrow (plunges, plunge) the Montagues and the Capulets.

Writing Application Write a brief dialogue between two of the characters in the play. Include five sentences with inverted word order.

◆ Reading Strategy

IDENTIFY CAUSES AND EFFECTS

A **cause** is an event that produces a result, or **effect**. This effect may then cause effects of its own. The plot of a play or other story consists of a chain of events linked by cause-and-effect relationships.

1. Describe the chain of events in Act V that lead up to the deaths of Paris, Romeo, and Juliet.
2. Summarize Friar Lawrence's monologue in Scene iii, lines 230–263 in a form similar to the one used on page 760.

◆ Build Vocabulary

USING THE PREFIX *ambi-*

The prefix *ambi-* means "both." Using the clues for help, complete each of the following sentences with one of the words below. Write your answers on a separate sheet of paper.

a. ambidextrous   **b.** ambilateral

1. An ____?____ person can use both hands with equal skill.
2. A condition affecting both sides of the body is ____?____.

CLUES

dexter: skillful   *later-:* side

USING THE WORD BANK

On a separate sheet of paper, write the letter of the word that is the best synonym of the first word.

1. remnants: (a) cloths, (b) remains, (c) factors
2. penury: (a) poverty, (b) currency, (c) disease
3. haughty: (a) timid, (b) friendly, (c) egotistical
4. sepulcher: (a) monument, (b) tomb, (c) cemetery
5. ambiguities: (a) courtesies, (b) details, (c) uncertainties
6. scourge: (a) sorrow, (b) whip, (c) hatred

Build Your Portfolio

 ## Idea Bank

Writing

1. **Summary** Imagine that Prince Escalus has asked you to brief him on the events leading up to the deaths of Romeo and Juliet. Write a short, factual account.

2. **Alternate Ending** Write a new version of Act V that develops naturally out of Acts I–IV. Your new ending can be happy or tragic, and it can involve the deaths of some or none of the characters.

3. **Response to Literary Criticism** W. H. Auden has said that *Romeo and Juliet* "is not simply a tragedy of two individuals, but the tragedy of a city. Everybody in the city is in one way or another involved in and responsible for what happens." Write a brief essay in which you explain why you agree or disagree with this statement.

Speaking and Listening

4. **Modern Scene** With a group, rewrite a scene from *Romeo and Juliet* to fit a contemporary setting of your choice. Rehearse your scene, then perform it for the class. **[Performing Arts Link]**

5. **Rap Song** Compose and perform a rap song about *Romeo and Juliet* that both summarizes the story and includes your reactions to it. **[Music Link; Performing Arts Link]**

Projects

6. **Set Design** Imagine that you and a group of classmates have been hired as set designers for a modern-day version of the play. Decide on an appropriate setting for the adaptation. Then create a description, with diagrams, of the set. **[Art Link]**

7. **Shakespeare Display** As a class, create a Shakespeare display. Include a variety of materials, such as biographies, versions of the plays, student compositions, and artwork.

 ## Writing Mini-Lesson

Persuasive Letter

If Friar Lawrence had tried to persuade both the Montagues and the Capulets to end their feud, Romeo and Juliet might have been saved. As Friar Lawrence, develop a letter to both families, written immediately after the wedding, to persuade them to end the feud.

Writing Skills Focus: Persuasive Appeals

To be persuasive, your letter must **appeal both to reason and to the emotions**. Emotional appeals attempt to touch the hearts of readers. You might touch the heart by asking both families if they want their children to be miserable. Appeals to reason present facts that support an argument. For example, you might cite the senseless bloodshed the feud has engendered. Note the appeal to reason the Nurse employs to try to persuade Juliet to marry Paris.

Model From the Selection

Romeo is banishèd; and all the world to nothing / That he dares ne'er come back to challenge you; / Or if he do, it needs must be by stealth. / Then, since the case so stands as now it doth, / I think it best you married with the County.

Prewriting Jot down all of the factual evidence and the emotional pleas you will present to persuade the families to end their feud.

Drafting Begin your letter by announcing the marriage ceremony you have just performed. Then arrange your persuasive points in a logical order. One method is to lead your readers up to your strongest argument.

Revising Read your draft as if you were a Montague or a Capulet. Does the letter present, in a logical order, arguments that appeal to reason and to the emotions? Might anything in the letter seem offensive to members of either family?

Editorial

Writing Process Workshop

In an **editorial**, a writer offers his or her personal views on an issue and provides facts and examples that support those views. Many newspapers and magazines carry editorials on a wide range of topics.

Write an editorial based on an idea in one of the plays in this section—for example, on dating or on resolving a long-standing feud—or on one of the plays itself. The following skills will help you write an editorial on any topic.

Writing Skills Focus

▶ **Make persuasive appeals to readers' emotions and to their reason.** In an emotional appeal, you attempt to touch the reader's heart and arouse a feeling such as pity or anger. In an appeal to reason, you present facts, details, and examples that support your argument. (See p. 777.)

▶ **Support your opinions with facts.** Facts are statements that can be proved true; opinions cannot be proved true or false. In your editorial, provide facts to support each of your opinions

In the following passage from an editorial, the writer uses these skills in trying to persuade readers to accept her point of view.

---

① The writer states her opinion early in the editorial.

② The writer appeals to reason by offering facts and examples to support her opinion.

③ The writer appeals to emotion by stirring readers' pride and anger.

MODEL FROM LITERATURE

Some publishers now print simplified versions of Shakespeare's plays. I feel that is very wrong. ① By not having the original text, readers are deprived of the beauty of the language. "Wherefore art thou Romeo?" becomes simply, "Why do you have to be Romeo?" Studies show that readers of such texts often don't go on to more challenging material. ② Soon publishers will be revising our Declaration of Independence! Is that what we want? I say stick to the original! ③

Prewriting

Choose a Topic Base your topic on an idea presented in either *The Dancers* or *Romeo and Juliet*, or write about one of the plays or playwrights. Choose an idea listed here or come up with your own idea.

Topic Ideas

- Should a parent tell a child whom to date?
- What is the best way to turn down a date?
- Should a long-standing feud be allowed to continue?
- Are Shakespeare's plays still relevant today?

Plan an Appeal to Reason Jot down your point of view on your topic, then list facts, examples, and details to support your point of view. First list the facts you already know. Then go to the library to find more information. Ask yourself:

▶ What supporting facts and examples can I find in books, encyclopedias, and almanacs?

▶ What information might I use from newspapers and magazines?

▶ What other sources might have useful information?

To help you distinguish facts from opinions, look at this chart:

Distinguishing Fact From Opinion

Opinions	Facts
This is a responsible newspaper.	This newspaper won a Pulitzer Prize for Meritorious Public Service.
Mr. Tsao isn't boring.	Mr. Tsao alternates between lectures and hands-on demonstrations.
We need more pet shelters.	Last year, more than 600 stray animals were destroyed because shelters had no room for them.
Americans eat too much fat.	The average American diet is 40 percent fat.

Plan an Appeal to Emotion On another piece of paper, identify the emotions you wish to stir in your readers. Do you want them to feel anger, fear, or sorrow? Take notes on emotional arguments you might use to achieve your goal. Also, consider how you might use pictures to arouse readers' feelings.

APPLYING LANGUAGE SKILLS: Compound-Complex Sentences

A **compound-complex sentence** has two or more independent clauses and one or more subordinate clauses:

The plays that Shakespeare wrote are great, but simplified texts ruin them.

The plays are great and *simplified texts ruin them* are independent clauses; *that Shakespeare wrote* is a subordinate clause.

Practice Rewrite each pair of sentences as a compound-complex sentence.

1. If you're treated like a child, you'll act like one. You'll never grow up.

2. The text is hard at first. If you read it long enough, it gets easier.

Writing Application As you draft your editorial, look for places where you can combine information into a compound-complex sentence.

Writer's Solution Connection Writing Lab

To help you gather evidence for your editorial, use the Pros and Cons organizer in the Prewriting section of the Persuasion tutorial.

APPLYING LANGUAGE SKILLS: Infinitives

An **infinitive** is a verb form preceded by the word *to*. Avoid splitting an infinitive by inserting a word between *to* and the verb.

Correct: It is hard to read Shakespeare quickly.

Incorrect: It is hard to quickly read Shakespeare.

Practice Rewrite each sentence to avoid a split infinitive.

1. Try to fully understand the text.
2. Don't be afraid to occasionally ask questions.
3. It feels good to bravely face a challenge.

Writing Application Review your editorial and check to see whether it contains any split infinitives. If it does, revise the sentences so the word *to* is not separated from its verb.

Writer's Solution Connection Writing Lab

For your additional help in revising your editorial, use the instruction and activities in the tutorial on Persuasion in the Writing Lab. You'll find an interactive student model and instruction on identifying faulty reasoning.

Drafting

Use a Solid Organization As you draft, be sure to use a solid organization to present the reasons that support your point of view. You might choose to go from the most important reasons to the least important, or do the reverse. You might also use a cause-and-effect organization, which will explain the reasons why something happened or will happen.

Write a Strong Introduction, Body, and Conclusion Begin your editorial with a strong statement that will capture readers' interest. In the body of your editorial, support your position with facts and examples. In the conclusion, restate your position and summarize your most important points.

Revising

Use a Peer Reviewer Ask a classmate to read your editorial, then answer the following questions:

▶ What is the writer's position?
▶ What details support the writer's position?
▶ What details do not support the writer's position?
▶ Has the writer appealed to reason? How?
▶ Has the writer appealed to emotion? How?

Use your peer reviewer's comments to guide your revision. However, use your judgment—you don't have to do everything your peer reviewer suggests.

Publishing

▶ **Classroom** Deliver your editorial in the form of a "live broadcast" to your class.
▶ **Newspaper** Send your editorial to your school newspaper or a local newspaper.
▶ **Magazine** Submit your editorial to a magazine that publishes editorials related to your topic.

Real-World Reading Skills Workshop

Strategies for Success

At times, you may be faced with reading a difficult selection, such as a play by William Shakespeare. Just looking at the material might discourage you, but don't lose hope! There are strategies for breaking down the text to make it easier to understand.

Get an Overview Whether the text is a long book, short story, poem, or play, first look at the overall selection. Note its title—it may signal the content of the selection. Next, note whether the text is divided into chapters, stanzas, or paragraphs. If there are subtitles, read them for clues to the content.

Tackle One Section at a Time Begin with the first section you plan to read. Look at captions or highlighted words that may appear in the section. Also, look for footnotes or glosses (notes in the side columns) that will illuminate the meaning. Next, go through the text line by line. If a sentence is long, break it into parts where a comma appears. Read the text once for general meaning. Then go back and reread those parts you didn't understand fully.

Do a Vocabulary Search As you read a difficult text, jot down any words that are unfamiliar. Try to get a sense of a word's meaning by its context—how it is used in the passage. If that doesn't work, look up the word in a dictionary before rereading the passage.

Apply the Strategy

Here is your chance to succeed with a challenging text. Read "The True Tragedy of Romeo and Juliet" article. Then answer these questions.

1. How is the text divided? What do you learn about the article from its title and subtitle?
2. What specific topic does the author discuss in each paragraph?
3. Which longer sentences did you break into parts? Where did you break them?
4. Which vocabulary words were you able to figure out from the context? What clues in the passage hinted at the meaning?

The True Tragedy of Romeo and Juliet

Shakespeare's tragedy *Romeo and Juliet* may be centuries old, yet its message is as timely as any contemporary tome. The two star-crossed lovers ultimately meet with tragedy because of a senseless feud between their clans.

A Message for Today

One only has to peruse today's newspaper headlines to conclude that baseless hatred remains rampant in modern society. Countries, armies, and families wage war with one another. If humans don't learn how to coexist in harmony, tragedy will continue to manifest itself with international, national, and personal repercussions.

> ✔ Here are other situations in which breaking down difficult text will help your understanding:
> ▶ Reading a scientific report
> ▶ Reading a contract
> ▶ Reading the results of a government study
> ▶ Reading a scholarly work

Speaking and Listening Workshop

Giving a Persuasive Speech

Imagine giving a speech in which you try to persuade the Capulets and the Montagues to give up their terrible feud. When you give a persuasive speech, your aim is to persuade listeners to accept your opinion about a subject. Knowing how to present yourself can help you to convince your listeners.

Appear Confident To persuade an audience, you must make them feel that you really believe what you're telling them. Speak in a tone of voice that is strong and confident. Also, be enthusiastic about your reasons. If you aren't excited about your views, chances are your listeners won't be, either.

Use Strong, Persuasive Language Choose words that will have an emotional impact on your listeners. Note the difference in these speeches. Which is more effective? Why?

> *This feud is harmful to everyone involved. I think you should give it up.*

> *Your ridiculous feud has sent your precious children to their graves. I urge you to make peace with each other—before more innocent lives are lost.*

Be Animated When you speak, don't stand stiffly. Also, don't look bored or tired. Move your arms or hands to emphasize a point you are making.

Tips for Giving a Persuasive Speech

✔ If you want to convince your audience to agree with your opinions, follow these strategies:
- ▶ Speak loudly and clearly.
- ▶ Use an enthusiastic tone of voice.
- ▶ Maintain good eye contact.
- ▶ Move your body effectively.

Apply the Strategies

Role-play these situations in front of your classmates. Then invite classmates to share feedback on how effective you were.

1. You plan to run for class office. Give a persuasive speech telling why students should vote for you.

2. Select an item of clothing you are wearing, such as your shoes. Try to convince your audience to buy the same product for themselves.

3. Think of a controversial school issue that many students are discussing. Give your personal opinion about the issue. Offer as many strong reasons as you can to support your view. Then, do a flip! Pretend you have the opposite opinion, and offer reasons to support *that* view.

Extended Reading Opportunities

As you read a play, try to envision the action, which is meant to be performed on stage. Following are just a few possibilities for extending your exploration of drama.

Suggested Titles

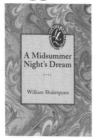

A Midsummer Night's Dream
William Shakespeare

In this comedy by William Shakespeare, the road to love is winding and rocky. Hermia loves Lysander, although she has been promised by her father to Demetrius—who is in turn adored by Helena. In the forest, where all the lovers flee, the merry fairy Puck further confuses matters by doling out a magic love potion that causes a person to fall asleep, then fall in love with the first object he or she sees upon awakening.

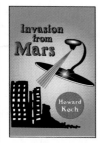

Invasion From Mars
Howard Koch

This radio play, based on *The War of the Worlds* by H. G. Wells, caused a huge sensation in 1938 when it first aired on Orson Welles's radio show, the *Mercury Theater*. At the time, many listeners thought it was an actual news report of a Martian landing! The play pretends to be an authentic evening of radio, including weather reports, musical interludes, and special news bulletins—which are accounts of an invasion by hostile beings from Mars.

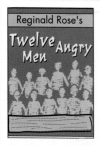

Twelve Angry Men
Reginald Rose

In this courtroom drama, the life of a young boy hangs in the balance as a jury deliberates whether or not to convict him for killing his father. Locked in the jury room, the jurors—twelve men of varying ages and temperaments—argue with increasing violence as they struggle to come to a unanimous decision. This teleplay, which won an Emmy Award and was later adapted into a movie, was inspired by Reginald Rose's own experience on a jury.

Other Possibilities

All the World's a Stage: Speeches, Poems and Songs from William Shakespeare   Dorothy Boux

Two Gentlemen of Verona   William Shakespeare
Calisto 5   Alan Ayckbourn

The Library, Jacob Lawrence, National Museum of American Art, Washington, D.C.

Poetry

In poetry, each word rings with meaning. In some poems, repetition and rhyme create musical rhythms. In other poems, figurative language can help you see the world in a whole new way. In this section, you'll encounter narrative poetry, which tells a story; lyric poetry, which expresses an emotional response toward a subject; haiku, which celebrates the wonders of nature; and several other types of poetry. Try reading some of the poems aloud to help you experience the full impact of what the poet is communicating.

Guide for Reading

William Wordsworth
(1770–1850)

Wordsworth began his career as a revolutionary firebrand and ended it as an honored, conservative member of England's establishment.

During all the stages of his long literary career, however, he made major contributions to British literature. In fact, Wordsworth is regarded as the father of the British Romantic Movement—a major literary movement of the early 1800's that emphasized the importance of the emotions, the imagination, and an appreciation of nature.

A Passion for Change Wordsworth was born on the northern edge of the rural Lake District in England. As a young man, he spent a period of time in France and became a supporter of the French Revolution's ideals of freedom, equality, and brotherhood. Although Wordsworth abandoned his desire for political change as the French Revolution grew increasingly bloody, he was able to bring about revolutionary changes in British literature.

Lyrical Ballads The revolution that Wordsworth prompted in British literature began in 1798 when he and fellow poet Samuel Taylor Coleridge published a book of poetry entitled *Lyrical Ballads*. Unlike the formal, highly intellectual poems that were popular at the time, the poems in the book used simple language to memorialize the remarkable moments of everyday life. In the preface, Wordsworth presented a definition of poetry that would influence the next generation of British poets.

Nature and Intuition Wordsworth's most memorable poetry, including much of the verse in *Lyrical Ballads*, rejoices in the powers of intuition and the kinship between people and nature. Written in 1804, his poem "I Wandered Lonely as a Cloud" was prompted by observations his sister Dorothy had made in her journal after she and William had suddenly come upon the sight of a field crowded with daffodils. Wordsworth took his sister's fragmented comments and turned them into this poem.

◆ Build Vocabulary

SPECIALIZED VOCABULARY: POETIC CONTRACTIONS

To maintain rhythm and rhyme, poets sometimes use **poetic contractions**—words in which a letter is replaced by an apostrophe. For example, you'll find the contraction *o'er* (over) in this poem. Notice the rhythm of this line: "That *floats* on *high* o'er *vales* and *hills*." The word *over* would have disrupted the iambic rhythm (soft/stressed), but the word *o'er* fits right in.

WORD BANK

host
glee
pensive
bliss

Before you read, preview this list of words from the poem.

◆ Build Grammar Skills

INVERTED WORD ORDER

"Ten thousand saw I at a glance...." What makes this sentence sound unusual is the **inverted word order**. Normal word order follows a subject-verb-complement pattern. In the sentence from Wordsworth's poem, the complement (*Ten thousand*) comes at the beginning, followed by the verb (*saw*) and then the subject (*I*). Wordsworth intentionally uses inverted word order to draw your attention to what he is seeing: ten thousand daffodils waving in a field. When you see other instances of inverted word order, imagine the sentence in normal order and think about what the writer hoped to do by inverting it.

I Wandered Lonely as a Cloud

◆ *Literature and Your Life*

CONNECT YOUR EXPERIENCE

You see the ocean for the first time. Your baby brother says your name and smiles. There are moments in your life that you replay in your memory, images that photographs and home videos can't do justice to because they can't capture your feelings. In this poem, Wordsworth captures both the images and the feelings connected to a special moment in his life when he and his sister came across a beautiful field of daffodils.

Journal Writing Make a list of natural scenes you've seen that stand out in your memory. What feelings do the scenes stir up in you?

THEMATIC FOCUS: OBSERVATIONS

Like many of the poems of Wordsworth and the other Romantic poets, this poem captures the poet's observations of the tranquil beauty of the natural world.

◆ Background for Understanding

LITERATURE

In his sister, Dorothy, William Wordsworth found not only a companion, but also a kindred spirit who shared his vision of life and his love of nature. Dorothy kept a daily journal of their activities, and, after their walks together through the hills and valleys of the Lake District, Dorothy would often record what they had seen. Sometimes her observations fed one of William's poems. "I Wandered Lonely as a Cloud" is probably the most famous example of this partnership of imagination. Here are Dorothy's observations on April 15, 1802:

> I never saw daffodils so beautiful they grew among the mossy stones about and about them, some rested their heads upon these stones as on a pillow for weariness and the rest tossed and reeled and danced and seemed as if they verily laughed when the wind that blew upon them over the lake, they looked so gay ever glancing, ever changing.

Compare Dorothy's observations with those presented in the poem you're about to read.

◆ Literary Focus

RHYME SCHEME

A **rhyme scheme** is a regular pattern of the rhyming words at the end of each line in a poem. You indicate the pattern of a poem's rhymes by using letters of the alphabet, assigning a new letter to each new rhyme. For example, the first stanza of "I Wandered Lonely as a Cloud" uses an *ababcc* rhyme scheme, which tells you that line 1 rhymes with line 3, line 2 with line 4, and line 5 with line 6.

As you read "I Wandered Lonely as a Cloud," see if Wordsworth keeps to this rhyme scheme in the other stanzas or if he tries something different. You might use a graphic organizer like this one to help you. Notice that the first stanza has been done for you.

Stanza	Rhyme Scheme
Stanza 1	ababcc
Stanza 2	
Stanza 3	
Stanza 4	

Reading for Success

Strategies for Reading Poetry

Getting into a poem may feel a little like getting into fancy clothes; you know from the start that you need to make a little extra effort. The process of reading a poem will be a little easier if you use the following strategies.

Identify the speaker.

When you read a poem, you hear a voice in your head. What you are hearing is the poem's speaker, the imaginary voice assumed by the poet. Sometimes the speaker is the poet, as in Wordsworth's poem, or is a part of the poet's personality. Other times, the speaker is a character created by the poet. Whenever you read a poem, identify its speaker and try to determine his or her outlook on life. How is that outlook reflected in the poem? How does the outlook compare with your own?

Pay attention to punctuation.

Keep in mind that even if a poem is shaped to fit a particular rhythm and rhyme, a poem's words are still put together and punctuated as sentences. For example, when you read "I Wandered Lonely as a Cloud," notice that Stanzas 1 and 2 are both complete sentences, each expressing a complete thought. When you read a poem, pay attention to the punctuation. Don't stop fully at the end of each line unless a punctuation mark (period, comma, colon, semicolon, or dash) stops you, and take special note of where each sentence ends. If you do this, you will take a big step toward understanding the poem's meaning.

Use your senses.

Once you have a basic idea of what is happening in the poem, use your senses to experience its pleasures. For instance, *see* the yellowness and greenness of Wordsworth's daffodils; *feel* the whoosh of the breeze; *hear* the waves of the nearby bay.

Paraphrase the poem.

Pause every so often and restate the speaker's experiences and feelings in your own words.

Respond to the poem.

Think about what the speaker has said, and put yourself in his or her place. How would the images in the poem—for example, the sight of the daffodils—affect you? Why would you remember this particular sight?

As you read "I Wandered Lonely as a Cloud," look at the notes along the sides of the pages. These notes demonstrate how to apply the strategies to a poem.

I Wandered Lonely as a Cloud

William Wordsworth

I wandered lonely as a cloud
That floats on high o'er vales[1] and hills,
When all at once I saw a crowd,
A <u>host</u>, of golden daffodils;
5   Beside the lake, beneath the trees,
Fluttering and dancing in the breeze.

Continuous as the stars that shine
And twinkle on the milky way,
They stretched in never-ending line
10   Along the margin of a bay:
Ten thousand saw I at a glance,
Tossing their heads in sprightly dance.

The waves beside them danced; but they
Outdid the sparkling waves in <u>glee</u>;
15   A poet could not but be gay,
In such a jocund[2] company;
I gazed—and gazed—but little thought
What wealth the show to me had brought:

---

1. **o'er vales:** Over valleys.
2. **jocund** (jak´ ənd) *adj.*: Cheerful.

◆ **Build Vocabulary**
host (hōst) *n.*: A great number
glee (glē) *n.*: Joy

fact that the
aker no longer
lonely when he
ounters the daf-
ls reveals his
connection to
re.

your senses to
re a field full
ousands of
odils.

can paraphrase
e two lines as,
oet can't help
g happy in such
rful company."

Notice that stanzas 3 and 4 can be read as a single sentence.

20

For oft, when on my couch I lie
In vacant or in <u>pensive</u> mood,
They flash upon that inward eye
Which is the <u>bliss</u> of solitude;
And then my heart with pleasure fills,
And dances with the daffodils.

◆ **Build Vocabulary**

pensive (pen´ siv) *adj.*: Thinking deeply
bliss (blis) *n.*: Great joy or happiness

Guide for Responding

◆ *Literature and Your Life*

Reader's Response Why do you think this experience created such a strong impression in Wordsworth's memory?

Thematic Focus Have you ever made an observation that caused you to feel the type of connection to nature that the poet describes? Explain.

Discussion With other students, create a "top ten" list of favorite (most beautiful, most powerful, strangest) scenes from nature.

☑ Check Your Comprehension

1. What terms does the speaker use to describe himself in the beginning of the poem?
2. Where are the daffodils, and what are they doing?
3. What does the speaker say happens when he is alone in a "pensive" mood?

Guide for Responding (continued)

◆ Critical Thinking

INTERPRET

1. (a) What does the speaker suggest by comparing himself to a cloud? (b) To what are the daffodils compared in Stanza 2, and what does the comparison suggest about the daffodils? **[Analyze]**
2. What effect does the scene have on the speaker while he is present? **[Synthesize]**
3. What "wealth" is he later aware of, according to the fourth stanza? **[Connect]**

APPLY

4. Of what value to people are natural scenes such as the one the poem presents? **[Apply]**

EXTEND

5. Wordsworth's poem paints a vivid portrait of the daffodils. What does his poem add that would not be conveyed by a photograph, videotape, or painting of the same scene? **[Art Link]**

◆ Reading for Success

STRATEGIES FOR READING POETRY

Review the reading strategies and the notes showing how to read poetry. Then apply these strategies to answer the following questions.

1. How does the speaker change from the beginning to the end of the poem?
2. Which sense(s) do you use most in reading this poem? Support your answer.
3. Review the structure of the poem. What idea does each stanza develop?

◆ Literary Focus

RHYME SCHEME

A **rhyme scheme** is a regular pattern of rhyming words at the end of each line in a poem. A sequence of letters is used to indicate rhyme scheme. For example, if every other line in each stanza rhymes, the rhyme scheme is *abab*.

1. What is the rhyme scheme of this poem?
2. How does the rhyme scheme help to set off the final two lines of each stanza?
3. How does setting off the final two lines of each stanza reinforce the meaning?

◆ Build Vocabulary

POETIC CONTRACTIONS

Poets sometimes use **poetic contractions**—words in which one or more letters are left out—to sustain a rhythm or rhyme scheme. For example, Wordsworth uses the contraction *o'er*—short for *over*—to maintain the rhythm of line 2.

Identify what these contractions actually mean. Then make up a line or two using each contraction.

1. 'twill   2. twasn't   3. fore'er   4. ne'er

USING THE WORD BANK

Choose the word whose meaning is most opposite to that of the first word.

1. glee: (a) intelligence, (b) happiness, (c) sorrow
2. pensive: (a) careless, (b) cheerful, (c) thoughtful
3. host: (a) guest, (b) small number, (c) parasite
4. bliss: (a) depression, (b) joy, (c) horror

◆ Build Grammar Skills

INVERTED WORD ORDER

Poets sometimes use **inverted word order** to emphasize words or to make their writing fit a rhythm. In the line, "Ten thousand saw I at a glance," Wordsworth uses inverted word order, following the pattern of complement-verb-subject. By inverting the words, he gives emphasis to the words *Ten thousand*.

> **Inverted word order** changes the subject-verb-complement pattern of normal word order in English.

Practice Find three other examples of inverted word order from Wordsworth's poem. Identify the pattern of each. Then, in each case, explain the effect Wordsworth created by using inverted word order.

Writing Application Rewrite these sentences, changing them from inverted to normal order or normal to inverted order, whichever applies.

1. Bright they were, and golden too.
2. I wandered lonely as a cloud.
3. A host of daffodils saw I.
4. They stretched in never-ending line along the margin of a bay.

Build Your Portfolio

Idea Bank

Writing

1. **Personal Response** Describe your reactions to this poem. Did you like it? Why or why not? What emotions did it evoke? What personal experiences did it call to mind?

2. **Poem With Similes** Wordworth's poem contains several similes—comparisons between strikingly different items, signaled by the words *like* or *as*. Using the poem as a model, write a poem in which you use similes to capture your feelings about a personal experience involving nature.

3. **Support for a Definition** Wordsworth defined poetry as "emotion recollected in tranquillity." How well does this poem illustrate his definition? Write an essay in which you apply Wordsworth's definition to the poem. Support your points.

Speaking and Listening

4. **Speech** Wordsworth freely shared his ideas about poetry with his audience. Share your ideas about poetry with your classmates by giving a brief speech in which you explain the qualities you think contribute to a good poem. Cite examples to support your opinion. **[Career Link]**

5. **Memorized Presentation** Memorize this poem and recite it to the class. Use the poem's rhymes to help you remember it. **[Performing Arts Link]**

Projects

6. **Anthology** Wordsworth is one of the most famous British Romantic poets. Find out about other Romantic poets. Collect examples of their poetry and put them together in an anthology. Include an explanation of each choice.

7. **Illustration** Create an illustration to accompany this poem. Show your illustration and explain how it connects to the poem. **[Art Link]**

Writing Mini-Lesson

Word Picture of a Natural Scene

In "I Wandered Lonely as a Cloud," Wordsworth uses words to create a vivid portrait of a natural scene. Create your own word picture—either in the form of a few paragraphs or in the form of a brief poem—of a beautiful natural scene that you've seen either in person or in photographs. Use the following tip to help you.

Writing Skills Focus: Avoiding Unnecessary Details

Too many details, especially details that don't fit together, can create a confusing picture. It's important to be selective when deciding which details to include in a description. Decide on your purpose in writing the word picture. Is it to create a particular mood or overall impression? To persuade the reader to visit the spot? **Avoid unnecessary details**—those that do not serve your purpose. For example, if you wanted to create a vivid impression of flowers bobbing in the wind, you wouldn't want to mention an earthworm you noticed or the taste of the crisp apple in your picnic lunch.

Prewriting Jot down as many details as you can think of that are related to the scene you've chosen. Next, decide on the purpose of your word picture. Then go through your details and eliminate those that don't fit your purpose.

Drafting Decide whether your word picture will take the form of a few paragraphs or a short poem. Then use the details you've gathered to write your first draft.

Revising Use these questions to help you revise: How well have you achieved your purpose? Have you left out important or memorable details? What details can you eliminate? Which words can you replace with ones that are more precise?

Part **1** *Meaning and Sound*

Fantastic Horse Cart, 1949, Marc Chagall, Blanden Memorial Art Museum

Guide for Reading

Alfred, Lord Tennyson *(1809–1892)*

The most popular of British poets during his lifetime, Tennyson rose from humble beginnings to the glory of being named poet laureate of England. Although he was enthralled by the technological advances of the Victorian era, Tennyson remained a poet of nature who brought both imagination and feeling to the landscape and its inhabitants.

Emily Dickinson *(1830–1886)*

Shy, solitary, and brilliant, Dickinson led a life of nearly piercing loneliness in Amherst, Massachusetts. Yet, despite her quiet exterior, an inner life raged, enabling her to produce at least 1,775 poems. A fly and a bird coming down a walk are among her deceptively simple subjects from nature. She also wrote about death, love, and some of her religious beliefs. No matter what her subject, however, Dickinson's treatment was imaginative, complex, and thought-provoking. (For more on Emily Dickinson, see p. 244.)

Langston Hughes *(1902–1967)*

Langston Hughes, born in Joplin, Missouri, was the first African American ever to have a strictly literary career. As a young man, he held a variety of jobs—teacher, ranch hand, farmer, seaman, and night-club cook, among others. He drew on all these experiences and, above all, on the experience of being an African American man to create his great body of literary work.

"Dream Deferred" and "Dreams" illustrate his ability to express the spirit of black America.

◆ Build Vocabulary

COLOR WORDS

Alfred, Lord Tennyson, uses the word *azure,* instead of its near-synonym, *blue,* to describe the sky that surrounds the eagle. Why doesn't Tennyson use *blue? Azure* says more, because it refers to the exact color of a clear blue sky, rather than to just any blue. Other specific color words, such as *vermilion,* which is a flaming red, help poets convey meaning with more exactness and feeling.

WORD BANK

Before you read, preview this list of words from the poems.

azure
sore
abash
deferred
fester
barren

◆ Build Grammar Skills

COORDINATING CONJUNCTIONS

Coordinating conjunctions join words, phrases, and clauses of equal rank. For example, when Hughes dramatically ends "Dream Deferred" with the question "Or does it explode?" he begins the question with the coordinating conjunction *or,* which presents an alternative. Tennyson ends "The Eagle" with a similar last line: "And like a thunderbolt he falls." This line begins with *and,* which signals an addition or, in a narrative sequence like this one, tells what happens next. Other coordinating conjunctions are *but* and *yet,* which show contrast or exception; *or* and *nor,* which signal an alternative; and *for,* which shows cause.

The Eagle ◆ "Hope" is the thing with feathers— Dream Deferred ◆ Dreams

◆ *Literature and Your Life*

CONNECT YOUR EXPERIENCE

In your dreams, you can accomplish anything. You can hit a game-winning home run, perform in a rock band in front of thousands of fans, or be the first person to set foot on Mars. Your hopes and dreams can provide you with the motivation you need to keep working toward a goal. These poems explore the significance of our hopes and dreams and look at what happens when dreams are shattered.

THEMATIC FOCUS: LOOKING INWARD

How do our hopes and dreams help define who we are?

Journal Writing Briefly describe one of your personal dreams.

◆ Background for Understanding

HISTORY

"Dream Deferred" begins with a reference to *Harlem*. Harlem has been a center for the African American population in New York City since about 1900. In the 1920's, a literary and cultural movement called the Harlem Renaissance flowered there. At the time this poem was written in 1951, however, a large percentage of the people in Harlem were living in extreme poverty and much of the neighborhood was in a state of decay. Furthermore, the advances of the civil rights era, though just around the corner, had not yet begun. As a result, many of those who lived in Harlem at the time felt a sense of hopelessness.

◆ Literary Focus

FIGURATIVE LANGUAGE

Figurative language is language that uses figures of speech. A figure of speech is a way of saying one thing and meaning another. Simile, metaphor, and personification are three common figures of speech. A **simile** compares one thing to another using the word *like* or *as*. Hughes uses a simile when he asks whether a dream deferred "stinks like rotten meat." A **metaphor** compares one thing to another without using *like* or *as*. Hughes uses a metaphor when he writes, "Life is a barren field." **Personification** gives human characteristics to an animal, object, or idea. Tennyson personifies an eagle by giving it "hands."

◆ Reading Strategy

PARAPHRASE

When you **paraphrase**, you use your own words to express what someone else has written. All of the following are examples of paraphrasing. Notice how each example uses simpler language to express ideas originally written in more complex language.

From "Dreams"

Hold fast to dreams

Paraphrased

Don't let go of dreams.

From "The Eagle"

Close to the sun in lonely lands,

Paraphrased

very high in the sky; alone

From "'Hope' is the thing with feathers—"

And sore must be the storm—/ That could abash the little Bird

Paraphrased

A storm would have to be really bad to stop the bird.

The Eagle

Alfred, Lord Tennyson

He clasps the crag[1] with crooked hands;
Close to the sun in lonely lands,
Ring'd with the <u>azure</u> world, he stands.

The wrinkled sea beneath him crawls;
5   He watches from his mountain walls,
And like a thunderbolt he falls.

---

1. crag (krag) *n.*: Steep, rugged rock that juts
out from a rock mass.

"Hope" is the thing with feathers— Emily Dickinson

"Hope" is the thing with feathers—
That perches in the soul—
And sings the tune without the words—
And never stops—at all—

5 And sweetest—in the Gale[1]—is heard—
And <u>sore</u> must be the storm—
That could <u>abash</u> the little Bird
That kept so many warm—

I've heard it in the chillest land—
10 And on the strangest Sea—
Yet, never, in Extremity,
It asked a crumb—of Me.

---

1. **Gale** (gāl) *n.*: Strong wind.

◆ **Build Vocabulary**
azure (azh´ ər) *adj.*: Blue
sore (sôr) *adj.*: Fierce; cruel
abash (ə bash´) *v.*: Embarrass

Guide for Responding

◆ Literature and Your Life

Reader's Response How do your views about hope compare with those expressed in Dickinson's poem?

Thematic Focus What is unique about Dickinson's definition of hope?

☑ Check Your Comprehension

1. What actions of the eagle are described in Tennyson's poem?
2. According to the speaker of Dickinson's poem, what does hope do?
3. Where has the speaker heard hope?

◆ Critical Thinking

INTERPRET
1. Why do you think Tennyson begins "The Eagle" by placing the eagle so high up? **[Analyze]**
2. Is *falls* the right word for the action of the eagle? Why or why not? **[Make a Judgment]**
3. Why do you think Dickinson compares hope to a bird? **[Speculate]**
4. According to the speaker, is it easy or difficult to lose hope? Support your answer. **[Interpret]**

EVALUATE
5. Why do you think Tennyson breaks up such a short poem into two stanzas? **[Evaluate]**
6. How does Dickinson define hope in a fresh and unexpected way? **[Synthesize; Evaluate]**

Dream Deferred

Langston Hughes

Harlem

What happens to a dream <u>deferred</u>?

Does it dry up
like a raisin in the sun?
5 Or <u>fester</u> like a sore—
And then run?
Does it stink like rotten meat?
Or crust and sugar over—
like a syrupy sweet?

10 Maybe it just sags
like a heavy load.

Or does it explode?

▲ **Critical Viewing** Explain why you do or do not think this piece of art is an effective illustration for the two poems. **[Support]**

◆ **Build Vocabulary**
deferred (di fʉrd´) *adj.*: Put off until a future time
fester (fes´ tər) *v.*: Form pus

Bernard's Daddy, Raymond Lark, Edward Smith and Company

Dreams

Langston Hughes

Hold fast to dreams
For if dreams die
Life is a broken-winged bird
That cannot fly.

5   Hold fast to dreams
For when dreams go
Life is a <u>barren</u> field
Frozen with snow.

◆ **Build Vocabulary**

barren (bar´ən) *adj.*: Empty

Guide for Responding

◆ *Literature and Your Life*

Reader's Response Describe what your life would be like if you were prevented from pursuing your dreams or goals.

Thematic Focus What types of qualities does it take for a person to hold onto dreams in the face of adversity?

Journal Entry Write about what you think people can do to hold onto their dreams when it seems that their dreams might never become a reality.

☑ Check Your Comprehension

1. List the verbs that Hughes uses to tell what can happen to a "dream deferred."
2. To what two things does the speaker in "Dreams" compare life?
3. Tell how the two poems are alike.

◆ Critical Thinking

INTERPRET

1. "Dream Deferred" is full of questions. Why do you think Hughes uses six questions and only one statement? **[Speculate]**
2. Interpret the last line of "Dream Deferred." **[Draw Conclusions]**
3. What is the message of "Dream Deferred"? **[Draw Conclusions]**
4. Restate in your own words the advice that "Dreams" offers. **[Interpret]**

APPLY

5. How might you apply the advice Hughes gives in "Dreams" to your own life? **[Apply]**

EXTEND

6. How might civil rights leaders have used these poems in support of their cause? **[Social Studies Link]**

Guide for Responding (continued)

◆ Literary Focus

FIGURATIVE LANGUAGE

These poems are filled with different types of **figurative language**—language that challenges us to look at things in fresh, unexpected ways.

1. How does Tennyson personify the sea?
2. Look at the simile in the last line of Tennyson's poem. In what ways is a swooping eagle similar to a thunderbolt?
3. Change the two metaphors in "Dreams" into similes by adding *like*. Does this change alter the effect or meaning of "Dreams"? Explain.
4. How does Hughes's use of metaphors contribute to the effectiveness of "Dreams"?
5. Although hope is compared to a bird in the Dickinson poem, hope is also, in some ways, personified. Tell how.

◆ Build Vocabulary

USING COLOR WORDS

Use a dictionary to find the meanings of these color words. Then, in your notebook, complete each of the following sentences with one color word.

    a. vermilion   **b.** emerald   **c.** ivory   **d.** ebony

1. Darkness fell like an ____?____ curtain.
2. Her ____?____ fingernails matched the color of her lipstick.
3. Her sparkling ____?____ teeth gleamed as she smiled.
4. His ____?____ eyes sparkled with happiness.

USING THE WORD BANK

On your paper, rewrite each sentence, substituting a word from the Word Bank for each italicized word or words.

1. The *miserable* treatment made the children cry.
2. The changes in the work calendar resulted in *delayed* vacations.
3. The clouds were bright white against the *blue* sky.
4. Kim was in such a good mood that nothing could *cause a feeling of shame* in him.
5. His cut began to *run with pus*.
6. The field behind the farmhouse seemed curiously *empty of life*.

◆ Reading Strategy

PARAPHRASE

When you **paraphrase**, you restate a writer's words in words of your own.

1. Paraphrase "The Eagle" line by line.
2. Paraphrase "Dreams." When you come to the similes, express the ideas in literal language. That is, do not use comparisons.
3. Go back to "'Hope' is the thing with feathers." Paraphrase the last stanza. Be sure to supply a noun to take the place of the pronoun *it*. If you don't know the meaning of *Extremity*, look it up.

◆ Build Grammar Skills

COORDINATING CONJUNCTIONS

Notice how Dickinson expands her definition of hope in each line by using the coordinating conjunction *and*:

> And sings the tune without the words—
> And never stops—at all—
> And sweetest—in the Gale—is heard—
> And sore must be the storm—

A **coordinating conjunction** joins words or groups of words of equal rank. **Coordinating Conjunctions Show** addition: *and* alternative: *or, nor* cause: *for* contrast or exception: *but, yet*

Writing Application Revise this paragraph by substituting a more accurate coordinating conjunction for each one given.

Langston Hughes gained fame as a writer, and he didn't have an easy life. At times, he received criticism from both African American or white reviewers. At times, he had to decide whether to keep writing but end his penniless state. Over time, he succeeded as a playwright or a poet. The work he created speaks to all people, and much of it is also specific to the African American experience.

Build Your Portfolio

 ## Idea Bank

Writing

1. **Advertisement** Write an ad for one of your favorite products using an interesting comparison. For example, you might write, "Tress shampoo is like ___?___" or "Running in Impala sneakers is as ___?___ as ___?___."

2. **Guidebook Description** Write a description of an eagle that could appear in a guidebook on birds. Tell what the eagle looks like and how it behaves. **[Science Link]**

3. **Analysis** Write an essay in which you interpret the message that the poet conveys in one of these poems. Support your interpretation by citing appropriate passages from the poem.

Speaking and Listening

4. **Inspirational Speech** Use the ideas of Dickinson and Hughes as the basis for an inspirational speech about the importance of hopes and dreams. Feel free to use quotations from the poems. Present your speech to the class. **[Performing Arts Link]**

5. **Oral Interpretation** With a partner or small group, practice and perform a dramatic reading of one of the poems. Use the volume and tone of your voice to help communicate meaning.

Projects

6. **Illustration** Draw or paint an illustration of an eagle that has the characteristics of Tennyson's eagle. **[Art Link]**

7. **Biographical Report** Research the life of one of these writers. Present your findings to the class.

 ## Writing Mini-Lesson

Comparison Poem

Create a poem of your own that presents either one detailed comparison or a series of comparisons. If you wish, write about hopes and dreams, or focus on an animal that interests you.

Writing Skills Focus: Using Figurative Language

The most effective, engaging comparisons present fresh ways of looking at things. Such comparisons are examples of **figurative language**—language that is intended to spark readers' imaginations. To make your poem as effective as possible, take the time to make your figurative language as interesting and thought-provoking as you possibly can. Think about Dickinson's poem. Why do you think she didn't simply write, "Hope is a bird"?

Prewriting Start by choosing your topic. Jot down descriptive details about your topic. Then brainstorm for a list of words and phrases to complete these sentence starters: "A (your topic) is like ___?___," and "A (your topic) is as ___?___ as ___?___."

Drafting Look at your sentence starters. Decide whether you want to develop a single comparison or present a series of comparisons. Then begin drafting. As you write, experiment with putting your ideas together in different ways—for example, try short and long lines or rhymed and unrhymed stanzas.

Revising Ask a classmate to identify the comparison or comparisons in your poem. Also, have the classmate suggest how you can improve your choice of words to make your figurative language more thought-provoking.

$\mathcal{G}$uide for Reading

Galway Kinnell
(1927–)

Galway Kinnell is an American poet concerned with the themes of the inevitability of death, selfhood, and the power of nature. He has taught at various universities and has been active in the civil rights movement.

Margaret Walker
(1915–)

A poet and a novelist, Walker is considered one of the legends of African American literature. As an artist, she focuses on the experiences and hardships of black people in America.

Julia Alvarez
(1950–)

Julia Alvarez moved from the Dominican Republic to New York City with her family when she was ten. She says that the complexity of the many cultures in America is "part of what makes us rich and makes us strong."

Gabriela Mistral
(1889–1957)

Born in Chile and named Lucila Godoy y Alcayaga, this writer formed her pen name from the names of two of her favorite writers, Gabriele D'Annunzio and Frederic Mistral. The 1945 recipient of the Nobel Prize for Literature, Mistral wrote many poems about children and motherhood.

Pattiann Rogers
(1940–)

Known for the scientifically exact language of her poems, Pattiann Rogers says that the natural world has always provided a way for her to consider the important questions of why we are here.

◆ Build Vocabulary

WORD ROOTS: *-primo-*

In her poem "Woman's Work," Julia Alvarez uses the phrase, "I was primed...." The word *prime* comes from the word root *-primo-*, which means "first in time or in importance." In this case, *primed* means "coached beforehand."

WORD BANK

Before you read, preview this list of words from the poems.

unbidden
sinister
primed
divine
meticulously

◆ Build Grammar Skills

PARALLEL STRUCTURE

In these poems, the poets use **parallel structure** to create rhythm and emphasize meaning. Parallel structure is the expression of similar ideas in similar grammatical form. Look at this example from Walker's poem:

Memory

I can remember wind-swept streets ...

I can remember seeing them alone ...

I can remember hearing all they said ...

By repeating the phrase "I can remember," Walker draws attention to the content of the speaker's memories and creates a pleasing rhythm.

Blackberry Eating ◆ Memory
Woman's Work ◆ Meciendo
◆ Eulogy for a Hermit Crab ◆

◆ *Literature and Your Life*

CONNECT YOUR EXPERIENCE

It's often possible to find deeper meaning in routine events and observations. For example, looking out at the ocean might make you think of the immensity and timelessness of nature. As these poems illustrate, one of the great qualities of poetry is that it can help lead you toward such insights.

Journal Writing Describe a time when you had an important insight that was inspired by a routine event or observation.

THEMATIC FOCUS: LOOKING INWARD

What role do the poets' experiences and attitudes play in shaping the insights that they gather from everyday occurrences and observations?

◆ Background for Understanding

SCIENCE

One of the poems is about a hermit crab, an animal that carries around an abandoned shell to cover its own unprotected abdomen. The hermit crab uses the tip of its tail to grip the inside of the shell. The claws of the crab are formed in such a way that when the crab withdraws into the shell, the claws close the opening. As the hermit crab grows, it becomes too big for the shell and must find a new one. There is a lot of competition among hermit crabs for suitable shells.

◆ Literary Focus

IMAGERY refers to language that paints pictures in readers' minds. An image may appeal to any one of the five senses. For example, when Margaret Walker speaks of "wind-swept streets of cities/on cold and blustery nights," she is using imagery that appeals to the senses of touch and sight. As you read, use a chart like this one to note memorable images and the senses to which each appeals. Note that one image is already included.

Image	Sight	Sound	Taste	Smell	Touch
fat, overripe, icy, black blackberries	X		X		X

◆ Reading Strategy

ENVISION THE IMAGERY

To appreciate the images that the poets use, form a mental picture of each image. Use your memory and imagination to *see, feel, hear, smell,* and *taste* what the poets describe. For example, when Kinnell refers to "fat, overripe, icy, black blackberries," try to imagine what the blackberries would look, feel, and taste like. Use the descriptive words to help you. For example, Kinnell's use of the word *black* in describing the blackberries clues you in to the fact that they're especially dark; his use of the word *icy* reveals that they're cold to the touch; and his use of the words *fat* and *overripe* suggest that the blackberries are large and swollen with flavor.

BLACKBERRY EATING

Galway Kinnell

I love to go out in late September
among the fat, overripe, icy, black blackberries
to eat blackberries for breakfast,
the stalks very prickly, a penalty
5   they earn for knowing the black art
of blackberry-making; and as I stand among them
lifting the stalks to my mouth, the ripest berries
fall almost <u>unbidden</u> to my tongue,
as words sometimes do, certain peculiar words
10 like *strengths* or *squinched*,
many-lettered, one-syllabled lumps,
which I squeeze, squinch open, and splurge well
in the silent, startled, icy, black language
of blackberry-eating in late September.

Memory
Margaret Walker

I can remember wind-swept streets of cities
on cold and blustery nights, on rainy days;
heads under shabby felts[1] and parasols
and shoulders hunched against a sharp concern;
5   seeing hurt bewilderment on poor faces,
smelling a deep and <u>sinister</u> unrest
these brooding people cautiously caress;
hearing ghostly marching on pavement stones
and closing fast around their squares of hate.
10 I can remember seeing them alone,
at work, and in their tenements at home.
I can remember hearing all they said:
their muttering protests their whispered oaths,
and all that spells their living in distress.

---

1. **felts:** Felt hats.

▶ **Critical Viewing** Why would the poem's first line make a good caption for this photograph? **[Explain]**

Guide for Responding

◆ Literature and Your Life

Reader's Response Which lines helped you to envision the blackberries in "Blackberry Eating"?

Thematic Focus What thoughts and feelings did "Memory" evoke in you? Explain.

☑ Check Your Comprehension

1. What words does Galway Kinnell use to describe the blackberries?
2. How does the speaker get the berries into his mouth?
3. In "Memory," what clues does the poet give that the people are poor?
4. How do you know that the people are unhappy?

◆ Critical Thinking

INTERPRET
1. What do "certain peculiar words" have in common with the blackberries? **[Interpret]**
2. What special meaning does eating blackberries have to the speaker of "Blackberry Eating"? **[Analyze]**
3. What kinds of lives do the people in "Memory" lead? **[Interpret]**
4. Explain how "Memory" can be seen as a poem that criticizes an injustice in society. **[Support]**

EVALUATE
5. W. H. Auden once said that to be a good poet, one had to "like to hang around words and overhear them talking to one another." How do these poems show that Kinnell and Walker fit this description? **[Evaluate]**

▲ Critical Viewing Which details in this painting connect it to Alvarez's poem? **[Connect]**

Woman's Work

Julia Alvarez

Who says a woman's work isn't high art?
She'd challenge as she scrubbed the bathroom tiles.
Keep house as if the address were your heart.

We'd clean the whole upstairs before we'd start
5   downstairs. I'd sigh, hearing my friends outside.
Doing her woman's work was a hard art

to practice when the summer sun would bar
the floor I swept till she was satisfied.
She kept me prisoner in her housebound heart.

10   She'd shine the tines of forks, the wheels of carts,
cut lacy lattices[1] for all her pies.
Her woman's work was nothing less than art.

And, I, her masterpiece since I was smart,
was <u>primed</u>, praised, polished, scolded and advised
15   to keep a house much better than my heart.

I did not want to be her counterpart!
I struck out . . . but became my mother's child:
a woman working at home on her art,
housekeeping paper as if it were her heart.

---

1. lattices (lat´ is əz): Narrow strips of pastry laid on the pie in a crisscross pattern.

◆ **Build Vocabulary**
primed (prīmd) *v*.: Made ready; prepared

Meciendo ("Rocking")
Gabriela Mistral
Translated by Doris Dana

El mar sus millares de olas
mece, divino.
Oyendo a los mares amantes,
mezo a mi niño.

5 El viento errabundo en la noche
mece a los trigos.
Oyendo a los vientos amantes,
mezo a mi niño.

Dios Padre sus miles de mundos
10 mece sin ruido.
Sintiendo su mano en la sombra,
mezo a mi niño.

The sea rocks her thousands of waves.
The sea is <u>divine</u>.
Hearing the loving sea
I rock my son.

5 The wind wandering by night
rocks the wheat.
Hearing the loving wind
I rock my son.

God, the Father, soundlessly rocks
10 His thousands of worlds.
Feeling His hand in the shadow
I rock my son.

◆ **Build Vocabulary**

divine (də vīn´) *adj*.: Holy; sacred

Guide for Responding

◆ Literature and Your Life

Reader's Response Do the images created in these poems appeal to you? Why or why not?

Thematic Focus What do these poems reveal about the poets' feelings toward motherhood?

☑ Check Your Comprehension

1. What ambition does the mother in "Woman's Work" have for her daughter?
2. How does the daughter react to her mother's wishes?
3. Whom is the speaker rocking in "Meciendo"?
4. In the third stanza, what does the speaker feel?

◆ Critical Thinking

INTERPRET
1. How can you tell that the daughter in "Woman's Work" both admires and resents her mother? **[Infer]**
2. Compare the mother's attitude toward housekeeping and her attitude toward the education of her daughter. **[Compare and Contrast]**
3. In "Meciendo," what is the connection between the image the speaker describes in each stanza and her rocking of her son? **[Connect]**

EVALUATE
4. What universal truths about motherhood do you think Mistral is addressing in "Meciendo"? **[Apply]**

Eulogy for a Hermit Crab

Pattiann Rogers

▲ Critical Viewing
What can you learn
about hermit crabs
from the photo-
graphs on these
two pages? **[Infer]**

You were consistently brave
On these surf-drenched rocks, in and out of their salty
Slough holes around which the entire expanse
Of the glinting grey sea and the single spotlight
5 Of the sun went spinning and spinning and spinning
In a tangle of blinding spume and spray
And pistol-shot collisions your whole life long.
You stayed. Even with the wet icy wind of the moon
Circling your silver case night after night after night
10 You were here.

And by the gritty orange curve of your claws,
By the soft, wormlike grip
Of your hinter body, by the unrelieved wonder

Of your black-pea eyes, by the mystified swing
15 And swing and swing of your touching antennae,
You maintained your name meticulously, you kept
Your name intact exactly, day after day after day.
No one could say you were less than perfect
In the hermitage of your crabness.

20 Now, beside the racing, incomprehensible racket
Of the sea stretching its great girth forever
Back and forth between this direction and another,
Please let the words of this proper praise I speak
Become the identical and proper sound
25 Of my mourning.

◆ **Build Vocabulary**

meticulously (mə tik′ yо̅о̅ ləs lē) *adv.*: Very carefully;
scrupulously

Guide for Responding

◆ *Literature and Your Life*

Reader's Response What image in the poem
do you like best? Explain.

Thematic Focus From the crab's point of view,
what is its life like?

Journal Entry Write a paragraph or two about a
day in the life of a hermit crab as the crab sees it.

☑ Check Your Comprehension

1. Where has the poet been observing the crab she
   describes?
2. What are the limits of the crab's world?

◆ Critical Thinking

INTERPRET
1. What evidence does the speaker use to prove
   the crab was "consistently brave"? **[Interpret]**
2. How was the crab's environment a constant challenge to it? **[Infer]**
3. As in any eulogy, the speaker praises the dead.
   For what qualities does the poet praise the dead
   hermit crab? **[Classify]**

APPLY
4. Based on the depiction of the crab in this poem,
   what lesson can people learn from hermit crabs?
   Support your answer. **[Relate]**

Guide for Responding (continued)

◆ Literary Focus

IMAGERY

These poems are filled with vivid **images**—groups of words that create pictures in our minds by appealing to one or more of our senses.

1. In "Blackberry Eating," find two words that appeal to your sense of touch.
2. Find three examples in "Memory" of images that appeal to your sense of hearing.
3. Find an image in "Woman's Work" that is especially appealing to your sense of sight.
4. Find an image in "Meciendo" that appeals to your sense of touch.
5. Find a particularly appealing image in "Eulogy for a Hermit Crab." To which of your senses does it appeal?

◆ Build Grammar Skills

PARALLEL STRUCTURE

Parallel structure is the expression of similar ideas in similar grammatical form. When you use parallel structure, be careful to use the same grammatical form for repeated elements.

Practice In your notebook, change one of each pair of italicized parts to match the other in grammatical form.

1. The prickly stalks knew the art of *blackberry making*. The man liked *to eat blackberries*.
2. *I can remember* all they said. *I also recall* their faces.
3. First she scrubbed *the bathroom tiles*. Then she washed *the floor of the kitchen*.

Writing Application In your notebook, rewrite this paragraph, replacing the underlined sections to achieve parallel structure.

> Julia Alvarez not only writes poetry, but she also <u>is a novelist</u>. Her first novel, *How the Garcia Girls Lost Their Accents*, is based on her own experience as an immigrant in America. <u>In the Time of the Butterflies is the title of her second novel. It is based on a true story about four sisters who remained in the Dominican Republic.</u>

◆ Reading Strategy

ENVISION THE IMAGERY

To appreciate the images in these poems, you have to create a mental picture of what each image describes.

1. Which image in these poems were you able to picture most clearly? Why?
2. Write a paragraph in which you expand on one of the images. Use the associations the image calls to mind to expand on what the writer describes.

◆ Build Vocabulary

USING THE WORD ROOT -primo-

In your notebook, write each sentence, completing it with one of these phrases.

a. prime witness b. prime minister c. prime coat

1. The ____?____ has a great deal of political power.
2. The ____?____ in the trial was nervous.
3. The painter had to wait for the ____?____ to dry.

USING THE WORD BANK

In your notebook, write the letter of the word that means about the same as the first word.

1. unbidden: (a) uninvited, (b) unusual, (c) ordered
2. sinister: (a) innocent, (b) evil, (c) sisterly
3. primed: (a) allowed, (b) coached, (c) followed
4. meticulously: (a) carefully, (b) sloppily, (c) quickly
5. divine: (a) godlike, (b) deep, (c) divided

Beyond Literature

Community Connection

Keeping the Past Alive Memories are worth saving. Personal memories (like those in Margaret Walker's poem) are often saved in photographs and journals. Historical memories are preserved in books, historical sites, and monuments. In many locations throughout America, historic buildings are preserved and monuments are erected to commemorate important people and events. What are some historic places in your area? Why is it important for a community to preserve its past?

Build Your Portfolio

 ## Idea Bank

Writing

1. **Menu** Imagine that you own a restaurant which serves crabs, blackberries, and other dishes of your choice. Write a menu in which you use vivid descriptive words to make the dishes sound appealing. **[Career Link]**

2. **Diary Entry** Write an entry that the mother in "Woman's Work" might have written in her diary. Have her comment on her daughter's behavior and attitude. **[Social Studies Link]**

3. **Evaluation** Write a critical evaluation of one of the poems. In your evaluation, discuss the effectiveness of the poet's word choice and use of imagery. Tell why you would or would not recommend the poem to readers. Cite lines from the poem to support your opinions.

Speaking and Listening

4. **Dramatic Reading** Deliver a dramatic reading of one of these poems. Use the tone and volume of your voice to emphasize key ideas and details. **[Performing Arts Link]**

5. **Monologue** Imagine that you're a politician representing the people described in "Memory." Deliver a speech in which you argue for better social services for the people who voted you into office. **[Career Link]**

Projects

6. **Concrete Image** Choose an image from one of the poems that appeals to the sense of sight. Draw a picture that shows what you see in your mind's eye. **[Art Link]**

7. **Research Project** Conduct research to learn how women's roles have changed over the past several decades. Share your findings with the class.

 ## Writing Mini-Lesson

Remember When . . .

The imagery used by Margaret Walker in "Memory" creates a main impression of despair, hopelessness, and poverty as the speaker reflects on her past. Choose a memorable moment or event from your own life and write a letter about it, using imagery to create a main impression.

Writing Skills Focus: Main Impression

Is your **main impression** of the event one of joy, fear, pride, or awe? Whatever it is, use imagery that contributes to that main impression. For example, if you want to convey a main impression of misery, use sensory details that support this main impression, and avoid details that contradict it.

Model From the Poem

I can remember wind-swept streets of cities
on cold and blustery nights, on rainy days;

Prewriting Once you've chosen an event to describe, list sensory details that contribute to your main impression of that event. What did you see, hear, taste, feel, and smell?

Drafting Using your prewriting notes, write a letter about the event you remember. Organize your details in order of time, space, or importance so your reader can follow your description. Refer to a grammar or etiquette book if you aren't sure about proper letter form.

Revising Put yourself in the place of your reader. Reread your letter, asking yourself whether the sensory details create your intended main impression. Revise as necessary. Check your work for proper letter form.

Guide for Reading

Christina Rossetti *(1830–1894)*

Christina Rossetti is considered by some critics to be the best female poet in English literature. Her father had come from Italy to live in England. The famous poet and painter Dante Gabriel Rossetti was her brother. Christina Rossetti's best-known work is the long poem "Goblin Market," a kind of supernatural fairy tale.

Many of her other poems, however, reflect concern for religion. A number of them, like "Uphill," deal with the theme of death.

Walter Dean Myers *(1937–)*

As a child, acclaimed author Walter Dean Myers never imagined himself becoming a writer. He was born into poverty in West Virginia, and even though he was writing award-winning poems and stories by his early teens, he believed his dream of becoming a professional writer would never be fulfilled. His dream became a reality, however, when he won a writing contest sponsored by the Council on Interracial Books for Children.

The King James Bible

The King James, or Authorized, Version of the Bible was published in 1611. It was the work of a committee of English churchmen led by Lancelot Andrews. The language of the King James Version is so beautiful that the Bible is ranked in English literature with the works of Shakespeare. According to tradition, Ecclesiastes, the section from which this selection is taken, was written by Solomon, the wise Hebrew king, who died around 932 B.C.

Edgar Allan Poe *(1809–1849)*

Edgar Allan Poe is best known for chilling tales like "The Cask of Amontillado." He was also a talented poet, however. As poems like "The Bells" illustrate, Poe was a master at using rhythm and sound effects to emphasize meaning and create a musical effect.

Many scholars believe that the idea for "The Bells" was suggested to Poe by Marie Louise Shew, a woman with medical training who treated Poe when his health began to fail during his final years. (For more on Edgar Allan Poe, see pp. 2 and 830.)

◆ Build Vocabulary

PREFIXES: *mono-*

In "The Bells," Poe describes the tolling of iron bells as a "muffled *monotone*." The word *monotone* contains the prefix *mono-*, which means "one." Knowing the meaning of the prefix, you might guess that the meaning of the word *monotone* is "one tone," which is close to the actual meaning, "uninterrupted repetition of the same tone."

| wayfarers |
| voluminously |
| palpitating |
| monotone |
| paean |

WORD BANK

Before you read, preview this list of words from the poems.

◆ Build Grammar Skills

END PUNCTUATION

End punctuation—the period, question mark, or exclamation mark at the end of a sentence—does more than merely signal the end of a sentence. These marks often indicate meaning or feeling. This is especially true in poetry, in which words and punctuation are used with precision. Notice how the exclamation mark adds terror and the question mark adds anxiety in these examples.

How they scream out their affright!

Shall I find comfort, travel-sore and weak?

Uphill ◆ Summer
Ecclesiastes 3:1–8 ◆ The Bells

◆ *Literature and Your Life*

CONNECT YOUR EXPERIENCE

You feel the heat of a steamy August day and you think about how the broiling heat of summer will change to the chill of autumn. You see parents and children enjoying the outdoors and realize that toddlers grow up to be adults. Nature and life have predictable cycles and stages. In the following poems, you will explore these cycles.

THEMATIC FOCUS: SEASONS AND CYCLES

As these poems illustrate, the world around us is filled with patterns and stages. What can you learn from the patterns of nature that you can apply to your life?

◆ Background for Understanding

SCIENCE AND LITERATURE

Poets through the ages have explored the variety, stages, and patterns found in life. For example, "The Bells" speaks of how different sounds made by bells signal the variety of life, while the poem "Uphill" concentrates on one particular stage of life. Cycles and seasons, stages and patterns: These are what comprise life. While each life is unique, each life can also be similar. People are born, then many grow to adulthood, grow old, and die. Advances in medicine have extended life expectancy far beyond what people centuries ago could have imagined. However, medicine has been unable to alter the basic cycles of life.

Journal Writing Jot down patterns or rhythms that you experience in your own life and that you see in the world around you.

◆ Literary Focus

LYRIC POETRY AND SOUND DEVICES

These poems are all examples of **lyric poetry**—highly musical verse that expresses the observations and feelings of a single speaker. In ancient times, lyric poems were sung to the accompaniment of the lyre, a type of stringed instrument. Modern lyric poems are not usually sung. However, they still have a musical quality that is achieved through various **sound devices** such as rhythm (the pattern of beats or stresses in language), alliteration (the repetition of initial consonant sounds), rhyme (the repetition of sounds at the ends of words), and onomatopoeia (the use of words that imitate the sounds).

◆ Reading Strategy

LISTEN

While the sound of words is important in all kinds of poetry, sound is especially significant in lyric poetry. To appreciate the musical quality of lyric poems, read them aloud and **listen** to your speech as you do so. For example, only by listening to the following lines from "The Bells" can you truly hear how onomatopoeia, rhyme, and rhythm combine to re-create the delightful sound and cheerful mood of sleigh bells.

> How they tinkle, tinkle, tinkle,
>   In the icy air of night!
> While the stars, that oversprinkle
> All the heavens, seem to twinkle
>   With a crystalline delight;

Read each of the following poems aloud to yourself or to a partner. Listen carefully for the musical effect created by the use of sound devices. Think about how the use of sound reinforces each poem's meaning.

Uphill

Christina Rossetti

Does the road wind uphill all the way?
    Yes, to the very end.
Will the day's journey take the whole long day?
    From morn to night, my friend.

5   But is there for the night a restingplace?
    A roof for when the slow dark hours begin.
May not the darkness hide it from my face?
    You cannot miss that inn.

Shall I meet other wayfarers at night?
10   Those who have gone before.
Then must I knock, or call when just in sight?
    They will not keep you standing at that door.

Shall I find comfort, travel-sore and weak?
    Of labor you shall find the sum.
15   Will there be beds for me and all who seek?
    Yea,[1] beds for all who come.

---

1. **yea** (yā): Indeed; truly.

◆ **Build Vocabulary**
wayfarers (wā´ fer ərz) *n.*: Travelers

Guide for Responding

◆ *Literature and Your Life*

Reader's Response How do you feel about the journey described in this poem? Why?

Thematic Focus The questions and answers in many ways reflect a typical journey in the world. What kind of journey does the poem describe?

☑ Check Your Comprehension

Cite four details of the journey.

◆ Critical Thinking

INTERPRET
1. What evidence is there that this journey is not just an ordinary trip? **[Analyze]**
2. What does the journey along a road symbolize, or represent? **[Interpret]**
3. What might the uphill winding represent? **[Interpret]**
4. What is the final destination of the journey? **[Infer]**

Summer

Walter Dean Myers

I like hot days, hot days
Sweat is what you got days
Bugs buzzin from cousin to cousin
Juices dripping
5   Running and ripping
Catch the one you love days

Birds peeping
Old men sleeping
Lazy days, daisies lay
10 Beaming and dreaming
Of hot days, hot days,
Sweat is what you got days

▶ **Critical Viewing** What feeling do these images of summer evoke in you? How are they similar to or different from the images evoked by the poem? **[Compare and Contrast]**

◆ Guide for Responding

◆ Literature and Your Life

Reader's Response Do you like hot summer days? Why or why not?

Thematic Focus Each season fills the world around us with an infinite number of images. What are some of your favorite images of summer?

☑ Check Your Comprehension

1. What happens to bugs and juices in the summer?
2. What do birds and old men do in summer?
3. What pair of lines sums up the way the speaker feels about summer?

◆ Critical Thinking

INTERPRET
1. What kinds of juices might be dripping? **[Interpret]**
2. What might the words "daisies lay beaming and dreaming" mean? **[Speculate]**
3. From what is said in the poem, how do people and living things from the world of nature act on hot days? **[Infer]**

EVALUATE
4. How does the poet use repetition to help communicate meaning? **[Evaluate]**

▲ **Critical Viewing** Why does this series of photographs effectively illustrate the poem? **[Connect]**

Ecclesiastes 3:1-8

(King James Version)

To every thing there is a season, and a time to
every purpose under the heaven:
A time to be born, and a time to die; a time to
plant, and a time to pluck up that which is planted;
A time to kill, and a time to heal; a time to break
down, and a time to build up;
A time to weep, and a time to laugh; a time to
mourn, and a time to dance;

5   A time to cast away stones, and a time to gather
stones together; a time to embrace, and a time to
refrain from embracing;
A time to get, and a time to lose; a time to keep,
and a time to cast away;
A time to rend,[1] and a time to sew; a time to keep
silence, and a time to speak;
A time to love, and a time to hate; a time of war,
and a time of peace.

---

1. **rend** (rend) *v*.: Tear.

Guide for Responding

◆ Literature and Your Life

Reader's Response Do you find this passage comforting? Why or why not?

Thematic Focus How does this poem connect the cycles of nature with the cycles of human life?

☑ Check Your Comprehension

1. Name four pairs of actions mentioned in the passage.
2. What verse contains the main idea?
3. How would you describe the way this passage is organized?

◆ Critical Thinking

INTERPRET

1. What does "To every thing there is a season" mean? **[Infer]**
2. What is the purpose of the repetition of the phrase "a time"? **[Speculate]**
3. What activity is suggested by the words "A time to cast away stones, and a time to gather stones together ..."? **[Infer]**

EVALUATE

4. This passage is balanced by pairs of phrases that are opposites. How does the pairing of opposite ideas help to communicate the message of the passage? **[Evaluate]**

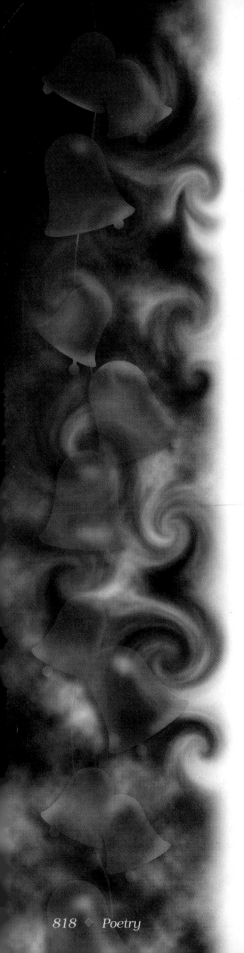

The Bells

Edgar Allan Poe

I

Hear the sledges[1] with the bells—
Silver bells!
What a world of merriment their melody foretells!
How they tinkle, tinkle, tinkle,
5   In the icy air of night!
While the stars, that oversprinkle
All the heavens, seem to twinkle
With a crystalline delight;
Keeping time, time, time,
10   In a sort of Runic[2] rhyme,
To the tintinnabulation[3] that so musically wells
From the bells, bells, bells, bells,
Bells, bells, bells—
From the jingling and the tinkling of the bells.

II

15   Hear the mellow wedding bells,
Golden bells!
What a world of happiness their harmony foretells!
Through the balmy air of night
How they ring out their delight!
20   From the molten golden-notes,
And all in tune,
What a liquid ditty[4] floats
To the turtle-dove[5] that listens, while she gloats
On the moon!
25   Oh, from out the sounding cells,
What a gush of euphony[6] voluminously wells!
How it swells!
How it dwells
On the future! how it tells
30   Of the rapture that impels
To the swinging and the ringing

---

1. **sledges** (slej ́ əz) *n.*: Sleighs.
2. **Runic** (r$\overline{oo}$ ́ nik) *adj.*: Songlike; poetical.
3. **tintinnabulation** (tin ti nab y$\overline{oo}$ la ́ shən) *n.*: Ringing of bells.
4. **ditty** (dit ́ ē) *n.*: Song.
5. **turtle-dove:** The turtle-dove is traditionally associated with love.
6. **euphony** (y$\overline{oo}$ ́ fə nē) *n.*: Pleasing sound.

Of the bells, bells, bells,
Of the bells, bells, bells, bells
Bells, bells, bells—
35   To the rhyming and the chiming of the bells!

III

Hear the loud alarum[7] bells!
Brazen[8] bells!
What a tale of terror now their turbulency tells!
In the startled ear of night
40   How they scream out their affright!
Too much horrified to speak,
They can only shriek, shriek,
Out of tune,
In a clamorous appealing to the mercy of the fire,
45 In a mad expostulation[9] with the deaf and frantic fire
Leaping higher, higher, higher,
With a desperate desire,
And a resolute endeavor
Now—now to sit or never,
50   By the side of the pale-faced moon.
Oh, the bells, bells, bells!
What a tale their terror tells
Of Despair!
How they clang, and clash, and roar!
55   What a horror they outpour
On the bosom of the <u>palpitating</u> air!
Yet the ear it fully knows,
By the twanging
And the clanging,
60   How the danger ebbs and flows;
Yet the ear distinctly tells,
In the jangling,
And the wrangling,
How the danger sinks and swells,
65 By the sinking or the swelling in the anger of the bells—
Of the bells—
Of the bells, bells, bells, bells,
Bells, bells, bells—
In the clamor and the clangor of the bells!

IV

70   Hear the tolling of the bells—
Iron bells!
What a world of solemn thought their monody[10] compels!
In the silence of the night,

---

7. **alarum** (ə ler´ əm) *adj.*: Sudden call to arms; alarm.
8. **brazen** (brā´ zən) *adj.*: Made of brass; having the sound of brass.
9. **expostulation** (ik späs chə lā´ shən) *n.*: Objection; complaint.
10. **monody** (män´ ə dē) *n.*: Poem of mourning; a steady sound; music in which one instrument or voice is dominant.

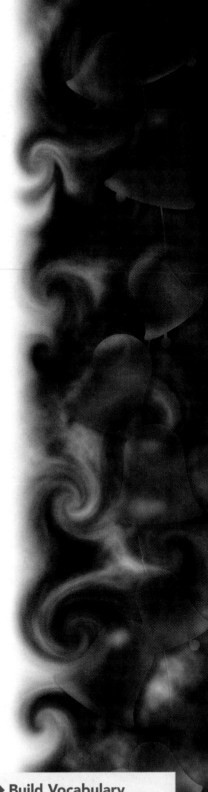

◆ **Build Vocabulary**

voluminously (və lo͞o´ mə nəs lē) *adv.*: Fully; in great volume

palpitating (pal´ pə tāt´ iŋ) *adj.*: Beating rapidly; throbbing

The Bells, Edmund Dulac, New York Public Library

▲ Critical
Viewing
How would
you describe
the mood of
this painting?
Does it
match the
mood of the
poem?
[Interpret]

How we shiver with affright
75   At the melancholy menace of their tone!
         For every sound that floats
         From the rust within their throats
                  Is a groan.
         And the people—ah, the people—
80   They that dwell up in the steeple,
                  All alone,
         And who tolling, tolling, tolling,
            In that muffled <u>monotone</u>,
         Feel a glory in so rolling
85   On the human heart a stone—
      They are neither man nor woman—
      They are neither brute nor human—
                  They are Ghouls:[11]
         And their king it is who tolls;
90   And he rolls, rolls, rolls,
                  Rolls

---

11. **Ghouls** (goolz) *n.*: Evil spirits that rob graves.

◆ Build
Vocabulary

monotone
(män´ ə tōn´) *n*
Uninterrupted
repetition of th
same tone

A pæan from the bells!
And his merry bosom swells
    With the pæan of the bells!
95   And he dances and he yells;
    Keeping time, time, time,
    In a sort of Runic rhyme,
        To the pæan of the bells—
            Of the bells:
100   Keeping time, time, time,
    In a sort of Runic rhyme,
        To the throbbing of the bells—
    Of the bells, bells, bells—
        To the sobbing of the bells;
105   Keeping time, time, time,
    As he knells, knells, knells,
    In a happy Runic rhyme,
        To the rolling of the bells—
            Of the bells, bells, bells—
110   To the tolling of the bells,
    Of the bells, bells, bells, bells,
        Bells, bells, bells—
To the moaning and the groaning of the bells.

◆ **Build Vocabulary**

pæan (pē´ ən) *n.*: Song of joy or triumph

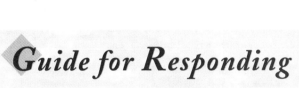

Guide for Responding

◆ Literature and Your Life

Reader's Response What feelings did each section of "The Bells" evoke in you?

Thematic Focus In "The Bells," the sounds of different kinds of bells evoke different scenes. What scenes or events from your world do the sounds of different kinds of bells evoke in you?

☑ Check Your Comprehension

1. What kinds of bells are described in each of the four sections of "The Bells"?
2. How many of the four sections of the poem speak of bells ringing in the night?
3. What similarities among the four sections do you see? Describe at least three.

◆ Critical Thinking

INTERPRET
1. What scene or situation is suggested in each of the sections? **[Infer]**
2. Why do you think Poe varies the length of the lines in "The Bells"? **[Draw Conclusions]**
3. Does the mood or spirit of the poem vary from one section to another or is it basically the same throughout? Explain. **[Compare and Contrast]**

EVALUATE
4. How successful is Poe in capturing the sounds of bells in words? Cite excerpts from one section of the poem to explain your answer. **[Criticize]**

APPLY
5. The poet T. S. Eliot once said that poetry can be enjoyed before it is understood. Could "The Bells" be used as evidence in support of this idea? Give reasons for your opinion. **[Synthesize]**

Although you may not have thought of it, song lyrics are a form of poetry. Like poetry, good song lyrics use sound devices, imagery, and figurative language. Among the most highly regarded modern songwriters are Paul McCartney and John Lennon, who were both members of the Beatles, a rock group that disbanded in 1970 but remain popular to this day. "The Long and Winding Road" is just one of their many hits.

The Long and Winding Road

The Beatles

John Lennon and Paul McCartney

The long and winding road that leads to your door,
Will never disappear,
I've seen that road before
It always leads me here,
Leads me to your door.

The wild and windy night the rain washed away,
Has left a pool of tears crying for the day.
Why leave me standing here, let me know the way.
Many times I've been alone and many times I've cried.
Anyway you'll never know the many ways I've tried, but
Still they lead me back to the long and winding road.
You left me standing here a long, long time ago.
Don't leave me waiting here, lead me to your door.

1. What might the "long and winding road" symbolize?
2. Find two especially effective images, and explain what each represents.
3. Compare and contrast this song with one of the poems you've just read.

Guide for Responding *(continued)*

◆ Literary Focus

LYRIC POETRY AND SOUND DEVICES

These poems are all examples of **lyric poetry**—highly musical verses that express the thoughts and feelings of a single speaker. The musical effect of the poems is created through the use of **sound devices** such as rhythm (the pattern of beats or stresses in language), alliteration (the repetition of initial consonant sounds), rhyme (the repetition of sounds at the ends of words), and onomatopoeia (the use of words that imitate sounds).

1. How does the speaker of "Uphill" feel about life's journey and its ultimate destination? Support your answer.
2. If you were to give "Summer" a different title, what would it be? Why?
3. The musical quality of "The Bells" is achieved in part through rhymes at the ends of lines and within lines. Point out three examples of rhymes within lines of "The Bells."
4. List at least four words in "The Bells" that are examples of onomatopoeia.
5. Much of the musical quality of Ecclesiastes 3:1–8 is achieved through the repetition of similarly constructed pairs of phrases opposite in meaning. List four such pairs of phrases.
6. Do all of the lines of Ecclesiastes 3:1–8 have the same rhythm or does the rhythm vary somewhat? Explain your answer.

◆ Reading Strategy

LISTEN

Because sound is so important in lyric poetry, reading a lyric poem aloud and **listening** as you do so is a good way to appreciate the poem fully. In a group, take turns reading sections from one or more of the four poems. Then answer these questions.

1. How does reading the poems aloud help you appreciate the use of rhyme in the poems?
2. How does reading the poems help draw your attention to the use of other sound devices such as alliteration and onomatopoeia?
3. How does reading aloud help you grasp each poem's meaning?

◆ Build Vocabulary

USING THE PREFIX *mono-*

Match each word containing the prefix *mono-*, meaning "one," with its definition on the right.

1. monorail   **a.** single large block of stone
2. monopoly   **b.** railway with a single rail as a track
3. monolith   **c.** exclusive control of the selling of something

USING THE WORD BANK

Write the paragraph in your notebook. Then complete it with words from the Word Bank.

Commuters, ____?____ heading home from work, ____?____ packed the railroad platform. With their hearts ____?____, they listened to an announcement delivered in a ____?____. When the voice proclaimed that their train was about to arrive, they sang a ____?____ as one!

◆ Build Grammar Skills

END PUNCTUATION

Beside signaling the end of a sentence, **end punctuation**—periods, question marks, and exclamation marks—often indicates meaning or feeling, especially in poetry. Notice how the end punctuation affects the meaning of these sentences:

The road winds uphill.

The road winds uphill?

The road winds uphill!

Practice Change the meaning or feeling of each sentence to that given in parentheses by changing only the end punctuation.

1. I will meet other wayfarers at night. (anxiety)
2. You like hot days. (disbelief)
3. Please, listen to the bells. (anger)
4. It's time to destroy what we've built. (resignation)

Writing Application Write a brief dialogue that might take place between you and your friends. Use each type of end mark within your dialogue to convey the emotions of the participants.

Build Your Portfolio

 ## Idea Bank

Writing

1. **Written Recommendation** If you had to recommend one of these poems to people interested in learning about lyric poetry, which poem would you choose? Write a short paper presenting and supporting your recommendation.

2. **Lyric Poem** Write a lyric poem about your favorite season of the year. Include vivid images that you associate with the season. In addition, be sure to express your feelings about the season clearly. As a challenge, try using musical devices, such as rhyming or alliteration.

3. **Comparison-and-Contrast Essay** Write an essay comparing and contrasting Sections III and IV of "The Bells." Explore similarities and differences in mood, word choice, rhythm, rhyme, and repetition. Use details from both for support.

Speaking and Listening

4. **Dramatic Reading** "The Bells" was meant to be read aloud. Practice and present a dramatic reading of the poem. Try to capture the poem's musical quality. **[Performing Arts Link]**

5. **Listening Activity** The rock group The Birds recorded a musical adaptation of Ecclesiastes 3:1–8 entitled "Turn, Turn, Turn." Find a recording of the song, share it with the class, and discuss whether the music adds to the poem. **[Music Link]**

Projects

6. **Illustration** Draw or paint a picture to illustrate the poem "Summer." Include as many of the images mentioned in the poem as possible. Also, try to capture the mood of the poem. **[Art Link]**

7. **Multimedia Presentation** Create a multimedia presentation on bells. The presentation should include both pictures and sounds.

 ## Writing Mini-Lesson

Rap Song

Like lyric poems, rap songs are musical expressions of a speaker's thoughts and feelings. Write a rap song that conveys your feelings about a season, a stage of life, or some other topic that interests you. Use repetition to emphasize your message.

Writing Skills Focus: Repetition

When you think about your favorite songs, certain repeated words or lines probably stand out in your mind. The **repetition** of key words, groups of words, or lines is one of the most effective ways of getting a message across to readers or listeners. In addition, repetition helps to create a musical effect. As you plan and write your rap song, use the repetition of sounds, words, and lines to leave a strong impression in the minds of your audience. Be careful not to overuse repetition, however. If you repeat too many different words or lines, none of them will stand out.

Prewriting Start by deciding on your topic and jotting down your thoughts about that topic. Decide which key ideas or messages you want to leave in the minds of your audience. Then think about which words or lines you could repeat to help drive home your points.

Drafting As you draft your rap song, focus on establishing a strong rhythm. Use rhymes at the ends of lines to help create a musical effect. In addition, establish a refrain—a line or group of lines that is repeated throughout the song.

Revising Read your rap song aloud to make sure that it has a strong rhythm and that your use of repetition highlights your main ideas. Make revisions to improve the sound and the meaning. Then perform your song for the class.

Writing Process Workshop

Songs may be described as "poetry set to music." Like poems, **song lyrics** often contain poetic elements such as rhythm, rhyme, repetition, and imagery. In addition, song lyrics also spark emotional reactions in listeners and often convey important messages about life.

Using your favorite songs as both models and sources of inspiration, write a set of song lyrics that conveys emotions as well as interesting ideas. The following skills, introduced in this section's Writing Mini-Lessons, will help you to write song lyrics.

Writing Skills Focus

▶ **Create a main impression** of your subject that will remain in listeners' minds. (See p. 811.)

▶ **Avoid unnecessary details in your writing.** Songs are brief, so every word counts. Use only those details that convey the ideas you wish to present. (See p. 792.)

▶ **Use figurative language,** such as similes and metaphors, to create interesting images and spark new ideas in listeners' minds. A simile compares one thing to another using the word *like* or *as*. A metaphor compares one thing to another without using *like* or *as*. (See p. 801.)

▶ **Use repetition of key words** to get your ideas across and to give the song a catchy sound. (See p. 824.)

The writer of the folk song "Clementine" uses these skills as he mourns the loss of his daughter.

MODEL

from "Clementine"

Oh, my darling, oh, my darling,
Oh, my darling Clementine, ①
You are lost and gone forever,
Dreadful sorry, Clementine. ②
Light she was and like a fairy, ③
And her shoes were number nine;
Herring boxes without topses,
Sandals were for Clementine. ④

① The phrase "Oh, my darling" is repeated several times, emphasizing the speaker's feelings.

② The writer focuses the song on his sorrow over the loss of Clementine.

③ Here, the writer uses a simile.

④ Notice the writer's use of rhyme.

Applying Language Skills: Figurative Language

Figurative language can include similes, metaphors, or personification, which gives human characteristics to an animal, object, or idea.

Simile: *Books are like a magic carpet ride.*

Metaphor: *Books are a magic carpet ride.*

Personification: *Books smile and take your hand.*

Notice how figurative language creates colorful images and new ways of looking at familiar things.

Practice On your paper, state each idea more colorfully by using figurative language.

1. Flowers are pretty.
2. Flowers smell good.
3. Flowers blow in the wind.
4. Flowers grow in a garden.

Writing Application As you draft your song lyrics, use figurative language such as simile, metaphor, and personification to create vivid images.

Writer's Solution Connection Writing Lab

To help you gather details for your songs, use the Word Bins activities in the Prewriting section of the tutorial on Creative Writing.

Prewriting

Choose a Topic Find a topic for your song lyrics by thinking of an idea or message about which you have strong feelings. You can also choose one of the topic ideas listed here.

Topic Ideas

- Something or someone you love
- A beautiful gift you have given or received
- A happy or special occasion
- An event that surprised you

Identify the Main Impression You'll Create Does your topic make you feel happy or sad? Fulfilled or empty? List words and phrases that describe the main impression of your topic. You may also wish to draw pictures that express your impression. Later, you can use the pictures as inspiration for your song lyrics.

Use of Figurative Language Next, make a list of similes or metaphors that convey the images you picture in your mind.

Similes	Metaphors
as red as a rose	the moon is a balloon
as fresh as morning dew	sun rays of happiness
blossomed like a flower	an explosion of love
as deep as the ocean	a chain around my heart

Choose the figurative language that you sense is most effective. Plan to use those phrases in your song.

Drafting

Choose a Tune To help you "hear" your lyrics in your head, set them to music. If you don't write music yourself, choose an existing song that you like, and use that tune.

Repeat Key Words and Phrases Popular lyrics often have a hook—a catchy phrase that is repeated throughout the song. As you write, find one or more phrases to repeat. The phrases should express the essence of your ideas and help convey the main impression you wish to share with readers.

Music Writing Tip Since song lyrics are set to music with a steady rhythmic beat, it is important that repeated words or phrases be easy to pronounce. Many phrases sound catchy because they contain a repeated consonant sound, as in "feeling foolish falling fast."

Avoid Unnecessary Details Be economical when using words to express your ideas. If your song is about love, stick to that idea. Don't introduce details that stray from your topic. If other subjects occur to you as you write, save them for another song.

Revising

Use a Checklist Go back to the Writing Skills Focus on the first page of this lesson to evaluate and revise your song lyrics.

▶ How well have I conveyed my main impression?
Invite a peer to read your song lyrics and describe his or her main impression. If the intended impression is not conveyed, revise the lyrics.

▶ How effective is my figurative language?
Find where you have used similes, metaphors, or personification. Does each phrase create a vivid image? If not, use different language.

▶ Have I repeated words and phrases?
Find the words that are repeated in your song. If they don't sound catchy or convey your main idea, revise them.

▶ Have I avoided unnecessary details?
Look for details that direct the focus away from your main idea, and remove them.

Publishing

▶ **Songbook** Collect lyrics from other students and create a class song book.
▶ **Performance** Recite or sing your lyrics for an audience. If you play a musical instrument, you may choose to accompany yourself. If your school has its own radio station, perform your song on the air.

APPLYING LANGUAGE SKILLS: Punctuating Song Lyrics

In a song, use a comma at the end of a line if there is a pause. Omit punctuation if there is no pause. Use a period at the end of a verse or stanza.

When sorrow or pain

Come close to me,

I try to flee.

Practice On your paper, add punctuation to these song lyrics:

Whether it's raining
Whether it's snowing
My love for you
Is always growing

Writing Application As you revise your song lyrics, note how you punctuated the lines. If you find a place where you used the wrong punctuation, make the necessary corrections.

Writer's Solution Connection Writing Lab

To help you revise, use the Language Variety Checker in the Revision section of the tutorial on Creative Writing.

Real-World Reading Skills Workshop

Strategies for Success

Songwriters, like poets, wish to convey to their audience a special feeling or idea. Consider the following points to help you interpret song lyrics.

What Is the Mood of the Music? Even before hearing a song's lyrics, the music can be a clue to their message. Is the melody lively and happy? Is it slow and sad? Remember that music is usually composed to match the feeling of the lyrics. The mood of the melody can signal the narrator's feelings.

Who Are the Speaker and the Audience? As you read song lyrics, consider who is narrating them. Is it one person, a pair, or a group? Also consider the intended audience. Is the song directed specifically to a male? To a female? To anyone at all? How easily could references to "he" in the lyrics be switched to "she," or vice versa?

What Is the Purpose? Consider the speaker's purpose in expressing his or her words. Is the person celebrating? Mourning? Giving a warning? Also consider the language that the speaker uses to express his or her message. What images do they create in your mind? The images you "see" are a clue to the narrator's purpose.

Apply the Strategy

Read carefully the lyrics to "Greensleeves." Then, if possible, listen to a recording of the song. Interpret the song lyrics by answering these questions.

1. Who is the speaker in the song? Whom is the speaker addressing?

2. What is the speaker's purpose in addressing Greensleeves? What is the speaker's message to her?

3. Why do you think the speaker is afraid of losing Greensleeves?

4. How relevant do you think this song is to modern-day audiences? To which lyrics can you relate the most? The least?

Greensleeves
Old English Folk Song (1620)

Alas, my love, you will do me wrong
If you cast me off so discourteously;
And I have loved you so very long
Delighted in your winning company.

Greensleeves, you were all my joy,
And you know, Greensleeves, you were my
 delight;
Greensleeves, you're my heart of gold,
No one else but my dear Lady Greensleeves.

✔ *Here are other situations in which interpreting song lyrics can be helpful:*
- ▶ Hearing a popular new song on the radio
- ▶ Interpreting the lyrics of a love song
- ▶ Appreciating a historical folk song
- ▶ Understanding the lyrics to a rap song

Transection #1, 1966, Clarence H. Carter, The Newark Museum

Guide for Reading

Edgar Allan Poe *(1809–1849)*

Although he is remembered mostly for his suspenseful, often horrifying, short stories, Edgar Allan Poe was also a gifted poet. "The Raven," his best-known poem, is haunting and mournful, reflecting the impact of the many misfortunes that Poe experienced during his brief, tragic life.

Early Life After losing both of his parents as a young boy, Poe was taken in by a wealthy Virginia merchant, John Allan. Poe had a stormy relationship with his stepfather, which completely disintegrated when Poe was a young man.

Literary Career Poe published numerous short stories, several collections of poetry, and a novel, but never achieved financial success as a writer. Despite his financial struggles, Poe experienced a period of happiness following his marriage to Virginia Clemm in 1835. This happiness was shattered, however, by his wife's death in 1847. (For more on Edgar Allan Poe, see pp. 2 and 812.)

William Shakespeare *(1564–1616)*

Theatergoers of Shakespeare's time expected to see action, humor, and passion played out on the stage. At a time when the English language was rapidly developing into a rich and powerful means of expression, they were also eager to hear impressive, fully developed speeches modeled on those in classical drama. Shakespeare was able to forge a perfect blend of high drama and exalted language that met his audience's twin expectations.

Memorable Speeches Altogether, Shakespeare wrote more than three dozen plays, most of which continue to be read and performed today. Because of the beauty of his language and the timelessness of the themes he addressed, speeches and scenes in his plays are quoted more often than the works of any other writer. "The Seven Ages of Man," from the play *As You Like It,* is considered one of his best speeches. (For more on William Shakespeare, see pp. 669 and 840.)

◆ Build Vocabulary

WORD ROOTS: *-sol-*

In "The Raven," the word *desolate* is used to help capture the speaker's state of mind as he struggles to come to terms with the death of the woman he loves. The word contains the root *-sol-*, which means "alone." How does the meaning of the root relate to the overall meaning of the word, which is "deserted" or "abandoned"?

WORD BANK

Here is a list of words from the selection. With a group of classmates, try to come up with a sentence using each of the words. If necessary, check meanings in the dictionary.

quaint
beguiling
respite
desolate
pallid
woeful
treble

◆ Build Grammar Skills

PARTICIPIAL PHRASES

Both poets use participial phrases (participles with modifiers and complements) to create detailed images. Participial phrases may be restrictive or nonrestrictive. A **restrictive participial phrase** is necessary to complete the meaning of the noun or pronoun it modifies. It is not set off by commas. A **nonrestrictive participial phrase** is not necessary but adds meaning. It is set off with commas.

Restrictive: . . . filled me with fantastic terrors *never felt before.*

Nonrestrictive: And then the whining schoolboy, with his satchel,
And shining morning face, *creeping like a snail*
Unwillingly to school.

The Raven ◆ The Seven Ages of Man

◆ *Literature and Your Life*

CONNECT YOUR EXPERIENCE

Why do people act the way they do? Adults often explain the behavior of young people by saying, "It's just a phase he or she is going through." In "The Seven Ages of Man," the speaker argues that each person goes through seven phases in a lifetime. "The Raven" presents a different perspective. It seems to suggest that the individual events of a person's life shape that person's behavior.

Journal Writing What do you think the "seven ages of man" might be? Jot down your ideas in your journal.

THEMATIC FOCUS: LOOKING INWARD

These two poems present different perspectives on human life. As you read, think about how the authors' perspectives compare with your own perspective.

◆ Background for Understanding

LITERATURE

"The Seven Ages of Man" is a speech from Shakespeare's comedy *As You Like It*. A comedy, in the Shakespearean sense, is a play in which humorous things are said and done, and in which a multitude of problems arise and are easily solved by the end of the play. Usually, Shakespeare's comedies end with one or more weddings.

As You Like It is about a duke who has been deprived of his rights and exiled to the forest by his own brother. "The Seven Ages of Man" is a speech addressed to the duke by his attendant, Jacques. The speech reveals the character and outlook on life of Jacques, who is a bitter realist.

◆ Literary Focus

NARRATIVE AND DRAMATIC POETRY

"The Raven" is a poem that has characters, a setting, and a plot. This makes it **narrative poetry**—poetry that tells a story. "The Seven Ages of Man," on the other hand, is an example of **dramatic poetry**—poetry in which the lines are spoken by one or more characters. When a dramatic poem has a single speaker who is a fictional character expressing his or her thoughts or feelings within a developing situation, it is called a **dramatic monologue**. "The Seven Ages of Man," which is a speech delivered by a character in a full-length play, is a dramatic monologue.

◆ Reading Strategy

MAKE INFERENCES ABOUT THE SPEAKER

Readers sometimes mistakenly assume that a poem's **speaker**—the voice of a poem—is always the poet. Though in some cases the speaker is in fact the poet, often the speaker is an imaginary voice assumed by the poet. To understand a poem, it is important to identify who the speaker is and then to **make inferences,** or draw conclusions, about his or her situation, attitudes, and personality traits by looking closely at the words and details. For example, from the first line of "The Raven"—"Once upon a midnight dreary, while I pondered, weak and weary"—you can infer that the speaker is in a gloomy, depressed state of mind. What does this knowledge of the speaker's situation lead you to expect in the rest of the poem?

Use a chart like this one to record words and details that reveal important information about each speaker. Jot down the inference you can make based on each detail.

Key Details	Inferences
——— ➤ ———	
——— ➤ ———	
——— ➤ ———	
——— ➤ ———	

The Raven

Edgar Allan Poe

Once upon a midnight dreary, while I pondered, weak and weary,
Over many a <u>quaint</u> and curious volume of forgotten lore,[1]
While I nodded, nearly napping, suddenly there came a tapping,
As of someone gently rapping, rapping at my chamber door.
5   "'Tis some visitor," I muttered, "tapping at my chamber door—
     Only this, and nothing more."

Ah, distinctly I remember it was in the bleak December,
And each separate dying ember wrought its ghost upon the floor.
Eagerly I wished the morrow—vainly I had tried to borrow
10 From my books surcease[2] of sorrow—sorrow for the lost Lenore—
For the rare and radiant maiden whom the angels name Lenore—
     Nameless here for evermore.

And the silken, sad, uncertain rustling of each purple curtain
Thrilled me—filled me with fantastic terrors never felt before;
15 So that now, to still the beating of my heart, I stood repeating
"'Tis some visitor entreating entrance at my chamber door—
Some late visitor entreating entrance at my chamber door—
     This it is and nothing more."

Presently my soul grew stronger; hesitating then no longer,
20 "Sir," said I, "or Madam, truly your forgiveness I implore;
But the fact is I was napping, and so gently you came rapping,
And so faintly you came tapping, tapping at my chamber door,
That I scarce was sure I heard you"—here I opened wide the door—
     Darkness there, and nothing more.

▲ **Critical Viewing**
Which adjectives applied to the speaker and the raven in the poem might also fit the pictures? **[Connect]**

---

1. **quaint . . . lore:** Strange book of ancient learning.
2. **surcease** (sʉr sēs´) *n.*: End.

◆ **Build Vocabulary**
quaint (kwānt) *adj.*: Strange; unusual

25 Deep into that darkness peering, long I stood there wondering, fearing,
    Doubting, dreaming dreams no mortal ever dared to dream before;
    But the silence was unbroken, and the darkness gave no token,[3]
    And the only word there spoken was the whispered word, "Lenore!"
    This *I* whispered, and an echo murmured back the word, "Lenore!"
30   Merely this, and nothing more.

    Then into the chamber turning, all my soul within me burning,
    Soon I heard again a tapping somewhat louder than before.
    "Surely," said I, "surely that is something at my window lattice;[4]
    Let me see, then, what thereat[5] is, and this mystery explore—
35 Let my heart be still a moment and this mystery explore—
          'Tis the wind, and nothing more!"

    Open here I flung the shutter, when, with many a flirt[6] and flutter,
    In there stepped a stately raven of the saintly days of yore;
    Not the least obeisance[7] made he; not an instant stopped or stayed he;
40 But, with mien[8] of lord or lady, perched above my chamber door—
    Perched upon a bust of Pallas[9] just above my chamber door—
          Perched, and sat, and nothing more.

    Then this ebony bird beguiling my sad fancy[10] into smiling,
    By the grave and stern decorum of the countenance[11] it wore,
45 "Though thy crest be shorn and shaven, thou," I said, "art sure no craven,[12]
    Ghastly grim and ancient raven wandering from the Nightly shore—
    Tell me what thy lordly name is on the Night's Plutonian[13] shore!"
          Quoth[14] the raven, "Nevermore."

    Much I marveled this ungainly fowl to hear discourse so plainly,
50 Though its answer little meaning—little relevancy bore;
    For we cannot help agreeing that no sublunary[15] being
    Ever yet was blessed with seeing bird above his chamber door—
    Bird or beast upon the sculptured bust above his chamber door,
          With such name as "Nevermore."

55 But the raven, sitting lonely on the placid bust, spoke only
    That one word, as if his soul in that one word he did outpour.

---

3. **token** (tō′ kən) *n*.: Sign.
4. **lattice** (lat′ is) *n*.: Framework of wood or metal.
5. **thereat** (ther at′) *adv*.: There.
6. **flirt** (flʉrt) *n*.: Quick, uneven movement.
7. **obeisance** (ō bā′ səns) *n*.: Bow or another sign of respect.
8. **mien** (mēn) *n*.: Manner.
9. **bust of Pallas** (pal′ əs): Sculpture of the head and shoulders of Pallas Athena (ə thē′ nə), the ancient Greek goddess of wisdom.
10. **fancy** (fan′ sē) *n*.: Imagination.
11. **countenance** (koun′ tə nəns) *n*.: Facial appearance.
12. **craven** (krā′ vən) *n*.: Coward (usually an adjective).
13. **Plutonian** (plo̅o̅ tō′ nē ən) *adj*.: Like the underworld, ruled over by the ancient Roman god Pluto.
14. **quoth** (kwōth) *v*.: Said.
15. **sublunary** (sub lo̅o̅n′ ər ē) *adj*.: Earthly.

Illustration to E.A. Poe's "The Raven,"
Edouard Manet, Museum of Fine Arts, Boston

Nothing farther then he uttered—not a feather then he fluttered—
Till I scarcely more than muttered, "Other friends have flown before—
On the morrow *he* will leave me, as my hopes have flown before."
60   Quoth the raven, "Nevermore."

Wondering at the stillness broken by reply so aptly spoken,
"Doubtless," said I, "what it utters is its only stock and store,
Caught from some unhappy master whom unmerciful Disaster
Followed fast and followed faster—so, when Hope he would adjure,[16]
65   Stern Despair returned, instead of the sweet Hope he dared adjure—
      That sad answer, 'Nevermore.' "

But the raven still beguiling all my sad soul into smiling,
Straight I wheeled a cushioned seat in front of bird, and bust, and door;
Then upon the velvet sinking, I betook myself to linking
70   Fancy unto fancy, thinking what this ominous bird of yore—
What this grim, ungainly, ghastly, gaunt, and ominous bird of yore
      Meant in croaking "Nevermore."

This I sat engaged in guessing, but no syllable expressing
To the fowl whose fiery eyes now burned into my bosom's core;
75   This and more I sat divining,[17] with my head at ease reclining
On the cushion's velvet lining that the lamplight gloated o'er,
But whose velvet violet lining with the lamplight gloating o'er,
      She shall press, ah, nevermore!

Then, methought, the air grew denser, perfumed from an unseen censer[18]
80   Swung by angels whose faint footfalls tinkled on the tufted floor.
"Wretch," I cried, "thy God hath lent thee—by these angels he hath sent thee
Respite—respite and Nepenthe[19] from thy memories of Lenore!
Let me quaff[20] this kind Nepenthe and forget this lost Lenore!"
      Quoth the raven, "Nevermore."

85   "Prophet!" said I, "thing of evil!—prophet still, if bird or devil!—
Whether Tempter[21] sent, or whether tempest tossed thee here ashore,
Desolate, yet all undaunted, on this desert land enchanted—
On this home by Horror haunted—tell me truly, I implore—
Is there—*is* there balm in Gilead?[22]—tell me—tell me, I implore!"
90   Quoth the raven, "Nevermore."

---

16. adjure (ə joor´) *v.*: Appeal to.
17. divining (də vīn´ iŋ) *v.*: Guessing.
18. censer (sen´ sər) *n.*: Container for burning incense.
19. Nepenthe (ni pen´ thē) *n.*: Drug used in ancient times to cause forgetfulness of sorrow.
20. quaff (kwäf) *v.*: Drink.
21. Tempter: Devil.
22. balm (bäm) **in Gilead** (gil´ ē əd): Cure for suffering; the Bible refers to a medicinal ointment, or balm, made in a region called Gilead.

◆ **Build Vocabulary**
beguiling (bi gīl´ iŋ) *adj.*: Tricking; charming
respite (res´ pit) *n.*: Rest; relief
desolate (des´ ə lit) *adj.*: Deserted; abandoned
pallid (pal´ id) *adj.*: Pale

"Prophet!" said I, "thing of evil!—prophet still, if bird or devil!
By that Heaven that bends above us—by that God we both adore—
Tell this soul with sorrow laden if, within the distant Aidenn,[23]
It shall clasp a sainted maiden whom the angels name Lenore—
95   Clasp a rare and radiant maiden whom the angels name Lenore."
       Quoth the raven, "Nevermore."

"Be that word our sign of parting, bird or fiend!" I shrieked, upstarting—
"Get thee back into the tempest and the Night's Plutonian shore!
Leave no black plume as a token of that lie thy soul hath spoken!
100   Leave my loneliness unbroken!—quit the bust above my door!
Take thy beak from out my heart, and take thy form from off my door!"
       Quoth the raven, "Nevermore."

And the raven, never flitting, still is sitting, still is sitting
On the pallid bust of Pallas just above my chamber door;
105   And his eyes have all the seeming of a demon that is dreaming,
And the lamplight o'er him streaming throws his shadow on the floor;
And my soul from out that shadow that lies floating on the floor
       Shall be lifted—nevermore!

---

23. Aidenn: Name meant to suggest Eden or paradise.

Guide for Responding

◆ Literature and Your Life

Reader's Response How do you feel about the speaker of the poem? Explain.

Thematic Focus How does the speaker's perspective on the raven change throughout the poem?

☑ Check Your Comprehension

1. What is the setting (time and place) of the poem?
2. Who is Lenore?
3. What one word does the raven speak?
4. What question does the speaker ask the raven near the end of the poem?

◆ Critical Thinking

INTERPRET
1. What can you infer, or conclude, about Lenore and the speaker's relationship with her? **[Infer]**
2. (a) Describe how your impression of the raven changes as the poem progresses. (b) What causes your impression to change? **[Connect]**
3. (a) How does the speaker's state of mind change as the poem progresses? (b) What causes these changes? **[Connect]**
4. What does the raven come to represent to the speaker? **[Draw Conclusions]**

EVALUATE
5. When Poe set out to write this poem, he thought of having a parrot repeat the word "Nevermore." Would the poem have been as effective if Poe had used a parrot instead of a raven? Explain. **[Evaluate]**

The Seven Ages of Man

William Shakespeare

The Seven Ages of Man, Folger Shakespeare Library, Washington, D.C.

All the world's a stage,
And all the men and women merely players:[1]
They have their exits and their entrances;
And one man in his time plays many parts,
His acts being seven ages.[2] At first the infant,
Mewling[3] and puking in the nurse's arms.
And then the whining schoolboy, with his satchel,
And shining morning face, creeping like snail
Unwillingly to school. And then the lover,
Sighing like furnace, with a <u>woeful</u> ballad
Made to his mistress' eyebrow. Then a soldier,
Full of strange oaths, and bearded like the pard,[4]
Jealous in honor,[5] sudden and quick in quarrel,
Seeking the bubble reputation
Even in the cannon's mouth. And then the justice,[6]
In fair round belly with good capon[7] lined,
With eyes severe and beard of formal cut,
Full of wise saws and modern instances;[8]

---

1. **players:** Actors.
2. **ages:** Periods of life.
3. **mewling** (myōōl´ in) *adj*.: Whimpering; crying like a baby.
4. **pard** (pärd) *n*.: Leopard or panther.
5. **Jealous in honor:** Very concerned about his honor.
6. **justice:** Judge.
7. **capon** (kā´ pän) *n*.: Roasted chicken.
8. **wise saws and modern instances:** Wise sayings and modern examples that show the truth of the sayings.

◆ **Build Vocabulary**

woeful (wō´ fəl) *adj*.: Full of sorrow
treble (treb´ əl) *n*.: High-pitched voice

And so he plays his part. The sixth age shifts
20 Into the lean and slippered pantaloon,[9]
With spectacles on nose and pouch on side,
His youthful hose[10] well saved, a world too wide
For his shrunk shank;[11] and his big manly voice,
Turning again toward childish <u>treble</u>, pipes
25 And whistles in his sound. Last scene of all,
That ends this strange eventful history,
Is second childishness, and mere oblivion,
Sans[12] teeth, sans eyes, sans taste, sans everything.

---

   9. pantaloon (pan´ təl oon´) *n.*: Thin, foolish old man—originally
a character in old comedies.
10. hose (hōz) *n.*: Stockings.
11. shank (shank) *n.*: Leg.
12. sans (sanz) *prep.*: Without; lacking.

◄ **Critical Viewing** How do the images in this
   stained glass window add to your understanding
   of the poem? **[Relate]**

Guide for Responding

◆ Literature and Your Life

Reader's Response Do you agree with the speaker's view of the seven ages of life? Explain.

Thematic Focus Does this poem in any way change your perspective about the stages of life? Why or why not?

Group Activity In a group, discuss how you would modernize this poem for today. What would the seven ages be?

☑ Check Your Comprehension

1. To what does the speaker compare the world?
2. What is the schoolboy's attitude toward school?
3. What is the soldier's main concern?
4. What is the last age of man?

◆ Critical Thinking

INTERPRET
1. What attitude does the speaker reveal by using the word *merely* in the second line? **[Analyze]**
2. What period of life does each person referred to in the poem represent? **[Interpret]**
3. What characterizes the periods of life represented by the soldier and the judge? **[Interpret]**
4. How does the last age bring us back full circle to the start? **[Interpret]**
5. What attitude toward life does the speaker seem to be expressing? **[Draw Conclusions]**

APPLY
6. Explain whether you think that most people who live long lives pass through seven periods similar to those described in the poem. **[Apply]**

Guide for Responding (continued)

◆ Reading Strategy

MAKE INFERENCES ABOUT THE SPEAKER

Making inferences about the **speaker** of a poem means seeing what is suggested about him or her through the choice of words and details. When, for example, the speaker of "The Raven" says, "Eagerly I wished the morrow—vainly I had tried to borrow/From my books surcease of sorrow . . . ," you can infer that he is sorrowful and that the night worsens the way he feels.

1. In "The Raven," what can you infer about the speaker's level of education and social class from the way he speaks throughout the poem?
2. What else can you infer about the speaker of "The Raven" from other details in the poem?
3. Look at lines 9 through 15 of "The Seven Ages of Man." What do the speaker's words reveal about his attitude toward lovers and soldiers?
4. Based on his ideas about the stages of life, what are your overall impressions of the speaker of "The Seven Ages of Man"? Support your answer.

◆ Build Vocabulary

USING THE WORD ROOT -sol-

Knowing that the root -sol- means "alone," write a definition of each italicized word.
1. Al was the *sole* owner of Al's Tackle Shop.
2. Maria enjoyed the *solitude* of a morning walk.
3. The *isolated* cottage at the end of the country road has been uninhabited for years.

USING THE WORD BANK

In your notebook, write the word from the Word Bank that belongs in each blank.

Entering the town, we thought to seek (1)___?___ from a long day of travel. A (2)___?___ inn tucked into a (3)___?___ corner far from the center of town caught our eye. The innkeeper, whose (4)___?___ complexion contrasted sharply with her black dress, launched into a (5)___?___ tale about a tragic event that had occurred in one of the rooms. When we looked dismayed, she broke into a (6)___?___ smile and admitted, in her high (7)___?___ voice, that the story wasn't really true.

◆ Literary Focus

NARRATIVE AND DRAMATIC POETRY

"The Raven" is a **narrative poem**—a poem that tells a story. "The Seven Ages of Man" is a **dramatic monologue**—a poem in which a fictional character directly expresses his or her thoughts in the midst of a developing situation.
1. How do the rhythm and rhyme scheme of "The Raven" enhance the telling of the story?
2. "The Seven Ages of Man" is from Shakespeare's play *As You Like It.* Tell why you think the poem is or is not clear and complete by itself.

◆ Build Grammar Skills

PARTICIPIAL PHRASES

Restrictive participial phrases are not set off by commas because they are necessary to the meaning of the word they modify. **Nonrestrictive participial phrases,** which are not necessary but add to the meaning, are set off by commas.

Writing Application Rewrite this paragraph:

At ten o'clock, I opened my literature book. "The Raven" assigned by my English teacher three nights earlier stared up at me from the page. With eyes tingling from sleep deprivation I began to read.

Beyond Literature

Cultural Connection

The Raven as a Symbol Through the ages, the raven has often been seen as a symbol of evil or negativity. For example, in Greek mythology, the raven is portrayed as indiscreetly revealing secrets, prompting the god Apollo to blacken the raven's white feathers as punishment. In many fairy tales, people who have had spells cast upon them have been depicted as ravens. In contrast, however, some Native American myths depict the raven more positively—as a creator of the natural world. What other birds might have made an effective symbol in Poe's poem?

Build Your Portfolio

Idea Bank

Writing

1. **Poem Summary** Write a summary of one of these poems. Capture the key details of the poem in the order in which they are presented.

2. **Story** Write a story about the relationship between Lenore and the speaker of "The Raven." End with the details of Lenore's death.

3. **Essay About the Stages of Life** Write an essay entitled "The Stages of Life." Like Shakespeare, choose a type of person to represent each stage. Begin with an introduction revealing the types of people you've chosen. Then write a paragraph explaining each choice.

Speaking and Listening

4. **Choral Reading** With a group of classmates, prepare a choral reading of "The Raven." Decide on the best arrangement of group and individual voices. For example, you might have a different person read the first five lines of each stanza and all read the last line. **[Performing Arts Link]**

5. **Debate** Stage a debate between a group of students supporting the views of the speaker of "The Seven Ages of Man" and a group with a more optimistic view. Each group should support its view with examples from real life.

Projects

6. **Photo Exhibit** Prepare a photo exhibit on the theme "Ages of Humankind." Decide what ages you will represent. Gather photos for each age. Then write a label for each photo. **[Art Link]**

7. **Fact Sheet** Gather information about ravens—what they look like, where they're found, and so on. Present your findings in an illustrated fact sheet. **[Science Link]**

Writing Mini-Lesson

Scene for a Movie

Imagine that you've been hired by a film studio to create a movie based on "The Raven." Come up with an idea for the movie's opening scene. Then write a detailed description of the scene that a scriptwriter could use as the basis for developing a script for the scene. In your description, provide detailed instructions about the setting, characters, and events in the scene. Pay special attention to the mood, or atmosphere, that should be established.

Writing Skills Focus: Setting a Mood

Edgar Allan Poe was a master at establishing specific **moods** through his careful choice of descriptive details. Follow his example by using precise details to describe the mood that you would like the scriptwriter to capture in your scene. Look at this example. Notice how Edgar Allan Poe uses the italicized words to establish a gloomy mood in the first line of "The Raven."

Model From the Selection
Once upon a midnight *dreary*, while I pondered, *weak* and *weary* . . .

Prewriting Start by thinking about how the poem could be expanded into a movie. Jot down the events that might take place in the opening scene. Then brainstorm for details related to the characters, setting, and mood. Keep in mind that the ideas you come up with must fit in with Poe's poem.

Drafting Using the ideas you've gathered, draft your description. Start with a paragraph describing the mood you want to establish. Then follow with paragraphs about the plot, characters, and setting.

Revising Have one of your classmates assume the role of the scriptwriter and read your description. Make sure that after reading your description, your classmate's impression of what the script should be like matches what you intended.

Guide for Reading

John Keats *(1795–1821)*

John Keats's poems are among the most admired in the English language. Remarkably, Keats accomplished this distinction in spite of his early death at the age of twenty-five.

Keats is considered one of the main poets of the Romantic Movement, a group of writers who stressed the importance of individual experience and the spiritual connection between people and nature.

William Shakespeare
(1564–1616)

William Shakespeare was as much a poet as a playwright. Not only are his 37 plays written in verse, he also composed 154 sonnets. Taken together, the sonnets seem to tell a story. The "plot" is not always clear, but it seems obvious that the main characters are a young nobleman, a lady, a poet (probably Shakespeare himself), and a rival poet. Some of the best sonnets, like "Sonnet 30," are addressed to the nobleman. (For more on William Shakespeare, see pp. 669 and 830.)

Bashō *(1644–1694)*

Bashō (bash´ō) is regarded as one of the greatest Japanese poets. In his youth, he knew luxury as the companion to the son of a lord. Later, however, he lived apart and devoted himself to writing haiku. Many of his best poems were inspired by travels in which he observed nature.

Chiyojo *(1887–1959)*

Chiyojo (chē yō´ jō) was the wife of a samurai's servant. When her husband died, she became a nun and she began studying poetry with a well-known teacher of haiku. Scholars value the lightness of spirit in her poems.

Richard Wright *(1908–1960)*

Richard Wright is best known for his acclaimed novel *Native Son* (1940), which chronicles the life of a boy raised in poverty in Chicago. However, Wright also produced a wide range of other types of works, including essays and poems. As a poet, Wright experimented with different forms, including the traditional Japanese haiku.

◆ Build Vocabulary

SUFFIXES: *-ness*

In his sonnet "On the Grasshopper and the Cricket," Keats describes a person half lost in drowsiness. *Drowsiness* ends in the suffix *-ness*, meaning "in the state or condition of." When added to the adjective *drowsy*, the suffix *-ness* forms the noun *drowsiness*, meaning "in the state of being drowsy or sleepy."

| ceasing |
| wrought |
| drowsiness |
| woes |

WORD BANK

Before you read, preview this list of words from the poems.

◆ Build Grammar Skills

CONCRETE AND ABSTRACT NOUNS

In his sonnet, Keats uses many concrete nouns to create images of grasshoppers and crickets in your mind. A **concrete noun** names something that can be perceived by the senses. The noun *birds,* for example, is a concrete noun. In "Sonnet 30," Shakespeare uses several abstract nouns to express ideas. An **abstract noun** names an idea, a belief, or a quality. The word *remembrance,* for example, is an abstract noun.

◆ On the Grasshopper and the Cricket ◆
Sonnet 30 ◆ Three Haiku ◆ Hokku Poems

◆ *Literature and Your Life*

CONNECT YOUR EXPERIENCE

Almost everyone has regrets—memories of losses, disappointments, and mistakes—that can ruin the enjoyment of the present. What can be done when regrets crowd out the present? In "Sonnet 30," Shakespeare offers a way to put aside regrets about the past. The other poems in this section present a way to keep focused on the present—through the careful observation of nature.

Journal Writing Nature includes animals, plants, weather, and more. List some aspects of nature you enjoy.

THEMATIC FOCUS: OBSERVATIONS

Each person experiences the world in a different way. As you read, think about how the poets' observations about the natural world compare with your own.

◆ Background for Understanding

SCIENCE

It is not surprising that Keats chose the cricket and the grasshopper when he wanted to write about the poetry of nature. These two members of the order Orthoptera are among the most musical of insects. The males of both groups produce sounds by rubbing one part of the body against another. Male crickets rub the rough surfaces of their wing covers together. Male grasshoppers usually rub a leg against a wing with a sawing motion.

◆ Literary Focus

SONNETS AND HAIKU

The poems in this section represent two poetic forms with strict rules. The poems by Shakespeare and Keats are sonnets. A **sonnet** is a lyric poem of fourteen lines, usually written in rhymed iambic pentameter (ten-syllable lines in which every second syllable is accented). This meter can be seen in the first line from Keats's poem.

The seven other poems in this section are haiku, a form of poetry developed in Japan. A **haiku** consists of three lines of verse. The first and third lines have five syllables each. The second line has seven syllables. In a very few words, the poet creates a dominant impression in the reader's mind with one or two striking images.

◆ Reading Strategy

READ IN SENTENCES

Like prose, many poems are written in sentences. They are also written in lines. However, poets don't always complete a sentence at the end of a line. A sentence may extend for several lines and then end in the middle of a line so that the poet can keep to the chosen rhythm and rhyme scheme.

To understand the literal meaning of a poem, **read in sentences**. Notice the punctuation. Don't make a full stop at the end of a line unless there is a period, comma, colon, semicolon, or dash. Notice where the stops are in the following lines from Keats's sonnet:

> That is the Grasshopper's—
>   he takes the lead
> In summer luxury,—he has
>   never done
> With his delights; for when
>   tired out with fun
> He rests at ease beneath
>   some pleasant weed.

On the Grasshopper and the Cricket

John Keats

The poetry of earth is never dead:
When all the birds are faint with the hot sun,
And hide in cooling trees, a voice will run
From hedge to hedge about the new-mown mead;[1]
5   That is the Grasshopper's—he takes the lead
In summer luxury,—he has never done
With his delights; for when tired out with fun
He rests at ease beneath some pleasant weed.
The poetry of earth is ceasing never:
10   On a lone winter evening, when the frost
Has wrought a silence, from the stove there shrills
The Cricket's song, in warmth increasing ever,
And seems to one in drowsiness half lost,
The Grasshopper's among some grassy hills.

---

1. **mead** (mēd) *n.*: Meadow.

Guide for Responding

◆ Literature and Your Life

Reader's Response Which scene painted by the poet appeals more to you? Why?

Thematic Focus What does the poet suggest about the world around us?

☑ Check Your Comprehension

1. What do birds do when summer gets too hot?
2. Who "takes the lead in summer luxury"?
3. Where does the cricket reside in winter?

◆ Critical Thinking

INTERPRET

1. How are the grasshopper and the cricket alike and different? **[Compare and Contrast]**
2. How are the two insects connected in the speaker's mind? **[Associate]**
3. What does the speaker mean when he says that the "poetry of earth is never dead"? **[Explain]**

APPLY

4. In your environment, what "poetry of nature" do you experience at different times of the year? **[Specify]**

EXTEND

5. How could you illustrate the theme of this poem in music? **[Music Link]**

Sonnet 30

William Shakespeare

When to the sessions of sweet silent thought
I summon up remembrance of things past,
I sigh the lack of many a thing I sought,
And with old <u>woes</u>' new wail my dear times waste:[1]
5   Then can I drown an eye, unused to flow,
For precious friends hid in death's dateless[2] night,
And weep afresh love's long since cancelled woe,
And moan the expense[3] of many a vanished sight:
Then can I grieve at grievances foregone,[4]
10 And heavily from woe to woe tell o'er[5]
The sad account of fore-bemoanèd moan,[6]
Which I new pay as if not paid before.
But if the while I think on thee, dear friend,
All losses are restored and sorrows end.

---

1. **And . . . waste:** And by grieving anew for past sorrows, ruin the precious present.
2. **dateless:** Endless.
3. **expense:** Loss.
4. **foregone:** Past and done with.
5. **tell o'er:** Count up.
6. **fore-bemoanèd moan:** Sorrows suffered in the past.

◆ **Build Vocabulary**

woes (wōz) *n.*: Great sorrows

Guide for Responding

◆ Literature and Your Life

Reader's Response Would you want the speaker of the poem as a friend? Explain.

Thematic Focus What two different "worlds" around him does the speaker describe?

☑ Check Your Comprehension

1. In general, what are the speaker's feelings when he recalls the past?
2. How does the speaker feel when he thinks of his friend?

◆ Critical Thinking

INTERPRET

1. What does "drown an eye" mean? **[Infer]**
2. In lines 10–12, the words "tell o'er" (count up) "account," "pay," and "paid" suggest someone going over bills. What action is the speaker describing through this metaphor, or implied comparison? **[Clarify]**
3. How is the metaphor extended in line 14? **[Identify]**
4. How does the poet's use of metaphor add interest to the sonnet? **[Explain]**

APPLY

5. What does the sonnet imply about the value of friendship? **[Generalize]**

Three Haiku

Temple bells die out.
The fragrant blossoms remain.
A perfect evening!
                    —Bashō

Dragonfly catcher,
How far have you gone today
In your wandering?
                    —Chiyojo

Bearing no flowers,
I am free to toss madly
Like the willow tree.
                    —Chiyojo

Girl With Lantern on a Balcony at Night, c. 1768 (detail), Suzuki Harunobu,
The Metropolitan Museum of Art

▲ Critical Viewing What inferences, or conclusions, can you
make about Japanese culture based on this painting? [Infer]

Hokku Poems

Richard Wright

Make up your mind snail!
You are half inside your house
And halfway out!

In the falling snow
A laughing boy holds out his palms
Until they are white

Keep straight down this block
Then turn right where you will find
A peach tree blooming

Whose town did you leave
O wild and drowning spring rain
And where do you go?

Guide for Responding

◆ Literature and Your Life

Reader's Response Which of the seven haiku do you like best? Why?

Thematic Focus Choose one of the haiku and explain how it heightens your awareness of the world around you.

Group Activity In a group, brainstorm to come up with a list of topics for a contemporary haiku.

☑ Check Your Comprehension

1. To which senses does Bashō's haiku appeal?
2. How does Chiyojo compare herself to the willow tree?
3. What two weather events does Richard Wright refer to in his haiku?

◆ Critical Thinking

INTERPRET
1. Describe the kind of evening that you imagine based on Bashō's haiku. **[Support]**
2. In Chiyojo's second haiku, what might the speaker be suggesting about herself? **[Analyze]**
3. What is the "house" in Wright's first haiku? **[Analyze]**
4. What feelings are stirred in you by the scene Wright depicts in his second haiku?
5. Compare the language of the three Japanese haiku with the language of Richard Wright's haiku. **[Compare and Contrast]**

EVALUATE
6. Which do you think are more effective—Wright's haiku or the Japanese haiku? Support your answer with details from the poems. **[Evaluate]**

Guide for Responding (continued)

◆ Reading Strategy

READ IN SENTENCES

You were better able to understand and appreciate these poems if you **read in sentences**—that is, if you paused or stopped only at punctuation marks rather than automatically at the ends of lines. The punctuation of the two sonnets may seem unusual by today's standards. In these poems, colons are used in place of periods to show a close connection between one sentence and the next.

1. In "Sonnet 30," why do lines 1 and 10 not end in punctuation marks?
2. In "On the Grasshopper and the Cricket," why do lines 1 and 9 end in colons rather than in periods?
3. Most of the lines in Shakespeare's sonnet end in punctuation marks. Several of the lines in Keats's poem do not end in punctuation marks. Explain the effect of the punctuation of each poem.

◆ Build Grammar Skills

CONCRETE AND ABSTRACT NOUNS

When Chiyojo writes about a dragonfly catcher, she creates a specific image in the reader's mind by using a **concrete noun**—one that names something that can be perceived by the senses. When Shakespeare writes about remembrance, he conveys an idea by using an **abstract noun**—one that names a concept, idea, belief, or quality.

Practice
1. List the nouns in the first eight lines of "On the Grasshopper and the Cricket." Label each one as concrete or abstract.
2. Why might Shakespeare's sonnet have more abstract nouns than the other poems?

Writing Application Rewrite these sentences, adding concrete nouns to paint a more vivid picture.
1. Though surrounded by luxury, the child was not happy.
2. His woes were many.
3. The family lacked the most basic necessities.
4. There was no want of beauty in her face.

◆ Literary Focus

SONNETS AND HAIKU

A **sonnet** is a lyric poem of fourteen lines, usually written in rhymed iambic pentameter. A **haiku** has three lines. The first and third lines have five syllables, and the second line has seven syllables.

A haiku generally consists of two concise, contrasting images that spark associations in the reader's mind. In a sonnet, the rhyme scheme reflects the content of the poem. A Shakespearean sonnet usually presents an idea or question in the first quatrain (four lines), explores the idea for the next two quatrains, and reaches a conclusion in the couplet (two lines) at the end. The rhyme scheme is *abab cdcd efef gg*. A Petrarchan sonnet, named for the Italian poet Petrarch, consists of an octave (eight lines) and a sestet (six lines). The octave always uses two rhymes in the pattern *abbaabba*. The rhyme scheme of the sestet can vary.

1. Can the thought content of "Sonnet 30" be divided into units that correspond to the divisions of three quatrains and a couplet? Explain.
2. In Keats's sonnet, how is the content of the octave related to that of the sestet?
3. What are the two main images in Wright's second haiku?

◆ Build Vocabulary

USING THE SUFFIX -ness

Rewrite each sentence by adding the suffix -*ness*, meaning "state of," to change the italicized adjective into a noun.

1. Elwood insisted that all he wanted was for me to be *happy*.
2. To become *drowsy* behind the wheel of a car can lead to a serious accident.
3. She was known throughout the town for being *friendly*.

USING THE WORD BANK

Identify the correct antonym for each first word.

1. wrought: (a) create, (b) seen, (c) destroyed
2. ceasing: (a) escaping, (b) rewarding, (c) beginning
3. drowsiness: (a) frankness, (b) alertness, (c) quietness
4. woe: (a) terror, (b) ease, (c) joy

$\it{B}$uild $\it{Y}$our $\it{P}$ortfolio

 ## Idea Bank

Writing

1. **Journal Entry** Write a journal entry describing something interesting in nature that you recently observed. **[Science Link]**

2. **Introduction** Write a brief passage that could serve as the introduction to one of these poems in a poetry collection. Offer your interpretation of the poem and explain why it is worth reading.

3. **Literary Analysis** Write an essay analyzing the relationship between the form and content of Shakespeare's sonnet. Explain how the thought content of the sonnet can be divided into sections that correspond to the sections of the sonnet. Cite details from the poem for support.

Speaking and Listening

4. **Poetry Reading** Prepare and deliver a reading of one of the sonnets that will help your audience understand its meaning.

5. **Dialogue** With a partner, write a dialogue between the grasshopper and the cricket in which they discuss the merits of summer and winter. Rehearse the dialogue and present it to the class.

Projects

6. **Illustrated Book** Put together an illustrated book of haiku. Choose three of the haiku you just read. Create an illustration or find a photograph to accompany each one. **[Art Link]**

7. **Internet Research** Conduct research on the Internet to learn more about haiku and their connection to Japanese culture. Gather examples of haiku, along with illustrations and background information. Present your findings to the class. **[Technology Link]**

 ## Writing Mini-Lesson

Haiku Series

Shakespeare wrote 154 sonnets with the same cast of characters. Yet each of the poems expresses a fresh new idea. Write three related haiku—either about the same subject or on the same theme. Remember that a haiku captures a feeling with one or two concrete images and follows a strict format: three lines of five, seven, and five syllables.

Writing Skills Focus: Keeping to a Format

When you write a poem that fits into a specific form, it is essential to **keep to the format** of that form. For example, when you write a haiku, you must compose three lines with the correct number of syllables in each line. This requires you to use one- or two-syllable words that spark strong associations. Notice how Bashō uses brief, evocative words in this haiku.

Model From the Selection

Temple bells die out.
The fragrant blossoms remain.
A perfect evening!

Prewriting Think of the topics for the three haiku and decide what will be the connection among them. Jot down a few images you will include.

Drafting In each haiku, capture one or two images and create one impression. Don't worry about getting exactly the right number of syllables as you draft.

Revising Count the syllables in each line. If you don't have the correct number, see what words you can change, leave out, or add to achieve the desired number of syllables. In addition, work with a classmate to make sure that your haiku convey the impression you intended.

Poem

Writing Process Workshop

Edgar Allan Poe once described poetry as "the rhythmical creation of beauty." When you write a **poem**, you express an image or idea in a special way that focuses on form, feeling, and sound. A poem requires far fewer words than a short story or a novel, yet its impact on readers can be just as great. Write your own poem, using the following skills introduced in this section's Writing Mini-Lessons.

Writing Skills Focus

▶ **Keep to the format of the type of poem you are writing.** You might choose to write a limerick, haiku, sonnet, or free verse, for example. Regardless of your choice, follow the form that the poem requires. (See p. 847.)

▶ **Set the mood in your poem through your choice of descriptive details.** Make your audience experience a specific feeling as they read—whether it's joy, sadness, fear, or surprise. (See p. 839.)

▶ **Use sound devices** such as rhythm, rhyme, and repetition to give your poem a musical quality and to emphasize your main ideas.

Japanese poets Bashō and Chiyojo use the above skills in haiku poetry, which celebrates the joys and wonders of life.

MODEL FROM LITERATURE

① Basho creates a mood of joy and satisfaction in his description of the evening.

② Chiyojo sticks to the format of haiku: three lines of verse with five, seven, and five syllables, respectively.

from "Three Haiku" by Bashō and Chiyojo

Temple bells die out.
The fragrant blossoms remain.
A perfect evening! ①

—BASHŌ

Dragonfly catcher,
How far have you gone today
In your wanderings? ②

—CHIYOJO

Prewriting

Analyze Formats Decide on a topic, then choose the type of poem you will compose. First, study a variety of poems to note how each is set up. Ask yourself these questions:

- ▶ How many lines are in the poem?
- ▶ How many syllables are in each line?
- ▶ How many stanzas are there?
- ▶ Does the poem rhyme? If so, in what order do the rhyming words appear?

After analyzing different formats, choose the one that you feel works best with your topic.

Choose Sensory Images Brainstorm for a list of sensory images that will describe how the subject of your poem looks, sounds, smells, tastes, and feels. The examples in the chart can help spark your own ideas.

Sensory Images

Sights	Sounds	Smells	Tastes	Physical Sensations
green fields	gurgling	roses	honey	hot sand
flashing neon	sobbing	garbage	salt water	velvet
towering tree	whispering	ocean air	bitterness	soft fur

Plan Your Mood The topic of your poem can help you determine the feeling, or mood, you wish to create, but topic alone is not enough. After all, a poem about love might be serious, sad, or funny. Ask yourself this question: If you read your poem aloud, what kind of music would you play in the background? Jot down details that will help create that mood.

Drafting

Develop Your Mood As you draft your poem, include the details you planned for creating the mood. Use colorful and powerful language to help readers form a precise picture of your subject in their minds. Pay particular attention to nouns, verbs, adjectives, and adverbs that you use.

Writing Tip If your poem rhymes, you may find it helpful to consult a rhyming dictionary. Make your rhymes conform to your ideas, however, not the other way around.

APPLYING LANGUAGE SKILLS: Concrete Nouns

A **concrete noun** is a word that names a person, place, or thing in a specific way, rather than in a general way.

General Noun:
I like music.

Concrete Noun:
I like rock-and-roll.

Notice how a concrete noun creates a clearer picture.

Practice On your paper, replace each general noun with a concrete noun.

1. I met a man.
2. I enjoyed the book.
3. The food is good.
4. The machine broke.
5. Your shoes look nice.

Writing Application As you draft your poem, use concrete nouns to name people, places, and things. Use nouns that readers can imagine clearly.

Writer's Solution Connection Writing Lab

For more on sensory images, use the Sensory Word Bin in the Prewriting section of the tutorial on Creative Writing.

APPLYING LANGUAGE SKILLS: Parallel Structure

In a sentence with **parallel structure,** details that are parallel in meaning are expressed in the same form.

Incorrect:

I love to swim, to run, and dancing.

Correct:

I love to swim, to run, and to dance.

or

I love swimming, running, and dancing.

Practice On your paper, rewrite each sentence so it has parallel structure.

1. The girl ran quickly, carefully, and with grace.

2. Running isn't the same as to jog.

3. She has confidence, pride, and is intelligent.

Writing Application Review your poem to see whether it contains any structure that is not parallel. If it does, rephrase the words so they become parallel.

Writer's Solution Connection
Writing Lab

For help revising your poem, use the instruction and activities in the Revision section of the tutorial on Creative Writing.

Stick to Your Format As you write, follow the rules for the style of poetry you have chosen. For example, if you've chosen haiku, do not deviate from its format. Remember that the way you express yourself is as important as what you say.

Revising

Use a Checklist Return to the Writing Skills Focus on the first page of this lesson, and use the items as a checklist to evaluate and revise your poem.

▶ Have I set a distinct mood in my poem?

Ask a classmate to read your poem and describe the mood he or she felt was expressed. If it isn't the mood you intended, consider details you can add, remove, or change to create the mood you want.

▶ Have I kept to the poem's format?

Check your poem for the number of lines, lines per stanza, syllables per line, and rhyme scheme. Compare it with a published poem of the same type. If you discover that you have not followed the format, make the necessary adjustments in your work.

REVISION MODEL

① Crackling! Booming!

See the many streaks of light!   ② attack the Thunderstorms

are attacking hard at night!

① The poet adds a line to help establish a mood of excitement and terror.

② The poet adjusts the words because the line can have only seven syllables.

Publishing

▶ **Classroom** Set up a Poetry Cafe in your classroom and read your poem to the audience.

▶ **Library** Collect your classmates' poems to make a poetry book that you donate to the school library.

▶ **Magazine** Submit your poem to a magazine that publishes poetry.

Real-World Reading Skills Workshop

Strategies for Success

You may read a newspaper for your own enjoyment or for a school assignment. The newspaper offers a vast amount of interesting information on a variety of topics. To help you find the information, use these strategies:

Look at the Headlines Most articles in a newspaper are preceded by a large headline in bold type. The headline gives a very brief summary of the information to follow. If you are in search of a particular story or news report, scan the various headlines until you find the reference you need.

Look at the Subheads Most newspaper articles are several paragraphs long. Often, a new paragraph or section is introduced with a subhead. The subhead, which appears in smaller type than the main headline, signals the specific information to come in that part of the article.

Look at the Section Headings Newspapers are usually divided into several sections. The first section often contains the international and national news stories. There may be other sections for features such as sports, entertainment, and comics. Often, an index tells you where each section is located within the newspaper.

Apply the Strategy

Use the newspaper to answer these questions:

1. What information can you learn about the new tax bill from the article's headline and subhead?
2. What do the plant workers seek?
3. How much money did the lottery winner get?
4. Where would you find the television listings?
5. Where would you learn about a death?

THE DAILY GAZETTE

President Signs New Tax Bill; House Approves

Benefits Both Rich and Poor

The President signed a bill today that will cut taxes across the board. The new bill, which was approved by the House by a vote of 246–188, is part of a long-term plan that calls for $70 billion in tax cuts over the next five years. Supporters have announced that Americans of all income levels will benefit from the new tax bill.

Resident Wins $3 Million Lottery

Inez Torres of Pine Hollow learned last night that she had won Monday's lottery jackpot of $3.2 million. "I've never won anything in my whole life!" an ecstatic Torres exclaimed to reporters. Torres said she plans to attend next month's High Rollers Ball, a yearly dinner dance for lottery winners and their families.

Workers Strike at Local Plant

Demand More Pay, Fewer Hours

Workers at the Orangewood Motors Plant announced their decision to strike last night. The decision followed the refusal of plant management to meet workers' demands for higher wages and shorter work shifts. A spokesperson for the workers told reporters that the strike will continue for as long as necessary. "We won't back down or settle for less than we deserve," said foreman Milton Lanier.

Section Index

International	A
National	A
City	B
Entertainment	B
Sports	C
Obituaries	D

✔ Here are other situations in which using headlines and text structure can be helpful:

▶ Reading a magazine
▶ Reading an encyclopedia article
▶ Using an almanac or yearbook

Speaking and Listening Workshop

At some point, you may have the opportunity to take part in a choral reading. A choral reading is a story presented by a chorus, in which some parts of the text may be sung and other parts may be spoken. During the spoken parts, music may play in the background. To give a successful presentation, follow these guidelines.

Read With the Appropriate Emotion In a choral reading, the selection you're reading helps determine the way in which you should speak. Is the selection loud or soft? Is it happy, sad, or scary? Make your tone of voice match the mood of the selection.

Concentrate on Timing Timing is very important in a choral reading. You may be required to recite your lines immediately after another chorus member finishes his or her part. Listen carefully as your turn approaches. Do not come in too early or too late.

Your reading portion may also need to coincide with music that is playing in the background. As you speak, listen to the music. Try not to read too quickly or too slowly.

Tips for Giving a Choral Reading

✔ If you want to present a memorable and effective choral reading, follow these strategies:
  ▶ Speak in the appropriate vocal tone
  ▶ Listen for musical cues
  ▶ Watch for signals from the conductor

Apply the Strategies

With a group of classmates, present each of these situations in a choral reading for the rest of the class.

1. Retell a story you have read in class or seen in a movie. Find appropriate music to play in the background as you tell the story. Alternate speaking parts with other members of your chorus.

2. Improvise a story together. Have one group member begin the story. Then have another continue, and pass it on to the next member. As each person speaks, have a classmate play different musical selections. Each speaker should speak in a tone that matches the mood of the music that's playing.

3. Read a story aloud while music plays in the background. Then recite the same story with music that expresses a completely different mood. How does the different musical mood affect each presentation?

Extended Reading Opportunities

Whether written in rhyming form or in blank verse, poetry is a highly charged form of literature in which every word is packed with meaning. Following are just a few possibilities for extending your exploration of poetry.

Suggested Titles

Old Possum's Book of Practical Cats
T. S. Eliot

Although widely considered a "serious" poet, T. S. Eliot had a playful side as well. In the 1930's, Eliot wrote a series of amusing poems about cats, which were later collected into this book. Here you'll meet fantastic felines like "Mr. Mistoffelees," "Growltiger," and "The Rum Tum Tugger"—all of whom have been brought to life on the stage in the hit musical *Cats.*

The Dream Keeper and Other Poems
Langston Hughes

Langston Hughes is best known for his powerful poetry, which celebrates the African American experience and often incorporates the rhythms of jazz and blues. In *The Dream Keeper and Other Poems,* you'll find some of Hughes's best poems about hopes, dreams, life, and love.

This Same Sky: A Collection of Poems From Around the World
Naomi Shihab Nye, editor

This book includes the work of 129 poets from 68 countries around the world. Writing about dreams, families, loss, and the world around us, these poets help us realize that although we may live far apart, the same sky connects us all.

Other Possibilities

Something Permanent

Soul Looks Back in Wonder
Final Harvest
Joyful Noise: Poems for Two Voices

Cynthia Rylant with photos by Walker Evans

Tom Feelings
Emily Dickinson
Paul Fleishman

Ulysses Deriding Polyphemus, 1819,
J. M. W. Turner, The National Gallery, London

The Epic

Turn the page to enter a world of heroes, gods, and sweeping adventures. In the *Odyssey*, Odysseus, a hero of the Trojan War, embarks on a journey home that takes him ten years to complete and brings him many thrilling and death-defying experiences. As you read the *Odyssey*, keep in mind that this epic poem began in the oral tradition and was passed down through word of mouth by wandering Greek minstrels. Can you think of a modern-day hero who could inspire stories that would span many generations?

Reading for Success

Strategies for Reading an Epic

In ancient societies, stories were passed from one person to another by word of mouth. Storytellers who arrived in a village, court, or camp would entertain eager listeners with tales of the gods or great heroes. The longer stories, now called epics, might be told over several days. To help the storytellers remember these lengthy pieces, the tales were composed in poetic lines and were often recited to the accompaniment of stringed instruments. Although these stories were filled with fantastic deeds and exploits, many were based on historical events and were accepted as fact by the listeners. Two epics, the *Iliad* and the *Odyssey*, had their roots in the events of the Trojan War, which occurred about 1200 B.C. While legend credits the abduction of Helen, the wife of a Greek king, as the reason for the war, most probably economic conflict over control of trade in the Aegean Sea was the cause.

As you read the *Odyssey*, you may find a few areas that cause some difficulty. Apply the following strategies to help you get the most from your reading.

Reread or read ahead.

If you don't understand a certain passage, reread it, looking for connections among the words or sentences. It might also help you to read ahead, because a word or idea may be clarified further on.

In the *Odyssey*, some of the long, involved, and ornate comparisons—called epic similes—may give you trouble. You might choose to skim through these on your first reading so that you don't lose the plot line. Later, reread the epic similes to appreciate their imagery.

Read in sentences, according to punctuation.

Although epics are written in poetic form, you should read the sentences according to the punctuation, instead of line by line. It might also help you to read parts aloud with your classmates.

Paraphrase.

As you read, pause periodically to restate in your own words what you have read. By doing this in your mind, you can check your own understanding of the key concepts and events in the epic.

Be aware of the historical context.

The *Odyssey* took place long ago and far away. Customs and attitudes in this epic are very different from those of today, and places may be unfamiliar. Being aware of the historical context of the epic will aid your understanding. Before you begin the *Odyssey*, familiarize yourself with the names of the characters. It will also help you to look at the map on p. 891.

By using these strategies as you read the *Odyssey*, you will be better able to follow the plot and apply your understanding to your own world.

Heroic Adventure

The Cyclops (Odysseus Series), 1977, Romare Bearden, collage, 14 x 11″
© 1997 Romare Bearden Foundation/Licensed by VAGA, New York, NY

Guide for Reading

Homer (circa 800 B.C.)

This legendary poet-historian is credited with writing two of the most famous and enduring epics of all time: the *Iliad* and the *Odyssey*. The length of these impressive works has resulted in an adjective being coined from the author's name.

> ### From Homer's name comes the adjective homeric, *meaning large-scale, massive, and enormous.*

Indeed, the *Iliad* and the *Odyssey*, which consist of thousands of lines of verse, are both homeric efforts.

Man of Mystery The facts about Homer's life have been lost in the mists of antiquity. In fact, scholars disagree about whether the *Iliad* and the *Odyssey* were written by the same person and even whether Homer existed at all! Homer is thought to have been born in western Asia Minor, the setting for many of the events in the *Iliad* and the *Odyssey*. According to tradition, he was blind. He did not write his two great epics as a modern novelist writes a novel. Rather, he composed them orally by assembling a number of earlier and shorter narrative songs. He probably traveled around the Greek-speaking world reciting them on many occasions. In later centuries, the two epics were the basis of Greek and Roman education.

◆ Build Vocabulary

WORD ORIGINS: WORDS FROM MYTHS

Many words and expressions in English come from Greek myths. For example, in line 496, a one-eyed giant is described as "titanic for the cast," as he prepares to hurl a boulder at Odysseus' fleeing ship. The word *titanic* comes from the mythical giants called Titans, who once ruled the world but were conquered by Zeus and the other Olympian deities. Like a mythical giant, anything enormous and powerful is described as titanic. From movies and musicals you might be familiar with the name *Titanic*—an enormous luxury ship that was sunk by an iceberg on its first voyage.

As you read, look for the myth behind other words, such as *siren* and *music* (muse).

plundered
squall
dispatched
mammoth
titanic
assuage
bereft
ardor
insidious

WORD BANK

Before you read, preview this list of words from the *Odyssey*.

◆ Build Grammar Skills

RESTRICTIVE AND NONRESTRICTIVE APPOSITIVES

An **appositive** is a noun or pronoun placed near another noun or pronoun to provide more information about it. An **appositive phrase** is a group of words that provides more information about a noun or pronoun. A **restrictive appositive** or appositive phrase is essential to the meaning of the sentence and is not set off by commas. A **nonrestrictive appositive** or appositive phrase provides additional information but is not necessary to the meaning of the sentence, and it is set off by commas.

nonrestrictive
The *Odyssey, an epic consisting of thousands of verses,*

restrictive
is attributed to the Greek poet *Homer.*

The nonrestrictive appositive phrase gives additional but unnecesary information about the *Odyssey*. The restrictive appositive is necessary to identify which Greek poet.

The Odyssey

◆ Literature and Your Life

CONNECT YOUR EXPERIENCE

Whether you're journeying across town or to another country, it sometimes seems to take forever to get to your destination. Getting there may not be half the fun—but it can be quite an adventure. In the *Odyssey*, you'll learn about a journey that took far longer than expected and experience the strange and exciting adventures that took place along the way.

Journal Writing Describe your own adventures—real, imaginary, or exaggerated—on a particularly long trip.

THEMATIC FOCUS: WORKING TOWARD A GOAL

Odysseus faces many challenges and adventures as he struggles to reach his goal—returning home to Ithaca. Why is returning home to one's loved ones after a long absence a goal worth fighting for?

◆ Background for Understanding

LITERATURE

The *Odyssey* describes what happened to one of the Greek heroes in the aftermath of the Trojan War. According to legend, the Trojan War was sparked when Paris, son of the king of Troy, ran off with Helen, the most beautiful woman in the world and daughter of the god Zeus. Unfortunately, Helen was already married to Menelaus of Sparta. To recapture the lovely Helen, Agamemnon, Menelaus' brother, led a Greek force to Troy. The seige of Troy dragged on for ten years and ended when the Greeks pretended to depart, leaving a giant wooden horse behind. Thinking themselves victorious, the Trojans dragged the horse within their city walls. That night, Greek warriors hiding within the horse crept out and opened the city gates to their waiting comrades, who then conquered the city.

◆ Reading Strategy

READ IN SENTENCES

To get the most out of a story told in verse, ignore the line breaks and **read in sentences**. Often, sentences flow from one line to the next or end in the middle of a line. Although the line breaks reveal the structure of the verse, they generally have little to do with the meaning of the author's words. Thus, you can read the *Odyssey* the same way you might read a magazine article or a novel. Ignore the line breaks, and let the words flow to you in complete sentences.

◆ Literary Focus

THE EPIC HERO

An epic is a long poem that tells the story about the adventures of gods or heroes. The central character of an epic, called the **epic hero,** is a figure of great, sometimes larger-than-life, stature. The hero may be a character from history or from legend and generally possesses the character traits that are most valued by the society in which the epic originates. Complete a cluster diagram similar to the one shown by filling in words and phrases you associate with the word *hero*.

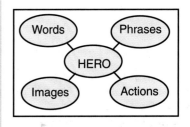

The Odyssey

Homer

Translated by Robert Fitzgerald

Part 1
The Adventures of Odysseus

In the opening verses, Homer addresses the muse of epic poetry. He asks her help in telling the tale of Odysseus.

Sing in me, Muse,[1] and through me tell the story
of that man skilled in all ways of contending,
the wanderer, harried for years on end,
after he plundered the stronghold
5   on the proud height of Troy.[2]
                    He saw the townlands and
learned the minds of many distant men,
and weathered many bitter nights and days
in his deep heart at sea, while he fought only
to save his life, to bring his shipmates home.

1. Muse (myoōz): Any one of the nine goddesses of the arts, literature, and the sciences.

2. Troy (troi): City in northwest Asia Minor, site of the Trojan War.

◆ **Build Vocabulary**

plundered (plun´ dərd) *v.*: Took goods by force from; looted

▲ Critical Viewing In the *Odyssey*, Telemachus searches for his father in a ship like this one. From what you observe in the painting, how does this ship compare with modern ships? [Compare and Contrast]

La Nef de Telemachus, The New York Public Library Picture Collection

CHARACTERS

Alcinous (al sin′ ō əs)—king of the Phaea-cians, to whom Odysseus tells his story

Odysseus (ō dis′ ē əs)—king of Ithaca

Calypso (kə lip′ sō)—sea goddess who loved Odysseus

Circe (sʉr′ se)—enchantress who helped Odysseus

Zeus (zo͞os)—king of the gods

Apollo (ə päl′ ō)—god of music, poetry, and medicine

Agamemnon (ag′ ə mem′ nän)—king and leader of Greek forces

Poseidon (pō sī′ dən)—god of sea and earth-quakes

Athena (ə thē′ nə)—goddess of wisdom, skills, and warfare

Polyphemus (päl′ ə fē′ məs)—the Cyclops who imprisoned Odysseus

Laertes (lā ʉr′ tēz)—Odysseus' father

Cronus (krō′ nəs)—Titan ruler of the uni-verse; father of Zeus

Perimedes (per′ ə mē′ dēz)—member of Odysseus' crew

Eurylochus (yo͞o ril′ ə kes)—another member of the crew

Tiresias (tī rē′ sē əs)—blind prophet who ad-vised Odysseus

Persephone (pər səf′ ə nē)—wife of Hades

Telemachus (tə lem′ ə kəs)—Odysseus and Penelope's son

Sirens (sī′ rənz)—creatures whose songs lure sailors to their deaths

Scylla (sil′ ə)—sea monster of gray rock

Charybdis (kə rib′ dis)—enormous and dan-gerous whirlpool

Lampetia (lam pē′ shə)—nymph

Hermes (hʉr′ mēz)—herald and messenger of the gods

Eumaeus (yo͞o me′ əs)—old swineherd and friend of Odysseus

Antinous (an tin′ ō əs)—leader among the suitors

Eurynome (yo͞o rin′ ə mē)—housekeeper for Penelope

Penelope (pə nel′ ə pē)—Odysseus' wife

Eurymachus (yo͞o rī′ mə kəs)—suitor

Amphinomus (am fin′ ə məs)—suitor

10 But not by will nor valor could he save them,
for their own recklessness destroyed them all—
children and fools, they killed and feasted on
the cattle of Lord Helios,[3] the Sun,
and he who moves all day through heaven
15 took from their eyes the dawn of their return.

Of these adventures, Muse, daughter of Zeus,[4]
tell us in our time, lift the great song again.

3. Helios (hē′ lē äs′): Sun god.

4. Zeus (zo͞os): King of the gods.

Sailing from Troy

*Ten years after the Trojan War, Odysseus departs
from the goddess Calypso's island. He arrives in
Phaeacia, ruled by Alcinous. Alcinous offers a ship to
Odysseus and asks him to tell of his adventures.*

"I am Laertes'[5] son, Odysseus.
                              Men hold me
    formidable for guile[6] in peace and war:
20 this fame has gone abroad to the sky's rim.

    My home is on the peaked sea-mark of Ithaca[7]
    under Mount Neion's wind-blown robe of leaves,
    in sight of other islands—Dulichium,
    Same, wooded Zacynthus—Ithaca
25 being most lofty in that coastal sea
    and northwest, while the rest lie east and south.
    A rocky isle, but good for a boy's training;
    I shall not see on earth a place more dear,
    though I have been detained long by Calypso,[8]
30 loveliest among goddesses, who held me
    in her smooth caves, to be her heart's delight,
    as Circe of Aeaea,[9] the enchantress,
    desired me, and detained me in her hall.
    But in my heart I never gave consent.
35 Where shall a man find sweetness to surpass
    his own home and his parents? In far lands
    he shall not, though he find a house of gold.

    What of my sailing, then, from Troy?
                              What of those years
    of rough adventure, weathered under Zeus?
40 The wind that carried west from Ilium[10]
    brought me to Ismarus, on the far shore,
    a strongpoint on the coast of Cicones.[11]
    I stormed that place and killed the men who fought.
    Plunder we took, and we enslaved the women,
45 to make division, equal shares to all—
    but on the spot I told them: 'Back, and quickly!

◆ **Reading Strategy**
Why do the opening
lines of Odysseus
sound more natural
when you ignore
the line breaks?

---

5. Laertes (lā ʉr´ tēz)
6. guile (gīl) *n.*:
Craftiness; cunning.
7. Ithaca (ith´ ə kə):
Island off the west coast of
Greece.
8. Calypso (kə lip´ sō)

9. Circe (sʉr´ sē) **of
Aeaea** (ē´ ē ə)

10. Ilium (il ē əm): Troy.

11. Cicones (si kō´ nēz)

Note: In his translation of the *Odyssey*, Fitzgerald spelled Greek names in a way that suggests the sound and flavor of the original Greek. In the excerpts included here, more familiar spellings have been used. Where, for example, Fitzgerald wrote "Kirkê," "Kyklops," and "Seirênês," you will here find "Circe," "Cyclops," and "Sirens."

Out to sea again!' My men were mutinous,[12]
fools, on stores of wine. Sheep after sheep
they butchered by the surf, and shambling cattle,
50 feasting,—while fugitives went inland, running
to call to arms the main force of Cicones.
This was an army trained to fight on horseback
or, where the ground required, on foot. They came
with dawn over that terrain like the leaves
55 and blades of spring. So doom appeared to us,
dark word of Zeus for us, our evil days.
My men stood up and made a fight of it—
backed on the ships, with lances kept in play,
from bright morning through the blaze of noon
60 holding our beach, although so far outnumbered;
but when the sun passed toward unyoking time,
then the Achaeans,[13] one by one, gave way.
Six benches were left empty in every ship
that evening when we pulled away from death.
65 And this new grief we bore with us to sea:
our precious lives we had, but not our friends.
No ship made sail next day until some shipmate
had raised a cry, three times, for each poor ghost
unfleshed by the Cicones on that field.

The Lotus-Eaters

70 Now Zeus the lord of cloud roused in the north
a storm against the ships, and driving veils
of squall moved down like night on land and sea.
The bows went plunging at the gust; sails
cracked and lashed out strips in the big wind.
75 We saw death in that fury, dropped the yards,
unshipped the oars, and pulled for the nearest lee:[14]
then two long days and nights we lay offshore
worn out and sick at heart, tasting our grief,
until a third Dawn came with ringlets shining.
80 Then we put up our masts, hauled sail, and rested,
letting the steersmen and the breeze take over.

I might have made it safely home, that time,
but as I came round Malea the current
took me out to sea, and from the north
85 a fresh gale drove me on, past Cythera.
Nine days I drifted on the teeming sea
before dangerous high winds. Upon the tenth
we came to the coastline of the Lotus-Eaters,
who live upon that flower. We landed there

12. mutinous (myo͞ot′ ən əs) *adj.*: Rebellious.

13. Achaeans (ə kē′ ənz): Greeks; here, Odysseus' men.

14. lee (lē) *n.*: Area sheltered from the wind.

◆ **Build Vocabulary**
squall (skwôl) *n.*: Brief, violent storm

90 to take on water. All ships' companies
    mustered alongside for the midday meal.
    Then I sent out two picked men and a runner
    to learn what race of men that land sustained.
    They fell in, soon enough, with Lotus-Eaters,
95 who showed no will to do us harm, only
    offering the sweet Lotus to our friends—
    but those who ate this honeyed plant, the Lotus,
    never cared to report, nor to return:
    they longed to stay forever, browsing on
100 that native bloom, forgetful of their homeland.
    I drove them, all three wailing, to the ships,
    tied them down under their rowing benches,
    and called the rest: 'All hands aboard;
    come, clear the beach and no one taste
105 the Lotus, or you lose your hope of home.'
    Filing in to their places by the rowlocks
    my oarsmen dipped their long oars in the surf,
    and we moved out again on our seafaring.

> ◆ **Literary Focus**
> What characteristics of a hero and leader does Odysseus show in the episode with the Lotus Eaters?

Guide for Responding

◆ *Literature and Your Life*

Reader's Response What is your first impression of Odysseus? Which of his qualities do you admire?

Thematic Focus Identify the conflicts represented by each of Odysseus' foes and explain how a person might work out these conflicts.

Journal Writing Describe a time when you were distracted from a goal by something that temporarily seemed more attractive. How did you overcome this distraction?

☑ Check Your Comprehension

1. Who is narrating these adventures?
2. Describe the events on Ismarus.
3. What keeps Odysseus from reaching home?
4. What happens to the men who eat the Lotus?

◆ Critical Thinking

INTERPRET
1. What were Odysseus' feelings when he was held captive by Calypso and Circe? **[Interpret]**
2. The third dawn after the storm is described as coming "with ringlets shining." What impression of the dawn does this image give you? **[Analyze]**
3. What does the episode with the Lotus-Eaters suggest about the kinds of problems Odysseus has with his men? **[Infer]**

EVALUATE
4. What lessons can be learned from the defeat of Odysseus and his men at Ismarus? **[Assess]**

APPLY
5. What impression do you have of the differences between the world of the *Odyssey* and today's world? **[Synthesize]**

The Cyclops

In the next land we found were Cyclopes,[15]
110   giants, louts, without a law to bless them.
In ignorance leaving the fruitage of the earth in
   mystery
to the immortal gods, they neither plow
nor sow by hand, nor till the ground, though
   grain—
wild wheat and barley—grows untended, and
115   wine grapes, in clusters, ripen in heaven's rains.
Cyclopes have no muster and no meeting,
no consultation or old tribal ways,
but each one dwells in his own mountain cave
dealing out rough justice to wife and child,
120   indifferent to what the others do. . . .

As we rowed on, and nearer to the mainland,
at one end of the bay, we saw a cavern
yawning above the water, screened with laurel,
and many rams and goats about the place
125   inside a sheepfold—made from slabs of stone
earthfast between tall trunks of pine and rugged
towering oak trees.
                 A prodigious[16] man
slept in this cave alone, and took his flocks
to graze afield—remote from all companions,
130   knowing none but savage ways, a brute
so huge, he seemed no man at all of those
who eat good wheaten bread; but he seemed rather
a shaggy mountain reared in solitude.
We beached there, and I told the crew
135   to stand by and keep watch over the ship:
as for myself I took my twelve best fighters
and went ahead. I had a goatskin full
of that sweet liquor that Euanthes' son,
Maron, had given me. He kept Apollo's[17]
140   holy grove at Ismarus; for kindness
we showed him there, and showed his wife and child,
he gave me seven shining golden talents[18]
perfectly formed, a solid silver winebowl,
and then this liquor—twelve two-handled jars
145   of brandy, pure and fiery. Not a slave
in Maron's household knew this drink; only
he, his wife and the storeroom mistress knew;
and they would put one cupful—ruby-colored
honey—smooth—in twenty more of water,

15. Cyclopes (sī klō′ pēz)
n.: Plural form of Cyclops
(sī′ kläps), a race of giants
with one eye in the middle
of the forehead.

◆ *Literature
and Your Life*
The description of
the Cyclopes reveals
what the ancient
Greeks regarded as
the benefits of civi-
lization. What in your
opinion are the ben-
efits of civilization?

16. prodigious (prə dij′ əs)
adj.: Enormous.

17. Apollo (ə päl′ ō): God
of music, poetry, prophecy,
and medicine.

18. talents: Units of
money in ancient Greece.

150   but still the sweet scent hovered like a fume
over the winebowl. No man turned away
when cups of this came round.

                           A wineskin full
I brought along, and victuals[19] in a bag,
for in my bones I knew some towering brute
155   would be upon us soon—all outward power,
a wild man, ignorant of civility.

We climbed, then, briskly to the cave. But Cyclops
had gone afield, to pasture his fat sheep,
so we looked round at everything inside:
160   a drying rack that sagged with cheeses, pens
crowded with lambs and kids,[20] each in its class:
firstlings apart from middlings, and the 'dewdrops,'
or newborn lambkins, penned apart from both.
And vessels full of whey[21] were brimming there—
165   bowls of earthenware and pails for milking.
My men came pressing round me, pleading:

                             'Why not
take these cheeses, get them stowed, come back,
throw open all the pens, and make a run for it?
We'll drive the kids and lambs aboard. We say
170   put out again on good salt water!'

                           Ah,
how sound that was! Yet I refused. I wished
to see the cave man, what he had to offer—
no pretty sight, it turned out, for my friends.
We lit a fire, burnt an offering,
175   and took some cheese to eat: then sat in silence
around the embers, waiting. When he came
he had a load of dry boughs[22] on his shoulder
to stoke his fire at suppertime. He dumped it
with a great crash into that hollow cave,
180   and we all scattered fast to the far wall.
Then over the broad cavern floor he ushered
the ewes he meant to milk. He left his rams
and he-goats in the yard outside, and swung
high overhead a slab of solid rock
185   to close the cave. Two dozen four-wheeled wagons,
with heaving wagon teams, could not have stirred
the tonnage of that rock from where he wedged it
over the doorsill. Next he took his seat
and milked his bleating ewes. A practiced job
190   he made of it, giving each ewe her suckling;

19. victuals (vit´ əls) *n.*: Food or other provisions.

20. kids (kids) *n.*: Young goats.

21. whey (hwā) *n.*: Thin, watery part of milk separated from the thicker curds.

22. boughs (bouz) *n.*: Tree branches.

thickened his milk, then, into curds and whey,
sieved out the curds to drip in withy²³ baskets,
and poured the whey to stand in bowls
cooling until he drank it for his supper.
195 When all these chores were done, he poked the fire,
heaping on brushwood. In the glare he saw us.

'Strangers,' he said, 'who are you? And where from?
What brings you here by seaways—a fair traffic?
Or are you wandering rogues, who cast your lives
200 like dice, and ravage other folk by sea?'

We felt a pressure on our hearts, in dread
of that deep rumble and that mighty man.
But all the same I spoke up in reply:

'We are from Troy, Achaeans, blown off course
205 by shifting gales on the Great South Sea;
homeward bound, but taking routes and ways
uncommon; so the will of Zeus would have it.
We served under Agamemnon,²⁴ son of Atreus—
the whole world knows what city
210 he laid waste, what armies he destroyed.
It was our luck to come here; here we stand,
beholden for your help, or any gifts
you give—as custom is to honor strangers.
We would entreat you, great Sir, have a care
215 for the gods' courtesy; Zeus will avenge
the unoffending guest.'

                          He answered this
from his brute chest, unmoved:

                          'You are a ninny,
or else you come from the other end of nowhere,
telling me, mind the gods! We Cyclopes
220 care not a whistle for your thundering Zeus
or all the gods in bliss; we have more force by far.
I would not let you go for fear of Zeus—
you or your friends—unless I had a whim²⁵ to.
Tell me, where was it, now, you left your ship—
225 around the point, or down the shore, I wonder?'

He thought he'd find out, but I saw through this,
and answered with a ready lie:

23. **withy** (with´ ē) *adj.*:
Tough, flexible twigs.

24. **Agamemnon** (ag´ ə
mem´ nän): King who led
the Greek army during the
Trojan War.

◆ **Literary Focus**
An epic hero like
Odysseus served as
a role model for
ancient Greeks.
What can be learned
about conduct and
respect for the gods
from Odysseus'
speech?

25. **whim** (hwim) *n.*: Sudden thought or wish to do
something.

◆ **Build Vocabulary**
dispatched (dis pacht´) *v.*:
Finished quickly

'My ship?

Poseidon[26] Lord, who sets the earth a-tremble,
broke it up on the rocks at your land's end.
230 A wind from seaward served him, drove us there.
We are survivors, these good men and I.'

Neither reply nor pity came from him,
but in one stride he clutched at my companions
and caught two in his hands like squirming puppies
235 to beat their brains out, spattering the floor.
Then he dismembered them and made his meal,
gaping and crunching like a mountain lion—
everything: innards, flesh, and marrow bones.
We cried aloud, lifting our hands to Zeus,
240 powerless, looking on at this, appalled;
but Cyclops went on filling up his belly
with manflesh and great gulps of whey,
then lay down like a mast among his sheep.
My heart beat high now at the chance of action,
245 and drawing the sharp sword from my hip I went
along his flank to stab him where the midriff
holds the liver. I had touched the spot
when sudden fear stayed me: if I killed him
we perished there as well, for we could never
250 move his ponderous doorway slab aside.
So we were left to groan and wait for morning.

When the young Dawn with fingertips of rose
lit up the world, the Cyclops built a fire
and milked his handsome ewes, all in due order,
255 putting the sucklings to the mothers. Then,
his chores being all dispatched, he caught
another brace[27] of men to make his breakfast,
and whisked away his great door slab
to let his sheep go through—but he, behind,
260 reset the stone as one would cap a quiver.[28]
There was a din[29] of whistling as the Cyclops
rounded his flock to higher ground, then stillness.
And now I pondered how to hurt him worst,
if but Athena[30] granted what I prayed for.
265 Here are the means I thought would serve my turn:

a club, or staff, lay there along the fold—
an olive tree, felled green and left to season[31]
for Cyclops' hand. And it was like a mast
a lugger[32] of twenty oars, broad in the beam—

26. Poseidon (pō sīˊ dən): God of the sea and of earthquakes.

◆ **Reading Strategy**
Read lines 244–250 in complete sentences, ignoring the line breaks. How does doing so help your understanding of the passage?

27. brace (brās) *n.*: Pair.

28. cap (kap) **a quiver** (kwivˊ ər): Close a case holding arrows.
29. din (din) *n.*: Loud, continuous noise; uproar.
30. Athena (ə thēˊ nə): Goddess of wisdom, skills, and warfare.

31. felled green and left to season: Chopped down and exposed to the weather to age the wood.
32. lugger (lugˊ ər) *n.*: Small sailing vessel.

270   a deep-sea-going craft—might carry:
       so long, so big around, it seemed. Now I
       chopped out a six foot section of this pole
       and set it down before my men, who scraped it;
       and when they had it smooth, I hewed again
275   to make a stake with pointed end. I held this
       in the fire's heart and turned it, toughening it,
       then hid it, well back in the cavern, under
       one of the dung piles in profusion there.
       Now came the time to toss for it: who ventured
280   along with me? whose hand could bear to thrust
       and grind that spike in Cyclops' eye, when mild
       sleep had mastered him? As luck would have it,
       the men I would have chosen won the toss—
       four strong men, and I made five as captain.

285   At evening came the shepherd with his flock,
       his woolly flock. The rams as well this time,
       entered the cave: by some sheepherding whim—
       or a god's bidding—none were left outside.
       He hefted his great boulder into place
290   and sat him down to milk the bleating ewes
       in proper order, put the lambs to suck,
       and swiftly ran through all his evening chores.
       Then he caught two more men and feasted on them.
       My moment was at hand, and I went forward
295   holding an ivy bowl of my dark drink,
       looking up, saying:

                              'Cyclops, try some wine.
       Here's liquor to wash down your scraps of men.
       Taste it, and see the kind of drink we carried
       under our planks. I meant it for an offering
300   if you would help us home. But you are mad,
       unbearable, a bloody monster! After this,
       will any other traveler come to see you?'

       He seized and drained the bowl, and it went down
       so fiery and smooth he called for more:
305   'Give me another, thank you kindly. Tell me,
       how are you called? I'll make a gift will please you.
       Even Cyclopes know the wine grapes grow
       out of grassland and loam in heaven's rain,
       but here's a bit of nectar and ambrosia!'[33]
310   Three bowls I brought him, and he poured them
          down.
       I saw the fuddle and flush come over him,

◆ Literary Focus
What heroic qualities
does Odysseus
reveal as he plots
against the Cyclops?

33. nectar (nek´ tər) and
ambrosia (am brō´ zhə):
Drink and food of the gods.

then I sang out in cordial tones:

'Cyclops,
you ask my honorable name? Remember
the gift you promised me, and I shall tell you.
315 My name is Nohbdy: mother, father, and friends,
everyone calls me Nohbdy.'

And he said:
"Nohbdy's my meat, then, after I eat his friends.
Others come first. There's a noble gift, now.'

Even as he spoke, he reeled and tumbled backward,
320 his great head lolling to one side; and sleep
took him like any creature. Drunk, hiccuping,
he dribbled streams of liquor and bits of men.

Now, by the gods, I drove my big hand spike
deep in the embers, charring it again,
325 and cheered my men along with battle talk
to keep their courage up; no quitting now.
The pike of olive, green though it had been,
reddened and glowed as if about to catch.
I drew it from the coals and my four fellows
330 gave me a hand, lugging it near the Cyclops
as more than natural force nerved them; straight
forward they sprinted, lefted it, and rammed it
deep in his crater eye, and leaned on it
turning it as a shipwright turns a drill
335 in planking, having men below to swing
the two-handled strap that spins it in the groove.
So with our brand we bored[34] that great eye socket
while blood ran out around the red-hot bar.
Eyelid and lash were seared; the pierced ball
340 hissed broiling, and the roots popped.

In a smithy
one sees a white-hot axhead or an adze
plunged and wrung in a cold tub, screeching steam—
the way they make soft iron hale and hard—:
just so that eyeball hissed around the spike.
345 The Cyclops bellowed and the rock roared round him,
and we fell back in fear. Clawing his face
he tugged the bloody spike out of his eye,
threw it away, and his wild hands went groping;
then he set up a howl for Cyclopes
350 who lived in caves on windy peaks nearby.

♦ **Reading Strategy**
How would you write
Odysseus' sly lie in
regular prose?

34. bored (bôrd) v.: Made
a hole in.

Some heard him; and they came by divers[35] ways
to clump around outside and call:

        'What ails you,
Polyphemus?[36] Why do you cry so sore
in the starry night? You will not let us sleep.
355 Sure no man's driving off your flock? No man
has tricked you, ruined you?'

        Out of the cave
the <u>mammoth</u> Polyphemus roared in answer:
'Nohbdy, Nohbdy's tricked me, Nohbdy's ruined me!'
To this rough shout they made a sage[37] reply:
360 'Ah well, if nobody has played you foul
there in your lonely bed, we are no use in pain
given by great Zeus. Let it be your father,
Poseidon Lord, to whom you pray.'
        So saying
they trailed away. And I was filled with laughter
365 to see how like a charm the name deceived them.
Now Cyclops, wheezing as the pain came on him,
fumbled to wrench away the great doorstone
and squatted in the breach with arms thrown wide
for any silly beast or man who bolted—
370 hoping somehow I might be such a fool.
But I kept thinking how to win the game:
death sat there huge; how could we slip away?
I drew on all my wits, and ran through tactics,
reasoning as a man will for dear life,
375 until a trick came—and it pleased me well.
The Cyclops' rams were handsome, fat, with heavy
fleeces, a dark violet.

        Three abreast
I tied them silently together, twining
cords of willow from the ogre's bed
380 then slung a man under each middle one
to ride there safely, shielded left and right.
So three sheep could convey each man. I took
the woolliest ram, the choicest of the flock,
and hung myself under his kinky belly,
385 pulled up tight, with fingers twisted deep
in sheepskin ringlets for an iron grip.
So, breathing hard, we waited until morning.

When Dawn spread out her fingertips of rose
the rams began to stir, moving for pasture,

35. divers (dī′ vərz) *adj.*:
Several; various.

36. Polyphemus (päl′ ə fē′
məs)

37. sage (sāj) *adj.*: Wise.

◆ **Build Vocabulary**
mammoth (mam′ əth) *adj.*: Enormous

390 and peals of bleating echoed round the pens
where dams with udders full called for a milking.
Blinded, and sick with pain from his head wound,
the master stroked each ram, then let it pass,
but my men riding on the pectoral[38] fleece
395 the giant's blind hands blundering never found.
Last of them all my ram, the leader, came,
weighted by wool and me with my meditations.
The Cyclops patted him, and then he said:

'Sweet cousin ram, why lag behind the rest
400 in the night cave? You never linger so,
but graze before them all, and go afar
to crop sweet grass, and take your stately way
leading along the streams, until at evening
you run to be the first one in the fold.
405 Why, now, so far behind? Can you be grieving
over your Master's eye? That carrion rogue[39]
and his accurst companions burnt it out
when he had conquered all my wits with wine.
Nohbdy will not get out alive, I swear.
410 Oh, had you brain and voice to tell
where he may be now, dodging all my fury!
Bashed by this hand and bashed on this rock wall
his brains would strew the floor, and I should have
rest from the outrage Nohbdy worked upon me.'

415 He sent us into the open, then. Close by,
I dropped and rolled clear of the ram's belly,
going this way and that to untie the men.
With many glances back, we rounded up
his fat, stiff-legged sheep to take aboard,
420 and drove them down to where the good ship lay.
We saw, as we came near, our fellows' faces
shining; then we saw them turn to grief
tallying those who had not fled from death.
I hushed them, jerking head and eyebrows up,
425 and in a low voice told them: 'Load this herd;
move fast, and put the ship's head toward the
 breakers.'
They all pitched in at loading, then embarked
and struck their oars into the sea. Far out,
as far offshore as shouted words would carry,
430 I sent a few back to the adversary:
'O Cyclops! Would you feast on my companions?
Puny, am I, in a cave man's hands?
How do you like the beating that we gave you,

38. pectoral (pek´ tər əl)
adj.: Located on the chest.

39. carrion (kar´ ē ən)
rogue (rōg): Repulsive
scoundrel.

◆ Literary Focus
An epic hero is
larger than life but
usually also has
some human failings.
What human weak-
ness does Odysseus'
behavior reveal?

you damned cannibal? Eater of guests
435 under your roof! Zeus and the gods have paid you!'

The blind thing in his doubled fury broke
a hilltop in his hands and heaved it after us.
Ahead of our black prow it struck and sank
whelmed in a spuming geyser, a giant wave
440 that washed the ship stern foremost back to shore.
I got the longest boathook out and stood
fending us off, with furious nods to all
to put their backs into a racing stroke—
row, row, or perish. So the long oars bent
445 kicking the foam sternward, making head
until we drew away, and twice as far.
Now when I cupped my hands I heard the crew
in low voices protesting:

                    'Godsake, Captain!
Why bait the beast again? Let him alone!'

450 'That tidal wave he made on the first throw
all but beached us.'

                          'All but stove us in!'
'Give him our bearing with your trumpeting,
he'll get the range and lob a boulder.'

                              'Aye
He'll smash our timbers and our heads together!'
455 I would not heed them in my glorying spirit,
but let my anger flare and yelled:

                              'Cyclops,
if ever mortal man inquire
how you were put to shame and blinded, tell him
Odysseus, raider of cities, took your eye:
460 Laertes' son, whose home's on Ithaca!'

At this he gave a mighty sob and rumbled:

'Now comes the weird[40] upon me, spoken of old.
A wizard, grand and wondrous, lived here—Telemus,[41]
a son of Eurymus;[42] great length of days
465 he had in wizardry among the Cyclopes,
and these things he foretold for time to come:
my great eye lost, and at Odysseus' hands.
Always I had in mind some giant, armed

> ◆ *Literature*
> *and Your Life*
> When they are
> angry or boasting,
> people sometimes
> say things that they
> later regret. How do
> Odysseus' words
> relate to your own
> observations of a
> person "having a
> big mouth"?

40. weird (wird) *n.*: Fate or destiny.
41. Telemus (tel e´ məs)
42. Eurymus (yōō rim´ əs)

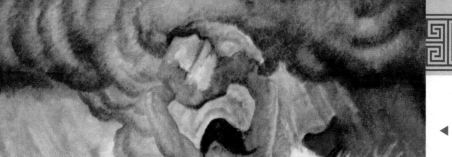

Polyphemus, The Cyclops, N. C. Wyeth, Delaware Art Museum

◄ **Critical Viewing**
Odysseus and his surviving men escape in their ship as the blinded Cyclops hurls boulders and curses. What events provoke this scene? **[Analyze]**

in giant force, would come against me here.
470 But this, but you—small, pitiful and twiggy—
you put me down with wine, you blinded me.
Come back, Odysseus, and I'll treat you well,
praying the god of earthquake⁴³ to befriend you—
his son I am, for he by his avowal
475 fathered me, and, if he will, he may
heal me of this black wound—he and no other
of all the happy gods or mortal men.'

Few words I shouted in reply to him:

'If I could take your life I would and take
480 your time away, and hurl you down to hell!

43. god of earthquake: Poseidon.

The god of earthquake could not heal you there!'

At this he stretched his hands out in the darkness
toward the sky of stars, and prayed Poseidon:

'O hear me, lord, blue girdler of the islands,
485   if I am thine indeed, and thou art father:
grant that Odysseus, raider of cities, never
see his home: Laertes' son, I mean,
who kept his hall on Ithaca. Should destiny
intend that he shall see his roof again
490   among his family in his father land,
far be that day, and dark the years between.
Let him lose all companions, and return
under strange sail to bitter days at home.'

In these words he prayed, and the god heard him.
495   Now he laid hands upon a bigger stone
and wheeled around, <u>titanic</u> for the cast,
to let it fly in the black-prowed vessel's track.
But it fell short, just aft the steering oar,
and whelming seas rose giant above the stone
500   to bear us onward toward the island.

                        There
as we ran in we saw the squadron waiting,
the trim ships drawn up side by side, and all
our troubled friends who waited, looking seaward.
We beached her, grinding keel in the soft sand,
505   and waded in, ourselves, on the sandy beach.
Then we unloaded all of Cyclops' flock
to make division, share and share alike.
Only my fighters voted that my ram,
the prize of all, should go to me. I slew him
510   by the seaside and burnt his long thighbones
to Zeus beyond the stormcloud, Cronus'[44] son,
who rules the world. But Zeus disdained my
   offering:
destruction for my ships he had in store
and death for those who sailed them, my
   companions.
515   Now all day long until the sun went down
we made our feast on mutton and sweet wine,
till after sunset in the gathering dark
we went to sleep above the wash of ripples.

When the young Dawn with fingertips of rose

◆ **Literary Focus**
What admirable qualities does Odysseus show in what he does with the stolen sheep?

44. Cronus (krō′ nəs): Titan who was ruler of the universe until he was overthrown by his son Zeus.

◆ **Build Vocabulary**
titanic (ti tan′ ik) *adj.*: Of great size or strength

520	touched the world, I roused the men, gave orders
	to man the ships, cast off the mooring lines:
	and filing in to sit beside the rowlocks
	oarsmen in line dipped oars in the gray sea.
	So we moved out, sad in the vast offing,[45]
525	having our precious lives, but not our friends.

45. offing (ôf´ əiŋ) *n.*:
Distant part of the sea
visible from the shore.

The Land of the Dead

*Odysseus and his men sail to Aeolia,[46] where Aeolus, king of the
winds, sends Odysseus on his way with a gift: a sack containing
all the winds except the favorable west wind. When they are near
home, Odysseus' men open the sack, letting loose a storm that drives them back to Aeolia. Aeolus casts them out, having decided
that they are detested by the gods. They sail seven days and arrive in the land of the Laestrygonians,[47] a race of cannibals. These
creatures destroy all of Odysseus' ships except the one he is sailing in. Odysseus and his reduced crew escape and reach Aeaea,
the island ruled by the sorceress-goddess Circe. She transforms
half of the men into swine. Protected by a magic herb, Odysseus
demands that Circe change his men back into human form. Before
Odysseus departs from the island a year later, Circe informs him
that in order to reach home he must journey to the land of the
dead, Hades, and consult the blind prophet Tiresias.*

46. Aeolia (ē ō´ li ə)

47. Laestrygonians (les tri
gō´ ni anz)

	We bore down on the ship at the sea's edge
	and launched her on the salt immortal sea,
	stepping our mast and spar in the black ship;
	embarked the ram and ewe and went aboard
530	in tears, with bitter and sore dread upon us.
	But now a breeze came up for us astern—
	a canvas-bellying land breeze, hale shipmate
	sent by the singing nymph with sunbright hair;[48]
	so we made fast the braces, took our thwarts,
535	and let the wind and steersman work the ship
	with full sail spread all day above our coursing,
	till the sun dipped, and all the ways grew dark
	upon the fathomless unresting sea.
	By night
	our ship ran onward toward the Ocean's bourn,
540	the realm and region of the Men of Winter,
	hidden in mist and cloud. Never the flaming
	eye of Helios lights on those men
	at morning, when he climbs the sky of stars,

**48. singing nymph . . .
hair:** Circe.

Odysseus in the Land of the Dead, N. C. Wyeth, Delaware Art Museum

◀ Critical Viewing What can you infer about ancient Greek beliefs about death and the afterlife from the text and this illustration? [Infer]

nor in descending earthward out of heaven;
545   ruinous night being rove over those wretches.
We made the land, put ram and ewe ashore,
and took our way along the Ocean stream
to find the place foretold for us by Circe.
There Perimedes and Eulylochus,[49]
550   pinioned[50] the sacred beasts. With my drawn blade
I spaded up the votive[51] pit, and poured
libations[52] round it to the unnumbered dead:
sweet milk and honey, then sweet wine, and last
clear water; and I scattered barley down.
555   Then I addressed the blurred and breathless dead,
vowing to slaughter my best heifer for them
before she calved, at home in Ithaca,
and burn the choice bits on the altar fire;
as for Tiresias, I swore to sacrifice
560   a black lamb, handsomest of all our flock.
Thus to assuage the nations of the dead
I pledged these rites, then slashed the lamb and
  ewe,
letting their black blood stream into the wellpit.

49. **Perimedes** (per´ ə mē´ dēz) **and Eurylochus** (yoo ril´ ə kas)
50. **pinioned** (pin´ yənd) *v.*: Confined or shackled.
51. **votive** (vōt´ iv) *adj.*: Done in fulfillment of a vow or pledge.
52. **libations** (lī bā´ shənz) *n.*: Wine or other liquids poured upon the ground as a sacrifice.

◆ **Build Vocabulary**

assuage (ə swāj´) *v.*: Calm; pacify

Now the souls gathered, stirring out of Erebus,[53]
565 brides and young men, and men grown old in pain,
and tender girls whose hearts were new to grief;
many were there, too, torn by brazen lanceheads,
battle-slain, bearing still their bloody gear.
From every side they came and sought the pit
570 with rustling cries; and I grew sick with fear.
But presently I gave command to my officers
to flay those sheep the bronze cut down, and make
burnt offerings of flesh to the gods below—
to sovereign Death, to pale Persephone.[54]
575 Meanwhile I crouched with my drawn sword to keep
the surging phantoms from the bloody pit
till I should know the presence of Tiresias.[55]

One shade came first—Elpenor, of our company,
who lay unburied still on the wide earth
580 as we had left him—dead in Circe's hall,
untouched, unmourned, when other cares compelled us.
Now when I saw him there I wept for pity
and called out to him:
                                  'How is this, Elpenor,
how could you journey to the western gloom
585 swifter afoot than I in the black lugger?'
He sighed, and answered:
                                  'Son of great Laertes,
Odysseus, master mariner and soldier,
bad luck shadowed me, and no kindly power;
ignoble death I drank with so much wine.
590 I slept on Circe's roof, then could not see
the long steep backward ladder, coming down,
and fell that height. My neckbone, buckled under,
snapped, and my spirit found this well of dark.
Now hear the grace I pray for, in the name
595 of those back in the world, not here—your wife
and father, he who gave you bread in childhood,
and your own child, your only son, Telemachus,[56]
long ago left at home.
                                  When you make sail
and put these lodgings of dim Death behind,
600 you will moor ship, I know, upon Aeaea Island;
there, O my lord, remember me, I pray,
do not abandon me unwept, unburied,
to tempt the gods' wrath, while you sail for home;
but fire my corpse, and all the gear I had,
605 and build a cairn[57] for me above the breakers—
an unknown sailor's mark for men to come.

53. Erebus (er´ ə bəs):
Dark region under the earth
through which the dead
pass before entering the
realm of Hades.

◆ **Literary Focus**
How is Odysseus'
courage revealed
even as he admits
to being "sick with
fear"?

54. Persephone (pər sef´
ə nē): Wife of Hades.
55. Tiresias (tī rē´ si as)

56. Telemachus
(tə lem´ ə kəs)

57. cairn (kern) n.: Conical
heap of stones built as a
monument.

Heap up the mound there, and implant upon it
the oar I pulled in life with my companions.'

He ceased, and I replied:

                         'Unhappy spirit,
610   I promise you the barrow and the burial.'

So we conversed, and grimly, at a distance,
with my long sword between, guarding the blood,
while the faint image of the lad spoke on.
Now came the soul of Anticlea, dead,
615   my mother, daughter of Autolycus,[58]
dead now, though living still when I took ship
for holy Troy. Seeing this ghost I grieved,
but held her off, through pang on pang of tears,
till I should know the presence of Tiresias.
620   Soon from the dark that prince of Thebes[59] came
       forward
bearing a golden staff; and he addressed me:

'Son of Laertes and the gods of old,
Odysseus, master of landways and seaways,
why leave the blazing sun, O man of woe,
625   to see the cold dead and the joyless region?
Stand clear, put up your sword;
let me but taste the blood, I shall speak true.'

At this I stepped aside, and in the scabbard
let my long sword ring home to the pommel silver,
630   as he bent down to the somber blood. Then spoke
the prince of those with gift of speech:

                        'Great captain,
a fair wind and the honey lights of home
are all you seek. But anguish lies ahead;
the god who thunders on the land prepares it,
635   not to be shaken from your track, implacable,
in rancor for the son whose eye you blinded.
One narrow strait may take you through his blows:
denial of yourself, restraint of shipmates.
When you make landfall on Thrinacia first
640   and quit the violet sea, dark on the land
you'll find the grazing herds of Helios
by whom all things are seen, all speech is known.
Avoid these kine,[60] hold fast to your intent,
and hard seafaring brings you all to Ithaca.
645   But if you raid the beeves, I see destruction

58. **Autolycus** (ô täl´ i kus)

59. **Thebes** (thēbz)

◆ **Reading Strategy**
Rephrase in ordinary language the verses about Odysseus putting his sword away. How can rephrasing Homer's verses help you read the *Odyssey* in sentences?

60. **kine** (kīn) *n.*: Cattle.

for ship and crew. Though you survive alone,
<u>bereft</u> of all companions, lost for years,
under strange sail shall you come home, to find
your own house filled with trouble: insolent men
650   eating your livestock as they court your lady.
Aye, you shall make those men atone in blood!
But after you have dealt out death—in open
combat or by stealth—to all the suitors,
go overland on foot, and take an oar,
655   until one day you come where men have lived
with meat unsalted, never known the sea,
nor seen seagoing ships, with crimson bows
and oars that fledge light hulls for dipping flight.
The spot will soon be plain to you, and I
660   can tell you how: some passerby will say,
'What winnowing fan is that upon your shoulder?'
Halt, and implant your smooth oar in the turf
and make fair sacrifice to Lord Poseidon:
a ram, a bull, a great buck boar: turn back,
665   and carry out pure hecatombs[61] at home
to all wide heaven's lords, the undying gods,
to each in order. Then a seaborne death
soft as this hand of mist will come upon you
when you are wearied out with rich old age,
670   your country folk in blessed peace around you.
And all this shall be just as I foretell.'

61. hecatombs (hek´ ə tōmz´) *n.*: Large-scale sacrifices: often the slaughter of 100 cattle at one time.

♦ **Build Vocabulary**
bereft (bi reft´) *adj.*: Deprived

Guide for Responding

♦ *Literature and Your Life*

Reader's Response What do you think of Odysseus' plan for escaping from Polyphemus?
Thematic Focus What are some constructive ways of working out conflicts with powerful or unreasonable opponents?

☑ Check Your Comprehension

1. What does Odysseus do to blind Polyphemus?
2. How do Odysseus and his companions ultimately escape from the Cyclops?
3. What does Tiresias foretell?

♦ Critical Thinking

INTERPRET
1. What does the encounter with Maron tell you about ancient Greek attitudes toward hospitality? **[Interpret]**
2. What "laws" of behavior and attitude does Polyphemus violate? Explain. **[Infer]**
EVALUATE
3. (a)What survival qualities does Odysseus exhibit in his conflict with Polyphemus? (b) What character trait does Odysseus display in "The Land of the Dead" that he did not reveal in his adventure with the Cyclops? **[Assess]**

The Sirens

*Odysseus returns to Circe's island. The goddess reveals his
course to him and gives advice on how to avoid the dangers
he will face: the Sirens, who lure sailors to their destruction;
the Wandering Rocks, sea rocks that destroy even birds in
flight; the perils of the sea monster Scylla and, nearby, the
whirlpool Charybdis;[62] and the cattle of the sun god, which
Tiresias has warned Odysseus not to harm.*

62. **Charybdis** (ka rib´ dis)

As Circe spoke, Dawn mounted her golden throne,
and on the first rays Circe left me, taking
her way like a great goddess up the island.
675   I made straight for the ship, roused up the men
to get aboard and cast off at the stern.
They scrambled to their places by the rowlocks
and all in line dipped oars in the gray sea.
But soon an offshore breeze blew to our liking—
680   a canvas-bellying breeze, a lusty shipmate
sent by the singing nymph with sunbright hair.
So we made fast the braces, and we rested,
letting the wind and steersman work the ship.
The crew being now silent before me, I
685   addressed them, sore at heart:

                    'Dear friends,
more than one man, or two, should know those
   things
Circe foresaw for us and shared with me,
so let me tell her forecast: then we die
with our eyes open, if we are going to die,
690   or know what death we baffle if we can. Sirens
weaving a haunting song over the sea
we are to shun, she said, and their green shore
all sweet with clover; yet she urged that I
alone should listen to their song. Therefore
695   you are to tie me up, tight as a splint,
erect along the mast, lashed to the mast,
and if I shout and beg to be untied,
take more turns of the rope to muffle me.'

I rather dwelt on this part of the forecast,
700   while our good ship made time, bound outward
   down
the wind for the strange island of Sirens.
Then all at once the wind fell, and a calm

> ◆ Literary Focus
> What does
> Odysseus reveal
> about his character
> by sharing informa-
> tion with his men?

882 ◆ *The Epic*

▲ **Critical Viewing** The beautiful sorceress Circe both helps and hinders Odysseus on his long journey home. What can you tell about Circe's character from this illustration? **[Deduce]**

came over all the sea, as though some power
lulled the swell.

              The crew were on their feet
705   briskly, to furl the sail, and stow it; then
each in place, they poised the smooth oar blades
and sent the white foam scudding by. I carved
a massive cake of beeswax into bits
and rolled them in my hands until they softened—
710   no long task, for a burning heat came down
from Helios, lord of high noon. Going forward
I carried wax along the line, and laid it
thick on their ears. They tied me up, then, plumb

amidships, back to the mast, lashed to the mast,
715 and took themselves again to rowing. Soon,
as we came smartly within hailing distance,
the two Sirens, noting our fast ship
off their point, made ready, and they sang:

     This way, oh turn your bows,
720   *Achaea's glory,*
     As all the world allows—
       Moor and be merry,

     Sweet coupled airs we sing.
       No lonely seafarer
725   *Holds clear of entering*
       Our green mirror.

     Pleased by each purling note
       Like honey twining
     From her throat and my throat,
730   *Who lies a-pining?*

     Sea rovers here take joy
       Voyaging onward,
     As from our song of Troy
     Graybeard and rower-boy
735   *Goeth more learnèd.*

     All feats on that great field
       In the long warfare,
     Dark days the bright gods willed,
       Wounds you bore there,

740   *Argos' old soldiery[63]*
       On Troy beach teeming.
     Charmed out of time we see.
     No life on earth can be
       Hid from our dreaming.

745 The lovely voices in <u>ardor</u> appealing over the water
made me crave to listen, and I tried to say
'Untie me!' to the crew, jerking my brows;
but they bent steady to the oars. Then Perimedes
got to his feet, he and Eurylochus,
750 and passed more line about, to hold me still.
So all rowed on, until the Sirens
dropped under the sea rim, and their singing
dwindled away.

◆ *Literature and Your Life*

Do you think the Sirens' song is the same for every listener? What might the Sirens sing to a real or fictional person you know?

63. Argos' old soldiery: Soldiers from Argos, a city in ancient Greece.

◆ **Build Vocabulary**

ardor (är´ dər) *n.:* Passion; enthusiasm

My faithful company
rested on their oars now, peeling off
755   the wax that I had laid thick on their ears:
then set me free.

Scylla and Charybdis

But scarcely had that island
faded in blue air than I saw smoke
and white water, with sound of waves in tumult—
a sound the men heard, and it terrified them.
760   Oars flew from their hands; the blades went
      knocking
wild alongside till the ship lost way,
with no oar blades to drive her through the water.

Well, I walked up and down from bow to stern,
trying to put heart into them, standing over
765   every oarsman, saying gently,

'Friends,
have we never been in danger before this?
More fearsome, is it now, than when the Cyclops
penned us in his cave? What power he had!
Did I not keep my nerve, and use my wits
770   to find a way out for us?

Now I say
by hook or crook this peril too shall be
something that we remember.

Heads up, lads!
We must obey the orders as I give them.
Get the oar shafts in your hands, and lay back
775   hard on your benches; hit these breaking seas.
Zeus help us pull away before we founder.
You at the tiller, listen, and take in
all that I say—the rudders are your duty;
keep her out of the combers and the smoke;[64]
780   steer for that headland; watch the drift, or we
fetch up in the smother, and you drown us.'

That was all, and it brought them round to action.
But as I sent them on toward Scylla,[65] I
told them nothing, as they could do nothing.
785   They would have dropped their oars again, in panic,

◆ Reading Strategy
How would you
rewrite Odysseus'
pep talk in paragraph
form without poetic
line breaks?

64. **the combers** (kōm′
ers) **and the smoke:** The
large waves that break on
the beach and the ocean
spray.

65. **Scylla** (sil′ ə)

to roll for cover under the decking. Circe's
bidding against arms had slipped my mind,
so I tied on my cuirass[66] and took up
two heavy spears, then made my way along
790   to the foredeck—thinking to see her first from there,
the monster of the gray rock, harboring
torment for my friends. I strained my eyes
upon the cliffside veiled in cloud, but nowhere
could I catch sight of her.

                            And all this time,
795   in travail,[67] sobbing, gaining on the current,
we rowed into the strait—Scylla to port
and on our starboard beam Charybdis,[68] dire
gorge[69] of the salt-sea tide. By heaven! when she
vomited, all the sea was like a cauldron
800   seething over intense fire, when the mixture
suddenly heaves and rises.

                       The shot spume
soared to the landside heights, and fell like rain.

But when she swallowed the sea water down
we saw the funnel of the maelstrom,[70] heard
805   the rock bellowing all around, and dark
sand raged on the bottom far below.
My men all blanched against the gloom, our eyes
were fixed upon that yawning mouth in fear
of being devoured.

                      Then Scylla made her strike,
810   whisking six of my best men from the ship.
I happened to glance aft at ship and oarsmen
and caught sight of their arms and legs, dangling
high overhead. Voices came down to me
in anguish, calling my name for the last time.

815   A man surfcasting on a point of rock
for bass or mackerel, whipping his long rod
to drop the sinker and the bait far out,
will hook a fish and rip it from the surface
to dangle wriggling through the air:

                             so these
820   were borne aloft in spasms toward the cliff.
She ate them as they shrieked there, in her den,
in the dire grapple, reaching still for me—

66. **cuirass** (kwi ras′) *n.*:
Armor for the upper body.

67. **travail** (trav āl′) *n.*:
Very hard work.

68. **Charybdis** (ka rib′ dis)

69. **gorge** (gôrj) *n.*: Hungry,
consuming mouth.

70. **maelstrom** (māl′
strəm) *n.*: Large, violent
whirlpool.

and deathly pity ran me through
at that sight—far the worst I ever suffered,
825 questing the passes of the strange sea.

                              We rowed on.
The Rocks were now behind; Charybdis, too,
and Scylla dropped astern. . . .

The Cattle of the Sun God

In the small hours of the third watch, when stars
that shone out in the first dusk of evening
830 had gone down to their setting, a giant wind
blew from heaven, and clouds driven by Zeus
shrouded land and sea in a night of storm;
so, just as Dawn with fingertips of rose
touched the windy world, we dragged our ship
835 to cover in a grotto, a sea cave
where nymphs had chairs of rock and sanded floors.
I mustered all the crew and said:

                         'Old shipmates,
Our stores are in the ship's hold, food and drink;
the cattle here are not for our provision,
840 or we pay dearly for it.

                    Fierce the god is
who cherishes these heifers and these sheep:
Helios; and no man avoids his eye.'

To this my fighters nodded. Yes. But now
we had a month of onshore gales, blowing
845 day in, day out—south winds, or south by east.
As long as bread and good red wine remained
to keep the men up, and appease their craving,
they would not touch the cattle. But in the end,
when all the barley in the ship was gone,
850 hunger drove them to scour the wild shore
with angling hooks, for fishes and seafowl,
whatever fell into their hands; and lean days
wore their bellies thin.

                    The storms continued.
So one day I withdrew to the interior
855 to pray the gods in solitude, for hope
that one might show me some way of salvation.
Slipping away, I struck across the island

> ◆ Literary Focus
> The characteristics of
> an epic hero reflect
> the values of his or
> her culture. What
> does this passage tell
> you about ancient
> Greek values?

to a sheltered spot, out of the driving gale.
I washed my hands there, and made supplication
860   to the gods who own Olympus,[71] all the gods—
but they, for answer, only closed my eyes
under slow drops of sleep.

71. **Olympus** (ō lim′ pəs): Mount Olympus, home of the gods.

                              Now on the shore Eurylochus
made his <u>insidious</u> plea:

                    'Comrades,' he said,
You've gone through everything; listen to what I say.
865   All deaths are hateful to us, mortal wretches,
but famine is the most pitiful, the worst
end that a man can come to.

                              Will you fight it?
Come, we'll cut out the noblest of these cattle
for sacrifice to the gods who own the sky;
870   and once at home, in the old country of Ithaca,
if ever that day comes—
we'll build a costly temple and adorn it
with every beauty for the Lord of Noon.[72]
But if he flares up over his heifers lost,
875   wishing our ship destroyed, and if the gods
make cause with him, why, then I say: Better
open your lungs to a big sea once for all
than waste to skin and bones on a lonely island!'

72. **Lord of Noon:** Helios.

Thus Eurylochus: and they murmered 'Aye!'
880   trooping away at once to round up heifers.
Now, that day tranquil cattle with broad brows
were gazing near, and soon the men drew up
around their chosen beasts in ceremony.
They plucked the leaves that shone on a tall oak—
885   having no barley meal—to strew the victims,
performed the prayers and ritual, knifed the kine
and flayed each carcass, cutting thighbones free
to wrap in double folds of fat. These offerings,
with strips of meat, were laid upon the fire.
890   Then, as they had no wine, they made libation
with clear spring water, broiling the entrails first;
and when the bones were burnt and tripes shared,
they spitted the carved meat.
                              Just then my slumber
left me in a rush, my eyes opened,
895   and I went down the seaward path. No sooner
had I caught sight of our black hull, than savory

◆ **Build Vocabulary**

insidious (in sid′ ē əs) *adj.*: Characterized by craftiness and betrayal

odors of burnt fat eddied around me;
grief took hold of me, and I cried aloud:

'O Father Zeus and gods in bliss forever,
900   you made me sleep away this day of mischief!
O cruel drowsing, in the evil hour!
Here they sat, and a great work they contrived.'[73]

Lampetia[74] in her long gown meanwhile
had borne swift word to the Overlord of Noon:

905   'They have killed your kine.'

                       And the Lord Helios
burst into angry speech amid the immortals:

'O Father Zeus and gods in bliss forever,
punish Odysseus' men! So overweening,
now they have killed my peaceful kine, my joy
910   at morning when I climbed the sky of stars,
and evening, when I bore westward from heaven.
Restitution or penalty they shall pay—
and pay in full—or I go down forever
to light the dead men in the underworld.'

915   Then Zeus who drives the stormcloud made reply:

'Peace, Helios: shine on among the gods,
shine over mortals in the fields of grain.
Let me throw down one white-hot bolt, and make
splinters of their ship in the winedark sea.'
920   —Calypso later told me of this exchange,
as she declared that Hermes[75] had told her.
Well, when I reached the sea cave and the ship,
I faced each man, and had it out; but where
could any remedy be found? There was none.
925   The silken beeves[76] of Helios were dead.
The gods, moreover, made queer signs appear:
cowhides began to crawl, and beef, both raw
and roasted, lowed like kine upon the spits.
Now six full days my gallant crew could feast
930   upon the prime beef they had marked for slaughter
from Helios' herd; and Zeus, the son of Cronus,
added one fine morning.

                      All the gales
had ceased, blown out, and with an offshore breeze
we launched again, stepping the mast and sail,
935   to make for the open sea. Astern of us

73. contrived (kən trīvd´)
v.: Thought up; devised.

74. Lampetia (lam pē´
shə): A nymph.

75. Hermes (hʉr´ mēz):
The herald and messenger
of the gods.

76. beeves (bēvz) *n.*:
Plural of beef.

the island coastline faded, and no land
showed anywhere, but only sea and heaven,
when Zeus Cronion piled a thunderhead
above the ship, while gloom spread on the ocean.
940 We held our course, but briefly. Then the squall
struck whining from the west, with gale force, breaking
both forestays, and the mast came toppling aft
along the ship's length, so the running rigging
showered into the bilge.

                           On the afterdeck
945 the mast had hit the steersman a slant blow
bashing the skull in, knocking him overside,
as the brave soul fled the body, like a diver.
With crack on crack of thunder, Zeus let fly
a bolt against the ship, a direct hit,
950 so that she bucked, in reeking fumes of sulphur,
and all the men were flung into the sea.
They came up 'round the wreck, bobbing awhile
like petrels[77] on the waves.

                        No more seafaring
homeward for these, no sweet day of return;
955 the god had turned his face from them.

                           I clambered
fore and aft my hulk until a comber
split her, keel from ribs, and the big timber
floated free; the mast, too, broke away.
A backstay floated dangling from it, stout
960 rawhide rope, and I used this for lashing
mast and keel together. These I straddled,
riding the frightful storm.

                          Nor had I yet
seen the worst of it: for now the west wind
dropped, and a southeast gale came on—one more
965 twist of the knife—taking me north again,
straight for Charybdis. All that night I drifted,
and in the sunrise, sure enough, I lay
off Scylla[78] mountain and Charybdis deep.
There, as the whirlpool drank the tide, a billow
970 tossed me, and I sprang for the great fig tree,
catching on like a bat under a bough.
Nowhere had I to stand, no way of climbing,
the root and bole[79] being far below, and far
above my head the branches and their leaves,
975 massed, overshadowing Charybdis pool.

◆ *Literature and Your Life*
How do these eerie occurrences create a sense of anticipation in you as you read?

77. **petrels** (pet′ rəlz): Small, dark sea birds.

78. **Scylla** (sil′ ə)

79. **bole** (bōl) *n.*: Tree trunk.

Real and Imaginary Places in the Odyssey

ITALY
CORSICA
SARDINIA
AEAEA (Circe)
Sirens' Island
Scylla and Charybdis
Land of the Laestrygones
Aeolus' Island
SICILY
Cyclopes' Land
THRINACIA (Cattle of the Sun God)
TUNISIA
Land of the Lotus Eaters
OGYGIA (Calypso)
Strait of Gibraltar
Land of the Dead
Phaeácia
ITHACA
GREECE
Mt. Olympus
Sparta
CYTHERA
Cape Malea
CRETE
Ismarus (Cicones)
Troy
TURKEY
Mediterranean Sea

0   150   300 mi
0   150   300 km

▲ **Critical Viewing** The entrance to the Land of the Dead is believed to be the Strait of Gibraltar. Why might the ancient Greeks have considered this location frightening? **[Analyze]**

Beyond ◆ *Literature*

Geography Connection

Tracing Odysseus' Route Odysseus' journey carries him to real places, such as Troy and Sparta, as well as to fictitious places, such as Aeolia and Aeaea. In modern times, historians and explorers have tried to retrace the epic journey of Odysseus to determine the actual locations of the places with fictional names and thus to determine Odysseus' exact route. What follows is just one of many theories of the actual route of Odysseus: From Troy in present-day Turkey, Odysseus proceeded briefly northward and then southwestward on the Aegean Sea, passing between the Greek lands of Peloponnesus and Crete. Then, sailing westward on the Mediterranean Sea, Odysseus traveled near Sicily, where he found the Cyclops and where nearby islands were homes to the Lotus Eaters, the Sirens, and Aeolus, among others. After circling Sicily clockwise, Odysseus sailed northeastward and finally reached the Ionian Islands of Greece and his home, Ithaca.

Activity Choose either another piece of literature or a movie in which one or more characters take a journey. Draw a map of that journey.

The Odyssey, Part 1, Cattle of the Sun God ◆ 891

But I clung grimly, thinking my mast and keel
would come back to the surface when she spouted.
And ah! how long, with what desire, I waited!
till, at the twilight hour, when one who hears
980 and judges pleas in the marketplace all day
between contentious men, goes home to supper,
the long poles at last reared from the sea.

Now I let go with hands and feet, plunging
straight into the foam beside the timbers,
985 pulled astride, and rowed hard with my hands
to pass by Scylla. Never could I have passed her
had not the Father of gods and men,[80] this time,
kept me from her eyes. Once through the strait,
nine days I drifted in the open sea
990 before I made shore, buoyed up by the gods,
upon Ogygia[81] Isle. The dangerous nymph
Calypso lives and sings there, in her beauty,
and she received me, loved me.

                                        But why tell
the same tale that I told last night in hall
995 to you and to your lady? Those adventures
made a long evening, and I do not hold
with tiresome repetition of a story."

80. Father . . . men:
Zeus.

81. Ogygia (o jij´ ĭ a).

Guide for Responding

◆ Literature and Your Life

Reader's Response In your opinion, when does Odysseus act most heroically? Explain.
Thematic Focus What personal qualities are useful when it comes to working out problems and reaching goals?

☑ Check Your Comprehension

1. (a) What does Tiresias foretell? (b) What directions and warnings does he give?
2. What does Odysseus do to protect his men from the Sirens?
3. How does Eurylochus persuade Odysseus' men to slaughter and eat Helios' cattle?
4. What is Zeus' response to Helios' demand for revenge?

◆ Critical Thinking

INTERPRET
1. Compare and contrast the peril of the Sirens and the peril of the Lotus-Eaters. **[Compare and Contrast]**
2. Why do you think Odysseus chooses to sail toward Scylla rather than Charybdis? **[Analyze]**
3. In these adventures, how does Odysseus show himself to be an effective leader? **[Draw Conclusions]**
EVALUATE
4. Is Odysseus right to keep his decision to sail toward Scylla a secret from his men? Give reasons for your opinion. **[Make a Judgment]**
APPLY
5. What is the meaning of the saying "caught between Scylla and Charybdis"? **[Apply]**

Guide for Responding (continued)

◆ Reading Strategy

READ IN SENTENCES

Read the words of an epic **in complete sentences**, without worrying about line breaks.

1. Copy Odysseus' description of preparing to meet the Sirens on pp. 883–884 from the second part of line 704 through the first part of line 713 as a single paragraph. Read your paragraph aloud.
2. Rewrite the paragraph in your own words.

◆ Literary Focus

THE EPIC HERO

The **epic hero**—the central character of an epic—possesses qualities superior to those of most people yet remains recognizably human.

1. (a) How is Odysseus different from ordinary men? (b) How is he similar to ordinary men?
2. Do you admire Odysseus? Explain.

◆ Build Vocabulary

USING WORDS FROM MYTHS

The words that follow come from mythology. Use one word to complete each sentence.

a. museum   **b.** odyssey   **c.** *Titanic*   **d.** siren

1. Because the enormous ocean liner was thought to be unsinkable, it was named the _____?_____.
2. The treasures from ancient Troy were housed in a _____?_____.
3. The archaeologist's study of ancient ruins took her on an _____?_____ across Turkey and Greece.
4. Unlike its mythical namesake, a modern _____?_____ makes an unpleasant warning sound.

USING THE WORD BANK

Match each word with its opposite.

1. dispatch	**a.** restore to its owner
2. bereft	**b.** finish slowly
3. plunder	**c.** joyfully acquiring
4. squall	**d.** tiny
5. mammoth	**e.** small and weak
6. assuage	**f.** calm, sunny weather
7. insidious	**g.** honest
8. titanic	**h.** aggravate
9. ardor	**i.** lack of interest

◆ Build Grammar Skills

RESTRICTIVE AND NONRESTRICTIVE APPOSITIVES

Appositives add information about the nouns and pronouns in a sentence. A **restrictive appositive** is essential to the meaning of the sentence and is not set off by commas. A **nonrestrictive appositive** or appositive phrase provides nonessential information and is set off with commas.

Practice In your notebook, identify the appositives in these phrases from the *Odyssey* and tell whether each is restrictive or nonrestrictive.

1. Of these adventures, Muse, daughter of Zeus, tell us in our time, lift the great song again.
2. Sweet cousin ram, why lag behind the rest in the night cave?
3. We Cyclopes care not a whistle for your thundering Zeus . . .
4. . . . grant that Odysseus, raider of cities, never see his home: Laertes' son, I mean, who kept his hall on Ithaca.
5. . . . a burning heat came down from Helios, lord of high noon.

Idea Bank

Writing

1. **Letter** Imagine that you are a sailor aboard Odysseus' ship. Write a letter home, telling your family about your adventures.

2. **Comparison-and-Contrast Essay** Write an essay in which you explore the concept of the hero. In your essay, compare and contrast Odysseus with other heroes, real or imaginary.

Speaking and Listening

3. **Play-by-Play Broadcast** Select an exciting, action-filled incident from Part 1 of the *Odyssey*. Using the text and your imagination, describe the action as it unfolds. When you have worked out all the details, perform your broadcast for an audience. **[Performing Arts Link; Career Link]**

Guide for Reading

◆ Review and Anticipate

In Part I of the *Odyssey*, Odysseus and his companions face many perils on their voyage from Troy to Ithaca, including the hypnotic Lotus, a man-eating Cyclops, the Sirens, and the monsters Scylla and Charybdis. Odysseus journeys to the Land of the Dead to consult the prophet Tiresias and learns of still more challenges to come. Although warned by the prophet to leave the cattle of the sun god Helios alone, Odysseus' men fail to heed this advice and are killed when a lightning bolt hurled by the god Zeus destroys their ship.

The events you will read about in Part 2 of the *Odyssey* take place in Ithaca, Odysseus' homeland and the goal of all his travels. Predict what you think will happen when Odysseus arrives home.

◆ Literary Focus

Epic Simile

An **epic simile,** sometimes called a Homeric simile, is an elaborate comparison that may extend for a number of lines. Epic similes may use the words, *like* or *as, just as,* or *so* to make the comparison. In lines 268–271, Odysseus uses an epic simile to describe the fallen tree from which he will create the weapon to blind the Cyclops.

> And it was like a mast
> a lugger of twenty oars, brood in the beam—
> a deep-sea-going craft—might carry:
> so long, so big around, it seemed.

◆ Reading Strategy

Summarize

You can better understand what is going on in an epic like the *Odyssey*—or in any other work of literature with a complicated plot—if you first **summarize** the events. When you summarize, you retell the plot briefly in your own words. Ideally, your summary should tell not only what happened but why it happened. To assist you in summarizing Part 2 of the *Odyssey*, you may find it helpful to jot down some notes about important events and their causes as you read.

◆ Build Vocabulary

Word Roots: *-equi-*

A disguised Odysseus, speaking to his wife Penelope, tells her that her good name is like the honor of a just king "who rules in equity." The word *equity* means "fairness" or "justice" and contains the word root *-equi-*, which means "same" or "equal." Thus, a king who rules in equity treats all his subjects the same.

dissemble
lithe
incredulity
bemusing
glowering
equity
maudlin
contempt

Word Bank

Preview these words from the selection.

◆ Build Grammar Skills

Participial Phrases

A participle is a verb form that is used as an adjective to modify a noun or pronoun. A **participial phrase** is a phrase that consists of a participle and the words that work with it. The entire participial phrase then serves as an adjective to modify a noun or pronoun. Here are some examples of participial phrases from the *Odyssey*.

> past participle
> This was an army *trained to fight on horseback* ...

> present participle
> So, *breathing hard*, we waited until morning.

Homer

Translated by Robert Fitzgerald

Part 2
The Return of Odysseus

"Twenty years gone, and I am back again"

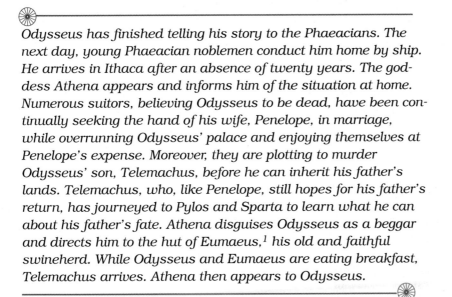

Odysseus has finished telling his story to the Phaeacians. The next day, young Phaeacian noblemen conduct him home by ship. He arrives in Ithaca after an absence of twenty years. The goddess Athena appears and informs him of the situation at home. Numerous suitors, believing Odysseus to be dead, have been continually seeking the hand of his wife, Penelope, in marriage, while overrunning Odysseus' palace and enjoying themselves at Penelope's expense. Moreover, they are plotting to murder Odysseus' son, Telemachus, before he can inherit his father's lands. Telemachus, who, like Penelope, still hopes for his father's return, has journeyed to Pylos and Sparta to learn what he can about his father's fate. Athena disguises Odysseus as a beggar and directs him to the hut of Eumaeus,[1] his old and faithful swineherd. While Odysseus and Eumaeus are eating breakfast, Telemachus arrives. Athena then appears to Odysseus.

1. **Eumaeus** (yo͞o mē´ əs)

    . . . . From the air
she walked, taking the form of a tall woman,
handsome and clever at her craft, and stood
1000 beyond the gate in plain sight of Odysseus,
unseen, though, by Telemachus, unguessed,
for not to everyone will gods appear.

Odysseus noticed her: so did the dogs,
who cowered whimpering away from her. She only
1005 nodded, signing to him with her brows,
a sign he recognized. Crossing the yard,
he passed out through the gate in the stockade
to face the goddess. There she said to him:

"Son of Laertes and the gods of old,
1010 Odysseus, master of landways and seaways,
<u>dissemble</u> to your son no longer now.
The time has come: tell him how you together
will bring doom on the suitors in the town.
I shall not be far distant then, for I
1015 myself desire battle."

                        Saying no more,
she tipped her golden wand upon the man,
making his cloak pure white, and the knit tunic
fresh around him. <u>Lithe</u> and young she made him,
ruddy with sun, his jawline clean, the beard
1020 no longer gray upon his chin. And she
withdrew when she had done.

                       Then Lord Odysseus
reappeared—and his son was thunderstruck.
Fear in his eyes, he looked down and away
as though it were a god, and whispered:

                       "Stranger,
1025 you are no longer what you were just now!
Your cloak is new; even your skin! You are
one of the gods who rule the sweep of heaven!
Be kind to us, we'll make you fair oblation[2]
and gifts of hammered gold. Have mercy on us!"

1030 The noble and enduring man replied:

"No god. Why take me for a god? No, no.
I am that father whom your boyhood lacked
and suffered pain for lack of. I am he."

Held back too long, the tears ran down his cheeks
1035 as he embraced his son.

                       Only Telemachus,
uncomprehending, wild
with <u>incredulity</u>, cried out:

2. **oblation** (ä blā´ shən) *n.*: Offering to a god.

◆ **Build Vocabulary**

dissemble (di sem´ bəl) *v.*: Conceal with false appearances; disguise

lithe (līth) *adj.*: Supple; limber

incredulity (in´ krə do͞o´ lə tē) *n.*: Inability to believe

Eumaeus, the Swineherd, N. C. Wyeth, Delaware Art Museum

◀ **Critical Viewing**
What can you tell about Eumaeus from this illustration? **[Infer]**

                                     "You cannot
be my father Odysseus! Meddling spirits
conceived this trick to twist the knife in me!
1040 No man of woman born could work these wonders
by his own craft, unless a god came into it
with ease to turn him young or old at will.
I swear you were in rags and old,
and here you stand like one of the immortals!"

1045 Odysseus brought his ranging mind to bear
and said:

◆ **Literature and Your Life**
How does Telemachus' reaction to his father compare with your own reaction to friends or relatives you haven't seen for a long time?

"This is not princely, to be swept
away by wonder at your father's presence.
No other Odysseus will ever come,
for he and I are one, the same; his bitter
1050   fortune and his wanderings are mine.
Twenty years gone, and I am back again
on my own island.

             As for my change of skin,
that is a charm Athena, Hope of Soldiers,
uses as she will; she has the knack
1055   to make me seem a beggar man sometimes
and sometimes young, with finer clothes about me.
It is no hard thing for the gods of heaven
to glorify a man or bring him low."

When he had spoken, down he sat.

                  Then, throwing
1060   his arms around this marvel of a father
Telemachus began to weep. Salt tears
rose from the wells of longing in both men,
and cries burst from both as keen and fluttering
as those of the great taloned hawk,
1065   whose nestlings farmers take before they fly.
So helplessly they cried, pouring out tears,
and might have gone on weeping so till sundown,
had not Telemachus said:

                "Dear father! Tell me
what kind of vessel put you here ashore
1070   on Ithaca? Your sailors, who were they?
I doubt you made it, walking on the sea!"

Then said Odysseus, who had borne the barren sea:

"Only plain truth shall I tell you, child.
Great seafarers, the Phaeacians, gave me passage
1075   as they give other wanderers. By night
over the open ocean, while I slept,
they brought me in their cutter,[3] set me down
on Ithaca, with gifts of bronze and gold
and stores of woven things. By the gods' will
1080   these lie all hidden in a cave. I came
to this wild place, directed by Athena,
so that we might lay plans to kill our enemies.
Count up the suitors for me, let me know
what men at arms are there, how many men.

◆ Literary Focus
What is being com-
pared in the epic
simile in lines
1063–1065?

3. **cutter** (kut´ər) *n.:*
Small, swift ship or boat.

1085 I must put all my mind to it, to see
if we two by ourselves can take them on
or if we should look round for help."

Telemachus

replied:

"O Father, all my life your fame
as a fighting man has echoed in my ears—
1090 your skill with weapons and the tricks of war—
but what you speak of is a staggering thing,
beyond imagining, for me. How can two men
do battle with a houseful in their prime?[4]
For I must tell you this is no affair
1095 of ten or even twice ten men, but scores,
throngs of them. You shall see, here and now.
The number from Dulichium alone
is fifty-two, picked men, with armorers,
a half dozen: twenty-four came from Same,
1100 twenty from Zacynthus; our own island
accounts for twelve, high-ranked, and their retainers,
Medon the crier, and the Master Harper,
besides a pair of handymen at feasts.
If we go in against all these
1105 I fear we pay in salt blood for your vengeance.
You must think hard if you would conjure up
the fighting strength to take us through."

Odysseus

who had endured the long war and the sea answered:

"I'll tell you now.
1110 Suppose Athena's arm is over us, and Zeus
her father's; must I rack my brains for more?"

Clearheaded Telemachus looked hard and said:

"Those two are great defenders, no one doubts it,
but throned in the serene clouds overhead;
1115 other affairs of men and gods they have
to rule over."

And the hero answered:
"Before long they will stand to right and left of us
in combat, in the shouting, when the test comes—
our nerve against the suitors' in my hall.
1120 Here is your part: at break of day tomorrow

4. in their prime: In the
best or most vigorous stage
of their lives.

home with you, go mingle with our princes.
The swineherd later on will take me down
the port-side trail—a beggar, by my looks,
hangdog and old. If they make fun of me
1125   in my own courtyard, let your ribs cage up
your springing heart, no matter what I suffer,
no matter if they pull me by the heels
or practice shots at me, to drive me out.
Look on, hold down your anger. You may even
1130   plead with them, by heaven! in gentle terms
to quit their horseplay—not that they will heed you,
rash as they are, facing their day of wrath.
Now fix the next step in your mind.

                                  Athena,
counseling me, will give me word, and I
1135   shall signal to you, nodding: at that point
round up all armor, lances, gear of war
left in our hall, and stow the lot away
back in the vaulted storeroom. When the suitors
miss those arms and question you, be soft
1140   in what you say: answer:

                         'I thought I'd move them
out of the smoke. They seemed no longer those
bright arms Odysseus left us years ago
when he went off to Troy. Here where the fire's
hot breath came, they had grown black and drear.
1145   One better reason, too, I had from Zeus:
suppose a brawl starts up when you are drunk,
you might be crazed and bloody one another,
and that would stain your feast, your courtship.
  Tempered
iron can magnetize a man.'

                              Say that
1150   But put aside two broadswords and two spears
for our own use, two oxhide shields nearby
when we go into action. Pallas Athena
and Zeus All-Provident will see you through,
bemusing our young friends.

                        Now one thing more.
1155   If son of mine you are and blood of mine,
let no one hear Odysseus is about.
Neither Laertes, nor the swineherd here,
nor any slave, nor even Penelope.
But you and I alone must learn how far
1160   the women are corrupted; we should know

◆ Reading Strategy
Summarize the
events of Odysseus'
reunion with
Telemachus.

how to locate good men among our hands,
the loyal and respectful, and the shirkers[5]
who take you lightly, as alone and young."

Argus

*Odysseus heads for town with Eumaeus. Outside the
palace, Odysseus' old dog, Argus, is lying at rest as his
long-absent master approaches.*

5. **shirkers** (shʉrk´ ərz)
n.: People who get out of
doing or leave undone
something that needs to be
done.

                                        While he spoke
an old hound, lying near, pricked up his ears
1165 and lifted up his muzzle. This was Argus,
trained as a puppy by Odysseus,
but never taken on a hunt before
his master sailed for Troy. The young men, afterward,
hunted wild goats with him, and hare, and deer,
1170 but he had grown old in his master's absence.
Treated as rubbish now, he lay at last
upon a mass of dung before the gates—
manure of mules and cows, piled there until
fieldhands could spread it on the king's estate.
1175 Abandoned there, and half destroyed with flies,
old Argus lay.

                        But when he knew he heard
Odysseus' voice nearby, he did his best
to wag his tail, nose down, with flattened ears,
having no strength to move nearer his master.
1180 And the man looked away,
wiping a salt tear from his cheek; but he
hid this from Eumaeus. Then he said:

"I marvel that they leave this hound to lie
here on the dung pile;
1185 he would have been a fine dog, from the look of him,
though I can't say as to his power and speed
when he was young. You find the same good build
in house dogs, table dogs landowners keep
all for style."

                        And you replied, Eumaeus:
1190 "A hunter owned him—but the man is dead
in some far place. If this old hound could show
the form he had when Lord Odysseus left him,
going to Troy, you'd see him swift and strong.

◆ **Build Vocabulary**

bemusing (bi myo͞o´ ziŋ)
adj.: Stupefying or muddling

He never shrank from any savage thing
1195 he'd brought to bay in the deep woods; on the scent
no other dog kept up with him. Now misery
has him in leash. His owner died abroad,
and here the women slaves will take no care of him.
You know how servants are: without a master
1200 they have no will to labor, or excel.
For Zeus who views the wide world takes away
half the manhood of a man, that day
he goes into captivity and slavery."

Eumaeus crossed the court and went straight forward
1205 into the megaron[6] among the suitors:
but death and darkness in that instant closed
the eyes of Argus, who had seen his master,
Odysseus, after twenty years.

The Suitors

Still disguised as a beggar, Odysseus enters his home.
He is confronted by the haughty[7] suitor Antinous.[8]

But here Antinous broke in, shouting:

                                        "God!

1210 What evil wind blew in this pest?
                            Get over,
stand in the passage! Nudge my table, will you?
Egyptian whips are sweet
to what you'll come to here, you nosing rat,
making your pitch to everyone!
1215 These men have bread to throw away on you
because it is not theirs. Who cares? Who spares
another's food, when he has more than plenty?"

With guile Odysseus drew away, then said:
"A pity that you have more looks than heart.
1220 You'd grudge a pinch of salt from your own larder
to your own handyman. You sit here, fat
on others' meats and cannot bring yourself
to rummage out a crust of bread for me!"

Then anger made Antinous' heart beat hard,
1225 and, glowering under his brows, he answered:

◆ *Literature*
and Your Life
Pet owners will
sometimes contend
that animals are
more perceptive
than people. How
does the story of
Argus support this
contention?

6. **megaron** (meg ə´ rön)
n.: Great, central hall of the
house, usually containing a
center hearth.

7. **haughty** (hôt´ ē) *adj.*:
Arrogant.
8. **Antinous** (an tin´ ō əs)

◆ **Build Vocabulary**
glowering (glou´ ər iŋ)
adj.: Staring with sullen
anger; scowling

"Now!
You think you'll shuffle off and get away
after that impudence?[9] Oh, no you don't!"

The stool he let fly hit the man's right shoulder
on the packed muscle under the shoulder blade—
1230 like solid rock, for all the effect one saw.
Odysseus only shook his head, containing
thoughts of bloody work, as he walked on,
then sat, and dropped his loaded bag again
upon the door sill. Facing the whole crowd
1235 he said, and eyed them all:

              "One word only,
my lords, and suitors of the famous queen.
One thing I have to say.
There is no pain, no burden for the heart
when blows come to a man, and he defending
1240 his own cattle—his own cows and lambs.
Here it was otherwise. Antinous
hit me for being driven on by hunger—
how many bitter seas men cross for hunger!
If beggars interest the gods, if there are Furies[10]
1245 pent in the dark to avenge a poor man's wrong, then may
Antinous meet his death before his wedding day!"

Then said Eupeithes' son, Antinous:

              "Enough.
Eat and be quiet where you are, or shamble elsewhere,
unless you want these lads to stop your mouth
1250 pulling you by the heels, or hands and feet,
over the whole floor, till your back is peeled!"

But now the rest were mortified, and someone
spoke from the crowd of young bucks to rebuke him:
"A poor show, that—hitting this famished tramp—
1255 bad business, if he happened to be a god.
You know they go in foreign guise, the gods do,
looking like strangers, turning up
in towns and settlements to keep an eye
on manners, good or bad."

              But at this notion
1260 Antinous only shrugged.

9. **impudence** (im´ pyoō dəns) n.: Quality of being shamelessly bold; disrespectful.

10. **Furies** (fyoōr´ ēz): Three terrible spirits who punish those whose crimes have not been avenged.

                                Telemachus,
after the blow his father bore, sat still
without a tear, though his heart felt the blow.
Slowly he shook his head from side to side,
containing murderous thoughts.
                               Penelope

1265   on the higher level of her room had heard
the blow, and knew who gave it. Now she murmured:

"Would god you could be hit yourself, Antinous—
hit by Apollo's bowshot!"

                       And Eurynome,[11]
her housekeeper, put in:

                    "He and no other?
1270   If all we pray for came to pass, not one
would live till dawn!"

                Her gentle mistress said:

"Oh, Nan, they are a bad lot; they intend
ruin for all of us; but Antinous
appears a blacker-hearted hound than any.
1275   Here is a poor man come, a wanderer,
driven by want to beg his bread, and everyone
in hall gave bits, to cram his bag—only
Antinous threw a stool, and banged his shoulder!"

So she described it, sitting in her chamber
1280   among her maids—while her true lord was eating.
Then she called in the forester and said:

"Go to that man on my behalf, Eumaeus,
and send him here, so I can greet and question him.
Abroad in the great world, he may have heard
1285   rumors about Odysseus—may have known him!"

11. **Eurynome:** (yo͞o rin´ əm ē)

Penelope

⊛————————————————————————⊛

In the evening. Penelope questions the old beggar about himself.

————————————————————⊛

"Friend, let me ask you first of all:
who are you, where do you come from, of what nation

and parents were you born?"

And he replied:
"My lady, never a man in the wide world

1290   should have a fault to find with you. Your name
has gone out under heaven like the sweet
honor of some god-fearing king, who rules
in equity over the strong: his black lands bear
both wheat and barley, fruit trees laden bright,
1295   new lambs at lambing time—and the deep sea
gives great hauls of fish by his good strategy,
so that his folk fare well.

O my dear lady,
this being so, let it suffice to ask me
of other matters—not my blood, my homeland.
1300   Do not enforce me to recall my pain.
My heart is sore; but I must not be found
sitting in tears here, in another's house:
it is not well forever to be grieving.
One of the maids might say—or you might think—
1305   I had got maudlin over cups of wine."

And Penelope replied:

"Stranger, my looks,
my face, my carriage,[12] were soon lost or faded
when the Achaeans crossed the sea to Troy,
Odysseus my lord among the rest.
1310   If he returned, if he were here to care for me,
I might be happily renowned!
But grief instead heaven sent me—years of pain.
Sons of the noblest families on the islands,
Dulichium, Same, wooded Zacynthus,[13]
1315   with native Ithacans, are here to court me,
against my wish; and they consume this house.
Can I give proper heed to guest or suppliant
or herald on the realm's affairs?

How could I?
wasted with longing for Odysseus, while here
1320   they press for marriage.

Ruses[14] served my turn
to draw the time out—first a close-grained web
I had the happy thought to set up weaving
on my big loom in hall. I said, that day:
'Young men—my suitors, now my lord is dead,

◆ Literary Focus
Identify the epic
simile in Odysseus'
response to Pene-
lope's question.

12. **carriage** (kar´ ij) *n.*:
Posture.

13. **Zacynthus** (za sin´
thus)

14. **Ruses** (rooz´ əz) *n.*:
Tricks.

◆ Build Vocabulary
equity (ek´ wit ē) *n.*: Fairness; impartiality; justice
maudlin (môd´ lin) *adj.*:
Tearfully or foolishly
sentimental

1325   let me finish my weaving before I marry,
       or else my thread will have been spun in vain.
       It is a shroud I weave for Lord Laertes
       when cold Death comes to lay him on his bier.
       The country wives would hold me in dishonor
1330   if he, with all his fortune, lay unshrouded.'
       I reached their hearts that way, and they agreed.
       So every day I wove on the great loom,
       but every night by torchlight I unwove it;
       and so for three years I deceived the Achaeans.
1335   But when the seasons brought a fourth year on,
       as long months waned, and the long days were spent,
       through impudent folly in the slinking maids
       they caught me—clamored up to me at night;
       I had no choice then but to finish it.
1340   And now, as matters stand at last,
       I have no strength left to evade a marriage,
       cannot find any further way; my parents
       urge it upon me, and my son
       will not stand by while they eat up his property.
1345   He comprehends it, being a man full-grown,
       able to oversee the kind of house
       Zeus would endow with honor.

                                    But you too

       confide in me, tell me your ancestry.
       You were not born of mythic oak or stone."

> ◆ Reading Strategy
> Summarize what Penelope tells the disguised Odysseus. How has she demonstrated her loyalty to her husband?

Penelope again asks the beggar to tell about himself. He makes up a tale in which Odysseus is mentioned and declares that Penelope's husband will soon be home.

1350   "You see, then, he is alive and well, and headed
       homeward now, no more to be abroad
       far from his island, his dear wife and son.
       Here is my sworn word for it. Witness this,
       god of the zenith, noblest of the gods,[15]
1355   and Lord Odysseus' hearthfire, now before me:
       I swear these things shall turn out as I say.
       Between this present dark and one day's ebb,
       after the wane, before the crescent moon,
       Odysseus will come."

15. **god of the zenith, noblest of the gods:** Zeus.

The Challenge

Pressed by the suitors to choose a husband from among them, Penelope says she will marry whoever can string Odysseus' bow and shoot an arrow through twelve axhandle sockets. The suitors try and fail. Still in disguise, Odysseus asks for a turn and gets it.

                    . . . And Odysseus took his time,
1360 turning the bow, tapping it, every inch,
      for borings that termites might have made
      while the master of the weapon was abroad.
      The suitors were now watching him, and some
      jested among themselves:

                              "A bow lover!"

1365 "Dealer in old bows!"

                        "Maybe he has one like it
      at home!"

            "Or has an itch to make one for himself."

      "See how he handles it, the sly old buzzard!"

      And one disdainful suitor added this:

      "May his fortune grow an inch for every inch he
          bends it!"
1370 But the man skilled in all ways of contending,
      satisfied by the great bow's look and heft,
      like a musician, like a harper, when
      with quiet hand upon his instrument
      he draws between his thumb and forefinger
1375 a sweet new string upon a peg: so effortlessly
      Odysseus in one motion strung the bow.
      Then slid his right hand down the cord and plucked it,
      so the taut gut vibrating hummed and sang
      a swallow's note.
                        In the hushed hall it smote the suitors
1380 and all their faces changed. Then Zeus thundered
      overhead, one loud crack for a sign.
      And Odysseus laughed within him that the son
      of crooked-minded Cronus had flung that omen down.

The Trial of the Bow, N. C. Wyeth, Delaware Art Museum

▲ **Critical Viewing** The winner of the archery contest will win Penelope's hand in marriage. How does the artist capture the tension in this scene? **[Interpret]**

He picked one ready arrow from his table
1385 where it lay bare: the rest were waiting still
in the quiver for the young men's turn to come.
He nocked[16] it, let it rest across the handgrip,
and drew the string and grooved butt of the arrow,
aiming from where he sat upon the stool.

                                        Now flashed
1390 arrow from twanging bow clean as a whistle
through every socket ring, and grazed not one,
to thud with heavy brazen head beyond.

                                        Then quietly

Odysseus said:

                        "Telemachus, the stranger
you welcomed in your hall has not disgraced you.
1395 I did not miss, neither did I take all day
stringing the bow. My hand and eye are sound,
not so contemptible as the young men say.
The hour has come to cook their lordships' mutton—
supper by daylight. Other amusements later,
1400 with song and harping that adorn a feast."

He dropped his eyes and nodded, and the prince
Telemachus, true son of King Odysseus,
belted his sword on, clapped hand to his spear,
and with a clink and glitter of keen bronze
1405 stood by his chair, in the forefront near his father.

16. **nocked:** Set an arrow against the bowstring.

Guide for Responding

◆ Literature and Your Life

Reader's Response How would you react if you were in Telemachus' or Penelope's place?

Thematic Focus How should Odysseus work to solve the problems caused by his long absence?

☑ Check Your Comprehension

1. How do Odysseus and Telemachus plan to handle Penelope's unwanted suitors?
2. What is Argus? What was he like in his youth?
3. Describe Antinous' treatment of Odysseus.
4. Describe the trick Penelope used to delay choosing a husband from among the suitors.

◆ Critical Thinking

INTERPRET
1. Compare Odysseus' emotions with Telemachus' when they are reunited. **[Compare and Contrast]**
2. Is Argus' death just when Odysseus returns a coincidence? Explain. **[Analyze]**
3. What impression of Penelope do you get from her conversation with the disguised Odysseus? **[Interpret]**

APPLY
4. Why do you think Odysseus chooses not to reveal his identity to his wife? **[Speculate]**

Odysseus' Revenge

Now shrugging off his rags the wiliest[17] fighter of the islands
leapt and stood on the broad doorsill, his own bow in his hand.
He poured out at his feet a rain of arrows from the quiver
and spoke to the crowd:

    "So much for that. Your clean-cut game is over.
1410 Now watch me hit a target that no man has hit before,
if I can make this shot. Help me, Apollo."
He drew to his fist the cruel head of an arrow for Antinous
just as the young man leaned to lift his beautiful drinking cup,
embossed, two-handled, golden: the cup was in his fingers:
1415 the wine was even at his lips: and did he dream of death?
How could he? In that revelry[18] amid his throng of friends
who would imagine a single foe—though a strong foe indeed—
could dare to bring death's pain on him and darkness on his eyes?
Odysseus' arrow hit him under the chin
1420 and punched up to the feathers through his throat.
Backward and down he went, letting the winecup fall
from his shocked hand. Like pipes his nostrils jetted
crimson runnels, a river of mortal red,
and one last kick upset his table
1425 knocking the bread and meat to soak in dusty blood.
Now as they craned to see their champion where he lay
the suitors jostled in uproar down the hall,
everyone on his feet. Wildly they turned and scanned
the walls in the long room for arms; but not a shield,
1430 not a good ashen spear was there for a man to take and throw.
All they could do was yell in outrage at Odysseus:
"Foul! to shoot at a man! That was your last shot!"
"Your own throat will be slit for this!"
      "Our finest lad is down!
You killed the best on Ithaca."
      "Buzzards will tear your eyes out!"
1435 For they imagined as they wished—that it was a wild shot,
an unintended killing—fools, not to comprehend
they were already in the grip of death.
But glaring under his brows Odysseus answered:

"You yellow dogs, you thought I'd never make it
1440 home from the land of Troy. You took my house to plunder.
. . . You dared
bid for my wife while I was still alive.
Contempt was all you had for the gods who rule wide heaven,
contempt for what men say of you hereafter.
Your last hour has come. You die in blood."

17. wiliest (wīl´ ə əst) *adj.*:
Most tricky.

18. revelry (rev´ əl rē) *n.*:
Boisterous festivity.

◆ **Reading Strategy**
Summarize Odysseus'
interactions with the
suitors to this point.
Why does he catch
them by surprise?
What do you think
will happen next?

◆ **Build Vocabulary**
contempt (kən tempt´) *n.*:
Actions or attitude of a
person toward someone
or something he or she
considers low or worthless

1445 As they all took this in, sickly green fear
pulled at their entrails, and their eyes flickered
looking for some hatch or hideaway from death.
Eurymachus[19] alone could speak. He said:

"If you are Odysseus of Ithaca come back,
1450 all that you say these men have done is true.
Rash actions, many here, more in the countryside.
But here he lies, the man who caused them all.
Antinous was the ringleader, he whipped us on
to do these things. He cared less for a marriage
1455 than for the power Cronion has denied him
as king of Ithaca. For that
he tried to trap your son and would have killed him.
He is dead now and has his portion. Spare
your own people. As for ourselves, we'll make
1460 restitution of wine and meat consumed,
and add, each one, a tithe of twenty oxen
with gifts of bronze and gold to warm your heart.
Meanwhile we cannot blame you for your anger."

Odysseus glowered under his black brows
1465 and said:

"Not for the whole treasure of your fathers,
all you enjoy, lands, flocks, or any gold
put up by others, would I hold my hand.
There will be killing till the score is paid.
You forced yourselves upon this house. Fight your way out,
1470 or run for it, if you think you'll escape death.
I doubt one man of you skins by."
They felt their knees fail, and their hearts—but heard
Eurymachus for the last time rallying them.

"Friends," he said, "the man is implacable.
1475 Now that he's got his hands on bow and quiver
he'll shoot from the big doorstone there
until he kills us to the last man.
                              Fight, I say,
let's remember the joy of it. Swords out!
Hold up your tables to deflect his arrows.
1480 After me, everyone: rush him where he stands.
If we can budge him from the door, if we can pass
into the town, we'll call out men to chase him.
This fellow with his bow will shoot no more."

He drew his own sword as he spoke, a broadsword of fine
  bronze,

19. **Eurymachus** (yoo ri´
mə kəs)

♦ Literature
and Your Life
What other "last
stands" from
movies and televi-
sion shows are
brought to mind
by Eurymachus'
brave but hollow
words?

1485   honed like a razor on either edge. Then crying hoarse and loud
he hurled himself at Odysseus. But the kingly man let fly
an arrow at that instant, and the quivering feathered butt
sprang to the nipple of his breast as the barb stuck in his liver.
The bright broadsword clanged down. He lurched and fell aside,
1490   pitching across his table. His cup, his bread and meat,
were spilt and scattered far and wide, and his head slammed
    on the ground.
Revulsion, anguish in his heart, with both feet kicking out,
he downed his chair, while the shrouding wave of mist closed on
    his eyes.

Amphinomus now came running at Odysseus,
1495   broadsword naked in his hand. He thought to make
the great soldier give way at the door.
But with a spear throw from behind Telemachus hit him
between the shoulders, and the lancehead drove
clear through his chest. He left his feet and fell
1500   forward, thudding, forehead against the ground.
Telemachus swerved around him, leaving the long dark spear
planted in Amphinomus. If he paused to yank it out
someone might jump him from behind or cut him down with a
    sword
at the moment he bent over. So he ran—ran from the tables
1505   to his father's side and halted, panting, saying:

"Father let me bring you a shield and spear,
a pair of spears, a helmet.
I can arm on the run myself; I'll give
outfits to Eumaeus and this cowherd.
1510   Better to have equipment."

                       Said Odysseus:

"Run then, while I hold them off with arrows
as long as the arrows last. When all are gone
if I'm alone they can dislodge me."

                       Quick
upon his father's word Telemachus
1515   ran to the room where spears and armor lay.
He caught up four light shields, four pairs of spears,
four helms of war high-plumed with flowing manes,
and ran back, loaded down, to his father's side.
He was the first to pull a helmet on
1520   and slide his bare arm in a buckler strap.
The servants armed themselves, and all three took their stand
beside the master of battle.

The Slaughter of the Suitors, N. C. Wyeth, Delaware Art Museum

◀ **Critical Viewing** Do you think the fight against the suitors was a "fair fight"? Why or why not? **[Make a Judgment; Support]**

       While he had arrows
he aimed and shot, and every shot brought down
one of his huddling enemies.
1525 But when all barbs had flown from the bowman's fist,
he leaned his bow in the bright entryway
beside the door, and armed: a four-ply shield
hard on his shoulder, and a crested helm,
horsetailed, nodding stormy upon his head,
1530 then took his tough and bronze-shod spears. . . .

*Aided by Athena, Odysseus, Telemachus, Eumaeus,
and another faithful herdsman kill all the suitors.*

And Odysseus looked around him, narrow eyed,
for any others who had lain hidden
while death's black fury passed.
       In blood and dust
he saw that crowd all fallen, many and many slain.

1535   Think of a catch that fishermen haul in to a half-moon bay
         in a fine-meshed net from the whitecaps of the sea:
         how all are poured out on the sand, in throes for the salt sea,
         twitching their cold lives away in Helios' fiery air:
         so lay the suitors heaped on one another.

Penelope's Test

*Penelope tests Odysseus to prove that he really is
her husband.*

◆ **Literary Focus**
How does the epic simile in lines 1535–1539 help you to picture the scene in your imagination?

1540   Greathearted Odysseus, home at last,
         was being bathed now by Eurynome
         and rubbed with golden oil, and clothed again
         in a fresh tunic and a cloak. Athena
         lent him beauty, head to foot. She made him
1545   taller, and massive, too, with crisping hair
         in curls like petals of wild hyacinth
         but all red-golden. Think of gold infused
         on silver by a craftsman, whose fine art
         Hephaestus[20] taught him, or Athena: one
1550   whose work moves to delight: just so she lavished
         beauty over Odysseus' head and shoulders.
         He sat then in the same chair by the pillar,
         facing his silent wife, and said:

                      "Strange woman,
         the immortals of Olympus made you hard,
1555   harder than any. Who else in the world
         would keep aloof as you do from her husband
         if he returned to her from years of trouble,
         cast on his own land in the twentieth year?

         Nurse, make up a bed for me to sleep on.
1560   Her heart is iron in her breast."

                      Penelope
         spoke to Odysseus now. She said:

                      "Strange man,
         if man you are . . . This is no pride on my part
         nor scorn for you—not even wonder, merely.
         I know so well how you—how he—appeared
1565   boarding the ship for Troy. But all the same . . .

         Make up his bed for him, Eurycleia.
         Place it outside the bedchamber my lord

20. Hephaestus (hi fes´ təs): God of fire and the forge and of metalworking.

built with his own hands. Pile the big bed
with fleeces, rugs, and sheets of purest linen."

1570 With this she tried him to the breaking point,
and he turned on her in a flash raging:
"Woman, by heaven you've stung me now!
Who dared to move my bed?
No builder had the skill for that—unless
1575 a god came down to turn the trick. No mortal
in his best days could budge it with a crowbar.
There is our pact and pledge, our secret sign,
built into that bed—my handiwork
and no one else's!
                                        An old trunk of olive
1580 grew like a pillar on the building plot,
and I laid out our bedroom round that tree,
lined up the stone walls, built the walls and roof,
gave it a doorway and smooth-fitting doors.
Then I lopped off the silvery leaves and branches,
1585 hewed and shaped that stump from the roots up
into a bedpost, drilled it, let it serve
as model for the rest. I planed them all,
inlaid them all with silver, gold and ivory,
and stretched a bed between—a pliant web
1590 of oxhide thongs dyed crimson.

                                    There's our sign!
I know no more. Could someone else's hand
have sawn that trunk and dragged the frame away?"

Their secret! as she heard it told, her knees
grew tremulous and weak, her heart failed her.
1595 With eyes brimming tears she ran to him,
throwing her arms around his neck, and kissed him,
murmuring:

                        "Do not rage at me, Odysseus!
No one ever matched your caution! Think
what difficulty the gods gave: they denied us
1600 life together in our prime and flowering years,
kept us from crossing into age together.
Forgive me, don't be angry. I could not
welcome you with love on sight! I armed myself
long ago against the frauds of men,
1605 impostors who might come—and all those many
whose underhanded ways bring evil on! . . .
But here and now, what sign could be so clear

Beyond Literature

Media Connection

Modern-Day Epics In film, the term *epic* applies to a movie of great scope and spectacle that features a heroic character who takes part in thrilling adventures. Lavish sets, enormous casts, and spectacular action—such as the parting of the Red Sea in the 1956 film *The Ten Commandments*—are hallmarks

Luke Skywalker, Princess Leia, and Han Solo in the epic film *Star Wars*.

of epic films. The advent of the wide screen in the 1950's ushered in a number of epics whose panoramic action was ideal for the new giant screens. Among those epics were *Ben Hur* (1959), *El Cid* (1961), *Cleopatra* (1963), and *Zulu* (1964). More recent epic films include *Roots* (1977), a chronicle of eighteenth- and nineteenth-century black life from enslavement to Reconstruction after the Civil War; *Star Wars* (1977), a depiction of adventures in a distant galaxy; and *Raiders of the Lost Ark* (1981), a film featuring the hair-raising adventures of Indiana Jones. What epic movies have you seen? What qualifies them to be called epic films?

as this of our own bed?
No other man has ever laid eyes on it—
1610   only my own slave, Actoris, that my father
sent with me as a gift—she kept our door.
You make my stiff heart know that I am yours."

Now from his breast into his eyes the ache
of longing mounted, and he wept at last,
1615   his dear wife, clear and faithful, in his arms,
longed for as the sunwarmed earth is longed for by a swimmer
spent in rough water where his ship went down
under Poseidon's blows, gale winds and tons of sea.
Few men can keep alive through a big surf
1620   to crawl, clotted with brine, on kindly beaches
in joy, in joy, knowing the abyss[21] behind:
and so she too rejoiced, her gaze upon her husband,
her white arms round him pressed as though forever.

◆ **Reading Strategy**
Summarize Penelope's test and Odysseus' reaction to what she says.

21. abyss (ə bis´) *n.*: Ocean depths.

The Ending

Odysseus is reunited with his father. Athena commands that peace prevail between Odysseus and the relatives of the slain suitors. Odysseus has regained his family and his kingdom.

Guide for Responding

◆ Literature and Your Life

Reader's Response Do you think Odysseus' revenge is justified? Why or why not?

Thematic Focus How do you think the problem of the suitors should have been handled?

Activity With a partner, role-play the exchange between Eurymachus and Odysseus.

☑ Check Your Comprehension

1. What is the suitors' reaction when Odysseus, still in disguise, takes up the bow?
2. Describe the immediate reaction of the suitors to the killing of Antinous.
3. How does Odysseus get revenge on the suitors?
4. What is Penelope's test, and how does Odysseus pass it?

Guide for Responding (continued)

◆ Critical Thinking

INTERPRET

1. What does Odysseus mean in "The Challenge" when he says, "The hour has come to cook their lordships' mutton—/supper by daylight"? **[Interpret]**
2. What are Odysseus' reasons for slaying all the suitors? **[Analyze]**
3. Since Odysseus has abandoned his disguise, why does Penelope still need to test him? **[Infer]**
4. Describe the mood of the scene at the end of "Penelope's Test." Is it altogether happy or does it include some sadness? Explain. **[Support]**

EVALUATE

5. Does Odysseus' success in the contest show that he is a skilled archer or merely that he has a god on his side? Support your answer. **[Assess]**

APPLY

6. Compare justice at the hands of Odysseus with justice in a modern society. **[Distinguish]**

◆ Reading Strategy

SUMMARIZE

Summarizing what you have read is a good way to check your understanding. It is also a useful skill when you need to demonstrate your knowledge on a test or when you want to share what you have learned with a friend.

1. List the main events in Part 2 in order.
2. For each event you listed, tell what caused it and what was the result of it.
3. Retell Part 2 of the *Odyssey* in a summary that explains why events occurred as they did.

◆ Literary Focus

EPIC SIMILE

An **epic simile** is a long, elaborate comparison between two dissimilar actions or objects. Many epic similes compare familiar objects and events with imaginative occurrences.

Identify three epic similes from Part 2 of the *Odyssey* and tell what two dissimilar objects or actions each one compares.

◆ Build Vocabulary

USING THE WORD ROOT -equi-

Keeping in mind that the word root -equi- means "equal," complete each sentence with one of these words.

  a. equinox   **b.** equivalent

1. Two nickels are _____?_____ to a dime.
2. At the _____?_____, the day and the night are of the same duration.

USING THE WORD BANK

Write the letter of the word or phrase that is the best synonym of the first word.

1. dissemble: (a) lie, (b) take apart, (c) disguise
2. lithe: (a) limber, (b) thin, (c) agile
3. incredulity: (a) disbelief, (b) naiveté, (c) anger
4. bemusing: (a) muddling, (b) entertaining, (c) allowing
5. glowering: (a) shining, (b) scowling, (c) laughing
6. equity: (a) fairness, (b) horses, (c) calmness
7. maudlin: (a) boring, (b) tired, (c) sentimental
8. contempt: (a) scorn, (b) pity, (c) pavillion

◆ Build Grammar Skills

PARTICIPIAL PHRASES

A **participial phrase** is a phrase that contains a participle and serves as an adjective to modify a noun or pronoun.

Practice Copy each excerpt below from Part 2 of the *Odyssey* in your notebook. Underline the participial phrase, identify the participle as *past* or *present*, and draw an arrow from the participial phrase to the noun or pronoun it modifies.

1. Crossing the yard, he passed out through the gate in the stockade to face the goddess.
2. Held back too long, the tears ran down his cheeks as he embraced his son.
3. Athena, counseling me, will give me word, and I shall signal to you, nodding . . .
4. Then anger made Antinous' heart beat hard, and, glowering under his brows, he answered . . .

Build Your Portfolio

Idea Bank

Writing

1. **Epic Simile** Describe an action by a hero—such as Odysseus or your favorite comic book superhero—using an epic simile to make the hero's action easy for your audience to imagine.

2. **Modern Heroic Poem** Write a narrative poem about a real-life modern-day hero.

3. **Literary Essay** Poet and critic W. H. Auden said: "Though it would be unfair to describe the Homeric hero as a mere puppet of the gods, his area of free choice and responsibility is pretty circumscribed. In the first place he is born, not made . . . so that though he does brave deeds, he cannot be called brave in our sense of the word because he never feels fear." Write an essay responding to this criticism.

Speaking and Listening

4. **Debate** Form two teams of two to four people each to debate the following issue: Should Odysseus be prosecuted for murder in the killing of Penelope's suitors?

5. **Oral Report** Odysseus is returning home from the Trojan War. Find out more about this conflict and, in an oral report, share your findings with the class. **[Social Studies Link]**

Projects

6. **Odyssey Map** Create a map that shows Odysseus' voyage. Calculate the actual straight-line distance from Troy to Ithaca. Based on your map, approximate how far Odysseus traveled. **[Social Studies Link; Math Link]**

7. **Board Game** Create a board game based on the *Odyssey*, decorating your board with scenes from the epic. **[Art Link]**

Writing Mini-Lesson

Letter Home

Imagine that Odysseus could have sent a letter home to Penelope and Telemachus. As Odysseus, write a letter home that vividly describes at least two of your adventures.

Writing Skills Focus: Sequence of Events

Your letters will be easier for your readers to understand if you pay attention to the **sequence of events**. Most of the time, you will want to recount events in chronological order—start off describing what happened first, then describe what happened next, and continue your narrative until you reach the final event.

Model

Dear Penelope and Telemachus,

   I hope this letter reaches you. Hermes promised he would deliver it. Anyway, it's been a busy week. First, I had to get past the Sirens. . . .

Prewriting Decide which adventures you will describe in your letter, then jot down the most important events on separate note cards, along with details about each event. Arrange the note cards in the proper order.

Drafting Using your prewriting notes as a guide, draft your letter in one sitting, without taking a break. Relate details about each adventure in chronological order. Don't worry that your draft isn't perfect. You can fix your letter in the revision stage.

Revising Read your letter aloud, noting where you need more details or where the order of events seems jumbled. Then revise your letter as needed. Make sure that participial phrases are close to the nouns and pronouns they modify so they do not seem to be modifying the wrong words.

Writing Process Workshop

Biographical Report

There are probably many people, living or deceased, who interest you greatly. They may fascinate you because of their unusual personalities or outstanding achievements. Perhaps you even feel they have influenced you as a person. Research and write a **biographical report** about an individual who interests you. In your report, describe the person's life, work, and the time in which he or she lived.

The following skill, introduced in this section's Writing Mini-Lesson, will help you write a biographical report about any individual.

Writing Skills Focus

▶ **Follow a sequence of events** in presenting your facts and details. Begin by describing the earliest significant events in the person's life. Then move on to describe the later significant events, all in the order in which they occurred in time. (See p. 918.)

In the following example, the writer practices the above skill by offering factual information about Homer's life in chronological order.

MODEL

Homer is thought to have been born somewhere between 1000 B.C. and 700 B.C., possibly in western Asia Minor. ① According to tradition, he was blind. He did not write his two great epics, the *Iliad* and the *Odyssey*, as a modern novelist writes a novel. Rather, he composed them orally by assembling a number of earlier and shorter narrative songs. ② He probably traveled around Greece reciting them on many occasions. ③ In later centuries, the two epics were the basis of Greek and Roman education. ④

① The writer begins with the earliest event: Homer's birth.

② The report continues by describing Homer's special method of writing.

③ The report tells what Homer did after composing his works.

④ The writer ends by telling what happened centuries later.

APPLYING LANGUAGE SKILLS: Using *Who* and *Whom*

When writing a biographical report, you'll find yourself frequently using pronouns. Make sure you use them correctly. Use *who* as the subject of a clause:

Homer is the person who wrote the Odyssey.

Use *whom* as the object in a clause:

Homer is a writer whom many critics praise.

Practice On your paper, complete each sentence using the correct word form.

1. Homer was a blind man (who, whom) told stories.
2. Do you know (who, whom) recorded his stories?
3. He was someone to (who, whom) scribes listened.
4. Odysseus is the hero of (who, whom) Homer speaks.

Writing Application As you draft your report, use *who* and *whom* correctly. Be sure to use *who* as a subject and *whom* as an object.

Writer's Solution Connection
Writing Lab

For additional support in gathering information for your report, use the instruction and activities in the Prewriting section of the tutorial on Research Writing.

Prewriting

Choose a Topic Think of a person from the past or present whom you admire or find interesting. You can also choose one of these topic ideas:

> ### Topic Ideas
> - Your favorite author
> - A famous political leader
> - A well-known artist
> - A famous scientist

Conduct Library Research List the information you need before going to the library. Take notes on what you learn.

Source	How to Find It
Nonfiction Books	Check library catalog, in card files or in electronic form
Newspapers and Magazines	Use indexes like *Readers' Guide to Periodical Literature*
Reference Works	Check library catalog for encyclopedias, atlases, and almanacs; some may be on CD-ROM

Organize Your Information Use an outline to help organize your ideas. Next to each Roman numeral, list your main points. Next to the capital letters, enter the topics you'll cover under each main point. Finally, list details about each topic next to the numbers.

> I. Homer's Life as a Storyteller
>   A. Creating the epics
>   1. Composing songs
>   B. Traveling throughout Greece

Drafting

Present Facts in Sequence As you draft your report, give information about the person's life in chronological order. Your first few sentences may be general statements about the person and why he or she is special. Afterward, begin presenting facts about the subject's early years.

End With a Summary At the end of your report, offer a brief summary of the person's accomplishments and his or her effects on you or on society in general. Although your report should be factual, your summary may offer your own theories or opinions about the person, based on facts you have already presented.

Revising

Use a Checklist The following checklist will help you revise:

▶ Have I followed the proper sequence for presenting my information?
  Read over your report. Make a timeline that lists the events you include. Does your timeline move in chronological order? If not, rearrange details as necessary.

▶ Have I included all of the key details of my subject's life?
  Your paper should present a complete picture of the person's life. Read over your work to see if there are any gaps. Then fill in these gaps by adding information. You may need to do some additional research to learn more about your subject.

▶ Will my paper capture the interest of my readers?
  Have a classmate read your paper and suggest ways that you can make it more interesting.

▶ Is all of the information in my report accurate?
  Ideally, you should be able to find each piece of information in your report in at least two sources. As you revise, take the time to verify any details that are found only in one source.

Publishing

▶ **Classroom** Share your biographical report with classmates by reading it aloud.

▶ **Library Book** Collect all class reports into a "Book of Biographies" to present to your school library.

▶ **Internet** Post your biographical report on the Internet.

APPLYING LANGUAGE SKILLS: Special Problems in Agreement

When a singular subject and a plural subject are joined by *or* or *nor*, the verb agrees with the closer subject.

Neither Homer nor his <u>critics</u> <u>have</u> left much information about him.

Neither Homer's critics nor <u>Homer</u> <u>has</u> left much information about him.

Practice On your paper, complete each sentence with the correct verb form.

1. Odysseus or his men (fare, fares) poorly.

2. Neither the poems nor the prose (is, are) accurate.

3. Homer's life or times (speak, speaks) for him.

Writing Application Review your draft and check your use of *or* or *nor* to join subjects. If the subject and verb do not agree, change the form of the verb.

Writer's Solution Connection
Writing Lab

For help revising your paper, use the Interactive Models provided in the Revising section of the tutorial on Research Writing.

Real-World Reading Skills Workshop

Strategies for Success

When you prepare a report, research is very important. You may find many books, magazines, and other materials that contain information on your topic. How do you know which resources contain the most useful information? Follow these guidelines for evaluating your sources.

Consider the Author The first thing to ask about a source is, Who wrote it? Is the author an expert on the subject? If you've never heard of the author, look for biographical information in the book.

Also note the company that published the book. Is it a reputable publisher? An older, larger publishing house may be more reliable than a newer, smaller company you don't know.

Consider the Date Look to see when a book was published. As a rule, books published more recently are more reliable than older books. A newer book may contain information that wasn't available previously. If it's a science book, it might correct misinformation that appeared in earlier books.

Compare Information Sometimes you find conflicting information in two different books—even in different encyclopedias. Check other sources to see what they say about the topic. In the end, let the majority opinion rule.

Apply the Strategy

Imagine you are doing research for a paper on nuclear fallout. Look at the sources available to you. Answer these questions:

1. Which would you prefer to use—the encyclopedia or the book of facts? Why?
2. Which of the two newspapers would you prefer to use? Why?
3. Which of the two books would you prefer to use? Why?
4. Of all the resources, which one do you consider most reliable? Why?

The World Book Encyclopedia, Volume N, © 1998

Dave's Book of Amazing Facts, by Dave Smith, © 1983

"New Studies on Nuclear Fallout," *The New York Times*, March 6, 1998

"Fallout," *Neighbor's Gazette*, May 9, 1999

Nuclear Fallout, by Dr. E. Baird, © 1998 by Prentice-Hall

✔ Here are other situations in which it is helpful to evaluate sources of information:
▶ Reading a political pamphlet
▶ Reading a newspaper editorial
▶ Investigating a rumor
▶ Reading a medical report

PART 2 *Responding to the Past*

The Fall of Troy **from *The Odysseus Suite*,** 1979, Romare Bearden, serigraph 18 x 24,
© Romare Bearden Foundation/Licensed by VAGA, New York, NY.

*G*uide for Reading

Edna St. Vincent Millay
(1892–1950)

Like many other American writers of her time, Millay is remembered for her artistic experimentation and her rebelliousness. She published several successful poetry collections, including *The Harp-Weaver, and Other Poems* (1923), which earned her a Pulitzer Prize.

Derek Walcott *(1930–   )*

Born on the Caribbean island of St. Lucia, this author writes poems that reflect the influence of his background. His work has won worldwide acclaim, and in 1992 he won the Nobel Prize for Literature. In addition to being a poet, Walcott is a successful playwright and director. "Prologue" and "Epilogue" are from his stage version of the *Odyssey*.

Margaret Atwood
(1939–   )

For almost forty years, this Canadian author has been writing about what it means to be a woman in a period of social change. Another of her central themes is the role of mythology in people's lives. These two concerns come together in "Siren Song," a startling new look at Homer's Sirens.

Constantine Cavafy
(1863–1933)

Considered the most important Greek poet of the first half of the twentieth century, Cavafy was born to Greek parents in Alexandria, Egypt. In "Ithaca," you can see his basic creative method—to use the world of Greek mythology to write poems that speak to today's reader.

◆ Build Vocabulary

SUFFIXES: *-esque*

In "Siren Song," one of the Sirens complains of having to look picturesque. You can easily determine the meaning of this word if you recognize that it is formed by adding the suffix *-esque,* meaning "like" or "having the quality of," to a familiar word—*picture*.

WORD BANK

As you read, you will encounter the words on this list. Each word is defined on the page where it first appears. Preview the list before you read.

beached
picturesque
tempests
amber
ebony
defrauded

◆ Build Grammar Skills

ADVERB CLAUSES

These poets sometimes show the relationships among ideas by using **adverb clauses,** which modify verbs, adjectives, and adverbs and show when, why, or under what conditions something happened. Adverb clauses may appear in the beginning, middle, or end of a sentence. Thus, they can be useful to poets who are trying to find just the right rhyme or rhythm for a line. Notice the placement of the adverb clause in this line from "An Ancient Gesture":

I thought, *as I wiped my eyes on the corner of my apron:* Penelope did this too.

An Ancient Gesture ◆ Siren Song
The Odyssey ◆ Ithaca

◆ *Literature and Your Life*

CONNECT YOUR EXPERIENCE
If you've ever listened to two people describe the same argument or the same traffic accident, you know that people can have very different perspectives of the same event. In these selections, four writers bring their own perspectives to the events in Homer's *Odyssey*.

Journal Writing Jot down each writer's reactions to the events and characters in the *Odyssey*.

THEMATIC FOCUS: LOOKING INWARD
As you read these selections, think about how the authors' own ideas and feelings shape each of their interpretations of Homer's *Odyssey*.

◆ Background for Understanding

HISTORY
"An Ancient Gesture" and "Siren Song" are both written by twentieth-century women whose perspectives on the role of women in society are very different from Homer's. For much of history in most cultures, women have had fewer legal rights and fewer educational and job opportunities than men. In fact, women in the United States didn't even have the right to vote until the passage of a constitutional amendment in 1920. Even after winning the right to vote, women didn't begin to gain better career and educational opportunities until the last few decades.

◆ Literary Focus

CONTEMPORARY INTERPRETATIONS
The characters and events of the *Odyssey* are timeless and universal in their interest and significance. They are so rich in meaning that every generation sees in them ideas and values relevant to the present. Hence, countless writers have mined the *Odyssey* for material to create original poems, plays, novels, and essays. Though these **contemporary interpretations** differ widely in purpose, theme, and artistic method, they usually have two features in common. They present persons, places, and events whose origins are in Homer's writings, but they use Homer's material in original ways to express contemporary thoughts, values, beliefs, and feelings.

◆ Reading Strategy

COMPARE AND CONTRAST
To fully understand a piece of writing based on an earlier work, it's important to **compare and contrast** the details, characters, and events in the updated work with those in the original. For example, when you read Margaret Atwood's poem "Siren Song," think about the way in which Atwood's portrayal of a Siren is similar to and different from Homer's portrayal. Once you've identified the similarities and differences, try to determine the reasons behind these similarities and differences. If, for instance, a writer has portrayed a character very differently from the way the character was portrayed originally, consider what the writer is trying to accomplish through the contrasting portrayal.

As you read, use a Venn diagram like this one to identify similarities and differences. Note differences in the outer sections of the two circles. Jot down similarities where the circles overlap.

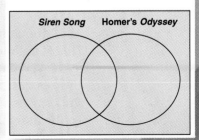

Siren Song   Homer's *Odyssey*

Penelope and The Suitors, 1912, J. M. Waterhouse, Aberdeen Art Gallery and Museum, Scotland

▲ **Critical Viewing** What is Penelope's attitude toward the suitors? How can you tell?
[Infer; Support]

An Ancient Gesture

Edna St. Vincent Millay

I thought, as I wiped my eyes on the corner of my apron:
Penelope did this too.
And more than once: you can't keep weaving all day
And undoing it all through the night;
5   Your arms get tired, and the back of your neck gets tight;
And along towards morning, when you think it will never be light,
And your husband has been gone, and you don't know where, for years,
Suddenly you burst into tears;
There is simply nothing else to do.

10   And I thought, as I wiped my eyes on the corner of my apron:
This is an ancient gesture, authentic, antique,
In the very best tradition, classic, Greek;
Ulysses did this too.
But only as a gesture,—a gesture which implied
15   To the assembled throng that he was much too moved to speak.
He learned it from Penelope . . .
Penelope, who really cried.

Siren Song

Margaret Atwood

This is the one song everyone
would like to learn: the song
that is irresistible:

the song that forces men
5   to leap overboard in squadrons
even though they see the <u>beached</u> skulls

the song nobody knows
because anyone who has heard it
is dead, and the others can't remember.

10   Shall I tell you the secret
and if I do, will you get me
out of this bird suit?[1]

I don't enjoy it here
squatting on this island
15   looking <u>picturesque</u> and mythical

with these two feathery maniacs,
I don't enjoy singing
this trio, fatal and valuable.

I will tell the secret to you,
20   to you, only to you.
Come closer. This song

is a cry for help: Help me!
Only you, only you can,
you are unique

25   at last. Alas
it is a boring song
but it works every time.

---

1. **bird suit:** Sirens are usually represented as half bird and half woman.

◆ Build Vocabulary

beached (bēcht) *adj.*: Washed up and lying on a beach

picturesque (pik´ chər esk´) *adj.*: Like or suggesting a picture

---

Guide for Responding

◆ *Literature and Your Life*

Reader's Response Do these poems make you feel more or less sympathetic to Penelope and the Sirens than the *Odyssey* did? Explain.

Thematic Focus How are these poets' perspectives different from Homer's?

Journal Writing Imagine that you are the speaker of "Siren Song." Write a journal entry about the encounter described in the poem.

✓ Check Your Comprehension

1. What similarity does the speaker of "An Ancient Gesture" see between herself and Penelope?
2. How does the speaker of "Siren Song" feel about being a Siren?

◆ Critical Thinking

INTERPRET

1. What is the "ancient gesture"? **[Infer]**
2. What difference between Penelope and Odysseus does the speaker point out? **[Compare and Contrast]**
3. To whom might the Siren in "Siren Song" be speaking? **[Infer]**
4. What is the speaker saying about some relationships between women and men? **[Draw Conclusions]**

EVALUATE

5. Do you agree with Millay's and Atwood's views of male/female relationships? **[Support]**

Prologue and Epilogue
from
The Odyssey

Derek Walcott

PROLOGUE

Sound of surf.

BILLY BLUE *(Sings)*
Gone sing 'bout that man because his stories please us,
Who saw trials and <u>tempests</u> for ten years after Troy.

I'm Blind Billy Blue, my main man's sea-smart Odysseus,
Who the God of the Sea drove crazy and tried to destroy.

5   Andra moi ennepe mousa polutropon hos mala polla . . .
The shuttle of the sea moves back and forth on this line,

All night, like the surf, she shuttles and doesn't fall
Asleep, then her rosy fingers at dawn unstitch the design.

When you hear this chord
(Chord)
10   Look for a swallow's wings,
A swallow arrowing seaward like a messenger

Passing smoke-blue islands, happy that the kings
Of Troy are going home and its ten years' siege is over.

So my blues drifts like smoke from the fire of that war,
15   Cause once Achilles was ashes, things sure fell apart.

Slow-striding Achilles, who put the hex on Hector
A swallow twitters in Troy. That's where we start.
(Exit.)

◆ **Build Vocabulary**

tempests (tem´ pists) *n.*: Violent storms with strong
winds

EPILOGUE

BILLY BLUE *(Sings)*
I sang of that man against whom the sea still rages,
Who escaped its terrors, that despair could not destroy,

20   Since that first blind singer, others will sing down the ages
Of the heart in its harbour, then long years after Troy, after Troy.

And a house, happy for good, from a swallow's omen,
Let the trees clap their hands, and the surf whisper amen.

For a rock, a rock, a rock, a rock-steady woman
25   Let the waves clap their hands and the surf whisper amen.

For that peace which, in their mercy, the gods allow men.
(Fade. Sound of surf.)

Guide for Responding

◆ *Literature and Your Life*

Reader's Response Is the narrator someone you would like to know? Explain.

Thematic Focus In what ways is this a contemporary perspective on the *Odyssey*?

☑ Check Your Comprehension

1. Who is the narrator?
2. According to the narrator, who is the main enemy of Odysseus?
3. Who is the "first blind singer" mentioned in the Epilogue?

◆ Critical Thinking

INTERPRET
1. Why does Billy Blue mention Achilles and Hector in the "Prologue"? **[Explain]**
2. What is the speaker's attitude toward Penelope? **[Infer]**
3. How faithful is this interpretation of the *Odyssey* to Homer? **[Associate]**

APPLY
4. Derek Walcott presents the Odysseus story in contemporary language. From your perspective, how is the story relevant to today's readers? **[Generalize]**

ITHACA

Constantine Cavafy

When you start on your journey to Ithaca,
then pray that the road is long,
full of adventure, full of knowledge.
Do not fear the Lestrygonians[1]
5 and the Cyclopes and the angry Poseidon.
You will never meet such as these on your path,
if your thoughts remain lofty, if a fine
emotion touches your body and your spirit.
You will never meet the Lestrygonians,
10 the Cyclopes and the fierce Poseidon,
if you do not carry them within your soul,
if your soul does not raise them up before you.

Then pray that the road is long.
That the summer mornings are many,
15 that you will enter ports seen for the first time
with such pleasure, with such joy!
Stop at Phoenician markets,
and purchase fine merchandise,
mother-of-pearl and corals, <u>amber</u> and <u>ebony</u>,
20 and pleasurable perfumes of all kinds,
buy as many pleasurable perfumes as you can;
visit hosts of Egyptian cities,
to learn and learn from those who have knowledge.

Always keep Ithaca fixed in your mind.
25 To arrive there is your ultimate goal.
But do not hurry the voyage at all.
It is better to let it last for long years;
and even to anchor at the isle when you are old,
rich with all that you have gained on the way,
30 not expecting that Ithaca will offer you riches.

Amphora with Grapes, Loran Speck, Loran Speck Art Gallery, Carmel, CA

▲ **Critical Viewing** The poet uses classical images from the *Odyssey*, like those pictured here, to make a connection to modern life. What experiences in *your* life could correspond to some of the classical images mentioned in the poem? **[Connect]**

---

1. Lestrygonians (les tri gō′ nē ənz): Cannibals who destroy all of Odysseus' ships except his own and kill the crews.

Ithaca has given you the beautiful voyage.
Without her you would never have taken the road.
But she has nothing more to give you.

And if you find her poor, Ithaca has not <u>defrauded</u> you.
35 With the great wisdom you have gained, with so much experience,
You must surely have understood by then what Ithaca means.

◆ Build Vocabulary

amber (am´ bər) *n.*: Yellowish resin used in jewelry

ebony (eb´ ə nē) *n.*: Hard, dark wood used for furniture

defrauded (di frôd´ əd) *v.*: Cheated

Guide for Responding

◆ *Literature and Your Life*

Reader's Response Does the journey to Ithaca as described in this poem appeal to you? Explain.

Thematic Focus Choose three or four words from the poem that symbolize the speaker's perspective on the journey to Ithaca.

☑ Check Your Comprehension

1. According to the speaker, how can you avoid meeting the Lestrygonians, the Cyclopes, and Poseidon on the road to Ithaca?
2. What two things should you pray for on the journey to Ithaca?
3. Why is Ithaca important?

◆ Critical Thinking

INTERPRET
1. What might the journey to Ithaca symbolize? **[Infer]**
2. What might Ithaca symbolize? **[Infer]**
3. In what way could a person carry the Lestrygonians, the Cyclopes, and the angry Poseidon in his or her own soul? **[Infer]**

APPLY
4. What do you think the speaker of this poem might have said to Odysseus if he could have advised him during his journey? **[Speculate]**

Guide for Responding (continued)

◆ Reading Strategy

COMPARE AND CONTRAST

As you read these poems, you were reminded of characters, events, or situations in Homer's *Odyssey*. **Comparing and contrasting**—seeing the likenesses and differences between—each poem and the *Odyssey* can not only add to your comprehension of the modern adaptations, but can also enhance your understanding of Homer's work.

1. What similarities do you see between Atwood's Siren and some contemporary women?
2. What does the speaker in Millay's poem imply about her life by comparing herself to Penelope?
3. Cavafy uses the journey to Ithaca as a metaphor— a comparison between two essentially unlike things. How is the journey he describes essentially different from the one Homer describes?

◆ Literary Focus

CONTEMPORARY INTERPRETATIONS

When modern writers **interpret** the *Odyssey* or some part of it creatively, they frequently use it to organize and express their own feelings, beliefs, and experiences. Atwood, for example, uses the Sirens to say something about women. Cavafy uses a basic plot thread of the *Odyssey*—the journey home of Odysseus—to say something about life and living. In the hands of these writers, Homer's subject matter takes on new meanings according to the special purpose of each artist.

1. What timeless theme does Edna St. Vincent Millay see in the *Odyssey*?
2. How does Margaret Atwood use similarities and differences between her Siren and Homer's to make a point about modern women?
3. How does Derek Walcott use language to bring Homer into the late twentieth century?
4. Why is Odysseus' journey home such excellent material for a literary work concerned with the course of human life?
5. What other literary works can you think of that are especially well suited for modern interpretations? Explain your answer.

◆ Build Vocabulary

USING THE SUFFIX -*esque*

Complete each sentence with one of the words containing the suffix -*esque*, meaning "like."

a. statuesque   **b.** arabesque   **c.** picturesque

1. The ____?____ mountain view lingered in my mind.
2. The carpet was covered in ____?____ designs resembling Moorish calligraphy.
3. The ____?____ actress commanded the attention of the audience by her regal bearing.

USING THE WORD BANK

On your paper, rewrite the paragraph, filling in the blanks with words from the Word Bank.

A ____?____ view could be seen from the rocky cliff that overlooked the entrance to the harbor. At dusk, tourists climbed the steep hills to watch an ____?____ sunset eventually fade to a deep ____?____ canopy dotted with twinkling stars. When ____?____ brewed, the sky turned a leaden gray. Afterwards, the townspeople would sometimes find a small boat ____?____ on the shore.

◆ Build Grammar Skills

ADVERB CLAUSES

An **adverb clause** is a subordinate clause that functions as an adverb, modifying a verb, adjective, or adverb in the main clause. These poets use adverb clauses to add important details to their poems.

Practice Identify the adverb clause in each sentence and tell what word it modifies.

1. When I read the *Odyssey*, I always dream of going on a long sea voyage.
2. I would sail first across the Pacific, because I would like to visit Hawaii.
3. If time permitted, I would spend time in Polynesia.
4. Unfortunately, this is probably not a realistic dream because I get seasick on all kinds of boats.

Writing Application Add details to each sentence by adding an adverb clause.

1. Odysseus left Troy with all his men.
2. The Cyclops might have destroyed their ship.
3. Penelope was besieged by suitors.

Build Your Portfolio

 ## Idea Bank

Writing

1. **Metaphor** Constantine Cavafy used Odysseus' journey to Ithaca as a metaphor for life. Come up with your own metaphor for life, and write a paragraph describing it.

2. **Comparison–and–Contrast Essay** Write an essay in which you compare and contrast one of the selections with the appropriate portion of Homer's original work. Support your points with passages from both selections.

3. **Adaptation** Follow the lead of these writers by creating your own adaptation of a section from the *Odyssey* in the form of a poem, a story, or a dramatic scene. You can either keep the original setting or use a more contemporary setting.

Speaking and Listening

4. **Monologue** Choose a character from the *Odyssey* and prepare a monologue modeled after "Siren Song." Show the character's innermost thoughts and feelings. Read your monologue aloud to the class. **[Performing Arts Link]**

5. **Choral Reading** Greek drama usually had a chorus that provided a commentary on events. With a group, prepare a choral reading of "Prologue" and "Epilogue." Rehearse several times so that you can read in unison. Then do your choral reading for the class. **[Performing Arts Link]**

Projects

6. **Illustration** Create a painting, collage, or drawing to illustrate one of these selections. Display your artwork for the class. **[Art Link]**

7. **Collection** Create a collection of literature inspired by the *Odyssey* or another famous work. Include an introduction to each piece.

 ## Writing Mini-Lesson

Now-and-Then Report

These poems remind readers that times have changed since the writing of the *Odyssey*—and so has Greece. Write a research report comparing ancient Greece and modern Greece. Of course, you won't be able to cover every aspect of life in Greece. Focus on just two or three—for example, government, the arts, or sports. Your report doesn't have to be all-encompassing, but the facts you do include should be accurate.

Writing Skills Focus: Accuracy

When you write a research report, it's essential that you make sure that your details are **accurate**—a true reflection of reality. To ensure accuracy, use as many sources as possible. Check each detail you find in another source. If a detail appears in two sources, you can generally be assured of its accuracy. Also, make sure that you are careful when recording the details you find. Do not change the meaning when you put the facts into your own words.

Prewriting Once you have chosen two or three areas to explore and have taken notes on note cards, make a comparison chart like this one and fill it in point by point.

Ancient Greece	Modern Greece
1.	
2.	

Drafting As you draft, use words that show points of comparison—*like, unlike, in contrast,* and so on.

Revising When you revise, make sure that your paper is clearly organized by points of comparison and contrast. Also, double-check your facts.

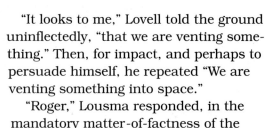

CONNECTIONS TO TODAY'S WORLD

In April 1970, the three-man crew of the *Apollo 13* spacecraft embarked on a modern-day odyssey to the moon. Like Odysseus, they set out with a spirit of anticipation and adventure. Their mission almost ended tragically, however, when an oxygen tank ruptured on board, but after several nerve-wracking days, the crew finally managed to return safely to Earth.

Jim Lovell, one of the astronauts on that flight, co-authored a book about this frightening adventure. The book, in turn, inspired a feature film. In this excerpt from the book, Lovell has just reported a gas leak to controllers on the ground.

From *APOLLO 13*

JIM LOVELL
AND
JEFFREY KLUGER

"It looks to me," Lovell told the ground uninflectedly, "that we are venting something." Then, for impact, and perhaps to persuade himself, he repeated "We are venting something into space."

"Roger," Lousma responded, in the mandatory matter-of-factness of the Capcom, "we copy your venting."

"It's a gas of some sort," Lovell said.

"Can you tell us anything about it? Where is it coming from?"

"It's coming out of window one right now, Jack," Lovell answered, offering only as much detail as his vantage point provided.

The understated report from the spacecraft tore through the control room like a bullet.

"Crew thinks they're venting something," Lousma said to the loop at large.

"I heard that," Kranz said.

"Copy that, Flight?" Lousma asked, just to be sure.

"Rog," Kranz assured him. "O.K. everybody, let's think of the kinds of things we'd be venting. GNC, you got anything that looks abnormal on your system?"

"Negative, Flight."

"How about you, EECOM? You see anything with the instrumentation you've got that could be venting?"

"That's affirmed, Flight," Liebergot said, thinking, of course, of oxygen tank two. If a tank of gas is suddenly reading empty and a cloud of gas is surrounding the spacecraft, it's a good bet the two are connected, especially if the whole mess had been preceded by a suspicious ship-shaking bang. "Let me look at the system as far as venting is concerned," Liebergot said to Flight.

"O.K., let's start scanning," Kranz agreed. "I assume you've called in your backup EECOM to see if we can get some brain power on this thing."

"We got one here."

"Rog."

The change on the loop and in the room

was palpable. No one said anything out loud, no one declared anything officially, but the controllers began to recognize that the *Apollo 13*, which had been launched in triumph just over two days earlier, might have just metamorphosed from a brilliant mission of exploration to one of simple survival.

1. In what ways is the flight of *Apollo 13* similar to the journey of Odysseus? In what ways is it different?

2. When the oxygen leak is detected, both the astronauts and the controllers try to think clearly and act calmly. How can keeping your head under pressure help you to achieve your goals?

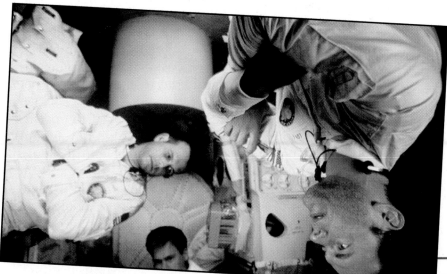

Writing Process Workshop

When you present factual information on a topic you've researched—such as the Trojan War or modern interpretations of the *Odyssey*—you're writing a **research paper**. A research paper usually includes an introduction that states the main idea of your topic; a body that offers information on all the subtopics in your report; and a conclusion that summarizes your main points. On each page, you cite the sources of your information in footnotes. You also include a bibliography at the end of the paper that lists all the sources you used.

Write a research paper on a topic that interests you. The following skill, introduced in this section's Writing Mini-Lesson, will help.

Writing Skills Focus

▶ **Be accurate** when researching and writing your paper. Make sure that you get your facts from reliable sources. Also be sure that you don't change the meaning of any information you rephrase in your own words. (See p. 933.)

In the following brief excerpt from a research paper, the writer uses the above skill when discussing modern interpretations of the *Odyssey*.

MODEL

① The writer clearly states her main idea.

② The writer offers details to support her main idea.

③ The names of the authors and their work are accurately recorded.

The characters and events in the *Odyssey* are timeless and universal in their interest and significance. ① They are so rich in meaning that every generation sees in them ideas and values relevant to the present. ② As a result, countless writers have mined the *Odyssey* for material to create original poems, plays, novels, and essays. Two such writers are Margaret Atwood, author of the poem "Siren Song," and Constantine Cavafy, author of the poem "Ithaca." ③ Though their interpretations differ widely in purpose and theme, they both use Homer's material in original ways to express contemporary thoughts, values, beliefs, and feelings.

Prewriting

Choose a Topic Pick a topic for your research paper by thinking of a subject that interests you. Your topic should also be one for which there is a good amount of information available. If you can't think of a topic on your own, consider one of the topic ideas listed here.

> ## Topic Ideas
> - An important historical event
> - A historic landmark
> - A famous scientific experiment
> - A highly regarded theory or philosophy

Find Accurate Sources In the library, locate the resources that will help you the most. These may include history books, newspapers, and magazines. Use the most up-to-date resources, because they may contain information not included in older materials. To further ensure accuracy, try to find the same facts or details in at least two different sources.

Use the Internet Use key words relating to your topic to search the Internet for additional information.

Take Accurate Notes Use note cards and source cards to record your information. Here are some tips:

Note Cards
- Enter only one piece of information on each card.
- Include the page number from which you obtained the information.
- Write a subhead at the top of each card telling on which aspect of your topic the note focuses.

Source Cards
- Create one source card for each source you use.
- List all the information you will need for crediting the source: author, title, publisher, date, and so on.

Drafting

Copy Your Notes Accurately Use your note cards to help you draft your research paper. Copy information accurately from each note card, double-checking to make sure you've rephrased all the information in your own words.

APPLYING LANGUAGE SKILLS: Citing Sources

When you quote a passage directly, **cite the source** in a footnote. Include the title of the work, the larger work it comes from, the city in which the publisher is located, the year of publication, and the page number of the quote.

Footnote:
1. Margaret Atwood, "Siren Song," You Are Happy (New York, 1974), p. 129.

Practice Identify the information that is missing in each footnote.
1. "Ithaca," (New York, 1976)
2. The World Book, Volume 4, p. 174.

Writing Application As you draft your paper, use a footnote at the bottom of the page to cite any passage on that page that you have quoted directly.

Writer's Solution Connection Writing Lab

For additional help in gathering information for your paper, use the instruction and activities in the Prewriting section of the tutorial on Research Writing.

APPLYING LANGUAGE SKILLS: Quotation Marks and Underlining

In a footnote, use **quotation marks** around the title of a poem, magazine article, or newspaper article. **Underline** or italicize the title of a book, magazine, or newspaper.

1. Constantine Cavafy, "Ithaca," The Complete Poems of Cavafy (New York, 1976), p. 59.

Practice On your paper, add quotation marks or underline where necessary.

1. E. Gray, The Hero Odysseus, Scholar's Magazine (Chicago, 1991), p. 32.
2. Colleges Drop Homer, The New York Times, May 3, 1988, p. B 7.

Writing Application As you review your research paper, check that you have written all footnotes correctly. Correct any errors you find.

Writer's Solution Connection Writing Lab

For additional help with revising, work through the Revision section of the tutorial on Research Writing. You'll find revision checkers for coherence and transitions that will help you improve your organizaiton.

Organize Your Ideas Begin with an introduction stating your thesis, the main point that you want to make about your topic. Follow with a series of body paragraphs, each focusing on a single subpoint and providing supporting details. End with a conclusion that drives home your main idea.

Quote Your Sources Accurately At some points in your paper, you will wish to quote a source directly. Be sure that you record those passages word for word. For each quotation, write a footnote that cites the author and source of the quote. List your source again in your bibliography.

Revising

Use a Checklist The following checklist will help you revise.

▶ Does my paper center around a thesis—a main point that I make about my topic?

Make sure that you've actually made a point about your topic, rather than just restating information you've gathered. For example, if you're writing a paper about Abraham Lincoln, you wouldn't simply state the facts of his life, you'd want to draw some conclusions about why he was a great leader.

▶ Have I accurately recorded my information?

Invite a peer to read your draft. If the reader questions the accuracy of any information, go back to your notes and check them. If you have copied something incorrectly, correct it.

▶ Have I accurately cited my sources of information?

Make sure that every passage that you haven't rephrased is marked with a footnote. If you have omitted a footnote, use your note cards to help you write one.

▶ Does my paper have a clear organization?

Read through your paper from start to finish, looking for any places where it seems to jump around or where one idea doesn't seem to flow logically from the previous one. Rearrange your ideas to make the organization clearer.

Publishing

▶ **Classroom** Share your research paper by presenting it to classmates as a special news report.

▶ **Audio Corner** Make an audiotape recording of your report. Create a classroom corner where classmates can listen to it.

Real-World Reading Skills Workshop

Strategies for Success

When you have access to the Internet, it's like having an entire library at your fingertips. The problem is that sometimes you can find so much information, it's hard to decide which is the most useful. How can you evaluate the information you find? Use these tips.

Don't Judge a Web Site by Its Appearance A Web site that looks slick and professional doesn't necessarily contain the most accurate information. Look past the flashy graphics to evaluate the information critically.

Try to Determine Why the Information Was Posted Sometimes companies and professional organizations post information that will promote their products, services, or philosophies. For example, a sneaker company will most likely promote their shoes as the best, without necessarily providing the facts about other brands. Look for objectivity in the information you uncover.

Verify the Information Elsewhere When evaluating any kind of information, try to verify facts in at least one, and preferably two, other sources.

Apply the Strategy

You can get more information about the reliability of a Web site by consulting a review guide that evaluates Web sites. Here are two you might want to try:

Argus Clearinghouse
http://www.clearinghouse.net/chhome.html

Mining Company
http://miningco.com

✔ Here are other situations in which sorting information on the Internet can be helpful:
- ▶ Learning about today's news
- ▶ Planning a vacation
- ▶ Finding want ads
- ▶ Locating a particular book

Speaking and Listening Workshop

Critically Viewing News Reports

Every day you encounter news reports on television, radio, and in the newspaper. Many of these reports offer an objective account of events, but it's not safe to assume that *every* news report is fair and accurate. Critically viewing news reports will help you to evaluate the information you learn through news media.

Know Your News There are different types of news reports. Straightforward "hard" news reports are meant to be objective. These reports address all sides of an issue. Feature stories offer a more personal, and therefore less objective look at a topic. A news feature may present only one side of an issue. Understanding which type of news you're viewing or listening to will help you be a more critical observer.

Listen to the Language Pay close attention to the language used in a news report. Listen for words that might sway the audience—that is, persuade viewers to think in a certain way.

> • *A roving pack of teenagers terrorized the mall today.*

> • *A group of teenagers overwhelmed the mall today.*

Which report sounds fairer to you?

Tips for Viewing News Reports Critically

✔ *If you want to be a good judge of a news report, consider these points as you listen:*
  ▶ *Who is reporting the news?*
  ▶ *Does the report address all sides of the issue?*
  ▶ *Is the language fair?*

Apply the Strategies

With a partner, perform each of these activities. Apply the strategies you have learned for critically viewing a news report.

1. Have your partner read you a news report from the newspaper. Listen carefully to analyze it for fairness. Stop your partner along the way to identify content that you question.

2. Tape a news broadcast from radio or television. Have your partner play the tape for you in class. When you hear content that you question, ask your partner to stop the tape, and then describe your concerns.

3. Have your partner write a news report on any topic, real or imaginary. As your partner reads the report to you, identify points at which you question the content.

After you and your partner have finished, switch roles and repeat each activity.

Extended Reading Opportunities

The world of the epic is the world of great heroes, classic struggles, and extraordinary deeds. Following are just a few possibilities for extending your exploration of the genre.

Suggested Titles

The Iliad
Homer

The *Iliad* is an epic poem that tells the story of the Trojan War. The fighting began after Paris, son of the king of Troy, ran off with the beautiful Helen, daughter of the god Zeus and wife of Menelaus of Sparta. The war between Troy and Greece dragged on for ten years and ended when the Greeks pretended to depart, leaving a giant wooden horse behind. The story of what lay waiting inside that horse, as well as many other thrilling events, has been engaging readers for centuries.

Mythology:
Timeless Tales
of Gods and Heroes
Edith Hamilton

This collection includes tales of the Greek and Roman gods and heroes, as well as the mythology of the Norse people. In it, Hamilton introduces Zeus and the other gods of Olympus and tells famous love stories, like that of Cupid and Psyche. In *Mythology*, readers also encounter thrilling tales of adventure, including Jason's perilous quest for the Golden Fleece, the epic story of the Trojan War, and the Norse legends of Signy and Sigurd.

Other Possibilities

The *Odyssey*   Homer
The Shining Company   Rosemary Sutcliff

Access Guide to Vocabulary

KEY TO PRONUNCIATION SYMBOLS USED

Symbol	Key Words	Symbol	Key Words
a	asp, fat, parrot	b	bed, fable, dub
ā	ape, date, play	d	dip, beadle, had
ä	ah, car, father	f	fall, after, off
e	elf, ten, berry	g	get, haggle, dog
ē	even, meet, money	h	he, head, hotel
i	is, hit, mirror	j	joy, agile, badge
ī	ice, bite, high	k	kill, tackle, bake
ō	open, tone, go	l	let, yellow, ball
ô	all, horn, law	m	met, camel, trim
o͞o	ooze, tool, crew	n	not, flannel, ton
o͝o	look, pull, moor	p	put, apple, tap
yo͞o	use, cute, few	r	red, port, dear
yo͝o	united, cure, globule	s	sell, castle, pass
oi	oil, point, toy	t	top, cattle, hat
ou	out, crowd, plow	v	vat, hovel, have
u	up, cut, color	w	will, always, swear
ʉr	urn, fur, deter	y	yet, onion, yard
ə	a in ago	z	zebra, dazzle, haze
	e in agent	ch	chin, catcher, arch
	i in sanity	sh	she, cushion, dash
	o in comply	th	thin, nothing, truth
	u in focus	th	then, father, lathe
ər	perhaps, murder	zh	azure, leisure
		ŋ	ring, anger, drink

abash, 795

acclaimed, 154

accosted, 6

acutely, 215

adept, 623

aerodynamics, 619

aesthetic, 604

afflicted, 6

aloofness, 573

amber, 931

ambiguities, 771

amicably, 168

anonymous, 310

arbitrary, 604

archaeologist, 113

archaic, 416

ardent, 478

ardor, 884

articulate, 239, 559

assuage, 878

astutely, 545

astuteness, 93

augmenting, 677

avail, 88

awry, 178

azure, 795

bafflement, 347

barren, 797

beached, 927

beguiling, 832

beleaguered, 437

bemusing, 901

benevolently, 229

bereft, 881

bizarre, 21

blandly, 25

blight, 432

bliss, 788

brazen, 239

buffet, 313

buffeted, 369

cannonading, 302

capacious, 387

cascade, 460

ceasing, 840

censure, 131

charged, 215

chasms, 445

chaste, 460

chattel, 129

chortled, 353

cipher, 131

circumvent, 398

cloister, 524

compelling, 623

complied, 144

concessions, 230

condescending, 593

condolence, 264

confer, 443

confounds, 415

console, 652

contempt, 910

conundrums, 93

covenant, 415, 445

creed, 141

cunning, 702

cur, 302

dallying, 171

déclassé, 537

decoy, 321

deferred, 796

defiance, 646

defrauded, 931

deity, 193

deleterious, 526

demure, 241

depravity, 347

depreciate, 460

derides, 621

derisive, 304

desolate, 832

despair, 189

despotic, 129

desultory, 528

determination, 145

detritus, 217

diffused, 560

disconsolately, 508

discreet, 463

disheveled, 540

dishevelment, 239

dismal, 752

dispatched, 868

disperse, 250

dissemble, 896

distraught, 301

diverged, 167

divine, 805

dogmas, 113

droll, 134

drowsiness, 840

ebony, 931

eddies, 560

eerie, 560

effervesce, 217

effigies, 250

eloquence, 727

elucidate, 216

encroaching, 471

endangered, 478

endeavoring, 365

endurance, 145

enigma, 591

enjoined, 750

entrails, 491

epiphany, 578

epithets, 250

equity, 905

erratic, 395

evanesced, 493

exalted, 141

exile, 726

explicit, 6

extrapolating, 562

extrapolation, 216

feint, 199

feline, 347

fester, 796

ideology, 445

iridescent, 489

monotone, 818

fetid, 506

imbued, 252

irradiated, 364

moribund, 433

fickle, 738

imminent, 489

jibed, 199

mortified, 189, 646

ford, 359

immortalized, 336

judicious, 528

muted, 560

forebears, 569

immutable, 595

keener, 246

myriad, 217

formality, 501

impassive, 506

kindred, 186

naive, 24

formidable, 93

imperative, 60, 180

laden, 272

novice, 560

fray, 725

imperialist, 113

lamentable, 708

oasis, 141

fretful, 67

impertinent, 371

languid, 284

obsessed, 604

furtive, 475

imperturbable, 395

languor, 264

obstinacy, 571

furtively, 60

implications, 588

larder, 347

omen, 371

futile, 27

impose, 6, 277

lassoed, 499

ominous, 170, 528, 560

gallant, 724

improbable, 621

lateral, 319

ominously, 366

garish, 50

improbably, 478

legacy, 591, 622

oppression, 141

gaunt, 133

inalienable, 445

legendary, 106

oracle, 395

genesis, 593

incognito, 310

levitation, 347

paean, 820

genteel, 645

incredulity, 896

lingered, 240

pagans, 524

glee, 787

indolently, 18

literally, 180

pallid, 504, 832

glowering, 902

indulged, 241

lithe, 896

pallor, 37

gossamer, 478

ineffable, 217

loathsome, 753

palpable, 17

grievance, 678

infallibility, 489

loitered, 365

palpitating, 817

grisly, 395

infrared, 387

longevity, 180

pandemonium, 154

grotesque, 25

ingeniously, 277

malevolence, 334

parched, 113

haggard, 301

insatiable, 369

malodorous, 229

parlance, 388

hamlet, 142

inscrutable, 304

mammoth, 872

pensive, 748, 788

harness, 171

insidious, 217, 888

manhandled, 144

penury, 762

harried, 239

insinuatingly, 302

marauders, 262

perennial, 428

harrowed, 543

insolent, 301

martial, 726

perish, 412

haughty, 766

instigates, 459

maudlin, 905

permeate, 577

heretics, 683

intent, 282

medley, 264

pernicious, 445, 677

hieroglyphics, 442

intercession, 706

menacing, 475

perpetuated, 252

hoax, 89

interpretation, 323

metaphors, 332

perplexed, 104

host, 787

interval, 9

metaphysical, 199

perplexes, 577

hurtling, 299

introspective, 92

meticulously, 168, 807

perverse, 239, 524

hydraulic, 619

intuition, 236

microcosms, 332

picturesque, 927

pilgrimage, 756

pinions, 442

pious, 571

placid, 47

placidly, 528

plaiting, 282

plundered, 860

poignant, 334, 588

portents, 153

postulated, 437

precariously, 491

precipitous, 262

precluded, 5

precursors, 387

predominant, 706

preposterous, 478

primed, 804

procure, 704

prodigious, 142, 526

prodigy, 229

profoundly, 540

projectiles, 351

pungent, 225

purged, 426

pursue, 621

pyre, 428

quaint, 830

rakishly, 299

rancor, 569, 595

ravages, 463

ravenous, 153

reciprocate, 476

recoiling, 9

reconcile, 115

reconciled, 193

reconnaissance, 63

recounted, 55

refrain, 359

remnants, 762

respite, 832

resplendent, 539

retort, 229

retribution, 5

revelry, 191

reverie, 238

riveting, 623

rueful, 537

ruminative, 623

sallow, 707

schism, 437

scourge, 774

scowling, 359

scruples, 24

sentimental, 593

sepulcher, 769

shard, 239

simultaneously, 385

singular, 84

sinister, 803

skeptical, 325

slouching, 131

sobriety, 177

sore, 795

specters, 170

spurn, 154

squall, 864

steeds, 416

stout, 283

strafing, 107

suavity, 349

subjugation, 115

submerged, 171

subsided, 9

subsidiary, 396

subtle, 560

succession, 9

succor, 267

suffice, 412

sullen, 56

surcease, 396

surge, 200

surpassed, 9

surreal, 559

tantalizing, 472

tempests, 928

termination, 9

thronging, 104

titanic, 876

transgression, 678

treble, 834

tremulous, 414

trundle, 310

tumult, 38

tumultuous, 587

unbidden, 802

unpalatable, 170

unrequited, 510

unwieldy, 714

valet, 312

vanquished, 504

venture, 180

vex, 93

vial, 749

vigorously, 9

vile, 153, 705

voluminously, 817

vortex, 489

warp, 249

waverer, 707

wavering, 191

wayfarers, 812

wayward, 750

woeful, 834

woes, 841

wreathed, 37

writhing, 37

wrought, 840

yearned, 321

LITERARY TERMS HANDBOOK

ACT *See* Drama.

ALLITERATION *Alliteration* is the repetition of initial consonant sounds. Writers use alliteration to give emphasis to words, to imitate sounds, and to create musical effects. Notice, in the following lines from Walter de la Mare's "The Listeners," how the s sound imitates a whisper:

> Ay, they heard his foot upon the stirrup,
>
> > And the sound of iron on stone,
>
> And how the silence surged softly backward,
>
> > When the plunging hoofs were gone.

Prose writers use alliteration too, but not as frequently as poets do. Jane Austen used the technique for the titles of her novels *Pride and Prejudice* and *Sense and Sensibility*. Notice, too, that alliteration is the basis of tongue twisters: She sells seashells by the seashore.

See Repetition.

ALLUSION An *allusion* is a reference to a well-known person, place, event, literary work, or work of art. In "The Gift of the Magi," on p. 459, O. Henry writes about a young couple and the Christmas gifts they give to each other. At the end of the story, the narrator explains the biblical allusion in the title: "The Magi, as you know, were wise men—wonderfully wise men—who brought gifts to the Babe in the manger. They invented the art of giving Christmas presents. Being wise, their gifts were no doubt wise ones. . . ."

ANECDOTE An *anecdote* is a brief story about an interesting, amusing, or strange event. Anecdotes are told to entertain or to make a point. In "A Lincoln Preface," on p. 129, Carl Sandburg tells anecdotes about Abraham Lincoln.

See Narrative.

ANTICLIMAX Like a climax, an *anticlimax* is the turning point in a story. However, an anticlimax is always a letdown. It's the point at which you learn that the story will not turn out the way you'd expected. In Thayer's "Casey at the Bat," the anticlimax occurs when Casey strikes out instead of hitting a game-winning run as everyone had expected.

ASIDE An *aside* is a short speech delivered by an actor in a play, expressing the character's thoughts. Traditionally, the aside is directed to the audience and is presumed to be inaudible to the other actors.

ASSONANCE *Assonance* is the repetition of vowel sounds followed by different consonants in two or more stressed syllables. Assonance is found in the phrase "weak and weary" in Edgar Allan Poe's "The Raven," on p. 832.

ATMOSPHERE *See* Mood.

AUTOBIOGRAPHY An *autobiography* is a form of nonfiction in which a person tells his or her own life story. An autobiography may tell about the person's whole life or only a part of it.

See Biography and Nonfiction.

BIOGRAPHY A *biography* is a form of nonfiction in which a writer tells the life story of another person. Biographies have been written about many famous people, historical and contemporary, but they can also be written about "ordinary" people.

A *biographical essay* is shorter than a biography. In "Georgia O'Keeffe," on p. 592, Joan Didion writes about the independent spirit of the famous painter.

See Autobiography and Nonfiction.

BLANK VERSE *Blank verse* is poetry written in unrhymed iambic pentameter lines. This verse form was widely used by Elizabethan dramatists like William Shakespeare.

See Meter.

CHARACTER A *character* is a person or an animal who takes part in the action of a literary work. The main character, or protagonist, is the most important character in a story. This character often changes in some important way as a result of the story's events. In Richard Connell's "The Most Dangerous Game," on p. 16, Rainsford is the main character and General Zaroff is the antagonist, or character who opposes the main character.

Characters are sometimes classified as round or flat, dynamic or static. A *round character* shows many different traits—faults as well as virtues. Walter Mitty, in James Thurber's "The Secret Life of Walter Mitty," on p. 299, is a round character. We know him not only as a

▲ Two of the most famous characters in literature are William Shakespeare's Romeo and Juliet.

mousy husband but also a man who has a means of escape: his fantasies. His wife is a *flat character*. We see her only as a shrew. A *dynamic character* develops and grows during the course of the story, as does Doodle's brother in "The Scarlet Ibis," on p. 484. A *static character* does not change. Walter Mitty, for example, is just as mousy and just as inclined to fantasize at the end of the story as he was at the beginning.

See Characterization and Motivation.

CHARACTERIZATION *Characterization* is the act of creating and developing a character. In *direct characterization*, the author directly states a character's traits. In "Uncle Marcos," for example, a character states that "Uncle Marcos's manners were those of a cannibal."

In *indirect characterization*, an author tells what a character looks like, does, and says, and how other characters react to him or her. It is up to the reader to draw conclusions about the character based on this indirect information. Toni Cade Bambara describes Granny Cain indirectly in the following

passages from her story, "Blues Ain't No Mockin Bird," on p. 498:

> "I don't know about the thing, the it, and the stuff," said Granny, still talkin with her eyebrows.

> Me and Cathy were waitin, too, cause Granny always got something to say. She teaches steady with no letup.

The most effective indirect characterizations usually result from showing characters acting or speaking. In Saki's "The Interlopers," on p. 262, two enemies lie trapped under a fallen tree. When one of them, Ulrich, suddenly offers a drink of wine to the other, the reader knows that Ulrich is beginning to change his mind about the old feud.

See Character.

CLIMAX The *climax* of a story, novel, or play is the high point of interest or suspense. The events that make up the rising action lead up to the climax. The events that make up the falling action follow the climax.

See Conflict, Plot, and Anticlimax.

CONFLICT A *conflict* is a struggle between opposing forces. Characters in conflict form the basis of stories, novels, and plays.

There are two kinds of conflict: external and internal. In an external conflict, the main character struggles against an outside force. This force may be another character, as in Richard Connell's "The Most Dangerous Game," on p. 16, in which Rainsford struggles with General Zaroff. The outside force could also be the standards or expectations of a group, such as the family prejudices that Romeo and Juliet struggle against. Their story, on p. 672, shows them in conflict with society. The outside force may be nature itself, a person-against-nature conflict. The two men trapped by a fallen tree in Saki's "The Interlopers," on p. 262, face such a conflict.

An *internal conflict* involves a character in conflict with himself or herself. An example is "Checkouts," on p. 236, in which two young people who meet by chance in a supermarket agonize over whether they should speak to each other.

A story may have more than one conflict. In addition to the person-against-nature conflict of "The Interlopers," there are also a person-against-nature conflict between the two men and an internal conflict for the main character, who must decide whether he should forgive his enemy.

See Plot.

CONNOTATION The *connotation* of a word is the set of ideas associated with it in addition to its explicit meaning. Paul Laurence Dunbar, in his poem "Sympathy," on p. 246, does not speak of a canary or a parakeet, both of which suggest pets and thus have positive connotations. Instead, he speaks of a "caged bird," which connotes a sad, trapped creature. The connotation of a word can be personal, based on individual experiences, but more often, cultural connotations—those recognizable by most people in a group—determine a writer's word choices.

See Denotation.

COUPLET A *couplet* is a pair of rhyming lines, usually of the same length and meter. A couplet generally expresses a single idea. In the following couplet from a poem by William Shakespeare, the speaker comforts himself with the thought of his love:

> For thy sweet love remember'd such wealth brings
>
> That then I scorn to change my state with kings.

See Stanza.

DENOTATION The *denotation* of a word is its dictionary meaning, independent of other associations that the word may have. The denotation of the word *lake*, for example, is an inland body of water. "Vacation spot" and "place where the fishing is good" are connotations of the word *lake*.

See Connotation.

DENOUEMENT See Plot.

DESCRIPTION A *description* is a portrait in words of a person, place, or object. Descriptive writing uses sensory details, those that appeal to the senses: sight, hearing, taste, smell, and touch. Description can be found in all types of writing. Rudolfo Anaya's essay, "A Celebration of Grandfathers," on p. 576, contains descriptive passages.

DEVELOPMENT See Plot.

DIALECT *Dialect* is the form of language spoken by people in a particular region or group. Pronunciation, vocabulary, and sentence structure are affected by dialect. In "The Invalid's Story," on p. 526, Mark Twain uses dialect:

> "Friends of *yourn*?"
>
> "Yes," I said with a sigh.

> "He's pretty ripe, *ain't* he!"

DIALOGUE A *dialogue* is a conversation between characters. It is used to reveal character and to advance action. In a story or novel, quotation marks are generally used to indicate a speaker's exact words. A new paragraph usually indicates a change of speaker. Look at an example from "The Scarlet Ibis" on p. 484. The narrator is a boy who is urging his frail younger brother, Doodle, to stand up and walk fast.

> "Aw, come on Doodle," I urged. "You can do it. Do you want to be different from everybody else when you start school?"
>
> "Does it make any difference?"
>
> "It certainly does," I said. "Now come on," and I helped him up.

A drama, of course, depends entirely on dialogue and actions. Quotation marks are not used in the *script*, which is the printed version of a play. Instead, the dialogue follows the name of the speaker. Here is an example from *The Dancers,* on p. 640.

HORACE. Miss . . .

WAITRESS. Yes?

HORACE. How much do I owe you?

WAITRESS. Twenty cents.

HORACE. Thank you.

He reaches in his pockets for the money.

DICTION *Diction* is word choice. To discuss a writer's diction is to consider the vocabulary used, the appropriateness of the words, and the vividness of the language. Both the *denotation,* or literal meaning, and the *connotation,* or associations, of words contribute to the overall effect. Diction can be formal, as in this excerpt from O. Henry's "The Gift of the Magi," which begins on p. 459:

> In the vestibule below was a letter-box into which no letter would go, and an electric button from which no mortal finger could coax a ring. Also appearing thereunto was a card bearing the name "Mr. Charles Dillingham Young."

Diction can also be informal and conversational, as in these lines from Ernest Lawrence Thayer's "Casey at the Bat," on p. 36:

> It looked extremely rocky for the Mudville nine that day;

The score stood two to four, with but an inning
left to play.

So, when Cooney died at second, and Burrows
did the same,

A pallor wreathed the features of the patrons of
the game.

See Connotation and Denotation.

DIRECT CHARACTERIZATION *See*
Characterization.

DRAMA
A *drama* is a story written to be performed by actors. The script of a drama is made up of
dialogue—the words the actors say—and stage directions, which are comments on how and where action
happens.

The drama's *setting* is the place where the action
occurs. It is indicated by one or more sets that suggest
interior or exterior scenes. *Props* are objects, such as a
sword or a cup of tea, that are used onstage.

At the beginning of most plays, a brief exposition
gives the audience some background information
about the characters and the situation. Just as in a
story or novel, the plot of a drama is built around characters in conflict.

Dramas are divided into large units called *acts* and
into smaller units called *scenes*. A long play may include
many sets that change with the scenes, or it may indicate a change of scene with lighting.

See Genre, Stage Directions, and Tragedy.

DRAMATIC IRONY *See* Irony.

DRAMATIC MONOLOGUE *See* Dramatic
Poetry.

DRAMATIC POETRY
Dramatic poetry is poetry
that utilizes the techniques of drama. The dialogue used
in Edgar Allan Poe's "The Raven," on p. 832, makes it
dramatic dialogue. A dramatic monologue is a poem
spoken by one person.

END RHYME *See* Rhyme.

EPIC
An *epic* is a long narrative poem about the
deeds of gods or heroes. Homer's the *Odyssey*, on
p. 860, is an example of epic poetry. It tells the story
of the Greek hero Odysseus, the king of Ithaca.

▲ One of the world's best-known epics is
Homer's *Odyssey*, which describes the perilous
journey homeward of Odysseus following the
Trojan War.

An epic is elevated in style and usually follows certain patterns. The poet begins by announcing the subject and asking a Muse, one of the nine goddesses of
the arts, literature, and sciences, to help. Early on, the
poet asks an epic question. The epic itself is the answer.
Odysseus asks,

> Where shall a man find sweetness to surpass
> his own home and his parents? In far lands
> he shall not, though he find a house of gold.
> What of my sailing, then, from Troy?

> What of those years of rough adventure, weathered
> under Zeus?

See Epic Simile and Narrative Poem.

EPIC SIMILE
An *epic simile*, also called *Homeric
simile*, is an elaborate comparison of unlike subjects. In
this example from the *Odyssey*, on p. 860, Homer compares the bodies of men killed by Odysseus to a fisherman's catch heaped up on the shore:

Think of a catch that fishermen haul in to a
 half-moon bay

in a fine-meshed net from the whitecaps of the sea:

how all are poured out on the sand, in throes
 for the salt sea,

twitching their cold lives away in Helios' fiery air:

so lay the suitors heaped on one another.

See Figurative Language and Simile.

ESSAY   An *essay* is a short nonfiction work about a
particular subject. While classification is difficult, four
types of essays are sometimes identified. A descriptive
essay seeks to convey an impression about a person,
place, or object. In "A Celebration of Grandfathers," on
p. 576, Rudolfo Anaya describes the cultural values that
his grandfather and other "old ones" from his childhood
passed down.

A *narrative essay* tells a true story. In "The Washwoman," I. B. Singer tells of his childhood in Poland, and
the hardworking woman who washed the family
clothes.

An *expository essay* gives information, discusses ideas,
or explains a process. In "Single Room, Earth View," on
p. 559, Sally Ride describes what it's like to be in outer
space.

A *persuasive essay* tries to convince readers to do

▲ In her essay "Single Room, Earth View," astronaut Sally Ride describes her observations of
Earth from the space shuttle.

something or to accept the writer's point of view. In
the essay, "To the Residents of 2029," on p. 434, Bryan
Woolley advises future generations on how to avoid
calamities.

A *visual essay* is an exploration of a topic that conveys its ideas through visual elements as well as language. Like a standard essay, a visual essay presents an
author's views of a single topic. Unlike other essays,
however, much of the meaning in a visual essay is conveyed through illustrations or photographs.

This classification of essays is loose at best. Most
essays contain passages that could be classified differently from the essay as a whole. For example, a
descriptive passage may be found in a narrative essay,
or a factual, expository section may be used to support
a persuasive argument.

See Description, Exposition, Genre, Narration, Nonfiction, and Persuasion.

EXPOSITION   *Exposition* is writing or speech that
explains a process or presents information. In the plot
of a story or drama, the exposition is the part of the
work that introduces the characters, the setting, and
the basic situation.

EXTENDED METAPHOR In an *extended metaphor*, as in regular metaphor, a subject is spoken or written of as though it were something else. However, extended metaphor differs from regular metaphor in that several comparisons are made. All extended metaphor sustains the comparison for several lines or for an entire poem. The "caged bird" of Paul Laurence Dunbar's "Sympathy," on p. 246, is an extended metaphor for a person who is not free.

See Figurative Language and Metaphor.

FALLING ACTION See Plot.

FANTASY A *fantasy* is highly imaginative writing that contains elements not found in real life. Examples of fantasy include stories that involve supernatural elements, stories that resemble fairy tales, and stories that deal with imaginary places and creatures, such as Ray Bradbury's "The Golden Kite, the Silver Wind," on p. 152.

Some writers consider science fiction a type of fantasy. Other writers make a distinction between the two kinds of writing.

See Science Fiction.

FICTION *Fiction* is prose writing that tells about imaginary characters and events. The term is usually used for novels and short stories, but it also applies to dramas and narrative poetry. Some writers rely on their imaginations alone to create their works of fiction. Others base their fiction on actual events and people, to which they add invented characters, dialogue, and plot situations.

See Genre, Narrative, and Nonfiction.

FIGURATIVE LANGUAGE *Figurative language* is writing or speech not meant to be interpreted literally.

Figurative language is often used to create vivid impressions by setting up comparisons between dissimilar things.

Though figures of speech are especially important in poetry, they are used in prose as well. Look, for example, at this description from James Hurst's "The Scarlet Ibis," on p. 484:

> . . . the oriole nest in the elm was untenanted and rocked back and forth like an empty cradle. The last graveyard flowers were blooming, and their smell drifted across the cotton field and through every room of our house, speaking softly the names of our dead.

Some frequently used figures of speech are *metaphors*, *similes*, and *personifications*.

See Literal Language.

FOOT See Meter.

FORESHADOWING *Foreshadowing* is the use in a literary work of clues that suggest events that have yet to occur. Use of this technique helps to create suspense, keeping readers wondering and speculating about what will happen next.

See Suspense.

FREE VERSE *Free verse* is poetry not written in a regular rhythmical pattern, or meter. Free verse seeks to capture the rhythms of speech. It is the dominant form of contemporary poetry.

See Meter.

GENRE A *genre* is a category or type of literature. Literature is commonly divided into three major genres: poetry, prose, and drama. Each major genre is in turn divided into smaller genres, as follows:

1. Poetry: Lyric Poetry, Concrete Poetry, Dramatic Poetry, Narrative Poetry, and Epic Poetry

2. Prose: Fiction (Novels and Short Stories) and Nonfiction (Biography, Autobiography, Letters, Essays, and Reports)

3. Drama: Serious Drama and Tragedy, Comic Drama, Melodrama, and Farce

See Drama, Poetry, and Prose.

HAIKU The *haiku* is a three-line verse form. The first and third lines of a haiku each have five syllables. The second line has seven syllables. A haiku seeks to convey a single vivid emotion by means of images from nature. The poems on p. 844 are haiku.

Translators of Japanese haiku try to maintain the syllabic requirements. Western writers, however, sometimes use the form more loosely.

HOMERIC SIMILE See Epic Simile.

IAMB See Meter.

IMAGE An *image* is a word or phrase that appeals to one or more of the five senses—sight, hearing, touch, taste, or smell. Writers use images to re-create

▲ In his lyric poem "The Eagle," Alfred, Lord Tennyson pays tribute to one of nature's creatures.

sensory experiences in words.
See Description.

IMAGERY *Imagery* is the descriptive or figurative language used in literature to create word pictures for the reader. These pictures, or images, are created by details of sight, sound, taste, touch, smell, or movement.

INDIRECT CHARACTERIZATION See Characterization.

INTERNAL RHYME *See* Rhyme.

IRONY *Irony* is the general term for literary techniques that portray differences between appearance and reality, expectation and result, or meaning and intention. In *verbal irony* words are used to suggest the opposite of what is meant. In *dramatic irony* there is a contradiction between what a character thinks and what the reader or audience knows to be true. In *irony of situation,* an event occurs that directly contradicts the expectations of the characters, the reader, or the audience. The humor in Ernest Laurence Thayer's "Casey at the Bat," on p. 36, derives in part from irony of situation. The speaker creates the expectation that Casey will save the day. However, at the end of the poem "there is no joy in Mudville" because "Mighty Casey has struck out."

LITERAL LANGUAGE *Literal language* uses words in their ordinary senses. It is the opposite of *figurative language*. If you tell someone standing on a diving board to jump in, you are speaking literally. If you tell someone standing on the street corner to jump in the lake, you are speaking figuratively.

See Figurative Language.

LYRIC POEM   A *lyric poem* is a highly musical verse that expresses the observations and feelings of a single speaker. In ancient times lyric poems were sung to the accompaniment of the lyre, a type of stringed instrument. Modern lyric poems are not usually sung. However, they still have a musical quality that is achieved through rhythm and other devices such as alliteration and rhyme. Alfred, Lord Tennyson's "The Eagle," on p. 796, is a lyric poem expressing the speaker's feeling of wonder as he watches an eagle dive from a cliff.

MAIN CHARACTER   See Character.

METAPHOR   A *metaphor* is a figure of speech in which one thing is spoken of as though it were something else. Unlike a simile, which compares two things using *like* or *as*, a metaphor implies a comparison between them. In "Dreams," on p. 799, Langston Hughes uses a metaphor to show what happens to a life without dreams:

> Hold fast to dreams
>
> For if dreams die
>
> Life is a broken-winged bird
>
> That cannot fly.

See Extended Metaphor and Figurative Language.

METER   The *meter* of a poem is its rhythmical pattern. This pattern is determined by the number and types of stresses, or beats, in each line. To describe the meter of a poem, you must *scan* its lines. *Scanning* involves marking the stressed and unstressed syllables, as shown with the following two lines from "I Wandered Lonely as a Cloud" by William Wordsworth, on p. 789.

> Ĭ wán|dĕred lóne|lў ás| ă clóud
>
> Thăt floáts | ŏn hígh | ŏ'er váles | ănd hílls.

As you can see, each strong stress is marked with a slanted line (´) and each unstressed syllable with a horseshoe symbol (˘). The stressed and unstressed syllables are then divided by vertical lines (|) into groups called feet. The following types of feet are common in English poetry:

1. *Iamb:* a foot with one unstressed syllable followed by a stressed syllable, as in the word "again"

2. *Trochee:* a foot with a stressed syllable followed by an unstressed syllable, as in the word "wonder"

3. *Anapest:* a foot with two unstressed syllables followed by one strong stress, as in the phrase "on the beach"

4. *Dactyl:* a foot with one strong stress followed by two unstressed syllables, as in the word "wonderful"

5. *Spondee:* a foot with two strong stresses, as in the word "spacewalk"

Depending on the type of foot that is most common in them, lines of poetry are described as *iambic, trochaic, anapestic,* and so forth.

Lines are also described in terms of the number of feet that occur in them, as follows:

1. *Monometer:* verse written in one-foot lines

   All things

   Must pass

   Away.

2. *Dimeter:* verse written in two-foot lines

   Thomas | Jefferson

   What do | you say

   Under the | gravestone

   Hidden | away?

   — Rosemary and Stephen Vincent Benet,

   "Thomas Jefferson 1743–1826"

3. *Trimeter:* verse written in three-foot lines

   I know | not whom | I meet

   I know | not where | I go.

4. *Tetrameter:* verse written in four-foot lines

5. *Pentameter:* verse written in five-foot lines

6. *Hexameter:* verse written in six-foot lines

7. *Heptameter:* verse written in seven-foot lines

Blank verse is poetry written in unrhymed iambic pentameter. Poetry that does not have a regular meter is called *free verse.*

MONOLOGUE A *monologue* is a speech by one character in a play, story, or poem. An example from Shakespeare's *Romeo and Juliet,* on p. 672, is the speech in which the Prince of Verona commands the Capulets and Montagues to cease feuding (Act 1, Scene I, lines 62–84).

See Dramatic Poetry and Soliloquy.

MONOMETER *See Meter.*

MOOD *Mood,* or *atmosphere,* is the feeling created in the reader by a literary work or passage. The mood is often suggested by descriptive details. Often the mood can be described in a single word such as lighthearted, frightening, or despairing. Notice how this passage from Edgar Allan Poe's "The Cask of Amontillado," on p. 5, contributes to an eerie, fearful mood:

> "The niter!" I said; "see, it increases. It hangs like moss upon the vaults. We are below the river's

bed. The drops of moisture trickle among the bones. Come, we will go back ere it is too late."

See Tone.

MORAL A *moral* is a lesson taught by a literary work. A fable usually ends with a moral that is directly stated.

MOTIVATION *Motivation* is a reason that explains or partially explains why a character thinks, feels, acts, or behaves in a certain way. Motivation results from a combination of the character's personality and the situation he or she must deal with. Nat Hocken, in "The Birds," on p. 46, is motivated by his fear of dying by bird attacks to board up windows and stay inside.

When the motives of a main character are not clear and logical, neither that character nor the story seems believable. Adventure stories often do not concern themselves much with the character's motivations. In contrast, serious fiction usually explores motivations in depth.

See Character and Characterization.

▼ Fear is the motivation for many of Nat Hocken's actions in "The Birds."

MYTH A *myth* is a fictional tale that explains the actions of gods or the causes of natural phenomena. Unlike legends, myths have little historical truth and involve supernatural elements. Every culture has its collections of myths. Among the most familiar are the myths of the ancient Greeks and Romans. The *Odyssey*, on p. 860, is a mythical story, attributed to the ancient poet Homer.

See Oral Tradition.

NARRATION *Narration* is writing that tells a story. The act of telling a story in speech is also called narration. Novels and short stories are fictional narratives. Nonfiction works such as news stories, biographies, and autobiographies are also narratives. A narrative poem tells a story in verse.

See Anecdote, Essay, Narrative Poem, Nonfiction, Novel, and Short Story.

NARRATIVE A *narrative* is a story told in fiction, nonfiction, poetry, or drama.

See Narration.

NARRATIVE POEM A *narrative poem* is one that tells a story. "Casey at the Bat," on p. 36, is a humorous narrative poem about the last inning of a baseball game. Edgar Allan Poe's "The Raven," on p. 832, is a serious narrative poem about a man's grief over the loss of a loved one.

See Dramatic Poetry, Epic, and Narration.

NARRATOR A *narrator* is a speaker or character who tells a story. The narrator may be either a character in the story or an outside observer. The writer's choice of narrator determines the story's *point of view*, which in turn determines the type and amount of information the writer can reveal.

When a character in the story tells the story, that character is a *first-person narrator*. This narrator may be a major character, a minor character, or just a witness. Readers see only what this character sees, hear only what he or she hears, and so on. The first-person narrator may or may not be reliable. We have reason, for example, to be suspicious of the first-person narrator of Edgar Allan Poe's "The Cask of Amontillado," on p. 5.

When a voice outside the story narrates, the story has a *third-person narrator*. An omniscient, or all-knowing, third-person narrator can tell readers what any character thinks and feels. For example, in Guy de

Maupassant's "The Necklace," on p. 536, we know the feelings of both Monsieur and Madame Loisel. A *limited* third-person narrator, on the other hand, sees the world through one character's eyes and reveals only that character's thoughts. For example, in James Thurber's "The Secret Life of Walter Mitty," on p. 299, we share only Mitty's experiences and feelings.

See Speaker.

NONFICTION *Nonfiction* is prose writing that presents and explains ideas or that tells about real people, places, objects, or events. Nonfiction narratives are about actual people, places, and events, unlike fictional narratives, which present imaginary characters and events. To be classified as nonfiction, a work must be true. Arthur C. Clarke's "If I Forget Thee, Oh Earth . . . ," on p. 426, presents a fictional account of the Earth as viewed from space. "Single Room, Earth View," on p. 559, presents a nonfictional account of the same subject.

Among nonfiction forms are essays, newspaper and magazine articles, journals, travelogues, biographies, and autobiographies. Historical, scientific, technical, political, and philosophical writings are also nonfiction.

See Autobiography, Biography, and Essay.

NOVEL A *novel* is a long work of fiction. Like a short story, a novel has a plot that explores characters in conflict. However, a novel is much longer than a short story and may have one or more subplots, or minor stories, and several themes.

OCTAVE See Stanza.

ONOMATOPOEIA *Onomatopoeia* is the use of words that imitate sounds. *Whirr, thud, sizzle,* and *hiss* are typical examples. Writers can deliberately choose words that contribute to a desired sound effect. In the following lines, from Edgar Allan Poe's "The Bells," on p. 818, *clang, crash, roar,* and *twang* are onomatopoeic:

Oh, the bells, bells, bells!

What a tale their terror tells

Of Despair!

How they clang, and clash, and roar!

What a horror they outpour

On the bosom of the palpitating air!

Yet the ear it fully knows,

By the twanging

And the clanging,

How the danger ebbs and flows

ORAL TRADITION The *oral tradition* is the passing of songs, stories, and poems from generation to generation by word of mouth. Many folk songs, ballads, fairy tales, legends, and myths originated in the oral tradition.

See Myth.

PENTAMETER *See Meter.*

PERSONIFICATION *Personification* is a type of figurative language in which a nonhuman subject is given human characteristics. When William Wordsworth describes daffodils, on p. 789, as "Tossing their heads in sprightly dance" he is personifying daffodils. In the poem below, "Soft Snow," William Blake personifies both the snow and winter:

I walked abroad in a snowy day;

I asked the soft snow with me to play;

She played and she melted in all her prime,

And the winter called it a dreadful crime.

See Figurative Language.

PERSUASION *Persuasion* is writing or speech that attempts to convince the reader to adopt a particular opinion or course of action. A newspaper editorial that says a city council decision was wrong is an example of persuasive writing attempting to mold opinion. A television commercial showing the benefits of a new toothpaste is meant to move viewers to act, in this case to buy toothpaste.

PLOT *Plot* is the sequence of events in a literary work. In most novels, dramas, short stories, and narrative poems, the plot involves both characters and a central conflict. The plot usually begins with an *exposition* that introduces the setting, the characters, and the basic situation. This is followed by the *inciting incident,* which introduces the central conflict. The conflict then increases during the *development* until it reaches a high point of interest or suspense, the *climax*. All the events leading up to the climax make up the *rising action*. The climax is followed by the *falling action,* which leads to the *resolution,* or end, of the central

conflict. Any events that occur after the resolution make up the *denouement*.

POETRY *Poetry* is one of the three major types of literature, the others being prose and drama. Most poems make use of highly concise, musical, and emotionally charged language. Many also make use of imagery, figurative language, and special devices of sound such as rhyme. Poems are often divided into lines and stanzas and often employ regular rhythmical patterns, or meters.

However, some poems are written out just like prose and some poems are written in free verse.

See Genre.

POINT OF VIEW *See Narrator.*

PROSE *Prose* is the ordinary form of written language. Most writing that is not poetry, drama, or song is considered prose. Prose is one of the major genres of literature and occurs in two forms: fiction and nonfiction.

See Fiction, Genre, and Nonfiction.

QUATRAIN A *quatrain* is a stanza or poem made up of four lines, usually with a definite rhythm and rhyme scheme. The following quatrain is from Ernest Lawrence Thayer's "Casey at the Bat":

Then from the gladdened multitude went up a
   joyous yell—

It rumbled in the mountaintops, it rattled in
   the dell;

It struck upon the hillside and rebounded on
 the flat;

For Casey, mighty Casey, was advancing to the bat.

See Stanza.

REPETITION *Repetition* is the use of any element
of language—a sound, a word, a phrase, a clause, or a
sentence—more than once. In his famous civil rights
speech, on p. 140, Martin Luther King, Jr., repeats the
words "I have a dream" eight times, each time in connection with a different image.

Poets use many kinds of repetition. Alliteration, assonance, rhyme, and rhythm are repetitions of certain
sounds and sound patterns. A refrain is a repeated line
or group of lines. In both prose and poetry, repetition is
used for musical effects and for emphasis.

See Alliteration, Assonance, Consonance, Rhyme, and
Rhythm.

RESOLUTION See *Plot.*

RHYME *Rhyme* is the repetition of sounds at the
ends of words. *End rhyme* occurs when the rhyming
words come at the ends of lines, as in "The Desired
Swan Song," by Samuel Taylor Coleridge:

Swans sing before they die—'twere no bad thing

Should certain persons die before they sing.

Internal rhyme occurs when the rhyming words
appear in the same line, as in lines 1 and 3 of Edgar
Allan Poe's "The Raven," on p. 832:

Once upon a midnight *dreary,* while I pondered,
 weak and *weary,*

Over many a quaint and curious volume of
 forgotten lore,

While I nodded, nearly *napping,* suddenly there
 came a *tapping,*

See Repetition and Rhyme Scheme.

RHYME SCHEME A *rhyme scheme* is a regular
pattern of rhyming words in a poem. The rhyme
scheme of a poem is indicated by using different letters
of the alphabet for each new rhyme. In an *aabb* stanza,
for example, line 1 rhymes with line 2 and line 3
rhymes with line 4. William Wordsworth's poem "I
Wandered Lonely as a Cloud," on p. 789, uses an
ababcc rhyme pattern:

I wandered lonely as a cloud	a
That floats on high o'er vales and hills,	b
When all at once I saw a crowd,	a
A host, of golden daffodils;	b
Beside the lake, beneath the trees,	c
Fluttering and dancing in the breeze.	c

Many poems use the same pattern of rhymes,
though not the same rhymes, in each stanza. The next
stanza of Wordsworth's poem, for example, has this
rhyme scheme: *dedeff*

See Rhyme.

RHYTHM *Rhythm* is the pattern of *beats,* or *stresses,*
in spoken or written language. Some poems have a
very specific pattern, or *meter,* whereas prose and free
verse use the natural rhythms of everyday speech.

See Meter.

RISING ACTION See Plot.

ROUND CHARACTER See Character.

SCENE See Drama.

SCIENCE FICTION *Science fiction* is writing that
tells about imaginary events that involve science or
technology. Many science-fiction stories are set in the
future. The setting can be on Earth, in space, on other
planets, or in a totally imaginary place. Arthur C.
Clarke's "If I Forget Thee, Oh Earth . . . ," on p. 426, is a
science-fiction story set on the moon after a nuclear
disaster on Earth.

See Fantasy.

SENSORY LANGUAGE *Sensory language* is writing or speech that appeals to one or more of the senses.

See Image.

SESTET See Stanza.

SETTING The *setting* of a literary work is the time
and place of the action. Time can include not only the historical period—past, present, or future—but also a specific
year, season, or time of day. Place may involve not only the
geographical place—a region, country, state, or town—but
also the social, economic, or cultural environment.

▲ Arthur C. Clarke uses the moon as the setting for his science-fiction story "If I Forget Thee, Oh Earth . . . "

In some stories, setting serves merely as a backdrop for action, a context in which the characters move and speak. In others, however, setting is a crucial element. Both the desert and Native American culture are important in Leslie Marmon Silko's "The Man to Send Rain Clouds," on p. 222, and the lunar landscape and the future are important in Arthur C. Clarke's "If I Forget Thee, Oh Earth . . . ," on p. 426.

Description of the setting often helps establish the mood of a story. For example, in Edgar Allan Poe's "The Cask of Amontillado," on p. 5, the setting contributes to the growing horror.

See Mood.

SHORT STORY A *short story* is a brief work of fiction. A *novel*, by contrast, is a long work of fiction. In most short stories, one main character faces a conflict that is resolved in the plot of the story. Great craftsmanship must go into the writing of a good story, for it has to accomplish its purpose in relatively few words.

The short story as a distinct literary form emerged in the nineteenth century. The American writers Edgar Allan Poe and Nathaniel Hawthorne were especially important in the development of the short story.

See Fiction and Genre.

SIMILE A *simile* is a figure of speech in which *like* or *as* is used to make a comparison between two basically unlike ideas. "Claire is as flighty as Roger" is a comparison, not a simile. "Claire is as flighty as a sparrow" is a simile.

Poets often use similes. The following example from William Wordsworth's "I Wandered Lonely as a Cloud," on p. 789, compares a mass of daffodils to a flood of stars:

Continuous as the stars that shine

And twinkle on the milky way,

They stretched in never-ending line

Along the margin of a bay.

▲ In his poem "I Wandered Lonely as a Cloud," William Wordsworth uses a simile to compare a field of daffodils to stars in the Milky Way.

Prose writers also use similes. Here is one from James Hurst's "The Scarlet Ibis," on p. 484:

> We were down in Old Woman Swamp and it was spring and the sick-sweet smell of bay flowers hung everywhere like a mournful song.

See Figurative Language.

SOLILOQUY A *soliloquy* is a long speech expressing the thoughts of a character alone on stage. In William Shakespeare's *Romeo and Juliet* (p. 672), Romeo gives a soliloquy after the servant has fled and Paris has died (Act V, Scene iii, lines 74–120).

See Monologue.

SONNET A *sonnet* is a fourteen-line lyric poem, usually written in rhymed iambic pentameter. The *English,* or *Shakespearean, sonnet* consists of three quatrains (four-line stanzas) and a couplet (two lines), usually rhyming *abab cdcd efef gg.* The couplet usually comments on the ideas contained in the preceding twelve lines. The sonnet is usually not printed with the stanzas divided, but a reader can see distinct ideas in each. See the English sonnet by William Shakespeare on p. 843.

The *Italian,* or *Petrarchan, sonnet* consists of an octave (eight-line stanza) and a sestet (six-line stanza). Often the octave rhymes *abbaabba* and the sestet rhymes *cdecde.* The octave states a theme or asks a question. The sestet comments on or answers the question.

The Petrarchan sonnet took its name from Petrarch, a fourteenth-century Italian poet. Once the form was introduced in England, it underwent change. The Shakespearean sonnet is, of course, named after William Shakespeare.

See Lyric Poem, Meter, and Stanza.

SPEAKER The *speaker* is the imaginary voice assumed by the writer of a poem. In many poems the speaker is not identified by name. When reading a poem, remember that the speaker within the poem may be a person, an animal, a thing, or an abstraction. The speaker in the following stanza by Emily Dickinson is a person who has died:

> Because I could not stop for Death—
>
> He kindly stopped for me—
>
> The Carriage held but just Ourselves—
>
> And Immortality.

STAGE DIRECTIONS *Stage directions* are notes included in a drama to describe how the work is to be performed or staged. These instructions are printed in italics and are not spoken aloud. They are used to describe sets, lighting, sound effects, and the appearance, personalities, and movements of characters.

See Drama.

STANZA A *stanza* is a formal division of lines in a poem, considered as a unit. Often the stanzas in a poem are separated by spaces.

Stanzas are sometimes named according to the number of lines found in them. A couplet, for example, is a two-line stanza. A tercet is a stanza with three lines. Other types of stanzas include the following:

1. Quatrain: a four-line stanza

2. Cinquain: a five-line stanza

3. Sestet: a six-line stanza

4. Heptastich: a seven-line stanza

5. Octave: an eight-line stanza

Sonnets, limericks, and haiku all have distinct stanza forms. A *sonnet* is a fourteen-line poem that is made up either of three quatrains and a couplet or of an octave followed by a sestet. A *limerick* consists of a single five-line stanza with a particular pattern of rhymes. A *haiku* is made up of a single three-line stanza.

See Haiku and Sonnet.

◄ A rare bird is the central symbol in James Hurst's story, "The Scarlet Ibis."

STATIC CHARACTER See Character.

SURPRISE ENDING A *surprise ending* is a conclusion that violates the expectations of the reader but in a way that is both logical and believable. O. Henry's "The Gift of the Magi," on p. 459, and Guy de Maupassant's "The Necklace," on p. 536, have surprise endings. Both authors were masters of this form.

SUSPENSE *Suspense* is a feeling of curiosity or uncertainty about the outcome of events in a literary work. Writers create suspense by raising questions in the minds of their readers.

SYMBOL A *symbol* is anything that stands for or represents something else. An object that serves as a symbol has its own meaning, but it also represents abstract ideas. Marks on paper can symbolize spoken words. A flag symbolizes a country. A flashy car may symbolize wealth. Writers sometimes use such conventional symbols in their work, but sometimes they also create symbols of their own through emphasis or repetition.

In James Hurst's "The Scarlet Ibis," on p. 484, the ibis symbolizes the character named Doodle. Doodle and the ibis have many traits in common. Both are beautiful and otherworldly. Both struggle against great odds. Both

meet an unfortunate fate. Since a story says something about life or people in general, the ibis, in a larger sense, becomes a symbol for those who struggle.

TETRAMETER See *Meter.*

THEME A *theme* is a central message or insight into life revealed through the literary work. The theme is not a condensed summary of the plot. Instead, it is a generalization about people or about life that is communicated through the literary work.

The theme of a literary work may be stated directly or implied. In James Hurst's "The Scarlet Ibis," on p. 484, the narrator directly states one theme of the story: ". . . pride is a wonderful, terrible thing, a seed that bears two vines, life and death."

When the theme of a work is implied, readers think about what the work seems to say about the nature of people or about life. The story or poem can be viewed as a specific example of the generalization the writer is trying to communicate.

Note that there is usually no single correct statement of a work's theme, though there can be incorrect ones. Also, a long work, like a novel or a full-length play, may have several themes. Finally, not all literary works have themes. A work meant only to entertain may have no theme at all.

TONE The *tone* of a literary work is the writer's attitude toward his or her audience and subject. The tone can often be described by a single adjective, such as *formal* or *informal, serious* or *playful, bitter,* or *ironic.* When O. Henry discusses the young married couple in "The Gift of the Magi," on p. 459, he uses a sympathetic tone. By contrast, Margaret Walker uses a grieving tone in her poem "Memory," on p. 805.

See Mood.

TRAGEDY A *tragedy* is a work of literature, especially a play, that results in a catastrophe for the main character. In ancient Greek drama, the main character was always a significant person, a king or a hero, and the cause of the tragedy was a tragic flaw, or weakness, in his or her character. In modern drama the main character can be an ordinary person, and the cause of the tragedy can be some evil in society itself. The purpose of tragedy is not only to arouse fear and pity in the audience, but also, in some cases, to convey a sense of the grandeur and nobility of the human spirit.

Shakespeare's *Romeo and Juliet,* on p. 672, is a tragedy. Romeo and Juliet both suffer from the tragic flaw of impulsiveness. This flaw ultimately leads to their deaths.

See Drama.

TRIMETER *See* Meter.

VERBAL IRONY *See* Irony.

VISUAL ESSAY A *visual essay* is an exploration of a topic that conveys its ideas through visual elements as well as language. Like a standard essay, a visual essay presents an author's views of a single topic. Unlike other essays, however, much of the meaning in a visual essay is conveyed through illustrations or photographs.

In her poem "Memory," Margaret Walker uses words and images that create a grieving tone.

WRITING HANDBOOK

THE WRITING PROCESS

A polished piece of writing can seem to have been effortlessly created, but most good writing is the result of a process of writing, rethinking, and rewriting. The process can be roughly divided into a series of stages: prewriting, drafting, revising, editing, proofreading, and publishing.

It's important to remember that the writing process is one that moves backward as well as forward. Even while you are moving forward in the creation of your composition, you may still return to a previous stage—to rethink or rewrite.

Following are stages of the writing process, with key points to address during each stage.

Prewriting

In this stage you plan out the work to be done. You prepare to write by exploring ideas, gathering information, and working out an organization. Following are the key steps to take at this stage.

Step 1: Analyze the writing situation. Start by clarifying your assignment, so that you know exactly what you are supposed to do.

- *Focus your topic.* If you need to, narrow the topic—the subject you are writing about—so that you can write about it fully in the space you have.
- *Know your purpose.* What is your goal for this paper? What do you want to accomplish? Your purpose will determine what you include in it.
- *Know your audience.* Who will read your paper influences what you say and how you say it.

Step 2: Gather ideas and information. You can do this in a number of ways:

- *Brainstorm.* When you brainstorm, either alone or with others, you come up with possible ideas to use in your paper. Not all of your brainstormed ideas will be useful or suitable. You'll need to evaluate them later.
- *Consult other people about your subject.* Speaking informally with others may suggest an idea or approach you did not see at first.
- *Make a list of questions about your topic.* Then find the answers to your questions.

- *Do research.* Your topic may require information that you don't have, so you will need to go to other sources to find information. There are numerous ways to find information on a topic. See the Research Handbook on p. 979 for suggestions.

The ideas and information you gather will become the content of your paper. Not all of the information you gather will be needed. As you develop and revise your paper, you will make further decisions about what to include and what to leave out.

Step 3: Organize. First, make a rough plan for how you want to present your information. Sort your ideas and notes; decide what goes with what, and which points are the most important. You can make an outline to show the order of ideas, or you can use some other organizing plan that works for you.

There are many ways in which you can organize and develop your material. Use a method that works for your topic. Following are common methods of organizing information in the development of a paper.

- *Chronological Order* In this method, events are presented in the order in which they occurred. This organization works best for presenting narrative material or explaining in a "how to."
- *Spatial Order* In spatial order, details are presented as seen in space, for example, from left to right or from foreground to background. This order is good for descriptive writing.
- *Order of Importance* This order helps readers see the relative importance of ideas. You present ideas from most to least important or from least to most important.
- *Main Idea and Details* This logical organization works well to support an idea or opinion.

Drafting

When you draft, you put down your ideas on paper in rough form. Working from your prewriting notes and your outline or plan, you develop and present your ideas in sentences and paragraphs.

Don't worry about getting everything perfect at the drafting stage. Concentrate on getting your ideas down.

Draft in a way that works for you. Some writers work best by writing a quick draft—putting down all their ideas without stopping to evaluate them. Other writers prefer to develop each paragraph carefully and thoughtfully, making sure each main idea is supported by details.

As you are developing a draft, keep in mind your purpose and your audience. These determine what you say and how you say it.

Don't be afraid to change your original plans during drafting. Some of the best ideas are those that were not planned at the beginning. Write as many drafts as you like. You can draft over and over until you've got it the way you like.

Most papers, regardless of the topic, are developed with an introduction, a body, and a conclusion. Here are tips for developing these parts.

Introduction In the introduction to a paper, you want to engage your readers' attention and let them know the purpose of your paper. You may use the following strategies in your introduction:

- State your main idea.
- Take a stand.
- Use an anecdote.
- Quote someone.
- Startle your readers.

Body of the paper In the body of your paper, you present your information and make your points. Your **organization** is an important factor in leading readers through your ideas. Your elaboration on your main ideas is also important. **Elaboration** is the development of ideas to make your written work precise and complete. You can use the following kinds of details to elaborate your main ideas:

- Facts and statistics
- Anecdotes
- Sensory details
- Examples
- Explanation and definition
- Quotations

Conclusion The ending of your paper is the final impression you leave with your readers. Your conclusion should give readers the sense that you have pulled everything together. Following are some effective ways to end your paper:

- Summarize and restate.
- Ask a question.
- State an opinion.
- Tell an anecdote.
- Call for action.

Revising

Once you have a draft, you can look at it critically or have others review it. This is the time to make changes—on many levels. Revising is the process of reworking what you have written to make it as good as it can be. You may change some details so that your ideas flow smoothly and are clearly supported. You may discover that some details don't work and you'll need to discard them. Two strategies may help you start the revising process:

1. Read your work aloud. This is an excellent way to catch any ideas or details that have been left out and to notice errors in logic.
2. Ask someone else to read your work. Choose someone who can point out its strengths as well as suggest how to improve it.

How do you know what to look for and what to change? Here is a checklist of major writing issues. If the answer to any of these questions is no, then that is an area that needs revision.

1. Does the writing achieve your purpose?
2. Does the paper have unity? That is, does it have a single focus, with all details and information contributing to that focus?
3. Is the arrangement of information clear and logical?
4. Have you elaborated enough to give your audience adequate enough information?

Editing

When you edit, you look more closely at the language you have used, so that the way you express your ideas is most effective.

- Replace dull language with vivid, precise words.
- Cut or change redundant expressions (unnecessary repetition).
- Cut empty words and phrases, those that do not add anything to the writing.
- Check passive voice. Usually active voice is more effective.
- Replace wordy expressions with shorter, more precise ones.

Proofreading

After you finish your final draft, the last step is to proofread the draft to make it ready for a reader. You may do this on your own or with the help of a partner.

It's useful to have handy both a dictionary and a usage handbook to help you check for correctness. Here are the tasks in proofreading:

- Correct errors in grammar and usage.
- Correct errors in punctuation and capitalization.
- Correct errors in spelling.

THE MODES OF WRITING

Description

Description is writing that creates a vivid picture for readers, draws readers into a scene, and makes readers feel as if they are meeting a character or experiencing an event firsthand. A description may stand on its own or be part of a longer work, such as a short story.

When you write a description, bring it to life with sensory details, which tell how your subject looks, smells, sounds, tastes, or feels. You'll want to choose your details carefully so that you create a single main impression of your subject. Avoid language and details that don't contribute to this main impression. Keep these guidelines in mind whenever you are assigned one of the following types of description:

Observation In an observation, you describe an event that you have witnessed firsthand, often over an extended period of time. You may focus on an aspect of daily life or on a scientific phenomenon, such as a storm or an eclipse.

Remembrance When you write a remembrance, you use vivid descriptive details to bring to life memorable people, places, or events from your past.

Description of a Place Often used to set the scene in a story or drama, your description of a place should convey the physical look and atmosphere of a scene—either interior or exterior.

Character Profile In a character profile, you capture a person's appearance and personality traits and reveal information about his or her life. Your subject may be a real person or a fictional character.

Narration

Whenever writers tell any type of story, they are using **narration**. While there are many kinds of narration, most narratives share certain elements—characters, a setting, a sequence of events (or plot, in fiction), and, often, a theme. You might be asked to try your hand at one of these types of narration:

Anecdote An anecdote, which may be oral or written, is a brief and often humorous narrative that is true or based on the truth. You may use an anecdote both to entertain and to make a general point about life.

Personal Narrative A personal narrative is a true story about a memorable experience or period in your life. In a personal narrative, your feelings about

events shape the way you tell the story—even the way you describe people and places.

Firsthand Biography A firsthand biography tells about the life (or a period in the life) of a person whom you know personally. You can use your close relationship with the person to help you include personal insights not found in biographies based solely on research.

Short Story Short stories are short fictional, or made-up, narratives in which a main character faces a conflict that is resolved by the end of the story. In planning a short story, you focus on developing the plot, the setting, and the characters. You must also decide on a point of view: Will your story be told by a character who participates in the action, or by someone who describes the action as an outside observer?

Exposition

Exposition is writing that informs or explains. The information you include in expository writing is factual or (when you're expressing an opinion) based on fact.

Your expository writing should reflect a well-thought-out organization—one that includes a clear introduction, body, and conclusion and is appropriate for the type of exposition you are writing. Here are some types of exposition you may be asked to write:

Cause-and-Effect Essay In a cause-and-effect essay, you consider the reasons something did happen or might happen. You may examine several causes of a single effect or several effects of a single cause.

Comparison-and-Contrast Essay When you write a comparison-and-contrast essay, you consider the similarities and differences between two or more subjects. You may organize your essay point by point—discussing each aspect of your subject in turn—or subject by subject—discussing all the qualities of one subject first, then the qualities of the next subject.

Problem-and-Solution Essay In a problem-and-solution essay, you identify a conflict or problem and offer a resolution. Begin with a clear statement of the problem and follow with a reasoned path to a solution.

Summary To write a summary or synopsis of an event or a literary work, you include only the details that your readers will need in order to understand the key features of the event or the literary work. Omit any personal opinions; include only factual details.

How-to Instructions You use how-to instructions to explain the steps involved in doing a particular task. In writing instructions it is also important to anticipate and answer questions the reader may have about why a particular procedure is being recommended.

Persuasion

Persuasion is writing or speaking that attempts to convince people to agree with a position or take a desired action. When used effectively, persuasive writing has the power to change people's lives. As a reader and a writer, you will find yourself engaged in many forms of persuasion. Here are a few of them:

Persuasive Essay In writing a persuasive essay, you build an argument, supporting your opinions with a variety of evidence: facts, statistics, examples, statements from experts. You also anticipate and develop counter-arguments to opposing opinions.

Advertisement When you write an advertisement, you present information in an appealing way to make the product or service seem desirable.

Position Paper In a position paper, you try to persuade readers to accept your views on a controversial issue. Most often, your audience will consist of people who have some power to shape policy related to the issue. Your views in a position paper should be supported with evidence.

Persuasive Speech A persuasive speech is a piece of persuasion that you present orally instead of in writing. As a persuasive speaker, you use a variety of techniques, such as repetition of key points, to capture your audience's interest and to add force to your argument.

Letter to the Editor When you write a letter to the editor, you may be responding to an article or an editorial published earlier, or you may be writing to express concern on an issue of importance to the community. Your letter should describe the issue briefly, present your views supported with evidence, and state any action you think should be taken.

Research Writing

Writers often use outside research to gather information and explore subjects of interest. The product of that research is called **research writing.** In connection with your reading, you may occasionally be assigned one of the following types of research writing:

Biographical Report In a biographical report, you examine a person's life and achievements. You include the dates and details of the main events in the person's life and, at times, make educated guesses about the reasons behind those events. For your biographical report, you may need to research not only the life of an individual but also the times in which he or she lived.

Research Paper A research paper uses information gathered from a variety of outside sources to explore a topic. In your research paper, you will usually include an introduction, in which your thesis, or main point, is stated; a body, in which you present support for the thesis; and a conclusion that summarizes, or restates, your main points. You should credit the sources of information, using footnotes or other types of citation, and include a bibliography, or general list of sources, at the end.

Multimedia Presentation In preparing a multimedia presentation, you will gather and organize information in a variety of media, or means of communication. You may use written materials, slides, videos, audio-cassettes, sound effects, art, photographs, models, charts, and diagrams.

Creative Writing

Creative writing blends imagination, ideas, and emotions, and allows you to present your own unique view of the world. Poems, plays, short stories, dramas, and even some cartoons are examples of creative writing. All are represented in this anthology and may provide inspiration for you to produce your own creative works, such as the following:

Lyric Poem In a lyric poem, you use sensory images, figurative language, and sound devices to express deep thoughts and feelings about a subject. To give your lyric poem a musical quality, employ sound devices, such as rhyme, rhythm, alliteration, and ono-matopoeia.

Narrative Poem Writing a narrative poem is similar to writing a short story, with a plot, characters, and a theme. However, your narrative poem, unlike a story, will be divided into stanzas (groups of lines that form a unit) usually composed of rhyming lines that have a definite rhythm, or beat.

Song Lyrics In writing lyrics, or words, for a song, you use many elements of poetry—rhyme, rhythm, repetition, and imagery. In addition, your song lyrics should convey emotions, as well as interesting ideas.

Drama When you write a drama or a dramatic scene, you are writing a story that is intended to be performed. Since a drama consists almost entirely of the words and actions of the characters, be sure to write dialogue that clearly shows the characters' personalities, thoughts, and emotions, and stage directions that convey your ideas about sets, props, sound effects, and the speaking style and movements of the characters.

Response to Literature

In a **response to literature,** you express your thoughts and feelings about a work and often, in so doing, gain a better understanding of what the work is all about. Your response to literature can take many forms—oral or written, formal or informal. During the course of your reading, you may be asked to respond to a work of literature in one of these forms:

Literary Analysis In a literary analysis, you take a critical look at various important elements in the work. You then attempt to explain how the author has used those elements and how they work together to convey the author's message.

Retelling of a Fairy Tale Most fairy tales—stories about good and evil characters, giants, and magic deeds—have been handed down from generation to generation, and often the original authors are unknown. When you retell a fairy tale in your own way, you can add to the original or change it. For example, you might set it in another place or time period or write it as a poem or a drama.

Reader's Response Journal Entry Your reader's response journal is a record of your thoughts and feelings about works you have read. Use it to remind you of writers and works that you particularly liked or disliked, or to provide a source of writing ideas.

Letter to an Author People sometimes respond to a work of literature by writing a letter to the author. You can praise the work, ask questions, or offer constructive criticism.

Critical Review In a critical review of a literary work, you discuss various elements in the work and offer opinions about them. You may also give a summary of the work and a recommendation to readers.

Practical and Technical Writing

Practical writing is fact-based writing that people do in the workplace or in their day-to-day lives. Business letters, memos, school forms, and job applications are examples of practical writing. **Technical writing,**

which is also based on facts, explains procedures, provides instructions, or presents specialized information. You encounter technical writing every time you read a manual or a set of instructions.

In the following descriptions, you'll find tips for tackling several types of practical and technical writing.

Letter Requesting Information In a letter requesting information, you state the information you're searching for and ask any specific questions you have. In your letter, include your name and address so that you can receive a response. Include the date, which can help you or the recipient keep track of correspondence. It is also customary to include the address of the party to whom you are writing. Use a formal greeting followed by a colon. Keep the body of the letter as brief and clear as possible. Use a polite closing, and remember to sign as well as type or print your name.

News Release News releases announce factual information about upcoming events. Also called press releases, they are usually sent to local newspapers, local radio stations, and other media. When you write a news release, use this format: Position your name and phone number in the upper right corner. Then capture your main point in a centered headline, which will allow the recipient to see at a glance what the news release is about. In the body, present factual information in a concise way. You may begin with an opening location tag that tells in which town or city the news release originated. The numeral 30 or number signs (###) customarily indicate the end of the news release.

Guidelines When you write guidelines, you give information about how people should act or you provide tips on how to do something. List guidelines one by one, using somewhat formal language. Your guidelines may or may not be numbered. In addition to factual information, which should be complete and accurate, guidelines may contain your opinions.

Process Explanation In a process explanation, you offer a step-by-step explanation of how to do something. Your explanation should be specific, using headings, labels, or numbers to make the process clear. You may also include diagrams or other illustrations to further clarify the process.

GRAMMAR AND MECHANICS HANDBOOK

Nouns A **noun** is the name of a person, place, or thing. A **common noun** names any one of a class of people, places, or things. A **proper noun** names a specific person, place, or thing.

Common Noun	Proper Noun
city	Washington, D.C.

Pronouns A **pronoun** is a word that stands for a noun or for a word that takes the place of a noun.

A **personal pronoun** refers to (1) the person speaking, (2) the person spoken to, or (3) the person, place, or thing spoken about.

	Singular	Plural
First Person	I, me, my, mine	we, us, our, ours
Second Person	you, your, yours	you, your, yours
Third Person	he, him, his, she, her, hers, it, its	they, them, their, theirs

A **reflexive pronoun** ends in -*self* or -*selves* and adds information to a sentence by pointing back to a noun or a pronoun earlier in the sentence.

> As I said these words I busied *myself* among the pile of bones of which I have before spoken.
> —"The Cask of Amontillado," Edgar Allan Poe, p. 9

An **intensive pronoun** ends in -*self* or -*selves* and simply adds emphasis to a noun or a pronoun in the same sentence.

> And Spring *herself,* when she woke at dawn, Would scarcely know that we were gone.
> —"There Will Come Soft Rains," Sara Teasdale, p. 414

A **demonstrative pronoun** directs attention to a specific person, place, or thing.

> this   these   that   those

> *These* are the juiciest pears I've ever tasted.

A **relative pronoun** begins a subordinate (relative) clause and connects it to another idea in the sentence.

> The poet *who* wrote "Fire and Ice" is Robert Frost.
> The president *whom* Sandburg admired was Lincoln.

An **indefinite pronoun** refers to a person, place, or thing, often without specifying which one.

> *Some* of the flowers were in bloom.
> *Everybody* chose something.

Verbs A **verb** is a word that expresses time while showing an action, a condition, or the fact that something exists.

An **action verb** indicates the action of someone or something.

An action verb is **transitive** if it directs action toward someone or something named in the same sentence.

> Henderson *shook* his head.
> — "The Machine That Won the War," Isaac Asimov, p. 396

An action verb is **intransitive** if it does not direct action toward something or someone named in the same sentence.

> Earth *had won* so all *had been* for the best.
> — "The Machine That Won the War," Isaac Asimov, p. 396

A **linking verb** is a verb that connects the subject of a sentence with a noun or pronoun that renames or describes the subject. All linking verbs are intransitive.

> Life *is* a broken-winged bird . . .
> — "Dreams," Langston Hughes, p. 799

A **helping verb** is a verb that can be added to another verb to make a verb phrase.

> Nor *did* I suspect that these experiences could be part of a novel's meaning.

Adjectives An **adjective** describes a noun or a pronoun or gives a noun or a pronoun a more specific meaning. Adjectives answer these questions:

What kind?	*blue* lamp, *large* tree
Which one?	*this* table, *those* books
How many?	*five* stars, *several* buses
How much?	*less* money, *enough* votes

The articles *the, a,* and *an* are adjectives. *An* is used before a word beginning with a vowel sound.

A noun may sometimes be used as an adjective.

> *diamond* necklace   *summer* vacation

Adverbs An **adverb** modifies a verb, an adjective, or another adverb. Adverbs answer the questions where? when? in what way? to what extent?

He could stand *there*. (modifies verb *stand*)
He was *blissfully* happy. (modifies adjective *happy*)
It ended *too* soon. (modifies adverb *soon*)

Prepositions A **preposition** relates a noun or a pronoun that appears with it to another word in the sentence.

before the end   *near* me   *inside* our fence

Conjunctions A **conjunction** connects other words or groups of words.

A **coordinating conjunction** connects similar kinds or groups of words.

mother *and* father   simple *yet* stylish

Correlative conjunctions are used in pairs to connect similar words or groups of words.

both Sue *and* Meg   *neither* he *nor* I

A **subordinating conjunction** connects two complete ideas by placing one idea below the other in rank or importance.

You would know him *if* you saw him.

Interjections An **interjection** expresses feeling or emotion and functions independently of a sentence.

"*Oh,* my poor, poor, Mathilde!"
— "The Necklace,"
Guy de Maupassant, p. 541

Sentences A **sentence** is a group of words with a subject and a predicate. Together, these parts express a complete thought.

I closed my eyes and pondered my next move.
— "Rules of the Game,"
Amy Tan, p. 231

A **fragment** is a group of words that does not express a complete thought.

The Swan Theater in London

Subject and Verb Agreement To make a subject and verb agree, make sure that both are singular or both are plural.

Many *storms are* the cause of beach erosion.
Either the *cats* or the *dog is* hungry.
Neither *Angie* nor her *sisters were* present.
The *conductor,* as well as the soloists, *was applauded.*

Phrase A **phrase** is a group of words, without a subject and a verb, that functions in a sentence as one part of speech.

A **prepositional phrase** is a group of words that includes a preposition and a noun or a pronoun that is the object of the preposition.

outside my window   below the counter

An **adjective phrase** is a prepositional phrase that modifies a noun or a pronoun by telling *what kind* or *which one.*

The wooden gates *of that lane* stood open.

An **adverb phrase** is a prepositional phrase that modifies a verb, an adjective, or an adverb by pointing out *where, when, in what way,* or *to what extent.*

On December the third, the wind changed overnight, and it was winter.
— "The Birds,"
Daphne du Maurier, p. 46

An **appositive phrase** is a noun or pronoun with modifiers, placed next to a noun or a pronoun to add information and details.

"It is a very great pleasure and honor to welcome Mr. Sanger Rainsford, *the celebrated hunter,* to my home."
— "The Most Dangerous Game,"
Richard Connell, p. 21

A **participial phrase** is a participle with its modifiers or complements. The entire phrase acts as an adjective.

"Try the settee," said Holmes, *relapsing into his armchair* . . .
— "The Red-headed League,"
Sir Arthur Conan Doyle, p. 82

A **gerund phrase** is a gerund with modifiers or a complement, all acting together as a noun.

The baying of the hounds drew nearer, . . .
— "The Most Dangerous Game,"
Richard Connell, p. 30

An **infinitive phrase** is an infinitive with modifiers, complements, or a subject, all acting together as a single part of speech.

I continued, as was my wont, *to smile in his face,* . . .
— "The Cask of Amontillado,"
Edgar Allan Poe, p. 5

Clauses A **clause** is a group of words with a subject and a verb.

An **independent clause** has a subject and a verb and can stand by itself as a complete sentence.

A **subordinate clause** has a subject and a verb but cannot stand by itself as a complete sentence; it can only be part of a sentence.

An **adjective clause** is a subordinate clause that modifies a noun or a pronoun by telling what kind or which one.

> Walter Mitty stopped the car in front of the building *where his wife went to have her hair done.*
>
> — "The Secret Life of Walter Mitty,"
> James Thurber, p. 299

An **adverb clause** modifies a verb, an adjective, an adverb, or a verbal by telling *where, when, in what way, to what extent, under what condition,* or *why.*

> The hunter shook his head several times, *as if he was puzzled.*
>
> — "The Most Dangerous Game,"
> Richard Connell, p. 28

A **noun clause** is a subordinate clause that acts as a noun.

> . . . I discovered *that the intoxication had worn off . . .*
>
> — "The Cask of Amontillado,"
> Edgar Allan Poe, p. 9

Summary of Capitalization and Punctuation

Capitalization

Capitalize the first word of a sentence and also the first word in a quotation if the quotation is a complete sentence.

> I said to him, "My dear Fortunato, you are luckily met."
>
> — "The Cask of Amontillado,"
> Edgar Allan Poe, p. 6

Capitalize all proper nouns and adjectives.

O. Henry   Ganges River   Great Wall of China

Capitalize a person's title when it is followed by the person's name or when it is used in direct address.

Madame   Dr. Mitty   General Zaroff

Capitalize titles showing family relationships when they refer to a specific person, unless they are preceded by a possessive noun or pronoun.

Uncle Marcos   Granddaddy Cain

Capitalize the first word and all other key words in the titles of books, periodicals, poems, stories, plays, paintings, and other works of art.

> *Rosa Parks: My Story*
> "I Wander'd Lonely as a Cloud"

Punctuation

End Marks Use a **period** to end a declarative sentence, an imperative sentence, an indirect question, and most abbreviations.

> Mr. Jabez Wilson laughed heavily.
>
> — "The Red-headed League,"
> Sir Arthur Conan Doyle, p. 85

Use a **question mark** to end a direct question, an incomplete question, or a statement that is intended as a question.

> Shall I meet other wayfarers at night?
>
> — "Uphill," Christina Rossetti, p. 814

Use an **exclamation mark** after a statement showing strong emotion, an urgent imperative sentence, or an interjection expressing strong emotion.

> Free at last! Free at last!
> Thank God almighty, we are Free at last!
>
> — "I Have a Dream,"
> Martin Luther King, Jr., p. 142

Commas Use a **comma** before the coordinating conjunction to separate two independent clauses in a compound sentence.

> All at once . . . she came upon a superb diamond necklace, and her heart started beating with overwhelming desire.
>
> — "The Necklace,"
> Guy de Maupassant, p. 538

Use commas to separate three or more words, phrases, or clauses in a series.

> My brothers and I would peer into the medicinal herb shop, watching old Li dole out onto a stiff sheet of white paper the right amount of insect shells, saffron-colored seeds, and pungent leaves for his ailing customers.
>
> — "Rules of the Game,"
> Amy Tan, p. 224

Use commas to separate adjectives of equal rank. Do not use commas to separate adjectives that must stay in a specific order.

> The big cottonwood tree stood apart from a small group of winterbare cottonwoods which grew in the wide, sandy arroyo.
> — "The Man to Send Rain Clouds,"
> Leslie Marmon Silko, p. 522

> In autumn those that had not migrated overseas . . . were caught up in the same driving urge . . .
> — "The Birds,"
> Daphne du Maurier, p. 46

Use a comma after an introductory word, phrase, or clause.

> When Marvin was ten years old, his father took him through the long, echoing corridors . . .
> — "If I Forget Thee, Oh Earth . . . ,"
> Arthur C. Clarke, p. 426

Use commas to set off parenthetical and nonessential expressions.

> An evil place can, so to speak, broadcast vibrations of evil.
> — "The Most Dangerous Game,"
> Richard Connell, p. 18

Use commas with places, dates, and titles.

> Poe was raised in Richmond, Virginia.
> On September 1, 1939, World War II began.
> Dr. Martin Luther King, Jr., was born in 1929.

Use a comma to indicate words left out of an elliptical sentence, to set off a direct quotation, and to prevent a sentence from being misunderstood.

> In the *Odyssey*, the Cyclops may symbolize brutishness; the Sirens, knowledge.

Semicolons Use a **semicolon** to join independent clauses that are not already joined by a conjunction.

> The lights of cities sparkle; on nights when there was no moon, it was difficult for me to tell the Earth from the sky. . . .
> — "Single Room, Earth View,"
> Sally Ride, p. 563

Use a semicolon to join independent clauses separated by either a conjunctive adverb or a transitional expression.

> Edward Way Teale wrote nearly thirty

books; moreover, he was also an artist and a naturalist.

Use semicolons to avoid confusion when independent clauses or items in a series already contain commas.

> Unable to afford jewelry, she dressed simply; but she was as wretched as a *déclassé*, for women have neither caste nor breeding— in them beauty, grace, and charm replace pride of birth.
> — "The Necklace,"
> Guy de Maupassant, p. 536

Colons Use a **colon** in order to introduce a list of items following an independent clause.

> The authors we are reading include a number of poets: Robert Frost, Lewis Carroll, and Emily Dickinson.

Use a colon to introduce a formal quotation.

> I have a dream that one day this nation will rise up and live out the true meaning of its creed: "We hold these truths to be self-evident; . . ."
> — "I Have a Dream,"
> Martin Luther King, Jr., p. 141

Quotation Marks A **direct quotation** represents a person's exact speech or thoughts and is enclosed in quotation marks.

> "Where I was born and where and how I have lived is unimportant," Georgia O'Keeffe told us in the book of paintings and words published in her ninetieth year on earth.
> — "Georgia O'Keeffe,"
> Joan Didion, p. 592

An **indirect quotation** reports only the general meaning of what a person said or thought and does not require quotation marks.

> The driver of the bus saw me still sitting there, and he asked was I going to stand up . . .
> — from *Rosa Parks: My Story*,
> Rosa Parks, p. 144

Always place a comma or a period inside the final quotation mark.

> "I don't know," he said slowly. "It says here the birds are hungry."
> — "The Birds,"
> Daphne du Maurier, p. 54

Place a question mark or an exclamation mark inside

the final quotation mark if the end mark is part of the quotation; if it is not part of the quotation, place it outside the final quotation mark.

> "That pig will devour us, greedily!"
>> —"The Golden Kite, the Silver Wind,"
>> Ray Bradbury, p. 153

> Have you ever read the poem "Dreams"?

Use single quotation marks for a quotation within a quotation.

> " 'But,' said I, 'there would be millions of red-headed men who would apply.' "
>> — "The Red-headed League,"
>> Sir Arthur Conan Doyle, p. 87

Use quotation marks around the titles of short written works, episodes in a series, songs, and titles of works mentioned as parts of a collection.

> "I Hear America Singing"   "Both Sides Now"

Dashes Use **dashes** to indicate an abrupt change of thought, a dramatic interrupting idea, or a summary statement.

> The streets were lined with people—lots and lots of people—the children all smiling, placards, confetti, people waving from windows.
>> —from *A White House Diary*,
>> Lady Bird Johnson, p. 586

Parentheses Use **parentheses** to set off asides and explanations only when the material is not essential or when it consists of one or more sentences.

> One last happy moment I had was looking up and seeing Mary Griffith . . . (Mary for many years had been in charge of altering the clothes which I purchased) . . .
>> —from *A White House Diary*,
>> Lady Bird Johnson, p. 586

Hyphens Use a **hyphen** with certain numbers, after certain prefixes, with two or more words used as one word, and with a compound modifier coming before a noun.

> seventy-six   Post-Modernist

Apostrophes Add an **apostrophe** and -s to show the possessive case of most singular nouns.

> Thurmond's wife   the playwright's craft

Add an apostrophe to show the possessive case of plural nouns ending in -s and -es.

> the sailors' ships   the Wattses' daughter

Add an apostrophe and -s to show the possessive case of plural nouns that do not end in -s or -es.

> the children's games   the people's friend

Use an apostrophe in a contraction to indicate the position of the missing letter or letters.

> You'll be lonely at first, they admitted, but you're so nice you'll make friends fast.
>> — "Checkouts," Cynthia Rylant, p. 236

GLOSSARY OF COMMON USAGE

among, between
Among is usually used with three or more items. *Between* is generally used with only two items.

> *Among* the poems we read this year, Margaret Walker's "Memory" was my favorite.

> Mark Twain's "The Invalid's Story" includes a humorous encounter *between* the narrator and a character named Thompson.

amount, number
Amount refers to a mass or a unit, whereas *number* refers to individual items that can be counted. Therefore, *amount* generally appears with a singular noun, and *number* appears with a plural noun.

> Annie Sullivan's work with Helen Keller must have required a huge *amount* of patience.

> In her poem, "Uphill," Christina Rossetti uses a *number* of intriguing symbols.

any, all
Any should not be used in place of *any other* or *all*.

> Rajika liked Amy Tan's "Rules of the Game" better than *any other* short story.

> Of *all* O. Henry's short stories, "The Gift of the Magi" is one of the most famous.

around
In formal writing, *around* should not be used to mean *approximately* or *about*. These usages are allowable, however, in informal writing or in colloquial dialogue.

> Shakespeare's *Romeo and Juliet* had its first performance in *approximately* 1595.

Shakespeare was *about* thirty when he wrote this play.

as, because, like, as to

The word *as* has several meanings and can function as several parts of speech. To avoid confusion, use *because* rather than *as* when you want to indicate cause and effect.

> *Because* Cyril was interested in the history of African American poetry, he decided to write his report on Paul Laurence Dunbar.

Do not use the preposition *like* to introduce a clause that requires the conjunction *as*.

> Dorothy Parker conversed *as* she wrote—wittily.

The use of *as to* for *about* is awkward and should be avoided.

> Rosa has an interesting theory *about* E. E. Cummings's unusual typography in his poems.

bad, badly

Use the predicate adjective *bad* after linking verbs such as *feel, look*, and *seem*. Use *badly* whenever an adverb is required.

> Sara Teasdale's poem "There Will Come Soft Rains" shows clearly that the author felt *bad* about the destruction of war.

> In O. Henry's "The Gift of the Magi," Della *badly* wants to buy a wonderful Christmas present for her husband, Jim.

because of, due to

Use *due to* if it can logically replace the phrase *caused by*. In introductory phrases, however, *because of* is better usage than *due to*.

> The popularity of Frank Stockton's "The Lady or the Tiger?" is largely *due to* the story's open ending.

> *Because* of her feeling that Bennie's mother had enough to worry about already, Bennie's grandmother keeps the doctor's conclusions to herself.

being as, being that

Avoid these expressions. Use *because* or *since* instead.

> *Because* the protagonist of James Hurst's "The Scarlet Ibis" is a dynamic character, he changes significantly in the course of the story.

> *Since* Romeo and Juliet were from feuding families, their relationship involved secrecy and risk.

beside, besides

Beside is a preposition meaning "at the side of" or "close to." Do not confuse beside with besides, which means "in addition to." Besides can be a preposition or an adverb.

> When our group discussed William Least Heat Moon's "Nameless, Tennessee," Luis sat *beside* Eileen.

> *Besides* "The Bells," can you think of any other poems by Edgar Allan Poe?

> John Updike is a celebrated novelist; he is a gifted poet and essayist, *besides*.

can, may

The verb *can* generally refers to the ability to do something. The verb *may* generally refers to permission to do something.

> The mysterious listeners in Walter de la Mare's poem *can* hear the words of the lonely traveler.

> *May* I tell you why I admire Edgar Lee Masters's "George Gray"?

compare, contrast

The verb *compare* can involve both similarities and differences. The verb *contrast* always involves differences. Use *to* or *with* after compare. Use *with* after contrast.

> Theo's paper *compared* James Weldon Johnson's style in "The Creation" with the style of African American sermons of the same period.

> In the opening lines of the famous speech in Shakespeare's *As You Like It*, the world is *compared* to a stage and men and women to actors or players.

> The speaker's tone of hysteria in the closing stanzas of Poe's "The Raven" *contrasts* with the quiet opening of the poem.

different from, different than

The preferred usage is *different from*.

> The structure of "The Meadow Mouse" is quite *different from* that of "I Wandered Lonely as a Cloud."

farther, further

Use *farther* when you refer to distance. Use *further* when you mean "to a greater degree" or "additional."

> The *farther* Rainsford traveled in the jungle in "The Most Dangerous Game," the nearer the baying of the hounds sounded.

> Despite his men's advice, Odysseus *further* insults the Cyclops and provokes the monster's curse.

fewer, less

Use *fewer* for things that can be counted. Use *less* for amounts or quantities that cannot be counted.

> Poetry often uses *fewer* words than prose to convey ideas and images.

> T. S. Eliot's humorous poems have received *less* critical attention than his serious verse has.

good, well

Use the adjective *good* after linking verbs such as *feel*, *look*, *smell*, *taste*, and *seem*. Use *well* whenever you need an adverb.

> In Walt Whitman's "I Hear America Singing," the "varied carols" sound *good* to the speaker.

> Dickens wrote especially *well* when he described eccentric characters.

hopefully

You should not loosely attach this adverb to a sentence, as in "*Hopefully*, the rain will stop by noon." Rewrite the sentence so that *hopefully* modifies a specific verb. Other possible ways of revising such sentences include using the adjective *hopeful* or a phrase such as, "everyone *hopes* that."

> Dr. Martin Luther King, Jr., wrote and spoke *hopefully* about his dream of racial harmony.

> Akko was *hopeful* that he could find some of the unusual words from Lewis Carroll's "Jabberwocky" in an unabridged dictionary.

> Everyone *hopes* that the class production of *Romeo and Juliet* will be a big success.

its, it's

Do not confuse the possessive pronoun *its* with the contraction *it's*, used in place of "it is" or "it has."

> Ancient Greek society must have recognized many of *its* ideal values in the *Odyssey*.

> In Walter de la Mare's "The Listeners," the traveler thinks *it's* strange that no one replies to his call.

just, only

When you use *just* as an adverb meaning "no more than," be sure you place it directly before the word it logically modifies. Likewise, be sure you place *only* before the word it logically modifies.

> Shakespeare's "Sonnet 30" offers *just* one remedy for the speaker's grief and depression: the thought of a dear friend.

> A stereotyped character exhibits *only* those traits or behavior patterns that are assumed to be typical.

kind of, sort of

In formal writing, you should not use these colloquial expressions. Instead, use a word such as *rather* or *somewhat*.

> Alfred is *rather* irresponsible in Morley Callaghan's story "All the Years of Her Life."

> In "The Secret Life of Walter Mitty," James Thurber characterizes Mitty as *somewhat* absent-minded.

lay, lie

Do not confuse these verbs. *Lay* is a transitive verb meaning "to set or put something down." Its principal parts are *lay, laying, laid, laid*. *Lie* is an intransitive verb meaning "to recline." Its principal parts are *lie, lying, lay, lain*.

> In Heyerdahl's *Kon-Tiki* the narrator says that after the ship hit the reef, Herman *lay* pressed flat across the ridge of the cabin roof.

> Homer describes the slaughtered suitors *lying* dead in a heap on the floor of Odysseus' hall.

leave, let

Be careful not to confuse these verbs. *Leave* means "to go away" or "to allow to remain." *Let* means "to permit."

> In Tennyson's "The Eagle," the bird *leaves* the crag and plunges like a thunderbolt toward the sea.

> The love-sick Romeo asks his friends to *leave* him alone while they go to Capulets' party.

> "*Let* wantons light of heart / Tickle the senseless rushes with their heels," he says.

literally, figuratively

Literally means "word for word" or "in fact." The opposite of *literally* is *figuratively*, meaning "metaphorically." Be careful not to use *literally* as a synonym for *nearly*, as in informal expressions like this: "He was *literally* beside himself with rage."

> Certain specific details in "I Hear an Army" show that James Joyce does not intend us to interpret the army *literally*; instead, the army and the speaker's nightmare are meant *figuratively* to suggest his despair at his abandonment by his love.

of, have

Do not use *of* in place of *have* after auxiliary verbs like *would, could, should, may,* or *might.*

> Sir Arthur Conan Doyle might *have* continued to practice medicine, but soon after the publication *of* his first Sherlock Holmes stories, he decided to write full time.

raise, rise

Raise is a transitive verb that usually takes a direct object. *Rise* is an intransitive verb and never takes a direct object.

> In "Casey at the Bat," Ernest Lawrence Thayer suspensefully *raises* the reader's expectations throughout the poem, only to end the narrative with a mighty anticlimax.

> Jorge *rose* to the challenge of interpreting Gabriel García Márquez's story "A Very Old Man With Enormous Wings."

set, sit

Do not confuse these verbs. *Set* is a transitive verb meaning "to put (something) in a certain place." Its principal parts are *set, setting, set, set. Sit* is an intransitive verb meaning "to be seated." Its principal parts are *sit, sitting, sat, sat.*

> The opening sentence of Saki's "The Interlopers" *sets* a tone of tension and conflict for the story.

> While Walter Mitty *sat* in a big leather chair in the hotel lobby, he picked up a copy of a magazine.

so, so that

Be careful not to use the coordinating conjunction *so* when your context requires *so that. So* means "accordingly" or "therefore" and expresses a cause-and-effect relationship. *So that* expresses purpose.

> He wanted to check the clues, *so* he read "The Red-headed League" again.

> The priest wanted to locate Teofilo's body *so that* he could give him the Last Rites.

than, then

The conjunction *than* is used to connect the two parts of a comparison. Do not confuse *than* with the adverb *then*, which usually refers to time.

> I enjoyed reading "Jacob Lawrence: American Painter" more *than* "Autumn Gardening."

> Sally Ride earned a doctorate in physics and *then* became the first American woman in space.

that, which, who

Use the relative pronoun *that* to refer to things or people. Use *which* only for things and *who* only for people.

> The phrase *that* James Thurber dislikes is "you know."

> Donald Justice wrote "Incident in a Rose Garden," *which* is a dramatic poem.

> The sea goddess *who* loved Odysseus was Calypso.

unique

Because *unique* means "one of a kind," you should not use it carelessly to mean "interesting" or "unusual." Avoid such illogical expressions as "most unique," "very unique," and "extremely unique."

> Homer occupies a *unique* position in the history of Western literature.

when, where

Do not directly follow a linking verb with *when* or *where.* Also, be careful not to use *where* when your context requires *that.*

> *Faulty:* Foreshadowing is *when* an author uses clues to suggest future events.

> *Revised:* In foreshadowing, an author uses clues to suggest future events.

> *Faulty:* Ithaca was *where* Penelope awaited Odysseus.

> *Revised:* Penelope awaited Odysseus on Ithaca.

who, whom

In formal writing, remember to use *who* only as a subject in clauses and sentences and *whom* only as an object.

> Richard Wright, *who* is widely admired for his novel *Native Son,* also wrote haiku verse.

> Leslie Marmon Silko, *whom* Mark quoted in his oral report, was raised on the Laguna Pueblo reservation in New Mexico.

SPEAKING AND LISTENING HANDBOOK

Language is both spoken and written. The literature in this book is written, which is one form of communication, but most of your communication is probably oral. Oral communication involves both speaking and listening. Having strong speaking and listening skills benefits you both in your school life and your life outside of school.

Many of the assignments accompanying the literature in this textbook involve speaking and listening. This handbook identifies some of the terminology related to speaking and listening, both the oral communication you experience every day and the assignments you may do in conjunction with the literature in this book.

Oral Communication

You use many different kinds of oral communication each day. When you communicate with your friends, when you communicate with your teachers or your parents, when you interact with a cashier in a store, you are communicating orally. In addition to ordinary, everyday conversation, oral communication includes class discussions, speeches, interviews, presentations, debates. When you communicate face to face, you usually use more than your voice to get your message across. If you communicate by telephone, however, you must rely solely on your verbal skills.

The following terms will give you a better understanding of the many elements that are part of oral communication.

ARTICULATION is the process of forming sounds into words; it is the way in which the tongue, teeth, lower jaw, and soft palate are used to produce speech sounds.

BODY LANGUAGE refers to the use of facial expressions, eye contact, gestures, posture, and movement to communicate a feeling or idea.

CONNOTATION is the set of associations a word calls to mind. The connotations of the words you choose influence the message you send. For example, most people respond more favorably to being described as "slim" rather than as "skinny." The connotation of *slim* is more appealing than that of *skinny*.

EYE CONTACT is direct visual contact with another person's eyes.

FEEDBACK is the set of verbal and nonverbal reactions that indicate to a speaker that a message has been received and understood.

GESTURES are the movements made with arms, hands, face, and fingers to communicate.

INFLECTION refers to the rise and fall in the pitch of the voice in speaking; it is also called **intonation.**

LISTENING is understanding and interpreting sound in a meaningful way. You listen differently for different purposes.

Listening for key information: For example, when a teacher gives an assignment, or when someone gives you directions to a place, you listen for key information.

Listening for main points: In a classroom exchange of ideas or information, or while watching a television documentary, you listen for main points.

Listening critically: When you evaluate a performance, song, or a persuasive or political speech, you listen critically, questioning and judging the speaker's message.

NONVERBAL COMMUNICATION is communication without the use of words. People communicate nonverbally through gestures, facial expressions, posture, and body movements. Sign language is an entire language based on nonverbal communication.

PROJECTION is speaking in such a way that the voice carries clearly to an audience. It's important to project your voice when speaking in a large space like a classroom or auditorium.

VOCAL DELIVERY is the way in which you present a message. Your vocal delivery involves all of the following elements:

Volume: the loudness or quietness of your voice
Pitch: the high or low quality of your voice
Rate: the speed at which you speak; also called pace
Stress: the amount of emphasis placed on different syllables in a word or on different words in a sentence

All of these elements individually, and the way in which they are combined, contribute to the meaning of a spoken message.

Speaking and Listening Situations

The following are some of the many types of situations in which you apply your speaking and listening skills.

AUDIENCE Your audience in any situation refers to the person or people to whom you direct your message. An audience can be a group of people sitting in a classroom or auditorium observing a performance or just one person to whom you address a question or a comment. When preparing for any speaking situation, it's useful to analyze your audience, learning what you can about their background, interests, and attitudes so that you can tailor your message to them.

DEBATE A debate is a formal public-speaking situation in which participants prepare and present arguments on opposing sides of a question, stated as a **proposition.** The proposition must be controversial: It must concern an issue that may be solved in two different, valid ways.

The two sides in a debate are the *affirmative* (pro) and the *negative* (con). The affirmative side argues in favor of the proposition, while the negative side argues against it. The affirmative side begins the debate, since it is seeking a change in belief or policy. The opposing sides take turns presenting their arguments, and each side has an opportunity for *rebuttal,* in which they may challenge or question the other side's argument.

GROUP DISCUSSION results when three or more people meet to solve a common problem, arrive at a decision, or answer a question of mutual interest. Group discussion is one of the most widely used forms of interpersonal communication in modern society. **Meetings** are a kind of organized group discussion for a specific purpose.

INTERVIEW An interview is a form of interaction in which one person, the interviewer, asks questions of another person, the interviewee. Interviews may take place for many purposes: to obtain information, to discover a person's suitability for a job or a college, or to inform the public of a notable person's opinions.

ORAL INTERPRETATION is the reading or speaking of a piece of literature aloud for an audience. Oral interpretation involves giving expression to the ideas, meaning, or even the structure of a piece of literature. The speaker interprets the piece through his or her vocal delivery. **Storytelling,** in which a speaker reads or tells a story expressively, is a form of oral interpretation.

PANEL DISCUSSION is a group discussion on a topic of interest common to all members of a panel and to a listening audience. A panel is usually composed of four to six experts on a particular topic who are brought together to share information and opinions.

PANTOMIME is a form of nonverbal communication in which an idea or a story is communicated completely through the use of gesture, body language, and facial expressions, without any words at all.

PARLIAMENTARY PROCEDURE refers to the set of rules used to conduct a meeting in an orderly manner. Parliamentary procedure makes discussions at meetings more efficient and productive, and protects the rights of individuals attending the meeting.

All of the business conducted according to parliamentary procedure is handled through motions. Motions are proposals for action made by members of the meeting. For example, besides main motions that set forth the items of business that will be considered, a motion can be made to adjourn—or end the meeting—or to amend, or alter the wording of a motion.

The following are the main principles of parliamentary procedure:

1. Only one item of business may be considered at a time.
2. Everyone has a right to express an opinion, and each opinion is treated as valuable.
3. Every member of the group has the right to vote, and each vote is counted as equal.
4. The group always follows the decision of the majority.

READERS' THEATER is a dramatic reading of a piece of literature in which participants take parts from a story or play and read aloud in expressive voices. Unlike a play, however, sets and costumes are not part of the performance, and the participants remain seated as they deliver their lines.

ROLE PLAY To role-play is to take the role of a person or character and, as that character, act out a given situation, speaking, acting, and responding in the manner of the character.

SPEECH A speech is a talk or address given to an audience. A speech may be **impromptu**—delivered on the spur of the moment with no preparation—or formally prepared and delivered for a specific purpose or occasion.

informative, as appropriate. The following are common occasions for speeches.

Introduction: Introducing a speaker or presenter at a meeting or assembly

Presentation: Giving an award or acknowledging the contributions of someone

Acceptance: Accepting an award or tribute

Keynote: Giving an inspirational address at a large meeting or convention

Commencement: Honoring the graduates of a school or university

- *Purposes:* The most common purposes of speeches are to persuade (for example, political speeches), to entertain, to explain, and to inform.

- *Occasions:* Different occasions call for different types of speeches. Speeches given on these occasions could be persuasive, entertaining, or

RESEARCH HANDBOOK

Many of the assignments and activities in this literature book require you to find out more about your topic. Whenever you need ideas, details, or information, you must conduct research. You can find information by using library resources and computer resources, as well as by interviewing experts in a field.

Before you begin, create a research plan that lists the questions you want answered about your topic. Then decide which sources will best provide answers to those questions. When gathering information, it is important to use a variety of sources and not to rely on one main source of information. It is also important to document where you find different pieces of information you use so that you can cite those sources in your work.

The suggestions that follow can help you locate your sources.

Library Resources

Libraries contain many sources of information in both print and electronic form. You'll save time if you plan your research before actually going to the library. Make a list of the information you think you will need, and for each item list possible sources for the information. Here are some sources to consider:

NONFICTION BOOKS An excellent starting point for researching your topic, nonfiction books can provide either broad coverage or specific details, depending on the book. To find appropriate nonfiction books, use the library catalog, which may be in card files or in electronic form on computers. In either case, you can search by author, title, or subject; in a computer catalog, you can also search by key word. When you find the listing for a book you want, print it out or copy down the title, author, and call number. The call number, which also appears on the book's spine, will help you locate the book in the library.

NEWSPAPERS AND MAGAZINES Books are often not the best places for finding up-to-the-minute information. Instead, you might try newspapers and magazines. To find information about an event that occurred on a specific date, go directly to newspapers and magazines for that date. To find articles on a particular topic, use indexes like the *Readers' Guide to Periodical Literature*, which lists magazine articles under subject

headings. For each article that you want, jot down the title, author (if given), page number or numbers, and the name and date of the magazine in which the article appears. If your library does not have the magazine you need, either as a separate issue or on microfilm, you may still be able to obtain photocopies of the article through an interlibrary loan.

REFERENCE WORKS The following important reference materials can also help you with your research.

- *General encyclopedias* have articles on thousands of topics and are a good starting point for your research, although they shouldn't be used as primary sources.
- *Specialized encyclopedias* contain articles in particular subject areas, such as science, music, or art.
- *Biographical dictionaries and indexes* contain brief articles on people and often suggest where to find more information.
- *Almanacs* provide statistics and data on current events and act as a calendar for the upcoming year.
- *Atlases*, or books of maps, usually include geographical facts and may also include information like population and weather statistics.
- *Indexes and bibliographies*, such as the *Readers' Guide to Periodical Literature*, tell you in what publications you can find specific information, articles, or shorter works (such as poems or essays).
- *Vertical files* (drawers in file cabinets) hold pamphlets, booklets, and government publications that often provide current information.

Computer Research

The Internet Use the Internet to get up-to-the-minute information on virtually any topic. The Internet provides access to a multitude of resource-rich sources such as news media, museums, colleges and universities, and government institutions. There are a number of indexes and directories organized by subject to help you locate information on the Internet, including Yahoo!, the World Wide Web Virtual Library, the Kids Web, and the Webcrawler. These indexes and directories will help you find direct links to information related to your topic.

Internet Sources and Addresses

- **Yahoo! Directory** allows you to do word searches or link directly to your topic by clicking on such subjects as the arts, computers, entertainment, or government.
  http://www.yahoo.com
- **World Wide Web Virtual Library** is a comprehensive and easy-to-use subject catalog that provides direct links to academic subjects in alphabetical order.
  http://celtic.stanford.edu/vlib/Overview.html
- **Kids Web** supplies links to reference materials, such as dictionaries, *Bartlett's Familiar Quotations*, a thesaurus, and a world fact book.
  http://www.npac.syr.edu/textbook/kidsweb/
- **Webcrawler** helps you to find links to information about your topic that are available on the Internet when you type in a concise term or key word.
  http://www.webcrawler.com

CD-ROM References

Other sources that you can access using a computer are available on CD-ROM. The Wilson Disk, Newsquest, the *Readers' Guide to Periodical Literature,* and many other useful indexes are available on CD-ROM, as are encyclopedias, almanacs, atlases, and other reference works. Check your library to see which are available.

Interviews as Research Sources

People who are experts in their field or who have experience or knowledge relevant to your topic are excellent sources for your research. If such people are available to you, the way to obtain information from them is through an interview. Follow these guidelines to make your interview successful and productive:

- Make an appointment at a time convenient to the person you want to interview, and arrange to meet in a place where he or she will feel comfortable talking freely.
- If necessary, do research in advance to help you prepare the questions you will ask.
- Before the interview, list the questions you will ask, wording them so that they encourage specific answers. Avoid questions that can be answered simply with *yes* or *no*.

- Make an audiotape or videotape of the interview if possible. If not, write down the answers as accurately as you can.
- Include the date of the interview at the top of your notes or on the tape.
- Follow up with a thank-you note or phone call to the person you interviewed.

Sources for a Multimedia Presentation

When preparing a multimedia presentation, keep in mind that you'll need to use some of your research findings to illustrate or support your main ideas when you actually give the presentation. Do research to find media support, such as visuals, CD's, and so on—in addition to those media you might create yourself. Here are some media that may be useful as both sources and illustrations:

- Musical recordings on audio cassette or compact disk (CD) (often available at libraries)
- Videos- that you prepare yourself
- Fine art reproductions (often available at libraries and museums)
- Photographs that you or others have taken
- Computer presentations using slide shows, graphics, and so on
- Video or audio cassette recordings of interviews that you conduct.

INDEX OF AUTHORS AND TITLES

INDEX OF SKILLS

GRAMMAR, USAGE, AND MECHANICS

VOCABULARY

CRITICAL THINKING AND VIEWING

WRITING

Writing Opportunities

INDEX OF FINE ART

ACKNOWLEDGMENTS (continued)

Arte Público Press
"The Harvest" from *La Cosecha* by Tomás Rivera, translated by Julián Olivares. Copyright © 1989 by Tomás Rivera Archives/Concepción Rivera. Reprinted by permission of Arte Público Press.

Atlantic Monthly Press
Book-jacket copy for *In These Girls, Hope Is a Muscle*, book written by Madeleine Blais, copyright © 1995 by Madeleine Blais. Reprinted by permission of Atlantic Monthly Press.

Margaret Atwood and Oxford University Press Canada
"Siren Song" from *You Are Happy* by Margaret Atwood. Copyright © 1974 by Margaret Atwood. Reprinted by permission of Margaret Atwood.

Bantam Books, a division of Bantam, Doubleday, Dell Publishing Group, Inc.
"One Ordinary Day, With Peanuts," excerpts from *Just an Ordinary Day: The Uncollected Stories* by Shirley Jackson. Copyright © 1997 by The Estate of Shirley Jackson. Used by permission of Bantam Books, a division of Bantam, Doubleday, Dell Publishing Group, Inc.

Elizabeth Barnett, literary executor
"An Ancient Gesture" by Edna St. Vincent Millay. From *Collected Poems,* HarperCollins. Copyright © 1954, 1982 by Norma Millay Ellis. All rights reserved. Reprinted by permission of Elizabeth Barnett, literary executor.

Brandt & Brandt Literary Agents, Inc.
"The Most Dangerous Game" by Richard Connell. Copyright, 1924 by Richard Connell. Copyright renewed © 1952 by Louise Fox Connell. "Sonata for Harp and Bicycle" from *The Green Flash* by Joan Aiken. Copyright © 1957, 1958, 1959, 1960, 1965, 1968, 1969, 1971 by Joan Aiken. Reprinted by permission of Brandt & Brandt Literary Agents, Inc.

Helen Brann Agency, Inc., agent for the author
"All Watched Over by Machines of Loving Grace," by Richard Brautigan, from *Trout Fishing in America, The Pill versus the Springhill Mine Disaster, and In Watermelon Sugar.* Copyright © 1967, 1968. Reprinted by permission of The Helen Brann Agency, Inc., agent for the author.

Abigail de Oliveria Carvalho
"Echo" by Henriqueta Lisboa, from *Poems Escolbidos: Chosen Poems,* translated by Helcio Veiga Costa, copyright © 1981 by Ed. Editora e Distribuidora, Ltda. Reprinted by permission of Abigail de Oliveira Carvalho, Henriqueta Lisboa's niece.

Arthur C. Clarke and Scott Meredith Literary Agency, Inc.
"If I Forget Thee, Oh Earth . . ." from *Expedition to Earth* by Arthur C. Clarke. Copyright © 1953, 1970 by Arthur C. Clarke; copyright 1951 by Columbia Publications, Inc. Reprinted by permission of the author and the author's agent, Scott Meredith Literary Agency, Inc., 845 Third Avenue, New York, NY 10022.

Coffee House Press
"Problems With Hurricanes" originally appeared in *Red Beans* by Victor Hernández Cruz, Coffee House Press, 1991. Copyright © 1991 by Victor Hernandez Cruz. Reprinted by permission of the publisher.

Don Congdon Associates
"The Golden Kite, the Silver Wind" by Ray Bradbury. Copyright © 1953 by Epoch Associates, renewed 1981 by Ray Bradbury. Reprinted by permission of Don Congdon Associates, Inc.

Richard Curtis Associates, Inc.
"Fly Away," from *The Beauty of the Beasts: Tales of Hollywood's Wild Animal Stars* by Ralph Helfer. Copyright © 1990 by Ralph Helfer. Reprinted by permission of Richard Curtis Associates, Inc.

Dial Books for Young Readers, a division of Penguin Books USA Inc.
From *Rosa Parks: My Story* by Rosa Parks with Jim Haskins. Copyright © 1992 by Rosa Parks. Used by permission of Dial Books for Young Readers, a division of Penguin Books USA Inc.

Doubleday, a division of Bantam, Doubleday, Dell Publishing Group, Inc.
"The Machine That Won the War," copyright © 1961 by Mercury Press, Inc. from *Nightfall and Other Stories* by Isaac Asimov. "The Gift of the Magi" by O. Henry from *The Complete Works of O. Henry.* Copyright © 1905 by Press Publications Company. "The Invalid's Story" by Mark Twain from *The Comic Mark Twain Reader,* edited by Charles Neider. Copyright © 1977 by Charles Neider. Used by permission of Doubleday, a division of Bantam, Doubleday, Dell Publishing Group, Inc.

Doubleday, a division of Bantam, Doubleday, Dell Publishing Group, Inc., and Curtis Brown Ltd.
"The Birds," copyright 1952 by Daphne du Maurier, from *Kiss Me Again Stranger* by Daphne du Maurier. Reprinted by permission of Doubleday, a division of Bantam, Doubleday, Dell Publishing Group, Inc., and Curtis Brown Ltd., London, on behalf of the Chichester Partnership.

EMI Music Publishing
"The Long and Winding Road" Words and Music by John Lennon and Paul McCartney © 1970 SONY/ATV SONGS LLC. Administered by EMI BLACKWOOD MUSIC INC. (BMI). All rights reserved. International copyright secured. Used by permission.

Farrar, Straus & Giroux, Inc.
"Georgia O'Keeffe" from *The White Album* by Joan Didion. Copyright © 1979 by Joan Didion. Prologue from *In My Place* by Charlayne Hunter-Gault. Copyright © 1992 by Charlayne Hunter-Gault. "The Washwoman" from *A Day of Pleasure* by Isaac Bashevis Singer. Copyright © 1969 by Isaac Bashevis Singer. The Prologue and The Epilogue from *The Odyssey: A Stage Version* by Derek Walcott. Copyright © 1993 by Derek Walcott. All rights reserved. Reprinted by permission of Farrar, Straus & Giroux, Inc.

Acknowledgments ◆ 991

Liveright Publishing Corporation
"maggie and milly and molly and may," copyright © 1956, 1984, 1991 by The Trustees for the E. E. Cummings Trust, from *Complete Poems: 1904–1962* by E. E. Cummings. Edited by George J. Firmage. Reprinted by permission of Liveright Publishing Corporation.

Marie-Christine MacAndrew
"The Necklace" from *Boule de Suif and Selected Stories* by Guy de Maupassant, translated by Andrew MacAndrew. Translation copyright © 1964 by Andrew MacAndrew. Reprinted by permission of Marie-Christine MacAndrew for the translator.

Macmillan Publishing Co.
"Jabberwocky" from *The Collected Verse of Lewis Carroll* (New York: Macmillan, 1933). "There Will Come Soft Rains" by Sara Teasdale. Reprinted from *Collected Poems by Sara Teasdale*. Copyright © 1920 by Macmillan Publishing Company, renewed 1948 by Mamie T. Wheless.

John McPhee
"Arthur Ashe Remembered" by John McPhee, first published in *The New Yorker,* March 1, 1993. Reprinted by permission of the author.

Manatt, Phelps & Phillips, LLP
"Both Sides Now" by Joni Mitchell from her album *Clouds*. Copyright © 1967 by Siquomb Publishing Corporation.

Milkweed Editions
"Eulogy for a Hermit Crab" by Pattiann Rogers was published in *Firekeeper: New and Selected Poems* (Milkweed, 1994). Copyright © 1994 by Pattiann Rogers. Reprinted with permission from Milkweed Editions.

National Public Radio, Inc.
"Amelia Earhart Redux" by Alex Chadwick. Copyright © National Public Radio 1997. The news report by NPR's Alex Chadwick was originally broadcast on NPR's "National Geographic Society Radio Expeditions" on March 17, 1997, and is used with the permission of National Public Radio. Any unauthorized duplication is strictly prohibited.

New American Library, a division of Penguin Books USA Inc.
From *The Tragedy of Romeo and Juliet* by William Shakespeare, edited by J. A. Bryant, Jr., copyright © 1964 by J. A. Bryant, Jr.

The New York Times Co.
"Woman's Work" by Julia Alvarez, published in *The New York Times,* September 5, 1994. Copyright © 1994 by The New York Times Co. Reprinted by permission.

North Point Press, a division of Farrar, Straus & Giroux, Inc.
"Gifts" by Shu Ting, reprinted from *A Splintered Mirror: Chinese Poetry from the Democracy Movement*, translated by Donald Finkel. Translation copyright © 1991 by Donald Finkel. Reprinted by permission of North Point Press, a division of Farrar, Straus & Giroux, Inc.

Naomi Shihab Nye
"Shoulders" from *Red Suitcase* by Naomi Shihab Nye. Copyright © 1994 Naomi Shihab Nye. All rights reserved. Reprinted by permission of the author.

Orchard Books
"Checkouts" from *A Couple of Kooks and Other Stories About Love* by Cynthia Rylant. Copyright © 1990 by Cynthia Rylant. Reprinted by permission of the publisher, Orchard Books, New York.

Oxford University Press and Faber and Faber Ltd.
"The Horses" from *Collected Poems* by Edwin Muir. Copyright © 1960 by Willa Muir. Used by permission of Oxford University Press, Inc. and Faber and Faber Ltd.

Playbill Magazine
"On Summer" by Lorraine Hansberry, reprinted from *Playbill Magazine,* June 1960. © Playbill, Inc. Playbill® is a registered trademark of Playbill Incorporated, NYC. All rights reserved. Used by permission.

Polygram International Music Publishing
"Pride (In the Name of Love)," lyrics by Bono and The Edge, music by U2. © 1984 Polygram International Music Publishing. Reprinted by permission of Polygram International Music Publishing.

G. P. Putnam & Sons
"Rules of the Game" from *The Joy Luck Club* by Amy Tan. Copyright © 1989 by Amy Tan. "Go Deep to the Sewer" is reprinted by permission of The Putnam Publishing Group from *Childhood* by Bill Cosby. Copyright © 1991 by William H. Cosby, Jr. Reprinted by permission of G. P. Putnam's sons.

Quarterly Review of Literature
"Astonishment" by Wislawa Szymborska, translated by Grazyna Drabik, Austin Flint, and Sharon Olds. Copyright *Quarterly Review of Literature Poetry Series,* Volume XXIII, edited by T. and R. Weiss. Reprinted by permission.

Random House, Inc.
"Blues Ain't No Mockin Bird" from *Gorilla, My Love* by Toni Cade Bambara. Copyright © 1971 by Toni Cade Bambara. "Caged Bird" from *Shaker, Why Don't You Sing?* by Maya Angelou. Copyright © 1983 by Maya Angelou. "New Directions" from *Wouldn't Take Nothin For My Journey Now* by Maya Angelou. Copyright © 1993 by Maya Angelou. "The Rug Merchant" from *The World Is My Home: A Memoir* by James A. Michener. Copyright © 1992 by James A. Michener. "Tonight, Tonight" from *West Side Story* by Arthur Laurents and Stephen Sondheim. Lyrics copyright © 1957 by Leonard Bernstein and Stephen Sondheim. Reprinted by permission of Random House, Inc.

Random House UK Ltd.
"The Inspector-General" from *The Sneeze* by Anton Chekhov, translated by Michael Frayn, published by Methuen Drama. Reprinted by permission of Random House UK Ltd.

Marian Reiner for Lillian Morrison
"The Spearthrower" from *The Sidewalk Racer and Other Poems of Sports and Motion* by Lillian Morrison. Copyright 1965, 1967, 1968, 1977 by Lillian Morrison. © Renewed Lillian Morrison. Reprinted by permission of Marian Reiner for the author.

Andrea Reynolds, attorney-in-fact for André Milos
"The Red-headed League" by Sir Arthur Conan Doyle. Reprinted by permission.

Dr. Sally K. Ride
"Single Room, Earth View" by Sally Ride, published in the April/May 1986 issue of *Air & Space/Smithsonian Magazine*, published by The Smithsonian Institution. Reprinted by permission of the author.

San Francisco Examiner
"Caucasian Mummies Mystify Chinese" by Keay Davidson, published March 13, 1994, © San Francisco Examiner. Reprinted by permission of the author.

Leslie Marmon Silko
"The Man to Send Rain Clouds" from *Storyteller* by Leslie Marmon Silko. Reprinted by permission of the author.

The Sporting News
Book review by Steve Gietschier of *In These Girls, Hope Is a Muscle* by Madeleine Blais, originally published in *The Sporting News*, May 15, 1995. Reprinted by permission of The Sporting News.

Kim Stafford for the Estate of William Stafford
"Fifteen" copyright © 1973 William Stafford from *Someday, Maybe* (Harper and Row). Reprinted by permission of The Estate of William Stafford.

Sterling Lord Literistic, Inc.
"Children in the Woods" from *Crossing Open Ground* by Barry Lopez. Copyright © 1988 by Barry Holstun Lopez. Reprinted by permission of Sterling Lord Literistic, Inc.

Stoddart Publishing Co. Limited
"There Is a Longing" from *My Heart Soars* by Chief Dan George. Reprinted with permission of Stoddart Publishing Co. Limited, Don Mills, Ontario.

Thacher Proffitt & Wood, as attorney-in-fact for Ishmael Reed
"Beware: Do Not Read This Poem" from *New and Collected Poems* by Ishmael Reed. Copyright © 1966, 1971, 1972, 1973, 1978, 1988 by Ishmael Reed. Reprinted by permission of the author.

Rosemary A. Thurber
"The Secret Life of Walter Mitty" copyright 1942 by James Thurber; copyright © 1970 Helen W. Thurber and Rosemary A. Thurber. From *My World—And Welcome To It*, published by Harcourt Brace Jovanovich, Inc. Reprinted by permission.

Viacom Consumer Products
"Data's Day" #40274-185 from *Star Trek: The Next Generation*, story by Harold Apter, Teleplay by Harold Apter and Ronald D. Moore. STAR TREK and Related Elements TM, & © 1998 Paramount Pictures. All Rights Reserved. Used by permission of Viacom Consumer Products.

Viking Penguin, A Division of Penguin Books USA Inc.
"Old Man of the Temple" from *Under the Banyan Tree* by R. K. Narayan. Copyright © 1985 by R. K. Narayan. From *The Road Ahead* by Bill Gates. Copyright © 1995 by William H. Gates III. "The Interlopers" from *The Complete Short Stories of Saki* by Saki (H. H. Munro). Copyright 1930, renewed 1958 by The Viking Press, Inc. Used by permission of Viking Penguin, a division of Penguin Books USA Inc.

Vintage Books, A Division of Random House, Inc.
Excerpts from *The Odyssey* by Homer, translated by R. Fitzgerald. Copyright © 1961, 1963 by Robert Fitzgerald and renewed 1989 by Benedict R. C. Fitzgerald. Reprinted by permission of Vintage Books, a Division of Random House, Inc.

Vital Speeches of the Day
"Glory and Hope" by Nelson Mandela, from *Vital Speeches of the Day*, June 1, 1994. Reprinted by permission of Vital Speeches of the Day.

Patricia Volk, and the Watkins/Loomis Agency
"An Entomological Study of Apartment 4A" by Patricia Volk, from *The New York Times Magazine*, March 5, 1995. Reprinted by permission of Patricia Volk and the Watkins/Loomis Agency.

Wesleyan University Press with University Press of New England
"Slam, Dunk, & Hook" from *Magic City* by Yusef Komunyakaa. © 1992 by Yusef Komunyakaa, Wesleyan University Press with University Press of New England. Reprinted by permission of Wesleyan University Press with University Press of New England.

Bryan Woolley
"To the Residents of A.D. 2029" from *The Time of My Life* by Bryan Woolley. © Bryan Woolley, 1984. Reprinted by permission of the author.

Note: Every effort has been made to locate the copyright owner of material reprinted in this book. Omissions brought to our attention will be corrected in subsequent editions.

ART CREDITS

Cover: Corel Professional Photos CD-ROM™; **vii:** (top) *Over and Above #13, 1964*, Clarence H. Carter, Oil on canvas, Courtesy of the Artist; (bottom) Jeffery Newbury/Discover Magazine **viii:** (top) *Coal (from AMERICA TODAY)*, 1920, Thomas Hart Benton, ©The Equitable Life Assurance Society of the United States, Collection, The Equitable Life Assurance Society, ©T.H. Benton and R.P. Benton Testamentary Trusts/Licensed by VAGA, New York, NY; (bottom) *Danae with young Perseus arriving on the island of Seripo*, Museo Archeologico, Ferrara, Italy. Scala/Art Resource, NY; **ix:** (top) Image © Copyright 1997 PhotoDisc, Inc.; (bottom) Corel Professional Photos CD-ROM™; **x:** (top) ©Danny Brass/Photo Researchers, Inc.; (center) ©Stephen Dalton/Photo Researchers, Inc.; (bottom) *The Jabberwock*, 1872, John Tenniel, The Granger Collection, New York; **xi:** Frank Whitney/The Image Bank; **xii:** (top) *Scarlet Ibis*, John James Audubon, Courtesy of The New York Historical Society, New York City; (bottom) *Farmworker de Califas*, Tony Ortega, Monotype, Courtesy of the artist; **xiii:** (top) *Cow's Skull: Red, White and Blue, 1931*, Georgia O'Keeffe, The Metropolitan Museum of Art, The Alfred Stieglitz Collection, 1949, Copyright © 1984 by The Metropolitan Museum of Art, Photograph by Malcolm Varon; (bottom) Monica Almeida/NYT Permissions; **xiv:** Photofest; **xv:** ©The Stock Market/Zefa Germany; **xvi:** (top) Corbis-Bettmann; (bottom) *Amphora with Grapes*, oil 15" by 19", Loran Speck, Loran Speck Art Gallery, Carmel CA; **xxiv–1:** *The Storm*, 1893, Edvard, Munch, Oil on canvas, 36 1/8 x 51 1/2" (91.8 x 130.8 cm). The Museum of Modern Art, New York, Gift of Mr. and Mrs. H. Irgens Larsen and acquired through the Lillie P. Bliss and Abby Aldrich Rockefeller Funds. ©1997 The Museum of Modern Art, New York; **2:** Corbis-Bettmann; **3:** Helga Lade/Peter Arnold, Inc.; **5:** Superstock; **7:** Brian Yarvin/Photo Researchers, Inc.; **9:** *Keying Up—The Court Jester* (detail), 1875, William Merritt Chase, Courtesy of the Pennsylvania Academy of the Fine Arts, Philadelphia, Gift of the Chapellier Galleries; **13:** *New Moon, New York*, 1945, George Ault, oil on canvas, 28 x 20" (71.1 x 50.8cm). The Museum of Modern Art, New York, Gift of Mr. and Mrs. Leslie Ault, Photograph © 1997 The Museum of Modern Art, New York; **14:** NYT Pictures; **16–17:** *Peering Through the Jungle*, Larry Noble, Sal Barracca & Associates; **18–19:** (background) Based on *Peering Through the Jungle* by Larry Noble, Sal Barracca & Associates; **19:** (tr) *Hat, Knife, and Gun in Woods*, David Mann, Sal Barracca & Associates; **20–23:** (background) *Based on Peering Through the Jungle* by Larry Noble, Sal Barracca & Associates; **24:** Grace Davies/Omni-Photo Communications, Inc.; **24–29:** (background) Based on *Peering Through the Jungle* by Larry Noble, Sal Barracca & Associates **30:** ©The Stock Market/John Dominis; **30–31:** (background) Based on *Peering Through the Jungle* by Larry Noble, Sal Barracca & Associates; **34:** National Baseball Library and Archive, Cooperstown, N.Y.; **37:** *Baseball Players Practicing*, 1875, Thomas Eakins, Museum of Art, Rhode Island School of Design, Jesse Metcalf Fund and Walter H. Kimball Fund; **41:** (background) NASA; **42:** Neil Leifer/Sports Illustrated; **42–43:** (background) NASA; **44:** AP/Wide World Photos; **46:** *Attack of the Birds, 1994*, Lev Tabenkin, Oil on canvas, 59" x 78", Maya Polsky Gallery; **52:** *Landscape from a Dream, 1936–38*, Paul Nash, Tate Gallery, London/Art Resource, NY; **59:** ©The Stock Market/Zefa Germany; **62–63:** *Wheatfield with Crows, 1890*, Vincent van Gogh, Van Gogh Museum, Amsterdam, The Netherlands, Art Resource, NY; **68:** *Over and*

Above #13, 1964, Clarence H. Carter, Oil on canvas, Courtesy of the Artist; **75:** ©The Stock Market/Tom Ives 1996; **79:** *La Réponse Imprévue, 1933*, Rene Magritte, Musées Royaux Des Beaux-Arts de Belgique, Bruxelles-Koninklijke Musea voor Schone Kunsten van Belgie, Brussel, ©1997 C. Herscovici, Brussels/Artists Rights Society (ARS), New York; **80:** *Sir Arthur Conan Doyle* (detail), H. L. Gates, The National Portrait Gallery, London; **83–98:** The Granger Collection, New York; **102:** (top) © Faber & Faber Ltd.; (center) ©1987 Costa Manos/Magnum Photos, Inc.; **103:** 1995 M.C. Escher/Cordon Art - Baarn - Holland. All rights reserved.; **104:** *Het Blinde Huis*, William Degouve de Nunques, State Museum, Kröller-Müller, Otterlo, The Netherlands; **107:** *Tropical Tree, 1990*, Grimanesa Amoros, 75 x 52", acrylic and mixed media on canvas, ©1997 Grimanesa Amoros/Licensed by VAGA, New York, NY; **110:** Courtesy of the author; **111–112:** Jeffery Newbury/Discover Magazine; **118:** D. Lloyd/Weatherstock; **121:** ©The Stock Market/Tom Stewart; **122:** © Phyllis Picardi/Stock South/PNI; **123:** (center) Reprinted by permission of Warner Books, Inc. from *To Kill a Mockingbird* by Harper Lee. All rights reserved.; **124–125:** *Human Achievement*, Tsing-Fang Chen, Lucia Gallery, New York City/SuperStock; **126:** *Carl Sandburg*, Miriam Svet, The National Portrait Gallery, Smithsonian Institution, Washington, D.C./Art Resource, New York; **127:** Courtesy of the Library of Congress; **130:** *Lincoln Proclaiming Thanksgiving*, Dean Cornwell, The Lincoln Museum, Fort Wayne, Indiana, a part of Lincoln National Corp.; **133:** *Peculiarsome Abe*, N. C. Wyeth, The Free Library of Philadelphia; **137:** *The Promise*, Paulette Peters, From the Permanent Collection of The Museum of American Folk Art, photograph courtesy of the Museum of American Folk Art, New York; **138:** (tl) & (bl) AP/Wide World Photos; (tr) Alan Markfield/Globe Photos; (br) The Granger Collection, New York; **140:** Corbis-Bettmann; **141:** (background) NASA; **143:** *The Beginning*, Artis Lane, mixed media, 36"x 36" Courtesy of the artist; **145:** *We the People*, Kathy Morrow, Original scratchboard painting with hand-loomed beadwork, Courtesy of the artist; **147:** *Coal (from AMERICA TODAY)*, 1920, Thomas Hart Benton, ©The Equitable Life Assurance Society of the United States, Collection, The Equitable Life Assurance Society, ©T.H. Benton and R.P. Benton Testamentary Trusts/Licensed by VAGA, New York, NY; **150:** Thomas Victor; **152–153:** *The Nymph of the Lo River*, section of a handscroll. (H.91/2") Attributed to Ku K'ai-chih, Courtesy of the Freer Gallery of Art, Smithsonian Institution, Washington, D.C. #14.53; **155:** Rectangular box, detail, Woven bamboo and painted lacquer, Late Ming Dynasty, early 17th century, H. 12.1 cm x W. 34.3 cm x L. 48.3 cm, H. 4 3/4" x W. 13 1/2" x L. 19", China, Avery Brundage Collection, #B60 M427, Asian Art Museum of San Francisco; **159:** AP/Wide World Photos; **163:** *Hole in Sky*, Monika Steinhoff, Egg tempera on panel 30" x 18" unframed, Photo by Dan Morse; **164:** (top) Dimitri Kessel/Life Magazine; (center) Henry McGee/Globe Photos; (bottom) AP/Wide World Photos; **166:** ©The Stock Market/Alan Goldsmith; **169:** *Mill Hand's Lunch Bucket, 1978*, Romare Bearden, From the Profile/Part I: The Twenties series (Pittsburgh Memories). Collage on board, 13 3/4 x 18 1/8". ©1997 Romare Bearden Foundation/Licensed by VAGA, New York, NY; **171:** Bob Firth/International Stock Photography, Ltd.; **174:** AP/Wide World Photos; **175:** Corel Professional Photos CD-ROM™; **176-177:** Charles Weckler/The Image Bank; **179:** Indian, Mughal, Leaf from a royal manuscript of the Shah-Jehan

Nameh: *A Procession in a Palace Courtyard,* gouache on paper, mid 17th century, 28.9 x19.7 cm. Kate S. Buckingham Endowment Fund, 1975.555. Photograph © 1996 The Art Institute of Chicago. All Rights Reserved.; **184:** UPI/Corbis–Bettmann; **185:** *Danae with young Perseus arriving on the island of Seripo,* Museo Archeologico, Ferrara, Italy. Scala/Art Resource, NY; **186–187:** *Andromeda Liberated,* Pierre Mignard, Louvre, Paris, France, Erich Lessing/Art Resource, NY; **189:** *Danae with young Perseus arriving on the island of Seripo,* Museo Archeologico, Ferrara, Italy. Scala/Art Resource, NY; **190:** Terre del Greco Ascione Collections/Superstock; **192:** *Perseus and Andromeda* (detail), Ca.1580, Paolo Veronese, Musee des Beaux-Arts, Rennes, France, Erich Lessing/Art Resource, NY; **196:** (top) Photo by Mandy Sayer; (center) Photo by Isidro Rodriquez; (bottom) Photo by Michael Nye; **199:** *Night Games,* Ernie Barnes, Oil on canvas, 48 x 24, Courtesy of The Company of Art, Los Angeles; **200:** ©Allsport/Tony Duffy; **204:** © Martin Rogers/Woodfin Camp & Associates/PNI; **208:** Ferguson/PhotoEdit; **209:** (left) Reprinted with the permission of Simon & Schuster Inc. from *The Old Man and the Sea* by Ernest Hemingway. Copyright © 1995 Scribner Paperback Fiction.; (center) Book cover of *The Miracle Worker* by William Gibson reprinted by special arrangement with Samuel French, Inc.; (right) "Cover" from *Rosa Parks: My Story* by Rosa Parks with Jim Haskins. Copyright © 1992 by Rosa Parks. Used by permission of Dial Books for Young Readers, a division of Penguin Books USA Inc.; **210–211:** "Thunder head" Serigraph, 19" x 18", from the two-piece suite "Full Circle," Frederick Philips, Atlas Galleries, Chicago; **212:** Thomas Victor; **213:** Corel Professional Photos CD-ROM™; **215–216:** ©The Stock Market/Mark Gamba; **217:** (background) ©The Stock Market/Mark Gamba; (bl) Corel Professional Photos CD-ROM™; **218:** (background) ©The Stock Market/Mark Gamba; **221:** *My Judy,* Mabel Martin Davidson, acrylic, 14" x 11"; **222:** Robert Foothorap; **224–226:** Image © Copyright 1997 PhotoDisc, Inc.; **227:** (tr) *Chess Mates,* 1992, Pamela Chin Lee, Courtesy of the artist, Photo by John Lei/Omni-Photo Communications, Inc.; (br) Image © Copyright 1997 PhotoDisc, Inc.; **228–230:** Image © Copyright 1997 PhotoDisc, Inc.; **234:** (right) Kit Stafford; **235:** Image ©Copyright 1997 PhotoDisc, Inc.; **236–237:** *Food City,* 1967, Richard Estes, Oil acrylic and graphite on fiberboard, 48" x 68", Collection of the Akron Art Museum, Akron, Ohio, Museum Acquisition Fund, © Richard Estes/Licensed by VAGA, New York, NY/Courtesy Marlborough Gallery, NY; **238:** NASA; **244:** (tl) & (tr) The Granger Collection, New York; (bl) & (br) AP/Wide World Photos; **247:** Horrillo Riola/A.G.E. FotoStock; **248:** *Bubbles,* watercolor, 39" x 29", Courtesy of Scott Burdick; **249:** Corel Professional Photos CD-ROM™; **251:** UPI/Corbis-Bettmann; **255:** (tr) & (br) Corel Professional Photos CD-ROM™; **259:** *Sunday School Boys,* (detail), 1990 Jonathan Green, Naples, Florida, Oil on canvas, 23 x 23", Photography by Tim Stamm; **260:** The Granger Collection, New York; **262:** R. Ashenbrenner/Stock Boston; **263:** David De Lossy/The Image Bank; **264–265:** Kenneth Redding/The Image Bank; **266:** David De Lossy/The Image Bank; **270:** Adam Scull/Globe Photos; **273:** Patrick Ward/Stock Boston; **274–275:** Tina Buckman/Index Stock Photography, Inc.; **280:** (tr) *E. E. Cummings* (detail), 1958, Self Portrait, The National Portrait Gallery, Smithsonian Institution, Washington, D.C./Art Resource, New York; (bl) Thomas Victor; (br) AP/Wide World Photos; **282:** *Woman Combing Girl's Hair,* 1989 (detail), Malcolm T. Liepke, pastel; **283:** *The Quiltmakers,* Paul

Goodnight, 22 11/16" x 24" Color Circle Art Publishing Inc.; **284:** Corel Professional Photos CD-ROM™; **288:** (top) ©Paul Fusco/Magnum/PNI; (bottom) © Joel W. Rogers/Allstock/PNI; **292:** Tony Freeman/PhotoEdit; **293:** (center) From *When the Legends Die* (Jacket Cover) by Hal Borland. Used by permission of Bantam Books, a division of Bantam Doubleday Dell Publishing Group, Inc.; (right) Vintage Books, Cover design by Lorraine Louie/Cover art by Nivia Gonzalez; **294–295:** *Scientist's Hobby: Failure #18 of the Anti-Gravity Pack, 1992,* Bruce Widdows, acrylic on canvas, 84 x 132 inches, Courtesy of George Adams Gallery, New York; **296:** UPI/Bettmann Newsphotos; **297 & 300:** *The Man With Three Masks,* John Rush, Courtesy of the artist; **303:** *New Orleans Fantasy 1985* (detail) Max Papart, Lithograph, Courtesy of Nahan Galleries, New York; **307:** © Fred Hilliard/Stock Illustration Source, Inc.; **308:** Corbis-Bettmann; **311:** *Valmondois Sous La Neige,* Maurice de Vlaminck, Superstock; **312:** *White Night,* 1901, Edvard Munch, oil on canvas, 45 1/2 x 43 1/2 in. (115.5 x 111 cm) Photo: J. Lathion ©Nasjonalgalleriet 1997; **316:** (left) Globe Photos; (right) Courtesy of the author; **318:** *Young Brothers in the Hood,* 17x22, Courtesy of the artist; **320:** Henry Horenstein/StockBoston; **326:** Chromosohm/Sohm/Stock Boston; **330:** Photo by Larry Sillen; **332:** (top) ©James H. Robinson/Photo Researchers, Inc.; (center) ©Stephen Dalton/Photo Researchers, Inc.; **333:** (top) ©Sturgis McKeever/Photo Researchers, Inc.; (bottom) ©Pat Lynch/Photo Researchers, Inc.; **334:** (tl) ©Louis Quitt/Photo Researchers, Inc.; (tr) ©Tom Branch/Photo Researchers, Inc.; (bottom) ©John M. Burnley/Photo Researchers, Inc.; **335:** (background) NASA; (tl) & (tr) *The Far Side* ©(1997) Farworks, Inc. Used by Permission of Universal Press Syndicate.; (bottom) ©R.J. Erwin/Photo Researchers, Inc.; **336:** ©Danny Brass/Photo Researchers, Inc.; **339:** Tony Freeman/PhotoEdit; **343:** © Dave Cutler/Stock Illustration Source, Inc.; **344:** (top) *T. S. Elliot* (detail), 1888–1965, Sir Gerald Kelly, National Portrait Gallery, Smithsonian Institution, Art Resource, New York; (center) Photo by William Lewis; (bottom) New York Public Library Picture Collection; **346 & 348:** From *Old Possum's Book of Practical Cats,* Copyright 1939 by T. S. Eliot: renewed 1967 by Esme Valerie Eliot, Reproduced by permission of Harcourt Brace Jovanovich, Inc., Illustration by Edward Gorey; **350 & 351:** Corel Professional Photos CD-ROM™; **352:** *The Jabberwock,* 1872, John Tenniel, The Granger Collection, New York; **356:** © 1966 by Michael Courlander; **362:** AP/Wide World Photos; **364:** Murray Wilson/Omni-Photo Communications, Inc.; **367:** UPI/Corbis-Bettmann; **368:** ©R. Gates/Archive Photos; **374:** David Young-Wolf/PhotoEdit; **377:** Michael Newman/PhotoEdit; **378:** Tony Freeman/PhotoEdit; **379:** (left) From *The Prince and the Pauper* (Jacket Cover) by Mark Twain. Used by permission of Bantam Books, a division of Bantam Doubleday Dell Publishing Group, Inc.; (center) From *Alice's Adventures in Wonderland* (Jacket Cover) by Lewis Carroll. Used by permission of © Oxford University Press Inc. and St. Martin's Press.; (right) Cover of *Childhood* by Bill Cosby. Reproduced by arrangement with The Berkley Publishing Group, a member of Penguin Putnam, Inc. All rights reserved.; **380–381:** Michael Agliolo/International Stock Photography, Ltd.; **382:** Andrea Renault/Globe Photos; **386:** Sanford/Agliolo/International Stock Photography, Ltd.; **387:** Index Stock Photography, Inc.; **391:** © Fred Otnes/Stock Illustration Source, Inc.; **392:** Thomas Victor; **395:** UPI/Corbis-Bettmann; **402:** NASA; **405–408:** Star Trek, Star Trek: The Next

Scott McCloud a 215 page analysis of comics in comics form. © and TM 1994 Scott McCloud; **616:** (left) Photo by Max Hirshfeld; (right) The Sporting News; **618:** P. DaSilva/Sygma; **621–622:** Monica Almeida/NYT Permissions; **626:** (background) NASA; **628:** Tom McCarthy/PhotoEdit; **631:** M. K. Denny/PhotoEdit; **632:** Ken Karp Photography; **633:** (center) Cover from *Blue Highways* by William Least Heat Moon. Reprinted with permission of Little, Brown & Co.; (right) From *All Things Bright and Beautiful* (Jacket Cover) by James Herriot. Used by permission of Bantam Books, a division of Bantam Doubleday Dell Publishing Group, Inc.; **634–635:** *The Sheridan Theatre, 1937,* Edward Hopper, Collection of the Newark Museum, 1940, Felix Fuld Bequest Fund/Art Resource, NY; **637:** *Balcony at the Alhambra, 1911,* Spencer Gore, oil on canvas, 19 x 14" York City Art Gallery, England; **638:** Photo by Eric H. Antoniou; **640:** Image © Copyright 1997 PhotoDisc, Inc.; **643:** FPG International Corp.; **644:** Footprints provided by The Arthur Murray Dance Studios; **646 & 648–649:** FPG International Corp.; **651, 652 & 654:** Footprints provided by The Arthur Murray Dance Studios; **654–655:** ©1996 Robert Brooks/FPG International Corp.; **656:** Footprints provided by The Arthur Murray Dance Studios; **661:** Tony Freeman/PhotoEdit; **665:** *Interior of the Theater of San Carlo in Naples,* (detail), 19th C. Musee Conde, Chantilly, France, Giraudon/Art Resource, NY; **667:** Illustration by Hugh Dixon from "Shakespeare in Performance" courtesy of Salmander Books, London; **668:** (background) NASA; (center) Photofest; **669:** *William Shakespeare,* (detail), Artist unknown, by courtesy of the National Portrait Gallery, London; **672 & 679:** Photofest; **685:** Culver Pictures, Inc.; **689:** Photofest; **691:** Movie Still Archives; **694:** Photofest; **702:** Culver Pictures, Inc.; **709 & 717:** Photofest; **725:** Memory Shop; **732:** Culver Pictures, Inc.; **740 & 753:** Memory Shop; **765, 767 & 772:** Photofest; **778:** Michael Newman/PhotoEdit; **782:** Tony Freeman/PhotoEdit; **784–785:** *The Library, 1960,* Jacob Lawrence, tempera on fiberboard, 60.9 x 75.8cm. National Museum of American Art, Smithsonian Institution, Washington, D.C., U.S.A., Gift of S.C. Johnson & Son, Inc./Art Resource, NY; **786:** The Granger Collection, New York; **789–790:** Corel Professional Photos CD-ROM™; **793:** *Fantastic Horse Cart, 1949,* Marc Chagall, Gauche and pastel, 23 1/4 x 18 1/8", Blanden Memorial Art Museum, ©1997 Artists Rights Society (ARS), New York/ADAGP, Paris; **794:** (top) *Alfred Lord Tennyson, c.1840,* S. Laurence, by courtesy of the National Portrait Gallery, London; (center) The Granger Collection, New York; (bottom) *Langston Hughes* (detail), c.1925, Winold Reiss, The National Portrait Gallery, Smithsonian Institution, Washington, D.C./Art Resource, New York; **796:** ©The Stock Market/Pete Saloutos; **796–797:** (background) Corel Professional Photos CD-ROM™; **798–799:** *Bernard's Daddy,* Raymond Lark, Master Drawing, graphite, 20 x 30 inches, Collection of Mary Moran, New Jersey. Photo courtesy of Edward Smith and Company; **802:** (tl) Andrea Renault/Globe Photos; (tr) UPI/Corbis-Bettmann; (bl) Prentice Hall; (br) Photo by Yvonne Mozee; **804:** Joel Glenn/The Image Bank; **805:** Barry Pribula/International Stock Photography, Ltd.; **806:** *The Broom, 1947,* Joseph Solman, oil on mat board, 20 x 16 inches, (50.8 c 40.6 cm) Acquired 1949, The Phillips Collection, Washington, D.C.; **807:** White/Pite/International Stock Photography, Ltd.; **808:** Corel Professional Photos CD-ROM™; **809:** Carolina Biological Supply Co./Phototake; **812:** (tl) & (right) Corbis-Bettmann; (bl) John Craig Photo; **814:** Index Stock Photography, Inc.; **815:** (top) Shelley Rotner/Omni-Photo Communications, Inc.; (center) Andre Gallant/The Image Bank; (bottom) Stephen Wilkes/The Image Bank; **816:** ©The Stock Market/Zefa Germany; **820:** (tc) *The Bells,* Edmund Dulac, New York Public Library; Astor, Lenox and Tilden Foundations; **821:** (background) NASA; **825:** Richard Hutchings/PhotoEdit; **829:** *Transection #1, 1966,* Clarence H. Carter, Acrylic on canvas, 77 x 54" Colletion of The Newark Museum/Art Resource, NY; **830:** (left) Corbis-Bettmann; (right) *William Shakespeare,* (detail), Artist unknown, by courtesy of the National Portrait Gallery, London; **832:** Detail: the raven, Illustration to E.A. Poe's "The Raven," 1875, Edouard Manet, lithograph, Gift of W.G. Russell Allen, Courtesy, Museum of Fine Arts, Boston; **833:** Illustration to E.A. Poe's "The Raven," Edouard Manet, Henry M. and Zoë Oliver Sherman Fund, Courtesy, Museum of Fine Arts, Boston, Gift of W. G. Russell Allen; **836–837:** The Folger Shakespeare Library, Washington, D.C.; **840:** (tl) & (tr) The Granger Collection, New York; (bl) *William Shakespeare,* (detail), Artist unknown, by courtesy of the National Portrait Gallery, London; (br) *Richard Wright* (detail), 1949, Miriam Troop, The National Portrait Gallery, Smithsonian Institution, Washington, D.C./Art Resource, New York; **841:** Luis Castaneda/The Image Bank; **842:** (tl) Luis Castaneda/The Image Bank; (tr) Stephen Frisch/Stock, Boston; **844:** *Girl with Lantern on a Balcony at Night, c. 1768* (detail), Suzuki Harunobu, The Metropolitan Museum of Art, Fletcher Fund, 1929, Copyright © by the Metropolitan Museum of Art; **848:** Corel Professional Photos CD-ROM™; **852:** Paul Conklin/PhotoEdit; **853:** (left) Book cover from *Old Possum's Book of Practical Cats,* Copyright 1939 by T. S. Eliot; renewed 1967 by Esme Valerie Eliot, Reproduced by permission of Harcourt Brace Jovanovich, Inc., Illustration ©1982 by Edward Gorey; (center) From *The Dream Keeper and Other Poems* by Langston Hughes, illustrated by Brian Pinkney. Illustrations copyright © 1994 by Brian Pinkney. Reprinted by permission of Alfred A. Knopf, Inc.; (right) Deborah Maverick Kelley; **854–855:** *Ulysses Deriding Polyphemus, 1819,* J. M.W. Turner, The National Gallery, London; **857:** *The Cyclops (Odysseus Series), 1977,* Romare Bearden, collage, 14 x 11" ©1997 Romare Bearden Foundation/Licensed by VAGA, New York, NY; **858:** Corbis-Bettmann; **861:** *La Nef De Telemachus (The Ship of Telemachus),* New York Public Library Picture Collection; **875:** *Polyphemous, the Cyclops* from Homer's *The Odyssey,* N.C. Wyeth, Delaware Art Museum, Photo by Jon Macdowell; **878:** *Odysseus in the Land of the Dead* from Homer's *The Odyssey,* N.C. Wyeth, Delaware Art Museum, Photo by Jon MacDowell; **883:** *Circe Meanwhile Had Gone Her Ways . . . , 1924,* William Russell Flint, Collection of the New York Public Library; Astor, Lenox and Tilden Foundations; **897:** *Eumaeus, the Swineherd* from Homer's *The Odyssey,* N.C. Wyeth, Delaware Art Museum, Photo by Jon MacDowell; **908:** *The Trial of the Bow* from Homer's *The Odyssey,* N.C. Wyeth, Delaware Art Museum, Photo by Jon MacDowell; **913:** *The Slaughter of the Suitors* from Homer's *The Odyssey,* N.C. Wyeth, Delaware Art Museum, photo by Jon MacDowell; **915:** Photofest; **919:** Corbis-Bettmann; **923:** *The Fall of Troy* from the *Odysseus Suite,* 1979, Romare Bearden, serigraph 18x24 , © Romare Bearden Foundation/Licensed by VAGA, New York, NY; **924:** (tl) *Edna St. Vincent Millay* (detail), Charles Ellis, The National Portrait Gallery, Smithsonian Institution, Washington, D.C./Art Resource, New York; (tr) Eugene Richards/Magnum Photos, Inc.; (bl) Thomas Victor; (br) The Granger Collection, New York; **926:** *Penelope and the Suitors, 1912,* J.M. Waterhouse, 51

1/2 x 75 in. (131 x 191 cm) City of Aberdeen Art Gallery and Museums Collections, Scotland; **929:** *Ulysses receives the wine with which he will make Polyphemus drunk,* Italiotic crater. Muiseo Eoliano, Lipari, Italy/ Scala/Art Resource, NY; **930:** *Amphora with Grapes,* oil 15" by 19", Loran Speck, Loran Speck Art Gallery, Carmel CA; **934:** (background) NASA; (bl) Ron Batzdorff/Photofest; **935:** Ron Batzdorff/Photofest; **936:** *La Nef De Telemachus (The Ship of Telemachus),* New York Public Library Picture Collection; **939:** Mary Kate Denny/PhotoEdit; **940:** Michelle Bridwell/PhotoEdit; **941:** (left) Cover from *The Iliad* by Homer, translated by W.H.D. Rouse. Published by Mentor, an imprint of Dutton Signet, a division of Penguin Books USA Inc.; (right) Cover from *Mythology* by Edith Hamilton. Illustrations by Steele Savage. Published by Meridian, the Penguin Group, a division of Penguin Books USA Inc.; **947:** Photofest; **949:** *Polyphemous, the Cyclops* from Homer's *The Odyssey,* N.C. Wyeth, Delaware Art Museum, Photo by Jon Macdowell; **950:** NASA; **952:** (background) Corel Professional Photos CD-ROM™; (center) ©The Stock Market/Pete Saloutos; **954:** ©The Stock Market/Zefa Germany; **958:** NASA; **959:** Corel Professional Photos CD-ROM™; **960:** *Scarlet Ibis,* John James Audubon, Courtesy of The New York Historical Society, New York City; **961:** Barry Pribula/International Stock Photography, Ltd.; **977:** Ken Karp Photography; **978:** AP/Wide World Photos; **980:** Mary Kate Denny/PhotoEdit.

ADDITIONAL CREDITS

Editorial: Tim Callahan, Elaine Goldman, Gregory Lynch, Laura Ring

Media Resources: Diane Alimena, Katty Gavilanes, Suzi Myers

Permissions: Rosalyn Arcilla, Jeanette Myers

Photo Research Service: Omni-Photo Communications, Inc.

PrePress Production: James D. Gwyn

Production: Claudia Dukeshire, Deborah O'Connell

Design and Page Layout: Ernest Albanese, Robert Aleman, Jane Alexander, Lisa Ann Arcuri, Penelope Baker, Anthony Barone, Linda Berniak, Elizabeth Bostwick, Emily Buckley, Chris Calloway, Rui Camarinha, Tara Campbell, Carlos Crespo, Thomas Davidson, Paul DelSignore, Robert Dobasczewski, Irene Ehrmann, Jeffrey Engel, Frederic Joe Galka, Diane Gerard, Pat Gilbanks, Florrie Gladson, Julie Goldstein, Alison Grabow, Leslie Greenberg, Greg Harrison, Ralph Henriquez, Kathleen Kennedy, Gregory Ludwig, Laura Maggio, Lynn Mandarino, John McClure, Deirdre Mitchell, Thomas Mitchell, Rebecca Myers, Karolyn Necco, Evelyn O'Shea, Harry Phillips, Linda Punskovsky, Ken Rosenblat, David Rosenthal, Phyllis Rosinsky, Janelle Roth, Irene Schwartz, Jan Schwartz, Rose Sievers, Dakota Smith, Scott Steinhardt, Tom Tedesco, Frances Turcott, Karen Vignola, Wendy Wolf

ILLUSTRATION CREDITS

45, 78, 207, 212, 222, 223, 258, 261, 271, 291, 317, 331, 342, 345, 357, 422, 425, 451, 457, 483, 496, 518, 535, 551, 600, 602, 664, 781, 828, 851, 922, 939: Ernest Albanese.
16-31: S.I. International representing Ted Enik; 394-395, 397: S.I. International representing Nick Jainschigg.
114, 444, 891: Ortelius Design.
358-359: Carol Bancroft representing Chi Chung.